Magill's
Cinema
Annual
2013

Magill's Cinema Annual 2013

32nd Edition
A Survey of the films of 2012

Brian Tallerico, Editor

A VideoHound® Reference

GALE
CENGAGE Learning®

Detroit • New York • San Francisco • New Haven, Conn • Waterville, Maine • London

Magill's Cinema Annual 2013
Brian Tallerico, Editor

Project Editor: Michael J. Tyrkus

Editorial Support Services: Wayne Fong

Composition and Electronic Prepress: Gary Leach, Evi Seoud

Manufacturing: Rhonda Dover

Gale, Cengage Learning
27500 Drake Rd.
Farmington Hills, MI, 48331-3535

ISBN-13: 978-1-55862-834-2
ISBN-10: 1-55862-834-7

ISSN: 0739-2141

Printed in Mexico
1 2 3 4 5 6 7 17 16 15 14 13

Contents

Preface

Magill's Cinema Annual 2013 continues the fine film reference tradition that defines the VideoHound® series of entertainment industry products published by Gale. The thirty-second annual volume in a series that developed from the twenty-one-volume core set, *Magill's Survey of Cinema,* the *Annual* was formerly published by Salem Press. Gale's seventeenth volume, as with the previous Salem volumes, contains essay-reviews of significant domestic and foreign films released in the United States during the preceding year.

The *Magill's* editorial staff at Gale, Cengage Learning, comprising the VideoHound® team and a host of *Magill's* contributors, continues to provide the enhancements that were added to the *Annual* when Gale acquired the line. These features include:

- More essay-length reviews of significant films released during the year
- Obituaries and book review sections
- Trivia and "fun facts" about the reviewed movies, their stars, the crew, and production
- Quotes and dialogue "soundbites" from reviewed movies, or from stars and crew about the film
- More complete awards and nominations listings, including the American Academy Awards®, the Golden Globes, and others (see the User's Guide for more information on awards coverage)
- Box office grosses, including year-end and other significant totals
- Publicity taglines featured in film reviews and advertisements

In addition to these elements, *Magill's Cinema Annual 2013* still features:

- An obituaries section profiling major contributors to the film industry who died in 2012
- An annotated list of selected film books published in 2012
- Nine indexes: Director, Screenwriter, Cinematographer, Editor, Art Director, Music Director, Performer, Subject, and Title (now cumulative)

COMPILATION METHODS

The *Magill's* editorial staff reviews a variety of entertainment industry publications, including trade magazines and newspapers, as well as online sources, on a daily and weekly basis to select significant films for review in *Magill's Cinema Annual*. *Magill's* staff and other contributing reviewers, including film scholars and university faculty, write the reviews included in the *Annual*.

MAGILL'S CINEMA ANNUAL: A VIDEOHOUND® REFERENCE

The *Magill's Survey of Cinema* series, now supplemented by the *Annual*, is the recipient of the Reference Book of the Year Award in Fine Arts by the American Library Association. Gale, an award-winning publisher of reference products, is proud to offer *Magill's Cinema Annual* as part of its popular VideoHound® product line, which includes *VideoHound®'s Golden Movie Retriever* and *The Video Source Book*. Other Gale film-related products include the four-volume *International Dictionary of Films and Filmmakers, Women Filmmakers & Their Films,* the *Contemporary Theatre, Film, and Television* series, and the four-volume *Schirmer Encyclopedia of Film*.

ACKNOWLEDGMENTS

The writing staff of *Magill's Cinema Annual 2013*, which consists of publishing professionals, freelance writers, and paid film critics (including nine members of the Chicago Film Critics Association, as well as one member of the Detroit Film Critics Society), brings love for cinema and sheer talent for writing about it to this year's book. Never losing their own voices while also representing the *Magill's* style as a collective, they worked independently and together to craft a comprehensive chronicle of the year in film. The staff continues to impress with their knowledge, dedication, and abilities. The staff at Gale Cengage—Mike Tyrkus and Jim Craddock—deserve thanks for their continued efforts on behalf of the book as well. *Magill's Cinema Annual 2013* was truly a collaboratively created work and would be nothing without not only the support of the writers assigned to it but the friends and family who so completely back its editor in every capacity. Nothing this exhaustive can be accomplished without widespread support and that is what the editor gets from his incredible wife Lauren and beautiful sons Lucas & Miles. They make this work not just possible but rewarding.

We at *Magill's* look forward to another exciting year in film and preparing the next edition of *Magill's Cinema Annual*. As always, we invite your comments, questions, and suggestions. Please direct them to:

Editor
Magill's Cinema Annual
Gale, Cengage Learning
27500 Drake Road
Farmington Hills, MI 48331-3535
Phone: (248) 699-4253
Toll-Free: (800) 347-GALE (4253)
Fax: (248) 699-8865

The Year in Film: An Introduction

While the major filmmakers of 2011 looked to the past nostalgically in films like *Midnight in Paris* (2011), *The Artist* (2011), and *Hugo* (2011), the transition to 2012 found celebrated directors looking to the history books more directly in acclaimed and award-winning works like *Argo* (2012), *Lincoln* (2012), and *Zero Dark Thirty* (2012). The comfort of knowing a predetermined, successful ending—the Iranian hostages get home, the slaves are freed, and Osama Bin Laden is killed—did not stop the works from Ben Affleck, Steven Spielberg, and Kathryn Bigelow from resonating artistically. In fact, one could argue that viewers living in the tumultuous reality of 2012 sought comfort in the cinematic confirmation that everything is going to be all right. Even blockbusters like *Marvel's The Avengers* (2012), *The Hunger Games* (2012), and *The Hobbit: An Unexpected Journey* (2012) come from a place of narrative comfort in that they were based on previously available work or had relatively predictable narratives (Joss Whedon was not about to kill Iron Man, for example). When filmmakers did throw viewers a narrative curve, it was often greeted with controversy as in Quentin Tarantino's *Django Unchained* (2012), Paul Thomas Anderson's challenging *The Master* (2012), or Ridley Scott's divisive *Prometheus* (2012). One could argue that it is even more remarkable for filmmakers to take the familiar or the known story and make it feel new. One could also argue that the world is scary enough in 2012 that the truly new has no place in blockbuster entertainment.

Perhaps the overall comfort of the familiar helps explain the notable dearth of interesting new filmmakers in 2012. One name rose high above all others in that department as Benh Zeitln's *Beasts of the Southern Wild* (2012) was a part of the cinematic conversation all year. From its Sundance Film Festival debut through a successful art-house run in the Summer to multiple Oscar® nominations, including Best Picture, Best Director, and Best Actress for Quvenzhane Wallis, the youngest nominee in that category in history, *Beasts of the Southern Wild* was the most memorable breakthrough of the year. Colin Trevorrow's *Safety Not Guaranteed* (2012), Drew Goddard's *Cabin in the Woods* (2012), Josh Trank's *Chronicle* (2012), Nicholas Jarecki's *Arbitrage* (2012), and, most of all, Stephen Chbosky's *The Perks of Being a Wallflower* (2012) were other debuts worth mentioning but the year in breakthroughs belonged to a little girl who lives in the bathtub with her daddy and too little else.

While filmmakers used history as a template, there was also a definite cinematic recognition that times in the real world are exceedingly difficult. Whether it was life in the Bathtub in *Beasts,* the stunning story of J.A. Bayona's *The Impossible* (2012), the man vs. nature tale of *The Grey* (2012), the basis of *The Hunger Games,* most of the characters in *Cloud Atlas* (2012), or dozens of economically challenged characters in indie films, it felt like movie characters this year were struggling to survive right along with viewers. Even the Summer season of escapism demanded superheroes who were willing to sacrifice as the national mood can always be reflected in the biggest box office hits.

What do the top financial successes of 2012 say about that national mood? Once again, families wanted to go to the theater as thirty percent of the top twenty films of the year domestically were animated kids movies. Captain America, Batman, James Bond, Bilbo Baggins, Spider-Man, Bella Cullen—viewers went back like clockwork to the characters they knew and loved. Once again, there seemed to be comfort in something predictable. People know what to expect from superheroes and book adaptations just as they know that Osama Bin Laden will be killed at the end of *Zero Dark Thirty,* itself a pretty massive financial hit, making over $100 million worldwide.

Box office statistics seemed to end the common lazy journalism of the financial failure of Hollywood as over 30 films broke $100 million domestically with 11 films over $200 million and 5 films cresting $300 million in the United States. (Only 7 films broke $200 million the year before.) And legendary characters often reached new and unexpected heights. James Bond's 50th anniversary was greeted with Sam Mendes's *Skyfall* (2012), not just one of the most critically acclaimed films in the franchise (and a double Oscar® winner) but a financial behemoth, grossing $304 million domestically (nearly double the second place film in terms of 007 grosses—*Quantum of Solace*) and a breathtaking $1.1 billion worldwide. In the worldwide arena, the Daniel Craig action flick is the seventh highest grossing film of all time.

But even Bond had to bow at the altar of the superhero one-two-three punch of Summer 2012, which began with *Marvel's The Avengers,* a film that grossed $623 million domestically and $1.5 billion worldwide, moved on to Sony's *The Amazing Spider-Man* (2012) ($262 million domestic, $752 million worldwide), and connected with Christopher Nolan's highly-anticipated *The Dark Knight Rises* ($448 million domestic, $1.1 billion worldwide). Fantasy, sci-fi, and superhero action served much the same purpose for teens and adults as the numerous animated films did for kids: escapism. They are cartoons for adults.

However, it should be noted that the gap between critics and commercial audiences seemed to shrink in 2012. It is not as if critics praised *Beasts of the Southern Wild* and audiences went to *The Avengers.* Seven out of nine Best Picture nominees broke $100 million in 2012, a remarkable total, especially after 2011, in which only one Best Picture nominee was also that popular of a favorite. Only Steven Spielberg and Tony Kushner could take the history lesson of Abraham Lincoln to the financial heights they did in *Lincoln* (13th place overall domestically), while Quentin Tarantino's quasi-historical and Oscar®-winning *Django Unchained* (2012) grossed more than any film in his impressive filmography. Films like *Argo, Life of Pi* (2012), *Magic Mike* (2012), *Silver Linings Playbook* (2012), *Flight* (2012), and *Zero Dark Thirty* connected with both critics and ticket buyers, proving there need not always be such distance between the two.

On the specialty market, Michael Haneke's devastating *Amour* (2012) garnered the most praise and awards (including the Oscar® for Best Foreign Language Film) but did not gross the most in an increasingly depleted foreign language market domestically. While the rest of the world seems to have little issue spending their movie-going dollar on films with subtitles, American audiences still do so in shockingly small numbers. The highest-grossing foreign language film of the year was the feel-good *The Intouchables* (2012) and even that could only muster $10 million domestically (on the heels of over $400 million worldwide). While critics fell in love with Leos Carax's *Holy Motors* (2012), Nuri Bilge Ceylan's *Once Upon a Time in Anatolia* (2012), and *Monsieur Lazhar* (2012), most American audiences were never even granted the chance to see them. On the documentary market, harsh times were reflected in dark films like *The Invisible War* (2012), *The Central Park Five* (2012), *The Gatekeepers* (2012), and *West of Memphis* (2012) but audiences and the Academy went with the feel-good story of the year in *Searching for Sugar Man* (2012), a tale that inspired viewers to think that they too could turn their passion and creativity into something fruitful long after it felt like that opportunity was missed.

Will filmmakers continue to look to history to provide entertainment for the present? Does the escapism of a certain ending provide comfort that simply cannot be found in more challenging works like P.T. Anderson's *The Master* (2012)? While audiences and critics were admiring predetermined narratives, Anderson offered a film with almost no traditional narrative at all. He dared suggest that viewers not only do not necessarily know where they are going but that this can be the source of art as much as historical fiction or inspirational heroes. Hollywood will never run out of filmmakers willing to make great movies out of well-known stories but one hopes the industry does not lose its mavericks, the men and women willing to craft their visions out of pure imagination in the process.

Brian Tallerico
Chicago, Illinois

Contributing Reviewers

Nick Allen
Professional Film Critic

David L. Boxerbaum
Freelance Reviewer

Tom Burns
Publishing Professional

Dave Canfield
Professional Film Critic

Erik Childress
Professional Film Critic

Mark Dujsik
Professional Film Critic

Matt Fagerholm
Professional Film Critic

Joanna MacKenzie
Freelance Reviewer

Locke Peterseim
Professional Film Critic

Matt Pais
Professional Film Critic

Matthew Priest
Freelance Reviewer

Brent Simon
Professional Film Critic

Peter Sobczynski
Professional Film Critic

Collin Souter
Professional Film Critic

Brian Tallerico
Professional Film Critic

Michael J. Tyrkus
Publishing Professional

Nathan Vercauteren
Freelance Reviewer

User's Guide

ALPHABETIZATION

Film titles and reviews are arranged on a word-by-word basis, including articles and prepositions. English leading articles (A, An, The) are ignored, as are foreign leading articles (El, Il, La, Las, Le, Les, Los). Other considerations:

- Acronyms appear alphabetically as if regular words.

- Common abbreviations in titles file as if they are spelled out, so *Mr. Death* will be found as if it was spelled *Mister Death*.

- Proper names in titles are alphabetized beginning with the individual's first name, for instance, *Gloria* will be found under "G."

- Titles with numbers, for instance, *200 Cigarettes,* are alphabetized as if the numbers were spelled out, in this case, "Two-Hundred." When numeric titles gather in close proximity to each other, the titles will be arranged in a low-to-high numeric sequence.

SPECIAL SECTIONS

The following sections that are designed to enhance the reader's examination of film are arranged alphabetically, they include:

- *List of Awards.* An annual list of awards bestowed upon the year's films by the following: Academy of Motion Picture Arts and Sciences, British Academy of Film and Television Arts Awards, Directors Guild of America Awards, Golden Globe Awards, Golden Raspberry Awards, Independent Spirit Awards, the Screen Actors Guild Awards, and the Writer's Guild Awards.

- *Obituaries.* Profiles major contributors to the film industry who died in 2012.

- *Selected Film Books of 2012.* An annotated list of selected film books published in 2011.

INDEXES

Film titles and artists are separated into nine indexes, allowing the reader to effectively approach a film from any one of several directions, including not only its credits but its subject matter.

- *Director, Screenwriter, Cinematographer, Editor, Art Director, Music Director,* and *Performer* indexes are arranged alphabetically according to artists appearing in this volume, followed by a list of the films on which they worked. In the *Performer* index, a (V) beside a movie title indicates voice-only work and an (N) beside a movie title indicates work as narrator.
- *Subject Index.* Films may be categorized under several of the subject terms arranged alphabetically in this section.
- *Title Index.* The title index is a cumulative alphabetical list of films covered in the thirty volumes of the *Magill's Cinema Annual,* including the films covered in this volume. Films reviewed in past volumes are cited with the year in which the film appeared in the *Annual;* films reviewed in this volume are cited with the film title and this year's edition in boldface. Original and alternate titles are cross-referenced to the American release title in the Title Index. Titles of retrospective films are followed by the year, in brackets, of their original release.

SAMPLE REVIEW

Each *Magill's* review contains up to sixteen items of information. A fictionalized composite sample review containing all the elements of information that may be included in a full-length review follows the outline on the facing page. The circled number following each element in the sample review designates an item of information that is explained in the outline.

1. **Title:** Film title as it was released in the United States.

2. **Foreign or alternate title(s):** The film's original title or titles as released outside the United States, or alternate film title or titles. Foreign and alternate titles also appear in the Title Index to facilitate user access.

3. **Taglines:** Up to ten publicity taglines for the film from advertisements or reviews.

4. **Box office information:** Year-end or other box office domestic revenues for the film.

5. **Film review:** A signed review of the film, including an analytic overview of the film and its critical reception.

6. **Reviewer byline:** The name of the reviewer who wrote the full-length review. A complete list of this volume's contributors appears in the "Contributing Reviewers" section which follows the Introduction.

7. **Principal characters:** Listings of the film's principal characters and the names of the actors who play them in the film.

8. **Country of origin:** The film's country or countries of origin and the languages featured in the film.

9. **Release date:** The year of the film's first general release.

10. **Production information:** This section typically includes the name(s) of the film's producer(s), production company, and distributor; director(s); screenwriter(s); cinematographer(s); editor(s); art director(s); production designer(s); music composer(s); and other credits such as visual effects, sound, costume design, and song(s) and songwriter(s).

11. **MPAA rating:** The film's rating by the Motion Picture Association of America. If there is no rating given, the line will read, "Unrated."

12. **Running time:** The film's running time in minutes.

13. **Reviews:** A list of brief citations of major newspaper and journal reviews of the film, including author, publication title, and date of review.

14. **Film quotes:** Memorable dialogue directly from the film, attributed to the character who spoke it, or comment from cast or crew members or reviewers about the film.

15. **Film trivia:** Interesting tidbits about the film, its cast, or production crew.

16. **Awards information:** Awards won by the film, followed by category and name of winning cast or crew member. Listings of the film's nominations follow the wins on a separate line for each award. Awards are arranged alphabetically. Information is listed for films that won or were nominated for the following awards: American Academy Awards®, British Academy of Film and Television Arts Awards, Directors Guild of America Awards, Golden Globe Awards, Golden Raspberry Awards, Independent Spirit Awards, the Screen Actors Guild Awards, and the Writers Guild of America Awards.

THE GUMP DIARIES ①
(Los Diarios del Gump) ②

Love means never having to say you're stupid.
—Movie tagline ③

Box Office: $10 million④

In writer/director Robert Zemeckis' *Back to the Future* trilogy (1985, 1989, 1990), Marty McFly (Michael J. Fox) and his scientist sidekick Doc Brown (Christopher Lloyd) journey backward and forward in time, attempting to smooth over some rough spots in their personal histories in order to remain true to their individual destinies. Throughout their time-travel adventures, Doc Brown insists that neither he nor Marty influence any major historical events, believing that to do so would result in catastrophic changes in humankind's ultimate destiny. By the end of the trilogy, however, Doc Brown has revised his thinking and tells Marty that, "Your future hasn't been written yet. No one's has. Your future is whatever you make it. So make it a good one."

In *Forrest Gump*, Zemeckis once again explores the theme of personal destiny and how an individual's life affects and is affected by his historical time period. This time, however, Zemeckis and screenwriter Eric Roth chronicle the life of a character who does nothing but meddle in the historical events of his time without even trying to do so. By the film's conclusion, however, it has become apparent that Zemeckis' main concern is something more than merely having fun with four decades of American history. In the process of re-creating significant moments in time, he has captured on celluloid something eternal and timeless—the soul of humanity personified by a nondescript simpleton from the deep South.

The film begins following the flight of a seemingly insignificant feather as it floats down from the sky and brushes against various objects and people before finally coming to rest at the feet of Forrest Gump (Tom Hanks). Forrest, who is sitting on a bus-stop bench, reaches down and picks up the feather, smooths it out, then opens his traveling case and carefully places the feather between the pages of his favorite book, *Curious George*.

In this simple but hauntingly beautiful opening scene, the filmmakers illustrate the film's principal concern: Is life a series of random events over which a person has no control, or is there an underlying order to things that leads to the fulfillment of an individual's destiny? The rest of the film is a humorous and moving attempt to prove that, underlying the random, chaotic events that make up a person's life, there exists a benign and simple order.

Forrest sits on the bench throughout most of the film, talking about various events of his life to others who happen to sit down next to him. It does not take long, however, for the audience to realize that Forrest's seemingly random chatter to a parade of strangers has a perfect chronological order to it. He tells his first story after looking down at the feet of his first bench partner and observing, "Mama always said that you can tell a lot about a person by the shoes they wear." Then, in a voice-over narration, Forrest begins the story of his life, first by telling about the first pair of shoes he can remember wearing.

The action shifts to the mid-1950s with Forrest as a young boy (Michael Humphreys) being fitted with leg braces to correct a curvature in his spine. Despite this traumatic handicap, Forrest remains unaffected, thanks to his mother (Sally Field) who reminds him on more than one occasion that he is no different from anyone else. Although this and most of Mrs. Gump's other words of advice are in the form of hackneyed cliches, Forrest, whose intelligence quotient is below normal, sincerely believes every one of them, namely because he instinctively knows they are sincere expressions of his mother's love and fierce devotion. ⑤

John Byline ⑥

CREDITS ⑦

Forrest Gump: Tom Hanks
Forrest's Mother: Sally Field
Young Forrest: Michael Humphreys
Origin: United States ⑧
Language: English, Spanish
Released: 1994 ⑨
Production: Liz Heller, John Manulis; New Line Cinema; released by Island Pictures ⑩
Directed by: Robert Zemeckis
Written by: Eric Roth
Cinematography by: David Phillips
Music by: Graeme Revell
Editing: Dana Congdon
Production Design: Danny Nowak
Sound: David Sarnoff
Costumes: David Robinson
MPAA rating: R ⑪
Running time: 102 minutes ⑫

REVIEWS (13)

Doe, Jane. *Los Angeles Times.* July 6, 1994.

Doe, John. *Entertainment Weekly.* July 15, 1994.

Reviewer, Paul. *Hollywood Reporter.* June 29, 1994.

Writer, Zach. *New York Times Online.* July 15, 1994.

QUOTES (14)

Forrest Gump (Tom Hanks): "The state of existence may be likened unto a receptacle containing cocoa-based confections, in that one may never predict that which one may receive."

TRIVIA (15)

Hanks was the first actor since Spencer Tracy to win back-to-back Oscars® for Best Actor. Hanks received the award in 1993 for his performance in *Philadelphia.* Tracy won Oscars® in 1937 for *Captains Courageous* and in 1938 for *Boys Town.*

AWARDS (16)

Academy Awards 1994: Film, Actor (Hanks), Special Effects, Cinematography

Nomination:

Golden Globes 1994: Film, Actor (Hanks), Supporting Actress (Field), Music.

A

ABRAHAM LINCOLN: VAMPIRE HUNTER

President by day. Hunter by night.
—Movie tagline

Are you a patriot or a vampire?
—Movie tagline

Box Office: $37.5 million

Among *Abraham Lincoln: Vampire Hunter*'s problems—and they are legion—is not its inherently goofy hook: The 16th president spent his early years dispatching (with his rail-splitting axe) the undead fiends who had infiltrated the new republic, only to later find himself back at odds with Confederate undead during his famed Civil War administration. In a year that also brought filmgoers another serious, high-minded Lincoln film full of award-ready performances and lofty ideas (Steven Spielberg's *Lincoln* [2012]), the notion of Abe slaying vampires is a perfectly fun and welcome basis for big, summer-blockbuster silliness.

However, screenwriter Seth Grahame-Smith (author of the cheeky historical-fantasy novel on which the film is based), producer Tim Burton, and most of all director Timur Bekmambetov take their Van Helsing version of Lincoln far too seriously, treating the vamp-dusting proceedings not like a cheesy, campy flick, but an essay prompt on a social studies exam. *Abraham Lincoln: Vampire Hunter* opens with a solemn quote from the Book of Genesis when it would have been better off taking a page from Roger Corman. Cleaved of a sense of humor or tongue-in-cheek camp, the film that follows is smothered in faux nobility as the Great Emancipator

mows down bloodsuckers (most of them part of the Antebellum South) with grim determination.

Bekmambetov's never been a model of stylistic restraint. First with his spastic Russian fantasy-action epics *Night Watch* (2004) and *Day Watch* (2006) and then in Hollywood's *Wanted* (2008), the director explored new ways of making his ADD-edited action films feel ponderous despite his trademark visual seizures and penchant for slow-mo, sped-up, slow-again action shots. That leaves *Abraham Lincoln: Vampire Hunter*, a film full of restless kinetic energy but no juice. There is an intentional artifice to Bekmambetov's cinema that gives it a faded one-dimensionality, as if his films are grim lithographs. They are full of spraying blood, but no beating heart, with no room for humanity amid the arch, monochromatic tableaus. (The normally extemporary cinematographer Caleb Deschanel fills scenes with smoke and moonshine and piles on the filters: blue for gothic nights, yellow-orange for dusty historical days.)

The director's much-ballyhooed fight visuals are impressive in small doses, and he can execute a dazzling batch of shots (a battle amid a horse stampede alongside a canyon, a midnight train crossing a bridge collapsing in flames), but there is no grasp of scene, and the CGI-staged stunts have no emotional heft—they are just eye popping tricks lacking a gut-punch. All is constant titillation with no giggling exploitation flavor—it is spectacle and sensation, epic chintz and chutzpah, none of it making much sense. Bekmambetov loves to pan over iconography, from stovepipe hats to the Washington Monument, but his characters feel as though they are also carved in the sides of granite tombs, frozen forever astride destiny but not really going anywhere. It is not the best approach for a film that must already carefully straddle and draw cinematic friction from two very different genres.

As Abe, Benjamin Walker keeps striving for charisma beneath the top hat, but is continually interrupted by training montages in which he learns to twirl his silver-edged axe. And Mary Elizabeth Winstead also does her best as a coquettish Mary Todd, but the moment she and Walker start to fan flames of courtship chemistry, Bekmambetov yanks Abe back to work at the frenzied, nonsensical vampire slaying. The cast is rounded out by Rufus Sewell easily tossing off snooty, aristocratic villainy without spilling his brandy. But as Abe's mysterious mentor in the vamp-combat arts, the very talented Dominic Cooper seems further doomed to play supporting caricatures in Hollywood fantasies. Anthony Mackie and Jimmi Simpson are also on hand as a couple of Lincoln's long-time compatriots.

As with so much Hollywood escapism these days, *Abraham Lincoln: Vampire Hunter* mistakes premise for plot—disjointed and scattershot, the film feels fuller of ideas than sense. About two-thirds of the way through, having run out of things to do, *Abraham Lincoln* gives up on the Young Man with an Axe routine and rushes through Lincoln's political rise—the narrative economy no doubt encouraged by a disappointing lack of beheadings during the Lincoln-Douglas debates.

Suddenly, the film arrives at the Civil War and Gettysburg where Bekmambetov plays at historical melodrama, slapping awkward faux glory on civil war scenes. There are also attempts throughout to blame the Southern slavery culture on the vampires, which might be offensive if the filmmakers cared about what they were saying. Offensive or not, played the right way, *Abraham Lincoln: Vampire Hunter* could have been howling, eye-rolling fun. But Bekmambetov cannot figure out how to wink at his audience through the deadpan, and so the film feels so much duller than its catchy title promises.

Released in June, *Abraham Lincoln: Vampire Hunter* stumbled at the North American box office, earning less than $40 million against its nearly $70 million production budget. It played better overseas, bringing in more than double its domestic haul. Most critics were unimpressed, but some were able to embrace the film's grand ambitions. *The Oregonian*'s Shawn Levy wrote, "this is a ludicrous premise, and it's sometimes played stiffly as to seem willfully inept. But when Bekmambetov is in full stride and the gore, oaths and silver bullets are flying, it's a kick. The title may sound like a joke, but *Abraham Lincoln: Vampire Hunter* is serious fun." However, more reviews were along the lines of Tasha Robinson's of *The Onion AV Club,* who said, "The story

is trying to ground fantasy in history, but neither one is used coherently enough to connect."

Locke Peterseim

CREDITS

Abraham Lincoln: Benjamin Walker
Henry Sturgess: Dominic Cooper
Will Johnson: Anthony Mackie
Mary Todd Lincoln: Mary Elizabeth Winstead
Adam: Rufus Sewell
Origin: United States
Language: English, French, Spanish
Released: 2012
Production: Tim Burton, Jim Lemley, Timur Bekmambetov; released by Tim Burton Productions, Blazelevs Production
Directed by: Timur Bekmambetov
Written by: Seth Graham-Smith
Cinematography by: Caleb Deschanel
Music by: Henry Jackman
Sound: Hugh Waddell
Editing: William Hoy
Art Direction: Beat Frutiger
Costumes: Carlo Poggioli; Varvara Avdyushko
Production Design: Francois Audouy
MPAA rating: R
Running time: 105 minutes

REVIEWS

Adams, James. *The Globe and Mail.* June 22, 2012.
Corliss, Richard. *Time.* June 21, 2012.
Dargis, Manohla. *New York Times.* June 21, 2012.
LaSalle, Mick. *San Francisco Chronicle.* June 22, 2012.
Levy, Shawn. *The Oregonian.* June 21, 2012.
O'Sullivan, Michael. *Washington Post.* June 22, 2012.
Robinson, Tasha. *AV Club.* June 21, 2012.
Rodriguez, Rene. *Miami Herald.* June 21, 2012.
Turan, Kenneth. *Los Angeles Times.* June 21, 2012.
Zacharek, Stephanie. *Movieline.* June 21, 2012.

QUOTES

Abraham Lincoln: "History prefers legends to men. It prefers nobility to brutality, soaring speeches to quiet deeds. History remembers the battle, but forgets the blood. However history remembers me before I was a President, it shall only remember a fraction of the truth."

TRIVIA

Tom Hardy was approached for the title role of Lincoln, but had to turn it down due to scheduling conflicts with *The Dark Knight Rises.*

ACT OF VALOR

The only easy day was yesterday.
—Movie tagline

Box Office: $70 million

The tricky thing about propaganda is that the more it is engaging and entertaining, the more effectively it sells its cause. The fictional action movie *Act of Valor* is pure propaganda—though not officially produced by the United States Navy, the project rose out of short Navy recruitment films created by co-directors Mike McCoy and Scott Waugh, the success of which led the filmmakers to ask the Navy to use not only real military equipment but also active-duty Navy SEALs in a feature-length narrative film.

Act of Valor exists for one purpose: To make the Navy, particularly its elite SEAL teams and their weapons and methods, seem so exciting, cool, and noble that viewers will, if not want to actually sign up, at least come away with an elevated opinion of and support for such military personnel and their country's endeavors. The film reinforces its message with plenty of visceral appeal, drawing both on the excitement and heroism of an action film and an emotional appeal based on the warrior tradition of honor, sacrifice, and brotherhood—all of it underscored by the fact these are actual SEALs using real tactics and weaponry.

As military action entertainment, *Act of Valor* comes with all the contrived premises and plot mechanics of the sub-genre. A Chechen Islamist (played with appropriate scowling menace and terrorist zealotry by Jason Cottle) has teamed with an opportunistic, hedonistic international smuggler (Alex Veadov) to launch a massive suicide-bombing campaign in the United States. The film's elite SEAL team heroes are called forth and sent rushing around the world to thwart the attack (using an impressive array of Navy transportation and arms). Peppered with military jargon and slang, the action unfolds either with awestruck panoramas of American firepower or from the gun-barrel point of view of a first-person shooter video game.

There are several visual moments in *Act of Valor* that grab—real Navy gunboats laying down a deadly field of fire, a real submarine slowly submerging—but they rely almost wholly on the filmmakers' access to genuine equipment operated by actual sailors (and supposedly often using live ammunition during the shoot) rather than any inherent skill from the directors. Otherwise, the movie is often a sub-par, uneven effort—for every scene that benefits from the verisimilitude, there are several that suffer from a lack of film-making and story telling skill and a slavish devotion to cliche. For the most part, McCoy and Waugh rely on an all-too-familiar excess of people, places, and things getting shot and/or blown up in big, orange fireballs and then making Big Speeches about the nobility of it all. Beyond the bullets and explosions, *Act of Valor*'s real message (presented just as ham-handedly by screenwriter Kurt Johnstad) is about the bravery and sacrifice of the men

and women operating all that cool weaponry, with plenty of solemn talk about codes of honor, tradition, and warrior blood being passed down through the generations. The film's plot and characters remind us, "There are threats everywhere," therefore America needs the men and women and military might and firepower so dazzlingly on display.

While *Act of Valor*'s brutal (child-killing, woman-torturing) villains are sneeringly played by professional actors, the film's Navy heroes, including its main protagonists "Chief Dave" and "Lieutenant Commander Rorke," are portrayed by unnamed, real-life "active-duty" SEALs reportedly ordered by the Navy to participate in the film for promotional purposes, despite a prior history of strict operational secrecy. The SEALs are not good actors, and the film's hagiographic context and deferential direction does not allow the sort of naturalism that might have let the non-professional actors come off less stilted. (Though in his handful of scenes, the SEAL playing Operations Officer and interrogator "Otto Miller" comes off with much more on-screen charisma than his peers.) The trade-off for using real SEALs and their to-be-expected lack of acting ability is that no one can accuse *Act of Valor* of sporting "pretty boy actors playing with guns," but everything the "real" characters say and do feels heavily filtered through both action-film tropes and the Pentagon's public relations department. As characters, Dave and Rorke are not just good men, but good family men—they have human problems, but no real weaknesses, flaws, or failings. The heroes and the actions of the nation they serve are completely sanitized in the flames of ideology, sacrifice, and honor.

While the dramatic interactions in *Act of Valor* feel as stiffly staged as a 1980s corporate training film, the combat scenes with all their visceral, manipulative power are intended to play at some emotional level as documentary—the film opens with the claim it is "based on real acts of valor" and closes with the names of every SEAL killed in action since September 11, 2001. As an action film, *Act of Valor* may be clunky and cliched, but the moments that do work as gut-level entertainment thrills only help sell the propaganda's message. For all the film's "realism" and talk about bravery and protecting American freedom, this is still a war fantasy, intended to sell combat as a thrillingly dangerous adventure where even those who make the ultimate sacrifice do so in beatific slow motion and are ushered into the hallowed halls of Valhalla, their names and memories draped in honor.

Act of Valor performed decently at the North American box office, where it earned $70 million against a relatively low budget of $12. Critical response was below average. Some like *The Boston Globe*'s Wesley

Morris applauded how the film's verisimilitude made it a "peculiarly entertaining exercise in bare-bones, Hollywood-style action heroism," and some wanted little to do with "A movie whose cinematic ineptitude is matched only by its ideological rottenness..." (*Slant Magazine*'s Andrew Schenker). For many, however, the film was stuck somewhere in the middle; Amy Biancolli of *The San Francisco Chronicle* felt the use of real SEALs, "...adds oomph to the proceedings, but the film gets snagged by its own narrative convention."

Locke Peterseim

CREDITS

Christo: Alex Veadov
Lisa Morales: Roselyn Sanchez
Abu Shabal: Jason Cottle
Walter Ross: Nestor Serrano
Sanchez: Emilio Rivera
Commander Pedros: Gonzalo Menendez
Lt. Rourke's Wife: Ailsa Marshall
Origin: United States
Language: English
Released: 2012
Production: Scott Waugh, Mike McCoy; Bandito Brothers; released by Relativity Media
Directed by: Scott Waugh; Mike McCoy
Written by: Kurt Johnstad
Cinematography by: Shane Hurlbut
Music by: Nathan Furst
Sound: Robert Webber
Music Supervisor: Peter Afterman
Editing: Scott Waugh; Siobhan Prior; Michael Tronick
Costumes: Erica Clum
Production Design: John Zachary
Running time: 110 minutes

REVIEWS

Baumgarten, Marjorie. *Austin Chronicle*. March 2, 2012.
Biancolli, Amy. *San Francisco Chronicle*. February 24, 2012.
Catsoulis, Jeannette. *New York Times*. February 23, 2012.
Ebert, Roger. *Chicago Sun-Times*. February 22, 2012.
Jenkins, Mark. *Washington Post*. February 24, 2012.
Levy, Shawn. *Oregonian*. February 23, 2012.
Morris, Wesley. *Boston Globe*. February 24, 2012.
Phillips, Michael. *Chicago Tribune*. February 23, 2012.
Pinkerton, Nick. *Village Voice*. February 22, 2012.
Schenker, Andrew. *Slant*. February 23, 2012.

QUOTES

Chief Dave: "That last night at home, you think about how you could of been a better dad, a better husband, that bedtime story you should of read, or that anniversary you forgot. You don't expect your family to understand what you're doing. You just hope they understand you're doing it for them, and when you get home you hope you can pick-up right where you left off."

TRIVIA

Due to the SEALS deployment cycles principal photography of the film took two and half years.

AWARDS

Nominations:
Golden Globes 2013: Song ("For You")

AI WEIWEI: NEVER SORRY

Can an artist change China?
—Movie tagline

Box Office: $534,100

At first glance, the cameras that surround the studio of Chinese artist Ai Weiwei appear to have been placed by the man himself as a mode of security. It is not until the lens of Beijing journalist Alison Klayman pulls in for a closer look that the troubling truth is revealed. These cameras in fact represent the ever-watchful eye of a frightened government that Ai Weiwei views as his opponent in an eternal chess match.

Moviegoers unfamiliar with the fearless titular muckraker of Klayman's invaluable documentary, *Ai Weiwei: Never Sorry*, are practically guaranteed to become instant fans after seeing this richly involving portrait. There is perhaps no greater champion of individuality and its inherent power than this controversial icon, whose distinctive works powerfully function as both art and political statements. Consider his famous photographs in which he shatters a Han Dynasty vase, thus conveying that the past, however sacred, must be done away with in order for necessary reform to be achieved.

Ai Weiwei's field of 100 million individually-made sunflower seeds represent the diversity of ideas that remain repressed by the bureaucratic regulations of his country's communist party. No doubt some of his revolutionary spirit rubbed off on Klayman, who utilizes various clips from Ai Weiwei's self-made documentaries that he distributed for free online. The footage chronicles his activism and the abuse that he has endured at the hands of government officials. Klayman has echoed her subject's philosophy by openly admitting in interviews that she hopes her film will be pirated, acknowledging that such a crime could help spread Ai Weiwei's message past the boundaries of American art houses.

This is not the sort of stuffy, pompously ponderous doc that audiences view as the cinematic equivalent of nutritious yet tasteless vegetables. Klayman has made an immensely entertaining picture that garners a great deal of its mileage from the irrepressible charisma of Ai Weiwei himself, who subsequently appeared in his own send-up of PSY's "Gangnam Style" video. He is not above poking fun at himself, but he is immensely serious when it comes to the messages that he intends to convey through his work. There is a visceral thrill in watching him thrust his middle finger at corrupted monuments such as the White House and the Bird's Nest Olympic Stadium for which he served as an artistic consultant. He quickly turned his back on the Olympic Games in protest upon learning of the migrant workers being forced out of Beijing prior to the festivities.

One of the most powerful sections in the film centers on Ai Weiwei's enraged response to his government's utter refusal to investigate the faulty construction that may have dramatically increased the number of schoolchildren who perished in the 2008 Sichuan earthquake. To further avoid sullying China's image, the government did not even make an effort to release the names of the deceased children, a disgrace that prompted Ai Weiwei to collect them himself. After posting the names on his blog to commemorate the one year anniversary of the tragedy, he displayed them in the form of a massive list accompanied by the audio recording of citizens reciting the names. Suddenly, the simple profession of the childrens' very existence became an act of rebellion in itself.

Klayman's film takes the form of a thriller as it explores Ai Weiwei's failed attempt to testify at the court hearing of Tan Zuoren, a fellow investigator of the student lives claimed by the earthquake. Audio was captured of the violence that occurred when Chengdu police broke into the artist's hotel room and bludgeoned his head, causing a cerebral hemorrhage that required emergency brain surgery. With a boldness evocative of vintage Michael Moore, Ai Weiwei confronts one of the officers who beat him while being followed by his trusted crew. It is as clear to him as it is to the viewer that justice will continually evade his grasp, but that is not reason enough for Ai Weiwei to give up on his righteous crusade. He may not receive an apology from the cop, but at least he will capture his sorry face on camera.

The story that Klayman unspools is so compelling that it registers as somewhat of a disappointment when it ultimately proves to be unfinished. Ai Weiwei's 81-day incarceration where he endured psychological torture at the hands of police received an international outcry in favor of the artist's release. Following his bail in 2011, Ai Weiwei was unable to give interviews and was not even permitted to leave the country. Klayman's decision to end her film in the midst of this dire crisis was perhaps unavoidable since the artist's unquenchable hunger to provoke ensures that his troubles with police will continue until his dying day. Though police claim that Ai Weiwei was arrested purely on the basis of tax evasion charges, Klayman's film makes a thoroughly convincing argument to the contrary.

At an effortlessly watchable 91 minutes, the film does leave certain aspects of Ai Weiwei's life underdeveloped, particularly his complex relationship with his devoted wife, who conspicuously vanishes from the film after it is revealed that her husband had a child with another woman. This detail may seem irrelevant to the film's central subject matter, but it is crucial in portraying Ai Weiwei as a flawed human rather than a larger-than-life saint. He has no desire to be worshipped, anyway. His single hope is that the vital truths his work illuminates will resonate with the multitudes, and that is precisely what has begun to happen. Ai Weiwei's status as a close runner-up for Time Magazine's Person of 2011 parallels the triumph of Chinese writer Liu Xiaobo, who was awarded the Nobel Peace Prize soon after being sentenced to 11 years in prison for "inciting subversion of state power." If these extraordinary activists prove anything at all, it is that one's power and influence can indeed transcend the boundaries of a governmental gag order. Ai Weiwei is more than a mere artist or activist. He is an indomitable force of nature.

Matt Fagerholm

CREDITS

Origin: United States, China
Language: English, Mandarin Chinese
Released: 2012
Production: Adam Schlesinger, Alison Klayman; United Expression Media; released by Sundance Selects
Directed by: Alison Klayman
Written by: Alison Klayman
Cinematography by: Alison Klayman
Music by: Ilan Isakov
Sound: Matt Gundy
Editing: Jennifer Fineran
MPAA rating: R
Running time: 91 minutes

REVIEWS

Burr, Ty. *Boston Globe*. August 2, 2012.
Dargis, Manohla. *New York Times*. July 26, 2012.

Gleiberman, Owen. *Entertainment Weekly.* July 25, 2012.
Lengel, Kerry. *Arizona Republic.* August 9, 2012.
Levy, Shawn. *Portland Oregonian.* August 2, 2012.
O'Hehir, Andrew. *Salon.com.* July 28, 2012.
Phipps, Keith. *AV Club.* July 25, 2012.
Schenker, Andrew. *Slant Magazine.* July 23, 2012.
Toro, Gabe. *The Playlist.* July 26, 2012.
Turan, Kenneth. *Los Angeles Times.* August 5, 2012.

AWARDS

Nominations:
Directors Guild 2012: Documentary Director (Klayman)

ALEX CROSS

Don't ever cross Alex Cross.
    —Movie tagline

Box Office: $25.9 million

Up to the release of the latest installment of the Alex Cross movie franchise, author James Patterson had already produced eighteen books in the series. By the time this film is available on DVD in early 2013, two more books—*Merry Christmas, Alex Cross* & *Alex Cross, Run*—will have been released. The films have not been nearly as steady, only getting its third cinematic treatment and the first since 2001's *Along Came a Spider.* Patterson's busily stalked protagonist did fairly well at the box office if not inspiring critics into believing he was worth following for another eighteen adventures. Fans of Patterson's airport fiction might disagree despite whatever objections they have had between the films and the varying text. New fans are being sought out for the franchise reboot though and they should be mostly pleased. Considering they are used to ham-handed acting, amateurish filmmaking, cartoonish villains, hypocritical motivations and a touch of old broad sass, they should be right at home watching Tyler Perry take the lead.

As the new era begins, Alex Cross (Tyler Perry) is once again chasing down another psychopath and saving a battered white girl. Along with his select team, childhood friend Tommy Kane (Edward Burns) and Monica Ashe (Rachel Nichols)—who are secretly hooking up behind the boss' back—they investigate crimes of some unspecified nature around the greater Detroit area. Their special unit is hardly defined by anything other than Alex being such a master of deduction that he can tell his wife (Carmen Ejogo) had coffee based on the blouse stain big enough to be spotted by a Fisher Price telescope from Pluto. Other than dealing with the occasional crime scene, life is good for "Detective Doctor" Alex Cross who is on the short list for an FBI job in Washington and he has just been told there's another little Cross on the way.

Also on the way is another psycho. This one, played by Matthew Fox, is a professional assassin who calls himself "The Butcher" but is referred to as "Picasso" by Tommy based on him leaving a drawing at a recent upscale massacre. There is a mystery benefactor behind The Butcher's recent spree which includes getting into underground MMA fights, paralyzing women with a special drug, and concocting elaborate break-ins to take out a French financial specialist. When Cross and Co. disrupt the latter, The Butcher takes to being bullet-grazed worse than being punched in the face.

There is a momentary fascination with the film in figuring out precisely what Fox's psychotic villain is really up to. How does buying one's way into a brutal fight connect to a stolen laptop, what's on it and how it leads to international finance? Just who is Jean Reno's one-scene millionaire if not the only superfluous suspect available to be funding The Butcher? Do professional mercenaries go off-script so often to take on personal vendettas after getting a little boo-boo from their adversary?

For every answer revealed in *Alex Cross*—and few are really offered—it opens up ten different logical conundrums over just how brilliant this particular cat and mouse really are. Loosely based on Patterson's prequel novel, *Cross*, the screenplay by first-timer Kerry Williamson and Marc Moss—whose only previous credit is the adaptation of Patterson's *Along Came a Spider* (2001)—actually gets less complicated and more boring as things get pieced together. What begins as a ludicrous police procedural becomes an even more ludicrous revenge thriller that asks viewers to believe this morally-principled Sherlock-wannabe is not just ready to turn into The Punisher but also possesses the superskills necessary for an overweight, out-of-shape, dopey, doughy detective to take on a cage fighter who overreacts to taking a single punch. There has not been a less convincing avenging angel than Tyler Perry's Alex Cross since Thomas Jane portrayed the comic world's Frank Castle by interrogating a suspect with a melting popsicle.

The stakes in *Alex Cross* are raised ever further with the kind of vengeful horror that most professional assassins would admit is against the code. Both of the *Taken* (2010, 2012) films pushed the boundaries of the ratings system but did so under a kind of unwritten guide that throat-punching is less graphic than the more macho-violent fare that Sylvester Stallone has done in his *Rambo* and *Expendables* films. *Alex Cross* will never be confused with those, but its violence quotient is shocking for an MPAA-rated "PG-13" mystery thriller. The connection between sexual fetish and murder is pushed during a torture scene. No less than two other crimes are committed towards women with one worthy of a funeral and the other nothing more than a cell phone snapshot. Patterson's specialty of bruising-up the fairer sex received an "R" rating when *Kiss the Girls* (1997) came out. Fifteen years later, viewers are apparently so numb that it can be extrapolated even while being dumbed down for those used to Perry's cartoonish portrayals of man-on-woman crimes.

All such shocking moments of *Alex Cross* could be all part of some calculated plan for Perry to prove that he is going hard in trying to prove what a serious, demonstrative actor he can be. Most would recommend a stint in acting classes for starters which co-star Matthew Fox is more than happy to teach. First lesson: Act with the eyes. Bug them out as far as possible to prove the depth of the character's villainy. The originally cast Idris Elba as Cross would have had to take the class on keeping a straight face in the middle of this nonsense. Lesson two goes to director Rob Cohen. With no competency as an action director and stars as wooden as Perry and Burns, shake the camera as much as humanly possible to justify urgency. James Cameron could not make a call to OnStar more dramatically riveting. Mainly because he would never create an action sequence around a call to OnStar (which actually exists in this movie). *Alex Cross* is equally silly, boring, offensive and implausible which are also its best qualities if the viewer is in a mocking kind of mood.

Erik Childress

CREDITS

Dr. Alex Cross: Tyler Perry
Picasso: Matthew Fox
Tommy Kane: Edward Burns
Monica Ashe: Rachel Nichols
Leon Mercier: Jean Reno
Nana Mamma: Cicely Tyson
Maria Cross: Carmen Ejogo
Origin: United States
Language: English
Released: 2012
Production: Bill Block, Paul Hanson, James Patterson, Steve Bowen, Randall Emmett, Leopoldo Gout; Emmett/Furla Films; released by Summit Entertainment
Directed by: Rob Cohen
Written by: Kerry Williamson; Marc Moss
Cinematography by: Ricardo Della Rosa
Music by: John Debney
Sound: Willie Burton
Editing: Thom Noble

Costumes: Abigail Murray
Production Design: Laura Fox
MPAA rating: PG-13
Running time: 101 minutes

REVIEWS

Bayer, Jeff. *The Scorecard Review*. October 25, 2012.
Ebert, Roger. *Chicago Sun-Times*. September 18, 2012.
Edelstein, David. *New York Magazine*. October 22, 2012.
Goss, William. *Film.com*. October 18, 2012.
Hynes, Eric. *Village Voice*. October 19, 2012.
Judy, Jim. *ScreenIt*. October 19, 2012.
Morgenstern, Joe. *Wall Street Journal*. October 18, 2012.
Sawin, Chris. *Examiner.com*. October 19, 2012.
Verniere, James. *Boston Herald*. October 19, 2012.
Westhoff, Jeffrey. *Northwest Herald*. November 2, 2012.

TRIVIA

Idris Elba had originally been considered to take over the role of Alex Cross from Morgan Freeman.

AWARDS

Nominations:

Golden Raspberries 2012: Worst Actor (Perry)

THE AMAZING SPIDER-MAN

The untold story begins.
—Movie tagline

His past was kept from him. His search for answers has just begun.
—Movie tagline

Box Office: $262 million

Five years after the third, final, and misjudged installment of director Sam Raimi's series of films about the superhero with abilities that make him akin to a spider, here is *The Amazing Spider-Man*, with a story that redoes the hero's origin—terrain already covered quite well in Rami's *Spider-Man* (2002). The temptation to engage in a kneejerk dismissal of a cinematic reboot—especially one that arrives only a decade after the film it retreads—is a strong one. There is precedent, though, if one looks to the source material. In the world of the comic books, Spider-Man has been "spectacular," "sensational," "astonishing," and "avenging," to list the modifiers of a few of the various series in which the superhero has starred.

Fortunately, the clumsy handling of practically every element of this reinterpretation of the character and the focus of the world which he inhabits renders null and void the initial skepticism of the movie based solely on its existence in relation to the previous films. Instead, *The Amazing Spider-Man* stands on its own as a lackadaisical and wholly unimpressive foray into revealing a far less appealing hero and relying on the tried and tired comic-book movie formula.

Peter Parker (Andrew Garfield) is something of a blank slate in this variation—a loner with no friends and with an interest in science, technology, and photography but who is not completely incompetent in relation to fitting in with others. He is less of a social outcast than he is socially overlooked (An amorous couple is kissing in front and in the way of his locker, and they do not even notice him when he attempts to open it). He is still incredibly awkward when it comes to the girl of his dreams; in this reincarnation, she is Gwen Stacy (Emma Stone), which is in line with the original mythos of the comic book.

Peter does not shy away from confrontation and, in fact, provokes one with the school's resident bully Flash (Chris Zylka) when he refuses to take a picture of the jock holding another student upside-down. Peter has the nerve to stand up for what is right; he simply does not have the physical ability to enforce it. The movie even gives him something approaching a rebellious streak with a skateboard, which he rides through the halls of his high school, much to the disapproval of the school's administrators.

This is not, in other words, the Peter Parker to whom the majority of the mainstream audience has become accustomed. The driving idea of Peter Parker as a nerd-turned-hero is that he garners immediate sympathy, a quality sorely absent from screenwriters James Vanderbilt, Alvin Sargent, and Steve Kloves' Peter, whose inconsistent characterization leans more toward a smug, off-putting personality. This becomes even more problematic when Peter dons his mask and red-and-blue suit.

Before that, though, the screenplay introduces a mysterious back story for Peter. His parents (Campbell Scott and Embeth Davidtz in brief appearances during the prologue) died in a plane crash after leaving their son with his aunt May (Sally Field) and his uncle Ben (Martin Sheen) when he was a boy. While exploring the basement, Peter discovers his father's old briefcase, which contains very little of importance, save for part of a mathematical formula and a newspaper clipping of his father with an old colleague named Dr. Curt Connors (Rhys Ifans). Peter sneaks his way into Connors' laboratory at a major corporation and learns that the scientist has been working on way to combine animal DNA with a human host in the hopes of discovering cures to degenerative diseases and to regenerate his missing right arm through the use of reptile genetic material.

The rest of Peter's transformation into Spider-Man plays out with only the specifics changed. A genetically altered spider bites him while he is exploring Connors laboratory. He begins to realize that a change has come over him, most notably in a scene on the subway when he overreacts out of instinct to a man placing a bottle on his forehead as Peter is passed out on the seat. The resulting fight is a piece of uncomfortably brutal slapstick, with Peter knocking out almost an entire train car full of people, including bashing some of them in the head with a metal pole he rips from its attachments to the floor and ceiling.

There is a montage of Peter testing out his new agility and climbing abilities in an abandoned warehouse. It is the only scene during his conversion that possesses a modicum of joy in discovery, even though director Marc Webb, who seems bored by the material, undermines that by placing a low-key pop song on the soundtrack, meant to tie into Peter finally gaining enough courage to awkwardly ask Gwen on a date. Their budding romance is the movie's highlight, particularly because Peter only briefly hesitates to inform her of his secret identity. Gwen knows the stakes and is equal parts impressed with and fearful of Peter's extracurricular excursions.

Most importantly, Peter allows a robber at a convenience store to escape after the cashier insults him; the thief kills Uncle Ben while fleeing. Peter spends his nights trying to hunt down the killer and, in the process, stops multiple crimes, turning him into a public hero and a nuisance for the police, especially Gwen's father Captain Stacy (Denis Leary), with whom Peter shares an on-the-nose conversation about the difference between vigilantism and justice over dinner.

If Peter is only barely sympathetic before the spider bite, he is downright obnoxious after donning the mask and suit—a punk with a bad attitude who taunts criminals (understandable but not exactly heroic) and spouts cringe-worthy one-liners while swinging, leaping, and fighting. The latter is anticipated, though Garfield's brash delivery lends a strange air of hostility to Spider-Man's deeds. An episode on a bridge, in which Spider-Man must rescue a child from inside a car dangling from the structure (simple enough until the car catches fire), allows the protagonist a transition from his less-appealing self to a bona fide do-gooder, though shortly after, the screenplay dismisses Peter's evolution almost immediately after it is suggested.

Just as that character development and the background of Peter's parents abruptly disappear from the narrative's equation, the screenplay disregards the through line of Peter tracking down Uncle Ben's killer for a more cliched route—a bigger battle with bigger stakes (The subplot only reemerges at the very end of the movie with a quick shot of a police sketch of the murderer). Connors' experimentation—hastened by a vague threat from the assistant (Irrfan Khan) of the company's dying, unseen CEO (yet another mystery omitted for—one supposes—the inevitable sequel)—does give him a new arm; it also mutates him into a human-lizard hybrid with a diabolical plan to release his chemical in the form of a gas in order to change everyone in New York City into human-lizard hybrids.

"The Lizard," as the creature is dubbed, is as unconvincing in appearance as his plan is in theory and in practice. He is a computer-generated creation of laughable design (The most prominent feature of his flat, oval head is an extended grin that only becomes more comical when he opens his mouth to growl) and poor execution (It makes one long for the campy relish of Raimi's first outing with Spider-Man—a suitable tone when presenting grown men who, of their volition, dress in ridiculous costumes and do battle in ludicrous setpieces). Spider-Man fights the lizard in the sewer, through the local high school, and atop a massive skyscraper, and no amount of random slow motion, first-person perspective shots, or gaudy neon-drenched cinematography from John Schwartzman can distract from or hide how generic these confrontations and the narrative rationale behind them are.

There need not be good reason to restart a franchise from the beginning, but there must be some creative impulse driving the implementation of that decision. *The Amazing Spider-Man* is the antithesis of that second thought—a lazy and completely ordinary superhero story that gets just about every facet of its central character and story wrong while failing to follow through on the few parts that show some promise in any satisfactory way.

Mark Dujsik

CREDITS

Peter Parker/Spider-Man: Andrew Garfield
Dr. Curt Connors/The Lizard: Rhys Ifans
Gwen Stacy: Emma Stone
Uncle Ben Parker: Martin Sheen
Aunt May Parker: Sally Field
George Stacy: Denis Leary
Rajit Ratha: Irrfan Khan
Flash Thompson: Chris Zylka
Richard Parker: Campbell Scott
Mary Parker: Embeth Davidtz

Origin: United States
Language: English
Released: 2012
Production: Laura Ziskin, Avi Arad, Matthew Tolmach; Columbia Pictures, Marvel Studios; released by Sony Pictures Home Entertainment Inc.
Directed by: Marc Webb
Written by: James Vanderbilt; Alvin Sargent; Steve Kloves
Cinematography by: John Schwartzman
Music by: James Horner
Sound: Shannon Mills; Addison Teague
Editing: Alan Edward Bell; Pietro Scalia
Costumes: Kym Barrett
Production Design: J. Michael Riva
MPAA rating: PG-13
Running time: 136 minutes

REVIEWS

Berardinelli, James. *ReelViews*. July 2, 2012.
Burr, Ty. *Boston Globe*. July 2, 2012.
Kenny, Glenn. *MSN Movies*. July 2, 2012.
Lacey, Liam. *Globe and Mail*. July 2, 2012.
Orndorf, Brian. *Blu-ray.com*. July 2, 2012.
Phillips, Michael. *Chicago Tribune*. June 29, 2012.
Phipps, Keith. *AV Club*. July 3, 2012.
Schager, Nick. *Slant Magazine*. June 29, 2012.
Sobczynski, Peter. *EFilmCritic.com*. July 1, 2012.
Tallerico, Brian. *HollywoodChicago.com*. July 3, 2012.

QUOTES

Spider-Man: "Ahem, you know, if you're going to steal cars, don't dress like a car thief."
Car Thief: "You a cop?"
Spider-Man: "You seriously think I'm a cop in a skintight red and blue suit?"

TRIVIA

When Peter first enters Gwen's room, there are several books stacked just inside the window through which Peter enters. The book at the top of the stack is the novel *Seabiscuit*. Tobey Maguire, who portrayed Peter/Spider-Man in the original film trilogy, also played the lead character in the film *Seabiscuit*.

AMERICAN REUNION

Save the best piece for last.
    —Movie tagline
The class of '99 returns for their high school reunion.
    —Movie tagline

Box Office: $57 million

There was no reason to expect anything positive from *American Reunion*. The fourth installment of the influential gross-out franchise arrives a distant nine years after the mediocre *American Wedding* (2003), which followed two years after the even-more excruciating *American Pie 2* (2001). A funny, character-driven film can quickly and easily become an obnoxious caricature of itself in sequels, and *American Wedding* likely left most viewers, including fans of the original *American Pie* (1999), grumbling, "If I never see these jokers again, it will be too soon."

What a pleasant surprise, then, that *American Reunion* turns out to be such a funny and unexpectedly emotionally satisfying trip back to East Great Falls, Michigan, the small town that started it all for a group of teenage guys just, like so many young onscreen horndogs before them, looking to get laid. Returning thirteen years later for their high school reunion (the planning committee clearly spent the past three years asleep at the wheel), none of the old gang enjoys the happy life they imagined in their senior year high school yearbook. New dad Jim (Jason Biggs) longed to have the sex life of—oops—Ricky Martin but instead, similar to other 2012 cinematic marital challenges in *Friends with Kids* and *Hope Springs,* finds himself in a sexual rut with his wife Michelle (Alyson Hannigan). Oz (Chris Klein) imagined having a family; instead he hosts an off-brand sports show, lost to Gilbert Gottfried in a TV celebrity dance competition and can barely keep up with his adventurous model-girlfriend (Katrina Bowden), whose hotness is now obscured by her personality. Kevin (Thomas Ian Nicholas) imagined happiness with Vicky (Tara Reid); now he mostly feels emasculated by his and his wife's (Charlene Amoia) TV-watching habits. Stifler (Seann William Scott) rarely hangs out with the boys, working as a temp and suffering the insults he prefers to dole out himself. Only world-traveled Finch (Eddie Kaye Thomas) has made his dreams a reality, though no one can corroborate his stories and he has yet to find the great love he seeks.

That is an effective place to start, particularly for a movie whose previous installment included, Stifler having sex with Jim's grandma. In the hands of *Harold and Kumar* writers/directors Jon Hurwitz and Hayden Schlossberg, *American Reunion* again becomes a casual and frequently very funny tour of the shenanigans that guys get themselves into and out of. The film does feature a few especially, uh, vivid images, such as pubic hair and vaginal secretions on Stifler's face after he goes down on an old classmate (Rebecca Field) long overdue for some sexual reciprocation. However, Hurwitz and Schlossberg are not nearly as crass as the relative no-names who helmed the last two *American* movies. *American Reunion*

coasts on a laid-back vibe along which some familiar faces (including Chris Owen as Sherman, aka the Sherminator, and John Cho, hilariously weird as MILF Guy #2) glide in and out. The experience of returning to a hometown and reverting back to childish ways with old friends seems as inevitable as the reunion itself.

That is not to say that the film does not offer several of the expected, over-the-top set pieces. After all, Jim still gets himself into a sticky situation, sometimes literally, seemingly every few hours, and he is caught absolutely every time. Whether he is trying to masturbate while his wife is taking a bath or spend time with Kara (Ali Cobrin), the girl next door for whom he used to baby-sit but who is now turning eighteen and ready for more adult activities, Jim seems to have an irresistible spell on him that taunts, "Yes, the last fifty times things have turned out awkwardly and embarrassing, but, hey, this could be fun, right?"

Yet part of what makes *American Reunion* rewarding is that the physical humor exists not just for the sake of a laugh/groan but to support a story about guys in their early thirties trying to reconcile their place in the world with their own expectations and perceptions. Among the errors: Oz's friends assume he must love having such a gorgeous girlfriend. Jim's friends assume he's having more sex than any of them. Kevin is happily married but cannot deny the feelings that are activated when he sees Vicky, who will always be his first love. Finch reconnects with a former classmate (Dania Ramirez) who has become stunningly beautiful but still cannot come clean about his current routine. Even Jim's dad (Eugene Levy), now a widower, feels dissatisfied, so Jim tries to help his dad get back into the dating game. (In return, dad offers some misguided sex advice: "Sometimes you can buy a little time with a well-placed thumb.")

This dose of adult melancholy suits these characters well and usefully modulates the outrageous behavior that ensues. Fortunately, most of it delivers the laughs. Hurwitz and Schlossberg include plenty of amusing visual gags, like Jim hiding links to his favorite Internet porn sites behind a bookmark labeled, "Boring work stuff," or funny exchanges like, after Stifler retaliates in traditionally extreme fashion against a bunch of high school punks, Kevin says, "You trashed their jetskis." "They splashed us, so..." responds Stifler, who, in Scott's performance that finds charm and vulnerability beneath the outer jerk, seems to recognize that this is one of many times that he has gone too far.

That, of course, is part of growing up, and a lesson that each guy learns in different ways in *American Reunion.* Yet these friends never stab each other in the back. They are there if a drunk, topless eighteen-year-old needs to be snuck back into her parents' house.

They are there if one of the guys stands outside in leather shorts and suspenders while facing a beat-down from a high school kid. And they are there if an ex's current flame—in this case, it's the cardiologist boyfriend (Jay Harrington) of Oz's ex, Heather (Mena Suvari)—needs to be put in his place. Rather than lamenting where they are, Jim and his pals discover how to reevaluate and enjoy being there together.

That feels so much truer and warmer than so many R-rated comedies, especially those starring Adam Sandler, which revolve around malicious deception and make light of various forms of insensitivity. In *American Reunion*, the heroes always mean well, and Stifler's idiocy only makes him look like someone with a lot of issues to work on. Clearly, being thirty-one does not automatically equal being thirteen years wiser and more mature than eighteen. Says Jessica (Natasha Lyonne) to Kevin at the reunion, "Be a real man; you have a beard now." If only it were that easy.

Matt Pais

CREDITS

Jim Levenstein: Jason Biggs
Michelle Flaherty-Levenstein: Alyson Hannigan
Chris "Oz" Ostreicher: Chris Klein
Kevin Myers: Thomas Ian Nicholas
Victoria "Vicky" Lathum: Tara Reid
Steve Stifler: Seann William Scott
Heather: Mena Suvari
Paul Finch: Eddie Kaye Thomas
Stifler's Mom: Jennifer Coolidge
Jim's Dad: Eugene Levy
Jessica: Natasha Lyonne
Nadia: Shannon Elizabeth
Chuck Sherman: Chris Owen
Origin: United States
Language: English
Released: 2012
Production: Adam Herz, Chris Moore, Craig Perry, Warren Zide; Practical Pictures, Relativity Media; released by Universal Pictures
Directed by: Jon Hurwitz; Hayden Schlossberg
Written by: Jon Hurwitz; Hayden Schlossberg
Cinematography by: Daryn Okada
Music by: Lyle Workman; JoJo Villanueva
Sound: Dave McMoyler
Music Supervisor: Angela Leus
Editing: Jeff Betancourt
Art Direction: Elliott Glick
Costumes: Mona May
Production Design: William Arnold

MPAA rating: R
Running time: 113 minutes

REVIEWS

Berardinelli, James. *ReelViews*. April 8, 2012.
Ebert, Roger. *Chicago Sun-Times*. April 4, 2012.
Gleiberman, Owen. *Entertainment Weekly*. April 4, 2012.
Chang, Justin. *Variety*. April 4, 2012.
Phipps, Keith. *AV Club*. April 4, 2012.
Puig, Claudia. *USA Today*. April 5, 2012.
Rothkopf, Joshua. *Time Out New York*. April 3, 2012.
Savlov, Marc. *Austin Chronicle*. April 4, 2012.
Schager, Nick. *Slant Magazine*. April 4, 2012.
Zacharek, Stephanie. *Movieline*. April 5, 2012.

QUOTES

Jim Levenstein: "Stifler's having a party tonight. Okay, I know that doesn't sound romantic or anything, but remember our first time was at a Stifler party. You made me your bitch."
Michelle: "Yes. Yes I did."

TRIVIA

At eight films, Eugene Levy has become the only actor to be in every film in the franchise.

AMOUR

Box Office: $5.1 million

In America, the elderly are typically relegated to secondary film roles that offer up saccharine sentimentality. Occasionally, filmmakers break through with something deeper. *Harold and Maude* (1971), *Going In Style* (1979), *Venus* (2006), and *Beginners* (2010) are all lovely films that offer insights about aging. But they are primarily about making the best out of what time is left. Even Sarah Polley's poignant *Away from Her* (2006), which finds some solace in the midst of Alzheimer's Disease is a walk in the park next to Michael Haneke's masterful *Amour* which sets the conversation about aging, quality of life, and death solidly in the confines of marriage and the limitations of human endurance.

Winner of the Cannes Film Festival 2012 Palme D'or, *Amour* has been called a radical departure for the Austrian director who is best known for controversial works like *Funny Games* (1997, 2007) but *Amour* signals itself as a Haneke film from the first few moments. A fire brigade breaks into an apartment to investigate a suspicious odor. They find a grim tableau over which Haneke superimposes the title of his film. The words disturbing, incongruous, will immediately leap to many viewers minds. Especially after they encounter the subject of the tableau in the next scene enjoying a concert with a loved one, enjoying a backstage meeting with the artist, and quietly riding the train home as the concert music continues to sound mellifluously on the soundtrack. It is only the beginning of the constant series of conscious juxtapositions that Haneke creates to illustrate the paradox of love.

Georges (Jean-Louis Trintignant) and Anne (Emmanuelle Riva), two elderly, retired music teachers arrive home to find a locked door that someone has tried to pry open during an attempted break-in. Unsettled they still simply go to bed, deciding to work on the problem after a good night's sleep. But what awaits them is unlike any other day they have experienced in their many years of wedded bliss. As Georges speaks to Anne over breakfast she suddenly stares off into space, unresponsive. Despite his efforts to gently coax her out of this state she only emerges minutes later and begins to pour coffee onto a saucer rather than into a cup.

Haneke does not dress up his characters in easy sentiment but in a raw reality that invites empathy. After it becomes fully apparent that Anne has suffered a stroke, Haneke has the courage to linger on the couple's darkened home, roaming room to room in a series of static shots that show it silent and empty though it is also clearly lived in and full of the possessions acquired over a shared lifetime. The moment provides transition not only through the couple's subsequent journey into the unknown but serves as a reminder that even a well-ordered personal universe can quickly empty out into a vacuum of unknowing. In the following sequence, the couple's daughter Eva (Isabelle Huppert) speaks privately to Georges. She is clearly upset over her mother's condition but the conversation turns to her husband's infidelity. She has taken him back. Concerned, Georges asks "But do you love him?," to which she replies "Yes, I think so." Clearly love is a mystery in Haneke's stark universe.

"Your mother and I have always coped" George assures Eva when she presses about what Anne's stroke will require. But of course coping is not the same thing as love. Neither is coping always what is best for all involved. Soon, Georges is overwhelmed and the film becomes a journey bordered by moments, small victories, light in tone and larger, more common defeats in which the moments of darkness slowly seems to swallow a once vibrant and happy couple. A surrender is underway. Describing a funeral to Anne, who has had to stay behind due to her being wheelchair bound, Georges lays out a scene relentlessly farcical, almost devoid of dignity. Staring into space, Anne simply asks whether it is perhaps time for her to die for both their sake, a sugges-

tion that Georges brushes off, but not without a shudder: the first major hint that Haneke is hinging his narrative upon notions of quality of life.

Anne is not alone in her doubts. Georges has, at her urging, promised his wife there will be no future hospitalizations, no extraordinary measures, and despite the help of nurses (some of whom prove inept and require dismissal amidst much argument and vitriol), he feels his own limitations grow with each passing day. Suddenly, their life together spares no one's feelings. Beauty, strength, ability, even memory, all become lost investments. To live is to age and finally to die. The relentlessness of it is a wearing down where menial tasks take on a weight that would require heroism if only that heroism was something more than debilitating. To hope becomes simply a point of view rooted in no particular reality. Reality subsumes, consumes. Every fiber of being, every bit of attention, must be put to the unsolvable problem, of survival.

It is startling how subdued *Amour* is. Almost all the cold mechanics of body fluid and function that Haneke could use to shock his audience are hidden largely from view yet he makes them felt more powerfully than can be elaborated here. The bathings, the toiletries, the feedings, and the ever growing difficulties in understanding one another are brought to life seemingly through a dearth of artifice and yet it is simply that Haneke is in such command of his medium that viewers simply never take notice of him, or his camera, his subtle framing. They are simply affected by it. Moved in a way that only a master can provoke.

There is something deeply poignant about watching acclaimed actor Jean-Louis Trintignant assay the part of Georges. In 1956 he became the object of intense scrutiny over rumor of an affair with Brigitte Bardot with whom he starred in ....*And God Created Woman* (1956). Other roles have included major parts in Costa Gravas' *Z* (1969), Bernardo Bertolucci's *The Conformist* (1970), and Krzysztof Kieslowski's *Three Colors: Red* (1994). *Amour* sees him full circle, as a man in a tortured and problematic relationship and he tackles the opportunity with every bit of power at his disposal.

Anne is played by the equally accomplished Emmanuelle Riva. After being discovered by Alain Resnais and cast as the lead in his historic French New Wave film *Hiroshima, mon amour* (1959) the future looked promising. But in the intervening decades she was rarely cast in material that was worthy of her. Roles in Jean-Pierre Melville's *Leon Morin, Priest* (1961) and *Three Colors: Blue* (1993) notwithstanding, it appeared she would never again rise to the heights her early career provided. But with *Amour* she is poised, to share an immense talent once again on a scale that befits her. It is worth remarking that Riva has the far harder job of the two leads as she is forced to convey meaning without dialogue for at least two thirds of the film. Her eyes haunted by the loss of the ability to communicate as her illness progresses sometimes devolve into a stupor. At times, she cries out mournfully and repeatedly "Hurts," when nothing is discernibly wrong. At others, she betrays no sign of her plight, singing along with her husband in a sing-song manner that has become virtually the only true verbal communication that has been left to them.

What becomes of Georges and Anne will challenge any thinking person to examine their own questions about marriage, death, dying, and even human community. Above all things, Haneke seems to suggest that love demands things of people that only they can understand. To love may be to go mad or at least appear mad to others. Haneke unsettles precisely because he does not make any value judgments on such questions. When he is pilloried by critics, which happens less and less these days, it is often for exactly this reason. The irony is that only this humility allows him to deal so masterfully with this subject matter at all.

Haneke has been busy making movies for the ages for a while now. *The Piano Teacher* (2001), *Time of the Wolf* (2003), *Cache (Hidden)* (2005), and *The White Ribbon* (2009) are films that offer timeless narrative. With each effort, he seems to deepen his ability to use his chosen artistic medium to communicate ever more complex observations about the human condition.

Dave Canfield

CREDITS

Georges Laurent: Jean-Louis Trintignant
Anne Laurent: Emmanuelle Riva
Eva: Isabelle Huppert
Alexandre: Alexandre Tharaud
Geoff: William Shimell
Origin: France, Austria
Language: French
Released: 2012
Production: Margaret Menegoz, Michael Katz, Veit Heiduschka, Stefan Arndt; released by Sony Pictures Classics
Directed by: Michael Haneke
Written by: Michael Haneke
Cinematography by: Darius Khondji
Music by: Cecile Lenoir
Sound: Guillaume Sciama
Editing: Monika Willi; Nadine Muse
Costumes: Catherine Leterrier
Production Design: Jean-Vincent Puzos
MPAA rating: PG-13
Running time: 125 minutes

REVIEWS

Andrews, Nigel. *Financial Times.* November 15, 2012.
Dargis, Manhola. *New York Times.* May 22, 2012.
Fragosa, Sam. *Fan The Fire.* September 18, 2012.
French, Philip. *Observer [UK].* November 18, 2012.
Robey, Tim. *Daily Telegraph.* November 15, 2012.
Taylor, Ella. *NPR.* December 18, 2012.
Turner, Matthew. *ViewLondon.* November 15, 2012.
Whitty, Stephen. *Newark Star-Ledger.* December 20, 2012.
Willmore, Alison. *Movieline.* December 12, 2012.

QUOTES

Anne: "What would you say if no one came to your funeral?"
Georges: "Nothing, presumably."

TRIVIA

According to Jean-Louis Trintignant, one of the biggest reasons the pigeon scenes took so long to shoot was due to the fact that Michael Haneke tried to constantly direct the animal.

AWARDS

Oscars 2012: Foreign Film
British Acad. 2012: Actress (Riva), Foreign Film
Golden Globes 2013: Foreign Film
Ind. Spirit 2013: Foreign Film
Nominations:
Oscars 2012: Actress (Riva), Director (Haneke), Film, Orig. Screenplay
British Acad. 2012: Director (Haneke), Orig. Screenplay

ANNA KARENINA

You can't ask why about love.
—Movie tagline

Box Office: $12.7 million

Director Joe Wright had to know he was strolling into a literary, cultural, and cinematic minefield when he decided to do yet another film version of Leo Tolstoy's classic 1877 novel *Anna Karenina*. The director, who in the past has taken on lofty literary endeavors such as *Pride and Prejudice* (2005) and *Atonement* (2007), also had to know that once he decided to stylistically set most of the action in screenwriter Tom Stoppard's crackling sharp adaptation on, behind, around, and above an imaginary theater stage it was akin to taking off running through said minefield.

After all, fans of Tolstoy are constantly on the lookout for ways in which *Anna Karenina* movies fail the Russian author's hefty and brilliant novel, especially when the book's characters—whose complex internal lives are so richly painted on the page—are misrepresented or cut out completely. Likewise, Wright's "theater stage" trick runs the risk of alienating both lovers of straight-forward period films and audiences and critics quick to pounce on any sense of misguided, off-putting aesthetic gimmickry.

But while this new *Anna Karenina* may still frustrate or alienate some members of all those parties, for the most part Wright's bold gamble works beautifully. Up front, the British director has assembled a strong cast, led by his *Pride and Prejudice* and *Atonement* star Keira Knightley as the title's doomed adulteress; with Aaron Taylor-Johnson as Vronsky, the dashing cavalry officer whose love ensnares Anna; and Jude Law as Anna's husband Karenin. The film is shored up by supporting work by a finely comic Matthew Macfadyen as Anna's philandering brother Oblonsky and an earnest Kelly Macdonald as his long-suffering wife Dolly.

Best of all, Wright and Stoppard have gone out of their way to make room for the existential-minded farmer Levin (Domhnall Gleeson) and his unrequited love for Dolly's younger sister Kitty (Alicia Vikander). Though Levin, a literary stand-in for Tolstoy himself, occupies fully half the novel, many film adaptations minimize or completely excise him and his philosophical quandaries in order to focus directly on the sexier, more melodramatic tale of Anna's scandalous, tragic love triangle. This time the filmmakers do not give Levin half the running time, but they do carefully fold him into the narrative and themes.

The inclusion of Levin, played by the open-faced Gleeson with the right mix of trust and frustration, is important, since Levin and Kitty's eventual tender and honest love is the book's redeeming embrace of what is "good" and "right," set in counterbalance to Anna and Vronsky's sensational but dangerous carnal passion. The new film understands that *Anna Karenina* is not a "love story" but rather a story about love. Wright makes it clear that Anna is denied her true love with Vronsky not just because the aristocratic society of the time felt she "broke the rules," but because she lets an idea of romantic love lead her down a foolish, impulsive, and ultimately self-destructive path.

A sometimes chilly actress, Knightley plays Anna more as the hopeless architect of her own crisis than a good-hearted innocent wronged; her welcoming smile at times bordering on a demure sneer, other times slightly aghast at others' and her own behavior. Taylor-Johnson's Vronsky is also intentionally no strapping, romantic

hero. Petulant in his bright uniforms, his predatory sullenness slinks around a selfishly entitled decadence. It can be hard to see what about this smug and callow Vronksy sweeps this Anna off her feet, but that is Wright's point: Presenting a perfectly matched Anna and Vronsky as ideal romantic specimens would have tilted the tale too far toward *Romeo and Juliet* territory.

Anna's cuckolded husband can be an even trickier character for modern audiences to accept. It is easy to dismiss Karenin as a stubborn foil to Anna and Vronsky's love, but Law's quiet, thoughtful version is no villain or sniveling victim. Instead, though stern and stuffy in his dutiful impotence, he is trying to let his faith in the laws of God and man guide his morality and honor.

But it is Wright's "stage" device that is the best thing about his *Anna Karenina*. This is not a filmed play, and the theater in which much of the action takes place (including the famous steeplechase) is not a fixed or even realistic space. Events spill over into the wider room, flowing through the seats and backstage as well as up into the fly. At one point, the theater's loft area transforms into a gritty Moscow street. And when focusing on Levin's farm, the theater is abandoned completely for a more naturalistic outdoor setting.

Not only does this allow Wright to move the story's many characters and narrative pieces around more quickly and smoothly (at one point Levin walks through the back of the stage into a genuine snowy St. Petersburg field), but the shifting sets strongly reinforce the themes. Yes, aristocratic Russian society is clearly presented as an artificial construction, but Anna also seems trapped in Karenin's mansion, especially in her beloved son's bedroom, which feels alternately like a warm, safe womb and a claustrophobic coffin. (Meanwhile, out in the "real" outdoors, Levin finds calming peace mowing alongside his farm's workers.)

Never frantic or silly, *Anna Karenina* deftly embraces this sort of artifice as Wright toys with the ways in which Tolstoy's story is both traditional and modern, both melodramatic and psychological. The stylistic conceit also keeps the director on his toes. The film never lulls into the easy, luxurious stupor of just another costume drama. Instead the proceedings are filled with cinematic energy from the constant, roving tension between the fake "fake" and the fake "real" and the stunning ways the action swings between the two. (Sometimes the fateful train from Petersburg to Moscow is obviously a miniature toy, sometimes it charges onto the stage life-size and covered in real snow.)

This is a sprawling story full of complicated characters and motivations, and Wright cannot capture it all perfectly. It could be argued that a familiarity with the novel and its persona dramatis is helpful when navigating the film's narrative (and who is who and related to whom), just as it could be argued that a film should stand on its own, free from its source material, no matter how canonical that material may be. But the director has taken a daring chance, neither abandoning fidelity to the novel nor sticking to the standard rules for classic-lit period films. The result is an *Anna Karenina* that is dazzling and invigorating both as cinema and as an adaptation.

Anna Karenina had a relatively wide art-house release and performed modestly at the box office (it did much better overseas), but the film's stylistic choices seemed to divide both audiences and critics. Ann Hornaday of the *Washington Post* felt that, "Like the masterpiece that inspired it, *Anna Karenina* poses some of life's toughest questions—about how to be good, how to be bad and the costs of both—but with nuance and sensuousness that make even its most profound truths levitate on flights of soaring imagination and pure poetry." On the opposite side, Mick LaSalle of the *San Francisco Chronicle* wrote, "*Anna Karenina* is a failure emotionally and dramatically...[Wright] adopts the strategy of telling the story at a distance, as a stylized piece, and along the way he comes up with beautiful compositions and seamless transitions. His work is audacious and at times impressive, but ultimately, bloodless. If you can't make an audience care about Anna Karenina in a movie called *Anna Karenina*, you haven't really made *Anna Karenina*."

Locke Peterseim

CREDITS

Anna Karenina: Keira Knightley
Alexei Karenin: Jude Law
Count Vronsky: Aaron Taylor-Johnson
Dolly: Kelly Macdonald
Oblonsky: Matthew MacFadyen
Countess Lydia: Emily Watson
Countess Vronskaya: Olivia Williams
Levin: Domhnall Gleeson
Kitty: Alicia Vikander
Origin: United Kingdom
Language: English
Released: 2012
Production: Tim Bevan, Paul Webster; Universal Pictures, Working Title; released by Focus Features
Directed by: Joe Wright
Written by: Tom Stoppard
Cinematography by: Seamus McGarvey
Music by: Dario Marianelli
Sound: Craig Berkey

Music Supervisor: Maggie Rodford
Editing: Melanie Oliver
Art Direction: Niall Moroney
Costumes: Jacqueline Durran
Production Design: Sarah Greenwood
MPAA rating: R
Running time: 130 minutes

REVIEWS

Hornaday, Ann. *Washington Post.* November 16, 2012.
LaSalle, Mick. *San Francisco Chronicle.* November 15, 2012.
O'Hehir, Andrew. *Salon.* November 15, 2012.
Phipps, Keith. *AV Club.* November 15, 2012.
Pinkerton, Nick. *Village Voice.* November 14, 2012.
Scott, A. O. *New York Times.* November 15, 2012.
Scott, Mike. *New Orleans Times-Picayune.* November 30, 2012.
Sharkey, Betsey. *Los Angeles Times.* November 15, 2012.
Willmore, Alison. *Movieline.* November 16, 2012.

QUOTES

Levin: "Sensual desire indulged for its own sake is the misuse of something sacred."

TRIVIA

At one point, Robert Pattinson was considered to play Count Vronsky.

AWARDS

Oscars 2012: Costume Des.
British Acad. 2012: Costume Des.
Nominations:
Oscars 2012: Cinematog., Orig. Score, Production Design
British Acad. 2012: Cinematog., Makeup, Orig. Score, Production Design
Golden Globes 2013: Orig. Score

THE APPARITION

Once you believe, you die.
—Movie tagline

Box Office: $4.9 million

With its slapdash nature, its tiresome reliance on the overused "found footage" gimmick and an ending so abrupt and unsatisfying that it signaled a basic contempt for anyone who paid money to bear witness to it, the cheapo horror film *The Devil Inside* (2012) was roundly derided by critics and audiences alike, although enough of the latter ignored enough of the former to give it a frighteningly lucrative opening weekend. That said, it did prove to be oddly comforting for legions of horror fans in a weird way—no matter what curve balls the genre might throw at them, there was no possibility that there could be a worse film of that type released in the remainder of 2012. Well, with a little more than four months left in the year, that promise was broken with the emergence of *The Apparition,* a spook story so bafflingly bad on every possible level that if one were to put it up against the legendarily klutzy likes of *Plan 9 from Outer Space* (1959) or *Manos: The Hands of Fate* (1966), there is an excellent chance that it would come out as being the poorer in the eyes of most viewers.

After no fewer than two introductory prologues—including one so incredibly superfluous to the rest of the proceedings that it seems to have been tacked on from another movie in a desperate bid to drag the film kicking and screaming to a feature length—the story proper opens as comely veterinary trainee Kelly (Ashley Greene) and her dopey techie boyfriend Ben (Sebastian Stan) head off to a remote housing development—the kind of place where one gets a definite moved-the-headstones-but-left-the-bodies vibe—to open up one of the homes for her mother to sell. They have hardly begun to settle in when the expected weird things begin to happen—doors open and close of their own accord, huge outbreaks of mold suddenly appear and the shower curtain becomes just opaque enough when Kelly turns up for an elongated rinsing to keep the proceedings well within the confines of a PG-13 rating. After this goes on for what feels like seventeen hours but which is probably only about seventeen minutes or so, Kelly discovers that Ben has not been honest about his past. It seems that a few years earlier, he took part in a college experiment engineered by colleague Patrick (Tom Felton) designed to lure and capture a spirit and prove once and for all that ghosts really exist. Unsurprisingly, things went gunny back then and now that same spirit has returned to destroy those that freed it, anyone that they love and any poor schmuck, neighborhood puppy or cactus that gets in the way.

The Apparition was presumably launched hurriedly into production in an effort to cash in on the popularity of the ridiculous and ridiculously popular *Paranormal Activity* series by ripping them off completely, but as shocking as it may sound (and this may be the only time in which the word "shocking" can legitimately be used in context with this movie), it actually does even less with them than the *PA* films. Aside from serving as a splendid showcase for Ashley Greene's legs, it not only fails to do anything right but does everything so spectacularly wrong that it appears to have been made by people who have only heard about what constitutes a proper horror film by osmosis. The story, for example, is such a mess in regards to even the most basic fundamen-

tals of narrative that it will no doubt give hope to many aspiring screenwriters on the basis that if something as half-assed and incoherent as this can get produced and released, imagine what might be done with something that makes sense.

The direction by Todd Lincoln is so incompetent that it seems as though it has been made by someone who has never even seen a film before—the entire thing seems like a random assemblage of footage mistakenly retrieved from the cutting room incinerator (such as the endless scenes of shopping for cacti and camping equipment at Costco that comprise the drowsy opening reel) and generates zero scares, tension, excitement or any known emotional reactions outside of incredulous laughter or unceasing boredom. "How boring is it?", one might ask. It is so boring that if you could magically transform this film into music, the entire thing would be a drum solo. It is so boring that a bit in which Kelly peels some linoleum off the floor is the closest that it comes to breakneck action.

Of course, when a movie gets reviews as bad as the ones that *The Apparition* generated, there is always a certain sector willing to embrace it as some kind of unintentionally hilarious camp classic—witness the cult fandom that has sprung up around the likes of the aforementioned *Plan 9* and *Manos* or the more recent *The Room* (2003). Do not be fooled for a minute, though, because this is one of the most excruciating wastes of 74 perfectly good minutes (not counting the protracted end credit roll) imaginable.

Peter Sobczynski

CREDITS

Kelly: Ashley Greene
Ben: Sebastian Stan
Patrick: Tom Felton
Lydia: Julianna Guill
Greg: Luke Pasqualino
Mike: Rick Gomez
Origin: United States
Language: English
Released: 2012
Production: Joel Silver, Andrew Rona, Alex Heineman, Todd Lincoln; Dark Castle Entertainment; released by Warner Bros.
Directed by: Todd Lincoln
Written by: Todd Lincoln
Cinematography by: Daniel Pearl
Music by: tomandandy
Sound: Mark Larry
Editing: Jeff Betancourt; Harold Parker

Costumes: Kimberly Adams-Galligan
Production Design: Steve Saklad
MPAA rating: PG-13
Running time: 82 minutes

REVIEWS

DeFore, John. *Hollywood Reporter.* August 24, 2012.
Dujsik, Mark. *Mark Reviews Movies.* August 23, 2012.
Kenigsberg, Ben. *Time Out New York.* August 24, 2012.
Leydon, Joe. *Variety.* August 24, 2012.
Miska, Brad. *Bloody Disgusting.* August 24, 2012.
Pais, Matt. *RedEye.* August 23, 2012.
Phipps, Keith. *AV Club.* August 24, 2012.
Tallerico, Brian. *HollywoodChicago.com.* August 23, 2012.
Verniere, James. *Boston Herald.* August 25, 2012.
Weinberg, Scott. *FEARnet.* August 24, 2012.

QUOTES

Maggie: "Your house killed my dog."

TRIVIA

The film's release was delayed for over two years after Warner Bros. ended its relationship with Dark Castle Entertainment. When finally released, the film was given the smallest wide-release Warner Bros. had ever given a major motion picture in its distribution history.

ARBITRAGE

> *Power is the best alibi.*
> —Movie tagline

Box Office: $7.9 million

Despite inhabiting two disparate genres—half tense crime thriller and half lifestyles-of-the-very-rich financial drama—*Arbitrage* succeeds admirably at them both. That success is in part due to first-time feature director Nicholas Jarecki's sure hand at juggling parallel cop and capitalism plotlines alongside hefty recession-era themes, but *Arbitrage* also owes a big "thanks" to its smoothly riveting star, Richard Gere.

Gere plays Robert Miller, the billionaire manager of a lucrative hedge fund who projects a burnished air of gently humble superiority over his lavish upper East Side home and well-comported family (including Susan Sarandon as his wife and Brit Marling as his daughter and business partner). No slimy, greedy plutocrat, Miller is presented as a hard-working and generous self-made man, but he is also in the middle of a shaky deal to sell his valuable hedge fund and has illegally shored up some losses in order to smooth the sale. And though he seems a loving husband and father, he slips out of his 60th birthday party early to visit his French mistress.

Even in a post-financial crash, Occupy Wall Street world, the viewer is inclined to root for Miller—Gere has built his career on playing morally complex (if not confused) characters, usually winning (and sometimes betraying) audience sympathy with his immense reserves of smoldering charisma. Age has not dulled those beguiling attributes—if anything, Gere has become more seductive, his once-dangerous edge now balanced with conniving life-experience that allows him to negotiate around morality.

Working from his own original screenplay, Jarecki puts Gere's duplicitous charms to good use, especially when Miller is involved in an accidental death that risks exposure of both his family and business illusions. Where *Arbitrage* opens amid the warm, fire-lit wine and whiskey commercial glow of safe and comfortable wealth, the film shifts into a crime and court procedural, drawing in Tim Roth as a rumpled and dogged detective and Nate Parker as a relatively innocent acquaintance of Miller's, now entangled in one of Robert's growing lies.

From there, *Arbitrage* takes on more visual grit and moral gray tone, Miller's perfect suits and disarming grin hiding legal troubles and a more tarnished principled duplicity and dishonesty. For all his insistences otherwise, to Miller money is not a thing to be had, to buy more things with, but rather a philosophical goal to be achieved, a race to be won. Jarecki beautifully creates a sense that lies also become living things, growing and taking on dangerous power.

Jarecki himself comes from a wealthy New York family—his father was an academic and later a commodity trader, and his older brothers Andrew and Eugene are smart, incisive feature and documentary film makers. As a result, the director navigates Miller's world with a deft understanding of both money's power and perks and its destructive magnetism. And Roth infuses his Detective Bryer with enough post-2008, justice-fueled, class anger to make the crime narrative sizzle.

Gere is at his silver-maned, cornered-lion best when mired in deepening moral compromises—he takes the audiences' affection for Richard Gere the movie star and uses it to grease Robert's slide from confident to concerned, his handsome face masking the growing number of lies even as the character is, literally, falling apart on the inside. The viewer still wants to root for him through both financial malfeasance and adultery, but once Jarecki has the audience hooked, he tests its allegiance, asking just how long Miller continues to deserve sympathy.

Meanwhile, deals and deadlines loom, negotiations and investigations proceed, and voices are raised louder in confrontations in bedrooms, boardrooms, and courtrooms. *Arbitrage* ultimately wants to meld the crime and finance themes together, making the not-so-subtle point that the rich believe they can get away with anything, no matter what kind of court they land in. Fronted by Gere and guided by Jarecki, *Arbitrage* is smart enough to be more than its parts, but it rarely overreaches in an attempt to ram home an overt message—the film seems satisfied to be a crackling crime drama, albeit one with a little class injustice on its mind.

Arbitrage received a limited North American release in the fall, coinciding with its home availability via Video on Demand. The film earned nearly $8 million in domestic theaters and another $14 million overseas, where Gere's international name-recognition remains strong. It fared even better with critics, earning mostly positive reviews. Bilge Ebiri of *Vulture* noted, "There are holes in the plot, to be sure, but somehow we don't mind, because for all the unbearable tension of Jarecki's script, the central attraction here is the man in the arena: Gere has been a punchline so often that it's kind of startling when he gets a chance to really act." On the other hand, Amy Nicholson of *Movieline* felt, "Gere does his best to give *Arbitrage* an agitated energy, but Jarecki's fatalism works against the film. We can't root for Miller; instead, we watch with dispassionate interest how the fallout of his misdeeds affects his friends, business partners and family."

Locke Peterseim

CREDITS

Robert Miller: Richard Gere
Ellen Miller: Susan Sarandon
Det. Michael Bryer: Tim Roth
Brooke Miller: Brit Marling
Julie Cote: Laetitia Casta
Jimmy Grant: Nate Parker
Origin: United States
Language: English
Released: 2012
Production: Laura Bickford, Robert Salerno, Kevin Turen, Justin Nappi; Alvernia Studios, Parlay Films, Lionsgate; released by Roadside Attractions
Directed by: Nicholas Jarecki
Written by: Nicholas Jarecki
Cinematography by: Yorick Le Saux
Music by: Cliff Martinez
Sound: Tod A. Maitland
Music Supervisor: Michael Perlmutter
Editing: Douglas Crise
Art Direction: Michael Ahern

Costumes: Joseph G. Aulisi
Production Design: Beth Mickle
MPAA rating: R
Running time: 107 minutes

REVIEWS

Burr, Ty. *Boston Globe*. September 13, 2012.
Dargis, Manohla. *New York Times*. September 13, 2012.
Ebert, Roger. *Chicago Sun-Times*. September 12, 2012.
Ebiri, Bilge. *Vulture*. September 13, 2012.
Hornaday, Ann. *Washington Post*. September 14, 2012.
Murray, Noel. *AV Club*. September 13, 2012.
Nicholson, Amy. *Movieline*. September 13, 2012.
Phillips, Michael. *Chicago Tribune*. September 13, 2012.
Pols, Mary. *Time*. September 13, 2012.
Sharkey, Betsey. *Los Angeles Times*. September 13, 2012.

QUOTES

Ellen Miller: "It's all going to be fine. It always is. Just follow the plan."
Robert Miller: "And what is that plan?"
Ellen Miller: "Confidence equals contract."
Robert Miller: "You sound like a fortune cookie."
Ellen Miller: "They are your words, actually."
Robert Miller: "Then you married an idiot."

TRIVIA

Richard Gere replaced Al Pacino in the role of Robert Miller.

AWARDS

Nominations:
Golden Globes 2013: Actor—Drama (Gere)

ARGO

The movie was fake. The mission was real.
    —Movie tagline
Based on the declassified true story.
    —Movie tagline

Box Office: $127. 4 million

Ben Affleck turned a notable corner in his effort to distinguish his work as a director to the same or higher degree as his on-screen level of success with the massively acclaimed and financially successful *Argo*, easily one of the best films of 2012 and a frontrunner for the Oscar for Best Picture despite Affleck's inexplicable absence from the list of nominees for Best Director. Despite missing out in that Academy category, Affleck won the Director's Guild of America Award for his work on the "recently declassified true story" and the film won the Producers Guild and Screen Actors Guild grand prizes. After an awards season in which it looked like Kathryn Bigelow's *Zero Dark Thirty* (2012) or Steven Spielberg's *Lincoln* (2012) would join the exclusive club of Academy Award winners for Best Picture, *Argo* snuck up and appears to be the likely winner at the time of this review's writing. How did Affleck's film become one of the most popular films for viewers and awards givers from 2012? It was the least divisive. Since its Toronto Film Festival and Telluride Film Festival premieres, it became the one film for which it seemed everyone could agree on its quality. Some dismissed it as not quite as good as their favorites of the year but everyone at least agreed that it was a notable film with fine-tuned direction from Affleck, as solid an ensemble as any film from the year, and an amazing true story. Sometimes a film needs to just be liked by all instead of loved by a few to be the consensus choice.

In November 1979, a group of insurgents stormed the U.S. Embassy in Tehran to protest the American asylum given the Shah of Iran after his dethroning following years of dictatorial rule. Before they could be taken hostage, six staff members (Tate Donovan, Clea DuVall, Christopher Denham, Scoot McNairy, Kerry Bishe, and Rory Cochrane) escaped out a back door. They made their way to the home of the Canadian Ambassador Ken Taylor (Victor Garber) and waited to be rescued. As the world watched the hostage crisis stretch on at the Embassy, a select group of exfiltration experts plotted to figure out how to get the six men and women home again.

Led by Tony Mendez (Ben Affleck) and his supervisor Jack O'Donnell (Bryan Cranston), the CIA devised an ingenious plan. How could they get the sextet through the airport without questions being asked as to how they were in Iran in the first place? Mendez, playing off his and his son's love for science fiction films, concocted a cover story in which the six would be members of a film production scouting locations. He went to a make-up artist who had helped the CIA in the past named John Chambers (John Goodman) and a film producer named Lester Siegel (Alan Arkin) and they built a back story and fictional future around a movie that did not exist. They grabbed a sci-fi script called *Argo,* opened a production office, and even staged a table read to get press in *Variety.* After the cover story was built, Mendez travelled to Iran and walked the men and women now masquerading as filmmakers on to a plane and home again.

Ben Affleck's previous two directorial efforts—*Gone Baby Gone* (2007) and *The Town* (2010)—displayed the fingerprints of a filmmaker clearly concerned with detail and atmosphere to a degree that drew comparisons to the gritty craftsmen of the '70s like William Friedkin, Francis Ford Coppola, and Sidney Lumet. While those works were undeniably accomplished pieces of directing, *Argo* is a step forward for Affleck the director in every way. Working with a perfectly structured script by Chris Terrio that moves seamlessly between the comedic underpinnings of Goodman and Arkin's skewering of Hollywood to the edge-of-seat tension of the action in Tehran, Affleck never misses a beat in terms of pace and tonal balance. *Argo* is one of those films that is always one step ahead of the viewer, switching genre unexpectedly while producing tension from the remarkable realism of the piece.

Affleck is ably assisted by a technical team that was among the best of the year. Master cinematographer Rodrigo Prieto has been somewhat flashy in works like *Babel* (2006) and *Brokeback Mountain* (2005) but he tones it down here, finding ways to express the claustrophobia of being prisoner in the Ambassador's house and even outside in a country where death could be imminent. Prieto shoots a scene in a crowded bazaar with the perfect balance of close-up and crowd shots to a tension-building degree that he has not been given nearly enough credit. The editing by William Goldenberg (who also co-edited *Zero Dark Thirty*), the lovely score by Alexandre Desplat, the perfect production design—Affleck uses all of his elements like a masterful conductor uses various instruments in his orchestra.

He also proves himself to be a stellar director in terms of his work with actors, drawing great supporting performances from Alan Arkin (who was nominated for the Oscar for Best Supporting Actor), Scoot McNairy, John Goodman, and Bryan Cranston. Even minor roles are fully fleshed out by great character actors like Richard Kind, Michael Parks, Kyle Chandler, and Victor Garber. There is not a single false performance in *Argo* and Affleck's DGA win was at least in part for the way he balanced a cast with dozens of notable speaking roles as much as it was for the way he used technical elements to produce tension.

As for Affleck the actor, his turn as Tony Mendez was incorrectly criticized by some for being too stolid but that misses the point of this character, who in reality was actually the subject of an episode of Errol Morris' *First Person* called "The Little Gray Man," in which it was detailed that Mendez was intentionally non-descript, the kind of guy who one could spend time with on an elevator but not be able to describe in any notable way. He must blend in with his environment to be a successful exfiltration expert. And so Affleck's reserved performance fits the character. It is not unlike Tom Hanks' work in *Apollo 13* (1995) in the way it is meant to guide the film almost as a straight man to the more vibrant personalities around him. Affleck is very good here both as director and actor. He got notable credit for the former but nowhere near enough for the latter.

Ultimately, *Argo* is like a well-made clock. Every piece fits. Every wheel, cog, screw of filmmaking connects in such a way that there is nary a flaw in the production. Some argued that Affleck's film was too distant, presenting tension without enough humanity or character but those critics know not of what they ask. An *Argo* that took more time for drama would lose out on tension. One that took more time for Hollywood satire would not be the thriller that this film ended up. Ben Affleck found in this story what so many other directors try to achieve their entire career—perfect tonal balance. The tension works, the comedy works, the characters work. It is all there and, when all was said and done, it made the film a worthy choice for the Oscar for the best of 2012.

Audiences fell in love with *Argo,* not only giving the film an "A" on Cinemascore but propelling it to over $120 million domestically at the time of this review (when it was still making money on an awards season re-release) and almost $200 million internationally. (Critics adored the film as well with numerous Critics Associations nominating and awarding the work and 242 out of 253 critics giving the film a "Fresh" rating on Rotten Tomatoes). It was actually Affleck's highest grosser as an actor in over a decade (2001's *Pearl Harbor*). The actor Ben Affleck has struggled for a few years to match the acclaim of his debut (1997's *Good Will Hunting*) or the peak of his popularity as a leading man. It turned out he needed to go behind the camera as well as the movie about a film that was never really made ended up the most important of his career.

Brian Tallerico

CREDITS

Tony Mendez: Ben Affleck
Lester Siegel: Alan Arkin
Jack O'Donnell: Bryan Cranston
John Chambers: John Goodman
Hamilton Jordan: Kyle Chandler
Lee Schatz: Rory Cochrane
Bob Anders: Tate Donovan
Jon Bates: Titus Welliver
Max Klein: Richard Kind
Ken Taylor: Victor Garber
Cora Lijek: Clea DuVall
Christine Mendez: Taylor Schilling
Origin: United States
Language: English
Released: 2012

Production: George Clooney, Grant Heslov, Ben Affleck; GK Films, Smokehouse Pictures; released by Warner Bros.
Directed by: Ben Affleck
Written by: Chris Terrio
Cinematography by: Rodrigo Prieto
Music by: Alexandre Desplat
Sound: Diana Ulzheimer
Editing: William Goldenberg
Art Direction: Peter Borck
Costumes: Jacqueline West
Production Design: Sharon Seymour
MPAA rating: R
Running time: 120 minutes

REVIEWS

Biancolli, Amy. *San Francisco Chronicle.* October 11, 2012.
Charity, Tom. *CNN.com.* January 4, 2013.
Hornaday, Ann. *Washington Post.* October 12, 2012.
Howell, Peter. *Toronto Star.* October 12, 2012.
Long, Tom. *Detroit News.* October 12, 2012.
Lumenick, Lou. *New York Post.* October 12, 2012.
Rea, Steven. *Philadelphia Inquirer.* October 11, 2012.
Rodriguez, Rene. *Miami Herald.* October 11, 2012.
Stevens, Dana. *Slate.* October 12, 2012.
Travers, Peter. *Rolling Stone.* October 11, 2012.

QUOTES

Lester Siegel: "If I'm going to make a fake movie, it's going to be a fake hit."

TRIVIA

The script for *Argo* (used by the CIA, not for this film) is from the unmade feature film *Lord of Light* based on the novel by Roger Zelazny.

AWARDS

Oscars 2012: Adapt. Screenplay, Film, Film Editing
British Acad. 2012: Director (Affleck), Film, Film Editing
Directors Guild 2012: Director (Affleck)
Golden Globes 2013: Director (Affleck), Film—Drama
Screen Actors Guild 2012: Cast
Writers Guild 2012: Adapt. Screenplay
Nominations:
Oscars 2012: Actor—Supporting (Arkin), Orig. Score, Sound, Sound FX Editing
British Acad. 2012: Actor (Affleck), Actor—Supporting (Arkin), Adapt. Screenplay, Orig. Score
Golden Globes 2013: Actor—Supporting (Arkin), Orig. Score, Screenplay
Screen Actors Guild 2012: Actor—Supporting (Arkin)

ATLAS SHRUGGED II: THE STRIKE

Everything has a breaking point.
—Movie tagline

Box Office: $3.3 million

Every year sees the release of any number of unnecessary movie sequels that were launched into production for reasons that defy most known notions of common sense—were there really enough unanswered questions at the end of something like the deathless *Weekend at Bernie's* (1989) to warrant *Weekend at Bernie's II* (1993)—but *Atlas Shrugged II: The Strike* may be the first such sequel to be produced despite challenging the very economic principles that the story itself espouses as well as the basic rules of common sense. After the total commercial and critical failure of *Atlas Shrugged—Part I* (2011), a rinky-dink attempt to bring Ayn Rand's controversial 1957 novel (or at least roughly its first third) to the screen, one might have expected that the producers would have just well enough alone but they instead decided to double down on their efforts with a second film covering the next third of the book with a mostly new cast and a moderately larger budget than before. And yet, as incredible as it may seem, *Atlas Shrugged II* is even cheesier and chintzier-looking than its predecessor in every possible way and one that even the staunchest of Objectivists will find themselves objecting to in the most strenuous manner imaginable.

Picking up pretty much right where the previous installment left off with nothing much to help orient any newcomers to the material (which means that viewers not only need to have already read the book or seen the first film, they need to have done it approximately five minutes before sitting down for this one), the film once again posits a nightmarish vision of an anticapitalist America circa-2016 in which gasoline is running at over $40 a gallon and more and more business leaders, chafing at increasing federal regulations designed solely to destroy their ability to turn a profit, are simply disappearing without a trace other than a note with the enigmatic question "Who is John Galt?" One industrialist who has not yet disappeared into the ether is railroad tycoon Dagny Taggart (Samantha Mathis), and, as the story kicks in, she is trying to puzzle out the apparently abandoned prototype for a new kind of motor that she and her married lover, two-fisted, steel-jawed steel magnate Hank Reardon (Jason Beghe), have discovered in an abandoned facility. For his part, Hank is battling government interference with his business regarding his ability to sell his patented brand of super-steel, a devastating explosion at one of his copper mines and the shrewish wife who will not grant him a divorce because of the scandal it will cause. Meanwhile, both Dagny and Hank are drawn further into the mystery of the identity of John Galt and his connection to all the disappearances, leading up to a cliffhanger finale that does little more than laboriously set up the next and presumably last entry in the franchise.

Rand's original novel has maintained legions of followers who have taken her critique of an America in which the haves are forced to share their creations and profits with the have-nots as pure gospel (a poll once ranked it as the second-most influential book following the Bible) but even they would be hard-pressed to derive any legitimate entertainment value out of this mess. It might have been possible to transform Rand's brand of lurid lunacy to the screen, as King Vidor did with his wild adaptation of her other popular novel, *The Fountainhead* (1949), but to do so would require a production large enough in size, scope and style to approximate her purple prose and actors with enough magnetism to fully embody her outsized characters. Needless to say, none of those attributes are on display here and while the end result this time around may not be as convulsively idiotic as the earlier film, its innate dullness makes it even more difficult to sit through. Despite transportation being a key visual motif throughout—characters are forever traveling from one place to another—the story is as propulsive as a dump truck struggling up a steep hill thanks to a never-ending parade of scenes in which the dialogue consists of either raw exposition or muddled economic theories and the inevitable wheel-spinning that comes with being the middle portion of a three-part saga. Director John Putch, hobbled with an unworkable screenplay and an inadequate budget, is unable to do much more than present the material in a clunky and utilitarian manner that displays all the flair of a middling junior high-level pageant. As for the actors, none of them are able to do anything with their virtually unplayable roles other than to stand around looking uncomfortable while waiting for a new team of actors to swoop in and replace them before *Part III* starts filming.

Outside of the bewildering appearance of a few familiar faces in cameo roles—running the gamut from conservative icons like Sean Hannity and Grover Norquist as themselves to the likes of stereotypical Diedrich Bader as one of America's few remaining geniuses and verbally reticent magician Teller in a brief speaking role as a security guard, *Atlas Shrugged II: The Strike* is a total wash that is too ridiculous to take seriously and too boring to work as inadvertent camp. In fact, the most interesting thing about its entire existence revolves around something that has practically nothing to do with the film itself. That would be the fact that around the time that it was appearing in theaters, one of the most notable Rand disciples—Wisconsin congressman Paul Ryan—was selected by Mitt Romney to be his running mate for the presidential election and frequently espoused how her theories inspired his own economic viewpoints (though he tended to play down her more inconvenient views regarding organized religion). In fact, when the film was eventually released just a few short weeks before the vote, the television commercials suggested that this was a movie that could actually influence the election due to the power of its message. To that end, let it be said that *Atlas Shrugged II* had approximately the same influence on the 2012 presidential election that Paul Ryan had on his political ticket—nada.

Peter Sobczynski

CREDITS

Dagny Taggart: Samantha Mathis
Henry Rearden: Jason Beghe
Francisco d'Anconia: Esai Morales
James Taggart: Patrick Fabian
Lillian Rearden: Kim Rhodes
Quentin Daniels: Diedrich Bader
Eddie Willers: Richard T. Jones
John Galt: D.B. Sweeney
Dr. Floyd Ferris: John Rubinstein
Dr. Robert Stadler: Robert Picardo
Origin: United States
Language: English
Released: 2012
Production: Jeff Freilich, Harmon Kaslow, John Aglialoro; released by Atlas Distribution Co.
Directed by: John Putch
Written by: Brian Patrick O'Toole; Duke Sandefur; Duncan Scott
Cinematography by: Ross Berryman
Music by: Chris Bacon
Sound: Craig Woods
Editing: John Gilbert
Art Direction: Mark Walters
Costumes: Bonnie Stauch
Production Design: Roland Rosenkranz
MPAA rating: PG-13
Running time: 111 minutes

REVIEWS

Baumgarten, Marjorie. *Austin Chronicle*. October 19, 2012.
Dargis, Manohla. *New York Times*. October 15, 2012.
Harvey, Dennis. *Variety*. October 13, 2012.
Jenkins, Mark. *Washington Post*. October 11, 2012.
Linden, Sheri. *Los Angeles Times*. October 15, 2012.
McCarthy, Todd. *Hollywood Reporter*. October 13, 2012.
Morris, Wesley. *Boston Globe*. October 12, 2012.
Orndorf, Brian. *Blu-ray.com*. October 14, 2012.
Scherstuhl, Alan. *Village Voice*. October 15, 2012.
Tobias, Scott. *AV Club*. October 12, 2012.

TRIVIA

Political commentator Bob Beckel appears as himself in this movie in a cameo role. His brother Graham Beckel played Ellis Wyatt in *Atlas Shrugged: Part I*. A picture of Graham Beckel as Ellis Wyatt appears in this film as part of a television news report on Wyatt's disappearance.

AWARDS

Nominations:

Golden Raspberries 2012: Worst Director (Putch), Worst Screenplay

THE AVENGERS
(Marvel's The Avengers)

Box Office: $623.4 million

In 2008, Marvel Studios launched an ambitious box-office gamble: a series of stand-alone super-hero movies (*Iron Man* [2008], *The Incredible Hulk* [2008], *Iron Man 2* [2010], *Thor* [2011], and *Captain America: The First Avenger* [2011]) that would cumulate with all their heroes uniting in a superhero team movie, *The Avengers*. The intention was to generate on the big screen the sort of team-up excitement that often plays out in printed comic book titles, but to do so without losing mainstream audiences who may not be as attentive to character back stories and cross-over continuity. When *The Avengers* finally arrived in theaters in 2012, Marvel's bold experiment turned out to be both a critical and box-office success.

The Avengers is little more—or less—than a really big superhero movie. But thanks to writer-director Joss Whedon's genre-savvy smarts, winning humor, and dazzling, action-sequence confidence, when it comes to pure entertainment value and enjoyableness, *The Avengers* is one of the most really big super-hero movies viewers could hope for.

It is not a perfect film—*The Avengers*' plot still follows the somewhat disjointed, one-thing-after-another formula of so many of its genre, and for those not up to speed on the other five "Avengers"-related films, this one can seem like a jumble of characters and back stories. McGuffin-wise, there's the Tesseract, a glowing blue energy cube everybody wants, including the villainous Loki (Tom Hiddleston) and the American security force S.H.I.E.L.D., led by the eye-patched Nick Fury (Samuel L. Jackson). Loki threatens the planet (specifically New York City) with an army of space aliens, and to protect it, Fury brings together a less-than-harmonious team of super-hero outsiders: Tony Stark/Iron Man (Robert Downey Jr), Captain America (Chris Evans), Thor (Chris Hemsworth), Bruce Banner/The Hulk (Mark

Ruffalo), The Black Widow (Scarlett Johanssen), and Hawkeye (Jeremy Renner).

What follows is also, in many ways, typical superhero movie fare, just super-sized for team impact. Much of *The Avengers* feels driven by what is expected from these kinds of films, and for a while, even as it steadily entertains, the movie keeps slipping sideways while working to round up the heroes and map out all the teams internal and external conflicts. As Tony Stark tells Loki later, "It takes us a while to get any traction."

Not all the parts mesh perfectly, but Whedon, with assistance from screenwriter Zak Penn, finds his way around the usual silliness of brightly colored capes and tights not by deconstructing it but by embracing it. There is none of Christopher Nolan's *Dark Knight* (2008) brooding here, nor any satire or subversion—just bright, shiny, four-color sincerity. (Though Whedon does find room to sneak in one of his favorite themes: distrust of government agencies and institutions.) Plus, never discount the simple comic-book joys of a giant, flying aircraft carrier.

Big flying toys aside, Whedon really gets cooking when it comes to dishing out group dynamics between seemingly incompatible personalities. A decade of creating and writing for film and television (on shows like *Buffy the Vampire Slayer* and *Firefly*) about bands of misfits learning to work together gives the writer-director a strong leg up when it comes to quickly crafting interesting, relatable, and witty characters and then pitting them against mettle-testing challenges. Much of the film's second act is solid face-to-face chats as the reluctant new Avengers teammates poke and prod each other (and their nemesis, Loki), the string of testy interactions made considerably more engaging by the work of Ruffalo and Downey.

At first, Downey, the biggest marquee star in the crowded cast, threatens to overpower the proceedings. Downey's an undeniably talented actor, but he rarely inhabits a role in big, franchise films like this—instead he seems to toss them off effortlessly from a vast reserve of on-screen charm and charisma. Still, even when Stark's constant belittling wise-cracking borders on too smugly glib, Downey's Whedon-penned zingers carry plenty of gleeful zip.

Luckily, Ruffalo is a master of bemused, knowing understatement, and his Bruce Banner provides a wryly brooding counterweight to Stark's braggadocio. Likewise, Evans once again pulls off the tough feat of making the ramrod, duty bound Steve Rogers both a naturally commanding presence and wryly humorous relief. The rest of the cast does admirable work, but it is British thespian Tom Hiddleston who truly gets it right. His Loki—an aloof, spoiled brat with classic timing and a perfect Euro-trash-smirk—is *The Avengers*' best blast of fresh comic-book flair.

The cast and Whedon keep *The Avengers* moving along even when the path is overly familiar. And where the previous pre-Avengers movies all had plenty of character but sported weak smash-pow finales, *The Avengers* fully delivers the pugilistic goods with a spectacular Big Battle in Manhattan against Loki's alien invaders. The third act's explosions and building-crumbling special effects are not anything new, but, unlike in the similarly large-scale destructive *Transformers* movies, Whedon's attention to character means audiences know and care about the heroes giving (and taking) the punches. The result is one of the rare blockbuster action movies where the massive, climactic fight is the best part.

At times *The Avengers* can feel like an over-large function of its own hype—as if it has been willed into existence by the fevered hopes and dreams of both comic-book fans and studio accountants. In the face of such grandiose expectations, Whedon hits all the expected notes, hauls out all the toys, and pauses now and then for speeches and lessons about true heroism and courage. However, he keeps it all chugging along with a whip-smart sense of humor, cleverly peppering the proceedings with wisecracks, quips, sarcasm, and wry deadpan. Best of all, *The Avengers* never wanders far from good clean, comic-book fun. It may still be "just" a superhero film and still an action-movie contraption, but if all superhero and action films were crafted with this much sincere love of the genre and provided such earnest enjoyment, maybe viewers would not have become so understandably weary of them.

Most critics were entertained. Keith Phipps of the *Onion A.V. Club* felt *The Avengers* joins its fellow Marvel films as "competent, well-polished pieces of product," but is also, "a heartfelt, exciting, and thematically resonant piece of big-screen mythmaking likely to please superhero geeks and general audiences alike." Others were more critical of those same aspects—*The Village Voice*'s Karina Longworth noted that, "Every time the movie hints at something rich and evocative, Whedon undercuts it with a punchline—his instincts as a big-picture storyteller crippled by his short-term need to please the crowd." For its part, the crowd was well-pleased: *The Avengers* earned a staggering $623 million in North America and more than one and a half billion dollars worldwide, putting it third behind only *Titanic* (1998) and *Avatar* (2009) on the all-time domestic and global box-office lists.

Locke Peterseim

CREDITS

Nick Fury: Samuel L. Jackson
Tony Stark/Iron Man: Robert Downey, Jr.
Steve Rogers/Captain America: Chris Evans
David Banner/The Incredible Hulk: Mark Ruffalo
Thor: Chris Hemsworth
Naasha Romanoff/Black Widow: Scarlett Johansson
Clint Barton/Hawkeye: Jeremy Renner
Prof. Erik Selvig: Stellan Skarsgard
Loki: Tom Hiddleston
Agent Phil Coulson: Clark Gregg
Agent Maria Hill: Cobie Smulders
Pepper Potts: Gwyneth Paltrow
Securty Guard: Harry Dean Stanton
Jarvis: Paul Bettany (Voice)
Origin: United States
Language: English
Released: 2012
Production: Kevin Feige; Marvel Studios, Paramount Pictures; released by Walt Disney Studios
Directed by: Joss Whedon
Written by: Zak Penn; Joss Whedon
Cinematography by: Seamus McGarvey
Music by: Alan Silvestri
Sound: Frank E. Evlner
Editing: Jeffrey Ford; Lisa Lassek
Costumes: Alexandra Byrne
Production Design: James Chinlund
MPAA rating: PG-13
Running time: 143 minutes

REVIEWS

Biancolli, Amy. *San Francisco Chronicle*. May 4, 2012.
Corliss, Richard. *Time*. April 25, 2012.
Ebert, Roger. *Chicago Sun-Times*. May 2, 2012.
Edelstein, David. *New York*. April 29, 2012.
O'Hehir, Andrew. *Salon*. May 1, 2012.
Hornaday, Ann. *Washington Post*. May 4, 2012.
Longworth, Karina. *Village Voice*. May 1, 2012.
Phipps, Keith. *AV Club*. May 2, 2012.
Stevens, Dana. *Slate*. May 3, 2012.
Zacharek, Stephanie. *Movieline*. May 1, 2012.

QUOTES

Pepper Potts: "Is this about the Avengers? Which I know nothing about."
Tony Stark: "The Avengers initiative was scrapped, I thought. And I didn't even qualify."
Pepper Potts: "I didn't know that either."
Tony Stark: "Apparently I'm volatile, self-obsessed, and don't play well with others."
Pepper Potts: "I knew that."

TRIVIA

Lou Ferrigno voices the Hulk in this film. He has played the Hulk in almost every live-action version since 1978 and has provided the voice for the Hulk in various animated productions.

AWARDS

Nominations:

Oscars 2012: Visual FX
British Acad. 2012: Visual FX

B

THE BABYMAKERS

She's fired up. He's firing blanks.
—Movie tagline

Box Office: $7,889

The Babymakers is a hopelessly sterile comedy from director Jay Chandrasekhar, known previously for helming the fraternal feature films orchestrated by his comedy troupe Broken Lizard (*Super Troopers* [2001], *Beerfest*, [2006]). Now, as he moves beyond Broken Lizard, Chandrasekhar (working from a script by Peter Gaulke and Gerry Swallow, writers of *Say It Isn't So* (2001), shows that his fixation on joking about boyish men has evolved from a state of arrested development and is now more like serving a life sentence in a frat house.

In the juvenile film, Paul Schneider plays Tommy Macklin, a middle-aged male entering into the next chapter of his existence as a man. He has already married Audrey, (Olivia Munn), the woman of his masturbatory dreams, and he has a house for the two of them to live their future, wedged into a suburban neighborhood populated by their friends. Now, on the third anniversary of his wedding, he is tasked by his wife with executing the next gender role related to his manhood—the act of conception (not performing anal sex, as he first presumes).

Plans to create new life from the couple's constant acts of sex are stilted when Audrey fails to get pregnant. After receiving useless advice methods from nosey family and friends, a trip to the doctor reveals that Tommy's sperm is sterile, despite his prideful insistence on otherwise. In a revelation that drives a frustrated Audrey away from him, he eventually confesses that in his past years he donated much of his sperm to help pay for her wedding ring, but that a series of spontaneous testicular injuries have left him without any strong sperm of his own. In a desperate act to save his marriage and his final remnant of reproductive manhood, Tommy enlists his friends Wade (Kevin Heffernan) and Zig-Zag (Oscar-winning screenwriter for *The Descendants* [2011] Nat Faxon), and a sketchy thug (an unamusing Jay Chandrasekhar), to help him break into the sperm bank at night and steal his last-remaining donation before it is given away to another couple.

Schneider, more recognized for revered independent dramas like David Gordon Green's *All The Real Girls* (2003) and Andrew Dominik's *The Assassination of Jesse James by the Coward Robert Ford* (2007) than comedies in which he is seen masturbating to the image of large cantaloupes acts like he at least deserves credit for trying, and he slightly does. But Schneider's input to the already weak comedy of *Babymakers* is non-existent except for his ability to take the script's abuse while maintaining bits of average-guy charisma. In similar fashion, *Babymakers* feels to be a pathetic joke played on Schneider, as the film is ultimately a failed attempt at a distinct comedic step away from drama (unless he intended on surprising his audience with a comedy as plain as this).

On top of a sloppy story that finds no charm in its course of events run by stupidity, the jokes in *The Babymakers* are consistently predictable. It is equally stunning and insulting that these mediocre jokes could be played earnestly, and one after the other. The only new spice that *The Babymakers* has to offer its audience in its absurd comedy is that many of its gags are centered on the act of masturbation or the presence of sperm. For example, in regards to the cliche of having a cartoonish character repeatedly slip up on a wet surface (often at the fault of a rogue banana peel), *The Babymakers* replaces the peel with an unimaginable amount of sperm. With such a visual in mind, the humor of this film is registered thoughtless, and becomes in desperate need of some fragment of maturity, regardless of how much this story revels in its juvenile perspective on the heterosexual American male's manhood.

The film's only funny sequence involves a common gag possibly best celebrated on the patriotic home video collage TV program *America's Funniest Home Videos*. It is a joke that could teach the rest of *The Babymakers* a useful lesson concerning how a classic gag can still show its vitality so long as it is placed within clever context. This bronze moment is, of course, when Schneider is subjected to a melee of shots to the groin in a montage that is more creative than the accidents seen on *AFHV*. Such a randomly placed, short-but-sweet montage provides a glimmer of laughter in a gross comedy that is otherwise unsuccessful with its comedic antiquing.

The script's angle of discussing sterility in manhood by shallow ways of masturbation jokes and sperm gags provides no comic relief to a serious subject. Instead, when lazily expressing the lengths a man's dedication will drive him to maintain his mark of masculinity and his marriage with the woman he loves, the intent of *Babymakers* becomes poor taste. And it becomes such regardless of this movie's drive to simply test audience's limits concerning what is gross-but-comical and what is simply gross.

Already reading like a script written by raunchy comedy Mad Libs, the weak jokes in this film feel like temporary placeholders that someone was too lazy to later change. Of course there is a joke about marijuana being used sheepishly for fake glaucoma, and, of course, there is a joke involving an adopted Asian baby receiving the name of "Jackie Chan" from her naive American parents. The list goes on, and, as it does, *Babymakers* grows to become even more dreadful.

Showing Chandrasekhar to be one of the worst slackers in the heavily populated class of American comedy, *The Babymakers* is a juvenile failure. It is the ugly offspring of a poor sense of humor and an empty sense of comedic comprehension.

Nick Allen

CREDITS

Tommy: Paul Schneider
Audrey: Olivia Munn

Wade: Kevin Heffernan
Darrell: Wood Harris
Zig-Zag: Nat Faxon
Karen: Aisha Tyler
Allison: Collette Wolfe
Leslie: Hayes Macarthur
Ron Jon: Jay Chandrasekhar
Origin: United States
Language: English
Released: 2012
Production: Jason Blum, Jay Chandrasekhar; Blumhouse Productions; released by Millennium Entertainment L.L.C.
Directed by: Jay Chandrasekhar
Written by: Peter Gaulke; Gerry Swallow
Cinematography by: Frank DeMarco
Music by: Ed Shearmur
Sound: Dan Gamache
Editing: Brad Katz
Costumes: Tricia Gray
Production Design: Katie Byron
MPAA rating: R
Running time: 93 minutes

REVIEWS

Anderson, Melissa. *Village Voice.* July 31, 2012.
Berardinelli, James. *ReelViews.* August 5, 2012.
Dujsik, Mark. *Mark Reviews Movies.* August 2, 2012.
Duralde, Alonso. *The Wrap.* August 3, 2012.
Ebert, Roger. *Chicago Sun-Times.* August 1, 2012.
Genzlinger, Neil. *New York Times.* August 2, 2012.
Gleiberman, Owen. *Entertainment Weekly.* August 1, 2012.
Leydon, Joe. *Variety.* August 2, 2012.
Tobias, Scott. *AV Club.* August 2, 2012.
VanDenburgh, Barbara. *Arizona Republic.* August 2, 2012.

QUOTES

Tommy: "Oh, I don't think I'm more important than Jesus, but unless he can miracle a baby up into my wife's vagina then I gotta take a pass."

BACHELORETTE

Box Office: $447,954

Leslye Headland's *Bachelorette* became a potential bellwether for the future of cinema delivery when it outdelivered all expectations On Demand before even opening in theaters. Hundreds of films have gone the On Demand route but few have charted as high on iTunes and other content delivery systems as Headland's starstudded raunchy comedy, a film with tones of *Brides-*

maids (2011) and *The Hangover* (2009) but not as creatively successful as either for a number of reasons including deeply unlikable characters, inconsistent plotting, awkward pacing, and unbelievable behavior. The talented cast comes out unscarred but the first massive On Demand pre-theatrical hit will mostly be remembered for its sales and not its quality.

The eve of a wedding and female leads allowed many critics to compare *Bachelorette* to Kristen Wiig's smash hit *Bridesmaids* but the film actually follows the arc of *The Hangover* more directly. It presents viewers with four semi-friends, the kind of people forced together by the unique dynamics that come pre-wedding, hides the actual future spouse for most of the action, and unleashes the other three characters into a profane world of drugs, strippers, and cheap sex. Some of the humor in *Bachelorette* connects thanks to the undeniable talents of its cast but Headland's script really falters when it attempts drama and character-based insight in the final act. As the film veers like a drunk at an open bar wedding from honest drama to physical comedy to sentimentality to gross-out humor, it can become head-spinning in its haphazard delivery. With a lesser cast, it could have been a complete disaster and so the most notable element of *Bachelorette* becomes how such talented actresses and actors can rescue a deeply flawed script and make it at least watchable.

Becky (Rebel Wilson, who popped up constantly in 2012, also appearing in *What to Expect When You're Expecting* and *Pitch Perfect,* among other) was the girl in high school who was always ridiculed by the more popular, prettier girls. Somehow, Becky still thinks they are friends, even when Regan (Kristen Dunst) greets the news of Becky's future nuptials with obvious disdain. Becky was once known as "Pigface," How could she possibly be married before the beautiful Regan? To join in her popular pity party, Regan calls former classmates Gena (Lizzy Caplan) and Katie (Isla Fisher), not knowing that the trio will end up being invited to Becky's wedding and the film jumps forward to the 24 hours of disaster before the big day.

Headland has already created a bizarre dynamic in that Regan, Gena, and Katie clearly mistreat and dislike Becky and so they become instantly hard to root for in any rational way. There is nothing wrong with comedic anti-heroes but these three are the kind of people most bar-goers would avoid after just a minute of conversation. They are petty, self-obsessed, and generally loathsome. Their behavior gets worse at a pre-wedding party on the night before the big event at which they behave so horrendously that they get un-invited from the wedding. The trio drowns their sorrow in cocaine, play around with Becky's dress, and rip the outfit. They spend the rest of the movie trying to get Becky's dress fixed, get

laid, and addressing their deep personality issues. Well, as much as people like this address the problems within. As in most comedies like this one, each of the three ladies gets a subplot and a beau—Regan flirts with the cocky Trevor (James Marsden), Katie attracts the eye of the sweet Joe (Kyle Bornheimer), and Gena deals with her ex-boyfriend Clyde (Adam Scott).

Headland is the kind of writer who believes that modern women call each other the c-word casually and that backstabbing and otherwise horrendous behavior is not only a fact of social existence but something that can typically be discarded with a smile and a hug. Regan is the kind of woman who is described, without irony, as a "good friend" because she does not let another woman overdose in a bathroom.

If Headland was really willing to push the pedal to the floor and fully embrace her Women Behaving Badly aesthetic, *Bachelorette* may have worked but she too often wants to play emotional cards as well. It is nearly impossible to care about the emotional catharsis of people this self-centered. Not only does it feel false on a character level but it requires an investment in the characters that the writing just does not engender.

Headland should send thank you cards to her cast every day because they are constantly pulling her comedy from the edge of total disaster through their sheer talent. Fisher and, especially, Dunst have well-known talent levels but Lizzy Caplan proves yet again that her under-the-radar status could change if she could only find the right part. She is the best thing here (and her interplay with the great Adam Scott further solidifies his status an actor who one really hopes gets better parts). Even small parts like those played by Marsden and Bornheimer feel fully inhabited. *Bachelorette* was adapted from Headland's own play and it feels like something that might have worked better on stage as the inherent, in-person likability of a cast, especially one as talented as this one, would have made their behavior more tolerable.

Brian Tallerico

CREDITS

Regan: Kirsten Dunst
Katie: Isla Fisher
Gena: Lizzy Caplan
Becky: Rebel Wilson
Trevor: James Marsden
Clyde: Adam Scott
Joe: Kyle Bornheimer
Dale: Hayes Macarthur
Origin: United States
Language: English

Released: 2012

Production: Brice Dal Farra, Claude Dal Farra, Jessica Elbaum, Will Ferrell, Adam McKay, Lauren Munsch; Gary Sanchez Productions, BCDF Pictures; released by Weinstein Company

Directed by: Leslye Headland

Written by: Leslye Headland

Cinematography by: Doug Emmett

Music by: Andrew Feltenstein; John Nau

Sound: John D'Aquino

Music Supervisor: Dana Sano; Libby Umstead

Editing: Jeffrey Wolf

Costumes: Anna Bingemann

Production Design: Richard Hoover

MPAA rating: R

Running time: 93 minutes

REVIEWS

Biancolli, Amy. *San Francisco Chronicle*. September 6, 2012.

Brody, Richard. *New Yorker*. September 17, 2012.

Puig, Claudia. *USA Today*. September 6, 2012.

Rainer, Peter. *Christian Science Monitor*. September 7, 2012.

Sharkey, Betsy. *Los Angeles Times*. September 6, 2012.

Simon, Brent. *Shared Darkness*. December 8, 2012.

Stevens, Dana. *Slate*. September 14, 2012.

Stewart, Sara. *New York Post*. September 7, 2012.

Verniere, James. *Boston Herald*. September 7, 2012.

Zacharek, Stephanie. *NPR*. September 6, 2012.

QUOTES

Clyde: "And you're wearing a dress?"

Gena: "No, actually it's a t-shirt."

Clyde: "Well, it's good to see you're still fighting the good fight against the tyranny of pants."

TRIVIA

Casey Wilson was set to play the role of Becky but dropped out for scheduling issues.

BATTLESHIP

The battle for Earth begins at sea.
—Movie tagline

Box Office: $65.4 million

The game is so simple that it began as something two people could play on just a piece of paper. Two opponents arrange their military forces, represented by spaces on a grid, and then proceed to fire upon each other with strategic guesses as to where the enemy is anchored. Pencil marks became pegs as it was turned into a popular board game in the 1960s, improved upon a decade later with electronic sound effects signifying the hit-and-miss nature of the competition. If that proved not to be realistic enough, the armchair Naval Captains can now see their precious dinner table fantasies brought to life by Hasbro, Universal Pictures, and director Peter Berg in the film version of the game *Battleship*. True to its title, viewers will get to see a real-life battleship. But, either inspired to advance the game into the 21st century from its last electronic talking addition or to capitalize on the enormous success of *The Transformers* franchise, the enemy is now from another planet. Of course, the true enemies are the people who made this film.

From the first encounter with Alex Hopper (Taylor Kitsch), the young man would appear to have no direction in life other than to hang in bars and hit on women. When his attempt to woo the very hungry Samantha (Brooklyn Decker) with a non-euphemistic burrito lands him tazed by police, his brother Commander Stone Hopper (Alexander Skarsgard) insists he saddle up and join the Navy. Despite Alex's hostile nature toward authority he quickly rises to the rank of Lieutenant, but still has trouble facing Admiral Shane (Liam Neeson), particularly when it comes to asking for his daughter Samantha's hand in marriage. When a confrontation during an intra-squad soccer game with Japanese Captain Yugi Nagata (Tadanobu Asano) spills over on the eve of their Hawaiian war games, Alex is quickly facing a dishonorable discharge once they get back to port.

Meanwhile, NASA or just some eager astronomers with big satellite dishes have sent out a signal deep into space and are now getting a response. An alien force has latched onto the signal, penetrated our atmosphere and have taken up base in the very waters that Alex and his brother have come to play pretend in. Soon enough one of the giant ships begins fortifying their position, attacking anything that appears as a threat and cutting off the outside world with a dome bubble so they may recreate the signal and launch reinforcements. Through circumstances that either require one to know military rankings or cinematic cliches, Alex is thrust into a commanding role to defeat the aliens before the Earth is destroyed.

Military strategy, particularly on the water, has surfaced through cinema with any number of claustrophobic, tension-filled standoffs. Up for discussion throughout viewing *Battleship* is exactly what proves to be the more failed tactic—Peter Berg's complete lack of providing a reasonable modicum of suspense, interest in any of the opponents, or why it was decided to go with extraterrestrials as the primary threat. The second part is easily answered as boys under the age of twelve would likely respond to aliens in Mighty Morphin' Halo-ish armor for their ground troops though their Amish facial look raises questions about their technological advances. As silly as board game adaptations are, *Battleship* still could have provided the whiz-bang excitement of giant explosions with a rogue military hero or nation waging war around the 70th anniversary of Pearl Harbor.

"We are the Indians," is a warning provided by geeky nerve-shattered scientist, Cal Zapata (Hamish Linklater) for those not up on their New World metaphors or understanding that Columbus was the visitor. Avoiding the obvious ironies of conquerors and occupiers, *Battleship*'s script by Jon & Erich Hoeber (also responsible for previous travesties, *Whiteout* [2009] and *Red* [2010]) triples down on a pro-military slant so thick that it bleeds red, white and blue. Shameless manipulation of the troops (both real and created) and the history of war (both foreign and domestic) are crassly forged into a film that should be deigned as no more than a pointless and potentially fun distraction. Since the aliens cannot even decide what is a true target and what is not (a little leaguer is a no-no, but highways with any number of commuting children are fair game) why should anyone expect the humans involved to stay on one.

While Berg and Universal took the trouble to hire Liam Neeson, one of the more reliable everyman action presences around these days, they have decided to barricade him away from the fight once it kicks into gear roughly forty minutes in. Plenty of numbing subplots to keep one busy though, including ground troops that will provide more time for Linklater's annoying scientist, Decker's physical (but not exactly mental) therapist and her patient, Mick (Gregory D. Gadson), a Lieutenant Colonel who unpleasantly reminds viewers in every scene how he can no longer be a soldier without his legs. Gadson, a real-life amputee and active Army Colonel, should project far more anger at *Battleship*'s deadly-serious-but-PG-13 version of casualties of war. The aliens kill several people in uniform in scenes of an "extinction-level event" that evoke not only 9/11 but Pearl Harbor as well. Like the current wars in Iraq and Afghanistan, the dead get very little air time and those that do survive are seen with burns and bloody cuts but no mangled limbs. Compare that to the introduction of Gadson's Mick in the rehab facility amidst shots of real veterans who paid the price in real battle. Insulting does not even begin to describe it. Though trotting out even more aging vets to get a put-out-to-pasture battleship functional for the finale to the strains of one of AC/DC's later unheralded tunes ("*Hard As a Rock*") takes it over-the-top.

If Berg had designed *Battleship* as the ultimate parody of Michael Bay's jingoistic effects-driven, blender-edited blockbusters, it could have been one of those rare wonders like *Shaun of the Dead* (2004) or *Hot Fuzz* (2006); servicing as both a goof and a genuine entry into its target genre. The most honest moment on

display derives from a plan of attack involving buoys and water ripples to create a grid similar to the game's original design. But even that is treated as a genuine inspiration into military strategy rather than someone bothering to comment it is just like that board game we used to play. No one ever gets to say the iconic catch phrase either. Then again after suffering through over two hours of this film, "you sunk my battleship" would have been pretty redundant.

Erik Childress

CREDITS

Alex Hopper: Taylor Kitsch
Stone Hopper: Alexander Skarsgard
Lt. Raikes: Rhianna
Samantha "Sam" Shane: Brooklyn Decker
Captain Yugi Nagata: Tadanobu Asano
Admiral Shane: Liam Neeson
Secretary of Defense: Peter MacNichol
Origin: United States
Language: English, French, Spanish
Released: 2012
Production: Sarah Aubrey, Peter Berg, Brian Goldner, Duncan Henderson, Scott Stuber, Bennett Schneir; Bluegrass Films, Film 44; released by Universal Pictures
Directed by: Peter Berg
Written by: Erich Hoeber; Jon Hoeber
Cinematography by: Tobias Schliessler
Music by: Steve Jablonsky
Sound: Darren King; Gregory King
Editing: Paul Rubell; Billy Rich; Colby Parker, Jr.
Art Direction: Aaron Haye; Scott P. Murphy; William Ladd (Bill) Skinner
Costumes: Louise Mingenbach; Kimberly Tillman
Production Design: Neil Spisak
MPAA rating: PG-13
Running time: 131 minutes

REVIEWS

Lybarger, Dan. *MovieMaker Magazine.* May 20, 2012.
McGranaghan, Mike. *Aisle Seat.* May 18, 2012.
Novikov, Eugene. *Film Blather.* May 19, 2012.
Nusair, David. *Reel Film Reviews.* May 20, 2012.
O'Connell, Sean. *CinemaBlend.com.* May 18, 2012.
Putman, Dustin. *DustinPutman.com.* May 17, 2012.
Rocchi, James. *AV Club.* May 16, 2012.
Sachs, Ben. *Chicago Reader.* May 24, 2012.
Tobias, Scott. *AV Club.* May 17, 2012.
Vaux, Rob. *Sci-Fi Movie Page.* September 6, 2012.

QUOTES

Cal Zapata: "If there is intelligent life out there and they come here, it's going to be like Columbus and the Indians, only we're the Indians."

TRIVIA

Jeremy Renner was cast as Alex Hopper, but dropped out to co-star in *The Master*, which he also subsequently dropped out of.

AWARDS

Golden Raspberries 2012: Worst Support. Actress (Rhianna)

Nominations:

Golden Raspberries 2012: Worst Director (Berg), Worst Ensemble Cast, Worst Picture, Worst Screenplay, Worst Support. Actor (Neeson), Worst Support. Actress (Decker)

THE BAY

Panic feeds on fear.
—Movie tagline

Box Office: $30,668

It is understandable when a genre's fan base bends over backwards to accept a luminary into its critically-derided world and overlooks the flaws of the work said filmmaker delivers. Such was the case with *The Bay*, a film that saw an Oscar winner and universally well-respected director named Barry Levinson (*Diner* [1982], *Rain Man* [1988], *Bugsy* [1991]) dive into a cinematic pool that is typically associated with a lack of filmmaking skill and not an abundance of it—the found-footage horror film. What drew an auteur like Levinson to the genre made popular by films like *Paranormal Activity* (2007) and *The Blair Witch Project* (1999)? And perhaps a more interesting question—why did so many horror fans simply embrace it without noting its serious flaws like a lack of tension and general genre failures? Levinson elevates what could have been a complete disaster in a lesser director's hands simply through his understanding of character and human interaction but that certainly does not make this very mediocre film the great one that some falsely professed it to be.

To be fair, Levinson gets to cheat quite a bit in terms of the rules of found footage films in the first place. *The Bay* is structured as a journalistic expose on "what really happened" in the small Oceanside town of Claridge over the Fourth of July weekend in which hundreds of residents die in gruesome, horrifying ways. The structure allows for footage that resembles home movies, news reports from that day, and film shot by a pair of oceanographers who just happen to find the genetic anomaly of the century in the murky waters. The very format of *The Bay* is one of its most interesting elements in that the source material—for example, some footage is supposed to resemble video shot on smart phones from the victims themselves while other

footage comes from the dash of a police car responding to the outbreak, and so on—is arguably the most unpredictable element. However, Levinson mistakenly does not play it straight enough as the film often fails the common tests of the found-footage genre including the commonly-asked "why would they be filming this" and just-as-essential "why would they then cut together their footage like a horror movie". The realism of the piece is often battling with the cliche of it and the former does not often win.

The plot is simple—general environmental poisoning of our world's oceans has created a man-eating parasite in the water and the steroids that the residents have Claridge have been feeding their chickens, which now run off into the ocean through their droppings, have made them big enough to cause a serious problem. As cute-as-a-button journalist Donna Thompson (Kether Donohue) learns the hard way, all of this is about to explode on to a quiet, family-oriented community during a Fourth of July weekend celebration. The first sign of something wrong is when a woman who had been dropping into a dunk tank starts to look like her skin is melting in the middle of the street. Sprinklers spray on people, revelers are swimming, a crab-eating contest is underway—it is all about to get very ugly. And Levinson spares nothing in terms of gore and the grotesque. People literally fall apart. The ick factor is respectably high.

The Bay works best when it operates under Levinson's gifts with "average people in an average town". Most of the best material comes in relatively throwaway moments like loved ones trying to communicate via Skype one final time. Watching a young girl Face Time with a friend about the lesions growing on her neck has visceral power. And there is a deep sadness in the material here that another director would have ignored.

Sadly, Levinson cannot keep the cliches at bay. Part of the problem is the general direction of the piece. Once people start melting, it becomes something of an exercise in the grotesque since there is nary a suggestion that people will be saved from this environmental nightmare. It becomes something of a found footage march to the gore chamber. Writer Michael Wallach tries to introduce some tension into a piece severely lacking it by often cutting to a couple who are heading to Claridge for the holiday via boat (Kristen Connolly & Christopher Denham). The roads may be closed but these poor souls do not know that and cannot get a hold of anyone on their phones. They are merely puttering into the nightmare of the movie and one wishes their arc was more completely developed instead of feeling too much like an afterthought. The viewers need to see themselves in these two, being drawn into the nightmare that the audience knows is there but the characters do not.

The Bay made a splash (please pardon a pun) in genre circles but failed to fully break through beyond the art house horror scene, grossing just over $31k overall and never expanding beyond 23 theaters. It is the kind of work that will surely find a longer and more loyal life on DVD. Cult horror movies often do. Even when they are not really all that good.

Brian Tallerico

CREDITS

Stephanie: Kristen Connolly
Donna: Kether Donohue
Sam: Christopher Denham
Dr. Jack Abrams: Stephen Kunken
Mayor Stockman: Frank Deal
Jacqueline: Nansi Aluka
Origin: United States
Language: English
Released: 2012
Production: Jason Blum, Steven Schneider; Automatik Entertainment, Hydraulx; released by Lionsgate, Roadside Attractions
Directed by: Barry Levinson
Written by: Michael Wallach
Cinematography by: Josh Nussbaum
Music by: Marcelo Zarvos
Sound: Mariusz Glabinski
Editing: Aaron Yanes
Art Direction: Stan Flint
Costumes: Emmie Holmes
Production Design: Lee Bonner
MPAA rating: R
Running time: 84 minutes

REVIEWS

Cabin, Chris. *Slant Magazine*. October 29, 2012.
Cox, David. *The Guardian*. October 29, 2012.
Longworth, Karina. *Village Voice*. November 1, 2012.
Lumenick, Lou. *New York Post*. November 1, 2012.
Morris, Andrew. *Boston Globe*. November 1, 2012.
O'Hehir, Andrew. *Salon.com*. November 4, 2012.
Olsen, Mark. *Los Angeles Times*. November 2, 2012.
Rothkopf, Joshua. *Time Out New York*. October 31, 2012.
Schwarzbaum, Lisa. *Entertainment Weekly*. November 1, 2012.
Scott, A. O. *New York Times*. November 1, 2012.

BEASTS OF THE SOUTHERN WILD

Box Office: $12.1 million

Most movies take place in worlds that have been seen many times on-screen. Even sci-fi and fantasy mov-

ies seem derivative of elements that have been explored time and time again. Contemporary, modern-day movies never seem to want to leave the suburbs, American small towns or well-worn cities like New York or Chicago. For a movie to take a serious detour from the banal, a filmmaker has to really dig deep within the crevices of the American landscape to find something wholly unique and unexplored. To achieve this successfully, the filmmaker cannot just utilize the landscape and forget about its inhabitants. The people must play a major role in its existence and should therefore dictate the story. Does such a place exist that has yet to be seen on American screens?

It would be understandable to guess not, but Benh Zeitlin's *Beasts of the Southern Wild* has probably the most unique vision and landscape of any movie in the last several years. It takes place on an island off the coast of Louisiana called The Bathtub, no doubt an appendage of sorts to New Orleans. The island exists on the fringes of the state itself, cut off but still attached. The inhabitants seem to be living off the land while taking whatever trash or treasures that wash ashore. There is beer and electricity here, but there is also squalor, alcoholism, and boats that are carved out of the backs of pick-up trucks, and this is the way they like it.

The central inhabitant of this peaceful place is a six-year-old African-American girl named Hushpuppy (Quvenzhane Wallis), who lives near her father, Wink (Dwight Henry). They live in separate quarters. He lives in a shack. She lives in a dilapidated trailer that is barely holding steady on stilts. Her father cooks chicken on an open grill while Hushpuppy passes the time trying to communicate with animals by holding them up to her ear and listening for heartbeats. "Mostly, they just speak in codes," she says. Hushpuppy introduces the viewer to The Bathtub by stating "we got the prettiest place on earth...more holidays than the rest of the world." Through her introduction, The Bathtub is seen as a magical place exploding with jubilant characters, fireworks, music and dance.

But Hushpuppy's life is not all celebratory. Her education exists on the streets and within her home where her father teaches her harsh lessons of survival. Her mother "swam away" one day and Hushpuppy hopes to see her again soon. To keep her mother's spirit alive, Hushpuppy talks to an old basketball jersey that once belonged to her. When she looks out at a lighthouse, Hushpuppy swears she sees her mother out there somewhere and sometimes calls out to her. Wink also has warm memories of this woman and recalls a story where when she walked into a room, the burners on the stove would just light up automatically. But for now, she exists as a ghost to the both of them.

Hushpuppy's relationship to her father is a troubled one, but not without love and respect. Wink talks to her like an equal, not as a child. He is not mindful about the logic of a child and tries to instill in her a logical mindset. But Hushpuppy sees the world through the eyes of many of her other elders, like the woman with the mastodon tattoo who uses it to explain to the children that the mastodon destroyed the cavemen, but not without a fight. "You're all meat," she says. Hushpuppy begins having hallucinations of these "beasts" just as it seems the world as she knows it is about to end.

The end of the world comes in the form of a big storm not unlike Hurricane Katrina. The movie never officially states whether or not it really is Katrina, but it may as well be. Many of the townspeople evacuate, but not Wink and Hushpuppy. Most of the Bathtub is buried underwater. To make matters worse, Wink is suffering from a life-threatening illness, for which he receives little treatment. Nevertheless, he still finds time to teach his daughter some new skills, like grabbing a catfish out of the river with her bare hands. Hushpuppy's survival instincts are put to the test and soon the "beasts" she imagines take on a whole new meaning.

Beasts of the Southern Wild is based on a stage play written by co-writer Lucy Alibar. Most movies based on plays become rather obvious about their source material. They often remain confined to the few rooms and settings a stage play will allow. But Zeitlin and Alibar's script seems to veer so far off the mainland and the actors are conveying their emotions with such great subtlety that it becomes a challenge to imagine this story taking place in one room with actors playing to the back of the hall. The movie opens up the viewer's world and depicts not just this microcosm, but its surroundings as well. The inhabitants of The Bathtub may be on the fringes of society, but they still have to view the factories and progress that exists outside their boundaries.

The performances here are more authentic and vibrant than in most mainstream movies. This is due in part to the fact that Zeitlin cast a lot of non-union Louisiana locals to play the roles instead of holding traditional auditions for professional actors. Dwight Henry was found at the last minute when Zeitlin was visiting a cafe in New Orleans, which Henry owns. A real-life Katrina survivor, Henry creates a father figure that is hard to love, but easy to understand. His rage is laced with sadness over the loss of his wife and loving care for his daughter.

Wallis is his perfect complement. At such a young age and with no prior acting experience, Wallis makes Hushpuppy a tough, old soul who lives a balanced existence between a child's imagination and a survivor of life's harshest ordeals. Her unrehearsed voiceovers put the viewer right into her thought process giving the feeling of a no-nonsense mind that is making life up as she goes along. Zeitlin and cinematographer Ben Richardson furthermore keep the camera at kid level, often shaky and looking up at the adult figures as they teach her their lessons. Wallace never comes off as conscious of being in a movie or "acting" the way most kids do. Hushpuppy becomes as real as anybody seen in a documentary.

The landscape here is equally remarkable. With a budget of just under $2 million, Zeitlin and his crew seem to have just arrived in the area and put this world together themselves with whatever scraps and metal they found laying around. It looks perfectly used and lived-in. Equally magical is the way in which one of the houses gets refurbished after the storm with large spikes sticking out of the roof so as to kill any bird that flies near it. It is the sort of absurdly beautiful image that can only exist in a child's imagination, but Zeitlin gives it an unusual logic and never tries to underscore its uniqueness, even with the lovely score, which he also co-wrote.

Beasts of the Southern Wild seems comprised of elements borrowed from David Gordon Green's debut *George Washington* (2000) combined with the storybook prose of Maurice Sendak and Spike Jonze's *Where the Wild things Are* (2009) as well as the lyrical, poetic narrative abandonment of Terrence Malick's *The Tree of Life* (2011). Yet, Zeitlin's film is truly his own and he clearly has an affection for this landscape and its inhabitants. Zeitlin says he plans to make more movies in this area. He has truly found an exciting niche and American cinema is all the better for it, if only so that when people think of the bayous of Louisiana, they will think of something other than the HBO series *True Blood*.

Collin Souter

CREDITS

Hushpuppy: Quvenzhane Wallis

Wink: Dwight Henry

Levy Easterly: Jean Battiste

Walrus: Lowell Landes

Origin: United States

Language: English

Released: 2012

Production: Michael Gottwald, Dan Janvey, Josh Penn; Journeyman Pictures, Cinereach, Court 13; released by Fox Searchlight

Directed by: Benh Zeitlin

Written by: Benh Zeitlin; Lucy Alibar

Cinematography by: Ben Richardson

Music by: Benh Zeitlin; Daniel Romer
Sound: Bob Edwards
Editing: Affonso Goncalves; Crocket Doob
Costumes: Stephani Lewis
Production Design: Alex DiGerlando
MPAA rating: PG-13
Running time: 93 minutes

REVIEWS

Anderson, Melissa. *Village Voice*. June 26, 2012.
Burr, Ty. *Boston Globe*. July 5, 2012.
Ebert, Roger. *Chicago Sun-Times*. July 5, 2012.
Lumenick, Lou. *New York Post*. June 29, 2012.
Murray, Noel. *AV Club*. January 25, 2012.
Neumaier, Joe. *New York Daily News*. June 28, 2012.
O'Hehir, Andrew. *Salon.com*. June 29, 2012.
Rea, Steven. *Philadelphia Inquirer*. July 12, 2012.
Schwarzbaum, Lisa. *Entertainment Weekly*. June 27, 2012.
Whitty, Stephen. *Newark Star-Ledger*. June 27, 2012.

QUOTES

Hushpuppy: "Sometimes you can break something so bad, that it can't get put back together."

TRIVIA

When Wink reaches down in the river to show Hushpuppy how to catch a fish with his bare hand, a member of the production crew almost died swimming under water to achieve this stunt.

AWARDS

Ind. Spirit 2013: Cinematog.

Nominations:

Oscars 2012: Actress (Wallis), Adapt. Screenplay, Director (Zeitlin), Film
British Acad. 2012: Adapt. Screenplay
Ind. Spirit 2013: Actress (Wallis), Director (Zeitlin), Film

BEING FLYNN

We're all works in progress.
—Movie tagline

Box Office: $540,152

The narrative conceit of *Being Flynn* is a clever one. It presents two narrators, a father and son who are both writers and both desperately want their story told. Their voice-overs essentially duel on the soundtrack; just as the audience settled into the son's story, the father breaks

in to assure that "You're back in the hands of a master storyteller."

The gimmick is not only clever but also appropriate. After all, these two have been fighting the entire time they have existed together. It is, though, a one-sided battle, since the father is of the absentee variety. The son never knew the man except through letters—a "non-presence," he calls him.

The fight is one-sided in another way, too. Both are trapped in the torment of circumstances of their own making: Nick Flynn (Paul Dano), the son, has let his demons—the absence of both parents and his fear of becoming like his father—control his life; Jonathan Flynn (Robert De Niro), the father, has psychological problems for which he has never considered seeking help. He assumes those issues are key to what makes him one of only three classic American writers, the other two being Mark Twain and J. D. Salinger. Unlike the other two, Jonathan has never had a book published; his only claim to the fame he imagines for himself is a letter from a publishing house stating that his work is a "virtuoso display of personality." He overlooks the fact that it is a rejection letter for the compliment, if it even is one in the first place.

Jonathan is a fascinating character who lives a delusion. He drives a taxi for a living (and many have connected his character here to the one he played in *Taxi Driver*, a hollow link if there ever was one) and lives in a squalid New York City apartment. He is a fervent racist and homophobe and also prone to fits of violence, like when he takes a board with nails sticking out of the end to attack his downstairs neighbors for conducting band practice in their apartment. Jonathan's life is a series of lies. When he first meets his son, he offers him a painting from his "personal friend" Jackson Pollock. It turns out to be a forgery, so the question remains: Does Jonathan know this and try to pass himself off as more important than he is or does he truly believe he was friends with the famous painter?

In its favor, the screenplay by director Paul Weitz (based on the real Nick Flynn's memoir *Another Bullshit Night in Suck City*, a far more illustrative title and the working title for this film until the studio panicked) refrains from outright psychoanalysis of these two characters for the most part. In the few instances it does, Weitz offers a counterpoint, like when Nick tells the story of how his mother (Julianne Moore) committed suicide after reading a short story he wrote about her. Jonathan offers that, while his son may have never told anyone else that story, Nick has been telling himself that he is cause of his mother's death for years. It has no basis in reality, but that does not matter to Nick.

Nick, as one could gather, has problems of his own. He is unemployed and, at the start of the movie, finds himself without a home after his current girlfriend (Katherine Waterston) kicks him out of her apartment when she discovers lipstick on a cigarette near the bed. When he offers that she had said their relationship was not going anywhere, she returns the blame to him. Before leaving, he stares into a mirror for a long beat before smashing his head into it.

Nick finds a new residence with low rent and meets Denise (Olivia Thirlby), a self-proclaimed "do-badder" who works at a homeless shelter. Nick begins working there, too, and they have a tremulous relationship based primarily on sex (she is not looking for anything more, until she hears some of his writing).

As Nick's life gets better, Jonathan's grows worse. Eventually, the father winds up at the homeless shelter where his son is employed, and as Jonathan's mental faculties deteriorate, Nick begins to believe what his father tells him: "You are me." His greatest fear becomes a self-fulfilling prophecy as Nick starts using cocaine.

Dano is fine as Nick in letting the inner turmoil show through, though there are some moments where the character's smugness suffocates sympathy for him. De Niro gives one of his better performances in recent years (although, considering his filmography during the last decade, that is not saying much), and while Jonathan is a character that could inspire a showy performance, De Niro is thankfully subdued.

The narrative itself is episodic and scattershot, blending flashbacks to Nick's childhood with the two present-day stories. Strangely, the most effective element is a background one. The depiction of the lives of the homeless in New York City is presented without any romanticism or nobility; it is simply a daily trial of trying to find food and staying warm in the harsh, winter nights. (A scene in which Jonathan finds warmth by sleeping on the vents that discard the excess heat from a library, matched with Nick's description of it as a kind of prison, is particularly disheartening). The shelter is considerably better, but, there, Nick sees the results: men needing delousing and new clothes because they have soiled themselves.

Being Flynn gradually shifts to Nick's story almost exclusively. Therein lies perhaps the most egregious misstep of the movie. He is simply not a particularly worthwhile character, and when juxtaposed with his father, he is downright dull.

Mark Dujsik

CREDITS

Jonathan Flynn: Robert De Niro

Nick Flynn: Paul Dano
Jody Flynn: Julianne Moore
Denise: Olivia Thirlby
Carlos: Eddie Rouse
Jeff: Steve Cirbus
Joy: Lili Taylor
Gabriel: Victor Rasuk
Origin: United States
Language: English
Released: 2012
Production: Andrew Miano, Michael Costigan, Paul Weitz; Depth of Field, Corduroy Films, Tribeca Films; released by Focus Features
Directed by: Paul Weitz
Written by: Paul Weitz
Cinematography by: Declan Quinn
Music by: Damon Gough
Sound: Ron Bochar
Music Supervisor: Linda Cohen
Editing: Joan Sobel
Art Direction: Ryan Heck
Costumes: Aude Bronson-Howard
Production Design: Sarah Knowles
MPAA rating: R
Running time: 102 minutes

REVIEWS

Burr, Ty. *Boston Globe*. March 9, 2012.
Ebert, Roger. *Chicago Sun-Times*. March 7, 2012.
Longworth, Karina. *Village Voice*. February 29, 2012.
Mondello, Bob. *NPR*. March 3, 2012.
Osenlund, R. Kurt. *Slant Magazine*. February 27, 2012.
Robinson, Tasha. *AV Club*. March 1, 2012.
Scott, A. O. *New York Times*. March 1, 2012.
Toumarkine, Doris. *Film Journal International*. March 1, 2012.
Whitty, Stephen. *Newark Star-Ledger*. March 1, 2012.
Zacharek, Stephanie. *Movieline*. March 1, 2012.

QUOTES

Jonathan Flynn: "There exists a striking association between creativity and manic depression. The only important thing, though, is to simply do the work."

TRIVIA

While taking a break from filming, Robert De Niro attempted to enter The Greenwich Hotel while still in costume. The hotel security did not recognize De Niro and turned him away, despite the fact that he co-owns the hotel.

BEL AMI

Possessed by love. Consumed by desire.
—Movie tagline

Temptation. Seduction. Obsession.
   —Movie tagline

Box Office: $120,462

French for the term "beautiful friend," the story of *Bel Ami*, as originally published in 1885 by author Guy de Maupassant, has become a passion for many filmmakers through a variety of cinematic eras. An indication of the storytelling fire this story can spark with its moments of sex and deception, *Bel Ami* has inspired adaptations that range from silent films (*Bel Ami* in 1919) to a same-titled, X-rated version starring *Deep Throat* (1972) lead Harry Reems in 1976. Any type of luminosity is bare to be found with this latest adaptation of *Bel Ami*, a film that sacrifices any spark by watering down its story to be an outdated soap opera, albeit one lead by one of the most currently sought after hunks in Hollywood, Robert Pattinson.

In the film, Pattinson plays George Dulroy, a former non-commissioned officer who served in Algeria, and has now made a dingy home for himself in 1890's Paris, France. While in Paris he runs into an old comrade, Charles de Forestier (Philip Glenister), a man who has gained his own wealth by writing for the political Parisian newspaper "La Vie Francaise" and advises Dulroy that "Paris is filthy with money...even the whores are getting rich." Tired of staring at bread scraps in his bug-infested apartment, Georges takes this comment to heart, and accepts his comrade's invitation to work at the newspaper, writing a piece called "Diary of a Calvary Officer." But because Georges secretly writes like "an errand boy," he receives a great amount of help with the article from Forestier's wife, the dominant Madeleine (Uma Thurman). Immediately into their working relationship, she advises Georges that she will not be his mistress.

This does not deter the manipulative goals of this penniless young buck, as he fixes his hormonal gaze on Clotilde de Marelle (Christina Ricci), a wealthy friend of the Forestiers whose husband is constantly absent. The two are able to hide their adulterous romps by using a secret getaway purchased by Clotilde solely to host their lovemaking. However, when Forestier dies of sickness, Dulroy ditches Clotilde to marry Madeleine. As Dulroy works on the paper (and is sometimes called "Forestier" by his snide colleagues), Madeleine continues to influence his political writings while having curious daytime visits from an older man, Comte de Vaudrec (Anthony Higgins), which makes Georges very jealous.

When Georges' newspaper boss Monseiur Rousset (Colm Meaney) pokes at Georges' jealousy about Madeleine, Georges aims to avenge his ego by sleeping with the chief's innocent wife Virginie (Kristin Scott Thomas). Turning the religious woman into a clingy

mess, Georges realizes the huge annoyance he has made for himself, but sees the ultimate prize after pulling his desperate housewife hat trick—the Rousset's romantically viable daughter, Suzanne, who will provide Georges the inheritance and revenge he has sought over these members of high society.

More than anything else, *Bel Ami* is vigilant about continuing Pattinson's momentary conquest as a sex symbol, while not proving that as an actor he is much more than another moody face to be lusted after. If it were a more serious venture for Pattinson to reach outside of his fan base (like David Cronenberg's *Cosmopolis* [2012]), perhaps he would be more proactive with his facial expressions, which are essentially interchangeable, and accumulatively too cold to bring this story of scandalous sex to even a simmer. Pattinson's gazes do not speak so much of lust as indifference, as if he had become a shoulder-shrugging captive of his own libido. With an exception of a freak-out moment in the third act, Pattinson's performance coasts on its presence alone, stripping the elements of curiosity or subsequent delicious deviousness necessary for such a character as he wages adultery on an interwoven group of powerful people.

The film's three female supporting performances are for the most part insignificant, with each of the actresses attempting to make the most out of their screen time with their lightly articulated characters opposite prime Hollywood hunk Pattinson. Thurman awkwardly chews her way through dramatic moments, while Thomas succeeds in adding some pitiful tragedy to her character's transformation from faithful wife to Georges' plaything. It is Ricci who comes out on top with the most compelling performance of the three, providing moments of perceptible chemistry between herself and Pattinson, and finding her way around a believable English accent to boot.

The richest attribute within *Bel Ami* is its string-heavy score, as composed by Lakshman Joseph de Saram and Rachel Portman. Covering the film wall-to-wall with delicate waltz melodies or chugging arrangements, the score is itself rapacious enough to add some desperately needed color to *Bel Ami*. Though the historical details are in place, the mise-en-scene of this film taking place in Paris but shot in London and Budapest lacks charm, or even an inspired camera by cinematographer Stefano Falivene to bask in the historic detail.

Bel Ami's most common visual tool, aside from close-ups on Pattinson, is white sunlight, which fills the privates spaces of the characters, but with little effect. Shining such a direct ray of sun, as filtered through a silk screen, only makes the actresses look older as examples of bad coverage. If this film is also out to beatify not only Pattinson but its supporting actresses, then such coverage is another example in which *Bel Ami* backfires, displaying an ugly dissonance between the makeup department and cinematography.

The story of *Bel Ami* has stayed viable in its age through its crafty ways of engaging sexual politics in the midst of a story of shattering manipulation. Although Georges is indeed a hound dog that needs to be put down, his cunning is fitting within the "rules" of this patriarchal high society, where women can influence their husbands, but have no power of their own. Such chewy bits of subtext are available in screenwriter Rachel Bennette's script adaptation, but this continuance of du Maupassant's previously laid territory is not interested in the gender discussion, so much as harvesting the plethora of juicy moments related to Georges' mischievous promiscuity, which do give this adaptation some energy, as it moves scandal to scandal, despite the lack of heat. However, such speediness negatively affects the script by undermining Dulroy's development, leaving him without a firmly planted explanation for his destructiveness, and also undermining the significance of his scandalous events themselves, along with a political subplot related to Dulroy's work at the newspaper. The film's only surviving bits of wit are buried in dialogue, which sporadically rise from the script's mental blandness to have a decently biting point.

The telling of simplified scandals with little zest from first time filmmakers Declan Donnellan and Nick Ormerod, *Bel Ami* has no more dramatic importance than a *People Magazine* report, focused on what who did what, or more accurately, who did who. Like guzzling down an aged wine simply because it is alcohol, *Bel Ami* is lowered from habituated literature to momentary amusement, constructed for the levels of attention that perceive Pattinson as a lead character most of all in celebrity gossip magazines.

Nick Allen

CREDITS

Georges Duroy: Robert Pattinson
Madeleine Forrestier: Uma Thurman
Virginie Rousset: Kristin Scott Thomas
Clotilde de Marelle: Christina Ricci
Rousset: Colm Meaney
Charles Forestier: Philip Glenister
Suzanne Rousset: Holliday Grainger
Origin: United Kingdom, Italy
Language: English, French
Released: 2012
Production: Uberto Pasolini; Redwave Films; released by Magnolia Pictures

Directed by: Declan Donnellan; Nick Ormerod
Written by: Rachel Bennette
Cinematography by: Stefano Falivene
Music by: Rachel Portman; Lakshman Joseph De Saram
Sound: Ian Wilson
Editing: Masahiro Hirakubo; Gavin Buckley
Costumes: Odile Dicks-Mireaux
Production Design: Attila Kovacs
MPAA rating: R
Running time: 102 minutes

REVIEWS

Anderson, John. *Newsday.* June 15, 2012.
Berardinelli, James. *Reel Views.* May 30, 2012.
Burr, Ty. *Boston Globe.* June 7, 2012.
Ebert, Roger. *Chicago Sun-Times.* June 21, 2012.
Hynes, Eric. *Village Voice.* June 5, 2012.
Kenny, Glenn. *MSN Movies.* June 5, 2012.
LaSalle, Mick. *San Francisco Chronicle.* June 8, 2012.
Linden, Sheri. *Los Angeles Times.* June 7, 2012.
Pols, Mary F. *Time.* June 7, 2012.
Weitzman, Elizabeth. *New York Daily News.* June 7, 2012.

QUOTES

Charles Forestier: "You couldn't have come at a better time. Paris is filthy with money, even the whores are getting rich."

TRIVIA

Nicole Kidman was offered Kristin Scott Thomas's role, but turned it down due to scheduling conflicts.

BERNIE

A story so unbelievable it must be true.
—Movie tagline

Box Office: $9.2 million

The entertaining, stranger-than-fiction true story of *Bernie* begins on a fittingly offbeat note: Affable, mustachioed Bernie (Jack Black) leads a demonstration of how to properly prepare a body to be dressed and casketed. Clip and shape the nails to suit the person. Adjust the hands (left over right) and carefully ensure the head position suggests neither navel gazing nor stargazing. Take note of the lip; it has a tendency to drift, and that can be disastrous. "You can not have grief tragically becoming comedy," Bernie says.

In fact, grief blends oddly and sometimes fascinatingly with comedy in the latest from Richard Linklater, who elevates his strong sense of place (best seen consecutively in the influential *Slacker* [1991], the raucous high school community of *Dazed and Confused* [1993], and the hopeful, bittersweet Vienna romance of *Before Sunrise* [1995]) to new heights. Set in Linklater's native Texas, *Bernie* incorporates many actual towns-people of Carthage, the small town where generous, lovable Bernie Tiede befriends widely-despised widow Marjorie Nugent (Shirley MacLaine). He also eventually kills her and then spends months trying to convince others that she remains alive, merely sick and unavailable. Much of the film consists of the towns folk speaking to an off-screen interviewer in a documentary style somewhat reminiscent of Errol Morris. They recount how Bernie made people feel good about themselves and how he became the most popular man in town after arriving to take a job as assistant funeral director. If the people in Carthage made a list of who would get into heaven, one person notes, Bernie would be at the top of the list.

On the other hand, Marjorie is someone that, as another local states, many would be glad to shoot for five dollars. She treats both strangers and family like garbage but takes a shine to Bernie, who brings her flowers and soaps after her husband passes away and treats her nicer than anyone has treated her for a long time. (She seems to have forgotten that what goes around often comes around.) Soon the two spend not just a high percentage of their time together but nearly $100,000 per year of Marjorie's money on exotic vacations to places like Belize. Marjorie enjoys Bernie's friendly companionship and so values him that she makes him priority number one in her will, though it is hard not to wonder at this point if Bernie is some sort of con artist. While he claims that in high school he wanted to be an evangelist to save his fellow students' souls, Bernie also proves to be quite a good salesman as he gently but manipulatively guides customers at the funeral parlor toward a more expensive casket than they initially intend to buy. He emphasizes how the least expensive option will fail to protect the deceased from burrowing animals and rainwater. Still, as someone who the people in town note has never shown interest in any women his age, Bernie does not seem to mind his platonic romance with a woman much older than him. His neighbors suspect Bernie is gay; Linklater does not seem to know for sure, so in Black's characterization Bernie seems merely effeminate and borderline asexual.

That is not the only thing these guys do not know. The big hole at the center of *Bernie* is the question of how Bernie tolerates Marjorie's pushiness for so long and why he snaps after so many years with a woman no one else can stand. Bernie knows what he did but acts as if it feels like someone else shot Marjorie, like her death resulted from a momentary, out-of-body lapse of reason. Unfortunately, *Bernie* fails to track the man's growing

resentment of his closest friend and meal ticket, other than a few instances of rising conflict between the two. "If I don't call her," he says, "She will give me living hell." It makes sense that he would not want to rid himself of someone who finances the most expensive items in his life, but the movie, co-written by Skip Hollandsworth, who wrote the *Texas Monthly* article on which *Bernie* is based, never depicts Bernie's thought process of being stuck between a rock and a rich person. Furthermore, during the months in which Bernie attempts to deceive Marjorie's stockbroker and the few others that care whether or not she is alive, Black's performance prevents viewers from determining how Bernie is feeling about his actions. Though the film concludes with a depiction of the real Bernie Tiede, he is not interviewed for *Bernie*, which possesses a better grasp of the man's actions than his motivations. Joel and Ethan Coen, directors long familiar with troubled people and their violent intentions, may have delivered a more insightful, less sunny version of this tale.

Nevertheless, *Bernie* remains a snappy slice of small-town weirdness. A good deal of responsibility for that comes from a terrific supporting turn from Matthew McConaughey (whom Linklater also used to great effect in *Dazed and Confused*) as district attorney Danny Buck. McConaughey delivers the perfect mix of charm and disbelief through this likable lawyer with unconventional methods of his own, such as rounding up deadbeat dads through a "Hands on a hard body" truck giveaway and spinning a "wheel of misfortune" to determine which suspected drug dealers he will go after next. Danny's case against Bernie seems as clear-cut as it comes, except for one bizarre truth: The people of Carthage do not seem to care that Marjorie is dead and do not want Bernie punished for her murder. He did not do it, one local woman insists. "He confessed!" Danny reminds her. This does not matter to the many people who have received selfless gifts from Bernie (who was also active in the community theater and church) and nothing but coldness from the woman he eliminates from their sight. It results in the unheard of need to request a change of venue for the trial on behalf of the prosecution, not the defense.

How unusual that the only other film titled for a character named Bernie that comes to mind is *Weekend at Bernie's*, another comedy about death featuring a mustached character who is not what he seems and a ruse that seems destined to fail. Of course, the story of two guys pretending a dead man is alive is pure fiction. The story of the man who encouraged the crushes of little old ladies and then crushed one into her own freezer is real. What exactly happened between Bernie and Marjorie, and, more importantly, why? Maybe a nice man reached his breaking point. Maybe he determined Carthage would be better off with Marjorie's money and not Marjorie. Perhaps the town's favorite person had secrets he shared with no one. *Bernie* only sort of knows the truth. In this account of emotion nearly trumping reason, Linklater makes it awfully amusing to wonder about the answers he leaves out.

Matt Pais

CREDITS

Bernie Tiede: Jack Black
Marjorie Nugent: Shirley MacLaine
Danny Buck: Matthew McConaughey
Scrappy Holmes: Brady Coleman
Lloyd Hornbuckle: Richard Robichaux
Don Leggett: Rick Dial
Sheriff Huckabee: Brandon Smith
Rev. Woodard: Larry Dotson
Origin: United States
Language: English
Released: 2012
Production: Liz Glotzer, David McFadzean, Dete Meserve, Judd Payne, Matt Williams, Ginger Sledge, Martin Shafer, Celine Rattray, Richard Linklater; Detour Filmproduction, Collins House Productions, Horsethief Pictures, Castle Rock Entertainment; released by Millenium Films
Directed by: Richard Linklater
Written by: Skip Hollandsworth; Richard Linklater
Cinematography by: Dick Pope
Music by: Graham Reynolds
Sound: Tom Hammond
Music Supervisor: Lisa Brown
Editing: Sandra Adair
Art Direction: Rodney Becker
Costumes: Kari Perkins
Production Design: Bruce Curtis
MPAA rating: PG-13
Running time: 104 minutes

REVIEWS

Burr, Ty. *Boston Globe*. May 17, 2012.
Chang, Justin. *Variety*. April 21, 2012.
Ebert, Roger. *Chicago Sun-Times*. May 2, 2012.
Edelstein, David. *New York Magazine*. May 11, 2012.
Morgenstern, Joe. *The Wall Street Journal*. April 26, 2012.
Pols, Mary. *Time*. April 26, 2012.
Rodriguez, Rene. *Miami Herald*. May 24, 2012.
Phillips, Michael. *Chicago Tribune*. May 17, 2012.
Weber, Bill. *Slant Magazine*. April 25, 2012.
Zacharek, Stephanie. *Movieline*. April 26, 2012.

QUOTES

Townsperson: "Well, I know the Bible says Jesus turned water into wine, but it didn't say liquor store wine. It had to have been non-alcoholic wine, because it didn't have time to ferment."

TRIVIA

In preparation for the film, Jack Black met with the real Bernie Tiede in Telford Unit State Prison. Shirley MacLaine also spoke with Tiede over the phone.

AWARDS

Nominations:

Golden Globes 2013: Actor—Mus./Comedy (Black)
Ind. Spirit 2013: Actor (Black), Film

THE BEST EXOTIC MARIGOLD HOTEL

Box Office: $46.4 million

The central question of *The Best Exotic Marigold Hotel*—beyond wondering which of these aging characters will die, a development that one character admits was an inevitability when it does happen—is how much and for how long can a cast of fine actors bolster material so slight on substance. The cast of the movie is an impressive lot, and their work is admirable in the face of a screenplay that spreads thin their characters' stories. Part of this is understandable, considering that the movie concerns seven characters of near-equal importance, and screenwriter Ol Parker (adapting Deborah Moggach's novel *These Foolish Things*) allows each of them at least one significant scene of insight—of varying degrees, naturally.

Although material of this variety can work as straight character study, one cannot help but feel that Parker and director John Madden are too eager to impart an optimistic message, too distracted by characters whose existence is only to provide ancillary conflict, and too enthralled with the movie's exotic setting, all at the expense of exploring the central septet's personal lives and the sense of community that sporadically emerges between these strangers in a foreign land. The latter element is especially missed, and there is no feeling of cohesion to the movie and the characters' disparate stories beyond the location and the fact that they are all men and women of a certain age range.

Each member of the group has come from different circumstances but has decided to travel from England to India in order to fill some hole or fix some problem in each of their lives. Evelyn Greenslade (Judi Dench) is a recent widow, her husband having died of a heart attack. The need to sell her house in order to cover the massive debt he left behind is only part of her decision to leave the country, as the opening scene, in which the camera slowly pulls back from the view of lives being lived outside Evelyn's window, reveals her trapped in a catch-22 with a customer service representative. Her life—the point is clear when the operator on the other end of the phone explains Evelyn can do nothing to solve the problem she is having without her husband—has never been her own.

Graham Dashwood (Tom Wilkinson) is a judge who finally has had enough of his career and wants to return to the country where he grew up in order to gain some closure on a secret chapter of his life. Douglas (Bill Nighy) and Jean Ainslie (Penelope Wilton) are also new retirees, and they need an inexpensive alternative to their original retirement plans after Douglas invested their savings in their daughter's startup company, which has yet to see a profit. The ill-tempered and racist Muriel Donnelly (Maggie Smith) must travel for hip surgery. Norman Cousins (Ronald Pickup) is tired of being disappointed with the local dating scene, Madge Hardcastle (Celia Imrie) wants freedom from her family in order to explore new romances.

Their destination is Jaipur, India, specifically the eponymous resort "for the Elderly and Beautiful" (also the movie's subtitle). As it happens, the accommodations are not anywhere near as impressive as the website promised, but everyone, save for Jean (She is the only character without an obstacle of some kind to overcome; in fact, she is the obstacle for her husband), either laughs about it or is too busy with his or her own goals to care much. They all go about their business, occasionally encounter each other in the process, and return at the end of the day to recount what has happened. Evelyn even starts a blog to detail her experiences, and it is also an excuse for a voice-over narration to fill in any blanks that the characters' assorted monologues leave in regards to the important lessons they have learned.

It becomes clear relatively quickly that there is little more to these characters than the successful prologue, which nimbly summarizes the essence of each character in pointed scenes, has already established. The only exception is Graham, whose story of a life filled with regret after abandoning his first—and, to the best of anyone's knowledge, only—love, a local boy his age whose family worked for his own when he was a young man. While the other characters all have some external gauge with which to measure their success in reinventing their lives, Graham's is far more introspective and honest. The result of the eventual conversation with the man is unimportant (Madden and Parker do not show it); it is simply enough that he has the chance.

The movie paints the rest of the characters' stories in broad strokes. Evelyn takes a job at a call center, teaching operators how to talk to the elderly, and begins a friendship with Douglas that is destined to become more. A visit to the family of a resort employee chal-

lenges Muriel's prejudices. Madge and Norman have varying success in trying to regain their sex lives. Most distracting of all is the series of subplots involving the hotel's manager Sonny (Dev Patel), who must try to impress his girlfriend (Tena Desae) and appease his overbearingly critical mother (Lillete Dubey), who wants to sell the property despite her son's protests.

The tone shifts radically from one thread to another—from regret-filled speeches to sex farce—and by the time the group must unite to save the hotel from sale or divide to return to their previous lives at home, the constant shifting of perspective and mood has all but forsaken the characters to a condition of stasis. *The Best Exotic Marigold Hotel* pummels the idea of adaptation yet feels stuck in an continual loop in which nothing actually changes for the characters until the plot allows.

Mark Dujsik

CREDITS

Evelyn Greenslade: Judi Dench
Muriel Donnelly: Maggie Smith
Douglas Ainslie: Bill Nighy
Jean Ainslie: Penelope Wilton
Graham Dashwood: Tom Wilkinson
Madge Hardcastle: Celia Imrie
Norman Cousins: Ronald Pickup
Sonny Kapoor: Dev Patel
Sunaina: Tena Desae
Origin: United Kingdom, United States
Language: English
Released: 2012
Production: Graham Broadbent, Peter Czernin; Participant Media, Blueprint Pictures; released by Fox Searchlight
Directed by: John Madden
Written by: Ol Parker
Cinematography by: Ben Davis
Music by: Thomas Newman
Sound: Ian Wilson
Editing: Chris Gill
Costumes: Louise Stjernsward
Production Design: Alan Macdonald
MPAA rating: PG-13
Running time: 124 minutes

REVIEWS

Berardinelli, James. *ReelViews*. May 3, 2012.
Burr, Ty. *Boston Globe*. May 4, 2012.
Ebert, Roger. *Chicago Sun-Times*. May 2, 2012.
Holden, Stephen. *New York Times*. May 3, 2012.

Kenny, Glenn. *MSN Movies*. May 1, 2012.
Lacey, Liam. *Globe and Mail*. September 4, 2012.
O'Sullivan, Michael. *Washington Post*. May 4, 2012.
Osenlund, R. Kurt. *Slant Magazine*. May 1, 2012.
Phillips, Michael. *Chicago Tribune*. May 3, 2012.
Phipps, Keith. *AV Club*. May 3, 2012.

QUOTES

Evelyn: "Nothing here has worked out quite as I expected."
Muriel: "Most things don't. But sometimes what happens instead is the good stuff."

TRIVIA

Bill Nighy and Penelope Wilton previously played husband and wife in *Shaun of the Dead*.

AWARDS

Nominations:

Golden Globes 2013: Actress—Mus./Comedy (Dench), Film—Mus./Comedy
Screen Actors Guild 2012: Actress—Supporting (Smith), Cast

BIG MIRACLE

Box Office: $20.2 million

Its rather nondescript title notwithstanding, *Big Miracle* is an agreeable drama of uplift about what begins as a seemingly unusual but one-off human interest story of the sort that typically closes local newscasts, and then snowballs into an international effort to rescue three California grey whales trapped in an Alaskan ice pack preventing them from making their annual migration south to warmer climes. Deploying a more expansive palette than many animal rescue movies of its ilk, the film, based on a true story from 1988 and originally titled *Everybody Loves Whales*, is a smart and amiable slice of family-friendly entertainment that nicely juggles a pinch of ambition with its more predictable feel-good impulses.

Big Miracle unfolds in Point Barrow, 300 miles from the North Arctic circle. News reporter Adam Carlson (John Krasinski) is the first to stumble across the lost, trapped whales, consisting of an adult male and female and their young offspring. He files a report explaining their congregation around a shrinking hole in the ice, and how they are unable to swim six miles underwater to safety. Los Angeles-based reporter Jill Jerard (Kristen Bell) has a feeling that the tale could have legs, an instinct which is quickly borne out. When the story goes national, and becomes a staple of the nightly network news broadcasts, suddenly everyone wants to get involved, for various self-serving reasons.

Oil company magnate J.W. McGraw (Ted Danson), looking for some good publicity to help prop up his pro-drilling agenda, agrees to loan an ice-smashing hover-barge to the efforts; a resolute National Guardsman, Colonel Scott Boyer (Dermot Mulroney), is tasked with the never-before-attempted duty of hauling the massive craft north, attached to a pair of helicopters. White House executive assistant Kelly Myers (Vinessa Shaw), looking to help burnish Republican administration environmental credentials during Vice President George Bush's run for the presidency, tries to marshal other government resources. Then there is Adam's ex-girlfriend and impassioned activist Rachel Kramer (Drew Barrymore), who, even if she will not admit it, in the plight of the whales sees a potential boon to her environmental advocacy group Greenpeace.

Adam has a friendly relationship with the local Inuits, including friendly young Nathan (Ahmaogak Sweeney), and understands their culture. But others are aghast at their initial plans to harvest the seemingly doomed whales for meat. The whale captains back down from their idea after consulting with elder Malik (John Pingayak), but a litany of solutions to free the whales still cannot cope with a newly formed ice ridge that would block their path out to sea. With time dwindling, finally and reluctantly, the motley coalition agrees to turn to the Soviets, who have a tanker in the area that they agree to send to help.

While logging occasional big screen credits, director Ken Kwapis spent a good portion of his early career on single-camera TV comedies, until experiencing something of a mini-breakthrough with his charming, airy, justifiably well-regarded adaptation of *The Sisterhood of the Traveling Pants* (2005). The diversity of those experiences—his familiarity with comedic timing as well as the tapestral narrative elements of the aforementioned movie—benefits *Big Miracle*. It has funny moments, but they are not discrete and forced; they instead flow from the quirks and foibles of the characters.

It no doubt helps, too, that Kwapis worked previously with his stars—Krasinski in *License to Wed* (2007), and Barrymore in *He's Just Not That Into You* (2009). But *Big Miracle* is more of an ensemble film with a broader narrative canvas than its marketing campaign conveyed. Given its meager, $20 million domestic theatrical gross when compared to similar movies like *Dolphin Tale* (2011) and *Free Willy* (1993), which each grossed four to five times as much, this box office shortfall perhaps reflects the reality of an erroneous public perception of a more streamlined, sappy story, centering around a nature-set, Krasinski-Barrymore romance.

Jack Amiel and Michael Begler's script, based on Tom Rose's 1989 book *Freeing the Whales*, reflects much tinkering and adjustment of multiple storylines, as one might expect from a work based on a true story. A bit of Rachel's dialogue is strident and too on-the-nose ("It's because whales can't vote, right? And they can't give big campaign contributions!" she rails at one point, in protest to the governor), and a couple other moments ring false—most notably a sit-down meeting, full of subset political speechifying, between Rachel, Adam, J.W., Kelly and Colonel Boyer. Yet the screenplay does a generally good job of driving and funneling the unfolding story naturally through its characters. There is a bit of dwindling Cold War-era political subplot, but never so much that it distracts from the core conflict of the fate of the whales.

Filming on location in Anchorage, Kwapis and cinematographer John Bailey make fantastic use of evocative outdoor vistas. Kwapis and his editor, Cara Silverman, also deftly integrate real news footage featuring Dan Rather, Peter Jennings, Tom Brokaw, Connie Chung and others, creating a solid foundation of believability for the dramatic recreations. The effects work, a blend of CGI and practical efforts, is also quite solid, and a good fit with the material.

Almost uniformly, the performances feed a story which is admirably free of scapegoating or side-taking in the name of cheap emotional reaction or catharsis. It is true that Barrymore imbues Rachel with some of the same sing-song cadence and demonstrative mannerisms she deploys in more overtly comedic fare, a fact that stands out in further contrast when stacked up against her costars. Krasinski, though, showcases professional aspiration that does not warp or pervert a core decency, and Bell plays professionally plucky but also shot through with uncertainty. In smaller roles, Rob Riggle and James LeGros shine as a pair of helpful, entrepreneurial, accented Minnesotans who arrive on the scene with a deicer. It is this array of pleasurable supporting performances that give the movie an especially palpable sense of rootedness.

It is certainly not a wildly adventurous tale, or even a particularly poetic one. *Big Miracle* is a conventionally structured story, and it lacks the expressive lyricism of something like New Zealand import *Whale Rider* (2003), another film (partially) about whales. But in depicting honestly the various ulterior motives of its many characters, and how they are nonetheless individually impacted and illuminated by this daunting group undertaking, *Big Miracle* is far more realistic and richly humanistic than one might expect, which is certainly its own miracle with respect to so much modern-day Hollywood product.

Brent Simon

CREDITS

Adam Carlson: John Krasinski
Rachel Kramer: Drew Barrymore
Jill Jerard: Kristen Bell
Colonel Scott Boyer: Dermot Mulroney
Pat Lafaytette: Tim Blake Nelson
J.W. McGraw: Ted Danson
Kelly Meyers: Vinessa Shaw
Governor Haskell: Stephen (Steve) Root
Porter Beckford: Michael Gaston
Dean Glowacki: Rob Riggle
Karl Hootkin: James LeGros
Malik: John Pingayak
Ruth Mcgraw: Kathy Baker
Origin: United States
Language: English
Released: 2012
Production: Tim Bevan, Liza Chasin, Eric Fellner, Steven Golin, Michael Sugar; Anonymous Content, Working Title Films; released by Universal Pictures
Directed by: Ken Kwapis
Written by: Jack Amiel; Michael Begler
Cinematography by: John Bailey
Music by: Cliff Eidelman
Sound: Geoffrey G. Rubay
Music Supervisor: Nick Angel
Editing: Cara Silverman
Art Direction: Scott Coates
Costumes: Shay Cunliffe
Production Design: Nelson Coates
MPAA rating: PG
Running time: 107 minutes

REVIEWS

Gleiberman, Owen. *Entertainment Weekly.* February 8, 2012.
Hazelton, John. *Screen International.* February 2, 2012.
Keogh, Tom. *Seattle Times.* February 2, 2012.
LaSalle, Mick. *San Francisco Chronicle.* February 2, 2012.
Page, Janice. *Boston Globe.* February 2, 2012.
Phillips, Michael. *Chicago Tribune.* February 2, 2012.
Puig, Claudia. *USA Today.* February 2, 2012.
Rechtshaffen, Michael. *Hollywood Reporter.* February 1, 2012.
Taylor, Ella. *NPR.* February 2, 2012.
Zacharek, Stephanie. *Movieline.* February 2, 2012.

QUOTES

Adam Carlson: "I usually get the breakfast burrito, which is fantastic. But the pile o' pancakes with a side of ham steak is tempting. What do you think I should get?"

Jill Jerard: "The name of a good cardiologist?"

TRIVIA

The sportscaster shown at the end of the archived news clip is Sarah Palin, before she became the Governor of Alaska and a nominee for Vice President, around two decades after the events depicted in the movie.

BLUE LIKE JAZZ

Everybody belongs somewhere.
—Movie tagline

Box Office: $595,018

Christian-based filmmaking, like any other filmmaking niche, often suffers from self-imposed limitations enforced by a lack of out-of-the-box thinking. *Blue Like Jazz* makes a concerted effort to push against this concept and go where no Christian film has gone before but fails to deliver the laughs, satirical smarts or emotional oomph of cinematic brethren like *Dogma* (1999) or *Saved* (2004). Still what it does deliver is important, and worth a look to anyone interested enough in the big questions to watch a simple, amusing story of a self-absorbed young man whose biggest spiritual need is the revelation of his true, relatively small, place in the universe.

Don Miller (Marshall Allman) is a firmly-ensconced Christian youth group type ready to head off to college. When his divorced mother (Jenny Littleton) winds up pregnant as the result of an affair with Don's Youth Pastor Kenny (Jason Marsden). Completely disillusioned he takes his father up on a surprise offer to attend Reed College in Portland, one of the most hedonistic campuses in America. What Don fails to understand is that his past will be immediately visible to everyone and his running away from it will surprise/impress no one. It also gets him nowhere but closer to where he began. A friendship with Lauren (Tania Raymonde), a hot lesbian he meets in the unisex bathroom, offers opportunity for introspection and small acts of kindness, an intense classroom debate showcases his rudeness and need to grow in compassion, and a crush on a girl named Penny (Claire Holt), a fellow student and social activist, uncovers his shallow motives for the little good he even bothers trying to do at school. Even the self-ordained Pope (Justin Welborn), who trundles down the street burning books in a shopping cart and partying with the best of them has nothing on Don, who ultimately unmasks mainly himself while taking confessions from others at the end-of-year, drunken, school bacchanal.

Reed College is an actual place and most of the quirky goings on showcased in the film are actually part of the day-to-day life on the campus. Tables full of other people's leftover food can be picked over for recycling by students not wanting to waste. Students chase each other around in mascot costumes as part of arcane symbolic rituals. But for all of the real-life zaniness of Reed that Taylor and company get up on the screen the realness of church experience eludes them. Viewers see two churches in the film, one of which is a near parody of how cliched Evangelical holy rollers are often portrayed while the other is a squeaky clean, more liturgically-based faith community that ends up having next to nothing to do with Don's journey. Instead, the script offers Penny as a surprise Christian stand-in to challenge Don about his shallowness and the audience is left wondering if they are supposed to root for the pair to become romantically involved.

The cast is good to very good here but they are working with uneven material that never quite finds its emotional locus. Don and Penny spend a great deal of the film in flux and by the time the script unwinds what it wants to say through them, they come off as dangerously thin characters. Kudos should go to Marshall Allman who gives Don a believably tortured sensibility and Justin Welborn who simply haunts as the self-appointed Pope of the school. Viewers will sense his big reveal coming from a mile away but Welborn sells every moment he is onscreen and gives what could have been a cartoonish character real depth when it most matters. The end confessional scene and any number of the other sequences work well in provoking laughs and even deep thought but in the end the difficulty is that *Blue Like Jazz* is merely an okay film rather than the dynamite one it might have been.

Steve Taylor (*The Second Chance* [2006]) has managed to distinguish himself as one of a new wave of Christian filmmakers more interested in telling stories that grapple with faith as lifestyle and mystery, setting up young heroes that have more questions than answers even by stories end. This is hardly the simple evangelistic stuff or overwrought apocalyptica, viewers will associate with dreadful films like *The Omega Code* (1999) or *Left Behind* (2001). The film wears its conscience on its sleeve, showcasing a young man coming of age and growing the hell up as much as coming back to faith. His argument, the central conflict in the film, is within himself, he is the problem, not those outside the faith or inside the faith. For those who see no problem within, or are unwilling to see that problem in spiritual terms, *Blue Like Jazz* will hardly be compelling. But for the judgmental, the self-important, the tempted, and those all too aware of their own fallenness, *Blue Like Jazz* will likely be well worth the time.

Dave Canfield

CREDITS

Don Miller: Marshall Allman
Penny: Claire Holt
Lauren: Tania Raymonde
The Pope: Justin Welborn
The Hobo: Eric Lange
Kenny: Jason Marsden
Origin: United States
Language: English
Released: 2012
Production: J. Clarke Gallivan, Coke Sams, Steve Taylor; RuckusFilm; released by Roadside Attractions
Directed by: Steve Taylor
Written by: Steve Taylor; Ben Pearson
Cinematography by: Ben Pearson
Music by: Danny Seim
Sound: Thomas Morrison
Editing: Matthew Sterling
Art Direction: David Hewlette
Costumes: Amy Patterson
Production Design: Cyndi Williams
MPAA rating: PG-13
Running time: 108 minutes

REVIEWS

Belfus, John. *Commercial Appeal*. May 4, 2012.
Burr, Ty. *Boston Globe*. April 12, 2012.
Judell, Brandon. *Culture Catch*. April 12, 2012.
Minnow, Nell. *Beliefnet*. April 19, 2012.
Nehme, Farran Smith. *New York Post*. April 13, 2012.
Osenlund, R. Kurt. *Slant Magazine*. April 10, 2012.
O'Sullivan, Michael. *Washington Post*. April 13, 2012.
Sachs, Ben. *Chicago Reader*. April 13, 2012.
Snider, Eric D. *Film.com*. April 13, 2012.
Swietek, Frank. *One Guy's Opinion*. April 14, 2012.

QUOTES

Donald Miller: "My dad says life is like jazz because it doesn't resolve. But what if we're not alone? What if all these stars are notes on a page of music, swirling in the blue, like jazz?"

TRIVIA

The movie was made possible by the efforts of fans that refused to let the project die. A campaign on KickStarter was started after a September 16th blog post by Donald Miller

stated that the project was dead due to a lack of backers. By the end of the funding period on October 25th, Save Blue Like Jazz had raised $345,992 (well over the $125,000 goal).

THE BOURNE LEGACY

There was never just one.
—Movie tagline

Box Office: $113.2 million

If there were an Oscar award for best agent, Jeremy Renner's job-finder would surely be entitled to one. After two decades in the salt mines of bit parts and low-budget movies, Renner exploded into stardom with his justly Oscar-nominated performance in *The Hurt Locker* (2009), the Best Picture Oscar winner of 2009. Since then, he has chosen his films very wisely: another Oscar-nominated turn in Ben Affleck's gritty *The Town* (2010), *Mission Impossible: Ghost Protocol* (2011), the best-and-highest-grossing entry in the franchise, and *The Avengers* (2012), the third highest-grossing film of all time. Now, he steps into the *Bourne* franchise which made Matt Damon into a worldwide household name and featured some of the most innovative action of the new century. Renner has had quite the 2012.

His success continues with *The Bourne Legacy,* which is surprisingly entertaining given that it is the fourth retread of the series' "super-agent-gone-rogue" storyline. This time around Jason Bourne is out of the story (Damon deemed *Bourne Supremacy* (2004) and *Bourne Ultimatum* (2007) director Paul Greengrass's participation so crucial that he declined to return to the franchise without him at the helm) but the sinister government agencies responsible for the super spy program which produced Bourne are alive and well and feverishly dealing with the fallout caused by Bourne in the first three films. Indeed, the film literally (and confusingly) begins where the last film left off. Without any explanatory text or exposition, CIA director Ezra Kramer (Scott Glenn) shows up at the home of retired admiral Mark Turso (Stacy Keach) and informs him that the efforts to eliminate Bourne have failed. Like a modern television show arc, the film assumes the viewer has seen the previous installments and makes no concessions if he or she has not. The Bourne mess is not Turso's only problem. In addition to Bourne being on the loose, Dr. Albert Hirsch (Albert Finney), a psychologist who oversaw the Operation Treadstone, the secret program that produced Bourne, has been indiscreet, threatening to expose a second, even-more-explosive secret project of genetically enhanced super spies, Operation Outcome.

Turso activates sociopathic clean-up operative Colonel Eric Byer (Ed Norton) and his team to protect

Outcome's secrecy. Unhindered by morality of any kind, Byer quickly decides that the only way to keep the program secret is to kill everyone involved and then start over again after everything blows over. This means that Hirsch, all the secret agents, all of the scientists administering the program and a pesky investigative journalist (Paddy Considine) have to be killed. In the logic of secret agent thrillers, it is always easier to maintain secrecy by murdering scores of people in spectacularly public fashion then just reminding them of their non-disclosure agreements and asking them to go underground. (These "kill 'em all" plots always bring to mind the old Universal Mummy movies where, in order to maintain the secrecy of the location of the pharaoh's tomb, the slaves constructing it are murdered on site after finishing building it, leaving open the question of how to ensure the silence of the soldiers who killed the slaves and so on and so forth). The super agents of the program are the easiest to kill because the program operates by supplying the agents with pills that enhance their mental and physical attributes until their genetic makeup changes permanently. So it is simply a matter of introducing a new pill for the subjects that kills them as far as closing the program down. Soon, super agents in various states of undercover investigations all over the world are collapsing dead in public with blood streaming out of their nostrils.

That is, all super agents but one. Aaron Cross (Jeremy Renner) is in the wilderness of Alaska engaging in solo training and so the death pill cannot be easily administered to him. Instead, a drone is sent to kill him. Through some rather daring work involving a homing device and a pack of wolves that has been pursuing him, Cross manages to make it look like he has been killed and is soon on the trail of those who want him dead. First, however, he needs to obtain more enhancement pills and to do so he goes after Dr. Marta Shearing (Rachel Weisz). He has to go to her because Dr. Shearing is the only remaining doctor involved in Operation Outcome who is still alive. Earlier in the week, her co-worker, Dr. Donald Foite (Zeljko Ivanek), went on a murder-suicide rampage to keep the program secret (one wonders if this potential job requirement was discussed with Dr. Foite at his job interview for the secret program) but was gunned down by security before he could finish the job by killing Dr. Shearing. In fact, when Cross arrives at Shearing's home, he interrupts the efforts of some scummy government operatives to murder Shearing and make it look like a suicide. Soon, Aaron and Shearing are on their way to Manila to obtain more drugs for Cross and they have a new generation of superspy, one that purposely lacks the cumbersome morality that has caused so much trouble with Bourne and Cross, in hot pursuit.

While it is fun to pick on *The Bourne Legacy's* absurd plot, plot is obviously not its point. One remembers the reason for seeing these films when Cross arrives at Shearing's house and, in one fluid and beautiful tracking shot, the camera follows him as he clambers up the side of the house, smashes through the glass sunroof and shoots an assassin dead. Director Tony Gilmore and editor John Gilmore deliver the trademark climbing, jumping, rooftop running, window smashing, and fist fighting with the whiplash editing that fans of the series expect. Gilroy's direction is crisp and invigorating and while he does not quite deliver the level of stunning action direction pioneered by Greengrass he does manage to generate more suspense than Greengrass's entries, particularly in scenes like Cross's interaction with a fellow agent in Alaska (who may or may not have been sent to kill him) and Dr. Shearer's (and the viewer's) slow, horrific realization that the "helpers" sent to her at her house are there to do anything but help her. Gilroy wrote and directed the supremely suspenseful *Michael Clayton* (2007) and his gift for building tension really pays off in *Legacy*. (It also helps that the *Bourne* series, unlike most of its action brethren, is not afraid to allow its characters to talk for more than 15-second intervals.)

Gilroy is also blessed, in Renner and Weisz, with superb actors who can sell the film's ridiculous dialogue. Renner is excellent and manages to invest his underwritten role with genuine humanity, reminding viewers why he was Oscar nominated. Oscar winner Weisz is also superb in what is essentially a stock damsel in distress role. Both actors manage to imbue their one-note characters with far more complexity than the characters have on the page and make the viewer care about them. And, most surprising of all, *Legacy's* script manages to come up with a genuinely novel twist. Cross's desperate need for more pills is not the threat of losing his super strength (that has already been hardwired in) but, like Cliff Robertson in the classic *Charly* (1968), his intelligence. In order to make his quota, Cross's army recruiter lied on his application and added 12 points to his IQ so he could make the bare minimum standards for an Army Private. In a welcome subversion of the usual action film emphasis, in which physical strength is everything, in *Legacy* Cross is racing against time to get the meds because otherwise he will not be *smart* enough to keep himself and Shearing alive.

One rumored possibility for the next film in the *Bourne* franchise is a team up between Jason Bourne and Aaron Cross. If that is the case, this viewer has one suggestion. It is time for a woman to be an agent. One of the agents slain in the shutdown of Operation Outcome is a female and it is a shame that the film did not get her into the action. *The Bourne Legacy* would have been a whole lot more fun if Cross and Weisz were both super agents and Rachel Weisz is simply too good an actress to waste on the ancient cliche of the damsel in distress. Otherwise, *The Bourne Legacy* is a successful and entertaining entry in the franchise and one hopes that in the inevitable sequel that the rogue agent protagonists can finally start tackling the guys at the top.

Nate Vercauteren

CREDITS

Aaron Cross: Jeremy Renner
Marta: Rachel Weisz
Byer: Edward Norton
Pamela Landy: Joan Allen
Dr. Albert Hirsch: Albert Finney
Noah Vosen: David Strathairn
Ezra Kramer: Scott Glenn
Origin: United States
Language: English
Released: 2012
Production: Frank Marshall, Patrick Crowley, Ben Smith, Jeffrey Weiner; Relativity Media; released by Universal Pictures
Directed by: Tony Gilroy
Written by: Tony Gilroy; Dan Gilroy
Cinematography by: Robert Elswit
Music by: James Newton Howard
Sound: Karen M. Baker; Per Hallberg
Editing: John Gilroy
Costumes: Shay Cunliffe
Production Design: Kevin Thompson
MPAA rating: PG-13
Running time: 125 minutes

REVIEWS

Atkinson, Michael. *Village Voice*. August 7, 2012.
Burr, Ty. *Boston Globe*. August 9, 2012.
Dargis, Manohla. *New York Times*. August 9, 2012.
DeBruge, Peter. *Variety*. August 6, 2012.
Ebert, Roger. *Chicago Sun-Times*. August 8, 2012.
Lumenick, Lou. *New York Post*. August 10, 2012.
Nathan, Ian. *Empire*. August 12, 2012.
Rothkopf, Joshua. *Time Out New York*. August 7, 2012.
Tobias, Scott. *AV Club*. August 8, 2012.
Turan, Kenneth. *Los Angeles Times*. August 9, 2012.

QUOTES

Aaron Cross: "Now, I've got a plan, and it's just not that complicated. What I'm going to do is wait for the next person to show up to kill you. Maybe they can help me."

TRIVIA

Before this movie was even considered, director Paul Greengrass had jokingly suggested making a fourth Bourne movie called *The Bourne Redundancy*.

BRAVE

Change your fate.
—Movie tagline

Box Office: $237.3 million

A film titled *Brave* should be expected to take significant risks. *Brave* takes a couple of narrative ones but fails to turn them into the sort of movie magic that will move most viewers to place it on the shelf with their very favorite Pixar films. Chief among its virtues are a resourceful heroine who navigates her destiny without the need of a male escort, and a coming-of-age narrative built around a fairly compelling mother-daughter conflict. Those elements alone put *Brave* a little off the beaten path. But they are locked in a story lacking in emotional punch. Viewers will experience *Brave* as standard animated family fare, slightly tweaked to a young female demographic, or, if they are inclined towards cynicism, they may see it as designed specifically to appeal to moms and dads who want the option of sitting the kiddies in front of a politically correct bit of consumerist flotsam. Always pretty to look at, often very funny, *Brave* plays it way too safe to inspire.

Since her youngest days in the Kingdom of Dun Broch, the Scottish Princess Merida (Kelly Macdonald) has longed for a life independent of her station. Though her father King Fergus (Billy Connolly) has nurtured her tomboy nature by, among other things, helping her become a first class archer, her mother Queen Elinor (Emma Thompson) is determined that her daughter will grow up to be a traditional royal companion. Familial unease reaches a boiling point when Merida refuses to be betrothed to any of the first-born of the lords of her kingdom, deeply insulting the clans of Lord Dingwall (Robbie Coltrane), Lord MacGuffin (Kevin McKidd), and Lord Macintosh (Craig Ferguson).

In a last ditch effort to avoid matrimony, Merida hires a witch (Julie Walters) and bargains for a spell that is supposed to change her mother's mind. Instead, it changes her mother into a bear, a creature already deeply feared in Dun Broch since the long ago day when King Fergus lost a leg to the monstrous bear Mor'Du. Smuggling her mother out of the castle, Merida learns she has only one day in which to change her mother back before the spell becomes permanent. Out in the wild, the pair must learn to communicate only to be pursued by both Mor'Du and the Lords of Dun Broch.

At heart, the story is age-old. Family dynamics are best served when everyone can meet in the middle, letting go of unrealistic expectations, and accept one another as individuals. But nobody in *Brave* is much more than a caricature. The characters who are more realistic in the way they are depicted follow predictable patterns and arcs ending up exactly where viewers will expect. Those that are less realistically rendered are done so as to provide comic bits of business that do little but distract from the story until the next plot point can reveal itself. This is especially worth noting since it breaks with the visual consistency that has been a hallmark of Pixar in all of its truly great films. As funny as Fergus and the Lords and the triplet princes are they seem like they belong in a different film, dragging down the narrative. But top-heaviness and quick fixes seem inevitable here since there are no fewer than three directors (Mark Andrews, Brenda Chapman, and Steve Purcell) sharing screenwriting credit with a fourth writer (Irene Mecchi).

The film is most effective when it relies on the stunning visuals the Pixar team creates. Landscapes, characters hair, the animal life of the film are all impossibly perfect and the directing team composes shot after epic shot, swooping the camera in and around the action. A good instance is the botched escape of Merida and her mother out of the castle. As their panic increases, the camera assumes their point of view and soon the scene becomes breathless. Yet, even in the visuals, Pixar is tripped up by the unnecessary use of 3D. There are some standout 3D sequences such as when Mor'Du chases Merida and her mother through the foggy moors. But mostly the 3D seems almost an afterthought. Truly great 3D films like *Hugo* (2011) or especially *Coraline* (2009) use the effect to tell the story, advance the viewer through characters' emotions. Here it is a novelty, used to enhance chase sequences in a story that lacks complexity and character development.

The score here by Patrick Doyle jumps and capers underneath everything, providing all the right touchstones without calling too much attention to itself. It is, in short, the very nature of what a film score should be, supportive, inspiring, and emotionally resonant. Most importantly, it feels authentic. This is no ersatz Celtic fluff. The score offers a rich tapestry of traditional instrumentation and sweeping power.

Voice work is absolutely first rate. Kelly Macdonald instills Merida with a fiery fierceness and Billy Connolly nails the cartoonish King Fergus. He is likewise supported by the buffoonery of the Lords and their sons. But then none of the men in this story matter much at all and the screenplay suffers for it. *Brave* seems to make excuses for the men simply because it is a convenient way to advance the story in the desired direction not because the men seem like they belong in this particular story or world. Amidst the gorgeous landscapes and environs, Fergus and company seem like cardboard theater puppets.

Mor'du is a thing of nightmarish intensity, so much so that parents may want to sample the film before they expose especially sensitive kids to *Brave*. But this is a thing the film does very well. It creates a sense of disorder in the natural world that only Merida, by virtue of her willingness to assume individual responsibility, can overcome and set right. As wildly beautiful as the forest is, Merida can only visit that place, allowing herself eventually to be tamed somewhat, so that she may build community with others and rightly assume her responsibility to more than just herself in the world.

Pixar will certainly make more compelling films than *Brave* and if every family film were as good as *Brave* family cinema would be a more sparkling place. But the film marks an interesting place in the history of the best animation studio ever. What kind of stories Pixar chooses to tell is what may make or break their track record for excellence. Hopefully, they will choose stories that are first and foremost compelling rather than merely marketable. No doubt the pressure to succeed has increased since they are well beyond the series of outlines proposed during the legendary luncheon that resulted in their first few huge hits. *Brave* is hardly a creative nadir but it embraces formula which is something that Pixar has largely avoided.

Dave Canfield

CREDITS

Merida: Kelly Macdonald (Voice)

Fergus: Billy Connolly (Voice)

Queen Elinor: Emma Thompson (Voice)

The Witch: Julie Walters (Voice)

Lord Dingwall: Robbie Coltrane (Voice)

Lord MacGuffin: Kevin McKidd (Voice)

Lord Macintosh: Craig Ferguson (Voice)

Origin: United States

Language: English, French, Spanish

Released: 2012

Production: Katherine Sarafian; Pixar; released by Walt Disney Studios

Directed by: Mark C. Andrews; Brenda Chapman; Steve Purcell

Written by: Mark C. Andrews; Brenda Chapman; Steve Purcell; Irene Mecchi

Music by: Patrick Doyle

Sound: Gwendolyn Yates Whittle

Music Supervisor: Tom MacDougall

Editing: Nicholas C. Smith
Production Design: Steve Pilcher
MPAA rating: PG
Running time: 100 minutes

REVIEWS

Brunson, Matt. *Creative Loafing*. June 23, 2012.
Ebert, Roger. *Chicago Sun-Times*. June 21, 2012.
DeKinder, Mathew. *St. Louis Post-Dispatch*. June 22, 2012.
Kennedy, Lisa. *Denver Post*. June 22, 2012.
Long, Tom. *Detroit News*. June 22, 2012.
Orr, Christopher. *The Atlantic*. June 22, 2012.
Overstreet, Jeffrey. *Response*. June 22, 2012.
Neish, Jamie. *HeyUGuys*. August 13, 2012.
Schwarzbaum, Lisa. *Entertainment Weekly*. June 20, 2012.
Stevens, Dana. *Slate*. June 21, 2012.

QUOTES

Princess Merida: "There are those who say fate is something beyond our command. That destiny is not our own, but I know better. Our fate lives within us, you only have to be brave enough to see it."

TRIVIA

None of the footage shown in the preview trailer is in the finished film.

AWARDS

Oscars 2012: Animated Film
British Acad. 2012: Animated Film
Golden Globes 2013: Animated Film

BROOKLYN CASTLE

Imagine a school where the cool kids are the chess team. Welcome to I.S.318.
—Movie tagline

Box Office: $213,074

In 2003, Jeffrey Blitz's documentary *Spellbound* practically made the case that a spelling bee could be every bit as compelling and intense as any football, baseball, basketball or hockey game. Since its release, national spelling bees have been popping up on ESPN and have become popular news items when the winning word gets revealed, sending everyone to their dictionaries to look it up. It helped that the movie had several fascinating and engaging characters to follow around for a year. *Brooklyn Castle,* a new documentary from director Katie Dellamagiore, seems to be making the same play in regards to chess. The characters are of roughly the same age as those in *Spellbound* (maybe a bit older), but the idea remains the same: Here at this school, the chess players (those who would normally be seen as outcasts at any other school) are the real athletes.

Brooklyn Castle takes place at Intermediate School 318 in Brooklyn, NY (also called I.S.318), a middle school in a low-income neighborhood that might not look like much on the outside, yet it holds the distinction for winning twenty-six national chess titles, more than any other middle school in the country. What started out as a little after-school experiment has since turned into a mini institution. The tournaments are held throughout the country in large banquet halls with as many as 5,500 players in attendance. At the start of the film, I.S.318 takes second place at a tournament in Nashville. Tears of disappointment come from some of the players at I.S.318, a few of who take center stage in Dellamagiore's film.

Pobo is an outspoken 7th grader with long-term goals of becoming a lawyer and eventually a surgeon general. Alexis is a male seventh grader who tries to get into one of New York's top public high schools, which has a lottery system for admittance, provided students can pass the exam. Justus is an incoming 6th grader who has the highest game rate of any kid his age. Patrick, who has ADHD, finds chess a great way to build his concentration. And Rochelle, an 8th grader, who might be on the verge of becoming the first African American female chess master in the history of the game. The only way for her to earn that title is to compete at every tournament and win. Rochelle, at the start of the film, has just graduated from I.S.318 and has been named "the hardest working, smartest girl I ever met" by John Gavin, the school's assistant principal.

Of course, schools need money to attend these tournaments year round and Dellamagiore's film makes clear how the economic downturn on Wall Street directly affects the school's ability to travel. Money must be raised somehow. Chess-In-The-Schools, a non-profit organization that helps out underfunded schools compete in chess tournaments, does what they can, while also helping out Rochelle by providing her a private chess master. Pobo makes a run for school president ("Vote for Poboma!") and makes a vow to raise the money that has been cut. A PTA meeting rallies parents to the cause and kick-starts an email campaign to get the money back.

Dellamagiore's film is made up of many such dramas, only a few of which occur at the actual tournaments. Pobo's run for class president has perhaps the comically suspenseful moment in the film as he awaits the campaign results. Dellamagiore also does a masterful job of putting everything in context with regards to the tournament and the scoring system. The film wisely never makes any attempts to explain the game itself, but explains that there are endless possibilities for how each game can turn out. That is enough for the uninitiated viewer to go on and goes a long way toward explaining the pressure these players put on themselves to win each and every game. The teachers themselves come off well, particularly Elizabeth Vicary, the school's chess coach, who explains how some of these students with academic difficulties find chess as their activity of choice because of the myriad of ways they can find their way into a problem that is worth solving. She is a comforting and encouraging voice for these students when they did not have a good day at the table.

There have been many documentaries like *Brooklyn Castle* before, but Dellamagiore's assured direction and Nelson Dellamagiore's editing keep the viewer from making quick comparisons. Dellamagiore and her team know exactly where to put the cameras, particularly during the tournaments themselves which have an uncommon smoothness about them (for a documentary). The tournaments convey the head-spinning complexity of the game, the frustration of hitting a mental brick wall and, of course, the unbearable agony of defeat. Chess is not for everyone and yet Dellamagiore has made a film to which just about anyone can relate, a staple of any great sports movie, whether they wear uniforms or not.

Collin Souter

CREDITS

Herself: Rochelle Ballantyne
Himself: Pobo Efokoro
Himself: John Galvin
Himself: Fred Rubino
Herself: Elizabeth Vicary
Origin: United States
Language: English
Released: 2012
Production: Katie Dellamaggiore, Brian Schulz, Nelson Dellamaggiore; Le Castle Film Works, Rescued Media; released by Producers Distribution Agency
Directed by: Katie Dellamaggiore
Cinematography by: Brian Schulz
Music by: Brian Satz
Editing: Nelson Dellamaggiore
MPAA rating: PG
Running time: 101 minutes

REVIEWS

Dargis, Manohla. *New York Times*. October 18, 2012.
Dowd, A. A. *Time Out Chicago*. October 15, 2012.
Ebert, Roger. *Chicago Sun-Times*. November 1, 2012.
Edelstein, David. *New York Magazine*. November 14, 2012.
Feeney, Mark. *Boston Globe*. November 15, 2012.
O'Hehir, Andrew. *Salon.com*. October 17, 2012.
Phillips, Michael. *Chicago Tribune*. November 1, 2012.
Sachs, Ben. *Chicago Reader*. November 1, 2012.
Schwarzbaum, Lisa. *Entertainment Weekly*. October 17, 2012.
Turan, Kenneth. *Los Angeles Times*. October 25, 2012.

BULLHEAD
(Rundskop)

Box Office: $151,840

Bullhead is a prime example of how a premise that could sound ridiculous on paper can be elevated to something approaching tragedy in the execution. The film, which was nominated for Best Foreign Language Film at the 2012 Academy Awards, is a crime drama about a seemingly less threatening crime syndicate known—according to a news report in the film—as "the hormone mafia." As one might suspect, their expertise is acquiring bovine growth hormones of questionable legal status and distributing them to their farming contacts. The result are large, juicy steaks that, at one point, are used as a gift to help incentivize a pair of men the group has contracted for a job. Their response is complete confusion, and despite the two not being anywhere near the smartest people in the film, it is the appropriate reaction.

Looking at it solely from its exterior, this is a strange film. It is also a surprisingly thoughtful one in which the particulars of the crime story only serve as the backdrop for the study of a complex character who believes his life is doomed (using a more colorful word himself in the opening narration) because of a defining event from his childhood—a physical, emotional, and psychological trauma of genuinely unbearable weight.

The man is Jacky Vanmarsenille (Matthias Schoenaerts, who also appeared in 2012's *Rust and Bone*), a low-rent thug for one branch of the hormone mafia whose primary job is to intimidate those people who cross the criminal enterprise's business. The first glimpse that there is more to the man than his hulking physical presence and efficiency at coercing people through brute force comes as he walks away from a farmer whom he has just manhandled and threatened. The soundtrack goes mostly silent as Jacky lumbers back toward his car; he raises his hand to his face in an outward sign of internal shame.

He lives on his family's farm with his infirm father (Kris Cuppens), mother (Sofie Sente), and brother Stieve

(Kristof Renson). Despite the constant source of potential company, Jacky spends his time at home alone for the most part. Director Michael R. Roskam, who also penned the screenplay, shows Jacky in the enclosed space of his bathroom as he prepares for the day. Framed by a window with the blinds closed to highlight the way he has shut himself off from the world, especially in these moments, he boxes the air and prepares a needle with what one assumes at first is a steroid. The actual identity of the drug is key to his sad story.

Roskam's screenplay takes its time in revealing the secret, painful center of Jacky's character and, in the meantime, paints a broad picture of the environment of lawlessness in which he lives. There is a hierarchy to the organization that remains vague.

The critical role of the upper level involves the murder of a police officer who had been investigating the crime ring. The identity of the killer is inconsequential, and the killing itself is only the impetus for a chain of events that will ultimately back Jacky into a corner where he can show of what stuff he is truly made (it also provides some much-needed comic respite in the form of two mechanics [Erico Salamone and Philippe Grand'Henry] who try to hide the luxury car in which the murder took place while still keeping its expensive tires to make a profit).

The main secondary character in Jacky's story is Diederik Maes (Jeroen Perceval), an old childhood friend who has turned police informant. As a child, Diederik (Baudoin Wolwertz) witnessed a local bully named Bruno (David Murgia) attack a young Jacky (Robin Valvekens). The assault ended with Bruno repeatedly hitting Jacky's testicles with a rock. The mafia labeled the entire thing an "accident." Those injections are of testosterone.

Roskam cuts back and forth between the modern events and the fracturing of Jacky and Diederik's friendship, giving the film an elegiac tone toward the innocence that has been lost. Diederik takes it upon himself to become something of a protector for his old friend, keeping his police contacts from looking too closely at Jacky.

The film's heart—a wounded and dangerous one—lies in the gradual exposure of the extent of the damage to Jacky's psyche. It also serves as a destruction of the prototypical alpha male—a man who only knows how to respond to challenge with violence. Roskam gives whatever sympathy he might show for his protagonist a hardened edge with the introduction of Lucia (Jeanne Dandoy), with whom Jacky was infatuated as a child based on only a few glances at her from a distance. She now owns and operates a perfume store; he knows this

because he keeps a book of photographs of and news clippings about her.

This is no longer a healthy, childish crush. He goes to her store to test the waters—to find out whether or not she knows who he is. He begins following her when she leaves home and eventually to a club one night. After their conversation is interrupted by a man asking her to dance, Jacky stalks the man as he walks home and beats him into a coma.

It is not the first time he has done something like this, either. Now a grown man, Bruno (Juda Goslinga) is in the hospital with brain damage; Roskam shows Jacky's fist coming down in an insert shot during his visit to his former tormentor to make the point clear. Bruno is also Lucia's brother, and during that visit, Jacky calls her from the phone in Bruno's hospital room. The question of Jacky's motivation for trying to connect with Lucia becomes hazy: He is either trying to live a normal life (he bemoans that he is like the bulls at his farm, unable to do what he is supposed to do—namely have and protect a family—because of circumstances) or further his revenge against Bruno. More than likely, even Jacky is uncertain of his reasons for pursuing her anymore.

The film moves inexorably toward calamity. In the climactic standoff of *Bullhead*, which favors tension over violence (although it is a prelude to bloodshed), Lucia calls Jacky an "animal." It is a description he denies, yet when Jacky is at the end of his journey through this bizarre world, Roskam and Schoenaerts prove the character wrong with a feral howl.

Mark Dujsik

CREDITS

Jacky: Matthias Schoenaerts
Marc De Kuyper: Sam Louwyck
Diederik: Jeroen Perceval
Lucia: Jeanne Dandoy
Eva: Barbara Sarafian
Sam: Frank Lammers
Origin: Belgium
Language: Dutch, French
Released: 2011
Production: Bart Van Langendonck; Eyeworks Film & TV Drama, Savage Film; released by Drafthouse Films
Directed by: Michael R. Roskam
Written by: Michael R. Roskam
Cinematography by: Nicolas Karakatsanis
Music by: Raf Keunen
Sound: Benoit De Clerck
Editing: Alain Dessauvage

Costumes: Margriet Procee
Production Design: Walter Brugmans
MPAA rating: R
Running time: 124 minutes

REVIEWS

Goss, William. *Film.com*. February 17, 2012.
Holden, Stephen. *New York Times*. February 16, 2012.
Marsh, Calum. *Slant Magazine*. February 15, 2012.
Morris, Wesley. *Boston Globe*. February 24, 2012.
Murray, Noel. *AV Club*. February 16, 2012.
Rocchi, James. *MSN Movies*. February 22, 2012.
Stevens, Dana. *Slate*. February 17, 2012.
Tallerico, Brian. *HollywoodChicago.com*. March 2, 2012.
Tobias, Scott. *NPR*. February 16, 2012.
Van Hoeij, Boyd. *Variety*. February 14, 2012.

QUOTES

Narrator: "Whatever you do, and whatever you think, one thing you can be sure of, you're always f**ked. Now, tomorrow, next week, and next year, until the end of time."

TRIVIA

According to Michael Roskam, the inspiration came from a crime scene in Belgium known as the Belgium Hormone Mafia.

AWARDS

Nominations:
Oscars 2011: Foreign Film

BULLY
(The Bully Project)

It's time to take a stand.
—Movie tagline

Be a hero. Take a stand.
—Movie tagline

Box Office: $3.5 million

The documentary *Bully* starts off with a series of shots from home movies about a boy named Tyler who committed suicide at the age of seventeen. The videos depict a boy whose life seemed unburdened. This was a happy child. But as he got older, his demeanor changed, and eventually he began to withdraw from those closest to him. His parents found him dead in his bedroom and now they use his story as a means of helping others who are victims of bullying. Thus sets the agenda for Lee Hirsch's documentary. This is not an even-handed piece of investigative journalism, but a personal, activist documentary that is meant to shed a light on a universal topic that has never been the subject of a mainstream documentary before.

The film follows several stories and occasionally stops to revisit Tyler's parents' story as they pick up the pieces of their child's tragically short life. One of the subjects is a twelve-year-old boy named Alex, who wears glasses, has protruding lips, and is hardly athletic. "People call me fish face," he says, "I don't mind." Alex seems to be in denial over his situation, or at least he does not want his parents to think he is being bullied. He downplays it, but admits "I feel like I belong somewhere else." When his parents ask how school was, he spaces out. His dad does not believe him when he says that the kids who refer to him as "a little bitch" are just joking around.

The film also follows a teenage girl named Kelby, who already knows she is gay and looks very boyish. She lives in an Oklahoma bible belt where even her teachers have picked on her about her appearance. Her parents have been receiving threats and hate mail. Her father, who once did not tolerate homosexuality of any kind, has since had a change of heart on the subject now that he has seen how his own daughter has been treated. Kelby was once suicidal, but now has a close group of friends whom she relies on every day.

Then there is fourteen-year-old Ja'Maya, who is in a juvenile home for retaliating against a bully. One day on a school bus, she withdrew a gun and threatened to use it, but never did. Since there were twenty-five students on the bus at the time, she faces twenty-five charges of kidnapping. Shots were never fired and a student did eventually apprehend her as the film shows in the video footage taken by the camera that was stationed in the bus at the time. The charges were dropped.

Bully never gets to know any of the bullies themselves, which feels like a major oversight on the part of its creators. This robs the film of a deeper impact and a broader means of discussion for its audience. What compels some kids to start picking on others? Are all parents whose kids are bullies in denial over their children's behavior? If so, that would go much further in advancing the film's agenda of bully prevention. If teachers and administrations should be held accountable (as the film suggests), then so should the parents.

The film captures moments of teachers and administrators in the act of trying to reconcile the bullies and the victims with pitiful results. When parents corner the dean of students at Alex's school about Alex being mercilessly bullied and physically harmed on a school bus, the dean reacts with skepticism and states that she has ridden on the bus with those kids before and they "are as good as gold." Never in a documentary has a teacher or faculty member ever looked so foolish and/or ignorant.

In a way, though, that moment in the film (and others like it) does the filmmakers' cause a disservice. By the end of *Bully,* the victims of cruel behavior are encouraged to step up and not be silent about their predicament. Yet the film never depicts a teacher or faculty member handling the situation of bullying in an effective or meaningful way. This suggests to the young viewers who might see this movie that nobody in the school system can help. Do the filmmakers honestly believe that all teachers and faculty are as incompetent as the ones they found for their film? To make matters worse, the film points out that after seventeen-year-old Tyler killed himself, nobody from the school board showed up at the town hall meeting a few days later to answer any questions.

But perhaps the film's most glaring oversight, especially in this day and age, is the lack of coverage on cyber-bullying. Many suicides have been reported as a result of kids being tormented on FaceBook or Youtube, but only once in *Bully* is cyber bullying ever mentioned and it is done so in passing. Perhaps this issue is best suited for another documentary unto itself and requires far more attention than a verite documentary can devote, but it seems like a form of bullying that can go viral in a matter of minutes amongst an entire student body would have been near the top of the agenda list for Hirsch and his crew.

Bully is a well-meaning, but troubling film. In spite of its flaws as a documentary (and there are many), it remains compelling and will no doubt stir emotions in people who have had a personal brush with bullying in their lives. The film was heavily marketed by The Weinstein Company as a film that every parent, teacher and child should see. This is hard to argue. The MPAA almost slapped the film with an R rating because of a few too many uses of the f-word. The film was released with some of those f-words removed and with a PG-13 rating so that young people had a better chance of seeing the film. The film's poor showing at the box office made it hardly worth the artistic compromise.

Collin Souter

CREDITS

Origin: United States

Language: English

Released: 2011

Production: Lee Hirsch, Cynthia Lowen; The Bully Project, Where We Live Films; released by Weinstein Company L.L.C.

Directed by: Lee Hirsch

Written by: Lee Hirsch; Cynthia Lowen

Cinematography by: Lee Hirsch

Music by: Michael Furjanic; Justin Rice; Christian Rudder

Sound: Christopher Barnett

Editing: Jenny Golden; Enat Sidi; Lindsay Utz

MPAA rating: PG-13

Running time: 98 minutes

REVIEWS

Ebert, Roger. *Chicago Sun-Times.* April 12, 2012.

Gleiberman, Owen. *Entertainment Weekly.* March 28, 2012.

Howell, Peter. *Toronto Star.* April 5, 2012.

Jones, J. R. *Chicago Reader.* April 13, 2012.

Long, Tom. *Detroit News.* April 13, 2012.

Lumenick, Lou. *New York Post.* March 30, 2012.

Morris, Wesley. *Boston Globe.* April 12, 2012.

Scott, A. O. *New York Times.* March 29, 2012.

Sobczynski, Peter. *eFilmcritic.com.* April 12, 2012.

Whitty, Stephen. *Newark Star-Ledger.* March 30, 2012.

QUOTES

Bullied Student: "Pretty much a good day for me would be people leaving their hands off of me."

TRIVIA

Anderson Cooper is a strong advocate of the film and the movement against bullying that it has stimulated. He featured the documentary on *Anderson Cooper 360°* in October 2011, at the "Bullying: It Stops Here" town hall program special.

BUTTER

There's going to be a meltdown!
—Movie tagline

A comedy about sex, power and spreading the wealth.
—Movie tagline

Box Office: $105,018

Jim Field Smith's toothless satire *Butter* employs a formula pioneered in classic films like *Election* (1999) and *Waiting for Guffman* (1996): invest a small town's low-stakes enterprise (an amateur historical play in *Guffman,* a student president election in *Election*) with the significance of the fall of the Soviet Union and add to it shallow and egotistical characters with delusions of grandeur. Churn and await side splitting laughter.

At least that is how it is supposed to work. The crucial difference for Smith's film is that it lacks the razor-sharp writing and unforgiving view of its characters that made those two films masterpieces.

The script's failure is a shame since the film features a lot of very talented actors who have been very funny in other places. Ty Burrell plays Bob Pickler, resident butter-sculpting champion of a small Iowa town. His wife, uptight Republican WASP Laura Pickler (Jennifer Garner), derives all of her self-worth out of her husband's champion status and believes, insanely, that it is the launching pad for her husband to run for governor. Destiny (Yara Shahidi) is a 10-year-old African-American orphan who has been passed from one foster home to another before finally landing in the excessively supportive home of local residents Ethan (Rob Corddry) and Jill (Alicia Silverstone). As soon as Destiny's ironic, world weary narration fills the soundtrack the viewer knows he is in trouble. The character, finely acted by Shahidi, is the kind of annoyingly precocious Diablo Codyish child that only exists on television and film who acts and talks like a hip 23-year-old at all times. When Ethan and Jill take their new daughter to the local fair, Destiny sneaks into Bob's award winning sculpture of the Last Supper and demonstrates her innate sculpting talent by improving upon it. An impressed Bob compliments her on her efforts and later in the day one of the competition's judges informs Bob that, after fifteen years of dominating the competition, it might be time to let someone else have a chance at winning. Bob agrees but an outraged Laura does not. After a big fight which sends Bob to the local strip club to sulk (and into the avaricious arms of an opportunistic stripper, Brooke [Olivia Wilde]), Laura vows to enter the contest herself.

Laura believes she will have little in the way of competition, however, on the day of the deadline to sign up for the competition, she and the deadly serious contest administrator (*The Office's* Phyllis Smith) watch in amazement as three other unlikely competitors show up: Brooke the stripper (who is after $600 Bob owes her for a half consummated sex act—they were interrupted by Laura ramming her SUV into Bob's car in the strip club parking lot), Carol-Ann (Kristen Schaal), a local cat enthusiast who has always dreamed of winning the competition, her complete lack of experience and talent notwithstanding, and, of course, the destined to win Destiny. Not content to compete fairly, Laura reignites a sexual relationship with her dim witted former high school boyfriend, used car salesman and cowboy hatted Boyd Bolton (Hugh Jackman in a role that seems to have been written for Matthew McConaughey). In return for sex, Bolton agrees to lie to county officials to discredit Destiny. Meanwhile Brooke seduces Bob's daughter, Kaitlen (Ashley Greene) to get her $600 which she then gives to Destiny so she can buy the perfect set of carving knives to defeat Laura in the climactic showdown.

As its very silly plot summary makes clear, *Butter* has the requisite madcap premise for a comedy and a bevy of talented comedic actors more than capable of capitalizing on that premise but first time screen writer Jason Micallef's weak script simply doesn't deliver the laughs. Premise and talented actors provide the opportunity for laughs, not the laughs themselves and *Butter* lacks the wicked bite crucial for a satire. *Election* was a pitch black comedy with a deeply dark view of human nature. None of its characters were likable. *Butter* fatally undercuts its humor by trying to have it both ways. Micallef's script wants to be sharply critical of its mostly shallow and hypocritical characters but also sweet and redemptive towards them as well. It's very difficult to be both snarkily funny and uplifting at the same time and *Butter* lacks the writing chops to pull it off. When it should be going in for the kill, it holds its punches. The result is a very slight and only mildly funny film.

Consequently, *Butter* squanders a ridiculously talented group of actors on a razor thin, halfhearted satire that the viewer will forget fifteen minutes after seeing it. There are some isolated funny moments, mostly involving Wilde and Jackman, (the latter, for example, conceals his Laura-authored accusation against Destiny in the brim of his cowboy hat and, reading it for the first time while he is making the accusation pronounces the second part of "conscience" like science class) but not nearly enough to recommend seeing the film. Smith and Micallef's film definitely lands buttered side down.

Nate Vercauteren

CREDITS

Laura Pickler: Jennifer Garner
Bob Pickler: Ty Burrell
Destiny: Yara Shahidi
Brooke: Olivia Wilde
Ethan: Rob Corddry
Boyd Bolton: Hugh Jackman
Kaitlen: Ashley Greene
Julie: Alicia Silverstone
Origin: United States
Language: English
Released: 2012
Production: Michael De Luca, Juliana Janes, Alissa Phillips, Jennifer Garner; Michael De Luca Productions, Vandalia Films; released by The Weinstein Company
Directed by: Jim Field Smith
Written by: Jason A. Micallef

Cinematography by: Jim Denault
Music by: Mateo (Matt) Messina
Sound: Andrew Decristofaro; Sean Garnhart
Editing: Matt Garner; Dan Schalk
Art Direction: Greg Richman
Costumes: Susie DeSanto
Production Design: Tony Fanning
MPAA rating: R
Running time: 90 minutes

REVIEWS

Anderson, John. *The Wall Street Journal*. October 4, 2012.
Arnold, Joel. *NPR*. October 5, 2012.
Burr, Ty. *Boston Globe*. October 4, 2012.
Catsoulis, Jeanette. *New York Times*. October 4, 2012.
Debruge, Peter. *Variety*. October 5, 2012.
Fear, David. *Time Out New York*. October 2, 2012.
Linden, Sheri. *Los Angeles Times*. October 4, 2012.
Schager, Nick. *Village Voice*. October 7, 2012.
Smith, Kyle. *New York Post*. October 5, 2012.
Travers, Peter. *Rolling Stone*. October 4, 2012.

QUOTES

Laura Pickler: "I plan on proudly bearing his children."

Brooke Swinkowski: "So, you want a cookie 'cause you're going to get pregnant? I get pregnant, like, once a month!"

TRIVIA

Kate Hudson was set to play Brooke, but dropped out to do *Something Borrowed* instead and was replaced by Olivia Wilde.

C

THE CABIN IN THE WOODS

You think you know the story.
—Movie tagline

Quaint abandoned property...sold.
—Movie tagline

If an old man warns you not to go there...make fun of him.
—Movie tagline

If you hear a strange sound outside...have sex.
—Movie tagline

If something is chasing you...split up.
—Movie tagline

Box Office: $42.1 million

Drew Goddard's *The Cabin in the Woods* (which he co-wrote with longtime collaborator and genre icon Joss Whedon) is a brilliant and fascinating examination of the entire tradition of horror storytelling as filtered through a tongue-in-cheek, modern approach to filmmaking. It is consistently clever, undeniably smart, and oh-so-much fun that it brings to mind the way Wes Craven deconstructed his own genre in the wildly influential *Scream* (1996), only Goddard and Whedon are examining a centuries-old tradition of man's need for sacrifice and horror that predates celluloid. For ages, man has recounted stories of bloody gifts to the Gods, ways to appease the demons below or beings above through, well, death. Has the virgin tied to the altar of the last millennium merely been replaced by the scream queen heroine who survives an assault in a slasher pic? At the same time, Goddard and Whedon are playing

with themes that they have examined for years in their TV work on shows like *Buffy the Vampire Slayer* (1997-2003) and *LOST* (2004-2010). Building on their strengths with an insightful and entertaining film in a genre for which both of those words have become increasingly difficult to apply, Whedon and Goddard deliver one of the best films of 2012.

The writers immediately throw audience expectations off their gauge by opening with a pair of wise-cracking gentlemen named Sitterson (Richard Jenkins) and Hadley (Bradley Whitford) discussing casual life stories over coffee like a workplace sitcom. What is going on? Who are these men? Isn't this a horror film? Where are the pretty girls and boneheaded jocks to die in gruesome ways? Instantly, Whedon and Goddard have viewers asking questions and approaching the genre from a unique angle as a viewer. Instead of just asking typical horror questions like the identity of the killer or the order or the carnage, one is questioning the very structure of the entire piece.

It is quickly revealed that Sitterson and Hadley work for an international organization that does nothing less than keep the world from being overrun by massive underground giants. The Gods need a sacrifice and teams of scientists (including architects like Sitterson and Hadley, explosive experts, and chemists like Amy Acker's Lin) must conduct elaborate scenarios to make sure the blood is spilled in just the right way. They increase pheromone levels to keep horny teens off their guard, mess with their hair dye and marijuana, and play other games to push their victims in the right direction without just outright burning them at the stake. The conceit is that the very genre of horror is a form of modern sacrifice. All of the boneheaded behavior (like splitting up when characters should stay together) is to the service of keeping the world from being overrun by angry Gods.

The five men and women who get sucked into this web of sacrifice could have been broadly sketched given the larger context of the piece but Whedon and Goddard do not skimp on character where they so easily could have done the bare minimum. Without all of the overarching themes of the piece, *Cabin* would have been a fun horror movie just with its quintet of unlucky vacationers. The lead would be Dana (Kristen Connolly), a sweet girl who is just getting over an ugly break-up with the college professor she was dating. Her best friend Jules (Anna Hutchison) invites her along on a weekend getaway to a cabin completely off the grid. Jules is bringing her hunky boyfriend Curt (Chris Hemsworth) and Curt has a cute friend named Holden (Jesse Williams), who might be just what Dana needs to get over her last love. The fifth wheel and comic relief is stoner Marty (Fran Kranz), whose rants about puppet masters might make him annoying but also make him the only one who actually knows what's going on.

After a tension-filled game of truth-or-dare, the door to the basement of the group's cabin opens up and it becomes time for them to pick their demise. As the team back at the mission control base takes bets on which enemy will be the one to perform the sacrifice this time around, the group looks through antiques, any one of which could call forth the tool of their death. After Dana reads from a journal, it is time for the Buckner family to rise from their shallow graves and unleash zombie carnage. As similar experiments around the world fail, it becomes clear that if the Buckners cannot get the job done then the results could be nothing short of the end of the world.

Whereas most horror films propel themselves toward a final act that will almost certainly be its least interesting given the inevitability of the hero/heroine's survival and the villain's demise, *Cabin in the Woods* contains one of the best final reels in horror film history. Whedon and Goddard do not just build to a typical climax, they deconstruct their entire film in an orgy of horror-movie-adoring carnage. Zombies, creatures from the deep, demons, ghosts, and even a deadly unicorn, *Cabin in the Woods* delivers the goods in a way that works for both horror fans and even those less familiar with the genre. It is one of the most fearless and notable conclusions in horror film history.

Whedon and Goddard's script is the true star of the film but the piece is also very well-cast and structured by its rookie director. As for the cast, Connolly is beautiful and charming, perfect traits for a piece like this one,

while Kranz brilliantly blends comic relief with the voice of the only guy who really knows what is going on. Jenkins and Whitford have a matching world-weariness that makes their sarcastic approach to the death of innocents even more unique. Even small roles like those played by Hemsworth and Acker are effective.

To be fair, one wishes that the middle act of *Cabin* had developed a few more actual scares. The best comedy/horror films of the last few years, like *Scream* or Edgar Wright's *Shaun of the Dead* (2004), worked because they became actually scary while commenting on their genre—being horror-comedies instead of just comedies. *Cabin* is more intellectual than visceral when a bit more of the latter could have made it a true genre masterpiece.

It is close enough that critics fell in love with the movie with some notable outlets (*San Francisco Chronicle*, *Tampa Bay Times*) even giving the film a perfect score, something nearly unheard of in the critically-maligned horror genre. After a financial collapse, MGM sat on *Cabin* for a few years (Hemsworth became Thor in a standalone Marvel film and *Marvel's The Avengers* [2012] while it was gathering dust) but waiting did nothing for the film's critical appeal. However, it could be argued that the movie disappointed at the box office, especially when one considers its critical adoration. Strong word-of-mouth carried it to $42 million domestically (and $66 million worldwide) but it is a lesser U.S. total than far-more-generic fare like *Resident Evil: Retribution* (2012), *Sinister* (2012), *The Possession* (2012), and *Paranormal Activity 4* (2012). Perhaps fans of the horror genre were not ready for an examination of why they so long to be told stories of sacrifice and why mankind has been conveying them for centuries. Whatever the reason, *The Cabin in the Woods* has already developed a loyal and appreciative following. Like the favorites of the genre and unlike its genetically-gifted stars, it will survive.

Brian Tallerico

CREDITS

Polk: Kristen Connolly
Curt: Chris Hemsworth
Jules: Anna Hutchison
Marty: Fran Kranz
Holden: Jesse Williams
Sitterson: Richard Jenkins
Hadley: Bradley Whitford
Truman: Brian White
Lin: Amy Acker
Origin: United States

Language: English, Spanish

Released: 2012

Production: Joss Whedon; Mutant Enemy; released by Lionsgate

Directed by: Drew Goddard

Written by: Drew Goddard; Joss Whedon

Cinematography by: Peter Deming

Music by: David Julyan

Sound: Dane A. Davis

Music Supervisor: Dana Sano

Editing: Lisa Lassek

Art Direction: Tom Reta

Costumes: Shawna Trpcic

Production Design: Martin Whist

MPAA rating: R

Running time: 95 minutes

REVIEWS

Burr, Ty. *Boston Globe*. April 12, 2012.

Ebert, Roger. *Chicago Sun-Times*. April 12, 2012.

Jones, J. R. *Chicago Reader*. April 13, 2012.

Kennedy, Lisa. *Denver Post*. April 13, 2012.

Long, Tom. *Detroit News*. April 13, 2012.

O'Hehir, Andrew. *Salon.com*. April 12, 2012.

Phillips, Michael. *Chicago Tribune*. April 12, 2012.

Puig, Claudia. *USA Today*. April 12, 2012.

Stevens, Dana. *Slate*. April 12, 2012.

Travers, Peter. *Rolling Stone*. April 13, 2012.

QUOTES

Wiry Girl: "That's not fair! I had zombies too!"

Sitterson: "Yes, you had 'Zombies.' But this is 'Zombie Redneck Torture Family.' Entirely separate thing. It's like the difference between an elephant and an elephant seal."

TRIVIA

The latin that Dana reads from the diary is: "Dolor supervivo caro. Dolor sublimus caro. Dolor ignio animus." It means: "Pain outlives the flesh. Pain raises the flesh. Pain ignites the spirit."

THE CAMPAIGN

May the best loser win.
—Movie tagline

Box Office: $86.9 million

The Campaign imagines the theater of politics as one of the absurd. The least silly thing in the film is the introductory quote from Ross Perot, and that is saying something.

The film was released in the middle of the preposterously long 2012 election cycle, before the candidates of the presidential election were "official" but when both of the inevitable candidates and the political action committees in each candidate's favor were busy slinging mud. At the time of this writing, the campaign proper has just started, after both political parties' respective national conventions; one can only prognosticate with certainty that the attacks will get worse.

Whether or not this prediction comes true is beside the point. The fact that one would immediately imagine the worst sort of political tactics to emerge from a hotly contested and, according to most polls, very close race is the most damning sign of the times. Cynicism about the political process has become so ingrained in the public's perception that *The Campaign* uses a set of billionaire brothers (modeled transparently after Charles and David Koch, who have become something of boogeymen in the eyes of certain groups), who invest a sizeable sum of money to mold a candidate that would act in their best interests in Congress, as the narrative's inciting incident. In another era, a story would treat this development as a shock worthy of outrage; here, it is merely a given.

The film, which is at heart a rude and crude comedy with only the broadest goals for political satire, winds up presenting a relatively accurate depiction of the contemporary political arena. Screenwriters Chris Henchy and Shawn Harwell merely take the proceedings up a notch to ensure that the film is still in the realm of fiction.

In the sleepy town of Hammond, North Carolina, Cam Brady (Will Ferrell, whose shtick serves the material instead of trying to overtake it, as the actor is sometimes wont to do), a four-term United States Congressman, is campaigning to serve yet another two years in office; once again, he is running unopposed. He is a serial philanderer of the desperate variety; taking a random woman he meets after a stump speech into a portable toilet to have sex. He has pictures of himself with Bill Clinton and Arnold Schwarzenegger in his office, just to drive the point home.

Brady's campaign slogan is three words: America, Jesus, and freedom. When his campaign manager Mitch (Jason Sudeikis) asks what that means, Brady admits he has no idea; the people love it, though. As a politician, the man is as hollow as his motto.

Despite this, he is not the ideal man for the Motch brothers, Glenn (John Lithgow) and Wade (Dan Akroyd), who need a lawmaker who will help introduce legislation in Congress that would allow the industrialists to open a factory in Hammond that would have working conditions comparable to the ones their business enjoys in China.

When one of Brady's affairs becomes public after he leaves a lurid message on the answering machine of a wrong number, the Motch brothers enlist the help of Marty Huggins (Zach Galifianakis, likeably daft with a soft-spoken Southern drawl), a decent family man who runs the local tourism board and desperately wants to impress his ever-disappointed father (Brian Cox, making the most of a small role). They even hire cutthroat campaign manager Tim Wattley (Dylan McDermott, whose character's tendency to appear unannounced eventually leads to him to skip a step by spending his time sitting in the Huggins family kitchen) to turn Huggins into a contender.

The film does not shy away from naming political parties (Brady is a "Blue Dog" or moderate Democrat, and Huggins is a Republican), but save for the most general traits (Brady's lack of fidelity and Huggins' endorsement from corporate entities), the screenplay also avoids stereotypical attacks on either. That is not to say the film is what some would dub an "equal-opportunity offender," seeing as there is no actual discussion of policy or political positions to be had. Perhaps unintentionally, the absence of actual ideas coming from either of its central characters is one of the screenplay's more astute observations (also unintentional is the way the film's episodic structure mirrors the way the media covers campaigns from one faux pas to the next).

The humor is split between random and often raunchy jokes and ones that are more specific to the premise and tie into the real world. The former are amusing enough (an extended riff in which Huggins' family tells their darkest secrets is a fine example of how a rambling, seemingly improvised string of jokes can work, and Brady punching a baby is an obvious twist on the campaign standby that really only pays off when he also punches the dog from *The Artist* [2011]), but the latter show a surprising level of research on the part of Henchy and Harwell.

Brady's team creates an attack ad that wonders if Huggins is "an Al-Qaeda" or "a Taliban" because he has facial hair. Some may recall a similar political ad in which a sitting Congressman called his opponent "Taliban Dan." As Brady waits for a judge to make his run official, he offers a throwaway line about posting a picture of his penis on a social networking website, which, of course, echoes the downfall of then-United States Representative Anthony Weiner. As an absurdist counterpoint, Brady later makes a sex tape with Huggins' wife Mitzi (Sarah Baker), airs it as an ad, and, to the shock of pundits, receives a boost in the polls.

When the two strands of comedy merge, the marriage is especially potent. Take a town hall debate that erupts into an all-out brawl. The impetus is Huggins us-ing a story Brady wrote as a child to suggest that his opponent is a Communist. With politicians throwing out words like "socialist" and "extremist" with such ease to brand someone to whom they are opposed, it is no wonder that the country is so divided. *The Campaign* is a genuinely funny and—in its own, strange way—a sobering reminder that most of those divisions are founded on nonsense.

Mark Dujsik

CREDITS

Cam Brady: Will Ferrell
Marty Huggins: Zach Galifianakis
Mitch: Jason Sudeikis
Tim Wattley: Dylan McDermott
Rose Brady: Katherine LaNasa
Mitzi Huggins: Sarah Baker
Glenn Motch: John Lithgow
Wade Motch: Dan Aykroyd
Raymond Huggins: Brian Cox
Origin: United States
Language: English
Released: 2012
Production: Will Ferrell, Jay Roach, Zach Galifianakis; Everyman Pictures; released by Warner Bros.
Directed by: Jay Roach
Written by: Chris Henchy; Shawn Harwell
Cinematography by: Jim Denault
Music by: Theodore Shapiro
Sound: Ken McLaughlin
Editing: Craig Alpert; Jon Poll
Costumes: Daniel Orlandi
Production Design: Michael Corenblith
MPAA rating: R
Running time: 85 minutes

REVIEWS

Burr, Ty. *Boston Globe.* August 9, 2012.
Hornaday, Ann. *Washington Post.* August 10, 2012.
McGranaghan, Mike. *Aisle Seat.* August 10, 2012.
Means, Sean P. *Salt Lake Tribune.* August 10, 2012.
O'Hehir, Andrew. *Salon.com.* August 12, 2012.
Phillips, Michael. *Chicago Tribune.* August 9, 2012.
Phipps, Keith. *AV Club.* August 9, 2012.
Putman, Dustin. *DustinPutman.com.* August 10, 2012.
Scott, A. O. *New York Times.* August 9, 2012.
Vaux, Rob. *Mania.com.* August 10, 2012.

QUOTES

Cam Brady: "People are taking this thing entirely out of context."

Mitch: "No. You did punch that baby."

Cam Brady: "Is anyone asking how my hand feels after punching that iron like jaw of that baby? I can barely make a fist!

TRIVIA

All cigarettes that the characters in the film smoke are Newports, which are manufactured by Lorillard Tobacco Company of Greensboro, North Carolina.

CASA DE MI PADRE

Funniest movie you'll ever read.
—Movie tagline

Box Office: $5.9 million

The project began with a press release. According to the rumors of the time, Will Ferrell was being sued by producer Gary Sanchez and to make amends he agreed to star in a Spanish-language production. With a reported "one month to teach him Spanish," the telenovela-style project now had a big American star and Sanchez's revenge would be sweet in reaping the profits or served cold in destroying the good will that Ferrell's name has brought to many successful projects in his native land. None of this was to be taken seriously, of course. It was all part of the absurdist ruse to explain why on Earth one of the most popular comedic stars of our time would be taking his talents to what could only be presumed arthouse cinema because of all the fancy reading audiences would have to partake in to understand it. However one interprets *Casa de mi Padre*— which means "House Of My Father"— consider it another attempt by a comedian to push the boundaries of his own curiosity and what he can get away with in trying to explore untapped sources of satire.

Sometime in the early '70s—assuming the film's copyright date is correct—Ferrell plays Armando Alvarez, a simple good-hearted rancher who is nevertheless not the apple of his father's eye. "If you were truly smart, you would know that you are dumb," says padre Miguel (Pedro Armendariz Jr.) and Armando later takes time to sing a song with his fellow rancheros about how little they know. The true apple is coming home though when the more successful brother, Raul (Diego Luna), arrives just in time to help save the ranch but brings with him his own package of trouble. His stunning girlfriend, Sonia (Genesis Rodriguez), is in tow, and, as she inspires thoughts of lust from the other ranch hands, Armando may have set eyes on a soul mate.

The Alvarez land is in greater crisis though with the presence of local drug dealer, Onza (Gael Garcia Bernal).

After Armando and his pals "hope nothing bad happens on the way home" from work, they witness Onza kill a man. When a second murder occurs, Armando discovers that the Alvarez land may be closer to the drug trade than his father even knows. Raul has been trafficking in product over the border onto the very turf that Onza controls. So within the rift between father and son, there is now another brewing between older and younger brother, between younger brother and drug lord and between older brother and bride-to-be who may already be part of the rift between husband-to-be and drug lord forever.

Understanding the brand of humor on display here is even more important than knowing the language being spoken. The obvious barbs in Andrew Steele's script are directed at telenovelas, the Spanish soap operas that do not last for decades but play more like an elongated mini-series with all the melodrama and plot twists one might expect. Soap operas, in general, are an easy target for comedy and a film committed to only taking jabs at overacting and implausible machinations would get stale quickly. Director Matt Piedmont, thankfully, is more interested in loading the film up with subtleties.

Indeed, *Casa de mi Padre* is a film that almost dares one to find the laughs. Since the film is rightfully played straight by all the actors, one must read between the line readings to construe the source of the humor in every scene. Sometimes it is obvious with animatronics and miniatures. Other instances it may take both ears to recognize broken Spanish or a third eye to realize just how they are filling in extras in the background. This may frustrate viewers, even those familiar with how off the beaten path Ferrell can go at times, but it does not mean everyone involved are not trying.

"If it sounds Spanish man, that's what it is, it's a Spanish movie," so says the opening narrator for those wondering if a transition to English is ever on the horizon. Viewers who take the leap of faith need not concern themselves with the historical ins and outs of the telenovela. A routine knowledge of American soap operas crossed with Robert Rodriguez's *El Mariachi* series will do just fine. The adversarial casting of Luna and Bernal, introduced to the U.S. through Alfonso Cuaron's *Y Tu Mama Tambien* (2001) is inspired on a variety of levels as was the late Pedro Armendariz Jr., a veteran of the telenovela. Most recognizable of all though is Ferrell. He has played both the arrogant and the naive throughout his film career and in real life it is unlikely that he was ever blackmailed into doing this project. Not because of the legal ramifications and the loose evidence of extortion detailed in a press release. It just seems that Ferrell is so naturally at home with this kind of stuff and is having so much fun that he would have done it for nothing.

Erik Childress

CREDITS

Armando: Will Ferrell
Onza: Gael Garcia Bernal
Raul: Diego Luna
Sonia: Genesis Rodriguez
Miguel Ernesto: Pedro Armendariz, Jr.
DEA Agent Parker: Nick Offerman
Esteban: Efren Ramirez
Manuel: Adrian Martinez
Origin: United States
Language: Spanish, English
Released: 2012
Production: Will Ferrell, Adam McKay, Emilio Deiz Barroso, Will Ferrell; Nala Films, Televisa Films; released by Pantelion Films
Directed by: Matt Piedmont
Written by: Andrew Steele
Cinematography by: Ramsay Nickell
Music by: Beacon Street Studios
Sound: Michael B. Koff
Editing: David Trachtenberg
Art Direction: Naaman Marshall
Costumes: Trayce Gigi Field; Marylou Lim
Production Design: Kevin Kavanaugh
MPAA rating: R
Running time: 84 minutes

REVIEWS

Bayer, Jeff. *Scorecard Review*. April 1, 2012.
Burr, Ty. *Boston Globe*. March 15, 2012.
Dargis, Manohla. *New York Times*. March 15, 2012.
Ebert, Roger. *Chicago Sun-Times*. March 15, 2012.
Nusair, David. *Reel Film Reviews*. March 18, 2012.
Rabin, Nathan. *AV Club*. March 15, 2012.
Rea, Steven. *Philadelphia Inquirer*. March 15, 2012.
Snider, Eric D. *Film.com*. March 17, 2012.
Swietek, Frank. *One Guy's Opinion*. March 15, 2012.
Verniere, James. *Boston Herald*. March 16, 2012.

QUOTES

Armando: (singing) "Why does the turtle move so slow?"
Backing singers: (singing) "I don't know!"

TRIVIA

Actor Will Ferrell spent a month learning and speaking Spanish with a dialect coach in preparation for his role.

CELESTE & JESSE FOREVER

A loved story.
—Movie tagline

For anyone who has to break up with their best friend.
—Movie tagline

Box Office: $3.1 million

Celeste & Jesse Forever takes place entirely in what many romantic comedies would consider the third act. This is the point in most films of this genre where the couple's relationship appears to be threatened or outright doomed unless one of the two people can make a serious compromise or adjustment in their lives. It usually takes a sassy best friend or two to talk some sense into the romantic leads or a revelation from a third party member (parent, boss, former lover, gay best friend) that causes one of the leads to go rushing back into the arms of the other lead whilst delivering an apology of sorts in a grandiose and/or humiliating fashion in front of many spectators.

Except that *Celeste & Jesse Forever* is not quite that conventional, but it comes close. At the start of the film, the titular characters Celeste (Rashida Jones) and Jesse (Andy Samberg) are a married couple who have decided to get a divorce. The news comes as a shock to their best friends Beth (Ari Graynor) and Tucker (Eric Christian Olsen). The divorce is not yet final and Jesse and Celeste live in separate quarters in the same general area. They also still like each other to the point that it appears as though they are still best friends who share inside jokes. Their friends are confused as to how Jesse and Celeste can still maintain this close, friendly rapport while going through something that is usually tormenting and emotionally draining.

Eventually, the two start to explore their lives separately from each other. Celeste has no intention of dating right away and she gets some help professionally from her gay boss (Elijah Wood), who actually points out his obvious role in the rom-com scheme of things when he tries to live up to the part ("Sorry, I was trying to be your savvy gay friend. It didn't feel right.") She works as a "trend predictor" and is now in charge of designing and marketing a new album by a vacuous teen pop sensation named Riley Banks (Emma Roberts), whom she openly despises. As the divorce looms, Celeste finds herself rummaging through Jesse's garbage and finding clues to his new life.

Jesse's new life involves a woman named Veronica (Rebecca Dayan), whom Jesse confesses he slept with in the last few months while the separation was taking place. One night, Jesse helps Celeste put together a piece of Ikea furniture, a favor that results in the two of them drinking a little too much wine and sleeping together once again. It appears as though the relationship might be rekindled, but complications arise when Jesse learns that Veronica is pregnant with his child and is not a U.S. citizen. This forces Jesse to reconsider the paths he has taken in his professional life (or lack thereof) and make more strides into being a responsible adult, something he could never really accomplish when he was with Veronica.

Rashida Jones co-wrote the script with Will McCormack. She claims that this story is based on a brief relationship they had a long time ago. It is obvious that *Celeste and Jesse Forever* comes from a personal place and Jones is well aware of the worn paths most movies in this genre have taken. But the script wants to have it both ways by not only commenting on rom-com conventions, but also embracing them. Some movies have pulled that off successfully (*Friends With Benefits* [2011] comes to mind), but *Celeste and Jesse Forever* comes off a bit awkwardly since the conventions far outweigh the knowing winks to the audience.

Still, there is an inherent charm in the film and that is large part due to the casting. Jones has been making a name for herself over the years both in the improvisational comedy field (a seasonal arc on TV's *The Office*) as well as an occasional dramatic role (*The Social Network* [2010]). She seems well suited to this kind of film and is able to balance the dignity as well as the humility of her character in much the same way Kristen Wiig did in *Bridesmaids* (2011). She makes the movie easily watchable, projecting an earthiness and vulnerability to which many will be able to relate. One hopes she will make some interesting choices in her career, which seems to be up for grabs in terms of what direction she could go in next.

The most interesting bit of casting, though, is, of course, Samberg. An alumni of *Saturday Night Live,* Samberg made quite a name for himself on that show with his Digital Shorts, the most famous being the rap video he did with Chris Parnell, "Lazy Sunday." Samberg has one of those faces that could have trapped him forever in one kind of film. Because of his weekly parody videos targeting all forms of over-the-top sincerity, he could have had a hard time convincing an audience of real sincerity, something that plagued Leslie Nielsen later in his career after he did the *Airplane!* and *Naked Gun* movies. But Samberg has no reason to worry. He pulls off a mostly dramatic performance with ease and now that he has left *SNL,* he might have just expanded his career horizons just a little more with this film (even if he certainly did not with the critically reviled *That's My Boy* [2012] earlier in the season).

Celeste and Jesse Forever is a movie that will not shake up the indie rom-com genre and it is no more original than its contemporary from the same summer, *Lola Versus* (2012). But it is at least a better film than that, if only because of the cast. Director Lee Toland

Kreiger does not call attention to the film with any kind of style, but it is not unwatchable either. *Celeste and Jesse Forever* would probably work better for someone who is actually going through a divorce and needs a couple of people to relate to for 92 minutes as a source of comfort food. The script is clearly written from the heart, but one wishes there were a little more brain sprinkled in for better measure.

Collin Souter

CREDITS

Celeste: Rashida Jones
Jesse: Andy Samberg
Paul: Chris Messina
Beth: Ari Gaynor
Skillz: Will McCormack
Scott: Elijah Wood
Veronica: Rebecca Dayan
Rupert: Rafi Gavron
Origin: United States
Language: English
Released: 2012
Production: Lee Nelson, Jennifer Todd, Suzanne Todd; Team Todd, Envision Media; released by Sony Pictures Classics
Directed by: Lee Toland Krieger
Written by: Rashida Jones; Will McCormack
Cinematography by: David Lazenberg
Music by: Sunny Levine; Zach Cowie
Sound: Matthew Nicolay
Editing: Yana Gorskaya
Costumes: Julia Caston
Production Design: Ian Phillips
MPAA rating: R
Running time: 92 minutes

REVIEWS

Burrr, Ty. *Boston Globe.* August 16, 2012.
Darlis, Manohla. *New York Times.* August 8, 2012.
Ebert, Roger. *Chicago Sun-Times.* August 9, 2012.
Gleiberman, Owen. *Entertainment Weekly.* August 1, 2012.
Longworth, Karina. *Village Voice.* July 31, 2012.
Lumenick, Lou. *New York Post.* August 3, 2012.
Morgenstern, Joe. *Wall Street Journal.* August 2, 2012.
Murray, Noel. *AV Club.* January 21, 2012.
Ogle, Connie. *Miami Herald.* August 23, 2012.
Whitty, Stephen. *Newark Star-Ledger.* August 3, 2012.

QUOTES

Riley: "You know what your problem is? Contempt before investigation. You think you're smarter than everybody else."

Nominations:

Ind. Spirit 2013: First Screenplay

THE CENTRAL PARK FIVE

Box Office: $325,653

Ken Burns, Sarah Burns, and David McMahon team to bring cinema one of the most insightful and timely documentaries about the injustice that can sprout from fear and racism in the stellar and award-winning *The Central Park Five*. Like most great documentarians, the trio does not simply present the shocking truth of the story they chose to capture but they place it in a new context, offering the definitive statement on their subject matter. The filmmakers brilliantly place this story of a stunning abuse of power within a time frame and location that virtually demanded it as the crime rate in an increasingly dangerous New York City in the '80s set the stage for something like this to happen. It was nearly inevitable.

On April 19, 1989, Trisha Meili was brutally raped and assaulted in Central Park. As she lay in a hospital bed, struggling to stay alive, the police rounded up suspects and the press shouted for justice. The same night that Meili was nearly killed, a group of teenagers had been "wilding" in the park. They ran around, causing problems that ranged from small-time vandalism to abuse of the elderly and homeless people they came across. Packs of angry, young, black men sent fear into the city of New York and police officers and prosecutors had to do something to stem that fear. They rounded up five of the teens who had admittedly been in Central Park that night—Anton McCray, Kevin Richardson, Raymond Santana, Kharey Wise, and Yusef Salaam.

All five young men were undeniably mentally abused in various New York police station interrogation rooms. Several of them were told that if they just confessed, they would be allowed to go home. Even as their stories did not come close to matching up, officers and prosecutors would bend the truth to make it fit what they thought happened that night. Hearing the men speak now in the film about their saga, one cannot help but feel a rising anger at a system that allowed something like this to happen. To try and bring justice to a horribly beaten woman and calm the fear of New Yorkers that their city was being overtaken by angry black men, people in powerful positions took actions that they knew were wrong. They would say that they were bending the truth to get the right men, but that

was clearly untrue, especially when the real serial rapist came forward in 2002 and the sentences of The Central Park Five were vacated.

The interviews with the now-grown men of The Central Park Five are emotionally devastating enough to make a worthwhile documentary. Their youth was taken from them and the wounds are clearly still open on a daily basis. The men and women responsible for their injustice will never truly pay for the country has a system that too easily dismisses stories like this one as faults of the system. The fact is that what happened to the Five, as presented in this excellent doc, was not just the fault of one or two people but an entire city and even country in increasing fear, especially of young African-Americans. The directors brilliantly use archival footage of powerful figures of the '80s, including Mayor Ed Koch and blowhard Donald Trump, in their calls for justice for the Central Park Jogger. They place the true crime story in cultural, societal, and historical context, elevating their film above the average injustice documentary (in much the same way Amy Berg did with another great 2012 doc, *West of Memphis*). Unlike other films like this, it is not so much a story of "this could happen again" as it is "this was bound to happen at least once."

Critics lauded *The Central Park Five* from coast to coast with the New York Film Critics even naming it the best non-fiction film of 2012 and the Chicago Film Critics Association nominating it in the same category (the Academy chose not to cite the film in its top five in what is notoriously the most snub-filled category of Oscar night). Eric Kohn of *indieWIRE* wrote, " With an editing approach that seamlessly blends past and present, [the film] contains a fluid, engaging storytelling that does away with the dry voiceover commentary and theatrical music choices that typically account for the narrative flow of most Burns films." Mark Jenkins added through *NPR*, "In addition to recent interviews with the five, the filmmakers deftly marshal news footage, clips from the supposed confessions, and trenchant analysis." Some critics thought the film was a bit too simplistic, not adding enough new to the true story, but they missed the new framing for what was a sadly familiar painting.

Brian Tallerico

CREDITS

Himself: Ed Koch
Himself: David Dinkins
Himself: Craig Steven Wilder
Himself: Calvin O. Butts, III
Himself: Jim Dwyer
Origin: United States

Language: English

Released: 2012

Production: Ken Burns, Sarah Burns, David McMahon; Florentine Films; released by Sundance Selects

Directed by: Ken Burns; Sarah Burns; David McMahon

Written by: Ken Burns; Sarah Burns; David McMahon

Cinematography by: Anthony Savini; Buddy Squires

Music by: Doug Wamble

Editing: Michael Levine

MPAA rating: Unrated

Running time: 119 minutes

REVIEWS

Denby, David. *New Yorker*. December 3, 2012.

Ebert, Roger. *Chicago Sun-Times*. December 6, 2012.

Jenkins, Mark. *NPR*. November 23, 2012.

Kohn, Eric. *indieWIRE*. November 20, 2012.

Morgenstern, Joe. *Wall Street Journal*. November 29, 2012.

Morris, Wesley. *Boston Globe*. December 13, 2012.

Phillips, Michael. *Chicago Tribune*. December 6, 2012.

Rainer, Peter. *Christian Science Monitor*. November 30, 2012.

Schwarzbaum, Lisa. *Entertainment Weekly*. November 20, 2012.

Turan, Kenneth. *Los Angeles Times*. November 29, 2012.

AWARDS

Nominations:

Ind. Spirit 2013: Feature Doc.

Writers Guild 2012: Documentary Screenplay

CHASING MAVERICKS
(Of Men and Mavericks)

Legends start somewhere.
—Movie tagline

Box Office: $6 million

An earnest underdog tale that could be considered a hagiography were its subject perhaps more well known, *Chasing Mavericks* is based on the real life of teenage surfing phenomenon Jay Moriarty. Co-directed by Curtis Hanson and Michael Apted (the latter of whom replaced Hanson when he was unable to complete filming due to complications from heart surgery), this well-photographed if familiar coming-of-age story bobs along on a rolling tidal swell somewhere between passable and tedious, lacking the level of nuance that would merit its running time of nearly two hours.

It is true that *Chasing Mavericks* is made with more care and precision than one expect given both its story proper and the circumstances of its production. But its sun-kissed cinematography and convincing surf staging cannot totally overcome the drabber elements of its frustratingly bland and programmatic screenplay, in which learned life lessons are literally repeated out loud when later applied.

A box office nonstarter upon its autumn release by distributor 20th Century Fox, *Chasing Mavericks* could not tap into the same sort of family-friendly, inspirational drama audience base as the $44 million-grossing *Soul Surfer* (2011), despite significant thematic similarities. After two weeks of release in over two thousand theaters, it quietly contracted and slunk back to shore with under $6 million in domestic receipts. A healthier life in targeted ancillary markets should await, however.

An opening sequence in 1987 in Santa Cruz, a comfortably sized beach town roughly midway up California's expansive coastline, gives way to the same setting seven years later. The product of a broken home, 15-year-old Jay (Jonny Weston) lives with his mom Kristy (Elisabeth Shue), a functional alcoholic who has trouble making it to her shifts on time. Their roles, in fact, are largely reversed. Jay cleans, cooks, wakes her up and even shares money from his job at a pizza parlor. In his spare time, though, he indulges in his true passion, surfing, with his best friend Blond (Devin Crittenden). He also nurses a crush on an older classmate, Kim (Leven Rambin).

A construction day laborer and odd-job specialist, Frosty Hesson (Gerard Butler, also a producer on the project) is a bit of a lay-about and a rather indifferent father who still sneaks away to pursue the thrill of big wave surfing, breaking promises to his wife Brenda (Abigail Spencer) to abandon that lifestyle. When Jay discovers that the huge waves of the so-called Mavericks surf break, some towering up to 50 feet, are not a myth and in fact are within driving distance, he hounds the initially reluctant Frosty into training him to take a crack at them. A mentorship ensues, but Frosty puts Jay through the paces for many months, assigning him written papers and lecturing him about the difference between fear and panic, as well as the dangers of Mavericks as compared to more traditional shoreline. "Big wave surfing is about performing when things go wrong," he says. Finally, of course, Jay gets his shot.

The final product, overseen by Apted and editor John Gilbert, though reportedly approved by Hanson, is surely something of a shared vision. But *Chasing Mavericks* owes most of its problems to a waterlogged script that never seems able to shake off its weighted collection of obligatory elements. Working from a story by Jim Meenaghan and Brandon Hooper, screenwriter Kario Salem delivers a work largely lacking in the sharp characterizations that are typically a hallmark of Hanson's other films.

There is a lot of fairly specific talk about tide and currents, which is good for believability. The surrogate father-son material has a natural pull to it, given Weston's vulnerability. And structurally, with the fixed goal of its seasonal training cycle, the movie has a clear end point on the horizon. But Salem shoehorns in some forced, tone-deaf narration ("We all come from the sea, but we are not all of the sea"), and his touch with nearly all the supporting characters is off. One feels the placeholders for catharsis, just not the honest emotions. Worst is a subplot with a laughably over-the-top bully, Sonny (Taylor Handley), who antagonizes Jay for seemingly no reason but then of course begrudgingly comes to respect him at the end.

If an array of mid-decade radio chart-toppers from the likes of Sponge, Matthew Sweet, The Offspring, Mazzy Star, Butthole Surfers and Cornershop give the movie an authentic 1990s alt-rock flavoring that makes certain scenes tangentially transportive, composer Chad Fischer's score is far less subtle about trying to cue emotions.

Otherwise, though, the film's polished technical package rates among its best qualities. Cinematographer Bill Pope has plenty of action movie experience, and he puts his smart sense of framing to excellent use here. Unnecessarily married to neither close-ups nor wide shots, he crafts a look and feel for the movie that is experiential without being showy about it.

The acting, too, is emblematic of *Chasing Mavericks'* somewhat choppy rhythms, in which the artificial abuts the meticulously constructed. Weston has an easygoing, unforced charm as Jay; a pair of naturally expressive eyes helps, along with the fact that he is playing a quieter and more reactive character. And both Shue and Spencer are lovely in thankless, woefully under-sketched roles.

Butler, though, plays Frosty as a beach bum variation on Donald Pleasance's Dr. Loomis from *Halloween* (1978)—a gruff, growly jerk who is sometimes almost unaccountably hostile. This would be fine, and even quite interesting, if it felt motivated by character, or the movie itself tilted away from melodrama and had a bit of a darker edge. But while some of the reasons for Frosty's gruff behavior are eventually meted out along with his backstory, they—along with his lectures about the four pillars of surfing, and its physical, emotional, mental and spiritual elements—feel less a consequence of his own experiences and more the product of some sort of *Fire in the Belly*-style pamphlet manifesto about modern-day manhood. *Chasing Mavericks* clearly believes in the transcendent nature of its lead characters—who are, after all, real people. It is just a shame that it is sell-ing, the foamy tragedies of its third-act and coda notwithstanding, overly polished versions of them.

Brent Simon

CREDITS

Jay Moriarty: Jonny Weston
Frosty Hesson: Gerard Butler
Christy Moriarty: Elisabeth Shue
Kim: Leven Rambin
Brenda Hesson: Abigail Spencer
Gordy: Scott Eastwood
Origin: United States
Language: English
Released: 2012
Production: Curtis Hanson, Brandon Hooper, Jim Meenaghan; Fox 2000 Pictures, Walden Media; released by 20th Century Fox Film Corp.
Directed by: Curtis Hanson; Michael Apted
Written by: Kario Salem
Cinematography by: Oliver Euclid; Bill Pope
Music by: Chad Fischer
Sound: Paul Apted
Editing: John Gilbert
Costumes: Sophie de Rakoff Carbonell
Production Design: Ida Random
MPAA rating: PG
Running time: 115 minutes

REVIEWS

Chang, Justin. *Variety*. October 25, 2012.
Conley, Mark. *San Jose Mercury News*. October 25, 2012.
Dargis, Manohla. *New York Times*. October 25, 2012.
Duralde, Alonso. *The Wrap*. October 25, 2012.
Ebert, Roger. *Chicago Sun-Times*. October 25, 2012.
LaSalle, Mick. *San Francisco Chronicle*. October 25, 2012.
O'Sullivan, Michael. *Washington Post*. October 26, 2012.
Rechtshaffen, Michael. *Hollywood Reporter*. October 25, 2012.
Sharkey, Betsy. *Los Angeles Times*. October 25, 2012.
Weitzman, Elizabeth. *New York Daily News*. October 25, 2012.

QUOTES

Frosty Hesson: "We all come from the sea, but we are not all of the sea. Those of us who are, we children of the tides, must return to it again and again, until the day we don't come back, leaving only that which was touched along the way."

TRIVIA

Michael Apted directed the last three weeks of principal photography when director Curtis Hanson had to pull out due to health reasons.

CHERNOBYL DIARIES

Experience the fallout.
—Movie tagline

Ten years ago, the Ukrainian government let tourists visit the area around Chernobyl. They said it was safe...it wasn't.
—Movie tagline

Box Office: $18.1 million

Chernobyl Diaries starts with a sly trick. The horror film opens with handheld video of cool, American twenty-somethings cavorting across Europe on vacation, and the viewer is led to believe that producer and co-writer Oren Peli (the creator of the *Paranormal Activity* [2007-2012] franchise) is serving up yet another "found footage" film. A dismissive groan from the audience would not be unwarranted in a year that saw *The Devil Inside, Chronicle, Project X, End of Watch,* and, of course, *Paranormal Activity 4* added to the genre's filmography. Except it is soon revealed that the video is being watched on a tablet computer, so technically *Chernobyl Diaries* quickly drops the found-footage gimmick.

The rest of the film, which follows that group of twenty-something "extreme tourists" as they discover something secret and terrible in an abandoned town near the titular doomed, radioactive nuclear power plant, is not told from a specific "found footage" point of view, which is to say, narrative-wise there is no one in the film making the film. The real joke, however, is that *Chernobyl Diaries* still looks and feels like found footage, complete with a shaky, handheld camera; a gray, washed-out "real-lighting" look; and meanderingly "unscripted" plot and dialogue that feels made up as it goes. So the film lazily gets the cheap effect of found-footage without having to conform to persnickety found-footage rules about who is holding the camera. Enjoy this little bit of cinematic slight of hand—it is the only semi-clever idea in this not-so-scary movie.

In fact, there are only two apparent reasons *Chernobyl Diaries* was released in theaters instead of going directly into the vast pile of direct-to-video horror films being dumped into video stores each year. One is the involvement of Peli, who, still riding his post-*Paranormal* wave of horror-film clout, co-wrote the script with Carey and Shane Van Dyke, based on his story. The other is its admittedly compelling location. Though shot in Hungary and Serbia, the film is set in the real city of Prypiat, Ukraine, whose 50,000 residents were forced to permanently evacuate it in a rush following the April 1986 radioactive accident at the nearby Chernobyl Nuclear Power Plant. The notion of an Eastern European city (already cloaked in the gray, concrete banality of Soviet-era architecture) abandoned for decades to the elements is a fine one. Unfortunately, Peli and *Chernobyl Diaries'* first-time director Bradley Parker do little with the premise visually, tonally, or plot-wise, other than

have their protagonists run around in empty buildings for an hour.

Those players, assembled only to be picked off one by one in the dark, include two brothers—responsible Chris (Jesse McCartney) and reckless Paul (Jonathan Sadowski)—Chris' smart, brunette girlfriend Natalie (Olivia Dudley); her flighty blonde friend Amanda (Devin Kelley); and two other random tourists, Australian Michael (Nathan Phillips) and his Scandinavian girlfriend Zoe (Ingrid Bolso; Berdal). The bland homogeny of both the film's writing and performances guarantees that the above descriptions are as close as a viewer will get to identifying or caring about these people. In terms of acting and character definition, *Chernobyl Diaries'* only stand out is Dimitri Diatchenko as the group's slightly shady tour guide, an ex-military opportunist named Uri.

Of course, their car and communication systems reliably break down, trapping the tourists in Prypiat after dark. But despite the survivalist premise, these uninteresting folks (and the film itself) roam the empty city with a listless lack of purpose. There is a giant bear, a pack of wild (radioactive?) dogs, and, most menacingly, a gang of "something elses" in the darkened ruins, but most of *Chernobyl Diaries'* running time involves characters engaging in seemingly improvised dialog that is intended to add verisimilitude and familiarize the viewer with their personalities and motives, but instead feels like time-killing filler.

When they are not speaking in banal, horror-film cliches, the characters wander foolishly into dark places and meet their respective fates, but as much as Parker aims for eeriness amid the too-quiet empty buildings, the director has no notion of how to create and cultivate the eerie. Lacking in both the imagination and aptitude for genuine chills, *Chernobyl Diaries* seems more like half an idea of a scary movie. The victims and their mysterious antagonists both play out like afterthoughts, and with no sense of a creative vision, the film does not seem to know where it is going or care whether or not it gets there. It never reaches a level of true awfulness because it never reaches for anything. *Chernobyl Diaries* aims only at the lowest "whatever" teenage date-night denominator.

Slipped into theaters in late May as counter programming to big, summer-action blockbusters, *Chernobyl Diaries* did not make much of a mark at the box office, with $18 million in North America, another $19 million overseas. Nor were critics kind to the horror film. Mark Olsen of the *Los Angeles Times* wrote, "The lack of suspense and surprise in this dispiritingly rote film becomes its own form of contamination." Others objected to the film makers using the real-life Chernobyl disaster and its lingering environmental effects as fodder for cheap scares, including *Slate*'s Dana Stevens who felt, "The movie is, without question, in atrociously poor taste."

Locke Peterseim

CREDITS

Paul: Jonathan Sadowski
Chris: Jesse McCartney
Amanda: Devin Kelley
Natalie: Olivia Taylor Dudley
Zoe: Ingrid Bolso Berdal
Michael: Nathan Phillips
Uri: Dimitri Diatchenko
Origin: United States
Language: English
Released: 2012
Production: Brian Witten, Oren Peli; Alcon Entertainment L.L.C.; released by Warner Bros.
Directed by: Bradley Parker
Written by: Oren Peli; Carey Van Dyke; Shane Van Dyke
Cinematography by: Morten Soborg
Music by: Diego Stocco
Sound: Ray Beckett
Editing: Stan Salfas
Costumes: Momirka Bailovic
Production Design: Aleksander Denic
MPAA rating: R
Running time: 88 minutes

REVIEWS

Goodykoontz, Bill. *Arizona Republic.* May 25, 2012.
Morris, Wesley. *Boston Globe.* May 26, 2012.
Olsen, Mark. *Los Angeles Times.* May 25, 2012.
O'Sullivan, Michael. *Washington Post.* May 26, 2012.
Schager, Nick. *Slant Magazine.* May 25, 2012.
Stevens, Dana. *Slate.* May 25, 2012.
Tobias, Scott. *AV Club.* May 25, 2012.
Vizcarrondo, Sara Maria. *Box Office Magazine.* May 25, 2012.
Webster, Andy. *New York Times.* May 25, 2012.
Willmore, Alison. *Movieline.* May 25, 2012.

QUOTES

Paul: "Have you heard of extreme tourism?"

TRIVIA

The film was shot on location in Hungary and Serbia.

CHICO & RITA

Box Office: $350,524

The Spanish animated film *Chico & Rita* was one of the most surprising nominees on the morning that the 84th Academy Award nominations were announced, beating out several other major studio films for a spot in the top five choices for the Best Animated Film of the Year. Having won awards around the world (including the Goya Award for Best Animated Film, Spain's equivalent of the Oscar) and placed on top ten lists after its European releases, the film was finally granted a U.S. theatrical release in 2012, where it rose to a very respectable (for an arthouse, foreign-language, adult-animated film) $350k and a total of $2.2 million worldwide. It is simple to see what the Academy saw in the film within minutes as this is a delightful, surprising, even sexy adult drama about music, love, loss, and the changing face of the world in the '40s and '50s. Employing gorgeous 2-D animation that reminds one of the great, frame-worthy art of Sylvain Chomet on *The Illusionist* (2010), *Chico & Rita* is mesmerizing.

An older gentleman in Havana is remembering his younger years and the one who got away as he goes through a memory box. The majority of *Chico & Rita* is a flashback film as Chico reminisces about the girl who changed his life and how he screwed it up. After the prologue, the film flashes back to Havana in the '40s. The world is vibrant, alive, and vital and the animation captures it in captivating ways. Music seems to be not just playing everywhere but keeping the city's heartbeat as its rhythm. There is beautiful music, glasses clinking, conversations happening, and people falling in love. It is a highly stylized world that somehow still resonates with honest emotion. These early scenes in Havana are so captivating that they allow flaws of later acts to be easily overlooked just as Chico never forgets the first time he sees Rita, singing across a crowded Cuban bar. He is in love.

Like so many instinct-driven musicians, Chico cannot keep his love for Rita in line. The two have a glorious working relationship, winning an important contest and creating beautiful music together at the piano and between the sheets. But Chico cannot restrain his jealousy. When he sees her talking to an admirer who turns out to be a music producer who could make her a star in New York, he explodes into a rage, not knowing that Rita was pushing to make sure he came with her to the States. She has had enough and leaves him behind.

Years later, Rita has become a star in the U.S. while Chico finally makes his way to Manhattan and crosses paths with her again. Here, *Chico & Rita* finds a new musical passion to balance with Havana. New York is just as alive with music and even appearances by Charlie Parker, Dizzy Gillespie, and Chano Pozo (whose real-life murder is fictionalized as an encounter that Chico witnesses). Music is not merely the backdrop of *Chico & Rita,* it is nearly a constant presence, driving the action and becoming part of the fabric of the narrative instead of mere storytelling device. It drives the plot instead of merely adding to it.

To be fair, said plot is pretty standard stuff. From the minute Chico meets Rita, it is clear they will fall in love, fall out of love, and probably fall back in again. Surprisingly for its genre, *Chico & Rita* is more of an atmosphere piece than a plot-driven one. With fluid animation that feels alive in ways that so many 3D computer-animated films do not, the filmmakers are more concerned with mood and tone than groundbreaking narrative. It is not the lyrics of the song that matter but the rhythm and the way it plays out. Everyone knows the tune but it is how well it is executed that matters.

Critics around the world fell in love with *Chico & Rita* with a few notable names, including Michael Philips of *The Chicago Tribune,* placing it on their top ten of the year. In fact, a year and a half before its stateside release, Stephen Farber wrote in *The Hollywood Reporter* that the work was "A visually hypnotic, musically electric film." In fact, it is perhaps most remarkable that the international pipeline of film distribution is so baffling that it took this great work so long to get to the U.S. And one wonders if it ever would have without the Academy Awards to give it a boost. The Academy is often criticizing for closing doors on smaller, independent, and foreign films in favor of works from studios that know how to play the political game. This is a case of the opposite, the opening of a door for a fantastic movie that may not have otherwise been as easy to see.

Brian Tallerico

CREDITS

Chico: Eman Xor Ona (Voice)
Rita: Liamara Meneses (Voice)
Ramon: Mario Guerra (Voice)
Origin: United Kingdom, Spain
Language: Spanish, English
Released: 2010
Production: Christina Huete, Santi Errando, Martin Pope, Michael Rose; CinemaNX, HanWay Films, Estdudio Mariscal, Isle of Man, Magic Light Pictures; released by GKIDS
Directed by: Fernando Trueba; Javier Mariscal; Tono Errando
Written by: Fernando Trueba; Ignacio Martinez de Pison
Music by: Bebo Waldes
Sound: Nacho Royo
Editing: Amau Quiles
MPAA rating: Unrated
Running time: 94 minutes

REVIEWS

Anderson, John. *Newsday.* March 16, 2012.
Ebert, Roger. *Chicago Sun-Times.* February 23, 2012.
Farber, Stephen. *Hollywood Reporter.* September 16, 2010.
Long, Tom. *Detroit News.* February 24, 2012.
Lumenick, Lou. *New York Post.* February 10, 2012.
Mondello, Bob. *NPR.* February 9, 2012.
Orange, Michelle. *Movieline.* February 7, 2012.
Rodriguez, Rene. *Miami Herald.* February 10, 2012.
Scott, A. O. *New York Times.* February 9, 2012.
Sharkey, Betsy. *Los Angeles Times.* March 8, 2012.

QUOTES

Chico: "Have you thought about your career? About your future?"
Rita: "Future, what future? The future never gave me anything! All my hopes are set on the past."

TRIVIA

To help accurately represent 1940s era Cuba, director Javier Mariscal went on a research trip to Cuba and was allowed to view government archive photographs from 1949.

AWARDS

Nominations:
Oscars 2011: Animated Film

CHRONICLE

What are you capable of?
    —Movie tagline
Boys will be boys.
    —Movie tagline
Not all heroes are super.
    —Movie tagline

Box Office: $64.6 million

After making an indelible impression on television and in the editing room, 27-year-old director Josh Trank became one of the youngest filmmakers to top the American box office with his splendid debut feature, *Chronicle,* a triumph of pop filmmaking on a limited budget. Made for a reported sum of $15 million, this modernized riff on superhero origins and telekinetic vengeance recharged the worn batteries of the found footage genre with inventive cinematography, fine performances and some truly stunning effects.

Yet the key to the film's success lies in its smart and infectiously playful script co-authored by Trank and Max Landis. Ever since Joshua Leonard's ad lib about the camera's function as a protective shield in Daniel Myrick and Eduardo Sanchez's game-changer, *The Blair Witch Project* (1999), filmmakers have been scrambling to justify their characters' need to keep the camera rolling. Aside from a few lines of self-conscious exposition, *Chronicle* has the most naturalistic camerawork of any found footage film since *Blair Witch*. Nearly every tilt of the lens and carefully chosen focal point is intrinsically linked to the angst-ridden protagonist's state of mind.

Seattle teen Andrew (Dane DeHaan, giving a mesmerizing performance reminiscent of the equally-disturbed youth he played on HBO's *In Treatment*) is first glimpsed through the mirror of a bedroom door, as his camera logs the ranting and fist-pounding of his abusive father, Richard (Michael Kelly). With his bedridden mother fading away at home and a passel of bullies waiting to torture him at school, Andrew looks to his camera as a source of comfort and companionship. When a popular-yet-genial peer, Steve (Michael B. Jordan), warns the weary-eyed outcast that he risks placing a barrier between himself and the world with his incessant camerawork, Andrew replies, "Maybe I need a barrier." As the young man's social life starts to open up, Trank allows other camera perspectives to frame the action, particularly that of Andrew's concerned cousin, Matt (Aussie thesp Alex Russell).

To the credit of Trank and Landis, no effort is made to explain the source of the boys' powers. Andrew, Matt, and Steve merely stumble upon a large, glowing object tucked inside an abnormally-large hole in the ground. In the next scene, the trio is experimenting with their newfound abilities. A more conventional narrative may have included cutaways to governmental bigwigs and media pundits reacting to these alarming events, but *Chronicle* wisely keeps the story confined within the world of its impressionable leading men.

Chronicle impeccably captures the exhilaration felt by these teens as they lift themselves off the ground for the first time. Expertly blending live action with digital trickery, Trank crafts sequences in which extraordinary consequences are fueled by the impulsiveness of youth. As the friends practice flexing their magic "muscle," they quickly discover the extent of their strength. When an irate driver ignites Andrew's volatile temper, he literally wipes him off the road, blowing out his headlights and sending the car over a guard rail with a wave of his hand.

Once Andrew realizes that he can make his camera levitate, cinematographer Matthew Jensen shifts from familiar handheld angles to beautifully fluid shots that freely move wherever Andrew's mind pleases. This solves the dilemma of characters begging to have the camera shut off, since it can easily wriggle out of their grasp. The technique also results in some fascinating imagery that illuminates the tormented hero's perception of himself. With great strength comes inevitable hubris, and Andrew begins to obsessively find ways to pound his enemies into the ground. After disposing of a few assorted thugs, the camera elegantly shifts to a god's eye perspective of the carnage, as Andrew observes the blood smeared on the pavement.

One of the most provocative aspects of the picture is the way in which Trank toys with audience sympathies. On one hand, Andrew is enormously sympathetic and his consuming anger is entirely justified by the hideous conditions of his life. The bullying that he faces is not portrayed with the slightest bit of self-aware snark. The extent to which the audience silently desires to see Andrew continue his path of destruction is as troubling here as it was in Brian De Palma's *Carrie* (1976).

If Matt were played by a bland straight arrow, *Chronicle* may have collapsed in its final act, but Russell matches DeHaan with his tender, endearing performance. His belief in altruism is apparent in his compassionate behavior throughout the film, thus causing him to resemble a hero just as Andrew descends into villainy. Even though Trank's use of superhero iconography is apparent in the film's final act, Matt and Andrew are never allowed to devolve into easy caricatures. Their altercations pack a real punch because they are the logical result of two vividly compelling characterizations. It is exciting to see a picture that allows audiences to have their sympathies split straight down the middle.

If the film falls just short of perfect, it's primarily due to the two-dimensional depiction of Richard, the Neanderthal-like father figure naturally detested by Andrew. He is such a monstrous wretch that it is difficult to believe him, even within the dangerous world conjured by Trank. His hatred for his son is spawned by far more than alcohol and depression, and seems to have been inspired directly by Piper Laurie's fanatical matriarch in *Carrie*. Whereas Laurie's performance perfectly emulated the jet-black satire that De Palma layered within his tale's tragic horrors, Kelly's portrayal feels as if it were lifted from an entirely different film altogether. Richard is the only true cardboard villain in the picture, but the character's scant screen time enables its flaws to register as little more than a quibble.

What ultimately makes *Chronicle* such an electrifying success is its unflinching portrait of adolescence, and the tumult that occurs when naive minds attempt to navigate their way through a hostile environment. Trank nails the fickleness of high school popularity, the violence spawned from teenage insecurity, the fear of losing a loving parent and the wrath provoked by a health care system that could not care less about the health of sick people. The authenticity of the film's central drama allows its flights of fancy to appear even more credible. Just as *Blair Witch* and Oren Peli's *Paranormal Activity* (2008) demonstrated the psychological impact of handheld horror, *Chronicle* illustrates the underutilized potential of found footage. It bypasses the cliches and contrivances that bog down so many Hollywood narratives while developing an intimate connection with its characters, enabling their frame of reference to dictate the cinematic language. Trank's supernaturally endowed teens are so relatable that when they gaze at their reflection in the mirror, viewers could easily see themselves.

Matt Fagerholm

CREDITS

Andrew Detmer: Dane DeHaan
Matt Garetty: Alex Russell
Steve Montgomery: Michael B. Jordan
Richard Detmer: Michael Kelly
Casey Letter: Ashley Hinshaw
Origin: United States
Language: English
Released: 2012
Production: John Davis, Adam Schroeder; Adam Schroeder Productions, Davis Entertainment, Film Afrika Worldwide; released by 21st Century Film Corporation
Directed by: Josh Trank
Written by: Max Landis
Cinematography by: Matthew Jensen
Sound: Kelly Oxford
Music Supervisor: Andrea von Foerster
Editing: Elliot Greenberg
Art Direction: Patrick O'Connor
Costumes: Dianna Cilliers
Production Design: Stephen Altman
MPAA rating: PG-13
Running time: 83 minutes

REVIEWS

Biancolli, Amy. *San Francisco Chronicle*. February 10, 2012.
Dargis, Manohla. *New York Times*. February 10, 2012.
Debrudge, Peter. *Variety*. February 10, 2012.
Dinning, Mark. *Empire*. February 10, 2012.
Ebert, Roger. *Chicago Sun-Times*. February 10, 2012.
Gleiberman, Owen. *Entertainment Weekly*. February 10, 2012.
Rea, Steven. *Philadelphia Inquirer*. February 10, 2012.
Sharkey, Betsy. *Los Angeles Times*. February 10, 2012.
Tobias, Scott. *AV Club*. February 10, 2012.
Uhlich, Keith. *Time Out New York*. February 10, 2012.

QUOTES

Matt Garetty: "There's something wrong with Andrew."

TRIVIA

The film features no original score, and instead utilizes sources such as radios and iPods to generate music.

CIRQUE DU SOLEIL: WORLDS AWAY

Box Office: $12.5 million

A greatest-hits sampler platter celebration of the physical artistry of everything that Cirque du Soleil is about, *Cirque du Soleil: Worlds Away* is the rare film that can be called both amazing and a bit wearisome. Visually lavish and featuring an array of undeniably mind-blowing acrobatic and gymnastic feats, the movie is a superb showcase for the well-regarded, Canadian-based circus troupe of its title, which brings in more than $800 million annually and has over the last several decades hosted audiences totaling an estimated 90 million people worldwide. As a standalone cinematic entity, however, *Worlds Away* buckles under the pressure of interweaving portions of seven different Cirque du Soleil productions. It dazzles fitfully throughout, but does not have a proper narrative hold all its own, so even at only ninety-one minutes it starts to drag mightily.

The framing device follows a young small town girl, Mia (Erica Linz), who comes across a flyer for a circus and crosses paths with a handsome trapeze artist (Igor Zaripov). Their flirtation is cut short, however, when he misses a catch and tumbles into a quicksand portal. Mia rushes to help him, but the ground gives way beneath her too. With a mysterious clown (John Clarke) initially acting as her guide, Mia then descends through a rabbit-hole of various states of limbo, each loosely manifested in the form of a separate Cirque du Soleil show.

As such, *Worlds Away* compares less to some of director Andrew Adamson's stated inspirations (like Lewis Carroll's *Alice in Wonderland* and Peter Tchaikovsky's *Swan Lake* ballet), or other stunt spectaculars, like *Jackass: The Movie* (2002), and more to those hundredth-episode clip shows of hit sitcoms, wherein a loose wraparound story is devised in order to serve up goosing, good-time highlight reminiscences from episodes past. To this end, it is necessary to if not judge *Worlds Away* on two different planes then at least acknowledge that for many viewers without the means to go to Las Vegas (where seven permanent shows currently play to many thousands of visitors per night) or catch one of the troupe's many traveling shows, this movie represents the best per-dollar entertainment value for a Cirque du Soleil staging.

Adamson has experience in both animation and live-action, which seems an obvious benefit for a unique project like this; he is able to think conceptually about space in a different way. Still, given the lack of dialogue, *Worlds Away* may have benefited from a less overtly telegraphed love story. There are advantages to such a familiar plot structure, but a more fanciful, less literal storyline could have complemented the choreography and given additional lift to the material as a truly dizzy slice of magical realism. The tweaked sequences from the shows that make up the movie—*O, Mystere, Ka, Love, Zumanity, Viva Elvis* and *Criss Angel Believe*—are so different in nature and tone that attempting to foist some cogence upon them seems like an exercise in folly.

The movie's main appeal, then, lies simply in its presentation of wondrous acts of contortion, tumbling and other feats of acrobatic prowess—in particular with respect to its aerial cinematography, captured by Brett Turnbull. James Cameron served as an executive producer on the project, and Adamson, Turnbull and 3D producer Vincent Pace used the Fusion 3D camera system developed by Cameron's company. The results effectively spotlight its performers' astounding physicality as well as the ingenuity of Cirque du Soleil's staging and costume design; viewers get a rather excellent sense of space from this smart, considered use of 3D. But *Worlds Away* also alternates between slow-motion and regular speed, which, along with some too-close camera angles and desultory editing choices by Sim Evan-Jones, occasionally undercut a fuller appreciation of the fluidity and difficulty of the trapeze-inspired sets in particular.

Some of the film's standout segments include acrobatic feats in a shallow, water-filled fishbowl (part of the *Zumanity* show), and a fun trampoline-inspired sequence from *Viva Elvis*. Several winning bits are also lifted from *Ka*, and interspersed throughout. The best of those moments, however, is a chase sequence that takes place on a pegboard which is lifted vertically into the air, and spins around. It is this imaginative combination of performance artistry and technological marvel that Cirque du Soleil does best, and the sort of set piece that in its own strange way rivals memorable action sequences from films like *The Matrix* (1999) and *Inception* (2010). It is even more amazing given the fact that it is not augmented by CGI or other post-production gimmickry.

Paradoxically, the movie's emotional grip loosens further as it segues into numbers from the Beatles-inspired *Love*, and builds toward its baldly romantic, straps-based aerial finale. Songs like "Lucy in the Sky With Diamonds," "Octopus' Garden" and "While My Guitar Gently Weeps" may have a greater emotional

investment for especially Boomer-aged viewers, but they only serve to underscore the production's discrete charms. In music, greatest hits packages are usually teased with additional new tracks for longtime fans, which *Worlds Away* does not really seem to offer in abundance. On the other hand, Cirque du Soleil neophytes will find plenty in the film at which to be astonished. And if anything, it is at least an atypically impressive display of human nimbleness and athletic ability, and a reminder that gymnastic artistry need not arrive only once every four years, with the Olympics.

Brent Simon

CREDITS

Mia: Erica Linz
The Aerialist: Igor Zaripov
Ringmaster: Lutz Halbhubner
Sad Clown: John Clarke
Boss: Dallas Barnett
Origin: United States
Language: English
Released: 2012
Production: Martin Bolduc, Aron Warner, Andrew Adamson; Reel FX Creative Studios, Strange Weather Films; released by Paramount Pictures
Directed by: Andrew Adamson
Written by: Andrew Adamson
Cinematography by: Brett Turnbull
Music by: Benoit Jutras
Sound: Tim Prebble
Editing: Sim Evan-Jones; Dirk Westervelt
Art Direction: Guy Barnes
Costumes: Josalene Ginn
MPAA rating: PG
Running time: 91 minutes

REVIEWS

Adams, Mark. *Screen International.* December 19, 2012.
Bell, Josh. *Las Vegas Weekly.* December 19, 2012.
Hartlaub, Peter. *San Francisco Chronicle.* December 20, 2012.
Jones, Kimberley. *Austin Chronicle.* December 28, 2012.
Lehmann, Megan. *Hollywood Reporter.* December 19, 2012.
MacDonald, Moira. *Seattle Times.* December 26, 2012.
Nelson, Rob. *Variety.* December 19, 2012.
O'Sullivan, Michael. *Washington Post.* December 21, 2012.
Rickey, Carrie. *Philadelphia Inquirer.* December 20, 2012.
Scherstuhl, Alan. *Village Voice.* December 19, 2012.

TRIVIA

In addition to the footage from the Las Vegas shows, shooting also took place in New Zealand and a New Zealand-style railway crossing sign can be seen in the film's first shot.

CITADEL

They see your fear.
—Movie tagline

Box Office: $13,377

Citadel first feels like it is a cousin of domestic horror films like *The Strangers* or *Them* but it then takes on more unique tones when it is revealed that the enemies pounding on the door and breaking the window are not traditional bad guys. What if the zombies in films like *Night of the Living Dead* or the bloodsuckers of *Fright Night* did not announce themselves with a flourish but crept up on their victims like a gang of harm-intending children in a bad part of town? Such is the premise of this clever, tension-filled piece, a movie that takes a bit too long and has some notable pacing issues given its brief running time but contains enough atmosphere and action to merit a look. Director Ciaran Foy is working with some interesting themes regarding fear of the other, especially a hooded teenager, but the movie does not do enough with its own clever concepts to really transcend its genre. Well-made and intriguing, but not as memorable as it could have been if its themes had been a bit more fully fleshed out.

Foy's film opens with Tommy's (Aneurin Barnard) final day of happiness. He leaves his very pregnant wife to take suitcases down to a car and returns to see her being assaulted by a trio of hooded figures that look about the size of pre-teens. They kill Tommy's wife but the baby survives. Now, Tommy is a single father who is literally crippled by intense agoraphobia. After what he witnessed with his spouse, he can barely leave his apartment, walks hunched and wide-eyed when he does, considers every sound a warning of imminent death, and speaks only to a social worker named Marie (Wunmi Mosaku).

At his wife's funeral, Tommy runs across a Priest (the perfectly gruff James Cosmo), who aggressively tells our reluctant hero that his bad days are far from over. He says something about the creatures who killed Tommy's wife coming back to get the child they left behind and Tommy is truly sent into a tailspin. Marie argues that the hooded figures who skirt the shadows of this urban landscape are just misunderstood teens but the religious leader argues that they are something entirely different—creatures of the night. Thematically, this is fascinating stuff. The idea that international fear of groups of young people meant to cause harm could be used as a foundation for a genre story. What if the lost boys of a society that increasingly dismisses them were more than just rebellious youth? And what if it is societal discarding of these troubled teens that makes turns them into something more (or less) than human?

The first act of *Citadel* has echoes of Roman Polanski's work of intense paranoia as Tommy is always looking over his shoulder as his baby is always crying. The film is aggressively foreboding and one leans forward to see where it goes. Sadly, it takes a bit too long to get there and the tension of the first act dissipates into something approaching tedium in the second. And then Foy really gets aggressive, turning *Citadel* into something less Polanski and more John Carpenter as Tommy and his religious counsel tackle the building that apparently houses these hooded creatures of the night. With tones of Carpenter's beloved, single-set masterpieces (and even notes that remind one of Gareth Evans' brilliant *The Raid: Redemption* [2012]), Foy proves to be not as deft at action as he is at tension. Too much of the final act feels routine and Foy fails to answer key questions about the action either physically or thematically. It is not as if he needs to wrap up every plot point and determine what is social statement is through this action-horror movie but the film's lack of doing so needed to be more refined itself. A film like *Citadel* does not need answers but it needs something more than this one's non-conclusion.

Small studio Cinedigm Entertainment could not get *Citadel* past the major cities and it only grossed just over $13,000 in domestic theaters, never playing wider than seven screens despite an audience-friendly genre and some positive reviews, including Roger Ebert, who wrote on his site, "This is a basic story, simply and directly told by Irish writer-director Ciaran Foy. He doesn't try to explain too much, he doesn't depend on special effects and stays just this side of the unbelievable." Joe Leydon wrote in *Variety,* "Writer-director Ciaran Foy skillfully taps into primal fears and urban paranoia to keep his audience consistently unsettled in Citadel, an intensely suspenseful horror-thriller." With praise from outlets that notable and a genre that always finds an audience on DVD, *Citadel* seems bound to be a cult classic.

Brian Tallerico

CREDITS

Tommy Cowley: Aneurin Barnard
Priest: James Cosmo
Marie: Wunmi Mosaku
Danny: Jake Wilson
Joanne: Amy Shiels
Origin: United Kingdom, Ireland

Language: English

Released: 2012

Production: Brian Coffey, Katie Holly; Blinder Films, Sigma Films; released by Cinedigm Entertainment Group

Directed by: Ciaran Foy

Written by: Ciaran Foy

Cinematography by: Tim Fleming

Music by: tomandandy

Sound: Steve Fanagan

Editing: Tony Kearns; Jake Roberts

Art Direction: Andy Thomson

Costumes: Anna Robbins

Production Design: Tom Sayer

MPAA rating: R

Running time: 84 minutes

REVIEWS

Catsoulis, Jeannette. *New York Times*. November 8, 2012.

DeFore, John. *Hollywood Reporter*. November 6, 2012.

Ebert, Roger. *Chicago Sun-Times*. December 6, 2012.

Groen, Rick. *The Globe and Mail*. November 16, 2012.

Leydon, Joe. *Variety*. November 6, 2012.

Olsen, Mark. *Los Angeles Times*. November 15, 2012.

Schager, Nick. *Slant Magazine*. November 6, 2012.

Taylor, Drew. *The Playlist*. November 8, 2012.

Toppman, Lawrence. *Charlotte Observer*. November 29, 2012.

Uhlich, Keith. *Time Out New York*. November 6, 2012.

TRIVIA

A set was built for the basement of the citadel.

CLOUD ATLAS

Everything is connected.
—Movie tagline

Box Office: $27.1 million

David Mitchell's *Cloud Atlas*, released to worldwide acclaim in 2004, is one of the best books of the new millennium. It is a challenging, daring piece of work in not only structure but theme. Composed like a series of Russian nesting dolls, the book contains six short stories conveyed in a remarkably unique structure. The reader gets the first half of each story and then the second in snake order—one through six, six through one. As the book reaches an amazing climax, all of the stories, told in different genre styles across different eras, have intertwined into one powerful piece of work. Tom Tykwer and Andy and Lana Wachowski's adaptation of Mitchell's work comes at the same concept from the other direction. The film opens with all six of the stories

and most of the major characters presented to the viewer in a series of quick-cut scenes. All of these people are thematically intertwined, and now the film will show you why. The decision to introduce this epic work in this manner is telling and the film's biggest problem—the dots are being connected for the viewer instead of a reader connecting them himself. Every theme in Mitchell's work has been underlined, highlighted, and bolded to the point that the viewer never really has to bring anything to it and, therefore, is never swept away in its relevance or emotional impact. The film has some undeniably strong technical elements and some interesting performances and critics should be careful not to completely dismiss works from Hollywood this ambitious or risk having nothing but multiplex fare, but it proves a point that many producers are not willing to realize—not all brilliant works in one medium can or should be adapted to another.

One decision was made early and it contributes to the sense that Mitchell's are being over-emphasized instead of allowed to organically grow from the source material. That is, instead of casting dozens of high- or low-profile actors in the film's many speaking roles, the producers actually kept their cast small, allowing performers to play multiple characters across the six stories and periods of the film. Relying on heavy makeup (that often distracts more than anything else), it was a daring move but it feels like a showy one. It is the filmmakers showing viewers that the human experience is the same across multiple genres and eras instead of telling them why that matters to this story or life in general. It is allowing makeup work to do the thematic highlighting.

The six stories of *Cloud Atlas* start in the South Pacific in 1849. A young man (Jim Sturgess) becomes the physical target of a cruel doctor on a ship, where he also befriends a runaway slave, who helps Sturgerss's character stay alive long enough to get home to his true love. Almost a hundred years later in England, a talented young composer (Ben Whishaw) is working with a legend (Jim Broadbent) while maintaining a series of love letters with his boyfriend. The composer slips into depression as happiness and success seem to evade him and his benefactor takes advantage of his good nature. In the 1970s, a journalist (Halle Berry) is investigating the criminal dealings of a major corporation (run by Hugh Grant) while also putting her own life at risk in the process. In the comedic story set in present day, a publisher (Broadbent) is held prisoner in a hospital after being committed by his jerk of a brother (Grant). Way in the future, a clone (Doona Bae) becomes self-aware and leads a revolution with the help of a unique stranger. Even further in the future (but with a cinematic look that could be way in the past), a simple villager (Tom

Hanks) works with a mysterious traveler (Berry) to possibly save the human race.

The themes of *Cloud Atlas* are dense enough to not only overwhelm any semblance of character or even storytelling but to invade most of the dialogue as well. Whether it is the 1800s or 2100s, people need people. It may sound simple, and a common theme of cinema, but Mitchell addresses it in a way that feels like a breakthrough. The issues that drive humanity transcend not just time but literary genres in his book. The power of love and human relationships to overcome virtually any hardship is a strong enough theme that it occasionally resonates here again. Whether it is in the delicate interplay between Hanks and Berry in the future story or the protective approach that Sturgess takes to Bae in the "sci-fi" story or the beautiful love story that carries Whishaw to the best performance in the film, there are moments of *Cloud Atlas* that truly convey the strength of Mitchell's book. The movie works best when it catches its breath and does not seem so intent on getting on to its next theme, character, storyline, etc. Some of the smaller moments, like two men sitting down to compose the piece of classical music that gives the film its title, have the power that one wishes the rest of the film contained. It is just so hurried. It is so insistent on moving on to the next subplot that one cannot take the time to actually care about the characters or what they are doing before trying to do so with others.

And yet it seems critically self-defeating to complain about a Hollywood film that is overloaded with themes and interesting ideas. The fact is that the machine of the blockbuster industry produces far more works completely barren of thematic interest that one wants to embrace what Tykwer and the Wachowskis have attempted here. It leads one to an inevitable question: Could David Mitchell's book ever have worked on the screen? Is this the best that could have been done? It's possible that the answer to the former is no and that the work should have stayed on the page or been adapted to a more long-form medium like the TV mini-series so its themes would not feel so rushed. Themes that pop up every twenty pages in Mitchell's work are naturally forced to the surface every two minutes in the film and likely would be no matter who adapted it. And while it is possible that another director (or trio of directors in this case) could have found a different way to crack this story, it is just as possible that this is, as many thought upon reading it, an "unfilmable book."

Technical elements deserve praise here, particularly the lovely score by co-director Tykwer, Johnny Klimek, and Reinhold Heil (it truly deserved an Oscar nomination, and the film's stellar editing should be cited as well). The cinematography maintains a consistency across all six periods that is hard to imagine given the

very different styles and tones in each and the fact that the directors split up to direct them. Overall, *Cloud Atlas* definitely feels like one coherent vision, a remarkable accomplishment given the different sets, characters, and even filmmakers involved. Much of the cast is worthy of praise as well, as there is not a lazy performer in the group. Most notable are Whishaw, Hanks, and the mesmerizing Doona Bae, so great in Park Chanwook's *Sympathy For Mr. Vengeance* (2002) and now possibly set for U.S. stardom.

One must use the word possibly for *Cloud Atlas* surely disappointed both commercially and critically. The film had a rather large budget (understandably so given its scope) but only mustered a pathetic $27 million domestically. Luckily, it grossed three times that internationally, but still fell short of expectations with $108 million worldwide. *Cloud Atlas* is the kind of film that audiences will embrace over time, many future viewers not understanding why critics did not embrace it more upon its initial release. And then maybe they will go back and read Mitchell's book and understand.

Brian Tallerico

CREDITS

Dr. Henry Goose/Hotel Manager/Isaac Sachs/Dermot Hoggins/Cavendish Look-a-Like Actor/Zachry: Tom Hanks

Native Woman/Jocasta Ayrs/Luisa Rey/Indian Party Guest/Ovid/Meronym: Halle Berry

Rev. Giles Horrox/Hotel Heavy/Lloyd Hooks/Denholme Cavendish/Seer Rhee/Kona Chief: Hugh Grant

Captain Molyneux/Vyvyan Ayrs/Timothy Cavendish/Korean Musician/Prescient 2: Jim Broadbent

Haskell Moore/Tadeusz Kesselring/Bill Smoke/Nurse Noakes/Boardman Mephi/Old Georgie: Hugo Weaving

Adam Ewing/Poor Hotel Guest/Megan's Dad/Highlander/Hae-Joo Chang/Adam/Zachry's Brother-in-Law: Jim Sturgess

Madame Horrox/Older Ursula/Yusouf Suleiman/Abbess: Susan Sarandon

Kupaka/Joe Napier/An-Kor Apis/Prescient: Keith David

Origin: United States

Language: English

Released: 2012

Production: Grant Hill, Stefan Arndt, Lana Wachowski, Tom Tykwer, Andy Wachowski; Anarchos Prods.; released by Warner Bros.

Directed by: Andy Wachowski; Lana Wachowski; Tom Tykwer

Written by: Andy Wachowski; Lana Wachowski; Tom Tykwer

Cinematography by: Frank Griebe; John Toll

Music by: Tom Tykwer; Reinhold Heil; Johnny Klimek

Sound: Ivan Sharrock

Editing: Alexander Berner
Costumes: Kym Barrett; Pierre-Yves Gayraud
Production Design: Uli Hanisch
MPAA rating: R
Running time: 164 minutes

REVIEWS

Berardinelli, James. *ReelViews*. October 27, 2012.
Debruge, Peter. *Variety*. September 9, 2012.
Ebert, Roger. *Chicago Sun-Times*. October 24, 2012.
LaSalle, Mick. *San Francisco Chronicle*. October 25, 2012.
Mohan, Marc. *Portland Oregonian*. October 25, 2012.
O'Hehir, Andrew. *Salon.com*. October 26, 2012.
Phipps, Keith. *AV Club*. October 24, 2012.
Savlov, Marc. *Austin Chronicle*. October 24, 2012.
Wilson, Calvin. *St. Louis Post-Dispatch*. October 25, 2012.
Willmore, Alison. *Movieline*. October 26, 2012.

QUOTES

Sonmi-451: "Our lives are not our own. From womb to tomb, we are bound to others. Past and present. And by each crime and every kindness, we birth our future."

TRIVIA

Andy Wachowski and Lana Wachowski directed the 1849, 2144, and 2321 segments of the film. Tom Tykwer directed the 1936, 1973 and 2012 segments.

AWARDS

Nominations:

Golden Globes 2013: Orig. Score

THE COLD LIGHT OF DAY

Instinct is his greatest weapon.
—Movie tagline

Box Office: $3.8 million

A boilerplate work of mock international intrigue, action thriller *The Cold Light of Day* stocks its yawningly familiar tale with a few well-known actors, but even they cannot save this tired, pointless exercise is genre calisthenics. Quietly dumped by distributor Summit Entertainment like a murder victim off a bridge from a moving vehicle—in only around 1,500 theaters, and without benefit of advance screenings for critics or much in the way of advertising support—the movie pulled in a meager $3.7 million domestically. To assail its stupidity with much lingering annoyance is hard to summon

the energy to do, however, given the film's steadfast commitment to all things bland and generic.

Trying to leave behind some economic worries, San Francisco financial trader Will Shaw (Henry Cavill, a bit drab) joins his family on vacation in Spain, only to have his mom Laurie (Caroline Goodall) and other loved ones taken hostage. After narrowly escaping capture himself by group of dirty cops who appear to have some connection to the disappearance, Will is rescued by his dad Martin (Bruce Willis, letting his goatee do the acting), who turns out not to be the career cultural attache he has portrayed himself to be but instead a top-secret government agent.

Will is shocked by this confession—along with the fact that he later finds out he has a half-sibling, Lucia Caldera (Veronica Echegui)—but has little time to process anything. Corrupt intelligence official Jean Carrack (Sigourney Weaver), who has some sort of connection to Will's father, desperately wants returned a mysterious briefcase swiped from her by some Middle Eastern spies, and so she tasks Will with tracking it down, in exchange for his family's freedom. Car chases and gunplay predictably ensue.

Director Mabrouk El Mechri helped spark a mini-renaissance for Jean-Claude van Damme with the slyly self-referential *JCVD* (2008), but the inventive stylishness of that film is wholly absent here. While cinematographer Remi Adefarasin does a decent job of capturing some of the natural environs that the movie's location shoot affords, there is not really an overriding template or vision for the look of the movie. All of the pedestrian action is staged in the most routine manner, with Lucas Vidal's goosing score—the aural equivalent of a liquored-up small town wedding singer—working overtime to try to convince viewers otherwise. Valerio Bonelli's slam-bang editing, meanwhile, largely undercuts any sense of jittery, stranger-in-a-strange-land tension that could arise from this novice being thrust into such incredible circumstances.

Written by Scott Wiper and John Petro, *The Cold Light of Day* deserves nominal credit for not magically recasting Will as a square-jawed, latent, sharpshooting superhero simply owing to his father's occupational prowess, but the script is otherwise marked most by rote characterizations and similarly inane dialogue that frequently reinforces the action unfolding on screen. In this sense the movie is reminiscent of *The Double* (2011), another spy movie distended with self-satisfaction over its air-quote clever twists and red herrings. When not cycling through poorly motivated chase rooftop chases and other sequences, *The Cold Light of Day* pulls the levers of double-cross and conspiracy so heartily that the story quickly ceases to mean anything.

Taking a step back from the actual onscreen analysis for a moment, it is all but certain that the behind-the-scenes wheeling and dealing that led to *The Cold Light of Day* getting made is just as if not more intriguing than the action that unfolds in the movie. A narrative retread through and through, *The Cold Light of Day*'s DNA is lifted almost entirely from the multi-billion dollar commercial success of the Jason Bourne series. Ergo, to cite surface similarities to something like *Ronin* (1998) or the much more adventurously structured *Vantage Point* (2010), to name but two other foreign-set action thrillers, is to miss the point.

With financing often cobbled together through territorial presales and by a half dozen or more companies seemingly designed to spread around executive producer credits as part of some international tax shelter scheme, faux-exotic European espionage and assassin action movies have, over the past decade-plus, carved out enough straight-to-DVD success—as Steven Seagal, Wesley Snipes (prior to his incarceration on tax evasion), the aforementioned Van Damme and Cuba Gooding, Jr. can all attest—that they almost merit their own subgenre grouping on Netflix. The stories for these tales are frequently extraordinarily cliched, and other resources threadbare, but there is enough money to land a couple recognizable faces and keep the production assembly line moving.

The Cold Light of Day, then, is like the sibling of this bunch that made good, and broke out of the direct-to-video ghetto. Nothing about its story or execution suggests a reason for a theatrical release, let alone its existence, and yet there are Weaver, Willis and the future Superman, all gamely attempting to put some sort of emotional spin on this hackneyed material.

To that point, the failures of *The Cold Light of Day* lie almost exclusively in its conception and technical execution, which are a bore. But if Weaver has a bit of fun gnashing her teeth as a whispery villainess, Cavill, set to star in Zack Snyder's *Man of Steel* (2013), does little other than display a handsome face to suggest that he is ready to don the cape of Superman and inherit Warner Bros. next great franchise hope. That is the cold, hard truth.

Brent Simon

CREDITS

Martin Shaw: Bruce Willis
Will Shaw: Henry Cavill
Laurie Shaw: Caroline Goodall
Meckler: Jim Piddock
Carrack: Sigourney Weaver

Zahir: Roschdy Zem
Maximo: Oscar Jaenada
Origin: United States
Language: English
Released: 2012
Production: Marc D. Evans, Trevor Macy; Film Rites, Picture Machine; released by Summit Entertainment
Directed by: Mabrouk El Mechri
Written by: Scott Wiper; John Petro
Cinematography by: Remi Adefarasin
Music by: Lucas Vidal
Sound: Oliver Tarney
Editing: Valerio Bonelli
Costumes: Bina Daigeler
Production Design: Benjamin Fernandez
MPAA rating: PG-13
Running time: 93 minutes

REVIEWS

Berardinelli, James. *ReelViews*. September 8, 2012.
Brunson, Matt. *Creative Loafing*. September 14, 2012.
Collis, Clark. *Entertainment Weekly*. September 11, 2012.
Duralde, Alonso. *The Wrap*. September 7, 2012.
Holden, Stephen. *New York Times*. September 7, 2012.
Jorgenson, Todd. *Cinemalogue.com*. September 7, 2012.
Linden, Sheri. *Los Angeles Times*. September 10, 2012.
Marsh, Calum. *Slant Magazine*. September 4, 2012.
Rabin, Nathan. *AV Club*. September 7, 2012.
Savlov, Marc. *Austin Chronicle*. September 14, 2012.

QUOTES

Lucia: "Sometimes I think, the more a parent is absent, the more you love them."

THE COLLECTION

Every great collector has a vision.
    —Movie tagline

Only one survivor. Only one chance to escape pure evil.
    —Movie tagline

Box Office: $6.8 million

Apparently, somebody somewhere made a movie called *The Collector* (2009) and enough people saw it and remembered it enough to warrant a sequel, *The Collection*. Where this cult developed and how the demand for a sequel became generated will forever remain a mystery, particularly since this sequel actually garnered a theatrical release (in December, no less) instead of a more-predictable straight-to-DVD unveiling.

The need to turn this thing into a lucrative and memorable franchise will likely be an uphill battle since the titular character relies so heavily on gadgets and devices and less on personality and presence. There is a reason that when people are asked about their favorite horror movie killers—Jason Voorhees, Freddy Krueger, Hannibal Lecter, Michael Myers, to name a few—The Collector never comes up.

Both *The Collector* and *The Collection* were written by Patrick Melton and Marcus Dunstan, both directed by Dunstan. Both involve a masked killer who wears a small, black potato sack over his head and who specializes in deadly booby traps and locking people in a chest. It comes from the creators of several of the *Saw* films and the two *Feast* films, the first of which was a clever and funny action/horror/comedy and the end-result of the third season of *Project: Greenlight*. The Collector movies are more on par with the *Saw* films, a form of torture porn that supposedly still has a devoted audience somewhere even though the franchise more than wore out its welcome years ago.

Unlike the first film, *The Collection* gets right to the carnage in an audacious way. The heroine, Elena (Emma Fitzpatrick), heads out to a club with her friends, a club where one needs a password for entrance. All appears normal for this club where the music blasts and the lights are blinding. There is some drama between the young characters about who likes who, but it means nothing. Elena wanders into a room where she sees the chest. Someone is trapped inside it. She opens it and somehow activates a device that results in a gigantic lawnmower-like apparatus that descends onto the club-goers and shreds them in hundreds of pieces, easily one of the bloodiest scenes in movie history. Elena becomes the next victim for the Collector as she gets kidnapped and taken to his lair.

Elena's father (Christopher McDonald) hires a group of mercenaries to go find his daughter. The group's leader, Lucello (Lee Tergesen), finds a man named Arkin (Josh Stewart), the lone survivor of the first film and the only one who knows what kind of unspeakable horror the group will find themselves in if they decide to go after her. Reluctantly, Arkin agrees to join them in helping to find Elena at an abandoned hotel called (what else?) Hotel Argento. The Collector uses people as bait so that mercenaries like these will try and come find him, which will result in a higher body count for his "collection."

Once they all enter the abandoned hotel, the body count slowly begins. Elena, meanwhile, manages to escape the chest using her bra strap. The Collector uses his spiders to lure her out of hiding, but she manages to not scream even though they crawl all over her. She eventually meets up with the mercenaries and Arkin, but the film remains a series of tortures, booby traps, explosives, carnage and dread. The survivors do their best to escape and try to lure the police outside to their whereabouts, but much of it predictably backfires.

The Collection clocks in at 82 minutes. A good seven minutes of that consists of closing credits where anybody who had a single line of dialogue received their own picture credit, in case any viewer out there wanted to know who that plucky young actress was who screamed "help!" during the opening scene before they were mauled down. The movie here exists as a laundry list of semi-clever traps and mutilations that Melton and Dunstan had in mind that they never got around to in the first film. *The Collector* at least made an attempt at a story. *The Collection* never holds together, becomes more apparently silly than scary and eventually just becomes an excuse for some interesting set design.

Still, it never gets boring and the amount of bloodshed on display here will definitely appease those looking for a mindless gore fest. It does become fun to try and imagine the Collector ordering his items from Home Depot and constructing them inside a building where, presumably, nobody ever enters to check up on things (and does this guy ever forget where his traps are hidden?). But nothing seems to motivate the Collector aside from the fact that he cannot get these body parts on eBay. Likewise, nothing seems to be motivating this sequel other than the fact that Melton and Dunstan felt the need to add another credit to their IMDB page.

Collin Souter

CREDITS

Arkin: Josh Stewart
Mr. Peters: Christopher Macdonald
Lisa: Navi Rawat
The Collector: Randall Archer
Elena: Emma Fitzpatrick
Origin: United States
Language: English
Released: 2012
Production: Patrick Rizzotti, Julie Richardson, Jennifer Monroe, Mickey Liddell, Brett Forbes; Fortress Features; released by LD Entertainment
Directed by: Marcus Dunstan
Written by: Marcus Dunstan; Patrick Melton
Cinematography by: Sam McCurdy
Music by: Charlie Clouser
Sound: Jon Ailetcher
Music Supervisor: Tricia Holloway
Editing: Mark Stevens; Kevin Greutert; Joseph Gonzalez

Art Direction: Douglas Fick
Costumes: Eulyn Womble
Production Design: Graham Walker
MPAA rating: R
Running time: 82 minutes

REVIEWS

Collis, Clark. *Entertainment Weekly*. November 28, 2012.
Goss, William. *Film.com*. November 27, 2012.
Graham, Adam. *Detroit News*. November 30, 2012.
Herrington, Nicole. *New York Times*. November 30, 2012.
LaSalle, Mick. *San Francisco Chronicle*. November 29, 2012.
Morris, Wesley. *Boston Globe*. November 29, 2012.
O'Sullivan, Michael. *Washington Post*. November 30, 2012.
Olsen, Mark. *Los Angeles Times*. November 29, 2012.
Phipps, Keith. *AV Club*. November 29, 2012.
Pinkerton, Nick. *Village Voice*. November 28, 2012.

TRIVIA

The Hotel Argento where the Collector keeps his victims is more than likely a nod to the Italian horror director Dario Argento.

COMPLIANCE

Box Office: $319,285

Not since Michael Haneke's *Funny Games* (1997) has a film actually dared its audience to leave the theater well before the end credits have begun to roll. Yet, unlike Haneke's film, which functions as more of a performance art piece than a cinematic narrative, Craig Zobel's *Compliance* triumphs as both a squirm-inducing drama and a riveting work of experimental theatre. While *Funny Games* punishes its audience for taking pleasure in the torture of its characters, *Compliance* plays directly into the viewer's darkest voyeuristic tendencies.

Perhaps that's why Zobel's film has had an uncanny knack for repelling audiences out of screening rooms during its festival run, while inspiring others to audibly shout words like, "Ridiculous!" If those viewers had bothered to stick around for the entire film rather than leave in an exasperated huff, they would have read the title card stating that the events portrayed on-screen have actually happened "over 70 times" in America alone. That galvanizing statistic may be initially hard to swallow, but it speaks to a larger, unsettlingly resonant truth illuminated by this vital, challenging picture.

The setting is a mundane fast food restaurant managed by Sandra (Ann Dowd), a middle-aged woman with a face lined by the disappointments of a listless life.

She is desperately grasping at what she considers to be her last chance at happiness by dating the mild-mannered yet thick-headed Van (Bill Camp). The opening scenes provide a key to everything that follows as Sandra displays a muted mixture of resentment and envy toward her petite, effortlessly pretty employee, Becky (Dreama Walker). When Sandra makes a pathetic stab at appearing hip in front of her young staff, her face burns with embarrassment as a chorus of snickers erupt behind her back.

An environment reliant on quick thinking and swift problem-solving is a natural setting for predators to wreak manipulative mischief, and that is precisely what occurs when a man identifying himself as "Officer Daniels" calls the restaurant. He shares with Sandra some alarming news: a former customer has reported a robbery to the police, and has identified Becky as the thief. The incredulity and disbelief in Sandra's expressions are present from the get-go, but they are ultimately overpowered by her need to obey the faceless yet imposing authority figure on the other line. "Daniels" strategically modulates his voice in order to flatter Sandra while threatening everyone else. He instructs the staff to confine Becky in a back room of the restaurant while searching her belongings. It is not long before the investigation includes a strip search.

Zobel's script makes no secret of the fact that "Daniels" is not at all who he appears to be. At about the halfway mark, Zobel allows the audience to not only view the perverse caller's face, but his warmly inviting house from which he makes the call (children's toys clutter the background of various shots). One of the film's great masterstrokes is casting character actor Pat Healy in the role of "Daniels." He memorably played the passive-aggressive pharmacist who triggers Julianne Moore's meltdown in *Magnolia* (1999), and here again proves adept at slyly pushing characters' nerves past their breaking point.

Cinematographer Adam Stone (*Take Shelter* [2011]) juxtaposes the horrifying events unfolding indoors with exterior footage of mud-caked snow and ever-deepening puddles that suggest a world in decay. The tightly-cramped framing mirrors the claustrophobic plight of Becky, as she is forced to undergo a series of increasingly sadistic sexual humiliations. Heather McIntosh's score wisely avoids dominating the emotional texture of each scene, while masterfully contributing to the mounting unease by forging a duet with Rich Bologna's peerless sound design.

Walker deserves praise for fearlessly enduring her character's grueling ordeal, though her nudity is never exploited by Stone's lens, nor granted explicit focus by Zobel. It is Healy's deadpan tone and the outrageous cooperation he receives from his victims that inspires equal amounts of uncomfortable laughter and dismayed groans. As a jet-black satire about the disaster that befalls those who fail to question authority, Zobel's film hinges greatly on the performance by Dowd, and it is an all-out winner. If her character's willful blind spot was the least bit unconvincing, the film would have fallen apart entirely. Dowd absolutely nails the jaded spirit of a woman whose need to overcome her daily obstacles overrides her desire to think them through. Early on, Dowd quietly sobs while facing the stripped and distraught Becky, but that emotion gradually hardens as the day progresses further and further into the realm of insanity.

The last ten minutes or so of *Compliance* are their most curious, as Zobel continues to follow his characters long after the central action has reached its conclusion. At first, this extended finale appears to be unnecessary, yet it leads to a moment of cross-examination that is flat-out bone-chilling, while providing an added peek into the psyche of a woman all-too-comfortable in following orders. The very final moments of Dowd's performance clinches its status as one of the year's best.

Matt Fagerholm

CREDITS

Sandra: Ann Dowd
Becky: Dreama Walker
Officer Daniels: Pat Healy
Van: Bill Camp
Kevin: Philip Ettinger
Detective Neals: James McCaffrey
Origin: United States
Language: English
Released: 2012
Production: Tyler Davidson, Theo Sena, Sophia Lin, Lisa Muskat, Craig Zobel; Bad Cop Film Productions, Dogfish Pictures; released by Magnolia Pictures
Directed by: Craig Zobel
Written by: Craig Zobel
Cinematography by: Adam Stone
Music by: Heather McIntosh
Sound: Rich Bologna
Editing: Jane Rizzo
Costumes: Karen Malecki
Production Design: Matthew Munn
MPAA rating: R
Running time: 90 minutes

REVIEWS

Chang, Justin. *Variety.* July 13, 2012.

Corliss, Richard. *Time.* August 20, 2012.
Denby, David. *New Yorker.* August 16, 2012.
Ebert, Roger. *Chicago Sun-Times.* August 29, 2012.
Hornaday, Ann. *Washington Post.* August 30, 2012.
Morgenstern, Joe. *Wall Street Journal.* August 12, 2012.
Nehme, Farran Smith. *New York Post.* August 17, 2012.
Phillips, Michael. *Chicago Tribune.* August 30, 2012.
Rabin, Nathan. *AV Club.* July 28, 2012.
Schwarzbaum, Lisa. *Entertainment Weekly.* August 8, 2012.

QUOTES

Supplier: "You're f**ked without bacon, I tell you that!"

AWARDS

Nominations:
Ind. Spirit 2013: Support. Actress (Dowd)

CONTRABAND

What would you hide to protect your family?
—Movie tagline

Box Office: $66.5 million

Mark Wahlberg has mixed it up fairly admirably throughout his career, and certainly found a successful and lucrative parallel calling as an executive producer of material in which he does not star. Wahlberg's go-to appeal as an actor has always laid in his credible touch with square-jawed, strong-but-silent Northeastern types (whether from New York or his native Boston), an inborn essence which he has poured into molded characters on each side of the law in a variety of dramatic efforts. Such is the case with *Contraband,* a cinematic offering with undercard punching power adapted by Aaron Guzikowski from Icelandic import *Reykjavik-Rotterdam* (2009). A moody, pedestrian crime thriller that winds its way through several preordained twists and turns before finally depositing its characters in a happy place, *Contraband* is the sort of movie that one has seen before, regardless of whether they have, you know, actually seen it.

Directed by Baltasar Kormakur and reset in New Orleans, the film centers around Chris Farraday (Wahlberg), an ex-smuggler who has given up crime and now lives a more peaceful life with his wife Kate (Kate Beckinsale) and their two young children, operating his own business installing alarm systems. When Kate's brother Andy (Caleb Landry Jones) has to dump a massive drug shipment into the harbor in order to avoid detection by the U.S. Customs Bureau during a surprise inspection, his volatile roughneck boss, Tim Briggs (Giovanni Ribisi), smashes his truck into Andy's car, putting Andy in the hospital.

Chris visits Briggs in an effort to smooth things over, but Briggs demands full repayment of all his money used to fund the purchase gone bad, and in only two weeks time. If he is not paid, the debt will fall first to Andy, and then Chris, says Briggs. Trying to come up with the cash, Chris, along with pal Danny Raymer (Lukas Haas), devises a scheme to join the crew of a cargo ship where his imprisoned father used to run contraband, and smuggle back $10 million in counterfeit bills from Panama. Captain Camp (J.K. Simmons) already has his eye on Chris, distrusting him because of his lineage and shady past, but things go even further sideways upon docking. The phony bills are not of high enough quality, and Chris has to take his case for replacements straight to another unstable hood, Gonzalo (Diego Luna). As Kate and his kids are threatened back home, Chris enlists the assistance of his best friend, Sebastian Abney (Ben Foster), to stave off Briggs. When Captain Camp is made aware of the possibility of smuggled goods aboard his ship, though, Chris finds himself caught up in a game much bigger than he previously realized, and is forced to improvise with his illicit cargo.

Whatever tinge of excitement one might feel at its foreign roots adding depth t o a cookie cutter concept more or less evaporates a couple reels into *Contraband*. Veering widely from the plotting of its source material, the film time and time again chooses conventional, puffed-up narrative gimmickry (even in its reversals) over lifelike details and emotional stakes more deeply rooted in character. Trite, placeholder-type dialogue ("You gotta do what you gotta do," and "Family is family") gives the movie a shrugging, come-what-may feeling, while the technical team labors overtime to impress sentiment upon the production that the script has not earned.

Contraband's camerawork is nervous and darkly lit, alternating between Steadicam work and more traditional modes of coverage. In theory, this tack is meant to alternate between action and more contemplative moments, but it comes off as poorly devised. In working in concert with editor Elizabet Ronalds and cinematographer Barry Ackroyd to deliver a movie that plays for specific, scene-by-scene stabs at audience attention, the quirkier aesthetic sensibilities of Kormakur (*101 Reykjavik* [2000], *The Sea* [2002]) get lost somewhere in the waters between Panama and New Orleans, rendering *Contraband* an anonymous, programmatic drama of underclass familial protection.

The acting is functional, though not illuminating. Foster, who has unleashed a string of frothy-mouthed

big screen psychos in recent years, is, admirably, a bit more restrained than one might surmise given the nature of his character. Beckinsale has little to do except look pretty and worried and terrorized, alternately, all of which she accomplishes. In his standard-issue tough-guy uniform of jeans and a fitted T-shirt, Wahlberg can crank out this sort of flinty, put-upon hero without much effort; to say that does so in *Contraband* is both a testament to his talents and an acknowledgment of how little work he does herein.

In fact, this entire project—or at least Wahlberg's involvement in it, which was undoubtedly a nice payday—is seemingly a sop to audiences who wanted to see that long-bandied-about sequel to *The Italian Job* (2003), in which Wahlberg co-starred. The problem is that *Contraband* lacks that movie's slickness and personality. There is neither any of the minimalist sizzle of *Drive* (2011), nor enough elevating pyrotechnics or pizzazz to give *Contraband* a memorable hold outside of the most forgiving genre fans.

The film is essentially a procedural, but it handles the specifics of cargo smuggling in such a cursory manner—a hollowed-out hold here, a bunch of eager bit player rogues there—that viewers do not get a true sense of vicarious thrill. There is a sense of can-do, analytical machismo to the proceedings, true, and a bit of a sense of humor to try to mitigate the misanthropic threat of violence against Kate and her children but *Contraband* is never particularly clever; it pulls all the most obvious levers.

Chris is posited as a character with a uniquely specialized set of skills, and a guy who has made a tremendous sacrifice ("Don't act like you don't enjoy this," says Andy to him at one point) in giving up this life of crime in order to "go legit," and raise his family in a safer fashion. But *Contraband* mostly tells rather than shows—Chris' prowess in this regard seems to consist of on-the-fly decision-making that conveniently breaks his way, paired with repeated reassurances to the ever-nervous Danny—and does little to genuinely earn its ludicrous closing twist, which reaps a considerable financial benefit out of left field.

If *Contraband* is just meant to illustrate that fortune favors the bold, so be it, but the more interesting film would have delved further into the world of smuggling, which surely holds much interest and intrigue. This movie is not offensively bad, it is just the cinematic equivalent of an ungarnished, microwaveable meat-and-potatoes dinner, or a batting cage's slow-pitch "fastball," lobbed straight down the middle of the plate. If nothing else, though, it provides filler material for future Wahlberg Blu-ray boxed sets, where there will reside better examples of his career's peaks.

Brent Simon

CREDITS

Chris Farraday: Mark Wahlberg
Sebastian Abney: Ben Foster
Tim Briggs: Giovanni Ribisi
Andy: Caleb Landry Jones
Kate Farraday: Kate Beckinsale
Danny Raymer: Lukas Haas
Gonzalo: Diego Luna
Captain Camp: J.K. Simmons
Bud Farraday: William Lucking
Origin: United States
Language: English
Released: 2012
Production: Stephen Levinson, Tim Bevan, Eric Fellner, Mark Wahlberg, Baltasar Kormakur; Leverage, Studio Canal, Farraday Films, Relativity Media, Working Title; released by Universal Pictures
Directed by: Baltasar Kormakur
Written by: Aaron Guzikowski
Cinematography by: Barry Ackroyd
Music by: Clinton Shorter
Sound: Pud Cusack
Editing: Elizabet Ronalds
Art Direction: Dennis Bradford
Costumes: Jenny Eagan
Production Design: Tony Fanning
MPAA rating: R
Running time: 110 minutes

REVIEWS

Chang, Justin. *Variety.* January 11, 2012.
Dargis, Manohla. *New York Times.* January 12, 2012.
Denby, David. *New Yorker.* January 24, 2012.
Ebert, Roger. *Chicago Sun-Times.* January 12, 2012.
McCarthy, Todd. *Hollywood Reporter.* January 12, 2012.
Morgenstern, Joe. *Wall Street Journal.* January 12, 2012.
O'Sullivan, Michael. *Washington Post.* January 13, 2012.
Puig, Claudia. *USA Today.* January 12, 2012.
Sharkey, Betsy. *Los Angeles Times.* January 13, 2012.
Stevens, Dana. *Slate.* January 12, 2012.

QUOTES

Chris Farraday: "I've got to try and fix this. Trust me, I know what I'm doing."

TRIVIA

Editor Elisabet Ronaldsdottir also edited the original *Reykjavik-Rotterdam.*

COSMOPOLIS

Box Office: $763,556

David Cronenberg has spent his entire career making films that some praise as thought-provoking masterpieces, others deride as pretentious and occasionally disgusting bores and leave everyone else wondering "What the hell was that?" And yet, even by those standards, his latest effort, *Cosmopolis,* is likely to go down as one of his most divisive entries. Based on the oddly prescient 2002 novel of the same name by Don DeLillo, this is a film that stands as a brilliant adaptation of a novel that most might have deemed to be unfilmable, an incisive and darkly funny evocation of the current socio-political climate and as a fascinating new exploration of some of the key themes that Cronenberg has been dealing with throughout his entire career. *Cosmopolis* is liable to have even some of the most devoted fans of the filmmaker scratching their heads at certain points and anyone lured into seeing it based solely on the presence of star Robert Pattinson is likely to walk away from it feeling confused and upset at the sight of their favorite vampiric glitterbomb in the midst of such a bizarre film. However, those able to wrap their heads around it will be rewarded with one of the most unique and challenging movies of the year and yet another standout effort from one of the best, if often underrated, filmmakers working today.

Robert Pattinson stars as Eric Packer, a Wall Street asset manager who has parlayed his gift for reading and understanding the markets into such perks as a billion-dollar fortune, a recent marriage to an equally beautiful billionaire (Sarah Gadon) and a ridiculously elongated and tricked-out white stretch limousine whose cork lining, tinted windows and computers constantly spitting out up-to-the-minute almost, but not quite, allow him to completely isolate himself from the world around him even when he is in the thick of it. However, the trouble with achieving such mammoth success so quickly and so early in life is that there is nowhere to go but down and indeed, Eric's reckless betting against the yuan in the financial markets has started to turn against him and as the story opens, his empire is in imminent danger of total and irrevocable collapse. His response to this is strangely subdued—instead of frantically battling to save his empire, he decides that this would be the perfect time to get a haircut at a place located on the other side of the city. Even ignoring his ongoing professional calamity, this seems like an insane idea—the combination of a presidential motorcade, the funeral procession of a recently deceased pop star and an Occupy-like protest featuring demonstrators flinging fake rats have brought traffic to a virtual standstill and chief of security Torval (Kevin Durand) warns of increasingly credible threats to his client's life—but Eric will not be denied and so he slips into his limo to make the crosstown journey.

With traffic at a virtual standstill for the most part, Eric manages to conduct a number of meetings and assignations along the way, many from within the confines of his limo. He has cryptic business chats with his chief technological advisor and currency analyst in which they offer dire warnings that he brushes aside. He has frequent meetings with his wife in which his short marriage pretty much crumbles away. He has sex with both an old girlfriend (Juliette Binoche), an art dealer who tries to sell him a recently acquired Rothko, and one of his bodyguards. He meets with his chief of business theory (Samantha Morton) and she finally admits that nothing that she is doing makes sense any more. At one point, he even multitasks by meeting with his financial chief (Emily Hampshire) while simultaneously getting a prostate examination. As the day goes on and turns to night, things get progressively stranger for Eric—he even finds himself the victim of a pie in the face a la Rupert Murdoch—and he more than responds in kind with a series of moves that find himself putting himself right into the crosshairs of the mysterious man (Paul Giamatti) who has been trying to kill him all day long.

In many of Cronenberg's previous literary adaptations, he has often changed much of the source material around in order to make things more personal and reflective of his concerns as a filmmaker. What is surprising about *Cosmopolis* is that, for the most part, Cronenberg (taking his first solo screenplay credit since *eXistenZ* [1999]) has translated DeLillo's novel in a surprisingly straightforward manner. Like the book, the film is largely a series of self-contained scenes that are almost entirely driven by dialogue that runs the gamut from financial jargon to metaphysical musings and occasionally punctuated by brief explosions of sex, violence or outright weirdness, all of which are told in a spare and deliberately alienating manner. Outside of the dropping of a couple of a couple vignettes and a slightly more ambiguous ending, Cronenberg has not only brought DeLillo's story to the screen in a relatively intact manner but has also pulled off the far more difficult trick of retaining his authorial voice as well. There is also a timeliness to the material, even though it was written a decade ago, that gives the material a certain kick and there are moments that so uncannily mirror current events that there are times in which it almost takes on the feel of a documentary. That said, the story as a whole is more timeless than timely when all is said and done and it is quite likely that the film as a whole will seem just as fresh and relevant three decades from now as the visionary *Videodrome* (1983) continues to feel thirty years after it first came out.

And yet, even as it pays honor to both the source novel and the subsequent current events that have come to further inform it, *Cosmopolis* is also a David Cronenberg film through and through that feels as distinct and personal as anything that he has done before. If there is one thread that links nearly all of Cronenberg's otherwise varied filmography, it is that they are about transitions—be they physical, mental, emotional, historical, sexual or technological—and how their characters either grow from or, more often, succumb to them. From the unexpected ways in which Eric reacts to the potential loss of his empire (suffice it to say, this is not one of those films where a rich guys loses his material possessions but regains his soul in the process) to its depiction of a world in which financial wizards look on in shock as the patterns that they have based their livelihoods upon suddenly go wildly askew, the films hits upon all of those variations and a few unexpected ones to boot. From a cinematic standpoint, it is also a piece with his other work—thanks in no small part to the contributions of such longtime collaborators as cinematographer Peter Suschitzky and composer Howard Shore, he presents a world that looks familiar enough on the surface, at least what we are privileged to see through the tinted windows or the limo as it cuts through the streets, but one in which nevertheless contains a strange undercurrent that gives an edge to everything.

One of the biggest keys to the success of *Cosmopolis,* as surprising as it may sound to some, is the performance by Robert Pattinson as Eric. When it was announced that Cronenberg had hired the guy best known for playing the world's blandest vampire in the *Twilight* series, reactions ranged from outright scoffing to people questioning the director's sanity. However, if there is one thing that Cronenberg does undeniably well, it is finding the perfect actors for his films and bringing great performances out of them—over the years, he has gotten career-best acting out of talents as diverse as James Woods, Jeff Goldblum, Jeremy Irons, Ralph Fiennes, Viggo Mortensen and Keira Knightley. If Cronenberg was going to take such a chance by casting Pattinson in the role, he must have seen something in his work to suggest that the teen idol was right for the part. Whatever it was, that instinct was correct because he nails every aspect of his performance perfectly and creates a character of pure, unadulterated arrogance who is always captivating to watch, even at his most callow, while still allowing some flickers of sympathetic behavior to occasionally bubble up from beneath his immaculately constructed surface. Consider the fact that most of the film consists of him performing one-on-one scenes with actors as accomplished as Juliette Binoche, Samantha Morton and Paul Giamatti and he more than holds own against them all. Casting him in a role was clearly a risky move on the part of Cronenberg but, much like *Cosmopolis* as a whole, it is one that pays off enormous dividends in the end.

Peter Sobczynski

CREDITS

Eric Packer: Robert Pattinson
Didi Fancher: Juliette Binoche
Elise Shifrin: Sarah Gadon
Andre Petrescu: Mathieu Amalric
Shiner: Jay Baruchel
Torval: Kevin Durand
Vija Kinski: Samantha Morton
Benno Levin: Paul Giamatti
Origin: Canada, France
Language: English
Released: 2012
Production: Paulo Branco, Martin Katz; Alfoma Films, Prospero Pictures; released by Entertainment One
Directed by: David Cronenberg
Written by: David Cronenberg

Cinematography by: Peter Suschitzky
Music by: Howard Shore
Sound: Jean-Paul Mugel
Editing: Ronald Sanders
Costumes: Denise Cronenberg
Production Design: Arv Greywal
MPAA rating: R
Running time: 109 minutes

REVIEWS

Dargis, Manohla. *New York Times*. August 16, 2012.
Denby, David. *New Yorker*. August 17, 2012.
Ebert, Roger. *Chicago Sun-Times*. August 23, 2012.
Orndorf, Brian. *BrianOrndorf.com*. August 23, 2012.
Pais, Matt. *RedEye*. August 23, 2012.
Phipps, Keith. *AV Club*. August 16, 2012.
Stevens, Dana. *Slate*. August 16, 2012.
Tallerico, Brian. *HollywoodChicago.com*. August 23, 2012.
Taubin, Amy. *Film Comment*. August 16, 2012.
Tobias, Scott. *NPR*. August 16, 2012.

QUOTES

Eric Packer: "My prostate is asymmetrical."

D

DAMSELS IN DISTRESS

Box Office: $1 million

Whatever crimes against cinema were committed in 2012, they could be at least partially redeemed by the fact that it was the year that writer-director Whit Stillman, the creator of the cult favorites *Metropolitan* (1990), *Barcelona* (1994) and *The Last Days of Disco* (1998) returned after a fourteen-year absence from the big screen—an event that was met with joy by auteurists of a certain age. Of course, after such a long absence, any initial returning effort has to face the burden of not only working on its own terms but of somehow living up to all of the inflated expectations of a fan base that has been waiting for so long that it will expect nothing less than absolute perfection. That said, it is doubtful that anyone was expecting something quite like *Damsels in Distress* a film as hilarious and delightful as his previous efforts but one that was so defiantly odd and off-kilter that even his most ardent fans found themselves scratching their heads over the bewilderments it offers.

The film is set at the fictional Seven Oaks College, where the faculty are largely non-existent, many of the guys have only a tenuous relationship to notions of personal grooming at best, and there is at least one student who, for reasons that turn out to be perfectly understandable, has somehow made it into the arms of higher education without even knowing what the different colors are. This is a college in need of a savior and, lo and behold, it has a self-appointed one in Violet (Greta Gerwig), a brutally efficient and borderline insane blonde who marches through the campus determined to help everyone that she can, albeit in the most skewed

ways imaginable. She recommends that girls should date boys who are their social, emotional, and intellectual inferiors because doing so will make them feel better about themselves. (Luckily, this is a campus where such people are at a premium.) She runs the suicide prevention center and is always there with a kind word and a donut for anyone who comes in with a sad story (though woe unto anyone that takes a donut without having any thoughts about self-extermination). She fervently believes in the therapeutic powers of dancing and her greatest dream in life, in fact, is to develop a dance called the Sambola and transform it into an international sensation.

As the film opens, Violet and her ever-present posse, Rose (Megalyn Echikunwoke) and Heather (Carrie MacLemore), stride into freshman orientation in the hopes of finding the perfect person to take under their collective wing, whether they like it or not. They quickly come across Lily (Analeigh Tipton) and before she knows what hits her, she now has an ever-present trio of friends who are always at her side and wiling to advise her on every possible situation, whether she wants it or not. Things start to go bad when Violet rescues the genuinely depressed Priss (Caitlin Fitzgerald) and she responds to the suggestion to date someone dumber and less attractive by taking up with Violet's own doltish sort-of boyfriend. This leads to an anxious night or two of the soul for Violet—well, a trip to a seedy diner far outside of town—and when she returns, she winds up making a play for Charlie (Adam Brody), who has been sort-of wooing Lily himself and who knows a thing or two about Violet as well. It all sounds as though it is fraught with portent but it all comes together in the end in what is perhaps the only possible way—the debut of the

Sambola and some of the funniest end credits to come along since the heyday of the Zucker Brothers.

Sometimes when a filmmaker takes such a long break between projects, their talents can get a little rusty and the end results can sometimes suffer as a result. In the case of Stillman, although this endeavor happens to be a little more overtly wacky than his previous efforts, the end result is so witty and charming that it hardly feels as if any time has passed at all in regards to his skills. Without ever pushing too hard for broad laughs, Stillman offers up a delightful array of non-sequiturs, diversions and the occasional sight gag (including such bits as a toga-clad campus brawl and one of the funnier on-screen suicide attempts of recent memory) that nearly all hit their marks. At times, it may seem like a jumble of outright weirdness that may put off even those viewers who have sparked to Stillman in the past, but those willing to embrace its droll deliriums are likely to absolutely fall in love with its quirky charms.

Besides Stillman's touch in the writing and directing departments, a good amount of the ultimate success of *Damsels in Distress* comes from the pitch-perfect performance by Greta Gerwig as Violet. The most visible face of the so-called "mumblecore" screen movement (largely because she was blonde, conventionally attractive and willing to take off her shirt at the drop of a hat), she has proven to be a polarizing figure for filmgoers, some of whom find her to be a charming and delightfully quirky breath of fresh air and some who actively flinch whenever she appears on the screen. That said, she knocks it out of the park here to such a degree that even those who actively dislike her will have to admit that her performance is a total success. Cynics might suggest that since her character here is meant to be deliberately off-putting and borderline nuts, that blandly obnoxious persona that she has developed has finally found a vehicle that it was perfectly suited to inhabit. That may be true, of course but regardless, she is really funny here and hell, maybe even strangely sympathetic to boot. Thanks in no small part to her efforts, *Damsels in Distress* is one of the most genuinely endearing films of the year and one that was just about worth the wait.

Peter Sobczynski

CREDITS

Violet: Greta Gerwig
Heather: Carrie Maclemore
Rose: Megalyn Echikunwoke
Lily: Analeigh Tipton
Thor: Billy Magnussen
Frank: Ryan Metcalf

Jimbo: Jermaine Crawford
Priss: Caitlin Fitzgerald
Xavier: Hugo Becker
Fred Packsenstacker/Charlie Walker: Adam Brody
Origin: United States
Language: English
Released: 2011
Production: Whit Stillman; Westerly Films; released by Sony Pictures Classics
Directed by: Whit Stillman
Written by: Whit Stillman
Cinematography by: Doug Emmett
Music by: Mark Suozzo
Sound: Tom Paul
Music Supervisor: Annie Pearlman
Editing: Andrew Hafitz
Art Direction: Brian Goodwin
Costumes: Ciera Wells
Production Design: Elizabeth J. Jones
MPAA rating: PG-13
Running time: 99 minutes

REVIEWS

Brody, Richard. *New Yorker*. April 9, 2012.
Corliss, Richard. *Time*. October 18, 2011.
Ebert, Roger. *Chicago Sun-Times*. April 12, 2012.
Edelstein, David. *New York*. April 2, 2012.
Goss, William. *Film.com*. April 27, 2012.
Hornaday, Ann. *Washington Post*. April 13, 2012.
Morris, Wesley. *Boston Globe*. April 19, 2012.
Pais, Matt. *RedEye*. April 12, 2012.
Scott, A. O. *New York Times*. April 5, 2012.
Stevens, Dana. *Slate*. April 6, 2012.

QUOTES

Violet: "Do you know what's the major problem in contemporary social life? The tendency to always seek someone cooler than yourself."

TRIVIA

Numerous characters in the film are named after flowers.

DARK HORSE

Box Office: $166,228

Todd Solondz is no stranger to the loser. While much of American society has written off the stories of masturbators, child molesters, manic—depressives and more by condemning them with the categorization of "taboo", Solondz has approached these uncomfortable subjects with genuine interest in their psychological tragedy, with hope to inspire his audience towards introspection concerning the flaws of these individuals.

It is only fitting, then, that Solondz would eventually find himself writing a treatise on the man-child, a common, much softer type of irresponsible loser seen in current American comedies, often celebrated by directors that range from Judd Apatow to Mark & Jay Duplass to Adam McKay. Working with a type of character that is much easier for viewers to immediately identify with than any of his dark individuals in a film of his like *Happiness* (1998), Solondz's latest is an emotionally persuasive warning against a goofy loser's destructive mindset, obtusely condemning the lighthearted attitudes of numerous American arrested development comedies with his own awakenings of dark reality.

With a wardrobe of t-shirts that say pithy puns like "Matzah Baller," Abe (Jordan Gelber) is a balding middle-aged man living with his parents in New Jersey, his childhood bedroom having now become a sanctuary of his youth (or a "man-cave" as arrested development comedies call it), featuring a collection of expensive toys (reminiscent of Steve Carell's title character in the man-child landmark *The 40-Year-Old Virgin* [2005]). In his one requirement of responsibility, Abe works for his father in an office, but is more interested in keeping up with the latest expensive toy on eBay than droll work (to the non-benefit of his maturity, he receives extra assistance from his father's secretary, Marie, played by Donna Murphy).

Abe is aware of his placement in life, especially compared to the status of his doctor brother (Justin Bartha), who has since moved out of the house, but his attitude displays comfort and optimism for his so-called "losing" qualities. He takes pride in the "dark horse" of the family, boasting, "I see myself as someone with a front runner mentality, but with dark horse qualities."

Abe's biggest competition as a supposed dark horse in life begins when he meets the vacuous Violet (Selma Blair) at wedding, and succeeds at inviting her out on a date by coasting on forced projected confidence. After their date has a late start (Miranda completely forgets about him), Abe eventually proposes to Miranda that night, an unforeseen invitation that she rejects. Later, after Abe has confided in Marie about his proposal and in turn warned by her that dating Miranda may not be a good idea, Miranda and Abe meet again. After discussing with Abe that she has been sad recently in her life, she tells Abe that perhaps marriage would be a positive solution for her. In one of the film's more direct moments of dark satire, the depressed Miranda confides, "I should stop trying to slit my wrists, give up on a literary career, give up on hope, ambition, self respect...I should just get married and have children."

Soon into their courtship, whilst Abe is making mental plans with Miranda to move into his parents' house together, she reveals her dark secret: she has Hepatitis B. This causes a downward spiral for Abe's winning attitude, especially when he meets Mahmoud (Aasif Mandvi) a man that Miranda constantly talks about, who may be her lover, and who may have given her Hepatitis B. Abe's focus is effected at work as well, when he is berated by his father for not following through on his responsibilities, and subsequently fired, causing him to leave in a huff ("How am I going to survive on my fucking Bar Mitzvah savings?!") which sends him recklessly into a brutal car accident (not shown, only heard).

From this point, *Dark Horse* takes a turn for the surreal, toying with the self-perception of the man-child through means of dream-within-a-dream in which Abe is confronted by the dark parts of his subconscious, which tell him (through the appearances of Richard, his mother Phyllis [Mia Farrow] and an over-sexed version of Donna) that "No one needs you," etc. Later in the dream, in a moment similar to when accused pedophile Mark Weiner (Matthew Faber) speaks out in *Palindromes* (2004), Mahmoud, taking the role of a toy store manager, speaks obscurely to the idea of the man-child, in which he points out to Abe that everyone has a receipt for their life, but that does not guarantee everything will add up.

Dark Horse is anchored by a truthful performance from Gelber, who embodies the small idiosyncrasies of a person who looks far older than they act. Gelber presents this archetype with striking authenticity, from the way in which he expresses Abe's emotions with the thoughtfulness of an angsty teenager, to Abe's facade of laid back cool, expressed through non-sequiturs that he displays to seem confident in a world he appears to be lost in. With the help of Solondz's tone, Abe becomes a strongly sobering representation of the characteristics touted by the men-children of various directors like Apatow, notably without the padding of fiction. Not a director who deals in sarcasm, Solondz plays an emotional moment from Abe with straight intent: "If it wasn't for my dad I could have been a singer. That's what I really wanted to be. But he said I had no future. Now I'm even too old for *American Idol*."

Continuing her character from Solondz's earlier film *Storytelling* (2001), Blair has a special wit to her representation of a depressed individual who suffers from her own self-involvement. *Dark Horse* also gets a striking performance from Murphy, who navigates both visions of her character, ultimately playing into a tragic being of her own.

Written from the heart and perspective of Solondz, a tender, non-sarcastic filmmaker, *Dark Horse* takes on the meaning of more than just the tragedy of the man-child, but a gloomy representation of other "losers," who are perhaps more true to fact than the archetype Abe is meant to be a realization of. With sunken-eyed characters like Jackie or Marie, the film solemnly presents living human beings who are fading away in drab offices, due to their own lack of ambition to defy their routines. Jackie returns home after work to watch television in silence with his wife; in the film's final scene, Marie daydreams of dancing with Abe in a warm apartment, but is jolted from this image by the monotony of her office job.

While Solondz has expressed great interest in the psychology of the suburbs before, (particularly with *Happiness* and *Storytelling*), *Dark Horse* is one of his more damning, albeit obscure critiques of the emptiness within a settled, expressionless life. Considering the tale of Abe as a prequel to the lives of many of the older adults around him, Solondz introduces a heartbreaking ambiguity related to the perceived definition of the word "loser," achieving a haunting melancholy between the losers who are dead by the end of the film, and those who are still living.

Nick Allen

CREDITS

Abe: Jordan Gelber
Miranda: Selma Blair
Phyllis: Mia Farrow
Jackie: Christopher Walken
Richard: Justin Bartha
Marie: Donna Murphy
Mahmoud: Aasif Mandvi
Origin: United States
Language: English
Released: 2011
Production: Ted Hope, Derrick Tseng; Double Hope Films; released by Brainstorm Media
Directed by: Todd Solondz
Written by: Todd Solondz
Cinematography by: Andrij Parekh
Sound: Jack Hutson
Editing: Kevin Messman
Art Direction: Dawn Masi
Costumes: Kurt and Bart
Production Design: Alex DiGerlando

MPAA rating: Unrated
Running time: 88 minutes

REVIEWS

Anderson, John. *Newsday.* June 22, 2012.
Corliss, Richard. *Time.* September 9, 2011.
Ebert, Roger. *Chicago Sun-Times.* June 21, 2012.
Gleiberman, Owen. *Entertainment Weekly.* June 20, 2012.
Hornaday, Ann. *Washington Post.* August 17, 2012.
McCarthy, Todd. *Hollywood Reporter.* September 7, 2011.
Pinkerton, Nick. *Village Voice.* June 5, 2012.
Scott, A. O. *New York Times.* June 7, 2012.
Stewart, Sara. *New York Post.* June 8, 2012.
Zacharek, Stephanie. *Los Angeles Times.* July 26, 2012.

TRIVIA

Estelle Harris, Jason Alexander, and Jerry Stiller were hired to do voice overs for the scenes where Mia Farrow and Christopher Walken are watching an unseen TV sitcom. Director Todd Solondz felt that the Costanzas on the TV series *Seinfeld* were a sitcom version of the family he was depicting, but he couldn't afford to use audio clips from actual *Seinfeld.* episodes.

THE DARK KNIGHT RISES

The legend ends.
    —Movie tagline
A fire will rise.
    —Movie tagline
Rise.
    —Movie tagline

Box Office: $448.1 million

In 2005, filmmaker Christopher Nolan was still a relative unknown when he was handed the keys to Warner Bros.' lucrative Batman franchise and asked to reboot it for a new generation. With only a highly regarded Sundance film, *Memento* (2001), drawing him recognition from both his peers in the Motion Picture Academy and the Director's Guild and the remake, *Insomnia* (2002), under his belt—as great as those were—there was speculation as to how he would handle such a beloved character with a large budget. All uncertainties were answered with *Batman Begins* (2005), an origin story that rose above all others while laying the groundwork for an interpretation of the legend that even comic book fans had to put aside their usual cries over faithful adherence. Nolan did not stop there though, upping the game even further with *The Dark*

Knight (2008), in both intensity and expanding on the inherent themes of good vs. evil and the gray duality in-between. But the story was not over, and like an honorable soldier gearing up for one final battle, Nolan was tasked with finishing what he had started. As methodical and consistently on point as both a social statement and a piece of entertainment, Christopher Nolan has now given fans a trilogy that will stand the test of time and be worthy of the argument that none can challenge its authority as the best ever.

As the final chapter begins, Batman has not been seen or heard from in eight years. Crime has been cleaned up, and, though Harvey Dent is dead, his martyred legacy has ensured that Gotham's streets will be safe for some time. Bruce Wayne (Christian Bale) has been left with nothing to do but become a Howard Hughes-like shut-in. Loyal family butler, Alfred (Michael Caine), is despondent with the direction his ward has taken but is even more troubled when a burglary on the grounds reinvigorates his friend's quest for justice. Commissioner Gordon (Gary Oldman), racked with guilt over the lie he has perpetuated over the truth about Dent's shift from righteousness to vengeance, longs for the day when Gotham's true crusader was not considered an enemy of the people. As does Officer John Blake (Joseph Gordon-Levitt), a young idealist on the force who is troubled at the city's youth being turned away from the unfunded orphanage and knows a little more about the Batman than even his superiors.

Selina Kyle (Anne Hathaway) is responsible for the robbery at the Wayne estate, but has greater plans for herself than merely stealing a set of pearls. A chance to wipe away her criminal past is afforded her by working with those hoping to strip the last scraps of power away from Bruce at Wayne Enterprises. His only chance at maintaining power is to reinstate a clean energy project that has remained dormant despite the funding of committed industrialist Miranda Tate (Marion Cotillard). A larger doom has come to Gotham though in the form of a mercenary called Bane (Tom Hardy). The hulking brute who speaks through a breathing apparatus is working from the ground up on a master plan to destroy the city and fulfill a destiny that was put in motion over a decade ago when Bruce betrayed the infamous League of Shadows in pursuit of a higher ideal of right and wrong.

The evolution of Nolan's Batman would be nothing without the adversaries to challenge not just his strength but the resolve to stay true to his own philosophy. A cadre of villains is inherent within any comic book character's universe, yet this is a series that has elevated it beyond just finding the next stronger, faster or cooler foe. Like any true trilogy there is an arc to the hero's journey and a full circle drawn back to the beginning, evident in Bane's connection to the very anarchists that

trained Bruce but could not assimilate him. Liam Neeson's mentor Ra's Al Ghul was the surrogate father figure that needed to be destroyed when his protege would not follow in his footsteps. Heath Ledger's Joker was the next stage of evil; a pure terror-monger that acted with no higher ideal in mind but "to see the world burn." Tom Hardy's Bane is the villain past the equal sign of this equation. Committed to fulfilling the destiny of a man who ex-communicated him through the extreme methods of Gotham's most apocalyptic terror, Bane takes to the guise of a liberator looking out for the people of a city who were forced to reject a hero.

Those desperate for Christopher Nolan to take a side through the perceived politicized content of Gotham will either be solely disappointed or unmasked as woefully misinformed. It is easy to point at a stockbroker throwing a dollar at the guy who shines his shoes and another commenting that there will be greater repercussions if the cops do nothing to prevent the robbery occurring within the market walls. Except it is far too crude to identify the Wall Street portion of the film as a mere potshot at the economic climate in the years since The Dark Knight last appeared. The post-9/11 actions of a gleefully destructive Joker designed to test the moral restitution of a society in crisis was just a bridge into the grander design began by the League of Shadows over a decade ago to use "economics" to divide and conquer the people. Gotham has become a territory of complacence. With the city's criminals at bay and law enforcement given nothing to do but celebrate the (wrong) fallen hero that put them there, the city elite is still chasing profits and those like Selina Kyle have to make their own compromises to stay afloat. Meanwhile good men like Bruce Wayne cannot even invest in the future without seeing the way it can be manipulated for negative gain by evil ones. Indeed his cynicism is evident even at fundraisers as nothing more than parties designed to feed the egos of their affluent benefactors. "If you want to save the world you have to start trusting it," Miranda tells him.

This is difficult with all the horror Bruce has experienced throughout his life. From losing his parents at a young age to the true love of his life, Rachel, it was the tragic downfall of Harvey Dent that was also Bruce's tragedy. Like Marshal Will Kane in *High Noon* (1952) he knew he was all alone in his fight and was forced to become the very symbol he always wanted for Gotham but at the cost of losing the man behind the mask. Bruce Wayne once lived large, hiding in plain sight as a selfish emblem of wealth and power, but can no longer stomach the desire to seek out such pleasures even at the insistence of his lifelong confidant, Alfred. The emotional roundabout that this inspires is an unexpected and welcome addition to this conclusion; one that should delight those who have miscalculated Nolan as a cold, detached filmmaker. Just as he did with *Inception* (2010), the casual puzzle-like setup turns into whiz-bang and hardened intensity that deviously is sprinkling in an poignant undercurrent destined for an affecting payoff at the end of the journey.

There are little reservations when it comes to Nolan's skills as a craftsman behind the camera. But it is the parallels within his screenplays and the themes he explores that are equally important to establishing him as, arguably, the best of his generation. Those gray dualities of the protagonists at the centers of *Memento*, *Insomnia* and *The Prestige* (2006) take on literal representation in the Batman trilogy, but also involve the peripheral players and the audience in our perception of what is really at stake when those dualities are tested. Bruce born to privilege and Bane born in "Hell on Earth," each keeping their pain at bay by using a mask, but one uses his resources for action and the other using them to make empty promises as a false idol. Bruce would rather believe in people—whether it be Selina's desire to start fresh (and earning it) to Blake's devotion to being more than just another badge patrolling the city—and that is the key attribute to his resolve as a guardian for those he can inspire to carry the torch.

Nolan is not alone here either with an assemblage of actors who have taken the term of "dream cast" to new heights. Michael Caine, in one of his best performances in years, is absolutely heartbreaking as a man who feels he is failing to protect the remaining legacy of the Wayne family. Gary Oldman continues to bring further dimension to the usually soft-spoken Jim Gordon who, like Batman, has made his own harsh discoveries of the cost of living up his own ethical standards. Anne Hathaway, though never referred to as Catwoman, is stepping into some symbolic high heels and she fills them admirably combining mischief with vulnerability (both real and manufactured) with a performance that could have been kitschy rather than as fully rounded as it is.

Tom Hardy is physically memorable as the hulking monster Bane but projects some unique facets the more we learn about him as a man prepared to give his life for the most basic and fragile of human emotions. That he's able to communicate as much without us ever seeing his face for all but one fleeting moment is a testament to his strengths as an actor. If Bane represents the body that is frequently represented as the flesh of Bruce Wayne's sacrifice for Gotham than John Blake is most definitely the soul; a mirror to the man who once flashed the same gritted-teeth smile to a group of orphans unable to hide his rage from at least one of them. Whether aware of it not, Blake is a protege quickly rising to his own heights and Joseph Gordon-Levitt wisely doesn't play him in the kind of vain spirit as if he knew the film was as much about him. Instead he is the audience's fabled window and his performance and image is the one we hope for ourselves in the best and worst of it.

Least of not in this impressive collection is Christian Bale, who some have suggested has almost become a supporting role in his own story between the ensuing carnage and subplots around him, nevertheless always makes his presence felt. From his gaunt-like emergence at the beginning here and through his defeats and triumphs, Bale is the first actor who stifles criticism that the role itself is its own duality with someone usually making a better Bruce Wayne than a Batman and vice versa. In his hands the character becomes an identifiable reflection of both halves and is a triumph in subtle artistry.

Judging *The Dark Knight Rises* strictly on its own is like arguing which act of a film is the most satisfying instead of recognizing which complements the others. And yet it is most definitely its own film, referencing the others through minor, but key flashbacks but building its own brand of intensity that is so unrelenting it is hard to breathe at times. This is a trilogy that will someday be studied in film classes scene-by-scene. Connections will be drawn not just within themselves but between the first and third, the second and third and so on. "One man's tool is another man's weapon," says Bruce in a line that can be drawn from his sonar phone spy device to the manner in which Batman and Bane use their own variation on the military's Skyhook tactic to even as a criticism towards contemporaries who have all the means at their disposal to create a lasting piece of entertainment but instead uses it for the very greed that haunts Hollywood's worst blockbusters. Like Bruce Wayne who has earned the peace he finally achieves, Christopher Nolan can move on to the next stage of his career knowing that he has given fans a true hero for their times and a trilogy that earns its own place right beside him.

Erik Childress

CREDITS

Bruce Wayne/Batman: Christian Bale
Bane: Thomas Hardy
Selina Kyle/Catwoman: Anne Hathaway
Miranda Tate: Marion Cotillard
Jon Blake: Joseph Gordon-Levitt
Alfred: Michael Caine
Commissioner Jim Gordon: Gary Oldman
Lucius Fox: Morgan Freeman
Holly Robinson: Juno Temple

Foley: Matthew Modine

Dr. Pavel: Alon Aboutboul

Daggett: Ben Mendelsohn

Stryver: Burn Gorman

Capt. Jones: Daniel Sunjata

Dr. Jonathan Crane/Scarecrow: Cillian Murphy

Mayor: Nestor Carbonell

Ra's al Ghul: Liam Neeson

Congressman: Brett Cullen

Doctor: Thomas Lennon

Prisoner: Tom Conti

President: William Devane

Bruce Wayne's lawyer: Tomas Arana

Origin: United States

Language: English

Released: 2012

Production: Charles Roven, Emma Thomas, Christopher Nolan; released by Warner Bros.

Directed by: Christopher Nolan

Written by: Christopher Nolan; Jonathan Nolan

Cinematography by: Wally Pfister

Music by: Hans Zimmer

Sound: Richard King

Editing: Lee Smith

Costumes: Lindy Hemming

Production Design: Nathan Crowley; Kevin Kavanaugh

MPAA rating: PG-13

Running time: 165 minutes

REVIEWS

Bell, Mark. *Film Threat.* July 17, 2012.

Berardinelli, James. *ReelViews.* July 17, 2012.

Fine, Marshall. *Hollywood & Fine.* July 16, 2012.

Johanson, MaryAnn. *Flick Filosopher.* July 16, 2012.

McWeeny, Drew. *HitFix.* July 16, 2012.

Morgenstern, Joe. *Wall Street Journal.* July 16, 2012.

Novikov, Eugene. *FilmBlather.* July 19, 2012.

Pfeiffer, Mark. *Reel Times.* July 19, 2012.

Tobias, Scott. *AV Club.* July 18, 2012.

Weinberg, Scott. *GeekNation.* July 20, 2012.

QUOTES

Selina Kyle: "There's a storm coming, Mr. Wayne. You and your friends better batten down the hatches, because when it hits, you're all gonna wonder how you ever thought you could live so large and leave so little for the rest of us."

TRIVIA

Christopher Nolan is the first director to complete a full trilogy of Batman films and the second to direct a full trilogy of films based on one superhero (Sam Raimi helmed the first three Spider-Man films). Similarly, actor Christian Bale is the first actor to portray Batman/Bruce Wayne in three films.

AWARDS

Nominations:

British Acad. 2012: Visual FX

DARK SHADOWS

Every family has its demons.
 —Movie tagline

Strange is relative.
 —Movie tagline

The legend bites back.
 —Movie tagline

Box Office: $79.7 million

The color would surely have drained from Barnabas Collins' face if it had had any to begin with, the vampire's shock upon seeing the dilapidated state of his family's once-magnificent mansion seeming almost enough to do in the undead. The black-rimmed eyes upon that corpse-like countenance clearly register disbelief, dismay and indignation, as the sight diverges so strikingly from his fond memories. "What have they done to you?" he exclaims, something uttered with at least as much emotion by those viewers of Tim Burton's *Dark Shadows* who nostalgically remember the highly-melodramatic, low-budgeted supernatural television soap opera upon which the film is based. (It ran weekdays on ABC from 1966-1971.) Most were astonished, disappointed, and as out for blood as the saga's plasma-pursuing protagonist due to what they saw as an irreverent revamping that makes light of their beloved *Dark Shadows*.

It had initially seemed promising to them that a couple of fellow fans were spearheading this big-screen adaptation, raising not only hopes but expectations of fidelity more than facetiousness. However, a stake was driven into many a fervent heart when it became clear that the aforementioned duo of devotees—director Burton and producer/star Johnny Depp, in their eighth collaboration—had given an unwanted twist to what had originally been played decidedly straight, mixing campy mirth with material that is seriously macabre. (The original only inadvertently—though not infrequently—elicited laughter, particularly because there was never enough money or time allotted to reshoot mishaps such as physical and verbal stumbling, uncooperative props, flies landing on foreheads, or crew members walking into plain view.) While screenwriter Seth Grahame-

Smith has enjoyed some success synthesizing disparate elements in his mashup novels, moviegoers old enough to remember the late Jonathan Frid as Collins (he shot a fleeting cameo along with other stars of the series shortly before his passing) as well as those only familiar with the more newfangled Cullens felt that the gloomy Gothic ghoulishness and grin that are spattered here and there throughout never satisfactorily coagulate into solidly-enjoyable entertainment.

Quite a bit in the original vein is the film's spellbinding prologue, which starts off with a forebodingly-enshrouded image of 1760's Liverpool and ends with two cursed lovers leaping down to their doom from a jagged Maine coastal cliff as startling lightning and ominous thunder emanate from a sinister sky above and dark waves well up from below as dramatically as Danny Elfman's highly-emotive score. The very shores off which the Collins family had enjoyed immense success in the fishing industry (so much so that the town in which they settled was named after them) are now the site of their once-promising heir's immeasurable suffering, as spurned servant and surreptitious sorceress Angelique Bouchard (a fetching yet frightening Eva Green) has not only cast the plunge-inducing spell that ripped away Barnabas' ethereal soul mate Josette (a blank if beautiful Bella Heathcote) but also cruelly made him into a vampire so he could feel the pain of his loss in perpetuity. Having sealed his fate, the same is done to his body within a chain-trussed casket that remains buried for nearly two hundred years.

Barnabas emerges in 1972 with such a powerful thirst that he gorily wets his whistle with eleven full-blooded excavators who have unknowingly unearthed him during a scene that grips viewers almost as forcefully as the parched (but apologetic) vampire does his hard-hatted beverage containers. While these unfortunate diggers are too drained to speak for themselves, one feels safe in asserting that they did not enjoy being grabbed. However, moviegoers caught up thus far in the creepiness felt quite the opposite, hoping that the film would be able to maintain this tight a hold on them. Unfortunately, that grip is all-too-palpably and quite disappointingly loosened soon after, as what was intriguingly portentous and chillingly baleful is undermined by far-from-hair-raising material bent on raising a smile instead. There is mild humor in watching this stiffly-walking, grandiloquently-talking, 18th-century aristocratic anachronism attempting to make sense of modernity, especially the era's lava lamps, troll dolls, and macrame that even middle-aged moviegoers looking back now find rather unfathomable. One merely smiles when Barnabas watches Karen Carpenter singing on television and demands that what he deems to be a sorcery-compressed songstress come on out. There are also

weakly wacky images like the vampire brushing his fangs or being found curled up in a cupboard until suitable, satin-lined sleeping accommodations can be acquired. Viewers may start to feel as if they are being repeatedly thwacked over the head with Barnabas' wolf's head cane as the film endlessly hammers-home that this 1700's vampire just out of his coffin is quite a fish out of water.

As for Barnabas' own letdown, it is hard to say whether Collinwood Manor (kudos to Oscar-winning production designer Rick Heinrichs), the family business, or the family itself is in a sadder state. The vampire seems less of an oddball amidst his idiosyncratic (if underwritten), fractured, and fractious folk: Proud, steely matriarch Elizabeth (Michelle Pfeiffer, yet another fan of the original series); her truculent teen daughter Carolyn (believable Chloe Grace Moretz); Roger, Elizabeth's selfish sleaze of a brother (Jonny Lee Miller); and his young son David (Gully McGrath), who has both literally and figuratively been haunted since his mother's death. Also on hand is Willie Loomis (Jackie Earle Haley), Collinwood's curmudgeonly and appropriately-creepy caretaker, and David's unprofessionally unbridled shrink prone to drink, Dr. Julia Hoffman (Burton's partner Helena Bonham Carter, apparently heir to some of the hair Depp wore in Burton's 2010 *Alice in Wonderland*). Two other faces seem quite familiar to Barnabas, as wide-eyed new governess Victoria Winters (Heathcote again) looks just like Josette for a very good reason and—for a reason that is anything but good—Angel Bay CEO Angie (Green redux), the blond knockout who has nearly scored just that against the Collins Cannery, is reminiscent of a certain vengeful witch. With the former he is smitten and the latter he would just as passionately love to smite. Angie vows to destroy Barnabas and his lady love all over again if he insists on picking wrong a second time.

While the misfortunes, misfit status, longing lovesickness, and oft-stated self-loathing of eminently-watchable Depp's Nosferatu-fingered Barnabas will probably make viewers feel for the character, they will likely care little during his efforts to restore the family's fortunes (which briefly feature Hammer Horror legend Christopher Lee). However, during some furious, flying fornication between Barnabas and Angie, the audience may also temporarily reconnect. After more unhelpful tone unevenness and a freakily-festive "happening" during which Barnabas is befuddled about the gender of performing Goth rocker Alice Cooper (playing himself), the film's climactic showdown (in which sudden-werewolf Carolyn's "Woof!" recalls Catwoman Pfeiffer's "Meow" in Burton's 1992 *Batman Returns*) ends with a fire that becomes as out of control as the scene itself. It does, admittedly, feature Burton's trademark visual flair. Still, this "director of moments rather than wholes," as

Los Angeles Times critic Kenneth Turan referred to Burton, simply fails to tell a cohesive, compelling tale. Made on a budget of $150 million, *Dark Shadows* grossed $79.7 million and received mixed reviews. Straining to keep up appearances, Elizabeth Collins Stoddard at one point states, "You'll have to imagine us on a better day." Fans of the series, thinking back, did just that.

David L. Boxerbaum

CREDITS

Barnabas Collins: Johnny Depp
Elizabeth Collins Stoddard: Michelle Pfeiffer
Dr. Julia Hoffman: Helena Bonham Carter
Angelique Bouchard: Eva Green
Willie Loomis: Jackie Earle Haley
Roger Collins: Jonny Lee Miller
Victoria Winters/ Josette Dupres: Bella Heathcote
Carolyn Stoddard: Chloe Grace Moretz
David Collins: Gulliver McGrath
Origin: United States
Language: English, French, Spanish
Released: 2012
Production: Christi Dembrowski, David Kennedy, Graham King, Richard D. Zanuck, Johnny Depp; Infinitum Nihil, GK Films; released by Warner Bros.
Directed by: Tim Burton
Written by: John August; Seth Graham-Smith
Cinematography by: Bruno Delbonnel
Music by: Danny Elfman
Sound: Julian Slater
Music Supervisor: Michael Higham
Editing: Chris Lebenzon
Art Direction: Chris Lowe
Costumes: Colleen Atwood
Production Design: Rick Heinrichs
MPAA rating: PG-13
Running time: 113 minutes

REVIEWS

Burr, Ty. *Boston Globe*. May 10, 2012.
Chang, Justin. *Variety*. May 8, 2012.
Corliss, Richard. *Time*. May 10, 2012.
Dargis, Manohla. *New York Times*. May 10, 2012.
Ebert, Roger. *Chicago Sun-Times*. May 9, 2012.
Gleiberman, Owen. *Entertainment Weekly*. May 9, 2012.
Hammond, Pete. *Boxoffice Magazine*. May 8, 2012.
Hornaday, Ann. *Washington Post*. May 10, 2012.
Lane, Anthony. *New Yorker*. May 18, 2012.
McCarthy, Todd. *Hollywood Reporter*. May 8, 2012.

QUOTES

Barnabas Collins: "ifteen, and no husband? You must put those child-bearing hips to good use, lest your womb shrivel up and die."

TRIVIA

In the original *Dark Shadows* television show, the character of Dr. Julia Hoffman was played by Grayson Hall, the wife of the show's head writer Sam Hall. In the film, Dr. Hoffman is played by Helena Bonham Carter, wife of director Tim Burton.

DARLING COMPANION

Box Office: $793,815

What happened to Lawrence Kasdan? After helping to write two of the most celebrated films in movie history, *The Empire Strikes Back* (1980) and *Raiders of the Lost Ark* (1981), he made an explosive directorial debut with the incredible *Body Heat* (1981), a searing adaptation of *Double Indemnity* (1944) which was one of the finest films of the 1980s or any decade. He followed with the baby boomer classic *The Big Chill* (1983) (a big budget reworking of John Sayles's classic *Return of Secaucus Seven* [1980]), made an old-fashioned cowboy movie, *Silverado* (1985), when no one in Hollywood except Clint Eastwood was making Westerns and closed the decade out with the Oscar-nominated *The Accidental Tourist* (1988). His early nineties films, *I Love you to Death* (1990), *Grand Canyon* (1991), and *Wyatt Earp* (1994) were not as good as his eighties work but interesting nonetheless. Starting in the late nineties, the gaps between films started to get greater and the films decidedly less interesting: *French Kiss* (1995), *Mumford* (1999) and the dreadful *Dreamcatcher* (2003).

Now, nearly a decade later, Kasdan returns with *Darling Companion,* a film that could have been written and directed by Nancy Meyers (*Father of the Bride* [1991],*What Woman Want* [2000], *It's Complicated* [2009]). Five family members and their housekeeper search the Colorado wilderness for the family dog, Freeway, who has run away while being walked by the self-involved patriarch Joseph (Kevin Kline). As the searchers pair up in different combinations to search for the beloved family mutt, they endure comedic hijinks and confront longstanding issues with one another. The one sentence pitch for the film was likely "In looking for Freeway they find themselves."

Unfortunately, this is not a journey that has been made remotely interesting or entertaining by Kasdan and his wife Meg's Hallmark Channel-level quality script. *Darling Companion* is the kind of made-for-TV movie that one might catch on a Tuesday afternoon, albeit with an exceptionally overqualified cast. Indeed, if Kasdan can no longer write he can certainly still attract an incredible cast and an amazing stable of fantastic actors are wasted on his trite film. Kline (in his sixth collaboration with Kasdan) plays Joseph, an egocentric spinal surgeon who has put his work ahead of his family for decades. Diane Keaton plays his long suffering wife, Beth, who has bottled up her frustration and is prone to emotional outbursts. Riding home one day, Beth and her adult daughter, Grace (a woefully underused Elisabeth Moss), spy an injured dog on the side of the road. They take him to a veterinarian where a nauseating meet-cute occurs between the dashing veterinarian/GQ model (Jay Ali) and Grace. The dog is taken home and then a musical montage fills in the next year: The initially skeptical Joseph is soon the dog's best friend, Freeway becomes a beloved part of the family, the camera pans up from Freeway sleeping beneath the dinner table to reveal Grace and the veterinarian holding hands while they eat with Joseph and Beth, culminating with their wedding at the family vacation home in the Rockies.

The wedding serves the dramatic purpose of getting the rest of the family together: Diane Wiest is Joseph's flakey sister, Penny, who shows up with her new fiancee, Russell (the great Richard Jenkins) who the rest of the family is meeting for the first time and who they do not trust, particularly after Penny and Russell reveal that they are planning on opening an Irish pub in the Midwest. Penny's surgeon son, Bryan (Mark Duplass) takes an immediate disliking to Russell, assuming that he is taking advantage of his mother. The group is rounded out by the most insufferable character of all, Carmen (Ayelet Zurer) a supermodel/psychic gypsy who is the caretaker for the vacation home. Carmen experiences visions which tell her where the family members should look for the dog and soon alternating combinations of family members are out searching for the dog. (For his part, Freeway the dog is adorable and steals every second of screen time he is given. Sadly that is very little time as he is a transparent plot device and has to promptly disappear to set the comedic searching/healing plot in motion).

Kasdan's script is bad in a way that only a vanity project from a well-established filmmaker can be bad. Traditional quality control mechanisms that would have disqualified or modified the script are absent due to the prestige of the filmmaker (See Lucas, George). The script's fatal flaw is a surprising one given Kasdan's long experience and talent as a screenwriter: his characters are shallow and underdeveloped. As a result their transformations are not believable and the viewer is never made to care about them. Joseph, the skeptical and scientific doctor who never wanted a dog in the first place and

who scoffs at the gypsy's hocus pocus predictions inexplicably delays his return to Denver (where his patients await) and rushes to and fro based on Carmen's string of psychic predictions. Joseph and Beth get lost in the woods, fall down a mudslide and bicker about his putting his work before the family and her reflexive hysteria. Suddenly, at the end of the 24-hour ordeal, they have resolved decades long marital issues. They even decide to invest in Penny and Russell's Irish pub despite having shown nothing but doubt and disdain for it up to the moment they decide to put money into it! "I suppose we should invest in the pub" says Joseph for no particular reason. Bryan and Russell have a mildly menacing encounter with a red neck dog breeder and suddenly Bryan is fine with Russell marrying his mother and opening a risky business with her money. Of course, Bryan and Carmen (the only two non-middle-aged characters) fall in love. None of these developments are remotely convincing. Characters make life-changing decisions, heal long-damaged relationships and fall in love because it is that point in the script. Sometimes talented actors can make the viewer care about their characters despite an inadequate script. This is not one of those films. It is a testament to how bad the Kasdans' script is that even actors as talented as Kevin Kline, Richard Jenkins, Diane Keaton, Diane Wiest, and Sam Shepard (as the local sheriff) cannot overcome it.

Having characters together in an isolated setting working out their emotional connections in a comedic manner is not a fatal conceit and has formed the basis for many a successful film (see Allen, Woody) but *Darling Companion* lacks the chops in the script department. The result is a listless mix of unfunny comedy and unconvincing drama. The film's direction is perfectly acceptable but totally generic. There is no hint of the master behind the camera. The caliber of *Darling Companion's* cast makes the viewer daydream about the movie that could have been. What if David Mamet had written and directed a film with the same actors? The sad thing is that once upon a time Kasdan would have been the screenwriter and director the viewer would have wished for.

Nate Vercauteren

CREDITS

Beth Winter: Diane Keaton
Dr. Joseph Winter: Kevin Kline
Russell: Richard Jenkins
Grace Winter: Elisabeth (Elissabeth, Elizabeth, Liz) Moss
Bryan Alexander: Mark Duplass
Penny Alexander: Dianne Wiest
Sheriff Morris: Sam Shepard

Carmen: Ayelet Zurer

Sam Bhoola: Jay Ali

Origin: United States

Language: English

Released: 2012

Production: Anthony Bregman, Elizabeth Redleaf, Lawrence Kasdan; Werc Werk Works, Kasdan Pictures, Likely Story; released by Sony Pictures Classics

Directed by: Lawrence Kasdan

Written by: Lawrence Kasdan; Meg Kasdan

Cinematography by: Michael McDonough

Music by: James Newton Howard

Sound: Robert Grieve

Editing: Dina Goldman

Art Direction: Christopher R. DeMuri

Costumes: Molly Maginnis

Production Design: Dina Goldman

MPAA rating: PG-13

Running time: 103 minutes

REVIEWS

Anderson, Melissa. *Village Voice*. April 17, 2012.

Burr, Ty. *Boston Globe*. May 17, 2012.

Ebert, Roger. *Chicago Sun Times*. April 25, 2012.

Lowenstein, Lael. *Variety*. April 15, 2012.

Lumenick, Lou. *New York Post*. April 20, 2012.

Rabin, Nathan. *AV Club*. April 25, 2012.

Rea, Steven. *Philadelphia Inquirer*. May 10, 2012.

Scott, A. O. *New York Times*. April 19, 2012.

Uhlich, Keith. *Time Out New York*. April 17, 2012.

Zacharek, Stephanie. *Movieline*. April 19, 2012.

TRIVIA

The film is Lawrence Kasdan's first directorial effort since the thriller *Dreamcatcher* nine years ago.

DEADFALL

Box Office: $66,351

Slow-burn atmosphere abounds in *Deadfall*, a snowy and noirish yet ultimately somewhat bewildering would-be thriller that lacks a unifying and defining dramaturgical touch, if not scope and originality within the boundaries of a genre setting. There is a certain literary quality to this Michigan-set crime drama ensemble, about the knotty roots of biology and bad decisions, and how they conspire to pervert sensible choices. If it falls more on the side of the fence of intriguing misfire than indisputable success, with an embrace defined by one's tolerance for finely sketched doom and violence over

keen psychology, *Deadfall* still has enough going for it to keep it engaging. It may not be the sort of movie people in large numbers seek out, but those who do will likely find enough of interest and reward that they will not feel their time was squandered.

It is not flashy in its telling, but *Deadfall* wastes absolutely no time in getting down to business. Having just robbed a casino of cash, siblings Addison (Eric Bana) and Liza (Olivia Wilde) are on the lam when they hit a snowdrift. Addison shoots and kills the state trooper who shows up at the scene of the single-car accident, so the pair split up, with loose plans to reconnect near or just over the Canadian border.

Meanwhile, ex-Olympic boxer Jay (Charlie Hunnam) has just been released from prison. After a nasty confrontation with his ex-trainer and promoter, he is reluctantly winding his way home for a Thanksgiving reunion with his parents, June (Sissy Spacek) and Chet (Kris Kristofferson), when he comes across a hitchhiking Liza. After holing up in a bar during a snowstorm, they enter into a play-acted seduction—a conceit that seems lifted from some movie Mickey Rourke and Kim Basinger never made in the 1980s—which in turn quickly morphs into something real.

Concurrent to all this, Addison is cutting a swath of violence across rural Michigan. On his trail is a police deputy, Hanna (Kate Mara), who has to suffer through a string of humiliations in front of her colleagues at the hands of her gruff father, Sheriff Marshall Becker (Treat Williams). Things come to a head when Addison and Liza finally again cross paths, and she is forced to consider breaking free from his sadistic grip, of which she has long been a willing enabler.

Director Stefan Ruzowitzky scored a Best Foreign Language Film Academy Award for *The Counterfeiters* (2008), a fictionalization, as told through the eyes of an imprisoned Jewish typographer, of the true-life Nazi German plan to destabilize the United Kingdom by forging currency notes. As in that movie, Ruzowitzky here juggles lots of characters and murky morality, and smartly keeps screenwriter Zach Dean's psychosexual sibling kink on slow boil, rather than let it overwhelm the film.

Deadfall lacks the dizzy twists and turns of icy capers with which it on the surface might seem to share a lot in common, like *The Ice Harvest* (2005) and *Thin Ice* (2012); it does not really play on that same field of wintry double-crosses. Yet it is not nasty and brutish enough, in the manner of *A Simple Plan* (1998), to really pack a wicked emotional wallop, or test one's scruples. In addition to the plot above, a whole lot happens, no doubt—Hanna gets an acceptance letter to the FBI Academy, there are knife fights and snowmobile chases, and a random domestic abuser is felled in order to throw another shade of ethical grey onto the proceedings—but in its mission to avoid being irresolute or overly predictable, *Deadfall* fails to do at least just one thing really well.

In fact, the bulk of its action seems adjunct to some plot that does not really come into focus. If films like *One False Movie* (1992), *Blood Simple* (1994) and *Red Rock West* (1994) were part of the inspiration for *Deadfall*, Dean got the characters right more than all the accumulated detail. There is a formal, stilted quality to some of Dean's dialogue ("Let's not dally," says Addison at one point) that does not seem to always jibe with the background and education of the characters, and backstory is revealed in chunky monologues of personal history. Additionally, the burgeoning love story between Jay and Liza is off by degrees, and once *Deadfall* settles into a talky standoff for its final reel it becomes clear that both Addison and the movie as a whole do not have any real game plan or ideas of resolution.

The recognizable cast, no doubt attracted to the material in some measure because of its ensemble nature and lack of fidelity to humdrum convention, for the most part all bring something interesting and worthwhile to the table. Spacek and Kristofferson have a nice, believable, well-worn rapport. And Hunnam and Wilde each ably communicate a certain amount of wounded neediness—they each desperately require healthier human connections, even if they do not yet realize it.

The diminutive Mara, though, struggles to pull off Hanna's authority, even if that shortcoming in her father's eyes is a defining trait of her character. And Bana, working with a sometimes tin and hokey rural accent of indeterminate origin, holds sway deceptively, owing more to his offscreen charisma than any hard-earned, legitimate insights or window into Addison's dark psychology.

Ruzowitzky and production designer Paul Denham Austerberry concoct an appealingly spare and chilly environment for the film. Cinematographer Shane Hurlbut, he of Christian Bale's infamously bombastic derision on the set of *Terminator Salvation* (2009), does a great job in making the environment an important extra character. Even without benefit of a visual scheme that really seeks to overtly play up its foreboding, Hurlbut locates a plan that slyly, effectively reinforces the film's bleak, downhearted tone. With Montreal and the surrounding snowy Quebec countryside doubling for Michigan's Upper Peninsula, *Deadfall* has a genuinely remote, frigid feeling that, along with its pulpy story, make it a rather fitting movie for predisposed genre fans

to curl up with, problems and all, at home on a cold night.

Brent Simon

CREDITS

Addison: Eric Bana
Liza: Olivia Wilde
Jay: Charlie Hunnam
June: Sissy Spacek
Chet: Kris Kristofferson
Origin: United States
Language: English
Released: 2012
Production: Shelly Clippard, Ben Cosgrove, Mark Cuban, Gary Levinsohn, Todd Wagner; released by Magnolia Pictures, Studio Canal
Directed by: Stefan Ruzowitsky
Written by: Zach Dean
Cinematography by: Shane Hurlbut
Music by: Marco Beltrami
Sound: Thomas O'Neil Younkman
Editing: Arthur Tarnowski; Dan Zimmerman
Art Direction: Michele Laliberte
Costumes: Odette Gadoury
Production Design: Paul Denham Austerberry
MPAA rating: R
Running time: 95 minutes

REVIEWS

Beck, Jeff. *Examiner.com*. December 6, 2012.
Burr, Ty. *Boston Globe*. December 6, 2012.
Corliss, Richard. *Time*. December 6, 2012.
Dargis, Manohla. *New York Times*. December 6, 2012.
Gleiberman, Owen. *Entertainment Weekly*. December 5, 2012.
Jenkins, Mark. *NPR*. December 6, 2012.
Legel, Laremy. *Film.com*. December 4, 2012.
O'Sullivan, Michael. *Washington Post*. December 7, 2012.
Rooney, David. *Hollywood Reporter*. April 27, 2012.
Sharkey, Betsy. *Los Angeles Times*. December 6, 2012.

QUOTES

Becker: "If you were one of my boys, I would hit you so f**kin' hard."
Hanna: "If I were one of your boys, you'd be proud of me."

TRIVIA

Olivia Wilde's first day of shooting was actually the scenes where her character almost freezes to death so she was wearing only a miniskirt during filming in Canada.

THE DEEP BLUE SEA

Box Office: $1.1 million

The greatest, and most unexpected, pleasure of Terence Davies's adaptation of Terence Rattigan's classic play *The Deep Blue Sea* is the sheer visual splendor he injects into what is essentially a dialogue between three characters. Davies's beautiful film is as much a visual valentine to post-war London as it is a vehicle for Rattigan's powerful meditation on obsessive love. Indeed the best scene in the film features no dialogue at all. The heroine, Hester Page (a superb Rachel Weisz in an Oscar-worthy performance), stands on the edge of a tube track as a train approaches, preparing to jump. Suddenly the scene flashes back to London during the blitz. Dust cascades down from the ceiling of a tube station as the city above is peppered with bombs. The camera slowly pans to the left in a long uninterrupted tracking shot of the civilians who have taken refuge on the platform as families huddle together, Bobbies patrol back and forth, and vendors wander the platform selling food and cigarettes. A lone member of the crowd is singing a haunting rendition of "Molly Malone." More voices join in as the camera slowly tracks across the platform until it is a deeply moving chorus. The camera finally stops at a man and woman clutching each other. It is Hester and her husband, Sir William Collyer (Simon Russell Beale), two-thirds of a love triangle that will play itself out a few years in the future, leading to Hester standing on a train platform deciding whether or not to jump.

This haunting sequence encapsulates both the great beauty of Davies's film and his success in recreating a lost world. He is aided greatly in both respects by Florian Hoffmeister's amazing cinematography. The texture of the film is grainy and faded, as though someone had touched up a black-and-white film reel with some primitive colorization. This authentic look is complemented by the small but fascinating details of post-war Britain that Davies provides like how all of the patrons of a pub spontaneously sing together as a form of communal entertainment in the days before television and cell phones. Davies's meticulously rendered and fascinating depiction of post-war London makes the film worth seeing all on its own.

Of course, *The Deep Blue Sea* is not simply a portrait of a time and place, it is a powerful study of passionate, self-destructive love. Hester, a lonely woman locked in a (for her) loveless marriage, has her passions unleashed with a vengeance by a roguish RAF pilot, Freddie Page (an excellent Tom Hiddleston). Having awakened to a passion she has never before experienced, Hester has fled her economically secure but passionless marriage for the penniless Page who she loves with a terrifying intensity. The problem is that Page does not feel the same passionate love for Hester that Hester feels for him. Hester is caught between the Devil and the Deep Blue Sea, forced to choose between two equally horrible choices (life with someone who does not love her as she loves him or suicide). What is most refreshing about these characters, particularly characters that were created sixty years ago, is how they are not reduced to the single dimensions that they would be in a lesser script. Though willing to sacrifice everything for her all-consuming love, Hester is not blinded by it and is keenly aware of her dilemma. Although she is irresistibly driven by uncontrollable passion she is also capable of recognizing that she is driven by it. She is by turns fiercely independent and needy, coolly rational and overcome with passion. Similarly, in a lesser script, Freddie the RAF pilot would simply be a shallow and self-absorbed opportunist, in the relationship for the short term physical rewards and out the door as soon as something better comes along. However, his character is more complicated. Freddie is shallow and self-absorbed but he is also reacting to being smothered by obsessive love. Would Freddie be more inclined to stay with Hester if she was not so overwhelmingly in love with him? How much of Freddie's character traits are due to his being smothered by an obsessive? And, the character most susceptible to being reduced to one dimension, Sir William Collyer, is not an evil mustache twirling villain intent on either possessing or destroying his adulterous wife but a confused man who loves Hester deeply and who has been deeply hurt but still wants to help her. The film sets up a heartbreaking and seemingly irreconcilable dynamic amongst its three characters: Simon loves Hester, Hester loves Freddie and Freddie loves himself. It is a recipe for misery for all involved. Or worse than misery as contemplated by Hester.

But does it have to be? Near the conclusion of *The Deep Blue Sea* Hester laments her dilemma of having to choose between two equally horrible choices to her no nonsense landlady Mrs. Elton (Ann Mitchell): "Sometimes it's tough to judge when you're caught between the devil and the deep blue sea." In response she receives the wisest words spoken by anyone in the film: "A lot of rubbish is talked about love. You know what real love is? It's wiping someone's ass, or changing the sheets when they've wet themselves, and letting 'em keep their dignity so you can both go on. Suicide? No one's worth it."

The suspense of Davies's haunting and emotionally wrenching film is whether or not Hester will realize that her options are not confined to those two horrible choices.

Nate Vercauteren

CREDITS

Hester Collyer: Rachel Weisz
Sir William Collyer: Simon Russell Beale
Freddie Page: Tom Hiddleston
Jackie Jackson: Harry Hadden-Paton

Mrs. Elton: Ann Mitchell
Mr. Miller: Karl Johnson
Origin: United States, British Virgin Islands
Language: English
Released: 2012
Production: Sean O'Connor, Kate Ogborn; Camberwell, Fly Films; released by Music Box Films
Directed by: Terence Davies
Written by: Terence Davies
Cinematography by: Florian Hoffmeister
Music by: Samuel Barber
Sound: Tim Barker
Music Supervisor: Ian Neil
Editing: David Charap
Art Direction: David Hindle; Sarah Pasquali
Costumes: Ruth Myers
Production Design: James Merifield
MPAA rating: R
Running time: 98 minutes

REVIEWS

Jones, J. R. *Chicago Reader*. March 29, 2012.
Zachareck, Stephanie. *Movieline*. March 22, 2012.
Weber, Bill. *Slant Magazine*. March 19, 2012.
Travers, Peter. *Rolling Stone*. March 22, 2012.
Scott, A. O. *New York Times*. March 22, 2012.
Morris, Wesley. *Boston Globe*. March 29, 2012.
Wise, Damon. *Empire*. March 16, 2012.
Lumenick, Lou. *New York Post*. March 23, 2012.
McCarthy, Todd. *Hollywood Reporter*. March 18, 2012.
Felperin, Leslie. *Variety*. March 18, 2012.

QUOTES

Collyer's Mother: "Beware of passion, Hester. It always leads to something ugly."
Hester Collyer: "What would you replace it with?"
Collyer's Mother: "A guarded enthusiasm. It's safer."

TRIVIA

This film is Barbara Jefford's first theatrical film in twelve years, the last being *The Ninth Gate*.

AWARDS

Nominations:

Golden Globes 2013: Actress—Drama (Weisz)

DETACHMENT

Box Office: $72,689

Eleven years after President George W. Bush signed the No Child Left Behind Act in an Ohio high school, American cinema responded to the act's successes and faults with three movies that crusaded for the art of teaching despite the dangerous assembly lines of the educational system. Two of these films, *Won't Back Down* and *Here Comes the Boom*, had an optimistic message about the spirit of teachers and their ability to make a difference for their students. These feel-good films were so in tune with one another that they even referred to the same Tom Petty song for inspiration (Petty's "I Won't Back Down."). Both of the films referred to school teachers as fighters. In *Won't Back Down*, Maggie Gyllenhaal played a single mother who teams up with a teacher (Viola Davis) in order to save a declining Pittsburgh school by taking it over themselves. In *Here Comes the Boom*, Kevin James was a science teacher who takes on the not-so-slick metaphorical cause of wrestling for his students by getting into matches of mixed martial arts in order to save his Boston-area public school's music program.

And then, gritting its teeth alone, there is *Detachment*, a limited release film about New York City teachers that featured a slew of notable faces playing instructors under the same roof, including Adrien Brody, Marcia Gay Harden, Christina Hendricks, James Caan, Lucy Liu, Tim Blake Nelson, and Blythe Danner. With this film, the teachers have indeed become a part of the "educational system" (dissected with great anxiety in the 2010 documentary *Waiting for Superman*), and their will to fight has waned.

Detachment is directed by Tony Kaye, who taught Americans a brutal lesson about the life-changing damage of hate with his scintillating debut film, *American History X* (1998). Here, Kaye channels that fire into a story about teachers, and while it may sit in its own dark corner, apoplectic to its own thoughts, it is a film with an angst that deserves to be heard.

In the movie, which is humbly billed in the credits as "A Tony Kaye Talkie," Adrien Brody plays Henry Barthes, a tough-minded teacher who has learned many difficult lessons from life itself, related to child trauma involving his grandfather and his mother's suicide. Living alone in a simple studio apartment, Henry is trying to funnel his energy into teaching. *Detachment* follows Henry as he is newly assigned to one of the city's forgotten high schools, instructing English. Some students treat him with respect, while others challenge his diligence to discipline.

Outside of the classroom, Henry worries about his grandfather, who is in an assisted living facility and suffering from his own mental conditions. One night when leaving the facility, he comes across Erica (Sami Gayle), a young woman of a high schooler's age who throws her fate into the streets by becoming a prostitute. After initially avoiding her, Henry decides to take her in with hopes of getting her cleaned up. This begins a paralleling story of Henry caring for this harmed individual while interacting with students in school, like the disturbed art student Meredith (Betty Kaye, daughter of the director), or other teachers, like Ms. Madison (Christina Hendricks).

The story takes breaks from Henry's gradual arc to show the other experiences of teachers, which are presented in brief moments by the script instead of mini narratives. Liu's guidance counselor Dr. Doris Parker freaks out on a student who has quit, Tim Blake Nelson's Mr. Wiatt just wants to be noticed as he clings to an outside school fence, etc. Frazzled but united, they are often showed being unappreciated, assaulted, or turned into scapegoats, either by violent students or screaming voices of their parents, who are embodied more often in the film as the violent red flashing of an answering machine more than a physical, involved presence.

While *Detachment* is a film about the power of teachers, and an audience's need to respect them as they attempt to whittle away at the potential angry adults of tomorrow, Kaye's film grabs its audience most of all through its grave cynicism. The teachers are decaying, the parents are not showing up on parent's night, and worst of all, as James Caan's character Mr. Seaboldt says, "Nobody says 'thank you.'"

Brody, a strong fit for a character worn on the inside and out, gives one of the strongest performances in an unbalanced acting filmography. Immediately conveying to his audience on his first day of class the type of darkness that he attempts to teach with, Brody provides compelling dimension to the character, and bigness to Henry despite his small stature. The way Brody uses his voice is a perfect fit as well, with a bassy rasp that delivers calmly but toughly to the young people he is attempting to level wth.

Kaye channels his anger through his aesthetics, which are fitfully chaotic, free-spirited expressions of themselves that are complicated, if not blinded, by the amount of emotion he feels for the subject (Kaye throws himself headfirst into the project as cinematographer). Characters move in and out of a camera's focus, or are thrown into the audience's face with extreme close ups, while dialogue overlaps itself in audio to create a feeling of the torrential downpour of stress faced by the film's characters. In terms of cutting, Kaye chops his examples of teacher hell with quickness, getting to the punch of the absurdity that these professionals are facing, but also reducing parents to squawking birds, as they claim that their child is the one being left behind etc. Mixed into this story of simple structure is the usage of fake documentary footage, which captures Harry at an unknown time, in an unknown place, which is also intermingled with weightless home movie film footage meant to provide point of view for his childhood. Throughout this visual melee, Kaye also utilizes animated chalkboard drawings (by Rebecca Foster) to display some commentary about any of the film's crazy moments, which can be the film's most on-the-nose artistic flourish.

If *Detachment* were to have one immediate fault, it would be that its sporadic collection of tough moments can nudge the film towards the emotional intent of teacher's humiliation porn. But yet, within this extreme darkness, *Detachment* does have a bizarre way of showing bits of hope, in the way that *American History X* did with Edward Norton's reformed neo-Nazi. Kaye, as much as he may fume about the unjust wrath dumped unto those who are in the nurturing position to directly influence the future of society, believes with full optimism in the potential of educators, and the importance in the experiences they have to teach. They endure through hellish moments, and they still show up to work, whether students, teachers, or state support is present or not. By presenting a tragedy of failure, Kaye, in his own backwards way, highlights the virtue of when the weary choose to persevere.

Detachment begins with a quote by Albert Camus, and it ends with a metaphor that may be heavy handed, but its presence speaks truth: one would not know what to make of a comparison between the spiritually crumbling educational system to Poe's "The Fall of the House of Usher" without the knowledge of a teacher.

Nick Allen

CREDITS

Henry Barthes: Adrien Brody
Ms. Sarah Madison: Christina Hendricks
Mr. Charles Seaboldt: James Caan
Principal Carol Dearden: Marcia Gay Harden
Dr. Doris Parker: Lucy Liu
Ms. Perkins: Blythe Danner
Mr. Wiatt: Tim Blake Nelson
Origin: United States
Language: English
Released: 2012
Production: Bingo Gubelmann, Benji Kohn, Chris Papavasiliou, Greg Shapiro, Carl Lund; Appian Way, Kingsgate Films, Paper Street Films; released by Tribeca Films
Directed by: Tony Kaye
Written by: Carl Lund

Cinematography by: Tony Kaye

Music by: The Newton Brothers

Sound: Chris Koch

Music Supervisor: Andy Gowen

Editing: Michelle Botticelli; Barry Alexander Brown; Geoffrey Richman

Costumes: Wendy Schecter

Production Design: Jade Healy

MPAA rating: Unrated

Running time: 97 minutes

REVIEWS

Abele, Robert. *Los Angeles Times*. March 22, 2012.

Holden, Stephen. *New York Times*. March 15, 2012.

Lane, Anthony. *New Yorker*. March 13, 2012.

O'Hehlr, Andrew. *Salon.com*. April 27, 2011.

Neumaier, Joe. *New York Daily News*. March 15, 2012.

Pols, Mary F. *Time*. March 22, 2012.

Reed, Rex. *New York Observer*. March 13, 2012.

Scheib, Ronnie. *Variety*. May 25, 2011.

Schenk, Frank. *Hollywood Reporter*. April 26, 2011.

Whitty, Stephen. *Newark Star-Ledger*. March 16, 2012.

QUOTES

Henry Barthes: "Whatever is on my mind, I say it as I feel it, I'm truthful to myself; I'm young and I'm old, I've been bought and I've been sold, so many times. I am hard-faced, I am gone. I am just like you."

TRIVIA

At one point, Michael Wincott was considered for a role in the film.

THE DEVIL INSIDE

No soul is safe.
—Movie tagline

Box Office: $53.3 million

Arriving at the dubious intersection of two increasingly played-out horror trends—"found footage" films and exorcism shockers—*The Devil Inside* manages to let down both sides thanks to an all-around lack of originality. (It is not even the first found-footage exorcism thriller—that would be 2010's *The Last Exorcism*.)

The Devil Inside follows Isabella Rossi (Fernanda Andrade), a gaunt, Gothic beauty searching for answers about the triple homicide her mother (Suzan Crowley) committed in 1989. The elder Rossi killed two priests and a nun during an attempted exorcism, but was found not guilty by reason of insanity and shipped off to Rome,

tucked away for decades in a Vatican-run mental hospital. Because these days nothing is worth doing if it is not captured on tape, Isabella enlists Michael (Ionut Grama), a young documentary maker to tag along to Italy and film her as she reconnects with her institutionalized mother.

Isabella's journey leads them first to a Vatican class on exorcism (where the film's plot points to come are neatly preordained in a lecture), then to two priests in the class. The young men of the cloth turn out to be renegades of sorts, performing unapproved exorcisms on the sly for the suffering who do not meet the Church's definition of "possession" (versus "mental illness"). Irish Father Ben (Simon Quarterman) is a scruffily handsome rebel out to defy Church bureaucracy; Father David (Evan Helmuth) is a doughy American fearful that all this rule-breaking might affect his future divine career inside said bureaucracy. Isabella and Michael accompany the exorcists to an eye-popping soul cleansing of a random young woman and then, with the film's quota of demonic swearing and body contortion fulfilled, tackle her mother's case.

The Devil Inside reminds us that exorcism film tropes have remained resolutely unchanged in the forty years since *The Exorcist* (1973). The possessing demons speak in dead, monotone voices; limbs and spines twist in grimace-inducing poses; and the afflicted spew profanity and sexual suggestions (not to mention nursery rhymes) at young priests already struggling with their faith. This latest entry does nothing to shake up any of these weary cliches. Instead it either counts on them appearing fresh to younger, more naive audiences or, more likely, that these now-familiar gags are part of the film's comforting appeal, acting as reassuring genre signposts for viewers.

All horror succeeds or fails on how well it draws the viewer in, how deeply the work puts him or her into the fleeing shoes or wide-spread eyes of the terrified protagonist. Add to that the fact that horror cinema has traditionally thrived in low-budget backwaters, free from studio interference and mainstream standards of decency and morality, and it is easy to see why the "found footage" horror craze caught fire with 1999's *The Blair Witch Project* and then experienced a Recession-era resurgence with 2009's *Paranormal Activity*. Cheaper than already cheap horror movies, in the YouTube and reality TV era, found-footage films can add an effective layer of authenticity as well as a direct and self-aware first-person point of view. Scenes are usually poorly lit and shakily filmed, with the lopsided framing and washed out murk of the handheld video camera often obscuring the action (and thus increasing the threat of the unknown). These aesthetic weaknesses become part of the films' emotion-wringing verisimilitude.

Found-footage films also lean toward brevity and a more self-contained, simplistic, straight-forward narrative—stripped of some of the usual structural and editing tactics used to create and juggle cinematic meaning and thematic layers, the horror sub-genre's conventions don't easily support multiple plotlines. However, while its slight premise and 83-minute running time would suggest more of a sketch than a full film, *The Devil Inside*'s director William Brent Bell and his co-writer Matthew Peterman have managed to convolute and render confusing what should have been a relatively simple scary story. Unnecessary themes and subplots are piled on haphazardly, clouding rather than enriching Isabella's central quest story until all the film makers seem able to do is slap on an abrupt ending. The "hands thrown in the air" result feels as if they ran out of either funding or ideas, rather than bring their story to a fulfilling finish.

For all its frenetic theological hand-wringing and demonic histrionics, there is nothing remotely compelling about *The Devil Inside*—it has zero imagination and even less respect for its audience. Though the characters are supernaturally forgettable, the acting is for the most part sub-par but not atrocious, nor is Bell completely incompetent on a scene-by-scene basis. Still, the film has not a single idea—philosophic, humanistic, or horrific—beyond its "found-footage exorcism movie" pitch. (Its only scare "trick" is to have possessed characters suddenly screech like banshees—unable to conjure up an honest sense of dread, the film almost literally resorts to yelling "boo!" at the audience.) It is not that *The Devil Inside* does not know what it wants to be or cannot fulfill its creative ambitions—it simply has none. It is an exercise in passive mediocrity.

Locke Peterseim

CREDITS

Maria Rossi: Suzan Crowley
Ben: Simon Quaterman
David: Evan Helmuth
Isabella Rossi: Fernanda Andrade
Lt. Dreyfus: Brian Johnson
Michael Schaefer: Ionut Grama
Rosa: Bonnie Morgan
Origin: United States
Language: English
Released: 2012
Production: Matthew Peterman, Morris Pawson, Matthew Peterman; Insurge Pictures, Prototype Production Inc.; released by Paramount Pictures
Directed by: William Brent Bell

Written by: William Brent Bell; Matthew Peterman
Cinematography by: Gonzalo Amat
Music by: Brett Detar; Ben Romans
Sound: Cristwea Mirel
Editing: Tim Mirkovich
Costumes: Terri Prescott
Production Design: Tony DeMille
MPAA rating: R
Running time: 83 minutes

REVIEWS

Dargis, Manohla. *New York Times*. January 6, 2012.
Edelstein, David. *Vulture*. January 6, 2012.
Jenkins, Mark. *Washington Post*. January 7, 2012.
Morris, Wesley. *Boston Globe*. January 7, 2012.
Olsen, Mark. *Los Angeles Times*. January 7, 2012.
Phillips, Michael. *V*. January 6, 2012.
Punter, Jennie. *The Globe and Mail*. January 5, 2012.
Rabin, Nathan. *AV Club*. January 6, 2012.
Vizcarrondo, Sara Maria. *Box Office Magazine*. January 6, 2012.
Willmore, Alison. *Movieline*. January 6, 2012.

QUOTES

Isabella Rossi: "Let my mother go."
Maria Rossi: "You'll burn."

TRIVIA

Filmmakers Matthew Peterman and William Brent Bell first came up with the idea for the movie after reading an article about the Vatican starting a school for exorcism.

DIARY OF A WIMPY KID: DOG DAYS

Box Office: $49 million

For viewers of a certain age—mostly parents who have been roped into taking their younger charges—watching *Diary of a Wimpy Kid: Dog Days* will no doubt bring back memories of their own childhoods. That said, these memories will be centered not so much on the awkwardness of early adolescence that author Jeff Kinney has made a fortune on illustrating in his series of best-selling children's books as on the equally awkward live-action family films that Disney cranked out in the moribund period between the death of Walt Disney and the revival of the studio's fortunes in the mid-eighties that usually involved place-kicking mules, dogs running for local office and sentient Volkswagens. On the one hand, this is not necessarily a bad thing because the worst one could say about those films is that they were aggressively innocuous and, unlike most of the movies aimed strictly at younger viewers today, it does not traffic in the gross-out humor, sloppy slapstick and tiresome pop-culture references that have come to dominate the genre in recent years. On the other hand, while there is nothing especially bad about it, there is nothing about it that is likely to inspire anyone outside of its immediate target audience to voluntarily sit through the entire thing.

The film follows the low-key misadventures of ordinary kid Greg Heffley (Zachary Gordon) as he makes a bunch of mistakes and learns valuable lessons as a result. This time around, school has just ended for the year and Greg plans on spending the next three months doing nothing but watching television and playing video games. This plan does not meet with the approval of his father (Steve Zahn), who wants him to spend his time outside playing sports or participating in scouting. Neither of these things hold much appeal to Greg but when best pal Rowley (Robert Capron) takes him as his guest to the ritzy country club that his family belongs to, the place has everything he could possibly want—uncrowded pools, endless smoothies and the presence of Holly (Peyton List), the cute classmate he has a crush on. Thus begins a series of lies and deceptions in which Greg spends all of his time at the country club and claims to his father that he has a job there, a charade that grows more involved when he and Rowley have a falling out and he needs to resort to trickier methods of getting inside. Adding to the complications, Greg's creepy older brother Roderick, who appears to be only one ill-advised birthday present away from transforming the film into *We Need to Talk About Kevin* (2011), discovers the ruse and insists on getting in on it as well or else he will squeal.

Dog Days marks the third entry in the *Wimpy Kid* film franchise, following *Diary of a Wimpy Kid* (2010) and *Diary of a Wimpy Kid: Roderick Rules* (2011) and one of the key problems is that while he is pleasant and ingratiating enough, Gordon is beginning to look a little too old for the role of Greg. On the page, the character can remain the same age, of course, but on the screen, it is impossible to ignore the fact that Greg looks as though he is well past his tween years. Under normal circumstances, that would be awkward enough but it makes his lies, deceptions and general ignorance about the ways of the world a little more off-putting because he looks as though he is old enough to know better. Of course, the whole point of the film is to teach younger viewers the importance about taking responsibility for their actions but that notion, as sincere as it may be, never quite comes across as well as it should because there is never any real sense that our hero has actually learned from his actions—everything just sort of works out for him in the end. In addition, there is also a weirdly unpleasant bit in which Greg's mom (Rachel Harris) tries to start a book club for him and his friends that only conveys the notions that reading is for nerds and chumps, an idea that seems especially odd considering the film's literary background. As for its cinematic qualities, they are negligible at best as the whole thing has the look and feel of a television show—on the bright side, this will allow it to have a smooth transition in its presumably quick journey to home video.

For younger audiences, *Diary of a Wimpy Kid: Dog Days* is serviceable enough, though it does seem at times to subconsciously suggesting that they would be better off playing outside than wasting their time watching it. For those of a somewhat advanced age—anyone reading this review, for example—it can be missed with impunity. However, it should be mentioned that while the film as a whole has nothing to offer older viewers, it does have a couple of amusing quirks that should keep them from completely hating it. There is the scene in which Dad threatens to disconnect the video games for the entire summer and realizes that he cannot discern which of the numerous cords emerging from the back of the television are the right ones. There is the amusingly squirmy moment in which Greg is forced to play a game called *I Love You Because* with Rowley and his oddball parents. Best of all, there is the bit in which father and son engineer a triumph of sorts at a scouting event and then simultaneously come to the realization that camping out is decidedly inferior to spending the night in a comfortable hotel room eating pizza. *Dog Days* may have a few mixed messages here and there but that one rings loud and clear.

Peter Sobczynski

CREDITS

Greg Heffley: Zachary Gordon
Rowley Jefferson: Robert Capron
Rodrick Heffley: Devon Bostick
Frank Heffley: Steve Zahn
Susan Heffley: Rachael Harris
Holly Hills: Peyton List
Patty Farrell: Laine MacNeil
Origin: United States
Language: English
Released: 2012
Production: Nina Jacobson, Brad Simpson; Fox 2000 Pictures, Color Force, Dune Entertainment; released by 20th Century-Fox
Directed by: David Bowers
Written by: Gabe Sachs

Cinematography by: Anthony B. Richmond
Music by: Edward Shearmur
Sound: Donald Sylvester
Editing: Troy Takaki
Costumes: Monique Prudhomme
Production Design: Brent Thomas
MPAA rating: PG
Running time: 99 minutes

REVIEWS

Bowles, Scott. *USA Today*. August 2, 2012.
Clarke, Donald. *Irish Times*. August 3, 2012.
Drake, Grae. *Movies.com*. August 7, 2012.
Genzlinger, Neil. *New York Times*. August 2, 2012.
Goss, William. *Film.com*. August 2, 2012.
Guzman, Rafer. *Newsday*. August 3, 2012.
Neumaier, Joe. *New York Daily News*. August 2, 2012.
Phillips, Michael. *Chicago Tribune*. August 2, 2012.
Pinkerton, Nick. *Village Voice*. August 3, 2012.
Rabin, Nathan. *AV Club*. August 2, 2012.

QUOTES

Greg Heffley: "I can't believe it's so crowded here. Maybe we should come back."
Rodrick Heffley: "How about never? Does never sound good?"

TRIVIA

Director David Bowers can be seen when Greg and his Father are laying on the bed in the Hotel room as Lil' Cute writer son.

THE DICTATOR

Box Office: $59.7 million

At his best, Sacha Baron Cohen is a daredevil satirist of the highest caliber. It is in the real world that his cheerfully offensive personas tend to truly come alive. When Borat tests the patience of a genial grocery store clerk by asking him to identify every individual piece of cheese in stock or when Bruno asks some raucous party boys to deliver their lines with "more energy" or when Ali G asks a Catholic priest whether he thinks God is "an over-hyped David Blaine," Cohen is in full command of his comedic genius.

The Dictator takes Cohen out of his comfort zone and into the realm of the scripted narrative, a realm that Cohen has not attempted to work within since his 2002 direct-to-DVD vehicle, *Ali G Indahouse*. Though *The Dictator* is not nearly as disastrous, it still falls short of the scathing hilarity audiences have come to expect from

his work. The opening title card that states, "In loving memory of Kim Jong-il" suggests a more pointed satire than the slapstick-heavy farce that follows. The humor here is less sociological than it is scatological.

Consider Cohen's new comic creation of General Aladeen, the impulsive tyrant who rules over the Republic of Wadiya with an iron fist. He delivers death sentences with a casual wave of his hand, but his childish impishness is meant to gloss over his detestable nature. Once Aladeen is thrust into the Big Apple and replaced at home by a clueless double (also played by Cohen), the film devolves into a strained fish-out-of-water comedy all too evocative of the botched *Arthur* remake. Just as Russell Brand hammered his trademark charisma into the ground, Cohen runs the risk of losing his audience by sticking to the same familiar formula.

While Borat and Bruno encountered real bigotry on the big screen, Aladeen meets a series of caricatures played too broadly to generate much momentum. Director and longtime Cohen collaborator Larry Charles seems to have taken his cue from anarchic Will Ferrell comedies where the gags fly so fast that the hits tend to overshadow the misses. Some of the jokes are so ludicrous that they inspire laughs of sheer incredulity. While under the glaringly false name of "Allison," Aladeen is asked by a compassionate liberal activist, Zoey (Anna Faris), for his last name. Aladeen's eyes search for a nearby word, landing on a sign advertising "Haffezi's Burgers." Naturally, Aladeen chooses "Burgers."

There are a handful of squirm-inducing sight gags, such as a terrorist video game with a level set during the Munich Olympics, but for the most part, *The Dictator* plays it too safe. That is especially surprising considering Cohen's fearlessness during his promotional appearances, which included dumping ashes on Ryan Seacrest, whose astonishing degree of vapid hollowness is arguably more offensive than anything Borat or Bruno have ever said. Not only does Cohen tiptoe around the provocative potential of his premise, but the script also recycles groan-inducing sketches that appear stolen from less ambitious fare like *Harold and Kumar 2* (2008) and *Scary Movie 4* (2006).

As usual, Cohen's goofball is paired with a straight-man sidekick in order to inspire some routine odd couple banter. Jason Mantzoukas does a fine job as the perturbed Wadiyan who convinces Aladeen to reclaim his rightful throne, while offering him a few sobering doses of reality. Aladeen is shocked, for example to learn that the entirety of his country did not, in fact, enjoy his performance in the alleged hit film, *You've Got Mail Bomb*. Yet there is an extended sketch onboard a helicopter that does not really work at all as Cohen and Mantzoukas proceed to indirectly play on the post-9/11 paranoia of a neurotic white couple. This gag was delivered far better and with much briefer screen time in *Harold and Kumar 2,* with Kal Penn paying homage to *Annie Hall* (1977) in the process.

This is perhaps the best showcase for the oft-miscast Faris since *Smiley Face* (2007), and her scenes with Cohen generate a comic energy of their own. The fervent conviction with which she defends the misunderstood "Allison Burgers" is disarmingly sweet, and Aladeen's unconventional work ethic at Zoey's organic food store leads to some inspired pratfalls. Though many of the raunchier set-pieces are gratuitous, there is a priceless moment when Zoey introduces Aladeen to the wonders of masturbation, thus providing him with a viable alternative to bedding countless women.

At a running time barely clocking in over 80 minutes, *The Dictator* is a very slight picture indeed. It is the sort of film that Cohen fans will undoubtedly purchase just to watch the supplemental material left on the cutting room floor, which is often funnier than anything in the final cut. Though it is a classic example of "too little too late," Aladeen does fire off a brilliant climactic monologue asking Americans to imagine the benefits of living under a dictatorship. "You could let one percent of the people have all the nation's wealth," Aladeen gushes. "You could help your rich friends get richer by cutting their taxes. And bailing them out when they gamble and lose." The monologue may be more Colbert than Cohen, but it will do.

Matt Fagerholm

CREDITS

Aladeen/Efawadh: Sacha Baron Cohen
Omar: Sayed Badreya
Tamir: Ben Kingsley
Herself: Megan Fox
Zoey: Anna Faris
Origin: United States
Language: English, French, Spanish
Released: 2012
Production: Anthony Hines, Scott Rudin, Todd Schulman, Sacha Baron Cohen, Alec Berg, David Mandel, Jeff Schaffer; Four by Two Film; released by Paramount Pictures
Directed by: Larry Charles
Written by: Sacha Baron Cohen; Alec Berg; David Mandel; Jeff Schaffer
Cinematography by: Lawrence Sher
Music by: Erran Baron Cohen
Sound: Andrew Decristofaro
Music Supervisor: Richard Henderson
Editing: Greg Hayden; Eric Kissack

Art Direction: Greg Berry
Costumes: Jeffrey Kurland
Production Design: Victor Kempster
MPAA rating: R
Running time: 83 minutes

REVIEWS

Corliss, Richard. *Time.* May 11, 2012.
Ebert, Roger. *Chicago Sun-Times.* May 11, 2012.
Jones, J. R. *Chicago Reader.* May 15, 2012.
Kohn, Eric. *indieWIRE.* May 14, 2012.
Lumenick, Lou. *New York Post.* May 16, 2012.
Schwarzbaum, Lisa. *Entertainment Weekly.* May 15, 2012.
Scott, A. O. *New York Times.* May 15, 2012.
Tobias, Scott. *AV Club.* May 14, 2012.
Williams, Joe. *St. Louis Post-Dispatch.* May 15, 2012.
Zacharek, Stephanie. *Movieline.* May 15, 2012.

QUOTES

General Aladeen: "I love it when women go to school. It's like seeing a monkey on rollerskates. It means nothing to them, but it's so adorable for us."

TRIVIA

The language that Aladeen and Nadal speak on the helicopter tour is actually Hebrew and not Arabic.

DJANGO UNCHAINED

Life, liberty, and the pursuit of vengeance.
—Movie tagline

This Christmas, Django is off the chain.
—Movie tagline

The "D" is silent. Payback won't be.
—Movie tagline

Box Office: $159.1 million

Quentin Tarantino's eighth film as a director turned out to be not only one of his most controversial (and the longest) but also the highest-grossing entry in an increasingly notable filmography. Every Tarantino film seems to matter now in much the way that late works by Stanley Kubrick resonated every time he chose to release one. He may not make movies that often (eight films in twenty years is a snail's pace compared to most of his contemporaries) but there is a sense that each film matters. This one did so to the tune of over $340 million worldwide (and counting; it was still in the top ten at the time of this review), nearly universal acclaim (despite controversies regarding race and movie violence), and an impressive five Oscar nominations. Tarantino's way with words and plotting are as honed as ever here and he proves yet again to work brilliantly with ensemble, drawing great performances from half a dozen actors and good ones from the rest. The film is smart, funny, action-packed, and as stylish as one would expect from a director whose obsessions seem to have settled in the Spaghetti Western genre. There is, to be fair, a feeling that this work was rushed to get it done in time for 2012 awards consideration and that another month in the editing bay could have resulted in a true masterpiece (and one missed Tarantino's longtime editor and collaborator, Sally Menke, who passed away in 2010 and had edited all of his previous films), but few can deny that this work comes awfully close to greatness, like most Tarantino films in his increasingly impressive career.

A chain gang of slaves crosses a wintery plain. Among them is a man named Django (Jamie Foxx), seemingly alike the other man to whom he is chained. A mysterious figure with a horse and carriage comes out of the darkness. It is Dr. King Schultz (Christoph Waltz), a bounty hunter masquerading as a dentist. Schultz makes clear that he does not believe in the practice of buying men but he needs Django's help and so he purchases the slave. Django used to be the slave of three men for whom Schultz has been assigned justice. The slave helps the bounty hunter and the two form a unique friendship. Schultz agrees to help Django complete his moral and emotional assignment: Finding his true love, Broomhilda (Kerry Washington), who has been purchased by the notoriously evil Calvin Candie (Leonardo DiCaprio). Tarantino's film builds to what is essentially a scene that takes up the entire third act at "Candie Land," a place where Django must pretend to be a Mandingo fighting expert before unleashing hot lead on his love's tormentors and owners. Samuel L. Jackson, Walton Goggins, and Don Johnson co-star in small but crucial roles.

While it is the writer/director's longest script, *Django Unchained* is also arguably Quentin Tarantino's most straightforward piece of work. There are not the chronological jumps of films like *Pulp Fiction* (1994) or *Kill Bill* (2003-04) and the story is relatively simple—two men devise a plan to save a slave in the name of love. It is what and how Tarantino builds on this simple story that matters. He had to answer too many questions about race (and the film's copious use of the n-word) and movie violence (especially as the topic rose in the national consciousness after gun violence became the most important subject of early 2013) but the fact is that the writer/director wove those questions into his film. He tried to dismiss some of them by arguing that *Django* was escapism but that too easily ignores the intellectual approach to race and violence that he is clearly taking here. Take for example that Candie is a fan of Mandingo fighting, brutally pitting his biggest slaves up against each other in fights that often result in death. While what Candie is doing is loathsome, he is using a situation (his power over slaves) to his entertainment. Is it not at least part of what Tarantino is doing as well—using slavery as a foundation for escapism? And Tarantino brilliantly handles his time period's emotional beats. A scene in which Broomhilda is removed from a hot box to the disgust of Django, Schultz, and the audience, has the greatest emotional impact of any in Tarantino's career. He can dismiss questions of serious subject matter with interviews to not have to address stupid queries but there is more going on here than pure escapism.

Django Unchained is a film that works on multiple levels. It features some daring tonal shifts that make the brutality of the action feel more honest than a lot of Tarantino's movies. In the final, incredible scenes at Candie Land, easily the peak of the film and some of the best scenes of the year, everyone on-screen is hiding something from Django pretending to be a Mandingo expert to Broomhilda pretending she does not know him to Samuel L. Jackson's memorable turn as a loyal butler with plenty to hide. No one is really who they purport to be and Tarantino has a blast here in something that plays not unlike an extended version of the scene in the bar in *Inglourious Basterds,* in which tension grows out of concern of a double agent's status being revealed.

While the final hour of *Django* is close to cinematic perfection, the middle one sags a bit, especially in scenes that go on too long or one that never should have made it in the first place. A sequence after Django and Schultz's first assignment in which Jonah Hill makes a cameo as a KKK member with a bag over his head that does not fit is a true embarrassment and one that probably would have ended up a DVD deleted scene in Sally Menke's editing room. Even without Menke, one can sometimes see truth in the rumors that Tarantino was rushed to get the film done by the end of 2012 and that he could have fine-tuned some of the pacing issues with more time to do so. The film also limps to its ending instead of providing a powerhouse one, as everything after Candie Land, particularly a nauseatingly bad bit of business with Tarantino cameo-ing as an Australian, could have been cut. Except for one great image of Candie Land's refugees walking down a moonlit street, it is all a waste of time.

Performances are stellar throughout, particularly Waltz, who shares nearly every scene with the more stoic Foxx and has five times the dialogue but was deemed eligible for the Academy Award for Best Supporting Actor in one of the most startling cases of miscategorization in the association's history. He is a co-lead in every way and a fantastic one at that. Dr. King

Schultz is a charismatic manipulator, a person who has a gift with words but starts to feel the weight of his conscience as the film goes on. It is a great character and Waltz knocks it out of the park. As for true supporting roles, Leonardo DiCaprio, Samuel Jackson, Walton Goggins (who reportedly took his small-but-crucial role after Kurt Russell dropped out), and Kerry Washington are all great.

Quentin Tarantino has revealed that he expects to only make one to two more films before retiring as a director, ending a career with ten great movies instead of two dozen modest ones. A decade ago, the assertion that anyone could make ten great movies with nary a misstep might have sounded like bragging. Now that Tarantino is eighty percent of the way there, it sounds likely.

Brian Tallerico

CREDITS

Django: Jamie Foxx
Calvin Candie: Leonardo DiCaprio
King Schultz: Christoph Waltz
Broomhilda von Shaft: Kerry Washington
Stephen: Samuel L. Jackson
Ace Speck: James Remar
Big Daddy: Don Johnson
Leonide Moguy: Dennis Christopher
Billy Crash: Walton Goggins
Mr. Stonesipher: David Steen
Lara Lee Candie-Fitzwilly: Laura Cayouette
D'Artagnan: Ato Essandoh
Bar Patron: Franco Nero
Dicky Speck: James Russo
U.S. Marshall Gill Tatum: Tom Wopat
Sheriff Bill Sharp: Don Stroud
Old Man Carrucan: Bruce Dern
Big John Brittle: M.C. Gainey
Lil' Raj Brittle: Cooper Huckabee
LeQuint Dickey Mining Co. employee: Michael Parks
Bag Head #2: Jonah Hill
Cora: Dana Michelle Gourrier
Betina: Miriam F. Glover
Sheba: Nichole Galicia
Son of a Gunfighter: Russ Tamblyn
Daughter of a Son of a Gunfighter: Amber Tamblyn
LeQuint Dickey Mining employee: Quentin Tarantino
Origin: United States
Language: English
Released: 2012
Production: Reginald Hudlin, Pilar Savone, Stacey Sher; Columbia Pictures; released by Weinstein Company

Directed by: Quentin Tarantino
Written by: Quentin Tarantino
Cinematography by: Robert Richardson
Sound: Wylie Stateman
Editing: Fred Raskin
Costumes: Sharen Davis
Production Design: J. Michael Riva
MPAA rating: R
Running time: 165 minutes

REVIEWS

Bradshaw, Peter. *The Guardian.* December 12, 2012.
Debruge, Peter. *Variety.* December 12, 2012.
Ebert, Roger. *Chicago Sun-Times.* January 8, 2013.
Foundas, Scott. *Village Voice.* December 18, 2012.
LaSalle, Mick. *San Francisco Chronicle.* December 26, 2012.
Morgenstern, Joe. *Wall Street Journal.* January 3, 2013.
Rabin, Nathan. *AV Club.* December 26, 2012.
Sharkey, Betsy. *Los Angeles Times.* December 26, 2012.
Williams, Joe. *St. Louis Post-Dispatch.* December 26, 2012.
Zacharek, Stephanie. *NPR.* December 27, 2012.

QUOTES

Calvin Candie: "Your boss looks a little green around the gills."
Django: "He just ain't used to seein' a man ripped apart by dogs is all."
Calvin Candie: "But you are used to it?"
Django: "I'm just a little more used to Americans than he is."

TRIVIA

Although the film is technically a part of the western genre, Quentin Tarantino prefers to refer to the film as a "southern" due to the film's setting in America's deep south.

AWARDS

Oscars 2012: Actor—Supporting (Waltz), Orig. Screenplay
British Acad. 2012: Actor—Supporting (Waltz), Orig. Screenplay
Golden Globes 2013: Actor—Supporting (Waltz), Screenplay
Nominations:
Oscars 2012: Cinematog., Film, Sound FX Editing
British Acad. 2012: Director (Tarantino), Film Editing, Sound
Golden Globes 2013: Actor—Supporting (DiCaprio), Director (Tarantino), Film—Drama

THE DO-DECA-PENTATHLON

25 Events, 2 Brothers, 1 Champion.
    —Movie tagline

Box Office: $10,000

After flirting with relative fame by making acclaimed works with John C. Reilly & Jonah Hill (*Cyrus* [2010]) and Ed Helms & Jason Segel (*Jeff, Who Lives at Home* [2012]), writer/directors/brothers Jay & Mark Duplass returned to their indie mumblecore roots (*The Puffy Chair* [2005], *Baghead* [2008]) with the personal, minor-key *The Do-Deca-Pentathlon* about two brothers and the competitive nature that can sometimes arise from sibling rivalry. The film was actually shot before the brothers' more high-profile comedies (but after their two mumblecore breakthroughs) but released after and one can easily see how it influenced *Cyrus* and *Jeff*, two films that also play with the way otherwise mature men can be reduced to children around each other. *Pentathlon* is a bit too slight for its own good, a work that might have worked better as a true short film (believe it or not, it does not have quite enough story or dramatic weight even to fill its brief 76-minute running time) but there is an honesty to the unique dynamic of brotherhood that makes it likable enough to serve as the bridge for Mark & Jay Duplass from indie respectability to relatively mainstream success.

The film is reportedly loosely based on actual brothers who lived down the street from the Duplass brothers as they grew up and the in-house competition they ran. Mark (Steve Zissis) is, like so many suburbanites, content more than he is happy. He is a relatively average guy who goes through the motions of work and married life. If someone asked him if he was happy, he would probably answer yes, but there does not seem to be an abundance of reasons to make him so. Mark has an estranged brother named Jeremy (Mark Kelly) who just happens to show up at their mom's house while Mark is visiting. Jeremy sparks something in Mark, something competitive and generally unhealthy but something that also seems to give more purpose to Mark's life. It turns out that reason that Mark and Jeremy are estranged can be traced back to "The Do-Deca-Pentathlon," a three-day competition that the pair devised when they were teenagers. With twenty-five events in all (like who can hold their breath longer underwater, arm wrestling, and basic sprints down the street), Mark & Jeremy find their competitive spirit awakened. It is almost as if they were both in some sort of paused life mode until they could resume the pentathlon that had been interrupted by a mother worried one would drown so many years earlier. Despite strong disapproval from Mark's wife (Jennifer Lafleur), a winner must be determined.

The best element of Duplass' work here, and it is true of most of their work, is the believability of the core relationships. Just as with Segel & Helms in *Jeff*, the most essential ingredient is that one believes the honesty of the brother dynamic. Siblings act differently than any other relationship. And it is clear that the real-

life brotherhood of Jay & Mark has deeply influenced their work. One instantly finds the competitive, bickering, and yet loving nature of Jeremy & Mark truthful and that cannot be underestimated as to how much it impacts the relative success of the film. If one does not "buy" these two men as brothers, the film collapses before anything else can be built on that foundation.

Sadly, the Duplass boys do not place what one hopes they would on that grounded foundation. There just is not much to *The Do-Deca-Pentathlon*. Brothers are competitive. Wives and mothers often do not understand the apparent lunacy of what goes on between boys raised in the same household. And the competitive drive of relatives to beat one another at silly games often hides a deeper sadness at being beaten down by life in general. These are pretty safe, borderline boring themes and *Pentathlon* accomplishes the remarkable feat of feeling long even at under 80 minutes. One wonders if the film would not have worked better as a short or if it needed a few more characters and a more notable final act plot turn to really resonate. As is, it too much feels like a movie that was not fully fleshed out and just sort of ends instead of having a notable conclusion.

Audiences barely had a chance to even see *The Do-Deca-Pentathlon* as the film made a stunningly miniscule $10k in theaters, never playing beyond eight screens, notably less than even *Baghead,* which made fourteen times as much. One gets the feeling that Jay & Mark Duplass have yet to really make the best works of their career. They continue to hone their craft as filmmakers and are likely to produce notable films in the '10s, '20s, and maybe even beyond. As they get more famous and dissected by critics, *The Do-Deca-Penathlon* will be more widely recognized as just a decent film but also an interesting bridge between their independent phase and the more Hollywood works they would do right after.

Brian Tallerico

CREDITS

Jeremy: Mark Kelly
Mark: Steve Zissis
Stephanie: Jennifer LaFleur
Alice: Julie Vorus
Origin: United States
Language: English
Released: 2012
Production: Stephanie Langhoff, Mark Duplass, Jay Duplass; Red Flag Releasing; released by Fox Searchlight
Directed by: Mark Duplass; Jay Duplass
Written by: Mark Duplass; Jay Duplass
Cinematography by: Jas Shelton

Music by: Julian Wass
Sound: John Chalfant
Editing: Jay Denby; Nat Sanders
Costumes: Ross Partridge; Marguerite Phillips
MPAA rating: R
Running time: 76 minutes

REVIEWS

Baumgarten, Marjorie. *Austin Chronicle.* July 6, 2012.
Fine, Marshall. *Hollywood & Fine.* July 9, 2012.
Grierson, Tim. *IFC.com.* July 9, 2012.
Hartl, John. *Seattle Times.* July 5, 2012.
Kohn, Eric. *indieWIRE.* July 9, 2012.
Levy, Shawn. *Oregonian.* July 9, 2012.
Neumaier, Joe. *New York Daily News.* July 9, 2012.
Rozen, Leah. *The Wrap.* July 9, 2012.
Simon, Brent. *Shockya.com.* July 15, 2012.
Smith, Kyle. *New York Post.* .

DR. SEUSS' THE LORAX
(The Lorax)

Box Office: $214 million

It is hard to imagine studio executives out there who would read a Dr. Seuss book and believe it would make for a great feature-length film. Yet, they do and they keep trying to turn these odd little poems and fables into cinematic gold. It has yet to really work. Aside from the classic TV adaptation of Dr. Seuss' *How The Grinch Stole Christmas,* the road from book-to-film for the Dr. Seuss library has been bumpy at best. Both *How the Grinch Stole Christmas* (2000) and *Cat in the Hat* (2003) had Jim Carrey and Mike Myers, respectively, buried in large costumes amidst an obnoxious array of empty-headed supporting characters, thin storylines and an overall feeling of desperation. They could not have been more lacking in charm. In spite of the fact that both films made money, nobody wanted to give a live-action adaptation another try.

The animated *Horton Hears a Who!* (2008) certainly faired better and it seemed to suit the material in a more faithful and appropriate manner. While still not great, at least it signaled how the Dr. Seuss movies should be done if they are to keep being used as a source for inspiration. Now, with *Dr. Seuss' The Lorax,* which made an impressive amount of money upon its release, it seems there is no stopping the Seuss adaptations. This film at least has meat on its bones in terms of storyline, which is a lot more than can be said for *Cat in the Hat.* This has a couple of stories going on as well as a message about the environment that is meant to encourage its young audience to plant more trees.

Who is The Lorax? It just so happens that The Lorax (voiced by Danny DeVito) introduces himself right at the outset against a red curtain backdrop. The Lorax is a short, roundish orange man with a big Wilford Brimley-like mustache. The story takes place in Thneedville, which is introduced to the viewer via a big musical number. Everything in Thneedville is up on the technology. Everything is processed, including the trees, which are inflatable. Nobody is suspicious when kids swim in a little pond and come out with a radioactive glow. The air in Thneedville comes via O'Hare Air, a corporation headed by the town's mayor, Aloysius O'Hare (voiced by Rob Riggle).

The story narrows in on a boy named Ted (voiced by Zac Efron) whose friend Audrey (voiced by Taylor Swift) is a girl he has a crush on and who is fascinated by growing real trees. He asks his mom if such a tree exists anywhere. His grandmother (voiced by Betty White) advises him to seek out a person called The Once-ler (voiced by Ed Helms). Ted has to venture far outside of Thneedville in order to find this person, which he eventually does. From there, the story goes into flashback mode as The Once-ler tells Ted about how there came to be no more trees in Thneedville. Turns out The Once-ler had invented a piece of clothing or apparel called the Thneed. All he needs to do in order to make them is get some wool from the cottony looking trees.

The Thneed turns out to be a big success and soon, all the trees are put to use as the demand grows for more Thneeds. The Once-ler and his invention turn in a huge profit and, suddenly, Thneedville becomes the thriving town it is today but not without protests from The Lorax, the little orange man who fights for the trees. Where The Once-ler sees major success, The Lorax sees an environmental catastrophe as thousands of animals go homeless, oil pollutes the rivers and nature takes a backseat to corporate greed. When the story shifts back to present day, Ted sees it has his responsibility to put things right in Thneedville, but not without a fight from Mayor O'Hare, who is selling a new brand of air.

Dr. Seuss' The Lorax has all the right ingredients to make a film that kids will find entertaining and thoughtful. A movie that encourages kids to plant more trees certainly has its heart in the right place. The film has a wonderfully detailed visual palette. Thneedville and the forests look like just the kind of bent reality in which Dr. Seuss characters typically exist. The musical numbers—and there are many—raise the energy of the narrative while stretching the film out to its 86 minute running time, even if they do not produce any songs really worth remembering. There are also plenty of cute, colorful and funny background critters and characters to amuse and delight the film's young target audience.

Adults, on the other hand, might not take to it as much. The film was written by Ken Daurio and directed by Chris Renaud and Kyle Balda. Daurio and Renaud wrote and directed *Despicable Me* (2010), respectively, which was equally madcap, inventive and had the comedic pace of a Tex Avery cartoon mixed with a Warner Bros. sensibility (particularly in its violence). While not entirely successful as a film, it had a good-sized heart. With *Dr. Seuss' The Lorax,* this writing-directing team too often overdo it one way or another. For instance, when the Lorax character is summoned after the chopping down of a tree, the movie awkwardly shifts from a big, hallucinatory musical number to a lament on the first fallen tree in the forest. Up to this point, the movie has been trying so hard to rattle the senses while going for broad laughs. To suddenly ask the audience to be moved by such a dramatic event feels a bit disingenuous.

It does not help matters that the character of Ted is voiced by Zac Efron, who sounds way too old to be giving voice to a nine-year-old boy, a distraction that makes it hard for the viewer to truly be engaged in the story. DeVito, of course, is perfectly cast as the wise-cracking, but determined Lorax. But Daurio's script might have benefited from another rewrite or two in order to balance out the comedy, music and pathos. Too much of everything with little regard for set-up, rhythm and pay-off can make for a truly disjointed viewing experience. A parent could do a lot worse than to have their kids watch a sometimes-charming fable on the importance of trees, but they could also do better by just reading them the book at an early, impressionable age.

Collin Souter

CREDITS

The Lorax: Danny DeVito (Voice)
Ted: Zac Efron (Voice)
Audrey: Taylor Swift (Voice)
Once-ler: Ed Helms (Voice)
O'Hare: Rob Riggle (Voice)
Grammy Norma: Betty White (Voice)
Marta: Willow Smith (Voice)
Origin: United States
Language: English
Released: 2012
Production: Janet Healy, Christopher Meledandri; Illumination Entertainment; released by Universal Pictures
Directed by: Chris Renaud; Kyle Balda
Written by: Cinco Paul; Ken Daurio
Music by: John Powell
Sound: Dennis Leonard

Music Supervisor: Massimo Ruberto
Editing: Claire Dodgson; Steven Lui; Ken Schretzmann
Art Direction: Eric Guillon
Production Design: Yarrow Cheney
MPAA rating: PG
Running time: 94 minutes

REVIEWS

Covert, Colin. *Minneapolis Star Tribune.* March 1, 2012.
Diones, Bruce. *New Yorker.* March 19, 2012.
Gleiberman, Owen. *Entertainment Weekly.* February 29, 2012.
Goodykoontz, Bill. *Arizona Republic.* March 1, 2012.
Guzman, Rafer. *Newsday.* March 2, 2012.
Morris, Wesley. *Boston Globe.* March 1, 2012.
O'Sullivan, Michael. *Washington Post.* March 2, 2012.
Sachs, Ben. *Chicago Reader.* March 2, 2012.
Smith, Kyle. *New York Post.* March 2, 2012.
Whitty, Stephen. *Newark Star-Ledger.* March 2, 2012.

QUOTES

Once-ler: "It's a girl, isn't it?"
Ted: "What? No!"
Once-ler: "Really? Because when a guy does something stupid once, well, that's because he's guy. But he does the same stupid thing twice, that's usually to impress some girl."

TRIVIA

This is the first film to feature Universal's 100th Anniversary logo.

DREDD

Judgment is coming.
—Movie tagline

Box Office: $13.4 million

To comic book fans, Judge Dredd is one of the later characters created not by rivals Marvel or DC but as part of a British anthology series. To movie fans, *Judge Dredd* (1995) is a notorious Sylvester Stallone film that all but sealed the fate that the character would not expand its fan base off the colored pages. Ironically, an enforcer that is not exactly fond of second chances with his brand of on-the-spot justice has been given just that. Seventeen years after the film which helped stall Stallone's mid-'90s momentum, the character has been put in the hands of even lesser-known names in the hopes that the only name that matters is the one in the title. Everyone knows Batman, Superman and Spider-Man. The run-off of films that led up to *The Avengers* (2012) familiarized uninitiated audiences and even those that missed one or all of them got more than the basic gist from just going in blind. Pete Travis' updating of Judge Joseph Dredd almost assumes that it is strictly for die-hard fans or those with faint memories of this uncomplicated law enforcer.

Those falling into neither category should know that in the future, an east coast metropolis known as Mega-City One is a crime-ridden wasteland that makes the Big Apple of *Escape from New York* (1981) look like Oz. Keeping order are the Judges who respond to whatever crimes they can find and then offer an immediate sentence that is usually death. On this particular day, Dredd (Karl Urban) has been given a temporary partner in Anderson (Olivia Thirlby). Actually he is tasked to observe her on the job seeing as how she has failed the necessary test to earn the title of a full Judge. Unfortunate that her added psychic skills could not show her the day they were in for.

Former prostitute turned drug lord, Madeline Madrigal or "Ma-Ma" for short (Lena Headey) has been taking control of a new drug called "Slo-Mo." After giving her competition a demonstration of the product before throwing their bodies down a 200-story high-rise, Dredd & Anderson make a psychic connection with one of Ma-Ma's chief enforcers, Kay (Wood Harris). As they try to remove their pre-judged suspect from the same building, Ma-Ma seals off the exits and orders a full-scale siege to track down the Judges and kill them.

Dredd has some bloody deaths for sure, but minus a build-up of excitement, tension and general rooting interest in an objective, the shock of a brutal demise is the only thing to hit the reaction button. The action sequences themselves are not well-designed or executed and that leaves *Dredd*'s "drop the mic" moments to have all the style inherent in qn average snuff film. Quality kills in movies that pride themselves on it—usually horror and action—are practically their own art form but Dredd lacks the needed satisfaction to at least partially justify its brutality.

The Dredd character himself is one designed to fantasize our own guarded bloodlust for vigilante justice in a world of semantics, technicalities, and corruption of the law on both sides. Naturally then his arc in a self-contained film exists to either justify or vilify his existence as an on-the-spot executioner. This was the conundrum in Stallone's version—and to far greater effect in *Minority Report* (2002)—as to what happens when the Judge becomes the judged, especially when they are innocent. This incarnation attempts to play within those boundaries around the more empathetic Anderson, but Dredd is such a non-entity of anything but force and a chin that one barely gets a handle on what he stands for and if it should be supported. Unlike

the best-if-unconnected version of Judge Dredd to date, Paul Verhoeven's *Robocop* (1987), *Dredd* makes no effort at the inherent satire of using violence to bring peace to a violent world nor audience acceptance of it as entertainment. After Zack Snyder took John Woo's slow-down of action beats into the digital effects age with *300* (2006), this would have been the perfect opportunity to satirize its effect on the visual cortex via the core drug that is being fought over.

Ang Lee's *Hulk* (2003) was trivialized by fans for its liberties with the storyline and lack of "Hulk Smash" action which led to the opportunity to claim Louis Leterrier's reboot *The Incredible Hulk* (2008) as the version they always wanted. Jonathan Hensleigh's *The Punisher* (2004) did not have a far trip to outclass Dolph Lundgren's 1989 attempt as the avenging Frank Castle, but still failed. The reboot of the reboot, *Punisher: War Zone* (2008), was mildly more successful in matching the violent nature of the comic and also featured a climax involving a trip through a leveled building to catch the bad guy. Is it conceivable that the detractors of *Spider-Man 3* (2007) then over praised the lackluster *The Amazing Spider-Man* (2012) out of pure spite? That is why comic books are comic books, television is television and why movies must stand on their own even when there is an earlier failure to measure it against.

Erik Childress

CREDITS

Judge Dredd: Karl Urban
Cassandra Anderson: Olivia Thirlby
Madeline "Ma-Ma" Madrigal: Lena Headey
Kay: Wood Harris
Judge Lex: Langley Kirkwood
Origin: United States
Language: English
Released: 2012
Production: Andrew Macdonald, Allon Reich, Alex Garland; DNA Films Ltd., Reliance Entertainment; released by Lionsgate
Directed by: Pete Travis
Written by: Alex Garland
Cinematography by: Anthony Dod Mantle
Music by: Paul Leonard-Morgan
Sound: Conrad Kuhne
Editing: Mark Eckersley
Costumes: Michael O'Connor
Production Design: Mark Digby
MPAA rating: R
Running time: 95 minutes

REVIEWS

Berardinelli, James. *ReelViews*. September 18, 2012.
Dargis, Manohla. *New York Times*. September 20, 2012.

Fine, Marshall. *Hollywood & Fine*. September 21, 2012.

Kohn, Eric. *Indiewire*. September 20, 2012.

McWeeny, Drew. *HitFix*. September 9, 2012.

Miller, Neil. *Film School Rejects*. September 21, 2012.

Orndorf, Brian. *Blu-ray.com*. September 21, 2012.

Phipps, Keith. *AV Club*. September 20, 2012.

Rocchi, James. *MSN Movies*. September 10, 2012.

Weinberg, Scott. *FearNet*. September 22, 2012.

QUOTES

Judge Dredd: "In case you have forgotten, this block operates under the same rules as the rest of the city. Ma-Ma is not the law. I am the law."

TRIVIA

With the exception of Peach Tree, the city blocks are all named after notable *2000 AD* creators and characters.

E

ELENA

Box Office: $233,380

Andrey Zvyagintsev's *Elena,* winner of the Special Jury Prize at the 2011 Cannes Film Festival, opens with such a deliberate and long shot of sunlight just starting to hit a Moscow apartment that one begins to think that the film has somehow paused itself. It is a slow, methodical pace that Zvyagintsev will continue throughout his noir, a work that contains very bad deeds but presents them in such a clinical, detached manner as to remove them of all melodrama or sentiment. It is the story of a woman who crosses cultural, economic, and social stratum in her new immediate family who finds herself at a moral crossroads and simply chooses a path to take, forever redefining her future and that of her family. Zvyagintsev's film is mesmerizing in its cool detachment from a subject that would typically be handled painted in melodramatic colors. With an incredible central performance from Nadezhda Markina, *Elena* became one of the most memorable title characters of 2012.

Elena (Markina) crosses social and economic strata. She is an average-looking, middle-aged woman, who is first met in the more luxurious half of her life. Years earlier, Elena was the nurse to a wealthy patient named Vladimir (Andrey Smirov) and is now his late-in-life wife. She clearly still tends to his needs. They sleep separately and much of her daily routine seems to be in service of Vladimir, although Zvyagintsev is careful to show that Elena is no mere servant. Elena and Vladimir still have a sex life and seem to enjoy each other's

company. In fact, if not for their children, they may go on living satisfied lives for years.

In what could be read as a subtle commentary on the current generation being problematic for the older generation in Russia, all of the problems in *Elena* stem from the children of Elena and Vladimir, both from previous relationships. Elena's son Sergei (Alexey Rozin) lives on the other side of Moscow (and Zvyagintsev is careful to track the journey Elena has to take to visit him, almost as if she is descending a ladder through the city's classes). Sergei is introduced playing video games as he awaits the cash being brought him by his mother, courtesy of her new relationship. The implication is clearly that Sergei is doing little to advance his own position in society in any way. He has a steady stream of what he needs from his new stepfather and that is where his ambition ends.

Problems arise when Sergei's son Sasha (Igor Ogurtsov) faces possibly being drafted into the Russian Army. He could go to school to avoid combat but that will require significantly more cash from dear old stepdad and Vladimir is hesitant to donate to the college fund. Perhaps the Army is just what the little brat needs.

Elena is understandably upset about the idea that her grandson could be killed in action but she seems even more off-put by Vladimir's refusal given that the man also gives money regularly to his wild-child daughter Katya (Elana Lyadova). Where Sergei and his family seem truly grateful, Katya acts almost as if she is owed every penny. Why give her money to waste on drugs instead of giving a troubled youth a chance to go to school?

One night, Vladimir reveals that he is going change his will to give Elena a stipend but most of his inheritance to Katya. It ends all conversation about Sasha possibly going to school and forces Elena to take drastic action. As Hollywood has displayed in noir after noir, one character telling another that their will is going to be changed the next morning often leads to murder.

Elena is a remarkable technical accomplishment in the way that Zvyagintsev uses a variety of elements together to form a cohesive, cool mood. The viewer can feel the chill in the air thanks to Mikhail Krichman's carefully refined cinematography, Philip Glass's perfectly modulated score, and sparse production and sound design that allows for fine detail. *Elena* is a film in which it feels every shot, every line, every detail was carefully considered for the way in which it not only pushes the plot forward but enhances the overall atmosphere of the claustrophobic piece.

Performances are solid throughout but the film belongs to Markina, who is in nearly every scene and delivers in a notably restrained, un-flashy way. Whereas most actresses, especially those in Hollywood, would dive into this role with reckless, scenery-chewing melodrama, Markina allows herself no easy acting crutches. Even the notable decision she makes is handled with cool detachment. And yet she never feels like a cold character. People make huge decisions every day and they do so without much external representation of the emotional and moral dilemmas going on within. Conveying that is what makes Markina's performance so memorable.

Elena ends on a similar note to its long, opening shot. Opulence is viewed through a long shot through a window, reminding the audience that they are mere observers. The bookends offer no emotional release as life goes on in increasingly class-divided mother Russia.

Brian Tallerico

CREDITS

Elena: Nadezhda Vasilievna Markina
Vladimir: Andrey Smirnov
Sergey: Aleksey Rozen
Katerina: Elena Lyadova
Tatyana: Evgeniya Konushkina
Origin: Russia
Language: Russian
Released: 2011
Production: Aleksandr Rodryanskiy; Non-Stop Productions L.L.C.; released by Zeitgeist Films Ltd.
Directed by: Andrey Zvyagintsev
Written by: Andrey Zvyagintsev; Oleg Negin

Cinematography by: Mikhail Krichman
Music by: Philip Glass
Sound: Andrey Dergachev
Editing: Anna Mass
MPAA rating: Unrated
Running time: 109 minutes

REVIEWS

Burr, Ty. *Boston Globe*. May 31, 2012.
Covert, Chris. *St. Paul Pioneer Press*. July 19, 2012.
Ebert, Roger. *Chicago Sun-Times*. July 12, 2012.
Goodykoontz, Bill. *Arizona Republic*. July 12, 2012.
Hartl, John. *Seattle Times*. July 12, 2012.
Jones, J. R. *Chicago Reader*. July 13, 2012.
LaSalle, Mick. *San Francisco Chronicle*. June 8, 2012.
Linden, Sheri. *Los Angeles Times*. May 24, 2012.
O'Sullivan, Michael. *Washington Post*. June 22, 2012.
Phillips, Michael. *Chicago Tribune*. July 12, 2012.

TRIVIA

During filming, Andrey Smirnov broke two ribs while playing with his son. He was ashamed to tell the truth while on set and instead said that he had slipped on the bathroom floor.

END OF WATCH

Every moment of your life they stand watch.
—Movie tagline
Watch your six September 28.
—Movie tagline

Box Office: $41 million

David Ayer's *End of Watch* is a good cop movie that could have been a great one. It goes to enormous lengths to capture the immediacy of an officer's day-to-day routine, yet frequently undermines much of its efforts by utilizing conventional cinematic techniques. Why do filmmakers bother aiming for documentary realism if they do not intend to sustain it? Every time Ayer's film threatens to become a genuine experience, a music cue or non-diegetic sound effect will break forth to remind audiences that they are indeed watching a movie.

The film's biggest assets are its two leading men, Jake Gyllenhaal and Michael Pena, who bring effortless gravity and charm to their roles as two Los Angeles officers. Many of the film's best moments take place in their police car, as longtime buddies Brian (Gyllenhaal) and Mike (Pena) engage in banter that is so candid and exuberant that it convincingly etches a relationship that appears to have lasted many years. They are like Butch and Sundance on the right side of the law, though they certainly are not opposed to engaging in a risky brawl in order to show criminals who is in charge. One of the film's early moments shows Mike engaging in hand-to-hand combat with a disrespectful thug while an amused Brian captures the fight on his handheld camera. The scene is effective, but it would have been even more intense if the visuals were not so incoherent.

Unfortunately, Brian's camera becomes a running gimmick throughout the film and adds a needless layer of confusion to the proceedings. Since the entire film appears to have been shot guerilla-style, there are various scenes that appear to have been shot on Brian's camera despite the fact that the camera placement is entirely illogical. Consider the scene where Brian takes a much-anticipated road trip with his lovely girlfriend, Janet (Anna Kendrick). As the couple drives down the road, a camera pans back and forth between them from the back seat. Who's operating the camera? Apparently no one, but the self-conscious camera movement suggests otherwise.

Ayer toys with the format of a found footage thriller but frequently abandons it. He should have either chosen to stick with it for the entirety of his film's running time or drop it altogether. The juxtaposition of Brian's camerawork and Roman Vasyanov's equally jittery cinematography becomes even more confounding when several other characters' cameras are added into the mix, such as the camera inexplicably carried by a member of the sinister Mexican drug cartel tracked down by the cops. Too many lines of dialogue are devoted to justifying the characters' determination to film everything, while David Sardy's score telegraphs danger before it arrives in the frame. Both of these demerits are classic examples of bona fide suspense-killers.

Yet Ayer still manages to keep the film reasonably taut by allowing smaller set-pieces to gradually connect before building to a head at the end. In a way, the film follows the structure of a found footage horror film by lining up various clues that eventually point toward a destination reeking with potential doom. The final act is at once inevitable and unexpected, as Brian and Mike suddenly find themselves in over their head. With different actors, the film's last third may have seemed too melodramatic to stomach, but Gyllenhaal and Pena are so plausible in their roles that they make the film's emotional stakes resonate on a truly wrenching level.

Unlike Ayer's overrated *Training Day* (2001), which offered a sensationalized portrait of a corrupted detective, *End of Watch* attempts to explore the brotherly bond between cops with the grounded observational detail of a fly-on-the-wall documentary. There is an almost "frat boy" camaraderie in the scenes set at the station as the friends attempt to lighten the mood with a few old school practical jokes. Though she does not have much screen time, America Ferrera makes an indelible impression as a strong-willed officer who occasionally tangles with the men during their increasingly eventful days. It is quite a departure from Ferrera's cuddly screen persona, hinting that the actress is capable of playing a far richer variety of roles. Too bad the film's other female characters function merely as sentimental diversions, while the villains are one-note stereotypes (the cartel's head honcho is given the laughably unsubtle name, "Big Evil").

While Ayer's film falls short of being first-rate cinema, it certainly succeeds as a heartfelt tribute to the personal sacrifices made by officers in the line of fire. Like Oliver Stone's *World Trade Center* (2006), the picture avoids politicizing its subject matter, opting instead to focus on the universally relatable humanity of its characters. Both films also stand as superb showcases for Pena, who continues to inspire a great deal of empathy in role after role. He remains one of the most engaging actors in modern American film, and *End of Watch* gives him one of his best roles to date. He and Gyllenhaal are so good that they ultimately cause viewers to forgive Ayer of his visual excesses, particularly the multiple video game-style shots that take the POV of the characters guns. These sequences are alarmingly reminiscent of the loathsome propaganda turkey known as *Act of Valor* (2012), but thankfully, that is the only element in this film reminiscent of *Act of Valor*.

Matt Fagerholm

CREDITS

Brian Taylor: Jake Gyllenhaal
Mike Zavala: Michael Pena
Janet: Anna Kendrick
Orozco: America Ferrera
Sarge: Frank Grillo
Davis: Cody Horn
Origin: United States
Language: English
Released: 2012
Production: Matt Jackson, John Lesher, Nigel Sinclair, David Ayer; Exclusive Media Group; released by Open Road Films
Directed by: David Ayer
Written by: David Ayer
Cinematography by: Roman Vasyanov
Music by: David Sardy
Sound: Michael D. Wilhoit
Music Supervisor: Gabe Hilfer; Season Kent
Editing: Dody Dorn
Art Direction: Kevin Constant

Costumes: Mary Claire Hannan
Production Design: Devorah Herbert
MPAA rating: R
Running time: 109 minutes

REVIEWS

Biancoli, Amy. *San Francisco Chronicle*. September 20, 2012.
Corliss, Richard. *Time*. September 24, 2012.
Denby, David. *New Yorker*. September 19, 2012.
Ebert, Roger. *Chicago Sun-Times*. September 19, 2012.
Goodykoontz, Bill. *Arizona Republic*. September 19, 2012.
Lumenick, Lou. *New York Post*. September 20, 2012.
Phillips, Michael. *Chicago Tribune*. September 20, 2012.
Rainer, Peter. *Christian Science Monitor*. September 21, 2012.
Schwarzbaum, Lisa. *Entertainment Weekly*. September 19, 2012.
Uhlich, Keith. *Time Out New York*. September 18, 2012.

QUOTES

Captain Reese: "An on-the-job shooting is still considered a homicide. It's never an easy ride. If you do the right thing, I'll always have your back. Do the wrong thing and cross me...I will personally throw you under the bus."

TRIVIA

The word "f**k" is used 326 times in the film, placing it sixth on the all time profanity list.

AWARDS

Nominations:

Ind. Spirit 2013: Actor—Supporting (Pena), Cinematog.

THE EXPENDABLES 2

Back for war.
—Movie tagline

Box Office: $85 million

Sylvester Stallone has made a career out of sticking around. Besides being the creator of the multi-film *Rocky* and *Rambo* franchises, he has also made at least one of almost every kind of genre film there is. Some of his non-action stuff has been very good although, more often than not, fans have been left wondering when he would return to that for which he is most famous. Having recently revived both his most notable franchises, hopes were riding high when he announced a new film project that would involve virtually all the famous action stars of the eighties. So reviewers could be excused for feeling that the *Expendables* films do not live up to the high standards suggested by the cast lists but only so long as they remember that most of the people on those cast lists have had a careers similar to Stallone's: A few good-to-great films and lots and lots of flops, mediocre genre romps and forgettable stabs at deeper stuff. *The Expendables 2* is every bit as enjoyable as *The Expendables* (2010) but not a whole lot different. An explosion of testosterone (and anything else that can explode) *The Expendables 2* delivers on its very simple mission.

The Expendables have been recruited to rescue a Chinese businessman in Nepal only to discover that fellow mercenary Trench (Arnold Schwarzenegger) is held captive there as well. After their successful rescue, Yin Yang (Jet Li) escorts the businessman back home. In New York, Barney Ross (Sylvester Stallone) finds out that his newest protege, sniper Billy the Kid (Liam Hemsworth), wants to leave the team, and retire to France with his girlfriend Sophia, while Ross and the rest of the team are commandeered by CIA Agent Mr. Church (Bruce Willis). Ross heads to Albania with Lee Christmas (Jason Statham), Hale Caesar (Terry Crews), Toll Road (Randy Couture), and Gunner Jensen (Dolph Lundgren).

Their mission involves retrieving an item from a safe in a downed aircraft. Securing the help of expert safe cracker Maggie Chen (Yu Nan), they get the item back only to be surprised by Jean Vilain (Jean-Claude Van Damme), who, together with his henchman Hector (Scott Adkins) and their rogue mercenary militia, the Sangs, have taken Billy hostage, demanding that the Expendables given him the mysterious item and hand over their own arsenal. In an attempt to save Billy's life, Ross and the team do as they are asked, only to be betrayed when Vilain kills Billy and makes his getaway, leaving Ross to swear vengeance.

It turns out that the object in question is a computer holding the whereabouts of tons of Soviet plutonium. Vilain wants to sell it, and with the Expendables in hot pursuit, helped by an old ally named Booker (Chuck Norris), whose additional firepower and intel help them to disable and track Vilain's gang, setting up the final confrontation in which a nearby village, who has had many of its members kidnapped and forced to work in the plutonium mines is ready to take a last stand. Helped by Trench to free the villagers, a series of mano a mano fights settle the score once and for all. The film ends with Sophia opening her door to discover a huge sum of money and a letter retrieved from Billy's body.

Director Simon West has had a steady career making movies an awful lot like this one. Some of those— *Con Air* (1997) and *Lara Croft: Tomb Raider* (2001)— have been good but, more often, his career has just seemed like busy work, seeing him at the helm of yawny horror remakes like *Black Christmas* (2006) and *When A*

Stranger Calls (2006). Only recently has he returned to the sort of action films that best take advantage of his slick style, turning in *The Mechanic* (2011) and *Stolen* (2012). He is completely at home here and knows exactly how to exploit the cast.

The main problem here is the script, which fails to do anything all that special with the mass assemblage of machismo. As in the previous film, there are no defining moments that revisit the past or place the aging action heroes in any current context. They are simply on display doing what they do best in a movie that has nothing in particular to challenge them. Only Stallone truly stands out here and, as in his recent Rocky and Rambo films, he shows that he is indeed a master of the strong hero. The second installment is proof that *The Expendables 3* would benefit from a smaller cast that offered everybody the chance to really shine instead of just bounce one-liners and short bits off one another.

Dave Canfield

CREDITS

Barney Ross: Sylvester Stallone
Lee Christmas: Jason Statham
Yin Yang: Jet Li
Gunnar Jensen: Dolph Lundgren
Toll Road: Randy Couture
Hale Caesar: Terry Crews
Bill "the Kid" Timmons: Liam Hemsworth
Mr. Church: Bruce Willis
Maggie: Yu Nan
Lacy: Charisma Carpenter
Jean Vilain: Jean-Claude Van Damme
Trench: Arnold Schwarzenegger
Booker: Chuck Norris
Origin: United States
Language: English

Released: 2012
Production: Avi Lerner, Danny Lerner, Kevin King Templeton, JOhn Thompson, Les Weldon; Millennium Films, Nu Image Films; released by Lionsgate
Directed by: Simon West
Written by: Sylvester Stallone
Cinematography by: Shelly Johnson
Music by: Brian Tyler
Sound: Christopher Eakins
Editing: Todd E. Miller
Costumes: Lizz Wolf
Production Design: Paul Cross
MPAA rating: R
Running time: 103 minutes

REVIEWS

Goss, William. *Film.com*. August 16, 2012.
Guzman, Rafer. *Newsday*. August 17, 2012.
Howell, Peter. *Toronto Star*. August 16, 2012.
Jones, Alan. *Radio Times*. August 23, 2012.
Keller, Louise. *Urban Cinefile*. August 27, 2012.
Lumenick, Lou. *New York Post*. August 17, 2012.
Pinkerton, Nick. *Village Voice*. August 14, 2012.
Schwarzbaum, Lisa. *Entertainment Weekly*. August 16, 2012.
Rodriguez, Rene. *Miami Herald*. August 15, 2012.
Russo, Tom. *Boston Globe*. August 23, 2012.

QUOTES

Barney Ross: "That's how we deal with death. We can't change what it is, so we keep it light until it's time to get dark. And then we get pitch black."

TRIVIA

One stuntman died and another was left in a critical condition while filming an action scene for the film in Bulgaria, that included an explosion on a rubber boat.

F

FAREWELL, MY QUEEN
(Les adieux a la reine)

Box Office: $1.3 million

Throughout the years, many filmmakers have attempted to put the life of the infamous Marie Antoinette on the big screen but in virtually every attempt, such films have tended to focus on two specific aspects of her life—the incredible opulence in which she lived her life as the wife of Louis XVI while the people of France starved in the streets and her grisly demise at the business end of the guillotine in the wake of the French Revolution. That said, the sudden transition from the one to the other has often been either ignored completely or quickly shuffled through in order to get to the gruesome stuff. In his latest film, *Farewell, My Queen*, the acclaimed French filmmaker Benoit Jacquot takes a look at those fateful days in July 1789 that marked the beginning of the end for the entire gilded era from a somewhat unusual perspective and the result is a real rarity—a film about a well-known and well-documented historical event that actually has something new to say about the subject at hand.

Adapting the novel by Chantal Thomas and utilizing a take that will remind some of the likes of such ruling class/working class mashups as *Upstairs, Downstairs* (1971) or *Gosford Park* (2001), Jacquot takes viewers on a tour of Versailles through the eyes of Sidonie (Lea Seydoux), a servant who has earned herself a certain position of privilege as the favorite reader of Marie Antoinette (Diane Kruger). However, as becomes obvious from the opening moments, in which a pesky mosquito can be heard merrily buzzing away, the bloom is

definitely off the rose that is Versailles—the furnishings are getting a bit on the tatty side, a gondola trip across the lake is likely to unveil dead rats in the water, and the entire place exudes a combination of seediness and opulence that suggests a luxury hotel that is still nice (provided one does not look too hard) but which has clearly seen better days. As the story opens, news begins to filter throughout the palace, via rumors and increasingly dire pamphlets, about some sort of unpleasantness that has just gone down at the Bastille and which may be heading towards Versailles itself before long.

At first, Sidonie is not particularly concerned with the news—after all, her lady does not look particularly worried and besides, if anything serious were to go down, Marie would no doubt do everything in her power to make sure that she was brought to safety and taken care of. As the atmosphere around the palace becomes more and more dire and even Marie has taken to digging jewels from their now-cumbersome settings in order to make sneaking them out during her planned escape much easier, Sidonie is forced to confront the fact that despite her elevated position amongst the help, she is still only that and nothing more. This becomes abundantly clear to her at last when she learns that her beloved Marie plans to use her as a decoy as part of a potentially dangerous plan to get someone she does genuinely care for—the mysterious and alluring Gabrielle de Polignac (Virginie Ledoyen)—to safety.

Shooting on location at Versailles itself, Jacquot does an excellent job of recreating those confused final days as rumors make the rounds, subjects and employees alike flee in droves and Sidonie rudely discovers just how important and valuable she is to the Queen for whom she has constantly pledged her love and loyalty. As he did in his earlier film *A Single Girl* (1995), he quietly and effectively depicts the class differences between the haves and have-nots through a character who finds herself straddling the two worlds without ever belonging to either of them. (Ironically, the chambermaid in that film was portrayed by Ledoyen). Jacquot is also aided immeasurably by the fine performances from his two lead actresses. Lea Seydoux, who is perhaps best known to American audiences as the sexy killer in *Mission Impossible: Ghost Protocol* (2011) and the record dealer in *Midnight in Paris* (2011), is excellent as Sidonie and makes her character compelling to watch even though everyone in the audience has a better idea of her ultimate fate than she. In the trickier role of Marie Antoinette, Diane Kruger, an actress who has rarely shown herself to be much more than a pretty face in her previous screen appearances, does a fairly astonishing job of showing all of the contrasting sides of the character—friendly and flighty at one moment and coldly conniving at the next—with a dexterity that is almost frightening to behold.

As stated earlier, *Farewell, My Queen* is less a standard-issue look at the world of Marie Antoinette and her eventual demise than it is *Downfall* (2006) with decolletage and since it does not revel in either the opulence of her life or the hideous circumstances of her demise, those looking for the same old thing are likely to be as aghast with what Jacquot has done here as they were with what Sofia Coppola offered up with her stunning and slyly subversive *Marie Antoinette* (2006). For those moviegoers, there are plenty of traditional takes on the subject that they can view but for those looking for something containing a new approach that might actually force them to rethink and reconsider their previously held notions while still working magnificently as a straightforward historical drama, *Farewell, My Queen* is an unqualified success.

Peter Sobczynski

CREDITS

Marie Antoinette: Diane Kruger
Sidonie Laborde: Lea Seydoux
Madame Henriette Campan: Noemie Lvovsky
Duchess Gabrielle de Polignac: Virginie Ledoyen
King Louis XVI: Xavier Beauvois
Jacob Nicolas Moreau: Michel Robin
Origin: France, Spain
Language: French
Released: 2012
Production: Jean-Pierre Guerin; GMT Productions S.A.S., Les Films du Lendemain, Morena Films; released by Cohen Media Group

Directed by: Benoit Jacquot
Written by: Benoit Jacquot; Gilles Taurand
Cinematography by: Romain Winding
Music by: Bruno Coulais
Sound: Francis Wargnier
Editing: Luc Barnier
Costumes: Christian Gasc; Valerie Ranchoux
Production Design: Katia Wyszkop
MPAA rating: R
Running time: 100 minutes

REVIEWS

Anderson, Jonathan. *Village Voice*. July 10, 2012.
Chang, Justin. *Variety*. July 9, 2012.
Dargis, Manohla. *New York Times*. July 12, 2012.
Ebert, Roger. *Chicago Sun-Times*. July 19, 2012.
Jenkins, Mark. *NPR*. July 12, 2012.
Kauffmann, Stanley. *The New Republic*. August 6, 2012.
McGavin, Patrick Z. *Boston Phoenix*. July 25, 2012.
Pais, Matt. *RedEye*. July 19, 2012.
Tobias, Scott. *AV Club*. July 2, 2012.
Turan, Kenneth. *Los Angeles Times*. July 12, 2012.

TRIVIA

Eva Green was originally cast as Marie Antoinette but had to drop out to do *Dark Shadows* and was replaced by Diane Kruger.

FIRST POSITION

6 dancers, 5 minutes on stage, 1 chance to make it.
—Movie tagline

Box Office: $1 million

The extraordinary art form of ballet is often recognized in cinema for the emotional and physical blisters it can leave on those who obsessively labor to meet the classical dance's demand for perfect manipulation of the human body. With such popular narrative films as the Academy Award-winning *Black Swan* (2010) and *Center Stage* (2000), the competitive nature of ballet has become a common theme for movies looking to express the strenuousness that becomes a commanding factor once one commits their life to ballet.

First-time filmmaker and former young Boston Ballet School dancer Bess Kargman responds to the heavy dramatics of these movies with her light documentary *First Position*, a film that does without psychologically troubled black swans and backstage back-stabbings and instead focuses on all idiosyncrasies within a ballet dancers' world. However, with such a preference towards a breezier presentation, this extreme lightness in the film eventually becomes overcompensation, sacrificing a proper conveyance of the anxious urgency undeniably felt by those performing with years of arduous work on the line.

First Position focuses on six different competitors entering into the Youth America Grand Prix Semi-Finals, an annual ballet competition that features 5,000 dancers from the ages nine to nineteen, competing in fifteen cities around the world. From that batch, 300 soloists are selected to audition for ballet companies and schools in the final round in New York City, vying for job contracts or scholarships that will further carry their dreams into professional realms.

Though these documentary subjects come from various economic and social backgrounds, they share the same aspirations to provide the exceptional alignment of body, technique and star-like presence that all companies are looking for in potential candidates. Aran Bell, age eleven, is a military child who lives with his family in Italy, and drives two hours to Rome to study ballet. Michaela DePrince, age fourteen, is a dancer who was rescued from an orphanage in Sierra Leone, and has dreamed of being a ballerina ever since seeing a ballet magazine cover since leaving her war-torn country. Joan Sebastian Zamora, age sixteen, is a young dancer who left his family in Colombia to live in New York City in order to pursue his dream of becoming a professional dancer, with hopes of achieving a scholarship to London's Royal Ballet School. Miko and Jules Fogarty, ages twelve and ten respectively, are a brother and sister duo who become homeschooled in order to commit more time to ballet. These dancers all go against the images created from the aforementioned films—even the "stereotypical" embodiment of a ballerina, an affluent white seventeen-year-old girl named Rebecca, makes a point to distance herself from previous media images of ballet dancers by pointing out that dance has not impeded her from having a social life, nor has it controlled the types of food she eats (Kargman is sure to include a shot in which Rebecca snacks on a Hot Pocket).

Kargman successfully challenges any presumptions viewers might have on the world of ballet, and does so by aptly presenting a thorough picture that could make anyone forget that such narrow preconceptions even existed in the first place. In between character-establishing chapters, there are informative segments in the film that convey such daily factors such as the constant physical injuries dancers endure (comparable to

that of a professional athlete), the popularity that ballet has amongst men either heterosexual or homosexual, and the importance that money has when embarking on a ballet career (so that one can afford the intricate costumes and tutus). In these regards, *First Position* justifies the specific arduous dedication by its subjects, expressing for these performers the factors that go underestimated when simply watching them dance.

There is, however, a lacking sense of audience attachment to the journey of many of these subjects, whose valuable emotional time is spread too thin by the filmmaker's attempts to properly portion the film's attention to all six of these dancers. *First Position* is able to provide concrete backgrounds for each of these subjects, but fails to instill a strong desire that their success is imperative for the state of a viewer's own emotions as well. Such a missing immediacy in the subjects' emotional state prevents the viewer from feeling the performers' anxieties in their pivotal moments, consequently making *First Position* improperly light for a non-fictional story about a competition that could change the life of anyone who works hard enough to even compete in it.

During the movie's climactic dance performances, the cinematography of *First Position* is stuck with the dancers' parents in the balconies, offering viewers flat presentations of otherwise impassioned performances. In some instances a secondary camera is able to capture the dances from the side of the stage, but neither of these angles provides the visual flair required to accurately translate a performer's energy from the power of dance to that of film. Instead, the cinematography becomes an example of how this documentary seems much more motivated by the idea of capturing ballet with a camera than it is filmmaking in general.

An inspired newcomer to the film world, Kargman has no other previous involvement with any type of filmmaking to her name. Instead, Kargman comes from a journalistic background, having contributed social and political stories in the past to publications like *National Public Radio* and the *Washington Post*. As for personal involvement with ballet, Kargman studied at Boston Ballet until the age of fourteen.

This background seems to provide a logical explanation for the perspective of *First Position*, a film that does succeed in thoroughly documenting a passionate picture of all things ballet. Yet, while the film is educational to those looking in from the outside on the world of ballet, this dry presentation of dancers, and the fleeting comprehensions of their competitive anxieties, functions more like an extensive news profile piece, and less that of something that makes for a generally engaging film watching experience.

Nick Allen

CREDITS

Origin: United States
Language: English
Released: 2011
Production: Bess Kargman; First Position Films; released by Sundance Selects
Directed by: Bess Kargman
Cinematography by: Nick Higgins
Music by: Chris Hajian
Sound: Eric Thomas
Editing: Bess Kargman
MPAA rating: Unrated
Running time: 90 minutes

REVIEWS

Dargis, Manohla. *New York Times.* May 3, 2012.
Dunkel, Ellen. *Philadelphia Inquirer.* May 10, 2012.
Hitt, Amy. *Washington Post.* May 11, 2012.
Holmes, Linda. *National Public Radio.* May 3, 2012.
Morgenstern, Joe. *Wall Street Journal.* May 5, 2012.
Pols, Mary F. *Time.* May 3, 2012.
Punter, Jennie. *Globe and Mail.* July 19, 2012.
Schwarzbaum, Lisa. *Entertainment Weekly.* May 2, 2012.
Simon, Alissa. *Variety.* February 23, 2012.
Stevens, Dana. *Slate.* May 4, 2012.

THE FIVE-YEAR ENGAGEMENT

A comedy about the journey between popping the question and tying the knot.
—Movie tagline

Box Office: $28.8 million

Writer/director Nicholas Stoller and co-writer/star Jason Segel located plenty of comedy in the arena of masculine doubt, and the difficulty in climbing back up on the romantic saddle in their previous collaboration, *Forgetting Sarah Marshall* (2008), a $105 million worldwide hit. A through-line of thematic follow-up can be traced to their new work, *The Five-Year Engagement,* a romantic dramedy that attempts to chart the turbulent, churned-up period of personal development and possibly divergent professional paths between a young betrothed couple's pledge for marriage and their eventual trip down the aisle. Alas, two appealing leads and plenty of recognizable and game supporting players (including

Mindy Kaling, Chris Parnell, Kevin Hart, and Brian Posehn) cannot save this bloated, hit-and-miss affair. It possesses the same basic nougat-y center of ribaldry and sentimentality in which producer Judd Apatow specializes, but falls victim to a sagging second act as well as an ending which feels more the product of test-marketing approval than genuine romantic rallying.

After having met-cute at a costume party one year earlier, San Francisco sous chef Tom Solomon (Segel) pops the question to his girlfriend, graduate student Violet Barnes (Emily Blunt), who happily accepts his proposal. At a party celebrating their engagement, Violet's sister Suzie (Alison Brie) hooks up with Tom's friend and colleague Alex (Chris Pratt), and later gets pregnant by him. That this odd-couple pair beat the career-minded duo to the altar is but the first of a string of hindrances and perhaps ominous warning signs for Tom and Violet.

When she is accepted to the University of Michigan, Tom follows Violet to snowy Ann Arbor, where he feels out of place and is unable to get a job anywhere commensurate with his skill level. As Violet forges bonds with her fellow students and rakish advising professor, Winton Childs (Rhys Ifans), Tom works his way into a funk, and seems to regress into a state of resentment and caveman-ish apathy. After several years of postponing the wedding, to pay down certain debts and keep other professional possibilities open and alive, Tom and Violet are faced with splitting up, and the realization that perhaps they are not meant for one another.

The Five-Year Engagement is reputedly rooted in, much like its predecessor, Segel's extended real-life relationship with his *Freaks and Geeks* costar Linda Cardellini. So in addition to its smart recognition and skewering of the male ego's fragility, the film also has *Forgetting Sarah Marshall*'s same desperate desire to span time and cram in lots of colorful complications. Ergo, it engenders lots of goodwill for the many things it does right—namely, it at least aims at a target a bit higher and off-center than the normal, unchallenging objectives of so many romantic comedies, even though its engagement framing seems like a sop for female viewers, and it dutifully ticks off the boxes of discrete relationship flashback. Stoller and Segel have a gift for capturing self-effacement through vulnerability, and how that frailty melts away into jocular shorthand when couples bond and fuse.

Yet for every bit of inspired, quirky lunacy (such as Alex's public forum ode to a string of Tom's exes, sung to the tune of Billy Joel's "We Didn't Start the Fire"), there are two or three unnecessary asides or outright farcical misfires that sap the film of any momentum—grand sketch comedy ideas that do not particularly comfortably fit in with the more established rhythms and efforts of character-based comedy. The idea of Tom's crisis in confidence manifesting itself physically after the couple decamps to Michigan is a good instinct, but rendered too broad by at least half when he grows a mountain-man beard and takes to homebrewing, hunting, smoking venison and keeping bees. Later, there is a scene in which two of Violet's colleagues icily toast everyone but one another, which plays very much like a *Saturday Night Live* bit. Worst, though, is a pointless and unfunny sequence in which Violet's niece shoots her in the leg with a crossbow.

Both Segel and especially Blunt can be charming performers, and they are not a bad match here, per se. But neither are they given material which demonstrates a genuine fusing (or are they able to conjure and fake the same), and so Tom and Violet's plight feels both less real and less funny than that of Vince Vaughn and Jennifer Aniston's characters in *The Break-Up* (2006), another movie which *The Five-Year Engagement* clearly wishes to emulate. That film, however, had the good sense and freshness to entertain the idea that its characters were not right for one another (its ultimate conclusion), but Stoller and Segel's effort, no matter its dip into acrimony, always seems preordained for the altar. The comedy and core conflict do not seem especially well integrated, and the increasing strain of that disconnection slows the movie to a crawl.

Still, it is not merely that *The Five-Year Engagement* is just long (clocking in at just over two hours), it is that so much of its time is misappropriated. Plot threads with Tom's parents (David Paymer and Mimi Kennedy) and Violet's mother (Jacki Weaver) could be jettisoned entirely, with that time freed up to examine in greater and more interesting detail Tom and Violet's emotional waywardness.

The Five-Year Engagement flirts with ideas both substantive and radical; it wants to assay contemporary life, and how the order and structure of relationships has changed, with so many couples living together before marriage. And it is likely, in its own easy, shambling way, to satisfy a certain baseline entertainment quotient for forgiving viewers. It will play comfortably as a stay-in date-night rental for twenty- and thirtysomething couples, in other words. But the film ultimately fades upon contact, when the snapshot of the turbulences of such a modern relationship could and should have left a much more indelible mark given more careful editorial pruning.

Brent Simon

CREDITS

Tom Solomon: Jason Segel

Violet Barnes: Emily Blunt
Alex Eilhauer: Chris Pratt
Suzie Barnes-Eilhauer: Alison Brie
Carol Solomon: Mimi Kennedy
Pete Solomon: David Paymer
George Barnes: Jim Piddock
Winton Childs: Rhys Ifans
Origin: United States
Language: English, French, Spanish
Released: 2012
Production: Judd Apatow, Rodney Rothman, Nicholas Stoller; Stoller Global Solutions, Apatow Productions; released by Universal Pictures Inc.
Directed by: Nicholas Stoller
Written by: Jason Segel; Nicholas Stoller
Cinematography by: Javier Aguirresarobe
Music by: Michael Andrews
Sound: George H. Anderson
Music Supervisor: Jonathan Karp
Editing: William Kerr; Peck Prior
Art Direction: John B. Josselyn
Costumes: Leesa Evans
Production Design: Julie Berghoff
MPAA rating: R
Running time: 124 minutes

REVIEWS

Anderson, John. *Variety.* April 19, 2012.
Denby, David. *New Yorker.* May 1, 2012.
Edelstein, David. *New York Magazine.* April 30, 2012.
Lemire, Christy. *Associated Press.* April 25, 2012.
Morgenstern, Joe. *Wall Street Journal.* April 26, 2012.
Puig, Claudia. *USA Today.* April 26, 2012.
Scott, A. O. *New York Times.* April 26, 2012.
Sharkey, Betsy. *Los Angeles Times.* April 26, 2012.
Stevens, Dana. *Slate.* April 26, 2012.
Weitzman, Elizabeth. *New York Daily News.* April 28, 2012.

QUOTES

George Barnes: "The first important thing to remember about marriage is that it requires commitment. The second important thing to remember about marriage is that so does insanity."

TRIVIA

Almost all of the restaurant scenes in the filem were shot inside the MGM Grand Detroit Casino.

FLIGHT

Box Office: $93.8 million

With *Flight,* Robert Zemeckis is making his return

to live-action filmmaking after over a decade exploring and testing the limits of animation that led many of his biggest supporters to wonder if he had lost his way connecting with humans. Similarly, Denzel Washington has spent the recent part of his resume in more commercially-viable enterprises and away from the kind of roles that made him one of the most acclaimed actors of our time. He arguably lost his humanity in the din of Hollywood blockbusters. As if brought together by fate, these two legends have come together at just the right moment in their careers to tell the tale of another, an alcoholic pilot named Whip Whitaker, a commercial airline pilot introduced as a hungover, deadbeat father, waking up less than two hours before his latest flight, having bedded down a member (Nadine Velazquez) of his crew, and using some cocaine as a pick-me-up. Onboard, he is ready to fly—with the help of a couple of mini-bottles of vodka—while his co-pilot (Brian Geraghty) is already weary of his questionable line of attack to bad weather. Just before final approach, their plane goes into an uncontrollable dive, and, through a daring combination of instinct and technique, Whip manages to get the plane down and save most of the souls onboard.

As the dust begins to settle and Whip keeps himself away from the media looking to speak with a hero, further details begin to come to light. Though Whip is steadfast in his conviction that he was put in a "broken plane," his good friend, Charlie (Bruce Greenwood), the head of the pilot's union, and their lawyer (Don Cheadle) are aware of the hospital's toxicology report which clearly shows the state he was in that morning. Now facing an investigation that could demand jail time, Whip, with help from his drug dealer, Harling (John Goodman), isolates himself at the family farm where he first learned to fly. He will not be alone for long though after meeting Nicole (Kelly Reilly), another recovering soul in the hospital who appears more mentally prepared to leave the worst of her past behind her.

This is far from the mystery thriller being sold to audiences throughout its trailer campaign. Come for the cool plane crash, stay for the self-destructive dependency. If the two were not directly connected, *Flight* might sound like an uneven narrative with which a casual viewer could get easily frustrated. Zemeckis is a far-more-skilled filmmaker than to just let his structure dangle and feel disjointed. How often has a tragic event, close call or signs of a coincidental nature point to a shift in how people should conduct our lives? Whip's flight begins as a resume of questionable risk-taking and poor behavior but ends as a wake-up call for a man who blankets himself in any excuse available to keep sleeping. Looking for mechanical failings may clear his conscience

and keep him out of jail, but Whip is a man who has already put up bars between everybody else in his life.

This is a character that needs an actor up to the challenge of suppressing all pretense of likability and casually leading an audience to the conclusion that Whip is more than just another guy who likes to drink. It helps that Denzel Washington is one of cinema's most dominant and instantly likable screen presences to ease us into our feelings about him. When Whip takes his immediate first step to better living, it looks like a clean slate. Like so many alcoholics, the pressures of life and the egocentric belief that they are alone in their view of the world around them throw Whip back into his old routines and this new spiral may just be the one of which he is unable to pull himself out. Denzel is beyond remarkable in towing the line between the actor's dream of digging into the tricks bag to play an out-of-control drunk and balancing perception of whether or not audiences feel Whip deserves care and concern. There are scenes of functionality during intoxication and a most uncomfortable visit with his estranged family that emphasizes the truth beyond the comical drunks viewers are used to seeing—and dismissing—in movies. But *Flight,* above all, is a film about the choices people make at the moment they need to make them. Whip's quick thinking under pressure is certainly the film's signature sequence but it is his stare down in an empty hotel room that may just be the most suspenseful; a "don't do it" moment of staggering intensity.

In an odd parallel that seems positively in line with the recurring themes of Zemeckis' career, Denzel's superior work here is a reminder of the earlier portion of his career that respectfully netted him five Oscar nominations and a cache of respect from the industry and critics as someone we all wanted to see again and again. Many of Denzel's own choices since winning his last Oscar for *Training Day* (2001)—also his last nomination—have gravitated toward more high-profile action pictures such as *The Book of Eli* (2010), *Safe House* (2012), and a continuing relationship with director Tony Scott that led to four more films of wildly varying quality—*Man On Fire* (2004), *Deja Vu* (2006), *The Taking of Pelham 123* (2009), *Unstoppable* (2010)—after their best collaboration back in 1995 with *Crimson Tide*. *Flight* is a film and a performance more in line with the award-caliber work—in both epic scale and small—and this reminder of that in a unique way plays like Denzel's own version of Dickens' *A Christmas Carol*.

Washington had not completely given up on more dramatic and less commercial ventures the way Nicolas Cage has, but *Flight* parades a variety of reminders that Denzel may have occasionally strayed too far from the path of promise. The first person Whip encounters in the hospital after the crash is Bruce Greenwood, a Jacob

Marley-esque representative from the pilot's union who looks a lot like the FBI agent who tried to take charge against him in *Deja Vu*. His next visitor is John Goodman's drug dealer; a past ghost he at first refuses but is nevertheless introduced with the Rolling Stones' "Sympathy for the Devil." That is the same song that closed their climactic scene in the possession thriller *Fallen* (1998), a film which just also happened to feature Denzel's character enter the next phase of his life through a tainted cigarette. Don Cheadle's breakout role was alongside Washington in *Devil in a Blue Dress* (1995) where he played the out-of-control one. Now he is the voice trying to get Whip to suppress his present situation to go on. Whip's evolving relationship with Kelly Reilly's Nicole was unthinkable to the man behind Whip in 1995 when he famously nixed the subplot of an interracial romance with Kelly Lynch in *Virtuosity*, stating that people "would not want to see him kiss a white woman." All of this is pure speculation naturally but when you consider all of the above and then watch the closing act as Whip/Denzel's Ghost of Christmas Future, the final line of John Gatin's screenplay holds even greater meaning.

Robert Zemeckis is such a precise craftsman—or just so naturally gifted he is not ever aware of the variations of his evolving themes—that it is impossible to completely dismiss the above theory. It alone as a follow-up to his animated interpretation of the Dickens classic falls in line with the anachronistic histories he has toyed with in *Who Framed Roger Rabbit* (1988), *Forrest Gump* (1994), and the *Back to the Future* trilogy. A plane crash as the trigger for a man to re-direct his rigidly-structured life calls back to Tom Hanks' journey in *Cast Away* (2000). Most notably, *Flight* again takes on Zemeckis' recurring exploration of a higher power and its place in people's lives as either personal fact or somebody else's fiction. God vs. science was right at the center of *Contact* (1997). The concept of destiny was imposed with wonder and melancholy in *Forrest Gump*. Did the tide bring in the sail in *Cast Away* just as it took a mechanical failure to put Whip on the road to salvation? Or does the remainder of the film play like the last temptation from someone more sinister? "If God be for us, who can be against us?" said the book of Romans and maybe the answer lies in ourselves.

Flight is not some personal statement on the filmmaker himself the way *Raging Bull* (1980) was for Martin Scorsese, though Zemeckis' own rite of passage through Catholic school certainly plays as a factor in his career. However one chooses to interpret the film in the many hours worth thinking about it afterwards, there is little doubt that Zemeckis is the higher power in control and—like with Noah, Moses, and Jonah—has given

Denzel a role that he can deliver like no other and may turn out to be the defining work of his life.

Erik Childress

CREDITS

Whip Whitaker: Denzel Washington
Hugh Lang: Don Cheadle
Nicole: Kelly Reilly
Harling Mays: John Goodman
Charlie Anderson: Bruce Greenwood
Ken Evans: Brian Geraghty
Margaret Thomason: Tamara Tunie
Deana: Gabrielle Beauvais
Origin: United States
Language: English
Released: 2012
Production: Walter F. Parkes, Laurie MacDonald, Steve Starkey, Jack Rapke, Robert Zemeckis; Imagemovers, Parkes/MacDonald Productions; released by Paramount Pictures
Directed by: Robert Zemeckis
Written by: John Gatins
Cinematography by: Don Burgess
Music by: Alan Silvestri
Sound: William B. Kaplan
Editing: Jeremiah O'Driscoll
Art Direction: David Lazan
Costumes: Louise Frogley
Production Design: Nelson Coates
MPAA rating: R
Running time: 138 minutes

REVIEWS

Berardinelli, James. *ReelViews*. November 4, 2012.
Dargis, Manohla. *New York Times*. November 1, 2012.
Edelstein, David. *New York Magazine*. October 29, 2012.
McGranaghan, Mike. *Aisle Seat*. November 2, 2012.
Morgenstern, Joe. *Wall Street Journal*. November 1, 2012.
O'Hehir, Andrew. *Salon*. October 31, 2012.
Phillips, Michael. *Chicago Tribune*. November 1, 2012.
Phipps, Keith. *AV Club*. November 1, 2012.
Tobias, Scott. *NPR*. November 1, 2012.
Vonder Haar, Pete. *Houston Press*. November 3, 2012.

QUOTES

Charlie Anderson: "Remember, if they ask you anything about your drinking, it's totally acceptable to say 'I don't recall.'"

Whip: "Hey, don't tell me how to lie about my drinking, okay? I know how to lie about my drinking. I've been lying about my drinking my whole life."

AWARDS

Nominations:

Oscars 2012: Actor (Washington), Orig. Screenplay
Golden Globes 2013: Actor—Drama (Washington)
Screen Actors Guild 2012: Actor (Washington)
Writers Guild 2012: Orig. Screenplay

FOOTNOTE
(Down the Hill)
(Hearat Shulayim)

Box Office: $2 million

Clashing ideologies in the realm of Talmudic scholarship hardly seems like cinematic, let alone accessible, subject matter. Yet in his acclaimed drama, *Footnote,* American-born Israeli filmmaker Joseph Cedar tackles the rivalry between a father and son with an exuberant craftsmanship often attributed to Hitchcockian thrillers. Amit Poznansky's taut score provides the first clue that this picture will center on far more than tedious bickering between stuffy intellectuals.

After receiving the Best Screenplay prize at Cannes, a truckload of accolades at the Ophir Awards and an Oscar nomination for Best Foreign Film, critics have been struggling to explain the film's unusual pleasures. Many have hailed it as a comedy, though it is doubtful that audiences will find themselves laughing very much. The tragic dimensions of the human drama are too heavy to dismiss, but there is enough wit in Cedar's script to offset the characters' escalating misery. Perhaps the best way to describe *Footnote* would be to categorize it as a drama with a disarming sense of playfulness.

What keeps the viewer mesmerized throughout are the powerhouse performances by its two leading men. One is fierce and impassioned, the other is quiet and morose, yet both men have an equally commanding presence. In the film's opening scene, they're witnessed sitting next to one another at a jubilant ceremony. Though they are seated mere inches from one another, there appears to be a cavernous distance separating them. As Uriel Shkolnik (Lior Ashkenazi) rises to deliver a heartfelt speech after being accepted into the National Israel Academy of Sciences, the camera remains fixed on the grim expression of his father, Eliezer (Shlomo Bar-Aba).

Throughout the first act, which functions as somewhat of a half-hour prologue, Cedar illustrates the duo's deep seated rivalry through the use of inventive yet tonally jarring stylistic montages. It's revealed that Uriel and Eliezer are both professors of Talmud studies at the Hebrew University of Jerusalem. Whereas Uriel continues to rake in praise, Eliezer's achievements has been ignored ever since a single discovery by his rival, Professor Grossman (Micah Lewensohn), rendered much of his work "unnecessary." This crushing blow to his ego has caused him to retreat behind a shell of stony indifference, while his colleagues continue to leave him feeling ostracized. One of the film's most darkly amusing moments occurs early on, as Eliezer is barred from the post-awards reception simply because he doesn't have the proper wristband ("Why don't you call the bomb squad?" he quips to the stubborn security guard).

The most potent and moving scene in the entire film occurs at the top of the second act, as Uriel is called in to a meeting with the voting board of the prestigious Israel Prize. With its absurdly cramped walls and oversized boardroom table, the meeting room seems designed to allow temperatures to rise through the roof during heated discussions. That's precisely what happens when Grossman breaks the unfortunate news that Eliezer received a false report that he had won the Israel Prize, when in fact the message was intended for Uriel. Despite his paternal estrangement, Uriel defends his father with a passionate zeal that startles everyone in the room, especially Grossman, whose craggy forehead causes him to resemble a simmering asteroid on the brink of catching fire.

As Uriel accuses the board of having a grudge against his father, while mocking their hypocritical championing of "transparency," Ashkenazi earns the audience's empathy. In light of his character's noted arrogance and obsession with public adoration, this selfless act of rebellion packs such a visceral punch that the rest of the picture has trouble living up to it. Within the claustrophobic confines of this room, Cedar creates such galvanizing tension that the scene threatens to explode (and, in some ways, it does). What happens next must be left for the viewer to discover, though it must be said that Cedar's interest in bitter ironies causes the plot to follow a certain nightmarish logic.

Nearly as great is the scene where Eliezer takes advantage of an opportunistic journalist's questions in order to trash his son's work, which he considers wildly overrated. In a brutally eloquent monologue, Eliezer argues that his pursuit of scientific truth is far more valuable than his son's writings on topics such as marital relations, which are pointlessly subjective. Editor Einat Glaser-Zarhin's juxtaposition of parallel action involving Uriel in this sequence is particularly poignant. Though

Uriel ultimately comes off as more sympathetic, his feelings of betrayal in light of his father's words cause him to display great cruelty toward his own son. There are many hints throughout the film that the contentious father-son dynamic is doomed to perpetuate for generations to come.

As good as *Footnote* is, it ultimately disappoints by lacking a satisfactory final act. The confrontation between Uriel and Eliezer that the film promises to be building toward never materializes. Instead, the picture devolves into a subtly surrealistic anti-climax that fails to expand beyond the revelations that took place in the previous scenes. The final fade out is guaranteed to elicit more frustrated howls than Joel and Ethan Coen's *A Serious Man,* which similarly stranded the viewer in the middle of a set piece that felt like the punchline to a karmic joke. Yet despite the frustrations of its last moments, Cedar's exploration of the generational gap between different methods of scholarship is undeniably provocative and resonant. Like Cedar's previous narrative feature, 2007's *Beaufort, Footnote* is a war film in the truest sense of the word, proving that familial battles cut the deepest.

Matt Fagerholm

CREDITS

Eliezer Shkolnik: Shlomo Bar-Aba
Uriel Shkolnik: Lior Loui Ashkenazi
Dikla Shkolnik: Alma Zack
Yehudit: Aliza Rosen
Josh: Daniel Marcovich
Yehuda Grossman: Micah Lewensohn
Noa: Yuval Scharf
Origin: Israel
Language: Hebrew
Released: 2011
Production: David Mandil, Moshe Edery, Leon Edery; United King Films, Movie Plus; released by Sony Pictures Classics
Directed by: Joseph Cedar
Written by: Joseph Cedar
Cinematography by: Yaron Scharf
Music by: Amit Poznansky
Sound: Tully Chen
Editing: Ernst Glasser
Costumes: Laura Sheim
Production Design: Arad Sawat
MPAA rating: PG
Running time: 103 minutes

REVIEWS

Biancolli, Amy. *San Francisco Chronicle.* March 22, 2012.
Denby, David. *New Yorker.* April 9, 2012.
Ebert, Roger. *Chicago Sun-Times.* March 14, 2012.
Jenkins, Mark. *NPR.* March 9, 2012.
Phillips, Michael. *Chicago Tribune.* March 8, 2012.
Schwarzbaum, Lisa. *Entertainment Weekly.* March 7, 2012.
Scott, A. O. *New York Times.* March 15, 2012.
Turan, Kenneth. *Los Angeles Times.* March 15, 2012.
Weissberg, Jay. *AV Club.* March 7, 2012.
Willmore, Alison. *Variety.* March 4, 2012.

TRIVIA

The film was Israel's official submission to the Best Foreign Language Film category for the 84th Academy Awards.

AWARDS

Nominations:

Oscars 2011: Foreign Film
Ind. Spirit 2012: Screenplay

FOR A GOOD TIME, CALL...

> *Lose your hang-ups. Find your calling.*
> —Movie tagline

Box Office: $1.3 million

Girls just wanna have a phone sex business in *For A Good Time, Call...,* a comedy that focuses on R-rated female friendships (a fertile comedic territory, recently traversed by Paul Feig's *Bridesmaids* [2011] and in 2012 by *Bachelorette,* directed by Leslye Headland). However, with this film's underwhelming gumption with its vulgar sexual humor, *For A Good Time, Call...* becomes an example itself that the flatness of weak raunchy humor is not only exclusive to boy's club movies.

Like the film's box office motivation *Bridesmaids, For A Good Time, Call ...* frames its characters in a current economic situation of high rent and low job availability, this time taking the money crunch to New York City. Lauren Miller's self-titled character is a young professional on the interview circuit looking to make something special of herself, especially after separating from her smug boyfriend Charlie (James Wolk) who criticized her for being predictable. At the ushering of mutual friend Jesse (Justin Long), Lauren moves in with college enemy Katie (Ari Graynor, in a lead role advantageous to her spunky charisma), who has been living in her late grandmother's very colorful Gramercy Park apartment.

While rooming with Katie amongst their differences, Lauren learns how her seemingly irresponsible roommate is able to pay her bills—she runs a phone sex business out of her bedroom, self-amusingly catering to horny clients while sprawled on her bed in her deceased relative's outdated clothes. After recovering from the initial stagger of this secret, Lauren decides to assist Katie strictly with the financial aspects of her business, until she discovers her own talent in working the phones herself.

For a distinct look for the film, first-time helmer Jamie Travis utilizes a neon palette inspired by modern hipster culture's flashy embrace of the 1980s, accelerated by his eye for expressive color as seen in his previous short *The Saddest Boy In the World* (2006). This aesthetic, a playful and fresh contrast to the often murky presentation of sex as a business, is reinforced by Katie's thoroughly retro costume design (by Maya Lieberman), which paints Katie as a woman in arrested development who has retreated from contemporary responsibility by expressing herself through past fashions of bell-bottoms and jumpsuits. And of course, there are the film's pink phones, a thorough reminder of the employee's omnipresent innocence behind their business.

Though both Graynor and Miller focus too heavily on servicing archetypes (Graynor the free-spirit, Miller the priss) than daring to challenge expectations, the two actresses do give the central unusual coupling an appealing sense to their juxtaposition. Should they have a more clever script centered on any profession, whether it is about construction workers, superhero cape designers, or fast food restaurant mascots, this duo's promising chemistry would still clash and/or match productively.

The film's phone sex humor unsuccessfully relies on its dialogue's shock potential, as it uses the type of X-rated sexual phrases one would not initially expect to be said by a clean cut lady such as Lauren. That being said, such supposedly bold humor often falls onto bored ears. It is vulgarity just for the sake of being vulgar, regardless as to who says it, or what bright color the character's bedroom workplace is.

Breezy perversion is not the only concept that this script struggles to productively toy with; the film's lacking cleverness is apparent in side characters, like Long's flamboyantly stereotypical gay character, played with little imagination through lisp riffs. And then there are Lauren's proper parents, (as played by Mimi Rogers and Don McManus) who are limply included in the story to provide disposable cover-up situations concerning Lauren's scrambling to hide evidence of her new job choice during apartment visits. However, Nia Vardalos, a comedian in need of a strong job herself, has an amusing cameo as a serious face potential employer for Lauren, in need of her own liberation from blandness.

Especially in an age of private entertainment like internet pornography, *For A Good Time, Call...* does not delve into why phone sex is a preferred method of casual intimacy for some clients. The script does however get a little giggly worth when expressing examples that depict the ridiculousness behind the usage of phone sex, as seen in the depiction of masturbating male customers who call the hotline in the middle of their workdays. These moments, featuring Kevin Smith, Ken Marino, and Seth Rogen in cameos, are where the script succeeds most with its goofy humor towards the phone sex business. It is a comedic setup that the film could benefit from more of (especially if more comedian cameos were included), while still maintaining the film's focus to be the unlikely camaraderie of Lauren and Katie, and their bond through a unique method of income. Showing males make perverted bozos of themselves in a predominantly female movie might be an easy gag, but it is surely a more-rounded tactic than solely relying on the shock value of a salacious phrase.

Co-written by Miller and Katie Ann Naylon, who plant their friendship's own autobiographical details within the film (and not only by the usage of their own names), *For A Good Time, Call...* is a serviceable comedy about two young ladies who reinstitute the concept of friendliness back into the Generation X term "frenemy." With such autobiographical inspiration highly evident, this comedy's general perspective is the offspring of that of its two main characters. Too often the brashness of this story flirts with being desperate, like Graynor's flamboyant Katie, who plays the extreme extrovert, the friend who uses loud laughs to inform all of those around her how happy she is. At the same time, *For A Good Time, Call...* is generically guiltless like Miller's Lauren, who decides to take on this strange venture to primarily flabbergast herself most of all. Combine these traits, and one is left with *For A Good Time, Call...*—a comedy that is surprised at the lecherous content that has spewed from its naughty mouth, and then laughs loudly with its innocent self, assuming everyone else thinks it is funny as well.

Nick Allen

CREDITS

Lauren Powell: Lauren Anne Miller
Katie Steele: Ari Graynor
Jesse: Justin Long
Charlie: James Wolk
Sean: Mark Webber
Scott Powell: Don McManus
Adele Powell: Mimi Rogers
Rachel Rodman: Nia Vardalos

Origin: United States

Language: English

Released: 2012

Production: Lauren Anne Miller, Katie Anne Naylon; AdScott; released by Focus Features

Directed by: Jamie Travis

Written by: Lauren Anne Miller; Katie Anne Naylon

Cinematography by: James Laxton

Music by: John Swihart

Sound: B.J. Lehn

Editing: Evan Henke

Art Direction: Dustin Cardwell

Costumes: Maya Lieberman

Production Design: Sue Tebbutt

MPAA rating: R

Running time: 86 minutes

REVIEWS

Covert, Colin. *Minneapolis Star Tribune*. September 6, 2012.

Ebert, Roger. *Chicago Sun-Times*. August 30, 2012.

Hunt, Drew. *Chicago Reader*. September 14, 2012.

Lemire, Christy. *Associated Press*. August 10, 2012.

Long, Tom. *Detroit News*. September 7, 2012.

Morris, Wesley. *Boston Globe*. August 30, 2012.

Rickey, Carrie. *Philadelphia Inquirer*. September 6, 2012.

Stevens, Dana. *Slate*. September 1, 2012.

Taylor, Ella. *NPR*. August 30, 2012.

Stewart, Sara. *New York Post*. August 31, 2012.

QUOTES

Katie Steele: "You know you're not better than me. You're not better than phone sex."

TRIVIA

The film was shot in just sixteen days.

FOR GREATER GLORY

He was the last man to believe in their cause.
But became the first willing to die for it.
—Movie tagline

Box Office: $5.7 million

There is an excellent film lurking in Dean Wright's *For Greater Glory* that longs to be free of the over-stuffed, ham-fisted tone in which it is trapped. Like John Singleton's *Rosewood* (1997), *For Greater Glory* is an example of a horrific and little known historical event that is the perfect subject for a film but fails because it is not conveyed with the subtly it requires.

That is unfortunate because the historical events chronicled in the film are inherently fascinating and lend themselves well to a drama. It is 1926 in Mexico and the recently elected President Calles (Reuben Blades) has declared war on Catholics. His Congress passes restrictive laws, which make it illegal for priests to conduct services or even say mass privately in the absence of a congregation. Unsurprisingly, this does not go over well with the Catholic population and clandestine services and pockets of resistance start opening up throughout the country. Calles meets this with murderous proto-Nazi measures. Soon, government troops are hanging priests in their churches, gunning them down against the walls of their cathedrals and Catholic resistance fighters are ambushing government troops in response.

For Greater Glory admirably seeks to depict the Cristeros War in it all it societal scope but bites off more than it can chew with too many characters and subplots. The most interesting and developed character is Andy Garcia as retired general Enrique Gorostieta. Gorostieta is lured out of retirement to lead the Catholic revolutionaries after a well-meaning but out of his depth priest accidentally kills hundreds of innocent people by ordering a train he thinks is empty to be set on fire. The revolutionaries consequently decide to recruit a leader with actual military experience to lead them. Enrique is not a Catholic and agrees to lead the rebels, at least initially, for the money. However, as the atrocities escalate he becomes more personally involved and views the rebellion as a matter of religious freedom. Screenwriter Michael Love gives Gorostieta some good speeches to deliver and Garcia has not been this good in anything in years. Garcia has made so many lackluster films for so many years that the viewer might forget that he is a decent actor when given a decent role to play. Unfortunately, his is the only memorable character in the film.

Eva Longoria plays Gorostieta's wife, Tulita, in a role that is little more than a cameo. She is wasted in the boring, predictable role of the wife who believes in the cause but fears for her husband's safety. Similarly squandered is the great Peter O'Toole who plays an elderly Catholic priest, Father Christopher, who represents the argument for non-violent resistance to the President's discriminatory laws. He declines to engage in or endorse violence but agrees to house the sick and poor and to continue to say mass, if only to himself. Shortly after being introduced he is facing a firing squad. Representing the opposing ideological extreme is Father Vega (Santiago Cabrera) who thinks the only way to fight violence is with violence. Very much agreeing with him is the pro Catholic bandito Victoriano Ramirez (Oscar Issac) nicknamed "El Catorce" (the Fourteen) because, as the film depicts in a sequence that would make Jason Statham proud, according to legend, he singlehandedly killed fourteen government agents in one engagement.

The film would have its work cut out for itself telling just these characters' stories but it also commits itself to telling the stories of the local mayor (*Lost's* Nestor Carbonell) and his teenage Godson Jose (Mauricio Kuri) who goes from thief to rebel to martyred saint. Then there is President Calles and his involvement with American president Calvin Coolidge (Bruce McGill) and Coolidge's Ambassador to Mexico Dwight Morrow (Bruce Greenwood) and the story of Dona Maria del Rio de Sanchez (Karyme Lozano) who is smuggling ammunition for the rebellion and her husband Anacleto Gonzalez Flores (Eduardo Verastegui) who is in a murkily depicted leadership position in the rebellion.

All of these true life stories have significant dramatic potential but they are fatally undercut by not enough running time (even at 145 minutes) to adequately do the individual stories justice. The film buckles under the weight of all of the stories it is trying to tell and as a result fails to tell any of them compellingly. As a consequence, *For Greater Glory* is an exercise of cross cutting from one story the viewer has not been made to care about to another story the viewer has not been made to care about. *For Greater Glory* feels like a six-hour mini-series chopped down to two-and-a-half. An HBO series would have been perhaps been a more appropriate venue for tackling such a complicated historical event with so many characters and subplots.

An HBO adaptation would have also helped with an even more fundamental problem, the script's total lack of subtly, something all the running time in the world cannot fix. The historical events depicted in the film are no doubt incendiary but one doubts they are as simplistic and black white as portrayed in the film. As Ambassador Morrow and representatives of the rebellion lunch on a train, murdered Catholics hang from telephone poles lining the tracks. The ne'er-do-well Jose goes from tossing dog feces at Father Christopher's head to martyred sainthood, walking to his execution by firing squad in a beyond over-the-top portrayal of Christ's walk to crucifixion. By the end of the film the atheist Gorostieta has converted to Catholicism. Far too much of *For Greater Glory* plays like an inspirational special on the Catholic Television Network EWTN.

As a result, there is little to recommend about *For Greater Glory*. With its inherently dramatic subject and ambitious narrative scope it is obvious that Wright and Love wanted *For Greater Glory* to be an epic film and the film certainly has all the trappings of such a production: A lush score by James Horner, lavish sets, exquisite period costumes, and battle scenes featuring hundreds of

extras. All that is missing is a focused and realistic script that does its compelling subject justice. It is as if Wright and Love looked at the outrageous historical facts and assumed that the story had written itself.

Nate Vercauteren

CREDITS

Enrique Gorotieta Velarde: Andy Garcia
Victoriano Ramirez: Oscar Isaac
President Plutarco Elias Calles: Ruben Blades
Father Christopher: Peter O'Toole
Ambassador Morrow: Bruce Greenwood
Tulita: Eva Longoria
Mayor Picazo: Nestor Carbonell
President Calvin Coolidge: Bruce McGill
Origin: United States
Language: English, Spanish
Released: 2012
Production: Pablo Jose Barroso; Dos Corazones Films, Newland Films; released by ARC Entertainment
Directed by: Dean Wright
Written by: Michael Love
Cinematography by: Eduardo Martinez Solares
Music by: James Horner
Sound: Dane A. Davis
Editing: Richard Francis-Bruce
Costumes: Maria Estela Fernandez
Production Design: Salvador Parra
MPAA rating: R
Running time: 145 minutes

REVIEWS

Adams, Sam. *Time Out New York*. May 29, 2012.
Baumgarten, Marjorie. *Austin Chronicle*. May 31, 2012.
Ebert, Roger. *Chicago Sun Times*. May 30, 2012.
Holden, Stephen. *New York Times*. May 31, 2012.
Leydon, Joe. *Variety*. May 31, 2012.
Lumenick, Lou. *New York Post*. June 1, 2012.
Morris, Wesley. *Boston Globe*. May 31, 2012.
Orange, Michelle. *Movieline*. May 31, 2012.
Pinkerton, Nick. *Village Voice*. May 29, 2012.
Rabin, Nathan. *AV Club*. May 30, 2012.

TRIVIA

Partially financed by the Knights of Columbus, whose American and Mexican members were an integral part of the actual Cristeros Rebellion.

FRANKENWEENIE

The electrifying dog is back from beyond the grave.
—Movie tagline

Box Office: $35.3 million

From director Tim Burton, who's more recent movies have been of the "adapted" variety—including not so original material like *Alice in Wonderland, Planet of the Apes, Charlie & the Chocolate Factory,* or even *Sweeney Todd: The Demon Barber of Fleet Street*—comes *Frankenweenie,* an expanded version of the far-superior half-hour live-action short of the same name that he made for Disney way back in 1984. Apparently in an effort to make clear once and for all that he is forever stuck in the past and hopelessly devoted to reworking old ideas, Burton's more recent incarnation of *Frankenweenie* is not only an homage to the golden era of the horror film, but it is also a remake of something much better he made a long time ago. Why tap the old idea well again? Perhaps it's as simple as it being a comfort-zone thing. Burton has been delivering his quirky, bizarre world vision for so long now maybe he can't do anything else. Or, it could be that the urge to make light of a pet dying by flippantly saying you can simply bring it back to life with a little electricity was just too great. Of course, that reduces the film to a base element that it might not deserve as I'm sure that was not the intent of the filmmakers, but the fact remains that *Frankenweenie* is a reminder of what was once so cool about the cinema of Tim Burton and what has since become tedious about it as well.

The film ostensibly begins as a heartwarming tale about a boy and his dog. When his beloved dog Sparky is hit by a car and killed, young Victor Frankenstein (Charlie Tahan) decides (as did his namesake) to play god and bring Sparky back from the dead. Inspired by a Vincent Price-like science teacher named Mr. Rzykruski (Martin Landeau), Victor harnesses the awesome power of electricity (via the old horror-film stand-by—the lightning storm) to bring his best friend back to life. As might be expected, Victor's experiment is a rousing success. In fact, Sparky seems to be Victor's same-old lovable pooch, albeit with a couple bolts sticking out of his neck and a few body parts that don't seem to want to stay attached. Perhaps this is the reason that Victor feels he has to hide Sparky from his parents (Catherine O'Hara and Martin Short) and the rest of the town. Regardless, no endeavor like this ever plays out without getting wildly complicated. This comes to pass when the town's other misfit children begin usurping Victor's reanimation technique by leaving out the key component of love and create a cadre of monsters that terrorize the spooky little hamlet, leaving Victor and his loyal friend Sparky to clean up the mess.

Much like Martin Scorsese's wonderful *Hugo* was a reflective love letter to early days of cinema, *Frankenweenie* is at times a clever and beautiful homage to the look and feel of the old Universal horror films. Unfortunately there's not much else to it. Sure, it looks great and anyone with even a passing knowledge of horror-film history will be delighted with all of the allusions and references buried within this movie. But the story plays out in an almost paint-by-numbers way that concludes with a colossal monster attack straight out of something like *Godzilla* or *The Beast from 20,000 Fathoms* designed to wrap everything up in a tight little storytelling package. But it doesn't. Screenwriter John August, who has done much better work with Burton in the past (including *Corpse Bride*), starts with the premise of Burton's 1984 short-film (which is more or less the film's first act) and adds very little in the way of anything worth caring about. For a tale that's supposedly about a boy and his beloved dog, there sure are a lot of weird peripheral characters and grotesque reanimated pets running around causing a lot of destruction and muddying up what should be a much simpler story. There's even an underlying message that encourages the viewer to embrace science so that mankind can move forward. Don't get me wrong, this is a great idea and at times, *Frankenweenie* proves to be a lot of fun exploring it, but spending time inside what Betsy Sharkey called, in the *Los Angeles Times,* the "darkly ironic mind" of Tim Burton, just doesn't hold the same cachet it once did. Essentially, the story was tighter and far more entertaining and poignant when it was just twenty minutes long and Burton had more to say than look how odd I am.

Despite all of this, the film does manage to entertain on a few levels, but it's an empty fulfillment. Ultimately, *Frankenweenie* is a reminder of how great Tim Burton used to be, if it is only a faint echo of what he once was. As Todd McCarthy wrote in the *Hollywood Reporter,* regardless of the reverence the film showers on the horror films of old, *Frankenweenie* feels "like second-generation photocopies of things Burton has done before. It all feels pretty rote and empty, drained of the old Burtonjuice."

Michael J. Tyrkus

CREDITS

Victor Frankenstein: Charlie Tahan (Voice)
Mr. Walsh: Martin Short (Voice)
Susan Frankenstein: Catherine O'Hara (Voice)
Elsa von Helsing: Winona Ryder (Voice)
Mr. Rzykruski: Martin Landau (Voice)
Bob: Robert Capron (Voice)
Bob's Mom: Conchata Ferrell (Voice)
Movie Dracula: Christopher Lee (Voice)
Origin: United States
Language: English
Released: 2012

Production: Tim Burton, Allison Abbate; released by Walt Disney Pictures

Directed by: Tim Burton

Written by: John August

Cinematography by: Peter Sorg

Music by: Danny Elfman

Sound: Oliver Tarney

Editing: Mark Solomon

Production Design: Rick Heinrichs

MPAA rating: PG

Running time: 87 minutes

REVIEWS

Baird, Kirk. *Toledo Blade.* October 4, 2012.

Burr, Ty. *Boston Globe.* October 4, 2012.

Corliss, Richard. *Time.* October 4, 2012.

Ebert, Roger. *Chicago Sun-Times.* October 3, 2012.

Puig, Claudia. *USA Today.* October 4, 2012.

McCarthy, Todd. *Hollywood Reporter.* September 20, 2012.

Schwarzbaum, Lisa. *Entertainment Weekly.* October 3, 2012.

Scott, A. O. *New York Times.* October 4, 2012.

Sharkey, Betsy. *Los Angeles Times.* October 4, 2012.

Travers, Peter. *Rolling Stone.* October 4, 2012.

QUOTES

Mr. Rzykruski: "Ladies and gentlemen. I think the confusion here is that you are all very ignorant. Is that right word, ignorant? I mean stupid, primitive, unenlightened. You do not understand science, so you are afraid of it. Like a dog is afraid of thunder or balloons. To you, science is magic and witchcraft because you have such small minds. I cannot make your heads bigger, but your children's heads, I can take them and crack them open. This is what I try to do, to get at their brains!"

TRIVIA

Persephone the poodle is named after the Greek goddess who was kidnapped by and then forcibly married to Hades.

AWARDS

Nominations:

Oscars 2012: Animated Film

British Acad. 2012: Animated Film

Golden Globes 2013: Animated Film

FRIENDS WITH KIDS

Love. Happiness. Kids. Pick two.
    —Movie tagline

Family doesn't always go according to plan.
    —Movie tagline

Box Office: $7.3 million

It is common knowledge that it is best to avoid assuming and judging the motives of two people's decision to have a child except in the case of *Friends with Kids,* which presents the audience with two, arrogant New Yorkers who decide to become parents for wholly selfish reasons. She wants to get a kid "out of the way" so that she might fastidiously start the process of looking for, what she calls, "my person"—the man she will meet who will sweep her off of her feet and live the rest of her life with her. He wants a child because he wants a child. Neither wants the other person for a relationship; they will simply have a baby and split custody.

The potential for disaster should be apparent to anyone with a basic knowledge of human behavior, the inherent complexity of any family structure, and, of course, the rules of middling romantic comedies such as this one. One's willingness to go along with the basic concept of Julie Keller (Jennifer Westfeldt, who also wrote and directed the movie) and Jason Fryman's (Adam Scott) choice will depend almost entirely on one's political persuasion. Some will see it as an example of the decline of the "traditional family" and an attack on the values that go along with that unrealistic notion; others will simply see it as progress—as the old cliche goes, "Different strokes for different folks."

On a theoretical level, there is nothing inherently wrong about the characters' decision. Westfeldt's screenplay, though, presents a scenario that is too specific to skirt by on an abstract concept. Its characters are too self-centered to escape disapproval, and the rose-tinted results of their plan are as naive as those critics of so-called "alternative families." The script takes far too long for reality to arrive for it to be authentic and for the characters to experience any humbleness about the gravity of the situation for them to be sympathetic.

Julie and Jason are an odd couple—friends who have known each other for so long that they feel comfortable playing a game in which they must choose between one hypothetical death or another. In a blatant bit of foreshadowing, Julie asks Jason if he would rather watch the person he loves die a slow, painful death or die himself. He answers the former, and it is only a matter of time before the question comes up again. They share the intimate details of the love lives, talking to each other late at night on the phone as their partners sleep beside them. Julie has not had a relationship of any kind in a while; Jason has had many of the short-term variety.

They meet with their friends for dinner. Leslie (Maya Rudolph) and Alex (Chris O'Dowd) are expecting their first child, the announcement of which embarrasses Julie and Jason after they ranted about bringing a kid to the fancy restaurant at which the friends meet. Ben (Jon Hamm) and Missy (Kristen Wiig) are recently married and are having sex in the bathroom at the restaurant when Julie and Jason arrive. Four years later, Leslie and Alex have had a second child, and Ben and Missy now have one of their own.

The plan comes to fruition during one of Julie and Jason's regular talks. They see how children have put a damper on their friends' respective marriages. Both dread the idea of loving a person (the child) more than the person with whom they will have decided to spend the rest of their lives. At this point, Westfeldt at least gives the audience a reasonable—if stereotypical—rationale for Julie to want a child. Jason's motive, though, is wholly inconsistent with the information she reveals about him. Here is a man who shirks emotional responsibility in his relationships without so much as a second thought, yet the idea to have a baby with Julie is his in the first place. Despite the erratic character logic, they decide to conceive the old-fashioned way, aided by alcohol to get over the jitters.

The actual child rearing is deceptively simple. The pair splits time evenly and enlists the aid of a nanny. After some time has passed, they invite their friends, who imagine the worst, over for a get-together; the group is shocked to see what looks like domestic bliss. Also of a suspiciously convenient nature is that both Julie and Jason meet people they believe are worthy of a serious relationship: Kurt (Edward Burns) for Julie and Mary Jane (Megan Fox) for Jason. Julie develops feelings for Jason, who has no intention of reciprocating.

The first half of the film relies primarily on situational comedy and the familiar characterization do the setup no favors. When Ben, whose collapsing marriage drives him to drink heavily, finally says what everyone has been thinking about Julie and Jason's situation, the honesty is refreshing (even if Westfeldt intends him to be a thoughtless jerk in the scene, given how passionately Jason defends their parenting). Soon after this point, the movie provides a transitional montage that shows the characters adjusting to new lives. It is a surprisingly effective sequence that finally addresses and resembles something approaching reality.

Unfortunately, the candor cannot last, and *Friends with Kids* resorts to the easiest of conflicts for its climax: Julie revealing her feelings and, after a lot of manipulative turns (including their son [Owen Bento] wondering why his dad does not live with them) and hemming and hawing, Jason coming to realize that she is "his person." Just as Westfeldt begins to explore the real complexity of this scenario, she falls back on formula.

Mark Dujsik

CREDITS

Julie Keller: Jennifer Westfeldt
Jason Fryman: Adam Scott

Ben: Jon Hamm
Missy: Kristen Wiig
Leslie: Maya Rudolph
Alex: Chris O'Dowd
Mary Jane: Megan Fox
Kurt: Edward Burns
Origin: United States
Language: English
Released: 2012
Production: Joshua Astrachan, Riza Aziz, Jon Hamm, Jake Kasdan, Lucy Barzun Donnelly, Jon Hamm; Locomotive, Points West Pictures, Red Granite Pictures; released by Roadside Attractions
Directed by: Jennifer Westfeldt
Written by: Jennifer Westfeldt
Cinematography by: William Rexer
Music by: Marcelo Zarvos
Sound: Ruy Garcia; Eliza Paley
Music Supervisor: Stephanie Diaz-Matos; Randall Poster
Editing: Tara Timpone
Costumes: Melissa Bruning
Production Design: Ray Kluga
MPAA rating: R
Running time: 100 minutes

REVIEWS

Anderson, Melissa. *Village Voice*. March 7, 2012.
Ebert, Roger. *Chicago Sun-Times*. March 7, 2012.
Edelstein, David. *New York Magazine*. March 4, 2012.
Hornaday, Ann. *Washington Post*. March 9, 2012.
Morris, Wesley. *Boston Globe*. March 9, 2012.
O'Hehir, Andrew. *Salon.com*. March 6, 2012.
Phillips, Michael. *Chicago Tribune*. March 8, 2012.
Robinson, Tasha. *AV Club*. March 8, 2012.
Stevens, Dana. *Slate*. March 9, 2012.
Zacharek, Stephanie. *Movieline*. March 6, 2012.

QUOTES

Jason Fryman: "Please, please, just let me f**k the sh*t out of you right now. And if you're not convinced afterwards that I am into you in every possible way a person can be into another person, then I promise I will never try to kiss you, or f**k you, or impregnate you ever again, as long as I live."

TRIVIA

Kristen Wiig shot most of her scenes on Sundays due to her role on *Saturday Night Live*.

FUN SIZE

Some people just can't handle Halloween.
—Movie tagline

Box Office: $9.4 million

Sorely missing the kid gloves comedic handling of a laugh track, *Fun Size* is a teen comedy made to slowly grow teen star Victoria Justice along with a fan base who would best recognize her from her canned laughter Nickelodeon sitcom, *Victorious*. Justice's tactic for staying relevant to her aging audience is to maintain her sitcom's wackiness while playing the *Project X* (2012) card, offering her own PG-13 demographic the shocking raucousness of that film, which itself was influenced by movies like *Superbad* (2007) and *Can't Hardly Wait* (1998). Whereas *Project X* has nonchalant usage of substances like the deadly ecstasy, all with the purpose of serving the hankering to experience "The Best Night Ever," *Fun Size* has the PG-13 equivalent, parading its underage characters on a night of breast-touching, humping mechanical chickens, and most importantly, make-out sessions. The film may be inspired by the truth expressed in the higher echelon of teen comedies, but *Fun Size's* lack of laughs and reliability on dated references has *Fun Size* destined to languish in the ranks of dated teen B-movies like *Valley Girl* (1983) (whereas *Valley Girl* has mall food courts, *Fun Size* has Facebook chat).

In her first wide release feature film performance, Justice plays Wren, a high school senior hoping to leave Cleveland ("The mistake by the lake," as she calls it) for New York University, even though she would be leaving behind her mother Joy and younger brother Albert, who mourn the loss of their husband/father. Each of them has taken on their own way of coping with the death—Wren wears her father's Def Jam Records jacket everyday (formerly worn by Mike D of the Beastie Boys), Albert has become mute, and Joy has started dating younger men with ridiculous names like Keevin (Josh Pence).

On the night of Halloween, when Wren is prepared to go to the popular Aaron Reilly's (Thomas McDonell) party, she is saddled with Albert babysitting duty, much to the dismay of her excited and socially conscious redhead friend April (Jane Levy). While taking Albert trick-or-treating, Wren loses her brother when he vanishes in a haunted house, in search of his own adventure. Such rebelliousness sends Wren and the annoyed April to ask the help of their friend Roosevelt, who can drive (played by Thomas Mann, also from *Project X*) and his pal Peng (Osric Chau, playing the stereotypical role of Goofy Asian Sidekick).

This sets up three different plots, unfurling at the same time: Albert is recruited by new friend Fuzzy (Thomas Middleditch), a convenience store employee who is trying to get revenge on Jorgen (Johnny Knoxville), the man who stole his former girlfriend. Meanwhile, Joy finds herself unhappy in her boyfriend's crowd of younger friends. All of this happens while Wren is on a wild brother chase through an assortment of wacky events, all to the displeasure of April, who would rather be at Aaron's party.

Lacking robust charisma, Justice's line delivery is not strong enough, something that avalanches into a banal performance; her innocence as a slightly dorky high-schooler (who initially considers Ruth Bader Ginsberg as a Halloween costume) mistaken for blandness. The actress' presence is aloof, and certainly missing any of the spark that makes for a successful teen comedy splash like Emma Stone's successful introduction in the similarly rambunctious *Easy A* (2010). Justice is a suitable filler of the shoes of a generic type (her character's name seems like the screenwriter's last attempt at making her remotely memorable), but she does not lay any claim in this performance as to why she should be able to keep this type of employment.

A further reminder of this movie's misplacement on the silver screen instead of television is the cinematography by Yaron Orbach, and the editing by Michael L. Sale, which make this film visually disposable. Save for the usage of slow motion (whether comedically, to show Chau making a humping gesture, or dramatically, when Justice runs through the night), the aesthetic work is barely serviceable, and insignificant at most. Schwartz's cheeky melding of scenes in which characters become very close to seeing each other, but ultimately do not, becomes a tired winking gag. A video that Albert edits at the end of the story has more attitude than any of the uninspired filmmaking by first-time director Josh Schwartz here (and not just because it features Auto-Tune work by YouTube-famous group The Gregory Brothers).

As contrived a story and deprived of cinematic quality the movie may be, the film's diehard desire to jostle parents' moral compasses while possibly winning over the relation of its teen viewers is admirable, if not fascinating. In a single scene, the rambunctious *Fun Size* makes references to cocaine (referring to "mainlining" a sugar stick) and pedophilia (when Fuzzy jokes to himself that he is inviting Albert into his car), all within the confines of the "La La La" thematic whimsy that this movie continuously carries itself on. Like *Big Shots*, the 1987 kid comedy about two Chicago pre-teens who accidentally steal a car with a dead body in it, *Fun Size* is a curious moment for PG-13 amorality, especially in an entertainment society that seems so invested in keeping a young demographic (and young characters) protected by politically correct representations of "adult" content. Whereas *Project X* touted ecstasy, *Fun Size* is the bubble gum cigarette equivalent—questionable as to whether it provides a damning moral influence to its young clients, or if it is embraced by its conscious target audience for allotting them a fleeting moment of mature vice.

While the film's recklessness might be its only spark of creativity, Max Werner's script does have a certain energy to it. With three separate stories unfolding at the same time, Werner loads his script with enough problems that it always feels busy, regardless as to whether viewers are invested in the characters' conflicts. It is in the third act, when all three stories are tied together for a tonally disastrous finale, that the movie bares itself true to its messiness, a shabby assemblance of butt jokes and dangerous kiddie shenanigans, motivated by the subconscious goal to educate viewers fresh to the PG-13 party about the dangers of cliches in teen comedies.

Nick Allen

CREDITS

Wren: Victoria Justice
Albert: Jackson Nicoll
April: Jane Levy
Joy: Chelsea Handler
Roosevelt: Thomas Mann
Peng: Osric Chau
Aaron Riley: Thomas A. McDonnell
Fuzzy: Thomas Middleditch
Jorgen: Johnny Knoxville
Origin: United States
Language: English
Released: 2012
Production: Bard Dorros, David Kanter, Stephanie Savage, Josh Schwartz; Anonymous Content, Fake Empire; released by Paramount Pictures Corp.
Directed by: Josh Schwartz
Written by: Max Werner

Cinematography by: Yaron Orbach
Music by: Deborah Lurie
Sound: Terry Rodman
Editing: Michael L. Sale
Art Direction: Lauren Fitzsimmons
Costumes: Eric Daman
Production Design: Mark White
MPAA rating: PG-13
Running time: 90 minutes

REVIEWS

Baker, Andrew. *Variety*. October 25, 2012.
Chaney, Jen. *Washington Post*. October 26, 2012.
Ebiri, Blige. *New York Magazine*. October 29, 2012.
Hartlaub, Peter. *San Francisco Chronicle*. October 25, 2012.
Linden, Sheri. *Hollywood Reporter*. October 26, 2012.
Longworth, Karina. *Village Voice*. October 23, 2012.
Moore, Roger. *McClatchy-Tribune News Service*. October 25, 2012.
Olsen, Mark. *Los Angeles Times*. October 25, 2012.
Smith, Kyle. *New York Post*. October 26, 2012.
Zacharek, Stephanie. *NPR*. October 25, 2012.

QUOTES

Jorgen: "Time to get elbow deep in a little Pepto-Bismol!"

TRIVIA

The film received a PG-13 rating from the MPAA, making it the second film from Nickelodeon Movies, after *Angus, Thongs and Perfect Snogging*, to receive this rating.

G

THE GATEKEEPERS
(Shomerei Ha'saf)

Box Office: $380,580

Dror Moreh's Oscar-nominated *The Gatekeepers* is a stunningly vital piece of work in the conversation about how countries deal with terrorism, the continuously volatile times in the Middle East, and the symbiotic relationship between people who cause violent acts and those who seek to stop them. Inspired by Errol Morris' stunning masterpiece *The Fog of War* (2003), Moreh casts a similarly-insightful light on every one of the men who have led one of Israel's intelligence agencies, Shin Bet, since its inception. The equivalent would be a film that featured one-on-one dissections of the Central Intelligence Agency and the decisions made in the name of America's safety with not only journalists and politicians but the people at the top of the power totem pole. Moreh's film has a stunningly forceful power as these men speak not only of changes in Israel and the way its government deals with violence but the gray areas that should be the focus of any ruling body, especially one that could take innocent lives. Dealing with civilian casualties, uncertainty about targets, and even the complex nature of vengeance, *The Gatekeepers* features a striking degree of honesty about decision-making in Israel, the constant interplay of choosing between two evils, and how these issues reflect on power structures around the world.

In *The Fog of War*, Robert McNamara looked back on the impact of his decisions on modern warfare. Inspired by the film and whether or not a similar piece could be built around Shin Bet, Moreh approached the six men who have led the agency through some of the most controversial and violence-filled times in the Middle East. The men seem somewhat reticent to talk about the most notable decisions of their regimes (understandably, they were most restrained when discussing the decisions that led to their forced retirements, especially for the older gentlemen), but, for the most part, they open up in breathtaking ways, discussing the concept of martyrdom (weighing the decision to let a terrorist live, knowing he may kill again, because taking him out might only make his cause seem more worth fighting), the importance of intelligence, failure of leadership in their own country, and the power of public and international perception. A major turning point in the history of Israel and a breathtaking sequence in the film, recreated through 3-D animations and archival photographs, revolves around an incident in which a bus of civilians was taken hostage by terrorists and how the evil-doers were brutally handled. The man in charge at the time practically admits that he does not consider the violent response under his orders was a mistake, instead the error was that the results were caught on camera. It is just one example in which Moreh copied the most important lesson from Morris' work—it is the interview that matters most of all. Moreh asks just the right questions, never pushing these men too far that they would shut down but also not allowing them to whitewash or rewrite important chapters in Israeli history.

The interviews form the bulk of *The Gatekeepers* but the documentary is masterful because of the way that Moreh then assembled his talking-head footage into a riveting film partitioned, in a very Morris-esque move, into seven segments. Not only does each segment generally cover one head of Shin Bet but they also illustrate the changing times in the country from the emergence of the organization altogether to the Oslo Accords to the assassination of Yitzhak Rabin to the growth of Hamas to the increasingly unstable atmosphere of violence in the country today. Throughout it all, as outlined in an introduction in which the (at the time of filming) current leader of Shin Bet describes the split-second decisions that could take innocent lives that often need to be made, the theme of the film seems to be common—there are no good options. There is no time for second guessing. It may be the wrong guy in the sight of that missile strike but if it is the right guy then he could get away and take hundreds of lives or even assassinate the Prime Minister. What percentage chance is worth taking? What degree of collateral damage is acceptable? And can all of these decisions be made in the blink of an eye?

The Gatekeepers is far from the first documentary about the turbulent, violent state of existence in Israel, but it is the best. Dror Moreh's work contains not only a heretofore unimaginable degree of personal insight from the men who shaped the policy of one of the most important country's in the world but features those insights shaped into a film by a masterful documentarian, one who was inspired by Errol Morris to make a work that deserves comparison with the work of arguably the best non-fiction filmmaker of the modern era.

Brian Tallerico

CREDITS

Origin: Israel

Language: Hebrew

Released: 2012

Production: Estelle Fialon, Dror Moreh, Philippa Kowarsky; Mac Guff Ligne, Cinephil, Les Films du Poisson; released by Sony Pictures Classics

Directed by: Dror Moreh

Cinematography by: Avner Shahaf

Music by: Ab Ovo; Daniel Meir

Sound: Alex Claude

Editing: Oron Adar

Production Design: Doron Koren

MPAA rating: PG-13

Running time: 95 minutes

REVIEWS

Chang, Justin. *Variety.* December 20, 2012.

McCarthy, Todd. *Hollywood Reporter.* December 20, 2012.

Morgenstern, Joe. *Wall Street Journal.* January 31, 2013.

Nehme, Farran Smith. *New York Post.* November 26, 2012.

Neumaier, Joe. *New York Daily News.* November 29, 2012.

Rainer, Peter. *Christian Science Monitor.* February 1, 2013.

Schwarzbaum, Lisa. *Entertainment Weekly.* February 6, 2013.

Scott, A. O. *New York Times.* November 26, 2012.

Semley, John. *Slant Magazine.* November 26, 2012.

Turan, Kenneth. *Los Angeles Times.* November 26, 2012.

AWARDS

Nominations:

Oscars 2012: Feature Doc.

GHOST RIDER: SPIRIT OF VENGEANCE
(Ghost Rider 2)

He rides again.
—Movie tagline

Box Office: $51.8 million

Two irresistible forces converged to green light *Ghost Rider: Spirit of Vengeance,* a sequel no one was waiting for: 1. Nicolas Cage's need for quick cash, and a lot of it, given his well publicized tax woes (resulting in his starring in a staggering seven films in 2011 and 2012) and 2. Hollywood's insatiable desire to adapt every comic book ever made into as many films as possible regardless of the comic's popularity or appropriateness for the screen. The result is a film as poorly written and disappointing as its 2007 predecessor.

In their excellent history of comic books, *The Comic Book Heroes,* Gerard Jones and Will Jacobs called the 1970s the "awkward age" for comic books for good reason. This was a decade where the historically dominant superheroes in tights found themselves playing second fiddle to comics about Dracula, werewolves, barbarians, kung fu, swamp creatures and, in the case of Ghost Rider, a leather clad, motor cycle riding bounty hunter for the devil with a flaming skull for a head. A very '70s brew of the occult, Evel Kneivel and the outlaw biker culture of the Hells Angels, anti-hero Ghost Rider is a "you won't like me when I'm angry" superhero in the vein of Dr. Jekyll & Mr. Hyde and The Incredible Hulk. By day he is Johnny Blaze, a motorcycle daredevil carnie; by night he is the Ghost Rider, tracking down sinners, demons and escapees from hell. The 2007 film recounted his origin story in which Blaze sells his soul to the devil to save his dying father's life and in return must work as the devil's henchman. *Ghost Rider* is not the most translatable premise in the history of comic-to-film adaptations but, as evidenced by Guillermo del Toro's similarly themed *Hellboy* (2004, 2008) films, excellent writing and an appropriately non-serious approach to the material can invest the viewer in even the most unusual of characters and situations. Unfortunately, as with its predecessor, *Spirit of Vengeance* has a terminally generic script and the viewer spends most of the film enduring some of the worst dialogue of 2012 waiting for the next action sequence, which are doled out far too sparingly in both films presumably due to budget limitations.

There are two types of sequels, planned sequels and unplanned sequels. In its purest form, the planned sequel is a single work of art consciously broken into multiple installments (see *Lord of the Rings* [2001-2003], or serialized television at its best like *The Wire* [2002-2008]). This type of sequel feels necessary and inevitable, concerned with continuity and continuing a story deliberately mapped from conception into carefully thought out parts. On the other end of extreme is the paycheck-star-vehicle sequel which retains the star from the first film and not much else. *Spirit of Vengeance* very much falls into the latter category and feels more like a reboot of *Ghost Rider* with the same star then an actual sequel to the 2007 film. *Spirit of Vengeance* makes no reference to the events of the first film (including Blaze's romantic relationship with Roxanne Simpson), re-sets the action to a new setting, Eastern Europe (one suspects filming was cheaper there), and features none of the supporting characters or actors from the first film.

That is a shame because the sole thing that made the original *Ghost Rider* slightly enjoyable was some pitch perfect casting in a few of the supporting roles. Sam Elliot was born to play the original Ghost Rider, an Old West cowboy (with a steed instead of a motorcycle) and the conscience of Johnny Blaze, and, in a delightfully inspired bit of casting, Peter Fonda was the perfect choice to play the devil to a motorcycle riding demon bounty hunter. They are both gone in *Spirit of Vengeance* along with love interest Eva Mendes. They have been replaced with Idris Elba in the sidekick role, Ciaran Hinds as the devil's earthly emissary, Roarke, and Violante Placido as the love interest. These talented actors do the best they can with their underwritten roles and terrible dialogue but there a limits to what even the best actors can do.

The most successful is Elba, one of the best actors working today, who manages to sell his ridiculous dialogue and even, incredibly, manages to generate some empathy for his character on the part of the viewer. Elba is by far the most interesting thing in the film and one wishes for an entire film to be spun off featuring his holy warrior character. The usually superb Hinds, however, falls uncharacteristically flat. Combining the devil and one of the best character actors working today would seem to be a recipe for an intriguing villain but Hinds simply cannot overcome a script that provides

him with nothing memorable to say or do. The script also fails spectacularly in creating a memorable villain out of Ghost Rider's main adversary in combat, Ray Carrigan (Johnny Whitworth, channeling a young Kurt Russell). As with his counterpart, Blackheart (Wes Bentley), in *Ghost Rider*, Carrigan is a generic pretty boy with no memorable qualities.

As Johnny Blaze, Cage works hard to make his generically written character memorable. A scene where he manically tries to keep from transforming into the Rider is crazy Cage at his trademark best ("he's scrapin' at the door!" he screams in the face of a terrified and uncomprehending baddie). However, this has the unfortunate effect of reminding the viewer of Cage's far more interesting over-the-top performances in many far superior films, particularly his brilliantly manic performance in Werner Herzog's *Bad Lieutenant: Port of Call-New Orleans* (2009). And, once he transforms into the Rider, Cage disappears from the film entirely. Cage trades a flaming skull for a face and when he speaks, it is in an unrecognizable computer enhanced voice. In these scenes, Cage might as well be (and may in fact be) a computer image. Like *Iron Man* (2008), *Spirit of Vengeance* is one of the few superhero movies where the film gets less interesting once the superhero part starts.

When the superhero part does start, the action it produces is nothing memorable. The action in *Spirit of Vengeance* is marginally better than its predecessor, mostly as a result of five years of advances in CGI. But compared to other comic book films it is merely serviceable, looks surprisingly cheap and is doled out rather scrooge-like considering the film's purpose for being is to depict the adventures of a motorcycle riding bounty hunter for Satan.

Cage's *Drive Angry* (2011) demonstrated that a film could get a lot of entertainment out of a modest budget and a ridiculous premise with halfway decent writing, a tongue-in-cheek attitude and wall to wall action. *Ghost Rider: Spirit of Vengeance* possesses none of these attributes and is animated by no spirit, other than the banal spirit of the quick buck. *Spirit of Vengeance* is a highly dispiriting affair for the viewer as a result.

Nate Vercauteren

CREDITS

Johnny Blaze/Ghost Rider: Nicolas Cage
Danny: Fergus Riordan
Roarke: Ciaran Hinds
Nadya: Violante Placido
Moreau: Idris Elba
Ray Carrigan: Johnny Whitworth

Origin: United States

Language: English

Released: 2012

Production: Ashok Amritraj, Ari Arad, Michael De Luca, Steven Paul; Hyde Park Entertainment, Imagenation Abu Dhabi FZ, Marvel Knights; released by Columbia Pictures

Directed by: Mark Neveldine; Brian Taylor

Written by: Scott Gimple; Seth Hoffman

Cinematography by: Brandon Trost

Music by: David Sardy

Sound: Steven Ticknor

Music Supervisor: Kier Lehman

Editing: Brian Berdan

Art Direction: Serban Porupca; Justin Warburton-Brown; Adrian Curelea

Costumes: Bojana Nikitovie

Production Design: Kevin Phipps

MPAA rating: PG-13

Running time: 95 minutes

REVIEWS

Barker, Andrew. *Variety*. February 20, 2012.

DeFore, John. *Hollywood Reporter*. February 17, 2012.

Genzlinger, Neil. *New York Times*. February 17, 2012.

Nordine, Michael. *Slant Magazine*. February 17, 2012.

O'Hara, Helen. *Empire*. February 16, 2012.

Sachs, Ben. *Chicago Reader*. February 23, 2012.

Savlov, Marc. *Austin Chronicle*. February 23, 2012.

Smith, Kyle. *New York Post*. February 17, 2012.

Travers, Peter. *Rolling Stone*. February 17, 2012.

Willmore, Allison. *Movieline*. February 17, 2012.

QUOTES

Johnny Blaze: [voiceover] "Why does the devil walk in human form anyway? I have no idea. Maybe he doesn't know either. Maybe he passes on from body to body, down through history, waiting for the perfect fit. But I know one thing, on Earth, he's weak. His powers are limited. He needs emissaries to do his dirty work, so he finds them or makes them, using his greatest power, the power of the deal."

TRIVIA

Unlike in the previous film, a full transformation from Johnny Blaze to Ghost Rider is never actually shown.

AWARDS

Nominations:

Golden Raspberries 2012: Worst Actor (Cage), Worst Remake/Sequel

GIRL IN PROGRESS

A tale of acting up, acting out, and acting your age.
—Movie tagline

Lessons in motherhood. Taught by a kid.
—Movie tagline

Box Office: $2.6 million

Girl in Progress seems to have been designed to subvert inherent familiarity with a genre a la *Scream* (1996) for the coming-of-age sub-genre by telling a story that wears its knowledge of its own narrative expectations on its sleeve throughout for all to see. The difference is that while Wes Craven's film cleverly skewered audience expectations at every turn by coming up with new ideas (which quickly became cliches themselves, of course) while cleverly skewering its cast, *Girl in Progress* announces its self-awareness of its generic tenets but instead of using them as a springboard for something new, it adheres to them with a narrative rigidity rarely seen outside of a Passover Seder.

Ansiedad (Cierra Ramirez) is a girl who is facing the onset of adolescence with no father, and a mother, Grace (Eva Mendes), who has little time for her between working two jobs (as a maid and a waitress) and carrying on an affair with the married gynecologist (Matthew Modine) whose house she cleans. One day, her English teacher (Patricia Arquette) begins a section on coming-of-age stories and Ansiedad hits upon a brilliant idea—she will self-generate her own coming-of-age tale by instigating the key moments of such tales on her own and get the painful process of growing up out of the way quickly and on her terms. Of course, her very existence—the result of Grace's teenage pregnancy—could serve as an argument against this particular line of thinking but that, of course, never occurs to Ansiedad as she sets about to instigate, in rough order, the dumping of her loyal best pal for a more popular classmate, her first kiss and the loss of her virginity. Meanwhile, Grace—who is still an adolescent in many ways herself—is slowly beginning to realize that her lover is probably not going to leave his wife and family for her, no matter how fetching she may look while wielding a duster.

From a conceptual standpoint, *Girl in Progress* sounds potentially intriguing and in the right hands, it could have been made into something special. The trouble here is that director Patricia Riggen (who previously made *Under the Same Moon* [2007]) and screenwriter Hiram Martinez have assembled all of the myriad elements but have no evident idea of what to do with them. By intertwining the tales of both mother and daughter, they clearly want to draw parallels between the two as they both grow to adulthood—one a little early in life and one fairly late—but they never manage to complement each other, due in no small part to the clash in tones between the serious-minded stuff involving Grace and the semi-comedic misadventures of Ansiedad. Another problem is the stuff involving Ansiedad jump-starting her own passage to maturity always feels kind of contrived and the bit involving her cruel behavior towards her former best friend is so jarringly unpleasant that it is nearly impossible to engage with her character for the rest of the story. And like most not-so-good movies of this sort, it all ends in an exceptionally melodramatic manner in which everything is miraculously resolved, largely due to screenplay contrivances rather than taking the time or effort to have any of the main characters actually learning anything of value.

The closest thing that *Girl in Progress* has to a saving grace (no pun intended) are a couple of bright and appealing actresses in the lead roles. Stepping away from the kind of pure sex bomb role that she is usually offered, Eva Mendes manages to dial down her considerable star wattage enough to reasonably pass herself off as an exhausted working-class stiff struggling to raise her daughter under daunting circumstances. As Ansiedad, Cierra Ramirez—making her first big-screen splash on the heels of a recurring role on the television series *The Secret Life of the American Teenager* (hey, it worked for Shailene Woodley)—is sweet and charming and comes across as being almost too smart for her character's actions to be fully believable. During the rare moments when the two are on-screen together and temporarily free of all the histrionics, the two demonstrate a nice rapport that one wishes that Riggen had made better use of. Alas, they are then split off once again to face their familiar narrative fates and while many words could be used to describe their respective journeys, "progress" is most certainly not one of them.

Peter Sobczynski

CREDITS

Grace: Eva Mendes
Ansiedad: Cierra Ramirez
Dr. Harford: Matthew Modine
Ms. Armstrong: Patricia Arquette
Trevor: Landon Liboiron
Origin: United States
Language: English, Spanish
Released: 2012
Production: John Fiedler, Ben Odell; Anxiety Productions, Latitude Entertainment, Pantelion Films; released by Pantelion Films
Directed by: Patricia Riggen
Written by: Hiram Martinez
Cinematography by: Checco Varese
Music by: Christopher Lennertz
Sound: Miguel Nunes

Editing: Dan Schalk
Costumes: Katia Stano
Production Design: Richard Paris
MPAA rating: PG-13
Running time: 90 minutes

REVIEWS

Anderson, Melissa. *Village Voice.* May 8, 2012.
Ebert, Roger. *Chicago Sun-Times.* May 10, 2012.
Goss, William. *Film.com.* May 11, 2012.
Linden, Sheri. *Los Angeles Times.* May 10, 2012.
Michel, Brett. *Boston Phoenix.* May 17, 2012.
Pais, Matt. *RedEye.* May 10, 2012.
Pols, Mary F. *Time.* May 10, 2012.
Rabin, Nathan. *AV Club.* May 11, 2012.
Savlov, Marc. *Austin Chronicle.* May 11, 2012.
Scott, A. O. *New York Times.* May 10, 2012.

QUOTES

Ansiedad: "I'm just here because I need somebody to recognize my potential and then watch helplessly as I throw it all away."

GOD BLESS AMERICA

Taking out the trash, one jerk at a time.
—Movie tagline

Box Office: $122,550

Sometime between the signing of the Declaration of Independence and the ascendancy of reality TV stars whose main talent is self-marketing, an overwhelming amount of Americans have made selfish interpretations of what the "pursuit of happiness" is meant to achieve. This is the case at least in the eyes of writer/director Bobcat Goldthwait as preaching from his manifesto *God Bless America,* a hit-and-miss charcoal black comedy of serial killer violence that expresses anger toward a cruel and stupid civilization with winding monologues and shocking slayings. Whereas every generation has probably wondered whether those following it are ruining humanity for everyone else, Goldthwait has decided that cruelty is at an all-time high, and that society is in need of someone to wipe out these negative forces who have highly contributed to its moral decay.

Cast as the mouthpiece for Goldthwait's teeth-gritting anger is the unassuming Joel Murray, who plays a divorced and middle-aged American man named Frank living in an amoral vacuum. When he turns on the TV, he cannot escape freak show idiocy, as his channel surfing brings upon an onslaught of grotesque reality TV imagery (including an "American Idol" parody called "American Superstarz") followed by sensationalistic news commentators who make immediate comparisons of President Obama to Adolf Hitler.

Frank's own interactions with the world are no less of a horror show. After a harmless gesture of sending flowers to a co-worker is considered to be harassment, he is fired from his office job. When Frank learns that he has a nearly inoperable brain tumor, he is told this by a disinterested doctor (Dan Spencer), who is more concerned with his cell phone than the gravity of such bad news. To make things worse, a phone call to his ex-wife and daughter reveals that the young girl has gained a monopoly of bratty demands over her mother.

With no hope left for niceness in humanity, Frank decides to kill himself while watching a show very similar to MTV's popular rich girl birthday party series "My Super Sweet 16." During this moment he has an epiphany, and decides instead to first kill the girl whining on-screen named Chloe (Maddie Hasson), who is seen complaining to her parents about getting the wrong luxury car as a present. After Frank completes this killing by shooting Chloe in a parking lot, he is talked out of completing his suicidal inclinations by a classmate of Chloe's named Roxy (Tara Lynne Barr). An instant admirer of Frank's attitude, she convinces him that there are more imbeciles to be killed in the world.

What ensues is a killing spree in the vein of Joel Schumacher's irritated underdog shoot 'em up *Falling Down* (1993) with Frank armed with both weapons and word. In between Frank's calculated diatribes about Lindsay Lohan, cell phones, and many more topics, the platonic duo embark on a carousal of (police investigation-less) shootings that leave no jerk unpunished. While trying to watch a documentary on the 1968 My Lai massacre in a movie theater, they shoot talkative audience members; their actions accompanied by Betty Hutton's rollicking 1951 big band tune "It's Oh So Quiet." Other demographics attacked in shocking comedic moments vary from Westboro Baptist Church-like protestors to people that carelessly take up two parking spaces.

Goldtwait's wild script receives strong support from its two lead performances, which play well against character type. Murray maintains his character's average man likeability, even when he shocks viewers with his potential for cold-blooded violence. Barr succeeds in providing a new interpretation of the fast-talking and violent schoolgirl, standing somewhere uniquely between Chloe Grace Moretz's Hit-Girl character from *Kick-Ass* (2010) and Ellen Page's Juno from the Jason Reitman film (2007) of the same name.

While the action of *God Bless America* might evoke the loud chaos of death metal music, Goldthwait does not ultimately feel this sentiment towards Frank's mission. There is a striking sense of melancholy underneath this story, as confirmed by his choice of music, which includes choosing tough guy acoustic ballad "I Never Cry" by heavy metal icon Alice Cooper to play over the closing credits. Killings in the film are not met with tunes of triumph, but instead composer Matt Kollar's score recalls both Carl Orff and solemn Americana hymns written during earlier and perhaps more civilized times in America.

A highly violent movie that ultimately asks people to be nice, *God Bless America* finds its most constructive criticism during the impassioned monologues that Murray delivers with magnetic ferocity. Though its guns may gain the film its viewers, the well-constructed statements that Goldthwait makes through Frank are bound to leave a larger impression concerning the topic of the importance of respect, especially when Frank asks out loud, "Why have a civilization anymore if we are no longer interested in being civilized?"

Sensationalistic in itself, Goldthwait's concept is flawed by its simple-minded means of catharsis. Lacking depth to its violence, the film's action often does not challenge viewers beyond the popular '90s bumper sticker sentiment, "Mean People Suck." Goldthwait's film aims to fulfill the anger inside Americans concerning those who rule the attention of pop culture with ugly fists, but does not fully accept (until a defeatist conclusion that marries "American Idol" to *Bonnie and Clyde* [1960]) that such disposable deities use attention (whether positive or violently negative) as their life-source. To slay these beasts, one must simply stop providing them such. Even by killing them gruesomely with surface-level violence in his story, Goldthwait is only making these characters of pop culture stronger.

While its name-drops and abrupt violence can be amusing or even quite funny, *God Bless America* continuously loses meaningful credibility as it succumbs to being what Frank hates—a piece of the "Oh No, You Didn't Say That!" shock jock mentality that makes viewers laugh with disbelief at such cruelness. As the kill count of *God Bless America* rises, it becomes clear that this violent fable which turns soapbox into sniper post would not be possible were its humor not enabled by an amoral society it is attempting to criticize.

Nick Allen

CREDITS

Frank: Joel Murray
Roxy: Tara Lynne Barr
Alison: Melinda Page Hamilton
Ava: Mackenzie Brooke Smith
Chloe: Maddie Hasson
Origin: United States

Language: English

Released: 2011

Production: Sean McKittrick, Jeff Culotta; Darko Entertainment, Jerkschool Prods.; released by Magnet Releasing

Directed by: Bobcat Goldthwait

Written by: Bobcat Goldthwait

Cinematography by: Bradley Stonesifer

Music by: Matt Kollar

Sound: Arran Murphy

Editing: Jason Stewart; David Hopper

Costumes: Sarah De Sa Rego

Production Design: Natalie Sanfilippo

MPAA rating: R

Running time: 105 minutes

REVIEWS

Ebert, Roger. *Chicago Sun-Times*. May 9, 2012.

Jones, J. R. *Chicago Reader*. May 9, 2012.

Snider, Eric D. *Film.com*. March 12, 2012.

Tobias, Scott. *AV Club*. May 10, 2012.

Pinkerton, Nick. *Village Voice*. May 8, 2012.

DeFore, John. *Hollywood Reporter*. September 10, 2011.

Sharkey, Betsy. *Los Angeles Times*. May 11, 2012.

Russo, Tom. *Boston Globe*. May 18, 2012.

Tallerico, Brian. *HollywoodChicago.com*. May 11, 2012.

Gleiberman, Owen. *Entertainment Weekly*. May 15, 2012.

QUOTES

Frank: [after finishing shooting practice] "You did a good job." Roxy: "I have a good coach. That and I was pretending the targets were the cast of *Glee*."

TRIVIA

The book that Frank lends the receptionist is *Pride and Prejudice and Zombies* by Jane Austen and Seth Grahame-Smith.

GONE

No one believes her. Nothing will stop her.
—Movie tagline

Box Office: $11.7 million

About halfway through *Gone,* one is left wondering which is more dubious: the exploitation of the heroine's post-traumatic stress disorder (never named as such in the movie but clear nonetheless) as a device to put her in harm's way again or the cheap thriller conventions through which she must maneuver to successfully make it from point A to point B. The screenplay by Allison Burnett is truly that simple—sister goes missing, heroine must find a serial killer to find her—and the process by which the protagonist goes about her search is equally straightforward.

The young woman at the center of the hunt is Jill Conway (Amanda Seyfried). A year ago, a man abducted her from her bed; she awoke in a hole in the middle of a forest outside of Portland, Oregon. Barely buried in the dirt at the bottom of the pit were human remains. She managed to escape, and despite her lucid statement, the police did not believe her story, dismissing it as a delusion after a search of the woods uncovered no trace of evidence.

Since then, Jill has become understandably paranoid. She crosses the street to avoid a man coming toward her on the sidewalk. She insists that she walk her co-worker Sharon (Jennifer Carpenter) to her car when their night shift at a local diner is finished (the screenplay gives no explanation for why she parks at a garage blocks away from her place of employment; the only logic is that it offers the false tension of her looking over her shoulder at the slightest of noises as she walks the rest of the way). She owns a handgun. The first glimpse of her is as she scours the forest looking for the place where she had been kept a prisoner; she marks off the areas she searches on a map.

Most of all, she is protective of her younger sister Molly (Emily Wickersham), who lives with Jill and has gotten into trouble because of excessive drinking and partying in the past. Upon coming home from work, Jill discovers that Molly is missing. The clothes she wore to bed are nowhere to be found, and Jill knows her sister would have left a note for her had she gone anywhere without Jill's knowledge. She is convinced the man who kidnapped and intended to kill her has taken Molly.

The story of Jill's past experience unfolds in flashbacks interspersed throughout the movie (visual cues, such as her seeing dog food in an apartment she's investigating, typically trigger them), and the majority of those sequences come across as afterthoughts (e.g., having to explain why Jill is upset when she sees the aforementioned dog food). The result is that Burnett and director Heitor Dhalia continuously pummel the audience with images of psychological torture for Jill for no other reason than to remind the audience of the already firmly established fact that she is a victim. The repetition of the imagery—with each subsequent segment revealing a new, traumatic detail of her ordeal—amounts to little more than wallowing in Jill's suffering for distasteful dramatic effect.

That impression is heightened by the presence of the local police, who had previously closed the file on Jill's kidnapping, in part, because she has a history of psychological problems, having been sent to a psychiatric institute years ago after the deaths of her parents. The possibility that she might be imagining the entire thing is ever-present, no matter how little sense that possibility makes. Sergeant Powers (Daniel Sunjata) and Detective Lonsdale (Katherine Moenning) are skeptical of Jill's theory about her sister's disappearance, as well, and do not even bother to check the any of the facts she brings to them. Given how wholly linear and trouble-free Jill's investigation turns out to be (she manages to find the killer's apartment after uncovering two pieces of evidence and making a few random detours), the police serve only as an impediment. Fortunately for her, the police are about as incompetent as can be. The only helpful one (played by Wes Bentley) is, naturally, overly helpful, making him a perfect red herring for a mystery that turns out neither to need a red herring nor be much of a mystery after all, as the killer is essentially a complete stranger to Jill.

Jill is not too bright, either, making such foolish moves as pulling a gun on a man in broad daylight and driving deep into the woods to meet with the man she suspects is the murderer without telling anyone where she is. That decision at least sets up the movie's one genuinely suspenseful scene, as she drives through the pitch-black forest toward unknown dangers—the calm voice of the killer guiding her over the phone. One might suspect something sinister at the end of this drive, and the result is a shock, if only because Burnett overcompensates for Jill's helpless frenzy throughout the movie with a cold-blooded act that instantly erases any sympathy she may have garnered. If the manipulative nature of the central character's psychological state in and the conventional execution of *Gone* are questionable, the conclusion is downright inexcusable.

Mark Dujsik

CREDITS

Jill Parrish: Amanda Seyfried
Molly: Emily Wickersham
Peter Hood: Wes Bentley
Powers: Daniel Sunjata
Lt. Ray Bozeman: Michael Pare
Nick Massey: Joel David Moore
Sharon Ames: Jennifer Carpenter
Billy: Sebastian Stan
Origin: United States
Language: English
Released: 2012
Production: Sidney Kimmel, Gary Lucchesi, Tom Rosenberg, Dan Abrams, Chris Salvaterra; Lakeshore Entertainment, Sidney Kimmel Entertainment; released by Summit Entertainment

Directed by: Heitor Dhalia
Written by: Allison Burnett
Cinematography by: Michael Grady
Music by: David Buckley
Sound: Thomas Cokran; Avram D. Gold
Music Supervisor: Eric Craig; Brian McNelis
Editing: John Axelrad
Art Direction: Sarah Contant
Costumes: Lindsay McKay
Production Design: Charisse Cardenas
MPAA rating: PG-13
Running time: 85 minutes

REVIEWS

Catsoulis, Jeannette. *New York Times*. February 24, 2012.
Ebiri, Bilge. *Vulture*. February 25, 2012.
Ehrlich, David. *Boxoffice Magazine*. February 24, 2012.
Johanson, MaryAnn. *Flick Filosopher*. April 23, 2012.
Leupp, Thomas. *Hollywood.com*. February 24, 201.
Orndorf, Brian. *Blu-ray.com*. February 24, 2012.
Osenlund, R. Kurt. *Slant Magazine*. February 25, 2012.
Robinson, Tasha. *AV Club*. February 24, 2012.
Whipp, Glenn. *Los Angeles Times*. February 27, 2012.
Zacharek, Stephanie. *Movieline*. February 24, 2012.

QUOTES

Jill: "What's a few meds between sisters?"

TRIVIA

WC Winks Hardware store is an actual store in Portland, OR and is located where it is shown in the film.

GOON

Meet Doug, The nicest guy You'll ever fight.
—Movie tagline

Box Office: $4.2 million

Goon is the story of a lovably dim minor-league hockey "enforcer" known as Doug "The Thug" Glatt (a terrific Seann William Scott). Despite his growing reputation as a brutally efficient fighter on the ice (he is there only to take out opposing players who have harmed or fouled his own teammates), Doug is really a large-hearted, small-brained guy who wants what everyone wants: to do something with his life and find love, friendship, and acceptance along the way.

The same is true of the film itself, co-written by Evan Goldberg and actor Jay Baruchel and loosely based on the 2002 book *Goon: The True Story of an Unlikely*

Journey into Minor League Hockey by Adam Frattasio and Doug Smith, detailing the Boston-born Smith's experience in the 1990s as a hockey enforcer known as "The Hammer." It is an obvious labor of love for Canadian Baruchel (who also stars as Doug's foul-mouthed, hyperactive pal), and as directed by his countryman Michael Dowse, *Goon* shares many of the fictional Doug's traits: Bloodied and raw, crude and obnoxious, and often thickheaded and flawed, *Goon* is also full of clear and sincere affection for both the sport of hockey and its many colorful characters.

Baruchel and Goldberg make no bones about following just about every sports-movie cliche available as the newcomer proves himself to cynical veterans while sparking his struggling team to win, with everything moving toward the climactic big-game showdown. Stylistically the only thing fresh about *Goon* is its gonzo devotion to its characters spilling blood and spewing increasingly crude sexual profanities. If that makes it sound a lot like 1977's *Slap Shot*, it is clear *Goon*'s filmmakers took plenty of inspiration from George Roy Hill's beloved cult classic, including less-than-heroic vignettes of team life in locker rooms, dive bars, and on crowded travel buses, all while mining rough-and-tumble humor from a glance at fighting and violence in professional hockey.

The sports film *Goon* most resembles, however, is the original *Rocky* (1976). Half the film revels with faux-epic glee in Doug's face-punching prowess as it counts down to an inevitable showdown with his hero Ross "The Boss" Rhea, a legendary enforcer. (As Rhea, Liev Schreiber flies a rugged handlebar mustache, but never goofs on the role, instead varnishing the aging brawler with weary authenticity. Peering over Ross' reading glasses, the always-excellent actor pulls much more gruff humanity out of the character than the script provides.) The other half of *Goon*'s story focuses on Doug's painfully awkward efforts to please his Jewish father (Eugene Levy); befriend his new room- and teammate, a jaded and gun-shy superstar (Marc-Andre Grondin); and woo a rough-around-the-edges hockey violence groupie (Alison Pill).

These characters are drawn with broad but earnest strokes, and *Goon* fumbles about with most of Doug's off-ice relationships—the romantic subplot especially is awkwardly sweet thanks to Scott and Pill, but as clumsy in its narrative beats as Doug is on skates. Scott, however, regularly picks the film up and carries it along on his portrayal of Doug. Since his 1999 breakout in *American Pie,* he has specialized in lunk heads, creating an ongoing cinematic essay on the Modern American Moron. Doug the Thug, however, continues Scott's move in recent years away from sneering jerks toward well-meaning simpletons. The actor's deceptively subtle work makes it clear Doug has learned to use his fists because his heart is so soft.

While the film received a very limited theatrical release, *Goon* was simultaneously available for home viewing via video on demand. Critical reaction was mixed, but leaned toward the positive, with many such as the *Austin Chronicle*'s Marc Savlov praising both the film's "exuberantly off-color, bloody, and frequently laugh-'til-you-choke" sense of humor and Scott's "layered" performance. Others were less amused by the same attributes—the *LA Times*' Robert Abele called *Goon* "monotonously lowbrow" and "a sloppy, unimaginative Cinderella story with more emphasis placed on profane locker room taunts than characterization or narrative."

It is true *Goon* is far from masterful, so it is sometimes hard to tell if what works so well in the film is by design or dumb luck. For example, to its credit there are no clear lines drawn on screen between glorifying the on-ice violence and off-ice vulgarity, wringing big laughs from them, and mocking them. The result continually feels like half-homage and half-satire. When the familiar, bombastic ache of Puccini's "Neesun dorma" from *Turandot* belts out over both tender courtship moments and bloody gladiatorial fight scenes (complete with teeth tumbling to the ice in slow motion) the opera aria feels like intentionally ironic overkill and yet also plays as genuine emotional uplift. Loose, gritty, and sometimes as ham-handed as its protagonist, *Goon* ends up succeeding because—not in spite—of the fact it simultaneously has its tongue in its cheek, its heart on its sleeve, and its fist in someone's face.

Locke Peterseim

CREDITS
Doug Glatt: Seann William Scott
Pat: Jay Baruchel
Eva: Alison Pill
Ross Rhea: Liev Schreiber
Dr. Glatt: Eugene Levy
Xavier LaFlamme: Marc-Andre Grondin
Ronnie Hortense: Kim Coates
Rollie Hortense: Nicholas (Nick) Campbell
Gord Ogilvey: Richard Clarkin
Origin: United States
Language: English
Released: 2012
Production: Andre Rouleau, David Gross, Ian Dimerman, Don Carmody, Jay Baruchel; released by Don Carmody Productions, Caramel Film
Directed by: Michael Dowse
Written by: Jay Baruchel; Evan Goldberg

Cinematography by: Bobby Shore
Music by: Ramachandra Borcar
Sound: Pierre-Jules Audet
Music Supervisor: Evan Dubinsky
Editing: Reginald Harkema
Costumes: Heather Neale
Production Design: Gordon Wilding
MPAA rating: R
Running time: 92 minutes

REVIEWS

Cole, Stephen. *The Globe and Mail.* February 24, 2012.
Ebert, Roger. *Chicago Sun-Times.* March 28, 2012.
Ebiri, Bilge. *Vulture.* March 30, 2012.
Holden, Stephen. *New York Times.* March 29, 2012.
La Salle, Mick. *Los Angeles Times.* April 5, 2012.
Levy, Shawn. *Portland Oregonian.* April 26, 2012.
Pinkerton, Nick. *Village Voice.* March 28, 2012.
Russo, Tom. *Boston Globe.* April 13, 2012.
Scott, Mike. *New Orleans Times-Picayune.* February 25, 2012.
Zacharek, Stephanie. *Movieline.* March 29, 2012.

QUOTES

Ronnie Hortense: "And for those of you who think you've got no practice tomorrow. 6AM, bag skate pussies! I wanna see every single one of you work your f**king asses off until you puke your guts out! This is not f**king baseball!"

TRIVIA

Jay Baruchel wanted to adapt the book into a film when he noticed a lack of hockey comedies in recent years.

THE GREY

Live or die on this day.
—Movie tagline

Box Office: $51.6 million

Common wisdom dictates that when a movie crash lands in the release date wasteland of January that hopes for critical survival are low. While history supported this thinking for years, the truth is that a steady stream of solidly entertaining films wind up in that predicament for all sorts of reasons from a studio's mishandling of a quality product to clever counterprogramming against Oscar fare. *The Grey*, which was released in this alleged dumping ground, is not only solidly entertaining, it is thought-provoking, well-acted, emotionally resonant, visually powerful, and one of actor Liam Neeson's best films.

John Ottway (Liam Neeson) is a hunter employed by an oil company in Alaska. His job is to protect the men from the wolves that plague their remote camp. At the close of the season, as the rest of the camp celebrate their last night at the bar, Ottway pens a goodbye note to his wife Ana (Anne Openshaw) and steps out into the darkness to shoot himself in the head. At the last moment, the sound of a wolf howling in the distance gives him pause, and Ottway is next seen boarding a plane that will take him and the other crewmen home.

The plane crashes in a blizzard somewhere in the Alaskan wilderness and Ottway finds himself de facto leader of a group of eight panicked survivors. He tends to the dying, defends the dignity of the dead by preventing looting, and does his best to band the group together. But even his grim faced stolidity may not be enough to lead them all to safety when a group of huge timber wolves descend on the wreckage to pick them off one-by-one in a show of territoriality. Determined, Ottway leads the men across the wilderness against all odds, strengthened by the memory of his wife and a strange poem left to him by his father.

In 2002, writer-director Joe Carnahan burst out of the gate with *Narc,* a muscular drama with an excellent cast that offered some surreal directorial choices and intense pacing. The man has an eye for how to tell a story but his other efforts have all failed in the screenwriting department. Hardly anything in *Smokin' Aces* (2006) or the enjoyable-but-clunky *The A-Team* (2010) could prepare viewers for *The Grey,* which seems like a calling card meant to declare that he has figured out what he does best and plans on making no future mistakes.

This is a classic survival story about men facing down death and finding out who they are in the process, and it plays both epic and intimate notes equally well, taking full advantage of the breathtaking scenery and action set-pieces with stunning cinematographic style. But just as often the camera trains in on the desperate men, suddenly dependent on one another, terrified, hungry, reaching inside for the bravery needed to take the next step. The best compliment may well be that viewers will be unaware of the camera even as they are carried along by it toward the heart of the drama over and over again.

The script offers plenty of opportunity for solid thrills containing, as it does, a plane crash, multiple wolf attacks and chases, fist fights, wild rapid rides, and literal cliffhangers. But the action goes hand-in-hand with a script that also is able to take familiar character types and breathe life into them precisely because of what it chooses to be about; the survival of not just physical life, but the human spirit. Like John Carpenter's *The Thing* (1983) or much of Howard Hawks' best work, the dialogue crackles as people talk over one another. These men are involved in a territorial dispute not just with the wolves but their fellow survivors.

The cast rises admirably to the challenge of what must have been a brutal shoot. Especially welcome is the presence of Frank Grillo, who takes the role of Diaz, a loud-mouthed ex-con who believes he has all the answers, and renders him semi-heroic, ultimately typified not by his generic braggadocio but by an ability to find peace. Dallas Roberts, who plays Hendrick, offers a fearlessly ordinary take on the man of conscience, a role that could have been thanklessly bland. As he is stretched and ultimately crushed by his situation there is is never a hint of melodrama. Dermot Mulroney also milks the uncertainty and long suffering nature of his character, Talget, for laughs, sympathy, and even a little awe, underplaying at just the right moments and thereby drawing the viewer into his predicament. The film forges no false bonds between these individuals. They remain each on their own journey, but they are powerfully brought to life in an ensemble piece where everyone is given an equal chance to shine.

Ultimately, however, the film is Neeson's. Those who have suffered through his recent work in clunkers like *Unknown* (2011) or *After.Life* (2009) and wondered if this would be just another gory action thriller a la the entertaining-but-rote action thriller *Taken* (2008) are treated to some of his best work as an actor. Ottway is a complexity, a man with a death wish, who chooses to comfort the dying; holding on to hope for reasons that become quite compelling by the end of the film. His ability to fight and physically survive is more than matched by a character that makes his despair a puzzle. Yet, ultimately, the film embraces him as anything but despairing, offering up a cinematic hero in the truest sense of Joseph Campbell's take on the concept.

The last major character in the film is death itself, given powerful representation by the wolves, both in a narrative and a visual sense. CGI wolves and wolf animatronics were inevitable here. In this sort of action adventure any such effects must be absolutely convincing if the film is to have any emotional power. At first the wolves in *The Grey* are relentless, shadowy figures, that when finally seen seem unassailable, undeniable engines of ferocity. They will be faced. They are a force of nature as sure as death itself.

One of the film's most compelling moments happens at the very end of the credits and involves a dark grace note on Carnahan's symphony of meaning apprehended through suffering. What should have been an over the top genre piece is a moving film, a story, full of unlikely heroes, their heroism largely unknown even to themselves.

Dave Canfield

CREDITS

Ottway: Liam Neeson
Diaz: Frank Grillo
Talget: Dermot Mulroney
Hendrick: Dallas Roberts
Flannery: Joe Anderson
Lewenden: James Badge Dale
Burke: Nonso Anozie
Hernandez: Ben Brey
Origin: United States
Language: English
Released: 2012
Production: Joe Carnahan, Jules Daly, Mickey Liddell, Ridley Scott, Tony Scott, Joe Carnahan; 1984 Private Defense Contractors, Liddell Entertainment, Scott Free Productions; released by Open Road Films
Directed by: Joe Carnahan
Written by: Joe Carnahan; Ian Mackenzie Jeffers
Cinematography by: Masanobu Takayanagi
Music by: Marc Streitenfeld
Sound: David Evans; Mark Gingras
Music Supervisor: Laura Katz; Andy Ross
Editing: Roger Barton; Jason Hellmann; Joseph Jett Sally
Art Direction: Ross Dempster
Costumes: Courtney Daniel
Production Design: John Willett
MPAA rating: R
Running time: 117 minutes

REVIEWS

Berardinelli, James. *ReelViews*. January 31, 2012.
Brayton, Tim. *Antaogny & Ecstacy*. February 3, 2012.
Ebert, Roger. *Chicago Sun-Times*. January 26, 2012.
French, Phillip. *Observer (UK)*. January 29, 2012.
Howell, Peter. *Toronto Star*. January 26, 2012.
Johnson, CJ. *ABC Radio (Australia)*. February 27, 2012.
Leydon, Joe. *Variety*. January 18, 2012.
Miraudo, Simon. *Quicklix*. February 15, 2012.
Scott, A. O. *New York Times*. January 26, 2012.
Smith, Kyle. *New York Post*. January 27, 2012.

QUOTES

Ottway: "Once more into the fray. Into the last good fight I'll ever know. Live and die on this day. Live and die on this day."

TRIVIA

Bradley Cooper was originally cast in the film but was replaced
with Liam Neeson.

THE GUILT TRIP

Get ready for one mother of a road trip.
—Movie tagline

Box Office: $37 million

The film career of Barbra Streisand is filled with
numerous variations of the same basic scene in which
some hunky guy tells her how charming and attractive
she is while she offers up a litany of "Who, me?" looks
because she just cannot believe that someone so handsome could possibly be interested in someone like her.
Therefore, it should come as no surprise to learn that
The Guilt Trip—in which she makes her return to the
big screen in a leading role (not counting her supporting
turns in *Meet the Fockers* (2004) and *Little Fockers*
(2010)) for the first time since *The Mirror Has Two
Faces* (1996)—contains just such a scene. What is
somewhat unexpected is that this particular version of
the familiar theme takes the form of her being wooed by
a rich Texas businessman who has just seen her chow
down on a four-and-a-half pound steak in order to win
an eating contest. It sounds like a joke but it is meant to
be taken seriously and the result is a scene that even
James Brolin himself might have some difficulty in
swallowing. The worst thing about this scene, however,
is that it is not even the worst scene in this dull and
crushingly depressing waste of the time and energy of
both those who were paid to make it and anyone who
pays to see it.

Streisand plays Joyce Brewster, the adorably over-
bearing widowed mother of son Andy (Seth Rogen), a
struggling inventor of eco-friendly household cleaners.
While on a last-ditch business trip to New York to
convince a chain to carry his product, he swings by for a
rare visit with mom and listens to her reminisce at length
about the long-long-lost love of her life. Using a
conspicuously non-Google-based search engine, he tracks
down someone with the same last name in San Francisco,
decides that this is the same person and invites Joyce to
accompany him on his road trip as part of a clandestine
plan to reunite her with the one that got away.
Inevitably, Andy quickly grows frustrated with his
mother's quirks and idiosyncrasies and tensions between
the two eventually boil over when she meddles with one
of his business pitches. Just as inevitably, however, the
two grow to appreciate and understand each other in
newer and deeper ways just in time for the multiple
denouements, all of which are delicately hinted at with

the subtlety of a brick to the face and which even
includes a stop at the Grand Canyon, which is to cross-
country road trip movies what prom is to a movie aimed
at teenagers.

The idea of a grown man and his mother reexamin-
ing their relationship was previously explored to brilliant
comedic effect by Albert Brooks in his hilarious *Mother*
(1996), so any film attempting to venture into the same
territory runs the risk of coming off as trite and pointless by comparison. In an unexpected move, *The Guilt
Trip* boldly answers this challenge by not making any
discernible effort at all to be original or insightful. There
is an aura of sheer laziness that looms over the proceedings that extends well beyond the reported insistence by
Streisand that the cross-country road trip be recreated in
locations no further than 45 minutes away from her
Malibu home (a move that reaches its dodgy extreme
during the painfully obvious attempts to simulate the
visit to the Grand Canyon). The screenplay by Dan
Fogelman feels like a pilot for an especially uninspired
sitcom with its overly broad stabs at humor and pathos,
its preference for caricatures over characters and the way
that it avoids messy truths with a series of patly
unconvincing homilies to wrap thing up in time for the
end credits. Living up/down to the standards of the
screenplay she has been given to work with, director
Anne Fletcher handles things from her end with all of
the style and elan that one might expect from a road
trip movie from the auteur of *27 Dresses* (2008) and *The
Proposal* (2009). As for the much-vaunted pairing of
personalities at its center, neither of its stars makes much
of an impression. Streisand is just going through the
motions with a performance that is just a slight variation of her character in the Focker films while Rogen
seems outright bored and hamstrung by his inability to
cut loose here as he has in his various collaborations
with Judd Apatow.

The best thing that one can say about *The Guilt
Trip* is that it is at least somewhat better than *Parental
Guidance* (2012), the other wacky cross-generational
family-oriented comedy that popped up at the multiplexes to compete for holiday movie-going dollars,
though that says more about the abysmal nature of the
latter film than anything else. Unlike *Parental Guidance*,
however, it failed to find much traction at the box-
office—instead of attracting two wildly different fan
bases, it turned out that Streisand followers did not
want to know from Rogen and vice-versa—and became
one of the bigger flops of the season instead.

Peter Sobczynski

CREDITS

Joyce Brewster: Barbra Streisand

Andy Brewster: Seth Rogen
Jessica: Yvonne Strahovski
Rob: Colin Hanks
Andrew Margolis Jr.: Adam Scott
Ben: Brett Cullen
Origin: United States
Language: English
Released: 2012
Production: Evan Goldberg, John Goldwyn, Lorne Michaels; Michaels-Goldwyn; released by Paramount Pictures
Directed by: Anne Fletcher
Written by: Dan Fogelman
Cinematography by: Oliver Stapleton
Music by: Christophe Beck
Sound: Karen M. Baker
Editing: Dana E. Glauberman; Priscilla Nedd Friendly
Art Direction: David Lazan
Costumes: Danny Glicker
Production Design: Nelson Coates
MPAA rating: PG-13
Running time: 95 minutes

REVIEWS

Barker, Andrew. *Variety*. December 17, 2012.

Black, Louis. *Austin Chronicle*. December 20, 2012.
Burr, Ty. *Boston Globe*. December 19, 2012.
Holden, Stephen. *New York Times*. December 18, 2012.
Morgenstern, Joe. *Wall Street Journal*. December 21, 2012.
Olsen, Mark. *Los Angeles Times*. December 18, 2012.
Orndorf, Brian. *Blu-ray.com*. December 19, 2012.
Packham, Chris. *Village Voice*. December 18, 2012.
Rabin, Nathan. *AV Club*. December 20, 2012.
Reed, Rex. *New York Observer*. December 19, 2012.

TRIVIA

The Paramount marketing department was so certain that Barbra Streisand would gain a Golden Globe nomination for her performance in this film, that not only did they put out an ad congratulating her on her nomination and posted it online moments before the nominations were announced, only to quickly retract in when she was not honored.

AWARDS

Nominations:

Golden Raspberries 2012: Worst Actress (Streisand)

H

HAYWIRE

They left her no choice.
—Movie tagline

Box Office: $18.9 million

Throughout his career, Steven Soderbergh has alternated between projects jam-packed with top-level stars (such as *Ocean's Eleven* [2001] and its sequels and the bio-thriller *Contagion* [2011]) with smaller-scale efforts centered around lesser-known talents (like *The Girlfriend Experience* [2009], which featured adult film star Sasha Grey in her first straightforward leading role) in accordance to the material. For his latest effort, the action-thriller *Haywire,* he has filled the supporting cast with many famous faces but for the lead, he has once again chosen to cast his net outside the usual pool of actors by recruiting Gina Carano, a mixed martial arts fighter whose most prominent previous role was as "Crush" on the short-lived revival of TV's *American Gladiators,* and creating an action film around her talents. Considering the meager number of athletes who have successfully made the transition to the big screen over the years—a feat that not even the likes of Muhammad Ali, Pele, or Michael Jordan could quite pull off—this would seem to be an act of pure foolishness on Soderbergh's part but whatever impulse it was that he was following this time around, it was once again the correct one because the end result is a breathlessly exciting and hugely entertaining action thriller and a good part of the reason for its success is due to its endlessly charismatic and compelling star.

The film starts off in the most ordinary manner possible as a young woman (Carano) steps into a remote diner in upstate New York and sits down for a cup of coffee. A few minutes later, a guy (Channing Tatum) walks in and sits down at her booth. They appear to be old acquaintances and engage in a bit of enigmatic chit-chat before he begins smacking her around and attempting to drag her out of the place. Good Samaritan bystander Scott (Michael Angarano) steps in and creates enough of a distraction for the woman to get the upper hand on her attacker and make her escape with Scott in his car. As they are speeding away, she begins to explain to Scott who she is and what led up to the events that he just witnessed. Her name is Mallory Kane and she is a highly trained combatant who left the military and who is now working for a shadowy security firm that goes in and does the kind of jobs that the government cannot officially be tied to in any way. For one of her most recent jobs, she and Aaron, the guy she was pounding on in the diner, were sent off by the mysterious Rodrigo (Antonio Banderas), on the recommendation of top government official Coblenz (Michael Douglas), to go to Barcelona and rescue a kidnapped Chinese journalist. From there, the story takes her to Ireland and back to the States and finds her mixed up with a duplicitous boss (Ewan McGregor) and a suave Irish agent (Michael Fassbender) in events that lead to the usual array of betrayals, double-crosses, fistfights, gun battles and the like as Mallory tries to discover who is responsible for betraying her and why.

On the surface, *Haywire* may not sound demonstrably different from most of the other genre product on cable at any given time. However, what sets this film apart is not the story so much as the way that the way that Soderbergh and screenwriter Lem Dobbs have chosen to tell it. As with their earlier collaboration, *The Limey* (1999), they have taken a fairly familiar genre premise and reinvigorated it by choosing a more elliptical approach that adds more of a sense of mystery to the proceedings and forces viewers to sit up and take more notice as to what is going on. At the same time, it allows Soderbergh, who is also once again acting as his own cinematographer and editor, to take a stab at the kind of purely kinetic action cinema that he has rarely indulged in with his past films. As it turns out, he has a real knack for it as he offers up any number of stunning set-pieces that deftly blend the balletic and the brutal in often startling and always watchable ways. In fact, these are some of the most impressive fight scenes to be seen in any American film in recent memory with the opening diner brawl being a highlight among highlights.

Haywire contains a better cast than one might normally expect from this kind of film and Soderbergh uses them effectively as guideposts to help drive the story along while preventing it from devolving into complete confusion. That said, the real standout in the cast is Gina Carano, the wild card of the deck, whose performance here is nothing short of a knockout, to use an extremely tired and hackneyed bit of wordplay that would be too embarrassing to use were it not so accurate. Whatever instinct Soderbergh must have had in casting her, it was indeed the correct one. Naturally, Carano is completely convincing as someone who possesses the ability to decimate opponents with her bare hands and she launches into the fight scenes with such ferocious determination that they have an extra edge that simply would not have existed in the hands of a more conventional performer. This is all to be expected given her background, but what comes as a surprise is the way that she is interesting even in the scenes that do not require her to beat people senseless. She has a compelling and likable personality, a casual ease in front of the camera, and more than holds her own in her scenes opposite her more experienced co-stars.

A lot of action films these days, for all the chases, explosions and gunfights they may offer up, tend to be real drags that do not keep their viewers on the edge of their seats as much as leave them slumped back out of sheer boredom. A film like *Haywire,* on the other hand, is special because, while it contains all of the expected ingredients, it mixes them up into the kind of cinematic stew that is worth savoring. Beautifully conceived and executed and featuring a star who it is virtually impossible to tear one's eyes away from (even as she is tearing away at the eyes of others), this is a fairly amazing piece of filmmaking—the kind of thing that will astound and dazzle art-house audiences and adrenaline junkies in equal measure.

Peter Sobczynski

CREDITS

Mallory Kane: Gina Carano
Aaron: Channing Tatum
Kenneth: Ewan McGregor
Paul: Michael Fassbender
Rodrigo: Antonio Banderas
John Kane: Bill Paxton
Coblenz: Michael Douglas
Scott: Michael Angarano
Origin: United States
Language: English
Released: 2012
Production: Gregory Jacobs; Irish Film Board; released by Relativity Media
Directed by: Steven Soderbergh
Written by: Lem Dobbs
Cinematography by: Steven Soderbergh
Music by: David Holmes
Sound: Larry Blake
Editing: Steven Soderbergh
Art Direction: Inigo Navarro; Jim Oberlander; Anna Rackard
Costumes: Shoshana Rubin
Production Design: Howard Cummings
MPAA rating: R
Running time: 93 minutes

REVIEWS

Corliss, Richard. *Time.* January 19, 2012.
Denby, Davd. *New Yorker.* January 24, 2012.
Ebert, Roger. *Chicago Sun-Times.* January 19, 2012.
Gonsalves, Rob. *eFilmcritic.com.* January 26, 2012.
Orndorf, Brian. *BrianOrndorf.com.* January 20, 2012.
Reed, Rex. *New York Observer.* January 17, 2012.
Scott, A. O. *New York Times.* January 19, 2012.
Snider, Eric D. *Film.com.* January 21, 2012.
Stevens, Dana. *Slate.* January 20, 2012.
Tallerico, Brian. *HollywoodChicago.com.* January 19, 2012.

QUOTES

Paul: "I've never done a woman before."
Kenneth: "Oh, you shouldn't think of her as being a woman. No, that would be a mistake."

TRIVIA

Gina Carano's voice was altered for the film, giving her character a deeper-sounding voice.

HEADHUNTERS
(Hodejegerne)

The hunt is on.
—Movie tagline

Box Office: $1.2 million

Genre films are often given too much credit for simply being "surprising," using twists, shocks, or extreme violence as the only markers of success or appeal. The truly surprising thing about director Morten Tyldum's snappy, startling, and sometimes cheeky Norwegian crime film *Headhunters* is that while it is chock full of twists, shocks, and very extreme violence, all those elements are serviced by (and in service to) interestingly nuanced characters and a solid plot that proceeds logically even as it veers into implausibility.

Headhunters has a sense of play right from the start—a good sign of a filmmaker sure enough of his genre skills to juggle tone and tropes. Tyldum also gets a major assist from his highly relatable star Aksel Hennie. The film opens with Hennie's Roger Brown giving the audience art-thievery lessons in voice over, and the loose, jazzy soundtrack music is clearly intended to suggest a breezy-cool *Ocean's Eleven* (2001) vibe. Brown wants the viewer to know: 1) He is an (adept, if not masterful) art thief; 2) He does it for the money, in order to live an impressive lifestyle beyond his means; and 3) He is short in stature, and fully admits that points 1 and 2 are his ways of over-compensating for 3.

Roger is married to another overcompensation: a strikingly tall blonde art gallery owner named Diana (Synnove Macody Lund) who, to Roger's swinging chagrin, wants a child with him. He also has a day job as a corporate recruiter, a clingy mistress on the side, and a cozy set up with his less-suave partner in art crime, Ove (Eivind Sander). Roger is something of a cad, always in search of the "big score" that will pay off his growing debts and let him retire early in style. And yet, Hennie and Tyldum have more in mind for Brown than just the lovable scoundrel—in a twist rarely seen in Hollywood films, Roger is trying, in fits and starts and with mixed results, to be a better person.

Enter Clas Greve, a wealthy, tall and strapping, ruggedly handsome corporate player with hints of a paramilitary past—in other words, as played with sly restraint by Nikolaj Coster-Waldau, Clas is Roger's exact opposite. Naturally, the smaller man decides to rob the alpha male. Specifics from there on out fall into "spoiler" territory, as Roger finds himself increasingly ensnared from all sides by plot twists and dastardly skullduggery

as the film's title embraces all its multiple meanings within and without the corporate world.

It is also from that point on that *Headhunters* deftly changes gears, ditching the smooth panache of an Ocean's heist film for the dry, darkly comic, and wildly violent rhythms of films by Quentin Tarantino or the Coen Brothers. If the rattling off of those influences sounds dismissive, know that one of the best things about Tyldum's film is that the director and screenwriters Lars Gudmestad and Ulf Ryberg (working from the 2008 novel *Hodejegerne* by Norwegian crime writer Jo Nesbo;) are fully aware of what they are swiping from whom.

Even as increasingly lurid trials and tribulations pile up around Roger, and the plot twists strain credibility, Hennie centers the film. He portrays Roger not as an action or crime hero rising to the cause, but as someone hopelessly outsmarted and outmatched by the circumstances. Brown becomes more resourceful, but for much of the movie he remains off-balance, struggling to survive, let alone catch up to the dire plots around him. The filmmakers drag their anti-hero through plenty of pain and humiliation, making Roger suffer for his earlier, relatively mild sins, and in the process, the audience goes from relating to him to actually caring and rooting for the poor guy.

In an effort to keep its audience on its toes, *Headhunters* continually changes up its plot lest viewers get too comfortable or think they have it all figured out. But as implausible as the narrative switch-ups sometimes are, Tyldum and the writers make sure even the wildest leaps are carefully seeded with narrative logic. Even as the film escalates into gruesome extremes (far from the comfortable heist film it pretended at first to be), it remains well-plotted—for all its nervy spins and turns, it moves forward with purpose, keeping its characters and storylines straight. Wild but never chaotic, *Headhunters* does not let its clever surprises cheat or cut corners, instead winning the viewer over with honestly crafted characters and plot.

Headhunters had a limited release in North America in the spring of 2012, but it was a big success in its native Norway when it was released there in the summer of 2011. It also did well in Denmark, Spain, and the United Kingdom, catching the attention of Hollywood, where an American remake was quickly green lit. Most critics responded positively to *Headhunters*, with Roger Ebert of the *Chicago Sun-Times* writing, "Unlike too many thrillers that depend on stunts, special effects and the Queasy-Cam, this one devises a plot where it matters what happens." Nicolas Rapold, however, writing for the *New York Times*, felt, "As black comedy, the film is crude and downright sloppy when compared with the clockwork machinations of the Coen brothers' creations."

Locke Peterseim

CREDITS

Roger Brown: Aksel Hennie
Clas Greve: Nikolaj Coster-Waldau
Diana Brown: Synnove Macody Lund
Ove Kjikerud: Eivind Sander
Origin: Norway
Language: Norwegian, English, Spanish
Released: 2011
Production: Marianne Gray, Asle Vatn; Yellow Bird Films, Nordisk Film A/S, ARD Degeto Film; released by Magnolia Pictures
Directed by: Morten Tyldum
Written by: Lars Gudmestad; Ulf Ryberg
Cinematography by: John Andreas Andersen
Music by: Jeppe Kaas; Trond Bjerknaes
Sound: Tormod Ringnes
Editing: Vidar Flataukan
Costumes: Karen Fabritius Gram
Production Design: Nina Bjerch Andresen
MPAA rating: R
Running time: 100 minutes

REVIEWS

Addiego, Walter. *San Francisco Chronicle.* May 4, 2012.
Burr, Ty. *Boston Globe.* May 10, 2012.
Ebert, Roger. *Chicago Sun-Times.* May 9, 2012.
Edelstein, David. *New York.* April 12, 2012.
Jones, Kimberley. *Austin Chronicle.* June 1, 2012.
Merry, Stephanie. *Washington Post.* May 11, 2012.
Morgenstern, Joe. *The Wall Street Journal.* April 26, 2012.
Rapold, Nicolas. *New York Times.* April 26, 2012.
Rodriguez, Rene. *Miami Herald.* May 31, 2012.
Turan, Kenneth. *Los Angeles Times.* April 27, 2012.

TRIVIA

Summit Entertainment bought the rights to produce an American version of this film, even before it was released.

AWARDS

Nominations:
British Acad. 2012: Foreign Film

HELLO I MUST BE GOING

Meet Amy Minsky. She's just getting over her divorce.
—Movie tagline

Box Office: $106,709

Driven by a strong, fearless performance from Melanie Lynskey, doing her best work since her breakthrough in Peter Jackson's *Heavenly Creatures* (1994), Todd Louiso's *Hello I Must Be Going* is almost a great movie. The truth of Lynskey's portrayal of a woman emotionally lost after a divorce allows one to forgive the cliches and genre trappings of Sarah Koskoff's sometimes pedestrian script. Strong supporting work by an eminently hateable Blythe Danner as one of the worst movie mothers in years and the great Christopher Abbott (HBO's *Girls*) further help a film that struggles with realism in terms of dialogue but finds truth through its performances.

Amy (Lynskey) is going through a rough time. She sleeps most of the morning and then watches TV in the bedroom she inhabits in her parents' (Blythe Danner & John Rubinstein) always-being-remodeled home. Recently divorced and notably emotionally adrift, Amy gets little support from her borderline abusive mother, the kind of psychological shrew who make jokes about how much her daughter likes desert in front of complete strangers at a family dinner. (Although even Amy's mother is given a bit of redemption later in the film when she notes how she is really just looking for some peace and quiet and has, somewhat understandably, grown tired of running a household. She is, nonetheless, an awful human being.) On the other hand, Amy's father is notably supportive, the kind of guy who tells his daughter that she can stay as long as she wants. With a loving father and a picky mother, Amy sees little hope for happiness. Then she meets a boy.

The boy is 19-year-old Jeremy (Abbott), the son of a pair that Amy's father is wooing in a business relationship. Jeremy is a young actor who does not really want to be an actor. His mother thinks he is gay, because that is what she expects him to be and he has just gone along with the misconception rather than correct her. He recognizes in Amy both another passionate soul and a person lost in crisis. Hers may be closer to a mid-life crisis (Lynskey is 35) while Jeremy's is more a quarter-life but they find passion in each other's arms and ways to relate. Both of them have parents who love them but do not quite understand them. They understand something about each other. And the way that Jeremy opens up Amy's life and allows her to deal with her own emotional and psychological issues is deftly handled.

Abbott is one of the most interesting actors of his generation and Danner simply destroys every time she is on-screen (she has long been one of the most underrated and under-utilized actresses in Hollywood) but *Hello I Must Be Going* belongs to Lynskey, an actress who appears in nearly every scene of the film and carries it fully with an emotionally daring turn. She perfectly captures a character who could have easily become little more than cliche, making Amy feel genuine in all of her emotions from the depression of the first act to the sexual awakening of the second to the catharsis of the final one. On paper, what Amy goes through in Koskoff's script could easily come off as just another generic Sundance art movie outline (the movie was the Opening Night selection for the 2012 Park City fest) but Lynskey single-handedly makes it interesting in every scene. She just feels honest.

Sadly, Koskoff cannot achieve quite the same honesty in terms of plotting. There is, of course, a scene where Amy and Jeremy are discovered (naked in a swimming pool) and it feels forced (although the parental response to their affair is not as predictable as it easily could have been in a lesser film) and the final act kind of meanders instead of building to an emotional climax. It is one of those films that kind of just ends instead of presenting any sort of solid conclusion. However, these are more minor complaints than they may sound.

Fledgling studio Oscilloscope picked up *Hello I Must Be Going* after Sundance and the film meandered its way to just over $100k, never expanding beyond fifteen theaters nationwide. It is a shame that more viewers did not get a chance to see *Hello* but it is the kind of film that will certainly carry itself far on DVD through good of word-of-mouth. Critics were certainly kind to the film with Brent Simon of *Shared Darkness* calling it "A fine and funny film balanced perfectly between heartbreak and uplift, anchored by a rich, superlative turn from Melanie Lynskey." Matt Pais of *RedEye* did note the film's final act problems by pointing out "Familiar messes that are somewhat too easily cleaned up."

Brian Tallerico

CREDITS

Amy Minsky: Melanie Lynskey
Ruth Minsky: Blythe Danner
Stan Minsky: John Rubinstein
Gwen: Julie White
Jeremy: Christopher Abbott
David: Dan Futterman
Origin: United States
Language: English
Released: 2012
Production: Hans C. Ritter, Mary Jane Skalski; Next Wednesday Productions, Skyscraper Content; released by Oscilloscope Films
Directed by: Todd Louiso
Written by: Sarah Koskoff
Cinematography by: Julie Kirkwood
Music by: Laura Veirs

Sound: Eric Raber
Music Supervisor: Holly Adams
Editing: Tom McArdle
Costumes: Bobby Frederick Tilley, II
Production Design: Russell Barnes
MPAA rating: R
Running time: 94 minutes

REVIEWS

Baumgarten, Marjorie. *Austin Chronicle*. September 28, 2012.
Burr, Ty. *Boston Globe*. October 18, 2012.
Ebert, Roger. *Chicago Sun-Times*. September 20, 2012.
Means, Sean. *Salt Lake Tribune*. November 3, 2012.
O'Sullivan, Michael. *Washington Post*. September 21, 2012.
Pais, Matt. *RedEye*. September 20, 2012.
Puig, Claudia. *USA Today*. September 13, 2012.
Sachs, Ben. *Chicago Reader*. September 21, 2012.
Simon, Brent. *Shared Darkness*. November 1, 2012.
Wilson, Calvin. *St. Louis Post-Dispatch*. October 18, 2012.

TRIVIA

The title of the film is a reference to a Groucho Marx song.

HERE COMES THE BOOM

No one will fight for his students like Mr. Voss.
—Movie tagline

One teacher still believes in fighting for his students.
—Movie tagline

Box Office: $45.3 million

For at least two movies, Kevin James tried. In previous family comedies made by Adam Sandler's production company Happy Madison, *Paul Blart: Mall Cop* (2009) and *Zookeeper* (2011), James played buffoonish working class men dedicated to their jobs and those he worked for (whether they were mall patrons or talking animals). But with *Here Comes the Boom*, in which James decides that taking a kick or punch to the face can be more lucrative than defending oneself with inspired offensive skill, he slyly celebrates the benefits of laziness. In some sort of meta-twist, James admits that along with his slacker character, he himself as co-writer has no problem giving in. In the end, he still gets paid just for showing up.

In the film James plays Scott Voss, a former "Teacher of the Year" who has become an unfortunate proponent in the American education system: his drive to share knowledge with his pupils has vanished, affecting the enthusiasm his students have for being in school as well. This laziness is not shared by an older colleague of James', Marty Streb (Henry Winkler), who teaches a popular music program in the same high school, and whimsically opines about the importance of music with the mysticism of a dorky wizard.

Conflict strikes the school as the music program is put on a list of budget cuts, leaving Marty scrambling to find a way to make the $48,000 necessary to save the program (the script does not seem to care about the other programs that are on the list). Aware of the students' enthusiasm for the music program and outraged that such a cut could happen to an inspired teacher, Scott seeks out a way to raise money in order to save the program. At night, Scott starts working as a citizenship teacher for immigrants looking to achieve American citizenship, a gig that he manages with the same level of indifference.

While tutoring a former mixed martial arts fighter named Niko (Bas Rutten), James discovers the money-making potential in participating in mixed martial arts fights—and is certainly appealed by the concept that losing fighters can be paid as much as $10,000 just to get into the ring. This sets off James on a hopeful scheme in which the not-so-athletic Scott trains to become eligible for small town MMA fights that he plans on losing, receiving athletic wisdom from Niko and useless emotional support of Marty. In the midst of Scott's training, the film also weakly entertains an "American Dream" subplot in which Scott continues to tutor Niko so that he may soon receive citizenship.

Considering his regular appearance as an overweight everyman, James' distinctive stomach size has certainly slimmed since *Paul Blart: Mall Cop* and *Zookeeper*, informing audiences immediately that the film's comedy will not entirely revolve around James' waist, at the very least. Still, the jokes about this average American man are with the same simple agenda—to have his brief projections of machismo reverted to emasculation, with many jokes of Scott's clumsiness playing into the actor's prowess as a silly slob. If anything, the newest addition to James' persona is a sense of crafty slyness, which makes this lazy teacher sound much more like one of his students than an adult; this is an immaturity that the film unfortunately does not repair in terms of possibly gaining sympathy for his character.

The two goofballs supporting James are not new to the rank of supporting a Happy Madison comedy. With music teacher Marty, Winkler channels his previous goofball coach from the Adam Sandler comedy *The Waterboy* (1998) as another daffy leader who becomes a goofy sidekick to the main character athlete. As in that

previous film, Winkler is here to be embraced with condescending laughter. At the same time, *Here Comes the Boom* has no problem embracing this character for his cliche sentiments ("You're mine," he says to James when talking about heroes) in moments where the film needs to try to force the audience to feel something.

Continuing his streak of appearing in Kevin James movies, Rutten has his biggest onscreen role yet (he previously voiced a sassy wolf that urinated on James in *Zookeeper*). Here, the actual former MMA fighter is a beefy bald man who does unexpected silly things, with a consistently animated attitude. Though he is still wildly funnier in his cult-favorite self-defense instructional videos than any of the two previous James movies he has been featured in, Rutten is the one positive goodie to take from *Here Comes the Boom*, if not for the bits of purity his presence maintains as a fairly new comedic face. But as has happened with the course of Kevin James' film acting career, one can be sure that if Rutten refuses to grow with these characteristics in following roles, his shtick will become much more tiresome than it is successfully comedic.

In a gross assumption that all viewers of the film already understand the rules of mixed martial arts fighting, (another example of the film's glowing laziness), the dialogue of *Here Comes the Boom* hardly provides a solid explanation as to the rules of MMA. For the uninformed, the sport appears like lawless hand-to-hand anarchy, with little sense of strategy indicated except for a few confident statements uttered by characters standing outside of the ring.

Phil Meheux's cinematography is equally uninspired, and unsure of what strong choices to make with its script other than utilizing desaturated dark colors. In an attempt to add a shred of grit to the film's fighting sequences, the movie changes film stock while using spare point-of-view shots, which hardly add any perceptible claustrophobia to the heavily physical fights at the center of the story. Immersion in these events is further prevented by the glaring skepticism of James' physical involvement, as the punches thrown at James lack any trace of anxious believability. And in a montage in which his character is apparently throwing a lot of punches, his face is conveniently hidden from the camera.

One would be hard-pressed to name a recent film with more phony inspiration than *Here Comes the Boom*, a spiritual element so prevalent in this story that the phrase must have been written in big bold letters as a mission over the screenwriters' desk when the script's predictable story events and generic characters were being cut and pasted together. An overwhelming amount of this film's attempts at comedy fall down in flat thuds, with no spark to their humor but the exhausted presence of a character's cartoonish qualities (as with the clowning by James, Winkler, and Rutten). The emotional elements of this story are hammered up, further cheapening the film's observance on the value of inspiration. This is especially the case with the movie's citizen subplot, which ends the movie with the forced sentiment of "Viva America!" being cheered as an American flag is captured glaringly in frame. Even the title of the movie slackly borrows from a decade—old song by rock group P.O.D., uselessly bringing back its chorus lyrics into pop culture consciousness.

While *Here Comes the Boom* digs into America's surplus of underdog script elements—the fight for teachers and the future of their students, music programs, and immigration—there is nothing to feel from this losing comedy. There is no pain, and there is certainly no gain. There are no laughs, either.

Nick Allen

CREDITS

Scott Voss: Kevin James
Marty: Henry Winkler
Bella Flores: Salma Hayek
Lauren Voss: Melissa Peterman
Origin: United States
Language: English
Released: 2012
Production: Todd Garner, Kevin James; Hey Eddie, Broken Road Productions, Happy Madison Productions, Sony Pictures Entertainment; released by Columbia Pictures
Directed by: Frank Coraci
Written by: Allan Loeb; Kevin James
Cinematography by: Phil Meheux
Music by: Rupert Gregson-Williams
Sound: Odin Benitez; Michael Hilkene
Editing: Scott Hill
Art Direction: Alan Au
Costumes: Hope Hanafin
Production Design: Perry Andelin Blake
MPAA rating: PG
Running time: 105 minutes

REVIEWS

Barnard, Linda. *Toronto Star*. October 12, 2012.
Covert, Colin. *Minneapolis Star Tribune*. October 13, 2012.
Genzlinger, Neil. *New York Times*. October 11, 2012.
Graham, Adam. *Detroit News*. October 12, 2012.
Lovece, Frank. *Newsday*. October 12, 2012.
Lumenick, Lou. *New York Post*. October 12, 2012.

Moore, Roger. *McClatchy-Tribune News Service*. October 10, 2012.
Phillips, Michael. *Chicago Tribune*. October 11, 2012.
Pinkerton, Nick. *Village Voice*. October 11, 2012.
Rocchi, James. *MSN Movies*. October 10, 2012.

QUOTES

Marty Streb: "If you're gonna lose, then I'm gonna help you lose. Deal?"
Scott Voss: "Deal. Let's do this. Let's lose."

TRIVIA

Kevin James started preparing himself physically for this role fourteen months before filming began by shedding around 80 pounds.

HIGH SCHOOL

Random drug tests? You just can't study for them.
—Movie tagline

Future going up in smoke? Make sure it's some primo sh*t.
—Movie tagline

Hit it June 1st.
—Movie tagline

Box Office: $139,034

Good pot comedies are hard to come by, it seems. For every *Pineapple Express* (2008), there are about a half-dozen Cheech & Chong movies that do not stand the test of time and a couple Harold & Kumar movies that never worked in the first place (save for the first one). Only occasionally does a *Dazed and Confused* (1993) or a *Smiley Face* (2007) come along to prove that, yes, with the right actors and the right sensibility, pot and/or potheads can be funny. The films that work do so because the characters are made to be funny and/or interesting with or without the substance. The audience does not have to be in on the joke in order to get it. Of course, that would be true of any sub-genre of comedy, but too often the writers of pot comedies labor under the delusion that the ideas were probably funny to them when they thought of it and they were probably high when they thought of it. Therefore, it will be funny.

Nothing could be further from the truth when it comes to *High School,* a pot comedy so devoid of wit, style or even the most guilty pleasure that one suspects that not only did the writers not get high while writing it, they have probably never smoked in their lives. *High School* feels as though it was made by people who were afraid to try pot, so they watched a bunch of bad high school comedies that had scenes of kids getting high and drew inspiration from that. Consider the title. "HIGH School! Get it? Because it's a school! And everyone is HIGH! " This is the level on which this movie operates.

The story concerns two hapless, less-than-popular guys, Henry (Matt Busch) and Travis (Sean Marquette), who meet in a detention where the principal is making the students watch an absurd scare film on the dangers of pot. Henry is thin, timid and gets 'A's in science. Travis is big, obnoxious and smokes a lot of weed with his friends. One day, they visit a treehouse from their youth and Travis gets Henry high for the first time. Henry hallucinates and becomes predictably paranoid. It is an unlikely friendship that is formed because the screenplay demands it.

Meanwhile, back at the school, Principal Dr. Leslie Gordon (Michael Chiklis) is instilling a mandatory drug test on every student in the school in order to combat some bad publicity in which a spelling bee contestant went on national television high as a kite. The mandatory drug test happens to be taking place shortly after Henry smoked his first joint. Henry is on his way to MIT, but will not be able to get in if he comes up positive for drug use. Coincidentally, the drug test is taking place on the same day as the PTA bake sale and, apparently, nobody in this town can bake anything but brownies. So, Henry and Travis hatch a plan to make as many pot brownies as they can to replace the regular brownies, thereby getting the entire school high (or at least everyone who eats a brownie, which almost everyone does).

The plan involves stealing a batch of a potent substance called "keef," which is a special kind of pot personally manufactured by a local whacked-out drug dealer named Psycho Ed (Adrien Brody), who is covered in tattoos and is easily distracted by his pet bullfrog who constantly says "what" to him, a gag that grows tiresome the minute it is introduced and plays ad nauseam through the rest of the film. Psycho Ed is named that for a reason and the plan to steal his stash is a dangerous one, indeed. The plan works, and everyone, including the teachers, administration, and members of a group who are taking a tour of the school, get high and talk like idiots through the rest of the film.

High School tries way too had to be reminiscent of *Superbad* (2007), but Busch and Marquette are a long way off from Michael Cera and Jonah Hill. This movie pretty much represents the downside of the success of Judd Apatow and Seth Rogen. No doubt, the film's writer and director John Stahlberg (who also co-wrote the film with Erik Linthorst and Stephen Susco) has an affection for '80s teen comedies, but everyone involved here seems to have studied the likes of *Zapped!* (1982), *Porky's 2: The Next Day* (1983) and *Hardbodies* (1984)

and ignored everything that made *Fast Times at Ridgemont High* (1982) work so well. The tone and execution are not dissimilar to the former and the desperation is just as excruciating to endure. Even a scene that references the suspenseful bathroom sequence in *Witness* (1985) cannot be bothered with a punchline.

The most shocking thing about the movie is the level of talent involved in the cast. Adrien Brody gives his most embarrassing performance since *The Village* (2004). It sure must have looked like it would be fun to play this role when he first read the screenplay, but unlike the kind of free-form improvisational vibe that permeates the set of an Apatow movie, Brody is given nothing to work with. He is cast adrift in a comedy where nobody has anything funny to say or do, even on a lark. Perhaps even more painful is the aggressively unfunny performance by Chiklis as the tyrannical principal who secretly masturbates in his office when his secretary enters and exits the room. Chiklis deserves better than this.

High School ends with a whiny rant from Henry in which he compares himself to Hamlet to a classroom of students who cheer him on. The speech is meant to convey Henry's disillusionment with college, high school and his own insecurities. It feels just as tacked-on as the coda at the end of the film that references Jerry Garcia concerts. It is a pathetic attempt at being relevant and substantial to teenagers. The movie might have gotten away with something like that if every gag were not so ham-fisted and tired. This movie just proves the old adage that if a person is *trying* to be funny, chances are they are not, even if the viewer is high while watching them.

Collin Souter

CREDITS

Psycho Ed: Adrien Brody
Travis Breaux: Sean Marquette
Henry Burke: Matthew Bush
Brandon Ellis: Colin Hanks
Dr. Leslie Gordon: Michael Chiklis
Sebastian Saleem: Adhir Kalyan
Mrs. Unger: Yeardley Smith
Origin: United States
Language: English
Released: 2010
Production: Warren Zide, Raymond J. Markovich; Parallel Media, FlipZide Pictures; released by Anchor Bay Entertainment Inc.
Directed by: Jon Stalberg, Jr.
Written by: Jon Stalberg, Jr.; Stephen Susco

Cinematography by: Mitchell Amundsen
Music by: The Newton Brothers
Sound: Beau Williams
Editing: Gabriel Wyre
Art Direction: Johnny Jos
Costumes: Marie France
Production Design: Seth Reed
MPAA rating: R
Running time: 99 minutes

REVIEWS

Ebert, Roger. *Chicago Sun-Times*. May 31, 2012.
Guzman, Rafer. *Newsday*. June 1, 2012.
Holden, Stephen. *New York Times*. May 31, 2012.
Long, Tom. *Detroit News*. June 1, 2012.
Olsen, Marc. *Los Angeles Times*. May 31, 2012.
Schenker, Andrew. *Village Voice*. May 29, 2012.
Sobczynski, Peter. *eFilmcritic.com*. May 31, 2012.
Stewart, Sara. *New York Post*. June 1, 2012.
Weinberg, Scott. *Cinematical*. April 6, 2012.
Whitty, Stepehen. *Newark Star-Ledger*. June 1, 2012.

QUOTES

Travis Breaux: "Be somebody!"

TRIVIA

Writer/director John Stalberg Jr. is the voice of Psycho Ed's frog.

HIT AND RUN

A comedy that never takes its foot off the gas.
   —Movie tagline

Box Office: $13.7 million

It is almost too easy for critics to play with the title/concept of Dax Shepard's tonally inconsistent *Hit and Run*. It loses the race, runs out of gas, blows a flat tire, and so on and so on and so on. Like a kid in a cliche candy store, Shepard seems to have taken the first opportunity at a major directorial project to make six movies instead of one. Clearly inspired by Quentin Tarantino's difficult-to-mimic gift with not just dialogue but multiple styles and tones, Shepard misses the mark by quite some margin, making a film that feels too much like the awful copies that followed the success of *Pulp Fiction* (1994). In the mid-'90s, Tarantino's star rose almost by virtue of how many filmmakers fell on their face trying to duplicate his tone. Shepard was just late to the twenty-car pile-up.

Charlie Bronson (Shepard, who also wrote and co-directed) was not born with such a kick-ass moniker. He took it when he entered the Witness Protection Program, a secret he has kept from his lovely girlfriend Annie (Kristen Bell), a girl who has clearly never seen *Death Wish* (1974). Charlie testified against a vile, notorious criminal played by Bradley Cooper, who is introduced in a scene where he literally ties a leash around an African-American man and drags him down the sidewalk like a dog. The only reason the scene did not get more negative attention in the press for being as remarkably insensitive as it is is because Shepard's film barely got any attention at all.

Charlie has a happy life with his sweet gal pal (in fact, their first scene of domestic bliss, is reminiscent of Shepard's work on the excellent *The Freebie* [2010]) and his friend Randy (Tom Arnold), who happens to be his clumsy WitSec Officer. His new existence is shattered when Annie gets an amazing job opportunity in Los Angeles and Charlie decides to leave his protective bubble to take her to the interview. Annie's slimy ex Gil (Michael Rosenbaum) wants to hurt Charlie and is suspicious of his questionable past and so he blows his cover online. The bad guys get wind of the Charlie and Annie road trip and something that kind of resembles *Death Proof* (2007) and *True Romance* (1993) with notes of *The Cannonball Run* (1981) ensues.

Hit and Run is a film with a few decent elements and moments that simply have not been sewn together into an entertaining whole by its creator. There is the aforementioned, strong opening scene of honest romance between the dating-in-real-life leads. Then, the film shifts gears and becomes a broad comedy with the lackluster timing of Mr. Arnold. Then, it switches again and becomes a race movie with extended chase and driving scenes (automobiles and the way the rev and spin are a personal passion of Shepard). It is a film constantly shifting gears in tone and style, something Tarantino has mastered but few have successfully copied.

The inconsistency of tone may not be as hard to take if the laughs actually connected in *Hit and Run*. This is the kind of film that thinks old naked people are funny...twice. And the movie's tone really blows out its clutch when Shepard's script gets bizarrely racist and homophobic on a few occasions. These hot-button issues have become a trademark of Tarantino's writing but are arguably the hardest element of his work to copy. Shepard falls flattest when he attempts to do so. There is a recurring bit about a Smart Phone app that can find gay people nearby that is one of the most aggravating and shockingly unfunny in a major film of the last several years.

The utter failure of *Hit and Run* is amplified by the talent sucked into this disaster. Shepard can be charming and funny in the right material, most notably on TV's *Parenthood* and Bell has a similar potential that the small-screen seems to have been the best medium to tap (she was great on *Veronica Mars*). Arnold is miscast here but is still likable while Cooper just looks lost, waiting for the better movie that would come (*Silver Linings Playbook* [2012]). He was clearly doing a favor for a friend. Most of the talented cast just looks lost.

In fact, the entire movie is lost. It jumps in style, tone, humor, genre, and everything like someone switching gears. Go try and drive around a course and shift gears randomly as the speedometer rises. The clutch will burn out, the car may hit the wall, and tragedy will ensue. *Hit and Run* is the equivalent experience on celluloid.

Some critics fell for Shepard's genre-jumping schtick as typically insightful Glenn Kenny called the film, "One of the summer's most enjoyable surprises, a consistently disarming romantic comedy..." On the other end of the spectrum, Chicago critics Richard Roeper and Michael Phillips (of *The Chicago Tribune*) put the film on their bottom ten of the year. Trust the city that helped produce a car-comedy classic (*The Blues Brothers* [1980]) to spot a cinematic lemon.

Brian Tallerico

CREDITS

Charlie Bronson/Yul Perrkins: Dax Shepard
Annie Bean: Kristen Bell
Alex Dmitri: Bradley Cooper
Randy Anderson: Tom Arnold
Clint Perrkins: Beau Bridges
Debby Kreeger: Kristin Chenoweth
Gil Rathbinn: Michael Rosenbaum
Neve Tatum: Joy Bryant
Origin: United States
Language: English
Released: 2012
Production: Andrew Panay, Nate Tuck, Kim Waltrip; Exclusive Media Group, Panay Films, Primal; released by Open Road Films
Directed by: Dax Shepard; David Palmer
Written by: Dax Shepard
Cinematography by: Bradley Stonesifer
Music by: Julian Wass
Sound: Sean O'Malley
Editing: Keith Croket
Costumes: Brooke Dulien
Production Design: Emily Bloom

MPAA rating: R
Running time: 100 minutes

REVIEWS

Ebert, Roger. *Chicago Sun-Times*. August 23, 2012.
Gleiberman, Owen. *Entertainment Weekly*. August 22, 2012.
Long, Tom. *Detroit News*. August 22, 2012.
Lumenick, Lou. *New York Post*. August 24, 2012.
Phillips, Michael. *Chicago Tribune*. August 23, 2012.
Roeper, Richard. *RichardRoeper.com*. August 30, 2012.
Sachs, Ben. *Chicago Reader*. August 23, 2012.
Sharkey, Betsy. *Los Angeles Times*. August 21, 2012.
Travers, Peter. *Rolling Stone*. August 23, 2012.
Zacharek, Stephanie. *NPR*. August 23, 2012.

QUOTES

Yul Perrkins a.k.a. Charles Bronson: "Close your eyes and take three deep breaths. This is the only moment you need to be worried about. There's no yesterday. There's no tomorrow. There's just right now. You're not late for anything. You aren't going to miss anything. You're exactly where you're supposed to be. And you're exactly who you're supposed to be. You're absolutely perfect. And whatever happens today is exactly what's supposed to happen. And if you want, I'll spend every moment with you for the rest of your life."

TRIVIA

Many of the cars featured in the film are from Dax Shepard's own collection.

HITCHCOCK

Behind every Psycho is a great woman.
　—Movie tagline
Good evening.
　—Movie tagline

Box Office: $6 million

Sacha Gervasi's *Hitchcock* is a film to be enjoyed in spite of itself. It moves along at a pleasingly crisp clip, features a jolly assortment of droll performances, and assembles enough cheeky one-liners and sly in-jokes to please the most casually invested of cinephiles. Yet viewers expecting an in-depth exploration of the iconic filmmaker are bound to be sorely disappointed by the blatant fabrications and sentimental flourishes in the script by *Black Swan* (2010) scribe John McLaughlin.

Rather than adapt Stephen Rebello's fine book, "Alfred Hitchcock and the Making of Psycho" for the screen, McLaughlin utilizes it as more of a loose inspiration. Gone are any insightful tidbits regarding the production of Hitchcock's game-changing 1960 masterpiece, nor is there any provocative examination of the director's distinctive genius. McLaughlin's script depicts Hitch as a mere mischievous oddball blessed with the good fortune of being married to a true visionary, Alma Reville. Though her largely unsung contributions to her husband's films certainly played a large role in their success, *Hitchcock* asks viewers to believe that Alma was the sole reason why *Psycho* (1960) worked as well as it did.

As played by the effervescent Helen Mirren, McLaughlin's Alma is the Alma of movie buff's dreams. Wily, witty, and never hesitant in expressing her bold opinions, this romanticized portrayal of Hitchcock's wife is fun to watch, but rings entirely false. If the real Alma were a fraction like Mirren, she would not have been so easily dwarfed in her husband's imposing shadow. Julian Jarrold's *The Girl* (2012), released on HBO roughly a month prior to *Hitchcock,* presents an altogether different and far better researched depiction of Alma, played by Imelda Staunton, who turns out to be an uncanny dead ringer.

Though *The Girl* is set only a few years after Gervasi's film, during the production of Hitch's ambitious *Psycho* follow-up, *The Birds* (1963), it appears to take place in an entirely different (and much darker) dimension from *Hitchcock.* With her beady orbs magnified by enlarged lenses, Staunton's Alma is resigned to turning a blind eye on her husband's increasingly unseemly infatuations with his blonde leading ladies. *Birds* star Tippi Hedren has often recalled how Alma took her aside and uttered the curious apology, "I'm sorry you have to go through this," a line included in Jarrold's film.

Mirren's idealized Alma is far too headstrong to put up with such behavior. As Hitch (Anthony Hopkins) ogles busty Janet Leigh (Scarlett Johansson), Alma entertains the advances of *Strangers on a Train* (1951) screenwriter, Whitfield Cook (Danny Huston). Far too much of the film's 91-minute running time is devoted to this contrived subplot, which grinds the film to a halt whenever it materializes on-screen. Yet this glaring deviation from the central action hints at a larger problem facing Gervasi's picture.

Perhaps because *Hitchcock* was a Fox Searchlight production, the filmmakers were forbidden by Universal to include or re-stage any scenes from *Psycho,* or use the still-standing set of the foreboding spook house inhabited by Norman Bates. In a way, Gervasi's crew were placed under infuriating limitations similar to those imposed on Hitch during the 1959 *Psycho* shoot. Whereas Hitch had to film the infamous shower scene while avoiding any images of nudity or knife-penetration, Gervasi did not have permission to use a single of frame of the movie that his own picture was allegedly about.

Imagine what *Hitchcock* could have been if the filmmakers had seized this limitation as an opportunity to evoke the director's brilliant method of playing on audience's imaginations. There is a multitude of ways in which Gervasi could have explored the revolutionary shooting days of *Psycho* without relying on reenactments of Joseph Stefano's script. Alas, Gervasi appears to be less interested in Hitchcock's artistic genius and more engaged in the business of churning out crowd-pleasers akin to his admittedly wonderful 2008 documentary, *Anvil: The Story of Anvil.* Thus, a more fitting title for Gervasi's behind-the-scenes trifle would be, "Hitchcock: The Story of Alma."

Instead of deepening the audience's understanding of a marriage that certainly stands as one of the most fascinating and mystifying in the history of show business, McLaughlin uses it as padding to fill the cavernous gaps left by Universal's censorship. Mirren transforms the modest, soft-spoken Alma into a fiercely independent feminist trailblazer tailor-made to land top-drawer actresses an Oscar nomination. Alma's impassioned monologue detailing her extravagant sacrifices includes the claim that she mortgaged her house to help fund the low-budget *Psycho,* deemed unpopular by Paramount. This eyebrow-raising detail is a key example of McLaughlin's willingness to stretch the truth (in actuality, Hitchcock funded the film through his company, Shamley Productions).

Equally preposterous are the film's revelations regarding the extent of Alma's vital alterations to *Psycho.* Not only did she give script approval (a detail confirmed by multiple accounts), she suggested Janet Leigh and Anthony Perkins for the lead roles, argued that the shower scene should be set to Bernard Herrmann's immortal score, came up with the idea to kill off leading lady Leigh a half-hour into the picture, stepped in to direct the spectacular murder of Detective Arbogast, and made invaluable edits to the film after suffering through the supposedly unwatchable first cut. These claims are so outlandish that they function as little more than a derisively amusing running gag.

However, McLaughlin's belittling of the contributions made by other key players is no laughing matter. If anyone deserves a round of applause for their efforts on *Hitchcock,* it's casting director Terri Taylor (*American Beauty* [1999]), who assembled an ensemble of such peerless perfection that their limited screen time turns out to be a grave disappointment. James D'Arcy's resemblance to Perkins, in both appearance and demeanor, is flat-out astonishing. Though his mannered quirks and stuttering speech may have been modeled after Perkins' performance as Bates (which ranks as one of cinema's finest), the accuracy of his portrayal transcends mere impersonation. The only other cast member who appears to be truly channeling the soul of his real-life counterpart is Ralph Macchio, who nails screenwriter Stefano's accent and endearing personality observed in countless archival interviews. It's a crime that Macchio's screen time is limited to a single scene.

As for Hopkins, he has a ball mimicking Hitchcock's cue-card delivery witnessed on his beloved TV show. He also scores many big laughs in scenes where the director takes pleasure in his signature brand of deviousness, such as when he horrifies an assortment of journalists gathered for the press unveiling of his top-secret *Psycho* project. Though Hopkins has not been this funny in years, he fails to disappear into the role. Jarrold's *The Girl* was bolstered by Toby Jones' exceedingly authentic performance, which is doomed to be forgotten not unlike the actor's staggering portrayal of Truman Capote in *Infamous* (2006) (which had the misfortune of being released soon after Philip Seymour Hoffman's Oscar-winning *Capote* [2005]).

Yet neither *Hitchcock* nor *The Girl* have a clue about what made Hitchcock's work so profoundly transfixing and infinitely rewarding. Both films are at their weakest when they pay lip-service to Hitch's complex psyche. Jarrold's film paints him as a boorish, self-loathing lecher, while Gervasi glosses over all troubling nuances, leaving audiences with a lovable eccentric who inexplicably fantasized about serial killer Ed Gein (featured in silly vignettes best left on the cutting room floor). McLaughlin's script is so eager to please that it turns everything into a punchline, such as when Production Code enforcer Geoffrey Shurlock (Kurtwood Smith) is appalled by Hitchcock's insistence on the inclusion of a toilet, which had never before been featured onscreen in American mainstream cinema. This scene inspires a cheap guffaw, but Gervasi refuses to explore precisely why the toilet was a crucial element in *Psycho*, foreshadowing the doomed heroine's resting place in a swamp. Just as the toilet coughs up incriminating evidence, the swamp is hesitant to bury the unwelcome corpse, which is guaranteed to not remain buried indefinitely.

Gervasi and McLaughlin's greatest failure is their complete misreading of the shower scene. According to their film, the brutality of the scene was motivated by Hitchcock's rage over his wife's supposed infidelity, an interpretation tantamount to rubbish. The single most believable moments in *Hitchcock* are the brief instances when Alma mothers Hitchcock, instructing him to finish his yard work or ordering him to lay off his prized junk food. In essence, Alma was the mother figure in Hitch's life, inspiring many of the sinister maternal figures in his films, leading all the way up to Mother Bates. The shower scene reflected Hitchcock's sexual frustration while functioning as a prelude to the rape scene in *Marnie*. It is one of the most revealing set-pieces in Hitchcock's oeuvre and warrants a much more thorough analysis than McLaughlin's simplistic nonsense. For a movie championing filmmaking on the cutting edge, *Hitchcock* plays it maddeningly safe.

Matt Fagerholm

CREDITS

Alfred Hitchcock: Anthony Hopkins
Alma Reville: Helen Mirren
Janet Leigh: Scarlett Johansson
Whitfield Cook: Danny Huston
Peggy Robertson: Toni Collette
Lew Wasserman: Michael Stuhlbarg
Ed Gein: Michael Wincott
Vera Miles: Jessica Biel
Anthony Perkins: James D'Arcy
Origin: United States
Language: English
Released: 2012
Production: Tom Thayer, Ivan Reitman, Tom Pollock, Joe Medjuck, Alan Barnette; Cold Spring Pictures, Montecito Picture Company L.L.C.; released by Fox Searchlight
Directed by: Sacha Gervasi
Written by: John J Mclaughlin
Cinematography by: Jeff Cronenweth
Music by: Danny Elfman
Sound: Mildred Iatrou; Ai-Ling Lee
Music Supervisor: David Norland
Editing: Pamela Martin
Art Direction: Alexander Wei
Costumes: Julie Weiss
Production Design: Judy Becker
MPAA rating: PG-13
Running time: 98 minutes

REVIEWS

Ebert, Roger. *Chicago Sun-Times*. November 20, 2012.
Gleiberman, Owen. *Entertainment Weekly*. November 20, 2012.
Longworth, Karina. *Village Voice*. November 20, 2012.
McCarthy, Todd. *Hollywood Reporter*. November 12, 2012.
Persall, Steve. *Tampa Bay Times*. December 5, 2012.
Phillips, Michael. *Chicago Tribune*. November 26, 2012.
Schenker, Andrew. *Slant Magazine*. November 16, 2012.
Tobias, Scott. *AV Club*. November 23, 2012.
Uhlich, Keith. *Time Out New York*. November 20, 2012.
Williams, Joe. *St. Louis Post-Dispatch*. November 30, 2012.

QUOTES

Alfred Hitchcock: "My contract guarantees me final cut on all of my pictures."

Barney Balaban: "It also states that Paramount doesn't have to release anything that might cause the studio embarrassment!"

Alfred Hitchcock: "As opposed to those last five Martin and Lewis pictures you're so proud of?"

TRIVIA

Anthony Hopkins is one of a number of several top British and American actors who pursued the title role.

AWARDS

Nominations:

Oscars 2012: Makeup
British Acad. 2012: Makeup
Golden Globes 2013: Actress—Drama (Mirren)
Screen Actors Guild 2012: Actress (Mirren)

THE HOBBIT: AN UNEXPECTED JOURNEY

From the smallest beginnings come the greatest legends.
      —Movie tagline

Box Office: $301 million

The act of adapting a book onto the big screen always, inevitably, ends up transforming the source material into something different. Even the most rigid book-to-film adaptations never quite capture the experience that the original author created on the page, often despite the filmmakers' best efforts. The key to success is whether the "something different" movie version delivers a new experience worth watching. This question of transformation definitely surrounded Peter Jackson's *The Hobbit: An Unexpected Journey,* quite possibly the most anticipated film adaptation of 2012.

Not only did Jackson task himself with turning one of the most beloved works of children's literature into a film, but he also chose to transform the novel into three films. *An Unexpected Journey* is merely part one—creating a new trilogy to follow his billion-dollar blockbuster *Lord of the Rings* (2001-03) trilogy, which concluded with 2003's *The Return of the King*. However, *The Hobbit* was the novel that started it all, where J.R.R. Tolkien's adventures of Middle-Earth first began, and pundits wondered how it would fit into Jackson's previously established movie universe. Would it feel like a *Lord of the Rings* movie? Could one short novel really be adequately stretched to create enough material for three full-length films? Would the younger, more juvenile tone of *The Hobbit* mesh with the epic hardships of the One

Ring's journey to Mordor? At the end of the day, *The Hobbit* was definitely transformed by Peter Jackson and the end result is something fairly unexpected—he transformed the novel into a movie prequel.

Some will argue that it is unfair to call *The Hobbit* a "prequel", given that the novel was published years before the other *Lord of the Rings* books. But that is the book version of *The Hobbit*. This movie version of *The Hobbit* is as much of a prequel as George Lucas' *Star Wars* prequel trilogy. In the same way that *The Phantom Menace* (1999) related to the original *Star Wars* films, *The Hobbit* is filled with references, allusions, and music cues entirely derived from Jackson's previous *Lord of the Rings* trilogy. The best word to describe *The Hobbit: An Unexpected Journey*—aside from "prequel"—is probably "familiar" because so much of its DNA seems practically cut and pasted straight out of 2001's *The Fellowship of The Ring*.

Much like in *The Fellowship of The Ring*, the story begins in The Shire, the home of the hobbits in Middle-Earth, where the aging Bilbo Baggins (Ian Holm) is writing his memoirs, specifically for his young nephew Frodo, the hero of the *Lord of the Rings* movies, once again played by Elijah Wood. Bilbo tells of how Smaug, a powerful, covetous dragon attacked a prosperous dwarf city in The Lonely Mountain, decimating and displacing the dwarf kingdom and installing itself as a sleeping watch-guard, perched atop the vast riches of the mountain stronghold. Wizard Gandalf the Grey (Ian McKellen) is inclined to help the heir to the dwarf kingdom, Thorin Oakenshield (Richard Armitage), reclaim the mountain for the dwarves and begins assembling a raiding party (or "fellowship") to steal back the treasure of the Lonely Mountain. Gandalf assembles a group of thirteen dwarves, Thorin included, and has them meet at the house of a young Bilbo (now played by Martin Freeman), who has no idea that Gandalf has chosen him to act as the team's official "burglar." (Hobbits, or Halflings, are apparently very good at not being noticed or, at the very least, being underestimated.) After considerable prodding, young Bilbo reluctantly agrees to join the dwarf fellowship and together they set off across Middle-Earth, headed towards their confrontation with Smaug at the Lonely Mountain.

It is no spoiler to say that they do not actually reach Smaug or the Lonely Mountain in *An Unexpected Journey*. Much like the original *LOTR* trilogy, this first chapter is all about set-up, more concerned with setting up the characters and the world than actually delivering any third-act closure. In fact, getting back to *The Hobbit*'s overt over-familiarity, one could argue that *The Hobbit* completely apes the plot structure of *Fellowship of the Ring*. In both movies, Gandalf the Grey convinces a Hobbit to go on a quest for the good of Middle-Earth.

Then the Hobbit and his fellowship set off on foot and find themselves pursued by evil orcs, barely escaping into an Elven stronghold where they take counsel from Lord Elrond (Hugo Weaving) and Galadriel (Cate Blanchett). Following that, the group attempts to cross a mountain pass and fails, leading them to journey under the ground where they encounter both foul creatures (orcs in *Fellowship of the Ring,* goblins in *The Hobbit*) and the pitiable Gollum, still breathtakingly portrayed via motion-capture CGI by Andy Serkis. It is all leading up to a knockdown-drag-out fight between the handsomest hero (in this case, Thorin) and a particularly nasty orc (this time, it is Azog the Defiler) and a vague ending where the travelling party acknowledges that they still have a lot more travelling to do.

Granted, the order of events does not exactly sync up and some of the encounters do have different results, but the overall structure of *The Hobbit* itself is staggeringly similar to *Fellowship of the Ring,* to the point where the term "carbon copy" could be used without much hesitation. At its heart, *The Hobbit* is a movie a bit like *Die Hard 2* (1990), where the primary concern of the filmmaker is to remind one of how much fun they had watching the original. *The Hobbit* is a movie made for people who loved the *Lord of the Rings* movies, which is a huge segment of the population (the film has already made a billion dollars worldwide). However, in his haste to please that overwhelming army of fans, Peter Jackson opted to re-create the wheel. *The Hobbit* is *Fellowship of the Rings*-lite. It is very ably told, it is well-crafted and meticulous, but, ultimately, thanks to the law of diminishing returns, it is nowhere near as engaging or thrilling as the original *Lord of the Rings* movies.

To his credit, Jackson has created a much more skillfully told prequel than any of George Lucas' *Star Wars* redos. Unlike Jar-Jar Binks, Andy Serkis' CGI Gollum is the highlight of his film and, while Lucas elicited some of the most wooden performances ever from some of the best actors of his generation, Jackson's cast comes off far more admirably in *The Hobbit.* Martin Freeman's Bilbo is a charismatic, complex lead and his gradual transformation into a willing adventurer is believable and winning. Jackson's band of dwarves are more of a mixed bag—some are overly dour, others far too silly—but, again, the actors behind the make-up (Richard Armitage, in particular) do find ways to shine through.

So, is *The Hobbit* an unexpected journey? No. It is unusual that Jackson chose to so closely emulate *Fellowship of the Ring,* but almost everything else about the movie just reeks of the familiar. Which, truth be told, is not all bad. *The Hobbit* is an over-long, big-budget redo, but it is earnest, visually appealing, and entertaining. There is nothing new or original about the movie in the slightest, which may turn new fans off, but, those who

love *Fellowship of the Ring* and can get over the deja vu, might find a lot to like in *The Hobbit.* But if one starts in on this trip back to Middle-Earth with the expectation of encountering the same big, brash, huge canvas storytelling that Peter Jackson so ably delivered with the *Lord of the Rings* trilogy, they will be sorely disappointed.

Tom Burns

CREDITS

Gandolf: Ian McKellen
Bilbo Baggins: Martin Freeman
Thorin Oakenshield: Richard Armitage
Frodo: Elijah Wood
Elrond: Hugo Weaving
Galadriel: Cate Blanchett
Saruman: Christopher Lee
Radagast: Sylvester McCoy
Azog: Manu Bennett
Gollum: Andy Serkis (Voice)
Origin: United States
Language: English
Released: 2012
Production: Carolynne Cunningham, Fran Walsh, Zane Weiner, Peter Jackson; Wing Nut Films, New Line Cinema, Metro-Goldwyn-Mayer Inc.; released by Warner Bros.
Directed by: Peter Jackson
Written by: Peter Jackson; Fran Walsh; Philippa Boyens; Guillermo del Toro
Cinematography by: Andrew Lesnie
Music by: Howard Shore
Sound: Brent Burge; Chris Ward
Editing: Jabez Olssen
Art Direction: Simon Bright
Costumes: Bob Buck; Ann Maskrey; Richard Taylor
Production Design: Dan Hennah
MPAA rating: PG-13
Running time: 169 minutes

REVIEWS

Burr, Ty. *Boston Globe.* December 12, 2012.
Debruge, Peter. *Variety.* December 3, 2012.
Gonzalez, Ed. *Slant Magazine.* December 8, 2012.
Kohn, Eric. *indieWIRE.* December 3, 2012.
Lane, Anthony. *New Yorker.* December 10, 2012.
Mondello, Bob. *NPR.* December 13, 2012.
Phillips, Michael. *Chicago Tribune.* December 13, 2012.
Robinson, Tasha. *AV Club.* December 12, 2012.
Scott, A. O. *New York Times.* December 13, 2012.
Williams, Joe. *St. Louis Post-Dispatch.* December 13, 2012.

Gandalf: "Well, why does it matter? He's back!"

Thorin Oakenshield: "It matters. I want to know. Why did you come back?"

Bilbo Baggins: "Look, I know you doubt me, I know you always have. And you're right. I often think of Bag End. I miss my books, and my armchair, and my garden. See, that's where I belong, that's home. That's why I came back. 'Cause you don't have one, a home. It was taken from you. But I will help you take it back if I can."

TRIVIA

Gollum only appears in one scene in the book. Andy Serkis completed work on that scene during the first week of production, but stayed on as the film's Second Unit Director.

AWARDS

Nominations:

Oscars 2012: Makeup, Production Design, Visual FX
British Acad. 2012: Makeup, Sound, Visual FX

HOLY MOTORS

Box Office: $641,100

Leos Carax (*The Lovers on the Bridge* [1991], *Pola X* [1999]) is one filmmaker who has never been accused of simply going through the motions when he steps onto the set. Here is a director who will only work on a project in which he passionately believes and that fervor can be felt in virtually every frame that he shoots. Granted, this inevitably means that he does not work nearly as often as other filmmakers—he has been working for nearly thirty years and only has five feature films to his name to date—but when he does get around to putting out a new movie, it takes on the patina of an event in world cinema circles because they know that, one way or another, he is going to give audiences something to talk and think about. That is certainly the case with the jaw-dropping *Holy Motors*, his latest effort and his first film (not counting his contribution to the anthology *Tokyo* (2008)) since the provocative *Pola X*. Combining the audacity of a newcomer all but vibrating with excitement at the prospect of getting the chance to express himself at last with the technical skill of a master filmmaker, Carax gives viewers one of the most memorable screen achievements of many years—a film so full-to-bursting with ideas and startling imagery that it practically pops off the screen even without the advent of 3-D photography.

Carax himself pops up during a brief prologue that sees him waking up from a deep sleep and passing through his bedroom wall into a forest that eventually leads him to a cinema filled with people watching the silent classic *The Crowd* (1928). From this point on, the film follows an immaculately groomed man known only as Monsieur Oscar (Denis Lavant) over the course of one long day as he leaves his fancy house to be chauffeured around Paris in a limousine piloted by the loyal Celine (French film legend Edith Scob) in order to fulfill a series of tasks for an unknown employer. It sounds like the set-up for some kind of crime thriller but that notion is quickly dissipated when Oscar steps out of the limo dressed as an elderly woman and proceeds to begin begging for spare change. All of Oscar's assignments, in fact, find him enacting strange scenarios with the aid of an elaborate array of outfits, wigs and assorted makeups that he applies from the back of his limo, a vehicle that, in terms of size and storage space, makes the one utilized by Robert Pattinson in *Cosmopolis* (2012) seem like a hatchback by comparison.

In one vignette, Oscar arrives at a movie soundstage in order to don a motion-capture suit that transforms his movements into a furious light show reminiscent of the *Tron* films. In another, he transforms himself into Mr. Merde—a grotesque, sewer-dwelling ogre first seen in *Tokyo*—in order to burst upon a fashion shoot at the famed Pere Lachaise cemetery, bite off the finger of a production assistant and lick the armpit of fashion model named Kay M (Eva Mendes) before spiriting her off to his underground lair. At one point, he is confronted by someone who appears to be his double and dispatches him and at another, he embodies a dying man saying a tearful goodbye to his daughter. In the most audacious section, he happens upon an old flame (Kylie Minogue) who also happens to be a performer. With a few minutes to spare before their next assignments, they roam the ruins of the abandoned La Samaritaine department store reminiscing about old times and at just the moment when some viewers may be thinking that the film seems poised to burst out into a musical number—at this point, it has done just about everything else imaginable *but* that—it does just that as Minogue breaks out into a heartbreaking song of lament (one penned by Carax himself) before bringing her story to a shocking conclusion. At long last, Oscar's day finally comes to an end but without giving anything away, let it be said that the film still has a couple of surprises up its sleeves.

In other words, *Holy Motors* is one of those films that contains practically everything but the kitchen sink and there is the distinct possibility that one of those might be revealed to be lurking in the margins on a second viewing. That said, those viewers who are not immediately taken by the film may suggest that one thing that Carax does not offer is some kind of explanation that ties all the various bits and pieces together and reveals what it is that he is trying to convey. Carax has never been one for telling simple, easy-to-digest stories— even such comparatively straightforward narratives as *Boy Meets Girl* (1984), *Mauvais Sang* (1986) and *The Lovers on the Bridge* were complex enough to lend themselves to any number of interpretations—and, with this film, he deliberately divests himself of such moorings to create something new and different and it is all the more exciting and fascinating as a result. Everything about the film is an enigma, to be sure, but Carax presents his admittedly outre collection of images and scenarios in a magnetic manner, aided in no small part by the lush digital photography from Caroline Champetier (although Carax has widely pronounced his preference for 35mm, this became his first digital film in order to lower costs as a way of attracting financiers), that it hardly matters that it does not always quite make any sort of literal sense. Besides, does anyone actually believe that the film would be improved markedly if there were a couple of added scenes explicitly describing Oscar and the nature of his assignments? If there are, there is the excellent possibility that they may not be the ideal audience for this film in the first place.

There are any number of way to interpret the goings-on in *Holy Motors*, of course. There are so many references to other films strewn throughout—ranging from movie clips to sound bites to in-jokes ranging from an explicit reference to Edith Scob's most famous film to the fact that the scenarios Oscar enacts have their basis in various genre tropes—that it could be Carax's meditation on the past and future of the art form that has consumed him for so long. Others could also read it as a comment on the increased mechanization of modern society and the like. However, the most likely explanation is that Carax conceived the film to serve as a crackpot tribute to his longtime collaborator Levant, with whom he has worked on all of his previous projects with the exception of *Pola X*. As dedicated to his craft as Carax is his, Levant throws himself into his role(s) with such zeal and dedication, no matter how bizarre the circumstances surrounding him, that someone walking into the film without any working knowledge of who he is might likely assume that the part of Oscar is being played by a number of different actors. While Levant is clearly the central focus here, Carax shows a keen interest here in the nature of performance in general and indeed, arguably the most memorable sequence in the entire film comes during the point when Carax and Levant cede the spotlight to Australian pop princess Kylie Minogue for her big scene. Sure, one could decode the meaning of this sequence in any number of ways or comment on how the deserted department store setting is reminiscent of the similarly abandoned bridge at the center of *The Lovers on the Bridge* or how Minogue is dressed up to resemble tragic cinema icon Jean Seberg. However, most people will not because they will be too swept up in the raw power that she conjures up while singing to notice that other stuff.

Holy Motors premiered at the 2012 Cannes Film Festival, where it was one of the most keenly anticipated titles, and while it lost the Palme d'Or to Michael Haneke's *Amour* (2012), its sheer strangeness ("Is 'Holy Motors' The Most Bonkers Film Ever?" asked *The Telegraph* in the headline of an article covering its premiere) won it instant acclaim from the moment it debuted and it went on to receive rave reviews around the world while *Cahiers du Cinema*, *Film Comment* and *Indiewire* all named it the best film of 2012. At the same time, those who do not find themselves on its wavelength are likely to find it to be one of the goofiest things they have ever seen. Whether one loves it or hates it—and few films of recent vintage will polarize viewers as completely—anyone who sees it will come away from it realizing that they have indeed seen something that they have never quite borne witness to before. Exactly *what* that something might actually be, on the other hand, is the kind of question that will no doubt fuel impassioned debates whenever it is shown for quite some time.

Peter Sobczynski

CREDITS

M. Oscar / Le banquier / La mendiante / L'OS de Motion-Capture / M. Merde / Le père / L'accordéoniste / Le tueur / Le tué / Le mourant / L'homme au foyer: Denis Lavant

Celine: Edith Scob

Kay M: Eva Mendes

Eva Grace (Jean): Kylie Minogue

Lea (Elise): Elise Lhomeau

Origin: France

Language: French

Released: 2012

Production: Martine Marignac, Albert Prevost, Maurice Tinchant; Pandora Filmproduktion, arte France Cinema, WDR/Arte, Pierre Grise Productions, Theo Films; released by Indomina Group

Directed by: Leos Carax

Written by: Leos Carax

Cinematography by: Caroline Champetier

Sound: Emmanuel Croset; Erwan Kerzanet

Editing: Nelly Quettier

Art Direction: Emmanuelle Cuillery

Costumes: Anais Romand

Production Design: Florian Sanson

MPAA rating: Unrated
Running time: 115 minutes

REVIEWS

Dargis, Manohla. *New York Times*. October 16, 2012.

Denby, David. *New Yorker*. October 22, 2012.

Ebert, Roger. *Chicago Sun-Times*. November 8, 2012.

Edelstein, David. *New York Magazine*. October 15, 2012.

Goss, William. *Film.com*. October 2, 2012.

Nelson, Rob. *Variety*. May 23, 2012.

Orndorf, Brian. *Blu-ray.com*. November 23, 2012.

Pais, Matt. *RedEye*. November 8, 2012.

Stevens, Dana. *Slate*. October 21, 2012.

Tallerico, Brian. *HollywoodChicago.com*. November 9, 2012.

TRIVIA

It was the French director Claire Denis who suggested that Leos Carax cast Kylie Minogue in the film.

HOPE SPRINGS

Fall in love again.
—Movie tagline

Box Office: $63.5 million

For obvious reasons, Hollywood rarely confronts the sex lives of people in their sixties. Audiences are far more likely to flock to love stories about characters one-third as old, played by tabloid cover boys and girls like Justin Timberlake and Mila Kunis, who, in fact, made a great pair in 2011's *Friends with Benefits*. So, it is both a pleasant surprise and an unexpected case of tunnel vision when *Hope Springs* focuses so tightly on the sex life of Kay (Meryl Streep) and Arnold (Tommy Lee Jones), who have been married for thirty-one years but have not had sex for nearly five. Their relationship has the intimacy of a day at the library, and not a library where everyone is reading *50 Shades of Grey*. Every day begins with Kay making Arnold bacon, eggs, and coffee, leaving him to read the paper before he kisses her on the cheek and goes to work. At night, Arnold falls asleep in front of the TV on a channel featuring people talking about golf. Eventually he and his wife retire to separate rooms, comfortable in a routine that offers predictability in place of happiness. At the start of *Hope Springs,* Kay gazes into the mirror and musses her hair, preparing to take a step that did not used to feel like a big deal. Satisfied with how she looks and her desirability, she goes into Arnold's room. "What are you doing?", he asks, clearly more interested in his Golf Instruction Annual than his bride standing in the doorway with a longing look on her face. She wants to sleep in the same bed for the first time in years. He stammers that he is not feeling well and sends Kay back to her room to spend the night alone once again.

In the script from first-time feature screenwriter Vanessa Taylor, Arnold and Kay's problems pretty much all boil down to sex—well, the lack of sex, a physical distance that resulted from years of poor communication and probably prevented any progress in or out of the bedroom. This husband and wife are terribly out of sync, which is why, despite her grouchy guy's complaints, Kay pushes these unsatisfied Nebraska folks to attend an intensive, week-long counseling session with Dr. Feld (Steve Carell), who then asks them questions almost exclusively focused on their sex life. Were he not played by Steve Carell as a bland sounding board for long-suppressed truths, Dr. Feld might come off as a professional whose professionalism comes into question from his unwillingness to talk about anything besides sex.

Seasoned pros like Streep and Jones, of course, almost always deliver when tasked with characters worthy of their talents. When Kay and Arnold finally put some effort into each other and spark a bond resembling the old days, the actors capture the history between two people in danger of depriving themselves of a present. Too often, though, *Hope Springs* feels like yet another story about a long-term relationship that has grown stale and can revive merely as a result of communication and increased appreciation.

The first step, of course, is admitting that there is a problem. Yet director David Frankel, who recently failed to articulate any vivid details in *The Big Year* (2011) and *Marley and Me* (2009), again rests on feelings and conflicts that exist extremely close to the surface. They are evident to the audience before they are recognized by characters who fail to change or develop in any imaginative way. Perhaps Arnold does have a limited musical vocabulary and would be inclined to put on Al Green's "Let's Stay Together" to seduce his wife, but moments like that make *Hope Springs* feel confined to the material everyone already knows, without a healthy curiosity about the unseen details that make each relationship unique and potentially complicated. Arnold's reservations notwithstanding, these two have nothing between them that cannot be resolved with a week's worth of therapy and a good old-fashioned rubbing away of the blurriness from the eyes.

Without any other major characters to broaden the situation, *Hope Springs* kills time through forgettable diversions like Kay asking her friend and clothing store co-worker Eileen (Jean Smart) if a marriage can be changed, to which Eileen responds, "You marry who you marry; you are who you are. Why would that change?"

In another absurdly small role, Elizabeth Shue plays Karen, a bartender to which Kay spills her story. This prompts Karen to survey the mostly overweight, unattractive men in the bar about who else is not getting any action. So Kay does not feel like the only one going through this problem, though she may not be as happy about the passengers in the same boat. In fact, roles like Eileen and Karen and many others are so insubstantial that the film credits almost every character besides Kay, Arnold and Dr. Feld as, for example, "Karen the bartender" or "Eileen, Kay's friend" or, in a nothing role played by Ben Rappaport, "Brad, their son".

It is a shame that *Hope Springs* does not open its arms to more characters and its mind to a deeper exploration of the great rewards of a long relationship and the specific challenges that come from being married and over sixty. Sarah Polley's *Away From Her* (2007) easily stands as the best recent example of a film that tapped into the intense love and heartbreak that can consume a relationship as two people age. *Hope Springs* does not aim at small-town cuteness like the outrageously corny *The Magic of Belle Isle* (2012). Still, its investigation into its characters hews closer to the simple than the true, exceptional chaos that exists between people whose decades together require more than a sentence or two to summarize.

Matt Pais

CREDITS

Kay: Meryl Streep
Arnold: Tommy Lee Jones
Dr. Feld: Steve Carell
Karen: Elisabeth Shue
Eileen: Jean Smart
Vince: Brett Rice
Carol: Mimi Rogers
Origin: United States
Language: English
Released: 2012
Production: Todd Black, Guymon Casady; Film 360, Escape Artists, Columbia Pictures, Mandate Pictures, Metro-Goldwyn-Mayer Pictures; released by Sony Pictures Entertainment
Directed by: David Frankel
Written by: Vanessa Taylor
Cinematography by: Florian Ballhaus
Music by: Theodore Shapiro
Sound: Danny Michael
Music Supervisor: Julia Michels
Editing: Steven Weisberg
Art Direction: Patricia Woodbridge

Costumes: Ann Roth
Production Design: Stuart Wurtzel
MPAA rating: PG-13
Running time: 100 minutes

REVIEWS

Berardinelli, James. *ReelViews*. August 8, 2012.
Chang, Justin. *Variety*. August 1, 2012.
Ebert, Roger. *Chicago Sun-Times*. August 7, 2012.
Fear, David. *Time Out New York*. August 7, 2012.
Groen, Rick. *The Globe and Mail*. August 8, 2012.
Tobias, Scott. *AV Club*. August 8, 2012.
Puig, Claudia. *USA Today*. August 7, 2012.
Rodriguez, Rene. *Miami Herald*. August 9, 2012.
Phillips, Michael. *Chicago Tribune*. August 7, 2012.
Schwarzbaum, Lisa. *Entertainment Weekly*. August 1, 2012.

QUOTES

Kay: "I hate golf. I do. I think it's boring. And watching it; that's even worse. It's like being married to ESPN or something. And when you eat ranch chips, your breath smells."

TRIVIA

Jeff Bridges was offered the leading male part in the film but turned it down.

AWARDS

Nominations:

Golden Globes 2013: Actress—Mus./Comedy (Streep)

HOTEL TRANSYLVANIA

Even monsters need a vacation.
    —Movie tagline
Where monsters go to get away from it all.
    —Movie tagline

Box Office: $148.3 million

It is in many ways surprising that Adam Sandler has not, sooner and more substantively, delved into the realm of animated features, given both the medium's enormous commercial popularity and his standing as the preeminent comedic box office draw of the last two decades. Perhaps he was licking his wounds from his only previous effort, the awkwardly marketed Hanukah tale *Eight Crazy Nights* (2002), which failed to capitalize on Sandler's name brand, and grossed under $24 million.

With the overly frenzied and thinly imagined *Hotel Transylvania,* however, producer-star Sandler finally has a foothold in the field. Vibrantly colored high-value animation gets wrapped around a slapdash story more suited to a Saturday morning cartoon in the film, which tries rather unsuccessfully to meld empty nest paternal anxiety with a curious, half-sketched tale about a getaway resort for monsters. Despite its broad, lazy storytelling and decidedly downbeat critical reception, though, the movie set a September opening weekend record, pulling in $42 million en route to over $130 million domestically and another $90 million overseas.

On her 118th birthday, headstrong vampire Mavis (Selena Gomez) is ready to finally go out and experience the world for herself. Her worried and overprotective single father, Count Dracula (Sandler), though, constructs an elaborate ruse about the scariness of humans to frighten her and keep her from leaving his side. They live together in a lavish hotel of Dracula's own design, a secluded "safe haven" from humans where an assortment of monsters—including the Invisible Man (David Spade), the Mummy (Cee Lo Green), the Werewolf (Steve Buscemi) and his wife (Molly Shannon), and Frankenstein (Kevin James) and his bride Eunice (Fran Drescher)—have all gathered to celebrate Mavis' benchmark birthday.

When a goofy human interloper, backpacker Jonathan (Andy Samberg), stumbles across Dracula's lair, the panicked Count endeavors to conceal his identity, lest it freak out his guests. He also works to douse the flickering flames of attraction between Mavis and this curious newcomer. When Jonathan's true nature is discovered, though, Dracula is forced to intervene, and his various deceits unravel around him.

In his feature film debut, Russian-born director Genndy Tartakovsky, best known for his spry and well received Cartoon Network television credits like *Dexter's Laboratory*, *Samurai Jack* and *Star Wars: Clone Wars*, tries to whip up audience connection chiefly through sound and movement. Together, he and editor Catherine Apple drive the movie at a blistering pace. But they are unable to impress a unifying vision upon the film, either in terms of tone or look. Visually, *Hotel Transylvania* lacks the stylized angularity for which Tartakovsky is best known. It is poppy but conventional, and while it has some standout sequences the bits that work best in 3-D, including a scene in which Dracula and Jonathan inadvertently bond during a swooping chase on flying dinner tables, feel like awkward inclusions shoehorned into the narrative as showcase set-pieces rather than moments that occur organically.

The screenplay is credited to Peter Baynham and frequent Sandler collaborator Robert Smigel, but there is a long list of "additional material contributors" in the end credits that includes relatives of Sandler. This uber-collaborative narrative practice is of course common in animated movies, but *Hotel Transylvania* feels especially beholden to the undisciplined rhythms of Sandler's more banal comedies, where digressive jocularity is valued above character consistency or narrative clarity.

Gags pop up in abundance, but *Hotel Transylvania* seems to be just playing a numbers game, as if laughs automatically derive from the sheer quantity of jokes. The many supporting monster characters in particular represent a big missed opportunity, since there is no real standout distinctness to them, nor much in the way of sly interplay rooted in their own proclivities. Everything revolves around manic but discrete bits staged for momentary effect, and nothing serving the characters or part of a deeper world.

Furthermore, holes in motivation and logic are common. First, with its human-vampire love story, for instance, the movie takes a page from the *Twilight* franchise, but puts no fresh spin on it nor has any spitfire fun. Mavis and Jonathan fall for one another because they happen to cross one another's fields of vision, it seems.

Next, though no real set-up or explanation of this power is given, Dracula can pause time. Ergo, when he employs this trick in certain situations but not others (for which it would make even more sense), it comes across as lacking discernment—just a cheap narrative gambit. And while a backstory reveals Dracula's reason for fearing and distrusting humans, all of the other characters merely seem to take him at his word that humans are ghastly creatures. There is no real reason for the hotel's existence, in other words; *Hotel Transylvania*'s inversion of monster cliches is about an inch deep but nowhere close to a mile wide.

Then there are the movie's vocal performances, which are fairly middling. The casting of singers (Gomez, Green) lends itself to a couple half-hearted musical numbers, which do not really connect emotionally or fit comfortably within the story. As Jonathan, Samberg wrings a couple smiles out of a bouncy, easygoing patois that recalls a dorky cousin of *Scooby-Doo*'s Shaggy. But Sandler's hokey and inconsistent Dracula accent is not exactly a meticulously crafted thing. In fact, it at times will remind some viewers of the foul-mouthed goat sketch from his old comedy album *What the Hell Happened To Me?* (1996), which may actually provide more diversionary amusement than what actually unfolds on screen.

The marketplace can sometimes place a crown on a pile of relative rubbish. When taking bets on which Sandler and Samberg collaboration would turn out to be a $200 million smash, most people would have guessed *That's My Boy* (2012). They were wrong, surprisingly.

Despite lacking the snap and distinctiveness of fellow autumnal animated entries like *ParaNorman* (2012), *Frankenweenie* (2012) and *Wreck-It Ralph* (2012), Sandler's snarky movie out-grossed all but the latter. Therefore, even though this tired, uninspired *Hotel* may not be worth checking into, its huge grosses all but assure that it will become another animated franchise property.

Brent Simon

CREDITS

Dracula: Adam Sandler (Voice)

Mavis: Selena Gomez (Voice)

Jonathan: Andy Samberg (Voice)

Frank/Frankenstein: Kevin James (Voice)

Murray the Mummy: Cee-Lo Green (Voice)

Griffin the Invisible Man: David Spade (Voice)

Quasimodo: David Koechner (Voice)

Wanda: Molly Shannon (Voice)

Eunice: Fran Drescher (Voice)

Wayne: Steve Buscemi (Voice)

Origin: United States

Language: English

Released: 2012

Production: Michelle Murdocca; Sony Pictures Home Entertainment Inc.; released by Columbia Pictures

Directed by: Genndy Tartakovsky

Written by: Dan Hageman; Kevin Hageman

Music by: Mark Mothersbaugh

Sound: Jason George; Geoffrey G. Rubay

Editing: Catherine Apple

Art Direction: Ron Lukas

Production Design: Marcelo Vignali

MPAA rating: PG

Running time: 91 minutes

REVIEWS

Biancolli, Amy. *San Francisco Chronicle*. August 28, 2012.

Buckwalter, Ian. *NPR*. August 27, 2012.

Debruge, Peter. *Variety*. September 7, 2012.

Minnow, Nell. *Chicago Sun-Times*. September 30, 2012.

O'Sullivan, Michael. *Washington Post*. September 28, 2012.

Puig, Claudia. *USA Today*. September 27, 2012.

Rechtshaffen, Michael. *Hollywood Reporter*. September 7, 2012.

Schwarzbaum, Lisa. *Entertainment Weekly*. September 26, 2012.

Sharkey, Betsy. *Los Angeles Times*. September 27, 2012.

Tallerico, Brian. *HollywoodChicago.com*. September 19, 2012.

QUOTES

Jonathan: "Are these monsters gonna kill me?"

Dracula: "Not as long as they think you're a monster."
Jonathan: "That's kinda racist."

TRIVIA

The film was released on September 28th, or World Rabies Day.

AWARDS

Nominations:

Golden Globes 2013: Animated Film

HOUSE AT THE END OF THE STREET

Fear reaches out...for the girl next door.
    —Movie tagline

Box Office: $31.6 million

Pedestrian director Mark Tonderai brings nothing but jump cuts and twitchy storytelling to an overcrowded genre with the truly lackluster *House at the End of the Street,* a cut-rate thriller that does little more than prove that the Oscar-nominated Jennifer Lawrence (*Winter's Bone* [2010]) is one of the best actresses of her generation...even in junk. Taking a role that could have been pure scream queen and investing it with some depth and realism, Lawrence is far-and-away too good for this film, a generic mess that only confuses when it should be thrilling; only annoys when it should be captivating. With a twist that is easy to see coming even though it makes almost zero sense in the real world, *House* borders on being offensively bad but its gorgeous and talented lead elevates it to merely forgettable.

David Loucka's script opens with what should be one of the film's most disturbing sequences in which a child kills her parents in the middle of the night. Almost immediately, one can sense that they are about to watch an inferiorly made film in that even this Lizzie Borden-lite scene is constructed and edited with such music video camera effects that it is drained of all of its inherent power (also perhaps to maintain the film's questionable PG-13 rating). With its inconsistent editing and structural mistakes, this is a work that does not just feel like it was made for a teenage audience but perhaps actually produced by teenagers.

Flash to years later as the titular house where the murders occurred has been left unoccupied. Or has it? Elissa (Jennifer Lawrence) and her mother Sarah (Elisabeth Shue) move in to the "House Just Before the End of the Street" and almost immediately hear the rumors. The girl who killed her parents was never found. Does she still live in the woods? And what of her brother, the reclusive Ryan (Max Theriot), who pops up in random places around town and it is quickly revealed is actually living in his family's former home. It is just-as-quickly revealed that Ryan is not alone. There's a girl trapped in the basement who Ryan has to keep sedated and stop from running to Elissa & Sarah's house. Is it his mentally deranged sister who Ryan is keeping under control or something more sinister? Who's the real danger to Elissa & Sarah? And how long will it be before that hapless Sheriff (Gil Bellows) becomes the requisite victim of this predictable piece?

It feels like there was a version of Tonderai's film that played purely as slow burn, not unlike the far-superior works of Ti West (*House of the Devil* [2010], *The Innkeepers* [2012]). Without that shocking open and a few red herring sequences of shadows in the woods, there is actually very little horror or tension in the first hour of the piece. Elissa meets new friends at school and bucks the general trend to mock Ryan. She competes in Battle of the Bands. She ignores the hands-y jock and makes a real friend. There is a sense that Loucka's script once contained a much-more-interesting narrative of the new girl who found her own way to fit and befriended the bullied, troubled soul only to learn that there was a reason the outsider remained on the fringe. And then that script was buried in cliches and generic thriller trappings that forced it out of the realm of realism and into total nonsense.

Through all of the bad writing and worse direction, one can still praise the work from Jennifer Lawrence, an actress swimming against the tide to ground her performance in something relatable and believable. In just a short career, Lawrence has reached the point where she can be counted on to deliver something interesting every single time she goes in front of the camera. This is certainly one of her lesser films but it is nearly as remarkable that she can do as much as she can with this character as with the ones in films like *The Hunger Games* (2012) and *Silver Linings Playbook* (2012), in which she was supported by a far-more-talented team. *House at the End of the Street* is a film about a new girl in town dealing with a loner but it is really Lawrence who is left stranded in this piece of work as the most talented player on a team that does not raise its game to her standards.

Audiences generally ignored *House at the End of the Street* to the extent that critics thought they should (the film notched a stunningly-low eleven percent on *Rotten Tomatoes,* indicating near-complete agreement that it was a waste of time) even if Lawrence's *Hunger Games* audience did push the film to a respectable $12 million opening weekend. It plummeted shortly thereafter on poor word of mouth and ended up just crossing the $30 million threshold. It turned out that no one wanted to visit this *House* even if its star survived her visit to it without her luminescence faded in the slightest.

Brian Tallerico

CREDITS

Elissa: Jennifer Lawrence
Ryan: Max Thieriot
Sarah: Elisabeth Shue
Weaver: Gil Bellows
Origin: United States
Language: English
Released: 2012
Production: Peter Block, Hal Lieberman, Aaron Ryder; FilmNation Entertainment, A Bigger Boat; released by Relativity Media
Directed by: Mark Tonderai
Written by: David Loucka
Cinematography by: Miroslaw Baszak
Music by: Theo Green
Sound: Mark Gingras
Music Supervisor: Steve Lindsey
Editing: Steve Mirkovich; Karen Porter
Art Direction: Shane Boucher
Costumes: Jennifer Stroud
Production Design: Lisa Soper
MPAA rating: PG-13
Running time: 101 minutes

REVIEWS

Berkshire, Geoff. *Variety*. September 21, 2012.
DeKiner, Mathew. *St. Louis Post-Dispatch*. September 21, 2012.
Gleiberman, Owen. *Entertainment Weekly*. September 21, 2012.
Holden, Stephen. *New York Times*. September 20, 2012.
Kenny, Glenn. *MSN Movies*. September 21, 2012.
Olsen, Mark. *Los Angeles Times*. September 21, 2012.
Orndorf, Brian. *Blu-ray.com*. September 21, 2012.
Pinkerton, Nick. *Village Voice*. September 22, 2012.
Rooney, David. *Hollywood Reporter*. September 21, 2012.
Tobias, Scott. *AV Club*. September 21, 2012.

QUOTES

Ryan: "People don't notice all the secrets around them. Even though they're right in front of them, just hiding, waiting to be found."

TRIVIA

The film was originally announced back in 2003 with Jonathan Mostow attached to direct and Richard Kelly providing the script.

HOW TO SURVIVE A PLAGUE

Box Office: $1 million

There is a tendency with documentaries, especially those tackling some of the most powerful and painful subjects of the times, to respond critically at first more to the emotional weight and impact of the film's subject than to the film itself. That is not a bad thing. After all, if a documentary fires its viewers up so much so they come away from it filled with righteous anger, wrenching sorrow, or uplifted hope, then it could be said the film has done its job.

First-time film maker David France's *How to Survive a Plague* is a chronicle from 1987 to 1996 of the activist group ACT UP's battle for more AIDS research and less homophobic institutional apathy about the disease. What makes the documentary so grippingly effective is that through his directorial choices and approach, France (with co-writers Todd Woody Richman and Tyler H. Walk) plugs his film so perfectly into its subject that both hum with righteous, outraged, symbiotic electricity.

Though there are some present-day talking-head interviews used throughout (as well as a computer animated segment that helpfully examines the close-up nature of the HIV virus itself) most of *How to Survive a Plague* is composed of on-the-scene videotape from the late 1980s and early 1990s. Some of the footage is from news reports and broadcast interviews at the time, but more often the tapes were made by guerilla videographers capturing street protests or simply people on the spot filming ACT UP's meetings and actions, including patients in drug trials and victims in hospitals. Also interspersed as an emotional counterweight are light-hearted home videos of the major players, many themselves AIDS sufferers, simply enjoying time with their families.

Spurred in part into existence by playwright and activist Larry Kramer, ACT UP was formed in New York City as a political action group to combat government indifference about the AIDS epidemic that was decimating the gay male population in the 1980s. *How to Survive a Plague* follows ACT UP's battles on multiple fronts including street protests and civil-disobedience sit-ins aimed at New York Mayor Ed Koch and outrage at national politicians like President George Bush and candidate Bill Clinton. But it also details the formation of ACT UP's Treatment and Data Committee, which, when the Food and Drug Administration dragged its bureaucratic feet on testing and approving possible AIDS drug treatments, took it on itself to educate ACT UP members on virology and research methods in order to knowledgably push for more scientific progress and pressure drug companies to provide cheaper medicine.

All of it—as filtered through the grainy, shaky, washed-out look of amateur video in the early days of the medium's public prevalence—crackles with a desperate drive. France's film succeeds so brilliantly because it makes the viewer feel the frustrated immediacy of the

time—it does not just report on a historical era, but brings it painfully, angrily to life. *How to Survive a Plague* focuses on a half dozen or so ACT UP leaders (including Kramer), but throughout, the film captures the immense social and scientific challenges facing all the men and women of ACT UP as they deal not only with governmental and scientific barriers, but also the cultural homophobia of the time (often personified, with dripping villainy, by clips of the late North Carolina Senator Jesse Helms), and the fact that so many of their friends, colleagues, and loved ones continued to die around them as many of them struggled themselves with infection and its increasingly debilitating effects.

Although *How to Survive a Plague* climaxes with the introduction of effective protease inhibitors for AIDS treatment in the mid-1990s, France did not set out make a hallowed look back at eventual triumphs. His film is not full of well-lit, noble, inspiring images and softly-swelling chamber music. Fueled by street energy, it documents anger and sometimes pushy rudeness and spends as much time with false hopes and internal conflicts as it does with successes. It shows ACT UP's fight, like all wars, did not follow a straight, heroic line, but rather was a constant, sometimes ugly battle in zig-zagging trenches. The film's demonstrates how anger can get things done, that there is strength in numbers, and that crisis can forge solidarity and exhausting attrition can break it down. But the film also shows the bittersweet grace and peace found in the good struggle, even amidst harrowing loss.

At the end of *How to Survive a Plague*, France features present-day interviews with several of the film's figures. Their tearful remembrances of the past 25 years are suggestive of a similar coda at the end of the World War II miniseries *Band of Brothers*. The message is clear: These people—complete with their grief, doubts, and humanity—have survived not just a plague but a war.

How to Survive a Plague was released in theaters in the fall, but it never exceeded more than 15 locations, and box office was minimal. However, it was met with great critical acclaim, and the documentary wound up on many critics' and critic groups' Best of 2012 lists. Sheri Linden of the *Los Angeles Times* wrote, "[France's] film succeeds not just as a vivid chronicle of recent history but as a primer in grassroots activism," and Scott Tobias of the *Onion A.V. Club* felt that, "Produced with sensitivity and a clear, dramatic recalling of events, *How to Survive a Plague* feels like an occasion for reconciliation." Writing for the *Washington Post*, Ann Hornaday said, "the film's limitations turn out to be appropriate to its gritty, often confrontational subject matter: Rather than a record of unexpected beauty, *How to Survive a Plague* is as direct as the men and women who used rage and militancy to fight for a treatment for a disease that was decimating their community."

Locke Peterseim

CREDITS

Origin: United States
Language: English
Released: 2012
Production: Howard Gertler, David France; Ninety Thousand Words, Public Square Films; released by Sundance Selects
Directed by: David France
Written by: David France; Todd Richman; Tyler H. Walk
Cinematography by: Derek Wiesehahn
Music by: Stuart Bogie
Sound: Stuart Deutsch; Lora Hirschberg; Topher Reifeiss
Editing: Todd Richman; Tyler H. Walk
MPAA rating: Unrated
Running time: 120 minutes

REVIEWS

Anderson, Melissa. *Village Voice*. September 19, 2012.
Biancolli, Amy. *San Francisco Chronicle*. September 20, 2012.
Holden, Stephen. *New York Times*. September 20, 2012.
Hornaday, Ann. *Washington Post*. October 12, 2012.
Linden, Sheri. *Los Angeles Times*. September 20, 2012.
Morgenstern, Joe. *The Wall Street Journal*. September 20, 2012.
Morris, Wesley. *Boston Globe*. September 27, 2012.
Osenlund, R. Kurt. *Slant Magazine*. March 22, 2012.
Phillips, Michael. *Chicago Tribune*. September 20, 2012.
Tobias, Scott. *AV Club*. September 20, 2012.

QUOTES

Larry Kramer: "Every single drug that's out there is because of ACT UP, I am convinced. It is the proudest achievement that the gay population of this world can ever claim."

AWARDS

Nominations:

Oscars 2012: Feature Doc.
Directors Guild 2012: Documentary Director (France)
Ind. Spirit 2013: Feature Doc.

THE HUNGER GAMES

May the odds be ever in your favor.
—Movie tagline
The games will change everyone.
—Movie tagline

The world will be watching.
—Movie tagline

Box Office: $408 million

After months, nay years, of expectation built on the cult of fame surrounding Suzanne Collins massively successful book *The Hunger Games,* the film adaptation from director Gary Ross rode a wave of publicity into theaters in the Spring of 2012 that is typically reserved for summer tentpole blockbusters spawned from comic books, nostalgic franchise reboots, or both. Not only did the move pay off financially as the film grossed a ridiculous $153 million in its first frame (on its way to almost $700 million worldwide and the 13th highest domestic gross of all time, more than any film in *The Twilight Saga*) but critics lauded the film's dramatic achievements as well. Unlike so many lackluster franchises based on young adult novels, Ross set out not to make a cash cow but an actual dramatic adaptation. The result is a work of art on multiple levels with fantastic technical elements and some of the best science fiction genre performances in years. The movie drags a bit and misses some character beats in the final act (although those are more likely flaws of Collins' work than the film's) but it is an undeniable achievement not only when compared to the onslaught of young adult junk that dominates the multiplex but as a film for all demographics.

It starts by taking its ridiculous concept seriously. It may sound simple but it is something that so few young adult films understand. Filmmakers who set out to make movies for teens often present and produce them as if they are looking on down on the very demographic that they hope will see their film multiple times. There is often a sense that the people who make these movies are above them, from the detached performances of the non-actors in the *Twilight* films to altogether lackluster fare like *Percy Jackson & The Lightning Thief* (2010). Ross, his screenwriters (he co-wrote with Collins and the great Billy Ray), his stellar ensemble, and his A-list technical team made a film that could serve as more than mere young adult escapism. Instead of making a film that gave kids an exaggerated universe in which to play, Ross and his team made a film that made that universe feel like their own. In every frame, there is a degree of craftsmanship rarely seen in blockbuster films that do not bear the name of Christopher Nolan or Joss Whedon.

It helps to have an A-list, Oscar-nominated actress like Jennifer Lawrence (who earned a nod for *Winter's Bone* [2010] and won an Academy Award for her performance in *Silver Linings Playbook* [2012]) in the lead. In fact, she is so good here that her work was largely underrated. She is just expected to be solid every time, a remarkable truth given her young age. She perfectly balances the strength and vulnerability of Katniss Everdeen, a young lady who is not chosen for the 74th Annual Hunger Games but steps into the place of her sister Prim when the younger, sure-to-be-killed girl has her number called. Every year, the twelve districts of this future world send a male and female "tribute" to The Hunger Games for a total of two dozen teenage contestants. From there, despite the fact that 23 of them are going to end up dead, the men and women become instant celebrities. Think of them as finalists on a show like *American Idol* or *Survivor* only ten times as famous and fated to die. They are trained in fighting techniques but also groomed in promotional events that teach them how to smile and speak as much as they are taught to kill. One of Collins' most ingenious plot twists is the idea that being able to promote oneself to sponsors is as important for survival in the increasingly celebrity-centered world as archery.

Of course, Katniss is not alone. She is partnered with a frightened young man from her district named Peeta Mellark (a perfect Josh Hutcherson) and the two run the gauntlet of preparation together including training by alcoholic former winner Haymitch (Woody Harrelson), interviews with Games host Caesar Flickerman (Stanley Tucci), assessment by producer Seneca Crane (Wes Bentley), image guidance by Cinna (Lenny Kravitz), and, well, something by the truly odd Effie Trinket (Elizabeth Banks). After this gauntlet of personality and power training, the Games begin. Can Katniss win a brutal fight to the death while maintaining her core of humanity? Can she be a good person who kills to survive? And what will happen when the film, as anyone who has seen a movie knows it will, gets to the point where Katniss and Peeta, who may be falling in love, are the final two?

The technical expertise of the team behind *The Hunger Games* is clear from frame one. Cinematographer Tom Stern (*Mystic River* [2003], *Flags of Our Fathers* [2006]) received some surprising critical flak for his work here but the gritty, handheld style he brings the film grounds the work in realism that it would have otherwise lacked. Those who wanted something a little less close-up and more stylized know not of what they ask. Composer James Newton Howard (nominated for Oscar eight times) does not provide the expected bombast in his score but offers a subtle and perfectly-used series of compositions. Editors Stephen Mirrione (a regular Steven Soderbergh collaborator and Oscar winners) and Juliette Welling find the beats of the drama and the tension of the action in perfectly cut ways.

If the film has a major problem, it is in length (although one can be certain that those greedy *Twilight* folks would have cut this into at least two, maybe three,

movies). There was likely a bit of temptation to trim the film's 142-minute running-time and the length can definitely be felt, especially in the set-up act which takes a bit too long to ramp up and get going. However, one of the greatest strengths of the film is in how Ross and his co-writers allow for so much character in between the more expected beats of youth melodrama and sci-fi action. There is also an amazing degree of visual storytelling, something almost always absent from the modern blockbuster, which increasingly feels the need to explain everything to its audience over and over again through dialogue, narration, title cards, and more overused devices.

As for performance, the film belongs to the young Ms. Lawrence, a superstar in the making who gives such a well-defined turn here that one can hardly imagine anyone else in the highly-coveted role. Like so many great performances, it is in what Lawrence does not do as much as what she does. She does not overplay the strength of this character, never turning her into a predictable tough chick heroine. And yet the softer, more dramatic moments are not overly underlined either. She finds the balance between the strength and vulnerability of this character in ways that Collins probably did not even imagine when she was conceived. In the process, she turns Katniss into a great role model for young girls, something all too rare in modern cinema.

There has been a small resurgence in the last few years of A-list blockbusters that also met with critical acclaim after years when projects budgeted at $100 million or more seemed almost entirely creatively bankrupt. Films like J.J. Abrams' *Star Trek* (2009) and *Super 8* (2011) ended up on many top ten lists at the end of their respective years while Christopher Nolan and Joss Whedon redefined the superhero genre. What all of these people have in common is a devotion to their subject matter that finds the truth in the escapist entertainment. And *The Hunger Games* joins this exclusive club of films trying to take back the blockbuster and no longer associate it with little more than profit.

Brian Tallerico

CREDITS

Katniss Everdeen: Jennifer Lawrence
Peeta Mellark: Josh Hutcherson
Gale Hawthorne: Liam Hemsworth
Seneca Crane: Wes Bentley
Effie Trinket: Elizabeth Banks
Caesar Flickerman: Stanley Tucci
Haymitch Abernathy: Woody Harrelson
Claudius Templesmith: Toby Jones

President Snow: Donald Sutherland

Cinna: Lenny Kravitz

Rue: Amandla Stenberg

Katniss's mother: Paula Malcomson

Cato: Alexander Ludwig

Clove: Isabelle Fuhrman

Octavia: Brooke Bundy

Prim Everdeen: Willow Shields

Venia: Kiniko Gelman

Flavius: Nelson Ascencio

Thresh: Dayo Okeniyi

Glimmer: Leven Rambin

Marvel: Jack Quaid

Portia: Latarsha Rose

Foxface: Jacqueline Emerson

Origin: United States

Language: English

Released: 2012

Production: Nina Jacobson, Jon Kilik; Color Force, Larger Than Life, Ludas Productions; released by Lionsgate

Directed by: Gary Ross

Written by: Gary Ross; Suzanne Collins; Billy Ray

Cinematography by: Tom Stern

Music by: James Newton Howard; T-Bone Burnett

Sound: Lon Bender

Editing: Christopher S. Capp; Stephen Mirrione; Juliette Welfing

Art Direction: John Collins

Costumes: Judianna Makovsky

Production Design: Philip Messina

MPAA rating: PG-13

Running time: 142 minutes

REVIEWS

Biancolli, Amy. *San Francisco Chronicle*. March 22, 2012.
Bowles, Scott. *USA Today*. March 22, 2012.
Brooks, Xan. *The Guardian*. March 16, 2012.
Mondello, Bob. *NPR*. March 23, 2012.
Neumaier, Joe. *New York Daily News*. March 20, 2012.
Rocchi, James. *Boxoffice Magazine*. March 16, 2012.
Schwarzbaum, Lisa. *Entertainment Weekly*. March 20, 2012.
Tobias, Scott. *AV Club*. March 21, 2012.
Turan, Kenneth. *Los Angeles Times*. March 21, 2012.
Zacharek, Stephanie. *Movieline*. March 20, 2012.

QUOTES

Peeta Mellark: "I just keep wishing I could think of a way to show them that they don't own me. If I'm gonna die, I wanna still be me. Does it make any sense?"

Katniss Everdeen: "Yeah. I just can't afford to think like that."

TRIVIA

Composer Danny Elfman left the film due to scheduling conflicts and was later replaced by James Newton Howard.

AWARDS

Nominations:

Golden Globes 2013: Song ("Safe and Sound")

THE HUNTER

Some mysteries should never be solved.
　　—Movie tagline

Box Office: $176,669

On the surface, *The Hunter* looks like a standard-issue cinematic depiction of the eternal battle twixt man and nature, something along the lines of *The Edge* (1997) or *The Grey* (2012)—it even goes so far as to bear a similarly perfunctory and non-nonsense title. As it turns out, there is far more going on in it than initially meets the eye thanks to a narrative that contains enough story elements to supply maybe two or three different features. The trouble with the film is that the elemental stuff involving man in the wild is so engrossing and so vividly captured that the rest feels like a distraction designed to appeal to audiences that might not otherwise want to see such a story. The end result plays like a lean and effective short story by the likes of Jack London or Ernest Hemingway that has been stretched out and dramatically diluted with several episode's worth of melodramatic soap operatics.

Willem Dafoe stars as Martin David, a quiet and resourceful mercenary who is hired by a biotech firm to go to Tasmania to track down and bring back samples from a Tasmanian tiger, an animal long thought to be extinct and which may contain a toxin in its bite that could have dark military purposes. Arriving at a small village near where the creature is rumored to lurk, Martin, posing as a university professor, winds up lodging with Lucy (Frances O'Connor), who has been zonked out on meds since the disappearance of her husband—a naturalist who was at constant odds with the local logging industry—and her two children, an adorable sass-mouthed girl (Morgana Davies) and an adorable mute boy (Finn Woodlock) who seems to have his own knowledge of the tiger. With the help of a friendly guide (Sam Neill), Martin heads into the wild to set his traps and begin his pursuit of the tiger but unexpectedly finds himself drawn towards Lucy and kids as well, a development that becomes even more complicated when it seems that there is more of a connection between them and his work than he previously imagined.

The Hunter is based on a 1999 novel by Julia Leigh, perhaps better known to cinephiles for writing and directing *Sleeping Beauty* (2011), an erotic drama so muddled on a narrative level that sitting through it was like watching naked paint dry. It is amusing, then, to note that the chief problem with this film is that it is so full of incident that it too is a bit of a mess. Not counting the essential plot thread of Martin tracking down the rare beast and confronting the moral and ethical questions involved with that, there are subplots involving the loner Martin coming out of his shell and becoming protective of the broken family unit that he has stumbled into, the local guide and his own unhealthy fascination with the woman, the conflict between the local loggers and environmentalists that Martin unwittingly falls into as a result of trying to maintain his cover and the mystery of what happened to Lucy's husband. Handled properly, these rather byzantine elements might have somehow made for an effective dramatic tapestry but screenwriter Alice Addison largely bungles the job as the numerous story lines never quite pull together into a cohesive whole and one enormous last-minute development is delivered in such an odd manner that it throws the entire film off-kilter. To be fair, a few of these moments have an individual power—most notably the one in which Lucy rises from a stupor and mistakes Martin for her long-lost husband—but there are not nearly enough of them to justify the clutter.

That said, *The Hunter* cannot be entirely dismissed because of the film's raw and adorned power when it focuses on its main story. Director Daniel Nettheim, a veteran of numerous Australian television shows, does an excellent job of capturing the wild in all of its majesty while still maintaining the aura of mystery that comes from being all alone in a place where few others have ever ventured to tread thanks to his slow-burn directorial approach. Nettheim is aided immeasurably in this by an excellent central performance from Willem Dafoe, who is highly convincing as a man who has learned to compartmentalize all of his natural emotions in order to do his specialized form of work. Even when the material threatens to get a bit sappy at times, he brings a gravitas to the material that helps to keep things grounded for the most part. Thanks to him, long scenes consisting of him simply sitting in the woods have more excitement than most normal thrillers. Unfortunately, whenever *The Hunter* strays from its main objective, the results are about as gripping as the average snipe hunt.

Peter Sobczynski

CREDITS

Martin David: Willem Dafoe
Jack Mindy: Sam Neill
Sass Armstrong: Morgana Davies
Lucy Armstrong: Frances O'Connor

Bike Armstrong: Finn Woodlock
Origin: Australia
Language: English, Spanish
Released: 2012
Production: Vincent Sheehan; released by Porchlight Films Prod., Screen Australia
Directed by: Daniel Nettheim
Written by: Alice Addison
Cinematography by: Robert Humphreys
Music by: Matteo Zingales; Andrew Lancaster; Michael Lira
Music Supervisor: Andrew Kotatko
Editing: Roland Gallois
Art Direction: Amanda Sallybanks
Costumes: Emily Seresin
Production Design: Steven Jones-Evans
MPAA rating: R
Running time: 101 minutes

REVIEWS

Burr, Ty. *Boston Globe.* May 17, 2012.
Holden, Stephen. *New York Times.* January 3, 2012.
Keough, Peter. *Boston Phoenix.* May 17, 2012.
Newman, Kim. *Empire Magazine.* July 1, 2012.
Olsen, Mark. *Los Angeles Times.* April 12, 2012.
Orndorf, Brian. *BrianOrndorf.com.* March 23, 2012.
Robey, Tim. *Daily Telegraph.* July 5, 2012.
Rothkopf, Joshua. *Time Out New York.* April 3, 2012.
Savlov, Marc. *Austin Chronicle.* April 6, 2012.
Tallerico, Brian. *HollywoodChicago.com.* April 26, 2012.

QUOTES

Jack Mindy: "So you can imagine when he arrived a few years back, he was about as popular as a snake in a sleeping bag."

TRIVIA

During the beginning of this film, archival footage is seen of the last Tasmanian Tiger living in captivity.

HYDE PARK ON HUDSON

The President. The First Lady. The King. The Queen. The Mother. The Mistress. One weekend would unite two great nations. After cocktails of course.
—Movie tagline

Box Office: $6.1 million

Sequels and genre franchises are a large part of the fuel on which Hollywood runs, but television, much more than film, has a rich history of weird and amusing little karmic spin-offs—projects that are not literal follow-ups, but re-positioned and re-imagined properties in which supporting characters are spun off to new environments, or new characters introduced to familiar settings.

That realization perhaps best explains the strange existence of *Hyde Park on Hudson*. *The King's Speech* (2010) was an enormous critical and commercial success, raking in over $410 million worldwide at the box office and counting Best Picture, Best Director and Best Screenplay Academy Award victories amongst its dozen nominations. Those factors almost certainly had something to do with the production go-ahead for director Roger Michell's wan dramedy and spiritual prequel, which prominently features the central character of that film, King George VI, in telling the tale of the first visit of a reigning British monarch to the United States, during which the so-called special relationship between the two countries was forged. The other main story strand: oh, just that of a good old affair between President Franklin Roosevelt and his sixth cousin.

Considerably spryer than most stuffy period pieces yet still comfortably, nonambitiously middlebrow, *Hyde Park on Hudson* is disjointed and rather formless. It is not a bad movie, but it is not particularly a good one either. From early on, it feels like an off-key and awkwardly matched treatment of two much more interesting separate stories, never quite rising above the level of oddball curio.

Like many presidents, Roosevelt (Bill Murray) enjoyed time outside of Washington, D.C., and was particularly fond of the upstate New York estate of his mother, Sara Delano (Elizabeth Wilson). So it was that in June of 1939, Roosevelt played host there to King George VI (Samuel West) and Queen Elizabeth (Olivia Colman), who, with Great Britain on the brink of war with Germany, were eager to stave off growing American isolationism and gain his pledged support.

Enter, too, Margaret "Daisy" Suckley (Laura Linney). Henpecked by his teetotaling mother and largely left untended by his sharp but hardly doting wife, Eleanor (Olivia Williams), Roosevelt needs human interaction to keep at bay the mounting pressures of leading the free world, which include this specific weekend a hotly debated public picnic with the royals. Daisy's company helps provide that balance. The pair goes on adventurous car rides together, and she tends to Roosevelt's tea and medications. In short order the relationship turns intimate. Daisy, however, is not the only mistress, as she eventually learns in a heartfelt confidence with Roosevelt's longtime secretary, Missy LeHand (Elizabeth Marvel).

Clearly, *Hyde Park on Hudson* is not a biopic of Roosevelt, but neither is it really a true ensemble piece. The movie focuses on but one event in his presidency, and in this regard is on the surface similar in structure to *Lincoln* (2012). Unfortunately, while a sense of his personality does come into focus, there is little sense of what drives Roosevelt's decision-making, and even less natural dramatic conflict. Ergo, *Hyde Park on Hudson* just sort of bobs along listlessly, the story of King George's visit clumsily abutting an under-sketched interpretation of his personal indiscretions.

Writer Richard Nelson originally adapted Suckley's private journals for a radio play of the same name that was broadcast in the United Kingdom in 2009, and it is this material that informs the screenplay for *Hyde Park on Hudson*, which is rather dryly comedic throughout (the line "I don't think your brother would eat a hot dog" actually sparks an argument).

Its fatal miscalculation, however, rests in an investment with a dreadful voiceover that is both misplaced and mind-numbingly obvious. With respect to the former, Daisy is not a character whom the average viewer knows, or has any emotional investment in, so it is a dubious act to tap her as the film's storyteller and doubly so when, in service of its brisk, 95-minute running time, the movie does not bother to introduce her well at all. Then there is the writing of the narration itself, which is utterly tedious when it is not risible. Were it not for Nelson's previous work, one would not surmise any extant material at all, so empty is his air-quote insight into his characters' lives and feelings. "Everyone was looking to him," says Daisy at one point, telling the audience what they already know of Roosevelt, even if they know nothing else. Later, to smooth a transition just prior to the royal arrival, she intones, "And all the while the King and Queen were getting closer." This device is lazy screenwriting, nothing more. It adds absolutely nothing to the story, and in fact unintentionally contributes to making Daisy seem quite daft.

At the movie's core, Murray's take on FDR—which garnered a Golden Globe nomination for Best Actor in a Motion Picture Musical or Comedy—is appealingly low-key, and without guile. He plays him as a simple man who craves the time for quiet reflection that poring over his stamp collection affords him. Murray of course remains best known for his work as a comedic actor in his heyday, but over the past 15 years—in Sofia Coppola's *Lost in Translation* (2003), as well as six collaborations with Wes Anderson and three more with Jim Jarmusch—he has shown a remarkable ease and indeed skill with shades of disaffected silence and loneliness. In *Hyde Park on Hudson*, Murray captures the rhythms of a man at ease with power but, oddly, neither worldly conflict nor himself.

With his chin jutted forward ever so slightly and his head tilted back jauntily for the frequently lingering photographers, part of what Murray does physically recalls the effusive brilliance of Christian McKay's superlative performance in *Me and Orson Welles* (2009)— playing a larger-than-life character who is, at times, knowingly trading on their own public persona, and "playing" themselves. But Murray otherwise does not invest much energy in either physical transformation or mimicry. He goes with a slight, generic patrician accent, and "is" Roosevelt only insofar as most citizens do not have a fixed perception of him beyond a few audio clips and speech quotations.

Importantly, however, Murray finds meaning in Roosevelt's silences. His performance is a deeply interior one, and not merely because he is mostly relegated to sitting. If part of the skill of a politician is in making someone feel important and the center of attention, that must certainly have been true of the four-term-elected Roosevelt. Murray captures both his character's natural inclusivity and mischievous instincts for leavening a situation with a humor (indeed, he sometimes recalls an amiable sitcom dad, trying to wrest a moment for himself amidst so much clamor). If *Hyde Park on Hudson* does not further develop upon and explore the basic characteristics of Roosevelt which Murray illuminates, it is not his fault.

In the same role for which Colin Firth won his Best Actor Oscar, West is a bit less wound up and standoffish, and a bit more aggrieved. If this portrait of the King and Queen does not align perfectly with *The King's Speech*, West and Colman, who is effectively chiding, make a nice pair, and show the personality jostling and horse-trading involved in marriage, royals or not. Linney, on the other hand, chafes at the limitations of her role. She is superb at conveying Daisy's wallflower soul, but little else; the film is as unquestioning as it is chaste, and does not demonstrate what binds her to Roosevelt.

In both *Morning Glory* (2010) and especially *Venus* (2006), Michell has rich directorial experience with folding prickly characters into the bosom of a cuddlier narrative, but *Hyde Park on Hudson* trends more toward his frothy work in *Notting Hill* (1999). Elizabeth is presented as headstrong, and Eleanor quite independent-minded, but the spats the movie does indulge never seem to harbor much weight or consequence.

All of Michell's more treacly, sentimental instincts manifest themselves, but without sense, proper set-up or benefit of special discernment. The initial outdoor greeting between King George and a sitting Roosevelt unfolds oddly under the Ink Spots' "I Don't Want to Set the World on Fire." Then there is Roosevelt and Daisy's first (and only shown) romantic interlude, a handjob sequence in an open field which cuts away from Daisy's reaction in its aftermath. Time and again, Nelson and Michell's collaboration pulls back rather than plumb its characters' deeper feelings and disappointments.

The striking exception to all of this is seven-minute scene in the film's middle, wherein Roosevelt and King George retire to his study after dinner. Having been fed a series of fancy talking points to woo the president, the king is terribly nervous. Roosevelt, however, puts him at ease, and establishes a personal connection by not only comparing the king's stuttering to his own polio, but also confiding how no one around him mentions the fact that he cannot walk. This sequence is a masterful one, full of subtle interplay and marked by strong and long shadows of reflected character. Yet it also comes in the midst of a long passage in which Daisy's tale is effectively banished from the front burner, which only reinforces the feeling that the film would be better off concentrating on one story.

Hyde Park on Hudson's technical package is decorous. Production designer Simon Bowles and costume designer Dinah Collin do a good job of summoning a rich and well-appointed rural atmosphere, even if cinematographer Lol Crawley's cramped frames sometimes evince the feeling of a made-for-television production. Still, at its core, *Hyde Park on Hudson* is too beset by narrative deficiencies to merit a recommendation outside of history buff cineastes. In trying to marry two storylines that might have made for more interesting standalone movies if explored separately, it flounders, succumbing to a Jekyll-and-Hyde feel.

Brent Simon

CREDITS

President Franklin Delano Roosevelt: Bill Murray
Margaret Suckley: Laura Linney
King George VI: Samuel West
Queen Elizabeth: Olivia Colman
Eleanor Roosevelt: Olivia Williams
Origin: United Kingdom
Language: English
Released: 2012
Production: David Aukin, Kevin Loader; Daybreak Pictures, Film Four International, Free Range Films; released by Focus Features
Directed by: Roger Michell
Written by: Richard Nelson
Cinematography by: Lol Crawley
Music by: Jeremy Sams
Sound: Danny Sheehan
Editing: Nicolas Gaster

Art Direction: Mark Raggett
Costumes: Dinah Collin
Production Design: Simon Bowles
MPAA rating: R
Running time: 94 minutes

REVIEWS

Dargis, Manohla. *New York Times*. December 6, 2012.
Debruge, Peter. *Variety*. September 2, 2012.
Ebert, Roger. *Chicago Sun-Times*. December 13, 2012.
Hornaday, Ann. *Washington Post*. December 14, 2012.
Kenny, Glenn. *MSN Movies*. December 6, 2012.
Puig, Claudia. *USA Today*. December 6, 2012.
McCarthy, Todd. *Hollywood Reporter*. August 31, 2012.
Phillips, Michael. *Chicago Tribune*. December 13, 2012.
Taylor, Ella. *NPR*. December 6, 2012.
Turan, Kenneth. *Los Angeles Times*. December 6, 2012.

TRIVIA

The car that FDR drove with special hand controls, a 1936 Ford Phaeton, is on display at the FDR Presidential Library in Hyde Park, NY.

AWARDS

Nominations:

Golden Globes 2013: Actor—Mus./Comedy (Murray)

HYSTERIA

A comedy about the birth of the vibrator in Victorian England.
  —Movie tagline

He created an invention that turned on half the world.
  —Movie tagline

Box Office: $1.8 million

Tanya Wexler's *Hysteria* takes place in Westminster, London in 1880 when things like "germs" were still only being debated and sometimes dismissed in the medical field. This was a time of great social upheaval and scientific discovery. The characters in *Hysteria* are all too aware of this sociological shift, none more so than the feminist, socialist woman at the heart of the story. The film opens with the caption that everything here is "based on a true story. Really." This promises the audience something intriguing, absurd, perhaps even scandalous. *Hysteria* is a movie with all the right ingredients to make good on that promise, but comes up with just merely "interesting." That it is, but like the

female characters that populate the film's opening sequence, the audience longs for something more.

The story concerns Mortimer Granville (Hugh Dancy), a young, aspiring doctor who is always up on the latest advances in medical science. So much so, that it costs him his job when he argues with an old skeptic about the importance of germs. Mortimer lives with his friend Edmund St. John-Smythe (Rupert Everett), an electrical specialist who is working on a design for an electric feather duster as well as experimenting with something called a telephone. Mortimer does his best to find work and ends up working for a female behavior specialist named Dr. Robert Dalrymple (Jonathan Pryce), whose female clientele frequent his office in order to be cured of "female hysteria," which he describes as erratic behavior made up of mood swings, depression and dissatisfaction. While this field of work is hardly Mortimer's specialty, he takes the job for the pay and the free room and board.

He meets Robert's two daughters who are both around Mortimer's age. Emily Dalrymple (Felicity Jones) is also loosely working in the field of medicine as a type of brain specialist. Mortimer is charmed by her and connects with her during a dinner scene in which Robert has a heated argument with his other daughter, Charlotte (Maggie Gyllenhaal). Charlotte is the head of a settlement house that is on constant need of funding. She proudly declares herself a socialist, an idealist and, though the word had not yet come into play, a feminist. Her father does what he can to get her out of this line of work and into something more proper and lucrative.

Meanwhile, Mortimer comes home from the office with a case of carpel tunnel syndrome after having spent the day inducing orgasms with his hands to his female patients who suffer from female hysteria. This purely clinical practice (done much like a gynecological exam) has become quite popular with the women in the area, but Mortimer cannot keep it up with his own physical ailments. One night, while fiddling with Edmund's electric feather duster, he hits on something extraordinary: The vibration of the gadget is just the thing to cure his wrist problem and if it can cure that, why not try it on the women who come to his office? Thus, the world's first vibrator was invented and female hysteria was cured.

Of course, the movie is about the misunderstanding of such a concept in that day and age. Women were just being women, but in Victorian England, anything remotely improper was inherently worth plenty of scrutiny. The screenplay by Stephen and Jonah Lisa Dyer insists on belaboring this point, particularly in the third act when the film settles in for one of the lazier screenwriting devices, a courtroom scene that serves as the film's climax. Here, the film all but loses whatever momentum it had in telling a juicy story about the invention of something unheard of. Who today would argue that women in Victorian England (and throughout most of the history of the world) lived confined and deeply unsatisfying existences? And why hire an American actress (Gyllenhaal) to give that speech?

While Gyllenhaal is always a charming presence in whatever film she appears, she looks a little too contemporary and physically perfect for this era. To work in a rustic settlement house in Victorian England and still have a perfect tan is a little hard to swallow. Hugh Dancy and Rupert Everett have the best scenes together and one wishes the movie were more about their partnership than the myriad of subplots the movie focuses on instead. Pryce is perfect as Dr. Dalrymple, conveying both an old world school of thought when it comes to status, but a progressive mindset when it comes to science.

Hysteria is meant to be a comedy of the invention of the vibrator and the fight for women's right to be complex individuals. As such, it certainly has its charm and it is easy to watch. Yet, it feels constrained and a bit unfocused. Mortimer's back-and-forth interest in both Dalrymple sisters feels unexplored and there is a sequence near the end of the film as the invention of the vibrator takes its hold over England that, in a more adventurous film, would have worked better in the second act, just as everything is about to get more interesting. *Hysteria* is not a bad movie by any stretch, but much like the invention itself, it works better when the switch is "on." Otherwise, it merely serves as a curiosity item.

Collin Souter

CREDITS

Dr. Mortimer Granville: Hugh Dancy
Charlotte Dalrymple: Maggie Gyllenhaal
Dr. Robert Dalrymple: Jonathan Pryce
Emily Dalrymple: Felicity Jones
Edmund St. John-Smythe: Rupert Everett

Fannie: Ashley Jensen
Origin: United Kingdom, France, Germany, Luxembourg
Language: English, French
Released: 2011
Production: Sarah Curtis, Judy Cairo, Tracey Becker; Informant Media, By Alternative Pictures, Delux Productions, arte France Cinema, Tatfilm, WDR/Arte; released by Sony Pictures Classics
Directed by: Tanya Wexler
Written by: Stephen Dyer; Jonah Lisa Dyer
Cinematography by: Sean Bobbitt
Music by: Gast Waltzing
Sound: Martin Trevis
Music Supervisor: Alison Wright
Editing: Jon Gregory
Art Direction: Bill Crutcher
Costumes: Nic Ede
Production Design: Sophie Becher
MPAA rating: R
Running time: 100 minutes

REVIEWS

Anderson, Melissa. *Village Voice*. May 15, 2012.
Holden, Stephen. *New York Times*. May 17, 2012.
Kenney, Glenn. *MSN Movies*. May 16, 2012.
Lane, Anthony. *New Yorker*. May 15, 2012.
LaSalle, Mark. *San Francisco Chronicle*. May 24, 2012.
Murray, Noel. *AV Club*. May 17, 2012.
O'Sullivan, Michael. *Washington Post*. May 25, 2012.
Schwarzbaum, Lisa. *Entertainment Weekly*. May 16, 2012.
Weitzman, Elizabeth. *New York Daily News*. May 17, 2012.
Whitty, Stephen. *Newark Star-Ledger*. May 17, 2012.

QUOTES

Mortimer Granville: "Sir, I would be enormously grateful for any position that allowed me to offer relief to my patients, with little chance of killing them."

TRIVIA

Dr. Granville's electromechanical vibrator was portable but also had a wet cell battery that weighed about 40 pounds.

I

I WISH
(Kiseki)

Box Office: $145,808

Sometimes, a movie simply lets the viewer just be with its characters, refusing to propel the audience along with traditional action. The greatest of these films, *Ikuru* (1952), *Floating Weeds* (1959), or perhaps, *The Straight Story* (1999), offer unforgettable characters, ones that change the audience as they themselves are shaped by the forces that drive their seemingly scant narratives. Few films have managed to do this with children as effectively as *I Wish*.

Starring real-life kid brothers Ohshiro Maeda and Koki Maeda, the film tells the story of a family separated by divorce. Their respective parents have chosen to live in different towns, leaving the siblings and best friends longing to be with one another and see their family reunited. The older and more serious Koichi (Koki Maeda) lives with his mother, Nozomi (Nene Ohtsuka), and her parents. The pair gett by on what she makes as a supermarket clerk. The always-smiling and hopeful younger brother, Ryunosuke (Ohshiro Meada), lives with his man-child dad Kenji (Jo Odagiri), a down-and-out (if likable) musician. Stuck communicating long distance, they hear of a local urban legend involving the bullet trains that traverse the distance between them every day. Supposedly, those wishing to have their fondest wishes come true can stand at the point where the two bullet trains first cross paths and shout their wish aloud. Joined by their other friends, who have their own list of wishes, the pair set off on an adventure that involves skipping school, tricking mom and dad, and raising money for the expensive tickets to get to the required location.

I Wish takes the truly magical point of view that getting there is half the fun and the journey is as much about preparing the heart to receive what it finds as it is getting what it wants. In some sense, almost everyone in the film is a child struggling with their emotions and insecurities. Nozomi is heartbroken by her family's dysfunction. Kenji, more of a realist, uses his selfish slacker attitude to shield himself from his responsibilities, refusing to recognize how he isolates himself from his family even as he stumbles from one job to another and half-heartedly postures himself as an artist.

Almost all of the characters need to break out, not of their familial bonds, but of their unwillingness to work within their limitations in relation to their ultimate hopes and dreams. The film's masterstroke is the way it finds hope and beauty in the middle ground between desire and practical reality. Like the grandfather's experimental rice cakes in the film, there is a subtlety at work here that will frustrate those who need immediate gratification. But for those willing to savor *I Wish*, moment to moment, the richness it has to offer will be much in evidence. Part comedy, part drama, the film jumps vibrantly to life in moments where children are relating to one another and their environments. Thoughts jump, conversations constantly shift mood and tone, and yet there is never anything less than a near complete sense of real life interaction. This is the way kids talk and act and think and hope and dream.

The Maeda brothers demonstrate an amazing degree of onscreen chemistry, coming across as not only individually winsome but truly connected, despite their obvious physical and emotional differences. They are individual too in their desires, struggling to accept one another. The complexity here really is comparable with the best work of Ozu or Kurasawa, but it is a complexity found in the simplicity that only children can bring to the table.

The supporting cast is very strong here even in the minor roles. Hiroshi Abe, known largely for his work in genre fare like *Godzilla 2000* (1999), *Survive Style 5* (2004), and *Chocolate* (2009), offers a surprisingly effective performance in a role that is almost a cameo, that of schoolteacher Mr. Sakagami, who is a slightly threatening symbol of discipline one moment and a reassuring father figure the next. Likewise, Isao Hashizume tackles the role of the rice cake-making grandfather with a naturalness that lifts him past the stereotypes that often render such characters mere plot devices.

The music here transports. Buttressed by well-chosen pop songs it avoids being syrupy, instead evoking understated moments of raw joy here, longing there, and when appropriate a strong melancholy. By the time the pop songs kick in the viewer will want to dance along with them, feel the wonder they provoke. The approach leads the viewer but is supported across the board by director Hirokazu Koreeda's slow and steady treatment of the story. Koreeda's prosaic visuals here belie the sense of magical realism that builds to the climactic arrival of the trains. Village life and Japanese society in general are offered up as seemingly unadorned by any effort to prettify or render it cinematic.

Koreeda has become identified with a slow burn, almost documentary-style that depends heavily on his actors to lend authenticity to the emotions he wants to evoke in his stories. *I Wish* may very well be his best film yet in a career that has included such grand successes as *Nobody Knows* (2004), which follows a group of children unsure of what to do when their mother leaves and does not return, and *Still Walking* (2008), which follows a family's struggle to cope with aging. These three works, the latter of which was picked up by the prestigious Criterion Collection for US release, signal Koreeda as a major talent in world cinema, able to grapple with complex human concerns, but with a penchant for doing so that seems rooted in faith; faith in the simple beauty of the human condition as brought out in gentle relief against the struggles and tiny triumphs that all humans experience. In *I Wish* especially, viewers are granted the privilege of seeing how faith, hope and love are, perhaps, the really important part of life after all.

Dave Canfield

CREDITS

Koichi: Koki Maeda
Ryunosuke: Oshiro Maeda
Nozomi: Nene Ohtsuka
Kenji: Joe Odagiri
Grandfather Shukichi: Isao Hashizume
Grandmother Hideko: Kirin Kiki
Origin: Japan
Language: Japanese
Released: 2011
Production: Kentaro Koike, Hijiri Taguchi; Shirogumi; released by Magnolia Pictures
Directed by: Hirokazu Kore-eda
Written by: Hirokazu Kore-eda
Cinematography by: Yutaka Yamasaki
Sound: Yatsuka Tsurumaki
Editing: Hirokazu Kore-eda
Costumes: Yatsuka Tsurumaki
Production Design: Ayako Matsuo
MPAA rating: PG
Running time: 128 minutes

REVIEWS

Benderev, Chris. *NPR*. May 10, 2012.
Dargis, Manhola. *New York Times*. May 10, 2012.
Ebert, Roger. *Chicago Sun-Times*. May 31, 2012.
Hewitt, Chris. *Minneapolis Star Tribune*. June 14, 2012.
Jenkins, Mark. *Washington Post*. May 25, 2012.
Levit, Donald J. *ReelTalk Movie Reviews*. May 11, 2012.
Morris, Wesley. *Boston Globe*. May 24, 2012.
Rea, Steven. *Philadelphia Inquirer*. May 24, 2012.
Urban, Andrew L. *Urban Cinefile*. September 29, 2012.
Williams, Joe. *St. Louis Post-Dispatch*. June 22, 2012.

ICE AGE: CONTINENTAL DRIFT

Box Office: $161.3 million

Everyone who went to a showing of *Ice Age: Continental Drift* was absolutely enchanted by the utterly fresh and inspired nature of what they saw upon the screen—and then the film began. The 3-D fourth installment of the profoundly-profitable, frigidly-titled franchise was preceded in theaters by a thoroughly beguiling *The Simpsons* short (also in 3D) entitled *Maggie Simpson in "The Longest Daycare,"* which mesmerized, melted hearts, and tickled funny bones (and was nominated for the Oscar for "Best Animated Short") far more during four-and-a-half dialog-free minutes than the entire mammothly-gabby feature that followed it. Between the time pacifier-sucking Maggie enters the Ayn Rand School for Tots to her sweet, touching rescue of an exquisite, azure butterfly from the murderous mallet of unibrowed Baby Gerald, one finds many witty and wondrous delights. A partial list includes the rack of "Raggedy Ayn Rand Dolls," the picture book entitled *The Drinking Fountainhead,* Maggie's rendition of Pagliacci's tragic aria "Vesti la giubba" when she thinks the poor mariposa has been mashed, and the pop-up, many-hued depiction of said insect's metamorphosis. At one point, Maggie is hooked up to a machine (manufactured by "Often-Wrong Technologies") that deems her intelligence to be merely average, and thus she is carried past the bright, well-appointed play area for gifted babies and off instead to a dreary niche for dolts. A banner on the wall there declares these tykes to be "Nothing Special," and since it was the short that satisfyingly lingered in one's memory long after watching *Ice Age: Continental Drift,* those two words seemed to aptly and succinctly sum up the quality of the full-length feature.

Whether triggered by the movement of molten rock beneath the planet's outer crust or a saber-toothed rat's red-hot pursuit of a deeply-desired acorn, the splitting apart of hypothetical supercontinent Pangaea millions of years ago supposedly sent its pieces spreading out this way and that ever since. (Here it is brought on by the urge rather than the surge.) This protracted plastic surgery upon the face of the Earth commences as the film itself begins, and while it took decades for some to agree with Alfred Wegener's theory that the continents are adrift, it took many moviegoers mere minutes to recognize that the same can safely be said of the *Ice Age* franchise. While this film's production notes refer to it as an "all-new chapter" in the saga, what is being offered-up here is actually akin to the things that Sid the Sloth (John Leguizamo) sickeningly spits out: material that has already been well chewed-over. This PG-rated franchise exalting all things familial has simply come to feel all too familiar.

Deja viewing begins at the outset, as not only does *Ice Age: Continental Drift* start off like all of its predecessors with Wile E. Coyote-esque Scrat (Chris Wedge) and his acorn ardor, but it is what many had seen two years prior in the appetite-whetting short entitled *Scrat's Continental Crack-Up.* (That had preceded Jack Black's negligible *Gulliver's Travels,* and those who also threw good money away on *Alvin and the Chipmunks: Chipwrecked* [2011] remembered a later stretch as what was

presented before that feature as *Scrat's Continental Crack-Up Part 2.*) Subsequently lumbering in is series regular Manny the Mammoth (Ray Romano), who is not only exceedingly wooly but worried once again about preserving the well-being of his wife, Ellie (Queen Latifah), and his daughter, the independence-asserting, adolescently-ripening Peaches (Keke Palmer). It is no surprise that the series' tightly bonded (but never tight-lipped) heterogeneous herd is temporarily cleaved apart again by dire, dramatic environmental events, sending Manny, Sid and saber-toothed tiger Diego (Dennis Leary) floating out to sea on an iceberg after a 3-D-prowess-exhibiting (and potentially tot-troubling) scene of continental division. Back on shore, there is the necessity for those left behind to embark on another arduous, uncertain mass exodus toward supposedly-safer territory. As usual, screw-up Sid needs saving, although he finally garners some respect for his role in rescuing everyone from ominously-named ape-ancestor pirate Capt. Gutt (enjoyably-odious Peter Dinklage). (The sloth both literally and figuratively gets a whale of an assist from his Granny, a cantankerous old-timer who has lost all of her teeth and seemingly many of her marbles and is portrayed by an either great or grating Wanda Sykes.) Just like Diego back in the 2002 original film, silver saber-tooth Shira (Jennifer Lopez) ends up seeing the light and quits slinking on the dark side, abandoning false, hard-hearted Gutt and his massive ice cube of a ship (a new twist on "Jenny from the Block"?) to join the true-blue herd and find love with the aforementioned tiger. All the expected chaotic reversals of fortune lead to a happy/sappy ending involving the reunification of Manny, Ellie and the fruit of their loins, as well as the reconciliation between Peaches and forlorn molehog Louis (Josh Gad), the faithful friend she had misguidedly ditched for cooler companions like Steffie (Nicki Minaj) and Katie (Heather Morris) and hormone-rousing hunk with a trunk Ethan (Drake). (Did those who enjoy the singing of Lopez, Drake, Minaj and Morris really end up flocking to see this film to experience their voiceover work, going home happily humming that credit-accompanying ditty everyone performs that rivals Kleenex in terms of disposability?)

There is also, of course, the endless pounding-home of preachy life lessons about love and loyalty that is characteristic of all the *Ice Age* films. When combined with the production's overall chattiness, one cannot help but wonder if seemingly-ceaseless yakking eventually led to exhaustion and ultimately to extinction for these Pleistocene pals. Listening to them can certainly get tiresome, and there a slew of new (and largely forgettable) characters here who are more than eager to pipe up. Viewers gets earnest assertions about a father's steadfast, dutiful devotion, how genuine caring means having the back of those who may sometimes get one's own back up, and, as Ellie wisely warns peer-pressured teen Peaches, "Don't let anyone change who you are." Despite the *Ice Age* films' sub-zero environs, such spouting of trite (if true) messages has grown rather stale.

How many other animated family adventure/comedies have attempted to mix references to the legendary lost city of Atlantis and literary masterpieces like Homer's *The Odyssey* and Coleridge's *The Rime of the Ancient Mariner* with booger jokes and gross, pre-masticated prune spittle depicted in glorious 3-D? (The film's creepy yet smile-inducing depictions of sirens who attempt to lure the seafaring characters is an inspired highlight.) While the continents break up during *Continental Drift*, neither younger nor older moviegoers ever quite seemed to do the same, remaining only modestly entertained. Nevertheless, despite being much more amiable than truly amusing, the $95 million-budgeted *Ice Age: Continental Drift* succeeded in grossing over $160 million in the U.S. and over $875 million worldwide despite mixed reviews, which spawned talk of a fifth film. Twentieth Century Fox and Blue Sky Studios are unlikely to stop the franchise or even change its formula when it keeps making them a fortune (over $2.5 billion worldwide, so far). Still, those moviegoers who have had enough cannot help but hope against hope for *Ice Age: Arrival of Cavemen with Clubs*.

David L. Boxerbaum

CREDITS

Manny: Ray Romano (Voice)
Diego: Denis Leary (Voice)
Sid: John Leguizamo (Voice)
Ellie: Queen Latifah (Voice)
Crash: Seann William Scott (Voice)
Eddie: Josh Peck (Voice)
Peaches: Keke Palmer (Voice)
Shira: Jennifer Lopez (Voice)
Granny: Wanda Sykes (Voice)
Captain Gutt: Peter Dinklage (Voice)
Origin: United States
Language: English
Released: 2012
Production: Lori Forte, John Donkin; Blue Sky Studios; released by 20th Century-Fox
Directed by: Steve Martino; Michael Thurmeier
Written by: Michael Berg; Jason Fuchs
Cinematography by: Renato Falcao
Music by: John Powell
Sound: Michael Silvers
Editing: David Ian Salter; James Palumbo

Art Direction: Nash Dunnigan
MPAA rating: PG
Running time: 88 minutes

REVIEWS

Debruge, Peter. *Variety*. June 28, 2012.
Ebert, Roger. *Chicago Sun-Times*. July 11, 2012.
Gleiberman, Owen. *Entertainment Weekly*. July 11, 2012.
Kiefer, Jonathan. *Village Voice*. July 13, 2012.
Lehmann, Megan. *Hollywood Reporter*. July 2, 2012.
O'Connell, Sean. *Washington Post*. July 12, 2012.
Phillips, Michael. *Chicago Tribune*. July 12, 2012.
Pols, Mary. *Time*. July 12, 2012.
Puig, Claudia. *USA Today*. July 12, 2012.
Rizov, Vadim. *Boxoffice Magazine*. July 10, 2012.

QUOTES

Manny: "I can't believe this, you slept through that storm?"
Granny: "Aah, I slept through the comet that killed the unicorns."

TRIVIA

The story was rumored to originally involve Manny, Sid, Diego, Ellie, and Scrat frozen solid and accidentally defrosted in a present-day museum. The movie was to be called *Ice Age: Th4w*.

THE IMPOSSIBLE

Nothing is more powerful than the human spirit.
—Movie tagline

Box Office: $18.1 million

An older woman (the timeless Geraldine Chaplin) speaks to a young stargazer who she knows is suffering something unimaginable. The seven-year-old is staring at the night sky with an even-younger boy cradled in his lap. The two children are alone because their parents are, in all likelihood, dead, victims of the devastating tsunami that struck Thailand the day before. She explains how some of the stars they see are actually already burned out. When asked how one can tell the difference, she offers that it is impossible to do so. The woman is clearly trying to comfort a boy whose brightest star may have burned out but the conversation works in the other direction as well. While it is impossible to tell if a star is dead, it is just as impossible to know that it may still be alive. Juan Antonio Bayona's *The Impossible* transports viewers to this hard-to-imagine chapter in world history, an absolute nightmare in which breathable air is replaced by rushing water, families are ripped apart, and lives hang on a razor's edge. Technically accomplished and emotionally complex at the same time, Bayona's film is a stunning achievement, a film that balances the unimaginable and the identifiable into one captivating piece.

Maria Belon (Naomi Watts) and her family are flying to one of the most gorgeous vacations spots in the world for Christmas. Henry (Ewan McGregor) is first portrayed as a worrywart, the kind who questions on the plane whether or not they locked the door when they left home. Maria is a stronger character but Bayona and writer Sergio Sanchez plant little bits about her possibly going back to work as a doctor, indicating that she is considering a major life change. While Henry's fears are more neurotic, Maria's are more practical, such as when turbulence hits the plane carrying them to paradise and she holds on tight. Maria and Henry have three sons—oldest Lucas (Tom Holland), who is clearly stronger than his two more fragile younger brothers, Thomas (Samuel Joslin) and Simon (Oaklee Pendergast). The family is having a typical (for the super-rich) vacation with a gorgeous room, veranda overlooking the ocean, and even a gift-filled Christmas morning. Everything is going well until the Earth cracks and sends a wall of water hurtling toward thousands of innocent lives.

The tsunami hits and Bayona cuts to moments later as Maria surfaces in a raging current of water. As it carries trees, debris, and even cars through the waves, she screams out for her son, who she happens to see being carried down the current. Through a miracle, Maria and Lucas get to each other and do not let go. They are somehow kept together but separated from Henry and the other two boys. When the water has rushed back to its home, Maria and Lucas hear the cry of another boy in the distance. Worried that another wave will kill them, especially given the fact that Maria is very badly hurt, Lucas wants to climb a large tree. Maria convinces him that they need to find the crying boy first. Even in times of extreme crisis when survival instinct should take over, one can always teach a child an important lesson— helping others is as important as helping yourself. It is a lesson that carries into the next act of the film. While Maria lies in a makeshift hospital hoping to cling to life for the sake of her son, Lucas helps others injured or separated from loved ones. Meanwhile, Henry refused to give up hope that the impossible could be true—his wife and eldest son may still be alive.

The Impossible is not an average story of an average family surviving or suffering crisis and so the too-common critical argument that the film tells too much of a white story and ignores the thousands of people who died that day seems remarkably naive or just critically lazy. Not only does the film set itself up as "one story" (the words are in the opening title card) but it makes clear that it is a miraculous one at that. Bayona and Sanchez also never ignore the fact that Maria and her family survived while so many others did not, such as in shots of bodies in a truck, square miles of injured people outside of a hospital, or bulletin boards with flyers for missing people. Three of the last four images in the film are: Two names of the likely dead on a piece of paper, another name of a likely dead on an arm, and of the devastation of the entire area. Yes, this is a story of a family who was privileged (something that is never ignored) but also one that was incredibly, ridiculously, impossibly lucky.

The film is a technical marvel in ways that were not nearly recognized enough in the American critical market. The fact that Bayona's stunning sound design team did not get an Oscar nomination is one of the year's most stunning snubs. The film opens with a wall of sound, the same aural nightmare that many survivors of the tsunami will probably hear for the rest of their lives. And the technical design—sound and visual—of the actual tsunami is jaw-dropping. It is even more so when one knows that there was no CGI used in the scenes with actors, as they filmed the tsunami crush in a giant water tank with debris on rigs to keep them safe. One marvels at the confidence it took in Bayona to jump from something as relatively low-concept as his excellent *The Orphanage* (2007) to something this ambitious. He is ably helped by great cinematography from Oscar Faura and an effective score by Fernando Velazquez, both of whom also worked on *The Orphanage.*

The technical achievements of Bayona's film are notable, but it is equally an accomplished acting piece. Watts, one of the best working actresses alive, feels so completely in the moment in every scene that one never even considers that she is retiring to a heated trailer after takes. Her pain and fear feel completely real. And she makes such smart decisions as an actress, ones that another performer would never make, such as in the way she interacts with Lucas, trying to keep strong for him but knowing that she will very likely die and that her son has already lost most of his family. She is a fearless performer and her work here landed her a second Oscar nomination (after *21 Grams* [2003]). Watts is nearly matched by great work from the young Tom Holland and the most emotionally revealing work from Ewan McGregor, possibly ever. It is the first time he has played a father and one wishes he would allow this emotionally raw side of his skill set out more often.

American audiences, perhaps swayed by the ludicrous misreadings of the film in some critical circles, largely dismissed *The Impossible,* as it made less than $18 million domestically. However, the film was an absolute phenomenon around the world, particularly in the home country of its director, crew, and subjects. Worldwide, *The Impossible* had broken $160 million at the time of this writing and it was still going strong. It is a film that will be found domestically through word of mouth over the years as people recommend it on Blu-ray and DVD. It is the kind of work that connects, resonates, and lingers so strongly with viewers willing to commit to this kind of emotional, inspirational story-telling without the cynicism that so often affects modern film criticism. Reminiscent of Steven Spielberg's most dramatic work, it is a piece that melds history and humanity, teaching something essential about both.

Brian Tallerico

CREDITS

Marie: Naomi Watts
Henry: Ewan McGregor
Lucas: Tom Holland
Thomas: Samuel Joslin
Simon: Oaklee Pendergast
Origin: Spain
Language: English
Released: 2012
Production: Belen Atienza, Alvaro Augustin, Ghislain Barrois, Enrique Lopez Lavine; Apaches Entertainment, Telecinco Cinema, Mediaset Espana Comunicacion S.A., Canal + Espana; released by Summit Entertainment
Directed by: Juan Antonio Bayona
Written by: Sergio G. Sanchez
Cinematography by: Oscar Faura
Music by: Fernando Velazquez
Sound: Oriol Tarrago
Editing: Bernat Vilaplana
Art Direction: Didac Bono
Costumes: Anna Bingemann; Sparka Lee Hall; Maria Reyes
Production Design: Eugenio Caballero
MPAA rating: PG-13
Running time: 114 minutes

REVIEWS

Chang, Justin. *Variety*. September 12, 2012.
Ebert, Roger. *Chicago Sun-Times*. December 19, 2012.
Mohan, Marc. *Portland Oregonian*. January 3, 2013.
Morgenstern, Joe. *Wall Street Journal*. December 20, 2012.
Pols, Mary. *Time*. December 20, 2012.
Puig, Claudia. *USA Today*. January 3, 2013.
Reed, Rex. *New York Observer*. December 12, 2012.
Toppman, Lawrence. *Charlotte Observer*. January 4, 2013.
Williams, Joe. *St. Louis Post-Dispatch*. January 3, 2013.
Young, Deborah. *Hollywood Reporter*. September 12, 2012.

QUOTES

Henry: "But you know, you know, the most scary bit for me?"
Thomas: "When the water hit?"
Henry: "No. After that, when I came up, I was on my own. That was the scariest part. And when I saw the two of you climbing to the tree, I didn't feel so scared anymore. I knew I wasn't on my own. You see?"

TRIVIA

Many of the extras used in the film are actual survivors of the tsunami.

AWARDS

Nominations:

Oscars 2012: Actress (Watts)
Golden Globes 2013: Actress—Drama (Watts)
Screen Actors Guild 2012: Actress (Watts)

THE IMPOSTER

There are two sides to every lie.
—Movie tagline

Box Office: $898,317

The Imposter is a documentary that tells a story so wild, so strange and so downright impossible to believe that if an enterprising filmmaker attempted to pitch a fictional project along the same lines to the moneymen at a major studio, he or she would be laughed out of the joint and admonished not to return until they came up with an idea that was a little more plausible. And yet, the story it tells is true and one of its considerable achievements is how it takes a situation that beggars belief and recounts it in such a way so that even the most cynical viewers will find themselves understanding how so many people could will themselves to believe a situation that many would deem to be a complete impossibility.

This particular story began in 1994 as a 13-year-old boy from San Antonio, Texas by the name of Nicholas Barclay left his friends to head back home and never arrived, having seemingly vanished into thin air. Three years later, it appeared as though a miracle had occurred when the Barclays were contacted with word that Nicholas had finally turned up in a Spanish children's home after what he claimed were years of physical and sexual abuse. When his sister arrived to collect him, however, the Nicholas she encountered bore little resemblance to the brother she once knew—among other things, he now had dark, receding hair and brown eyes instead of being blonde and blue-eyed as he had been, he now spoke with more than a hint of a French accent and he now looked several years north of sixteen. However, these differences were chalked up to the horrifying experiences that he underwent during the three previous years and, thanks in part to a mistake involving a family photo, everyone is convinced enough to send him home to a family too overjoyed to question his changes.

What they don't know (or at least refuse to admit)—but which viewers learn early on (and the title is a bit of a spoiler to boot, after all)—is that the person claiming to be Nicholas is really a 23-year-old Frenchman named Frederic Bourdin who, thanks to a combination of audacity and sheer luck, is able to pass himself off as Nicholas. After a while, however, even he seems baffled by the way that his "family" is willing to simply accept his claims at face value and indeed, it is up to a couple of outsiders—most notably a private investigator by the name of Charlie Parker (a man that the Coen Brothers should base a film around as soon as possible)—to point out that there is no possible way that this "Nicholas" could possibly be who he claims to be. And yet, the willingness of the Barclay family to believe the unbelievable raises a number of unsettling questions of its own that are just as disturbing as anything else and which Bourdin attempts to fan even as the startling depths of his own deceptions are gradually revealed.

Using a wide variety of documentarian tools—multiple perspectives, old photos, videos and news clips that suggest an endless array of possibilities without actually confirming anything and even dramatic recreations of key moments in the story with the performers lip-synching the words of Bourdin himself—British filmmaker Bart Layton takes a story that seems to be completely inexplicable on the surface and while he does not quite manage to tie all the bits and pieces of the increasingly convoluted story together, he does manage to do some things that are far more complicated than that. He manages to let viewers understand why the personal losses of the Barclay family and Bourdin transformed their lives in such startling ways that they almost seemed tailor-made to fill the vacancies in each other's lives in the ways that they seem to need each other even as they appear to be exploiting each other for their own respective gains. In an even trickier move, he lets viewers know practically from the outset that Bourdin is a lying sack of filth, largely by letting him hang himself via his own words and attitude, but does so in a way that still manages to invoke a certain amount of sympathy towards him, especially when the tables begin to turn and he becomes convinced that he has unwittingly become a player in a con game even more elaborate than any he could ever devise and one with more devastating consequences.

Although *The Imposter* is as compulsively fascinating a tale as one could ever hope to see, either as documentary or as conventional fiction (the story did get a straightforward-though-fictionalized narrative treatment in the little-seen *The Chameleon* [2010]), some viewers may be a little put off by the way that it lets a few key plot developments sort of drift away without any proper resolution. Also, while Layton recounts and explores the mystery at hand in a technically and creatively audacious manner, students of the form may find themselves wondering idly about what might have resulted if the project had landed in the hands of Errol Morris, who has demonstrated himself to be a keen investigator of criminal activity and human behavior throughout his own celebrated documentaries such as *The Thin Blue Line* (1988). Regardless, the film as a whole is a dark, despairing and endlessly fascinating work that cannot, in the end, simply be shaken off with the refrain that "it is only a movie."

Peter Sobczynski

CREDITS

Origin: United Kingdom
Language: English
Released: 2012
Production: Dimitri Doganis; Film4 Library, A&E Indiefilms, Protagonist Pictures, RAW; released by Indomina Releasing
Directed by: Bart Layton
Cinematography by: Erik Alexander Wilson; Lynda Hall
Music by: Anne Nikitin
Sound: Andrew Stirk
Editing: Andrew Hulme
MPAA rating: R
Running time: 95 minutes

REVIEWS

Atkinson, Michael. *Village Voice*. July 10, 2012.
Barnard, Linda. *Toronto Star*. October 11, 2012.
Catsoulis, Jeannette. *New York Times*. July 12, 2012.
Denby, David. *New Yorker*. July 23, 2012.
Feeny, Mark. *Boston Globe*. August 16, 2012.
Orndorf, Brian. *Blu-Ray.com*. August 16, 2012.
Rothkopf, Joshua. *Time Out New York*. July 10, 2012.
Tallerico, Brian. *HollywoodChicago.com*. August 24, 2012.
Tobias, Scott. *NPR*. July 12, 2012.
Verniere, James. *Boston Herald*. August 17, 2012.

AWARDS

Nominations:
British Acad. 2012: Feature Doc.

IN DARKNESS

Box Office: $1 million

In Darkness carries on a time-honored tradition in cinema, that of the Holocaust drama, in this case, the kind in which Jews escape their camps thanks to the help of a gentile or two. Steven Spielberg's enduring *Schindler's List* (1993) is the most notable and popular in this genre, but in the last decade or so there have been more than enough stories to go around explaining (and sometimes over-explaining) just how horrible the Holocaust was for all involved. In the last decade, films such as *The Pianist* (2002), *The Reader* (2008), and *A Film Unfinished* (2011) (and plenty more) garnered some degree of arthouse success and, in the case of *The Pianist* and *The Reader,* managed to nab a couple Oscars. As if compassion fatigue could never possibly set in after such an onslaught of despair, now comes the appropriately named *In Darkness.*

The film opens with several scenes of naked women running helplessly through the woods while being followed by German soldiers, Jewish men in the ghettos having their beards pulled out of their skin and home invasions in Poland. Much of the film takes place in the sewers underneath the Warsaw ghettos, where a group of Jewish men have managed to dig a tunnel with plans to escape. Hordes of more men, women and children soon follow. Among them are two sisters who eventually become separated. When one sister tries to leave the sewers to find her, she is advised to stay put. To leave is to risk certain death.

Time is passed underground by reading scripture as well as articles stating the progress (or lack thereof) by the German armies. The group is led by Leopold Socha (Robert Wieckiewicz), a gentile sewer worker who knows the sewers backwards and forwards. He tells this massive following that he can only take eleven people and that everyone else will have to stay behind. Socha is not doing this out of any pure kindness. These prisoners are paying him and he still carries a lot of resentment toward the Jews and he makes that known. "Give a Yid a finger and they take an arm," he says as they try to bargain for more people to take with him. Socha has only so much money to use to help feed these people, which he does by going above ground as a regular citizen and staying out of the watchful eyes of the soldiers.

But the soldiers are suspicious of Jews hiding in the sewers even though all the Jews who were above ground have been moved to another camp or ghetto. At one point, Socha takes an officer named Bortnik (Michal Zurawski) below and assures him that no one is hiding. Bortnik is Socha's main obstacle for not getting caught. While the Jews in the sewers pass the time during the day, Socha keeps the ruse up above ground by going

about his routine. The claustrophobia, dampness, rats and overall stench eventually take its toll on the group and a lot of in-fighting inevitably occurs. There are moments of levity as the kids in the group perform songs as a way of lifting spirits.

In Darkness takes place almost entirely where its title suggests. Jolanta Dylewska's cinematography and Erwin Prib's production design explicitly captures the cold harshness of the sewers as well as the decaying of humanity taking place at ground level. The scenes in the sewers are trickier, of course. There could not possibly be so much light coming through the holes in the ground or even the lanterns they use, but Dylewska has to show the audience as much as possible with as little light as possible. A good percentage of shots are surrounded by pure blackness as hope fades day by day for these tortured individuals.

The film is based on a book by Robert Marshall and, of course, it is a true story. Director Agnieszka Holland gets fine performances from the cast and a great deal of production value to help tell this story, but the one thing that *In Darkness* lacks is a clear sense of purpose. Holland tries to get by on nobility alone and while it may very well be noble to make a film about the persecution of the Jewish people during World War II, it would be even better if one were to do so in a way that either sheds new light on the topic or breaks cinematic ground. Holland does neither. The small dramas that unfold between all the characters feel like obligatory plot points inserted to help make the audience just feel worse. Even discussions about Jesus being a Jew and the uselessness of prayer feel like bullet point dissertations.

It takes a lot for an audience to want to sit through a film such as this and it is a shame that *In Darkness,* for all it has going for it with the performances and production, does not offer much more than "See? The Holocaust was awful, but sometimes people tried to do good" as its central thesis. These stories have been told before and not all of them had happy endings, of course, and one should not necessarily expect that going into a film like this. But once the nobility factor has been covered, there should be more than just opera music accompanying the horrors and more than just a light or a crying baby at the end of the dark, dark tunnel.

Collin Souter

CREDITS

Mundek Margolies: Benno Furmann
Leopold Socha: Robert Wieckiewicz
Szezepek: Krzysztof Skonieczny
Yanek Grossmann: Marcin Bosak

Chaja: Julia Kijowska
Klara Keller: Agnieszka Grochowska
Paulina Chiger: Maria Schrader
Ignacy Chiger: Herbert Knaup
Bortnik: Michal Zurawski
Origin: Poland
Language: Polish, German, Yiddish
Released: 2011
Production: Marc-Daniel Dichant, Eric Jordan, Juliusz Machulski, Paul Stephens, Steffen Reuter, Patrick Knippel, Leander Carell; The Film Works Ltd., Schmidtz Katze Filmkollektv; released by Sony Pictures Classics
Directed by: Agnieszka Holland
Written by: David F. Shamoon
Cinematography by: Jolanta Dylewska
Music by: Antoni Komasa-Lazarkiewicz
Sound: Robert Fletcher
Editing: Michael Czarnecki
Art Direction: Katarzyna Sobanska
Costumes: Katarzyna Lewinska
Production Design: Erwin W. Prib
MPAA rating: R
Running time: 145 minutes

REVIEWS

Anderson, John. *Newsday*. March 2, 2012.
Atkinson, Michael. *Village Voice*. February 7, 2012.
Burr, Ty. *Boston Globe*. March 1, 2012.
Denby, David. *New Yorker*. February 26, 2012.
Ebert, Roger. *Chicago Sun-Times*. February 16, 2012.
Jones, J. R. *Chicago Reader*. February 17, 2012.
Kennedy, Lisa. *Denver Post*. March 2, 2012.
LaSalle, Mick. *San Francisco Chronicle*. February 23, 2012.
Schwarzbaum, Lisa. *Entertainment Weekly*. February 8, 2012.
Turan, Kenneth. *Los Angeles Times*. December 8, 2011.

TRIVIA

The film was Poland's candidate to compete for Best Foreign Language Film at the 2012 Academy Awards.

AWARDS

Nominations:
Oscars 2011: Foreign Film

THE INNKEEPERS

Some guests never check out.
    —Movie tagline

A Ghost story for the minimum wage.
    —Movie tagline

Come stay at the Yankee Pedlar for a night you will never forget.
    —Movie tagline

Box Office: $78,396

The horror film can be approached many ways and achieve many different affects; the stark terror of the inescapable encounter, dread of the unknown, disgust with the abject, the disturbing quality of displacement. Even irony is strongly connected to the genre offering opportunities for unexpected twists that can lead to any of the above. When a film accomplishes all of the above it can safely be said to be a masterpiece of horror. Such a film is *The Innkeepers* by Ti West who has proven with this feature that he is both a master of the slow burn and the sense of utter panic that fuels the very best the genre has to offer.

Asthmatic Claire (Sara Paxton) and geeky Luke (Pat Healey) are desk clerks at The Yankee Peddler Inn, a quaint little historic hotel located in a small New England town that happens to be closing. The film opens as the pair prepares to man the last 24 hours of hotel operations, ready to say goodbye to each other and the grand old Peddler. Meanwhile, Luke is trying to use what little time he has left looking for definitive proof of spooks in the supposedly haunted inn and finishing up his ghost hunters website. Claire, who he secretly has a crush on, helps by manning recording equipment. In between giving each other the heebie-jeebies and practical jokes they attend to the various guests that populate the soon-to-be defunct business: the mother and child on the run from a bad relationship, the old man who just wants to stay in the room he honeymooned in decades ago, and the one-time TV star turned psychic, Leanne Rease-Jones (Kelly McGillis) whom Claire dotes on, despite the fact that she is mean as hell. The night drones on, but during their separate shifts Luke and Claire begin to believe someone or something else is in the hotel with them and the guests. What remains to be seen is whether or not they are right or simply the victims of their own anxious personalities. It could be said the film plays like a mumblecore version of Robert Wise' *The Haunting* (1963) but such comparisons might invite misunderstanding. West's film encourages viewers at every turn to use their own imaginations, to bond with the characters over the simple of motivations and to give themselves over to the most fundamental human emotions.

There are so many things to praise about *The Innkeepers* that the hard part of doing so is prioritization. For a screenplay that has its characters walking down dark hallways an awful lot *The Innkeepers* nonetheless offers a complex is-it-real-or-just-in-their-imaginations narrative offering a perfect structure for West and cinematographer Eliot Rockett (who also worked with West on the dynamite *The House of the Devil* [2009]) to create atmosphere. The pair takes advantage of that at every turn utilizing the simplest techniques to the greatest effect prowling through darkened hallways and timing their scares. By the film's end they achieve a near unbearable sense of shrieking panic but the achievement has as much to do with the solid screenplay than anything else. This is a film that will literally keep viewers guessing until far past the ending.

The cast is uniformly excellent. Both Paxton and Healy generate tension, get laughs and exude real screen presence and chemistry together. Supporting player Kelly McGillis, last seen in the excellent *Stakeland* (2010), also makes the most of her role. McGillis uses her former household name status (from films like *Witness* [1985] and *Top Gun* [1986]) to full advantage, channeling a jaded spinster who still has a little bit of her soul left to share when Claire needs it most. The film even features a fun cameo by noted mumblecore filmmaker Lena Dunham as a self-absorbed diner clerk.

If *The Innkeepers* proves anything at all about the horror genre and ghost stories in particular it is that they are truly universal, appealing to deep-rooted needs that viewers feel to see their anxieties expressed as potently as possible. In an age of wanton shock-til-ya-drop extreme movies West, despite his young age, is a throwback to the days when viewers were forced to confront themselves rather than simply react to and then forget what was on the screen. This is cinema that stays, creeps into the backseat of the car, and surprises viewers in the garage just when they think everything is safe.

Dave Canfield

CREDITS

Claire: Sara Paxton
Luke: Pat Healy
Leanne Rease-Jones: Kelly McGillis
Barista: Lena Durham
Gayle the Angry Mom: Alison Bartlett
Boy: Jake Ryan
Origin: United States
Language: English
Released: 2011
Production: Derek Curl, Larry Fessenden, Peter Phok, Ti West, Ti West; Dark Sky Films, Glass Eye Pix; released by MPI Media Group
Directed by: Ti West
Written by: Ti West
Cinematography by: Eliot Rockett

Music by: Jeff Grace
Sound: Tom Efinger; Graham Reznick
Music Supervisor: Marguerite Phillips
Editing: Ti West
Art Direction: Scott Kuzio; Chris Trujillo
Costumes: Elisabeth Vastola
Production Design: Jade Healy
MPAA rating: R
Running time: 100 minutes

REVIEWS

Berardinelli, James. *ReelViews.* February 2, 2012.
Drake, Grae. *Movies.com.* February 7, 2012.
Ebert, Roger. *Chicago Sun-Times.* February 2, 2012.
Holcomb, Brian. *CinemaBlend.com.* May 1, 2012.
Huddleston, Tom. *Time Out.* June 6, 2012.
Leydon, Joe. *Variety.* March 17, 2012.
Morris, Wesley. *Boston Globe.* February 2, 2012.
Newman, Kim. *Empire Magazine.* June 3, 2012.
Pinkerton, Nick. *Village Voice.* January 31, 2012.
Scott, A. O. *New York Times.* February 2, 2012.

QUOTES

Claire: "Never skimp on bread; you'll always regret it."

TRIVIA

The movie was filmed at the actual Yankee Pedlar Inn, in Torrington, Connecticut.

THE INTOUCHABLES

Sometimes you have to reach into someone else's world to find out what's missing in your own.
—Movie tagline

One man brought a family together...and changed their lives forever.
—Movie tagline

Box Office: $10.2 million

Olivier Nakache and Eric Toledano's *The Intouchables* was an international phenomenon, an old-fashioned crowd-pleaser that American audiences may have grown weary of seeing in the multiplex but the rest of the planet clearly was not as the film made a stunning $416 million in foreign gross. Its worldwide gross ranks above smash hits like *Twilight* (2008), *Star Trek* (2009), and *Live Free or Die Hard* (2007). In fact, its $10 million domestic gross may first seem like a pittance compared to the rest of the world until one realizes that it says more about the market for subtitles in the U.S. than anything else. *The Intouchables* was actually the highest-grossing foreign-language film at the domestic market in 2012 and #24 in movie history. Americans just do not see foreign films. And in the case of *The Intouchables,* other than the fascinating international story, they may not have missed much that they had not seen before.

The Intouchables plays with so many buddy movie cliches that went out of American movie fashion years ago that it almost feels like a film from another era. A paraplegic man named Philippe (the great Francois Cluzet) is seeking to hire a caregiver. The interviews are going relatively routinely—boring professionals who handle all assignments by the numbers—until a force of nature named Driss (Omar Sy) comes barreling in just to get a signature to prove that he interviewed so he can get his welfare benefits. Driss does not treat Philippe like a freak, even going as far as to shameless flirt with Phillipe's stunning assistant Magalie (Audrey Fleurot). Of course, Philippe wants to give Driss a shot at the job instead of just signing his paperwork. The strong, young black man and the crippled, older white man will surely change each other, learning from their unique friendship. While the film is based on a true story, it may as well have been created by a screenwriting program designed for cross-demographic buddy comedy production.

When the phone rings, Driss hands it to Philippe, forgetting he cannot use his arms. This is charming and annoying. When Philippe takes Driss to art sales and operas, the latter may seem perturbed but he is secretly enjoying the culture. The idea that a rich white man gives a poor black one culture (Driss even becomes an artist, selling an awful painting that should insult all aspiring painters) and that a poor black man teaches a rich white one how to find his soul (often through American R&B music) truly borders on the offensive. The film's script often brings to mind works like *The Green Mile* (1999) and *The Legend of Bagger Vance* (2000) in the way a nearly-magical black man saves a white one. One wishes that the cultural, racial, economic, and social issues were more subtle and refined instead of so clearly on-the-nose in ways that remind one of TV sitcom writing.

However, despite the script's notable flaws, the two gentlemen cast in the lead roles (and even most of the ensemble in the smaller ones, particularly the mesmerizing Fleurot) truly deliver captivating work. Omar Sy won several awards for his breakthrough performance, including the French equivalent of the Oscar for Best Actor. So many viewers in so many different countries fell in love with this film not because of its groundbreaking screenplay or unique story but the two men who convey it. Every single thing that works about *The Intouchables,* all of the reasons that it is easy to overlook the cliche and just enjoy the comedy, comes down to

performance. Sy is the laugh-getter and the vibrant personality that was most associated with the film's success but Cluzet matches him in subtlety and smart decisions. So great in *Tell No One* (2006), Cluzet has become one of France's most interesting actors.

While the film was a smash success around the world, critics were more divided. Some U.K. critics were notably harsh while American critics seemed more able to accept *The Intouchables* for the crowd-pleasing, heartwarming fare it always set out to be (although it is wise that most U.S. critical bodies did not go overboard as the film missed out on most Best Foreign Language Film prizes and missed the cut for the big five at the Academy Awards. It is an OK film and one is glad that it did not beat out more ambitious fare like *Amour* [2012], *Holy Motors* [2012], and *Once Upon a Time in Anatolia* [2012]). Not every film needs to break new ground. *The Intouchables* is a familiar story, well-told, and as its phenomenal success makes clear, sometimes that is all one needs to connect with audiences around the world.

Brian Tallerico

CREDITS

Philippe: Francois Cluzet
Driss: Omar Sy
Yvonne: Anne LeNy
Magalie: Audrey Fleurot
Adama: Cyril Mendy
Albert: Christian Ameri
Antoine: Gregoire Oestermann
Origin: France
Language: French
Released: 2012
Production: Yann Zenou, Laurent Zeitoun, Nicolas Duval-Adassovsky; Quad Productions; released by Weinstein Company L.L.C.
Directed by: Oliver Nakache; Eric Toledano
Written by: Oliver Nakache; Eric Toledano
Cinematography by: Mathieu Vadepied
Music by: Ludovico Einaudi
Editing: Dorian Rigal-Ansous
Costumes: Isabelle Pannetier
Production Design: Francois Emmanuelli
MPAA rating: R
Running time: 112 minutes

REVIEWS

Berardinelli, James. *ReelViews*. May 23, 2012.
Cole, Stephen. *The Globe and Mail*. May 31, 2012.

Corliss, Richard. *Time*. May 26, 2012.

Goodykoontz, Bill. *Arizona Republic*. May 31, 2012.

Morgenstern, Joe. *Wall Street Journal*. May 24, 2012.

O'Hehir, Andrew. *Salon.com*. May 23, 2012.

Puig, Claudia. *USA Today*. May 24, 2012.

Rainer, Peter. *Christian Science Monitor*. May 26, 2012.

Reed, Rex. *New York Observer*. May 24, 2012.

Williams, Joe. *St. Louis Post-Dispatch*. June 1, 2012.

QUOTES

Philippe: "My true disability is not having to be in a wheelchair. It's having to be without her."

TRIVIA

The sports car Driss is driving for Philippe is a Maserati Quattroporte.

AWARDS

Nominations:

British Acad. 2012: Foreign Film
Golden Globes 2013: Foreign Film

INTRUDERS

The nightmare is real.
—Movie tagline

Box Office: $69,136

Two intertwined stories from different time periods, one in English and the other in Spanish, come together in the tony but utterly inert *Intruders,* a putative psychological thriller and horror movie wrapped up in some of the dark fears of parenthood, both internalized and externally manifested. Directed by Juan Carlos Fresnadillo, the movie is by turns derivative and deadly dull—hinging on a convoluted and absurd twist ending that somehow attempts to justify its baroque contortions of ambiguity. The cold, hard truth is that *Intruders* ultimately never stirs up enough passion to even be bewildering or confounding in an interesting way.

The story centers around Hollow Face, a ghastly, cloaked figure conjured by or somehow connected to stories two different children in two different eras scribble down in notebooks before bedtime. In Madrid, more than three decades ago, single mom Luisa (Pilar Lopez de Ayala) is unnerved by the story her son Juan (Izan Corchero) tells her about a shadowy, hooded ghoul who slips into children's rooms at night and takes their faces, so that he may be recognized and loved. She tries to comfort young Juan, but eventually confides her fears

in her priest, Father Antonio (Daniel Bruhl), who tries to arrange a sort of exorcism/intervention.

In present-day London, meanwhile, 12-year-old Mia (Ella Purnell) is, improbably enough, somehow tormented and assaulted by the same figure as Juan, after finding a faded manuscript hidden in the hole of a tree. Her dad, John (Clive Owen), is the only other person who can see the figure. He tries to protect Mia, chasing Hollow Face away and even burning an effigy of him in the backyard, while his wife and Mia's mother, Susanna (Carice van Houten), becomes more and more worried about the state of her family. Eventually the seemingly impossible connections between these two discrete stories are revealed.

Almost every genre film has influences that it wears fairly readily on its sleeve, but the antecedents that visually and thematically inform *Intruders* is a list that runs deep, and without much artful disguise: *The Exorcist* (1973), *The Frighteners* (1996), *The Sixth Sense* (1999), *The Others* (2001), *Pan's Labyrinth* (2006), *Mirrors* (2008) and *Don't Be Afraid of the Dark* (2011). Snatched bits of inspiration from all these and more are trotted out, and ladled over a movie that has little in the way of a unifying psychological forethought and imagination.

Cinema, especially when attempting to evoke dread and discomfort, may lean heavily on visual vocabulary, but the screenplay is still the thing, and this, in a nutshell, is the problem with *Intruders*. Its self-satisfied script, by Nicolas Casariego and Jaime Marques, thinks it is clever (among other tidbits John's surname is Farrow, making his daughter, yes, Mia Farrow), and that merely by restraining from much in the way of blood or gore it is original and gripping. But the big to-do attached to its "ta-da" moment is undeserved, not because of the legitimately potentially interesting questions this twist attempts to raise about nature versus nurture, fear, mental health and the legacy of denial, but because of the overly coy and ham-fisted way in which it goes about telling that story.

On a macro level, it is easy to understand the roots of Fresnadillo's attraction to the material, since it shares some fanciful pinch and blend of big ideas and moody telling with his *Intacto* (2001), about a world where luck can be amassed, traded and stolen like any other commodity. So stylistically, Fresnadillo really presses down on the peddle with *Intruders*. To compensate for a narrative lack of more concretely defined menace and fright, he aims for scares via vertiginous low-angle framing and goosed-up, bump-in-the-night sound design, the latter of which has to contend with composer Roque Banos' alternately creaky and dissonant string score.

For a while, this pays certain dividends. Early on, before much of the story is settled, *Intruders* works in scene-to-scene fashion as an exercise in eerie atmospherics. Hollow Face is rendered in CGI, but Fresnadillo and cinematographer Enrique Chediak also make savvy use of deep shadow. Quick cuts, orchestrated by editor Nacho Ruiz Capillas, underscore the uncertainty that feed adolescent nightmares. Untethered to much of earned intrigue, however, Fresnadillo's grand flourishes (and the aforementioned jarring score) quickly become grating, a bag of tricks in service of an empty vessel.

While Owen is an eminently watchable actor who characteristically invests a lot of energy as the increasingly panicked and confused John, he cannot save *Intruders*. The other performances, too, are hampered by the two-dimensionality of the characters, as written. It is young Purnell who emerges as the real standout here; she possesses a sympathetic yet vague visage that helps sustain the movie's ambiguousness, at least in its early passages.

Long before its silly wrap-up arrives, though, Fresnadillo's movie proves most unwelcome, simply by way of its mannered tediousness and smug belief that it is peddling a smarter brand of horror, which it is not. Viewers are advised not to let these *Intruders* into their homes.

Brent Simon

CREDITS

John Farrow: Clive Owen
Mia Farrow: Ella Purnell
Juan: Izan Corchero
Luisa: Pilar Lopez de Ayala
Susanna Farrow: Carice van Houten
Father Antonio: Daniel Bruhl
Dr. Rachel: Kerry Fox
Origin: Spain
Language: English, Spanish
Released: 2011
Production: Belen Atienza, Mercedes Gamero, Enrique Lopez Lavigne; Antena 3 Films, Apaches Entertainment, Canal+ Espana, Ministerio de Cultura, Universal Pictures International; released by Millennium Entertainment
Directed by: Juan Carlos Fresnadillo
Written by: Nicolas Casariego; Jaime Marques
Cinematography by: Enrique Chediak
Music by: Roque Banos
Sound: James Munoz
Editing: Nacho Ruiz Capillas
Art Direction: Inigo Navarro
Costumes: Tatiana Hernandez
Production Design: Alain Bainee
MPAA rating: R
Running time: 100 minutes

REVIEWS

Biancolli, Amy. *San Francisco Chronicle*. March 29, 2012.
Dargis, Manohla. *New York Times*. March 29, 2012.
Gilsdorf, Ethan. *Boston Globe*. March 29, 2012.
Goodykoontz, Bill. *Arizona Republic*. March 29, 2012.
Klein, Andy. *Christian Science Monitor*. March 30, 2012.
Orange, Michelle. *Movieline*. March 28, 2012.
Rooney, David. *Hollywood Reporter*. September 16, 2011.
Snider, Eric. *Film.com*. March 30, 2012.
Tobias, Scott. *AV Club*. September 14, 2011.
White, Dave. *Movies.com*. March 30, 2012.

QUOTES

John Farrow: "Monsters are cowards. You stand up to them, they run away."
Mia: "Not this one."

TRIVIA

The film's director has said that editing the film was a big challenge, stating that it was a long, complex process because of the story's dual structure.

THE INVISIBLE WAR

Box Office: $69,190

Kirby Dick knows how to incite with his skill as a documentary filmmaker. His brilliant works *Twist of Faith* (2004), *This Film is Not Yet Rated* (2006), and *Outrage* (2009) tackled the cover-up of child abuse in the church, the deeply-flawed MPAA rating system, and closeted politicians who take action against gay rights, respectively. His best work was yet to come. Dick is doing the work that this country's investigative journalism industry stopped doing when all cable news networks decided to take political sides for ratings and all broadcast news ones started interviewing celebrities more than politicians. With *The Invisible War*, Dick delivers a heartfelt, moving, emotionally devastating expose of what should be an internationally known story and shame on the United States: Over 20

of the women who have volunteered to serve and protect their country in some capacity have been sexually assaulted. The brilliance of Dick's work is that he does not reduce the story to what could have been a series of shocking statistics. He finds the human stories beneath them and, in doing so, illuminates the lives of some true heroes: Women willing to step forward and fix a system that seems virtually designed for this kind of horror to take place.

Of course, that is not meant to imply that the Army, Navy, Coast Guard, or Marines are encouraging sexual assault. However, they are not doing nearly enough to stop it. And what they are doing is often either misguided or simply ludicrous. How else can one describe a structure that inherently protects the supervisor who sexually assaults one of his cadets by making him the person that must process the paperwork to report it? How can one look at the instructional videos that encourage female soldiers to always bring a buddy when they are facing the possibility of walking home alone at night and not realize that it is little more than a form of victim blaming? And how does one even fathom the fact that one of the true heroes in Dick's film fails to get medical service through the V.A. for her broken jaw suffered during her rape because she did not complete her service in the Coast Guard (because, of course, she had a broken jaw)? Dick does not just illuminate the fact that over 16,000 men and women were sexually assaulted in 2011 alone (and that is a Department of Defense number, so one can presume it is probably much higher), he illustrates how the system supports such a tragic situation.

Dick's main subject, although that is meant as no slight to the other men and women he carefully and respectfully chronicles, is Michigan Coast Guard Veteran Kori Cioca, a woman struck with a litany of post-traumatic issues related to her assault. She barely sleeps because she prefers the quiet of the night. She carries a knife when she leaves her home. She cannot eat solid foods because of her jaw. She opens up to the filmmaker in emotionally raw and devastating ways and becomes the catalyst for change. By the end, the viewer wants to stand with her as she fights in Washington to try and change a system that too often sweeps these problems under the rug and too often makes them easy to take place initially.

This is when Dick's film surpasses all other documentaries in 2012 and becomes a true work of art for it is not a sob story. It is not merely a document of horror, it is also one of heroism. Like "Twist of Faith" (another masterpiece of the documentary genre), it is about healing and progress as much as it is pain. Kori Cioca's bravery to come forward and tell her stories on film is virtually unmatched in recent non-fiction film. She is unforgettable. Her story is hard to take and hard to sit through but investigative journalism like this sometimes should be difficult to swallow. The only way to fix the truly shameful aspects of our society is to address them head-on. Thank God there are filmmakers like Kirby Dick and heroes like Kori Cioca willing to do so.

At the time of this review, *The Invisible War* had won several high-profile awards, including the Sundance Film Festival prize and Chicago Film Critics Association Award for Best Documentary, and was considered a strong contender to win the Oscar for the same category

in a few weeks' time. Sadly, the fact that documentary films simply do not play in most film markets (the movie never played wider than seven screens at one time) and the financial strength of a small company like Cinedigm Entertainment meant that *The Invisible War* could not even crack $65k at the domestic box office. Like a lot of battle cries, it is a film that will take time, building through press and word-of-mouth. Films this powerful do not just go away.

Brian Tallerico

CREDITS

Origin: United States
Language: English
Released: 2012
Production: Amy Ziering, Tanner King Barklow; Chain Camera Pictures, Girls Club Entertainment; released by Cinedigm Entertainment Group
Directed by: Kirby Dick
Written by: Kirby Dick
Cinematography by: Kirsten Johnson; Thaddeus Wadleigh
Sound: Tom Casetta; Aaron DelGrosso
Editing: Douglas Blush; Derek Boonstra
MPAA rating: Unrated
Running time: 98 minutes

REVIEWS

Corliss, Richard. *Time.* June 21, 2012.
Ebert, Roger. *Chicago Sun-Times.* June 27, 2012.
Hornaday, Ann. *Washington Post.* June 28, 2012.
Rooney, David. *Hollywood Reporter.* June 16, 2012.
Schwarzbaum, Lisa. *Entertainment Weekly.* June 21, 2012.
Scott, A. O. *New York Times.* June 21, 2012.
Stewart, Sara. *New York Post.* June 22, 2012.
Tobias, Scott. *AV Club.* June 20, 2012.
Weitzman, Elizabeth. *New York Daily News.* June 21, 2012.
Willmore, Alison. *Movieline.* June 25, 2012.

TRIVIA

In a rare example of a film actually influencing government/military policy, the end credits state that "On April 14, 2012, Secretary of Defense Leon Panetta, watched this film. Two days later, he took the decision to prosecute away from unit commanders." It was also noted that "this is not enough."

AWARDS

Ind. Spirit 2013: Feature Doc.
Nominations:
Oscars 2012: Feature Doc.
Directors Guild 2012: Documentary Director (Dick)
Writers Guild 2012: Documentary Screenplay

J

JACK REACHER
(One Shot)

The law has limits. He does not.
—Movie tagline

Box Office: $79.5 million

Cinematic franchises come in all shapes and sizes. There are those dependent on the worlds, universes, and sprawling landscapes conjured up in the minds of science fiction and fantasy. Occasionally, lightning strikes and all-of-a-sudden one is born out of consumer demand, studio greed, and lack of imagination. Sometimes all one needs is a name—Jason Bourne, Rambo, or Rocky Balboa. James Bond has been going strong for fifty years. Hollywood searches far and wide trying to find the next great franchise name and the latest was hopefully found in the books of Lee Child. The pen name of British author Jim Grant is responsible for seventeen Jack Reacher novels and it has taken fifteen years for someone to step up to the plate and take a shot at the cult hero. Interestingly enough though, the name one is likely to be remembering at the end of his first adventure is not that of the titular protagonist but of the moviestar who made it work—Tom Cruise.

The film opens with a sniper meticulously putting into motion a plan to commit a seemingly random act of terror—five people gunned down in cold blood. A trained military gunman arrested in less than a day. His one written statement is "Get Jack Reacher." Before District Attorney Rodin (Richard Jenkins) and lead investigator Emerson (David Oyelowo) have a chance to start searching, Reacher (Tom Cruise) appears in their office. With the suspect beaten unconscious in the hospital and unavailable for questioning, Reacher is nevertheless convinced that he is guilty based on a previous incident of the accused that he personally investigated while still on staff with the U.S. Army. Defense Attorney Helen Rodin (Rosamund Pike) is not sure what to believe in.

At first, Helen is convinced she is just doing her job to give her client the defense necessary for justice to be served. After being convinced to stick around, Reacher pushes her to look at the crime through the eyes of the victims. It is here where even he begins to question the facts of the case. While the "why" is far from focused, the "who" becomes a bit clearer to the audience as we become closer to a variety of henchmen and lackeys determined to keep their plans under wrap. Charlie (Jai Courtney) and his five o'clock shadow is easily recognized as the actual shooter and the orders he takes come from a mysterious German known only as The Zec (Werner Herzog). The further Reacher digs the more attempts to scare him out of town arrive and the greater his need for justice becomes.

Reacher's investigative skills are not going to earn him a place alongside Sherlock Holmes or, to a much lesser extent, Alex Cross. What he knows and what he keeps to himself until he is ready to reveal it is presented in nice, clean fashion but will be far from people's minds once he begins negotiating his fists into other people's bodies. Violence seems to find Reacher and he is more than capable of defending himself despite this being a tale where the concept of justice is flipped towards the aggressors. When Helen is asked to confront a father of one of the fallen we are met with the uneasy convergence of grief dictating the potential for further violence.

Reacher seeks what is right and is not afraid to beat the remorseless or eliminate them entirely from a system that might prosecute the taking of an eye only to serve them a paper cut. Jack would rather have an eye.

Any weighty moral conundrums are shoved to the side in favor of piecing together the mystery and a series of solid action sequences that circumvent the need to fully understand the bare intricacies of the villainous plot. Director Christopher McQuarrie more than delivers in this area from a breakdown of a five-on-one street fight to a most amusing attempt by henchmen to land the necessary kill blow in a tiny space. Standing out above all is an extended car chase that puts us right on the hood of Reacher's revving engine as he tries to escape pursuers while chasing down those who put him in this precarious situation. Expertly filmed with the kind of editing and sound design that calls back some of the great chases that defined the cinematic adrenaline rush.

Try as McQuarrie does to bring some of the signature dialogue he injected into his screenplays for *The Usual Suspects* (1995) and *The Way of the Gun* (2000), the material is still airport bookstore fodder; just another quick page-turner with a plot as quickly disposable as any weekly television whodunit. Courtney's henchman is clearly a very bad man but is just one of a revolving door of personality-free lackeys. Werner Herzog, in a rare appearance in front of the camera, has all the capabilities of delivering a memorable Christopher Walken-esque villain full of off-kilter speechifying. Though getting a solid introduction and some freakish traits he is kept off-screen until the climax where it is unlikely he will go fist-to-fist with Reacher and instead just gets to sit in a chair.

The first hour has a layer of unpredictability until the second half needs the domination of its action scenes to snuff the increasingly ludicrous plotting. Rosamund Pike goes deep into the bug-eyed, clueless and scared facial tics that are part of her formal training and is so unconvincing at times it is hard to fathom how she got past the first class of law school when the professor asked her name. Richard Jenkins is left with a thankless part that extends only as far as to whether or not he is going to be the surprise conspirator or not. When one villain simply replies that they had no other choice, the surprise nature of his villainy immediately leaps one's mind to a half-dozen questions of why that was the case.

Jack Reacher has a lot of adventures that can still be turned into movies, but with a recently reinvigorated Ethan Hunt franchise in *Mission: Impossible—Ghost Protocol* (2011) still afloat it seems superfluous. Do people really remember the character more than the action? Indiana Jones and James Bond he is not. But Tom Cruise is every bit Tom Cruise and the sort of authoritative confidence and likability that he displays as this character is the very reason that he is a movie star.

Erik Childress

CREDITS

Jack Reacher: Tom Cruise
Helen Rodin: Rosamund Pike
Alex Rodin: Richard Jenkins
Emerson: David Oyelowo
The Zec: Werner Herzog
Sandy: Alexia Fast
Cash: Robert Duvall
Origin: United States
Language: English
Released: 2012
Production: David Ellison, Dana Goldberg, Dan Granger, Gary Levinsohn, Kevin J. Messick, Paula Wagner, Tom Cruise; Mutual Film Company, Skydance Productions, TC Productions; released by Paramount Pictures
Directed by: Christopher McQuarrie
Written by: Christopher McQuarrie
Cinematography by: Caleb Deschanel
Music by: Joe Kraemer
Sound: Alan Rankin; Mark Stoeckinger
Editing: Kevin Stitt
Art Direction: Christa Munro
Costumes: Susan Matheson
Production Design: James Bissell
MPAA rating: PG-13
Running time: 130 minutes

REVIEWS

Berardinelli, James. *ReelViews*. December 24, 2012.
Edelstein, David. *Vulture*. December 24, 2012.
McGranaghan, Mike. *Aisle Seat*. December 22, 2012.
Morgenstern, Joe. *Wall Street Journal*. December 21, 2012.
Phillips, Michael. *Chicago Tribune*. December 20, 2012.
Putman, Dustin. *DustinPutman.com*. December 20, 2012.
Sachs, Ben. *Chicago Reader*. December 21, 2012.
Singer, Matt. *ScreenCrush*. December 20, 2012.
Scott, A. O. *New York Times*. December 20, 2012.
Vaux, Rob. *Chicago Sun-Times*. December 21, 2012.

QUOTES

Jack Reacher: "You think I'm a hero? I am not a hero. I'm a drifter with nothing to lose. Now you killed that girl to put me in a frame. I mean to beat you to death and drink your blood from a boot! Now this is how it's gonna work. You're gonna give me the address and I'll be along when I'm damn good and ready. If she doesn't answer the phone when I call this number, if I even think you've hurt her, I disappear. And if you're smart, that scares you. Because I'm in your blind spot. And I have nothing better to do."

TRIVIA

The sales person behind the counter selling Nancy Holt (the blonde female victim) was Tom Cruise's stand-in for the movie.

JEFF, WHO LIVES AT HOME

The first step to finding your destiny is leaving your mother's basement.
—Movie tagline

Box Office: $4.3 million

Jay and Mark Duplass made their feature film debut with the independently produced *The Puffy Chair* (2005), which screened at the Sundance Film Festival and picked up the Audience Award at the SXSW Festival that same year. While other would-be auteurs who made their mark around the same time either slipped into the welcome-but-gear-jammed embrace of the studio development tract or fiddled endlessly with follow-ups, the Duplass brothers cranked out four narrative features in basically six years—in addition to a documentary, a short film, myriad acting projects for Mark, and a steady stream of script-doctoring jobs on studio material.

It almost goes without saying, then, that there is a limberness and dexterity to the Duplass' filmmaking absent in much mainstream Hollywood cinema these days. The pair are rigid and brutally on point with respect to structure. But they are otherwise not overly precious about their work, preferring to dig down into character and spin off focused improvisations—like miniature controlled explosions—in search of the humor and awkwardness within things that are inherently dramatic.

It does not quite match to say that their most recent film, *Jeff, Who Lives at Home,* is a work of magical realism, but it is certainly much different, and smarter, than it was peddled in its advertising. Trailers and television ads for the movie (as well as its disarmingly forthright title) made it seem like a stoner version of *Failure to Launch* (2006), combined with maybe a pinch of fraternal slap-fighting—the same sort of warped, testosteronized rivalry that has informed the Duplass brothers' canon in films like *Cyrus* (2010) and *The Do-Deca-Pentathlon* (2012). In reality, *Jeff, Who Lives at Home* is a sly, endearing work that radically subverts expectations about where it is headed; it is a paean to fraternity and family and worldly engagement. To the extent that there is a macro statement in this sputtering yet sincere and intimately observed little comedy, it is this: It is far better to live in the real world, with all its messiness and complications, than to seek refuge in a protected but false castle of solitude.

Jason Segel stars as the title character, an oafish, early-thirties slacker who has been stuck in a state of arrested development seemingly a decade-plus, ever since the death of his father. Jeff still lives in the basement of his childhood home in Baton Rouge, where he exists in a state of responsibility-free stoner wonderment, whiling away the hours watching TV and philosophizing from behind a bong. His mother Sharon (Susan Sarandon) tolerates this with benign exasperation, but on the day over which the movie unfolds tasks her younger son with tracking down some wood glue from a hardware store, in order to fix a busted kitchen shutter. This is, she says, all she wants for her birthday.

After receiving a wrong-number phone call asking for someone named Kevin, Jeff, seizing upon a unified theory ethos drawn from his favorite movie, *Signs* (2002), shuffles into action, convinced that this is indeed a day to venture outside and perhaps find out exactly who this mysterious Kevin is. If Jeff is the sensitive, brooding thinker of the family, the doer is his jerky older brother Pat (Ed Helms), whose wife Linda (Judy Greer) is infuriated by his recent purchase of a Porsche they cannot afford. While Sharon confides the existence of a workplace secret admirer to colleague and friend Carol (Rae Dawn Chong)—a development that has her both a bit titillated and on guard, feeling that it might be a joke—Jeff and Pat cross paths, and see Linda in the company of another man. Misadventures ensue, as the two brothers investigate into whether she is having an affair.

There is a kind of hokey, unabashed simplicity to *Jeff, Who Lives at Home* (the wood glue is a metaphor, you see), and yet enormous engagement and amusement from the manner in which it slyly draws knowing smiles of recognition. This is not a comedy in the traditional sense of joke-setup-punchline, but rather a movie which invites viewers to laugh through the refracted prism of its characters' reaction to the banal. The Duplass brothers are quite comfortable in the grey. For them, truth is often found in seriocomic digression (hence Jeff's obsession with finding someone named Kevin, and the entire investigation of Linda's affair), and character revealed in moments of absurd conflict or stress. So the livewire, almost electric connection here comes from a collection of characters who wear some combination of their wants, needs and desperation on their sleeves.

The film's performances certainly feed this character-rooted bond. The radiant Sarandon captures Sharon's circumspect nature in graceful strokes, while a goatee and short-sleeve-and-tie combination (along with the fact that Pat holds business meetings at Hooters) go a long way toward helping Helms succeed against type, as a character who projects some of his own unhappiness on his brother. And Segel's imposing physicality definitely helps sell the man-child qualities of Jeff, in exaggerated fashion; one of the movie's more amusing bits finds him having to don a too-small suit jacket and cram himself into a seat while eavesdropping on Linda in a fancy restaurant.

In keeping with both the Duplass' brothers overall aesthetic sensibility and the movie's simple narrative framework, the production value in *Jeff, Who Lives at Home* is almost downright spartan, in order to underscore its Everyman qualities. Working with cinematographer Jas Shelton, the brothers craft a visual palette defined by the absence of clutter, and use quick pans and zooms to simultaneously track characters' emotions and render subtle authorial statements about them—whether of support and identification or chiding dissent.

If its finale, an amusing slice of affirmation, might strike some as too pat, *Jeff, Who Lives at Home* is still a movie of recognizable characters, considerable empathy and some surprising, gut-punch emotional connection. It locates the treasure and pleasure of life, amidst the mundanity and pain.

Brent Simon

CREDITS

Jeff: Jason Segel
Pat: Ed Helms
Sharon: Susan Sarandon
Linda: Judy Greer
Carol: Rae Dawn Chong
Steve: Steve Zissis
Kevin: Evan Ross
Origin: United States
Language: English
Released: 2012
Production: Lianne Halfon, Russell Smith, Jason Reitman; Indian Paintbrush, Mr. Mudd, Right of Way Films; released by Paramount Pictures
Directed by: Jay Duplass; Mark Duplass
Written by: Jay Duplass; Mark Duplass
Cinematography by: Jas Shelton
Music by: Michael Andrews
Sound: Robert Sharman
Editing: Jay Deuby

Costumes: Ashley Martin
Production Design: Chris Spellman
MPAA rating: R
Running time: 83 minutes

REVIEWS

Debruge, Peter. *Variety.* September 15, 2011.
Ebert, Roger. *Chicago Sun-Times.* March 15, 2012.
Jones, Kimberley. *Austin Chronicle.* March 16, 2012.
Lemire, Christy. *Associated Press.* March 14, 2012.
Morgenstern, Joe. *Wall Street Journal.* March 15, 2012.
Morris, Wesley. *Boston Globe.* March 15, 2012.
Schwarzbaum, Lisa. *Entertainment Weekly.* March 15, 2012.
Sharkey, Betsy. *Los Angeles Times.* March 15, 2012.
White, Dave. *Movies.com.* March 16, 2012.
Zacharek, Stephanie. *Movieline.* March 16, 2012.

QUOTES

Sharon: "Jeff, what do you do in the basement? You're not cleaning it."
Jeff: "You really want to know? You didn't like it last time we had this conversation."
Sharon: "Okay no, you're right, I don't."

TRIVIA

Directors Jay and Mark Duplass claim to have cried through the entire premiere of this film.

JIRO DREAMS OF SUSHI
(Jiro sni o sushi)

Box Office: $2.6 million

"It is beautiful to create," says Jiro Ono, Japan's sensei of sushi. As shown in the documentary *Jiro Dreams of Sushi*, there is also a certain beauty in laying witness to a person's impassioned creativity, and to hear them talk romantically about an act of love that they have been able to happily devote their entire life to. To observe such pure devotion to a job that provides endless happiness is equally inspiring and fulfilling to a witness' own soul. Here is a human being who has found how to make the most out of his life. He has unlocked the mystery of harmony between life, love, and employment that everyone tries to figure out when forming how one wants to spend their time alive. Here is a man who is living his dream.

Working from early in the morning until late at night, 85-year-old Jiro Ono is considered by many to be the world's greatest sushi chef. Fitting to his humbling personality, his sole restaurant Sukiyabashi Jiro only serves ten customers at a time and is located under Tokyo in a subway stop. However, with such a worldwide prominence (and a rare three-star Michelin review), Ono's business requires reservations to be made months in advance, with each entree from the restaurant's sushi-only menu coming at a very high price.

Jiro Dreams of Sushi captures sushi-making as an art form, and finds a wealthy amount of tantalizing content to be shared about both the art and the artist. Many of these different perspectives provide a picture of how Jiro's massive passion has heavily influenced the work ethic of others.

With the help of a small group of apprentices, Jiro makes much of the delicacies himself, in front of his customers. Meticulous enough to massage an octopus for forty-five minutes to make sure its texture is chewy enough, Jiro's kitchen schooling runs with the same intensity—ten years of experience is required before any chef can handle the eggs. Jiro's influence is certainly felt on his inheritors, as interviews with Jiro's sons Yoshikazu and Takashi provide an intimate perspective on how Jiro's love for sushi-making affected the relationship he had with them as a father. The focus on the sons (the youngest, Takashi has his own restaurant, while the eldest Yoshikazu still works for his father) provides *Jiro Dreams of Sushi* with an appealing desire for an epilogue. This documentary is not only about a man's dominant desire to make perfect sushi, but the intimidating height of the bar that even his sons may not ever reach.

The pieces de resistance of *Jiro Dreams of Sushi* are the spellbinding moments in which one watches Jiro handcraft his award-winning sushi. These delicious moments are filmed with a strongly cinematic sense, utilizing slow motion and acute focus, as accompanied by a very Philip Glass-y Philip Glass score (with rushing string arpeggios and all). The amount of these segments is even properly portioned so as to not leave the viewer desiring more or less. Witnessing these scenes, viewers can see director Gelb pursuing the same perfection within his craft that so presents such a subject. Just as Jiro carefully uses his hands in a specific manner to mold each specialized piece of sushi, so does Gelb find the fitting aesthetic for which to present the dreamy food's creation.

As the film progresses, a glaring sloppiness (especially when compared to Jiro's skill) becomes apparent as Gelb tries to fill his 81-minute time frame with fatty chapters in the Jiro story that could have been cut off entirely. A scene that rants about the lowering numbers in the fish population feels structurally out of place (even for a film about sushi), and a meeting with old school friends only conveys Jiro as a regular adorable old Japanese man, with adorable old friends. For rookie measure, there is even a dull shot of weak poetry that captures Jiro walking in slow motion, against the crowd; it is easily the cheapest shot in a film that is otherwise visually rich. Even for a running time of 81 minutes, *Jiro Dreams of Sushi* manages to be overlong with extraneous scenes that do not immediately correlate to the movie's thesis of passion.

Jiro Ono embodies the concept of how the never-ending pursuit for perfection will always lead to improvement, regardless of how many years he has been making sushi, or how much praise he has been given for his work. Though lovingly crafted in some parts, this rookie director's documentary about Jiro's immeasurable pursuit for extreme quality becomes an example itself of the focus required on the journey towards excellence.

Nick Allen

CREDITS

Himself: Jiro Ono
Himself: Yoshikazu Ono
Origin: United States
Language: Japanese
Released: 2012
Production: Tom Pelligrini, Kevin Iwashina; released by Preferred Content
Directed by: David Gelb
Cinematography by: David Gelb
Sound: Darren Wain
Editing: Brandon Driscoll-Luttringer
MPAA rating: PG
Running time: 81 minutes

REVIEWS

Anderson, John. *Newsday*. April 5, 2012.
Burr, Ty. *Boston Globe*. April 5, 2012.
Ebert, Roger. *Chicago Sun-Times*. April 5, 2012.
Falperin, Leslie. *Variety*. May 14, 2011.
Gleiberman, Owen. *Entertainment Weekly*. March 21, 2012.
Mercer, Benjamin. *Village Voice*. March 6, 2012.
Merry, Stephanie. *Washington Post*. March 23, 2012.
Phillips, Michael. *Chicago Tribune*. April 5, 2012.
Pols, Mary F. *Time*. March 9, 2012.
Rapold, Nicolas. *New York Times*. March 8, 2012.

QUOTES

Jiro Ono: "Once you decide on your occupation, you must immerse yourself in your work. You have to fall in love with your work. Never complain about your job. You must dedicate your life to mastering your skill. That's the secret of success, and is the key to being regarded honorably."

JOHN CARTER

Lost in our world. Found in another.
—Movie tagline

Box Office: $73.1 million

As a film, Disney's would-be epic *John Carter* is a plodding muddle of mediocrity that feels more like a failed promotional campaign than an actual work of cinema. Studios now try to create "event" movies—would-be blockbusters that are marketed to not just appeal to a broad audience base but also to feel like cultural must-sees. Although analysis or criticism of film usually avoids discussing such marketing and box-office matters, preferring to focus solely on the artistic effort on the screen, studio efforts on behalf of the bottom line are not completely separate from the merits (or lack thereof) of the film itself. *John Carter* has quite a few problems, but many seem to stem from creative meddling-by-studio-committee and marketing-driven "adjustments."

Directed and co-written by Pixar's Andrew Stanton and starring Taylor Kitsch as the eponymous Civil War veteran, this adaptation of Edgar Rice Burrough's 1917 novel *A Princess of Mars* has all the right pieces. There are dazzlingly pretty CGI effects, including soaring airships and a slowly crawling city presented with glorious Steampunk gears and wheels. There are genuinely talented actors like Lynn Collins, Mark Strong, Dominic West, and Ciaran Hinds, plus Willem Dafoe voicing and acting out the CGI-rendered (green, tall, and extra-limbed) Thark leader Tars Tarkas. And there are several semi-impressive action scenes scattered throughout the two-hour-plus movie. However, like most giant-sized event movies these days, where studio bookkeeping and demographic pandering drive major artistic decisions, everything else about *John Carter* feels both under-cooked and over-baked.

As the story and Carter journey to Mars in the late 1800s and explore the Red Planet's battling species, there are glimpses here and there of Stanton earnestly trying to capture Burroughs' pulp spirit, but the spastic narrative requirements of this kind of film, with a disastrously large budget of $250 million hanging around its neck, quickly extinguish any possible flames. Stanton is not a bad or unintuitive director, and there is a sense he understands and aspires to Burroughs' adventurous heart, but his efforts feel stymied by the studio's need to make *John Carter* an all-things-to-all-audiences box-office hit. Ironically, the more the film seems to have been fussed over and watered down to broaden its demographic appeal, the more convoluted and unnatural it feels.

The special effects are big and impressive, but, as in any fantasy film, engaging human actors are required to emotionally sell the spectacle. Instead, *John Carter* sports decent actors in silly costumes doing their best with stilted dialogue and propped-up characters. Kitsch tries to play Carter's broken stoicism, but the movie does not give him time to meaningfully brood. (Too often during its over-long running time *John Carter* drags when it should move and rushes when it should linger.) Kitsch grimaces with a laconic, Eastwood squint, but Carter's potentially interesting layers—a cynical and self-loathing "hero" with a haunted past—would be too complicated for a Disney "family" film.

Likewise, as the film's villains, British thespians West and Strong play their characters as if they are just that: villains being played by go-to British thespians who have by now been hired for so many of these roles in big genre movies it must be impossible to feign any sort of enthusiasm for the work anymore. Among the on-screen cast, only Collins as Martian princess Dejah Thoris energetically embraces her character. However, while Dejah is built up as a strong female and given important things to do, there is no real sense of an independent character—she is a scientist and a leader, but in the end she still breaks down crying and needs a strong man to save her. (Ironically, performing as a CGI creation, Dafoe is the only actor truly comfortable with it all.)

It is no surprise the cast members often seem confused about their purpose. *John Carter* winds up feeling like every other over-sized "tent-pole" movie of its bloated, overly busy ilk—lots of action, but very little true excitement or emotion. The screenplay is credited to Stanton, Mark Andrews, and novelist Michael Chabon, but it shows the choppy, contrived marks of what must have been an army of writers and studio executives. The film's plot is a jumbled, connect-the-dots affair full of meaningless busy work quests, maps, puzzles and locks. Little remains of Burroughs' swashbuckling glee—just a convoluted, stuffy, hollow portentousness, and a flat, faux "urgency" driven by yet another intrusive, non-stop music score instead of interesting character motivations. (Why do we care about John Carter, other than the fact he is at the center of a big action movie?) Like its fish-out-of-water hero, *John Carter* the film has no idea what or where it is. Just as the Earthman looks awkward and unreal as he uses Mars' weaker gravity to bound across the crimson desert-scape, the film feels off; carefully constructed and contrived with a forced sense of wonderment.

Potential audiences appear to have shared the film's discomfort with itself: *John Carter* floundered at the North American box office, earning only $73 million, though it did much better (three times, in fact) overseas with $210 million. Still, a worldwide total of $283 million comes nowhere close to justifying the film's hefty costs. Likewise, critical reviews were extremely mixed—some writers enjoyed the film for its entertainment value (the *Village Voice*'s Mark Holcomb found it "a lively, visually crafty pleasure" and the *New York Time*'s A.O. Scott deemed it "messy and chaotic...but also colorful and kind of fun"), but others like the *San Francisco Chronicle*'s Mick LaSalle declared *John Carter* "a dud... There's nothing to see, nothing to think about, nothing to care about, and nothing to feel, just emptiness."

Locke Peterseim

CREDITS

John Carter: Taylor Kitsch
Tars Tarkas: Willem Dafoe
Princess Dejah Thoris: Lynn Collins
Sola: Samantha Morton
Matai Shang: Mark Strong
Tandos Mors: Ciaran Hinds
Sab Than: Dominic West
Kantos Khan: James Purefoy
Sarkoja: Polly Walker
Powell: Bryan Cranston
Tal Hajus: Thomas Haden Church
Origin: United States
Language: English
Released: 2012
Production: Jim Morris, Colin Wilson, Lindsey Collins; released by Walt Disney Pictures
Directed by: Andrew Stanton
Written by: Andrew Stanton; Mark C. Andrews; Michael Chabon
Cinematography by: Dan(iel) Mindel
Music by: Michael Giacchino
Sound: Timothy Nielsen; Jonathan Null
Editing: Eric Zumbrunnen
Art Direction: James Hambidge
Costumes: Mayes C. Rubeo
Production Design: Nathan Crowley
MPAA rating: PG-13
Running time: 132 minutes

REVIEWS

Corliss, Richard. *Time.* March 8, 2012.
Ebert, Roger. *Chicago Sun-Times.* March 7, 2012.
Holcomb, Mark. *Village Voice.* March 7, 2012.
Hornaday, Ann. *Washington Post.* March 9, 2012.
LaSalle, Mick. *San Francisco Chronicle.* March 8, 2012.
Phipps, Keith. *AV Club.* March 8, 2012.
Scott, A. O. *New York Times.* March 8, 2012.
Sharkey, Betsy. *Los Angeles Times.* March 9, 2012.
Stevens, Dana. *Slate.* March 8, 2012.
Zacharek, Stephanie. *Movieline.* March 8, 2012.

QUOTES

Matai Shang: "We do not cause the destruction of a world, Captain Carter. We simply manage it. Feed off it, if you like."

TRIVIA

Both Jon Hamm and Josh Duhamel were considered for the role of John Carter.

JOURNEY 2: THE MYSTERIOUS ISLAND

Believe the impossible. Discover the incredible.
—Movie tagline

Box Office: $103.9 million

The tag line for the posters hyping *Journey 2: The Mysterious Island,* an incredibly loose adaptation of the Jules Verne classic *Mysterious Island* that also serves as the sequel to *Journey to the Center of the Earth* (2007), the equally promiscuous adaptation of another Verne favorite and one of the initial entries in the current 3-D boom, reads "Believe The Impossible. Discover The Incredible." As it turns out, the statements on the poster are indeed true, though perhaps not in the way that one might have hoped or expected. While it might seem impossible to believe, the filmmakers have somehow managed to take Verne's vivid and imaginative work and transform it into the cinematic equivalent of the kind of buggy and excitement-free video game that comes free with the purchase of one of those systems that disappears from shelves after only a few months. Older viewers may find it incredible to discover that Michael Caine has at long last managed to appear in a movie with the word "island" in the title that is even worse than *The Island* (1980) Finally, as impossible and incredible as it may seem, the absence of Brendan Fraser, who starred in the previous film, from this go-around indicates that there are apparently some things that the star of *Monkeybone* (2001), *Inkheart* (2009), and *Furry Vengeance* (2010) will not do for money after all.

Without Fraser, viewers are left with only the supremely unlikable Josh Hutcherson to serve as the connective tissue between the two films as Sean, the obnoxious teen and budding Verne obsessive who intercepts a radio signal that may have been sent from his long-lost grandfather from the seemingly mythical Mysterious Island. Perhaps realizing that Hutcherson's appeal would be somewhat limited, the producers have made an effort to beef up the film with other familiar faces/pectorals. There is Dwayne "The Rock" Johnson as Hank, the well-meaning stepdad who agrees to take Sean on a jaunt to the Hawaiian islands to find the Mysterious Island as a bonding experience and supplies both the muscles and the kind of oddly specific knowledge that comes in useful when one is faced with being trapped on a sinking island with an ancient submarine in need of an instant jump-start. There is the usually invaluable Luis Guzman as Gabato, the helicopter pilot hired to help them find the island and supply the kind of wacky ethnic humor that might be deemed offensive if it could be determined just what ethnicity he was impugning in the first place. There is Vanessa Hudgens as Gabato's daughter Kailani and she is there to supply...well, you know. Finally, there is none other than Michael Caine, no doubt trying to find a way to kill time between Christopher Nolan joints, as wacky grandfather Alexander Anderson, who has devoted thirty years of his life to finding the island and, having done so, appears to be spending the rest of his days being an insufferable jerk to everyone but Sean as a result.

For reasons too labored to go into, the island—a bizarre land in which small creatures like bees and spider are ginormous while elephants are pocket-sized—is about to collapse into the ocean and our heroes must traverse it in order to escape it before they go into the drink. Along the way, viewers are treated to sights that we have seen before in other, better films and some that few rational people would have ever dreamed that they would one day bear witness to, such as Luis Guzman getting covered with a giant load of bird poop or The Rock singing "What a Wonderful World" with special novelty lyrics. Alas, these elements fail to distract from the film's more pressing problems, such as the fact that absolutely nothing about it works—it is neither funny nor exciting, the 3-D effects are ho-hum and it plunges into levels of stupidity that even the little kids it is being aimed at will find insulting. (If Sean is such an ambitious and brilliant student and explorer, for example, how is it that he is somehow unfamiliar with the concepts of latitude and longitude?) And while it is understandable how such a thing would have gone over the heads of virtually every member of the target audience, how is it possible that a film could include a scene involving Michael Caine riding a giant bee through the sky and not work in at least one reference to *The Swarm* (1978), the infamous disaster movie that is now only the second-worst bee-related film in his oeuvre? Not helping matters much is director Brad Peyton's bizarre decision to interrupt most of his big action beats with shifts into slo-mo that are so prevalent after a while that even Brian De Palma himself might question their overuse.

The biggest failing of *Journey 2,* especially considering the basic source material, is its absolute lack of imagination when it comes to depicting the magical world of the mysterious island. There are some fantasy films, like *Avatar* (2009) and the *Lord of the Rings* and *Harry Potter* franchises, in which enormous sums of money have been dedicated to creating astonishingly detailed worlds that almost feel real. Then there are fantasy films in which the level of verisimilitude is somewhat reduced—remember those cut-rate 1970's films where Doug McClure would stumble amidst cardboard rocks to save Caroline Munro from a demonstrably fake giant insect while Peter Cushing furrowed his brow in the background? For a film like this, either approach would have sufficed—a deliberately tacky take might have actually been refreshing—but *Journey 2: The Mysterious Island* (and one can only pray that the dope who dreamed up that ungodly title was summarily whipped with reeds as a result) winds up splitting the difference by giving us a world that is meant to dazzle us with all of its digital wizardry but it has been deployed in such a shabby manner that the whole thing just looks like the kind of messy green-screen effects that will leave most viewers just feeling green when all is said and done.

Peter Sobczynski

CREDITS

Sean Anderson: Josh Hutcherson
Hank Parsons: Dwayne "The Rock" Johnson
Kailani: Vanessa Anne Hudgens
Gabato: Luis Guzman
Alexander: Michael Caine
Liz Anderson: Kristin Davis
Origin: United States
Language: English
Released: 2012
Production: Beau Flynn, Charlotte Clay Huggins, Tripp Vinson; Contrafilm, New Line Cinema, Walden Media; released by Warner Bros.
Directed by: Brad Peyton
Written by: Mark Gunn; Brian Gunn
Cinematography by: David Tattersall
Music by: Andrew Lockington
Sound: Al Nelson

Music Supervisor: Andrea Von Foerster
Editing: David Rennie
Art Direction: Bruce Robert Hill
Costumes: Denise Wingate
Production Design: Bill Boes
MPAA rating: PG
Running time: 94 minutes

REVIEWS

Anderson, Melissa. *Village Voice*. February 7, 2012.
Ebert, Roger. *Chicago Sun-Times*. February 9, 2012.
Genzlinger, Neil. *New York Times*. February 9, 2012.
Maltin, Leonard. *Leonard Maltin's Picks*. February 10, 2012.
Orndorf, Brian. *BrianOrndorf.com*. February 10, 2012.
Pais, Matt. *Red Eye*. February 9, 2012.
Pols, Mary F. *Time*. February 9, 2012.
Rabin, Nathan. *AV Club*. February 9, 2012.
Snider, Eric D. *EricDSnider.com*. February 11, 2012.
Tallerico, Brian. *HollywoodChicago.com*. February 10, 2012.

QUOTES

Hank: "What in the blue heck is that?"
Gabato: "That is the finest helicopter in Palau!"
Sean: "I'd hate to see the worst."

TRIVIA

Michael Caine searches for Captain Nemo's Nautilus submarine through the latter half of this movie. In the 1997 remake of *20,000 Leagues Under the Sea*, Caine played Captain Nemo.

JOYFUL NOISE

Dream a whole lot louder.
—Movie tagline

The film was shipped to theaters under the code name "Choir Practice."
—Movie tagline

Box Office: $31 million

Despite some charms, *Joyful Noise* smacks more of focus group research than it does organic storytelling. Queen Latifah and Dolly Parton are Vi Rose Hill and G.G. Sparrow, two larger-than-life, warring queen bees whose personal conflicts might run the Sacred Divinity Choir of Pacashau, Georgia into the ground. To start, Vi Rose is poor and pious while G. G. is rich and bombastic. But it is when Vi Rose takes over the choir after G.G.'s husband Bernard (Kris Kristofferson) succumbs to a fatal heart attack in the first few minutes of the movie (but not before leading the choir to victory at

the semifinals of the Joyful Noise signing competition) that the pecan pie really hits the fan. Vi Rose and G.G. butt heads over the choir's future: Vi Rose intending to keep the choir's repertoire firmly rooted in gospel classics, while G.G. is sure a modern song list is the key to winning the state championship. To further complicate matters, G.G.'s musically-gifted bad boy grandson, the appropriately named Randy (Jeremy Jordan), develops a thing for Vi Rose's golden-voiced teenage daughter Olivia (Keke Palmer). Olivia has been trained by her mother to keep her pride in check, not to belt out the tunes unless she is sure God is singing through her, while Randy, like his Grandma, is a born exhibitionist. Naturally, they make beautiful, forbidden music together.

Someone, during the course of plotting out this story, must have noted that a *West Side Story* (1961) romance was too easy. To appeal to the widest possible audience *Joyful Noise* was given a *Bring It On* (2000) underdog subplot: The choir only gets to Nationals after another team is disqualified. The pressure intensifies when viewers see just how down on its luck Pacashau is; full of "going out of business" signs the town *needs* the Sacred Divinity choir to give them something to believe in again. And of course there are the secondary and tertiary choir members who also have their own stories to investigate: The vivacious and curvy Earla (Angela Grovey) sets her sights on the long and lean Mr. Hsu (Francis Jue), while Caleb (Andy Karl) has a crisis of faith after his family-owned hardware store goes under. And then there is Vi Rose's extra baggage: a military husband who's been gone for two years, and a son, Walter (Dexter Darden), with Asperger's syndrome who does not understand how his mother can keep the faith despite, what he deems to be, his God-given condition.

With all of these subplots, *Joyful Noise* runs itself off the rails into a ditch of cliches and trite wrap-ups in many ways. Randy is so smitten for Olivia that he is all goofy smiles and pretty much trips over his feet when she is around. Not at all the suave approach one would expect from a New York musician. G.G. is the butt of many plastic surgery jokes and refuses to drive anywhere near the speed limit. When Vi Rose and G.G. finally have it out, it is with a weak-effort food fight at a local diner. And then there is the music. Peppered with gospel greats, audiences in the know will appreciate the nod to veterans of the genre. The rest of the audience will cringe when Usher's "Yeah" is twisted to include the lyrics "Now Jesus is my homey." But like the Sacred Divinity choir, *Joyful Noise* perseveres.

Everything about the movie is so earnest, it is hard not to love it. One can actually start to believe that a win at Nationals will somehow reinvigorate the town's economy—something that could not possibly happen since an economic stimulus plan does not come with the title. But this small detail (along with some of the bigger puzzles) does not faze any of the actors. Each of them seems to really be having fun and enjoying being part of the film. They do not see anything wrong with the cheesy song lyrics or the fact that none of them get enough screen time to really round out their characters, so why should viewers? Jordan plays Randy as more cute than corny, with an infectious, genuine smile. Latifah does not let a complicated character back-story get her down; rather she owns Vi Rose's rigid mama bear, providing one of the movie's best fight scenes with her daughter. And Parton embraces playing a kitschy, calculating Southern Belle with gusto. Watching Walter find an outlet for his frustrations in music is so touching you forget to question if it is medically plausible. And when Caleb's subplot is wrapped up like an afterthought—still searching for God's grace, he finally sees the light midway through the group's final concert—the warmth and joy he feels is, like a lot of *Joyful Noise*, utterly contagious.

Joanna Topor MacKenzie

CREDITS

Vi Rose Hill: Queen Latifah
G.G. Sparrow: Dolly Parton
Bernard Sparrow: Kris Kristofferson
Olivia Hill: Keke Palmer
Randy Garrity: Jeremy Jordan
Pastor Dale: Courtney B. Vance
Walter Hill: Dexter Darden
Marcus Hill: Jesse L. Martin
Baylor Skyes: Kirk Franklin

Origin: United States
Language: English
Released: 2012
Production: Michael Nathanson, Joseph Farrell, Catherine Paura, Broderick Johnson; Alcon Entertainment, ONC Entertainment; released by Warner Bros.
Directed by: Todd Graff
Written by: Todd Graff
Cinematography by: David Byrd
Music by: Mervyn Warren
Sound: Mary Ellis
Music Supervisor: Linda Cohen
Editing: Kathryn Himoff
Art Direction: G. Victoria Ruskin
Costumes: Tom Broecker
Production Design: Jeff Knipp
MPAA rating: PG-13
Running time: 118 minutes

REVIEWS

Biancolli, Amy. *San Francisco Chronicle*. January 12, 2012.
Edelstein, David. *New York Magazine*. January 15, 2012.
Guzman, Rafer. *Newsday*. January 13, 2012.
Holden, Stephen. *New York Times*. January 12, 2012.
Kennedy, Lisa. *Denver Post*. January 13, 2012.
Kenny, Glenn. *MSN Movies*. January 13, 2012.
Puig, Claudia. *USA Today*. January 12, 2012.
Roeper, Richard. *RichardRoeper.com*. January 13, 2012.
Sachs, Ben. *Chicago Reader*. January 12, 2012.
Travers, Peter. *Rolling Stone*. January 13, 2012.

QUOTES

G.G. Sparrow: "Who cares if I've had a few little nips and tucks? God didn't make plastic surgeons so they could starve!"

K

KATY PERRY: PART OF ME

Be yourself and you can be anything.
—Movie tagline

Box Office: $25.3 million

With *Katy Perry: Part of Me,* the enormously successful singer takes her first big stab at crossover success (unless you count her voiceover work in *The Smurfs* [2011]) with her own rockumentary and while there is no mistaking the film for anything other than a naked cash grab, there was at least some reason to believe that it might have been something better than the lazily-made likes of *Glee 3-D* (2011). For starters, her fusing of the key personality traits of the two great pop princesses of the Eighties—the up-front sexiness of Madonna and the cheerful silliness of Cyndi Lauper—is undeniably appealing and she has an uncanny ability to craft gorgeously catchy pieces of ear candy that still manages to retain its flavor even after approximately a half-billion times. More importantly, she has somehow managed to maintain a certain down-to-earth charm, or at least the simulacrum of same, that allows her to come across as more likable and relatable than most of the current parade of pop stars. Therefore, it comes as a shock to discover that her film is nothing more than a slapdash bit of self-aggrandizement that claims to display the singer blemishes and all but which turns out to be as heavily Clearasil-ed as its presumed target audience.

The film is essentially a behind-the-scenes look at Perry as she sets out on her "California Dreams" concert tour, a worldwide jaunt designed to promote *Teenage Dream,* her eagerly anticipated 2010 sophomore album and her shot at proving that the success of her 2008 debut *One of the Boys* and her monster hit single "I Kissed a Girl" were not simply flukes. As she journeys across the globe while racking up record-breaking sales (eventually becoming the first person to have five #1 singles off of the same album) performing her wildly gaudy revue—a cotton candy-hued fantasia featuring elaborate choreography, special effects and a seemingly endless line of dessert-inspired costumes that could single-handedly give her audiences Type 2 diabetes just by looking at them for more than a few seconds—viewers see her on-stage running through such hits as "Hot & Cold," odqThe One That Got Away," "Not Like the Movies," and the inspirational anthem "Firework" along with covers of "I Wanna Dance with Somebody" (a reasonably inspired choice) and "Hey Jude" (perhaps not so much) for her adoring audiences. She is also shot offstage as she meets with her fans, hangs out with her new husband (comedian Russell Brand) and other members of her real and professional families, and recounts her meteoric rise from the largely sheltered daughter of a Pentecostal minister to one of the reigning stars of the pop-culture firmament.

Yes, a successful pop star generally maintains a healthy ego—especially one willing to have a movie made about them after releasing only two albums to date—but Perry's wonderfulness is stressed so repeatedly and without even the slightest deviation from the hagiographic nature of the enterprise. Instead of asking any serious-minded questions of its subject or even showing full performances of any of her songs, it consists mostly of fans, hangers-on and even competitors like Adele, Rihanna, and Lady Gaga talking about how wonderful she is, how she was able to triumph over every adversity that the music world threw at her by not immediately recognizing her genius, and generally making a case for her immediate sainthood while Perry occasionally prattles on and on about not much of anything at all. After a while, the whole thing takes on the aura of an exceptionally fawning magazine cover story and when she responds to a little kid with lots of questions at a backstage meet & greet by telling him that she has given him more information than she ever has to a regular reporter, it is meant to be a joke but by the time the film ends, one may feel otherwise. The only fly in the ointment comes as the film ends up chronicling (albeit from a carefully cultivated distance) the eventual dissolution of Perry's marriage to Brand, despite her Herculean efforts to keep it going, and even that turns out to have a silver lining.

When all is said and done, there is only one brief moment in *Katy Perry: Part of Me* that breaks through the sales pitch in order to show something real. Throughout the film, viewers are treated to a repeated image of Perry as she is preparing to pop out on stage for her first number in a dress covered with motorized spinning circles. Most of the time, she is cheerful enough but at the point in question, the combination of sheer exhaustion and the news of the end of her marriage has taken its toll and as she gets ready to emerge, she looks utterly crushed until the ever-increasing cheers of her fans help her to literally put on her game face and do the show once again. The smile may be fake but the whole bit is, ironically enough, the closest the film ever gets to true authenticity. Make no mistake, Perry is an undeniably engaging performer but this film has all the depth of a souvenir program and for the sake of her fans, one can only hope that this shamefully shallow effort may one day inspire her to make a better and smarter film that is infinitely more worthy of her talents and accomplishments.

Peter Sobczynski

CREDITS

Katy Perry: Katy Perry
Himself: Adam Marcello
Himself: Casey Hopper
Himself: Patrick Matera
Himself: Max Hart
Himself: Joseph Moreau
Origin: United States
Language: English
Released: 2012
Production: Emer Patten, Martin Kirkup, Ted Kenney, Steven Jensen, Ron Howard, Brian Grazer, Bradford Cobb, Katy Perry; released by MTV Films

Directed by: Dan Cutforth; Jane Lipsitz
Music by: Deborah Lurie
Sound: Tim Chau
Editing: Scott Evans; Scott Richter; Brian David Lazarte
Costumes: Johnny Wujek
Production Design: Baz Halpin
MPAA rating: PG
Running time: 93 minutes

REVIEWS

Guzman, Rafer. *Newsday.* July 5, 2012.
Longworth, Karina. *Village Voice.* July 3, 2012.
Orange, Michelle. *Movieline.* July 5, 2012.
Pais, Matt. *RedEye.* July 3, 2012.
Savlov, Marc. *Austin Chronicle.* July 6, 2012.
Scott, A. O. *New York Times.* July 4, 2012.
Shanahan, Mark. *Boston Globe.* July 5, 2012.
Sharkey, Betsy. *Los Angeles Times.* July 4, 2012.
Stevens, Dana. *Slate.* July 6, 2012.
Stewart, Sara. *New York Post.* July 5, 2012.

QUOTES

Katy Perry: "How was the concert, Grandma?"
Ann Hudson: "Loud!"

TRIVIA

This film received a PG rating, making it the second film from MTV Films to receive that rating, and the first documentary film from the studio to do so.

KEEP THE LIGHTS ON

Box Office: $246,112

A semi-autobiographical drama, writer-director Ira Sachs' melancholic *Keep the Lights On* delves into the slow unraveling of a long-term but troubled gay love affair, plagued by sexual compulsions and drug abuse. The fidgety nature of its narrative—its refusal to submit to the hoariest cliches of its genre forebears, and the manner in which it spans nine years mostly indifferent to the usual markers of relationship dramas—give the movie a lingering hold, along with its nuanced lead performances.

But its placeholder characterizations and overall muteness largely dampen any emotional catharsis for viewers. The result is at once sensitive and a bit mesmeric in snatches and patches, but also frequently confounding. After premiering at the Sundance Film Festival, the movie was picked up for distribution by Music Box Films, through which it received a modest autumnal theatrical release and parlayed solid critical notices into an arthouse box office haul of just under $250,000.

The movie opens in 1998, in New York City. Danish-born Erik Rothman (Thure Lindhardt) is a would-be filmmaker slowly pecking his way through a documentary on an obscure avant-garde artist in the gay community. His more practical older sister Karen (Paprika Steen) advises Erik that being up-and-coming is attractive in one's twenties but not in their thirties.

Cruising for phone sex one night, Erik meets Paul Lucy (Zachary Booth), a lawyer for a respected publishing house who, though he has slept with other men, has only dated women. They meet up for a tryst, their brief time together sparks an infatuation in Erik, and the two eventually fall into a relationship.

The film flashes forward several years at various times. Things happen, though they are not rigorously connected in the usual causal fashion. Erik and Paul move in together. Erik's friend Claire (Julianne Nicholson) posits that they should have a baby together if she does not find someone else suitable. Erik finally finishes his film. He keeps having phone sex (and more) with various strangers. Paul's drug use intensifies; his friends and family stage an intervention, after which he goes to rehab. Through it all, Erik and Paul remain together, even as the flickering flame of their relationship seems to drive each man to more self-destructive extremes.

The best moments of Sachs' well observed movie—the intimacy of its raw love scenes, and its touch with furtive glances and wounded silences—recall films like *The Anniversary Party* (2001), *Rachel Getting Married* (2008), *Blue Valentine* (2011) and other cinematic works where handheld camerawork and an up-close-and-personal mode of storytelling intersects with narratives of rubbed-raw familial and romantic tension. In its own restless way, by opting for a collection of isolated moments over only important ones, *Keep the Lights On* charts its doomed romance in a demonstrably truer fashion than any number of more traditional and argumentative divorce dramas.

But its characters are ciphers, essentially. In order for Erik and Paul to ring true, and their turbulent relationship to mean something, one needs to see or at least understand how an obvious mutual regard has been worn down by the cutting winds of life, and perhaps disapproval over some of the other's choices. But the script for *Keep the Lights On*, co-written by Sachs and Mauricio Zacharias, eschews any deeper examination of Erik's (undiagnosed but self-evident) codependency, and is sometimes so abstruse as to seemingly willfully invite ridicule. This latter problem is most illustrated in a baffling sequence where Erik, having finally tracked down Paul at an upscale hotel after another drug bender,

submits wordlessly to a cuckolding between Paul and a male escort.

What holds *Keep the Lights On* together is its acting and the artful manner of its telling. Long tracking shots underscore the film's aching melancholy, while other tightly captured sequences are at times quite imaginatively framed by cinematographer Thimios Bakatakis. And its warm lighting leans toward saturated and grainy as the intensity of Erik and Paul's relationship glows and recedes. (On the downside, the movie is hampered by a low-quality audio mix that sacrifices the dialogue track to too much ambient clatter.)

Sachs won the Grand Jury Prize at the Sundance Film Festival with *40 Shades of Blue* (2005), but had something of a misstep with his follow-up, the Douglas Sirkian crime dramedy *Married Life* (2007). Throughout his canon, however, he has always evidenced a solid touch with actors, something that is certainly present here as well. There is a mannered neatness to Booth, in both appearance and performance, which intriguingly hints at hidden reservoirs of pent-up pain. If Sachs quite never fully exploits it, it is still there, just underneath the surface. The star, and revelation, of *Keep the Lights On*, though, is Lindhardt, who communicates much about Erik's self-esteem without saying a word. This pair's naturalistic performances ground this material, and are at the core of any sympathetic reading.

The things that most mark *Keep the Lights On* as a delicate and unique work are in the end some of the same things that prevent it from taking hold as something greater than the sum of its parts—as a tale of romantic obsession, addiction or depression. Perhaps because it is so personal, Sachs does not wish to force diagnosis upon his characters. A bit of that would have been welcome, though, and greatly benefited *Keep the Lights On*.

Brent Simon

CREDITS

Erik Rothman: Thure Lindhardt
Paul: Zachary Booth
Claire: Julianne Nicholson
Karen: Paprika Steen
Russ: Sebastian La Cause
Origin: United States
Language: English
Released: 2012
Production: Ira Sachs, Lucas Joaquin, Marie Therese Guirgis; Parts&Labor, Alarum Pictures, Tiny Dancer Films; released by Music Box Films
Directed by: Ira Sachs
Written by: Ira Sachs; Mauricio Zacharias

Cinematography by: Thimios Bakatakis
Music by: Arthur Russell
Sound: Mariusz Glabinski; Damian Volpe
Editing: Affonso Goncalves
Art Direction: Laura Miller
Costumes: Liz Vastola
Production Design: Amy Williams
MPAA rating: Unrated
Running time: 101 minutes

REVIEWS

Chang, Justin. *Variety.* January 24, 2012.

Duralde, Alonso. *The Wrap.* September 6, 2012.

Ebert, Roger. *Chicago Sun-Times.* October 25, 2012.

Edelstein, David. *New York Magazine.* September 4, 2012.

Greene, Ray. *Boxoffice Magazine.* January 27, 2012.

Hornaday, Ann. *Washington Post.* September 21, 2012.

Kohn, Eric. *IndieWIRE.* August 28, 2012.

Morris, Wesley. *Boston Globe.* October 11, 2012.

O'Hehir, Andrew. *Salon.com.* January 28, 2012.

Tallerico, Brian. *HollywoodChicago.com.* October 26, 2012.

AWARDS

Nominations:

Ind. Spirit 2013: Actor (Lindhardt), Director (Sachs), Film, Screenplay

THE KID WITH A BIKE
(Le gamin au velo)

Box Office: $1.5 million

Restless, angry, alienated and always on the run— these words aptly describe the type of protagonist favored by Belgian auteurs Jean-Pierre and Luc Dardenne, and their 2012 effort, *The Kid with a Bike,* is no exception. In a way, this film brings the directing duo full circle to their 1996 breakthrough drama, *La Promesse,* which catapulted them to the ranks of internationally renowned masters of cinema.

The Dardenne brothers' distinctive brand of realism was spawned organically from their two-decade career in documentary filmmaking. The interviews they conducted with members of Belgium's lower class in various nonfiction pictures largely served as the inspiration for the characters in their subsequent scripted features. Perhaps that is why their stories are bereft of banal cliches and the reassuring illusion of closure.

Both *La Promesse* and *The Kid with a Bike* center on young boys who threaten to devolve into destructive

products of their environment. The psychological abuse they received at the hands of their remote father figures have forced them to grow up much more quickly than the majority of their peers. Their eyes are unclouded by the phony promises that their society is poised to break, yet whereas *Promesse* charts the moral awakening of a boy, Igor (Jeremie Renier), *Bike* follows Cyril (Thomas Doret) as he tilts precariously on the edge of a doom-laden void.

To Igor and Cyril, bike (or moped) riding is not just a form of transportation. It provides them with a mode of escape from their claustrophobic traps, allowing them to taste the momentary exhilaration of freedom, as the red hues of their clothing leave an arresting streak of color on the sullen, gray landscape. These boys seem to share the same troubled, resilient soul, which is why it makes perfect sense for Renier to play Doret's father in *Bike.* There are distinctive echoes of Renier's astonishing debut performance in Doret's uncannily authentic work. It is clear that both of these young performers were under the guidance of directorial geniuses.

Rather than wax intellectually on character motivations, the Dardennes aim to immerse their actors so completely within the lives of their characters that the nuances of their psyches are naturally conveyed through their body language. The brothers' disinterest in psychoanalyzing their characters for the sake of their actors is a trait strikingly similar to that of Alfred Hitchcock. The Dardennes are among the very few modern filmmakers worthy of comparison to the Master of Suspense, though the life-or-death stakes in their films are much starker, devoid of Hitch's comforting morbid wit.

Like *Rosetta,* the titular heroine of the Dardenne's 1999 Cannes prize-winner, Cyril is desperate to find his place in a world that appears to have little need for him. Abandoned by his father, Guy (Renier), in a state-run youth farm, Cyril furiously attempts to track him down. The boy earns such visceral empathy from the audience that it is little wonder why a childless hairdresser, Samantha (the radiant Cecile De France), would want to adopt him. She respects his budding manhood but is adamant about keeping him far away from trouble, particularly the trouble embodied by Wes (Egon Di Mateo), a charismatic gang leader intent on recruiting wayward youth to carry out his crimes. The more susceptible Cyril becomes to Wes's advances, the more viewers are bound to be perched on the edge of their seats.

This is an excruciatingly suspenseful film, but it is also a deeply powerful meditation on the vitality of human connection in an unforgiving universe. In a rare break from their minimalist aesthetic, the Dardennes utilize non-diagetic music in the form of Beethoven's "Adagio un poco mosso." Even a classic piece such as this risks sullying the purity of the Dardennes' technique, yet the melancholic warmth of Beethoven's notes could not have been more impeccably matched to the on-screen action.

Nowhere is this more apparent than during Cyril's shocking breakdown following his devastating reunion with Guy, who finally removes any shred of doubt that he is out of his son's life for good. Overcome with rage and disbelief, Cyril begins to slam his head into the window of Samantha's car as she drives him back to her home. Rather than react in alarm, Samantha forcibly places Cyril at her side, and the struggle gradually transforms into a deep, tearful embrace. This scene is every bit as potently moving as the moment in *La Promesse,* when Igor wraps his arms tightly around the fiery woman whose life he is attempting to save. The galvanizing series of haphazard events that led to each of these unlikely embraces reflect the Dardennes' peerless mastery in portraying a chaotic world where love is somehow within our grasp.

Matt Fagerholm

CREDITS

Cyril Catoul: Thomas Doret
Samantha: Cecile de France
Guy Catoul: Jeremie Renier
Wes: Egon Di Mateo
Origin: Belgium, France
Language: French
Released: 2011
Production: Jean-Pierre Dardenne, Luc Dardenne, Denis Freyd, Jean-Pierre Dardenne, Luc Dardenne; Archipel 35, France 2 Cinema, Les Films du Fleuve, Lucky Red; released by Sundance Selects
Directed by: Jean-Pierre Dardenne; Luc Dardenne
Written by: Jean-Pierre Dardenne; Luc Dardenne
Cinematography by: Alain Marcoen
Sound: Thomas Gauder
Editing: Marie-Helene Dozo
Costumes: Maira Ramedhan-Levi
MPAA rating: Unrated
Running time: 87 minutes

REVIEWS

Burr, Ty. *Boston Globe*. March 29, 2012.
Dargis, Manohla. *New York Times*. March 15, 2012.
Ebert, Roger. *Chicago Sun-Times*. March 21, 2012.
Hornaday, Ann. *Washington Post*. April 5, 2012.
Lane, Anthony. *New Yorker*. March 12, 2012.
Longworth, Karina. *Village Voice*. March 13, 2012.
Morgenstern, Joe. *Wall Street Journal*. March 15, 2012.
Phillips, Michael. *Chicago Tribune*. March 22, 2012.
Schwarzbaum, Lisa. *Entertainment Weekly*. March 18, 2012.
Tobias, Scott. *AV Club*. March 14, 2012.

TRIVIA

The script was structured with a fairytale in mind, wherein the boy would lose his illusions and Samantha would appear as a fairy-like figure.

AWARDS

Nominations:

Golden Globes 2012: Foreign Film
Ind. Spirit 2012: Foreign Film

KILL LIST

Box Office: $29,063

Writer/director Ben Wheatley can be said to have specialized in the horror of the mundane, always a neat trick. His three feature films all skirt neat genre labels. *Down Terrace* (2011) was ostensibly a crime drama while *Sightseers* (2012) was a black comedy. Only *Kill List* could be called an out-and-out genre film and yet there is little doubt such labels miss the point. As different as all three of these films seem, they are all unmistakably the work of a single creative vision. Deep character studies, visceral violence, and a dark sense of humor combine with keen observations about the nature of family and social contracts to help all three films accomplish complex narrative goals. *Down Terrace* plays like an inversion of Scorsese's *Good Fellas* (1990) in which instead of success bringing chaos, crime is downwardly mobile to all but a chosen few even as it is deeply analogous to family dysfunction and a soulless consumer vision. *Sightseers* wears horror conventions on its sleeve but certainly goes far beyond them in telling the tale of a seemingly affable couple who are criminally insane in their willingness to shape the world around them to maintain their own emotional comfort zones. *Kill List* presents horrors natural and unnatural in devastatingly effective fashion, reshaping the crime drama into something darker than ever before, tracing a particular type of evil back to something that seems undeniably a part of everyone rather than an outside agency.

Jay (Neil Maskell) appears to be a normal middle-aged husband and father. But a spate of unemployment is causing stress at home and the family needs money badly. Determined to get him back to work, his wife

Shel (MyAnna Buring) invites his business partner Gal (Michael Smiley) over for a dinner party. Between drinks, viewers discover that Gal and Jay are indeed business partners but of a different sort, having become hit men after meeting in the military. Jay is unemployed because a botched job has left him badly shaken. Gal convinces Jay to take a new very lucrative job they have been offered and the next day the pair meet their mysterious client and receive their kill list, but only after the client cuts both his own and Jay's hand so the contract can be signed in blood.

Following this disturbing event, the two embark on what seems to be a perfectly run-of-the-mill mission. Their first victim, a priest, goes down without a hitch, although he thanks them just prior to being shot. The second name on the list leads them to a man who is involved in child pornography, which completely unhinges Jay, who tortures the man to death in order to track down the rest of the gang. When they find them, Jay goes berserk and Gal discovers a file on himself and Jay, including details of the last job that went bad. Gal, fearing the mission has spun out of control arranges a meeting with their client who demands they finish the job, which involves a member of parliament. As they stake the job out in the woods near the victim's home they discover a strange occult ritual. Enraged by an apparent human sacrifice, Jay opens fire on the seemingly unconcerned cult members who pursue the hit men into woods where Gal is killed. Jay barely escapes making his way to the remote safe house where his wife and son have hidden away. Pursued by the occultists the family makes a last stand at the house.

Kill List, could be said to metaphorically pick up where *Down Terrace* left off, as it provides viewers a judgment on all of its wrongdoers. It is a tale that slowly reveals itself as first family drama, then criminal character study, then psychological conspiracy thriller, and finally occult horror. Along the way, it powerfully echoes Robin Hardy's *The Wicker Man* (1973), in which a man certain of his own moral standing falls victim to his inability to truly see himself and thus becomes blind to the dark powers arrayed against him.

But the scariest thing about *Kill List* is hardly the violence, which, though stomach churning, is always put to the exact purpose to which it is intended. Minus any horror elements at all, viewers would still be left with the presentation of murder as being no different than any other career, employing people who are skilled at little else and consider themselves happy to be able to apply those skills to finance a hot tub in the backyard or invite friends over for a backyard soiree. It seems less like greed or malice and that makes it scary as hell because that is what almost anyone wants: To simply get by, have a good life, not even an extravagant one. Yet,

what Jay and Shel are willing to sacrifice to get it is nothing less than their souls.

Wheatley has a keen eye for symbolic detail as in one sequence where a rabbit killed by the family cat ends up devoured by Jay out of desire to show dominance as much as out of hunger. Viewers constantly hear references to the need Jay feels to punish evil. A foam sword battle between Shel and Jay and their son is prescient.

Three dynamic tales into his career Ben Wheatley is emerging as a very important filmmaker. He transcends genre and finds the power of his tales in the human heart. Given the amount of physical confrontation, argument and sheer terror onscreen *Kill List* is most remarkable in that it manages to smolder rather than scream.

Dave Canfield

CREDITS

Jay: Neil Maskell
Gal: Michael Smiley
Shel: MyAnna Buring
Fiona: Emma Fryer
Origin: British Virgin Islands
Language: English
Released: 2012
Production: Claire Jones, Andy Starke; Rook Films, Warp X; released by IFC Films
Directed by: Ben Wheatley
Written by: Ben Wheatley; Amy Jump
Cinematography by: Laurie Rose
Music by: Jim Williams
Sound: Martin Pavey
Editing: Robin Hill
Art Direction: Julie Ann Horan
Costumes: Lance Milligan
Production Design: David Butterworth
MPAA rating: Unrated
Running time: 95 minutes

REVIEWS

Burr, Ty. *Boston Globe*. March 1, 2012.
Catsoulis, Jeannette. *New York Times*. February 2, 2012.
Christley, Jaime N. *Slant Magazine*. January 30, 2012.
Ebert, Roger. *Chicago Sun-Times*. March 15, 2012.
Lemire, Christy. *Associated Press*. January 31, 2012.
MacDonlad, Moira. *Seattle Times*. March 1, 2012.
McDonagh, Maitland. *Film Journal International*. February 3, 2012.
Newman, Kim. *Empire Magazine*. August 29, 2011.
Tobias, Scott. *NPR*. February 3, 2012.
Weinberg, Scott. *FEARnet*. September 5, 2011.

TRIVIA

A Wilhelm Scream is featured in the film when Gal fires his shotgun at the masked pursuers just after the hanging.

KILLER JOE
(Killer Joe: A Twisted Redneck Trailer Park Murder Story)

A totally twisted deep-fried Texas redneck trailer park murder story.
—Movie tagline

Murder never tasted so good.
—Movie tagline

Available for hire. Terms and conditions will apply.
—Movie tagline

Box Office: $2 million

Before there was Colin Farrell or Channing Tatum, there was the original modern-era big screen beefcake, Matthew McConaughey, who gave a memorable supporting turn in *Dazed and Confused* (1993), but really rocketed to notoriety in the sweaty adaptation of John Grisham's bestselling, Mississippi-set novel *A Time to Kill* (1996). The young actor was frequently shirtless in that movie, and over the better part of the next decade he sustained a career that, while studded with some occasionally interesting work, mostly traded on his tan, well-toned body and pin-up looks. After a string of wan, seemingly interchangeable romantic comedies and adventure movies, there was an extended period of time when McConaughey was known seemingly as much for tabloid photos of beach cavorting with his pal Lance Armstrong as anything he did on screen. He was on his way to becoming the living embodiment of the curious marketing slogan stamped across the front of Johnson's Baby Powder: "clinically proven mildness."

Over the last two years, however, McConaughey seemed to go out of his way to tackle more challenging work, and reconnect with auteur-minded filmmakers. He did not completely button up (notably appearing shirtless in Steven Soderbergh's *Magic Mike* [2012], a movie about male strippers), but garnered a string of positive notices for his very different performances in *The Lincoln Lawyer* (2011) and a trio of other 2012 releases—Richard Linklater's *Bernie*, Jeff Nichols' *Mud*, and Lee Daniels' *The Paperboy*.

The funky, crusty jewel in McConaughey's comeback crown, though, just may be *Killer Joe*, a blackly comedic white trash masterpiece from director William Friedkin. Garish and shocking (it is rated NC-17, in what is most assuredly not a gimmick), gripping and more than a bit perverse, Friedkin's movie—adapted by Pulitzer Prize-winning playwright Tracy Letts from his own stage play of the same name—is also darkly funny, if the mutual comeuppance of scuzzy idiots is entertaining to viewers.

Panicked and in problematic debt to a local thug, 22-year-old Chris Smith (Emile Hirsch) turns to his henpecked father Ansel (Thomas Haden Church) and domineering stepmother Sharla (Gina Gershon) for help. He does not have the greatest relationship with either of them but soon a twisted plan begins to take shape. Having heard about Joe Cooper (McConaughey), a Dallas police officer who moonlights as a contract killer, Chris pitches his dad on a plot to kill his biological mother and split up a $50,000 life insurance policy that benefits Chris' younger sister, Dottie (Juno Temple). Chris and Ansel arrange a meeting, but, lacking the money for the necessary down payment of $20,000, seem to hit an impasse. For the first time, though, Joe makes an exception to one of his rules, setting his sights on the virginal Dottie as "retainer" for his services, and entering into a warped relationship with her. Naturally, all does not go smoothly in either love or death for this collection of distasteful characters.

Killer Joe summons up memories of fellow noir-ish works like *Blood Simple* (1985), *Red Rock West* (1994), and *The Killer Inside Me* (2010), as well as true crime tales *Alpha Dog* (2007) and the aforementioned *Bernie*. It is a movie about victimhood and vengeance, but one that that unfolds in a pulpy, lurid world of singular construction. Friedkin and Letts previously collaborated on the underrated *Bug* (2006), and their obvious rapport and lockstep sensibilities benefit this follow-up. (The movie's opening credits even offer up an unusual double-possessive title: "William Friedkin's Film of Tracy Letts' *Killer Joe*.") Trace amounts of inspirations as diverse as Tennessee Williams and Quentin Tarantino come bubbling to the surface of this Southern Gothic.

Admirably, there is no attempt to soften the edges of any of the characters in *Killer Joe*; everyone is kind of scummy, desperate and despicable ("Maybe it'll do her some good," rationalizes Ansel at pimping out his daughter), or at the very least under-educated to an almost wince-inducing degree. Only Dottie remains a bit of a cipher and plot device. Early on in the film's running time she claims her mother tried to kill her as a baby by smothering her with a pillow, but the intrigue and promise of greater elucidation of her motivations dances beyond the movie's grasp, and the range of

Temple's performance. This ambiguity may have worked better on the stage, but in the adaptation it feels like a chip not cashed in.

Killer Joe is instead more interested in baroque grotesqueries, and this surely relates to its reception amongst older critics. While the film scored a 76 percent fresh rating on Rotten Tomatoes (and an 80 percent rating with audiences), its 63 percent score amongst top critics indicates a bit of institutional/generational resistance to the movie's undomesticated rhythms. Writing for the *Wall Street Journal*, Joe Morgenstern called the movie "ugly and vile," while Anthony Lane, in his *New Yorker* review, said the film skirted "abusive farce." To read some of this criticism—almost all of which harps on a couple scenes of unpleasant humiliation, and in particular a destined-to-be-remembered scene of degradation involving a fried chicken leg—would lead one to think the actors were somehow rounded up off the street and forced into participation against their will.

The film is nasty, yes, and peppered with some outrageous sequences. But its characters often react in believably simple ways to the pressures around them, at first with lots of bumbling and then with farfetched delusion. (At one point Chris considers escaping by driving to Peru.) Joe's psychotic behavior, meanwhile, is informed by a latent disgust with the rest of the extended Smith family, and their willingness to pimp out Dottie; his care for her is genuine, but measures he takes seem designed to mete out some Old Testament-type punishment. He is morally empty and a dealer of death in multiple ways, and Dottie becomes a strange vessel for his salvation. *Killer Joe* always feels grounded, in its own sick, misshapen way.

Abetting this well-bound feeling is the pulpy look of the film, cast in luxurious shadows by cinematographer Caleb Deschanel, and, most of all, its delicious performances. Church is spot-on as the dim and suggestible Ansel, while Gershon is fearless as Sharla, a sort of uncouth, trailer park Lady MacBeth. It is McConaughey, however, as the title character, who achieves a scary and unlikely reinvention. Its other wicked delights notwithstanding, *Killer Joe* serves as a reminder that he has notable gifts other than just killer abs.

Brent Simon

CREDITS

Killer Joe Cooper: Matthew McConaughey
Chris Smith: Emile Hirsch
Dottie Smith: Juno Temple
Ansel Smith: Thomas Haden Church
Sharla Smith: Gina Gershon

Origin: United States
Language: English
Released: 2011
Production: Nicolas Chartier, Scott Einbinder; Voltage Pictures; released by Lions Gate Entertainment Corp.
Directed by: William Friedkin
Written by: Tracy Letts
Cinematography by: Caleb Deschanel
Music by: Tyler Bates
Sound: Jeffrey Haupt
Editing: Darrin Navarro
Costumes: Peggy Anita Schnitzer
Production Design: Franco-Giacomo Carbone
MPAA rating: R
Running time: 102 minutes

REVIEWS

Dargis, Manohla. *New York Times*. July 26, 2012.
Ebert, Roger. *Chicago Sun-Times*. August 2, 2012.
Edelstein, David. *New York Magazine*. July 30, 2012.
Lemire, Christy. *Associated Press*. July 27, 2012.
Morgenstern, Joe. *Wall Street Journal*. July 26, 2012.
Puig, Claudia. *USA Today*. August 2, 2012.
Rodriguez, Rene. *Miami Herald*. August 23, 2012.
Sharkey, Betsy. *Los Angeles Times*. August 2, 2012.
Stevens, Dana. *Slate*. July 27, 2012.
Tallerico, Brian. *HollywoodChicago.com*. August 2, 2012.

QUOTES

Killer Joe Cooper: "You insult me again, and I'll cut your face off and wear it over my own."

TRIVIA

Near the end of the movie, Joe tells Chris, "caveat emptor." This is Latin for "let the buyer beware."

AWARDS

Nominations:
Ind. Spirit 2013: Actor (McConaughey)

KILLING THEM SOFTLY

In America you're on your own.
   —Movie tagline

Box Office: $15 million

A Molotov cocktail of economic misanthropy amassed for an angry country, *Killing Them Softly* is the work of Australian director Andrew Dominik, who uses a simple crime story as the stage to display rage against the bailout of numerous American companies in 2008—especially in a capitalist society of thugs of all economic backgrounds who are steered by their selfish pursuit of money. With its pulpy focus that assuages Dominik's inclination towards genre filmmaking (tough guys in leather jackets) just as much it does its direct metaphor, the film discusses with its tale of a heist's revenge the cost of money and the subsequent cost of taking money, while utilizing actual bailout era speeches from politicians like President George W. Bush in scattered sound bites, which play out like stage directions for the hard-boiled action presented onscreen. The film's crime speaks to those of the bailout, and vice versa.

Based on the 1974 novel *Cogan's Trade* from Boston crime novelist George V. Higgins, Ben Mendelsohn and Scoot McNairy play Russell and Frankie, two greasy guys who are hired by an underworld organize nicknamed Johnny "Squirrel" Amato (Vincent Curatola) to rob a crime ring's card game. The gambling session is run by Markie Trattman (Ray Liotta), who proves a unique target—he has knocked over one of his own card games before and been forgiven for it, and is thus a perfect scapegoat. Despite the thugs' clumsiness in the heist, the robbery ends efficiently, with the two also taking money from the wallets of gambling participants, to which Frankie jokes to them, "It's only money."

Into town rides clean-up killer Jackie Cogan (Brad Pitt), as hired by the unassuming business man Driver (Richard Jenkins) who serves as messenger for unseen crime bosses with a "total corporate mentality," in the words of Driver. "I have to guide them through everything like retarded children," he confides to Jackie, as they conduct business in a sedan. First to be dealt with is Trattman, who is beat to a bleeding pulp one night amidst his howls of innocence. Soon after, it is revealed by Russell (who is now dealing heroin while looking grungier than ever) to cleaned-up Frankie that a hit is out on both of them and Amato, because Russell idiotically bragged about his involvement in the heist to the wrong person.

Meanwhile, having heard this information, Cogan deduces that four people must be killed for this heist—Trattman, Frankie, Russell and Squirrel. Jackie takes on the responsibility to assassinate the robbers, but he can not kill Amato, as the crime organizer would recognize him. Driver then decides to hire veteran hit man Mickey (James Gandolfini) to kill Amato. Per Driver's insistence, Mickey files in on coach.

When Mickey meets up with Jackie, the worn-out criminal proves to be a big mess in front of Jackie. He is in trouble for some felony charges involving hunting shotguns, and confides that he should not be out of state without court permission. Days later, with Mickey spending his time with hookers and not doing his job, Jackie speaks to Mickey about getting work done, but it is of no use. Mickey is insulted, and barks at him. Jackie goes to Driver, who agrees with him that Mickey has to be removed from the situation. It then becomes Jackie's direct responsibility to clean up the quartet of crooks, working within what Driver calls, "A business of relationships."

Providing an appealing ratty performance is McNairy, who uses his low weasel-like rasp to great effect as this character, a man who would not be intimidating were it not for his guns. In this sense, he is reminiscent of Casey Affleck's representation of anti-masculinity in Dominik's previous *The Assassination of Jesse James by the Coward Robert Ford* (2007), but in comparison McNairy does not find as much weight in his characters' meekness.

Essentially, playing the lead in the movie (despite his introduction in the second act), Pitt does get to carry some of the film's finer moments, which he does deliver with the chill needed by Dominik's script. With his prettier, more polished look, Pitt does use his large presence as both character and superstar to menacingly overshadow other characters in a couple of intimidating moments (much as he did as heroic villain Jesse James in Dominik's previous film). Still, when he is shooting someone point blank, Pitt's performance, and the power inferred to this role because Brad Pitt is playing it, still carries a light waft of the side of the star's onscreen persona that is also able to sell perfume as well.

In a small-yet-effective role of only a few scenes, Gandolfini provides an acute embodiment of the spiritual deterioration of the society presented in *Killing Them Softly*, as a hit man who has lost an idea of integrity due to his fleeting, gluttonous vices, like Russell and his heroin. Gandolfini shows the smallness of a man when he has lost his job focus, and his crankiness and the sunglasses that cover his face cannot express beyond the idea that this thug is another loser, in need of more than just a nap.

Continuing the attitude of the story, the cinematography by Greig Fraser (also of *Zero Dark Thirty* [2012]) achieves a fitfully visually involving aesthetic to the film's coldness, especially when the camera often follows behind walking characters in extensive long takes. Fraser's camera certainly includes the viewer into its startling bursts of aggressively realistic violence, which comes at the audience point blank, whether it be a slow-motion bullet ripping through a character's body, or the sight of a man's brain as it explodes out of the back of his skull.

Though its title refers to Jackie's philosophy of killing contracts at a distance, *Killing Them Softly* very actively attempts to distance itself from the Roberta

Flack track "Killing Me Softly With His Song," (later famously covered by the Fugees), for which viewers could easily associate its title with, by having a very active, mostly soundtrack that plays many of its songs out in full. Characters are personified by their accompanying tunes, like when Jackie Cogan rolls into the movie with the sounds of "When the Man Comes Around" by Johnny Cash, the song providing a mythic quality as Cogan's car rides in on echoing piano bass notes. For the most part, the soundtrack proves to be a diverse addition to its story, further complicating the tone of its simple structure with sarcastically used tunes like "Life Is Just A Bowl of Cherries" by Jack Hylton & His Orchestra, or "It's Only a Paper Moon" by Cliff 'Ukelele Ike' Edwards. In a couple of other instances, the soundtrack is more direct with its song choices, like when "Heroin" by the Velvet Underground is used to accompany an extensive scene of Russell's heroin usage, or when "Money (That's What I Want)" by Barrett Strong accompanies the film's conclusive thoughts.

Dominik paces his movie with great patience, letting the fire within the film burn with a cool flame. With this, Dominik does not hesitate to vamp with sequences that drag, even considering the film's relatively small running time of 97 minutes. However compelling Dominik's metaphor may be, especially in such a raw film, and however up-close its moments of action may be, the editing still highlights the truth that the movie's destitute atmosphere still is not any more accessible, especially as its story is continually obscured from its finite shape. This film is not only bitter to its characters, but its audience. Dominik sacrifices the tightness of a small story to stretch it out, gambling his pacing on the idea that audiences will embrace this tale as a much larger director's statement—a choice that robs the film of even the simplest element of tension.

Acting with a free spirit more common in untamed first-time directors, and certainly playing under the magnificence of his previously masterful *The Assassination of Jesse James By the Coward Robert Ford*, Dominik warps his lucid story to an obscure shape, and then paints it with a glaring metaphor that requires control in terms of its limits of interpretation of symbolism. It is unclear as to whether characters or events are being used to represent entire non-fictional elements in the bailout crisis, represent various clashing mentalities, or simply stand as products themselves of the daily financial climate. In this sense, the story becomes even more shabby; its slow pacing already difficult for the viewer to become involved in, the film's obvious metaphor subsequently all the more challenging to completely interpret.

Through his displays of brutal violence, Dominik's anger towards a cannibalistic economy is expressed to how justice is achieved, as the film makes a point to focus its crime story around the choleric vengeance brought against those who take the money. In this regard, *Killing Them Softly* preaches to its own frustration, while reveling in its bleak vision of the world seen through the eyes of pulpy tough guys, hustlers of a financial ideology no different from those who crumbled a nation's economy into a recession. Though the film does have a palpable Coen Brothers-esque black comedy humor to its story of flawed criminals, *Killing Them Softly* does not speak to anything outside of its pessimism, nor find it even useful to provide any answers as to how the troublesome system of capitalism could somehow save itself. Instead, *Killing Them Softly* is best seen as the passionate bottling of combustible cynicism for an era that desires the vengeful aim of a non-fictional Jackie Cogan.

Nick Allen

CREDITS

Jackie Cogan: Brad Pitt
Frankie: Scoot McNairy
Russell: Ben Mendelsohn
Markie: Ray Liotta
Mickey: James Gandolfini
Dillon: Sam Shepard
Driver: Richard Jenkins
Johnny: Vincent Curatola
Origin: United States
Language: English
Released: 2012
Production: Dede Gardner, Anthony G. Katagas, Paula Mae Schwartz, Steve Schwartz, Brad Pitt; Annapurna Pictures, Chockstone Pictures, Inferno Entertainment, Plan B Entertainment; released by Weinstein Company
Directed by: Andrew Dominik
Written by: Andrew Dominik
Cinematography by: Greig Fraser
Music by: Rachel Fox
Sound: Kirk Francis
Editing: Brian A. Kates
Costumes: Patricia Norris
Production Design: Patricia Norris
MPAA rating: R
Running time: 97 minutes

REVIEWS

Burr, Ty. *Boston Globe*. November 29, 2012.
Chang, Justin. *Variety*. November 30, 2012.
Ebert, Roger. *Chicago Sun-Times*. November 29, 2012.
McCarthy, Todd. *Hollywood Reporter*. May 22, 2012.

Morgenstern, Joe. *Wall Street Journal.* November 29, 2012.

Reed, Rex. *New York Observer.* November 28, 2012.

Scott, A. O. *New York Times.* November 29, 2012.

Stevens, Dana. *Slate.* November 29, 2012.

Whitty, Stephen. *Newark Star-Ledger.* November 30, 2012.

Zacharek, Stephanie. *NPR.* November 29, 2012.

QUOTES

Jackie Cogan: "America is not a country it's a business."

TRIVIA

This is the first feature film to use Kodak's 500T 5230 film stock.

L

THE LADY

Wife. Mother. Prisoner. Hero.
—Movie tagline

From house arrest to Parliament.
—Movie tagline

The Lady contains virtually everything that any self-respecting biopic needs in order to succeed. It has, in the life of Burmese political activist Aung San Suu Kyi, a stirring narrative involving a woman who overcame violence, oppression and separation from her family due to the courage of her convictions, a powerful narrative that will also serve as an eye-opener to a portion of recent world history of which many may not be fully aware. At its center, it contains a powerful career-best performance by Michelle Yeoh. Most importantly, it has been made with impeccable skill and with enormous and obvious respect for its subject. The only problem is that while *The Lady* is as well-meaning and sincere as can be, it is also a bit of a drag—a passion project without any noticeable demonstration of genuine passion.

For those unfamiliar with the story of Suu Kyi, it begins here with a prologue set in 1947 when her father, a popular general and a leader in the movement to bring democracy to Burma, was murdered by a military death squad when she was only three. When the story picks up again in 1988, Burma is under the thumb of a brutal military dictatorship and Suu Kyi is living in Oxford with her professor husband, Michael Aris (David Thewlis) and their two sons. When she gets word that her mother has had a stroke, she returns to Burma to be at her side and while at the hospital, she finds herself in the middle of a violent crackdown against those protesting the government. When word gets out that she is in the country, she is pressed into service as a leader of the burgeoning reform movement in the hopes that she can continue her father's work and lead Burma to freedom. The military tries to intimidate her into stepping away—even going so far as to point a gun straight at her head during a protest—but she refuses to back down and forms a political party that unites much of the country.

In 1990, her party sweeps the Burmese elections in a landslide. Inevitably, the current dictatorship is less than enthused with the results and responds by ignoring the vote and placing Suu Kyi under house arrest while forbidding her family from visiting. For the next decade, Suu Kyi is stuck in her house with only minimal contact with the outside world while Michael struggles to call attention to her plight in the hopes that the eyes of the world ensure that she will not suddenly "disappear" one day. Eventually, Michael's efforts result in Suu Kyi winning the Nobel Peace Prize in 1991, an event that she cannot attend because she knows she will never be let back into the country if she does. To make matters worse, the government continues to forbid her family from visiting her, even after Michael develops prostate cancer and has only a short time to live. Because of this, Suu Kyi finds herself literally forced to choose between her family and her country and no matter which one she picks, she may lose the other forever.

Oddly enough, *The Lady* has been directed by none other than Luc Besson, the French director who specializes in wild and borderline cartoonish (in the best possible way) action-fantasies like *La Femme Nikita* (1990), *Leon* (1994) and *The Fifth Element* (1997) not to mention the dozens and dozens of titles that he has written or produced such as the *Transporter* and *Taken* films. One might think that Besson's typically nutball cinematic approach would seem to be a profound mismatch with parameters of the life story of Suu Kyi, whose ass-kicking was of the dignified and metaphorical kind, and it seems as though Besson felt the same way as not even the most finely tuned auteur radar would be able to detect his handiwork based on the on-screen evidence. Even his previous biopic, the Joan of Arc epic *The Messenger* (1999) found him indulging in his cheerfully childish side during the scenes in which he frankly embraced the mythical aspects of his heroine both dramatically and cinematically. None of that is to be found here—no bits of goofball humor, no wild camera moves, no flashy editing or any of the other things that have made Besson's films such a joy to watch in the past.

The trouble is that in the process of delivering his most staid and straightforward work as a director so as to presumably avoid showing any disrespect to his subject, he has overcompensated to such a degree that a story that should have been electrifying instead comes across as kind of dull and dramatically inert. Besson does not do anything dramatically wrong and the contributions from key collaborators like cinematographer Thierry Arbogast and composer Eric Serra are top-notch as usual but after a while, the whole thing begins to really drag. To be fair to Besson, the screenplay by Rebecca Frayn that he is working from is too reverential by half and inexplicably frames the story with material surrounding Michael's cancer that weirdly steals the focus away from its subject as the film comes to its conclusion. As a result, a film about a woman who became famous for putting the needs of her country before herself ends up playing like just the kind of hagiography that seems totally out of character with what she represents.

What almost makes *The Lady* work, despite its misfired good intentions, is the performance by Michelle Yeoh as Aung San Suu Kyi. For years, Yeoh was marketed as an action babe thanks to her appearances in films like *Supercop* (1992), *Tomorrow Never Dies* (1997) and *Crouching Tiger, Hidden Dragon* (2000), but even when she was doing wild stunts and intricate fight choreography, she brought a quiet dignity and serenity to the proceedings that was striking enough to suggest that she would continue to flourish in roles that did not require her to deliver beatings on a regular basis. Alas, her recent filmography has been somewhat uneven, to put it politely, but whatever she is in (even a disaster like *Memoirs of a Geisha* [2005]), she has always been the best thing about whatever project which with she has been involved and that is certainly the case here. Yeoh is

a dead ringer for Suu Kyi and might have easily been cast in the role based on that aspect alone but unlike so many performances in biopics these days she is doing something far deeper and truer than a mere impersonation. Without ever succumbing to the temptation to deliver the big, showy performance that might have earned her an Oscar nomination, she instead goes inward to find Suu Kyi's soul—what it was that made her tick and carry on in the face of such adversity—and her representation of that is fascinating to watch. It does not quite balance out all of the other flaws of *The Lady* in the end but it comes very close to doing just that.

Peter Sobczynski

CREDITS

Aung San Suu Kyi: Michelle Yeoh
Michael Aris: David Thewlis
Kim Aris: Jonathan Raggett
Alexander Aris: Jonathan Woodhouse
General Ne Win: Htun Lin
Origin: France, United Kingdom
Language: English
Released: 2011
Production: Virginie Besson-Silla, Andy Harries; Left Bank Pictures, France 2 Cinema; released by Cohen Media Group
Directed by: Luc Besson
Written by: Rebecca Frayn
Cinematography by: Thierry Arbogast
Music by: Eric Serra
Sound: Didier Lozahic
Editing: Julien Rey
Costumes: Olivier Beriot
Production Design: Hugues Tissandier
MPAA rating: R
Running time: 128 minutes

REVIEWS

Anderson, John. *Newsday*. April 27, 2012.
Burr, Ty. *Boston Globe*. April 12, 2012.
Chang, Justin. *Variety*. November 10, 2011.
Corliss, Richard. *Time*. April 12, 2012.
Ebert, Roger. *Chicago Sun-Times*. April 19, 2012.
Murray, Noel. *AV Club*. April 12, 2012.
Scott, A. O. *New York Times*. April 10, 2012.
Smith, Kyle. *New York Post*. April 13, 2012.
Tallerico, Brian. *HollywoodChicago.com*. April 12, 2012.
Taylor, Ella. *NPR*. April 12, 2012.

TRIVIA

At on point, Giuseppe Tornatore was considered to serve as the film's director.

A LATE QUARTET

*No arrangement is more beautiful...or more
complicated.*
—Movie tagline

Box Office: $1.5 million

It is, perhaps, necessary for the musical quartet at the heart of *A Late Quartet* to split, though one wonders if the move comes too early in the proceedings. One also wonders if the series of conflicts that follows as a result is worthy of the characters and what they represent. Here are four people who share an unrequited love of music and a kind of conversational shorthand when they discuss it. A few of the best moments in the movie are either wordless or short on speech: The short view of the group's rehearsals, in which they only briefly pause in their communication through notes on their stringed instruments for verbal notes on pacing and a man listening to the singing of his deceased wife on an old record, remembering everything he loved about her and every moment he has regretted being without her.

When the members of the quartet go their separate ways, they might as well not be musicians; in addition to their careers, the screenplay puts their craft on hold. Their private lives become the stuff of soap opera (a debilitating disease here, an extramarital affair there), and it is only the strong and—in light of the material—restrained performances from the four leading actors that manage to keep writer/director Yaron Zilberman's more melodramatic touches (a marriage dissolving into constant fights here, a romance between a young woman and a man a couple decades her senior there) from becoming too overwhelming.

The Fugue, as the quartet is called, has achieved much success; it is about to enter its 25th season. The de facto leader and cellist of the group is Peter Mitchell (Christopher Walken), and, as they rehearse in his spacious home, he has trouble keeping up with the others. It a problem that Peter himself says is common with Beethoven's Late String Quartets, which are meant to be played without any breaks in between the movements and can cause nightmares in terms of the musicians keeping in tune with each other. Zilberman uses the lesson as a prologue, just so the metaphor of the ensuing disharmony within the company is not lost.

After a visit to the doctor, Peter learns he has the early signs of Parkinson's disease. If the medication starts to work, he wants a final, farewell performance with the Fugue and, afterwards, that it continues with a replacement for him.

The announcement is the catalyst for chain reaction of interpersonal conflicts for the other three musicians. With the inevitable change to the group, second violin

Robert Gelbart (Philip Seymour Hoffman) believes it is time for him to occasionally perform the role of first violin on certain pieces, alternating with current first violin Daniel Lerner (Mark Ivanir). Robert's wife Juliette (Catherine Keener), whom Peter and his late wife raised as their own daughter since she was a child, does not agree with her husband, and the tension between them starts. When Robert raises the idea to Daniel at an inopportune moment, the conflict between the two of them begins, and it is only heightened when Robert discovers that Peter and Juliette have been having secret meetings to discuss quartet issues without him.

At least these power struggles and Robert's wounded ego are organic to the movie's setup; from there, though, things begin to devolve. Robert has a one-night stand with a dancer (Liraz Charhi) whom he talks to while out on his morning jogs. Juliette discovers the transgression after she contacts him about his violin, which he left behind at her apartment. Meanwhile, Daniel tutors Robert and Juliette's daughter Alexandra (Imogen Poots) on the violin. They are antagonistic at first, so, obviously, the relationship will become romantic. In one of the movie's unfortunately unintentional punch lines to these complications, Robert tells Daniel to follow his passion, after which he disposes of his hesitation to moving forward with Alexandra. The result, of course, is even more strain on the already unstable dynamic of the quartet.

Music and its performance are not so much driving forces for the characters or the story but opportunities for trite metaphors and—for the performance aspect—a means to bookend the movie (The climax offers only insignificant sections of the piece in question). The few exceptions involve Peter, who remains out of the loop of the drama unfolding with his colleagues while trying to secure a replacement and adjust to his new life. Two scenes in particular stand out entirely because of Walken's presence. One is the aforementioned scene in which Peter listens to a record of his wife singing, and Zilberman's camera simply holds on Walken's face and allows the actor to revel in the cathartic emotions of the scene (when the camera cuts to a vision of Peter's wife [Anne Sofie von Otter], Zilberman almost ruins the moment). In the other scene, he tells his class about playing for a musician he greatly admired as a young man and sums up the essence of his character in the process.

In retrospect, that story, in which the lesson is to the emphasize the positives—allowing one to be open to recognizing moments of "transcendence"—instead of picking apart faults, could also be aimed at the audience. When *A Late Quartet* observes the characters talking about and doing what they love, the movie offers a few moments that border on the word chosen by the musician in Peter's story; the trudge through the screenplay's transparent conflicts is not worth the few glimmers of honesty.

Mark Dujsik

CREDITS

Peter Mitchell: Christopher Walken
Robert Gelbart: Philip Seymour Hoffman
Juliette Gelbart: Catherine Keener
Alexandra Gelbart: Imogen Poots
Gideon Rosen: Wallace Shawn
Daniel Lerner: Mark Ivanir
Dr. Nadir: Madhur Jaffrey
Origin: United States
Language: English
Released: 2012
Production: Vanessa Coifman, David Faigenblum, Emanuel Michael, Tamar Sela, Mandy Tagger, Yaron Zilberman; Concept Entertainment, Unison Films; released by RKO Pictures
Directed by: Yaron Zilberman
Written by: Yaron Zilberman; Seth Grossman
Cinematography by: Frederick Elmes
Music by: Angelo Badalamenti
Sound: Robert Hein
Music Supervisor: Maureen Crowe
Editing: Yuval Shar
Art Direction: Rumiko Ishii
Costumes: Joseph G. Aulisi
Production Design: John Kasarda
MPAA rating: R
Running time: 105 minutes

REVIEWS

Berardinelli, James. *ReelViews*. November 10, 2012.
Burr, Ty. *Boston Globe*. November 1, 2012.
Ebert, Roger. *Chicago Sun-Times*. October 31, 2012.
Holden, Stephen. *New York Times*. November 1, 2012.
Holmes, Linda. *NPR*. September 9, 2012.
Hornaday, Ann. *Washington Post*. November 2, 2012.
Kenny, Glenn. *MSN Movies*. November 2, 2012.
McCarthy, Nick. *Slant Magazine*. October 29, 2012.
Orndorf, Brian. *Blu-ray.com*. October 23, 2012.
Sharkey, Betsy. *Los Angeles Times*. November 1, 2012.

QUOTES

Juliette Gelbart: "Why are you so angry with me? What did I do to cause you to talk to me in this way? I mean, did we just spoil you too much? Is that what it is?"
Alexandra Gelbart: "Do you think I had fun? Do you think it was fun growing up with two roving quartet players as

parents? Who were gone seven months of the year and I was always taking a back seat to a violin and a viola? Always. Is that fun? Does that seem fun to you?"
Juliette Gelbart: "You have always been our first priority."
Alexandra Gelbart: "That is bullshit! That's bullshit, that's just words. That's nothing."

LAWLESS
(The Wettest County in the World)

When the law became corrupt, outlaws became heroes.
—Movie tagline

Box Office: $37.4 million

Appalling things are happening amidst the Appalachians in *Lawless*, with a savage throat-slitting, a rape, a castration, the snapping of a sweet, crippled teen's neck, a tar and feathering, and numerous brutal beatings all leading up to a climactic tit for rat-a-tat-tat that turns a gorgeous setting grisly. Yes, the hills are alive with the sound of gunfire and agonized groans in Prohibition-era Franklin County, Virginia, dubbed "The Wettest County in the World" because it was singularly awash with illicit moonshine but seems as if it might also qualify on account of all the bloodshed. The moniker is also the name of the 2008 novel by Matt Bondurant that combines fact and fancy to tell of the harrowing mountain mayhem that resulted when his notoriously-formidable bootlegging ancestors refused to kowtow to corruption. While famed local lawyer T. Keister Greer emphasized that The Bondurant Boys "plainly were not saints," this cinematic adaptation of their story does its best to at least elevate them to the status of heroes. Like the firmly-rooted and towering trees featured in shot after awe-inspiring shot of their neck of the woods, the Bondurants are meant to stand almost as tall in moviegoers' eyes, to be admired for the way they chose to defiantly plant their feet and rise up impressively in the face of those unfairly aiming to cut them down.

Although they themselves are involved in criminal activity, brothers Forrest (Tom Hardy), Howard (Jason Clarke), and Jack (Shia LaBeouf) are, along with their fellow makers of moonshine, to be thought of as intrepid entrepreneurs in a struggle to endure, simply resourceful and resilient rustic poor folk who had needed to find some way—any way—to get by in tough times. Clearly, it is hoped that their ingenuity can thus be appreciated despite its illegality, especially considering that the Constitutional amendment that made them lawbreakers would eventually be recognized as misguided and repealed. In the meantime, even the local sheriff (Bill Camp) is wholly content to accept what they are doing—or, to be more specific, accept complimentary cases of the Bonderants' finest brew in exchange for turning a blind eye to their illicit activities.

During the decimating 1918 flu pandemic, Forrest had been brought to death's door and yet somehow managed at the last minute to defiantly slam it shut. The (ultimately incorrect) story circulates that he endured a twelve mile winter hike to a hospital while pressing together the aforementioned gurgling neck gash that enemies had inflicted. Howard was the only member of his regiment to return alive from World War I. These things have not only given the family a tremendously emboldening sense of invincibility, but also an aura that has exceedingly intimidated those who might wish to interfere in, or encroach upon, their operations. The general consensus became that anyone thinking of doing so should have their head examined, and *Lawless* certainly puts forth a version of Special Deputy Charley Rakes (Guy Pearce) that is in manifest need of psychological evaluation. In real life, he was a crooked and brutish Franklin County lawman, but Rakes has been converted here to something much less conventional, not just corrupt but a rather effete, maniacally fastidious, and enthusiastically sadistic freak who has malignantly metastasized from the big, bad city of Chicago. He is as vain as he is volatile, getting terribly upset if his meticulously-parted and slicked-back hair gets mussed up in a tussle, or if the pristine nature of his gloves is marred while beating someone to a pulp. Rakes also quickly corrects those who address him merely as "deputy" without the "special." He so thoroughly douses himself with a perfumy scent that putrid pigs two counties downwind are likely complaining about a stench. Rakes sometimes erupts in the unnerving giggle of the unhinged. Peace's flamboyant performance is unquestionably riveting, although this character that is inexplicably and bizarrely devoid of eyebrows is so odd and odious that he comes within an eyelash of being a mere caricature.

Clearly, there is a method to this portrayal of Rakes' madness, as the crazed, outrageous relentlessness with which he wages a war of attrition against the Bonderants purposefully shoves audiences' sympathies toward the backwoods bootleggers with equal potency. By comparison, the Bondurant brothers seem infinitely more likeable and relatable. Likewise, the fact that Rakes is not just sick but a city slicker enables the presentation of a character who refers to the Bonderants and their ilk with cool, cruel disdain as "hicks" who are "ignorant." The lawman is a fine one to talk about anyone being "animalistic" considering the ferociously beastly manner in which he himself attempts to achieve dominance over

the Bonderants, frustratedly attacking and killing due to their steadfast refusal to submit—the lone, stouthearted holdouts to his extortion demands. Sure, moviegoers may want to look the other way when the Bondurants gorily resort to castration, but it seems clear that the audience is fully expected to do so in the figurative sense because the bootleggers' barbarism is not just retaliatory but chivalrous, performed on a representative of Rakes who had raped Forrest's girlfriend, Maggie Beauford (Jessica Chastain).

Especially after a fuming, frenzied Rakes gets around to the fully-expected and cold blooded murder of gentle, angelic, and rickets-ravaged Bondurant associate Cricket Pate (highly-promising Dane DeHaan), it was obviously hoped that profoundly-manipulated audience members would be wanting to climb up into the frame and help the bootleggers exact vengeance. When it comes, it is desired that the showdown be viewed as not only satisfying but something grand and gloriously impressive, an event worthy of being remembered with appreciation. Reinforcing their uncanny, legendary indestructibility, this laudably-loyal band of moonshine-making brothers are the ones who have rightly and intrepidly liberated Franklin County from this vile, disdainful outsider's wildly-unbridled oppression. The film's posters state it succinctly: "When the law became corrupt, outlaws became heroes." After such an effort to make the Bondurants loom large, it is strange that the choice was made to undercut them in the film's coda. Hardy's Forrest is a commanding presence throughout, a hushed hulk predominantly emitting mere guttural utterances who is diffident with women and yet also powerful, intimidating and seemingly indestructible. The reality, of course, is that he is mortal like everyone else, but making that point as *Lawless* ends seems counterproductive to its nearly two-hour endeavor to add luster to a legend.

Unfortunately, *Lawless* also has a fundamental problem from the start. Like Matt Bondurant's book, much of the film deals with Jack's straining to impress, yearning to command respect like his older, bolder brothers. He starts out as a boy derisively laughed at by Forrest and Howard because he has too much heart and not enough nerve to slay a hog. Years later, when Rakes stingingly refers to Jack as "the runt of the litter" while beating him severely, one notes how the young man warns of his brothers' future vengeance instead of his own. Enthralled and exhilarated upon seeing big shot Chicago gangster Floyd Banner (a regrettably-underused Gary Oldman) brazenly terminate someone with a Tommy gun in the middle of town in broad daylight, Jack emulates the feared man's style in striving to win over Bertha (Mia Wasikowska), a pious Dunkard minister's daughter whose strait-laced demeanor he is gradually able to loosen. (LaBeouf and Wasikowska have precious little palpable chemistry.) During the film's climactic confrontation, as Jack strides across a covered bridge to fire upon Rakes, it is as if he is crossing over into manhood, no longer that kid who was too reticent when something needed to be killed. The trouble is that every time *Lawless* predominantly focuses on overeager Jack's coming of age, one's interest in the proceedings tends to go away. The film keeps becoming listless whenever it veers away from what is gripping and toward what comparatively seems so much more mundane. (Another thing not able to be sustained throughout are the accents.) Compared to Hardy, who magnetically draws viewers in with his intense underplaying, and Pearce, who fascinatingly bursts forth in borderline over-the-top fashion, LaBeouf too often seems akin to the sepia-colored background in shots dominated by alluring Maggie in her vibrantly-colorful dresses. (Incidentally, even though Chastain is nude in one scene, her character is unfortunately never as satisfactorily fleshed-out.)

There is much more beauty to behold in *Lawless* beyond Chastain, such as the snowflakes drifting down out of a night's sky that are captured with commendable skill by French cinematographer Benoit Delhomme. Kudos must also go to production designer Chris Kennedy and costume designer Margot Wilson for their work to evoke period and place. Originally there was a prologue montage that attempted to connect the present to past, comparing the U.S.. government's continued war on drugs and the county's current economic downturn to Prohibition and the Great Depression. While this was decided to be too heavy-handed, an effort was made to suggest these correlations through music, such as having eighty-five-year-old bluegrass legend Ralph Stanley sing the Velvet Underground's "White Light/White Heat" so that a composition about methamphetamines seems as if it was written many years ago about moonshine. Such songs were chosen by rocker Nick Cave before he even wrote the score and screenplay for *Lawless*, the second script that the Bad Seeds frontman has penned for a film directed by long-time friend and fellow Aussie John Hillcoat. The other was for *The Proposition* (2005), a memorable Down Under Western which also pits less-than-law-abiding brothers against a lawman determined to succeed. Despite its impressive cast, this collaboration that Hillcoat enjoyed calling his "Wangster" (a combination of the Western and gangster genres) is nowhere near as noteworthy. It unquestionably falls woefully short of *Bonnie and Clyde* (1967), which the director said was his greatest cinematic influence for this production. The film earned $37 million and garnered mixed reviews. Publicity material for the film crowed that the Bondurants and other moonshine-manufacturing hill folk "helped build the American

Dream," and LaBeouf enthused that "the bootlegger was the superhero of that period." With Rakes being not only such a weird and dastardly dandy here but also from that mean metropolis on Lake Michigan, the same sinister site responsible for unsavory Bannister and the unspeakable horrors from which Maggie has fled in search of pastoral peacefulness, a clear-cut contrast has been drawn between urban depravity and the admirable fundamental righteousness of struggling but ever-stalwart country dwellers like the Bondurants. It is all about as subtle as the taste of white lightning.

David L. Boxerbaum

CREDITS

Forrest Bondurant: Thomas Hardy
Howard Bondurant: Jason Clarke
Jack Bondurant: Shia LaBeouf
Special Agent Charlie Rakes: Guy Pearce
Maggie Beauford: Jessica Chastain
Bertha Minnix: Mia Wasikowska
Floyd Banner: Gary Oldman
Gummy Walsh: Noah Taylor
Origin: United States
Language: English
Released: 2012
Production: Douglas Wick, Michael Benaroya, Megan Ellison, Lucy Fisher; Pie Films Inc., Red Wagon Productions, Benaroya Pictures; released by Weinstein Company L.L.C.
Directed by: John Hillcoat
Written by: Nick Cave
Cinematography by: Benoit Delhomme
Music by: Nick Cave; Warren Ellis
Sound: Christopher Eakins, Robert Jackson
Editing: Dylan Tichenor
Costumes: Margot Wilson
Production Design: Chris Kennedy
MPAA rating: R
Running time: 115 minutes

REVIEWS

Abele, Robert. *Los Angeles Times.* August 29, 2012.
Corliss, Richard. *Time.* August 11, 2012.
Ebert, Roger. *Chicago Sun-Times.* August 29, 2012.
Gleiberman, Owen. *Entertainment Weekly.* August 29, 2012.
Lane, Anthony. *New Yorker.* August 27, 2012.
Phillips, Michael. *Chicago Tribune.* August 28, 2012.
Puig, Claudia. *USA Today.* August 29, 2012.
Rooney, David. *Hollywood Reporter.* August 11, 2012.
Scott, A. O. *New York Times.* August 28, 2012.
Travers, Peter. *Rolling Stone.* August 30, 2012.

TRIVIA

Tom Hardy's character was originally supposed to be slimmer but Hardy had to bulk up for his role in *The Dark Knight Rises*.

LES MISERABLES

The dream lives.
—Movie tagline

Fight. Dream. Hope. Love.
—Movie tagline

The dream lives this Christmas.
—Movie tagline

Box Office: $146.9 million

Based on the 1862 novel by Victor Hugo, the musical version of *Les Miserables* was first launched as a short-run French language show in 1980, only to be revived as a full-length English speaking musical on Broadway in 1985. It became a worldwide phenomenon and currently boasts of being the longest-running musical ever. The idea of making it into a film has been around almost since day one. After all, the novel has been filmed many times with solid success and the songs the musical version brings to the table are so strong that a little competent direction and even a moderately talented group of actor/singers should have been able to bring it to life onscreen. Yet this all-star, lavishly-mounted movie version of *Les Miserables* the musical suffers from a myriad of problems. Miscasting and even a few missed notes keep it from reaching the dizzying heights the show continually reaches for, and, worst of all, director Tom Hooper is only occasionally up to the challenge of balancing the story's need for scope and intimacy. What ends up on-screen is too long and not a little boring at times, a shame given the film's ability to maintain much of the inherent strength in its powerhouse musical numbers.

In 1815, Frenchman Jean Valjean (Hugh Jackman) is released on parole after five years hard labor for stealing bread and fourteen years for trying to escape. Jean, aka Prisoner 24601, is sternly cautioned by his overseer, Inspector Javert (Russell Crowe), to live under the onerous terms of his release despite the fact that no matter where Valjean turns for work he is beaten and vilified as a convict. Starving, he shows up on the steps of a church where the local Bishop (Colm Wilkinson) feeds and shelters him. Unmoved, Valjean rises in the middle of the night to steal the silver from the church only to be caught on the run by the police. Lying to the police, the Bishop insists the silver was a gift, which humbles Valjean so that he pledges to live a better life, and, within eight years, elevates himself, under a false name, to the position of mayor of a small town, Montreuil-sur-Mer, where he also owns a factory which employs poor indigent women. When one of his workers, Fantine (Anne Hathaway) is unjustly fired and forced into prostitution to be able to send money to her illegitimate daughter, Valjean realizes he had missed an opportunity to help her and takes her to a local hospital. But by now Javert has arrested an innocent man and accused him of being AWOL Prisoner 24601 and Valjean realizes that he must confess his true identity. Rushing to the court he makes a quick confession, then dives back to Fantine's dying bed to pledge he will find and care for her daughter Cosette. Javert arrives and the two embark on a fierce battle as Valjean vainly cries for the time he needs to ensure the safety of the child. Narrowly escaping, Valjean makes his way to the Thenardiers Inn and bargains the child away from the two slimy innkeepers (Sacha Baron Cohen and Helena Bonham Carter) setting off for parts unknown to make yet another new life for himself and his new family.

Ten years later, the country is deeply divided by class and on the brink of civil war as a group of young would-be revolutionaries prepare a revolt meant to inspire the masses. One of those young men, Marius (Eddie Redmayne) meets and falls immediately in love with the older Cosette (Amanda Seyfried) just as she and Valjean are discovered yet again by Javert and preparing to leave. Unaware that his own best friend, the beautiful Eponine (Samantha Barks), daughter of the Thenadiers, is in love with him, he pursues and woos Cosette only to be drawn, along with Javert and Valjean into the revolt. As characters sacrifice themselves for one another, for country and for love, the grand narrative of judgment, forgiveness and redemption that has carried *Les Miserables* through many mediums reveals itself.

It was decided early on that, rather than have the actors dub their singing later in studio, they would be recorded during the actual shooting. The technique produces a very present effect making it impossible to separate the singing from the acting when evaluating the overall effectiveness of individual performances. Most of the cast shines. Hugh Jackman, an accomplished Broadway performer, does fine, although at times he seems a tiny bit out of his vocal range. Even then, his portrayal is spot-on, lending Jean Valjean a sense of desperation, frustration, and nobility.

On the other hand, Russell Crowe is clearly out of his musical depth as Inspector Javert. He strains during almost every scene simply to hit the notes his part demands and the resulting vocal performance is weak, airy, and anything but Javert-like. Worse yet, the strain of having to sing seems to have stilted his performance significantly. Viewers are likely to notice him thinking his choices through rather than simply being in the moment.

Anne Hathaway wrenches every bit of pathos from the part of Fantine and her version of "I Dreamed A Dream," one of *Les Miserables* signature tunes, is definitive, full of wistful disillusionment, bitterness, and despair. Some will accuse her of chewing the scenery but they are ignoring the way *Les Miserables* is written.

Of the remaining cast members, Eddie Redmayne, best known for his role in last year's exemplary historical horror film *Black Death* (2011) and co-starring with Michelle Williams in *My Week with Marilyn* (2011), has the strongest voice. His rich baritone wafts through the part of Marius in the most natural way possible, working hand in hand with his special gift for emotional transparency to create the perfect wide-eyed youth in love. Samantha Barks as Eponine is simply perfect. Sacha Baron Cohen and Helena Bonham Carter are a delight as Mr. and Mrs. Thenardier, bouncing decadently through roles that are quite similar in many ways to those they assayed in Tim Burton's version of *Sweeney Todd: The Demon Barber of Fleet Street* (2007). Lastly, it was heartening to see the important part of the Bishop of Digne who frees Jean Valjean at the beginning of the film played by none other than Colm Wilkinson, who originated the role of Jean Valjean on Broadway.

But the casting of Javert aside, the film suffers much through the frenetic third act. Instead of gelling together, things feel episodic and forced. This is a real difficulty with the source material provided by the original stage version which is over reliant, in general, on the audience filling in the blanks as it lopes from, admittedly stunning song to song. But whatever the perils of adaptation, the problems of Tom Hooper's approach to direction must also be noted. For all of the film's endless close-ups that draw viewers into the singing, it lacks a certain intimacy, a sense of closeness to the characters as something other than vehicles for the spectacle that Hooper seems bent on showcasing. The end result seems like a reaction to finally being turned loose from the drawing room limitations of *The King's Speech* (2010). Unforgettable musical numbers are pulled off with some panache here but in the main *Les Miserables* suffers from a variety of visual ills despite stunning art direction. Tops of heads are cut off in some shots, and the cinema verite stylings of scenes on location fail to mesh with the overt theatricality of other sequences creating a stylistic hodge-podge.

Les Miserables has always been at its strongest in the way it plugs tiny people into the vast movement of history. In the end, it is a tale about the hope for a better world and the responsibility of those who hear it share in the work of bringing that about. Many talented people came together to build a *Les Miserables* for the screen but the result is just not revolutionary enough.

Dave Canfield

CREDITS

Jean Valjean: Hugh Jackman
Javert: Russell Crowe
Fantine: Anne Hathaway
Cosette: Amanda Seyfried
Thenardier: Sacha Baron Cohen
Madame Thenardier: Helena Bonham Carter
Marius: Eddie Redmayne
Young Cosette: Isabelle Allen
Origin: United Kingdom
Language: English
Released: 2012
Production: Tim Bevan, Eric Fellner, Debra Hayward, Cameron Mackintosh; Working Title Films; released by Universal Pictures Inc.
Directed by: Tom Hooper
Written by: William Nicholson
Cinematography by: Danny Cohen
Music by: Claude-Michel Schonberg
Sound: Lee Walpole; John Warhurst
Music Supervisor: Becky Bentham
Editing: Chris Dickens; Melanie Oliver
Art Direction: Grant Armstrong
Costumes: Paco Delgado
Production Design: Eve Stewart
MPAA rating: PG-13
Running time: 157 minutes

REVIEWS

Baird, Kirk. *Toledo Blade.* December 24, 2012.
Chang, Justin. *Variety.* December 6, 2012.
D'Souza, Karen. *San Jose Mercury News.* December 12, 2012.
Dargis, Manhola. *New York Times.* December 25, 2012.
Edelstein, David. *New York Magazine.* December 10, 2012.
Guzman, Rafer. *Newsday.* December 24, 2012.
Lacey, Liam. *Globe and Mail.* December 21, 2012.
Lumenick, Lou. *New York Post.* December 20, 2012.
Robinson, Tasha. *AV Club.* December 24, 2012.
Turan, Kenneth. *Los Angeles Times.* December 25, 2012.

QUOTES

Fantine: "I had a dream my life would be so different from this hell I'm living!"

TRIVIA

Paul Bettany was considered for the role of Inspector Javert before Russell Crowe was cast.

AWARDS

Oscars 2012: Actress—Supporting (Hathaway), Makeup, Sound

British Acad. 2012: Actress—Supporting (Hathaway), Makeup, Production Design, Sound

Golden Globes 2013: Actor—Mus./Comedy (Jackman), Actress—Supporting (Hathaway), Film—Mus./Comedy

Screen Actors Guild 2012: Actress—Supporting (Hathaway)

Nominations:

Oscars 2012: Actor (Jackman), Costume Des., Film, Production Design, Song ("Suddenly")

British Acad. 2012: Actor (Jackman), Cinematog., Costume Des., Film

Directors Guild 2012: Director (Hooper)

Golden Globes 2013: Song ("Suddenly")

Screen Actors Guild 2012: Actor (Jackman), Cast

LIBERAL ARTS

Sometimes students make the best teachers.
—Movie tagline

Box Office: $327,345

In very different ways, two films released in September 2012 identify the specific sensations of being a particular age at a particular time in a particular place.

In writer-director Stephen Chbosky's largely effective adaptation of his 1999 novel *The Perks of Being a Wallflower,* the casting of now-twenty-year-old Logan Lerman as a high school freshman greatly undermines that character's challenges and growth. Lerman does not look the part of a shy teenager, who will experience a great deal of physical and emotional transformations before turning twenty. Certainly it is nothing new to cast an actor a few years older than a character, but in this case, young Charlie never seems as much of a vulnerable wallflower as he should as a result of the casting. On the other hand, *Liberal Arts,* writer/director Josh Radnor's funny, insightful reflection on college and life after college, taps precisely into both the collegiate mentality and the point of view of a man in his mid-30s who longs for the old, campus days of studying romantic literature and engaging in intellectual conversations until jaws grow sore.

Radnor stars as 35-year-old Jesse, who is less than fulfilled by his job as an admissions officer for a New York university. The way he tells prospective students that they could have the greatest city in the world as a

backdrop suggests he does not really mean it. Perhaps this is because of his routine job or relationship that has recently come to an end; regardless, Jesse is not happy, so he embraces the chance to return to his Ohio alma mater when his favored former professor Hoberg (Richard Jenkins) calls and invites Jesse to a retirement dinner on campus. There, Jesse takes in the setting like a man given chocolate for the first time in years. He lies in the grass. He walks with the energy of an adult who feels at home again. He asks "How are you?" to students, who look back at him as if to say, "Who is this old guy, and what is he so happy about?"

So much of *Liberal Arts* zeroes in on the notion of perspective—both in the challenge of appreciating a time to think and laugh and love without the pressures of a mortgage or a full-time job as well as the danger of romanticizing the past or attempting to transform adulthood into a collegiate state of mind. These issues play out with great warmth and poignancy in Jesse's relationship with 19-year-old sophomore Zibby (Elizabeth Olsen). She is not written as a contrived fantasy girl, and Olsen does not play her as one. Zibby is simply a girl eager to seem older than her age and smart enough to pull it off. Fortunately, Radnor does not craft her as overly intellectual, though; Zibby's fondness for an un-challenging series of novels about vampires (the books, clearly meant to reference Stephenie Meyer's *Twilight* series, have amusingly redundant titles like "Solar Sun" and "Lunar Moon") plays a key role in Jesse coming to terms with his own judgmental tendencies. He also childishly still believes that a person's pop culture tastes speak louder than their character while trying, consciously or subconsciously, to find fault with a young girl who deep down makes him uncomfortable, even as they enjoy an instant ease and rapport soon after meeting during Jesse's trip back to school.

Radnor shot *Liberal Arts* at his own alma mater, Kenyon College, and obviously possesses a great respect for the academic pursuits of youth. He also effectively confronts some of the issues plaguing Ted Mosby, his character on *How I Met Your Mother,* with an honesty about the downsides of Jesse spending so much time in his own head. Like Ted, he feels continually off balance in work and love, but Jesse perceives one particular place as the location of his greatest happiness. It is a view that prevents him from moving forward, just as professor Hoberg struggles to confront the next step of his life, futilely begging his superior for a few more years on the job. His fear of returning to the outside world recalls that of paroled inmate Brooks Hatlen (James Whitmore) in *The Shawshank Redemption,* shortly before he takes his own life.

Where his filmmaking debut *Happythankyoumoreplease* (2011) boiled down to frustratingly simple notions of, "Anyone who wants to be happy should just be happy!" *Liberal Arts* reflects on a far more complicated version of contentment. Sure, Nat (Zac Efron), an amusing hippie Jesse befriends on campus, seems at peace with himself and the world. Yet he also appears to have few ambitions outside of living on his own, laid-back wave of positivity. Jesse wants to feel how he felt in college, inspired by his British romantic literature professor (Allison Janney) and free to wallow in the cognitive alleys of his mind, either with a classmate or alone with a book. When he meets Zibby, their connection at first suggests a link to the past that could translate to the present. Yet his hilarious, on-paper evaluation of their age difference suggests a truth he must admit to himself: In a few years, 50-year-old Jesse and 34-year-old Zibby may be right for each other. By the time they are 87 and 71, the difference is negligible. Now, Jesse cannot force himself to feel right about the different places he and Zibby are in their lives no matter how much they enjoy each other's company. Heck, having to worry about Zibby's roommate coming in only heightens Jesse's unease about being on Zibby's bed. He delights in discovering a new appreciation for classical music through her, but there is sadness in it too, the expressly collegiate concept of sharing mixtapes and fueling infatuations over chuckles on the quad or a beer in a red plastic cup. Meanwhile, Jesse sees some of himself—perhaps in both the college and current version of himself—in Dean (John Magaro), a moody, smart kid who desperately needs someone to help him stay afloat.

Change is not easy, especially as time passes by. Students become advisors. Camp counselors become professors. Children become adults, at least according to their birth certificate and calendar. This process rarely occurs without a bittersweet acceptance of the past being the past, however, made all the more confusing by the truth, as delivered by Hoberg, "Nobody feels like an adult; it's the world's dirty secret." Eventually, maybe some people feel settled into adulthood, without always sensing that young, uncertain confusion tapping on the shoulder. For anyone interested in that struggle, *Liberal Arts* plants a personal, thoughtful kiss on the formative years while saluting the future those years are meant to inform.

Matt Pais

CREDITS

Jesse: Josh Radnor
Zibby: Elizabeth Olsen
Peter: Richard Jenkins
Judith: Allison Janney
Ana: Elizabeth Reaser

Dean: John Magaro
Susan: Kate Burton
David: Robert Desiderio
Nat: Zac Efron
Origin: United States
Language: English
Released: 2012
Production: Brice Dal Farra, Claude Dal Farra, Jesse Hara, Lauren Munsch, Josh Radnor; IFC Films; released by Strategic Motion Ventures
Directed by: Josh Radnor
Written by: Josh Radnor
Cinematography by: Seamus Tierney
Music by: Ben Toth
Sound: Henry Auerbach
Music Supervisor: Andrew Gowan
Editing: Michael R. Miller
Art Direction: Scott Kuzio
Costumes: Deborah Newhall
Production Design: Jade Healy
MPAA rating: PG-13
Running time: 97 minutes

REVIEWS

Burr, Ty. *Boston Globe*. September 20, 2012.
Chang, Justin. *Variety*. September 20, 2012.
Ebert, Roger. *Chicago Sun-Times*. September 20, 2012.
Edelstein, David. *New York Magazine*. September 20, 2012.
Morgenstern, Joe. *Wall Street Journal*. September 20, 2012.
Pols, Mary. *Time*. September 20, 2012.
Rodriguez, Rene. *Miami Herald*. September 20, 2012.
Phillips, Michael. *Chicago Tribune*. September 20, 2012.
Weber, Bill. *Slant Magazine*. September 20, 2012.
Zacharek, Stephanie. *Movieline*. September 20, 2012.

QUOTES

Zibby: "How can you hate something if you've never read it? I mean, isn't that like what repressive regimes do? You want to burn books you don't like?"

TRIVIA

The book Jesse discusses with Dean in the coffee house and hospital is David Foster Wallace's *Infinite Jest*.

LIFE OF PI

Box Office: $114.1 million

Ang Lee's *The Life of Pi* is based on a novel by Yann Martel, a novel many considered to be unfilmable. The center of the film is a survivalist story, the kind that has been made before, but the ideas explored within the narrative as well as its somewhat ambiguous ending are deeper and more meaningful than the usual adventure fare tends to offer. The story of a boy trapped on a boat with a Bengal tiger seems a natural place to start for a thrilling tale of survival and friendship, but when religion, surrealism and deep introspection come into the fray, it hardly seems like the recipe for a big studio picture. But Martel's novel reached many readers, as did the equally (if not more) complex *Cloud Atlas* by David Mitchell, released just a month prior. One has to imagine that those who embraced Martel's fiction did so not just because of the inherently exciting storyline, but also because of the deeper questions explored by the story's protagonist.

The story is told in flashback by a man named Pi Patel (played as an older man by Irrfan Khan). He tells his story to a novelist who has been told by others that Pi's story is so good, it will make him believe in God. Pi now lives in Montreal, but the story begins in India when he was eleven. His father (Adil Hussain) named him after a swimming pool, but because his first full name is Piscine (often pronounced "pissing"), he gets mercilessly teased. He instead refers to himself as Pi for his unique ability to write the endless mathematical number. His family owns a zoo and they appear perplexed by Pi's interest in religion. Not any particular religion, but all religions. He considers himself a Catholic Hindu. "I feel guilty in front of hundreds of Gods, not just one." His father suggests that "religion is darkness" and that science and reason carries more fulfillment.

Years later, when Pi is a teenager (now played by Suraj Sharma), the family faces financial hardships and the father decides to move the zoo to Canada. Not at all pleased with the idea of leaving his friends and the life he has always known, Pi joins his parents and his brother Ravi (Vibish Sivakumar) for a treacherous journey by ship as all the caged animals must be transported from India to Montreal. One night, while traveling through the Marianas Trench, a storm rages and causes the boat to capsize, killing almost every human and animal on board. Miraculously, Pi makes it onto a lifeboat, along with a zebra and (he later finds out), a hyena, an orangutan and, of course, the Bengal tiger. Luckily, the boat is loaded with such handy tools as extra oars, life jackets, food, rope and other such amenities that will aid in his survival.

But he still has a tiger and a hyena to worry about. Pi, for the most part, keeps himself on the other side of the boat from the other animals who luckily have trouble navigating the giant tarp that covers his side. The other three animals eventually do themselves in, but the tiger remains at the top of the food chain and soon only he

and Pi remain. Due to a clerical error at the zoo, the tiger has been given the name Richard Parker. Pi and Richard Parker, on the surface, see themselves as each other's possible last meal, but Pi must somehow overcome his biggest fears and to train the tiger not to eat him so they can coexist in this predicament.

Pi and Richard Parker are not always alone, of course. The ocean offers plenty of food and natural wonders to fill the days and nights. Pi reads from a survival manual that gives tips on how to pass the time. He constructs a makeshift raft tethered to the boat by a rope, often used as a means of escape when the tiger gets too vicious. There are also great sights of whales, dolphins, flying fish and a horizon that seems to have no line. Occasional moments of hope and rescue are soon thwarted until there is nothing left to do but to tend to the tiger and its needs.

The journey is a long one and it is pretty much a one-man show for Sharma, much in the same way Tom Hanks singlehandedly commanded the narrative in *Cast Away* (2000). Both go through the same transformation as the feeling of isolation and malnourishment take its toll on their physical, emotional and spiritual well-being. Sharma has the extra task of acting alongside a dangerous predator that actually never existed on the set (aside from a few shots). Sharma gives a strong, believable performance that is never less than engaging and, at times, heartbreaking. The manifestation of the tiger, likewise, always looks convincing and their scenes together flow seamlessly.

But Lee has such command over the medium as a storyteller that he is able to once again keep the viewer for looking at the cracks in the seams. Just as he did with *Crouching Tiger, Hidden Dragon* (2000), Lee never lets the high concept get in the way of the characters and the story. Many fanciful elements come into play once the story centers entirely on Pi and Richard Parker. Lee often employs overhead shots of the boat lying still in the water as the sky's reflection in the water fills the screen. Lee has always given into these still moments and long silences that they have almost become trademarks of his. Lee does not intend to always keep the audience on edge. The beauty of this film comes not just from the relationship between the boy and the tiger, but in the natural wonders around them, some merciless, some ethereal.

This also marks the first time Lee has employed 3-D and he does so with the same artistry and restraint Martin Scorsese did a year prior with *Hugo* (2011). Lee does not let every single choice become dictated by the format. The movie works well enough in 2-D. But there are moments when Lee and cinematographer Claudio Miranda adjust the aspect ratio so that the objects or creatures flying toward the audience do so in a way that they look as though they really are flying into the theater. It has to be seen to be appreciated and the moments are few and far between, but it remains a testament to Lee's adventurous filmmaking spirit to try and play with the conventions and form of commercial filmmaking, something he has not fully attempted since his underappreciated *Hulk* (2003).

The film is far from perfect. It would have been wiser to cut back on the voiceover narration and there is a feeling of redundancy to it once the story centers around the boy, the tiger and the hallucinatory images of being lost at sea. The monotony is thankfully broken at just the right time, however, as the journey takes Pi and Richard Parker to an island that appears to be a kind of savior, but eventually reveals itself to be a dead end in more ways than one. But much like *Cast Away*, there occurs a jarring, awkward narrative shift toward the third act once the camera cuts away from the ocean and back into present day (or normal life).

Life of Pi had many appreciators (mostly people who read the novel), but it also had serious detractors, many of whom hated the ending, one that challenges viewers to question everything they had just seen. But for this character, who is often preoccupied with religion, folklore and philosophy, his ability to conjure up an alternative narrative makes perfect sense. In order to relate a fantastical story to a new pair of ears, there needs to be consideration for their ability to take in such an absurd story. It may be frustrating to learn that other angles and meanings exist within this storyline, but is that not the basis for most religious stories and folklore? As his father taught him, there must be room in life for science and reason. Pi simply maintains that balance between the two and *Life of Pi* makes the case that stories such as this carry more weight when applied to real-life lessons and situations, whether they actually happen or not.

Collin Souter

CREDITS

Pi Patel: Suraj Sharma
Adult Pi: Irrfan Khan
Gita Patel: Tabu
Santosh Patel: Adil Hussain
Writer: Rafe Spall
Pi (11/12 years): Ayush Tandon
Origin: United States
Language: English
Released: 2012
Production: Gil Netter, David Womark, Ang Lee; Fox 2000 Pictures, Dune Entertainment; released by Fox 2000 Pictures

Directed by: Ang Lee
Written by: David Magee
Cinematography by: Claudio Miranda
Music by: Mychael Danna
Sound: Philip Stockton; Eugene Gearty
Editing: Tim Squyres
Costumes: Arjun Bhasin
Production Design: David Gropman
MPAA rating: PG
Running time: 127 minutes

REVIEWS

Ebert, Roger. *Chicago Sun-Times.* November 21, 2012.
LaSalle, Mick. *San Francisco Chronicle.* November 21, 2012.
Long, Tom. *Detroit News.* November 21, 2012.
Morgenstern, Joe. *Wall Street Journal.* November 22, 2012.
Neumaier, Joe. *New York Daily News.* November 21, 2012.
O'Hehir, Andrew. *Salon.com.* November 19, 2012.
Schager, Nick. *Village Voice.* November 20, 2012.
Schwarzbaum, Lisa. *Entertainment Weekly.* November 21, 2012.
Scott, A. O. *New York Times.* November 20, 2012.
Stevens, Dana. *Slate.* November 21, 2012.

QUOTES

Santosh Patel: "You think tiger is your friend, he is an animal, not a playmate."
Pi Patel: "Animals have souls. I have seen it in their eyes."

TRIVIA

At one point M. Night Shyamalan was attached to write and direct the film.

AWARDS

Oscars 2012: Cinematog., Orig. Score, Visual FX
British Acad. 2012: Cinematog., Visual FX
Directors Guild 2012: Director (Lee)
Golden Globes 2013: Orig. Score
Nominations:
Oscars 2012: Adapt. Screenplay, Director (Lee), Film, Film Editing, Production Design, Song ("Pi's Lullaby"), Sound, Sound FX Editing
British Acad. 2012: Adapt. Screenplay, Director (Lee), Film, Film Editing, Orig. Score, Production Design, Sound
Golden Globes 2013: Film—Drama
Writers Guild 2012: Adapt. Screenplay

LINCOLN

Box Office: $178.9 million

Reverently placed into many an album in 1865 was a carte de visite entitled "The Apotheosis of Washington

& Lincoln," which depicts the supremely-esteemed Father of Our Country gratefully embracing its newly-martyred savior and approvingly bestowing upon him a halo wreath after the latter's ascension through the clouds to rarified air. The idolatrous image is pretty lofty stuff, and while it appears that the slain, sublimely-benevolent, and eloquent, secular saint has come to be more beloved than even the "Indispensible Man" of the War for Independence and precedent-setting first president, he still can sometimes seem rather elevated beyond one's reach. Sitting on high in his hallowed and respectfully-hushed memorial with the far-off look known to have often crossed the onerously-burdened man's careworn face in life, this colossal, immaculately-white striver for "a new birth of freedom" who felt "malice toward none" and "charity for all" appears as if he is still engaged in righteous rumination. Nevertheless, what was left long ago upon a pillow in the Petersen House all-too-evidently proved that this icon had been a magnificent but mortal man of flesh and blood, and one's appreciation of him is anything but diminished when he is assessed as such. With the late president seemingly resurrected by an awe-inspiring Daniel Day-Lewis, lifelike complexity permits an unusual level of accessibility during most of Steven Spielberg's laudable *Lincoln,* one of the best pictures of 2012.

Although the former rail-splitter does not surprise here by heroically wielding designed-to-be-deadly axes in nimble ninja fashion as in this year's made-up mashup *Abraham Lincoln: Vampire Hunter* (2012), the formidable but fact-based finesse with which Honest Abe bests his opposition in *Lincoln* seemed almost as startlingly incongruous to what most people know of the man. Focusing on the first months of 1865 that would be the last of both his presidency and his life, this film enlightened those in the dark about the consummate, pragmatic craftiness of this idealist who was also an inveterate lover of the rough-and-tumble political process. While unquestionably upright, Lincoln was not above stooping to the strategic use of somewhat fishy tactics, such as what he fascinatingly does to reel in enough legislative support to pass a virtuous constitutional amendment abolishing villainous slavery.

As his bold 1863 Emancipation Proclamation that freed slaves within the rebelling states was a wartime measure that might be challenged by Southerners and counteracted in the courts once fighting ceased and Reconstruction began, Lincoln urgently aimed to prevent that possibility by at long last achieving all-encompassing, Constitutionally-cemented abolition for the country as a whole—before it became whole again. While the Senate had given its approval to the proposed Thirteenth Amendment, it was truly a House divided, with Lincoln's progressively-inclined fellow Republicans

and their more conservative Democratic counterparts embroiled in a decidedly-uncivil war of words on the touchy subject, featuring the lobbing of highly acerbic (and just as amusing) insults and the shooting of deliciously-contemptuous looks. While some members of his own Cabinet, as well as Lincoln's wife Mary (an appropriately potent and pained Sally Field), could not see how this rushed ramrodding-through of ratification could possibly succeed and advised against it, an unshakably-resolved Lincoln kept his eye fixedly on the prize. His expressed determination to press on in the face of the political firestorm that will surely result seems to be visually represented by a shot of him concurrently poking purposefully at burning logs in the fireplace, which then flare up.

This prodding may be seen as having further meaning, however, for if Lincoln's objective cannot be accomplished solely by direct appeals to what he called "the better angels of our nature" in his second inaugural address, he would approve the use of more circumspect and somewhat suspect methods. Secretary of State William Seward (a perfectly-cast David Strathairn), who was once a condescending doubter but now a close coworker and loyal confidant, surreptitiously retains the services of a tricky triumvirate (John Hawkes, Tim Blake Nelson, and a delightfully-pungent James Spader) for "shady work" that, as a prudent Seward emphasizes, should be "nothing strictly illegal." They mainly try to tantalizingly dangle patronage positions in front of imminently-departing lame duck Democrats to see if they can be lured into biting the bait and in turn be on the hook to vote for the amendment. Besides all the partisan bickering, the debatable methods of these 19th Century lobbyists is certainly relatable.

As both president and commander-in-chief, Lincoln has been striving so strenuously to end the killing that it has aged him noticeably, and he is palpably haunted by sights like one scene's battlefield covered with drifts of the dead. Nevertheless, he grapples (as does the audience) with what seems to be an unavoidable, potently distressing necessity: nothing can be done to finally stop the already-staggering corpse count from rising until after the number of "ayes" for this amendment does the same and can be adopted before a reabsorbed South has the chance to thwart it—perhaps permanently. Thus, when Confederate peace negotiators head for Washington before the vote, Lincoln telegraphs that they are to be delayed en route until further notice. When rumors that such a party is on the way are used by opponents to try and indefinitely postpone voting, the former circuit lawyer sends slickly-composed word that he knows of no such group currently either in Washington or imminently arriving. Thus, after a vote that is suspenseful despite viewers' knowledge of the outcome, abolition is attained thanks to an eye-opening kind of acumen exhibited by Artful Abe.

Also on display but much better known to most moviegoers is the painstaking skillfulness of Day-Lewis, who is so thoroughly convincing (in a role previously set to be played by Liam Neeson) that it quickly seems as if one's ticket had been for a seat in a time machine instead of a movie theater. Especially in profile, the degree of verisimilitude is quite striking, capable of eliciting a strange yet unmistakable sense of gratitude in Lincoln lovers who felt as if they had been granted the opportunity to actually spend time in his presence. The actor's alchemy came up with the reedy tenor voice that contemporary "earwitness accounts" uniformly describe. Day-Lewis also adopts Lincoln's stooped posture and the awkward walk of this sure-footed leader. Quite clearly conveyed is how Lincoln could so often be all alone with his thoughts in a room full of people, often deliberately weighing the weightiest of matters and wisely endeavoring to consider things from every viewpoint and not just his own. Moviegoers could feel Lincoln's melancholic world-weariness born of bearing the horrible heft of the load that is ceaselessly upon him, which includes his enduring grief over the loss of idolized, precocious son Willie in 1862, the fear of losing a third child (Edward had died back in 1850) when eldest boy Robert (Joseph Gordon-Levitt) strains to leave his books behind for battle, and the mercurialness of Mary, who is sometimes a helpmate and other times a profoundly-wounded, wild hellcat. (The scene in which what has been tamped down flares up between husband and wife, accentuated by an equally-tempestuous thunderstorm, seems stagy but, sadly, is most likely not overdone.) One witnesses Lincoln's well-tempered steel ("I am the President of the United States, clothed in immense power," he bellows, "You will procure me these votes!") as well as the hushed, gentle sweetness with which he curls up next to sleeping youngest son Tad (Gulliver McGrath) and lovingly caresses the lad's locks. Last but certainly not least, there is Lincoln's characteristic incessant scanning of his memory for any anecdote that might help get across a point or break a situation's—or his own—tenseness. (It is quite humorous to watch Bruce McGill's Secretary of War Edwin Stanton roll his eyes and later sputteringly flee from hearing yet another story.) Day-Lewis's multifaceted metamorphosis is endlessly Oscar-worthy.

Also Academy Award bait is Tommy Lee Jones' flame-throwing fulminator Thaddeus Stevens, a Radical Republican who comes to agree that it will be smart (if quite a strain) to douse his fiery assertions of complete equality of the races in order to prevent the scaring-off of support specific to the amendment. At least part of reason for his zeal is revealed when he presents the of-ficial copy of the approved legislation to the mulatto housekeeper (S. Epatha Merkerson) who is actually the longtime love of his life, listening with evident satisfaction as she reads it aloud from the other side of their bed.

Additional praise is particularly due for cinematographer Janusz Kaminski, composer John Williams, and production designer Rick Carter. Made on a budget of $65 million, *Lincoln* grossed well at the box office and justly received both widespread critical acclaim (especially for Day-Lewis) and numerous nominations. It is based in part on Pulitzer Prize-winning historian Doris Kearns Goodwin's insightful 2005 bestseller *Team of Rivals: The Political Genius of Abraham Lincoln*, and is a fleshed-out portion of Pulitzer-winning playwright Anthony Kushner's original unwieldy, whole-life-encompassing draft that Spielberg singled out as particularly engrossing, freshly-illuminating, and inspiring. For the most part, he was correct. (At times, the two-and-half-hour production drags a little.) As Ty Burr of *The Boston Globe* wrote, "It's possible you may think *Lincoln* is too talky, too full of characters and ideas, too taxing to our Twitter-pated attention span. Consider, then, that it may not be the movie that's unworthy of your time. You may not be worthy of it." Somewhat testy; rather true.

One thing many thought *Lincoln* does indeed have in excess are moments that seem like its last: the film's final fade really should have followed an eerie extended view of the president tramping down a White House hall toward tragedy at Ford's Theatre that elicits a mounting urge to protectively grab him back before it is too late. What also could not be held back during what actually ends the film is sentimental Spielberg's urge to make tears well up in viewers' eyes amidst images that unabashedly and all-too-fervently foist Lincoln up for adoration. After a glimpse of his being pronounced dead, an image of the president speaks out from within a bedside candle-turned-eternal-flame, followed still further by the sight of this visionary, murdered on Good Friday, standing at the conclusion of his second inaugural address with arms extended like Jesus on the cross. Since Spielberg repeatedly insisted that he aimed to afford access to a complex, deeply human man rather than endeavor to lift him up for some glorious hero-worship, it seems that the otherwise estimable film joins its real-life namesake in coming to an unfortunate end.

David L. Boxerbaum

CREDITS

Abrahm Lincoln: Daniel Day-Lewis
Mary Todd Lincoln: Sally Field
William Seward: David Strathairn

Robert Todd Lincoln: Joseph Gordon-Levitt
Preston Blair: Hal Holbrook
Thaddeus Stevens: Tommy Lee Jones
Robert Latham: John Hawkes
Alexander Stephens: Jackie Earle Haley
Edwin Stanton: Bruce McGill
Richard Schell: Tim Blake Nelson
John Hay: Joseph Cross
Ulysses S. Grant: Jared Harris
Fernando Wood: Lee Pace
George Pendleton: Peter McRobbie
Tad Lincoln: Gulliver McGrath
Elizabeth Keckley: Gloria Reuben
John Nicolay: Jeremy Strong
George Yeaman: Michael Stuhlbarg
Asa Vintner Litton: Stephen Spinella
Clay Hutchins: Walton Goggins
Cpl. Ira Clark: David Oyelowo
Montgomery Blair: Byron Jennings
Elizabeth Blair Lee: Julie White
Sen. "Beanpole" Burton: Raynor Scheine
Judge John A. Campbell: Gregory Itzin
Lydia Smith: S. Epatha Merkerson
John Usher: Dakin Matthews
Origin: United States
Language: English
Released: 2012
Production: Kathleen Kennedy, Steven Spielberg; Amblin Entertainment; released by DreamWorks SKG
Directed by: Steven Spielberg
Written by: Tony Kushner
Cinematography by: Janusz Kaminski
Music by: John Williams
Sound: Richard Hymns
Music Supervisor: Alejandro de la Llosa
Editing: Michael Kahn
Art Direction: Curt Beech; David Crank; Leslie McDonald
Costumes: Joanna Johnston
Production Design: Rick Carter
MPAA rating: PG-13
Running time: 150 minutes

REVIEWS

Lane, Anthony. *New Yorker*. November 12, 2012.
McCarthy, Todd. *Hollywood Reporter*. November 2, 2012.
Morgenstern, Joe. *Wall Street Journal*. November 8, 2012.
Packham, Chris. *Village Voice*. November 7, 2012.
Phillips, Michael. *Chicago Tribune*. November 8, 2012.
Puig, Claudia. *USA Today*. November 8, 2012.
Rainer, Peter. *Christian Science Monitor*. November 9, 2012.
Scott, A. O. *New York Times*. November 8, 2012.
Travers, Peter. *Rolling Stone*. November 8, 2012.
Turan, Kenneth. *Los Angeles Times*. November 8, 2012.

QUOTES

Abraham Lincoln: "I can't listen to this anymore. I can't accomplish a goddamn thing of any worth until we cure ourselves of slavery and end this pestilential war! I wonder if any of you or anyone else knows it. I know! I need this! This amendment is that cure! We've stepped out upon the world stage now. Now! With the fate of human dignity in our hands. Blood's been spilled to afford us this moment now!"

TRIVIA

Once actor Daniel Day-Lewis decided on the voice that he would use as Lincoln, he sent an audiotape of it to director Steven Spielberg in a box with a skull and crossbones on it to ensure that only he would hear it.

AWARDS

Oscars 2012: Actor (Day-Lewis), Production Design
British Acad. 2012: Actor (Day-Lewis)
Golden Globes 2013: Actor—Drama (Day-Lewis)
Screen Actors Guild 2012: Actor (Day-Lewis), Actor—Supporting (Jones)

Nominations:

Oscars 2012: Actor—Supporting (Jones), Actress—Supporting (Field), Adapt. Screenplay, Cinematog., Costume Des., Director (Spielberg), Film, Film Editing, Orig. Score, Sound
British Acad. 2012: Actor—Supporting (Jones), Adapt. Screenplay, Cinematog., Costume Des., Film, Makeup, Orig. Score, Production Design
Directors Guild 2012: Director (Spielberg)
Golden Globes 2013: Actor—Supporting (Jones), Actress—Supporting (Field), Director (Spielberg), Film, Screenplay
Screen Actors Guild 2012: Actress—Supporting (Field), Cast
Writers Guild 2012: Adapt. Screenplay

A LITTLE BIT OF HEAVEN

Life starts now.
—Movie tagline

Box Office: $15,375

Kate Hudson burst out of the gate at a fairly young age. Since then, though, the flame of her career has flickered more than dazzlingly glowed. Certainly two pregnancies and motherhood cut into her productivity a bit. But Hudson's waning fortunes (she has not had a movie gross more than $100 million domestically since *How To Lose a Guy in 10 Days* [2003]) was not entirely a case of a voluntary surrender of the limelight. A string of wan, almost indistinguishable (and frequently barely mediocre, if that) romantic comedies sullied the eye-opening shine of Hudson's Academy Award-nominated turn in *Almost Famous* (2000), to the point that her name became virtually synonymous with humdrum.

A Little Bit of Heaven, then, is a step up for Hudson, and a small step in the right direction—even if the film did not get a fair shake at the box office. Though it lacks the depth and shaded personality of the thematically similar *50/50* (2011), it does offer up Hudson's most credible and charming work in years, and therefore connects as a slightly above-average dramedy of terminal life lessons. Shot in early 2010 under the title *Earthbound,* the movie opened in a few foreign territories in early 2011. Finally, more than a year later, *A Little Bit of Heaven* was given a quiet, cursory theatrical stateside release in early May by Millennium Entertainment, in only a couple cities and eleven total theaters. Peripatetic fans of the actress feeling burned by her last several big screen starring efforts would do well to track it down.

The film centers on Marley Corbett (Hudson), a young and beautiful New Orleans advertising executive who uses humor as a well-manicured hedge to help protect her from life's seriousness. After she is diagnosed with an aggressive and terminal form of colon cancer, however, the relationship-phobic Marley develops something of a crush on her doctor, Julian Goldstein (Gael Garcia Bernal), who harbors similar feelings. As she begins medical treatment to try to stem the encroachment of her disease, Marley leans on her best pal Sarah (Lucy Punch) and good friend and neighbor Peter (Romany Malco), the latter of whom half-jokingly secures her the services of Vinnie (Peter Dinklage), a rakish dwarf gigolo (and the film's namesake, actually) who dispenses surprising wisdom. More stress arrives for Marley via her mother Beverly (Kathy Bates), who moves in to help take care of her, and her married sister Renee (Rosemarie DeWitt), whose pregnancy is a looming, contrasting reminder of her own mortality. As Marley grows closer to Julian than she anticipated, she must also grapple with her innate inclination for self-sabotage, informed by her relationships with her mom and estranged father, Jack (Treat Williams).

A Little Bit of Heaven is seemingly a strange thematic match for director Nicole Kassell, who made her debut with *The Woodsman* (2004), and has since worked in episodic television. Yet she and cinematographer Russell Carpenter make fine use of the movie's New Orleans locations, giving the movie a bit more authentic regional color than the deluge of other projects shot in coastal Louisiana in the aftermath of Hurricane Katrina, ever since a massive tax incentive program has turned the area into a veritable Hollywood South. Yes, it leans

heavily on French Quarter flavoring, but also incorporates and spotlights other areas of the city.

In some respect, *A Little Bit of Heaven* benefits from a paucity of expectation as much as anything else. With the programmatic feel these days of so much big screen working-girl-comes-to-find-balance-in-life claptrap—derivative films that followed in the wake of *Bridget Jones's Diary* (2001), but with neither the grace nor sharpness of wit that film and its 2004 sequel provided—Gren Wells' first produced screenplay has the advantage of a distinguishing downbeat characteristic. Viewers might not initially know that it bears more in common with *Sweet November* (2001) than many of Hudson's execrable comedies, but they will reap that reward.

Critical reaction to *A Little Bit of Heaven* was unduly harsh, perhaps because of the stigma of its minuscule theatrical release. In his May 1, 2012 ReelViews review, James Beradinelli characterized the movie as lacking in honesty, which he said was "supplanted by artifice." On the surface, this might seem true. In the smothering mom and gay best friend, it certainly leans on very familiar characterizations; ditto car-sing-along and shopping montages, which collectively skirt disaster in their flirtations with pat emotional manipulation. A half-hearted plot device about wishes is little more than an excuse to shoehorn in some winking moments of self-discovery. And when the movie dips into a hallucinatory dream sequence in which Marley converses with God (Whoopi Goldberg) during a colonoscopy, it feels like it has lost its way, without question—veering off into parody-world caricature of this sort of genre effort.

But to dismiss *A Little Bit of Heaven* outright simply for what is recognizable about it is to ignore what it gets right. Hudson exudes a unifying hold over the proceedings, even if the film's basic romantic chemistry remains a bit suspect. Her usual effervescent charm is present, but the real gift of Hudson's performance lies in the manner that she plays a bit off-center of the material, and its set-ups. It is to the movie's credit that it does not fundamentally alter the nature of Marley's personality once she learns of her disease. Her world is rocked, yes, and she is racked with uncertainty, but Marley remains as she was before—complicated and more than a bit obstinate. There is a clear and consistent throughline to Marley, and Hudson threads the needle of her joint soulful awakening and discontent in something approaching sublime fashion.

Perhaps paradoxically, it is *A Little Bit of Heaven's* sense of tonal unsettledness and jumbled purpose that most recommends it. In lieu of massively re-imagining the character of Julian, the movie features rather than fixes the absurdity of casting Bernal ("Yeah, I'm Jewish," he simply says, "from Mexico"), shrugging off the cultural disconnect and setting the scene for some enjoyable banter down the line, wherein Marley suggests getting some "gefilte fish tacos." And while many films would feel obliged to make a stronger commitment to either its "illness-of-the-week" narrative or its burgeoning romance, Wells' script bobs and weaves, adamantly trying to serve multiple masters.

Like its headstrong protagonist, *A Little Bit of Heaven* has a mulish desire to cram in as much as possible; in this regard, the film feels stuffed with contrasting feelings, just like real life. For fans of Hudson eager to see her stretch a bit more, as well as those who have a soft spot for slightly maudlin familial-rooted movies like *Sweet November*, *Dying Young* (1991), *A Walk in the Clouds* (1995), *One True Thing* (1998), *In Her Shoes* (2005) and *The Family Stone* (2005), this canted love story may not reinvent the wheel, but it gets more right than it does not.

Brent Simon

CREDITS

Marley Corbett: Kate Hudson
Julian Goldstein: Gael Garcia Bernal
Beverly Corbett: Kathy Bates
Sarah Walker: Lucy Punch
Peter Cooper: Romany Malco
Renee Blair: Rosemarie DeWitt
God: Whoopi Goldberg
Jack Corbett: Treat Williams
Rob Randolf: Steven Weber
Vinnie: Peter Dinklage
Dr. Sanders: Alan Dale
Thomas Blair: Jason Davis
Cammie Blair: Bailey Bass
Cammie Blair: Charlotte Bass
Origin: United States
Language: English
Released: 2012
Production: Robert Katz, Mark Gil, John Davis, Adam Schroeder, Neil Sacker; Davis Entertainment; released by The Film Department
Directed by: Nicole Kassell
Written by: Gren Wells
Cinematography by: Russell Carpenter
Music by: Heitor Pereira
Sound: Kelly Oxford; Michael D. Wilhoit
Music Supervisor: Jim Black; Rebekah Touma
Editing: Stephen A. Rotter
Art Direction: W. Steven Graham
Costumes: Ann Roth
Production Design: Stuart Wurtzel

MPAA rating: PG-13
Running time: 106 minutes

REVIEWS

Adams, Mark. *Screen International.* February 1, 2011.
Dargis, Manohla. *New York Times.* May 3, 2012.
Duralde, Alonso. *The Wrap.* May 3, 2012.
LaSalle, Mick. *San Francisco Chronicle.* May 3, 2012.
Linden, Sheri. *Los Angeles Times.* May 3, 2012.
Ogle, Connie. *Miami Herald.* May 4, 2012.
Rea, Steven. *Philadelphia Inquirer.* May 3, 2012.
Scheck, Roger. *Hollywood Reporter.* May 4, 2012.
Schenker, Andrew. *Slant Magazine.* May 3, 2012.
Schwarzbaum, Lisa. *Entertainment Weekly.* May 2, 2012.

QUOTES

Marley Corbett: "What I would give to experience, just one more time; to feel that incredible sensation, when he looked at me, and then I felt alive."

LOCKOUT
(MS One: Maximum Security)

Take no prisoners.
—Movie tagline

Box Office: $14.3 million

Lockout is a futuristic action extravaganza so deranged, so cartoonish, and so preposterous that it takes all basic and long-cherished notions of plausibility and common sense and goes after them like the guy with the fire extinguisher in the opening scene of *Irreversible* (2002) went after the poor dope he was pursuing and with most of the same results. The film is so shamelessly ridiculous and nonsensical that the only hope that it has of coming across as anything other than borderline insulting gibberish rests entirely on the prospect that that it somehow manages to be as wildly entertaining as it is completely ludicrous and amazingly enough, it somehow manages to do just that.

Set in the not-too distant future of 2079, the film begins as winsome presidential daughter Emilie (Maggie Grace) is flying off to MS1—a maximum-security prison orbiting the Earth and housing America's deadliest criminals in states of suspended animation—on a goodwill mission to ensure that the incarcerated are not in any way being exploited by the huge, multi-national corporation that helped to fund the program. Unfortunately, as soon as she arrives, everything goes gunny as the inmates break loose and take over the joint and with a full assault on the prison an impossibility, the president and his advisors realize that there is only one man for the job—tough-talking ex-CIA operative Snow (Guy Pearce). Even better, he is about to be sent to that very same prison after being accused of espionage after a sting he was involved with resulted in the death of a key agent and the disappearance of a briefcase apparently filled with important secrets. Against his better judgment, Snow eventually agrees to take the job and soon finds himself in the bowels of MS1 trying to track down the feisty Emilie before the bad guys—led by one rational-but-indecipherable madman and his totally-psychotic-yet-equally-indecipherable brother—can find her and discover who she really is.

Of course, this is all just prelude to a series of increasingly insane action set-pieces that test all the bounds of logic. For example, there is a motorcycle chase that is so overlaid with CGI effects that it literally veers between live-action and animation in the blink of an eye. There is a zero-gravity fistfight over giant grinding gears that is impressive, though perhaps not as much as it might have been had there not been a similar bit in *Mission Impossible: Ghost Protocol* (2011) There is much more, of course, and it all leads up to a finale that is so amazingly over-the-top that it not only redefines the term for future generations, it makes the loony interstellar antics of *Moonraker* (1979) seem scientifically sound by comparison. Seriously, the only thing preventing the revelation of said moment in these pages in order to prove its outlandishness is that it is so far beyond the pale that most readers simply would not believe it.

Lockout is the latest model from the one-man-moviemaking empire that is Luc Besson, a man so tireless that he has directed four films and worked on the screenplays for another eight (with two more currently in pre-production) since 2006, the year that he announced that he was formally retiring from filmmaking altogether. Here, he not only produced and co-wrote the screenplay, he is also credited separately (and repeatedly) with supplying the "original idea" for the film. Considering the fact that the whole thing is essentially a mash-up of the classic *Escape from New York* (1981) and his own *Taken* (2009) (right down to having Maggie Grace return as the damsel in distress), this credit may well inspire some of the biggest laughs to be had. That said, while he has turned over the directorial reins to Stephen St. Leger and James Mather, it sure feels like a full-blown Besson film through and through with its combination of outrageous action sequences, flashy visual style, and a storyline so cheerfully cartoonish that it feels like a couple of wired ten-year-old kids are making it up in a sandbox as it goes along. It is that weird sense of child-like exuberance that Besson brings to the proceedings

that gives his films their distinct personality and it is why a film like *Lockout* turns out to be so much fun to watch despite all of the obvious idiocies on display.

There are plenty of reasons why many sane and sober-minded critics might lambaste a film like *Lockout*. The bad guys are bores with accents so thick that it seems as though they escaped from a Ken Loach film instead of an interstellar prison. Guy Pearce's relentless quips and one-liners grow somewhat monotonous after a while, although his opening interrogation scene is pretty hilarious for all the right reasons. Maggie Grace has nothing to do except look pretty and then, after disguising herself, to look less pretty. Strangest of all, after pulling off its audacious climactic stunt, the film inexplicably goes on for another ten minutes or so in order to wrap up all the suitcase nonsense. And yet, *Lockout* is so cheerfully ridiculous that these flaws almost become virtues because they are deployed in a completely guileless manner. Yes, it is dumb but it is of the kind of dumbness that makes for strangely compelling viewing for those willing to embrace its pop-art insanities all the way to the moon and back.

Peter Sobczynski

CREDITS

Snow: Guy Pearce
Emilie Warnock: Maggie Grace
Alex: Vincent Regan
Hydell: Joe Gilgun
Harry Shaw: Lennie James
Scott Langral: Peter Stormare
John James Mace: Tim Plester
Origin: France
Language: English, Italian, Portuguese, Spanish
Released: 2012
Production: Marc Libert, Leila Smith; Europa Corp.; released by Open Road Films
Directed by: Stephanie Leger; James Mather
Written by: Stephanie Leger; James Mather; Luc Besson
Cinematography by: James Mather
Music by: Alexandre Azaria
Sound: Paul Davies
Editing: Eamonn Power; Camille Delamarre
Art Direction: Frank Walsh
Costumes: Olivier Beriot
Production Design: Romek Delmata
MPAA rating: PG-13
Running time: 95 minutes

REVIEWS

Childress, Erik. *eFilmcritic.com*. April 13, 2012.

Dargis, Manohla. *New York Times*. April 12, 2012.
Denby, David. *New Yorker*. April 23, 2012.
Dujsik, Mark. *Mark Reviews Movies*. April 12, 2012.
Ebert, Roger. *Chicago Sun-Times*. April 12, 2012.
Goss, William. *Film.com*. April 13, 2012.
Pais, Matt. *RedEye*. April 12, 2012.
Russo, Tom. *Boston Globe*. April 12, 2012.
Tallerico, Brian. *HollywoodChicago.com*. April 13, 2012.
Tobias, Scott. *AV Club*. April 12, 2012.

QUOTES

Langral: "I don't like hurting you, Snow."

Snow: "Is that why you're having him do it?"

Langral: "I can have Rupert bludgeon you all night."

Snow: "I'm being beaten up by a guy called Rupert?"

TRIVIA

There is a Wilhelm Screeam used when the inmate trips and falls right after coming out of stasis.

LOLA VERSUS

(Lola gegen den rest der welt)

Lola vs. sex, love, Lola, the world.
—Movie tagline

Box Office: $252,603

The word ambivalent is often misused, and interchangeably associated with being uncertain—the connotation being a blithe lack of weight or emotional investment in a situation. In real life, however, that is not true. Ambivalence is more than mere indecision. It is heavier. It can feel like a weight on one's chest, stifling decision-making, creativity, even movement.

Director Daryl Wein's offbeat romantic dramedy *Lola Versus* grasps this. On the one hand, with its comfortably ramshackle plotting and character archetypes, it is just another showcase for fairly solid joke-writing but with a watchability that stems chiefly from a collection of nuanced observations about human frailty rather than any lip-nibbling, cutesy set-ups, the film exists and unfolds in a realistic miasma of bewilderment and late-twenty-something confusion. It is a serially silly movie about the serious discombobulation of change in life—the shock and fear attached to it, and the swirl of, yes, ambivalence that rushes in to fill the void of old habits and routines. Given a lackluster summer counter-programming run by distributor Fox Searchlight, where it pulled in under $1 million at the box office, the film

should only grow in value and reputation with time, as wider mainstream audiences become more familiar with the rising star of Greta Gerwig.

The actress stars as the title character, a New York grad student working on a dissertation about society's discomfort with silence. When her fiance Luke (Joel Kinnaman), a painter, nervously dissolves their engagement just weeks before their destination wedding, Lola is devastated. Her parents (Bill Pullman and Debra Winger) swoop in to help bolster her spirits, and Lola also leans on her best friends—Alice (co-writer Zoe Lister-Jones), a manic singleton, and Henry (Hamish Linklater), a sensitive indie rocker whose relationship with Lola extends back to their adolescence. Over the course of the next year, as Lola cycles through some bad decision-making and various love triangles form and dissipate both inside of her social circle and outside of it, Lola tries to locate her personal compass and get it situated upwards.

There is a gathering middling critical consensus around the film—where it tops out at just over fifty percent on Rotten Tomatoes amongst top critics—that its sole saving grace is really Gerwig and her sunny, offbeat charm. And it is true both that she is great and that the grander narrative arcs of the movie eventually devolve into a collection of discrete bits: a pregnancy scare, a hypnotherapy appointment, and a couple bits involving Nick (Ebon Moss-Bachrach), a one-time sexual coupling that Lola comes to regret. But there is a funky energy here that helps the material transcend its navel-gazing roots, even if its final resting place of self-actualization is somewhat predetermined.

Lister-Jones and director Wein previously collaborated on *Breaking Upwards* (2009), a slyly autobiographical tale of a New York couple who, battling codependency, meticulously plot out their own separation. Their off-screen lives clearly also inform the backdrop and flavorings of *Lola Versus*, shot through with little bohemian asides.

The pair also crafts dialogue that crackles. Lola and Alice's patter ("Is your Match.com log-in still let-me-be-your-hole?" and "Who puts your sentences together? Honestly, it's like your brain is a bad deejay") capture the easy rhythms of a friendship in which niceties are not paramount, while other bits ("This is number one on Yelp for best bar in a scary neighborhood") score simply as one-liners. There are also some funny gags (like Alice confusing Oxycontin with Oxytocin) that are smoothly interwoven into the scenes surrounding them.

While the film's visual scheme, concocted by Wein and cinematographer Jakob Ihre, on more than several occasions opts for very simple, flatly conceived set-ups that do little to belie the sitcom-friendly nature of its banter, Teresa Mastropierro's production design is solid—kind of grungy but elegant at the same time, without overplaying its indie hipster credentials. Meanwhile, with its catchy yet bittersweet musical contributions to this and Ry Russo-Young's *Nobody Walks* (2012), Fall on Your Sword, consisting of composer Will Bates and guitarist Phil Mossman, are fast making a name for themselves as go-to purveyors of soundtrack nostalgia and heartbreak.

The acting, though, is what really elevates *Lola Versus*, trumping a fairly meandering narrative and making it such a treat. Zoe-Lister is quite fun, and gifted with an innate sense of comedic timing, proving that her success on the small-screen *Whitney* is no fluke. And as Lola's liberal-minded parents, Pullman and Winger are also delightful, beautifully filling in a backstory which is only hinted at.

Then there is Gerwig, whose expressive reactions and skillfully embodied vulnerability anchors the movie. Her beauty may not tick all the conventional boxes, but Gerwig has a guileless naturalness that comes from her off-screen education and curiosity about the world, and that makes her supremely attractive. Her choices are always interesting, conveying the choppy, at-odds inner cadences of a character who tries to argue her way out of a bad decision by exclaiming, "I'm slutty, but a good person!" She makes the film both funny and a bit heartrending.

Lola Versus lacks the adventurousness and certainly the stylishness of *(500) Days of Summer* (2009), but it is a sort of more femme-centric version of that, crossed with Lena Dunham's *Tiny Furniture* (2005). One of those movies hit it big at the box office and the latter, like *Lola Versus*, disappeared with the tiny "plunk!" of a small pebble tossed off a pier into the ocean. But Dunham's star rose again with HBO's zeitgeist smash *Girls*, and the incandescence of Gerwig, who gives this movie so much, is such that it only remains a matter of time until her mainstream breakthrough.

Brent Simon

CREDITS

Lola: Greta Gerwig
Luke: Joel Kinnaman
Alice: Zoe Lister Jones
Henry: Hamish Linklater
Lenny: Bill Pullman
Robin: Debra Winger
Origin: United States
Language: English
Released: 2012

Production: Janice Williams, Michael London, Jocelyn Hayes; released by Groundswell Productions
Directed by: Daryl Wein
Written by: Zoe Lister Jones; Daryl Wein
Cinematography by: Jakob Ihre
Sound: Michael Feuser
Editing: Suzy Elmiger; Susan Littenberg
Art Direction: Peter Baran
Costumes: Jenny Gering
Production Design: Teresa Mastropierro
MPAA rating: R
Running time: 87 minutes

REVIEWS

Debruge, Peter. *Variety.* April 25, 2012.
Ebert, Roger. *Chicago Sun-Times.* June 14, 2012.
Goodykoontz, Bill. *Arizona Republic.* June 21, 2012.
Hornaday, Ann. *Washington Post.* June 15, 2012.
LaSalle, Wesley. *San Francisco Chronicle.* June 14, 2012.
Longworth, Karina. *Village Voice.* June 5, 2012.
Rickey, Carrie. *Philadelphia Inquirer.* June 14, 2012.
Rocchi, James. *MSN Movies.* June 6, 2012.
Sharkey, Betsy. *Los Angeles Times.* June 7, 2012.
Weitzman, Elizabeth. *New York Daily News.* June 7, 2012.

TRIVIA

Orlando Bloom was originally cast in the film's lead role but dropped out before filming started.

LOOPER

Face your future. Fight your past.
  —Movie tagline

Hunted by your future. Haunted by your past.
  —Movie tagline

Box Office: $66.5 million

The best science-fiction films, the ones that do not just hide behind robots and flying cars, the kind of sci-fi movies that stick with audiences for years to come, take wild, speculative, mind-bending ideas and create very personal stories around them. Because science fiction should not just be about robots, it should be about what robots say about human beings, right smack dab in the here and now. Fortunately, writer-director Rian Johnson, the creative mind behind the underrated *Brick* (2005) and *The Brothers Bloom* (2008), understands the sci-fi genre and, with *Looper,* he delivers the most captivating, textured time travel movie since Shane Carruth's *Primer* (2004).

Even though the world of *Looper* is set in the future, where time travel, solar-powered cars, and telekinetic mutants are all a reality, the central conceit behind the film is a relatively simple one. A brash young man is forced to hunt down his future self. It's very high concept, but, in the quiet moments, when a twenty-five-year old man is sitting in a diner booth looking at himself in thirty years—and that fifty-five-year-old man looks back—*Looper* really shows how something as flashy as time travel can be used to reveal very real truths about humanity, morality, and regret.

As the film opens, viewers are introduced to Joe (Joseph Gordon-Levitt), a Mafia-connected hitman living in Kansas City in 2044. Rian Johnson's future is a bleak reflection of the present day, where poverty is achingly high (a domestic Vagrant War is referenced) and cars still look the same, albeit with tacky solar panels now affixed to their sides. Joe is a very particular kind of hitman called a "Looper." The way it works is that in the even-farther future (around 2074), time travel has been both perfected and outlawed. But organized crime figures have obtained access to it and use the technology to dispose of bodies, throwing their targets thirty years into the past. (Apparently, forensic science in 2074 is really, really good.) The mob bosses send their victims back to 2044, a Looper shoots them, destroys the bodies, and collects a bounty of gold sent back in time, strapped to the victim's back. The name "Looper" comes from the fact that, eventually, these hitmen will have to murder their own future selves to, in effect, "close the loop" of evidence.

Thus Joe and his fellow Loopers live decadent, shallow lives, although Joe is more introspective than most, stashing away his earnings and dreaming of running away with his favorite showgirl/call girl Suzie (Piper Perabo). Regrettably, Joe runs into the very situation that all Loopers dread. His future self, Old Joe (Bruce Willis), arrives from the future and promptly escapes. The penalties for not closing your own loop are strictly enforced by mob boss Abe (Jeff Daniels), so Joe has to run for his life, knowing that the only way to remove the bounty from his own head is to kill his older self. However, Old Joe has returned to the past with a purpose: Seeking to hunt down a legendary mob boss from the future known as The Rainmaker. Old Joe plans to find and kill The Rainmaker as a child, Terminator-style, to stop the crime lord from ruining his life in the future. (A montage showing Gordon-Levitt gradually age and transform into Willis, while living abroad in China, is one of the film's strongest sequences.)

The cat-and-mouse game between young Joe and old Joe eventually leads them to the Dust Bowl-esque farm of Sara (Emily Blunt), a shotgun-totting survivor who's determined to protect her young son Cid (Pierce Gagnon) from the horrors of their dystopian present. Young Joe eventually warms to the grounded Sara and finds himself cast in the role of her protector as Sara's farm becomes a staging ground for a bloody battle between both Joes, the mob, and, potentially, the Rainmaker himself.

To call *Looper* an ambitious movie would be an understatement. It is a movie bursting at the seams with texture, tricky plot turns, revealing character moments, and big, widescreen ideas. Visually, it is the most striking movie that Johnson has made to date. He finds a dignified beauty in the future ruins of rural America, making every day landscapes seem positively futuristic in similar way to how Andrew Niccol transformed classic modernist architecture into bleeding edge sci-fi in 1997's *Gattaca*. Johnson is also extremely skilled at drawing vivacious, nuanced work from his actors. Not only does he draw out yet another fine performance from Gordon-Levitt, but he additionally gives Emily Blunt a career-best role and brings an emotional weight to Bruce Willis that audiences have not seen since Terry Gilliam's *12 Monkeys* (2006).

Not every decision Johnson makes in *Looper* works. There are segments in the second act where the film becomes too ponderous by half, briefly derailing its narrative drive, and a few of Johnson's technical choices occasionally underwhelm. (There is a flying motorcycle that probably seemed like a great idea in theory, but the clumsy FX when it flies stands out like a sore thumb against Johnson's otherwise assured visual palette.) However, possibly the worst choice that Johnson made in *Looper* was his decision to have Joseph Gordon-Levitt wear extensive facial prosthetics to more closely resemble Bruce Willis. While one has to applaud Johnson's desire for accuracy, the end result is that Gordon-Levitt looks strikingly odd throughout the entire movie. The prosthetics make his face look so stylized and unreal that, at times, he does not seem to fit in with the visual landscape of the rest of the film. (His new, exaggerated profile would be better suited for a film like Robert Rodriguez's *Sin City* [2005].) Gordon-Levitt performs admirably under all of that make-up, but, at the end of the day, it was unnecessary. Johnson should have trusted that his audience could handle the artifice of a young movie star playing the past self of an older movie star and left it at that.

But these few flaws do not a masterpiece ruin. For the handful of misguided technical moments in *Looper*, Johnson makes a million other dead-on choices that elevate his film far beyond the lion's share of most modern sci-fi. He brilliantly employs time travel to tell a powerful story of a young man nervous about his future and an old man consumed by his regretful past. And, as these two men circle each other in an endless bloody loop, one is reminded of just how perceptive and relevant science fiction can be.

Tom Burns

CREDITS

Joe: Joseph Gordon-Levitt
Older Joe: Bruce Willis
Sara: Emily Blunt
Seth: Paul Dano
Suzie: Piper Perabo
Jesse: Garret Dillahunt
Beatrix: Tracie Thoms
Origin: United States
Language: English
Released: 2012
Production: Ram Bergman, James D. Stern; Endgame Entertainment, FilmDistrict, Ram Bergman Productions; released by TriStar Pictures
Directed by: Rian Johnson
Written by: Rian Johnson
Cinematography by: Steve Yedlin
Music by: Nathan Johnson
Sound: Jeremy Peirson
Editing: Bob Ducsay
Costumes: Sharen Davis
Production Design: Ed Verreaux
MPAA rating: R
Running time: 119 minutes

REVIEWS

Hornaday, Ann. *Washington Post*. September 28, 2012.
Lane, Anthony. *New Yorker*. October 1, 2012.
Morgenstern, Joe. *Wall Street Journal*. September 27, 2012.
Murray, Noel. *AV Club*. September 26, 2012.
Newman, Kim. *Empire*. September 17, 2012.
Nicholson, Amy. *Boxoffice Magazine*. September 7, 2012.
O'Hehir, Andrew. *Salon.com*. September 28, 2012.
Puig, Claudia. *USA Today*. September 27, 2012.
Turan, Kenneth. *Los Angeles Times*. September 27, 2012.
Willmore, Allison. *Movieline*. September 26, 2012.

QUOTES

Joe: "Then I saw it, I saw a mom who would die for her son, a man who would kill for his wife, a boy, angry and alone, laid out in front of him the bad path. I saw it and the path was a circle, round and round. So I changed it."

TRIVIA

This movie marks the third collaboration between director Rian Johnson and lead actor Joseph Gordon-Levitt, the first

being *Brick*, and the second being a cameo in *The Brothers Bloom* as a bar patron with a guitar.

AWARDS

Nominations:
Writers Guild 2012: Orig. Screenplay

THE LUCKY ONE

Box Office: $60.5 million

Nicholas Sparks wrote his first novel in 1985. The title of any of his books should automatically be followed by the words "Spoiler Alert" before announcing its authorship because the chances are that someone in the story is not going to make it out alive. It could be the heroine with leukemia. It might be the damaged gentleman caller who gets caught in a sea storm or a mudslide only to have a third party deliver final letters to the heroine. Sometimes Sparks gives one of them Alzheimer's and kills them both anyway. Does it come down to irony or gall that Sparks would name one of his books, *The Lucky One*? The title certainly does not apply to anyone who had to sit through the seventh cinematic adaptation of his work.

"You know, the smallest thing can change your life. In the blink of an eye something happens by chance when you least expect it, sets you on a course you never planned into a future you never imagined. Where will it take you? That's the journey of our lives. Our search for the light. But sometimes finding the light means you must pass through the deepest darkness. At least that is how it was for me."

Those are the words of Nicholas Sparks, or at least, his protagonist U.S. Marine Logan Thibault (Zac Efron). Amidst the chaos and rubble of Iraq, he finds a picture of a pretty girl just a few feet away from where his fellow soldiers are ambushed and killed. Referred to as a guardian angel—even before a second incident—Logan now feels obligated to track down the person in the picture with the words "keep safe" inscribed on the back. Thanks to a one-stop Google search of lighthouses, Logan takes his trusty dog and walks his way from Colorado to Louisiana to find her. Beth Clayton (Taylor Schilling) is her name, and, as luck would have it, she owns a dog kennel where he applies for a job without announcing his true intentions. It is amazing how coincidences and interruptions can delay destiny in the Sparks universe.

Beth's grandmother (Blythe Danner) hires him despite Beth's reservations. The harmless, hard-working Thibault (pronounced "TE-BOW") instantly draws the ire of the town's Sheriff Deputy Keith Clayton (Jay R. Ferguson) who gives Logan a cooler welcome upon first meet than Brian Dennehy does John Rambo in *First Blood* (1982). Keith is Beth's ex and the little boy around the kennel is theirs, but his suspicion reaches sociopathic levels over a guy who "likes to walk," "likes to read," and quotes Dr. Seuss. Logan also possesses more of the genteel, supportive traits of a father figure to Beth's son, Ben (Riley Thomas Stewart), that can no longer be provided by her brother—a fellow Marine who died in action.

One day a famous philosopher will surmise that "War is hell, but Nicholas Sparks owns the waiting room." Flipping through his pages or going scene-to-scene is like sitting there knowing that bad news awaits you on the other side and all you have to keep you busy are the same old magazines. Secrets will turn into revelations that will temporarily derail the burgeoning romance of potentially star-crossed lovers. Antagonists will be defined without a single shade of grey. And someone is going to die. Sparks and screenwriter Will Fetters tease viewers by introducing grandma with the line "Did you take your medication?" The parody potential alone of turning the next Sparks screenplay into a mystery centered around a game of Spin the Bottle is either too tempting or too unbearable to consider.

A film as hopelessly meandering as *The Lucky One* could momentarily survive if the central relationship produced worthwhile chemistry but neither Efron nor Schilling can do much more than to look lifelessly beautiful and produce the button-pushing emotions on cue for those star-crossed readers and viewers who respond to nothing more. Neither is interesting as individuals and even less so together. Director Scott Hicks does nothing to help matters but to instill as many montages as possible to get through those awkward passages of developing characters as people rather than caricatures. The only true curiosity is how many antagonistic cliches Sparks can apply to one character in "Deputy Enemy": An offspring of a rich family put into a position of power still trying to impress daddy while being a bad daddy and husband himself who is also bad at the job he uses to keep throwing monkey wrenches into the love story that is supposed to make us cry. To Nicholas Sparks' credit though, practicing violin in a treehouse is the most interesting bit of foreshadowing he has come up with yet.

Erik Childress

CREDITS

Logan: Zac Efron
Beth Clayton: Taylor Schilling
Nana: Blythe Danner
Ben: Riley Thomas Stewart
Keith Clayton: Jay Ferguson
Origin: United States
Language: English, French, Spanish
Released: 2012
Production: Denise Di Novi, Kevin McCormick; Di Novi Pictures, Langley Park Productions; released by Warner Bros.
Directed by: Scott Hicks
Written by: Will Fetters
Cinematography by: Alar Kivilo
Music by: Mark Isham; Hal Lindes
Sound: Curt Schulkey; Aaron Glascock
Music Supervisor: John Bissell
Editing: Scott Gray
Art Direction: Paul D. Kelly
Costumes: Dayna Pink
Production Design: Barbara C. Ling
MPAA rating: PG-13
Running time: 101 minutes

REVIEWS

Bayer, Jeff. *Scorecard Review.* April 29, 2012.
Dequina, Michael. *TheMovieReport.com.* May 6, 2012.
Ebert, Roger. *Chicago Sun-Times.* April 19, 2012.
Erbland, Kate. *Film School Rejects.* April 21, 2012.
Goss, William. *Film.com.* April 20, 2012.
Minow, Nell. *Beliefnet.* April 19, 2012.
Nusair, David. *Reel Film Reviews.* April 20, 2012.
Puccio, John J. *Movie Metropolis.* August 24, 2012.
Scott, A. O. *New York Times.* April 19, 2012.
Snider, Eric D. *EricDSnider.com.* April 20, 2012.

QUOTES

Logan: "You should be kissed every day, every hour, every minute."

TRIVIA

Theaters on military installations were given an advanced showing of this film.

M

MADAGASCAR 3: EUROPE'S MOST WANTED

Six years ago, they disappeared without a trace. Next summer, they finally resurface.
—Movie tagline

Box Office: $216.4 million

For a moment it seemed like *Deep Impact* (1998) and *Armageddon* (1998) all over again, except with anthropomorphic creatures instead of sci-fi doomsday scenarios. After overlapping development tracks, *Madagascar* (2005) beat the similarly themed *The Wild* (2006), another animated story of loosed zoo animals, to theaters by a significant amount of time. Perhaps owing partially to that, *The Wild* crashed at the box office, but big returns greeted *Madagascar*, and a lucrative film franchise was born.

Madagascar: Europe's Most Wanted, the third movie in the series, underscores the spoils of sometimes just arriving first. A box office smash (it pulled in over $730 million worldwide, including a domestic-best for the series of $216 million) that somehow extracted positive critical response through the sheer force of its manic overload, the movie is in reality a bewildering and irrationally strung together bunch of noise and color. In this respect, *Madagascar: Europe's Most Wanted* is "funny" or "cute" in the same way as a toddler thrown into a crib of feathers and finger paint: it makes an impression, all right, but not a particularly nuanced or clever one.

Somewhere, an executive involved in the development of *The Wild* sits clench-jawed with envy, studying *Madagascar*'s staying power and residual payouts.

Directed by Conrad Vernon, Tom McGrath and co-writer Eric Darnell, the third installment of *Madagascar* again centers mainly around lion Alex (Ben Stiller), zebra Marty (Chris Rock), hippopotamus Gloria (Jada Pinkett Smith), and giraffe Melman (David Schwimmer), a gang of pampered Central Park Zoo animals who have found themselves a long way from home. Picking up where the second film, which ported the action to Africa, left off, *Madagascar: Europe's Most Wanted* finds Alex plagued by a nightmare in which he and all his friends have gotten old.

Heading to Monte Carlo to try to get their crafty penguin pals and vainglorious lemur friend, King Julien (Sacha Baron Cohen), to fly them back to New York, the aforementioned quartet find themselves trailed by a mad, dogged French animal control officer, Chantel DuBois (Frances McDormand). The gang then comes across a band of circus performers, including embittered Siberian tiger Vitaly (Bryan Cranston), slinky jaguar Gia (Jessica Chastain), and excitable sea lion Stefano (Martin Short). Wild performances and friendships ensue, and their initial plan—to bide their time as circus stowaways in an effort to get back to New York City—starts to fall by the wayside when they realize that they have perhaps grown too much in spirit to return to captivity.

Madagascar: Europe's Most Wanted may run 93 minutes, but even if one shaves off the dozen minutes of credits there is still only about 20 to 25 minutes of actual story to cover the rest of the movie's running time, which is expanded to feature length with all the skill and savvy of a self-taught accordion player. The screenplay is by Darnell and Noah Baumbach, the independent-minded writer-director team who collaborated with Wes Anderson on *Fantastic Mr. Fox* (2009). Any trace amount of off-kilter pixie dust from that critically lauded animated effort, however, is swallowed here by over-caffeinated impulsivity.

There is no cogent tone or sense of scale and crafted payoff to the movie, as evidenced by its cycling through of grab-bag music cues from the likes of the Spice Girls and C+C Music Factory. Referential jokes of supposedly highbrow or at least sly quality (when the action shifts to Rome, Alex riffs, "My ancestors used to perform here. Every show had a captive audience—apparently it killed!") are delivered with a bit too much forthrightness, but mostly buried under tossed-out one-liners, mock-clever quips ("When in Rome, viva la France!"), and non sequiturs ("Was that the sound of my HP printer printing?"). In his *Hollywood Reporter* review, Todd McCarthy beautifully encapsulated the film's wearying problems when he described it as "conspicuously unmodulated, with the volume set on high and the pacing all but pushed to fast-forward."

What redeems *Madagascar: Europe's Most Wanted*, to the extent that word applies, is its visual audaciousness. This is the focal point of every positive review, which basically seems to boil down to: "Yes, it is a frenzied avalanche of disconnected jokes and only half-sketched ideas, but it looks great." There is some truth to the latter consideration. The movie's use of everything from whip-pans, dizzying tracking shots and point-of-view framing keeps one engaged on a purely sensory level, and its 3-D presentation is often imaginative to boot. A neon-lit trapeze bit set to Katy Perry's "Firework" may be the film's most eye-popping achievement on a purely technical level. But in the end it has no deeper expressive connection. And when it dips into slow-motion theatrics during a comedic machine-gun firing of bananas at Chantel, the movie so lacks concentration that it cannot even stick to a clarifying wide shot for a proper send-up of the groundbreaking action sequence of *The Matrix* (1999).

The vocal performances offer some piecemeal delights for fans of the actors, but these are not so much characters as vessels for jokes that suit the moment. When Alex chides Vitaly and the other circus animals about having gotten stuck in a rut, stopped pushing and taking risks, it is a critique that might well apply to the film as a whole. Its makers no doubt think and feel that in their willful embrace of exuberant freneticism, their movie is breaking exciting new ground. To a viewer craving some semblance of honest emotional mooring, however, *Madagascar: Europe's Most Wanted* is nothing but a clamorous cash-grab. It abandons sense and any unifying ability because it does not respect its audience.

Brent Simon

CREDITS

Alex: Ben Stiller (Voice)
Marty: Chris Rock (Voice)
Melman: David Schwimmer (Voice)
Gloria: Jada Pinkett Smith (Voice)
Julien: Sacha Baron Cohen (Voice)
Maurice: Cedric the Entertainer (Voice)
Mort: Andy Richter (Voice)
Capt. Chantel DuBois: Frances McDormand (Voice)
Origin: United States
Language: English, French, Spanish
Released: 2012
Production: Mark Swift, Mireille Soria; DreamWorks Animation; released by Paramount Pictures
Directed by: Eric Darnell; Tom McGrath; Conrad Vernon
Written by: Eric Darnell; Noah Baumbach
Music by: Hans Zimmer
Sound: Dennis Leonard
Editing: Nick Fletcher
Art Direction: Shannon Jeffries
Production Design: Kendal Cronkhite-Shaindlin
MPAA rating: PG
Running time: 93 minutes

REVIEWS

Biancolli, Amy. *San Francisco Chronicle*. June 8, 2012.
Chang, Justin. *Variety*. May 18, 2012.
Duralde, Alonso. *The Wrap*. June 6, 2012.
Gleiberman, Owen. *Entertainment Weekly*. June 6, 2012.
Hynes, Eric. *Village Voice*. June 5, 2012.
Kennedy, Lisa. *Denver Post*. June 8, 2012.
McCarthy, Todd. *Hollywood Reporter*. May 18, 2012.
O'Sullivan, Michael. *Washington Post*. June 8, 2012.
Sharkey, Betsy. *Los Angeles Times*. June 7, 2012.
Willmore, Alison. *AV Club*. June 7, 2012.

QUOTES

Alex: "Well, I say they can take the animals out of the circus, but they can't take the animals out of the circus! Uh, you know what I mean!"

TRIVIA

A Wilhelm Scream can be heard, in the international version of the film, when a motor cycle driver screams as he flies out of the freeway.

MADEA'S WITNESS PROTECTION

(Tyler Perry's Madea's Witness Protection)

Believe it or not, they know too much.
—Movie tagline

New look. New York. New Madea.
—Movie tagline

Box Office: $65.7 million

Tyler Perry is a storyteller first, a mogul second, an actor third, and maybe somewhere down the list, a filmmaker fourteenth or fifteenth. This order of professional priorities is evident with the overall quality of any of his projects; his authorship is constructed of shabbily made narratives with cardboard characters, as glued together by laughable melodrama (which has made *Good Deeds* [2012], *Why Did I Get Married Too?* [2010] and *For Colored Girls* [2010], critically condemned, among others). Often working from his own original screenplays, which would be first drafts for many other writers, Perry remains a fiercely prolific force on his level, creating a surplus of storytelling about middle-aged African-Americans for the mediums of television, film, and the stage, where Perry's unrivaled enterprise was first conceived.

Through many stories, often featuring themes of forgiveness leading to redemption and usually dramatically steered by sharp turns more commonplace in soap operas than mainstream American films, one of Perry's most successful contributions to American film culture has been the rambunctious character Madea, a senior African-American woman that has Perry wearing stuffy flower dresses over a junky bodysuit, topping his head with a cheap gray wig, and completing the look with a sharp, high-pitched voice. Yet, despite Madea's accessibility as a familiar archetype to a general mainstream audiences buttered by the previous transvestite slapstick of Martin Lawrence and Eddie Murphy, Madea has always run secondary to Perry's stuffy sermonizing, often utilized to lure viewers unaware of the shallow spiritual waters they are about to tread (as with *Madea Goes to Jail* [2009] or *I Can Do Bad All By Myself* [2009], movies that could have certainly used more Madea). While *Madea's Witness Protection* might be yet another cheaply-assembled preaching product from the Tyler Perry Studios factory, this particular film stands out for being the first time that Perry allows the comedic freewheeling strength of Madea to ultimately drive the story.

In the film, a very twitchy Eugene Levy plays George Needleman, a CFO of an investment firm who was duped into a Ponzi scheme that laundered money from the mob to fake charities. One of the investment

funds lost in the scheme belongs to former thug Jake (Romeo Miller), who initially invested funds to save his father's (John Amos) church, and is left to his own naive devices to get the money back.

While the company is under investigation by friendly prosecutor Brian (Tyler Perry), George, and his wife Kate (Denise Richards), son Howie (Devan Leos), daughter Cindy (Danielle Campbell), and mother Barbara (Doris Roberts) are put into a witness protection program. With the involved mob considered a serious threat to the Needlemans (despite their bare appearance in the story), Brian comes up with the idea that they will stay at his Aunt Madea's place under witness protection, where his father Joe also lives. This begins a collection of events that lead to wisdom imparted on the family by Madea and Joe as they all live together, with the uptight family learning to cherish the time they spend with each other, without the distraction of work (as with George) or technology (as with Howie and Cindy). There is also a running joke in the movie that Barbara and conceived George years ago when they coincidentally met 52 years prior.

George and Brian find a break in the case when the fake name of "Precious Jackson" is revealed to be that of a codename for a nonexistent account holder. In a move that is inspired by something Whoopi Goldberg did in *Ghost* (1990), Madea is secretly enlisted by George to pretend that she is Precious Jackson, so that she can travel to New York City and transfer the remaining funds back to the real clients (which includes Jake's church money).

Perry is a storyteller who knows the value of serving his niche; and if Perry's most faithful demographic is indeed middle-aged, churchgoing African-American women, then Madea is their id; a high-tempered, Bible-illiterate sinner with wild back stories involving episodes of "hookin', strippin', robbin'" in her younger life. And yet, she can still be embraced by her audience for her foundational advocacy for second chances, especially when it comes to young men and women.

Whether Perry's machine gun improvising hits comedic targets or not, this character is still his most inspired aspect of his films, making the cheap-but-heavy drama surrounding Madea's shenanigans dead weight by comparison. In the case of *Madea's Witness Protection*, it is a relief that Perry resolves his preaching at the end of the second act, and concedes the third act to be mindless, more propelled by the spirit of Perry's desire to improvise as much as possible than an interest in preaching from his own moral compass. Often presenting this woman living in "the dark ages" at odds with technology ("Madea vs. The TSA") or high brow vacationing ("Madea vs. Fancy Hotels"), Perry allows *Madea's Witness*

Protection to be a more direct serving of what outsiders may expect from a title (and the film's advertising, which suggests Madea might be under witness protection herself). Such servings may be high in fat, but the occasional laugh keeps them from being regrettable.

Acting is still a challenge for Perry himself, despite his stubbornness in playing three roles in the film, and writing loose scenes for himself in which all three of his characters interact with one another at the same time (with Joe and Madea squawking at each other). When he is not hiding behind old age makeup, an exaggerated impersonation and saucy elderly attitude (either for Madea or Joe), his plain face character Brian is completely barren of charisma, his own perfection mistaken for lifelessness.

Perry certainly lacks a gauge for what make a rich performance in others, and leaves the work up to his actors, whether they care to make anything of their job or not (Loretta Devine stepped up to the challenge with a memorable turn in *For Colored Girls*). With such breezy direction, performances become unhinged—Levy's fidgety neuroses are overloaded until the actor's genuineness is unrecognizable, and the adolescent acting of Campbell and Miller comes at the quality of an unprepared audition, rushing past the concept of emotional control. Interactions between characters are often be filled with unintentional beats, with actors putting the bare organization of the script on embarrassing display.

With *Madea's Witness Protection*, Perry demonstrates a little improvement visually from his past films, but it is not by much. For example, he does not dare toy with glaring negative space as he did with *Good Deeds*, an aesthetic choice that made dull scenes even more aesthetically lifeless (both films use cinematographer Alexander Gruszynski). Yet at the same time, this film does reinforce his sloppy attitude towards editing, with shots lingering too long between his different characters, a breaking of the fourth wall that constantly reminds the audience of who is behind the makeup; frequent Perry editor Maysie Hoy is so in tune with the mogul's filmmaking laziness that she may as well be another Perry personality.

While Madea presents Perry's flailing strength at improvising, the structure that Perry's script sets for himself is no more concrete than his previous work, with cheaply constructed characters speaking flat dialogue that delivers exposition with the force of a 2X4, achieving the general impression such writing would be more at home in PSAs than Hollywood drama. The story itself is nothing significant, taking viewers from a post-Recession tale of betrayal to Madea's church to a light third act. While Perry has been accused in the past of constructing characters from ugly stereotypes, it becomes all the more likely, especially with the depthless characters and the events they face in this story, that Perry simply has little imagination.

Unlike his other efforts, *Madea's Witness Protection* does not pretend for too long that it is anything more than the same biannual sermon, repackaging the same themes as previous. As a filmmaker continually bumbling through cinematography, editing, writing, and most certainly directing, Perry still has a lot of work to do should he ever want to be taken seriously as a filmmaker, and not just a multi-millioniare. Amongst a critically challenging filmography, *Madea's Witness Protection* can be seen as a winking indication of Perry's strongest suit, embodying Madea—he certainly knows the profit of a good disguise.

Nick Allen

CREDITS

Madea/Joe/Brian: Tyler Perry
George Needleman: Eugene Levy
Kate Needleman: Denise Richards
Barbara: Doris Roberts
Cindy Needleman: Danielle Campbell
Howie Needleman: Devan Leos
Jake: Romeo Miller
Walter: Tom Arnold
Pastor Nelson: John Amos
Hattie: Marla Gibbs
Origin: United States
Language: English
Released: 2012
Production: Ozzie Areu, Paul Hall, Tyler Perry; Tyler Perry Studios; released by Lionsgate
Directed by: Tyler Perry
Written by: Tyler Perry
Cinematography by: Alexander Gruszynski
Music by: Aaron Zigman
Sound: Whit Norris
Editing: Maysie Hoy
Art Direction: Dane Moore
Costumes: Carol Oditz
Production Design: Eloise Stammerjohn
MPAA rating: PG-13
Running time: 115 minutes

REVIEWS

Feeney, Mark. *Boston Globe.* July 1, 2012.
Genzlinger, Neil. *New York Times.* June 29, 2012.
Gleiberman, Owen. *Entertainment Weekly.* July 4, 2012.

Howell, Peter. *Toronto Star*. June 29, 2012.
Lengel, Kerry. *Arizona Republic*. July 1, 2012.
Leydon, Joe. *Variety*. June 29, 2012.
Moore, Roger. *McClatchy-Tribune News Service*. July 6, 2012.
Olsen, Mark. *Los Angeles Times*. June 29, 2012.
Pinkerton, Nick. *Village Voice*. June 29, 2012.
Schenk, Frank. *Hollywood Reporter*. June 29, 2012.

TRIVIA

Uncle Joe, when reminiscing about the Army nurses that followed Company B to their barracks, says their names were Blanche, Rose, and Dorothy. These are the names of the title characters of the television show *The Golden Girls*.

AWARDS

Nominations:

Golden Raspberries 2012: Worst Actress (Perry), Worst Director (Perry), Worst Ensemble Cast, Worst Remake/Sequel

MAGIC MIKE

Work all day. Work it all night.
—Movie tagline

Box Office: $113.7 million

2012 was a champion year for actor Channing Tatum, having starred in three different genre films that grossed over $100 million domestically (which includes *The Vow* [$125 million] and *21 Jump Street* [$138 million]). His most successful effort of the year artistically was *Magic Mike,* Tatum's own take on what former boxer Sylvester Stallone expressed with the landmark film *Rocky* (1976), and a shoo-in bid for People Magazine's title of "Sexiest Man Alive" (which he received on November 15, 2012). In the hands of prolific director Steven Soderbergh, this story of Tatum's true tales as a male stripper in Florida is beefed up with as much delicious meta meat as man meat, introducing the career evolution of Tatum from objectified *Step Up* (2006) hunk to an inspired artist.

Reuniting Tatum with Soderbergh after *Haywire* (2012), Tatum plays Mike, a young, self-proclaimed "entrepreneur" who hustles through the economic recession with the ultimate goal of starting his own custom-made furniture company. His most lucrative employment, however, is in a business that deals strictly in cash: male stripping. Along with a few other dancers (played by Matt Bomer, Kevin Nash, Adam Rodriguez, and Joe Manganiello), Mike works under the leadership of head honcho veteran stripper Dallas (Matthew Mc-Conaughey) at Club Xquisite, where they have deemed themselves "The Cock-Rocking Kings of Tampa," performing for clamoring crowds of women while temporarily dressed as firemen, cave men, cowboys, and more.

While working as a roofer, Mike finds the next Club Xquisite recruit in Adam (Alex Pettyfer, who plays naive a little too close to the chest), an underage ruffian unqualified for roofing, if not many other adult responsibilities. With his parents out of the picture, and his troublesome college past behind him, Adam lives with his sister Brooke (Cody Horn).

After tricking Adam into recruiting two 21-year-olds (Camryn Grimes and Kate Easton) by schmoozing them so that Mike can give them flyers, Adam witnesses for himself the spectacle of male stripping, observing as Mike and others tear off their clothes to a dubstep rendition of "It's Raining Men." Later on in the night, when Tarzan (Nash) is incapacitated by substance usage, the green Adam is pushed on stage by Mike to perform his own impromptu strip performance, fitfully accompanied by the tune "Like A Virgin." This becomes an eye-opening experience for Adam, revealing to him the power bestowed onto him for having a handsome smile and decent body, which turns him into Dallas' next protege, as Mike had once been before.

With the stage set, the story takes a darker direction as a cautionary tale. As Adam becomes a larger part of Club Xquisite and begins living a faster life involving the selling of ecstasy, Dallas plans a move for the kings to Miami. Unable to be taken seriously by the banks or by Brooke, Mike begins to ponder his own direction, especially in regards to whether stripping is going to lead him towards his goals, or towards a relationship in which he is not objectified.

The film's script is written by Reid Carolin, who also produced this and 2012's *10 Years* alongside Tatum. Sometimes giving viewers geared for a cinematic strip show too much to tune out, Reid's script too casually leans on predictability with story, borrowing from any expected moment in a performer's drama, including the presentation of downfall by reckless behavior. This certainly causes for slack moments in the film, regardless as to whatever big artistic picture is being serviced. Though the script does have strong moments of dialogue, the story structure too readily agrees much of its audience did not exactly come to *Magic Mike* for a story.

Tatum sells himself here as a hard worker, a full-on entertainer who commits to his work even if the job does not service his personal goal. Armed with machine gun hip thrusts and a million-dollar grin, Tatum is a brimming package here in *Magic Mike,* able to win over the audiences from either the art house or the multiplex.

As he strips and grinds, Tatum is a thrilling spectacle, a giddy centerpiece to the movie's main attraction. In other moments, in which the film is going through dramatic moments of airy plot, in which Tatum continually expresses his desire to be an artist and not just a performer, the rising actor carries the audience's attention, making for an all the more image-changing moment when he stutters to say in the third act, "I am not my goddamn job. It is what I do, but it's not who I am." This role is Tatum's chance to speak to both sides, those who come for the nudity, and those who come for the subtext—Tatum is so effective with this statement as Magic Mike that he turns this movie into his victory lap, a celebration for the next chapters of his career where his accolades will certainly be beyond "Sexiest Man Alive."

The experience of watching this mesmerizing title character is best embodied by the acting of Horn, a blank canvas masterfully colored up by Soderbergh's interest in the observer. Horn's stiffness here, potentially painfully average in the hands of other directors, proves to work gracefully with her character's reserved expressions, especially in an incredible scene in which Brooke watches Mike perform for the first time, unsure of whether to indulge in the potentially arousing spectacle, or to maintain her fortitude by passing judgment with averted eyes—she blushes without actually blushing.

No one may be having more fun in this party movie than McConaughey, who takes this freewheeling opportunity to cheekily reference images associated with his persona (the primal banging of bongos, the drawl of "Alright, alright, alright...") while occasionally exploring the darker side of aging into the business end of hunk-hunting. There is darkness to McConaughey's portrayal of Dallas as a veteran performer who has decided to make an immortal persona out of aging sex appeal. And yet McConaughey, with a thunderous unscripted strip performance of his own in the third act, and a couple of staggering moments in which his dramatic chops do ring dead serious, basks in the attention, whether it is positive or negative. As Dallas, and possibly also as McConaughey, he is invigorated by the lifeblood that is his audience's acceptance.

Aside from Tatum, the other shining star of *Magic Mike* is Soderbergh, who uniquely deepens the potential of this potentially trashy plot concept. Indeed "another Steven Soderbergh experience" (to take the tagline from his unique 2005 film *Bubble*), *Magic Mike* is specialized by its director's handling, as he continues to show giddiness in observing what happens when he plays with the persona of his stars, like with his star studded cast *Ocean's Eleven* (2001), or the film most similar to *Magic Mike*, *The Girlfriend Experience* (2009).

As storyteller, Soderbergh keeps an air between him and the story, allowing plot turns to provide some of the furniture to an otherwise atmospheric movie. As cinematographer, (under the name Peter Andrews), Soderbergh enables the environments involved to breathe naturally, capturing conversing characters as life continues around them, whether they are in a kitchen-turned-dressing room at Club Xquisite, or on a boardwalk. The one aspect in which Soderbergh's eye for observational cinematography undermines *Magic Mike* is with the stripping sequences, which are shot flatly, and maintain a slightly sobering reality to them, as opposed to having flair of their own. Yet whereas Soderbergh's camera may be like his attachment to his stories, thoroughly an outsider, he continues to be an involved editor (under the name Mary Ann Bernard), slicing his jackpot stripping moments into slick montages, while also allowing other moments in the film to breathe naturally.

A bottling of the Tatum zeitgeist and a display of his talents relevant to both past and future, *Magic Mike* is a giddy art film masquerading as a fun night for audience members who do not often find themselves at male strip clubs (though Soderbergh certainly welcomes these viewers). Under the observing eye of a director who can fortify a sturdy bridge between the art house and the multiplex, *Magic Mike* is a rare treat, a rich film inspired by male stripping as much as it is artistic integrity.

Nick Allen

CREDITS

Dallas: Matthew McConaughey
Magic Mike: Channing Tatum
Joanna: Olivia Munn
Adam: Alex Pettyfer
Brooke: Cody Horn
Big Dick Richie: Joe Manganiello
Ken: Matt Bomer
Origin: United States
Language: English, French, Spanish
Released: 2012
Production: Nick Wechsler, Gregory Jacobs, Channing Tatum, Reid Carolin; Iron Horse, Extension 765; released by Warner Bros.
Directed by: Steven Soderbergh
Written by: Reid Carolin
Cinematography by: Steven Soderbergh
Sound: Larry Blake
Music Supervisor: Frankie Pine
Editing: Steven Soderbergh
Art Direction: Christopher Dileo

Costumes: Christopher Peterson
Production Design: Howard Cummings
MPAA rating: R
Running time: 110 minutes

REVIEWS

Brody, Richard. *New Yorker*. July 2, 2012.
Burr, Ty. *Boston Globe*. June 28, 2012.
Dargis, Manohla. *New York Times*. June 28, 2012.
Debruge, Peter. *Variety*. June 25, 2012.
Ebert, Roger. *Chicago Sun-Times*. June 28, 2012.
Gleiberman, Owen. *Entertainment Weekly*. June 29, 2012.
Longworth, Karina. *Village Voice*. June 26, 2012.
Snider, Eric D. *Film.com*. June 29, 2012.
Stevens, Dana. *Slate*. June 28, 2012.
Turan, Kenneth. *Los Angeles Times*. June 28, 2012.

QUOTES

Dallas: "You are the husband they never had! You are that dreamboat guy that never came along!"

TRIVIA

Film director Joe Johnston can be seen as one of Mike's phone contacts.

AWARDS

Ind. Spirit 2013: Actor—Supporting (McConaughey)

THE MAGIC OF BELLE ISLE

A re-coming of age story.
—Movie tagline

Box Office: $102,388

When almost everything about a movie invites adjectives like cloying and syrupy almost nothing else about it tends to matter. A great cast, which *The Magic of Belle Isle* has, just sinks into the background, only occasionally emerging above the white noise of unearned sentimentality to remind viewers that they are there struggling to make something out of a lifeless affair.

Over a montage of small town views and overused vintage pop, well-known writer Monte Wildhorn is being driven to his temporary summer digs by his nephew Henry (Kenan Thompson). A taciturn, despairing soul, he has given up both writing and living since his wife died and wants nothing more than to find a quiet place to drink himself into oblivion. His next-door neighbors, the O'Neills, consist of Charlotte (Virginia Madsen) and her three daughters, Finnegan (Emma Fuhrmann), Wil-low (Madeline Carroll) and Flora (Nicolette Pierini), who are all doing their best to cope with the tragedy of mom and dad's recent divorce. Wildhorn does his best to sequester himself but is inevitably drawn into the lives of the O'Neil's and the other oh-so-folksy townies, who eventually inspire him to start writing again. He moves away to Mexico near the story's end (like any good Western novelist would) but ultimately finds his muse back in Belle Isle where he purchases the house where he was reborn.

Morgan Freeman is well cast as Monte Wildhorn a character weighed down by grief and alcohol. Too bad his eloquent delivery and gravitas is put to use at the service of a script weighed down so heavily with cliche and clunky soulfulness. As written, Wildhorn is a combination of cultured sage, grump, alcoholic, and softie with an acerbic sense of humor. In other words a caricature of a real human being who would be slightly less interesting, far less self-assured, and far more resistant to the sort of feel-good change the script demands by the end of the film's runtime. Freeman's performance is predictably excellent, however. In fact, he almost makes Wildhorn interesting enough to keep the story interesting.

Virginia Madsen, always dependable, offers a winsome widow in the person of Charlotte but is, like everyone else, saddled with that atrociously overwritten dialogue. She mainly stands as a reminder that there are two Academy Award winners acting in this film and a nominated director. The end result is a veneer of class, and a bare smidgen of nuance, that quickly cease to be of any importance. Once the characters are all introduced and Rob Reiner signals his intention to milk the sentiment, viewers will realize no one is going to save them from just how bad this can be.

Generally speaking, actors have a rough job. They often must take bad material and attempt to infuse it with life. If they are not quite up to the level of a Freeman they can hardly be blamed. Few are. But watching the downright embarrassing character of Carl lope his way across the screen is apt to irritate anybody. The town's token mentally handicapped man-child, Carl (Ash Christian) is just one of the far-too-facile components of a screenplay that knows where it wants to get but takes the easy road at every turn. In fact, this character is not merely poorly conceived but deeply offensive, coming more as broad caricature than truth. Written by Guy Thomas, whose only other feature film credit is *Wholly Moses* (1980), this film plays exactly like a Hallmark Hall of Fame remake of *Tender Mercies* (1983) minus every bit of merit.

Lastly, this film is directed by Rob Reiner who has made a living the last few years churning out one forgettable romantic comedy and family drama after another. He and Freeman both worked together on his last decent movie, *The Bucket List* (2007), but seeing Reiner's name above the credits here will invoke mourning in the heart of anyone who has enjoyed the several truly great films from his golden period. Only Reiner's name coupled with Freeman and Madsen's explains how this actually made it into theaters.

The Magic of Belle Isle is as unlikely to kill viewers as it is to inspire them. It exists in that middle ground of films that viewers might leave on TV if they were too distracted to change the channel. It is, in essence, harmless, except that it wastes the time of all those who wrote, directed, acted in it or worked on it. Those who watch it may incur the benefit of being lulled into a needed nap but even then the film is likely to work into their subconscious where who knows what havoc might result. God forbid anyone actually lived, acted, or thought like the characters in this claptrap.

Several times in the film, Wildhorn addresses a dog for which he has been forced to care. He lays down the rules of the house: No farting, no begging, no humping the other neighborhood dogs. It is the sort of empty moralizing that the film itself seems most interested in delivering, as if the audience itself were a dog that needed to be spoken to, slowly and without artifice.

Dave Canfield

CREDITS

Monte Wildhorn: Morgan Freeman
Charlotte O'Neil: Virginia Madsen
Willow O'Neil: Madeline Carroll
Finnegan O'Neil: Emma Fuhrmann
Flora O'Neil: Nicolette Pierini
Henry: Kenan Thompson
Al Kaiser: Fred Willard
Joe Viola: Kevin Pollak
Carl Loop: Ash Christian
Origin: United States
Language: English
Released: 2012
Production: Nicolas Chartier, Alan Greisman, Lori McCreary, Salli Newman, Rob Reiner, David Valdes; Castle Rock Entertainment, Revelations Entertainment, Summer Magic, Firebrand, Voltage Pictures; released by Magnolia Pictures
Directed by: Rob Reiner
Written by: Guy Thomas
Cinematography by: Reed Morano
Music by: Marc Shaiman
Sound: Lon Bender
Editing: Dorian Harris
Art Direction: Kevin Bird
Costumes: Shawn Holly Cookson
Production Design: Tom Lisowski
MPAA rating: PG
Running time: 109 minutes

REVIEWS

Chen, Sandie Angulo. *Common Sense Media.* July 6, 2012.
Goss, William. *Film.com.* July 6, 2012.
Holden, Stephen. *New York Times.* July 5, 2012.
Olsen, Mark. *Los Angeles Times.* July 5, 2012.
Lumenick, Lou. *New York Post.* July 6, 2012.
Reed, Rex. *New York Observer.* July 12, 2012.
Roten, Robert. *Laramie Movie Scope.* November 27, 2012.
Schager, Nick. *Village Voice.* July 3, 2012.
Whitty, Stephen. *Newark Star-Ledger.* July 6, 2012.
Willmore, Allison. *Movieline.* July 6, 2012.

QUOTES

Monte Wildhorn: "Drinking is a very demanding profession, and I can't hold down two jobs at once."

TRIVIA

Annette Bening was originally cast as the female lead but dropped out and was replaced by Virginia Madsen.

MAN ON A LEDGE

You can only push an innocent man so far.
—Movie tagline

Box Office: $18.6 million

"To jump or not to jump," Nick Cassidy (Sam Worthington) openly ponders during one of his many confrontations with the police in *Man on a Ledge.* The audience, meanwhile, is left to wonder how screenwriter Pablo F. Fenjves will work himself out of the corner into which he intentionally has written himself. Nick will inevitably get off that ledge; the only question is how.

The setup is simplicity itself: Nick, as the title suggests, is stuck on the ledge of the 21st floor of a hotel in New York City. Behind him in the hotel room where he stepped out the window and on to the ledge (in a neat bit of editing, the camera passes in a continuous motion through a closed window as Nick climbs through an open one), the police are waiting to arrest him—end of story. In front of him, there is sometimes only six inches of concrete, and beyond that is an over-200-foot drop to the street below—end of story, again. In a way, the central question is less how Fenjves will save Nick from the ledge and more how the screenwriter will manage to keep his protagonist in such a precarious situation for the length of a feature-length movie. That is where things become far more convoluted than need be.

The story of Nick's self-imposed peril is the movie's strong point, if only because it relies entirely on the visceral chill of seeing a person standing on a narrow outcrop hundreds of feet in the air with nothing to break his fall (There is a decent-sized air mattress on the ground, but even the police who place it there can only say, "Good luck hitting that;" as it turns out, Nick is exceptionally, inhumanly lucky). Director Asger Leth (directing his first narrative feature) recognizes the primal nature of a fear of high places, especially when confronted with no practical protection from falling. He and cinematographer Paul Cameron ensure the audience sees Nick from every imaginable angle—from crane shots at just enough distance to appreciate the void of nothing immediately in front of him to overhead shots that will challenge any vertigo-prone viewer.

Leth and his crew accomplished the effect using digital effects, replicated sets on a soundstage, and, of course, the real location; it is seamless. With the illusion complete, one need only see a few looks of the drop to recognize the urgency of the scenario.

After establishing the premise during a prologue that starts *in medias res,* the script reveals how Nick arrived at the ledge. He was at the Sing Sing Correctional Facility for a 25-year sentence; before that, he was a police officer in the city. The details of his crime at first are sketchy, though Fenjves does provide a psychiatrist (J. Smith-Cameron) who quite blatantly reveals back story—one of serveral characters to serve this purpose (the most egregious example is a news reporter played by Kyra Sedgwick, who exists only to iterate key plot points). Much of the dialogue is unnatural in its expository nature. Another such character is his former partner Mike Ackerman (Anthony Mackie), who visits to tell Nick his father is dying.

At the burial, Nick escapes by stealing his brother Joey's (Jamie Bell) car; the police pursue him. In the first instance of extremely fortunate and highly unlikely events within the story, Nick manages to walk away with only a few cuts and bruises after a train collides with the car and sends it—and him—flipping through the air. After a few stops, the narrative eventually catches up with itself and finds Nick where he started. The police arrive at the hotel; he demands that they bring in Lydia Mercer (Elizabeth Banks), a police negotiator who became infamous after a man she tried to save from a suicide attempt on a bridge jumped with television cameras capturing the whole thing, to talk him down from the ledge.

Nick's antics at the hotel are only a distraction so that Joey and his girlfriend Angie (Genesis Rodriguez) can bicker while breaking into a building across the street where Nick believes the powerful David Englander (Ed Harris) is hiding a diamond. Nick was in prison for stealing said diamond; he is convinced Englander faked the robbery as an insurance scheme to recover from losses during the economic crisis. Harris has little to do in the movie other than to look intimidating and shout throwaway lines like, "Get me the mayor's office," to show he has influence.

The heist consists of Joey and Angie avoiding various security measures and guards, who always miss detecting them by just a matter of seconds (Just as Joey blocks a camera with a picture of the room, a guard turns his head toward the monitor; Angie climbs into an air duct just before guards enter the room). It becomes increasingly ridiculous, particularly when the pair learns the diamond is not in the central safe of Englander's vault. The backup plan is to let Englander take the diamond out of its hidden vault and take it from him when he brings it to his office. This plan, of course, depends upon Nick's rival being incredibly and unbelievably dense—taking the diamond out of an otherwise impenetrable safe for no discernable reason except that he must for the plot to move forward.

Man on a Ledge continues to spiral into the realm of the preposterous as the climax becomes a generic chase, with Nick leaping away from and outrunning police along the side of the building, through hotel rooms, and up a stairwell. A police corruption subplot concludes with a whimper, and Nick's final descent from the building is only believable if one were to dismiss the laws of physics. It is as if Leth completely forgot all those shots establishing the long way down.

Mark Dujsik

CREDITS

Nick Cassidy: Sam Worthin
Editing: Kevin Stitt
Art Direction: David Swayze
Costumes: Susan Lyall
    gton
Lydia Mercer: Elizabeth Banks
Joey Cassidy: Jamie Bell
Mike Ackerman: Anthony Mackie
Angie: Genesis Rodriguez
David Englander: Ed Harris
Jack Dougherty: Ed Burns
Dante Marcus: Titus Welliver
Suzie Morales: Kyra Sedgwick
Origin: United States
Language: English
Released: 2012
Production: Mark Vahradian; di Bonaventura Pictures; released by Summit Entertainment
Directed by: Asger Leth
Written by: Pablo F. Fenjves
Cinematography by: Paul Cameron

Music by: Henry Jackman
Sound: Jon Johnson
Editing: Kevin Stitt
Art Direction: David Swayze
Costumes: Susan Lyall
Production Design: Alec Hammond
MPAA rating: PG-13
Running time: 102 minutes

REVIEWS

Anderson, John. *Wall Street Journal.* January 27, 2012.
Holden, Stephen. *New York Times.* January 26, 2012.
LaSalle, Mick. *San Francisco Chronicle.* January 27, 2012.
Morris, Wesley. *Boston Globe.* January 27, 2012.
Phillips, Michael. *Chicago Tribune.* January 26, 2012.
Orndorf, Brian. *Blu-ray.com.* January 26, 2012.
Pols, Mary. *Time.* January 26, 2012.
Putman, Dustin. *DustinPutman.com.* January 5, 2012.
Vaux, Rob. *Mania.com.* January 26, 2012.
Zacharek, Stephanie. *Movie Line.* January 26, 2012.

QUOTES

David Englander: "That's what's great about this county. If you want it bad enough, you can make it back. Hmm? In this city, on this island, we don't go to work, we go to war! And if somebody takes something from you, you take it back. And more."

TRIVIA

All of the wide shots of the actors on the ledge were real. Restraining cables were either hidden from camera view or removed during post production.

THE MAN WITH THE IRON FISTS

You can't spell Kung Fu without F and U.
—Movie tagline

Seven clans, a fortune in gold. Let the battle begin.
—Movie tagline

They put the F.U. in Kung Fu.
—Movie tagline

Box Office: $15.6 million

Throughout his career, Quentin Tarantino has been trying to re-introduce all manner of '70s Grindhouse Cinema to new generations of filmgoers who missed out on the golden age of exploitation films. His cohort Robert Rodriguez has also been building a career from the influences of Z-grade sci-fi and bloody revenge films. Their collaboration on *Grindhouse* (2007), in which they concocted a three-hour double feature (they each directed a film) and linked them with hilarious fake grindhouse movie trailers made by Edgar Wright, Eli Roth, and Rob Zombie, was one of the top bargains at

the box office that year and won mostly good reviews from the press. It was also a major box office disappointment, as was Rodriguez' *Machete* (2010), a feature-length take on one of the trailers from *Grindhouse*. It might have to do with the fact that Rodriguez has little to say as a filmmaker and remains a cinematic man-child while Tarantino possesses real talent and always has something to say while delving into grindhouse conventions and tributes. After all, Tarantino's own follow-up, *Inglourious Basterds* (2009), was a major success.

The recent wave of grindhouse revivals has not caught on with the mainstream public but there are still mainstream films being produced for the cult following that has embraced the movement. RZA's directorial debut *The Man with the Iron Fists* might well be a third part to Tarantino/Rodriguez' *Grindhouse* and it pretty much announces itself that way. It arrives on the screen blazing with scratchy film grain, subtitled credits over large Japanese type, and a promise to deliver all sorts of bloody mayhem. With the unconventional addition of rap music, it also calls attention to be viewed as a hybrid of sorts, mixing martial arts with spaghetti westerns and hip-hop. It is a familiar recipe, but RZA clearly has a lot of enthusiasm for it regardless.

The story lacks a clear center, but basically it involves a warrior out for revenge, a Man-With-No-Name-like stranger who wanders into town and an all-seeing blacksmith who serves as the narrator. The unnamed Blacksmith (played by RZA himself) is known for manufacturing most of the weapons used in the fictional Jungle Village. Although he does not appear in every scene in the film, he somehow knows everything. He sets up the story of the Lion Clan, Wolf Clan, and the Hyena Clan and the wars that erupted out of betrayal and lust for power and money. Out of this war came the death of a man at the hands of Gold Lion (Kuan Tai Chen), the leader of the Lion Clan. The man's son, Zen Yi (Rick Yune), has vowed revenge for the killing and eventually makes himself into a human pocket knife. No matter what contraption he is in, chances are he will get out of it with a random blade hidden somewhere on his person.

Meanwhile, at a brothel called the Pink Blossom, run by Madame Blossom (Lucy Liu), a man (Russell Crowe) enters Clint Eastwood style and takes a few women into his room and spends the night having his way with them until a fight breaks out that ends with him killing a large beast of a man with a combination gun/knife. "My name is Mr. Knife," he says to everyone. "You can call me Jack. I'm on vacation." Eventually, he gets roped into this story of Zen Yi and his vow for revenge and the bigger story involving a transfer of the King's Gold, which the Lion Clan plans to ambush so long as they can get past the Gemini Killers who are doing the transporting.

The Lion Clan has also learned of Zen Yi's powers and abilities to get himself out of any jam, so they hire a seemingly invincible barbarian named Brass Body (Dave Bautista) whose skin cannot be penetrated by any blade, no matter how sharp. It would stand to reason that this is the titular Man with the Iron Fists (but maybe not). Furthermore, the Lion Clan captures the blacksmith and tries to convince him to conceive the same kind of weaponry he has been making for Zen Yi. Eventually, all of these characters and storylines result in a typically bloody climax that bring in some unlikely allies, all of whom help the movie make good on its promise of murder and mayhem.

On the surface, *The Man with the Iron Fists* serves its purpose of being a throw-away piece of malice-minded entertainment, but RZA (whose real name is Robert Fitzgerald Diggs and who is better known as being a co-founder of the rap group Wu-Tang Clan) has little more to offer than a re-hash of a tribute that has been warmed over a few times already. RZA is a self-proclaimed student of Tarantino, who served as his mentor while developing the project. RZA also worked with Eli Roth who ended up co-writing the screenplay. The influences here are obvious. There are attempts at ponderous monologues and the movie definitely delivers on gore and grizzly murders, but it all comes off as little more than an imitation with some misplaced rap music thrown in.

As such, *The Man with the Iron Fists* is not a chore to sit through. Crowe seems to be having fun playing an anti-hero with a strange sexual bathtub fetish in a curiously horrifying sight gag, but RZA too often settles on wooden performances from the rest of his cast, even himself (just because someone can rap, it does not mean they should narrate). The fight sequences are choreographed and cut together well enough to keep them interesting and the movie's pace is just about right and has few lags to drag it down. RZA just needs to find a style that is his own instead of just mimicking someone else's, no matter how much fun it might be for him.

Collin Souter

CREDITS

The Blacksmith: RZA
Jack Knife: Russell Crowe
Madame Blossom: Lucy Liu
Zen Yi: Rick Yune
Lady Silk: Jamie Chung
Poison Dagger: Daniel Wu

Brass Body: Dave Bautista
Bronze Lion: Cung Le
Origin: United States
Language: English
Released: 2012
Production: Marc Abraham, Eric Newman, Eli Roth; Strike Entertainment, Arcade Pictures; released by Universal Pictures
Directed by: RZA
Written by: RZA; Eli Roth
Cinematography by: Chi Ying Chan
Music by: RZA; Howard Drossin
Sound: Odin Benitez; John Marquis
Editing: Joe D'Augustine
Costumes: Thomas Chong
Production Design: Drew Boughton
MPAA rating: R
Running time: 95 minutes

REVIEWS

Burr, Ty. *Boston Globe*. November 4, 2012.
Dargis, Manohla. *New York Times*. November 1, 2012.
Gibbs, Ed. *The National*. November 21, 2012.
Hoffman, Jordan. *Film.com*. November 2, 2012.
Howell, Peter. *Toronto Star*. November 2, 2012.
Kenigsberg, Ben. *Time Out New York*. November 6, 2012.
McCarthy, Todd. *Hollywood Reporter*. November 1, 2012.
Pinkerton, Nick. *Village Voice*. November 2, 2012.
Rabin, Nathan. *AV Club*. November 2, 2012.
Smith, Kyle. *New York Post*. November 2, 2012.

QUOTES

Poison Dagger: "I'll see you in hell!"
Jackknife: "Yes, I suppose you will. I'll save you a spot by the fire."

TRIVIA

RZA and Eli Roth worked on the screenplay together over two years, discussing every aspect of the story, down to the detail of every weapon used throughout the film.

MARLEY

Box Office: $1.4 million

Bob Marley was not merely a hugely popular and influential singer-songwriter, but one who veritably introduced reggae music to much of its now-worldwide audience. As such, any nonfiction exploration of his life and legacy has a lot of ground to cover, and director Kevin Macdonald's sprawling, exhaustive biopic does that, giving a great overview of his days on this Earth, and the things that mattered to him. If its soft-spoken subject retains more than a pinch of elusiveness at the end of its running time of nearly two-and-a-half hours, *Marley* still aptly celebrates a figure whose predominant message of love and unity could use a little amplification in the present day.

The son of a Jamaican teenager, Cedella Malcolm, and a 60-year-old British philanderer, Norval Sinclair Marley, Bob Marley was born in the small village of Nine Mile in February, 1945. Derided by some as a half-caste, Marley "had to earn his ebony," as stepbrother Bunny Wailer notes. A decade later, he and his mother moved to Kingston, seeking more opportunity. Marley became interested in music, and after a brief stab at a solo career, in 1963 he formed The Wailers, with Wailer and Peter Tosh. Later, in 1974, after they left the group in a dispute over touring and payment from their record company, The Wailers became Bob Marley & The Wailers, with a new roster of band members.

Rooted in sociopolitical issues, Rastafarianism, African repatriation and, more broadly, social justice and equality, their songs and standout live performances would light a fire under the world music scene generally, and the burgeoning reggae genre quite specifically. In his personal life, Marley would father three children by wife Rita—daughter Cedella and sons Ziggy and Stephen—as well as at least eight others by a string of mistresses, including Cindy Breakspeare, the former Miss World 1976. Initially diagnosed in 1977 with malignant melanoma under the nail of one of his toes, Marley dismissed recommendations to have either his foot or entire leg amputated (stories vary); the cancer would eventually spread throughout his entire body, including his lungs and brain, and fell him at age 36 in 1981.

There is an overall professorial tone to the chronologically plotted *Marley*, along with a certain unsettled quality, perhaps appropriate for a man who eschewed writing a will in the final months of his battle with cancer, not wanting to cede anything to mortality. While meticulously crafted, the movie achieves notional truth rather than deep-seated illumination on a couple key matters, most namely Marley's Rastafarian religion and sprawling, atypical family.

Marley was originally to be directed by Martin Scorsese, who dropped out due to scheduling problems, and was replaced by Jonathan Demme. Subsequently, Demme left over creative differences with producer Steve Bing, and the aforementioned Macdonald came onboard. Macdonald has alternated in his career between fiction and nonfiction features, and even won an Academy Award for his documentary *One Day in September* (1999), so it is ridiculous to suggest he was not up to

the task. But perhaps the circuitous development track that led to his attachment to *Marley* influenced its narrative shape, as did the fact that Ziggy Marley and Island Records founder Chris Blackwell (whose label released much of Marley's music) each serve as executive producers.

It is most assuredly not a hagiography, but *Marley* does oddly lack much in the way of dynamism considering its subject, and also fails to completely bridge the gap between idealistic social warrior and commercially-minded musician. It charts things in a straightforward and somewhat dispassionate manner. (Notably under-addressed are the wounds caused by Tosh and Wailer's exits from the group, and how if at all this impacted its musical direction.) These shortcomings illustrate the difference between a movie that is more admired, and one that inspires deep, rapturous love. Understandably, the film's music is an undeniable high point (a two-disc soundtrack was released concurrent with its April 2012 theatrical debut), but it often comes in snippets, unlike Don McGlynn's similarly comprehensive gospel documentary *Rejoice and Shout* (2011), which is built around much lengthier performances.

There is archival interview footage of Marley, speaking about music as well as God and politics. But it is broad, and does not elucidate Rastafarianism, and its connection to the sacramental use of marijuana. *Marley* also touches on the fact that its subject's music connected predominantly with white audiences once he became an international superstar, but—symptomatic of its lack of an analytical look at the wider cultural significance of said music—it does not dig down quite as deeply as one wishes into how Marley felt about that, and why it was so. Blackwell notes reggae's penchant for off-accent ska beats, and its touches of calypso and rhythm and blues, but there are critics out there capable of giving more eloquent voice to just how high Marley lifted the torch of reggae. Macdonald does not tap these voices.

A large part of what one gleans from *Marley* about the psychological makeup of its star, then, is extra-textual—which is to say it exists in the eye of the beholder, from a latent reading of the material. The quiet, reserved Marley was a man of few words and little self-explanation off stage. Still, there is the sense that, not unlike President Barack Obama, his biracial roots and absentee father had a powerful influence on his worldview. One of the movie's most emotionally poignant passages concerns being turned away during a trip to the offices of his father's eponymous construction firm, which, even though Norval passed away when Marley was ten years old, still did significant business in Jamaica. The sting of rejection would inform the 1970 song "Cornerstone," in which Marley sings, "The stone that the builder refused/Will always be the head cornerstone." The truth of that is self-evident; Marley's hold on his surname surpasses any accomplishments of his biological father. Three decades since his untimely passing, one need only check college dorm room walls for evidence.

Brent Simon

CREDITSBOB MARLEY

Origin: United States

Language: English

Released: 2012

Production: Steve Bing, Charles Steel; Shangri-La Entertainment, Tuff Gong Pictures, Cowboy Films; released by Magnolia Pictures

Directed by: Kevin MacDonald

Cinematography by: Alwin Kuchler; Mike Eley

Music by: Bob Marley

Sound: Glenn Freemantle

Editing: Dan Glendenning

MPAA rating: PG-13

Running time: 145 minutes

REVIEWS

Ebert, Roger. *Chicago Sun-Times*. April 19, 2012.
Lane, Anthony. *New Yorker*. April 17, 2012.
LaSalle, Mick. *San Francisco Chronicle*. April 20, 2012.
Lodge, Guy. *Variety*. February 23, 2012.
Morgenstern, Joe. *Wall Street Journal*. April 19, 2012.
Phillips, Michael. *Chicago Tribune*. April 19, 2012.
Phipps, Keith. *AV Club*. April 19, 2012.
Stevens, Dana. *Slate*. April 19, 2012.
Turan, Kenneth. *Los Angeles Times*. April 19, 2012.
Whitty, Stephen. *Newark Star-Ledger*. April 20, 2012.

TRIVIA

Both Martin Scorsese and Jonathan Demme were attached to direct the film at one point.

AWARDS

Nominations:

British Acad. 2012: Feature Doc.

THE MASTER

Box Office: $16.3 million

What is Paul Thomas Anderson's *The Master*? Before it screened publicly, the film's advance buzz was tied closely to how much of the story related to the history of Scientology, the controversial religion so popular among Hollywood power players. There were rumors that the highly acclaimed writer/director of *Boogie Nights* (1997) and *There Will Be Blood* (2007) had shown the film to his friend and star of *Magnolia* (1999), Tom Cruise, the virtual figurehead for Scientology. While the film contains definite allusions to L. Ron Hubbard and the birth of Scientology, it is a far more complex work than the historical drama that could still come from that true story. *The Master* is to Scientology as *There Will Be Blood* is to oil. It is merely the backdrop, the canvas on which Anderson paints his story. This work is about international, all-religion issues such as free will vs. destiny, instinct vs. religion, animal vs. wrangler, and more. There is a lack of narrative cohesion but it is in pursuit of a stunning work that emphasizes theme over plot. Thematically fascinating, technically remarkable, and with several of the best performances of 2012, *The Master* is an achievement on multiple levels, a work that will continue to grow in esteem and historical prominence as the years go on.

Just as *There Will Be Blood* opened with a series of dialogue-free scenes to set tone and character, *The Master* starts with imagery rather than plot. A young soldier named Freddie (Joaquin Phoenix) looks lost. He stares into the distance (his dead eyes telling viewers more about his hollow character than dialogue ever could), chops a coconut with a machete, masturbates into the ocean, pretends to have sex with a woman made of sand, and makes alcohol out of anything he can distill down to liquor. He is pure instinct. He sleeps with whom he wants, fights with whom he wants, drinks what he wants, etc. In ways that could have been cliched or overdone but absolutely are not here, Freddie is presented as a borderline animal who does not consider issues other than what he wants at that specific moment. This selfish worldview is shattered when one of Freddie's homemade batches of alcohol may have killed a man, and he runs and stows away on a boat filled with well-dressed party goers.

The next morning, Freddie wakes up to learn that the man who owns the boat is a respected author named Lancaster Dodd (Phillip Seymour Hoffman). The charismatic leader heads a new religion, a quasi-cult built around "The Cause." The true design of this cult is not clear and Anderson really only hints at it over the course of the entire film but it is intended as the opposite of how Freddie has been presented. Freddie is forced to listen to recordings about animal nature, deal with the possibility of past lives, and even undergo hypnosis. A game begins in which Dodd tries to take more and more control from Freddie. However, the cult leader has his own insecurities, some of which are ironed out by a supportive wife (Amy Adams), who may be as much the leader of this group as its figurehead.

The game really begins in a scene of breathtaking acting as Freddie undergoes Dodd's "processing." Dodd asks the young man a series of repetitive questions not unlike the cut-rate psychology approach of word association, trying to get as quick and honest a response as possible. The questions get more probative as the scene goes on and Freddie spits back answers rapid fire. The scene becomes a mini-masterpiece on its own as the two actors deliver the kind of breathtaking character dissection that is all too rare. It is a scene in which Dodd is trying to assert intellectual control over Freddie and it is beautifully matched by a later scene in a jailhouse in which the two men battle in more physical, emotional ways—the very human tools that Dodd is trying to suppress. Many things in *The Master* (characters, themes, even scenes) have a match and this pair—the processing scene and the jailhouse one—define so much about the movie and serve as proof that these two performances were well-deserving of their accolades, including matching Oscar nominations (Adams received a nomination as well).

Where *The Master* goes from here would not really be worth recapping since it is so defiantly not a plot-driven film. In fact, the film gets more obtuse as it goes along, which pushed some viewers away and even polarized critics groups (who more often went with Kathryn Bigelow's *Zero Dark Thirty* [2012]) during awards season. Anderson has crafted a film about a man who seeks to and thrives from the control of others that gets more free-form and less controlled as it goes along. The result is a film that lingers through its themes instead of instantly satisfying through its plot. In the moment, Anderson's daring storytelling decisions keep the viewer at arms' length, resulting in the director's coolest film in emotional terms. But the film has a lingering power that has often been missing from Anderson's more immediate works. It defies typical analysis and the cinematic world could use more films for which that statement is true.

Whether its themes work for the viewer or it pushes them out of the experience, no one can deny the stunning technical accomplishments of *The Master*. The cinematography from Mihai Milaimare Jr. (*Youth Without Youth* [2007]) is gasp-inducing, especially in 70MM, the increasingly-rare format in which the film was shot and premiered in Chicago. Anderson's staging is often breathtaking—whether it is a simple unbroken shot of a woman showing off a fur in a department store or whom he chooses to shoot during the soon-to-be-legendary processing scene. Anderson has reached a perfect balance of visual storytelling and thematic composition (aided ably by another great score from *Blood* composer Jonny Greenwood, which practically becomes a character in its own right). He tells a story but does so with the strength of his imagery instead of in a traditional way. He is the embodiment of the timeless dictum "show, don't tell." For most people, Anderson does not tell enough but what he shows is undeniably beautiful.

Anderson is no mere visual master however. He has never worked more successfully with ensemble as he does here. Phoenix plays Freddie as such a primal creature that he can be uncomfortable to watch. He is nearly hunched over and in a perpetual sneer that seems to get more pronounced based on his blood alcohol percentage. One of the reasons Freddie seems drawn to Lancaster is that the latter is one of the few people who does not seem uncomfortable in his presence. Phoenix is matched by Hoffman, who finds the balance of confidence, which allows a man like Dodd to build his following, and insecurity that forces his son (Jesse Plemons) to say "he makes it up as he goes along."

That line, which may seem throwaway to some, is the theme that this viewer takes away from Anderson's entire film. Everyone makes it up as they go along. Freddie is making it up in ways that are too instinctual, too driven by base desire. Lancaster is trying to control how others make it up. One makes booze from paint thinner another makes a community from his own insecurity but both make it up. In the end, who does the title even refer to? Lancaster Dodd may seem the obvious choice given his cult-like control but is Anderson saying that Freddie Quell is just as much the master as those who try to control him? His film offers no inarguable answers, allowing viewers to dissect, discuss, and analyze. One wishes there were more films willing to take that chance.

Brian Tallerico

CREDITS

Lancaster Dodd: Philip Seymour Hoffman

Freddie Sutton: Joaquin Rafael (Leaf) Phoenix

Peggy Dodd: Amy Adams

Val Dodd: Jesse Plemons

Helen Sullivan: Laura Dern

Origin: United States

Language: English

Released: 2012

Production: Megan Ellison, Daniel Lupi, Joanne Sellar, Paul Thomas Anderson; Ghoulardi Film Co., Annapurna Pictures; released by Weinstein Company

Directed by: Paul Thomas Anderson

Written by: Paul Thomas Anderson

Cinematography by: Mihai Malaimare, Jr.

Music by: Jonny Greenwood
Sound: Christopher Scarabosio
Music Supervisor: Linda Cohen
Editing: Leslie Jones; Peter McNulty
Costumes: Mark Bridges
Production Design: David Crank; Jack Fisk
MPAA rating: R
Running time: 138 minutes

REVIEWS

Dibdin, Emma. *Total Film*. November 4, 202.
Lacey, Liam. *The Globe and Mail*. September 20, 2012.
Morris, Wesley. *Boston Globe*. September 20, 2012.
Persall, Steve. *Tampa Bay Times*. September 19, 2012.
Phillips, Michael. *Chicago Tribune*. September 20, 2012.
Schwarzbaum, Lisa. *Entertainment Weekly*. September 14, 2012.
Scott, A. O. *New York Times*. September 13, 2012.
Turan, Kenneth. *Los Angeles Times*. September 14, 2012.
Williams, Joe. *St. Louis Post-Dispatch*. September 20, 2012.
Wise, Damon. *Empire*. October 29, 2012.

QUOTES

Lancaster Dodd: "If you figure a way to live without serving a master, any master, then let the rest of us know, will you? For you'd be the first person in the history of the world."

TRIVIA

The ship carrying the cult is called the Alithia, which is the Greek word for "truth."

AWARDS

Nominations:

Oscars 2012: Actor (Phoenix), Actor—Supporting (Hoffman), Actress—Supporting (Adams)
British Acad. 2012: Actor (Phoenix), Actor—Supporting (Hoffman), Actress—Supporting (Adams), Orig. Screenplay
Golden Globes 2013: Actor—Drama (Phoenix), Actor—Supporting (Hoffman), Actress—Supporting (Adams)
Screen Actors Guild 2012: Actor—Supporting (Hoffman)
Writers Guild 2012: Orig. Screenplay

MEN IN BLACK 3

They are back... in time.
—Movie tagline

Back to the past...to save the future.
—Movie tagline

Back in time to save the future.
—Movie tagline

This summer, he'll have to find the answers...in time.
—Movie tagline

Box Office: $179 million

Less of a traditional sequel than an attempt to further flesh out the characters' back stories, *Men in Black 3* is a film that wears its heart on its sleeve, conveyed by a series of good-to-excellent special effects action sequences. Filled with sci-fi cliches and broad humor, *Men in Black 3* manages to earn some emotional weight as it uses time travel to showcase the idea that human choice is still relevant in a world where forces larger than mankind constantly threaten to crush the things it holds most near and dear.

In present day, Agent K's (Tommy Lee Jones) ultimate nemesis and last of the Boglodite's, Boris the Animal (Jemaine Clement), escapes LunarMax prison fortress in hopes of time traveling to 1969 at a point just before K arrested him. When K learns of the assassination plot, he is full of regret for not having killed Boris when he had the chance. Closing ranks and shutting out his partner Agent J (Will Smith), K sets up an ambush only to mysteriously disappear. When J goes to work the next day, everyone at MIB headquarters tells him they remember Agent K dying on that fateful day back in 1969.

K convinces Agent O (Emma Thompson), who has taken over since the passing of Zed (Rip Torn in the first two films), that a space-time fracture has occurred leading her to believe the new timeline they are living in will lead to a deadly Boglodite invasion. Acquiring a similar time -jump mechanism, J travels back to 1969, where, after encountering some amusing challenges due to his skin color, he is arrested by a young Agent K (Josh Brolin). Finally persuaded of the importance of J's mission, a skeptical K agrees to set out with him. With the help of a prescient alien named Griffin (Michael Stuhlbarg), who can see all possible futures, they stalk and finally confront Boris with the fate of Earth hanging on the outcome.

The plotting here invites all sorts of criticism. A full synopsis would lead the reader through so many twists and turns that the thought of it making sense onscreen might seem highly unlikely. Incorporated into the above are Andy Warhol's Factory, The Apollo 11 Moon launch, the arc-net defense system, and a complicated series of events during the climax that suggests a warm-hearted if implausible and as yet unrevealed relationship between J and K. Yet the emotional touchstones and fine casting make this an above average bit of sci-fi fluff.

Jones and Smith certainly convince as J and K. But when the film puts Josh Brolin onscreen, his impersonation of Tommy Lee Jones is one of the most entertaining and winsome things the actor has ever done. It goes far beyond spot-on into some weird surreality every bit as unsettling as the idea that Earth is a hostel for aliens hidden among the rest of us. Curiously, the *Men in*

Black 3 aliens themselves are the least interesting in the series, with a couple of notable exceptions. Little of the alien designs or effects create anything approaching the wonder of those in the first film. The special effects work best here when applied to the action sequences, such as when J jumps off the Chrysler building to move through time.

Boris is brought wonderfully to life by Jemaine Clement who growls and grimaces his way through a marvelously over-the-top bit of villainy. But Michael Stuhlbarg steals every scene he has as Griffin. Stuhlbarg is as yet a vastly underrated actor whose appearance as the lead in Joel and Ethan Coen's *A Simple Man* (2009) earned him numerous awards and nominations. Here he carries viewers into a wide-eyed hopeful view of the universe and space time, reveling in what is and what could be. He is a sort of child Yoda figure and the effect is simply enchanting.

Director Barry Sonnenfeld has had a curious career. He was Director of Photography on a large number of classic films that are simply too numerous to list here, doing some of his best work with the Coen Brothers during their early period. But his subsequent move into the director's chair has shown him, more often than not, in need of better material with which to work. His wonderfully entertaining debut *The Addams Family* (1991), *Addams Family Values* (1993), *Get Shorty* (1995) and *Men in Black* (1997) represent the best of a resume that also includes the execrable *Wild Wild West* (1999), and little else of note.

The *Men in Black* franchise has been a long-running comic book and could potentially make a good TV series. But as a series of films it has only managed to strike creative gold once, with the first film. Viewers will recall that *Men in Black* ended on a curious note. A huger-than-huge alien playing with the planets picks up Earth and prepares to hurtle it in a cosmic game of marbles. As a statement about man's place in the universe, viewers were thus offered an uneasy mix of whimsy and cynicism. Curious then that *Men in Black 3* offers man a more-assured sense of destiny. Humanity matters somehow, even in the face of uncertainty about his place. It is worth it to love one another, sacrifice for one another. In the vast cosmos the view to take is the hopeful one of Griffin, not a luxury but a deep and abiding revelation.

Dave Canfield

CREDITS

Agent J: Will Smith
Agent K: Tommy Lee Jones
Young Agent K: Josh Brolin
Boris the Animal: Jemaine Clement
Agent O: Emma Thompson
Young Agent O: Alice Eve
Agent X: David Rasche
Griffin: Michael Stuhlbarg
Origin: United States
Language: English, French
Released: 2012
Production: Laurie MacDonald, Walter F. Parkes; Columbia Pictures; released by Amblin Entertainment
Directed by: Barry Sonnenfeld
Written by: Etan Cohen; David Koepp
Cinematography by: Bill Pope
Music by: Danny Elfman
Sound: Junior Cyrus Baron
Editing: Don Zimmerman
Art Direction: Maya Shimoguchi; W. Steven Graham
Costumes: Mary Vogt
Production Design: Bo Welch
MPAA rating: PG-13
Running time: 106 minutes

REVIEWS

Barker, Andrew. *Variety*. May 22, 2012.
Burr, Ty. *Boston Globe*. May 23, 2012.
Ebert, Roger. *Chicago Sun-Times*. May 24, 2012.
Gibson, Brian. *Vue Weekly*. July 24, 2012.
Kendrick, James. *Q Network Film Desk*. May 30, 2012.
Kenny, Glenn. *MSN Movies*. May 22, 2012.
Morgenstern, Joe. *Wall Street Journal*. May 24, 2012.
Orr, Christopher. *The Atlantic*. May 25, 2012.
Ross, Adam. *The Aristocrat*. September 27, 2012.
Scott, A. O. *New York Times*. May 24, 2012.

QUOTES

Griffin: "A miracle is something that seems impossible but happens anyway."

TRIVIA

At one point, Michael Bay expressed interest in directing the film.

MIDDLE OF NOWHERE

Love can lead us where we least expect.
    —Movie tagline
You never know where love will take you.
    —Movie tagline

Box Office: $236,806

Ava DuVernay's *Middle of Nowhere* may seem at first to be another standard Sundance Film Festival drama—a character piece that hits predictable beats in the indie arthouse scene and seems a little stale outside of the thin mountain air of Park City, Utah. It is nearly a subgenre of its own: The drama that wins awards at Sundance but disappears without much noise once the actual festival ends. In this case, the story turned unexpectedly once *Nowhere* hit theaters in the Fall as some critics even went as far as to suggest that its breakthrough star, the stunningly good Emayatzy Corinealdi, should be nominated for a Best Actress Oscar for her genuine, moving work. The performances throughout DuVernay's resonate even when the movie's melodramatic, on-the-nose dialogue holds the work back from its true potential overall. Due to its stellar ensemble, *Middle of Nowhere* finds honesty, compassion, and genuine emotion in a genre that too often feels like it is going through the indie film motions. The film features two of the most striking debuts of 2012 from writer/director DuVernay and star Corinealdi and one hopes they work together again sooner than later.

The success of *Middle of Nowhere* comes down to truth of character over the many potential pitfalls of cliche into which the story could have easily fallen. It is a sense of realism that sometimes leads to some overdrawn story beats but the clear emphasis on character over melodrama pays off. It is a testament to the trust that DuVernay places in Corinealdi that the latter so completely feels three-dimensional and genuine in a role that could have turned into pure Lifetime Channel TV movie in the hands of the wrong actress.

Said role is that of Ruby, a woman who, like so many in today's prison culture, has a husband behind bars. Derek (Omari Hardwick) is something of a cipher to even his own wife. She visits him regularly and clearly works hard to finance his legal defense but Derek is pulling away from Ruby with each subsequent meeting. He grows increasingly distant and cold, clearly withholding the difficulty of life in prison and perhaps less clearly, maybe even subconsciously, pushing the woman he loves away to distance her from his mounting mental and physical problems. And it is here, early on, in which DuVernay begins asking daring questions as a filmmaker in that *Middle of Nowhere* quickly becomes a complex issue of audience desires for its protagonist. Why should Ruby stay loyal to a man who is pushing her away? Perhaps it would be best for her if she took the push? A revelation makes the temptation to forever sever ties with Derek more enticing and Ruby is faced with a tough decision—is it better for her to stay with the man she still clearly loves or give up on him for her own good? And can one forgive someone for something if that person is behind bars and cannot even be consoling through touch?

Matters are complicated for Ruby even further when she meets a kind bus driver named Brian (David Oyelowo), someone who has noticed this beautiful woman more than most of the passengers on his daily route. It feels good for Ruby to be noticed. And it feels good to be desired. Should she stand by her man or take a ride with the new one. It is a believable story of a genuine woman in a tough situation.

With a clear emphasis on truth over contrivance, DuVernay draws genuinely moving performances from her entire cast, particularly in the quieter moments. When the story gets deeper into its love triangle, some of the dialogue feels a bit too on-the-nose as realism is replaced by melodrama but DuVernay finds a way to direct her actors to believable performances despite her occasional weaknesses with dialogue. The work by Corinealdi, Hardwick, and Oyelowo is uniformly strong enough to make any screenwriting issues easy to overlook.

Middle of Nowhere builds to an artistic success through the cumulative emotional power of small moments: A disapproving look from a mother who has been asked to pay the retainer for her son-in-law's counsel, a confrontation with one of Derek's friends who believes that Ruby has betrayed her mate, the look on Ruby's face when she realizes that Brian has been noticing her, etc. DuVernay has a gift with these scenes in a way that makes it easy to believe that she could become one of the most interesting voices in American cinema over the next decade. This is one of the recent Sundance Film Festival critical smashes that lives up to its hype.

Middle of Nowhere could only muster up a few dollars under $240k at the box office, a reasonable number for an independent film but nowhere near the peaks it could have hit with better marketing and studio support. The film never played wider than twenty-five theaters but earned Independent Spirit Award nominations for Best Actress, Best Supporting Actress, and Best Supporting Actor. It is the kind of work with which audiences will catch up on DVD and wonder why it did not make a bigger splash in theaters.

Brian Tallerico

CREDITS

Ruby: Emayatzy Corinealdi
Derek: Omari Hardwick
Brian: David Oyelowo
Fraine: Sharon Lawrence

Littleton: Dondre T. Whitfield
Ruth: Lorraine Toussaint
Gina: Maya Gilbert
Origin: United States
Language: English
Released: 2012
Production: Howard Barish, Paul Garnes, Ava DuVernay; Forward Movement Films, Kandoo Films; released by Participant Media
Directed by: Ava DuVernay
Written by: Ava DuVernay
Cinematography by: Bradford Young
Music by: Kathryn Bostic
Sound: Kunal Rajan
Editing: Spencer Averick
Costumes: Stacy Beverly
MPAA rating: R
Running time: 97 minutes

REVIEWS

Baumgarten, Marjorie. *Austin Chronicle.* October 26, 2012.

Cane, Clay. *BET.com.* October 18, 2012.

Kennedy, Lisa. *Denver Post.* November 30, 2012.

LaSalle, Mick. *San Francisco Chronicle.* October 18, 2012.

Long, Tom. *Detroit News.* October 19, 2012.

Macdonald, Moira. *Seattle Times.* October 18, 2012.

Meyers, Jeff. *Metro Times.* October 26, 2012.

Puig, Claudia. *USA Today.* October 18, 2012.

Sachs, Ben. *Chicago Reader.* October 18, 2012.

Schwarzbaum, Lisa. *Entertainment Weekly.* October 24, 2012.

AWARDS

Nominations:

Ind. Spirit 2013: Actor—Supporting (Oyelowo), Actress (Corinealdi), Actress—Supporting (Toussaint)

MIRROR MIRROR

(Snow White)

One bad apple.
 —Movie tagline

The Snow White legend comes alive.
 —Movie tagline

Army of one.
 —Movie tagline

Snow wonder.
 —Movie tagline

Box Office: $64.9 million

Snow White (Lily Collins) has lived most of her life without a father and in the shadow of her stepmother, the Queen (Julia Roberts). Having lived a sheltered existence in the palace, Snow White has been unaware of how the world outside the kingdom has faltered under the Queen's rule or her second mother's true feelings towards her. On a visit to one of the downtrodden villages, Snow runs into Prince Alcott (Armie Hammer) who has been victimized by local bandits. Little does she know that despite their instant connection to one another, his journey is toward the palace at the bequest of the Queen who has plans for him as well.

As another glorious ball is undertaken under her roof, Snow voices her displeasure with the Queen's ruling techniques. Words from her newly blossomed stepdaughter are of less concern to the Queen than the ones from her magic mirror; a younger reflection of herself that advises a quick marriage to wealth. Not just to save her kingdom but someday she will ask "who the fairest of them all is" and she "will not like the answer." The Queen then orders her loyal servant, Brighton (Nathan Lane), to take Snow White into the woods and have her fed to the feared beast that resides there. Brighton takes mercy on the girl and releases her to whatever fate claims in the dark forest. Instead of death she is led to the doorstep of seven tiny little men with their own grudge against her evil stepmother.

Is "evil" really a fair label for the Queen though? *Mirror Mirror* makes no qualms that she is indeed the resident antagonist, but wavers in the approach of just how loud viewers are meant to hiss at her. Director Tarsem Singh begins the story as pure fairy tale with the fanciful touch of animation, puppetry, and Alan Menken's wistful score. Listening to the opening narration though, one may feel they have walked into a snarky parody. The Queen's voice shifts from the dulcet tone of a mother reading a bedtime story about Snow White to a sarcastic drawl about how probably "that was the most pretentious name they could come up with." Live-action versions over the years have shifted to the more horrific elements of the story, so in the middle of an overload including a darker competitor at the theaters in *Snow White and the Huntsman* (2012) plus television's *Once Upon a Time,* the tale is ripe for a classical interpretation even if the intent was nothing more than to goof on its child-like principles. With no Yellow Brick Road to lead him however, Tarsem tries to do both and skewers the tone past viewer patience.

"This is my story, not hers," says the Queen in the prologue. Funny then that most of our time is spent directly with Snow White on her journey—surviving the forest, getting to know her new dwarf friends and preparing for the final confrontation to permanently remove the Queen from her narrating duties. Whenever the story shifts back to the Queen, the scenes are played for laughs—mostly at the expense of the Prince's humiliation. Even the Queen's evil laugh is sarcastic. Julia Roberts might seem like an inspired casting choice given her once prominent standing as "America's sweetheart" reduced to that of another fading box office draw except it is her performance that interferes every time the film begins to pick up some momentum. Without following through with even an attitude towards the tale's many elements, Roberts' Queen comes off more like a jealous teenager than a force that needs to be overcome to ensure the happiness of the heroine.

The Princess Bride (1987), *Shrek* (2001) or even *Enchanted* (2007) are benchmarks that *Mirror Mirror* cannot reach, but it is not entirely without its charms. Lily Collins is an ideal Snow White with a graceful appeal that well outdoes Kristen Stewart's perpetual poker-faced performance in the rival 2012 film. The seven dwarves are given real personality—not the kind that can be summed up by the mere names that Disney gave them—and the actors—Ronald Lee Clark, Joe Gnoffo, Martin Klebba, Mark Povinelli, Jordan Prentice, Sebastian Saraceno, Danny Woodburn—are the one group that does strike the right balance with their work. Tarsem Singh's visual stylings have always trumped his storytelling—as seen in *The Cell* (2000), *The Fall* (2006) and *Immortals* (2011)—and this is the last time viewers will be able to enjoy his work with the stunning costume designer Eiko Ishioka who passed away before the film's release. Her contributions as well as that of Singh's art directors and cinematographers were the only things to make his films stand apart from the spate of filmmakers who work so hard on the show that they forget just how to tell.

Erik Childress

CREDITS

Snow White: Lynn Collins
Evil Queen: Julia Roberts
Prince Andrew Alcott: Armie Hammer
Brighton: Nathan Lane
The King: Sean Bean
Margaret: Mare Winningham
Origin: United States
Language: English
Released: 2012
Production: Bernie Goldmann, Ryan Kavanaugh, Brett Ratner; Goldmann Pictures, Rat Entertainment, Misha Films; released by Relativity Media
Directed by: Tarsem
Written by: Melisa Wallack; Jason Keller

Cinematography by: Brendan Galvin
Music by: Alan Menken
Sound: Robert C. Jackson; Martyn Zub
Editing: Robert Duffy; Nick Moore
Costumes: Eiko Ishioka
Production Design: Tom Foden
Running time: 106 minutes

REVIEWS

Bell, Josh. *Las Vegas Weekly*. March 30, 2012.
Berardinelli, James. *ReelViews*. March 29, 2012.
Johanson, MaryAnn. *Washington Post*. March 30, 2012.
Jones, J. R. *Chicago Reader*. March 30, 2012.
Lovell, Wesley. *Oscar Guy*. June 13, 2012.
McWeeny, Drew. *HitFix*. March 30, 2012.
Nusair, David. *Reel Film Reviews*. April 20, 2012.
Robinson, Tasha. *AV Club*. March 29, 2012.
Snider, Eric D. *Film.com*. March 30, 2012.
Verniere, James. *Boston Herald*. March 30, 2012.

QUOTES

Brighton: "Snow White is dead. One of God's great mysteries is his plan for each and every one of us."
The Queen: "Speed it up."
Brighton: "Snow White lived, she died, God rest her soul, Amen. There will be a buffet lunch served at two."

TRIVIA

This was the last film of costume designer Eiko Ishioka before her death.

AWARDS

Nominations:
Oscars 2012: Costume Des.

MONSIEUR LAZHAR
(Bachir Lazhar)

Box Office: $2 million

From *The Blackboard Jungle* (1955) to *Won't Back Down* (2012), the "inspirational teacher" film has become a genre of its own, replete with its own conventions and cliches: The "unteachable class," the unreachable class clown, the unorthodox teacher who tricks, cajoles and ultimately inspires his students to learn. Fortunately, director and screenwriter Philippe Falardeau's subtle and perceptive *Monsieur Lazhar* avoids all of these of these cliches and succeeds in telling a story about dealing with tragic loss that simply happens to take place in a classroom. In a genre characterized by cartoon characterizations and black-and-white solutions to complicated questions, *Monsieur Lazhar* is complex and ambiguous, providing the viewer with no easy answers.

The film begins with a shocking event. Elementary age children play in the snow outside of their Montreal school before the school day begins. Comrades Simon (Emilien Neron) and Alice (Sophie Nelisse) share a snack and childish barbs. Simon is on milk duty that day and therefore enters the school before his fellow students to pick up the milk and transport it to his class room. As he approaches the door he sees his teacher hanging from the ceiling, having just committed suicide. The fallout of this shattering event defines the remainder of the film.

Into this volatile situation steps the titular Monsieur Lazhar (Mohamed Fellag). Since the school year has already begun, replacement teachers are scarce and the hard-pressed principal (Danielle Proulx) eagerly hires Lazhar, even though his approach to acquiring the job is unconventional to say the least. No advertisement has been made for the teaching position but Lazhar shows up in her office, indicates that he read about the tragedy in the newspaper and presents his resume. Though he has only taught in his native Algeria, the administrator, desperate for a body, takes him on. Lazhar the teacher proves to be as unconventional as his approach to interviews. His methods range from unfashionable (changing the student's desks from a new age-y circle of chairs to straight rows) to the unusual (having 11-year-olds learn diction by reading Balzac) to the highly unorthodox (batting an unruly Simon on the head when he is misbehaving). He is also skeptical of the effectiveness of the psychologist who has been assigned to the class to help them deal with the suicide of their previous teacher.

In a more conventional film, the students would first be completely against their new teacher and then, after some magical teaching (perhaps via musical montage), completely on his side. In *Monsieur Lazhar*, their reaction is the mixed response that it would be with any group of people in real life: Alice takes to her new instructor and she quickly becomes his favorite. Soon, in recognition of her advanced intellect, he is giving her adult literature to read. Simon, struggling to deal with the horror he witnessed (and the fact that his manic depressive teacher specifically picked the time and place of her suicide because she knew Simon would be the first to find her), becomes the class clown and an ever present thorn in Lazhar's side. Meanwhile, the decidedly by-the-book student Marie-Frederique (Marie-Eve Beauregard) is not won over in the least and is deeply suspicious of her new teacher's antiquated grammatical terms ("Personal adjectives don't exist any more!" she lectures him in front of the class) and his toss-the-book-out-the-window approach to teaching.

And her suspicions are well-warranted. Lazhar is more complicated then he appears and harbors a secret that explains his unorthodox methods and conceals an exceptionally painful past. His students are not the only ones who are dealing with a tragic loss and his is by far the greater. Why does such a seemingly kind and generous man not share anything about his past with his students or coworkers? Why does he shy away from the pretty young co-teacher, Claire, (Brigitte Poupart) who is obviously attracted to him? As the film progresses, it becomes clear that Lazhar is in as much need of healing as the class he is attempting to heal.

Such a one-sentence summary, however, threatens to over simplify the subtle complexity of Falardeau's film. The key to the film's power is its commitment to realism.The film steadfastly avoids sentimentalism and admirably avoids the easy answers supplied by nearly all the rest of its sub-genre. Lazhar is not a miracle worker and his students are not magically healed overnight. The romance with Claire that would be automatic in a more traditional film does not occur because Lazhar is too deeply wounded by what has happened in his past. The principal, his fellow teachers, his student's parents and government officials are not the one-dimensional heroes or villains they are in nearly all of the films in the genre. They are all normal, flawed human beings trying to deal, in different ways, with an exceptionally emotional situation. A tragic event has occurred in the lives of the students and in the life of their new teacher and the film chronicles the *beginning* of their addressing their grief, a process that will presumably take years if not the rest of their lives. Thanks to Falardeau's subtle script and restrained direction, this process feels absolutely authentic. Also key to the film's authenticity is a superbly nuanced performance by Fellag (himself an immigrant from Algiers) and amazing performances from Neron, Nelisse, and the rest of the children playing the students. Their and Falardeau's greatest achievement (in what is a sad commentary on the state of the genre) is simply creating children that actually look and sound like children. Indeed, the greatest pleasure of Falardeau's wonderful film is simply basking in the world of a realistically depicted classroom, something that is sorely missing from American cinema.

Nate Vercauteren

CREDITS

Bachir Lazhar: Mohamed Fellag
Alice L'Ecuyer: Sophie Nelisse

Simon: Emilien Neron

Mrs. Vaillancourt: Danielle Proulx

Claire: Brigitte Poupart

Origin: Canada

Language: French, English

Released: 2011

Production: Luc Dery, Kim McCraw; MicroScope, Seville Pictures; released by micro_scope, Music Box Films

Directed by: Philippe Falardeau

Written by: Philippe Falardeau

Cinematography by: Ronald Plante

Music by: Martin Leon

Sound: Sylvain Bellemare; Mathieu Beaudin

Music Supervisor: Sebastian Lepine

Editing: Stephane Lafleur

Costumes: Francesca Chamberland

Production Design: Emmanuel Frechette

MPAA rating: PG-13

Running time: 94 minutes

REVIEWS

Burr, Ty. *Boston Globe*. April 19, 2012.

Ebert, Roger. *Chicago Sun Times*. April 25, 2012.

Holden, Stephen. *New York Times*. April 12, 2012.

Hynes, Eric. *Time Out New York*. April 10, 2012.

Jones, J. R. *Chicago Reader*. April 26, 2012.

Mondello, Bob. *NPR*. April 16, 2012.

Orange, Michelle. *Village Voice*. April 10, 2012.

Semley, John. *AV Club*. April 12, 2012.

Smith, Kyle. *New York Post*. April 13, 2012.

van Hoeij, Boyd. *Variety*. April 9, 2012.

TRIVIA

The film was Canada's official submission to the Best Foreign Language Film category of the 84th Academy Awards in 2012.

AWARDS

Nominations:

Oscars 2011: Foreign Film

MOONRISE KINGDOM

Box Office: $45.5 million

Wes Anderson approaches filmmaking with such an increasingly definable style that anyone who has seen his previous films can recognize even a commercial directed by the auteur in just a few seconds time. However, his wonderful *Moonrise Kingdom* eschews much of the cyni-cism that had recently infected works like *The Life Aquatic with Steve Zissou* (2004) and *The Darjeeling Limited* (2007) in favor of a truly delightful story of young love, injected with whimsy to be sure but not weighed down by the cynicism that had arguably derailed the filmmaker since his masterful one-two punch of *Rushmore* (1998) and *The Royal Tenenbaums* (2001). Before the highest-grossing film of his career in over a decade (*Moonrise* grossed $67 million worldwide, only $4 million less than *Tenenbaums*), Anderson shot the highly acclaimed *The Fantastic Mr. Fox* (2009) and it feels like the writer/director's journey into childhood storytelling reawakened the youthful spirit within the filmmaker.

One thing that is immediately notable about *Moonrise Kingdom* is the complete lack of bloat or extended running time in the production. It is as streamlined as an action film, coming in just a hair over 90 minutes and not wasting a single one of them. Part of that streamlined approach can certainly be credited to the relative simplicity of the plot, which can be summed up in an awfully succinct pitch: Two love-struck kids run away from home. Well, one runs away from home and the other runs away from Khaki Scouts Camp. The former is the sweet, somewhat awkward Suzy (Kara Hayward), who has three younger brothers (who all appear to be the same, annoying-to-an-older-sister age) and relatively distant parents (Frances McDormand and Bill Murray), who communicate more often through bull-horn announcements echoing through their home than in a normal human way. The Khaki Scout is the unpopular Sam (Jared Gilman), who, technically, does not run away from home as it is quickly learned that he has no home to go back to. His foster parents have decided not to take him back in. It makes complete sense that the borderline-OCD kid with no family and no friends would fall for the girl more obsessed with the books she steals from the library than other people.

A year after spotting Suzy at a church show about Noah's Ark, Sam breaks free from the Khaki Scouts Camp run by Scout Master Ward (Edward Norton) and crosses an island to find the girl that he has been corresponding with since she shook him from the boredom of his life in a homemade raven costume. The two trace an old Indian path across the island they call home, reading her favorite books, listening to records on the battery-powered player that Suzy stole from her brother, sucking on rocks to create saliva to stave off thirst, and even getting physically involved in awkward ways that teen boys and girls often do, especially in the 1960s when the film is set. They are tracked by an increasing number of odd characters, including Suzy's parents, a sad-sack police officer named Captain Sharp (Bruce Willis), and the rest of the Scouts led by Scout Master Ward.

The behavior of the children seems to spark a bit of lunacy in the adults as Sharp and Suzy's mother flirt and Scout Master Ward seems to grow some backbone in defense of the boy that neither parents nor fellow scouts wanted around. They, ultimately, grow protective of Suzy and Sam as Social Services (Tilda Swinton, and, yes, her character is brilliantly known only as and referred to as "Social Services") looms on the horizon to take Sam back to make him a ward of the system.

Anderson's best works offer a worldview filtered through the eyes of either a child or a man-child. Dignan in *Bottle Rocket* (1996) and Max Fischer in *Rushmore* are clear creative ancestors of Sam Shakusky. They approach the world from their own unique viewpoint in much the same way that Anderson's cinematic style is so uniquely his own. He has discarded the pretension that marred recent work and replaced it with that sense of committed wonder that made Dignan, Max, and, now, Sam such memorable protagonists. But he does so with enough edge to make it still feel like a filmmaker who has not completely sold out to young love. There is little sentimentality in the piece (a poor dog even gets an arrow through the neck) and the beachside, underwear-clad scene between Sam and Suzy borders on making the audience uncomfortable in its exploration of teenage sexuality. And Anderson wisely sidesteps emotional manipulation, finding as much joy in the details as he does the broad strokes of his story. When Sam pauses a story so he can inventory what he has brought on their adventure, one can sense that Anderson sides with the kid when it comes to chronicling as much as experiencing.

Arguably more so than any film in Anderson's career, the technical elements here are beyond criticism. The use of natural light by cinematographer Robert D. Yeoman clearly thinks in unison in terms of visuals with the director for whom he has collaborated on every film. Yeoman and Anderson have a definable look by now, never more so than when they are deftly sliding their camera around Suzy's home as if it is a larger-than-life diorama in a school classroom. And that house has been perfectly designed by Adam Stockhausen, Gerald Sullivan, and Kris Moran, who found the perfect wallpaper, artwork, and even tent designs for the tone of the piece. The film should have been an Oscar nominee for Best Art Direction (it was for Best Original Screenplay), and won that category for the Chicago Film Critics Association. Costume design by Kasia Walicka Maimone, editing by Andrew Weisblum, and music by Alexandre Desplat are also tonally of a piece.

Anderson also excels with ensemble here more than he has in years, drawing more joy-filled performances from Bruce Willis and Edward Norton than they have given in years. McDormand, Murray, and cameos by Jason Schwartzman, Harvey Keitel, and Bob Balaban are as much fun as one would expect them to be in a Wes Anderson film while the two young actors are more than adequate although so heavily stylized that it is hard to discern the true caliber of their acting ability. One can easily say that the entire cast clicks with a similar cadence and rhythm that has become a trademark of the Wes Anderson universe.

It could be argued that such a heavily stylized approach keeps *Moonrise Kingdom* from truly connecting emotionally; that it is like a diorama in terms of humanity as well as art direction. While this is a natural first response, Anderson's film is one that only improves with memory. It is not unlike a reminiscence of first love in the viewer's mind in that the true flaws of it all get smoothed out by the erosion of memory.

Brian Tallerico

CREDITS

Captain Sharp: Bruce Willis
Scout Master Ward: Edward Norton
Walt Bishop: Bill Murray
Laura Bishop: Frances McDormand
Social Services: Tilda Swinton
Sam: Jared Gilman
Suzy: Kara Hayward
Cousin Ben: Jason Schwartzman
Origin: United States
Language: English, French, Spanish
Released: 2012
Production: Jeremy Dawson, Scott Rudin, Steven M. Rales, Wes Anderson; American Empirical Pictures, Scott Rudin Productions; released by Focus Features
Directed by: Wes Anderson
Written by: Wes Anderson; Roman Coppola
Cinematography by: Robert Yeoman
Music by: Alexandre Desplat
Sound: Craig Henighan
Editing: Andrew Weisblum
Art Direction: Gerald Sullivan
Costumes: Kasia Walicka-Maimone
Production Design: Adam Stockhausen
MPAA rating: PG-13
Running time: 94 minutes

REVIEWS

Biancolli, Amy. *San Francisco Chronicle*. May 31, 2012.
Dargis, Manohla. *New York Times*. May 24, 2012.
Goodykoontz, Bill. *Arizona Republic*. June 7, 2012.

Morris, Wesley. *Boston Globe.* May 31, 2012.

O'Hehir, Andrew. *Salon.com.* May 23, 2012.

Rea, Steven. *Philadelphia Inquirer.* June 7, 2012.

Rodriguez, Rene. *Miami Herald.* June 21, 2012.

Scott, Mike. *New Orleans Times-Picayune.* June 22, 2012.

Tobias, Scott. *AV Club.* May 23, 2012.

Williams, Joe. *St. Louis Post-Dispatch.* June 8, 2012.

QUOTES

Social Services: "You two are the most appallingly incompetent custodial guardians Social Services has ever had the misfortune to encounter in a twenty-seven year career!"

TRIVIA

An abandoned Linens 'n Things retail store outside of Newport, Rhode Island was used as the sound stage for the film.

AWARDS

Nominations:

Oscars 2012: Orig. Screenplay

British Acad. 2012: Orig. Screenplay

Golden Globes 2013: Film—Mus./Comedy

Ind. Spirit 2013: Actor—Supporting (Willis), Cinematog., Director (Anderson), Film, Screenplay

Writers Guild 2012: Orig. Screenplay

N

NEIL YOUNG JOURNEYS

Box Office: $215,026

As one of the few veteran rockers who has consistently chosen to move forward with new and challenging works instead of simply resting on past laurels with endless greatest hits tours and the like, the year 2012 found Neil Young in an unusually reflective mood from an artistic standpoint. On the musical side of things, he reunited with his longtime off-and-on backup band Crazy Horse to release two new albums—one of which had them covering a collection of classic American folk tunes like "O Susannah," "This Land is Your Land," and "Get a Job." On a more personal front, he also published *Waging Heavy Peace,* a fascinating and quirky memoir that found the normally reticent Young musing on his life and work, not to mention his obsessions with model train collecting and finding a decent alternative to current digital musical distribution systems. His artistic journey through the past even extended to the world of film—a medium in which he has increasingly dabbled in recent years via the likes of *Greendale* (2004), *Neil Young: Heart of Gold* (2006), *CSNY/Deja Vu* (2008) and *Neil Young Trunk Show* (2009)—with the release of his latest cinematic effort, *Neil Young Journeys,* the third in a loose-knit trilogy of concert documentaries that he has done in conjunction with director Jonathan Demme, following *Heart of Gold* and *Trunk Show,* and while some might wonder what the two of them could possibly have to say with a third film of this type in a little more than six years, it once again offers viewers a fascinating portrait of a true musical legend who is equally compelling both onstage and off.

This time around, intimacy is the key as Young appears on the stage of Toronto's Massey Hall to perform the final shows of a solo tour promoting *Le Noise,* a 2010 release featuring a series of tunes in which he accompanied himself via electric or acoustic guitar with not a single other musicians to be had. From a musical standpoint, Young is seen in peak form here as he runs through a lineup that includes most of the songs from *Le Noise* mixed in with a few classics ("Ohio", complete with archival footage of the Kent State tragedy that inspired him to write it, "After the Gold Rush" and "I Believe in You") and even a couple of previously unreleased tunes, the most notable of which is the lovely "Leia". Interspersed between the songs is footage of a road trip that Young and Demme took through Ontario to get to the concert that finds Young piloting his 1956 Ford Crown Victoria through the streets of the rural town of Omemee, where he spent many of his formative years, while reminiscing about the days that used to be.

Although the idea of Young performing solo may cause people to assume that the music leans closer to his quieter, folkier material, he proves right from the start that this is not the case. He may be up there by himself but he attacks the songs with such power (augmented by a sound mix that brings the music front and center to such a degree that even the acoustic numbers have the speakers practically rumbling off the walls) that any additional instrumentation would come across as superfluous. In keeping with the intimate nature of the proceedings, Demme smartly repeats the trick that helped make his previous concert movie masterpiece *Stop Making Sense* (1984) work so wonderfully and keeps the presence of the audience to an absolute minimum by keep them off-screen for the most part and even minimizing them on the soundtrack as much as possible. He keeps things focused squarely on Young—literally at some points thanks to cameras aimed so closely at Young that a bit of spittle hits the lens at one point—and lets his songs speak for themselves instead of offering up inane shots of fans clapping and cheering in ecstasy. He utilizes the same approach for the most part during the road trip segments and between that and his pre-existing friendship with Young, he gets the often-taciturn singer to open up quite a bit and while the memories may not seem especially revelatory on the surface, it is fascinating to watch him muse upon his memories of how things were back in the day and how things have changed.

For viewers who are somehow unfamiliar with Neil Young and his extensive songbook, *Neil Young Journeys* is not exactly the best way of exposing yourself to his work for the first time—the much gentler *Heart of Gold* is a far more effective gateway to his music for newcomers. For his fan base, which now stretches across several generations, the film works brilliantly both as an individual portrait of an artist who still finds himself grappling with the ideas that first inspired him even after a career that few could possibly hope to equal in either length or artistic relevance and as the eminently satisfying conclusion to one of the most unexpectedly rewarding film trilogies in recent memory. And, yet, there is no sense of finality in anything that we see and hear. In fact, the last scene in the film follows Young as he leaves the stage at Massey Hall for his tour bus and once more sets off down the road for parts unknown. Where he winds up next is anybody's guess but wherever he winds up, here is hoping that he remembers to invite Demme along for the ride as well.

Peter Sobczynski

CREDITSNEIL YOUNG

Origin: Canada, United States
Language: English
Released: 2011
Production: Elliot Rabinowitz, Jonathan Demme; Shakey Pictures, Clinica Estetico; released by Sony Pictures Classics
Directed by: Jonathan Demme
Cinematography by: Declan Quinn
Music by: Neil Young
Editing: Glenn Allen
MPAA rating: PG
Running time: 86 minutes

REVIEWS

Adams, Sam. *AV Club*. June 28, 2012.
Baumgarten, Marjorie. *Austin Chronicle*. September 7, 2012.
Burr, Ty. *Boston Globe*. July 12, 2012.

Ebert, Roger. *Chicago Sun-Times*. July 12, 2012.
Henely, Kalvin. *Slant Magazine*. June 29, 2012.
Hillis, Aaron. *Village Voice*. June 26, 2012.
Holden, Stephen. *New York Times*. June 28, 2012.
Keough, Peter. *Boston Phoenix*. July 10, 2012.
Phillips, Michael. *Chicago Tribune*. July 12, 2012.
Smith, Kyle. *New York Post*. June 29, 2012.

NOBODY WALKS

Box Office: $25,342

Ry-Russo Young's abysmal *Nobody Walks* is the kind of film that people hold up as an example of the pretentious dreck that often emerges from the Sundance Film Festival. What Magnolia saw in this totally false domestic drama other than some beautiful faces to put on a poster or Blu-ray case is beyond comprehension. The only thing less understandable is how such a talented case of actors and actresses or a writer as insightful as Lena Dunham (*Tiny Furniture* [2010], HBO's *Girls*) could get sucked into something that never once feels true. Even common interactions feel overly scripted and the actual drama sounds like something that *Family Guy* would use in a spoof of arthouse movies that snowbound audiences eat up in Park City but die like plucked flowers outside of Utah.

One of the many problems in Dunham and Russo-Young's script is that its central character, Martine (Olivia Thirlby), is an enigma of a character used purely for sexual titillation. She makes out with three different me in the first act alone, almost as if every male she encounters would throw their life away just to stick their tongue down her throat. In fact, the film opens with Martine having a groping encounter with a stranger she met on the plane on her way to Los Angeles. She has headed to the city of angels to work with a filmmaker named Peter (John Krasinski of *The Office*) who is helping her mix sound on a project about bugs. Before long, the film within a film, which seems to consist solely of bug movement and inner monologues become more interesting than the human action of *Nobody Walks*.

Like the old saying of never bringing a gun on stage unless it is going to be used, it is inevitable that Peter and Martine will hook up (with hum-dinger lines like "Marriage is complicated.") but Russo-Young handles it with all the subtlety of a teen girl's diary. In this world, sexuality underpins every interaction. Martine flirts with Peter's assistant David (Rhys Wakefield). Peter's wife Julie (Rosemarie DeWitt) flirts with a patient (Justin Kirk). Julie's daughter Koly (India Ennenga) flirts with David and her Italian teacher. *Nobody Walks* is one of those films that purports that every social interaction is merely a masquerade for pent-up sexual frustration waiting to be acted upon.

The most cardinal sin committed by *Nobody Walks* is in how it completely wastes such a talented cast. Thirlby once seemed like the next great young actress after scene-stealing turns in *Snow Angels* (2007) and *Juno* (2007). She is not so much wasted here as given nothing worthwhile on a character level with which to play. She is so deeply sexualized from her opening scene parking garage heavy petting to scenes in which she is shown in a bra, nightie, bathing suit, etc. that she becomes a caricature of the indie movie girl who sexually awakens an average home. Thirlby deserves better. As do the rest of the talented supporting cast, including the always-great Rosemarie DeWitt, solid-if-not-spectacular John Krasinski, and even a few notable faces in the extended cast, including Jane Levy (TV's *Suburgatory*) and Dylan McDermott. The newcomer here, India Ennenga, is also very solid, actually delivering the most engaging performance in that her awkward, sexually-driven behavior seems more genuine given her teen age. It is believable for her character, just not for the adults around her. *Nobody Walks* is one of those ridiculous films in which a wife sees her husband flirting with a girl and chooses to go flirt herself with her handsome patient before confronting him. That does not happen in the real world. It rarely even happens in movies outside of Sundance. Ultimately, the film has numerous problems but perhaps they can best be boiled down to one declarative sentence—there is not a single, spoiled, obnoxious character that one does not wish would be hit by an L.A. bus by the film's merciful final walk.

After picking it up at Sundance, Magnolia debuted *Nobody Walks* in their new On-Demand platform that gives viewers access to films while they are still in theaters and even debuts them on HDNet for one-time only. The buzz-building strategy has worked for some of their films but others have died on the vine and such was the case with *Nobody Walks,* a work that barely surpassed $25k in its entire domestic theatrical run, never playing on more than seven screens nationwide. Most critics were understandably vicious to the film with Ben Sachs of *The Chicago Reader* noting "This dreary independent drama is essentially an art-world soap opera, but without the melodramatic verve that makes some soap operas interesting." Amanda Mae Meyncke was crueler (but also correct) when she called the film "...a self-important nightmare...shallow script and boring situations. Perhaps that is the simplest way to sum up the film, boring. Offensively boring."

Brian Tallerico

CREDITS

Martine: Olivia Thirlby
Peter: John Krasinski
Julie: Rosemarie DeWitt
Leroy: Dylan McDermott
Billy: Justin Kirk
Kolt: India Ennenga
David: Rhys Wakefield
Origin: United States
Language: English, Italian
Released: 2012
Production: Jonathan Schwartz, Andrea Sperling, Warren Fischer, Alicia Van Couvering; Super Crispy Entertainment; released by Magnolia Pictures
Directed by: Ry Russo-Young
Written by: Ry Russo-Young; Lena Dunham
Cinematography by: Christopher Blauvelt
Music by: Fall on Your Sword; Tiffany Anders
Sound: Rich Bologna
Editing: John W. Walter
Art Direction: Mando Lopez
Costumes: Kim Wilcox
Production Design: Linda Sena
MPAA rating: R
Running time: 83 minutes

REVIEWS

Addiego, Walter V. *San Francisco Chronicle.* October 26, 2012.
Corliss, Richard. *Time.* October 18, 2012.
Debruge, Peter. *Variety.* January 24, 2012.
Ebert, Roger. *Chicago Sun-Times.* November 8, 2012.
McCarthy, Todd. *Hollywood Reporter.* February 10, 2012.
Meyncke, Amanda Mae. *Film.com.* November 4, 2012.
Rabin, Nathan. *AV Club.* October 18, 2012.
Sachs, Ben. *Chicago Reader.* November 8, 2012.
Sharkey, Betsy. *Los Angeles Times.* October 18, 2012.
Smith, Kyle. *New York Post.* October 19, 2012.

QUOTES

Kolt: "Every morning I say drive away, I'm reaching back for you. It is a helpless feeling, this wishing, this wanting, this knowing you will arrive, just minutes after I've gone."

NOT FADE AWAY

Box Office: $610,792

In the wake of the massive critical and commercial success of his ground-breaking television series *The Sopranos*, it was perhaps only a matter of time before creator David Chase, made his move from the world of cable to the big screen. Although some may have hoped for a feature film that would continue the saga of mobster Tony Soprano and his extended families, if only in the hopes of getting some clarification regarding the enigmatic cut to black that ended the show on a much-discussed note, he chose instead to make *Not Fade Away*, a semi-autobiographical and fully engaging tale of a group of kids from the suburbs of New Jersey trying to make it with their rock band during the Sixties, a time when it seemed that rock and roll really could change both the world and the lives of those who practiced it.

Although the film starts with a recreation of one of the pivotal moments in the history of rock—the fateful day in 1961 in which former classmates Mick Jagger and Keith Richards happened to reunite on a train and sowed the seeds for what would eventually become the Rolling Stones—the story it tells, as young narrator Evelyn (Meg Guzulescu) informs us, is about one of the literally countless number of garage bands that never quite made it beyond the garage. This group will eventually be called The Lord Byrons and will be formed by Evelyn's older brother, Doug (John Magaro), and his friends Gene (Jack Huston) and Wells (Will Brill) in the wake of the success of groups like the Beatles and the Stones with the purest of motives—to make music and get girls. At first, Doug is content to simply be the drummer but when an accident involving lead singer Gene forces him to take center stage, he discovers that he likes it, especially when he finally attracts the attention of longtime crush Grace (Bella Heathcoate). Having tasted a bit of musical glory, no matter how minor and fleeting, Doug is forever changed.

This becomes apparent when he returns home from his first semester of college with a Dylanesque head of hair, Cuban heels on his feet and a decision to drop out of school to concentrate on the band full-time. None of this sits particularly well with his working-class father (James Gandolfini) and the rift that already exists between the two of them grows larger as a result. On the musical front, he tries to expand the horizons of the band by insisting that they need to write their own material instead of relying on covers and eventually voices the opinion that he would be a better lead singer than Gene. By comparison, neither Gene nor Wells share his ambitions and would rather continue to be big fish in a very tiny pond that taking a chance on going to the next level, though they try to disguise their insecurity by claiming that they don't want to ruin the "mystique" the group has allegedly developed. As time goes by, Doug's relationships with his father, Grace and his bandmates grow in unanticipated ways and while he may not quite achieve his dreams of rock stardom, his adventures do give him the courage to finally take charge of his own life at last.

At first glance, viewers of *Not Fade Away* may liken it to such films as Cameron Crowe's *Almost Famous* (2000) and Woody Allen's *Radio Days* (1987), two autobiographical films that sought to recreate the effect that popular culture had on the populace in general and themselves in particular. That element is undeniably on display (Chase did play drums in a band before breaking into television) but while those other films were frankly nostalgic in the way that they evoked their particular eras, Chase resolutely refuses to romanticize the era in telling his story. Instead, he evokes the period in a realistic and low-key manner that is both striking and refreshing. Like most stories of this type, it involves a generation gap between parent and child but instead of playing out in the expected ways before a pat resolution, Chase approaches it in a manner that breathes new life into a potentially tired narrative trap. Meanwhile, without rubbing it in the faces of viewers, Chase also quietly and effectively explores other social gaps of the era—class, race and gender—without ever letting them bog down the proceedings. If there is a flaw to his work here, it is in the fact that, having been given the opportunity to spin out a story of the course of several years and dozens of hours on television, he attempts to do the same thing here within the confines of a two-hour running time and the result is a number of subplots, such as the tragedy involving Grace's wild older sister, that are introduced but never completely resolved. (It is fairly evident that Chase shot a lot more material than he could have possibly used and hopefully it will turn up when the film hits Blu-ray.)

Although one might have expected that the first major post-*Sopranos* project from David Chase would get some degree of attention upon its release, *Not Fade Away* failed to make much of an impression when it hit theaters, no doubt due to a combination of its laid-back nature, no-star cast and competition from any number of awards-bait behemoths. Once all the smoke clears, however, there is a very good chance that it will be discovered and embraced by audiences because whatever its flaws, there is much to love about the film. The screenplay offers up a gallery of compelling characters and any number of moments that are both comedic and poignant without coming across as too written. The performances from the largely unknown cast are also impressive—Magaro is so convincing in his transformation as Doug that it almost feels as if the role is being played by different actors and Gandolfini has a couple of moments (including a dinnertime confession to Doug) that are among the best that he has ever played. The soundtrack that Chase has compiled with the assistance of Jersey music legend/*Sopranos* alum Steven van Zandt is a killer collection of lesser-known but enormously catchy period songs filled out with a couple of nifty new tunes. And for all of those worried about Chase and his ability to stick the landing in the wake of the controversy surrounding his last project, let it be known that he concludes *Not Fade Away* with an image that is absolutely dead-on perfect.

Peter Sobczynski

CREDITS

Douglas: John Magaro
Eugene: Jack Huston
Wells: Will Brill
Pat: James Gandolfini
Grace Dietz: Bella Heathcote
Jack Dietz: Christopher McDonald
Jerry Ragavoy: Brad Garrett
Origin: United States
Language: English
Released: 2012
Production: Mark Johnson, David Chase; Chase Films, Gran Via Productions, Indian Paintbrush, Weinstein Company; released by Paramount Vantage
Directed by: David Chase
Written by: David Chase

Cinematography by: Eigil Bryld
Sound: Nerses Gezalyan
Music Supervisor: Steven Van Zandt
Editing: Sidney Wolinsky
Art Direction: Henry Dunn
Costumes: Catherine Marie Thomas
Production Design: Ford Wheeler
MPAA rating: R
Running time: 112 minutes

REVIEWS

Burr, Ty. *Boston Globe*. December 27, 2012.
Foundas, Scott. *Village Voice*. December 11, 2012.
Goldstein, Gary. *Los Angeles Times*. December 20, 2012.
Holden, Stephen. *New York Times*. December 20, 2012.
Jenkins, Mark. *NPR*. December 20, 2012.
Kohn, Eric. *indieWIRE*. October 6, 2012.
Murray, Noel. *AV Club*. December 20, 2012.
Orndorf, Brian. *Blu-ray.com*. October 23, 2012.
Pais, Matt. *RedEye*. December 27, 2012.
Rooney, David. *Hollywood Reporter*. October 5, 2012.

O

OCTOBER BABY

Every life is beautiful.
—Movie tagline

Box Office: $5.4 million

Aside from *The Hunger Games*, there was another Hollywood miracle that opened huge the weekend of March 23, 2012—that movie was *October Baby*, which collected $1.7 million, a surprising feat that put it in the number eight spot of the American box office. Opening in only 390 theaters nationwide, the film earned an average of $4,352, which helped cover in a single weekend the film's approximate budget of one million dollars.

Co-written and directed by brothers Andrew and Jon Erwin, *October Baby* receives certain inspiration from the life story of Gianna Jessen, an abortion survivor who has cerebral palsy and currently speaks internationally for the pro-life cause. The script proves to be very passionate about this cause as well, but unfortunately the troublesome film is not as equally inspired by the desire to tell a spirited story, or carry *October Baby* beyond the boundaries of juvenile maudlin evangelism.

Newcomer Rachel Hendrix plays a variation on Jessen named Hannah, a home-schooled nineteen-year-old who was raised Baptist. After she collapses during her lead performance in a school play, Hannah is sent to the hospital, where her symptoms of seizures and dramatic scribbles in her diary ("I am drowning") are diagnosed as the result of her premature birth, which was caused by a failed abortion attempt by her biological mother (Shari Rigby). Feeling completely lost about her identity and worth, she receives assistance from her male friend from childhood, Jason (Jason Burkey), who is able to finagle his upcoming road trip with friends to include a pit stop at Mobile, Alabama, the town in which Hannah was born.

What ensues is a quarter road-trip movie, all pro-life melodrama that leads Hannah to the disturbed abortion clinic nurse (Jasmine Guy) who ultimately delivered her and the twin brother whom Hannah was unaware of (he was born with one arm and low-functioning brain activity), and most importantly, the abandoning mother who refuses to acknowledge their shared past.

Shortly after being ignored by her birth mother, Hannah is scooped up by her father (John Schneider, who played Bo Duke on *Dukes of Hazzard*) who brings her back home in hopes to continue healing. Hannah begins to find comfort when she hears the story about how her adopted mother lost two twins of her own, but soon after had heard in a cathedral's church bulletin about the availability of two prematurely born twins who survived an abortion attempt. This inspires Hannah to go to that cathedral, where she has a brief conversation with a priest who tells her that since God has forgiven us, we have the power to forgive others, and that "anger is a burden." With support from her father, Hannah goes back to her birth mother's office building, and leaves a simple note that says "I forgive you."

Though under the control of sappy direction that believes drama is best achieved by squeezing tears out of actors or having them look off into the distance, the cast of *October Baby* collectively provides genuine performances that breathe some life into their cardboard structuring of character. Hendrix and Guy, sharing the film's most confident scene, come out as the two who are best able to make their archetypes believable.

A fine service to the movie (and those who like soft rock groups like The Fray or Coldplay) the *October Baby* soundtrack is populated by musicians and singer-songwriters that share the movie's wholesome optimism, and express such in often pretty tunes that use gentle voices with climactic piano and/or guitar accompaniments. Key inspiration Jessen even has her own song, "Ocean Floor," appear in the film during the montage in which Hannah walks to the cathedral and subsequently has her epiphany about forgiveness. The song "Life is Beautiful" by The Afters becomes a ringing jingle for the end of the movie, and opines with such a quasi-generic statement about what indeed makes life beautiful: the specialty of "fireworks," "New Year's Eve dreams," "a mother's prayer," "Christmas lights," among others.

Aside from a solid selection of songs, *October Baby* can also take aesthetic kudos for its sunny cinematography, as coordinated by credited cinematographer Erwin brother Jon. The heavy usage of bright sun might be appear within sappy scenes, but such light becomes effective in a warming spiritual sense, combined with hopeful southern American afternoons (the film was shot in Alabama) to create the general presence of the "sun" that is eluded to by the priest during Hannah's cathedral visit (that moment being a sequence in which the cathedral is lit like it is noontime, despite the priest himself indicating it is closing time for the day). With some lens flare added in for stylistic measure, this type of cinematic camerawork that elevates *October Baby* beyond TV quality would at least bring a tear to Michael Bay's eye.

The third act is especially troublesome in that it surprisingly adds a devastating tragedy to the story, but tries to comfort the viewer that such a surprise in the story is believable because it is an example of a miracle by God. This might as well be on the same level of fabrication, if not even more so, than the sequence in which Hannah is able to excuse her road tripping friends from a $5,000 parking fine by saying she is looking for her birth mother, or the entire concept of a girl of Hannah's age not knowing she was born prematurely, adopted, or that she had a brother. Considering the other phony dramatic plot components that fill this film, *October Baby* does not earn the right from the viewer to be able to credibly pull something like this off—instead, the viewer is more likely to feel that last stab at the heart as more melodrama for this movie, with its closing example being its most shameless sermon yet. No positive testament to the message it is trying to

convey, the implementation of God's miracles is handled like another one of *October Baby's* egregious contrivances.

With such a direct fixation on preaching to those who already believe in its cause, this film is not open to start a discussion about the difficult issue itself. *October Baby* is blandly wholesome pro-life propaganda that deserves its fate of only preaching to its choir.

Nick Allen

CREDITS

Hannah: Rachel Hendrix
Jason: Jason Burke
Jacob: John Schneider
Grace: Jennifer Price
Alanna: Colleen Trussler
Origin: United States
Language: English
Released: 2012
Production: Justin Tolley, Dan Atchison, Jon Erwin, Cecil Stokes; Gravitas; released by Samuel Goldwyn Films
Directed by: Andrew Erwin; Jon Erwin
Written by: Andrew Erwin; Jon Erwin; Cecil Stokes; Theresa Preston
Cinematography by: Jon Erwin
Music by: Paul Mills
Editing: Andrew Erwin
Sound: Stephen Preston
Costumes: Anna Redmon
Production Design: Edward Gurney, Jr.
MPAA rating: PG-13
Running time: 107 minutes

REVIEWS

Catsoulis, Jeannette. *New York Times*. March 22, 2012.
Ebert, Roger. *Chicago Sun-Times*. March 22, 2012.
Feeney, Mark. *Boston Globe*. April 12, 2012.
Goldstein, Gary. *Los Angeles Times*. March 22, 2012.
Leydon, Joe. *Variety*. March 22, 2012.
Long, Tom. *Detroit News*. March 23, 2012.
Merry, Stephanie. *Washington Post*. March 23, 2012.
Orange, Michelle. *Village Voice*. March 20, 2012.
Scheck, Frank. *Hollywood Reporter*. March 23, 2012.
Smith, Kyle. *New York Post*. March 23, 2012.

QUOTES

Hannah: "I have so many unanswered questions, questions I feel but can't even begin to speak because there are no words to express them."

TRIVIA

This film is inspired by the true story of Gianna Jessen, who survived a saline abortion in 1977.

THE ODD LIFE OF TIMOTHY GREEN

He's a force of nature.
—Movie tagline

Box Office: $51.9 million

Fables are an eternal part of storytelling. One may even be so inclined to refer to them as the adult's version of fairy tales. But even that would be so erroneous in misleading those who believe they had grown out of stories like *Jack and the Beanstalk* and done their best to remove George Orwell's *Animal Farm* from their psyche. Fable is a fanciful word that is too often mistaken for tales of mere magical fantasies. A fable is not a fable if said magical properties involve just mere humans and a deus ex machina. The adoption headquarters at which one particularly odd story is told by a prospective couple could easily have been interrupted to dismiss its metaphorical implications in the real world. If only the child welfare officers on hand had enough knowledge of the meaning of the term "fable" they could have stopped this story dead in its tracks and thrown its narrators into the nearest lock-up.

The story in question is being told by Jim and Cindy Green (Joel Edgerton and Jennifer Garner). In an effort to prove themselves as worthy candidates for an adoption, they provide an epilogue to their application with the story of a fateful night that they swear to be true. Having exhausted their medical options for having a kid the old-fashioned way, the couple decides to put the matter behind them in a wine-fueled effort to create the perfect child. With slips of paper in hand they write down each endearing quality they want their little miracle to have from simple manners to life accomplishments. They bury the scraps in the backyard, a rainstorm appears in the middle of a drought just over them, and, the next thing they know, a muddy ten-year-old boy is wandering around their house.

With little choice in the matter, Jim and Cindy announce the newcomer, Timothy (CJ Adams), as their own while hiding the boy's curious deformity of leaves growing out of his ankles. His oddness certainly cannot be covered up entirely though. Despite assuming every one of their wishes came true, Jim and Cindy may begin to feel as if they made a deal with a devious genie. Timothy's lack of musical prowess hardly impresses Cindy's sister (Rosemarie DeWitt), a model of a braggart parent. Scoring the winning goal is a bit difficult if he

does not understand how to play the game. Honest to a fault seems like a great quality until you are exposing the warts and all of mommy's hard-nosed boss (Dianne Wiest); though mostly the warts. Only a new classmate (Odeya Rush) of Timothy's seems not to mind that he is prone to make like a tree sometimes, literally and figuratively, thus giving his tale the fable-like quality it seeks.

Young children with magical capabilities have immediate appeal to kids interested in fiction which puts the words to their own escapist fantasies. *Harry Potter* certainly proved that. Disney had their *Witch Mountain* films in the '70s. Even *The Twilight Zone* on television and its 1983 film likely sparked a few cool, if wicked, ideas with its tale of a young boy who can have whatever he wants just by thinking of it. Bet Timothy Green wishes he had such authority and kids in the audience may be confused about his purpose in this world. Their moms and dads on the other hand may be more interested in Jim and Cindy's side of the story as the couple going through the growing pains of being unexpectant parents. With their expectations of a fantasy world where their child is just as they had imagined, Hedges' screenplay has potential deeper implications over the true exertion of shaping a new human being to becoming a perfect fit for this world. As this is exposed to be as perplexing as the magical portion of the tale, one must be inclined to ask—Just who is this film supposed to be for?

What is soon discovered about Timothy's preciously attached foliage is that they cannot be plucked nor removed by sharp botanist tools. When he does begin to lose them, one is left to wonder if it is because he has completed some task of destiny, learned a valuable lesson or simply because autumn is going full bloom. Timothy experiencing his own growing pains through varying displays of empathy and understanding would be a positive lesson for kids too confused by his sun-worshipping recharge. Without a justification of Timothy's purpose though, Hedges' screenplay falls back on the old axiom of how a miraculous protagonist makes a difference in every character that needs a friend or a midstream change-of-heart. A nice sentiment, except maybe for those who walk into an adoption agency everyday without a story like this or the gullible advisors willing to accept it as strong parenting rather than putting them in straitjackets.

All of this maddening bewilderment into the lessons of parenthood makes the kidnapping couple at the center of *Raising Arizona* (1987) seem stable. Even the adoption advisors are so behind in the concept of how to best counter bullying that they seemed shocked that public social interaction would be a positive in a child's growth. Peter Hedges is responsible for the adaptation of his novel, *What's Eating Gilbert Grape?* (1993) and has committed himself admirably enough with the directorial efforts of his original scripts, *Pieces of April* (2002) and *Dan In Real Life* (2007). *The Odd Life of Timothy Green* feels like it came from the same head with its themes of familial outsiders and general quirk to its lessons of bonding, but written as if for another planet; one actually less advanced in child-rearing. It is enough to check out of even before Hedges succumbs to further complications about unemployment and the patenting of an idea so wacky that adults and kids alike are liable to leave fashioning more jokes about what number two pencils are really made out of. Possibly the same thing as this screenplay.

Erik Childress

CREDITS

Timothy Green: CJ Adams
Cindy Green: Jennifer Garner
Jim Green: Joel Edgerton
Franklin Crudstaff: Ron Livingston
Ms. Crudstaff: Dianne Wiest
Brenda Best: Rosemarie DeWitt
James Green Sr.: David Morse
Uncle Bub: M. M. Emmet Walsh
Aunt Mel: Lois Smith
Origin: United States
Language: English
Released: 2012
Production: Ahmet Zappa, Scott Sanders, James Whitaker; Scott Sanders Productions, Monsterfoot Productions; released by Walt Disney Pictures
Directed by: Peter Hedges
Written by: Peter Hedges
Cinematography by: John Toll
Music by: Geoff Zanelli
Sound: Michael Kirchberger
Editing: Andrew Mondshein
Costumes: Susie DeSanto
Production Design: Wynn Thomas
MPAA rating: PG
Running time: 100 minutes

REVIEWS

Bell, Josh. *Las Vegas Weekly.* August 15, 2012.
Burr, Ty. *Boston Globe.* August 15, 2012.
Ebert, Roger. *Chicago Sun-Times.* August 15, 2012.
Kenigsberg, Ben. *Time Out Chicago.* August 14, 2012.
Minow, Nell. *Beliefnet.* August 16, 2012.
Nusair, David. *Reel Film Reviews.* August 15, 2012.
Orndorf, Brian. *Blu-ray.com.* August 17, 2012.
Phipps, Keith. *AV Club.* August 14, 2012.
Rocchi, James. *MSN Movies.* August 14, 2012.
Scott, A. O. *New York Times.* August 15, 2012.

QUOTES

Uncle Bub: "Did you know that I invented the peanut butter and jelly sandwich?"
Timothy Green: "Did you know that I'm a big fan of your work?"

TRIVIA

The role of Cindy was originally offered to Sandra Bullock.

ON THE ROAD

The best teacher is experience.
    —Movie tagline

Box Office: $154,250

Ever since the publication of Jack Kerouac's *On the Road* in 1957, there have been attempts to bring his ground-breaking chronicle of the Beat Generation to the big screen. Soon after its initial publication, Kerouac himself lobbied Marlon Brando in a letter to star in one proposed version, and after acquiring the rights to the project in the late 1970s, Francis Ford Coppola spearheaded a number of attempts that, at various times, featured the likes of himself, Joel Schumacher, and Gus van Sant behind the camera and potential stars such as Brad Pitt, Ethan Hawke, and Billy Crudup in front of it. None of these versions panned out, of course, and for a long time, the book was deemed by many to simply be unfilmable. Finally, after countless delays and false starts, *On the Road* has finally made the transition from the page to the screen via screenwriter Jose Rivera and director Walter Salles, who previously collaborated on *The Motorcycle Diaries* (2004)—another period drama featuring an enigmatic duo on a life-changing road trip—but after sitting through this misfired adaptation, most people will come away from it wondering why they bothered to in the first place if the end result was going to be a lifeless waxwork of this sort.

Beginning in 1947, the film opens as aspiring writer Sal Paradise (Sam Riley) is introduced, via poet friend Carlo Marx (Tom Sturridge), to charismatic, pot-smoking, car-stealing rebel Dean Moriarity (Garret Hedlund) and his underage wife Marylou (Kristen Stewart). Caught up in the thrall of Dean's considerable personality, Sal agrees to venture out west to visit and after hitchhiking all the way to Denver, he discovers that Dean is also carrying on, with Marylou's full knowledge (if not necessarily her approval), with the upper-class Camille (Kirsten Dunst). Over the next couple of years, Sal, Dean and sometimes Marylou will bounce in and out of the lives and beds of themselves and a wide array of associates of Dean, the most notable being his junkie mentor Old Bull Lee (Viggo Mortensen) and his wife (Amy Adams), in jaunts taking them to such locales as New York, San Francisco, New Orleans and Mexico. After a while, the heedlessness that dictates Dean and his entire existence begins to weary the others—especially when he marries Camille but thoughtlessly leaves her alone with their baby while he goes out to whoop it up with Sal—and before long, the party is over. For Dean, this leaves the former life of the party on the outside looking in but for Sal, these misadventures are just the spark that he needs to begin penning the semi-autobiographical book that will immortalize his friends forever in the annals of literary history.

One of the key problems with bringing *On the Road* to the screen is the inescapable fact that for all of its literary merits (some of which are admittedly debatable), the book simply does not possess much in the way of a narrative spine with which to build a film. Perhaps in recognition of this, Salles and Rivera have included other materials into the mix, including correspondence and bits from the original version of the book that Kerouac famously wrote on a scroll as one unbroken piece before reworking it into the version that was eventually published, but even with this additional material to draw on, there is still precious little that one might consider to be a plot. As a result, anyone charged with making a successful film out of this material has to accomplish two things—they have to figure out a way of reconceptualizing the distinct and revolutionary prose stylings of Kerouac into purely cinematic terms and they have to find actors magnetic enough to properly embody the characters, especially in regards to the role of Dean Moriarty.

Alas, the movie utterly fails in regards to both counts. Salles stages the scenes in a respectful enough manner but that proves to be the incorrect approach. The film cries out for a messier, edgier take that takes chances with the material but outside of including a little more nudity than is usually seen in American films these days, Salles is far too safe and sensible for its own good and there are long stretches where the whole enterprise feels less like an adaptation of *On the Road* than it does a series of Gap ads vaguely inspired by it. Stripped of the magic of Kerouac's voice, the film quickly devolves into a seemingly endless series of monotonous misadventures that, even after being shorn of nearly fifteen minutes following its tepidly-received world premiere at Cannes, will eventually test the patience of most viewers.

On the performance end, the film is further hobbled by the fact that Garret Hedlund is a complete bore in the crucial role of Dean—despite his obvious efforts and willingness to drop his pants at a moment's notice, he is such a blank that it strains credibility to the breaking point when the other characters talk about his powerful personality. Things are a little better in regards to the smaller supporting turns—Viggo Mortensen and Amy Adams make a vivid impression in their brief appearances, and as Marylou, Kristen Stewart gives her liveliest performance in years and once again reminds viewers of the undeniable talent that kind of got pushed to the wayside amidst all the hype surrounding the *Twilight* series.

Although *On the Road* was considered unfilmable by many, that did not necessarily mean that a movie version was inherently doomed to failure. After all, many people said the same thing about the William Burroughs classic *Naked Lunch* and that was transformed into a pretty extraordinary movie. In that case, however, everyone lucked out because the property was placed in the hands of a director, David Cronenberg, who was able to make it work as cinema while still staying true to the spirit of the book by taking the same kind of audacious risks that Burroughs himself did on the page. By comparison, Salles seems to have been so overwhelmed by the notion of making a film that would satisfy longtime fans of the book while at the same time introducing it to a new generation that he decided to take the safest route possible so as to avoid upsetting either group. The result, perhaps inevitably, is a film that winds up satisfying no one—fans of the book and Kerouac will bemoan it as one long missed opportunity while those who have heard of the book before but who have never actually read it will come away from the film wondering what all the fuss was about.

Peter Sobczynski

CREDITS

Sal Paradise: Sam Riley
Dean Moriarty: Garrett Hedlund
Marylou: Kristen Stewart
Jane: Amy Adams
Carlo Marx: Tom Sturridge
Terry: Alice Braga
Galatea Dunkel: Elisabeth (Elissabeth, Elizabeth, Liz) Moss
Ed Dunkel: Danny Morgan
Camille: Kirsten Dunst
Old Bull Lee: Viggo Mortensen
Origin: Brazil, France
Language: English

Released: 2012

Production: Charles Gillibert, Nathanael Karmitz, Rebecca Yeldham; MK2, American Zoetrope; released by IFC Films

Directed by: Walter Salles

Written by: Jose Rivera

Cinematography by: Eric Gautier

Music by: Gustavo Santaolalla

Sound: Martin Hernandez

Music Supervisor: Lynn Fainchtein

Editing: Francois Gedigier

Art Direction: Martin Gendron

Costumes: Danny Glicker

Production Design: Carlos Conti

MPAA rating: R

Running time: 124 minutes

REVIEWS

Brady, Tara. *Irish Times*. October 13, 2012.

Corliss, Richard. *Time*. December 24, 2012.

Haglund, David. *Slate*. December 20, 2012.

Holden, Stephen. *New York Times*. December 20, 2012.

Holmes, Linda. *NPR*. November 7, 2012.

Kenny, Glenn. *MSN News*. December 19, 2012.

Murray, Noel. *AV Club*. December 20, 2012.

Orndorf, Brian. *Blu-ray.com*. December 19, 2012.

Pinkerton, Nick. *Village Voice*. December 18, 2012.

Turan, Kenneth. *Los Angeles Times*. December 20, 2012.

TRIVIA

Johnny Depp turned down the role of Sal Paradise when the film was in development in the early 1990s.

ONCE UPON A TIME IN ANATOLIA

(Bir zamanlar Anadolu'da)

Box Office: $152,408

With masterworks like *Distant* (2002), *Climates* (2006), and *Three Monkeys* (2008), Turkish director Nuri Bilge Ceylan established himself as one of the most interesting and admired filmmakers on the international scene. His latest, *Once Upon a Time in Anatolia*, earned him even more accolades, taking the prize as the co-winner of the Grand Prix at the 2011 Cannes Film Festival with the Dardenne Brothers' stunning *The Kid with a Bike* (which recorded a 2012 theatrical domestic release as well with the vagaries of international distribution...it takes an inordinate amount of time for Cannes successes to make their way across the pond).

Occupying one of the smallest genres in film history—the philosophical procedural—with Bong Joon-ho's amazing *Memories of Murder* (2003) and David Fincher's masterpiece *Zodiac* (2007), *Anatolia* is the work of a filmmaker who finds depth in the mundane. It is a film about a murder that becomes about everything BUT the actual crime as Ceylan finds gravity, depth, and beauty in the people scouring the Turkish countryside on a lonely night instead of the mere facts of the crime. Beautiful and haunting, it is one of the best foreign language films of 2012.

The plot of *Anatolia* is so simple that it would probably be told in its entirety before the bum-bum sound that opens an episode of NBC's long-running *Law & Order*. A group of average-looking Turkish police officers are driving around a haggard, mumbling prisoner in the middle of the night. They talk about everything but what they are doing. They talk about smoking. They talk about yogurt. They get calls from loved ones. They yawn, nod off, laugh at inside jokes, etc. Then it is almost as if they remember that they are working on a case. The man in the back seat killed someone and buried the body. He is either screwing with them as he claims to not know where the body is that he is supposed to be leading them to or was honestly too drunk to remember. Either way, it becomes clear very early that Ceylan's film is mostly about the people driving around trying to find a body and not how the body got there in the first place.

The cops and their criminal are not alone. It is a caravan of crime-solvers as the officers are joined by gravediggers in one car and a prosecutor, doctor, and the handicapped brother of the accused in another. Each group has a unique angle and perspective on the crime and it is interesting how Ceylan often sticks with those not searching the latest tree or gulley for the body as he is more interested in their dialogue than the action.

In many ways, *Anatolia* is actually more narratively conventional than the even-more-obscure works of Ceylan's past. Those were almost entirely mood pieces with long scenes of no dialogue at all. *Anatolia* is actually pretty dialogue heavy as the men on this long night get more philosophical as time goes on. Ceylan seems more honestly interested in these characters than the ones he has used more as devices in the past. He knows and likes these characters and tells viewers so much about them and their worlds just through their dialogue and action on one chilly night.

There is a fluidity to the shooting of *Anatolia* by Ceylan regular collaborator Gokhan Tiryaki that gives the film a lyrical tone without ever over-emphasizing it in the flashier, more poetic style of Ceylan's previous work. At one point, an apple falls from a tree and the camera follows it down a hill and into a river as a conversation takes place closer to the tree. It is almost as if the viewer is a traveler on this journey, looking at the apple or watching a train go by while others talk. As people do, the focus is not always on the faces of the people speaking and Ceylan creates atmosphere and realism with Tiryaki in the way they combine the realistic and the poetic, often in the same shot. It is a gift with visual composition that Ceylan has used in the past for more obviously gorgeous visual storytelling but that is no less powerful here although it is arguably much more subtle. It is the way that Ceylan weaves in and out of conversation and groups of characters until he settles on the doctor and the prosecutor, who will drive the entire the final act. Like the apple ends up in the river, the film merely ends up with them.

To be fair, *Once Upon a Time in Anatolia* is missing something of the emotional resonance that Ceylan found in his previous works. Those had a more heartfelt immediacy to them, if purely through the breathtaking composition of their visuals. This work is more of a slow burn, the kind of work that does not immediately take one's breath away but lingers in the mind much longer than just a pretty picture.

Brian Tallerico

CREDITS

Kenan: Firat Tanis
Ramazan: Burhan Yildiz
Commissar Naci: Yilmaz Erdogan
Nusret: Taner Birsel
Dr. Cemal: Muhammet Uzuner
Origin: Turkey
Language: Turkish
Released: 2012
Production: Zeynep Ozbatur Atakan; 1000 Volt, Zeyno Film; released by The Cinema Guild
Directed by: Nuri Bilge Ceylan
Written by: Nuri Bilge Ceylan; Ercan Kesal; Ebru Ceylan
Cinematography by: Gokhan Tiryaki
Sound: Thomas Robert
Editing: Bora Goksingol
Art Direction: Dilek Yapkuoz Ayaztuna
Production Design: Cagri Erdogan
MPAA rating: Unrated
Running time: 150 minutes

REVIEWS

Bradshaw, Peter. *The Guardian*. March 16, 2012.
Dargis, Manohla. *New York Times*. January 3, 2012.
Ebert, Roger. *Chicago Sun-Times*. March 7, 2012.
Kohn, Eric. *indieWIRE*. December 31, 2011.
Lacey, Liam. *The Globe and Mail*. March 1, 2012.
Morris, Wesley. *Boston Globe*. May 17, 2012.
O'Hehir, Andrew. *Salon.com*. January 4, 2012.
Orange, Michelle. *Movieline*. January 5, 2012.
Phillips, Michael. *Chicago Tribune*. March 10, 2012.
Tobias, Scott. *AV Club*. January 4, 2012.

TRIVIA

This film was Turkey's official submission to the Best Foreign Language Film category of the 84th Academy Awards.

AWARDS

Nominations:

Ind. Spirit 2013: Foreign Film

ONE FOR THE MONEY

She's looking for a few not-so-good men.
    —Movie tagline

Box Office: $26.4 million

One for the Money was in a twenty-year gestation period before finally making it to the big screen in 2012. The film would have been the first in a series of adaptations of Janet Evanovich's popular novels about Stephanie Plum. It is easy to understand why a high-profile, if limited, actress would want to jump at the chance to start a franchise for themselves with this series. Popular lines of books have been known to be quite profitable when finally translated to screen. It stands to reason that fans will show up regardless of quality. And it could be a fun, juicy part if the material is up to the task of creating a believable and interesting enough character to warrant a full series of movie adaptations.

But that is not the case here. Fans of the books stayed away in droves upon the release of *One for the Money*. Lions Gate, the studio that distributed the film, did so with little to no fanfare, much to the bewilderment of critics who had no idea the movie existed until just days before its release and to fans who suddenly saw that their heroine was given the big-screen treatment without their knowledge or approval. It is apparent from the first five minutes why nobody had any interest in making this film a success. It is the cinematic equivalent of Nutraloaf, the stunningly bland food served to prisoners as a form of punishment that many say is worse than solitary confinement.

The movie opens with Stephanie (Katherine Heigl), a divorcee, visiting her parents and informing them that she has been laid off from Macy's where she was a lingerie manager. One day, she goes to her cousin Vinny's bail bond office and instantly lands a job as a freelance bounty hunter. Her first case is to apprehend Joe Morelli (Jason O'Mara), a former police officer on bail for committing first-degree murder. It just so happens these two characters have a past. Of course, they are both good-looking and attracted to each other. He all but seduces her within minutes of meeting her again and ends up escaping from her. If she actually does get him, she gets a cut of the $50,000 he is worth.

She enlists the help of Ranger (Daniel Sunjata), a far-more-experienced bounty hunter who takes her under his wing, buys her a gun, takes her target shooting and introduces her to all forms of bounty hunter terminology. She tries to get help from other people, including Morelli's mother, a distant relative who happens to be a cop, a couple of stereotypical Jersey hookers and a boxing gym owner (John Leguizamo). An altercation at the boxing gym leads to Stephanie and Joe joining up again for another meet-cute. Again, she fails to take him in. The film then jumps to another subplot in which Stephanie's parents try to fix her up with an appliance salesman who miraculously has inside information for Stephanie to help her try and nab Morelli (so she can lose him again?).

She does manage to get Morelli's car keys. She steals his car and uses it to get around. She eventually tries to find someone more instantly lucrative and easier to nab. She gets assigned to track down an old nudist who missed a court appearance, which leads to another run-in with Morelli who sees that she stole his car. One rainy night, he tries to steal his car back, but she knows how to remove fuses from engines, which she regards as strictly a New Jersey trick. Apparently, no other car in the U.S. has this feature. She spends much of the rest of the movie looking for someone named Carmen, Morelli's informant who has disappeared.

There is a moment where Stephanie's grandmother (Debbie Reynolds) tells her that she "lacks vision," which pretty much sums up every aspect of *One for the Money*. Director Julie Anne Robinson seems to relate all too well to Stephanie Plum's plight of needing to make money quickly, no matter what it takes to make it. The film has the feeling of being slapped together with nary a trace of passion or feeling for the characters or storyline. Screenwriters Stacy Sherman, Karen Ray and Liz Brixius, likewise, seemed to have turned in a first draft in hopes that the actors would maybe mess around with it, cut loose with it and make it their own. That may have worked for Heigl's only decent foray into film acting with Judd Apatow's *Knocked Up* (2007), but left to her own devices, she has nothing to offer.

This lack of ambition is further evidenced by overnarration from Stephanie Plum, a device that adds nothing in terms of insight or wit. The delivery alone sounds as though Heigl had already spent the money she made for making the film and had no interest in trying to make it better. At one point in the film, Stephanie is handcuffed naked to a shower stall by Morelli and set free by Ranger. She narrates: "That's two men in one evening who saw me naked and walked away. Should I be worried?" Judging by the lack of talent to make this film and the lack of audience to come out and see it, it is safe to say that, yes, Katherine Heigl should be worried.

Collin Souter

CREDITS

Stephanie Plum: Katherine Heigl
Joe Morelli: Jason O'Mara
Ranger: Daniel Sunjata
Jimmy Alpaca: John Leguizamo
Lula: Sherri Shepherd
Grandma Mazur: Debbie Reynolds
Origin: United States
Language: English
Released: 2012
Production: Wendy Finerman, Sidney Kimmel, Gary Lucchesi, Tom Rosenberg; Lakeshore Entertainment, Sidney Kimmel Entertainment; released by Lionsgate
Directed by: Julie Anne Robinson
Written by: Stacy Sherman; Karen Ray; Liz Brixius
Cinematography by: Jim Whitaker
Music by: Deborah Lurie
Sound: Michael Babcock
Music Supervisor: Eric Craig
Editing: Lisa Zeno Churgin
Costumes: Michael Dennison
Production Design: Franco-Giacomo Carbone
MPAA rating: PG-13
Running time: 106 minutes

REVIEWS

Barker, Andrew. *Variety*. January 27, 2012.
Gleiberman, Owen. *Entertainment Weekly*. January 27, 2012.
Howell, Peter. *Toronto Star*. January 26, 2012.
Lacey, Liam. *Globe and Mail*. January 27, 2012.
Linden, Sheri. *Los Angeles Times*. January 30, 2012.
Schager, Nick. *Time Out New York*. January 30, 2012.
Scott, A. O. *New York Times*. January 27, 2012.
Sobczynski, Peter. *eFilmcritic.com*. January 27, 2012.
Weitzman, Elizabeth. *New York Daily News*. January 27, 2012.
Whitty, Stephen. *Newark Star-Ledger*. January 27, 2012.

QUOTES

Ranger: "I'm busy."
Stephanie Plum: "I'm naked."
Ranger: "I'll be right there."

TRIVIA

Author Janet Evanovich told *USA Today* that "Katherine Heigl

is the perfect Stephanie Plum" and that now, whenever she writes about Stephanie Plum, she sees visualizes Heigl.

AWARDS

Nominations:

Golden Raspberries 2012: Worst Actress (Heigl)

P

THE PAPERBOY

Box Office: $693,286

When Lee Daniels' *The Paperboy* premiered at the 2012 Cannes Film Festival, it almost became the stuff of legend thanks to a critical reaction that either denounced it as one of the worst, most over-the-top movies to ever play the festival or praising it as some kind of trash masterpiece. Such reaction tends to overshadow everything else at such high prestige festivals where the prizes given out tend to shift the entire dynamic of the year-end awards season. *The Paperboy*, while it did not win the Palme d'Or, ended up being one of the top curiosity items in recent years, generating a reputation as a movie everyone has to see to believe. Given Daniels' previous movie *Precious: Based on the Novel Push by Sapphire* (2009) and its desperate attempts to thoroughly depress everyone in its path, it comes as no surprise that Daniels would turn heads again in a bigger, broader fashion.

The reputation, however, is not earned, at least not in the film that ended up being released to the general public. *The Paperboy* wants to be trashy, over-the-top, pulpy and permanently engrained in the memories of every viewer who sits through the entire thing, but in the end, it is little more than an average crime drama with a scene of someone urinating on someone else to give it a boost as a curiosity item. It has small moments of audaciousness, but most of it is in large part due to the big name cast and their willingness to do Daniels' bidding. Were it not for the cast, the movie would have arrived and disappeared into obscurity.

The story takes place in Moat County, Florida in 1969. Zac Efron plays the titular Paperboy, a young budding journalist named Jack Jansen whose father, W.W. Jansen (Scott Glenn), runs the local paper. Living with Jack is his stepmom-to-be and their maid, Anita Chester (Macy Gray), who narrates the story through flashback as she gives an interview for a book written about the story the film is about to tell. Jack's brother, Ward Jansen (Matthew McConaughey), is a Pulitzer Prize-winning journalist who comes back to town to investigate the conviction of an alleged killer named Hillary Van Wetter (John Cusack). With him is a Brit of African descent named Yardley (David Oyelowo), who works as his assistant and who adds to the racial tension already present in the area.

The key to this investigation is a sultry woman named Charlotte Bless (Nicole Kidman), a waitress who has a weakness for men behind bars. She and Hillary have been trading steamy, passionate love letters since his incarceration and when she offers to use these letters to help Ward with the investigation, it results in a heated sexual exchange in a prison visiting room where they are forbidden to touch each other. Hillary is suspected of killing a police officer, and, given his temperament and erratic behavior, it would come as no surprise to anyone if he actually did it. To avoid further distractions, Ward tries to get Hillary to talk without the aide of Charlotte.

Jack is also attracted to Charlotte and she knows it, but her heart belongs permanently to Hillary. One day at a beach, Jack goes in for a swim and is attacked by jellyfish. When he comes back, he has markings all over his skin and is in incredible pain. In order to alleviate the pain and keep the bites from getting worse, Charlotte urinates on him, an incident that makes national headlines, although it never once advances the storyline.

The whole scene seems to exist so that the viewer will have something to talk about afterwards. Jack and Charlotte's relationship is not quite as interesting as the relationship Jack has with his maid, Anita, who has become a friend and mother figure to Jack and who is also the most interesting character in the entire film.

It would be easy to brush off the criticisms of this film with the notion that it is intended to be viewed as a pulpy trash novel with despicable characters and an absurd storyline, except that most of the film's intentions in that area either come off as muted or forced. Either the reaction from Cannes caused major editing changes or Daniels has no handle on what he wants to accomplish with the film's tone or execution (or both). Most of the film is played straight, but with occasionally interesting stylistic flourishes as Daniels tries to emulate romance movies from the '50s and '60s. Most of the time, though, the movie sits waiting to take off, but it never really does.

So the flaws stick. Daniels' screenplay has these characters all existing in a vacuum. Efron and McConaughey are supposed to have a brotherly bond, but the bond is not grounded in anything. The characters seem miles away from each other. Furthermore, Ward Jansen is supposed to eventually become so obsessed with this case that it consumes him completely, but it is never established why this case would be any different from any other crime story. Hillary is not a good guy nor is he someone whom society would wrongly demonize. To make matters worse, the role is completely miscast with John Cusack in it, trying desperately to play against type.

The rest of the cast tries their best as well, but the movie lacks an assured hand to make them memorable or interesting. There might be some who would declare this movie an "instant cult film," except that such a thing could never actually occur. Cult films have to be nurtured and discovered by a devoted group of fans who generate the word-of-mouth. One of the problems with *The Paperboy* is that it wants to be a cult film, but it also wants to be taken seriously (much like *Precious*), but the movie too often wears its desperation on its sleeve. A movie cannot get by on atmosphere alone, but it is the only thing *The Paperboy* has going for it. The film earned some pre-release buzz as a so-bad-it's-good kind of film, but when finally released to the public, they rightfully shrugged it off as nothing to get excited about.

Collin Souter

CREDITS

Charlotte Bliss: Nicole Kidman
Jack Jensen: Zac Efron
Ward Jensen: Matthew McConaughey
Hillary Van Wetter: John Cusack
Anita Chester: Macy Gray
Yardley Acheman: David Oyelowo
Origin: United States
Language: English
Released: 2012
Production: Ed Cathell, III, Cassian Elwes, Hilary Shor, Lee Daniels; Benaroya Pictures, Lee Daniels Entertainment, Millenium Films, Nu Image Films; released by Millennium Entertainment L.L.C.
Directed by: Lee Daniels
Written by: Lee Daniels
Cinematography by: Roberto Schaefer
Music by: Mario Grigorov
Sound: Jay Meagher
Editing: Joe Klotz
Costumes: Caroline Eselin
Production Design: Daniel T. Dorrance
MPAA rating: R
Running time: 107 minutes

REVIEWS

Corliss, Mary. *Time.* May 25, 2012.
Covert, Colin. *Minneapolis Star Tribune.* October 11, 2012.
Denby, David. *New Yorker.* October 8, 2012.
Howell, Peter. *Toronto Star.* October 18, 2012.
Morris, Wesley. *Boston Globe.* October 11, 2012.
O'Hehir, Andrew. *Salon.com.* October 4, 2012.
Rea, Steven. *Philadelphia Inquirer.* October 11, 2012.
Scott, A. O. *New York Times.* October 4, 2012.
Tobias, Scott. *AV Club.* May 25, 2012.
Whitty, Stephen. *Newark Star-Ledger.* October 5, 2012.

QUOTES

Charlotte Bless: "I'm not gonna blow a friendship over a stupid little blowjob."

TRIVIA

Actor Tobey Maguire was originally cast as Ward but had to drop out due to scheduling conflicts.

AWARDS

Nominations:
Golden Globes 2013: Actress—Supporting (Kidman)
Screen Actors Guild 2012: Actress—Supporting (Kidman)

PARANORMAL ACTIVITY 4

All the activity has led to this.
—Movie tagline

It's closer than you think.
—Movie tagline

Box Office: $53.9 million

The only thing seriously wrong with *Paranormal Activity 4* is the number on the end of the title. The plain truth is that despite some sincere efforts to expand the mythos of the original, none of the *Paranormal Activity* films differ much from each other. Viewers, even those who count themselves as staunch fans of the franchise, go see these movies precisely because of the dependable way they go about setting up and delivering predictably styled scares not because of the minor changes in the storyline that take place with each new installment. But if *Paranormal Activity 4* is enough like its predecessor to annoy critics, it is still entertaining enough to rise head and shoulders above the generally forgettable American horror films that have risen to crowd the market with the found-footage aesthetic.

Typical suburban teen Alex (Kathryn Newton) and her boyfriend Ben (Matt Shively) are surprised in the garden tree house by Robbie (Brady Allen), a younger, unusually quiet neighbor boy whom they escort back home. But early the following morning, Robbie is back courtesy of Alex's mom who has offered to watch him while his mom recovers in the hospital. Soon, Robbie has established an odd relationship with Wyatt (Aiden Lovekamp), Alex's younger brother, and introduced him to his imaginary friend. Courtesy of Ben's filming of an impromptu dance session in the living room, it becomes apparent to viewers that Robbie's friend is anything but imaginary.

After reviewing footage captured by his computer during web-chats with Alex, Ben, with Alex's help, sets up laptops around the house to act as surveillance cameras. What follows is different enough from other *Paranormal* films to be considered somewhat divergent. Yet the scares remain basically the same until the end of the film, which is very effective, conjuring favorable comparisons with *The Wicker Man* (1973) and even *Gakko no kaidan G* (1998), the original made-for-TV film that inspired the Japanese *Ju-on* franchise. The fun, of course, is still in getting there and a host of strange symbols, shadowy figures and crashing banging household goods do a fine job of keeping the tension high.

Katie Featherston makes another appearance as Katie, the demonized woman from the first film, and the way she is included here is truly unsettling, incorporating some of the most ghastly imagery in which the series has yet dabbled. The parents (played by real-life couple Stephen Dunham and Alexondra Lee) are used as plot devices rather than real characters with no real chance to develop character or become much of a presence. But Kathryn Newtown really owns the part of

Alex, emerging as a strong player able to register intelligence, strength, and real terror as the young teenager fending off the advances of her older boyfriend even as she delves into the mystery of who Robbie and his mother really are.

Henry Joost and Ariel Schulman are on their second *Paranormal* film but they remain best known for their own controversial documentary *Catfish* (2010). Yet the very thing that made *Catfish* controversial (the re-staging of events which were then presented as having been originally captured on film) points to strengths that are well evident here. *Catfish* is nothing if not compelling in truth or fictionalization and viewers should have no trouble realizing that *Paranormal Activity 4* has the power to scare the living hell out of newcomers to the horror genre, and even unnerve horror fans simply because Joost and Schulman know how to project a sense of reality to the found-footage medium.

In fact, as written by Christopher Landon, the plot twists, even the less convincing ones, are generally more effective than in the third film, and the film lags far less than either the first, second or third installments. If, as has been duly noted, the story is full of moments that seem almost cliche, they do build on one another to a fever pitch. As a suburban nightmare, *Paranormal Activity 4* generally overcomes the derivative treatment Landon gives to character and plotting which should come as no surprise since his only feature screenplay credit outside this franchise, which includes all of the sequels, is for the thinly veiled *Rear Window* (1954) remake *Disturbia* (2007).

The special effects of the *Paranormal* series have generally been given the short shrift by reviewers who feel like they already have these film's scares figured out and that such knowledge gives them the right to be cynical. But knowing how an effect is done hardly makes the sight of a shrieking little girl being dragged by invisible hands across a room less unsettling. No doubt, many of the effects in the series are accomplished via computer manipulation and cheaply accomplished theatrics. But beyond techniques involving the actual effects themselves are the filmmaking skills involved in leading the viewer to them, breathlessly, one step at a time. All the *Paranormal* films contain such moments. *Paranormal Activity 4* contains more than its share.

The likelihood of more *Paranormal Activity* films has been decided by the success of this one and yet another sequel is already in the works. The effectiveness of future sequels seems contingent on the truly unnerving possibility that it will become ineffective at even the simple things it has done well. Luckily for all concerned, viewers are scared of these things for a reason, scared of the dark, scared of the unknown, and the relentless sense that evil stalks, unseen just outside the corner of the eye.

Dave Canfield

CREDITS

Alex: Kathryn Newton
Ben: Matt Shively
Wyatt: Aiden Lovekamp
Robbie: Brady Allen
Doug: Stephen Dunham
Holly: Alexondra Lee
Katie: Katie Featherston
Origin: United States
Language: English
Released: 2012
Production: Oren Peli, Jason Blum; Blumhouse Productions, Solana Films, Room 101; released by Paramount Pictures
Directed by: Henry Joost; Ariel Schulman
Written by: Christopher Landon
Cinematography by: Doug Emmett
Sound: Walter Anderson
Editing: Gregory Plotkin
Art Direction: Jason Garner
Costumes: Leah Butler
Production Design: Jennifer Spence
MPAA rating: R
Running time: 88 minutes

REVIEWS

Berkshire, Geoff. *Variety*. October 17, 2012.
Bumbray, Chris. *JoBlo's Movie Emporium*. October 19, 2012.
Gilchrist, Todd. *Chiller TV*. October 19, 2012.
McWeeny, Drew. *HitFix*. October 1, 2012.
Olsen, Mark. *Los Angeles Times*. October 18, 2012.
Orndorf, Brian. *Blu-ray.com*. October 19, 2012.
Seibold, Whitney. *CraveOnline*. October 24, 2012.
Tobias, Scott. *AV Club*. October 19, 2012.
Willmore, Allison. *Movieline*. October 18, 2012.
Weinberg, Scott. *FEARnet*. September 29, 2012.

QUOTES

Robbie: "He does not like you."
Ben: "What? Who? Who does not like me?"
Robbie: "You'll find out."

TRIVIA

Following the credits, there is an easter egg for the Latino spin-off of the franchise.

PARANORMAN

You don't become a hero by being normal.
—Movie tagline

It's all fun and games until someone raises the dead.
—Movie tagline

Box Office: $56 million

The ads for *ParaNorman* suggest a harmless, comedic romp with a bunch of kids through a mystery involving zombies and paranormal hijinks. It looked like Saturday morning kid fodder with a bigger budget, but not much in the way of sophistication. With their animated films, studios often either have to play it safe by emphasizing all the humor and mayhem (as is often the case) or risk making it look too smart and sophisticated and completely baffle the parents by making them wonder "will my kid get this?" When a movie has to be dumbed down a bit for the trailer just to get people to come see it, that is clearly a business decision, but sometimes a movie can look too childish and scare off a bigger audience that might embrace it.

At the end of the day, though, ads are irrelevant, but they can leave a lasting imprint on the film's reception as a whole. People to this day still scoff at the notion that George Miller's *Babe: Pig In the City* (1998) is some kind of masterpiece (it is). *ParaNorman* might suffer the same fate, but it most definitely deserves its high praise. The ads for the film do it a disservice, but then an editor would be hard-pressed to convey all the film's perfect details, grand gestures and emotional beauty in just two and a half minutes. And why spoil it anyway? One of the best things to happen to a viewer when watching a film for the first time is the element of surprise and exceeded expectations.

The movie hits the ground running with its wit, intelligence and style. It opens with an academy ratio, old-fashioned "Feature Presentation" banner then proceeds with an old-school type of slasher film, complete with film grain. The film is being watched by Norman (voiced by Kodi Smit-McPhee), an eleven-year-old who enjoys horror movies. With him is his Grandmother (voiced by Elaine Stritch), who is revealed later on to be dead. Norman can see and talk to dead people. His parents, Harry (voiced by Jeff Garlin) and Sandra (voiced by Leslie Mann) think he is rather odd and is making all this up. Even the kids at school know about Norman's tendency to talk to nobody in particular. He is bullied at school by Alvin (voiced by Christopher Mintz-Plasse), but befriended by another outsider, Neil (voiced by Tucker Albrizzi), who takes his bullying in stride.

The town they live in, Blithe Hollow, is not unlike Salem, Massachusetts. This year, they are celebrating the 300th anniversary of the hanging of a witch after a famous trial. Norman plays a part in the school play about this trial, where he hallucinates the actual event, no doubt a side effect of paranormal abilities. This happens after he and Neil are paid a visit in a park by Norman's estranged (and deranged) uncle, Mr. Prenderghast (voiced by John Goodman), who warns them that there is not much time and tells Norman to watch for the signs of the witch's curse. None of this really makes a lick of sense to either of them.

Nevertheless, it is up to Norman to take a book that was about to be given to him by Mr. Prenderghast before he suddenly dropped dead. Mr. Prendergrast's ghost instructs Norman to take the book and read it out loud at the graveyard where the seven victims of the witch's curse rest. For tonight, the witch intends to raise the dead. A series of unfortunate events keep this plan from panning out and Norman must find a way to save the town from complete destruction. Joining him are Neil, Alvin, Norman's gum-popping, teenage sister Courtney (voiced by Anna Kendrick) and Neil's weight-lifting, doofus older brother, Mitch (voiced by Casey Affleck).

When talking about an animated film's merits, usually the technical achievements get first mention, but for *ParaNorman,* what sets it apart first and foremost are the performances by the voice actors and the animators who bring the stop-motion characters to life. The faces on these figures have more than just a stock pile of general emotions at their disposal. These seem like real, living characters with deep emotions and complex thought processes. The voice actors, especially the talented Smit-McPhee, never just say their lines when prompted to do so. They bring these characters to life in a way that seems to go above and beyond the call of duty. This may seem easy to pull off with a computer animated film and the similarly executed *Coraline* (2009) also accomplished this feat, but *ParaNorman* goes even further and helps to give the film an emotionally satisfying conclusion.

The film is directed by Sam Fell (who also wrote the screenplay) and Chris Butler. Both are making their directorial debut. Fell has a great ear for the way kids talk and is able to cram in as many jokes on the screen as possible without overwhelming the audience. One of the things that makes *ParaNorman* more worthy of notice than many other animated films is how much it accomplishes thematically and emotionally. The final third of the film takes an interesting look at revisionist history and how often complexities of character are left out of the narrative when taught to children, as the Salem witch trials rears its ugly head once again with mob mentality taking over rational behavior. The film also accomplishes more when addressing bullying than *Bully* (2012), the much-publicized documentary from the same year, did. This is a great film to show to kids to teach them a lesson or two on the subject.

Make no mistake, though. *ParaNorman* has many big laughs, payoffs and movie in-jokes, as well as a nifty little post-credits coda. The film makes a wonderful companion piece to *Monster House* (2006) and *Coraline* (2009), two of the best animated films of the last decade. Butler and Fell have made a name for themselves as major talents to watch. Their instincts for when to cut and when to use music are impeccable. They would also probably do well in the live-action realm, but for now, they have picked up the slack for 2012 after Pixar played it way too safe with their summer offering, *Brave,* which was also mis-advertised, but in the opposite way. If these two movies switched ad campaigns, there would be more truth in advertising and the final box office numbers would be better justified.

Collin Souter

CREDITS

Norman: Kodi Smit-McPhee (Voice)
Mitch: Casey Affleck (Voice)
Mr. Prenderghast: John Goodman (Voice)
Perry Babcock: Jeff Garlin (Voice)
Sandra Babcock: Leslie Mann (Voice)
Grandma: Elaine Stritch (Voice)
Courtney: Anna Kendrick (Voice)
Sheriff Hooper: Tempestt Bledsoe (Voice)
Origin: United States
Language: English
Released: 2012
Production: Travis Knight, Arianne Sutner; Laika Entertainment; released by Focus Features
Directed by: Sam Fell; Chris Butler
Written by: Chris Butler
Cinematography by: Tristan Oliver
Music by: Jon Brion
Sound: Ronald Eng
Editing: Christopher Murrie
Production Design: Nelson Lowry
MPAA rating: PG
Running time: 92 minutes

REVIEWS

Burr, Ty. *Boston Globe.* August 16, 2012.
Coveert, Colin. *Minneapolis Star Tribune.* August 16, 2012.
Goodykoontz, Bill. *Arizona Republic.* August 15, 2012.
Goss, William. *Orlando Weekly.* August 15, 2012.
Guzman, Rafer. *Newsday.* August 17, 2012.
Jones, J. R. *Chicago Reader.* August 16, 2012.
Long, Tom. *Detroit News.* August 17, 2012.
Robinson, Tasha. *AV Club.* August 16, 2012.

Rodriguez, Rene. *Miami Herald*. August 16, 2012.
Schwarzbaum, Lisa. *Entertainment Weekly*. August 8, 2012.

QUOTES

Sandra Babcock: "Not believing in an afterlife is like not
believing in astrology."

TRIVIA

A candy bar inside a vending machine has the name
"Cuj-Oh's" and features a picture of a dog on the wrapper,
this is a reference to the novel *Cujo* by Stephen King.

AWARDS

Nominations:

Oscars 2012: Animated Film
British Acad. 2012: Animated Film

PARENTAL GUIDANCE

Here come the grandparents. There go the rules.
   —Movie tagline
This Christmas it's a battle for the ages.
   —Movie tagline

Box Office: $75.8 million

Parental Guidance came out during the holiday
season as the family-friendly alternative to the big,
prestigious award contenders that normally populate the
moviegoing landscape. This would be the one film
parents could take their kids to see and not have to
worry about being offended or uncomfortable. And yet,
there could not be a worse movie about parenting or
child rearing. *Parental Guidance* basically points the
finger to all parents of all types and tells them what a
horrible job they are doing. It does so with the aid of
urine, vomit and poo-poo jokes that do little more than
provide mindless entertainment for parents who just
want to plop their kids down in front of a screen that
will babysit them for a long period of time. Supposedly,
there are lessons for kids to learn from this film, but
they come out of nowhere and not out of selfless acts.

The film stars Billy Crystal and Bette Midler, two
comedians whose acts had their time and place a couple
decades ago, but who now have to channel those same
energies into a story that has them playing doddering,
old boneheads who can barely work a cordless phone.
How the mighty have fallen. The whole film seems to
be a metaphor for Crystal's career. At the beginning of
the film, he gets fired from his job as a minor league
baseball sportscaster and by the end of the film ends up
even lower on the sportscaster totem poll, his dignity

just barely intact. Midler does not fair any better as it
remains unclear just what her character is all about. She
simply exists to react to everything Crystal has to say.

Crystal and Midler play Artie and Diane Decker,
grandparents to their daughter Alice's (Marisa Tomei)
three precocious kids, Harper (Bailee Madison), Turner
(Joshua Rush) and Barker (Kyle Harrison Breitkopf).
Alice's husband Phil (Tom Everett Scott) has to go out
of town to help sell his household invention, the R-Life,
a voice activated device that opens doors, greets incoming visitors and starts any electronic appliance in the
house. Both parents want to go out of town for this so
they can spend some alone time together, but the
grandparents on Phil's side of he family are unavailable.
They reluctantly call upon Artie and Diane, who fear
they will somehow corrupt their kids by not abiding by
their style of new-age parenting. Both know they are not
the favored pair of grandparents in the family. "We're
the *other* grandparents," Artie says.

The two have their hands full with the grandkids.
Harper is a struggling violinist who is due to audition
for a prestigious prep school that will prepare her for
Julliard. Turner is a boy with a stutter who gets bullied
at school and has an obsession with being able to watch
all of the *Saw* movies. Barker, the youngest, has a
myriad of problems, not the least of which is his imaginary
friend, Carl, whom everyone around him treats as a real
being. Unable to see her parents as being capable of
dealing with such problems, Alice turns around at the
last minute and cancels her trip so she can help watch
the kids.

Even with her authoritative presence, wackiness
ensues. The R-Life machine refers to Artie as "Farty."
Artie gives ice cream cake to the otherwise sugar-
deprived youngsters, which results in a sugar rush that
makes an unspeakable mess in the kitchen. Artie attempts to change the ways of the neighborhood softball
game, which results in him getting hit in the crotch
with a baseball bat. Artie then vomits on the kid who
hit him in the crotch with a baseball bat. Barker has to
pee, so he urinates on a skateboard slide where Tony
Hawk is about to do a stunt. Barker has to poop, but he
cannot go unless his father sings to him, so Artie and
Barker sit in a men's restroom stall. Grandpa sings, kid
poops. The family goes to a classical music concert where
Barker runs off and Artie has to catch him and almost
spanks him in front of the entire audience, but not
before stopping the show and lecturing everyone in the
place on how new age, touchy-feely parents have ruined
everything.

Amidst this desperation for a laugh, lessons must be
learned. Harper learns that she must not be obsessed
with being perfect at the violin if she does not enjoy it

in the first place. Turner learns that if he just listens to the famous play-by-play of "The Shot Heard Around The World," he will lose his stutter. Barker learns that he can have everything he wants as long as he is given money to shut his mouth by his Grandpa Artie. Alice, an only child who still holds a grudge against her father for being negligent, learns that her parenting skills will lead to her kids being resentful of her if she does not change her ways. All of these moments come through in awkward and obligatory ways with a script (by Lisa Addario and Joe Syracuse) that forces more unearned sentiment than a Hallmark card and has no forward momentum. The film seems to be made up of nothing but deleted scenes.

Crystal has always had a reputation for being a "nice" comedian, an offspring of the Catskills-era comics. Yet, he has never appeared in anything this sloppy, mean-spirited and culturally backwards. Marisa Tomei, on the other hand, has been enjoying a career resurgence as of late. How she managed to get roped into a film from the director of *She's the Man* (2006) is both baffling and sad. Director Andy Fickman underscores every lame gag with an aggressive score, a common misconception by directors of his type that audiences will not laugh until the music tells them to, much like the kids in the film who are told by their parents to just laugh every time one of their grandparents makes a joke, even if they do not understand it or think it is very funny. Crystal and Midler seem to be begging the audience for this film to do the same thing.

Collin Souter

CREDITS

Artie Decker: Billy Crystal
Diane Decker: Bette Midler
Alice: Marisa Tomei
Phil Simmons: Tom Everett Scott
Harper Decker Simmons: Bailee Madison
Turner Decker Simmons: Joshua Rush
Barker Decker Simmons: Kyle Harrison Breitkopf
Origin: United States
Language: English
Released: 2012
Production: Peter Chernin, Samantha Sprecher, Lianne Halfon, John Malkovich, Billy Crystal; Chernin Entertainment, Walden Media; released by 20th Century Fox Film Corp.
Directed by: Andy Flickman
Written by: Lisa Addario; Joe Syracuse
Cinematography by: Dean Semler
Music by: Marc Shaiman
Sound: Robert L. Sephton

Music Supervisor: Julia Michels
Editing: Kent Beyda
Art Direction: John R. Jensen
Costumes: Genevieve Tyrrell
Production Design: David J. Bomba
MPAA rating: PG
Running time: 104 minutes

REVIEWS

Gleiberman, Owen. *Entertainment Weekly*. December 26, 2012.
Goodykoontz, Bill. *Arizona Republic*. December 25, 2012.
Guzman, Rafer. *Newsday*. December 24, 2012.
Lacey, Liam. *Globe and Mail*. December 28, 2012.
Morris, Wesley. *Boston Globe*. December 24, 2012.
O'Sullivan, Michael. *Washington Post*. December 25, 2012.
Packham, Chris. *Village Voice*. December 27, 2012.
Rickey, Carrie. *Philadelphia Inquirer*. December 25, 2012.
Weitzman, Elizabeth. *New York Daily News*. December 25, 2012.
Whitty, Stephen. *Newark Star-Ledger*. December 24, 2012.

QUOTES

Harper Decker Simmons: "Yogurt not like ice cream! You lied!"

TRIVIA

Because of the time of year the movie was shot during—late fall early winter—the grass at the home in Atlanta was dead and had to be digitally colored to look green.

PEACE, LOVE & MISUNDERSTANDING

Life is a journey. Family is a trip.
—Movie tagline

Box Office: $560,700

Every cultural era has its fads and foibles, but few hang over and permeate the consciousness of future generations who did not live them out quite like the free-love, hippie-dippy 1960s and early 1970s. The latest case in point: *Peace, Love & Misunderstanding*, a multi-generational film set in the present day, but built around and designed to exploit a comfortably relatable stereotype associated with that time, the free-spirited Earth mother. A limp, upstate-New-York-set comedy of familial reconciliation for the Teva-sandal-and-patchouli set, director Bruce Beresford's film, in offering up little pockets of punctured mood, aims for feeling more than rigorous plot, with decidedly mixed results.

When uptight Manhattan lawyer Diane Hudson (Catherine Keener) breaks the news of her impending divorce from husband Mark (Kyle MacLachlan), her teenage son Jake (Nat Wolff) responds simply with, "It's about time." College-age Zoe (Elizabeth Olsen) is a bit more concerned, but there is not much time for an in-depth explanation since Diane has whisked her kids away for an impromptu road trip upstate to introduce them to their hippie grandmother they have never met, Grace (Jane Fonda). Diane has not spoken to her mom in two decades, and everything about her anxious and conservative disposition is in stark contrast (and response) to Grace's nature.

This grand and sudden gesture of reconnection would seem to open itself up to a lot of angsty soul-searching, but rather than dig too heartily into how sins of the past might be tethered to heartache of the present, *Peace, Love & Misunderstanding* prefers to keep things fairly light. Grace is presented as openhearted and forthright, if somewhat kooky. She smokes (and grows) pot; howls at the moon once a month with some of her goddess-worshipping girlfriends; has a gentleman friend of much younger age, in the form of guitar-strumming carpenter Jude (Jeffrey Dean Morgan); and doles out romantic advice ("The art of seduction lies in the convergence of timing and atmosphere") to her grandkids. So while vegan Zoe wrestles with her attraction to local butcher Cole (Chace Crawford), Jake, a would-be future filmmaker, takes nervous, tentative steps toward lip-lock with Tara (Marissa O'Donnell), a sweet-faced barista. Soon enough, though, as the responsible Diane finds herself gravitating toward the superior stubble of Jude, mother-daughter complications arise and old recriminations come bubbling to the surface.

Still, there is mostly a loose and groovy vibe to the movie. Its script, by Christina Mengert and Joseph Muszynski, gets into Diane and Grace's issues with one another a bit, but elides any substantive analysis of the psychological impact of this forced separation from their grandmother on Jake and Zoe. This seems like a bit of a cheat. Kids in adolescence and even their early tweens can shrug off an imposed excommunication and go with the flow if it is all they have known. But the lack of a deeper curiosity (and latent resentment) seems a bit less likely with older, more mature kids.

Similarly, the casting of Fonda would seem to indicate an attempt to tap into her counterculture credibility, and the heated feelings she still arouses for a certain portion of the population. Yet the movie does not sketch out Grace to be much of a true radical, but instead just a holistic adherent of go-with-the-flow positivism. Mengert and Muszynski, and by extension Beresford, are more interested and invested in make-nice rosiness, light humor and bromidic life lessons ("You're so busy fighting everyone that you don't realize they're not fighting back," Jude tells Diane) that escape risibility

chiefly through the skill of a cast who imbue them with an unfussy simplicity.

This fact, and especially the aforementioned dodge on a deeper exploration of swallowed adolescent bitterness, give *Peace, Love & Misunderstanding* a strong feeling of narrative predetermination, of coasting downhill to an already marked resting spot. Scene to scene, it is pleasant and engaging enough, but it lacks an illuminating depth. The film trades in overly pat connective shorthand (Zoe and Cole bond in unlikely fashion over poetry, in this case Walt Whitman), and a full-blown acoustic rock montage sequence achingly yearns to whip up sentiments that the story does not earn.

A two-time Academy Award nominee, Australian-born director Beresford oversees a technical package that underscores the movie's down-to-earth qualities. He and cinematographer Andre Fleuren select earthy tones and make copious use of diffuse naturalistic lighting and open spaces within frames—choices that, along with the work of composer Spencer David Hutchings (and the screenplay's musical sing-along selection of The Band's "The Weight"), highlight the story's sense of candidness and burgeoning possibility. Carl Sprague's production design (inclusive of protest signs, woodcraft and other artistry, and hens in Grace's kitchen) further check almost all the boxes of hippiedom which even younger viewers have culturally absorbed.

Peace, Love & Misunderstanding's attractive collection of ensemble players is certainly its strongest selling point—something that the savvy casting of Olsen, in her first screen role, will only help bolster over time, giving it a certain catalogue curio value. Keener has an endlessly fascinating visage, and the inherent ability to communicate roiled inner landscapes even when the script does not meaningfully dig into them. Fonda, meanwhile, is more relaxed and appealing than in years; Morgan is not required to do much more than again drag out his ample scruffy charm. And if the feeling of glide-path inevitability of the twin young romances elicits mostly shrugs, one does not hold it against the young actors; Olsen, Wolff and O'Donnell are all amiable. One merely wishes they had a lot more with which to work, and that *Peace, Love & Misunderstanding* included a more significant communicated understanding of its characters.

Brent Simon

CREDITS

Diane: Catherine Keener
Jake: Nat Wolff
Mark: Kyle MacLachlan

Zoe: Elizabeth Olsen
Grace: Jane Fonda
Jude: Jeffrey Dean Morgan
Tara: Marissa O'Donnell
Cole: Chace Crawford
Origin: United States
Language: English
Released: 2011
Production: Jonathan Burkhart, Lauren Munsch, Brice Dal Farra, Claude Dal Farra; released by BCDF Pictures
Directed by: Bruce Beresford
Written by: Christina Mengert; Joseph Muszynski
Cinematography by: Andre Fleuren
Music by: Spencer David Hutchings
Sound: Robert Hein
Editing: John David Allen
Art Direction: Elise Viola
Costumes: Johann Stegmeir
Production Design: Carl Sprague
MPAA rating: R
Running time: 92 minutes

REVIEWS

Debruge, Peter. *Variety.* September 15, 2011.
Ellingson, Annlee. *Paste Magazine.* June 8, 2012.
Holden, Stephen. *New York Times.* June 7, 2012.
Honeycutt, Kirk. *Hollywood Reporter.* September 15, 2011.
Lemire, Christy. *Associated Press.* June 6, 2012.
Ogle, Connie. *Miami Herald.* June 8, 2012.
O'Sullivan, Michael. *Washington Post.* June 8, 2012.
Phillips, Michael. *Chicago Tribune.* June 7, 2012.
Rainer, Peter. *Christian Science Monitor.* June 8, 2012.
Sharkey, Betsy. *Los Angeles Times.* June 7, 2012.

QUOTES

Zoe: "Where does the perpetuation of fragmentation lead us? You know, it seems like we should be finding a way back into harmony with one another rather than representing, and therefore replicating our division."

TRIVIA

Jane Fonda's character in the movie attended the Woodstock Festival in 1969 while pregnant; her water broke during Jimi Hendrix's rendition of "The Star-Spangled Banner." Fonda actually knew little about Woodstock (at the time, she was already over 30 and living in Europe), and didn't relate to this part of the story, until shown a documentary by co-star Catherine Keener. Watching Hendrix's set in the documentary, Fonda said, "I got it."

PEOPLE LIKE US

Find your family.
—Movie tagline

Box Office: $12.4 million

There is an unfortunate factor of creepiness to *People Like Us* that is unavoidable, given how screenwriters Alex Kurtzman (who also directed), Roberto Orci, and Jody Lambert implement a dramatic conceit that allows a scenario in which a man and woman who share the same father begin to look and act a lot like characters in a romantic comedy. The formula is essentially the same: One character keeps quiet about his feelings for a woman and eventually she begins to see the man in a new, romantic light. In this instance, the man knows he is the woman's half-brother, and for no discernible reason—despite the fact that the entire plot depends on his silence—he does not share this information with her.

It takes a while for the half-sister to begin toying with the idea of what is—unbeknownst to her—an incestuous relationship with a man who, from her point of view, coincidentally shows up with a sketchy story about himself just after the death of the father who abandoned her so many years ago. That section of the movie provides a series of scenes that are equal parts disquieting and laughable. Even before that, though, the screenplay has established a frustrating sort of no-win scenario for itself. Instead of dealing with the thorny emotions of two people dealing with different forms of rejection by their father and the difficult process of forming a familial bond with a person who shares one's genes but for all intents and purposes is a stranger (in another word, "reality"), the screenwriters have devised a lazy narrative apparatus that provides no insight into the characters and only annoys with its ongoing wait for the half-brother to finally reveal his real identity to his half-sister.

The man is Sam (Chris Pine), an irresponsible man-child with an unclear job of taking and re-selling overstocked inventory from a wide variety of vendors. He is late for everything and always has a lame excuse for his tardiness. Upon coming home from work after learning that a shipment to Mexico he organized put the company for which he works under federal investigation (The constant phone messages from a Federal Trade Commission investigator provide an especially useless through line and additional point of conflict), his girlfriend Hannah (Olivia Wilde) informs Sam that his father has died. To ensure that his callousness is clear, he asks, "What's for dinner?"

Sam tries to avoid returning home for the funeral—downplaying plans for buying plane tickets to his hometown of Los Angeles and hiding his driver's license in the glove compartment so he cannot get to the plane—but Hannah insists, not noticing his avoidance. He and Hannah arrive after the services and reception, where his mother Lillian (Michelle Pfeiffer) is waiting with passive-aggressive responses to his every statement and slap across the face for good measure.

Later, his father's attorney (Philip Baker Hall) meets with Sam at a diner to go over the will. His father, a music producer, leaves Sam with little—some memorabilia and records—save for a final task: to deliver $150,000 to a woman he does not know. She is Frankie (Elizabeth Banks), a single mother of Josh (Michael Hall D'Addario) and a recovering alcoholic. They meet after Sam follows her to an Alcoholics Anonymous meeting, where he discovers that his father is also her own from a speech she gives at the meeting decrying the fact that she was not mentioned in her father's obituary.

The not-so-subtle point to all of this is to observe Sam's growth from a selfish, immature human being into one who thinks of others, accepts responsibility for his own actions, and learns to deal with the past. Considering the way the plot is based on Sam's necessity to lie at every turn, that sense of progress is far too much to ask of or see in him. He must hide Frankie's existence from his mother to spare her feelings—or, more likely, avoid a fight. For some reason, Kurtzman includes an insert shot of Lillian watching from her window and apparently overhearing a conversation between Sam and Hannah in which he explains Frankie's lineage to his girlfriend. Nothing comes of this point, as Lillian is surprised to learn her son knows about his half-sister. The movie's single, semi-effective scene features mother-son bonding over their complicated relationships with the deceased; even this turns into histrionics.

He must also, obviously, keep the information from Frankie, although the reason for this is unclear to the point infuriation. The only possible rationale for his secrecy is a warped logic that Sam is attempting to determine if Frankie and her son deserve the money—money he could use to pay off a debt to his employer and to which he might feel entitled. Sam begins spending time with Frankie and Josh, and soon enough, Frankie begins looking at him with a level of affection that should stop his deception immediately.

Not one of the characters in the dysfunctional family unit—especially Sam—is sympathetic because the screenplay has no concern for them outside of creating excuses to extend what is an easily resolvable situation. Uncomfortable moments in the final act aside, *People Like Us* does finally touch upon the realities of Sam and Frankie's relationship, but by then the movie is too entangled in its need for conflict to do anything of substance with it. This is a movie that ends just as the story with any actual interest begins.

Mark Dujsik

CREDITS

Sam: Chris Pine
Frankie: Elizabeth Banks
Josh: Michael Hall D'Addario
Lillian: Michelle Pfeiffer
Hannah: Olivia Wilde
Ted: Mark Duplass
Ike Rafferty: Philip Baker Hall
Origin: United States
Language: English, French, Spanish
Released: 2012
Production: Bobby Cohen, Roberto Orci, Clayton Townsend; released by DreamWorks SKG, Touchstone Pictures
Directed by: Alex Kurtzman
Written by: Alex Kurtzman; Roberto Orci; Jody Lambert
Cinematography by: Salvatore Totino
Music by: A.R. Rahman
Sound: Gwendolyn Yates Whittle; Christopher Scarabosio
Music Supervisor: Liza Richardson
Editing: Robert Leighton
Art Direction: James E. Tocci
Costumes: Mary Zophres
Production Design: Ida Random
MPAA rating: PG-13
Running time: 113 minutes

REVIEWS

Holden, Stephen. *New York Times*. June 28, 2012.
Lacey, Liam. *Globe and Mail*. June 29, 2012.
Orndorf, Brian. *Blu-ray.com*. June 28, 2012.
Phillips, Michael. *Chicago Tribune*. June 28, 2012.
Phipps, Keith. *AV Club*. June 28, 2012.
Putman, Dustin. *DustinPutman.com*. June 25, 2012.
Rocchi, James. *MSN Movies*. June 27, 2012.
Schenker, Andrew. *Slant Magazine*. June 24, 2012.
Sobczynski, Peter. *EFilmCritic.com*. June 29, 2012.
Zacharek, Stephanie. *Movieline*. June 27, 2012.

QUOTES

Sam: "It means that the outcome doesn't matter. What matters is that you were there for it, whatever it is, good or bad, kind of like right now."

TRIVIA

Hilary Swank read the script and pursued a role in the film, but was turned down.

THE PERKS OF BEING A WALLFLOWER

We are infinite.
—Movie tagline

We accept the love we think we deserve.
—Movie tagline

Box Office: $17.7 million

"We accept the love we think we deserve," says the hero of *The Perks of Being A Wallflower*. Such sentiment is often reserved for Oprah self-help Book of the Month discussions, but in this coming of age film, it is the basis for some of the most complex relationships seen in a movie about high school. The titular "Wallflower" is a high school freshman who is welcomed by a group of friends, but the one he has his eye on is a senior and perhaps the most beautiful soul he has ever met. A lesser film would have made that the plot and ended with a platitude about love conquering all, age be damned. But in this wise and assured directorial debut by the film's writer (as well as the author of the book) Stephen Chbosky, life is more complicated than that. Chbosky remembers what that time was like and how small people often feel when first cast adrift into the new world that is high school.

Chbosky's book was told as a series of letters to an undisclosed recipient and the film takes the same narrative approach in its narration, although it is smart to keep these passages to a minimum. Charlie (Logan Lerman) is a freshman in high school and without many friends. The only person he attempts to make a connection with is his English teacher, Mr. Anderson (Paul Rudd). That is until he tries talking to Patrick (Ezra Miller), a flamboyant senior who is taking a freshman shop class. Patrick seems like the kind of safe friend to try and make for Charlie. A bit of an outsider himself, Patrick has the unfortunate curse of being called "Nothing" all year by his classmates thanks to a war of words with the shop teacher (Tom Savini).

Patrick has a step-sister named Sam (Emma Watson), a beautiful free spirit who is probably Patrick's one and only friend for life. Soon, Charlie finds himself swept up in a group of close outsider friends who create fanzines, make mix tapes and who perform on stage in the local *Rocky Horror Picture Show*. It is clear to the audience that Charlie loves Sam, but the movie is not about whether or not he will confess this or pursue it at all costs. She tells him flat out "I like Craig," an older guy whose parties they often attend. As a consolation, Charlie ends up the unwitting boyfriend of Mary Elizabeth (Mae Whitman), one of the members of their clique who enjoys having him around a bit too much. Charlie does not feel as though he deserves that kind of attention, nor does he wish it.

Charlie's life and problems are not dealt with in the traditional way you might see in, say, an *American Pie* movie. Charlie attends mass with his parents and appears to take it seriously. The film shifts to the past in startling jump cuts to Charlie's Aunt Helen (Melanie Lynskey), who dies when he was much younger and with whom he seemed to have a very meaningful relationship. Her death has changed him and most of that is dealt with head-on in the film's third act, a courageous act of screenwriting that could have easily derailed the whole project. As soulfully acted by Lerman, Charlie becomes worthy of the viewer's sympathies from the outset and the journey from the perils of high school to the perils of confronting one's past plays effortlessly and with an emotional payoff that is truly earned.

To describe *The Perks of Being A Wallflower* is to almost make it sound as though it were constructed of nothing but cliches from other high school movies and it is true that there are dynamics, characters and situations that are not new to the genre. But miraculously, everything here feels fresh, exciting and, most importantly, truthful. Chbosky finds new ways to deal with the material where it could have been uninspired. There are a couple scenes involving drugs that are not strictly played for laughs. No character is treated like a caricature. Chbosky remembers these moments of adolescence as major turning points in life, from the first unrequited love to the first time hearing a David Bowie song that was never on the radar until a friend introduced it personally.

The film takes place in 1992 and Chbosky never goes to the trouble of calling too much attention to that fact. So many movies that tale place in the '80s or '90s want to show off how much they remember from that time period by underscoring certain technologies or pop culture references. Could the movie have taken place in the present day and be just as powerful? Perhaps, but the time period, which is obviously personal to Chbosky, reminds one of the time in which a wallflower *had* to leave the house in order to make a true connection. It is perfect that Charlie and his friends wind up at the *Rocky Horror Picture Show* every weekend, discover songs on the radio and make fanzines by hand. There are quaint reminders such as that of an almost bygone era that is rarely seen in American films and yet they exist as strong pieces of character development rather than just a humorous aside.

While the title suggests a bit of self-indulgence and/or neurosis, the movie never once comes off that way. There are big laughs in the film as well as melancholia, aided greatly by Andrew Dunn's darkly beautiful cinematography. The performances are across-the-board perfect, particularly Watson, who is never portrayed as the typical, quirky, free-spirited pixie girl who exists solely to break the protagonist from his awkward shell. Her poise, confidence and warmth become hurdles for Charlie to be noticed by her and when she does notice him, it carries with it the sense of being truly alive, much like how the viewer feels when the movie ends.

Collin Souter

CREDITS

Charlie: Logan Lerman
Sam: Emma Watson
Patrick: Ezra Miller
Mary Elizabeth: Mae Whitman
Candace: Nina Dobrev
Brad: Johnny Simmons
Aunt Helen: Melanie Lynskey
Father: Dylan McDermott
Mother: Kate Walsh
Origin: United States
Language: English
Released: 2012
Production: Lianne Halforn, John Malkovich, Russell Smith; Summit Entertainment, Mr. Mudd; released by Summit Entertainment
Directed by: Stephen Chbosky
Written by: Stephen Chbosky
Cinematography by: Andrew Dunn
Music by: Michael Brook
Sound: Perry Robertson; Scott Sanders
Editing: Mary Jo Markey
Costumes: David C. Robinson
Production Design: Inbal Weinberg
MPAA rating: PG-13
Running time: 103 minutes

REVIEWS

Anderson, John. *Newsday.* October 4, 2012.
Biancolli, Amy. *San Francisco Chronicle.* September 28, 2012.
Burr, Ty. *Boston Globe.* September 27, 2012.
Ebert, Roger. *Chicago Sun-Times.* September 27, 2012.
Long, Tom. *Detroit News.* September 28, 2012.
Lomnhworth, Karina. *Village Voice.* September 4, 2012.
Lumenick, Lou. *New York Post.* September 21, 2012.
O'Hehir, Andrew. *Salon.com.* September 19, 2012.
Rickey, Carrie. *Philadelphia Inquirer.* September 27, 2012.
Sachs, Ben. *Chicago Reader.* September 27, 2012.

QUOTES

Charlie: "Right now we are alive and in this moment I swear we are infinite."

TRIVIA

When Patrick holds up his report card, the name at the top reads "Patrick Nothing," which is a reference to his nickname in the book and the film.

AWARDS

Ind. Spirit 2013: First Feature
Nominations:
Writers Guild 2012: Adapt. Screenplay

PIRANHA 3DD

Double the action. Double the terror. Double the D's.
—Movie tagline
Twice the Teeth. Twice the Terror.
—Movie tagline
Terror lurks where you least expect it.
—Movie tagline
No body is safe.
—Movie tagline

Box Office: $376,512

Expectations really are everything. It may seem baffling why anyone would pay attention to, much less expect anything but the worst from a cheap exploitation sequel about killer piranha attacking a topless water park. Or from a film that wears its extreme nudity, gore, and D-list stunt casting (sometimes all three at once) proudly on its blood-soaked, chewed-off sleeve. Except that *Piranha 3DD* is a sequel to 2010's *Piranha 3D*. And although that earlier film also reveled in extreme nudity and gore, thanks to director Alexandre Aja, the first *Piranha 3D* was extremely well-crafted with a genuinely gross-funny sense of dark humor. As a result, it found the perfect sweet spot between satire and exploitation. So when the sequel is released, as the lady says, attention must be paid.

If *Piranha 3D* had not been so cleverly, deliciously enjoyable in its over-the-top transgressions, *Piranha 3DD* could have been dismissed as little more than a schlocky, stupid-for-stupid's-sake direct-to-video or cable-TV creature feature. As it is, given its sloppy production values (even by cheap horror standards), minimalist theatrical release (three weeks in less than 100 theaters), and 83-minute running time (13 of which are given over to blooper clips during the credits—that math is correct: the credits are one-sixth of the film) by any rational standard, *Piranha 3DD* can barely be considered a "feature film."

What *Piranha 3DD*, like so many sequels, is is a quick cash grab tossed together with sub-standard materials. Aja has been replaced by John Gulager, a low-budget horror film maker who, after winning the 2005 *Project Greenlight* reality competition TV show, displayed some raggedly gonzo potential in his first film, *Feast* (2005). After that came *Feast II: Sloppy Seconds* (2008), and then *Feast III: The Happy Finish* (2009), and by that point it was clear the raggedly gonzo potential was going to remain just that, potential. For *Piranha 3DD*, Gulager brought along the *Feast* screenwriters, Patrick Melton and Marcus Dunstan, the writing team also responsible for four out of seven of the *Saw* films.

Story-wise, *Piranha 3DD* does not deviate from its predecessor: The vicious prehistoric, aquatic carnivores that tore up, *en masse*, topless spring breakers at a lake in the first film migrate over to an "adult" water park in the second film and tear up, *en masse*, the topless strippers employed there. Along the way, the usual gang of clueless, sex-crazed youth are also chewed up one-by-one by the hyperactive fish, as Melton, Dunstan, and Gulager push for extreme gross-out sex and death scenes purely for their own "look what we did!" sake.

Where *Piranha 3D* had its share of party-naked youth, it also had at its center grown-up actors like Elizabeth Shue and Adam Scott playing grown-up characters. Although *Piranha 3D* alums Ving Rhames and Christopher Lloyd pop up briefly and David Koechner takes over the sleaze-merchant role from Jerry O'Connell, for the most part *Piranha 3DD* forgoes the adult supervision. The sequel's younger characters run down the usual checklist of types: Danielle Panabaker as the smart girl; Katrina Bowden as the blonde; Meagan Tandy as the brunette; Jean-Luc Bilodeau and Paul James Jordan as the male-model boyfriends; Chris Zylka as a smugly unctuous cop; and Matt Bush as the nerdy good guy.

That those descriptions are about as deeply as the film makers care about or bother to make the audience care about the characters, is supposed to be part of the "meta" joke. However, as with the sequel's campy casting of self-inflicted punch-line actors like Gary Busey and David Hasselhoff, the fact that none of this is meant to be taken seriously is used not as leverage for satire, but simply a lazy excuse.

The same goes for the film's giggling, puerile use of sex and gore. There is a sleazy shoddiness to *Piranha 3DD* that detaches its gratuitousness nudity and violence (including severed heads and self-mutilated genitals in 3D) from any sort of ironic filter or creative context, using it to pander to the lowest common denominator rather than making it the joke. Think of it as the aesthetic difference between a retro burlesque show and a dead-end strip club. Watching Gulager and company plod gracelessly through their paces is like watching no-talent orchestras play Mozart: they dutifully bang it out as loudly as they can, but with no understanding of the notes' relationship to each other. Or a worse example, the clod who thinks he is funny, but whose telling of a joke strips it of all nuance, rendering it cruel and dull instead of comedic.

During its three week North American release, *Piranha 3DD* made less than $400,000, but it made just over $8 million overseas. Still, it was among the worst-reviewed theatrical releases of the year. Rare critical tolerance came from Mark Olsen of the *Los Angeles Times* who wrote, "*Piranha 3D*...went for full-bore in-the-know badness by ramping up the bare breasts, blood and ridiculousness. *DD* director John Gulager keeps that tone for the sequel and winds up with a fairly fun, basically passable, could-be-better bad movie." Most critics shared opinions similar to that of the *New York Times'* Neil Genzlinger, who felt, "John Gulager, has no idea how to mix his ingredients to create a savvy self-parody. Instead he flings comic bits and gross-out gags around desperately," or Stephen Cole of *The Globe and Mail*, who described the film as, "overcrowded and pointlessly mean."

Locke Peterseim

CREDITS

Maddy: Danielle Panabaker
Barry: Matthew Bush
Clayton: Gary Busey
Shelby: Katrina Bowden
Josh: Jean-Luc Bilodeau
Chet: David Koechner
Kyle: Chris Zylka
Ashley: Meagan Tandy
Mr. Goodman: Christopher Lloyd
Deputy Fallon: Ving Rhames
Himself: David Hasselhoff
Origin: United States
Language: English, Spanish
Released: 2011
Production: Mark Canton, Mark Toberoff, Joel Soisson; Mark Canton Productions, IPW; released by Dimension Films
Directed by: John Gulager
Written by: Marcus Dunstan; Patrick Melton; Joel Soisson
Cinematography by: Alexandre Lehmann
Music by: Elia Cmiral
Sound: Trip Brock
Music Supervisor: Richard Glasser
Editing: Martin Bernfeld; Devin C. Lussier; Kirk Morri
Costumes: Carol Cutshall
Production Design: Ermanno Di Febo-Orsini
MPAA rating: R
Running time: 83 minutes

REVIEWS

Cole, Stephen. *The Globe and Mail.* June 1, 2012.
Genzlinger, Neil. *New York Times.* June 1, 2012.

Gilchrist, Todd. *Box Office Magazine.* May 31, 2012.
Gonzalez, Ed. *Slant Magazine.* May 27, 2012.
Olsen, Mark. *Los Angeles Times.* June 4, 2012.
Pinkerton, Nick. *Village Voice.* May 30, 2012.
Robinson, Tasha. *AV Club.* June 1, 2012.
Savlov, Marc. *Austin Chronicle.* June 1, 2012.
Smith, Neil. *Total Film.* May 15, 2012.
Zacharek, Stephanie. *Movieline.* June 1, 2012.

QUOTES

Deputy Fallon: "Bring me my legs."

TRIVIA

A Chihuahua dog was used to record the piranha growls.

AWARDS

Nominations:

Golden Raspberries 2012: Worst Remake/Sequel, Worst Support. Actor (Hasselhoff)

THE PIRATES! BAND OF MISFITS

(The Pirates! In an Adventure with Scientists!)

> *It's a plunderful life.*
> —Movie tagline

> *Laugh your booty off.*
> —Movie tagline

> *Join the crew and kick some booty.*
> —Movie tagline

> *Prepare for a new breed of pirates.*
> —Movie tagline

> *Let's go plundering.*
> —Movie tagline

> *Places to pillage. People to skewer.*
> —Movie tagline

Box Office: $31 million

While extinction-expediting entrees like panda face fritters and pygmy elephant nuggets can rightly be referred to as inadvisable fare, the same cannot be said of another rare treat: *The Pirates! Band of Misfits.* Indeed, it can be heartily recommended as a delicacy to be savored without reservation. It was prepared for one's pleasure by England's Aardman Animations, the stop-motion masters embraced with fervency and fondness for their *Wallace & Gromit* efforts and films like *Chicken Run* (2000), and is the first such production they have served up in 3D. Though perhaps not quite rising to the level of those acclaimed achievements, *The Pirates!* is, from bow to aft, a daft delight. While there is mention of an understandably bummed-out baboon whose kidneys now reside in a specimen jar, the film itself lacks neither heart nor, most notably, a brain. Instead of lazily sinking to the depths for a predominance of lowbrow humor or immersing audiences in a flood of destined-to-be-dated pop culture references, Aardman chooses to jauntily offer up deliciously droll and dry quirky cleverness with an unmistakable British accent that can be universally understood. With this wittiness combined with the wackiness of its sight gags and action sequences, there is plenty to satiate the appetite for fun of all ages.

In 1837, a motley crew of pirates appears to be both figuratively and literally at sea as they try to pinpoint the best thing about their line of work. Dashing outfits, looting, encounters with mermaids, or the chance to catch exotic diseases (hopefully not from one of the mermaids) are all asserted to be the correct answer by crew members identified solely by chuckle-inducing monikers like The Surprisingly Curvaceous Pirate (Ashley Jensen) and The Pirate Who Likes Sunsets and Kittens (jovial NBC weatherman Al Roker). The pinnacle of piracy is declared to be "Ham Nite" by The Pirate Captain (a top-notch Hugh Grant), who is arguably the highlight of the film itself. In his first appearance, viewers learn that there is unexpectedly more to this marauder than meets the eye. Indeed, the kind of person The Pirate Captain is at heart is apparent the minute he reaches into the luxuriant beard of which he often understandably boasts (notice its wave-like pattern) and reveals he has kept beloved (and surprisingly big-boned) Polly the Parrott protectively nestled within. The fervency of his subsequent nuzzling is even striking to the men (and one disguised woman) who know and love him well. It is thus easy to embrace The Pirate Captain himself from the outset, and even moreso once one comes to realize that demoralization lies below all his determined buoyancy and bravado. In short, he has a lot of panache but precious little prowess when it comes to pirating. For twenty years, The Pirate Captain has coveted the Pirate of the Year Award, profoundly driven to garner the validation that would come with such recognition. When The Pirate Captain is ridiculed for even thinking of entering again by formidable challengers like Black Bellamy (Jeremy Piven) and fetching Cutlass Liz (Salma Hayek), a close-up captures the touching wounded look in the character's eyes. Anyone who fails to feel for him and root for his ultimate triumph should be made to walk the plank.

Spurred on by such stinging mockery, The Pirate Captain aims to finally prove himself by besting his detractors, and his attempts to obtain loot are a hoot.

Despite feeling sorry for him, one cannot help but grin when The Pirate Captain and his crew make buccaneering booty calls on vessels devoid of valuables, including boats replete with plague sufferers, schoolchildren on a field trip, and nudists without even a pocket to pinch. Eventually, they happen upon a forlorn, pre-famous Charles Darwin (admirable David Tennant) on his HMS Beagle, and find the scientist less interested in how monkeys evolved into man than in how he himself can be turned into the kind of man that no lady would dismiss. Darwin's deflated ego and yearning to impress mirror that of The Pirate Captain, minus the latter's facade. Thanks to Darwin's sharp eyes (located below a humorously simian brow), Polly is recognized as an anything-but-extinct Dodo, an astonishing find that, while flightless, could nonetheless be the means by which both men can finally soar to lofty levels of much-needed approbation.

All of this enjoyable nautical nonsense heads for the shores of London, where a duplicitous Darwin and his flash card-flipping chimpanzee servant Mr. Bobo (silent yet superiorly insightful a la Gromit) vie with The Pirate Captain for possession of Polly in order to win the award for Best Scientific Discovery at the Royal Academy. "Chuck" desires the romantic affections of "Vicki" (that is Queen Victoria to the rest of us), but she is only salivating over Polly for a reprehensible repast. It is disappointing when The Pirate Captain gives up the beloved bird in exchange for a haul of royal riches that could make him Pirate of the Year, but he wins back the approval of both the audience and his crew when he rescues her in the film's frantic finale, and his winning of the award at long last is gratifying to behold.

In typical Aardman fashion, there are not only a slew of quick quips but also no dearth of detail within a mise-en-scene packed like a treasure chest brimming with alluring pieces of eight. Eyes scanning the frame for delightful treasures are richly rewarded. A sign is glimpsed on the back of the ship that reads "Honk if you're seasick." One in the streets of London advertises "Urchin throwing, Cockney baiting," and a wanted poster embarrassingly offers a measly amount of doubloons and a free pen for The Pirate Captain's capture. Also, a gold Wallace can be spotted in the Queen's vault. The pause button will be much-appreciated during DVD viewings. Other details also impress: twenty-four shots of slightly-altered plasticine puppets make up each second of film, with approximately three seconds completed per day over eighteen months; 340 puppets were used, including over thirty Pirate Captains simultaneously used by thirty to forty units; and over 8,000 hard-substanced mouths that could be continually swapped out to match letter sounds and express emotions with painstaking precision. Computer generated imagery is seamlessly used for waves, skies and other background details.

The Pirates! Band of Misfits was released in the UK as *The Pirates! In an Adventure with Scientists!*, the title of the 2004 book by Gideon Defoe that became a cult favorite there and has been improved upon for the screen by the author himself. The film is deftly directed by Peter Lord, the co-founder of Aardman who last helmed the aforementioned (and Oscar-nominated) *Chicken Run*. "This is our most educational adventure ever," proclaims one of the pirates, but while it is intelligently told, *The Pirates!* aims for absurdity rather than accuracy when it comes to the representation of historical personages like Darwin and Queen Victoria: verisimilitude would not have been very funny. There has also never been much serious debate over whether pigs can be correctly classified as fruit. The assertion that London reeks of a mustiness reminiscent of one's grandmother is, one supposes, open to question, as it depends upon each person's subjective assessment of his or her own ancestor's aroma. Nevertheless, most viewers agreed on the message *Pirates!* imparts: the friends one dearly holds onto possess a value that no monetary riches can match. Still, its makers would likely have appreciated more money than the $31 million that their positively-reviewed, $55 million-budgeted film grossed in the United States. Regardless, while Queen Victoria rants "I HATE pirates!" throughout the production, few people were moved by the film to exclaim the same.

David L. Boxerbaum

CREDITS

Pirate Captain: Hugh Grant (Voice)
Pirate with a Scarf: Martin Freeman (Voice)
Queen Victoria: Imelda Staunton (Voice)
Charles Darwin: David Tennant (Voice)
Black Bellamy: Jeremy Piven (Voice)
Cutlass Liz: Salma Hayek (Voice)
Pirate King: Brian Blessed (Voice)
The Albino Pirate: Anton Yelchin (Voice)
The Pirate with Gout: Brendan Gleeson (Voice)
Peg Leg Hastings: Lenny Henry (Voice)
Origin: United Kingdom, United States
Language: English, Spanish
Released: 2012
Production: Julie Lockhart, Peter Lord, David Sproxton; Columbia Pictures; released by Sony Pictures Home Entertainment Inc., Aardman Animations Ltd.
Directed by: Peter Lord; Jeff Newitt
Written by: Gideon Defoe
Cinematography by: Frank Passingham

Music by: Theodore Shapiro
Sound: Adrian Rhodes
Editing: Justin Krish
Art Direction: Matt Perry
Production Design: Norman Garwood
MPAA rating: PG
Running time: 88 minutes

REVIEWS

Corliss, Richard. *Time*. April 26, 2012.
Dargis, Manohla. *New York Times*. April 26, 2012.
DeFore, John. *Hollywood Reporter*. March 26, 2012.
Felperin, Leslie. *Variety*. March 26, 2012.
Hammond, Pete. *Boxoffice Magazine*. April 27, 2012.
Markovitz, Adam. *Entertainment Weekly*. April 25, 2012.
O'Sullivan, Michael. *Washington Post*. April 26, 2012.
Phillips, Michael. *Chicago Tribune*. April 26, 2012.
Pinkerton, Nick. *Village Voice*. April 24, 2012.
Puig, Claudia. *USA Today*. April 26, 2012.
Russo, Tom. *Boston Globe*. April 26, 2012.
Turan, Kenneth. *Los Angeles Times*. April 26, 2012.

QUOTES

Pirate Captain: "And that's why, in a straight fight, a shark would probably beat a Dracula."

TRIVIA

The film is primarily stop-motion animation, but computer-generated animation was used for much of the scenery.

AWARDS

Nominations:

Oscars 2012: Animated Film

PITCH PERFECT

Get pitch slapped.
—Movie tagline

Box Office: $65 million

Anyone (okay, maybe any girl) who came of age in the early aughts would agree that a person's cool factor could be determined by just how many *Bring It On* (2000) quotes they could insert into a regular conversation. Without question, the movie was a ridiculous, out-of-this-world experience that left most viewers debating the merits of national, ESPN-worthy cheerleading competitions, but it also left a lot of viewers jazzed and wondering if they could still do the splits.

Bring It On was a butterfly story-romantic comedy hybrid that brought fans into the world of competitive high school cheerleading and it worked because it committed fiercely to said world. These cheer-obsessed schools might not exist in most back yards, but after watching the movie, it was easy to think that they were out there. And if the schools existed, so did the characters and they were lovable in all their vapid weirdness. Thanks to a similar commitment to world building, coupled with delightful characters and a charming love story, *Pitch Perfect* is destined to do for the tens what *Bring It On* did for the aughts: galvanize an age group around a pop-culture phenomenon (teen a cappella groups) and weed out uncool members if they do not catch on to aca-jokes. That it further gives props to musical theatre lovers everywhere is just an added bonus.

Beca (Anna Kendrick) is a hip college freshman, and uber talented D.J., who wants to move to L.A. and start working her way up in the music biz. Her father, a professor at Barden University values traditional education and strikes a deal with his perpetually-plugged-into-her-oversized-headphones daughter: If she commits to one year of run-of-the-mill college and still wants to move to the West Coast, he will help her out. Beca agrees. But of course Barden is not your standard, run-of-the-mill college. Barden is so into a cappella that the school has not one, but four rival groups. Although she greets this information with a huge eye roll we soon learn that Beca can not only sing, her mixing skills might be the one chance for the school's all-female act, The Bellas, to redeem themselves at nationals. Of course, to do so, she is going to have to match wits with the group's ice princess leader, who does not want to move The Bellas' repertoire past Ace of Base's 1993 "The Sign," while also keeping her feelings for Jesse (Skylar Austin), a wannabe movie scorer and member of the rival all-boys group The Trebelmakers, a secret since cavorting with the enemy is strictly verboten.

The basic set-up is reminiscent of television's super successful *Glee,* and rightfully so. *Pitch Perfect* owes its box office take to the show's breakout fans, but thanks to its motion picture running time, *Pitch Perfect* does not have to worry about running out of source material, nor does it have to be appropriate for primetime family viewing. The mash-ups, which cleverly weave Simple Minds' "Don't You (Forget About Me)" with Miley Cyrus' "Party In The U.S.A." and Vickie Sue Robinson's "Turn The Beat Around" are memorable. So too are the over-the-top puke gags. Both work to turn this predictable plot into a true crowd pleaser. And there is no denying that it is predictable. Just like *Bring It On, Pitch Perfect* is a classic underdog story. From the get-go, as The Barden Bellas blow it in last year's finals during the movie's opening minutes, audiences know the kind of story that will unfold. But as *Bring It On* showed, predictable does not have to be boring. And, in the right hands, predictable allows a screenwriter such as Kay Cannon (*30 Rock*) to focus on hitting the audience where it counts: in the heart and in the funny bone.

The witty, in-tune script nails the Millennial tongue-in-cheek banter while also providing heartfelt subplots for the leading characters—Beca and Jesse have a charming meet-cute, a sad emoticon-worthy breakup and a sweet, YouTube-worthy make-up. But it is the energetic cast that solidifies *Pitch Perfect* as a hit. Rebel Wilson as Fat Amy, a self-prescribed moniker to ward off the nicknames made up by skinny girls, steals the show with raunchy asides, perfect one-liners and a grounding air of indifference to the whole, ridiculous a cappella scene. The banter between the disgruntled a cappella competition commentators, played by Elizabeth Banks and John Michael Higgins, is priceless, and Hana Mae Lee as soft, barely-audible Bella member Lilly provides one the film's more quotable lines. Brittany Snow is delightful as Chloe, the Bellas overly emotional second in command. And 27-year-old Kendrick exceeds expectations as alt rock chick Beca. Though the shedding of her tough girl exterior is the ultimate trajectory for Beca, it is her ability to throw down with Blackstreet's "No Diggity" at a late-night riff-off that will have audiences cheering.

Joanna Topor MacKenzie

CREDITS

Beca: Anna Kendrick
Fat Amy: Rebel Wilson
Chloe: Brittany Snow
Bumper: Adam DeVine
Aubrey: Anna Camp
Stacie: Alexis Knapp
Luke: Freddie Stroma
Gail: Elizabeth Banks
Tommy: Christopher Mintz-Plasse
Origin: United States
Language: English
Released: 2012
Production: Paul Brooks, Max Handelman, Elizabeth Banks; Gold Circle Films; released by Universal Pictures
Directed by: Jason Moore
Written by: Kay Cannon
Cinematography by: Julio Macat
Music by: Christophe Beck
Sound: Lee Orloff; Paul Ledford
Editing: Lisa Zeno Churgin

Art Direction: Jeremy Woolsey
Costumes: Salvador Perez
Production Design: Barry Robinson
MPAA rating: PG-13
Running time: 112 minutes

REVIEWS

Beck, Laura. *Village Voice*. October 8, 2012.

Diones, Bruce. *New Yorker*. October 8, 2012.

Edelstein, David. *New York Magazine*. October 1, 2012.

Guzman, Rafer. *Newsday*. September 28, 2012.

Howell, Peter. *Toronto Star*. September 28, 2012.

O'Sullivan, Michael. *Washington Post*. September 28, 2012.

Puig, Claudia. *USA Today*. September 27, 2012.

Roeper, Richard. *RichardRoeper.com*. October 5, 2012.

Smith, Kyle. *New York Post*. September 28, 2012.

Whitty, Stephen. *Newark Star-Ledger*. September 29, 2012.

QUOTES

Fat Amy: "I'm gonna kill him! I'm gonna finish him like a cheesecake!"

TRIVIA

The role of Gail was originally written for Kristen Wiig but she when declined due to scheduling conflicts, Elizabeth Banks, one of the film's producers, took on the role.

PLAYING FOR KEEPS
(Playing the Field)

Box Office: $13.1 million

Like Tom Shadyac's *Liar Liar* (1997) sans any of the Frank Capra cuteness, *Playing for Keeps* is the father fantasy of a washed-up former soccer star named George (Gerard Butler) who has to put his life back together before it completely falls apart. He is running low on money to pay rent on his guesthouse residency, and his ex-wife that he still has feelings for (Jessica Biel) is about to be married off to another man. His relationship with his young son Lewis (Noah Lomax) is strained, due to the fact that he abandoned the boy at a young age, and since being back in his life has become the "I'm Sorry I'm Late" type of dad (much like Jim Carrey in *Liar Liar*, or Arnold Schwarzengger in Brian Levant's *Jingle All the Way* [1996]). To make his revival even more of a challenge, his hopes of rejuvenating his career in soccer by becoming a sportscaster are stilted by his inability to have a good audition tape or gain the interest of any potential employers.

One day when he takes Lewis to soccer practice, George witnesses the uninspired work of his son's preoccupied coach, and decides to kick the ball around with his son and the team himself. This prompts on-looking parents to immediately recognize the chemistry George has with a soccer ball and their children, which immediately elects him to the position of head coach.

While becoming head coach gives him the advantage of spending more time with his son, and showing to his ex-wife that he is on course to being a different man, it also features the "disadvantage" of the individuals on the sidelines, namely the overzealous suburban parents (like Dennis Quaid's bribing Carl) or the procreant moms (Judy Greer's Barb, Uma Thurman's Patti, and Catherine Zeta-Jones' Denise) who want to turn this former athlete/single dad into their cathartic sexual bed shreds.

Produced by Butler, *Playing for Keeps* shows that he is pathetically out of touch with his viewers, and not only because it attempts to negotiate Butler's forceful insistence of being recognized for his apparently undeniable sex appeal with the image of being a good father. In one of the film's many disagreeable choices, soccer is chosen as the main focus, despite its lack of popularity in America, especially compared to its lifeblood importance in other countries. Somewhere on the list of "Sports Americans Care About," "soccer" is certainly towards the bottom, with "planking" and "being on the internet" above it. Which brings the question: Why soccer? Is it possible that Scottish actor Butler and Italian director Gabriele Muccino stubbornly insisted on the sport being a centerpiece for the story, over something considered thoroughly American (and subsequently likely more box office friendly) such as baseball?

The focus of soccer admittedly does prove to be solely useful for the fitting metaphor it provides for the movie's supporting performances, full of hyper actors (Zeta-Jones, Quaid, and Thurman) looking to turn this insignificant moment in their filmography into a pebble of gold (if not a comeback for their onscreen personas), fighting for the audience's attention like little ones chaotically clamoring for a rolling soccer ball. Thurman and Zeta-Jones each make a lunge for the title of the movie's top cougar, with Thurman getting an extended scene in her underwear, and Zeta-Jones adding as much sultriness as possible to typical sideline chats between that of coach and concerned parent.

The champion of this supporting cast, however, is Quaid, who barrels through this movie with enthusiasm most comparable to a giddy sociopath to win this film's useless designation. In some glimmers of the story, his embodiment of a suburban dad hyper on his own insanity provides a couple of amusing giggles, much like his appearance in *What To Expect When You're Expecting*, or Michael Shannon's zealous villain in *Premium Rush*, both from 2012.

The film's other "sport," the sexual pursuit of middle-aged women, reveals itself to be a cashing-in on the media revolution of the "cougar," in which the hormonal liberation of housewives and soccer moms is promoted by various television shows like *Cougar Town* or *Desperate Housewives*. With the film's sexual content providing nothing to the story but limp comedic bits and more macho ego chips for Butler's onscreen persona, *Playing for Keeps* shows that it does not need the restraints of a PG-13 rating to reduce any zest to its grown up humor. Add the cougar hunting with the story's tale of a man trying to be a good father and exhusband, and one is left with the grossest type of fantasy porn for bad dads—a man not only gets to show up on time to preserve his relevancy to his family unit, but he also gets to be seen with various enamored soccer moms as well.

Butler's barometer for audience sympathy is still malfunctioning, as he fails to present a character who is both believably desirable but still a good person. It is quite a challenge for a character to draw heavy attention to their sex appeal, and then turn around and proclaim that such is not one of their truer traits, and that one should be sympathized for their burdening uncontrollable attractiveness. Michael Fassbender was able to accomplish this feat of pity with Steve McQueen's 2011 film *Shame*, but certainly with the assistance of a dark story of sex addiction, where his character was pitied for the heavy depths of despair to which he sunk. This particular film, without even being compared to *Shame*, is simply the story of a burned-out bad dad who screwed up being a husband, and is now just considering possibly putting a stop to his promiscuous ways.

Such a lack of attachment to Butler's character becomes a strong factor in the emotionally empty experience of *Playing for Keeps*, a movie that prods along with its helping of dramatic moments (often involving Jessica Biel, and tears that are believable enough). Robbie Fox's script is inspired more by suburban blandness than the emotions it is attempting to put on display. Lacking spirit or a shred of sweetness, the film ultimately leaves audiences with nothing to root for—not the sport involved, not the happiness at stake, and certainly not the work of Butler. *Playing for Keeps* is a losing shot at a romantic comedy for parents; they deserve better on a night away from their kids.

Nick Allen

CREDITS

George: Gerard Butler
Stacie: Jessica Biel

Lewis: Noah Lomax

Carl: Dennis Quaid

Patti: Uma Thurman

Denise: Catherine Zeta-Jones

Matt: James Tupper

Barb: Judy Greer

Origin: United States

Language: English

Released: 2012

Production: Heidi Jo Markel, Kevin Misher, Jonathan Mostow, Alan Siegel, John Siegel, Gerard Butler; Eclectic Pictures, Evil Twins, Millenium Films, Misher Films, Nu Image Films; released by FilmDistrict

Directed by: Gabriele Muccino

Written by: Robbie Fox

Cinematography by: Peter Menzies, Jr.

Music by: Andrea Guerra

Sound: Robert Jackson

Music Supervisor: Selena Arizanovic

Editing: Padraic McKinley

Art Direction: Bob Danyla

Costumes: Angelica Russo

Production Design: Daniel T. Dorrance

MPAA rating: PG-13

Running time: 105 minutes

REVIEWS

Anderson, Melissa. *Village Voice*. December 7, 2012.

Dargis, Manohla. *New York Times*. December 6, 2012.

Ebert, Roger. *Chicago Sun-Times*. December 7, 2012.

Guzman, Rafer. *Newsday*. December 6, 2012.

Hornaday, Ann. *Washington Post*. December 7, 2012.

Jones, J. R. *Chicago Reader*. December 14, 2012.

Lemire, Christy. *Associated Press*. December 5, 2012.

Long, Tom. *Detroit News*. December 7, 2012.

Morris, Wesley. *Boston Globe*. December 6, 2012.

Sharkey, Betsy. *Los Angeles Times*. December 6, 2012.

AWARDS

Nominations:

Golden Raspberries 2012: Worst Support. Actress (Biel)

THE POSSESSION

Pray for her.
—Movie tagline

Fear the demon that doesn't fear God.
—Movie tagline

Box Office: $49.1 million

There are some films that not only strike audiences at the right time but which are so overwhelmingly the last word on the subject that any such attempts at revisiting the material in the future seem superfluous at best and who-are-they-kidding at worst. *Titanic* (1997) is one of those films. Christopher Nolan's trilogy stamp on the Batman legend is another. Certainly William Friedkin and William Peter Blatty's *The Exorcist* (1974) has to be the end-all of possession films. Sequels, prequels and direct remakes of said prequels aside, films about demonic interference of one's anatomy were mainly brushed aside until the success of *The Exorcism of Emily Rose* (2005). Now it seems theaters have been overrun with the premise in films as pleasantly surprising as *The Last Exorcism* (2010) to some of the worst on record in *The Rite* (2011) and *The Devil Inside* (2012). Now it is the turn for director Ole Bornedal, no stranger to revisions having re-directed his Danish thriller, *Nightwatch* (1994), for American audiences in 1997. *The Possession* is his first English film since then and he has chosen to make it in the most familiar language possible understood by those who know what to expect from generic PG-13 horror films.

The Brenek family is adjusting to a new divorce. Clyde (Jeffrey Dean Morgan) has moved out but shares joint custody with his ex, Stephanie (Kyra Sedgwick). Weekend visits have their fair share of rules for daughters Hannah (Madison Davenport) and Emily (Natasha Calis) such as no pizza or restrictions on making dad feel bad for their predicament. Clyde does his best though including splurging on them at a local yard sale where Emily takes a liking to an old wine box that appears designed to not be opened. Or not meant to be opened as dad rightly deduces.

Soon after, Clyde's new house is being invaded by giant moths and something raiding his refrigerator. Is it a raccoon, E.T. or something else? More curious though is Emily's shift in behavior. She is withdrawn, prone to blackouts, and has an insatiable appetite that, if interrupted, will get one the business end of a fork. Concerned but dismissive of it as a side effect of the separation, it is not until a tragedy at school that Clyde begins to suspect Emily's new security blanket may not be there to protect her.

After some shuffling around of the film's release scheduled, it was re-titled from *Dybbuk Box*, presumably because audiences know what a possession is but not the lore of dislocated Jewish spirits. The history of the box which led to the true story Bornedal's film purports to be based on is infinitely more fascinating than concocting just another endangered child to save from it. As maybe the only film to draw its inspiration from an eBay auction—turned into a 2004 article by Leslie Gornstein—the screenplay by Juliet Snowden and Stiles White (also responsible for the Nostradamus-in-a-time-capsule film, *Knowing* [2009]) hedges its own bets on how far it wants to take gentile audiences into a Jewish Exorcist film.

It is not the only frustrating element of *The Possession* as it becomes yet another film with supernatural bumps in the night where nobody stops to ask the right questions or explain it in a matter that does not make them look like a nut. Closed rooms do not just fill up with moths. Teeth do not just begin falling out by the mouthful. When you throw something out across town, it is also very likely that someone would leave the house in the middle of the night and find it. That is a rather strange phenomenon that might be worth bringing up when you are accused of being a bad father in court. Clyde finally begins believing in a higher power and seeks out help. First, to a professor who mocks him and also the audience by having his blackboard emphasized with big capital letters—"SELF POSSESSION THROUGH TRANSFORMATION"—just in case someone was in the bathroom for the previous forty-five minutes. Up next comes the Hassidic community, which all but abandons Clyde except for Rabbi Tzadok (Matisyahu) who is on hand to provide more exposition and a climax that feels more like a cheerleading chant than an exorcism.

The Possession was produced by Sam Raimi and every once in a while, Bornedal strays from the abject terror and takes a cheekier approach to the material that recalls Raimi's own *Drag Me To Hell* (2009) and the kind of winking eye he has brought to all genres. Becoming a contradiction onto itself, it instead becomes its own parody with recognizable moments from previous entries and a heavy-handed music score that manages to combine the familiar strains of *Jaws* (1975) with the untoward vibe created by the piano at an *Eyes Wide Shut* (1999) party. Every scare sequence is more noteworthy for its sound design than what is actually happening on screen. The volume is raised to a deafening roar, then a moment of complete silence followed by a single piano note. This constant melodic sequence of white noise and general avoidance of any theological originality diverts from the film's one standout in the performance of Natasha Calis. She holds the screen with her struggle in a manner to where she appears to be the only one truly believing in the material, which is rather essential when all an audience is really left to suppose is that all dislocated Jewish spirits really want is a vessel to enjoy a good meal.

Erik Childress

CREDITS

Clyde: Jeffrey Dean Morgan
Stephanie: Kyra Sedgwick

Em: Natasha Calis
Brett: Grant Show
Professor McMannis: Jay Brazeau
Hannah: Madison Davenport
Tzadok: Matisyahu
Origin: United States
Language: English
Released: 2012
Production: J. R. Young, Sam Raimi, Robert G. Tapert; Ghost House Pictures, North Box Productions; released by Lionsgate
Directed by: Ole Bornedal
Written by: Juliet Snowden; Stiles White
Cinematography by: Dan Laustsen
Music by: Anton Sanko
Sound: Jussi Tegelman
Editing: Anders Villadsen
Costumes: Carla Hetland
Production Design: Rachel O'Toole
MPAA rating: PG-13
Running time: 91 minutes

REVIEWS

Kaplan, Dave. *Kaplan vs. Kaplan.* August 31, 2012.
Kenny, Glenn. *MSN Movies.* August 30, 2012.
Levin, Robert. *Film School Rejects.* September 1, 2012.
McGranaghan, Mike. *Aisle Seat.* August 31, 2012.
O'Hehir, Andrew. *Salon.com.* August 30, 2012.
Putman, Dustin. *DustinPutman.com.* August 31, 2012.
Rabin, Nathan. *AV Club.* August 30, 2012.
Swietek, Frank. *One Guy's Opinion.* August 31, 2012.
Weinberg, Scott. *FEARnet.* August 31, 2012.
Wilkinson, Ron. *Monsters and Critics.* September 3, 2012.

QUOTES

Tzadok: "I hate hospitals. People die here."

TRIVIA

The demon in the box speaks Polish.

PREMIUM RUSH

Ride like hell.
—Movie tagline

Box Office: $20.3 million

David Koepp has had an extraordinarily lucrative career as a screenwriter, penning scripts for big-budget action adventures and thrillers like *Jurassic Park* (1993),

Carlito's Way (1993), *Mission: Impossible* (1996), *Spider-Man* (2002), *Panic Room* (2002), and *War of the Worlds* (2005). This success as a writer-for-hire has afforded him a parallel livelihood as a screenwriter-director of more typically compact genre fare, where Koepp has carved out a successful niche as the peddler of genre dramas like *The Trigger Effect* (1996), *Stir of Echoes* (1999) and *Secret Window* (2004). His latest film is *Premium Rush,* a streamlined, espresso shot of unpretentious and relatively unsophisticated fun which has the benefit of a pair of perfectly contrasted lead performances from Joseph Gordon-Levitt and Michael Shannon.

Generally positive critical response failed to lift the movie much at the box office; it grossed only a bit over $20 million domestically in theaters. But if other films, blockbusters like *The Dark Knight Rises* (2012) for Gordon-Levitt and the impending *Man of Steel* (2013) for Shannon, are where these actors will perhaps most make their name (and money), *Premium Rush* is a crafty thrill ride that will enjoy sustained catalogue appeal owing to their rising, burnished stars. This is a movie that will age well, and find an audience through warm word-of-mouth.

The film's tale centers on New York City bike messenger Wilee (Gordon-Levitt), an irrepressible speed junkie for whom "brakes are death." When approaching jammed intersections, he surveys minute openings and possible routes with a precognitive clarity, visualizing the disaster of potential choices. Other riders cycle with great focus and effort, but an eye also on the bottom line; for Wilee, who nets less per delivery than a waitress at a popular restaurant might in tips per hour, his job is about his love of riding and its Zen purity.

Wilee's ex-girlfriend Vanessa (Dania Ramirez) also bikes for the same company, and has a connection to Nima (Jamie Chung), from whom Wilee gets a rush pick-up dispatch from his boss Raj (Aasif Mandvi). This order sends Wilee from the far reaches of Manhattan's Upper West Side to Chinatown, and it also nets him a ruthless antagonist, in the form of dirty cop Bobby Monday (Shannon). Unbeknownst to Wilee, Nima's nondescript delivery is a piece of paper that serves as a payment marker on a mysterious transaction, and the cash-strapped Monday will stop at nothing to intercept it. When authoritative cajoling fails, he starts chasing Wilee across the city. Further complicating matters for Wilee are a competitive coworker, Manny (Wole Parks), who works himself into the situation, and an unnamed but dogged NYPD bike patrolman (Christopher Place) who seems to always find himself on the wrong end of Wilee's crafty escapes.

In addition to the rather significant physical demands of his role—and in performing most of his own stunts he definitely takes a beating, as an end credits outtake that shows the aftereffects of a crash through the back windshield of a taxi makes abundantly clear—Gordon-Levitt also brings a grounded yet rakish leading man quality to *Premium Rush*. He has a perfect sense of its entertainment-value mandate. Shannon, meanwhile, is in stark contrast a scene-chewing delight—an unhinged, theatrical lunatic loosely in the mold of Gary Oldman's bad guy from *The Professional* (1994). Koepp grants Monday an ongoing dental problem, and Shannon teases Monday's ever-increasing aching-jaw misery into a collection of often amusing tics, twitches and yelps. Together, this pair elevate *Premium Rush*, and give it a crackling, electric energy.

Working with cinematographer Mitchell Amundsen and editors Derek Ambrosi and Jill Savitt, Koepp deftly keeps the action breakneck without it ever becoming overwhelming or wildly unrealistic. Whereas a lot of action movies attempt to conjure experiential audience identification through frenetic cutting and canted angles, Koepp wants viewers to feel the peddling, muscle-straining effort of his actors, and does so by making smart use of both wide-angle and tracking shots.

An emphasis on practical effects versus augmented CGI is of importance, too; the latter is utilized fairly sparingly and mostly in the aforementioned slow-motion sequences which illustrate Wilee's mental dexterity and lightning quick reflexes. Koepp also keeps his characters connected with one another through the use of hands-free cell phones, and utilizes smart, modern ways (aerial mapping) to communicate distance and space to his audience. Perhaps most significantly, however, all this action fits the narrative hand-in-glove. While a lot of films bend over backwards to cram in action sequences, *Premium Rush* is all about a mad, multi-layered chase to begin with, so it flows quite naturally. It has a fixed gear, but its manic singularity works.

The only times *Premium Rush* really struggles or flags are when it dips into flashback—whether further explaining Vanessa and Nima's connection, or other bits related to Nima's circumstances. Here, there is a tug against the movie's pounding immediacy, which is one of its most appealing qualities. *Premium Rush* also does not really have the time to devote to an honest subcultural exploration of urban biking, which makes a part of its ending more than a bit silly. Still, if one forgives *Premium Rush* its definitely original but still complicated and unlikely motivating plot device (from the less-is-more school of thought, a simple MacGuffin would have perhaps worked better), Koepp succeeds in crafting a slick, forward-leaning thriller that both cycling enthusiasts and those who have never ridden a bike can enjoy in equal measure.

Brent Simon

CREDITS

Wilee: Joseph Gordon-Levitt
Bobby Monday: Michael Shannon
Nima: Jamie Chung
Raj: Aasif Mandvi
Origin: United States
Language: English
Released: 2012
Production: Gavin Polone; Pariah Films; released by Columbia Pictures
Directed by: David Koepp
Written by: David Koepp; John Kamps
Cinematography by: Mitchell Amundsen
Music by: David Sardy
Editing: Jill Savitt; Derek Ambrosi
Costumes: Luca Mosca
Production Design: Therese DePrez
MPAA rating: PG-13
Running time: 90 minutes

REVIEWS

Barker, Andrew. *Variety.* August 23, 2012.
Dargis, Manohla. *New York Times.* August 23, 2012.
Ebert, Roger. *Chicago Sun-Times.* August 23, 2012.
Gang, Alison. *San Diego Union-Tribune.* August 24, 2012.
Mondello, Bob. *NPR.* August 24, 2012.
Phillips, Michael. *Chicago Tribune.* August 23, 2012.
Schenker, Andrew. *Slant Magazine.* August 23, 2012.
Sharkey, Betsy. *Los Angeles Times.* August 23, 2012.
Toppman, Lawrence. *Charlotte Observer.* August 24, 2012.
Willmore, Alison. *Movieline.* August 23, 2012.

QUOTES

Raj: "What is it with this envelope? People love it, they hate it, they gotta have it, they gotta get rid of it. It's like cigarettes or Democrats."

TRIVIA

Bobby Monday's alias Forrest J. Ackerman is a tribute to Forey Ackerman, a noted science fiction and horror movie fan and memorabilia collector.

PROJECT X

You are invited.
    —Movie tagline

Witness it.
    —Movie tagline
The party you've only dreamed about.
    —Movie tagline

Box Office: $54.7 million

The party movie has been done over and over again, whether it is *Animal House* (1978) or *PCU* (1994) or *The Hangover* (2009). Inevitably, filmmakers must find a way to raise an even bigger ruckus than the last one while avoiding the law of diminishing returns. In the overly-maligned, R-rated *Project X*, that means throwing a party so huge and out-of-control that it takes over an entire street. In real life, of course, a bash so loud and reckless (and underage) would be shut down within minutes, hopefully before anyone could get hurt. In fact, the film inspired several copycat parties in the weeks after its release, one resulting in the death of a Houston teenager and another nearby party thwarted before it could get going. In the latter case, a teen charged with trying to throw a *Project X*-style party arrived to court in a T-shirt and shorts and was consequently told he could not go before a judge until he came back in appropriate attire at a later date. That does not exactly suggest positive things about the youth of America, or the notion that people would recognize the mayhem that ensues in *Project X*, rather than just the freewheeling bash that precedes it.

Perhaps that stems from a certain sense that no matter how out of hand things become in *Project X,* the characters still think that the debauchery is worth the destruction. Technically the occasion for the party is the seventeenth birthday of Thomas Kub (Thomas Mann). It is clear, though, that Thomas' friend Costa (Oliver Cooper), a loudmouth who frequently references how much better and more sexually fulfilling his life in New York was compared to his current status in Pasadena, would take any opportunity to throw a huge, popularity-increasing bash before it is too late. If Thomas' parents were going out of town on Flag Day, Costa would ensure that every good-looking young woman in Southern California suddenly wanted to toast Flag Day in the grandest possible fashion.

Plotwise, *Project X* has little on its mind but the party—and its beer bongs and bouncy castle, drugs and DJs and unbridled excess. There is a sporadic emphasis on Thomas' gradually revealing affections for his best female friend Kirby (Kirby Bliss Blanton). These, of course become compromised by his lust for the hottest girl in school (Alexis Knapp), whose newfound attraction to Thomas suggests either a young girl's generosity toward men celebrating their birthdays or, more likely, the social cachet that comes from being the centerpiece of a party that exists somewhere between a suburbanite's recreation of a rap video and *Girls Gone Wild.* There is no denying that *Project X,* like several other movies with the Todd Phillips stamp on them (including *The Hangover, Road Trip* [2000], and *Old School* [2003]) possesses a limited interest in its female characters outside the context of sexual or romantic opportunity, while sometimes unfolding as pure male fantasy. A crucial difference, however, is that of the aforementioned movies, only *Project X* focuses on 17-year-old high school boys, who can pretty much be expected to operate at the whim of their hormones and see the opposite sex in a less-enlightened manner than they might at a later, more mature time in their lives. (*Project X* also does not bare the same stink of misogyny as much of Phillips' work.) Similarly, many of the film's negative reviews claimed that Thomas, Costa and, J.B. (Jonathan Daniel Brown), the third leg of this convincingly bonded tripod, are obnoxious. Yes, sometimes they are, especially Costa. So is Jonah Hill's character in *Superbad,* and many other characters in teen party movies. Teenagers can be obnoxious. In other news, rain is wet.

In many ways and with a pulsing rhythm that truly feels as if a party is unfolding in real time, the sexy, chaotic *Project X* becomes a delirious and exhausting experience that taps into the adolescent mind yearning to turn one night into, as Costa, puts it, a "game-changer." Despite the trio's wishes to be seen as more than soft-spoken outsiders, the script by Matt Drake and Michael Bacall (who also co-wrote the entertaining 2012 reboot of *21 Jump Street*) does not overemphasize notions of geeks and cool kids. As the party becomes louder and sweatier and, eventually, graced with a flamethrower-wielding drug dealer (Rick Shapiro) seeking revenge after Costa steals his lawn gnome, Thomas' house is not filled with various cliques but merely hundreds upon hundreds of young people who want to have a good time, regardless of their grades or future plans. That the cops cannot control the party and must wait for the fire to burn out serves as a useful metaphor for parents who do their best to contain teenage children but also must often police a one-man or one-woman show in danger of losing it.

The movie could certainly use more jokes. Even viewers happy to vicariously return to a youth without responsibilities will recognize that *Project X* exists more as a teenage disaster movie than a comedy, aside from awful stabs at humor like a little person who is stuffed into an oven and then punches several people in the groin. The film's found-footage approach, as the entire film plays out as a home movie being made to document Thomas' birthday, certainly arrives long after *The Blair Witch Project* (1999) rode the style to shockingly profitable success. Yet this does provide the necessary sensation that those watching *Project X* on screen are also right in the center of the party, living it instead of just watching it, longing to take a shot and jump in a pool full of topless women and run before anyone's hair gets set on fire. Thomas, Costa, and J.B. may not be the most likable kids all the time, but a well-handled late scene, when Costa calms the party's pre-teen security guards' lust for vengeance against a justifiably unhappy neighbor, shows that they are not without a conscience, at least after sleeping off the night before for a few hours.

In reality, the consequences for this party would be enormous, financially and legally. The movie largely brushes off the impact that these penalties have on its apologetic kids, who cannot help but celebrate the benefits that the party generates in their social standing. In a few days, or a few months, or a few years, they will probably look back on the party that they threw, which the police could not contain and the news covered via helicopter, and regret throwing away countless opportunities and dollars for the sake of a few hours of fun. That, however, is the thought-process of an adult with the power of hindsight. For a teenager trying to survive one day at a time, tomorrow is a million miles away, irrelevant to the fact that last night, for best friends who created and endured the whole mess together, was legendary.

Matt Pais

CREDITS

Brendan: Brendan Miller
J.B.: Jonathan Daniel Brown
Alexis: Alexis Knapp
Kirby: Kirby Bliss Blanton
Thomas: Thomas Mann
Astin Martin: Martin Klebba
Costa: Oliver Cooper
Dax: Dax Flame
Miles: Miles Teller
Origin: United States
Language: English
Released: 2011
Production: Todd Phillips; Green Hat Films, Silver Pictures; released by Warner Bros.
Directed by: Nima Nourizadeh
Written by: Matt Drake; Michael Bacall
Cinematography by: Ken Seng
Sound: Mark Larry
Music Supervisor: Gabe Hilfer
Editing: Jeff Groth
Art Direction: Desma Murphy
Costumes: Alison McCosh

Production Design: Bill Brzeski
MPAA rating: R
Running time: 87 minutes

REVIEWS

Berardinelli, James. *ReelViews*. March 3, 2012.

Genzlinger, Neil. *New York Times*. March 1, 2012.

Gleiberman, Owen. *Entertainment Weekly*. March 1, 2012.

Lapin, Andrew. *NPR*. March 2, 2012.

Morris, Wesley. *Boston Globe*. March 1, 2012.

Phipps, Keith. *AV Club*. February 29, 2012.

Rodriguez, Rene. *Miami Herald*. February 29, 2012.

Rothkopf, Joshua. *Time Out New York*. March 2, 2012.

Stewart, Sara. *New York Post*. March 1, 2012.

Weitzman, Elizabeth. *New York Daily News*. March 1, 2012.

QUOTES

Costa: "Mr. Kub, how cool is it that Thomas was born on your anniversary, yeah? What a great anniversary gift. A baby."

TRIVIA

Although the party seems to have more than a thousand people attending, only around 200 extras were used during actual filming.

PROMETHEUS

> *The search for our beginning could lead to our end.*
> —Movie tagline

> *They went looking for our beginning. What they found could be our end.*
> —Movie tagline

> *We came from them. They will come for us.*
> —Movie tagline

Box Office: $126.5 million

Partly because it marked the return of director Ridley Scott to the genre that he revolutionized decades earlier with the one-two punch of *Alien* (1979) and *Blade Runner* (1982) and partly because of rumors that it might be a prequel of sorts to the former film, *Prometheus* came into theaters with an enormous amount of anticipation from audiences and critics alike. And yet, after the film was finally unleashed for its initial press screenings, the internet was practically humming for hours with people offering their oblique murmurs of discontent/disappointment with what they had just seen—even those who had been recently given passing grades to such multiplex meatballs as *Men in Black III* (2012) and *Snow White and the Huntsman* (2012) were

muttering about how the film just did not work for them to such a degree that one might have thought that George Lucas had directed it instead of Ridley Scott. Once it started showing publicly, the response was largely the same—it was a hit at the box-office (though not quite as big as some had predicted) and some viewers really responded to it but for the most part, there was a vague sense of dissatisfaction amongst its core audience. One can only hope that the lukewarm response was because the combination of Scott returning to science-fiction and the possibility of doing so within the context of the *Alien* universe jacked up expectations to such gigantic proportions that anything other than an instant, unambiguous masterpiece would be considered a failure in their eyes. Otherwise, the alternative—that a film as crazily ambitious and audacious as this can be rejected by moviegoers despite its obvious qualities simply because it failed to follow all the rules of contemporary blockbuster filmmaking—is far too depressing of a notion to contemplate.

Following one of the more startling opening sequences to grace the screen in a long time, the story launches forward to the year 2089 as archaeologists Elizabeth Shaw (Noomi Rapace) and Charlie Holloway (Logan Marshall-Green) discover a cave in the Scottish highlands containing drawings that appear to indicate that beings from another world once visited our planet and a map showing where they can be found in return. This is amazing enough but it turns out that similar findings have been made throughout the world in the ruins of ancient cultures that couldn't have possibly known about each other or traded such information. Theorizing that these beings, whom they dub "Engineers," are our actual creators, Shaw (who is interested in them in both a scientific and spiritual sense) and Holloway (who is all about the science and nothing more) inspire aging and incredibly wealthy industrialist Peter Weyland (Guy Pearce) to fund the construction of a mammoth ship, dubbed Prometheus, that will take them and a team of scientists on a journey to where the Engineers supposedly reside in order to see if they still exist and, if so, to legitimately meet their maker.

Four years later, the ship arrives at the planet, dubbed LV-233, and the crew, after awakening from cryogenic sleep, learn the details of their mission and also discover that Weyland has passed away in the interim. Representing the company on board is human-looking android David (Michael Fassbender), who has passed the time controlling the ship's functions, practicing his basketball shots and watching *Lawrence of Arabia* (1962) and the cold-as-space-itself corporate stooge Meredith Vickers (Charlize Theron). She makes it perfectly clear from the get-go that she considers the mission a complete waste of time and that if they do happen to encounter the Engineers, none of the Prometheus crew are to engage them in any way. Eventually, they touch down on the planet near a mysterious structure and a group of them disembark in order to investigate it and discover the corpse of a being presumed to be an Engineer, a giant statue of a humanoid head and numerous stone cylinders. When more bodies are discovered, the crew assumes that the Engineers are now extinct but when a dangerous storm suddenly brews up, most of them make it back to the ship in time while a couple are forced to stay behind in the structure until the next morning. What no one notices in the confusion is that David has grabbed one of the cylinders to take back to the ship and the others are now beginning to leak an icky black fluid. There is much that happens from this point on and little of it is very good for most of the people involved.

Obviously, the question on everyone's mind in regards to *Prometheus* is about whether it does serve as a prequel to *Alien* or not and the answer is "sort of but not really." It clearly does take place within the same universe as the *Alien* films and there are the occasional off-hand references to names and locations that will resonate with the hard-core fans of the series. Towards the end, the connections become a little more overt and for the most part, these are the parts of the film that are the least successful because they almost seem designed as a sop to satisfy viewers who might be pissed off that they spent their $12 on—gasp!—an original film and not a long-running series now on either its fifth or seventh installment, depending on whether one counts the *Alien vs. Predator* spin-offs or not (and one most certainly should not). For the most part, however, it is not a literal prequel to the films—instead of ending in a way that directly leads into *Alien,* it charts its own distinct narrative that can co-exist with the other films without contradicting them.

Where it is most like the original *Alien* is in the way that Scott approaches the material. Instead of flinging monsters and goo at viewers from the outset, as one might expect, he has instead chosen to replicate the structure of the original in that he keeps a lid on the overt shocks and scares in order to slowly build up a sense of tension and dread while at the same time acknowledging the fact that his audience has a better working idea of what the characters can possibly expect to discover and playing around with those very expectations as well. This is a risky move to take—if it goes wrong, the film runs the risk of spinning its wheels for an hour while everyone grows increasingly impatient— but it turns out to be surprisingly easy to once again get completely caught up in the proceedings while dreading the possibilities lurking around each and every darkened corner.

However, unlike last year's unnecessary and fairly misbegotten *The Thing* (2011), a film that could not decide if it wanted to be a remake or a prequel of the 1982 cult favorite and instead wound up being nothing more than an expensive piece of fan fiction, *Prometheus* is more than able to stand on its own and in fact, it is at his best when Scott and screenwriters Jon Spaihts and Damon Lindelof are exploring both the new universe they have created and the intriguing metaphysical questions that they raise in their screenplay. Throughout his career, Scott has become an expert at providing viewers with lavishly detailed worlds to frame his narratives (which may be one reason why such frankly contemporary works like *Someone to Watch Over Me* (1987) and *Matchstick Men* (2002) tend to be somewhat wanting) and *Prometheus* is no exception—this is one of those films where everything is designed in such an imaginatively detailed manner that one can easily imagine pausing the Blu-Ray simply just to investigate the incredible visuals in further detail. (Scott even manages to wrestle the dreaded 3-D gimmick into submission with a deployment of the format that is, for once, worth shelling out the extra money to experience.)

The storyline is also fascinating in the way that, like *Blade Runner,* it uses what could have simply been a straightforward genre exercise as a way of grappling with heady metaphysical questions. Admittedly, the film never quite answers all the questions that it raises but in a funny way, this does not really matter, partly because it seems silly to expect a movie to fully answer the basic questions of existence that have haunted mankind throughout its existence and partly because it forces the viewer to engage with what is going on in a more direct manner rather than having everything spoon-fed to them. Besides, by leaving things open-ended, the film leaves the door open for future installments that further grapple with the concepts it raises.

This is not to say that *Prometheus* is just an extended meditation on the existence of mankind and its relationship to the universe—something like *Tree of Life* (2011) with spacesuits—because once the film starts going for the more overtly horrific in the second half, it works perfectly well on those terms and then some. Veering effortlessly between jumbo-sized action beats and smaller moments in which we are never quite sure what is out there in the darkness, Scott keeps the excitement and tension going throughout in ways that strike an interesting balance between the haunted house thrills of *Alien* and the hardware-heavy action that James Cameron brought to *Aliens* (1986). There is one crackerjack sequence that imaginatively mixes up action and tension along with our knowledge of what the alien creatures are capable of doing, tosses in a nifty new bit of hardware to complicate things and the end result is a bit of pure filmmaking of such a bravura nature that even the nay-sayers grudgingly admitted that it was a true highlight. Also helping to drive along the excitement is the strong and muscular lead performance from Noomi Rapace as Shaw. Happily, while the character is no mere Ripley clone—she has her own unique backstory and quirks to play with—she does share an intelligence and fierce determination that is rarely found in female sci-fi characters and Rapace, like Sigourney Weaver before her, is just the right actress to bring those elements out while still coming across like a real person. Her performances in the *Girl with the Dragon Tattoo* movies may have made her an international sensation but this film confirms once and for all that she is indeed a star.

Prometheus is not without its flaws—the Charlize Theron character could have been given more to do, some of the expository dialogue delivered by the ship's captain (Idris Elba) could have been a little less on the nose, and a certain participant's name could have been eliminated from the opening credits for reasons that will be understood after seeing the film. However, when a film comes around that takes as many risks as this one—both in terms of its own narrative and its place in the entire *Alien* franchise—and pulls off most of them to boot, those stumbles are easy to overlook. (Who knows, maybe Scott will rethink them in some future cut of the film as he has done some times before in the past?) As for the hostile reaction from some of the early reviews, there is some small comfort to be had in the fact that neither the original *Alien* nor *Blade Runner* received universal critical acclaim when they were first released (and the latter was a notorious non-starter at the box-office as well) and only became canonized as classics a few years down the line. While it is too soon to elevate *Prometheus* to their level quite yet, there is an excellent chance that history may repeat itself because for all its admitted flaws, this is the kind of bold, visionary film-making that has a better chance of standing the test of time when memories of most of its competitors have faded from memory. More importantly, it leaves viewers genuinely wanting more and when was the last time that a film generated that sensation?

Peter Sobczynski

CREDITS

Elizabeth Shaw: Noomi Rapace
David: Michael Fassbender
Peter Wayland: Guy Pearce
Captain Janek: Idris Elba
Charlie Holloway: Logan Marshall-Green
Meredith Vickers: Charlize Theron
Milburn: Rafe Spall

Origin: United States
Language: English
Released: 2012
Production: David Giler, Walter Hill, Ridley Scott; Dune Entertainment, Scott Free Productions; released by 20th Century-Fox
Directed by: Ridley Scott
Written by: Damon Lindelof; Jon Spaihts
Cinematography by: Dariusz Wolski
Music by: Marc Streitenfeld
Sound: Victor Ray Ennis; Mark P. Stoeckinger
Editing: Pietro Scalia
Costumes: Janty Yates
Production Design: Arthur Marx
MPAA rating: R
Running time: 124 minutes

REVIEWS

Corliss, Richard. *Time.* June 7, 2012.
Denby, David. *New Yorker.* June 18, 2012.
Ebert, Roger. *Chicago Sun-Times.* June 7, 2012.
Edelstein, David. *New York.* June 8, 2012.
Goss, William. *Film.com.* June 8, 2012.
Maltin, Leonard. *Indiewire.* June 14, 2012.
Phillips, Michael. *Chicago Tribune.* June 7, 2012.
Scott, A. O. *New York Times.* June 7, 2012.
Stevens, Dana. *Slate.* June 7, 2012.
Tallerico, Brian. *HollywoodChicago.com.* June 7, 2012.

QUOTES

David: "Big things have small beginnings."

TRIVIA

Gemma Arterton, Carey Mulligan, Olivia Wilde, Anne Hathaway, Abbie Cornish, and Natalie Portman were all considered for the role of Elizabeth Shaw.

AWARDS

Nominations:
Oscars 2012: Visual FX
British Acad. 2012: Visual FX

PROMISED LAND

What's your price?
—Movie tagline

Box Office: $7.6 million

On November 27, almost one month to the day before the opening of *Promised Land,* the Atlanta Falcons played against the New Orleans Saints. It seemed like a match-up guaranteed to spark high drama: The 10-1 Falcons' only loss of the season was to the Saints, so obviously Atlanta was not a sure thing in this game. And 5-6 New Orleans would be almost certainly out of the playoff picture with a loss, ending their shot to play in a Super Bowl in their own city. Then the game was played, and besides for some sporadic tension and threat of something great, it turned out to be a mild entertainment that was never as good or exciting as it might have been.

Oddly enough, *Promised Land*, a drama about natural gas that marks director Gus Van Sant's reunion with *Good Will Hunting* (1997) writer/star Matt Damon (this time collaborating with co-writer/co-star John Krasinski), unfolds just like that game. The film presents a similarly stacked showdown between a powerful favorite and an underdog with a lot on the line. Steve Butler (Damon) and Sue Thomason (Frances McDormand) specialize in traveling around the country, popping into small, financially struggling towns and convincing them that their company should begin the fracking process in order to gather natural gas. They foster dreams of blue-collar citizens becoming millionaires and bribe officials when necessary. (Damon earns a good laugh as Steve, somewhat condescendingly trying to dress like a local, forgets to take off the tag from his new outfit.) It is easy to see why people unable to pay their bills or keep their farm afloat, in a town full of neighbors feeling the same, would ignore any possible complications behind fracking—which involves drilling into the ground to inject high-pressure fluid so shale rocks will fracture and release natural gas—and vote to bring on the gas.

McKinley, Pennsylvania seems like another slam dunk for Steve and Sue, but it is not. That becomes clear during a town meeting in a high school gym when Frank Yates (Hal Holbrook), who now teaches science for fun years after earning a Ph.D in physics from Cornell University and doing research and development for Boeing, stands up and advocates for the people to weigh the benefits and risks of natural gas and vote after everyone has had time to think, and let the dollar signs disappear from their eyes. Steve, a native of farming-heavy Eldridge, Iowa himself, tries to dispel Frank's concerns and questions of safety to the land and the people, but Steve, is clearly rattled. Most of the time, obviously, he is not asked to make much of a case, which is why he frequently relies on the same endearing sales pitch that begins by charmingly assuming a child playing outside is the owner of a house and farm.

Steve's troubles triple with the appearance of Dustin Noble (Krasinski), who represents small environmental group Superior Athena. He brings pictures of dead cows and a story of how the problems caused by fracking and

natural gas took only nine months to shut down his father's nearly 200-year-old farm. These anecdotes, plus Dustin's amusing karaoke take on Bruce Springsteen's *Dancing in the Dark*, pose a threat for which Steve and Sue are obviously not prepared. Yet *Promised Land* rarely allows this conflict to boil in a way that broadens across every character in the film. Steve grows frustrated and threatens to punch Dustin. Damon is very good at being likable even when his character is not, and in the conflict between the newly promoted vice president of land management and a lone protestor with a surprising amount of confidence, Damon and Krasinski represent an effective, watchable contrast.

However, neither Steve nor the townspeople ever fully delve into real, concrete examples of benefits or risks behind fracking. So many of the debates in the film, which comes from a story by Dave Eggers, feel more theoretical than informed. Paul Geary (Lucas Black) cannot wait to embrace Steve and boost his bank account; Jeff Dennon (Scott McNairy) despises Steve's presence in his town and on his property and, later, drunkenly approaches Steve at the bar, perhaps looking to extend his confrontational nature into something more physical. At no point does it seem like anyone here has the full picture of the big issues, only a general concept of whether or not it is worth turning the page toward new technology and greater funds or sticking to an assumedly safer, cash-poor status quo.

Perhaps that is, on some level, the point, particularly when a late-movie twist shows this was never a fair fight in the first place. Damon and Krasinski's script may merely intend to suggest that no one fully grasps what is involved in fracking, and no one should blindly go along with promises of fortune without considering possible consequences. That feels like an old lesson, though, bringing to mind the classic *Simpsons* episode "Marge vs. the Monorail" (1993), which itself was a nod to *The Music Man* (1962). Steve may not be a con artist exactly, but he is someone who may or may not buy the product he is selling if he really stepped back and thought about what came along with it.

Disappointingly, *Promised Land* fails to construct a crisis of conscience for Steve, instead setting aside time for his flirtation with a local woman named Alice (Rosemarie DeWitt), a relationship that is both charming and not especially useful to the story. In a film that suggests small-town Americans, who represent the bulk of the nation—Steve notes that two hours outside of any city looks like Kentucky—should not be underestimated, Van Sant, Damon and Krasinski treat Alice like exactly the type of broadly conceived, beautiful-but-available local woman a single, good-looking guy like Steve would hope to meet on these trips.

In 2011, *The Descendants* also entertained without properly engaging its plotline about the emotional value of land versus the value of changing what it is used for. Two years after the acclaimed documentary *GasLand* (2010) and five years after Paul Thomas Anderson's stunning *There Will Be Blood* (2007), which more than accentuated the clash between personal ideals and risky commerce, *Promised Land* comes along to add, "Let us also include natural gas in the conversation." The cows, the farmers and the frackers surely would all support a film that captures that whole conversation, not just the opening statements.

Matt Pais

CREDITS

Steve Butler: Matt Damon
David Churchill: Terry Kinney
Michael Downey: Joe Coyle
Frank Yates: Hal Holbrook
Sue Thomason: Frances McDormand
Dustin Noble: John Krasinski
Origin: United States
Language: English
Released: 2012
Production: Chris Moore; Participant Media, Pearl Street Films, Imagenation Abu Dhabi FZ; released by Focus Features
Directed by: Gus Van Sant

Written by: Matt Damon; John Krasinski; Dave Eggers
Cinematography by: Linus Sandgren
Music by: Danny Elfman
Sound: Robert Jackson
Music Supervisor: Brian Reitzell
Editing: Billy Rich
Art Direction: Gregory A. Weimerskirch
Costumes: Juliet Polcsa
Production Design: Daniel Clancy
MPAA rating: R
Running time: 106 minutes

REVIEWS

Adams, Sam. *AV Club*. June 6, 2012.
Chang, Justin. *Variety*. June 4, 2012.
Ebert, Roger. *Chicago Sun-Times*. June 13, 2012.
Goodykoontz, Bill. *Arizona Republic*. June 14, 2012.
Phillips, Michael. *Chicago Tribune*. June 14, 2012.
Pols, Mary. *Time*. June 7, 2012.
Puig, Claudia. *USA Today*. June 14, 2012.
Rea, Stephen. *Philadelphia Inquirer*. June 14, 2012.
Scott, Mike. *New Orleans Times-Picayune*. June 22, 2012.
Williams, Joe. *St. Louis Post-Dispatch*. June 22, 2012.

TRIVIA

This is second film co-starring John Krasinski with major contribution by writer David Eggers. Eggers also wrote *Away We Go* which starred Krasinski.

Q

QUARTET

Four friends looking for a little harmony.
—Movie tagline

Every diva deserves an encore.
—Movie tagline

Box Office: $9.1 million

Dustin Hoffman has always been one of the most respected and consistent actors of his generation. Since his star-turning performance in *The Graduate* (1967), he has given several of the most memorable performances of the last forty years, earning seven Academy Award nominations and winning the Best Actor award for *Kramer vs. Kramer* (1979) and *Rain Man* (1988), at which time he famously derided the idea that anybody can be the "Best" at anything. He has been known to take the Method approach to acting, wherein an actor stays in character throughout most of the shoot. Even in films where he and the other actors seem to be phoning in their performances (*Sphere* [1998], for example), he has lent an air of dignity to the project that otherwise might not have existed. As he enters his fiftieth year in the business, Hoffman has finally taken a seat in the director's chair.

He attempted this once before for the film *Straight Time* (1978), but after a few days of shooting he hired Ulu Grosbard to direct it. Hoffman starred in the film, which was badly treated by Warner Bros., which could be one reason why Hoffman did not attempt another directing job until now. With *Quartet,* Hoffman has decided to stay off-screen altogether and let his generous ensemble do the honors. It is a low-key, charming comedy/drama that takes place mostly in one central location (a retirement home). Prior to the film's release, Hoffman was a recipient at the Kennedy Center Honors in Washington D.C., where his friend Robert De Niro spoke about him being a "world-class, spectacular, colossal pain in the ass." That may be true of his temperament when working on the set as an actor, but as the director of this sweet, gentle little movie, Hoffman shows no sign of strain or ego.

The film takes place at a retirement home for musicians and opera singers. The film opens with many of the residents practicing their vocal strengths under the cantankerous direction of Cedric (Michael Gambon). They prepare for a show coming up in a month, a birthday celebration of Italian Romantic composer Giuseppe Verdi. The title refers to three of the current residents: Wilf (Billy Connolly), the irrepressible, flirtatious charmer has all but lost whatever filter he once had when speaking to anyone; Cissy (Pauline Collins), easily charmed, but also in the very early stages of Alzheimer's; Reginald (Tom Courtenay), the most straight-laced of the group who had once been married to a fourth member.

But that fourth member, Jean (Maggie Smith) will soon be a resident. When Jean approaches the home, she has a feeling of being taken prisoner against her will. Her arrival comes as a big surprise to everyone there, particularly Reginald. Yet in spite of this hardship, she is greeted warmly by the residents with heartfelt applause. But Reginald, who also teaches music classes to young people, sees her arrival as the end of his well-being at the home and considers relocating. The four have most famously recorded together on Verdi's Rigoletto opera.

But when Reginald first sees Jean during one of his classes, he treats her as a stranger.

Jean appears to want to put the past behind them and does her best to make apologies. He coldly brushes her off, but eventually, they get together on a park bench and catch up in as friendly a manner as can be expected. They reveal to each other why they stopped singing professionally. But as the Verdi concert approaches and various singers drop out, the need for these people to perform the quartet from the Rigoletto together becomes greater. Cedric begs them to consider the idea, but convincing Jean becomes the biggest hurdle toward making it happen. The concert, if they can get enough people to attend, will help keep he retirement home open.

The entire cast shines in this film, but most eyes will be drawn to Smith, whose character seems the most conflicted with everything surrounding her, from the first moment when she is seen in her old, now-empty house to confronting every aspect of her past, professionally and personally. Smith has always had an authoritative way about her. In a shouting match, she would be the most likely to have the last word. That authority is on display here as well, but her vulnerability and internal struggles will be more memorable than anything else. The same can be said for Courtenay, who similarly struggles to put the past behind him and move forward. Collins and Connelly are perfectly cast as the two who have to act as personal referees while trying to maintain retirement without having to retire from life.

Quartet is based on a play by Ronald Harwood, who also wrote the screenplay. Harwood and Hoffman do what they can to open up the play on screen so that the central location does not feel constricting to the material. The wonderful cast also make the dialogue flow naturally like conversation instead of trying to make the author's words take center stage, a common trap for play-to-screen adaptations. Those hoping to hear the quartet that is cast here will be disappointed when the movie sidesteps actually hearing them sing. But this story really has nothing to do with singing and everything to do with the people who must sing, even in the face of old age and deteriorating vocal cords. But those hoping to hear some fine classical music as a background track will not be disappointed. The film loves music as much as it loves its cast.

It comes as no surprise that Hoffman is clearly an actor's director. Like many actors-turned-directors before him, he is more concerned with the story of the people and getting the performances just right than with showcasing any visual flair. The film has no stamp of an auteur, just a genuine affection for the people on the screen. So much so that during the film's closing credits,

Hoffman acknowledges each and every cast member's past work by underlining their most famous roles, either on stage or on screen (many real-life opera singers appear in the film). Even Andrew Sachs gets a shout-out for playing TV's most famous waiter, Manuel from *Fawlty Towers*. Such admiration shows Hoffman as a true fan, admirer and maybe not quite a total curmudgeon when it comes to awards and accolades.

Collin Souter

CREDITS

Jean Horton: Maggie Smith
Reginald Paget: Tom Courtenay
Wilf Bond: Billy Connolly
Cissy Robson: Pauline Collins
Cedric Livingston: Michael Gambon
Dr. Lucy Cogan: Sheridan Smith
George: Trevor Peacock
Origin: United Kingdom
Language: English
Released: 2012
Production: Finola Dwyer, Stewart Mackinnon; Headline Pictures, DCM Productions, Finola Dwyer Productions, BBC Films; released by The Weinstein Company
Directed by: Dustin Hoffman
Written by: Ronald Harwood
Cinematography by: John de Borman
Music by: Dario Marianelli
Sound: Glenn Freemantle
Editing: Barney Pilling
Costumes: Nigel Egerton
Production Design: Andrew McAlpine
MPAA rating: PG-13
Running time: 98 minutes

REVIEWS

Bradshaw, Peter. *Guardian (UK)*. December 27, 2012.
Calhoun, David. *Time Out*. December 26, 2012.
Gibbs, Ed. *The Sun Herald*. December 23, 2012.
Kartin, Harvey S. *Compuserve*. November 17, 2012.
Osenlund, R. Kurt. *Slant Magazine*. December 2, 2012.
Pols, Mary F. *Time*. December 24, 2012.
Robey, Tim. *Daily Telegraph*. October 16, 2012.
Sharkey, Betsy. *Los Angeles Times*. December 5, 2012.
Smith, Neil. *Total Film*. December 11, 2012.
Taylor, Ella. *NPR*. December 4, 2012.

QUOTES

Jean: "This is not a retirement home, it is a madhouse!"

THE QUEEN OF VERSAILLES

Box Office: $2.4 million

One by one, the children enter the gloom-filled room to appease their formidable father. His wrinkled features cause him to resemble an ancient relic from another time, while his voice is in the form of a cantankerous wheeze. He has spent much of his life embracing the boundless material pleasures granted to him by his exorbitant wealth. But now that the subprime mortgage crisis has thrown his business into a tailspin, the prideful giant of a man has been forced to live within his newly restricted means.

As the owner of Westgate Estates, David Siegel was among the many one-percenters hit hardest by America's financial meltdown. Among the many delicious ironies unearthed by Lauren Greenfield's morbidly fascinating documentary is that David had once boasted about his efforts to elect the man arguably responsible for the crisis, George W. Bush, by utilizing methods that "may not have been legal." In a splendid example of poetic justice, David's questionable deeds have indirectly caused him to worry about previously trivial matters such as the electricity bill.

It is with a mixture of amusement and aggravation that the audience regards David as he sits stubbornly in his room while his endless parade of children make failed attempts at dragging him out of his funk. When one of his young sons recites the magic words, "I love you," David bitterly retorts, "Thank you. If you love me, you'll turn off the lights."

David's eldest child, it must be said, is his wife, Jackie, who scampers away from the morose grouch while whispering, "I know it's nothing that I did." She met David when she was a beauty contestant, and though he was three decades older, he provided the sort of stability and adoration that she desired in the aftermath of her abusive marriage. Even now, with her Botox-injected features and tight-fitting attire designed to frame her buxom cleavage, Jackie appears to be a hair's breadth away from breaking into a runway pose. Her need to be loved is so crucial to her well-being that

she has acquired a Von Trapp-sized family (totaling eight youngsters and a plethora of animals).

These endearing character details make *The Queen of Versailles* a cut above the hideous mockery and exploitation of so-called educational programs on TLC. It is nowhere near as excruciating as "Honey Boo Boo" or "My Super Sweet 16," though there are times when viewers may feel compelled to change the channel. For the first act of Greenfield's film, the audience is treated to a tour of the 90,000 square foot palace where the family intends to move. Apparently, their puny 26,000 square foot mansion couldn't house the entirety of their possessions. When a friend points toward an enormous self-contained space in the unfinished castle and asks, "Is that your room?" the pampered queen-to-be responds, "No, that's my closet!"

The conspicuous absence of irony in Jackie's voice causes her to sound like a skilled deadpan comedian, but it becomes quickly apparent that she is blind to the absurdities of her existence. Her delusional state is so impenetrable that she truly does not seem to understand what has caused her husband to have become so cranky. Though she laughs off her husband's plans to trade her in for two 20-year-olds, it is difficult to tell whether the old man is joking (the sexual harassment charge launched against him in 2008 was certainly no laughing matter). When asked whether he finds any strength in his marriage, David answers with a resounding "no."

It is clear that Greenfield's intentions were to devise a metaphor for the decaying state of capitalism, which is epitomized in the form of the hollow would-be mega-home, which was modeled after Versailles. At a time when the middle class is teetering on the edge of collapse, the Siegel's "problems" are flat-out laughable. The children are forced to switch from private to public schools while Jackie is stunned to find herself shopping for Christmas presents at Wal-Mart. David's timeshare company, which had thrived on selling ordinary couples the temporary opportunity to "feel rich," is suddenly in jeopardy, as is his publicized goal of funding the new Las Vegas resort, PH Towers Westgate. Meanwhile, the family is forced to put their empty, incomplete palace on the market for a mere $75 million.

What routinely keeps the film more watchable than reprehensible is cinematographer Tom Hurwitz's keen eye for the inane. In preparation for a fancy holiday soiree, one of the family's most dedicated nannies is required to don a humiliating Rudolph costume complete with an electronic blinking nose. There is also a fabulous shot of the Siegel girls seated on a playground roundabout that's being pushed by their little brother, who huffs and puffs into the lens before collapsing onto the ground. Apart from being laugh-out-loud funny, the moment could also be read as a comment on the faceless working class multitudes whose exhaustive labors keep families like the Siegels perched comfortably atop the consumerist food chain.

Greenfield earned her Best Director prize at Sundance for creating perhaps the most compassionate portrait that could've been made of this family. The fact that David threatened to sue Greenfield and Magnolia Pictures for their "gross misrepresentation" of his clan speaks to his disconnect from reality. When he chides the filmmakers for their tagline, "A riches to rags story," he seems to have forgotten that the words came straight from his mouth.

Matt Fagerholm

CREDITS

Origin: United States
Language: English
Released: 2012
Production: Lauren Greenfield; Evergreen Pictures; released by Magnolia Pictures
Directed by: Lauren Greenfield

Cinematography by: Tom Hurwitz
Music by: Jeff Beal
Sound: Michael Jones
Editing: Victor Livingston
MPAA rating: PG
Running time: 100 minutes

REVIEWS

Chang, Justin. *Variety*. July 11, 2012.
Ebert, Roger. *Chicago Sun-Times*. August 1, 2012.
Gleiberman, Owen. *Entertainment Weekly*. July 11, 2012.
Kohn, Eric. *indieWIRE*. July 19, 2012.
Longworth, Karina. *Village Voice*. July 17, 2012.
Lumenick, Lou. *New York Post*. July 20, 2012.
Murray, Noel. *Variety*. July 11, 2012.
Phillips, Michael. *Chicago Tribune*. August 2, 2012.
Pols, Mary. *Time*. July 19, 2012.
Scott, A. O. *New York Times*. July 19, 2012.

AWARDS

Nominations:

Directors Guild 2012: Documentary Director (Greenfield)

R

—•—

THE RAID: REDEMPTION

(Serbuan maut)

1 ruthless crime lord, 20 elite cops, 30 floors of hell.
—Movie tagline

When there's nowhere left to run or hide, you fight or die.
—Movie tagline

Box Office: $4.1 million

Action films are usually, but not always, typified by broad narrative strokes allowing for quick character movement between stunt set pieces. Simply-stated relationships and characters that operate within typical good-guy-bad-guy conventions are the norm. Whether or not an action film can be said to succeed depends largely on how well it takes advantage of what this approach to filmmaking allows for in the way of spectacle. But *The Raid: Redemption* goes several steps further, packing so much dread and suspense into its runtime that though it could be favorably compared to many of the best action films the genre of Asian action films has to offer (*Eastern Condors* [1987], *Hard Boiled* [1992], *Ong Bak* [2003] and *Born To Fight* [2004]) it also bears comparison to relentless siege horrors like *Assault on Precinct Thirteen* (1976). Full of riveting fight sequences, gun battles, intense action, and a ghastly visceral quality, *The Raid: Redemption* will stand up to multiple viewings like most action films fail to do.

A twenty-man SWAT team descends on a huge apartment building in the center of Jakarta's slums to take down the land/crime lord: Tama Riyadi (Ray Sahetapy), who has turned the structure into a safe house for the city's worst criminals. Long-considered unassailable, the thirty-floor building, packed with those loyal to Tama, has held back rival gangs, and even the police, for so long that the mission feels doomed to fail from the start. The inexperienced team is initially able to maintain the element of surprise by quietly forcing their way into the building and subduing a number of the residents. Sure enough, those advantages are lost when a young lookout raises the alarm, alerting Tama to the SWAT team's presence. Using the building's public broadcast system, Tama offers lifetime, rent-free residence to anyone in the building that can eliminate the intruders. The SWAT team must fight for its life against the worst-of-the-worst of the city's criminal underground. To complicate matters, it is revealed that one of Tama's right hand men, Andi, is the estranged brother of the SWAT squad member and expectant father, Rama (Iko Uwais), while the de facto leader of the SWAT squad Lieutenant Wahyu (Pierre Gruno) is found to have called the raid for his own corrupt reasons.

The action in the film truly is relentless and often wince-inducing. Director Gareth Evans, along with stars/fight choreographers Iko Uwais and Yayan Ruhian, consistently ups the ante moment to moment, finding new ways to introduce mayhem. In one scene, a tank of propane and a refrigerator are used as a makeshift bomb. In another, the team must cut holes to drop from floor-to-floor as they are pursued by a seemingly endless series of assassins. The shooting style is quick-cut but bullet hits, falls, punches and the like are up close and personal. In one shot, a stuntman (it had to be a stuntman) is thrown off of a concrete balcony, somersaults and lands square on his back on the lip edge of a concrete balcony in front.

But most impressively the traditional Indonesian martial art Pencak Silat is showcased every bit as effectively as Tony Jaa showcased the then-unknown Muay Thai style in his breakout films. This is unbelievably quick stuff, almost too quick for the eye. A series of fights leads up to a final showdown between brothers Andi and Rama against the vicious gangster Mad Dog (Yayan Ruhian) which in and of itself nearly redefines the fight scene in modern action cinema. Not only does Mad Dog stand in for all his henchman predecessors in past martial arts films but he takes that type and extends it in terms of what viewers expect from it. This fight to the death is unbelievably brutal, impossible to watch without wincing and yet it sings with a vibrant life, reaffirming the struggle it represents in its own genre where men attempt to retain their own humanity via some sort of honor code in combat.

It should be noted Ray Sahetapy makes the character of Tama sing. In his electrifying introduction, one sees the boss executing a row of bound men. His gun suddenly empty, he gently places it on the shoulder of his intended victim asking him to hold it while he searches through his desk for bullets. All through the film, his leering, tired face offers a weird counterpoint to the constant barrage of action.

Gareth Evans makes a choice that is worth noting. At the beginning of the film, Rama is shown in prayer. He is a Muslim. He then exercises, kisses his pregnant wife, and leaves. Nowhere else in the film do we see him reference his religion except in his basic treatment of other human beings. It would be ironic that such a violent film has a Muslim hero if the film made any effort at all to preach or to link his Muslim heritage to his actions as a police officer. But the film does not do this. There is no irony here. Just a man of principled faith, and it could be any faith, trapped in a violent world, meeting it blow-by-blow and hanging on to his humanity in the process.

Dave Canfield

CREDITS

Rama: Iko Uwais
Jaka: Joe Taslim
Andi: Doni Alamsyah
Mad Dog: Yayan Ruhian
Wahyu: Pierre Gruno
Bowo: Tegar Satrya
Tama: Ray Sahetapy

Origin: United States
Language: English
Released: 2011
Production: Ario Sagantoro; Celluloid Nightmares, PT Merantau Films, XYZ Films; released by Sony Pictures Classics
Directed by: Gareth Evans
Written by: Gareth Evans
Cinematography by: Matt Flannery; Dimas Imam Subhono
Music by: Fajar Yuskemal; Aria Prayogi
Sound: Suhadi Yuskemal
Editing: Gareth Evans
Costumes: Upay Maryani
Production Design: Moti D. Setyanto
MPAA rating: R
Running time: 101 minutes

REVIEWS

Accomando, Beth. *KPBS.org*. March 31, 2012.
Clifford, Laura. *Reeling Reviews*. March 28, 2012.
Dargis, Manhola. *New York Times*. March 22, 2012.
Diones, Bruce. *New Yorker*. April 9, 2012.
Ebert, Roger. *Chicago Sun-Times*. March 22, 2012.
Fear, David. *Time Out New York*. March 20, 2012.
Goldstein, Gary. *Los Angeles Times*. March 22, 2012.
Hardy, Ernest. *Village Voice*. March 20, 2012.
Howell, Peter. *Toronto Star*. March 22, 2012.
Koehker, Robert. *Variety*. September 13, 2011.

QUOTES

Mad Dog: "Pulling a trigger is like ordering a takeout."

TRIVIA

All the guns used in the film are Airsoft replicas and not functioning firearms, which meant that all the shots of the guns' actions—cycling, muzzle flashes and casings ejecting—were added digitally.

THE RAVEN

The only one who can stop a serial killer is the man who inspired him.
—Movie tagline

Box Office: $16 million

The repurposing of noted historical figures for genre entertainment is nothing new. Sometimes it works well, especially when the character is repurposed rather than entirely recast. For instance, Abraham Lincoln is easy to imagine as an axe-slinging defender of American democracy against vampires because in some sense his known physicality supports it and his strength and determination is a bit Van Helsing-like. But Edgar Allan Poe as a turn of the century action hero is just a bad idea. Part of the problem is that Poe's popular image is of a rather slight figure, sickly, depressed. He is hardly the type that runs around with a pistol, looking heroic. But *The Raven* is only cursorily interested in what has made Poe an iconic figure ripe for re-envisioning. Instead it shoehorns the inventor of the detective story into a half-baked adventure that conjures little mystery or excitement.

In 19th century Baltimore, Maryland a group of policeman follow hideous screams to an apartment, where they discover an uncommonly grisly mother-daughter murder scene. When Detective Emmett Fields (Luke Evans) arrives to assist in the investigation he notices similarities to events in a short story, *The Murders in the Rue Morgue* by local author Edgar Allan Poe (John Cusack). When approached, Poe is horrified. The meager pittance he earns from his writing is barely enough to keep him in the alcoholic stupor he uses to distract from his other problems and he hardly needs this kind of attention. Largely ignored as a writer, taken advantage of when he is published, Poe must also contend with a Captain Hamilton (Brendan Gleeson) who has threatened violence if Poe does not stay away from his daughter Emily (Alice Eve). Seeing no way out, Poe agrees to help the police track the killer down using his own short stories as a map.

James McTeigue does his best to pour on the atmosphere that viewers will hunger for but no amount of fake fog or number of gory still-life tableaus make up for the completely forgettable story here. The pity is that McTeigue is hardly a bad director. He managed to make the best adaptation of an Alan Moore work yet, *V For Vendetta* (2005), a film that, while it had problems, made ample and very effective use of truly epic source material. Another film, *Ninja Assassin* (2009) offered stylish visual thrills and dynamic action. But more importantly, as different as they were, those films offered a world the viewer could get lost in. Here the director conjures no such magic, ladling ersatz atmosphere onto a forgettable script that offers a miscast lead.

Writers Ben Livingston and Hannah Shakespeare have constructed a mystery that offers no mystery. Of course Poe offers to help the police, of course his own lady love is endangered, of course the villain emerges completely out of left field as the movie attempts to make some sort of statement about the nature of the recognition which Poe has been so embittered about not receiving. Worst of all, Poe is presented as a far more capable man of action than his drunken, irresponsible, self-pitying ways would allow for in a film that even attempted to make sense of him. But, then again, the real

Poe, with his John Waters creeper mustache would hardly have been as attractive for the marketing department as Cusack with a dashing goatee.

Lastly, there is no getting around the fact that Cusack is badly miscast. His Poe is not only too good looking and capable but also far too energetic. Cusack can hardly be blamed for having to follow the script in creating a Poe in name only but there is absolutely no connection to the historical or mythic figure of Poe in his approach beyond the general character and historical references the film embraces for the sake of plot gimmickry.

Better is Brendan Gleeson, who chews the scenery as Poe's romantic block Captain Hamilton. The dynamic Gleeson is perfectly cast to play the part of the baleful blowhard emerging as slightly more sympathetic by stories' end. But his basically bilious nature underscores the fact that there are no really likable characters here at all except for Emily and she is so clearly a mere plot device that she is utterly uninteresting. Poe is ultimately a good-looking victim at best, the villain is a cardboard denouement; Hamilton and inspector Reynolds mere character types.

The end result of all of this is that *The Raven* feels as cobbled together as the streets of any small town the characters could inhabit making for a very bumpy ride, unforgiving to the concept of sustained thought or any particular enjoyment. If Poe had written commercials for a living he could have thrown this one off in an hour or two. *The Raven* is a lifeless corpse that no one but investors will mourn and not even they would be inspired to write a tragic ode to what it could have been. A sequel? Nevermore.

Dave Canfield

CREDITS

Edgar Allan Poe: John Cusack
Detective Fields: Luke Evans
Emily Hamilton: Alice Eve
Captain Hamilton: Brendan Gleeson
Cantrell: Oliver Jackson-Cohen
Mrs. Bradley: Pam Ferris
Origin: United States
Language: English, Spanish
Released: 2012
Production: Marc D. Evans, Trevor Macy, Aaron Ryder; Intrepid Pictures, FilmNation Entertainment, Galavis Film, Pioneer Pictures, Relativity Media; released by Rogue Pictures
Directed by: James McTeigue
Written by: Ben Livingston; Hannah Shakespeare

Cinematography by: Danny Ruhlmann
Music by: Lucas Vidal
Sound: Eric Lindemann
Music Supervisor: Del Spiva
Editing: Niven Howie
Art Direction: Frank Walsh
Costumes: Carlo Poggioli
Production Design: Roger Ford
MPAA rating: R
Running time: 110 minutes

REVIEWS

Alter, Ethan. *Television Without Pity.* April 27, 2012.
Bibbiani, William. *CraveOnline.* August 22, 2012.
Ebert, Roger. *Chicago Sun-Times.* April 26, 2012.
Felperin, Leslie. *Variety.* March 9, 2012.
Fuchs, Cynthia. *PopMatters.* May 2, 2012.
Kendrick, Ben. *ScreenRant.* September 27, 2012.
Means, Sean. *Salt Lake Tribune.* May 4, 2012.
Phillips, Michael. *Chicago Tribune.* April 26, 2012.
Scott, A. O. *New York Times.* April 26, 2012.
Snider, Erik D. *Film.com.* April 27, 2012.

QUOTES

Ivan: "The idea of drinking something that will kill you, but having time to carry on a conversation is, as they say, fraught with dramatic possibilities."

TRIVIA

Noomi Rapace was offered the role of Emily at one point.

RED DAWN

Welcome to the home of the brave.
    —Movie tagline

This Thanksgiving, the fight begins at dawn.
    —Movie tagline

Heroes are made in America.
    —Movie tagline

When Marines die, we go to hell and regroup!
    —Movie tagline

Box Office: $44.8 mllion

It is always fun when a film taps into the cultural zeitgeist. When the right film comes around at the right time and connects in a very real, very in-the-moment way with audiences. John Milius' *Red Dawn* (1984) was definitely a zeitgeist movie. Released during the height of the Reagan Cold War era, it ably created an escapist fantasy out of Middle America's nationalistic anxieties about the Soviet Union and turned "Wolverines!" into a bona fide pop culture catchphrase. Granted, it is a flawed movie that does not particularly stand the test of time, but, in 1984, it was the perfect movie for its day. Unfortunately, the same thing cannot be said about director Dan Bradley's 2012 remake of *Red Dawn,* a plodding, boring action flick that fails to tap into anything even mildly relevant or interesting.

It is actually almost an impressive achievement to watch a film with such a loaded premise—a foreign country invades the United States—squander said premise in such a remarkable fashion. At its core, *Red Dawn* is a movie that constantly straddles the line between being earnestly boring and patently ridiculous. The film opens with an intriguing montage demonstrating the weakening of America's defenses due to the global economic crisis and the mass of American troops deployed abroad. It is a semi-intriguing conceit until the film makes a sharp left turn and casts a North Korean/Russian alliance as the invading force. Not to downplay North Korea's powerfully dangerous role in world politics, but it is next to impossible to take the small nation seriously as a candidate for overthrowing the United States via invasion. North Korea might be a plausible nuclear threat, but there is just no way that audiences can feel the same assimilating dread towards North Korea that '80s Americans felt towards the Soviet Union. It is a perfect example of a filmmaker getting the zeitgeist dead wrong. (It should be noted that, when the movie was filmed, China was actually the invading force in question, but, due to fears of alienating the growing Chinese film market, the studio chose to change the invaders into North Koreans in post-production. This is a shame because American audiences might actually have felt some anxiety towards China and its growing role as the world's dominant super-power, but *Red Dawn* is so inept in its portrayal of global politics anyway that it probably would not have made much of a difference.)

Following the opening montage, viewers are introduced to All-American Jed Eckert (Chris Hemsworth), a Marine returning home to Spokane, Washington, after a long deployment in Afghanistan. The next morning, however, the power goes out and Eckert's family witnesses hordes of North Korean paratroopers descending onto Spokane from the sky. Jed's policeman father Tom (Brett Cullen) sends Jed and his brother Matt (Josh Peck) to the family's cabin in the woods while he stays to fight the invaders. Jed and Matt hide out in the woods with their friends until the North Korean soldiers admonish them to surrender, ultimately trying to flush them out by murdering Jed's father. But this only inspires professional soldier Jed to organize a resistance movement, which means stealing some guns, having a training montage, and the inevitable screaming of "Wolverines!"

After a few skirmishes with the North Korean troops, the Wolverines meet up with a small squad of Marines, led by Sergeant Major Andrew Tanner (Jeffrey Dean Morgan), who introduce the film's central MacGuffin. Apparently, the North Koreans shut down the US power grid with an electromagnetic pulse weapon—EMPs are among the most hacky film plot devices this side of clones and nanobots—and invaded both the East and West Coasts. The US Military still controls the central states, but, thanks to the all-too-convenient EMP, they cannot contact their forces abroad to stage a counter-offensive. Thus, the Wolverines must steal the only EMP-shielded telephone around, which, again, is conveniently held by the evil Captain Cho (Will Yun Lee), the invader who also murdered Pa Eckert. That is right. The key to saving America is stealing a telephone—not exactly thrilling.

This is the odd duality of *Red Dawn*. For most of its run time, it follows a series of photogenic young actors (Hemsworth, Peck, and Adrianne Palicki are the best of the bunch) pensively scowling as they struggle to save their homeland. But, every time the film gets too serious, Bradley hits the audience with either silly, overblown action moments or laugh-out-loud improbable plot developments. This is a film that desperately, desperately wants to be taken seriously. It really does think it is saying something profound about patriotism and the American spirit. Unfortunately, while *Red Dawn*'s heart is clearly on its sleeve, its brain is nowhere to be found.

For a film like *Red Dawn* to succeed, the audience has to believe that somehow "this could happen one day." But everything *Red Dawn* tries to accomplish is just so improbable, over-wrought, and downright silly that it has no impact at all. It feels like a commercial for the Marines dreamed up by a junior high student who did not quite finish their social studies reading. It is not surprising that someone tried to remake John Milius' *Red Dawn*—it is probably the best known Invasion U.S.A. movie to date—but it is surprising that the film-makers took Milius' winning premise and botched it so completely.

Tom Burns

CREDITS

Jed Eckert: Chris Hemsworth
Matt Eckert: Josh Peck
Robert: Josh Hutcherson
Toni: Adrianne Palicki

Erica: Isabel Lucas
Daryl: Connor Cruise
Danny: Edwin Hodge
Tom Eckert: Brett Cullen
Julie: Alyssa Diaz
Col. Andy Tanner: Jeffrey Dean Morgan
Lt. Pak: Fernando Chien
Origin: United States
Language: English
Released: 2012
Production: Beau Flynn, Vincent Newman; Contrafilm, Vincent Newman Entertainment; released by MGM
Directed by: Dan Bradley
Written by: Carl Ellsworth; Jeremy Passmore
Cinematography by: Mitchell Amundsen
Music by: Ramin Djawadi
Sound: Christopher T. Silvermann
Music Supervisor: Dana Sano
Editing: Richard Pearson
Art Direction: Gina B. Cranham; Tom Reta
Costumes: Catherine George
Production Design: Dominic Watkins
MPAA rating: PG-13
Running time: 93 minutes

REVIEWS

Dargis, Manohla. *New York Times*. November 20, 2012.
Leydon, Joe. *Variety*. September 30, 2012.
O'Sullivan, Michael. *Washington Post*. November 20, 2012.
Olsen, Mark. *Los Angeles Times*. November 20, 2012.
Phillips, Michael. *Chicago Tribune*. November 20, 2012.
Pinkerton, Nick. *Village Voice*. November 20, 2012.
Puig, Claudia. *USA Today*. November 20, 2012.
Russo, Tom. *Boston Globe*. November 20, 2012.
Scheck, Frank. *Hollywood Reporter*. November 16, 2012.
Schwarzbaum, Lisa. *Entertainment Weekly*. November 20, 2012.

QUOTES

Robert: "They're not gonna keep their uber box in the freaking couch."
Daryl Jenkins: "How do you know?"
Robert: "It's vital piece of military equipment, not your porn stash."

TRIVIA

Chris Hemsworth and Isabel Lucas were both in the Australian soap opera *Home and Away* and dated each other in real life.

AWARDS

Nominations:
Golden Raspberries 2012: Worst Remake/Sequel

RED HOOK SUMMER

Box Office: $338,803

Before *Red Hook Summer,* the only sequels to Spike Lee's challenging masterpiece of racial harmony *Do the Right Thing* (1989) had been written by the successive events of American history; the biggest sequel being the true story of a man who would once take his future wife on a first date to *Do the Right Thing* and later become the country's first black president.

Hopscotch many years later and Lee himself has only made spiritual spin-offs of the film through a colorful filmography that shows his ability to cultivate the personal aspects in any of his narratives, regardless of their film genre or budget size. Even Lee's last theatrical release, the failed *Miracle At St. Anna* (2008), reminisced the tensions between post Reagan-era African-Americans and Italian-Americans in Sal's Famous Pizzeria in *Do the Right Thing*.

Now, *Red Hook Summer* stands as the only possible direct sequel to *Do the Right Thing*, and at its best is a follow-up of the 1989 movie's soul. Yet surprisingly, though this film takes Lee back to the type of environment that inspires a special storytelling groove, Lee lacks an immediate attachment to the story, his storytelling focus more now directly comparable to a spotty amateur than the same poet of cinema who forced audiences to question right and wrong with *Do the Right Thing*. Lee is happy to be home, but his best perceptions have not come with him.

In the film, newcomer Jules Brown plays Flik Royale, a young boy from Atlanta who is dropped off by his mother for the summer at New York City's Red Hook neighborhood. To his distaste, the teenage vegan begrudgingly lives with his grandfather, Da Good Bishop Enoch Rouse (Clarke Peters), who introduces Flik to various members of his neighborhood, while also hoping to convince him to accept God. While working at Bishop Enoch's church (called Little Heaven), he starts a friendship with a girl of a similar age named Chazz Morningstar (Toni Lysaith). The two get into some trouble, including plundering food from the church's pantry, and defiling the wet cement outside of a ferociously angry Caucasian woman's (Patty Simmons) home (which provides the movie its only example of the mentioned gentrification).

Flik's directionless summer story slowly leads the focus of the plot to be on his grandfather, who is shown giving extensive sermons that opine on the state of religion in today's crumbling state of morality ("This is my gangsta; this is my Internet!" he says, holding his Bible in the air). In the classic fashion of Lee, an instigator as both a storyteller and Hollywood personality, he toys with the audiences, ebbing them to a certain

slumber with these lanky gospel sermons, and character monologues that might as well be sermons, both of which unnecessarily stretch the film's running time. But lest ye think that Lee is completely resigned to seeing the world (or in this case, religion) in black or white, he seductively changes his ways in the third act with a surprise revealing of a disturbing moment in Bishop Enoch's past. An invigorating twist, it unveils the facade in the *Red Hook Summer's* initially convincing religious fortitude, and boldly introduces the film's primary discussion (especially with the viewers who might have assumed this film was steering a pure religious course) about the relationship between the questionable existence of God related to the act of sin.

The young acting in the movie has a distracting quality of cheapness to it, as Lee uses first-time performers who are not well versed in variation of emotion; they are only able to express themselves physically. Brown is stilted; his bored eyes a glaring fault whenever he is attempting to express angst. A more frustrating example of first-time acting rockiness is with Lysaith, who must have been cast by Lee simply for the flamboyance she can add to the words "STOOPID!" and "NAAAH!" As the story moves on, it becomes increasingly obvious that Lee is not that interested in these caricatures of teenagers either, with an exception of one scene in which the two youths share their own junior conversation about the existence of God.

Although Bishop Rouse's story comes with drowsy monologues, he eventually has the most interesting angle of the story, as presented with believable finesse by Peters. Able to stand away from the easy comparison of Ossie Davis' wise Mr. Mayor character in *Do the Right Thing*, Peters is able to flourish in the high and low points of such a character.

The film's paramount performance undoubtedly comes from Colman Domingo, who sets a fire under this film and leaves the emotional scar that redeems *Red Hook Summer* from soft preaching, as boosted aesthetically by the inclusion of Lee's trademark dolly shot (in which an actor stands still on a camera cart, as if the character is being pulled towards the viewer by emotional gravity). With amazing management of his face (particularly the sides of his trembling mouth and his fixated eyes, which drop perfectly-timed tears), this moment becomes a fire and brimstone revelation in itself, and then explodes into chaos as Domingo takes on intense physical reactionary form, as a howling messenger with his own word of truth to be shared with the members of Little Heaven. It is a fantastically impacting moment that sends this movie to its most captivating dark corners.

Though the film's soundtrack uses electric piano ditties by Bruce Hornsby and features nearly full performances of a handful of lyrically repetitive Negro spirituals, the movie's aesthetic sense is more akin to the compositional shift by jazz musician Miles Davis starting in the late '60s when he embraced acid rock for his "electric years" (a fruitful period that would lead to the creation of fusion jazz). Uniting cinematography and editing under a nature of inconsistency and unpredictability, Lee uses grotesque jump cuts, blatant discontinuity errors, fourth wall breaks, abrupt handheld camera movements, and even switches to 8mm film stock quality to take a break from the cinematography's overall ugly and cheap digital look (the snark of Lee using household brand cameras to parody Hollywood falsity in 2000's *Bamboozled* has vanished now). Yet, whereas Davis was able to find an obtuse beauty in such unsteadiness, Lee's aesthetics, often used to make things look uglier, plays upon the artistic quality of the interchangeable perception of a dissonant note to that of a simply wrong note. These aesthetics become another oft-putting commodity to a film that already tests its audience with rambling sermons and directionless storytelling.

With only a cameo appearance as his *Do the Right Thing* character Mookie in this film, Lee's most significant personal touch as storyteller now is to be distant from the story, instigating the film's confrontations from the outside and letting his embedded audience struggle with these characters themselves. Even the title for this movie suggests ambivalence as opposed to the name *Do the Right Thing* (a phrase only heard here during scenes inside Little Heaven). Instead, *Red Hook Summer* is a fitfully sedentary name for a movie that can not be identified by one strong moral quandary.

Such a detachment does betray any intention of heart with this story, and affects the resonating charm of the location and its inhabitants, something that worked efficaciously with *Do the Right Thing* and its theatrical setting of Bed-Stuy, New York. The side characters of *Red Hook Summer* are physically colored with the same bright colors as those from Bed-Stuy (Nate Parker's character Box's devil-red gang colors, or Lillie Marshall's character Miss Marshal and her purple dress), but Lee's lack of attention to make these characters interesting leaves them emotionally drab.

As for his new Bed-Stuy, Lee is able to convey the physicality of Red Hook, with long-take cinematography that has free reign over the apartment courtyard and sidewalks, and brief documentary-like snippets of nameless areas. But, this neighborhood simply does not breathe. It becomes a generic microcosm, as opposed to a unique locale for Lee's homegrown sentimentality to flourish.

Though featuring a couple notable performances that make for a magnetically caustic third act, *Red Hook Summer* is a heavily flawed homecoming for a filmmaker underplaying his cleverness. The film is ultimately betrayed by its absent focus, and lacks the proper palpability for something of such personal intent, a la *Do the Right Thing*. But regardless as to whether *Red Hook Summer* is held next to that triumphant film or not, this is a messy expression composed of too many of the wrong choices.

Nick Allen

CREDITS

Silas "Flik" Royale: Jules Brown
Colleen Royale: De'Adre Azziza
Enoch Rouse: Clarke Peters
Box: Nate Parker
Deacon Zee: Thomas Jefferson Byrd
Sister Sharon Morningstar: Heather Alicia Simms
Chazz Morningstar: Toni Lysaith
Mr. Kevin: James E. Ransome
Mr. Mookie: Spike Lee
Origin: United States
Language: English
Released: 2012
Production: Spike Lee; Forty Acres and A Mule Filmworks Inc.; released by Variance Films
Directed by: Spike Lee
Written by: Spike Lee; James McBride
Cinematography by: Kerwin Devonish
Music by: Bruce Hornsby
Sound: Philip Stockton
Editing: Hye Mee Na
Costumes: Emilio Sosa
Production Design: Sarah Frank
MPAA rating: R
Running time: 121 minutes

REVIEWS

Corliss, Richard. *Time.* August 9, 2012.
Denby, David. *New Yorker.* August 9, 2012.
Ebert, Roger. *Chicago Sun-Times.* August 23, 2012.
Holden, Stephen. *New York Times.* August 9, 2012.
Hornaday, Ann. *Washington Post.* August 24, 2012.
LaSalle, Mick. *San Francisco Chronicle.* August 31, 2012.
Rooney, David. *Hollywood Reporter.* January 23, 2012.
Smith, Kyle. *New York Post.* August 10, 2012.
Stevens, Dana. *Slate.* August 10, 2012.
Weitzman, Elizabeth. *New York Daily News.* August 9, 2012.

RED LIGHTS

How much do you want to believe?
—Movie tagline

Box Office: $52,624

There are many ways a film can disappoint, but one of the most frustrating is when a genre movie of relatively modest ambitions has all the pieces it needs to succeed, to thrill and entertain on its own merits, but the filmmakers let it get away from them, squandering decent amounts of potential along the way. Writer and director Rodrigo Cortes does not just let his psychological suspense film *Red Lights* get away from him, he actively flings it aside.

The Spanish-born Cortes, whose first English-language feature was the taut thriller *Buried* (2010), spends the front half of *Red Lights* crafting a moody, enthralling exploration of paranormal con artists and the scientists out to debunk them, but then sends it all spinning madly, wildly out of control in the second half. Not, it should be noted, into a fascinating, exciting sort cinematic madness, but rather into a parade of overwrought, laughably serious silliness.

Red Lights follows two paranormal skeptics and university researchers, Dr. Margaret Matheson (a suitably stern-but-wounded Sigourney Weaver) and Dr. Tom Buckley (the always eerily detached Cillian Murphy). With Dr. Buckley in tow, Dr. Matheson is out to debunk pseudo-science faith healers, mentalists, mediums and their like—a personal and scientific crusade that raises the ire of the hucksters whose livelihood she is messing with. (The film's title refers to the skeptics' term for discordant tell-tale signs that point to fakery.) Elizabeth Olsen and Toby Jones are also on hand as, respectively, a research assistant/love interest for Tom and Margaret's institutional foil, a fellow scientist who wants to believe.

One such possible con man is the mysterious psychic Simon Silver (Robert DeNiro, hauling out his unfortunately all-too-familiar lazy histrionics), a Uri Geller-like ESP superstar from the 1970s recently emerged from seclusion. That makes the first half of *Red Lights* a solid skeptical crime investigation, adorned with steely lectures from Weaver's Matheson about not just the parlor tricks, but also the dangers of believing in pseudo-science clap trap.

For a while, this premise and its execution make for a fairly compelling film. Cortes and his cinematographer Xavi Gimenez drape the proceedings in cold, dreary, rainy grays, and Anton Laguna's production design gives *Red Lights*, which is clearly set in the present day, a nicely displaced late '70s/early '80s feel (when talk-show psychics like Geller were at their cultural peak). Weaver and Murphy are surprisingly well-paired, with Weaver's portrayal of world-weary obsession balanced by Murphy's deep-running and chilly still waters. All of this fills the film with an oddly stilted but compelling sense of being out of time and off-balance.

In the post-*Sixth Sense* landscape of psychological thrillers, however, a film cannot just be a solid, well-told, character-driven genre story. So, in the second half, Cortes piles on more contrived paranormal melodramas while letting once-carefully crafted plot and character motivations slip and slide off the rails. (In the film, the skeptics must have a deep, painful personal reason for doubting and debunking—it can never be simply because they believe in reason and science over self-deluding mumbo jumbo.)

Further smothering any hope of a genuine thrill, *Red Lights*' third-act narrative ridiculousness is wrapped in dourly earnest gravitas and over-the-top sermonizing. There is a lot of dramatic potential in why people believe what they believe, but as the film maker pumps up the theatrics, what should have been an intricate, intelligent genre film instead begins to feel like children's blocks tossed clumsily into a pile. The film starts to feel like a long, infuriating haul, the slog not helped by DeNiro's increasingly loud, crass caricature mugging. Murphy, with his odd, almost alien appearance and manner, can be a mesmerizing central presence, but his willowy passivity cannot anchor the film when DeNiro starts tugging it off its axis.

Worst of all, the now de rigueur twist ending not only fails to enrich the film, but negates it entirely, devaluing and hollowing out the first half's message. *Red Lights* twists and turns so completely that it ends up pandering to the very hocus-pocus pabulum its heroes once set out to debunk. A muddled and less-than-thrilling thriller that cannot figure out what it wants to be, the film has a wasted premise, wasted smarts, wasted talent, and most of all, wastes the viewer's time.

Despite pandering to the tastes of a wider audience, *Red Lights* was given a very limited theatrical release in late July and quickly vanished with only $52,624 earned in North America. (It performed better over seas, bringing in nearly $10 million.) Most critics were equally unkind, though William Goss, writing for *The Playlist,* felt, "It's a bold effort by Cortes to step up his directorial game, equal parts deft and daft, that coyly addresses the divide between seeing and believing." The *Chicago Sun-Times'* Roger Ebert summed up many critics' complaints, however, when he noted, "most audiences would prefer a film with an ending that plays by the same rules as the rest of the story." And Rene Rodriquez of the *Miami Herald* dismissed *Red Lights* as, "a movie about highly intelligent people in pursuit of trivial nonsense."

Locke Peterseim

CREDITS

Tom Buckley: Cillian Murphy
Margaret Matheson: Sigourney Weaver
Simon Silver: Robert De Niro
Paul Shackleton: Toby Jones
Monica Hanson: Joely Richardson
Sally Owen: Elizabeth Olsen
Origin: United States, Spain
Language: English
Released: 2012
Production: Adrian Guerra, Rodrigo Cortes; released by Nostromo Pictures
Directed by: Rodrigo Cortes
Written by: Rodrigo Cortes
Cinematography by: Xavi Gimenez
Music by: Victor Reyes
Editing: Rodrigo Cortes
Art Direction: Edward S. Bonutto
Costumes: Patricia Monne
Production Design: Anton Laguna
MPAA rating: R
Running time: 113 minutes

REVIEWS

Biancolli, Amy. *San Francisco Chronicle.* August 2, 2012.
Ebert, Roger M. *Chicago Sun-Times.* July 25, 2012.
Ebiri, Bilge. *Vulture.* July 13, 2012.
Goodykoontz, Bill. *Arizona Republic.* August 2, 2012.
Goss, William. *The Playlist.* July 11, 2012.
Litovitz, Adam. *The Globe and Mail.* January 5, 2012.
Pinkerton, Nick. *Village Voice.* July 11, 2012.
Pols, Mary. *Time.* July 11, 2012.
Rodriguez, Rene. *Miami Herald.* August 2, 2012.
Willmore, Alison. *Movieline.* July 12, 2012.

QUOTES

Margaret Matheson: "There are two kinds of people out there with a special gift. The ones who really think they have some kind of power. And the other guys, who think we can't figure them out. They're both wrong."

TRIVIA

Spanish director Eugenio Mira plays Robert De Niro's character in his early thirties.

RED TAILS

High-octane action and daring dogfights!
   —Movie tagline

Courage has no color.
   —Movie tagline

Box Office: $49.9 million

The real-life story of the Tuskegee Airmen, an emotionally resonant, compelling one, is a story of men in war, not just the spectacle of combat itself. *Red Tails* fails to connect those two elements and also fails to make the national stakes of World War II deeply felt, delivering instead a somewhat old-fashioned thrill ride pieced together with scenes of tired classic wartime melodrama. Producer George Lucas, the driving force behind the project, has even called the film jingoistic. He is being too generous, though many reviewers have felt the same. The jingoism argument rests, in the main, on whether or not the film celebrates belligerent foreign policy or nationalistic hubris. *Red Tails* projects hardly enough energy to celebrate anything. Blandly played out in the confines of the "good war," the worst that can be said of *Red Tails* is that anything it does is mostly by the accident of cramming cliches and genre conventions together.

The year is 1944 and viewers are introduced to a group of disgruntled young African-American fighter pilots. Part of an experimental training program allowing "Negroes" to fly, the men face a glass ceiling set by the politics and incipient racism of the white bureaucracy blocking their participation in combat. Instead they are forced to fly junk planes, and sent on mop-up missions. Viewers meet the hot-headed Lightning (David Oyelowo), loose-tongued Joker (Elijah Kelley), team leader and closet alcoholic Easy (Nate Parker), and would-be hotshot Raygun (Tristan Wilds), referred to by his team as Junior. The young men are led by Major Stance (Cuba Gooding Jr., ironically a cast member of the far superior HBO film, *The Tuskegee Airmen* [1995]), who does his best to maintain morale and discipline, and Col. Bullard (Terrence Howard), who is in the unenviable position of having to go to bat for the program in Washington.

What transpires could be predicted by anyone who has watched any amount of classic wartime B-movie cinema. Cliches pile up on one another until the whole movie grinds to an emotional halt under the weight. Stance secures a combat mission that must be successful in order for the team to remain in the air. Lightning meets a girl (by visiting her house after she waves to him from the ground). Raygun, who has been visually impaired, begs Easy to keep him in the air, which Easy does against his better judgment. Lightning makes a deal with Easy to obey orders in the air if Easy will lay off the bottle. One of the pilots, the one with the most to lose, dies at the end of the film.

The script is full of corny dialogue as none of the men ever does or says anything unexpected. Their character defects feel mostly like narrative devices rather than emotionally compelling traits. In short, they have nothing to overcome except the script itself. Even the way the script deals with racism is suspect, delivering short vignettes that have no strong impact. One has to believe that John Ridley (story credit) and Aaron McGruder (screenplay) had better, more compelling stories available to them in the film's source material, the book *Red Tails: An Oral History of the Tuskegee Airmen* by John B. Holway. But the incidents of racism depicted seem almost shoehorned in. Viewers never feel in the shoes of these men and their struggle to be seen simply as men who want to serve their country. For a film that was in development for so long (Lucas first launched the project in 1998), *Red Tails* bears the marks of a seriously underdeveloped narrative.

Performances it should be mentioned are as good as they are in almost any recent Lucas project. Lucas did not direct here but first-time director Anthony Hemingway virtually channels him in producing a blander-than-bland aesthetic which seems to have no interest in the presence of the actors onscreen. The sad irony is that Lucas championed the project over the long haul despite studio indifference stemming from the presence of an all-black cast. In interviews, he made the rejection sound like exactly the sort of racism one associates with Hollywood studios, but viewers may well wonder if, after reading the script, studios simply realized how unremarkable the final product was bound to be.

Some have felt the action scenes lift the film into a sort of effects-driven reverie. Sadly though, they are only initially thrilling. About midway through, a sameness quickly takes hold, dashing the hope that *Red Tails* may develop into a tolerably entertaining time-waster. Planes shoot planes, pilots banter (almost always in close-up), and the outcomes of the battles seem predetermined. The end result is a series of CGI dog-fight sequences that are as cold-looking as they are digital. From the moment the planes leave the ground they never feel real. Battles never provide a sense of danger or risk. The film also has the very bad habit of leading viewers emotionally with an annoyingly obvious score. In short, nothing about *Red Tails,* nothing at all, stands out as being anything other than forgettable, the entire film passes by and fades away like a far-off vapor trail.

Dave Canfield

CREDITS

Col. A.J. Bullard: Terrence Howard
Maj. Emanuelle Stance: Cuba Gooding, Jr.

Martin "Easy" Julian: Nate Parker
Joe "Lightning" Little: David Oyelowo
Andrew "Smoky" Salem: Ne-Yo
Ray "Junior" Gannon: Tristan Wilds
Maj. William Mortamus: Bryan Cranston
Maj. Col. Jack Tomilson: Lee Terjesen
Origin: United States
Language: English
Released: 2012
Production: Rick McCallum; Lucasfilm Ltd., Partnership Films; released by 20th Century-Fox
Directed by: Anthony Hemingway
Written by: John Ridley; Aaron McGruder
Cinematography by: John Aronson
Music by: Terence Blanchard
Sound: Matthew Wood
Editing: Michael O'Halloran; Ben Burtt
Art Direction: Jindrich Koci
Costumes: Alison Mitchell
Production Design: Michael Carlin; Nick Palmer
MPAA rating: PG-13
Running time: 125 minutes

REVIEWS

Alexandria, Michelle. *Eclipse Magazine.* January 22, 2012.
Bradshaw, Paul M. *Total Film.* May 29, 2012.
Brady, Tara. *Irish Times.* June 11, 2012.
Clark, Bill. *FromTheBalcony.* January 22, 2012.
Debruge, Peter. *Variety.* January 19, 2012.
Ebert, Roger. *Chicago Sun-Times.* January 19, 2012.
Holden, Stephen. *New York Times.* January 19, 2012.
McCarthy, Todd. *Hollywood Reporter.* January 19, 2012.
Rozen, Leah. *The Wrap.* March 2, 2012.
Snider, Eric D. *Film.com.* January 21, 2012.

QUOTES

Colonel A.J. Bullard: "Politics is the art of postponing a decision until it is no longer relevant."

TRIVIA

Samuel L. Jackson was in talks with George Lucas at one point to star in and possibly direct the film.

RESIDENT EVIL: RETRIBUTION

Evil goes global.
    —Movie tagline
Think global. Kill local.
    —Movie tagline
The ultimate battle begins.
    —Movie tagline

Box Office: $42.3 million

The *Resident Evil* films have never had much use for such archaic concepts as plot, character or dramatic tension but with *Resident Evil: Retribution*, such elements are cast away to such a degree that what might appear to be little more than an especially crass commercial enterprise takes on the hallucinatory nature of an exceptionally surreal art-house experiment worthy of being celebrated in the pages of *Film Comment* or *Cahiers du Cinema* instead of *Fangoria*. In theory, this sounds like little more than the kind of deliberately outrageous commentary that one might expect from the likes of Armond White but in the case of this fifth installment of the popular film franchise inspired by the equally successful video game series, it is a concept worth considering. This is a film that, either by design or by a disinterest in presenting anything other than pure sensation, so completely slips the bonds of the requirements of commercial filmmaking, thanks to such elements as constantly shifting locations, a narrative that doubles and sometimes triples back on itself with endless plot change-ups, scenes that may or may not be dream sequences, and actors often playing radically different versions of their characters from scene to scene, that there are times when it suggests what *The Discreet Charm of the Bourgeoisie* (1972) might have been like had it contained mutants and zombies instead of Fernando Rey.

Taking place before, during, after, and occasionally parallel to the events of the previous episodes, *RE: Retribution* finds the seemingly indestructible Alice (Milla Jovovich) on yet another adventure that finds her doing battle against the endless hordes of mutated zombies that have overrun the Earth thanks to the depravations of the malevolent Umbrella Corporation while searching for fellow survivors and/or safety. Although the ads suggest that the action will be taking place all over the world this time around, it turns out that her trek only consists of a couple of underground sound stages designed by Umbrella to resembles places like New York, Tokyo, Moscow and other places that could help bump up the international box-office take. As Alice makes her way from place to place, the backgrounds change so abruptly (a laboratory door opening into what appears to be downtown Tokyo) and presumably dead characters from earlier installments turn up with such frequency that the proceedings take on a hallucinatory edge that makes one wonder if Anderson had actually designed the film to be a feature-length homage to the classic Chuck Jones cartoon *Duck Amuck* (1953) in which Daffy Duck was driven to distraction by the shifting surroundings supplied by a sadistic and largely unseen animator—one almost expects that in the final shot, the camera would pull back to reveal Luc Besson at an AVID machine remarking "Ain't un salaud je?"

The movie is, of course, one of the most preposterous things ever projected on the silver screen and any critic with even a modicum of shame or a tenuous grasp on their critical faculties would decry it incoherent junk more in need of a Ritalin prescription than a cogent analysis—that is, unless they having too much fun watching it get especially upset with its blatant idiocies. Look, the *Resident Evil* movies are cinematic junk food—and *Resident Evil: Retribution* certainly falls under that heading—meant to appeal to the 14-year-old boy inside everyone with its cacophony of ear-splitting noise, CGI gore, big guns, tiny dresses, fabulous-looking babes, and a screenplay that contains less dialogue than the average Terrence Malick film, and of that, roughly fify percent consists of expository ejaculations and the other fifty percent consists of the characters repeating said ejaculations so that no one in the audience gets confused.

While this kind of base cinema can be pure torture in most cases (such as the wretched *Underworld* films), the *Resident Evil* films manage to pull it off. Part of this is because the series seems to have a healthy sense of its own inherent silliness and plays up to it in ever-inventive ways. For example, while most movies of this type might come up with the concept of Stalinist zombies chasing our heroes on a fleet of motorcycles through the streets of fake Moscow, only this film would dare add the lunatic touch of ensuring that all the cyclists were wearing safety helmets. Part of it is because while the fight scenes consistently defy the laws of gravity, physics, and common sense, they are such a gorgeous riot of sound and image that the entire film could be put on a constant loop in a trendy art gallery and it would seem perfectly at home in those surroundings. A large chunk of it is due to the undeniably magnetic screen presence of Milla Jovovich, who kicks, jumps and struts her way through the proceedings with a kind of droll panache that is just as fetching and alluring as the two thin sheets of paper that make up her entire wardrobe for several minutes of screen time. More importantly, unlike Kate Beckinsale in the *Underworld* films (not to beat up on those clinkers once again), who goes through her paces with a palpable sense of condescension towards the material, Jovovich still seems to be having fun with the material and that feeling can be sensed by the audience as well.

Look, this book is chock-full of movies that, good or bad, were made with the noblest of intentions and with the hope of communicating something of value to their audiences. *Resident Evil: Retribution,* on the other hand, was clearly made for one reason and one reason only—the four previous films made tons of money for Sony throughout the world and a fifth would be pretty much guaranteed to do the same. This may not be the most profound or radical rationale for making a movie but what it may lack in so-called artistic integrity, it more than makes up for in terms of sheer silly fun, the kind of film for which the phrase "guilty pleasure" was all but invented. Thanks to its combination of wild action, pretty faces, cheerful absurdity and a finale that will leave fans salivating for a sixth installment (even as they recall that the films have always ended on stunning final notes that the subsequent installments never quite follow up on), *Resident Evil: Retribution* more than delivers its admittedly low-rent goods and quite frankly, that is more than can be said for most of the titles in this volume.

Peter Sobczynski

CREDITS

Alice: Milla Jovovich
Jill Valentine: Sienna Guillory
Rain Ocampo: Michelle Rodriquez
Ada Wong: Bingbing Li
Luther West: Boris Kodjoe
Leon Kennedy: Johann Urb
Barry Burton: Kevin Durand
Carlos Oliveira/Todd: Oded Fehr
James "One" Shade: Colin Salmon
Albert Weskler: Shawn Roberts
Origin: Canada, Germany
Language: English
Released: 2012
Production: Samuel Hadida, Jeremy Bolt, Robert Kulzer, Don Carmody, Paul W.S. Anderson; Constantin Film, Screen Gems; released by Sony Pictures Home Entertainment Inc.
Directed by: Paul W.S. Anderson
Written by: Paul W.S. Anderson
Cinematography by: Glen MacPherson
Music by: tomandandy
Sound: Stephen Barden
Editing: Niven Howie
Costumes: Wendy Partridge
Production Design: Kevin Phipps
MPAA rating: R
Running time: 96 minutes

REVIEWS

Abele, Robert. *Los Angeles Times*. September 14, 2012.
Catsoulis, Jeanette. *New York Times*. September 15, 2012.
Guzman, Rafer. *Newsday*. September 17, 2012.
Leydon, Joe. *Variety*. September 17, 2012.
Orndorf, Brian. *Blu-Ray.com*. September 14, 2012.
Pinkerton, Nick. *Village Voice*. September 14, 2012.
Robinson, Tasha. *AV Club*. September 14, 2012.
Savlov, Marc. *Austin Chronicle*. September 21, 2012.
Scheck, Frank. *Hollywood Reporter*. September 14, 2012.
Willmore, Alison. *Movieline*. September 14, 2012.

QUOTES

Rain: "I'm coming for you!"
Alice: "Good luck with that."

TRIVIA

This is the first movie of the series not to feature undead dogs.

AWARDS

Nominations:

Golden Raspberries 2012: Worst Actress (Jovovich)

RISE OF THE GUARDIANS

Legends unite.
   —Movie tagline

Naughty, nice. You better believe.
   —Movie tagline

Santa Claus is more than a legend.
   —Movie tagline

The Sandman is more than a dream.
   —Movie tagline

When darkness falls, the Guardians will rise.
   —Movie tagline

The Easter Bunny is more than a fable.
   —Movie tagline

Jack Frost is more than a myth.
   —Movie tagline

The Tooth Fairy is more than a fairy tale.
   —Movie tagline

Box Office: $102.1 million

Upon first glance, DreamWorks Animation's *Rise of the Guardians* seemed to be built around a genius concept. Much in the same way that Alan Moore and Kevin O'Neill's acclaimed comic book series *The League of Extraordinary Gentlemen* brought together public domain literary heroes like Captain Nemo and the Invisible Man into an unstoppable supergroup, *Rise of the Guardians* creates its own legendary super-team built around some of the most famous icons of childhood— legends like Santa Claus, the Easter Bunny, the Sandman, and the Tooth Fairy. The concept reads like The Avengers for the elementary school crowd and the fact that it was based on a continuing book series by author and Academy Award-winning filmmaker William Joyce only adds to the project's pedigree.

Unfortunately, as was the case with the film adaptation of *The League of Extraordinary Gentlemen* (2003), there was a major disconnect between *Rise of the Guardians'* genius concept and the resulting movie, a film that somehow found a way to mangle Joyce's inspired conceit into something breathtakingly bland.

There is no easy way to explain why *Rise of the Guardians* simply does not work. DreamWorks had delivered popular animated adaptations before, most notably *How to Train Your Dragon* (2010). William Joyce was heavily involved in the film as was executive producer Guillermo Del Toro. The script was authored by David Lindsay-Abaire, the Pulitzer Prize-winning playwright responsible for *Rabbit Hole* (2010). The voice cast featured Alec Baldwin, Hugh Jackman, and Chris Pine. And how do you find more appealing, more recognizable lead characters than Santa Claus and the Easter Bunny? *Rise of the Guardians* should have been a four-quadrant movie guaranteed to play endlessly on TV every holiday season. And yet...that did not happen.

Many of the problems with *Rise of the Guardians* revolve around the film's protagonist, Jack Frost (Chris Pine), a minor mythological figure who is transformed into the Luke Skywalker of this by-the-book hero's journey. While most people only know Jack Frost as the guy "nipping at your nose" in Christmas carols, *Rise of the Guardians* gambled on making Frost its lead, a decision that ultimately backfired. Frost, as written by Lindsay-Abaire, is far too vague and navel-gazing to be an engaging lead, and centering the film around him was a bad call.

As the film opens, viewers are introduced to Jack, who tells us of how, hundreds of years ago, the mysterious Man on the Moon pulled him out of a frozen lake and turned the young man into the mythological embodiment of winter. The only problem is that people cannot see Jack unless they believe in him and, once again, whoever mentions Jack Frost outside of a Christmas carol anyway? This gives Jack some serious Man on the Moon issues and makes him jealous of the childhood icon heavy-hitters, The Guardians. This group of four—Santa Claus (Alec Baldwin), the Easter Bunny (Hugh Jackman), the Tooth Fairy (Isla Fisher), and the pleasantly mute Sandman—protects the innocence of children around the world and vaguely takes orders from the never-seen Man on the Moon, as if they were the Angels to the Moon Man's ethereal Charlie.

When a fear-spewing bogeyman named Pitch (Jude Law) begins an assault on children's dreams, intent on transforming them all into nightmares, the Guardians jump into action, only to get a surprise message from the Man on the Moon, instructing them that Jack Frost is the key to their success. The surprised Guardians try to induct the even-more-surprised Frost into their group, but Jack is filled with self-doubt and misplaced anger towards the Man on the Moon and refuses to join. Santa fills the Obi-Wan Kenobi role of mentor for Jack, instructing him to "find his center," but the group (with Jack tagging along) quickly has to rush off to the Tooth Fairy's kingdom where Pitch has stolen all of the world's collected baby teeth. (Happy childhood memories are, apparently, stored in the teeth.) Pitch uses the teeth to assault the dreams of children everywhere, which causes kids around the world to lose their faith. The Guardians and Jack Frost decide to combat this global lack of belief by helping the Easter Bunny deliver the best Easter ever, but, after Pitch disrupts their plans, children stop believing in the holiday and the tall, lithe warrior rabbit shrinks into a tiny, ineffective bunny.

Jack then exiles himself to Antarctica where he's tempted by Pitch and eventually discovers the truth surrounding his origins, which helps him "find his center" and organize the dejected Guardians for one final attack against the powerful nightmare king.

"Finding your center" is an exceptionally vague quest for a hero to go on and, ultimately, it seems to just be an analog for the evergreen "just believe in yourself" plot device. Along those lines, *Rise of the Guardians* consistently takes some of the most famous characters of all time and gives them nothing that exciting to do. Alec Baldwin's Santa is a fun reinterpretation of the character as a sword-wielding Baltic barbarian, but, aside from a few sword swings, sleigh rides, and some cut-rate mentoring, he does not actually DO much to move the story forward. The same goes for the other Guardians, who are all given some legitimately interesting characteristics, but, as characters, they never really go anywhere. The bunny hops, the fairy is obsessed with teeth, and the Sandman weaves dreams. If the Guardians were more central to the story for *Rise of the Guardians,* it might have been a more engaging experience, but the actual journey of the film pits Jack against Pitch, who both fall into generic hero-villain mode at the drop of a hat.

Jack is conflicted until the plot demands that he not be. Pitch is unstoppable until he is stopped. Nothing feels earned in *Rise of the Guardians,* it just happens. The generic storyline could have been overlooked if the film itself was more freewheeling and fun, but, regrettably, *Rise of the Guardians* alternates between being deadly serious and trying to force whimsy in ways that never really work.

How do you bungle a billion-dollar idea? You saddle it with a dead-weight lead character, a vague quest, a ponderous, self-important tone, and a supporting cast of inch-deep cultural icons. *Rise of the Guardians* should have risen at the box office—Is Santa and the Tooth Fairy teaming up that different than Iron Man and Thor teaming up?—but, at the end of the day, these legends of childhood simply were not all that interesting when removed from their respective holidays. This league of extraordinary holidays just was not extraordinary enough.

Tom Burns

CREDITS

Jack Frost: Chris Pine (Voice)
North/Santa Claus: Alec Baldwin (Voice)
Pitch: Jude Law (Voice)
Tooth Fairy: Isla Fisher (Voice)
E. Aster Bunnymund/Easter Bunny: Hugh Jackman (Voice)
Origin: United States
Language: English
Released: 2012
Production: Nancy Bernstein, Christina Steinberg; DreamWorks Animation; released by Paramount Pictures
Directed by: Peter Ramsey
Written by: David Lindsay-Abaire
Music by: Alexandre Desplat
Sound: Richard King
Editing: Joyce Arrastia
Art Direction: Max Boas
Production Design: Patrick Mark Hanenberger
MPAA rating: PG
Running time: 97 minutes

REVIEWS

Ebert, Roger. *Chicago Sun-Times.* November 20, 2012.
Ebiri, Bilge. *New York Magazine.* November 21, 2012.
Gleiberman, Owen. *Entertainment Weekly.* November 20, 2012.
O'Sullivan, Michael. *Washington Post.* November 20, 2012.
Packham, Chris. *Village Voice.* November 20, 2012.
Richards, Olly. *Empire.* November 26, 2012.
Robinson, Tasha. *AV Club.* November 21, 2012.
Rocchi, James. *Boxoffice Magazine.* November 20, 2012.
Scott, A. O. *New York Times.* November 20, 2012.
Whitty, Stephen. *Portland Oregonian.* November 23, 2012.

QUOTES

North: "It is our job to protect the children of the world. For as long as they believe in us, we will guard them with our lives."

TRIVIA

In his workshop at the beginning of the film, North is listening to and humming Igor Stravinsky's "Firebird" suite.

AWARDS

Nominations:
Golden Globes 2013: Animated Film

ROBOT & FRANK

Friendship doesn't have an off switch.
—Movie tagline

Box Office: $3.3 million

There are far worse cinematic sins than the attempted commingling of hijinks and heartwarming uplift but the two impulses seem especially at odds in *Robot & Frank,* a sweet-natured and mostly agreeable dramedy built around a solid performance from Frank Langella that massively stumbles via misplaced plotting in its second and third acts. The feature film debut of commercial director Jake Schreier, *Robot & Frank* premiered at the Sundance Film Festival, where it shared the Alfred P. Sloan Feature Film Prize, which is awarded to movies that spotlight science and technology. Picked up for distribution by Samuel Goldwyn and released in the autumn, it rang up decent arthouse returns of $3.2 million.

Robot & Frank unfolds in the near future, in upstate New York, where retired cat burglar Frank Weld (Frank Langella) lives by himself, under a cloud of Alzheimer's-like conditions that have impinged upon his memory. His daughter Madison (Liv Tyler) is caught up in travel abroad, but shares concerns with her brother Hunter (James Marsden) about their dad's isolation. Not wanting to place him in a nursing home, Hunter buys, against Frank's wishes, a walking, talking humanoid caregiver robot (voiced by Peter Sarsgaard) programmed to administer to his dietary needs and improve his physical and mental health.

Frank is at first gruff and dismissive of the robot. He views it as unnecessary and emasculating. Slowly, though, he warms to the companionship it provides. And as Frank's health improves, so too do his ambitions. He begins a stilted courtship with Jennifer (Susan Sarandon), the local librarian whose branch is set to undergo a complete digitalization, and also finds his old occupational instincts awakened, wanting to steal a valuable rare book from said library. Since the robot lacks any moral encoding, it enters into a tentative pact with Frank to assist him, built around various benchmarks of health.

Robot & Frank originated as the thesis short film of Schreier's New York University film school friend, Christopher Ford. When he had an opportunity to direct his first movie, Schreier tapped screenwriter Ford to flesh it out to feature-length. Given their limited budgetary means, the pair eschews much deeper exploration of the near-future setting and robots' place in it, except for noting that it is a matter of some cultural conflict. This is science fiction in only the loosest sense. Instead, Ford and Schreier opt for a more low-key story of beaten-back loneliness, laced with a parallel thematic exploration of memory, which is obviously of huge importance to Frank but no consideration at all to his robot companion. Given the unusual nature of its core relationship, this is a tack that certainly works for much of the movie's running time.

Working with director of photography Matthew Lloyd, Schreier roots the look of his film in the comedy of composition, and thankfully avoids flashy stylistic gambits. Visually, he constructs his movie in wide shots and longer takes, attempting to wring maximum effect out of sequences that present the contrast of a lurking Frank and his much shorter robot.

It is in fact this interplay of its two title characters which provides *Robot & Frank* with its emotional connection and most memorable moments. Alterian Effects (also responsible for designing Daft Punk's helmets, among other costumes) crafted the robot's white, bubble-headed suit—sort of a less overtly comedic, more utilitarian version of Marvin the Paranoid Android from *The Hitchhiker's Guide to the Galaxy* (2005)—which was worn on set by performer Rachael Ma. Sarsgaard's lines, meanwhile, recorded after shooting, are at once clipped and sympathetic, and have an appealingly naive quality that stands in frequent contrast to Frank's exasperation and dismissiveness.

The other component of that equation, of course, is Langella. Though he had been juggling fairly notable film, stage and television work for years, *Frost/Nixon* (2008), for which he received a Best Actor Oscar nomination, catapulted Langella back into the limelight as a top-lining talent. *Robot & Frank*, however, is much more of a piece with *Starting Out in the Evening* (2007), another intimately scaled movie in which his character's walls of ornery self-preservation melt away. In that film, Langella plays a once-famous author given to small, pedestrian rituals, unwilling or unable to cope with change. While the films' respective tones and stories are quite different, both feature finely modulated performances from Langella that showcase managed disappointment.

The main difference is that *Robot & Frank* goes off the tracks, narratively speaking. The film touches on mortality and political themes, but in a fairly elemental and haphazard way. Its sedate, inwardly reflective rhythms—which are its most convincing parts—are mortally compromised by an ill conceived and awkwardly rendered twist that first pops up in the second act and winds its way through to its conclusion. The movie could have kept the same basic storyline, but its inclusion of cartoonishly antagonistic Jake (Jeremy Strong), Jennifer's library boss, is ridiculous. He is a metaphor for modernism, but written in rather ham-handed fashion. Even more pointless and unbelievable is Sheriff Rowlings (Jeremy Sisto), the local lawman who so does Jake's bidding that he allows Jake to accompany him on a trip to question Frank about a break-in.

This clumsy, forced imprinting of outside drama, meant to heighten the film's stakes, instead just comes across as implausible, and lessens its overall emotional hold and impact. *Robot & Frank* is best when it is chronicling familial fissures, and how this robot—and more broadly, technology in general—bridge some but not all of those gaps. Unfortunately, Schreier and Ford bite off more than they can reasonably chew, erroneously assuming the audience wants a more complicated tale.

Brent Simon

CREDITS

Frank: Frank Langella
Hunter: James Marsden
Madison: Liv Tyler
Jennifer: Susan Sarandon
Jake: Jeremy Strong
Sheriff Rowlings: Jeremy Sisto
Robot: Peter Sarsgaard (Voice)
Origin: United States
Language: English
Released: 2012
Production: Lance Acord, Jackie Kelman Bisbee, Galt Niederhoffer, Sam Bisbee; Dog Run Pictures, TBB, White Hat, Park Pictures; released by Samuel Goldwyn Films
Directed by: Jake Schreier
Written by: Christopher D. Ford
Cinematography by: Matthew Lloyd
Music by: Francis and the Lights
Sound: Antonio Arroyo
Editing: Jacob Craycroft
Costumes: Erika Munro
Production Design: Sharon Lomofsky
MPAA rating: PG-13
Running time: 90 minutes

REVIEWS

Bell, Josh. *Las Vegas Weekly*. August 29, 2012.
Buckwalter, Ian. *NPR*. August 23, 2012.

Dargis, Manohla. *New York Times.* August 16, 2012.

Gang, Alison. *San Diego Union-Tribune.* August 24, 2012.

Greene, Ray. *Boxoffice Magazine.* January 24, 2012.

Jones, Kimberley. *Austin Chronicle.* August 31, 2012.

LaSalle, Mick. *San Francisco Chronicle.* August 23, 2012.

O'Hehir, Andrew. *Salon.com.* August 16, 2012.

Stevens, Dana. *Slate.* August 17, 2012.

Turan, Kenneth. *Los Angeles Times.* August 23, 2012.

QUOTES

Robot: "Hello, Frank. It is a pleasure to meet you."
Frank: "How do you know?"

TRIVIA

The vehicle that passes Frank when he is walking down the road is an available production car—Tango by Commuter Cars.

AWARDS

Nominations:

Ind. Spirit 2013: First Screenplay

ROCK OF AGES

Nothin' but a good time.
—Movie tagline

Box Office: $38.5 million

From the moment that Sherrie (Julianne Hough) belts out her little-girl-lost version of Night Ranger's "Sister Christian" on a bus headed from Oklahoma to Los Angeles, and from the moment the other passengers join in, it is obvious what kind of a movie *Rock of Ages* is going to be: a tongue-in-cheek homage to scraggly long-haired, tight leather pant wearing 1980s rock. That it picked its soundtrack with sing-along-ability as opposed to chronological accuracy (one could point out that Extreme's "More Than Words" was not even released in the 1980s, when the film is set) just goes to show that *Rock of Ages* is only about one thing: shameless, self-reflective fun. This is the kind of movie where characters break into song at the slightest provocation, where plot twists can be seen from a mile away, and where the boy always gets the girl (even if she goes slumming at a strip club for a while). Anyone looking for a more serious musical need not apply.

When viewers meet her, Sherrie has just left Tulsa for life in the City of Angels. Armed with a couple of bucks and her collection of record albums, she is determined to make her dreams of singing stardom come true. She is pin-up gorgeous, blonde, wide-eyed, and she

has a great voice. Too bad the big city is going to eat her alive, right? Well, sort of. She gets mugged right off the bat, but she also happens to meet Drew (Diego Boneta) a rocker wannabe who moonlights as a bar back at the Bourbon Room, the hottest club on the sunset strip. Their relationship is the thing that tween day dreams are made of: full of deep eye gazing and perfectly harmonized duets, without any real substance. But that is okay because, even though they headline the film's cast credits, these two are not the stars of the show. Neither is Catherine Zeta-Jones, who plays Patricia Whitmore, the uber-conservative mayor's wife determined to rid Los Angeles of the devil's music and the sex that comes with it. Though the supporting cast members all absolutely shine on screen, they too are not the real magic behind *Rock of Ages*. Tom Cruise kills as Stacee Jaxx, an aging Axl Rose-type rocker who commands a legion of swooning fans with his diamond encrusted thong, to be sure. Alec Baldwin and Russell Brand as the Bourbon Room managers with benefits are hilarious. Paul Giamatti as Jaxx's oily manager is spot on, Malin Akerman as the sexually repressed *Rolling Stone* reporter let loose on Stacee Jaxx is stellar, and Mary J. Blige as the strip club madame cum oracle with a heart of gold is spectacular. But as thrilling as it is to see this powerhouse line-up of stars onscreen together, the real magic starts when they open their mouths and sing. That is where *Rock of Ages* comes together, in the music. Cruise belting out Def Leppard's "Pour Some Sugar On Me" to Blige throwing down with Journey's "Any Way You Want It," every song in *Rock of Ages* is recognizable to children of the 1980s, avid movie watchers (some of these are standard go-tos for many montage sequences), or people who just happen to own a radio. The actors here were chosen as much for their singing and dancing ability as they were for their acting chops. *Rock of Ages* is about the novelty of Tom Cruise playing a rock god as it is about the Hough-Boneta love story. The mash-ups are also fresh, which is saying a lot in a culture that has seen just about everything paired-up and mixed-up thanks to the likes of TV's *Glee* and hits like *Pitch Perfect* (2012). *Rock of Ages* boasts a particularly impressive collision between Starship's "We Built This City" and Twisted Sister's "We're Not Going To Take It".

It goes without saying that *Rock of Ages* has some quirks. For all their talk about rock stardom, Sherrie never actually performs. Drew does not seem to "make it" as much as he gets rich writing songs for other people. But these missteps are quickly forgotten in light of a pretty funny highlight reel featuring Cruise's ability to make every Stacee Jaxx scene about his penis, Zeta-Jones' awkward succumbing to Jaxx's power, and Baldwin and Brand's duet of REO Speedwagon's "Can't

Fight This Feeling." *Rock of Ages* also gets props for a cute sub-story about the attempted assassination of real, hard core rock 'n' roll by Backstreet Boys-esque boy bands, and how the music industry has a mandate to shatter the illusions of honest, talented folk like Sherrie and Drew. Sure, it is a stretch that everything works out for the dimpled, awe-struck duo, but the sweet, albeit shallow, redemptive message is just a cherry on a really frilly, really fun sundae.

Joanna Topor MacKenzie

CREDITS

Sherrie Christian: Julianne Hough
Drew Boley: Diego Boneta
Lonny: Russell Brand
Dennis Dupree: Alec Baldwin
Mike Whitmore: Bryan Cranston
Patricia Whitmore: Catherine Zeta-Jones
Paul Gill: Paul Giamatti
Stacee Jaxx: Tom Cruise
Origin: United States
Language: English, French, Portuguese, Spanish
Released: 2012
Production: Matthew Weaver, Adam Shankman, Scott Prisand, Tobey Maguire, Carl Levin, Garrett Grant, Jennifer Gibgot; New Line Cinema, Corner Store Entertainment, released by Warner Bros.
Directed by: Adam Shankman
Written by: Chris D'Arienzo; Allan Loeb; Justin Theroux
Cinematography by: Bojan Bazelli
Music by: Adam Anders; Peer Astrom
Sound: Mildred Iatrou; John A. Larson
Music Supervisor: Matthew Rush Sullivan
Editing: Emma E. Hickox
Costumes: Rita Ryack
Production Design: Jon Hutman
MPAA rating: PG-13
Running time: 123 minutes

REVIEWS

Berardinelli, James. *ReelViews*. June 14, 2012.
Biancolli, Amy. *San Francisco Chronicle*. June 14, 2012.
Burr, Ty. *Boston Globe*. June 14, 2012.
Ebert, Roger. *Chicago Sun-Times*. June 13, 2012.
Hammond, Pete. *Boxoffice Magazine*. June 13, 2012.
Jones, J. R. *Chicago Reader*. June 13, 2012.
O'Hehir, Andrew. *Salon.com*. June 13, 2012.
Travers, Peter. *Rolling Stone*. June 14, 2012.
Turan, Kenneth. *Los Angeles Times*. June 14, 2012.
Zacharek, Stephanie. *Movieline*. June 14, 2012.

QUOTES

Dennis Dupree: "This place is about to become a sea of sweat, ear-shattering music and puke."

TRIVIA

The scene set beneath the Hollywood sign was actually shot on a garbage dump landfill in Pompano Beach, Florida.

A ROYAL AFFAIR
(En kongelig affaere)

They changed a nation forever.
—Movie tagline
Their love affair would divide a nation.
—Movie tagline

Box Office: $1.3 million

The heaving bosoms of period piece romance have political ramifications in Nikolaj Arcel's highly acclaimed and accomplished *A Royal Affair,* a nominee for the 2013 Academy Award for Best Foreign Language Film. Arcel follows up his international smash original version of *The Girl with the Dragon Tattoo* (2009), which he co-wrote, with a film that is much warmer, passionate, and historically relevant. The cool calculations of that work have been replaced by the heat of candlelight. The film not only chronicles a love affair between an intellectual doctor and a passionate Queen but the emergence of the Enlightenment in 18th-century Europe. With a pair of strikingly good central performances matched with top-level design from Arcel's entire technical team, *A Royal Affair* is not the stuffy, dusty period drama that it would have been in lesser talent's hands.

Caroline Mathilde (Alicia Vikander, who also appeared in another 2012 costume drama, *Anna Karenina*) is being given to King Christian VII (Mikkel Boe Folsgaard) as a political gift in marriage. She shall be the lovely young Queen of Denmark, which does not seem like too awful a fate until Caroline realizes that young Christian is totally crazy. He hides behind a tree on their first meeting, can be aggressively violent, and does not understand the plight of his people nor his new wife's disgust towards him. In fact, Christian thinks that Caroline should see a doctor to stop her bad moods. He is a child in royal's clothing and the new doctor, Struensee (Mads Mikkelsen) is anything but a boy. With his striking features, deep voice, and clear intellect, Mikkelsen is perfectly cast as the polar opposite of Christian. Naturally, the young Queen falls for the enlightened doctor. The two begin a passionate affair, inspired by their mutual desire for change in Denmark, a country increasingly damaged by divisions between the haves and the have-nots, disease that is not being adequately treated, and an overly religious approach to rule.

As might be clear by now, this is no mere period piece romance. Struensee has been named the King's doctor in the first place by men hoping to enact political change. So while he is sleeping with the Queen, he is also manipulating the feeble-minded and crazy Royal to change his country. Captivated by the ideals expressed by Voltaire, Caroline joins in the political games even as personal and primal issues threaten to destroy them. As Caroline and Struensee push the crazy King to a position he is clearly entitled but has been understandably taken away from him by the political machine, they risk their entire country falling apart and their romance being exposed.

Arcel takes his time with *A Royal Affair,* which never feels rushed but neither over-long at a notable 137 minutes. More importantly, it never comes across, as so many works like this do, as a history lesson, nothing more than pretty people playing dress-up in the name of a film production. These characters feel real, as does the urgency of their situation, in no small part due to incredibly accomplished technical elements all around. The costumes are lavish without feeling ridiculous. The sets are perfectly constructed to feel both genuine and cinematic. Even the score and cinematography are above average. Credit to Arcel for tackling such an ambitious project with numerous locations and dozens of major speaking roles.

The two most important speaking roles, of course, belong to Vikander and Mikkelsen, both perfectly cast and simply stellar here. Mikkelsen has become something of an international superstar, appearing in works as diverse as *Casino Royale* (2006), *Clash of the Titans* (2010), and the title role in NBC's *Hannibal*. He has a strong screen presence, but also allows for an amazing degree of vulnerability, coming across as truly human instead of merely the cliche of the other man. A scene in which he sees his love child with Caroline is one of the most subtle of his career. Vikander is newer to the acting scene but also conveys a perfect balance of strength and naivete. She seems honestly hopeful that her relationship with King Christian will work out but unafraid to find other routes to happiness when it is clear that it will not.

A Royal Affair made a modest $7 million internationally on the back of some very strong reviews from critics around the world. Joe Morgenstern correctly opined in the *Wall Street Journal,* "With its sumptuous settings, urgent romance and intellectual substance, *A Royal Affair* is a mind-opener crossed with a bodice-ripper." Joe Williams added in the *St. Louis Post-Dispatch,*

"Although the brazen lovers, bellicose ministers and backstabbing handmaidens are familiar elements, the film is so handsomely mounted that we happily endure the ride until the turning of the screws in the tragic last act."

Brian Tallerico

CREDITS

Caroline Mathilde: Alicia Vikander
Johann Friedrich Struensee: Mads Mikkelsen
Christian VII: Mikkel Boe Folsgaard
Juliane Marie: Trine Dyrholm
Ove Hoegh-Guldberg: David Dencik
Origin: Denmark, Sweden, Czech Republic
Language: Danish, English, German, French
Released: 2012
Production: Sisse Graum Jorgensen, Meta Louise Foldager, Louise Vesth; Zentropa Entertainment, Film i Vast; released by Magnolia Pictures
Directed by: Nikolaj Arcel
Written by: Nikolaj Arcel; Rasmus Heisterberg
Cinematography by: Rasmus Videbaek
Music by: Cyrille Aufort; Gabriel Yared; Mikkel E.G. Nielsen
Sound: Hans Christian Kock; Claus Lynge
Music Supervisor: Mikkel Maltha; Nicolas Koch Futtrup
Editing: Kasper Leick
Costumes: Manon Rasmussen
Production Design: Niels Sejer
MPAA rating: R
Running time: 137 minutes

REVIEWS

Adams, Sam. *AV Club.* November 7, 2012.
Ebert, Roger. *Chicago Sun-Times.* November 7, 2012.
Goodykoontz, Bill. *Arizona Republic.* November 15, 2012.
Morgenstern, Joe. *Wall Street Journal.* November 8, 2012.
Puig, Claudia. *USA Today.* November 29, 2012.
Rea, Steven. *Philadelphia Inquirer.* November 15, 2012.
Taylor, Ella. *NPR.* November 8, 2012.
Toppman, Lawrence. *Charlotte Observer.* December 6, 2012.
Turan, Kenneth. *Los Angeles Times.* November 8, 2012.
Williams, Joe. *St. Louis Post-Dispatch.* January 17, 2013.

TRIVIA

This film was Denmark's official submission for the Foreign Language Film category of the 85th Academy Awards.

AWARDS

Nominations:

Oscars 2012: Foreign Film
Golden Globes 2013: Foreign Film

RUBY SPARKS

She's out of his mind.
—Movie tagline

Box Office: $2.5 mllion

She is every man's dream, a vision of perfection as earthy as she is unattainable. Her world revolves entirely around her lover, whom she worships even when he treats her poorly. She will freely sacrifice her own dreams as long as his are achieved, which is hardly a problem considered her interests are identical to his own. She is everything a brooding, directionless, single man could ever want. In fact, that is all she is.

Ever since "The Onion AV Club" critic Nathan Rabin coined the phrase, "Manic Pixie Dream Girl," that term has been applied to a variety of screen beauties whose sole purpose in life is to get their men out of a psychological rut. It is the latest sexist archetype to plague mainstream Hollywood, which has a rich and varied history in manufacturing heroines that embody the idealized dream girl of countless male screenwriters. Even the most spunky female characters have routinely crumbled at the very thought of a life without her man. Scarlett O'Hara is required to weep and moan about the dismal plight of her relationship, while Rhett Butler is free to not give a damn.

The genius of Zoe Kazan's first screenplay, *Ruby Sparks,* lies not only in its sly deconstruction of the Manic Pixie persona, but in its seriocomic exploration of the alienated male mind that brought her to life. In the film's opening moments, a young writer named Calvin (Paul Dano) is seen walking his dog before retreating to his oversized apartment. The white walls that remain largely unadorned in his bachelor pad mirror the blankness of the page staring at him from his typewriter. After achieving widespread acclaim with his first novel, lofty expectations have been weighing on him like a ten-ton weight.

It is worth wondering whether filmmakers Jonathan Dayton and Valerie Faris felt similar pressure after their feature debut, 2006's marvelous crowd-pleaser *Little Miss Sunshine,* became one of the most celebrated sleeper hits of the last decade. Anyone familiar with the directing duo's past work in TV and music videos is well aware of their artistic integrity and refusal to remain within the safe constraints of a formula. It is clear that Dayton and Faris had no intention of merely repeating their earlier success, and favored scripts because of their content rather than their marketability. Like Michael Arndt's Oscar-winning *Sunshine* script, *Sparks* is the work of a rookie screenwriter, and both films share a freshness and unpredictability that is utterly beguiling. It goes without saying that Dayton and Faris chose wisely,

and that their second feature effort is more than worth the wait.

Whereas the central ensemble of *Sunshine* was thoroughly lovable, flaws and all, Calvin is a tougher creature to embrace. At first, his childlike self-absorption is charming in a Woody Allen-esque sense, and Dano captures his befuddlement in several priceless double takes. Writer's block coupled with the heartache of a failed relationship has caused Calvin to spend most of his time fantasizing about an ideal companion. She is 26-years-old, drop-dead gorgeous, sexually sophisticated, and totally available. Plus, she really digs zombie flicks. Pretty soon, Calvin finds that all he can write about is this girl, carrying the whimsical name of Ruby Sparks. He is not writing with any particular end goal in mind. He is writing to spend time with her. And that is when Ruby (Zoe Kazan) suddenly materializes in his apartment.

This is where the picture could have flown off the rails by indulging in Calvin's wish-fulfillment while halting his character from growing past the boundaries of his own arrested fantasies. Yet Kazan probes further, opting neither for the fish-out-of-water sweetness of *Splash* (1984) nor the brilliant-yet-pessimistic sourness of *The Purple Rose of Cairo* (1985). What she creates instead is a universally relatable metaphor for the tendency of lovers to maintain control over one another, thus limiting their ability to truly connect with the other person. One of the key lines in the film occurs during a tense conversation between Calvin and his ex, who flatly states, "The only person you wanted a relationship with was you." The words sting like an open wound, and Kazan does not shy away from their implications.

To Calvin, Ruby is a psychological comfort on the page. However, once she becomes a member of the real world, she gradually starts to develop a mind of her own. As Ruby's world grows beyond the boundaries of the apartment, she starts to enjoy the company of others and Calvin's jealousy is instantly inflamed. Suddenly, Ruby is articulating opinions around which he cannot fully wrap his head. She starts claiming that she is too tired for sex and decides one night to stay out late with friends. As Calvin starts to protest, Ruby tells him that space is healthy in a relationship, otherwise "it's like we're the same person." And that is when the frustrated puppet master decides to turn to the typewriter for revisions.

Earlier on, Calvin exploited the manipulative power of his typewriter keys by proving to his disbelieving brother, Harry (Chris Messina), that Ruby is for real, a clever gag that earns some of the film's biggest laughs. Though the film offers juicy roles for supporting players including Annette Bening, Antonio Banderas, Steve

Coogan, Elliott Gould and Alia Shawkat, it is Messina who resonates the most. Though his uber-masculine bravado has been a turn-off in past films (such as 2009's *Julie & Julia*), it fits perfectly in the role of Harry, who urges his brother to take full advantage of his newfound powers, despite its elements of "mindcest." Messina sports expert comic timing in his scenes with Dano, yet is also grounded enough to function as the film's skeptical everyman.

As for Dano and Kazan, their off-screen chemistry as a couple is apparent in their ease with each other in front of the lens. The flair for physical comedy Dano displayed in *Sunshine* as the oft-silent Dwayne has not diminished one iota. His euphoric reaction to Ruby's inexplicable (and mercifully unexplained) flesh-and-blood existence is so infectious that the audience shares in it, at least for the first act. Kazan is remarkable in the way she suggests and gauges Ruby's growing individuality in countless small nuances. She also proves quite adept at physical comedy in the scenes where Calvin desperately alters her personality and discovers that every vision of heaven contains its own built-in hell. Composer Nick Urata, whose quartet DeVotchka provided the memorable score for *Sunshine,* brings a soulful quality to each scene, enabling the audience to become more emotionally in tune with the characters without making blatant attempts at eliciting a particular emotional response.

Though *Sparks* has a wealth of playful and funny moments, it is a much more thoughtful and affecting film than one might expect. Dayton and Faris are not aiming for the wall-to-wall hilarity that made their last film such a kick, and audiences expecting a similar experience will be let down. Kazan plumbs the depths of Calvin's possessiveness to such an unsettling degree that she risks losing the rom-com base that the ads have targeted, yet her film is all the stronger for it. Without honestly exploring the most disturbing aspects of its central relationship, the film would've been little more than an entertaining trifle. Calvin's pursuit for perfection mirrors Richard's obsession with winning in *Sunshine,* and both men must ultimately learn to embrace the inherent imperfections of life. Yet whereas Richard's journey climaxed with an exhilarating act of irreverent rebelliousness, Calvin plunges toward the frightening core of his self-deception, resulting in a stunning sequence that plays like the emotional equivalent of a train wreck.

In an image-driven society hellbent on profiting off one's own feelings of inadequacy, a film like *Ruby Sparks* is an utterly refreshing palate cleanser. It renews one's faith in the power of cinema, and its unique ability to simultaneously provide viewers with an escape route from their problems and a heightened perch from which to examine them. After earning raves for her work both onstage and onscreen, Kazan has officially solidified her status as a major voice in modern American cinema, while Dayton and Faris have once again masterfully exposed the foibles and absurdities that are intrinsically linked with the passions of the human heart. This is one of the year's best films.

Matt Fagerholm

CREDITS

Ruby Sparks: Zoe Kazan
Calvin Weir-Fields: Paul Dano
Dr. Rosenthal: Elliott Gould
Harry: Chris Messina
Gertrude: Annette Bening
Mort: Antonio Banderas
Langdon Tharp: Steve Coogan
Mabel: Alia Shawkat
Cyrus Modi: Aasif Mandvi
Origin: United States
Language: English
Released: 2012
Production: Albert Berger, Ron Yerxa; Bona Fide; released by Fox Searchlight
Directed by: Jonathan Dayton; Valerie Faris
Written by: Zoe Kazan
Cinematography by: Matthew Libatique
Music by: Nick Urata
Sound: Edward Tise
Editing: Pamela Martin
Costumes: Nancy Steiner
Production Design: Judy Becker
MPAA rating: R
Running time: 105 minutes

REVIEWS

Berardinelli, James. *ReelViews.* July 24, 2012.
Chang, Justin. *Variety.* July 13, 2012.
Ebert, Roger. *Chicago Sun-Times.* July 25, 2012.
Gleiberman, Owen. *Entertainment Weekly.* July 25, 2012.
Holden, Stephen. *New York Times.* July 25, 2012.
Kohn, Eric. *indieWIRE.* July 23, 2012.
McCarthy, Todd. *Hollywood Reporter.* July 13, 2012.
Osenlund, R. Kurt. *Slant Magazine.* July 25, 2012.
Robinson, Tasha. *AV Club.* July 25, 2012.
Walsh, Katie. *The Playlist.* July 23, 2012.

QUOTES

Ruby Sparks: "What's your dog's name?"

Calvin Weir-Fields: "Uh, Scotty. I named him for F. Scott Fitzgerald."

Ruby Sparks: "Isn't that disrespectful?"

Calvin Weir-Fields: "What?"

Ruby Sparks: "Naming your dog after him? It's a little disrespectful. Think about it. You're a novelist. You think this guy's the greatest. So you name your dog after him to cut him down to size. This way, you can put him on a leash and yell, 'Bad Scotty' and feel all superior because you pee inside. Kill your idols, man. I'm all or it."

TRIVIA

The book that has been torn apart by Scotty the dog is a copy of *The Catcher in the Rye* by J.D. Salinger.

AWARDS

Nominations:

Ind. Spirit 2013: Screenplay

RUST AND BONE
(De rouille et d'os)

Box Office: $2 million

An indistinct series of images involving the sea, a sleeping child, and outstretched arms greets the viewer as *Rust and Bone* opens, along with light snoring and a lilting and somewhat sad bit of what sounded like shanty tune. Then, viewers find themselves in the company of a pair of legs walking along a busy road. The legs belong to Alain van Versch (Matthias Schoenaerts) and his son Sam (Armand Verdure) who are trekking cross-country, their footsteps, hitchhiking, and train rides (during which they scrounge for food left behind by other passengers) are their only modes of transport. Petty thievery is their only means of raising money.

When the pair seeks refuge with Alain's estranged sister Anna (Corinne Masiero) and her husband Richard, viewers learn that Sam was being used by Alain's ex-wife to smuggle drugs, hence the road trip. As they build toward a new future, Alain gets a job as a security guard at a local club and while breaking up a fight he rescues a beautiful yet strangely unhappy young woman named Stephanie (Marion Cotillard) only to drive her back to her apartment, where after learning that she is an Orca trainer (and insulting her choice of club wear) he is met by her ungrateful, jealous boyfriend and leaves. Soon after that fateful night Stephanie loses her lower legs in an accident involving the whales and as she despondently begins the process of rehabilitation, Alain, unaware, becomes a security guard, begins sparring at the gym with other boxers, and rekindles his social life, a social

life that does not mesh well with his responsibilities as a single father. He is almost a child himself, more concerned with easy sex, and easier money than finding a stable career or being a father. When he gets a call from Stephanie suggesting they meet, he eagerly accepts. He arrives at her darkened apartment and is stunned. There she sits in a wheelchair, abandoned and having all but abandoned herself.

As they speak, Alain betrays nothing except his desire to help. Surprisingly, even to himself, he is no mere hunk on the make. Her response is incremental. Edging out of her depression, the once beautiful-now-disheveled Stephanie agrees to go outside, donning sunglasses as the sun spills light onto her scary journey back into the world of other people. But this is not enough for Alain, who invites her into the surf at a local beach and dives in even after she refuses to join him. Persuaded, she undresses and allows herself to be carried into the water. In the waves, able to move about freely she moans in delight and returns home anew. The pair continues in their platonic get-togethers and Stephanie learns that Alain has started boxing on the side in a brutal last-man-standing under-the-table operation.

When Stephanie attends the match with him she is forced to watch from the car window at the male-only event. She has never seen him this way before. Clearly in his element, caught up in the joys and pain of his sport, he is alive. But even as he races to the store on the way home to buy a toy she is surprised to find out that he has a son as he has never mentioned it before. She is equally surprised when he peremptorily asks if she wants have sex.

And thus begins the story's most delicate dance. Two people, both deeply wounded, connect with one another, but what those first instincts lead to gives the film's primary revelations about love, relationships, commitment, friendship and personal growth the air of an exploratory dialogue. This is not a simple boy-meets-girl story, it is almost a fable. The strong become weak and the weak become strong. Unlikely alliances form and relationships that seemed built on firm foundations falter.

The film presents a haunting array of images, juxtaposing elements in a cinematographic dance that is often deeply moving. Sequences of Alain engaged in mindless, lustful sex with one woman are counterpointed with his gentle halting exploration of Stephanie's body during which he asks when and where she wants to be touched. Of course, later, viewers see Stephanie haltingly climbing down the steps of Marine Land on her new prosthetic legs to commune with one of the Orcas, speaking with her hands in the code she formerly used to control the animals as a trainer. Love is a language we all speak in code, even to ourselves. Just as Stephanie has had the courage to face and once again befriend the Orca there is the sense that Alain must face and embrace what the ring allows him to avoid, a fierceness, beyond and yet somehow connected to his physicality, a mystery within himself.

Marion Cotillard is, of course, transcendentally beautiful but also fully believable in her role, evoking a complex mix of shyness, arrogance, despair, hope, and determination. In the best use of the B52's "Love Shack" ever she dances in circles in her wheelchair after her first day at the beach. Later, she is shown back at the club where she and Alain first met. She registers intense disgust at a man who suddenly becomes embarrassed after hitting on her when he realizes she is handicapped. Most of all, as she moves through all these modes, viewers will have a sense that she is reclaiming not only what has been lost but becoming something utterly new.

Matthias Schoenaerts is most recently known for his star turn as another troubled tough guy in the masterful *Bullhead* (2012), directed by Michael R. Roskam. His ability to project complex emotions through a strong silent persona is impressive. Here, he walks a fine line between hinting that he may be a cad and yet may be on the cusp of revelation, ready to emerge and fight for his own character. Or he may truly be as faceless and nameless as his opponents in the ring. But the road to realizing how his actions can affect others may also demand too much of him. He underplays brilliantly.

Writer/director Jacques Audiard excels here in the quiet yet forceful characterization and storytelling that has made him one of the great directors currently working. Coming off the brilliant one-two punch of *A Prophet* (2009) he must be credited here for coaxing incredible performances out of his leads. His story meanders a bit, hints at devolving into a doomed-love sort of noir tale but is never less than cautionary, inspiring, and beautiful to contemplate.

Dave Canfield

CREDITS

Stephanie: Marion Cotillard
Alain van Versch: Matthias Schoenaerts
Sam: Armand Verdure
Louise: Celine Sallette
Anna: Corinne Masiero
Martial: Bouli Lanners
Richard: Jean-Michel Correia

Foued: Mourad Frarema
Simon: Yanick Choirat
Origin: France, Belgium
Language: French
Released: 2012
Production: Pascal Caucheteux, Martine Cassinelli, Jacques Audiard; Page 114, France 2 Cinema, Les Films du Fleuve, RTBF (Television Belge), Lunanime, Why Not Productions, Lumiere; released by Sony Pictures Classics
Directed by: Jacques Audiard
Written by: Jacques Audiard; Thomas Bidegain; Craig Davison
Cinematography by: Stephanie Fontaine
Music by: Alexandre Desplat
Sound: Pascal Villard
Music Supervisor: Frederic Junqua
Editing: Juliette Welfling
Art Direction: Yann Megard
Costumes: Virginie Montel
Production Design: Michel Barthelemy
MPAA rating: R
Running time: 120 minutes

REVIEWS

Anderson, Melissa. *Village Voice*. November 20, 2012.
Barnard, Linda. *Toronto Star*. December 20, 2012.
Corliss, Richard. *Time*. May 17, 2012.
Debruge, Peter. *Variety*. May 17, 2012.
Frosch, Jon. *The Atlantic*. May 30, 2012.
Lane, Anthony. *New Yorker*. November 28, 2012.
O'Hehir, Andrew. *Salon.com*. November 22, 2012.
Rea, Steven. *Philadelphia Inquirer*. December 20, 2012.
Scott, A. O. *New York Times*. November 22, 2012.
Stevens, Dana. *Slate*. November 30, 2012.

QUOTES

Stephanie: "What have you done with my legs?"

TRIVIA

Actors Marion Cotillard and Matthias Schoenaerts met for the first time three weeks before shooting began during the script reading at Jacques Audiard's house.

AWARDS

Nominations:

British Acad. 2012: Actress (Cotillard), Foreign Film
Golden Globes 2013: Actress—Drama (Cotillard), Foreign Film
Ind. Spirit 2013: Foreign Film
Screen Actors Guild 2012: Actress (Cotillard)

S

SAFE

She has the code. He is the key.
—Movie tagline

Box Office: $17.1 million

There are times when *Safe* feels less like a movie and more like the cinematic equivalent of a greatest hits album that an artist puts out between real projects as a way of making a quick bundle of cash without putting in much of anything resembling an effort. In this case, the artist in question is British action star Jason Statham and while the film is technically original, virtually every scene in it will remind his fans of similar moments found throughout his filmography. This is not so much a criticism as it is a mere observation because even though there is nothing particularly unique about the film, it serves up the familiar stuff in a reasonably energetic and entertaining manner.

Statham plays Luke, a former hotshot New York cop whose was drummed off the force by his corrupt colleagues and whose second career as a small-potatoes cage fighter fell apart when his refusal to take a dive for the Russian mob led to the murder of his beloved wife. At the end of his rope and with nowhere to go, he is about to end it all when he rescues a ten-year-old Chinese girl (Catherine Chan) from some no-goodniks. It turns out that the girl is a math prodigy brought to America by a Chinese crime boss who uses her ability to memorize and crack long numerical codes for his own nefarious purposes and the code that she now has in her head is of value not only to him but to the Russian gangsters and the corrupt cops that ruined Luke's life. Needless to say, Luke takes it upon himself to protect the girl in the best way that he knows how—by pounding the crap out of every bad guy who comes his way.

Written and directed by Boaz Yakin, whose career has veered between ambitious dramas like *Fresh* (1994) and *A Price Above Rubies* (1998) and formulaic silliness like *Remember the Titans* (2000) and *Uptown Girls* (2003), *Safe* is the kind of action film that is so predictable that not only will most viewers be able to see where the story is going, they will even be able to plot the trajectories of the flying fists, feet and bullets as well. And yet, while no one will mistake his efforts here as among his finest hours as a filmmaker, he does deliver the goods in a straightforward manner that is not entirely reliant on the kind of hyperkinetic editing and violations of the laws of physics that are pretty much standard for the genre these days. Refreshingly, he does not attempt to milk the relationship between the kid and her protector for maximum pathos—there is a prickly edge to their byplay that helps to enliven things. Yakin also manages to squeeze in a few welcome moments of humor into the proceedings without turning them into too much of a distraction—one bit in which a tough guy gets run over by the same car twice is staged in such a clever manner that each hit inspires a laugh.

The best thing about *Safe*, perhaps not surprisingly, is the presence of Jason Statham. After first coming to the attention of moviegoers with his appearances in the early Guy Ritchie vehicles *Lock, Stock and Two Smoking Barrels* (1998) and *Snatch* (2000), he has been working steadily in films ranging from smash hits like the *Transporter* and *Expendables* franchises to disposable junk like the remakes of *Death Race* (2008) and *The Mechanic* (2011) and numerous weirdo cult favorites like the deeply deranged *Crank* (2006) and *In the Name of the King: A Dungeon Siege Tale* (2008). Although he has occasionally chosen projects that would allow him to show more of a dramatic range—sometimes successfully (*The Bank Job* [2008]) and sometimes not so much (*London* [2005])—he has generally stuck to the action genre and while he has not yet had the vehicle that would launch him into the superstardom that he has been on the cusp of for the last few years, his work here shows that he has everything he needs to achieve that goal, with the possible exception of a more selective method of vetting screenplays; he is intensely charismatic, possesses a winningly dry sense of wit and pulls off the difficult task of coming across like an ordinary guy while still being fearsomely convincing during the action scenes. In the hands of most other performers, a film like *Safe* would have come across as little more than derivative junk but with Statham on board...okay, it is still derivative junk but thanks to his efforts, most genre fans will not mind that so much.

Peter Sobczynski

CREDITS

Luke Wright: Jason Statham
Mei: Catherine Chan
Captain Wolf: Robert John Burke
Han Jiao: James Hong
Alex Rosen: Anson Mount
Origin: United States
Language: English, Spanish
Released: 2012
Production: Lawrence Bender, Dana Brunetti; IM Global, Lawrence Bender Productions; released by Lionsgate
Directed by: Boaz Yakin
Written by: Boaz Yakin
Cinematography by: Stefan Czapsky
Music by: Mark Mothersbaugh
Sound: Wylie Stateman; Dror Mohar
Music Supervisor: Liz Gallacher
Editing: Frederic Thoraval
Art Direction: Jesse Rosenthal
Costumes: Ann Roth; Michelle Matland
Production Design: Joseph C. Nemec, III
MPAA rating: R
Running time: 119 minutes

REVIEWS

Adams, Sam. *AV Club*. April 27, 2012.
Dalton, Stephen. *Hollywood Reporter*. April 27, 2012.
Goss, William. *Film.com*. April 27, 2012.

Hillis, Aaron. *Village Voice*. April 24, 2012.
Lowry, Brian. *Variety*. April 23, 2012.
Neumaier, Joe. *New York Daily News*. April 26, 2012.
Newman, Kim. *Empire Magazine*. April 29, 2012.
Pais, Matt. *RedEye*. April 26, 2012.
Russo, Tom. *Boston Globe*. April 28, 2012.
Webster, Andy. *New York Times*. April 26, 2012.

QUOTES

Alex Rosen: "What is she to you?"
Luke Wright: "Life."

TRIVIA

The Dekalb Ave. subway station and Canal St. station were filmed at the Cortlandt St. station.

SAFE HOUSE

No one is safe.
—Movie tagline

Box Office: $126.4 million

A technically polished action thriller that starts off strong but rather quickly succumbs to a grinding monotony, *Safe House* plays it safe throughout, offering up placebo thrills in telling the story of a young CIA agent desperately trying to keep custody of a high-value target in the face of a furious assault. Starring Denzel Washington and Ryan Reynolds, the movie has a pinch of distinctness courtesy of its South African setting, but otherwise feels dutifully stitched together out of wellworn genre elements.

Though it only connected in middling fashion with critics, ranking just above 50 percent on Rotten Tomatoes, *Safe House* reaffirmed Washington's box office star power, ringing up more than $40 million its opening weekend en route to $126 million domestically and another $76 million abroad. Adult audiences in particular seemed to respond in Pavlovian fashion to the movie's smooth blend of familiar components.

When notorious traitor and ex-spy Tobin Frost (Washington) turns himself in at an American embassy in Johannesburg, it confounds the CIA. They quickly order him remanded to a little-used safe house overseen by Sam Weston (Reynolds), an untried, low-level operative sure that he is ready for a more important posting. When that fortified secret location is subsequently attacked by a gang of heavily armed mercenaries, Weston barely escapes with Frost in his custody.

Frost has an important file that he is aiming to sell, and he does not submit easily and comfortably to being in Weston's charge. But while the CIA, who ostensibly has such a high interest in Frost because of his past crimes of treason, scrambles to get another extraction team to South Africa in around twelve hours, Weston begins to wonder if perhaps some in the agency have a more concentrated and nefarious investment in the specifics of Frost's latest piece of purloined intelligence.

Minus the amnesiac elements, *Safe House* comes across in significant ways as a long-in-the-tooth *The Bourne Identity* (2002), complete with rooftop chases, close-quarters fisticuffs, a foreign-born love interest (Nora Arnezeder) and scrambling bureaucrats—in this case a pair of at-odds higher-ups, David Barlow (Brendan Gleeson) and Catherine Linklater (Vera Farmiga), and a CIA Deputy Director, Harlan Whitford (Sam Shepard), who are all looking to cover their own asses just as much if not more than actually getting to the bottom of Frost's sudden and mysterious reappearance. The reason: a cover-up, of course. (Suffice to say that Frost's valuable item strongly recalls the NOC list of *Mission: Impossible* [1996]).

While *Safe House* is not explicitly a movie about terrorism or war, it does fall within the broader context of a wide range of sociopolitical action thrillers that over the past decade have sought to capitalize on American curiosity (and indeed, anxiety) about real-world events and threats from abroad—movies like *The Kingdom* (2007), *Body of Lies* (2008), *Vantage Point* (2008) and *Green Zone* (2010). The film's super-saturated and at times jittery camerawork, meanwhile, also seems to take as its source of inspiration many of Washington's previous collaborations with director Tony Scott, like *Man on Fire* (2004), *Deja Vu* (2006) and *Unstoppable* (2010).

But it is a ripe self-awareness, and maybe even a pinch of defensiveness, over the obviousness of all these antecedents that seems to inform the narrative direction of *Safe House* as much as anything else. The fight sequences and shootouts, of which there are many, pack a brawny wallop—perhaps unsurprisingly, since the movie is shot in a hyperactive visual style akin to the first three *Bourne* films prior to spin-off *The Bourne Legacy* (2012), all of which cinematographer Oliver Wood worked on before his work here. And when Weston needs to pick up directions to a new safe house, he is dispatched to a crowded Green Point Stadium during a soccer match, a nonsensical choice seemingly designed to wring some differentiating production value out of staging a big chase sequence in and around the distinct structure new built for the 2010 FIFA World Cup.

The script, the first produced work from screenwriter David Guggenheim, simply feels thin and lacking in psychological perspicacity, perhaps whittled down to

broad strokes conflict by a consensus committee. The background shading of both Frost and Weston arrives in chunky case-file exposition that does not even have the pop or sizzle of delicious phrasing. (When someone describes Frost as having "gone off the reservation," it is but the first of several times viewers might be able to recite along descriptions while watching the movie for the first time.) *Safe House* barely scratches the surface of Frost's past sins, too, seemingly so as to not sully his character too much. And when its final, nominal twists come, they arrive with a shrugging inevitability.

Most problematically, the movie gives its audience, in Frost and Weston, a cat and mouse, and then spends most of its overblown 115-minute running time keeping them from truly mentally playing with one another. The basic emotional trajectory of *Safe House* tracks closely to Washington's *Training Day* (2001), offering up an equally antagonistic but less explicitly personal clash of well-worn and corrupted occupational cynicism with wide-eyed, do-right optimism. But while Washington has a proven track record in playing these sorts of morally dubious, darkly charismatic characters, *Safe House* does not have enough going for it in terms of the depth of its character sketches to convincingly depict the caffeinated, enemy-of-my-enemy-is-my-momentary-friend logic that powers its action. Consequently, Washington and Reynolds' performances, however scrupulously professional and emotionally invested, have a hollow resonance.

In his fourth feature film but first work for a major Hollywood studio, director Daniel Espinosa, a Swedish-born filmmaker of Chilean origin, ably puts his actors through the paces but does little outside of location shooting to impress a more pronounced sense of dislocation upon the proceedings. (When nabbed by security forces, Weston speaks Afrikaans; later, he intuitively tracks down Frost after he escapes, knowing the neighborhoods.)

Then again, one does not feel much with respect to *Safe House*, a movie of tidy, plotted conflicts and to-scale bluster. It does not offend mightily, but neither does it exhibit any capacity or appetite for great risk. Its aims seem entirely meager, which means that its hold is correspondingly trivial and insignificant. Even those with an overall more generous opinion of *Safe House* will be more apt to recall the generalized contented feeling it elicits rather than any manner of specifics. Even store-brand generic snacks, after all, can fill one up.

Brent Simon

CREDITS

Tobin Frost: Denzel Washington

Matt Weston: Ryan Reynolds
David Barlow: Brendan Gleeson
Harlan Whitford: Sam Shepard
Daniel Kiefer: Robert Patrick
Alec Wade: Liam Cunningham
Catherine Linklater: Vera Farmiga
Carlos Villar: Ruben Blades
Ana Moreau: Nora Arnezeder
Origin: United States
Language: English
Released: 2012
Production: Scott Stuber; Intrepid Pictures, Moonlighting Films, Relativity Media, Stuber Productions; released by Universal Pictures
Directed by: Daniel Espinosa
Written by: Davis Guggenheim
Cinematography by: Oliver Wood
Music by: Ramin Djawadi
Sound: Per Hallberg
Editing: Richard Pearson
Art Direction: Jonathan Hely-Hutchinson; Shira Hockman; Pablo Maestre Galli; Erik Polczwartek
Costumes: Susan Matheson
Production Design: Brigitte Broch
MPAA rating: R
Running time: 115 minutes

REVIEWS

Chang, Justin. *Variety*. February 9, 2012.
Dargis, Manohla. *New York Times*. February 9, 2012.
Goodykoontz, Bill. *Arizona Republic*. February 9, 2012.
Hazelton, John. *Screen International*. February 9, 2012.
Lemire, Christy. *Associated Press*. February 9, 2012.
McCarthy, Todd. *Hollywood Reporter*. February 8, 2012.
Puig, Claudia. *USA Today*. February 9, 2012.
Rabin, Nathan. *AV Club*. February 9, 2012.
Tallerico, Brian. *HollywoodChicago.com*. February 9, 2012.
Turan, Kenneth. *Los Angeles Times*. February 9, 2012.

QUOTES

Tobin Frost: "You practice anything a long time, you get good at it. You tell a hundred lies a day, is sounds like the truth. Everyone betrays everyone."

TRIVIA

Actor Denzel Washington was actually waterboarded while filming some of the torture scene, though only for a few seconds per take.

SAFETY NOT GUARANTEED

Box Office: $4 million

Just because people cannot time travel does not mean they do not often live in the past, whether deliberately or unintentionally. The past may be behind everyone, but it can just as easily be a distant memory as an anchor.

In the unexpectedly romantic *Safety Not Guaranteed*, three characters struggle to establish a stable life in the present due to years-old pain or pleasure. Darius (Aubrey Plaza) has never found a sense of place or peace of mind since her mother died when Darius was 14, in a car accident about which Darius still feels responsible. Jeff (Jake M. Johnson), Darius' superior during her internship at Seattle Magazine, longs for the carefree, physical and emotional satisfaction he had during a fling when he was eighteen. And Kenneth (Mark Duplass) so fixates on the love he lost that he plans to go back in time and reconnect with the woman, who may or may not be the reason he currently seems to spend most of his time alone.

Most so-called rational people would read an ad like the one posted by Kenneth searching for a partner on his time-travel mission and assume that it is the work of a deluded fool with no chance of success. That arrogant condescension is why Kenneth immediately sees through Jeff when the reporter tries to make contact, hoping to dive into the Oceanview, Washington resident's unusual goal and do a story for the magazine. That leaves the task to Darius—which is fine by Jeff; he prefers to reconnect with old flame Liz (Jenica Bergere) anyway —who approaches Kenneth at the grocery store where he works and acts as if she knows as much as he does about time-travel. She calls his ad sloppy and notes, "I hope you worked harder on your calibrations." Kenneth will need more time to decide that he trusts Darius to be by his side, but she passes his first test.

Admittedly, this plot does not hold much credibility from a journalistic perspective. Darius unethically does not reveal to Kenneth that she is reporting on him (and a story in which she is progressively involved). It is also unlikely that a publication like Seattle Magazine would be able to pay for a several-days-long trip for Jeff, Darius and fellow intern Arnau (Karan Soni) in service of a story that may turn out to be a borderline farce in the first place. Perhaps for that reason *Safety Not Guaranteed* mostly brushes aside the importance of the article in favor of the development of the relationship between Kenneth and Darius, who sees him as not some misguided crackpot but a man bold enough to pursue something others do not believe exists. When her colleagues want to focus on what could be wrong with Kenneth, Darius defends him, referencing innovators like Albert Einstein and David Bowie and noting that pursuing something new does not mean a person has something wrong with him or her.

With compassionate performances from Plaza and Duplass, the film becomes an entertaining study of cynicism and belief. First-time feature writer Derek Connolly refrains from coating the film in glossy optimism, detached from reality. Jeff learns this the hard way as he bonds with Liz, who is both surprisingly available and quietly wounded, and learns that he cannot will happy memories into a promising future. At first he is reluctant to admit that she has grown up, wanting to see her as the 18-year-old who gave him the best oral sex of his life. He eventually must admit that just because she still excels in the bedroom, and now bakes a mean strawberry rhubarb pie, does not mean that she is automatically the answer to what is missing in his life.

Likewise, *Safety Not Guaranteed* does not labor to explain the intricacies of time-travel science, though Kenneth does make more mentions of lasers and diagrams than anyone in *Looper,* the better of 2012's movies in which time travel is a vehicle for a deeper, more emotional story. *Safety* does, however, have a sense of humor about its characters' oddities, including Arnau's social awkwardness that Jeff suggests may be partially a result of his poorly chosen glasses. A good script makes good use out of supporting characters without over-relying on them for comic relief or dramatic impact, and Arnau is a perfect wallflower, sweetly attempting to hit on Darius and later discovering, with Jeff's advice, that a fun night and romantic conquest may only be an attitude adjustment away. And no one gets a second chance to be young and scar-free.

At times, *Safety Not Guaranteed* feels like a familiar indie drama, barely edging past the 80-minute mark and incorporating an obscure instrument (in a late, heartbreaking scene, Kenneth sings a song while playing the zither for Darius), recently seen in 2011's *Another Earth* and a performance on the saw. Yet the fragile nature of its characters and their relationships lead to a story in which faith in unique personalities and troubled people looks a lot better than an aversion to those who take an unpaved path to happiness.

After all, Jeff at first seems like one of the more stable characters, yet his statement about his job, "It's all one school year now. No start, no finish," reveals an emptiness that foreshadows his indifference to the professional task at hand in Oceanview. Many people see adulthood as a time to zone out, get through the day without enthusiasm and forget any inclination toward something special or wondrous. "Have you ever stared fear and danger in the eye and said yes?" Kenneth asks. How many average Americans can say they do that even once in a given year?

That does not mean anyone should feel encouraged to embrace great risk at all times. Yet through the bond of two people at least open to the possibility that they could go back in time, *Safety Not Guaranteed* sweetly taps into the open-minded trust required for any couple to move forward together into uncharted territory.

Matt Pais

CREDITS

Darius: Aubrey Plaza
Jeff: Jake M. Johnson
Arnau: Karan Soni
Kenneth: Mark Duplass
Liz: Jenica Bergere
Origin: United States
Language: English
Released: 2012
Production: Stephanie Langhoff, Peter Saraf, Marc Turtletaub, Colin Trevorrow, Derek Connolly; released by Duplass Brothers Productions, Big Beach Films
Directed by: Colin Trevorrow
Written by: Derek Connolly
Cinematography by: Benjamin Kasulke
Music by: Ryan Miller
Sound: Eric Johnson
Music Supervisor: Marguerite Phillips
Editing: Joe Landauer; Franklin Peterson
Art Direction: Lisa B. Hammond
Costumes: Rebecca Luke
Production Design: Ben Blankenship
MPAA rating: R
Running time: 86 minutes

REVIEWS

Adams, Sam. *AV Club.* June 6, 2012.
Chang, Justin. *Variety.* June 4, 2012.
Ebert, Roger. *Chicago Sun-Times.* June 13, 2012.
Goodykoontz, Bill. *Arizona Republic.* June 14, 2012.
Phillips, Michael. *Chicago Tribune.* June 14, 2012.
Pols, Mary. *Time.* June 7, 2012.
Puig, Claudia. *USA Today.* June 14, 2012.
Rea, Stephen. *Philadelphia Inquirer.* June 14, 2012.
Scott, Mike. *New Orleans Times-Picayune.* June 22, 2012.
Williams, Joe. *St. Louis Post-Dispatch.* June 22, 2012.

QUOTES

Darius: "I have no funk. I'm totally funkless."

TRIVIA

The part of Darius was written specifically for Aubrey Plaza, because writer Derek Connolly wanted to work with her.

AWARDS

Ind. Spirit 2013: First Screenplay
Nominations:
Ind. Spirit 2013: First Feature

SALMON FISHING IN THE YEMEN

Box Office: $9 millon

For the better part of a decade the name Lasse Hallstrom used to mean something very specific, if also a bit ethereal. Though *My Life as a Dog* (1987), for which he received the first of his two Best Director Academy Award nominations, was the Swedish-born filmmaker's introduction to many American arthouse fans, it was his sensitive touch with actors, as evidenced in *What's Eating Gilbert Grape* (1993) and *Something to Talk About* (1995), that helped make him an in-demand commodity. Five movies over the next seven years, starting with his adaptations of *The Cider House Rules* (1999) and the treacly *Chocolat* (2000) and ending with the bloated farce *Casanova* (2005), made Hallstrom perhaps the go-to filmmaker for awards-bait-type projects of precious sentimentality and literary leanings. If he did not quite have the stamp of an auteur who wrote his own projects, he certainly had a similar imprimatur.

The confines of that perhaps self-imposed perception of Hallstrom began to change, by degrees, with the roguish *The Hoax* (2007), based on the true story of an author, Clifford Irving (Richard Gere), who in the early 1970s faked a collaborative autobiography of the reclusive Howard Hughes. Though not a hit, the movie was spry and darkly comedic, and actually fun. For the first time in many years, Hallstrom seemed able to marshal and orchestrate bittersweet, dramatic and even cheeky elements in a meaningful and believable way.

Salmon Fishing in the Yemen, Hallstrom's latest movie, is an additional example of the director's gift with commingled tonalities when given a strong script. A lovely little story told in equally lovely fashion, it is another adaptation, in this case of British author Paul Torday's critically acclaimed 2006 debut novel. But it feels loose-limbed, genuine and alive in a manner absent from much of Hallstrom's stuffy mid-career work. While it did not set the Stateside box office on fire during its spring theatrical exhibition via neophyte distributor CBS Films, topping out at just over $9 million in a platform release that included 524 theaters at its peak, the film grossed a robust $25 million overseas, and should certainly remain a popular catalogue title, owing to its appealing cast and wistful romantic charm, if not its unusual title.

The story centers on Dr. Alfred Jones (Ewan McGregor), a fisheries expert with the British Civil Service who is tasked with overseeing an unlikely international outreach project that the Prime Minister's hard-charging press secretary, Patricia Maxwell (Kristin Scott Thomas), believes will simultaneously serve as a feel-good human interest story of ever-improving relations with an Arab nation while also distracting the public from dark and troubling news related to ongoing war in the Middle East. Visionary Sheik Muhammed (Amr Waked) is a passionate salmon fly-fisher. Believing that importing this pastime can help enrich the lives of his people and promote peace and spiritual reflection, he desires to construct a damned freshwater tributary in the not-so-friendly Yemeni desert, and tasks his special representative, Harriet Chetwode-Talbot (Emily Blunt), to spare no expense in turning his outlandish dream into a reality.

Practical-minded and somewhat posh, Alfred initially does not see how any of this is possible, but Patricia exerts bureaucratic pressure that keeps him assigned to the job, and eventually Alfred starts to warm to the steep challenges the undertaking presents. When they begin working together, both Alfred and Harriet also have significant others—in the form of Alfred's wife, Mary (Rachael Stirling), and Robert Mayers (Tom Mison), an air force captain with whom Harriet is involved who gets sent to fight in Afghanistan. But as they spend longer periods of time on site trying to help bring Sheik Muhammed's vision to life, they start to develop an attraction to one another.

Some of the book's merrily satirical assault on political hypocrisy is sacrificed for the gauzy, soft-centered amorous awakening between Alfred and Harriet—something of a specialty for Hallstrom. And McGregor's character is older in the novel, while Thomas' character is a man. But Oscar-winning screenwriter Simon Beaufoy wonderfully juggles a clutch of disparate elements, in part because he seems to have such a good grasp of these wildly different worlds. A pinch of throwback chastity and spitfire dialogue further enlivens the conceit, giving the clashing-of-wills jousting and eventual romantic bloom between Alfred and Harriet depth and vigor. This is not a lazy romance where boy and girl merely fall into one another's arms.

Beaufoy also nails the material's connection to the real world; *Salmon Fishing in the Yemen* is just as political as it needs to be, and not an ounce more. He shows the sheik grappling with fundamentalists who view his efforts as an affront to God, but does not get bogged down in deep religious or cultural divides, instead sketching out faith in parallel metaphorical fashion, through Alfred's growing belief that farm-raised salmon can and eventually will actually "run," and swim impulsively upstream. In assaying whether money really can buy everything, the movie tacitly underscores whether that capitalistic tack is always right, without tipping over into heavy-handed speechifying.

The film's technical package is also quite handsome and accomplished. Cinematographer Terry Stacey has a unique way of capturing wide open vistas without contravening or compromising character, most notably on display previously in writer-director Bart Freundlich's *World Traveler* (2001), and here he delivers an inviting, visually pleasing balance of point-of-view cinematography and wide shots. The movie's location shooting—in England and Scotland, with Morocco substituting for Yemen—gives it an authentic flavor and production value, and Hallstrom and production designer Michael Carlin furthermore find smart, economical ways to contrast Alfred's old office life with the great outdoors.

Also worth mentioning is the fact that it is revealed that Alfred has Asperger Syndrome. McGregor wonderfully embodies the social awkwardness that comes along with this diagnosis. Refreshingly, though, Hallstrom's film does not pivot and over-invest in this trait, morphing into a mawkish, malady-of-the-month movie. Blunt is a delight, and has a great rapport and chemistry with McGregor. Given the degree to which the more assertive Harriet drives and defines their relationship, the movie provides another showcase for her equally adept touch with drama and comedy.

It may not quite track along the most conventional romantic comedy lines, and at first blush neither does its setting sound like something in which mainstream American audiences might have much interest. But *Salmon Fishing in the Yemen* is a movie whose currents and rhythms feel always legitimate and true, reflective of the complications of real life, and how unlikely adventure can lie just around the bend. Adults and art-house fans will be hard-pressed to find a more winning and sophisticated romantic dramedy from this year.

Brent Simon

CREDITS

Dr. Alfred Jones: Ewan McGregor
Harriet Chetwode-Talbot: Emily Blunt
Patricia Maxwell: Kristin Scott Thomas
Sheikh: Amr Waked
Mary Jones: Rachael Stirling
Origin: British Virgin Islands
Language: English
Released: 2011
Production: Paul Webster; BBC Films, Davis Films, Kudos Film and Televison, Lionsgate, U.K. Film Council; released by CBS Films

Directed by: Lasse Hallstrom
Written by: Simon Beaufoy
Cinematography by: Terry Stacey
Music by: Dario Marianelli
Sound: Harry Barnes
Music Supervisor: Maggie Rodford
Editing: Lisa Gunning
Art Direction: Steve Carter; Nicki McCallum
Costumes: Jane Marcantonio
Production Design: Michael Carlin
MPAA rating: PG-13
Running time: 112 minutes

REVIEWS

Anderson, John. *Newsday.* March 16, 2012.
Bowles, Scott. *USA Today.* March 15, 2012.
Debruge, Peter. *Variety.* March 5, 2012.
Gleiberman, Owen. *Entertainment Weekly.* March 7, 2012.
Holden, Stephen. *New York Times.* March 8, 2012.
Hornaday, Ann. *Washington Post.* March 8, 2012.
Morris, Wesley. *Boston Globe.* March 8, 2012.
Phillips, Michael. *Chicago Tribune.* March 8, 2012.
Rainer, Peter. *Christian Science Monitor.* March 9, 2012.
Taylor, Ella. *NPR.* March 8, 2012.

QUOTES

Dr. Alfred Jones: "When things get tricky in my life, I talk to my fish."

TRIVIA

Actor Ewan McGregor had to learn the art of fly fishing for his role as Dr. Alfred Jones.

AWARDS

Nominations:

Golden Globes 2013: Actor—Mus./Comedy (McGregor), Actress—Mus./Comedy (Blunt), Film—Mus./Comedy

SAMSARA

Box Office: $2.7 million

A passion project inspired by the ambitiousness of planet Earth, *Samsara* is a rare, massive movie that is able to wrap itself around the hugeness of this world. Titled after the Sanskrit word for "the ever-turning wheel of life," *Samsara* is a highly cinematic documentary with only its poetic connections between its building block images creating a driving "narrative" based on the movie's themes. In this regard, it is similar to something like composer Franz Liszt's tone poems, in which he made music not to conceive a specific thought in the audience, but to inspire meditation on the thematic association of juxtaposing elements being put together as one. Educating viewers with worldwide truths of modern existence without indicating by text the location being shown, *Samsara* widens the audience's perspective to a sense of universality between these subjects of extremely different backgrounds.

Filmed in twenty five different countries over the course of five years, *Samsara* is the most successful film to be released by budding independent company Oscilloscope Laboratories, topping *We Need to Talk About Kevin*'s (2011) domestic total of $1.7 million. It is the work of filmmaker duo director/cinematographer Ron Fricke and producer Mark Magidson, whose previous project together was *Baraka*, released in 1992. Their first collaboration was the shorter *Chronos* (1985), which marked Fricke's first time as director, having previously worked as writer, editor and cinematographer for the landmark film *Koyaanisqatsi* (1982). That cult hit reignited the landscape for documentaries like *Chronos* and *Baraka*, establishing a following for filmgoers interested in catching glimpses of extremely diverse cultures, often with the presentation of time-lapse cinematography.

Setting its meditative scene with images of a sand mandala being meticulously created grain-by-grain by Buddhist monks in Ladakh, India, *Samsara* soon takes its vamping on life, death, and rebirth to worldwide perspective. With wholly gorgeous cinematography in which no shot is wasted, *Samsara* captures the wordless grandiosity of stunning sights like domestic buildings eroded by Hurricane Katrina, the busy shuffling of factory workers as they enter the gates for another day at a Chinese food packaging plant, or an African funeral in which a man's coffin is the shape of a revolver. Mixing in images of human beings staring into the camera (and only "performing" for it when doing performance art, such as the Dance of 1000 Hands, or the wild work of Olivier de Sagazan), *Samsara* becomes a hypnotic survey of worldwide landscapes, those of man and nature.

Amongst its many observances, *Samsara* takes an effectively eerie look into the growing reach that artificiality has in modern society, mixing together images of androids that are clones of their creators, headless sex dolls, and dancing Thai transvestites (credited as "The Ladyboys of Cascade Bar"). This becomes one of the leading fascinations of the film that sets it apart from its predecessors, as it enhances the interest Fricke seems to have with assembly lines, and the general image compositions of the masses moving back and forth in specific directions.

Samsara receives distinctness in its sequences with its choice of music, as led by musical director Michael Sterns. The soundtrack for the film goes beyond the atmospheric mush in *Baraka*, and allows sequences to have contrasting, unique colors. For example, the usage of the mournful, simple song "Kothbiro" by Ayub Ogada has particularly haunting usage in a sequence that presents a world ready for war, as the film mourns a society of death that has many clenching their guns, or standing on one side of a dividing wall with tight fists. In a different moment, an opposing strong pigment is achieved from a driving percussion beat that adds great urgency to one of the film's assembly line sequences. And in the same film, there is the presence of loud dance music, accompanied by a performance by hundreds of inmates at the Cebu Detention Center in the Philippines.

Such scenes show maturity in the authorship of Fricke, as with *Samsara* he has learned what any successful technical filmmaker seems to realize—that emotion is inherently more resonant than spectacle. Though packed with their own beauty, Fricke's films before *Samsara* can be too guilty of mood monotony, focused too much on presenting the labored aesthetic more than anything else. *Samsara* even returns to images captured in previous films (some of the same pyramids, cathedrals, and canyons make cameos), but with stronger emotional context. Thus, while *Samsara* is the most universal, it is also the most admiring of Fricke's heavily labored films.

Though it is a unique film in style, *Samsara* is still a documentary constructed by select point of view. As encompassing as the film may be, it is certainly still a project that specifically selects its imagery, and how to connect them all together. Thus, whereas the images are captured by matter-of-fact cinematography, the editing of the film has strongly opinionated moments, which could be polarizing to some viewers. In two sequences, one involving the manufacturing of pistols and the other featuring the manufacturing of food for a massive population, the scenes are sure to have codas in which the destructiveness of such elements are presented—a hard cut shows a wounded soldier in a war graveyard, and an obese trio of Burger King customers are shown eating large servings in a time lapse, respectively. More so than other moments, these sequences (however beautiful) are driving towards a specific point which may be distracting to the uninhibited meditative quality the movie, or on the other hand, such could be empowering to those who see *Samsara* as fully expressive of truth.

As it photographs such unofficial wonders of the world, *Samsara* is itself an incredible spectacle to witness. Similar to its images of hundreds of children performing syncopated karate moves at China's Shao Lin Academy, or thousands of worshippers swirling around the Kaaba in Mecca, Saudi Arabia, the cinematic capturing of such wonders in such unique environments holds an equally artistic impressiveness. The phenomena are entirely natural, their presentation in *Samsara* subsequently unmodified. *Samsara* is artwork of extreme dedication, as the film uses man-made elements like natural lighting, precise framing, and time-lapses, achieving visuals considered only to be possible with the help of special effects and elaborate production design.

In a filmmaking era in which many cinematographers of various budget and set sizes are painting their artificial landscapes with digital cameras, *Samsara* is photographed entirely on the rich format of 65mm film, shot by Super Panavision 70 cameras. This is a thoroughly cinematic choice previously utilized by *West Side Story* (1961), *Lawrence of Arabia* (1962), and *2001: A Space Odyssey* (1968) before it; this technique recently received unique utilization in 2012 by director Paul Thomas Anderson for his film *The Master* (though a dwindling amount of theaters can project these films as originally intended). While *Samsara* is widely shown in the digital format of Sony 4K, the grit of the original film image is not lost in the presentation, allowing the sharp contrasts in lighting to stand true, making the choice of classic 65mm not a stubborn one, but another element of *Samsara's* contribution to purist cinema.

With no immediate parallel but to its predecessors *Baraka* and *Chronos*, *Samsara* is a film that best condenses the diversity and simultaneous universality of existence on our planet, all while triumphantly showing the remarkable potentials of human beings to create, destroy, and re-create. It is just, then, that *Samsara* would be a monumental earthly expression presented by the most encompassing and greatest form of art created by man.

Nick Allen

CREDITS

Origin: United States
Language: English
Released: 2012
Production: Mark Magidson; Magidson Films; released by Oscilloscope Films
Directed by: Ron Fricke
Written by: Ron Fricke; Mark Magidson
Cinematography by: Ron Fricke
Music by: Marcello De Francisci; Lisa Gerrard; Michael Stearns
Sound: Miguel Rivera
Editing: Ron Fricke; Mark Magidson
MPAA rating: PG-13
Running time: 102 minutes

REVIEWS

Anderson, John. *Wall Street Journal*. August 30, 2012.
Covert, Colin. *Minneapolis Star Tribune*. September 6, 2012.
Demara, Bruce. *Toronto Star*. October 4, 2012.
Ebert, Roger. *Chicago Sun-Times*. September 6, 2012.
Feeney, Mark. *Boston Globe*. September 6, 2012.
Holcomb, Mark. *Village Voice*. August 21, 2012.
Jenkins, Mark. *Washington Post*. September 14, 2012.
Marks, Ken. *New Yorker*. September 24, 2012.
Turan, Kenneth. *Los Angeles Times*. August 30, 2012.
Weitzman, Elizabeth. *New York Daily News*. August 23, 2012.

TRIVIA

This is the first feature-length film since Kenneth Branagh's *Hamlet* to be shot entirely on 70mm film.

SAVAGES

Box Office: $47.4 million

Since the massive critical and commercial failure of his wildly ambitious historical epic *Alexander* (2004), Oliver Stone has been working on a smaller scale with films that almost seem to be going out of their way to be non-controversial—films like the bland *World Trade Center* (2006), the confused *W* (2008) and the painfully unnecessary sequel *Wall Street: Money Never Sleeps* (2010). With his latest film, *Savages*, the Stone of old returns with a vengeance with this brutally violent and morally ambiguous action-drama involving a couple of freelance dope dealers, the woman that they both love (and who responds in turn), and the violent Mexican drug cartel with whom they become involved in a dark and extremely bloody battle for survival. Eschewing incisive political commentary for the kind of giddy B-movie trashiness that he brought to his cheerfully sleazy *U-Turn* (1997), Stone more than makes up for his recent mildness by packing enough bad behavior into its 133 minutes to fuel an entire slate of ordinary films. The results are not perfect and those who have never warmed to his bombastic approach in the past are unlikely to find that much has changed in the ensuing years but for everyone else, *Savages* will come across like the work of a real filmmaker and not merely the uninspired effort of someone trying to get a movie in the can in the quickest and least controversial manner imaginable.

Based on the 2010 novel of the same name by Don Winslow, *Savages* tells the story of a pair of high school buddies who have pooled their respective skill sets together to use in the drug trade. Chon (Taylor Kitsch) is a hotheaded former Navy SEAL who returned from duty in Afghanistan with a cache of high-quality marijuana seeds while Ben (Aaron Johnson) has deployed his double majors in botany and business to cultivate and market strains of dope with an almost unheard-of THC content that wins them a loyal customer base willing to pay top dollar for their product. One thing they do have in common is O (Blake Lively), the flighty beach bunny with whom they have set up an idyllic *menage a trois*. This hedonistic paradise—or at least as hedonistic as it can get when the girl involved clearly has a "no nudity" clause in her contract—is eventually interrupted when the representatives of a violent Mexican drug cartel led by the fearsome Elena (Salma Hayek) come a-calling with an offer that they probably should not refuse to acquire their boutique operation. Things are at a standstill until Elena discovers their weak spot and has O snatched from a final pilgrimage to the mall by her brutal enforcer Lado (Benicio Del Toro). From this point on, the story becomes increasingly twisted and involves such peripheral characters as a cheerfully corrupt DEA agent (John Travolta), Elena's legal representative (Demian Bachir), her estranged daughter (Sandra Echeverria) and an ending that many people are going to flat-out hate with the same passion that they brought to the abrupt finale of *The Devil Inside* (2012).

Right from the start, *Savages* finds Oliver Stone once again swinging for the fences and, as people who have been following his career over the years can no doubt attest, that is not always a good thing. The major flaw this time around is a question of finding the correct tone. There are a couple of different ways in which Stone and co-writers Winslow and Shane Salerno could have approached the material—they could have used it to explore the realities of the increasingly violent Mexican drug cartels and the continued failures of the so-called war on drugs or they could have conceived it as a blackly comic exploration of same that could have also taken to task the self-absorbed mindset of its heroes for ignoring the harsh realities just beyond the edges of their dream-like existence. Instead, the film tries to negotiate a middle ground between the two approaches in a move that cannot help but weaken it dramatically. On the one hand, there is a certain amount of political/social commentary to be had here and there (such as the notion of using techniques learned in Iraq to fight the drug wars back home) but since that is not the major thrust of the film, such comments, when they are made, wind up coming across as more gratuitous than incisive. On the other hand, there are plenty of opportunities for dark social satire as well but Stone seems to want us to actually like these characters to the point that he pulls these punches as well and as a result, when O narrates the events in the most air-headed manner imaginable, it appears that Stone wants viewers to take her meanderings at least semi-seriously instead of laughing them off as nothing more than drug-induced babble.

And yet, while the film does stumble in regards to the big stuff, it does have a lot going for it nevertheless. Stone is clearly having a blast making this film and that sense of fun and reckless energy can be felt throughout. This is the snappiest work that he has done in a long time and even though it clocks in at 133 minutes, the whole thing has the breakneck pace of a roller-coaster to the degree that it never feels as though it is running long. He seems to be getting an exceptionally big charge out of the scenes involving the big action beats or the grotesque tortures devised by Lado as a way of extracting information or getting rid of the competition—the few minutes of the assault on the safe house alone feature more excitement and crackerjack stunt choreography than the likes of *Battleship* (2012) and *The Amazing Spider-Man* (2012) combined. Perhaps recognizing that his lead characters (and the actors playing them) were pretty but a little dull when all was said and done, Stone has populated the supporting cast with a group of strong actors who gleefully chew the scenery throughout in the best possible way—Del Toro is both fiendish and fiendishly amusing as the enforcer, Travolta is equally amusing as the sleazy DEA agent who is constantly trying to talk himself in and out of one deal or another and Hayek, in the best part she has had in a while, is quite memorable as the bewigged cartel head with a will of iron that nevertheless has at least one soft spot after all.

Dark, deranged and very bloody, *Savages* is an example of an increasingly rare breed of film—a profoundly "R"-rated work that is aimed strictly at adults—and if nothing else, it deserves a certain amount of consideration simply because it isn't just another expensive comic-book movie, either figuratively or literally. It may be messy and ungainly in parts and it could probably use some slightly more charismatic people in the lead roles but in its best moments, it really is something to see, even if more sensitive viewers are forced to do so behind covered eyes. More importantly, it helps to serve as a reminder that Oliver Stone, despite his own weak spots and unfortunate tendencies, is still one of the most captivating pure filmmakers working today when he is fully engaged in his work. *Savages* may not be among his best films but it is the first one in a long time to hint at the peaks that he once regularly hit and the first to suggest that he could be re-ascending to those heights in the very near future.

Peter Sobczynski

CREDITS

O: Blake Lively
Chon: Taylor Kitsch

Ben: Aaron Taylor-Johnson
Lado: Benicio Del Toro
Dennis: John Travolta
Alex: Demian Bichir
Elena: Salma Hayek
Origin: United States
Language: English, French, Spanish
Released: 2012
Production: Moritz Borman, Eric Kopeloff; Relativity Media, Ixtlan Production, Onda Entertainment; released by Universal Pictures
Directed by: Oliver Stone
Written by: Oliver Stone; Shane Salerno; Don Winslow
Cinematography by: Dan(iel) Mindel
Music by: Adam Peters
Sound: Wylie Stateman; Renee Tondelli
Music Supervisor: Budd Carr
Editing: Stuart Levy; Joe Hutshing; Alex Marquez
Art Direction: Lisa Vasconcellos
Costumes: Cindy Evans
Production Design: Tomas Voth
MPAA rating: R
Running time: 131 minutes

REVIEWS

Burr, Ty. *Boston Globe*. July 5, 2012.
Corliss, Richard. *Time*. July 5, 2012.
Denby, David. *New Yorker*. July 23, 2012.
Ebert, Roger. *Chicago Sun-Times*. July 5, 2012.
Edelstein, David. *New York*. July 6, 2012.
Pais, Matt. *RedEye*. July 5, 2012.
Reed, Rex. *New York Observer*. July 12, 2012.
Rothkopf, Joshua. *Time Out New York*. July 3, 2012.
Snider, Eric D. *Film.com*. July 5, 2012.
Turan, Kenneth. *Los Angeles Times*. July 5, 2012.

QUOTES

Chon: "You're already dead. You're dead from the moment you're born. If you can accept that, you can accept anything."

TRIVIA

Oliver Stone began working on the screenplay adaptation before the book was even published.

SEARCHING FOR SUGAR MAN

Box Office: $3.3 million

Malik Bendjelloul's *Searching For Sugar Man* was as surprising a critical and commercial smash as the story it chronicled, that of a legendary folk singer who reportedly died (maybe even on stage) before he could see his star rise internationally and finally find at least a modicum of the fame that his talent dictated he should find. With an Oscar nomination for Best Documentary and a win in the same category from the Broadcast Film Critics Association, the film made over $3 million domestically, a large number for this often under-exposed genre. It was the fifth-highest grossing non-fiction film of 2012 after a deeply political piece about President Barack Obama, a family movie with the Disney label, a Katy Perry concert film, and a hot-topic film about bullying. The story of Rodriguez, an undeniable talent who disappeared in the '70s after never finding the level of fame to which he should have climbed, is undeniably fascinating. It is a fun story with great music and so has broad appeal but the filmmaker fails to address some serious questions and the final result feels a little slighter than it otherwise might have and it is surprising that it competed critically with some of the more notable documentaries of 2012 like *The Invisible War*, *The Central Park Five*, and *West of Memphis*.

Sixto Diaz Rodriguez, who would go by only his last name as a recording artist, was born in Detroit, Michigan in the '40s. After working clubs and honing his craft, Rodriguez released two albums, *Cold Fact* (1970) and *Coming From Reality* (1971). Bendjelloul does an excellent job in the opening scenes of *Searching For Sugar Man* of making the case that Rodriguez was a true talent. He allows large sections of Rodriguez's music to play, often over animated scenes of a solitary figure walking through a snowy, urban landscape. The implication is that Rodriguez was a singer/songwriting talent on the level of Bob Dylan and songs like "Crucify My Mind," "Cause," and "Inner City Blues" make that case better on their own more than any talking head interview possibly could do.

Searching For Sugar Man quickly turns from the music to the legend. Stories abounded that Rodriguez killed himself on stage but no one knew exactly where he had gone or who he really was in the first place. It is likely that the legend of Rodriguez would have stayed myth if the man's two recordings had not become massive hits in, of all places, South Africa. Rodriguez's music became anthemic in the fight against apartheid and his songwriting skills spoke to an entire generation of young people battling old beliefs. A few South African men tried to pin down the man who inspired their country, trying to trace the money from sales of Rodriguez's work back to the man or at least his family but hitting a brick wall. They even started to parse his lyrics for signs of where he grew up or where he might be. Ultimately, they discovered the truth about Rodriguez and started another amazing chapter in his story.

There are some elements of Rodriguez's story that feel inherently cinematic and they go a long way to making *Searching For Sugar Man* an artistic success. Bendjelloul makes some very smart decisions, including focusing heavily on Rodriguez's music (actual songs make up at least forty percent of the film) and allowing a lot of screen time to interviews with the man's well-spoken, beautiful daughters. However, one cannot help shake the feeling that it is the story of *Sugar Man* and not the filmmaking that distinguishes it. Great documentarians shape their story and do not merely film it, and it feels like a few notes were missed here including questions as to where royalties from Rodriguez's South African fame went, why he never became famous in the States (some raise the specter of racism given his name but it is never followed up on), and why he walked away. Ultimately, the focus seems to be on a very heartwarming idea—staying true to oneself is all that matters and that the cream will always rise to the top... or, in this case, the sugar.

Critics fell in love with *Searching For Sugar Man* with some notable names even placing it on their top ten films of 2012. Michael Phillips of the *Chicago Tribune* put it on his best of the year, saying in his review, "At 85 minutes, it's a tight, sharp achievement, yet one of the things I love about it is simple: It moves to a relaxed rhythm, in sync with its slightly otherworldly subject." Roger Ebert said in the *Chicago Sun-Times*, "I hope you're able to see this film. You deserve to. And yes, it exists because we need for it to." Mr. Ebert is getting at something essential about the success of *Sugar Man* in that it is as heartwarming as documentaries get. Everyone hopes that true talent will someday be recognized, even if it is halfway around the world.

Brian Tallerico

CREDITS

Origin: United States
Language: English
Released: 2012
Production: Simon Chinn, Malik Bendjelloul; Red Box Films, Passion Pictures; released by Sony Pictures Classics
Directed by: Malik Bendjelloul
Written by: Malik Bendjelloul
Cinematography by: Camilla Skagerstrom
Sound: Malik Bendjelloul
Editing: Malik Bendjelloul
MPAA rating: PG-13
Running time: 85 minutes

REVIEWS

Burr, Ty. *Boston Globe.* August 9, 2012.

Dargis, Manohla. *New York Times.* July 26, 2012.
Ebert, Roger. *Chicago Sun-Times.* August 9, 2012.
Goss, William. *Film.com.* March 20, 2012.
Puig, Claudia. *USA Today.* July 26, 2012.
Sachs, Ben. *Chicago Reader.* August 9, 2012.
Schwarzbaum, Lisa. *Entertainment Weekly.* July 25, 2012.
Sharkey, Betsy. *Los Angeles Times.* July 26, 2012.
Taylor, Ella. *NPR.* July 26, 2012.
Travers, Peter. *Rolling Stone.* July 26, 2012.

QUOTES

Rick Emmerson: "He had this kind of magical quality that all the genuine poets and artists have: to elevate things. To get above the mundane, the prosaic. All the bullsh*t. All the mediocrity that's everywhere. The artist, the artist is the pioneer."

TRIVIA

Some parts of the documentary were shot on an iPhone App called 8mm Vintage Camera after the producers ran out of film for an expensive real 8mm camera.

AWARDS

Oscars 2012: Feature Doc.
British Acad. 2012: Feature Doc.
Directors Guild 2012: Documentary Director (Bendjelloul)
Writers Guild 2012: Documentary Screenplay

THE SECRET WORLD OF ARRIETTY

(Kari-gurashi no Arietti)

Do not be seen by humans. That's been the law of children of the underfloor.
—Movie tagline

Box Office: $19.2 million

In this day and age when animation has made such gigantic leaps and bounds in terms of technology, it is a bit of a miracle that something as old-fashioned as Studio Ghibli exists. The Japanese animation studio has been responsible for some of the most poetic and startling animated movies of the last twenty or thirty years and to this day it has not broken stride from its ability to make thought-provoking, gentle and moving animated films. Not content to just pander to children's most base interests or to gain mainstream relevance by utilizing a hip soundtrack or clever sight gags (as their contemporaries often do), Ghibli exists on more of an intellectual level that is both engaging to children and challenging to grown-ups who might not be used to such flights of fancy dictating the storylines.

Even more miraculous is their ability to maintain this vision while still utilizing single cell animation instead of computer based images. Every frame is hand-drawn by a human being with a pen or marker in their hand. They continue to craft stories concerned with family bonding, love, the environment, adolescent growth, and community, and they do so with simplicity, grace, and a respect for all audiences.

The Secret World of Arrietty is based on the beloved book *The Borrowers* by Mary Norton. It tells the story of a house where there lives a family of tiny people about the size of crickets who live in secret within the walls and crevices. When they need food, clothing or a small, handy household item, they "borrow" it and the regular-sized humans who inhabit the house are left to wonder where their clothespins are or why their salt shakers are slightly less full even though they have not used them in weeks. The borrowers see it as their right to take whatever they need and that human beings (or "human beans," as they call them) exist on this earth to serve them even though the borrowers must stay out of their sight.

The story centers around Shawn (voiced by David Henrie), a boy who has just moved into this particular house. His Aunt Jessica (voiced by Gracie Poletti) brings him to live with her and Miss Hara (voiced by Carol Burnett) where he can get better treatment for his heart condition. His parents, as he tells it, are too busy to deal with his current state. They are in the midst of a divorce and he spends most of his time in bed. Miss Hara is suspicious that something odd is happening in the house. She enlists the help of an exterminator. Still, Aunt Jessica and Miss Hara know a thing or two about the borrowers.

The borrowers consist of Homily (voiced by Amy Poehler), Pod (voiced by Will Arnett) and Arrietty (voiced by Bridgit Mendler), their 14-year-old daughter. They have made a comfortable life for themselves within this house. Arrietty is about to have a rite-of-passage, her first borrowing. Her parents are understandably worried about letting her go out on her own, especially after she is almost seen by Shawn. While on her first borrowing mission with her father, they happen upon a doll-house that would fit them perfectly if they could inhabit it. "Borrowers only take what they need," her father tells her.

Later on, she and her father come in contact with Shawn in his bedroom, but flee before he can actually see them. Shawn calls out to them that he knows they are there and that his mother used to tell him stories about "the little people." The next day, Shawn goes out

to an area of the house where he believes the borrowers reside and leaves a sugar cube for them as a way of inviting them into the open. The adventurous Arrietty is all too eager to accept the invitation even as her parents forbid her to make anymore contact. Arrietty tells Shawn to leave them alone and that they will have to move if too many people know about them. Shawn means well and wants them to stay. A friendship between Arrietty and Shawn develops while Arrietty's parents talk of moving away.

The director, Hiromasa Yonebayashi, making his debut after years in the Ghibli art department, tells a gentle fable in which so many things conspire to keep Arrietty and Shawn from developing a lasting friendship. Even as the story deals with elements of fantasy, danger and enchantment, the overall sadness of the story is never far from sight. Studio Ghibli have often let their stories venture into the surreal, sometimes at the expense of the audience's ability to understand everything at face value. *The Secret World of Arrietty* is one of their more straightforward efforts, but that is not to say it lacks depth. It has the feeling of an old-fashioned storybook fantasy that one's parents might read before bedtime.

Yonebayashi's film is more in tune with Mary Norton's first book than the live action *The Borrowers* (1997) staring John Goodman. That film, which was cute, but forgettable, was more comedic in tone. This is a far richer and faithful film. The American voice work for these films is usually pretty strong and consists of big name actors to help lure people into the multiplexes. The only bit of miscasting is that of Henri as Shawn, who sounds a little too old for this part. Still, it is a minor hiccup in an otherwise beautiful and rewarding film that serves as another gift from a studio that remains true to its origins while never resting on their laurels.

Collin Souter

CREDITS

Arrietty Clock: Bridgit Mendler (Voice)
Shawn: David Henrie (Voice)
Homily Clock: Amy Poehler (Voice)
Pod Clock: Will Arnett (Voice)
Hara: Carol Burnett (Voice)
Spiller: Moises Arias (Voice)
Origin: Japan, United States
Language: English
Released: 2010
Production: Frank Marshall, Kathleen Kennedy, Toshio Suzuki; Dentsu, Hakuhodo DY Media Partners, Nippon Television Network, Studio Ghibli; released by Walt Disney Pictures
Directed by: Gary Rydstrom; Hiromasa Yonebayashi

Written by: Karey Kirkpatrick; Hayao Miyazaki; Keiko Niwa
Cinematography by: Atsushi Okui
Music by: Cecile Corbel
Sound: Koji Kasamatsu
Editing: Rie Matsuhara
Art Direction: Youji Takeshige; Noboru Yoshida
MPAA rating: G
Running time: 94 minutes

REVIEWS

Buckwalter, Ian. *The Atlantic*. February 7, 2012.
Burr, Ty. *Boston Globe*. February 16, 2012.
Guzman, Rafer. *Newsday*. February 17, 2012.
Hills, Aaron. *Village Voice*. February 14, 2012.
Long, Tom. *Detroit News*. February 17, 2012.
Lumenick, Lou. *New York Post*. February 17, 2012.
Robinson, Tahsa. *AV Club*. February 16, 2012.
Schwarzbaum, Lisa. *Entertainment Weekly*. February 15, 2012.
Sobczynski, Peter. *eFilmcritic.com*. February 16, 2012.
Turan, Kenneth. *Los Angeles Times*. February 16, 2012.

QUOTES

Sho: "You came back. Wait, don't go."
Arietty: "Please, leave us alone. I wanted to tell you that."
Sho: "I want to talk to you."
Arietty: "Human beings are dangerous. If we're seen, we have to leave. My parents said so."

TRIVIA

This is the fourth feature film from Studio Ghibli to not be directed by either Hayao Miyazaki or studio co-founder Isao Takahata.

SEEKING A FRIEND FOR THE END OF THE WORLD

Nice knowing you.
—Movie tagline

The end is coming soon.
—Movie tagline

The first comedy about the end of it all.
—Movie tagline

Box Office: $7.1 million

Incredulity would be an understandable reaction to news that a colossal asteroid is about to collide with Earth, potently punctuating the story of mankind with one very final period. It is also a wholly reasonable response to the excessively-effusive sentiments exchanged by *Seeking a Friend for the End of the World*'s ephemeral odd couple as just such a catastrophe is about to occur. At the eleventh hour, a middle-aged, listless sad sack filled with regret by the name of Dodge (Steve Carell) finds his lucky Penny (Keira Knightley), a younger, ebullient, bohemian Brit, and it is like pairing a Mourning Dove with the Bluebird of Happiness. It is not impossible to accept that the two could fortuitously become "Best Friends Forever" while facing such disconcertingly-finite circumstances together, deeply appreciating the other's presence during their mutually-beneficial road trip before arriving with the rest of the world at a truly dead end. However, when their journey bypasses fond, compassionate and convivial companionship and winds up skidding on syrupy declarations of romantic devotion, even those who had been moderately enjoying the ride up to that point were likely stopped short by such unctuousness.

Seeking a Friend for the End of the World is not a nail-biter during which a grand, gallant Hail Mary attempt to save the planet is launched skyward as the days dwindle down. It does not try to blow viewers away with jaw-droppingly-rendered depictions of cities submerged under towering tidal waves or engulfed in cataclysmic conflagrations. "Oceans rise. Cities fall. Hope survives." was the melodramatic tagline for *Deep Impact* (1998), but *Seeking a Friend* takes place just as last-ditch efforts have failed and all hope is gone. The film zeroes-in to hypothesize about the effects of another profound jolt: the discombobulating blow to the human psyche upon learning that Armageddon imminently, inexorably approaches.

While humanity learns that it has precious little to look forward to as *Seeking a Friend for the End of the World* begins, most moviegoers found themselves cautiously optimistic about what was to come. A deft characterization is drawn of Dodge, a man who likely looked like the world was coming to an end even before it actually was. After hearing on his car radio that there will be no avoiding the asteroid (listeners are enticed to stay tuned for a countdown of their all-time favorite songs during the countdown to the end of days), Dodge's wife contemptuously shoots him a glacial glance before abruptly ditching her drag of a husband and heading off to her heart's desire. Time is unquestionably of the essence, and the woman apparently cannot bear to settle a second longer for dull decency and secure stagnancy. (One chuckles upon learning that not only is she played by Carell's real-life wife, Nancy, but that the scene was filmed on their wedding anniversary).

What follows are effectively-satirical scenes that contrast the very different ways in which people might attempt to cope. Some shut down, robotically trudging on in denial with their usual day-to-day tasks if they do not simply dive despondently off a balcony. (Viewers will likely scoff at the absurd futility of those arduously pumping iron to preserve buff physiques or carefully maintaining lawns with eco-friendly mowers.) Others act up, either going out to rampage and loot or inviting friends over for no-holds-barred bacchanalian abandon as casually as they used to for backyard barbeques. Dodge, ironically employed in the insurance industry, belongs to the first group, dutifully droning on to potential customers about the "Armageddon Package" until he cannot keep his tamped-down angst from surfacing along with his lunch. His friends Warren (Rob Corddry) and Diane (Connie Britton), a couple decidedly belonging in the second category, throw an unbridled bash replete with heroin, vodka, and fireworks that affords their minor children the opportunity to try and handle at least two of the three. Along with Roache (Patton Oswalt), who comically if crudely details how women's standards are plummeting as precipitously as the asteroid, the pair urge Dodge to amorously seize more than just the day. However, the devastatingly-timed desertion of his wife and the subsequent revelation of her adultery have been earth-shattering in terms of Dodge's own world, and thus his broken heart would just not be in it. True to his name, decent, carefully-contained, cuckolded Dodge plays it safe and resists any licentious involvement.

Dodge obviously needs to come alive before he dies, and the symbolism is clear when he decides to open a window in his apartment and lets in Penny, the stranger who will be a delightful, revivifying breath of fresh air. She has a medical condition that makes it exceedingly difficult for Dodge to wake her up, and one guesses that it will likely be as daunting a task for her to rouse this yawn of a man who has essentially been sleepwalking through his life. Yet the eyes of both characters gradually open to see each other in a way that neither had expected during their intermittently-involving, contrivance-assisted quest that proceeds down a rom-com route with surprisingly little urgency. Dodge wants to end up in the arms of the high school sweetheart he regretfully opted not to marry, and drives to the woman's home in a loaner Penny procures from a handily-located ex-boyfriend (Derek Luke) who is set to hunker down in a bunker. Penny's hope to be with her beloved family back in England hinges on Dodge's possible procurement of a private plane, which turns out to be piloted by the estranged father (an uncredited Martin Sheen) with whom he will all-too-smoothly and sappily reconcile in the nick of time. (Another visit along the way is a much better scene: Dodge and Penny stop at Friendsy's, a raucous restaurant that has ditched all decorum in anticipation of doomsday and now more than lives up to its name. There, a wanton waitress at-

tempts to also provide service under the table to an uncomfortable, unwilling Dodge, but the only rise she gets out of him is when he jumps up to flee.)

After a hastily-ditched note on an old love's doorstep and a sudden U-turn over the Atlantic, Dodge and Penny decide instead to curl up together for a final scene that delivers a disconcerting wallop after first wallowing in the depths of mushiness. Assertions like "You were the love of my life" and "I couldn't live without you—no matter how long!" gush forth, and while the two may simply be caught up in the moment, more than a few in the audience were unable to do the same. Some viewers did indeed find themselves gulping hard to deal with poignancy-induced lumps in their throats, but many others simply had a tough time swallowing a sudden force-feeding of too-fervent gooiness. Granted, Dodge and Penny have clearly come to enjoy and care about each other. They are deeply grateful for the indispensable solace and serenity that their time together has provided. At one point, proximity has understandably led to passion. However, while these last days have unquestionably been meaningful to both, it was easy to balk at believing that they quite meant what screenwriter/ first-time director Lorene Scafaria wants viewers to think that they did. Made on a budget of $10 million, *Seeking a Friend for the End of the World* only succeeded in grossing $6.6 million. Critical reaction was mixed. While Dodge and Penny have achieved peaceful acceptance when the end comes, it was a stretch to ask many of those watching to arrive at the same.

David L. Boxerbaum

CREDITS

Dodge: Steve Carell
Penny: Keira Knightley
Owen: Adam Brody
Diane: Connie Britton
Warren: Rob Corddry
Karen: Melanie Lynskey
Roache: Patton Oswalt
Origin: United States
Language: English, French, Spanish
Released: 2012
Production: Steven Golin, Joy Gorman, Mark Roybal, Steven M. Rales; Anonymous Content; released by Focus Features
Directed by: Lorene Scafaria
Written by: Lorene Scafaria
Cinematography by: Tim Orr
Music by: Rob Simonsen; Jonathan Sadoff
Sound: Perry Robertson
Editing: Zene Baker

Costumes: Kristin Burke
Production Design: Chris Spellman
MPAA rating: R
Running time: 101 minutes

REVIEWS

Burr, Ty. *Boston Globe.* June 21, 2012.

Debruge, Peter. *Variety.* June 19, 2012.

Ebert, Roger. *Chicago Sun-Times.* June 20, 2012.

Holcomb, Mark. *Village Voice.* June 19, 2012.

Hornaday, Ann. *Washington Post.* June 21, 2012.

Phillips, Michael. *Chicago Tribune.* June 21, 2012.

Pols, Mary. *Time.* June 21, 2012.

Puig, Claudia. *USA Today.* June 21, 2012.

Schwarzbaum, Lisa. *Entertainment Weekly.* June 20, 2012.

Scott, A. O. *New York Times.* June 21, 2012.

QUOTES

Roache: "So, you wanna double stuff that cookie with me?"

TRIVIA

Director Lorene Scafaria appears in still photos as Olivia, the lost love of Dodge.

SEEKING JUSTICE

Vengeance always has a price.
—Movie tagline

Box Office: $411,746

It has gotten to the point where Nicolas Cage's very name carries the sure promise of bargain-basement dreck. In 2011 and 2012, Cage was featured in a total of five turkeys, including Roger Donaldson's wholly ignored action flick, *Seeking Justice.* To say the film is Cage's most watchable vehicle of this dark period, clearly driven by paycheck roles due to the actor's tax payment problems, is to say very little, considering its competition is *Season of the Witch* (2011), *Drive Angry* (2011), *Trespass* (2011), and *Ghost Rider: Spirit of Vengeance* (2012).

The Oscar-winning actor is no stranger to taking gambles with projects, but perhaps his judgment is too undiscerning. Here is a man who can bring down the house merely by reciting the alphabet (as in 1988's *Vampire's Kiss*) or staring at a hallucinated pair of iguanas (in Werner Herzog's 2009 comic masterpiece, *Bad Lieutenant: Port of Call New Orleans*). He has no business wasting his talents on a bland hybrid of the *Taken* (2008) vigilante formula and the conspiracy thriller genre.

In *Seeking Justice,* Cage is in the jittery, paranoid mode of 2006's *The Wicker Man,* albeit without the gloriously hammy, B-movie excesses. He plays Will, a New Orleans English teacher and all-around everyman who is tempted to break his moral code after his wife, Laura (January Jones), is raped and savagely beaten. At the hospital, Will is approached by a slickly shady character named Simon (played with bald-headed malevolence by Guy Pearce), who offers to have his underground vigilante group track down and murder the rapist.

Simon is so menacing in this scene that it is difficult to believe that Will would enlist his services. And yet, after an initial moment of hesitation, Will decides to make a pact with the smooth-talking devil. In order to prove that he wants Simon's help, Will is ordered to purchase two Forever Bars from a nearby vending machine within the hour. After Simon leaves, Will purchases the bars under the scrutinizing gaze of a security camera. Who is on the other end of the camera? The film does not specify.

That scene is an early example of the multitudinous lazy contrivances in Robert Tanner's screenplay. Simon's vigilante group is apparently so widespread that they can literally be anywhere at any given moment, especially if their presence is needed to conveniently advance the plot. The audience is expected to believe that Simon's cronies can repeatedly sneak silently into Will's apartment and rearrange his refrigerator magnets in order to spell out threatening messages. It soon becomes clear that Will is not the target of diabolical intruders so much as he is the victim of a script so wildly illogical that it neuters any sense of urgency or suspense.

Six months after the dirty deed is done, Simon confronts Will and asks him to murder the latest undesirable on his hit list. When Will declines, Simon warns him that "a promise is a promise." Of course, no such promise was articulated (*Strangers on a Train* [1951] this is not), thus immediately outing Simon as the psychopath that he so clearly is. It is only a matter of time before the rest of the expected plot twists fall neatly into place. Simon frames Will for murder, which requires the tireless protagonist to do a lot of running, ducking and (in the film's only memorable stunt) jumping out of the path of an oncoming truck.

This role could have benefited from some of Cage's campy flourishes, but the actor plays it with a straight face, and his humorlessness ends up contributing to the film's tedium. Yet his work is riveting when contrasted with the utter hollowness of Jones, whose blankness is passed off as "inner strength." Aside from a single instance of lip-trembling, Jones makes no attempt to convey the emotional duress of a woman attempting to

348

recuperate in the aftermath of such horrendous trauma. She is so expressionless that when she is placed in a room populated with mannequins, it is difficult to pick her out from the crowd.

Only a few choice moments in the film hint at the humor that could have been milked from this lame premise. A sequence where Will turns the tables on Simon by barking orders to him over the phone verges on self-parody. Will sternly instructs him to perform menial tasks like, "Buy a hot dog" and "Go to the men's room and take a piss," while Simon leers with aggravation. Where do these pointless instructions lead? Nowhere. Will simply approaches Simon at the hot dog stand and the scene ends. If this film were a hit, a decent *SNL* skit could have easily been inspired by this silliness.

The final scenes exploit the town's post-Katrina decay by staging a climactic gunfight in the abandoned New Orleans Centre next to the Superdome. Cage fans will undoubtedly be praying for the worlds of *Bad Lieutenant* and *Seeking Justice* to merge, thus enabling drug-addled Terence McDonagh to blow away the bad guys while musing on whether fish have dreams. Only a brilliant oddball like Herzog could have possibly made this material interesting, let alone credible. Like Cage's deadly dud, *Trespass,* this film barely registered with audiences. It opened at number twenty-seven at the U.S. box office, and went on to gross a mere $12.3 million worldwide.

Matt Fagerholm

CREDITS

Will Gerard: Nicolas Cage
Laura Gerard: January Jones
Simon: Guy Pearce
Jimmy: Harold Perrineau, Jr.
Trudy: Jennifer Carpenter
Lt. Dugan: Xander Berkeley
Alan Marsh: Jason Davis
Det. Green: Marcus Lyle Brown
Det. Rudenski: Joseph Chrest
Origin: United States
Language: English
Released: 2012
Production: James Stern, Ram Bergman, Tobey Maguire; Endgame Entertainment, Material Entertainment; released by Anchor Bay Entertainment
Directed by: Roger Donaldson
Written by: Robert Tannen; Yuri Zeltser
Cinematography by: David Tattersall
Music by: J. Peter Robinson
Sound: Pavel Wdowczak

Music Supervisor: John Houlihan
Editing: Jay Cassidy
Art Direction: Kelly Curley
Costumes: Caroline Eselin
Production Design: Dennis Washington
MPAA rating: R
Running time: 104 minutes

REVIEWS

Abele, Robert. *Los Angeles Times*. March 16, 2012.
Ebert, Roger. *Chicago Sun-Times*. March 14, 2012.
Gleiberman, Owen. *Entertainment Weekly*. March 18, 2012.
Lumenick, Lou. *New York Post*. March 16, 2012.
Rabin, Nathan. *AV Club*. March 14, 2012.
Reed, Rex. *New York Observer*. March 13, 2012.
Sachs, Ben. *Chicago Reader*. March 15, 2012.
Schager, Nick. *Slant Magazine*. March 11, 2012.
Tobias, Scott. *NPR*. March 19, 2012.
Willmore, Alison. *Movieline*. March 15, 2012.

QUOTES

Simon: "Well, if we hand him over to the police it'll take at least six months for DNA tests to be completed. Ultimately there'd be a trial, and your wife, assuming she didn't drop the charges, would be dragged through this nightmare over and over. She'd be in court, she'd be questioned by lawyers. Even if the D.A. gets a conviction, which is not guaranteed, a rapist can serve as little as eleven months, which is half the time you get for tax evasion."

AWARDS

Nominations:

Golden Raspberries 2012: Worst Actor (Cage)

THE SESSIONS
(The Surrogate)

The festival hit of the year!
—Movie tagline

Box Office: $6 million

American indies routinely favor protagonists faced with the daunting task of breaking out of their shell. For 36-year-old Mark O'Brien, his shell is more literal than most. Stricken with polio, O'Brien spends much of his days confined in an iron lung. The very notion of intimacy is as alien to him as the concept of walking. Thus, it comes as little surprise that the accomplished yet perpetually alienated man would harbor an innate desire to get laid.

Such is the set-up for Ben Lewin's *The Sessions,* a crowd-pleasing festival smash (it won the Audience Award at the 2012 Sundance Film Festival when it was titled *The Surrogate*) with a story rooted firmly in reality. The real-life O'Brien was a journalist who had no qualms about sharing his daily struggles and triumphs with readers. As a polio survivor himself, Lewin is an ideal filmmaker to tell this tale from the perspective of O'Brien, who died in 1999 at age 49. It is a heartfelt and poignant effort that manages to satisfy regardless of its flaws.

Crucial to the picture's success is its central performance from the tirelessly versatile John Hawkes. He inhabits the role of O'Brien with the same astonishing level of commitment that Daniel Day-Lewis brought to *My Left Foot* (1989). He studied Jessica Yu's Oscar-winning 1996 documentary short, *Breathing Lessons: The Life and Work of Mark O'Brien,* which he later cited as a great source of inspiration. He even attempted to replicate his character's contorted spine by lying on a large ball of foam during his scenes. Considering that Hawkes' last major role was the physically imposing, sexually predatory cult leader in Sean Durkin's *Martha Marcy May Marlene* (2011), the virginal, genial O'Brien couldn't be a further leap in the opposite direction.

Largely based on O'Brien's 1990 article, "On Seeing a Sex Surrogate," Lewin's script serves as a pleasing antidote to the sniggering sex farces designed for America's puritanical sensibilities. Sex is viewed as neither shameful nor scandalous, but as a necessity that remains essential regardless of one's disabilities. Though Fox Searchlight paid a hefty sum to distribute the picture following its spectacular success at Sundance, the studio ultimately failed to give it the wide release it deserved. An initial glance at the film's subject matter may indicate box office poison, yet the considerable achievement of *The Sessions* is its deft method for making potentially distressing material effortlessly accessible, for better and worse.

Despite his penchant for good-natured witticisms, O'Brien's paralysis has made him unable to develop much of a love life. With his desire for connection at a fever pitch, he enlists the aid of a sex surrogate after seeking the approval of his Catholic priest, Father Brendan (played with droll charm by William H. Macy). One of the film's forced comic conceits is the sight gag of O'Brien candidly confessing his primal urges to Father Brendan as his voice echoes through the church while eliciting shocked reactions from nearby worshippers. Yet the character of Father Brendan is refreshingly devoid of the smarm that accompanies so many cinematic men of the cloth. He thoughtfully contemplates O'Brien's bold request before confidently concluding that God will grant him "a free pass on this one."

The real heart of the film lies in the scenes between O'Brien and his surrogate, Cheryl Cohen-Greene (Helen Hunt), a middle-aged mother and wife who appears at her most confident and comfortable sans clothing. She treats her clients like humans rather than laboratory projects and responds to O'Brien's yelps of insecurity by gently telling him, "It's not sexy when you yell at me." She understands that sex is not merely a physical need, but an emotional and psychological one as well, though she risks leaving more than a few mental scars on her client once their six sessions have run their course. Lewin's tidily brisk denouement avoids the more troubling repercussions of Cohen-Greene's temporary union with O'Brien, while Marco Beltrami's score telegraphs every emotion with dutiful precision rendered entirely unnecessary by the uniformly fine performances.

Throwing caution to the wind with a performance that is nakedly authentic in every sense of the word, Hunt proves to be utterly luminous when she is at her most uninhibited. Moon Bloodgood is equally effective as O'Brien's devoted medical orderly who matches her client's frankness during their disarmingly honest conversations. Even character actor Ming Lo scores big laughs as a hotel clerk curious about the precise nature of O'Brien and Cohen-Greene's therapy sessions. The film is so funny and touching that many viewers will overlook its tendency to sentimentalize the material in ways that threaten to become dramatically dishonest. The obstacles and heartache that O'Brien faces are softened and skimmed over in order to keep the film's overall tone upbeat. A scene in which O'Brien is rejected by his beloved infatuation falls flat, especially when juxtaposed with the wrenching power of Day-Lewis' infamous restaurant scene in *My Left Foot.* It is a real shame since Hawkes is clearly capable of delivering a similarly well-rounded portrayal.

The Sessions is far more commercial than one would expect, especially considering how it has been virtually shut out of suburban multiplexes. The script may fall short of greatness, but it is bolstered significantly by the brilliant work of Hawkes and Hunt. Their scenes unfold like a tender comic duet tinged with bittersweet beauty. Rarely has sex appeared as endearing, empowering and vital as it does here. Critics may get caught up in its shortcomings, but most mainstream audiences are bound to give it a free pass.

Matt Fagerholm

CREDITS

Mark O'Brien: John Hawkes
Cheryl Cohen-Green: Helen Hunt
Father Brendan: William H. Macy

Vera: Moon Bloodgood
Rod: W. Earl Brown
Amanda: Annika Marks
Origin: United States
Language: English
Released: 2012
Production: Stephen Nemeth, Judith Levine, Ben Lewin; So Much Films, Rhino Films; released by Fox Searchlight
Directed by: Ben Lewin
Written by: Ben Lewin
Cinematography by: Geoffrey Simpson
Music by: Marco Beltrami
Sound: Marty Kasparian
Editing: Lisa Bromwell
Costumes: Justine Seymour
Production Design: John Mott
MPAA rating: R
Running time: 95 minutes

REVIEWS

Debruge, Peter. *Variety*. October 13, 2012.
Ebert, Roger. *Chicago Sun-Times*. October 24, 2012.
Edelstein, David. *New York Magazine (Vulture)*. October 15, 2012.
Kohn, Eric. *indieWIRE*. October 18, 2012.
LaSalle, Mick. *San Francisco Chronicle*. October 25, 2012.
Lumenick, Lou. *New York Post*. October 19, 2012.
McCarthy, Todd. *Hollywood Reporter*. October 13, 2012.
Persall, Steve. *Tampa Bay Times*. November 14, 2012.
Phillips, Michael. *Chicago Tribune*. October 25, 2012.
Rabin, Nathan. *AV Club*. October 13, 2012.

QUOTES

Mark O'Brien: "I believe in a God with a sense of humor. I would find it absolutely intolerable not to be to able blame someone for all this."

TRIVIA

Actor John Hawkes had to use a cushion under one side of his back in order have the appearance of an arched and distorted spine.

AWARDS

Ind. Spirit 2013: Actor (Hawkes), Actress—Supporting (Hunt)
Nominations:
Oscars 2012: Actress—Supporting (Hunt)
British Acad. 2012: Actress—Supporting (Hunt)
Golden Globes 2013: Actor—Drama (Hawkes), Actress—Supporting (Hunt)
Screen Actors Guild 2012: Actor (Hawkes), Actress—Supporting (Hunt)

SEVEN PSYCHOPATHS

They won't take any shih-tzu.
—Movie tagline

No te metas con el perro (Don't mess with the dog).
—Movie tagline

Box Office: $15 million

Martin McDonagh has made a successful career exploring darkly comic situations involving violence on the English stage. After numerous awards and Tony nominations, he brought his talents to film with *Six Shooter* (2006), which won the Oscar for Best Live Action Short Film. Two years later he would team up again with the star of that short, Brendan Gleeson, for his feature debut, *In Bruges* (2008), a standard hitman thriller in the hands of most directors. But in McDonagh's it felt like a melange of quirk, inventiveness and unexpected pathos that earned him another Oscar nomination for Best Original Screenplay. One would imagine that such an acclaimed resume would leave little room for self-doubt in McDonagh's abilities. Though in his sophomore effort, McDonagh explores just that while leaving very little doubt in his new audience that he is the real deal.

Marty (Colin Farrell) is having a little trouble starting his new screenplay. He has the title, *Seven Psychopaths,* but it would help to know just precisely who those magnificent bastards were. His best friend, Billy (Sam Rockwell), is a struggling actor who would like nothing more than to help Marty, though his friend's reluctance gives him time for his day job—kidnapping dogs. Along with his partner, Hans (Christopher Walken), Billy nabs the pooches in broad daylight and, after waiting for a reward to be posted, show up with the pet unharmed and humbly collect the money. One day, however, they nab the wrong dog.

This cute little Shih Tzu belongs to Charlie (Woody Harrelson), a gangster who loves his doggie even more than the unscrupulous manner in which he dispatches those who cross him. As the net closes in on them, Billy, Hans and Marty must hit the road in order to survive while fiction and reality also begin to collide in their own minds. Marty already has his own set of problems including a tired girlfriend (Abbie Cornish), another potential real-life psychopath (Tom Waits) willing to provide inspiration, and a love of the drink that is a constant source of intervention for his friends. Billy, meanwhile, has his own lady on the side to appease (Olga Kurylenko) and believes a local avenger taking out bad guys left and right could be the key to sparking Marty's inspiration.

McDonagh's screenplay takes some time in comforting audiences that it has a grander direction than just a series of seemingly random events of violence. After a hilariously off-kilter opening scene, McDonagh keeps the plotting to a minimum while cleverly establishing the relationship to his three protagonists. Much the same way he did with *In Bruges*, he is beholden to his characters first and foremost and then allows the story to find itself. In the case of *Seven Psychopaths*, he does it literally.

Marty's writer's block leads him to not just individual stories within the greater collective of his own screenplay but even the legendary tales of those folks he has surrounded himself with. With a prime number of psychopaths to fill, one is easily open to draw inspiration from avenging serial killers—or even take advice from them. It is too much of a coincidence that Farrell is playing an Irish screenwriter with the same name as his creator. Once a stable objective is created in the journey of Marty and Co., McDonagh is free again to play with the expectations of the genre's tradition. Almost as if borrowing a cue from the more commercially-minded Donald Kaufman of Charlie Kaufman's script for *Adaptation* (2002), *Seven Psychopaths* begins predicting its own fate and changing its course at the whim of the writers who are now taking control of their destiny.

Many of *Seven Psychopaths'* most enjoyable scenes simply involve Farrell, Rockwell and Walken riffing on their next moves. It becomes a blended exercise of watching McDonagh's screenplay evolve and a chance to watch three gifted actors sell it no matter how absurd it gets. Farrell is playing a more confused set of nerves than his high-strung, reactionary character from *In Bruges* and winds up playing the straight man to the always-energetic Rockwell and a surprisingly restrained counterpart. Christopher Walken has developed a unique reputation over the years for his frequently lampooned speech affectations and bizarre methods of delivering eccentric monologues. That is all very much on display as Hans here along with a childlike sentimentality that is projected from a character racked with grief and guilt. He is a man uncertain of when to repress, when to give into his anger, and when to just give up. It is easily Walken's most well-rounded performance since *Catch Me If You Can* (2002).

Seven Psychopaths is quite the delight for those who do not mind a little red-blooded macabre with their comedy. McDonagh achieved such a range of cinematic satisfactions with *In Bruges* that his standard may not have been topped but has clearly become the norm. Too many filmmakers crafting comic gangster tales will find one strength and beat it into the ground. It could be tough-guy dialogue, creative kills or outright irony to prove that they are really above the material they are presenting. McDonagh's work so far has shown none of that. Though some could craft an easy argument that the fantasy sequences of *Seven Psychopaths* shows precisely that, they are more representative of the uncertainty of

man's casual delusions of being more important to the universe's grand plan than an attempt to dismiss their worthiness of existence in the first place. There is too much empathy in McDonagh's work to lump him into the same category.

Erik Childress

CREDITS

Marty: Colin Farrell

Charlie: Woody Harrelson

Billy: Sam Rockwell

Hans: Christopher Walken

Zachariah: Tom Waits

Kaya: Abbie Cornish

Paulo: Zeljko Ivanek

Origin: United States, United Kingdom

Language: English

Released: 2012

Production: Graham Broadbent, Pete Czernin, Martin McDonagh; Blueprint Pictures, Film4 Library; released by CBS Films

Directed by: Martin McDonagh

Written by: Martin McDonagh

Cinematography by: Ben Davis

Music by: Carter Burwell

Sound: Geoffrey Patterson

Editing: Lisa Gunning

Costumes: Karen Patch

Production Design: David Wasco

MPAA rating: R

Running time: 110 minutes

REVIEWS

Bayer, Jeff. *The Scorecard Review*. October 16, 2012.

Berardinelli, James. *ReelViews*. October 12, 2012.

Dargis, Manohla. *New York Times*. October 11, 2012.

Ebert, Roger. *Chicago Sun-Times*. October 11, 2012.

Lybarger, Dan. *Arkansas Democrat-Gazette*. October 14, 2012.

Orndorf, Brian. *Blu-ray.com*. October 12, 2012.

Phillips, Michael. *Chicago Tribune*. October 11, 2012.

Turan, Kenneth. *Los Angeles Times*. October 11, 2012.

Vaux, Rob. *Mania.com*. October 12, 2012.

Verniere, James. *Boston Herald*. October 12, 2012.

QUOTES

Hans: "An eye for an eye leaves the whole world blind."

Billy: "No, it doesn't. There'll be one guy left with one eye. How's the last blind guy gonna take out the eye of the last guy left?"

In the graveyard scene, the grave that the Jack of Diamonds killer is hiding behind is named "Rourke." Mickey Rourke was initially cast in the movie, but dropped out after disagreements with the director.

AWARDS

Nominations:

Ind. Spirit 2013: Actor—Supporting (Rockwell), Cinematog.

SIDE BY SIDE

A documentary about the science, art, and
impact of digital cinema.
—Movie tagline

Box Office: $58,825

Everything one hopes to learn about the vociferous debate between film vs. digital is seemingly summed up in the first five minutes of the documentary *Side by Side* and put in motion by Keanu Reeves. A shiny new technology or anything that challenges the status quo will always be met with the stubbornness of the old guard unwilling to adapt to a new era. The questions raised within this examination extend further than the mere quality of the image. Through the trickle-down effects to all the elements that go into making a movie, those asking the questions hope to provide a clearer picture on just why there is such resistance even while many of the cinema pioneers of our time are ready to embrace it.

In the digital world, film is the analog format that requires more time and ulcers to mold into a final product. The giant room-filling machines of the past and the cut-and-splice intimacy of the Moviola have all been simplified through computers and tiny chips instead of giant film magazines. Going by the wayside is the waiting game involved in processing multiple ten-minute reels. "Dailies" are now "immediacies," allowing filmmakers to see if the fruits of their labor match their mind's eye on the spot rather than knowing they have lost a day's work the next morning. The image is crisper than ever and the technological advances have allowed more young filmmakers the dream of making an inexpensive motion picture. So what is the problem?

Ego for starters. The first act of *Side by Side* is not just about generating the conflict but exposing it as more than just old fuddy-duddies unwilling to learn how to use a new toy. Some actors like Robert Downey Jr. were not used to the constant shooting schedule allowed by digital cameras while others trained in the theater like John Malkovich welcomed it. Cinematogra-

phers in many circles shared a similar power to their director bosses in knowing just how to manipulate images and light. As we see during one session with lauded director of photography Roger Deakins, a touch of a keyboard can now color-correct anything from its natural state. As one of the first films to experiment with this process, the golden hues of *O Brother, Where Art Thou?* (2000) represented the end of a golden era of filmmaking.

In 1993, after James Cameron had accelerated the use of CGI effects in place of traditional VFX, the work on the dinosaurs in *Jurassic Park* (1993) inspired model-makers and other practical artists to ironically coin that they were the ones who were now extinct. George Lucas' ILM division was at the forefront of computer-based editing—the dubbed EditDroid eventually gave way to the AVID—and when he announced "film is dead" when deciding to shoot *Star Wars Episode II: Attack of the Clones* (2002) digitally, the film community shared a moment of panic and outrage. Robert Rodriguez who launched his career with the famously ultra-low budget *El Mariachi* (1992), boldly claimed "I'm following Obi-Wan" and it led to creating his vision for *Sin City* (2005). Quentin Tarantino, on the other hand, has recently linked his own retirement to the disappearance of film and concocted the climax of *Inglourious Basterds* (2009) where the burning of celluloid prints led to the downfall of Hitler.

Extreme reactions are balanced out by those like Christopher Nolan who still shoots on film and calls the advances "seductive, but hollow" and Martin Scorsese who sees value but still enjoys the romantic notion of film. The direction of Christopher Kenneally's documentary transfers from history to the future just as quickly as many of cinema's most celebrated directors have done. Timing of editing is also questioned in the same mold of visual effects taking away the ingenuity of having to work with a ceiling. At the touch of a button, a screenplay can take an entirely new direction and the ease of use can lead to over-editing—though the film does not get interviews with Michael Bay, Paul W.S. Anderson, or McG to defend such styles. David Lynch says that the increase of digital cameras and their affordability is akin to everyone having a piece of paper to write stories. Yet, how many truly great stories have been written?

The clarity expanse of pixels from 720 to nearly 2,000 has now led to 4,000 restorations of classics that have never looked better in a theater or on a Blu-ray disc, but also criticism of Peter Jackson's decision to shoot *The Hobbit: An Unexpected Journey* (2012) in 48 frames per second for additional clarity. The smooth elimination of motion blurs also provides acceleration to natural movement which feeds into one of the ultimate questions that *Side By Side* asks: Is anything real anymore? James Cameron may flippantly dismiss it since the reality of movies is all an illusion anyway but in an era when amateur filmmakers can so easily manipulate the truth, does the artistry become lost, or worse, can it lead to greater mis-truths?

The paranoia of the latter is all part of the slippery slope debate when it all basically comes down to the eye of the beholder. If the naysayers believe there truly is "no tastemaker" maybe film criticism becomes more important than ever. As seen here, many major films are still shot on film from Best Picture nominees like *Moneyball* (2011), *The Tree of Life* (2011), and *War Horse* (2011) to blockbusters like *The Hunger Games* (2012), *Mission Impossible: Ghost Protocol* (2011), and *The Dark Knight Rises* (2012). Advancements have far from stunted the creative process. *Side by Side* does a solid job of exploring so many aspects of the issue about which the average moviegoer may never have dreamed or even cared. Though the highly technical document may play better in film schools where it truly is a must-see, if Keanu Reeves can grasp the understanding of all its intricacies then maybe viewers can too.

Erik Childress

CREDITS

Himself: Richard Linklater
Himself: Martin Scorsese
Himself: David Lynch
Himself: Steven Soderbergh
    Keanu Reeves
Origin: United States
Language: English
Released: 2012
Production: Justin Szlasa, Keanu Reeves; Company Films; released by Tribeca Films
Directed by: Christopher Kenneally
Written by: Christopher Kenneally
Cinematography by: Chris Cassidy
Music by: Billy Ryan; Brendan Ryan
Sound: Lewis Goldstein
Editing: Mike Long; Malcolm Hearn
MPAA rating: Unrated
Running time: 99 minutes

REVIEWS

Adams, Mark. *Screen International.* May 15, 2012.
Bowles, Scott. *USA Today.* August 30, 2012.
Fine, Marshall. *Hollywood & Fine.* August 30, 2012.
Kohn, Eric. *IndieWire.* September 5, 2012.

Murray, Noel. *AV Club.* August 30, 2012.
Orndorf, Brian. *Blu-ray.com.* September 13, 2012.
Rodriguez, Rene. *Miami Herald.* September 23, 2012.
Scott, A. O. *New York Times.* August 30, 2012.
Verniere, James. *Boston Herald.* September 5, 2012.
Whitty, Stephen. *Newark Star-Ledger.* August 31, 2012.
Wilkinson, Ron. *Monsters & Critics.* September 3, 2012.

SILENT HILL: REVELATION 3D

Box Office: $17.5 million

Some movies, especially horror films, video game adaptations and patently unnecessary sequels to barely-remembered titles, are so sloppily made that it feels as if each individual scene was stuck into the mix at random without any concern with how it might fit with what came before or after it. *Silent Hill: Revelations,* the patently unnecessary sequel to *Silent Hill* (2006), the big-screen adaptation of the popular horror video game franchise, is, on the other hand, a film so completely confused and confusing that each individual frame seems to have been haphazardly inserted without any thought of how it might fit with the surrounding material. With the possible exception of *Holy Motors* (2012), this is easily the single most baffling movie of 2012. The difference between the two is that the former was made by someone with such deft control of the cinematic medium that his lunacies still managed to maintain a style and internal logic that made them fascinating to watch while the latter is a movie that has been slapped together by people with only the vaguest apparent notions of what such a thing is supposed to look, sound or feel like.

Having survived the horrors of the first *Silent Hill* that she endured as a little girl with no concrete memory of what actually happened (much like the vast majority of the audience), the now-grown-and-renamed Heather (Adelaide Clemens) has spent the last few years moving from town to town with her father (Sean Bean) for reasons that she cannot begin to comprehend (again, much like the vast majority of the audience). She barely has time to settle into her new town when mysterious forces kidnap Dad and leave behind a message demanding that she return to Silent Hill if she ever wants to see him again. With the aid of rebel-classmate-with-a-secret (Kit Harrington), Heather makes the journey back to Silent Hill—a remote burg where the constant snowfall is really ash from an underground fire which seems to have been burning since the invention of fire and which is populated entirely by the tortured souls of the damned (though their milkshakes are to die for)—and while searching for her father, she discovers that her presence could allow the local evil spirits to be set free to destroy the world or something equally dire. Along the way, she runs into a number of familiar faces that include series veterans Radha Mitchell and Deborah Kara Unger (both making appearances that all but scream "Contractual Obligation!" all over them) and newcomers Carrie-Anne Moss, Martin Donovan and Malcolm McDowell. Put it this way—this is the kind of movie where it would actually be more startling and shocking if Malcolm McDowell was *not* in the cast.

Truth be told, the original *Silent Hill* was just as mystifying from a narrative standpoint as this film is—even more so, it could be argued, since those who saw the first one at least have a couple things that they can grab on to this time around, no matter how futile their efforts towards understanding might be in the long run. The difference is that the original had, in Christophe Gans, the French director behind the deliriously enjoyable kung-fu/werewolf epic *Brotherhood of the Wolf* (2001), a filmmaker who knew how to create a compelling piece of pure cinematic eye candy—even though none of it made any sense when all was said and done, every scene was so spectacular from a visual standpoint that it hardly mattered that none of it added up. This time around, the story is just as inscrutable as ever—even the numerous moments in which everything stops dead so that the characters can explain what is going on to each other only serve to muddy the waters further—but this time around, the visual scheme provided by writer-director Michael J. Bassett is just as murky as his screenplay. While the first film had one hallucinatory vision after another up its sleeves, this film has all the cinematic panache of a video of a haunted house set up haphazardly in a local warehouse and staffed by people who are simply too bored with their tasks to put in even a token effort anymore. Put it this way—the author of this review caught the film immediately after a viewing of the kid-oriented Halloween comedy *Fun Size* (2012) and even *that* had more genuine tension than this one. Adding to the muddiness is the so-called miracle of 3-D, an attraction that, save for a couple of interesting compositions involving the that-isn't-snow-fall, only serves to take scenes that, because they are set either at night or in dimly-lit areas, are hard enough to see as is and, thanks to the reduced brightness that is part and parcel with the process, make the film a bigger chore to watch than it already is.

To give *Silent Hill: Revelations* its due, there is one sequence—involving some mannequins and a particularly nasty spider-like creature—that is fairly creepy and effective and while she hardly has anything to do other than look scared and/or confused by her surroundings, Adelaide Clemens is sweet and sympathetic enough to make one want to see her in another film as soon as possible. For the most part, though, the film is little more than a string of barf-bag moments put together by people with nothing else on their minds than creating a cheapo exploitation film that will score a quick buck or two regardless of how brutally incoherent the end result might be to anyone dumb enough to fork over their money to endure what they have wrought. Of course, there may well be people out there for whom every single moment of this film makes perfectly logical sense and who would, given the chance, gladly spend hours and hours explaining each and every detail to one and all. Ironically, the very idea of sitting next to such a person on a cross-town bus for more than twenty minutes is a notion far more frightening than anything to be found here.

Peter Sobczynski

CREDITS

Heather/Alessa: Adelaide Clemens
Vincent: Kit Harington
Claudia Wolf: Carrie-Anne Moss
Harry: Sean Bean
Rose Da Silva: Radha Mitchell
Leonard: Malcolm McDowell
Douglas: Martin Donovan
Dahlia: Deborah Kara Unger
Red Pyramid: Roberto Campanella
Travis Grady: Peter Outerbridge
Detective Santini: Jefferson Brown
Detective Cable: Milton Barnes
Origin: France, United States, Canada
Language: English
Released: 2012
Production: Samuel Hadida, Don Carmody; released by Davis Films, Anibrain Digital Technologies Private Ltd.
Directed by: Michael J. Bassett
Written by: Michael J. Bassett
Cinematography by: Maxime Alexandre
Music by: Jeff Danna; Akira Yamaoka
Sound: Jane Tattersall; David Mccallum
Editing: Michele Conroy
Art Direction: Anthony Ianni
Costumes: Wendy Partridge
Production Design: Alicia Keywan
MPAA rating: R
Running time: 94 minutes

REVIEWS

Brady, Tara. *Irish Times*. November 2, 2012.

Goss, William. *Film.com*. October 26, 2012.

Harvey, Dennis. *Variety*. October 26, 2012.

Michel, Brett. *Boston Phoenix*. October 31, 2012.

Olsen, Mark. *Los Angeles Times*. October 26, 2012.

Rabin, Nathan. *AV Club*. October 26, 2012.

Savlov, Marc. *Austin Chronicle*. October 2, 2012.

Schager, Nick. *Village Voice*. October 26, 2012.

Webster, Andy. *New York Times*. October 26, 2012.

Weinberg, Scott. *FEARnet*. October 26, 2012.

QUOTES

Heather Mason: "Go to hell!"

Alessa: "Can't you see? We're already here."

TRIVIA

Red Pyramid is a full body costume that was blended at Roberto Campanella wrists, requiring only 25 minutes of preparation for each scene, as opposed to the three hours it took to prep in the first film.

SILENT HOUSE

Box Office: $12.8 million

While the big-screen careers of her two eldest sisters lasted no longer than a "New York Minute," it was clear during Sundance 2011 that Elizabeth Olsen would be far more than a flash in the pan. Not only was the camera obviously in love with her radiant features, but it lingered on them long enough for Olsen's remarkably nuanced portrayals to be fully appreciated. In both of her Sundance entries that year, the vast majority of dialogue that Olsen delivered was through her eyes rather than her mouth.

The first film was Sean Durkin's masterful psychodrama, *Martha Marcy May Marlene* (2011), which effortlessly blended parallel timelines, fusing memories, nightmares and reality into a mesmerizing brew fraught with paranoia. Olsen played a girl who escapes from a cult and reenters the life of her older sister, while silently fearing that her captors may not be far behind. Durkin's film builds such an overwhelming sense of dread that audiences may find themselves looking over their own shoulders after the final fade-out. By refusing to provide the audience with traditional closure, it triumphantly immersed them within the unsettled psyche of its heroine.

Olsen's other star-vehicle at her breakout festival debut was Chris Kentis and Laura Lau's *Silent House* (2011), which is a vastly different picture than *Martha*, but does share some notable similarities. Both films

require Olsen to be in an increasingly frantic state, while the camera's almost predatory gaze accentuates her characters' fear of sexual abuse. Each of these thrillers are about the phobia of being followed, though whereas *Martha* allows much of the terror to take place within its character's mind, *House* externalizes it with standard horror set-pieces, an intrusive score and loud clangs on the soundtrack. It is nowhere near as frightening, but for its first two-thirds, Olsen forges a rather hypnotic duet with an extraordinarily athletic camera crew headed by cinematographer Igor Martinovic (*Man on Wire* [2008]).

Based on Gustavo Hernandez's 2010 Uruguayan horror show, *La casa muda*, *House* borrows the stylistic conceit of its predecessor by staging the action in several long takes stitched together to resemble a single continuous shot. As a technical achievement, the film is quite impressive, though there are a handful of moments when the deliriously shaky cameras render the action incoherent (while possibly obscuring the edits). Yet such shakiness is to be expected when the cameramen are literally chasing Olsen through a field while keeping the lens as close to her face as possible. The most remarkable shot is the very first one, which observes Olsen from a god's eye perspective before lowering to the ground and following her on foot. This required the cinematographer to keep his camera steady while being lowered in a crane and stepping off onto the ground. For students of cinema, it is difficult to not be dazzled by this feat.

Olsen plays Sarah, a luminously lovely young woman who is first seen navigating her way through the murky corridors of a lakeside retreat that her father (Adam Trese) and uncle (Eric Sheffer Steven) intend on selling. As the men punch holes in the walls while bickering amongst themselves, a woman (Julia Taylor Ross) suddenly appears on their porch. She identifies herself as a childhood friend of Sarah's, while exuding a confidence that is rather troubling. As Sarah struggles to recall the woman's face, Lau's script builds a palpable sense of unease. It is not long after this ominous encounter that Sarah suddenly finds herself trapped within the house. The windows are boarded, the doors are inexplicably locked and there seems to be a threatening creak emanating from behind every corner. When Sarah finds her father bloodied and unconscious, she desperately attempts to escape her ever-encroaching doom. As blurred figures start to materialize in various shots, the film provides a great deal of time for the audience to consider what could be happening. Is the house haunted or is Sarah going mad? Or are there really homicidal home invaders masterminding this game of torture? All three options are far-fetched, but nowhere near as outlandish as the twist that reveals itself in the final minutes.

Whereas Kentis and Lau's bone-chilling 2003 effort, *Open Water,* followed the plight of two divers abandoned in shark-infested waters to its logical conclusion, *House* hurls logic out the window in its last act. Upon second viewing, it is easier to perceive how the filmmakers offered clues about its surrealistic flourishes throughout, though that does not make them any less difficult to swallow. Lau has cited Donald Kalsched's "The Inner World of Trauma" as an influence on the Lynchian dreamscape that she attempted to construct, but it causes the narrative to become so far-fetched that it kills off all semblance of tension precisely at the moment when the film should be at its scariest. Even the eerier sequences preceding this disastrous finale reek of gimmickry. With only a flashbulb to light her way through a particularly dark room, Sarah can only view her surroundings in sporadic freeze frames. This technique was utilized to far better effect in countless other films, most recently Gonzalo Lopez-Gallego's 2011 found-footage gem, *Apollo 18,* and the startling imagery that it illuminates are all predictable cliches.

What ultimately keeps the film afloat, even during its weakest passages, is the viscerally affecting performance by Olsen. Though most of her lines are in the form of screams, the actress finds endless fresh ways to convey her mounting hysteria. When she spots a menacing figure in her rearview mirror, Sarah's shock causes her to briefly choke on her own frightened shrieks. It is a small touch, but it makes the moment infinitely more memorable. It is a shame that the scares themselves are not nearly as inspired as her reactions. While *Martha* burrowed deep within the skin of its audience, *House* leaves viewers with nothing to haunt their dreams.

Matt Fagerholm

CREDITS

Sarah: Elizabeth Olsen
John: Adam Trese
Peter: Eric Sheffer Stevens
Sophia: Julia Taylor Ross
Little Girl: Haley Murphy
Stalking Man: Adam Barnett
Origin: United States
Language: English
Released: 2012
Production: Agnes Mentre, Laura Lau; Elle Driver, Eye for an Eye Filmworks, Tazora Films; released by Open Road Films
Directed by: Chris Kentis; Laura Lau
Written by: Laura Lau
Cinematography by: Igor Martinovic
Music by: Nathan Larson

Sound: Noah Vivekanand Timan
Art Direction: Katya Debear
Costumes: Lynn Falconer
Production Design: Roshelle Berliner
MPAA rating: R
Running time: 88 minutes

REVIEWS

Bradshaw, Peter. *The Guardian.* March 7, 2012.
Ebert, Roger. *Chicago Sun-Times.* March 7, 2012.
Erbland, Kate. *Boxoffice Magazine.* March 2, 2012.
Gonzalez, Ed. *Slant Magazine.* March 4, 2012.
Kohn, Eric. *indieWIRE.* March 7, 2012.
McCarthy, Todd. *Hollywood Reporter.* March 2, 2012.
Nelson, Rob. *Variety.* March 3, 2012.
Pinkerton, Nick. *Village Voice.* March 3, 2012.
Schwarzbaum, Lisa. *Entertainment Weekly.* March 7, 2012.
Uhlich, Keith. *Time Out New York.* March 6, 2012.

TRIVIA

The entire movie was shot to mimic one continuous real-time take, with no cuts from start to finish. It was shot in approxiamtely 10-minute segments and then edited to blend the cuts.

SILVER LININGS PLAYBOOK

Watch for the signs.
　　—Movie tagline

Box Office: $108.4 million

David O. Russell's *Silver Linings Playbook* was the critical crowd-pleaser of 2012, a film that Harvey Weinstein rode like a runaway train from the 2012 Toronto Film Festival through awards season all the way to a remarkable number of Oscar nominations, including not just nods for Best Picture, Best Director, and Best Adapted Screenplay, but all four of the acting categories, a feat that had not been accomplished since before Jennifer Lawrence, was born (with Warren Beatty's *Reds* [1981]). The film wowed both critics and audiences (to the tune of $130 million and rising worldwide) largely through the strength of its notable ensemble. Every year there is an adult comedy that has its flaws easily overlooked because it is so much smarter, edgier, and character-driven than the average junk that crowds the marketplace (past Best Picture nominees that fit the description include *Up in the Air* [2009], *As Good As It Gets* [1997], *Jerry Maguire* [1996], and *Sideways* [2004]). *Silver Linings Playbook* is that film that crosses from crowd-pleaser to critical darling for 2012.

Working from the novel by Matthew Quick, Russell the screenwriter takes what could have easily been a generic comedy in another writer's hands and makes it much more than that, although arguably not AS much as some critics gave him credit for doing. The story of *SLP* is thin and its weakest element. In fact, the greatest accomplishment of Russell's skill here is how much he built on the generic frame of a male fantasy given him by the source material. The performances are so solid throughout and the dialogue so crisp, one does not even really notice the general nonsense of the plot and how easily it dismisses mental illness and family problems with cliche until second viewing.

Pat Solatano (Bradley Cooper) is being released from a mental hospital and is being picked up by his sweet, old-fashioned mother Dolores (Jacki Weaver). His buddy Danny (Chris Tucker, in his first performance outside of the *Rush Hour* films since 1997) could use a ride home too. In a comedic moment that shines light on Pat's mental state, it is revealed on the drive home that Danny was not actually released from the hospital. Pat is not willing to accept what is right in front of him. Just going home to his family is not enough. Just moving on is not enough. He wants more. Whether it is taking Danny home before he is released or trying to contact his ex-wife despite the restraining order, Pat does not often see reality. And when reality confronts him, he often responds violently, as he did the day that he came home and found his wife in the shower with another man.

Medicated and counseled, Pat returns to his family home, ready to convince his wife that the two should reunite. He simply does not understand the restraining order placed on him and works his way through the syllabus for the class his wife is teaching in one of many misguided efforts to impress her. He stays up late in the attic of the home of his mom and Pat Sr. (Robert De Niro) and rekindles a friendship with Ronnie (John Ortiz) and his wife Veronica (Julia Stiles), who just so happens to be friends with Pat's ex. Every move on Pat's part feels manipulative, even as he starts to get close to Veronica's sister Tiffany (Jennifer Lawrence), seeing in her another road to getting back together with his wife. He has a playbook and he is going to make his own happy ending. Of course, as is often the theme in films like this one, Pat learns that playbooks need to be rewritten.

Tiffany has some mental and emotional problems of her own. She has been made a widow at far too young an age (Lawrence was only twenty-one at the time of the film's shoot although the character seems to have been written as older, and her age nor the fifteen year difference between her and Cooper is never made an issue in

the film). The depression related to the loss of her police officer husband has made Tiffany promiscuous to a degree that borders on dangerous. And she is angry. She meets Pat's outbursts with her own and sees a way to use him as he is using her. She agrees to help Pat if he will be her dance partner for an upcoming contest. In her, Pat starts to see a kindred spirit—a damaged soul without the filter that stops people from the kind of expressive outbursts that could hurt. In Pat, Tiffany sees someone willing to commit who is not just in it for sex. However, the scales do seem a bit imbalanced. In the inevitable coupling, Pat gets a beautiful, outspoken, sex-crazed dancer and Tiffany gets a rage-aholic who lives in his parent's attic. (There is the aforementioned male fantasy aspect—beat up your wife's lover, take some pills, reconcile with your distant dad, and get a hot girlfriend.)

Two messed up people in a dance contest who fall in love. It sounds like a subplot in one of Garry Marshall's nauseating star-packed, holiday-based rom-coms. And yet Russell works wonders with what could have been overly light, fluffy material, grounding it in realistic, foul-mouthed characters with whom audiences can easily identify and love. Russell allows his cast to be likable without ever feeling desperate. Most romantic comedies feature characters the producers are desperate to make likable, pushing their sweetness, cuteness, and romantic ideals on the audience like a carnival barker making a sale. Russell never takes that route and it is why so many people fell in love with his film. Because he never begs them to do so.

Having one of the best ensembles of 2012 helps. Russell is quite simply one of the best working directors in terms of performance, as evidenced by the 2010 Oscar wins of two stars of his last film *The Fighter*. Bradley Cooper does the best work of his career and Lawrence matches him at every turn. It is the lack of artifice that elevates the performance here as one so quickly sees not Cooper and Lawrence but Pat and Tiffany. And then there is Robert De Niro, an actor most critics thought was lost to lazy performances in awful comedies and action pics over the last two decades. Most wondered if there would ever be another great turn from the man once considered in the conversation for the best actors of all time. From the first minute he graces the screen, there is a light in De Niro's eyes here that has been absent for dozens of films. It is his best work since the '90s and resulted in his first Oscar nomination since 1991's *Cape Fear*. The nomination for Jacki Weaver was merely an indication of the wave of support for the film overall. Even the very talented Ms. Weaver would probably admit she did not deserve it but the weakness of the category carried her in. She is solid but entirely unremarkable. In many ways, Julia Stiles is just as deserving.

Silver Linings Playbook certainly does not break any new ground. It is Russell's least ambitious film in that regard. It is a mere character study, wonderfully told. The best scenes take place in familiar places—living rooms watching football, dining rooms for a family meal, diners, movie theaters, football stadium parking lots. It is a film that invites viewers to spend time with its characters and merely enjoy their company instead of leaving with a definitive message—an accomplishment in cinematic storytelling that is harder to pull off than one may first presume.

Brian Tallerico

CREDITS

Pat Solitano: Bradley Cooper
Tiffany: Jennifer Lawrence
Pat Solitano Sr.: Robert De Niro
Dolores Solitano: Jacki Weaver
Danny: Chris Tucker
Dr. Patel: Anupam Kher
Ronnie: John Ortiz
Jake: Shea Whigham
Veronica: Julia Stiles
Officer Keogh: Dash Mihok
Origin: United States
Language: English
Released: 2012
Production: Bruce Cohen, Donna Gigliotti, Jonathan Gordon; Mirage Enterprises; released by Weinstein Company
Directed by: David O. Russell
Written by: David O. Russell
Cinematography by: Masanobu Takayanagi
Music by: Danny Elfman
Sound: Odin Benitez
Music Supervisor: Susan Jacobs
Editing: Jay Cassidy; Crispin Struthers
Art Direction: Jesse Rosenthal
Costumes: Mark Bridges
Production Design: Judy Becker
MPAA rating: R
Running time: 122 minutes

REVIEWS

Dargis, Manohla. *New York Times*. November 15, 2012.
Hornaday, Ann. *Washington Post*. November 15, 2012.
Kohn, Eric. *indieWIRE*. September 18, 2012.
Morgenstern, Joe. *Wall Street Journal*. November 15, 2012.
O'Hehir, Andrew. *Salon.com*. November 16, 2012.
Rea, Steven. *Philadelphia Inquirer*. October 18, 2012.
Rooney, David. *Hollywood Reporter*. September 18, 2012.
Schwarzbaum, Lisa. *Entertainment Weekly*. November 14, 2012.
Travers, Peter. *Rolling Stone*. November 15, 2012.
Turan, Kenneth. *Los Angeles Times*. November 15, 2012.

QUOTES

Pat: "The only way to beat my crazy was by doing something even crazier. Thank you. I love you. I knew it from the moment I saw you. I'm sorry it took me so long to catch up."

TRIVIA

After Anne Hathaway dropped out of the role that eventually went to Jennifer Lawrence due to scheduling conflicts, Rachel McAdams, Olivia Wilde, Elizabeth Banks, Blake Lively, Rooney Mara, Kirsten Dunst, and Andrea Riseborough were all considered for the part.

AWARDS

Oscars 2012: Actress (Lawrence)
British Acad. 2012: Adapt. Screenplay
Golden Globes 2013: Actress—Mus./Comedy (Lawrence)
Ind. Spirit 2013: Actress (Lawrence), Director (Russell), Film, Screenplay
Screen Actors Guild 2012: Actress (Lawrence)

Nominations:

Oscars 2012: Actor (Cooper), Actor—Supporting (De Niro), Actress—Supporting (Weaver), Adapt. Screenplay, Director (Russell), Film, Film Editing
British Acad. 2012: Actor (Cooper), Actress (Lawrence)
Golden Globes 2013: Actor—Mus./Comedy (Cooper), Film—Mus./Comedy, Screenplay
Ind. Spirit 2013: Actor (Cooper)
Screen Actors Guild 2012: Actor (Cooper), Actor—Supporting (De Niro), Cast
Writers Guild 2012: Adapt. Screenplay

SINISTER

Once you see him, nothing can save you.
    —Movie tagline
Be the first to see the year's most terrifying film.
    —Movie tagline

Box Office: $48.1 million

Sinister may be a slave to horror-movie movie formula, but it also contains a genuinely unsettling premise—one that connects a series of apparently ritualized murders with the ritual of watching movies. The movie's focus on the deteriorating psyche of its protagonist also helps to make the screenplay's abundant cliches easier to swallow.

This is, at its heart, a story about obsession—a search for truth that attempts to find it in the unspooling of film reels through a projector. The films in question are of the snuff variety, and their impact permeates the rest of the otherwise routine trappings of the movie, giving everything that unfolds an air of impending doom. Here, like in so many genre entries, the protagonist wanders through a darkened house (without ever turning on a light switch, despite their prevalence on the walls), and it is only partially about the possibility of a killer or a false scare appearing to frighten him and the audience. Just as the man is compelled to repeatedly watch and intensely scrutinize the mysterious box of films documenting murder, so too does he feel obligated to track down each and every noise in his house—equally hoping and fearing that he will find an answer.

Ellison Oswalt (Ethan Hawke, achieving the gradual rise in terror necessary for performances of this sort to work) was once a popular author of true crime books until the well of worthwhile stories and eager readers ran dry. He teaches now and is looking for a subject that will help him win back his fame. He believes the key lies in an unsolved quadruple homicide committed in the backyard of an ordinary house, on an ordinary street, in an ordinary town.

The opening scene relates the crime in the form of a "found" document—an 8mm film. It shows the family standing beneath a tree—hoods over their heads and nooses around their necks. A saw, seemingly without anyone guiding it, begins to move back and forth against another branch; as the one branch falls, the other, with the family connected via the ropes, rises. On its own, the scene is utterly chilling; in terms of setting the tone for everything that follows, it lingers.

Director Scott Derrickson (who also co-wrote the screenplay with C. Robert Cargill) incorporates several of these faux home movies, each of them with seemingly innocent titles (The first is labeled "Family Hanging Out," and when Ellison arrives at one called "Yard Work," there is a preemptive chill up the spine). The author comes across the film canisters in the attic of the house into which he and his family—wife Tracy (Juliet Rylance), son Trevor (Michael Hall D'Addario), and daughter Ashley (Clare Foley)—recently moved. Tracy is skeptical of her husband's reason for moving, given his history of moving the family into neighborhoods where murders have been committed. He insists this is not the case; the tree in the back yard—the same as from the opening scene—is the only sign needed to know he is lying.

The story moves back and forth between Ellison watching one of the film reels and wandering his new home, investigating some strange noise coming from some shadowy recess of the house. This is a repetitive process, for certain, and the scenes of Ellison in darkened halls and rooms are shallow on the surface. What keeps those sequences from tedium are the preludes—those haunting snuff films showing drowning, slashing, immolation, and, in the movie's most shocking moment, the absolute worst use of a lawnmower imaginable. Christopher Young's score incorporates eerie atonal chanting like howling, industrial-sounding screeches, and modulated vocal and music tracks. It is over-the-top yet unnerving.

The movie's central question is the presence of a strange figure, dressed in black and with blacked-out eyes and mouth, in each of the movies. He hides somewhere in the background, or Ellison manages to spot him in reflection when going frame by frame through the movies. The shared occurrence points to all of these crimes being connected, although since they span over four decades, it is unlikely that the killer is the same in each or that the man with the hollow face is the same person in each one. At least, that is the opinion of a college professor (an uncredited Vincent D'Onofrio), whose expertise just happens to be in "occult criminology." He theorizes that these murders are likely part of some kind of cult activity.

It is a perfectly logical, real-world explanation (at least in terms of horror-movie logic and realism) for everything that Ellison has uncovered and experienced—that a group of people are essentially toying with him for some nefarious purpose. The other possibility, of course, is that he is going insane, which the movie touches upon while never quite making the option seem likely. Instead, the screenplay takes a detour into the realm of the supernatural, as Ellison learns about a demonic spirit that takes children. Derrickson's grasp on the narrative's view of events as Ellison perceives them loosens, as ghosts and phantoms that he cannot see populate the screen and a closer look at the demon from the movies renders him almost comical.

The third act's headlong dive into this realm manages to undermine not only what occurs throughout the rest of the movie but also everything that has come before it. *Sinister* manages create an atmosphere of unease for so much of its running time that the greatest shock of all within the movie is how quickly it deflates.

Mark Dujsik

CREDITS

Ellison: Ethan Hawke
Professor James: Vincent D'Onofrio

Ashley: Claire Foley

Stephanie: Victoria Leigh

Tracy: Juliet Rylance

Origin: United States

Language: English

Released: 2012

Production: Jason Blum, Brian Kavanaugh-Jones; Alliance Films, Possessed Pictures, Blumhouse Productions, Automatik Entertainment; released by Summit Entertainment

Directed by: Scott Derrickson

Written by: Scott Derrickson; C. Robert Cargill

Cinematography by: Christopher Norr

Music by: Christopher Young

Sound: Dane A. Davis

Editing: Frederic Thoraval

Costumes: Abby O'Sullivan

Production Design: David Brisbin

MPAA rating: R

Running time: 110 minutes

REVIEWS

Berardinelli, James. *ReelViews*. October 11, 2012.

Ebert, Roger. *Chicago Sun-Times*. October 10, 2012.

Kohn, Eric. *IndieWIRE*. March 11, 2012.

Lacey, Liam. *Globe and Mail*. October 12, 2012.

McCarthy, Nick. *Slant Magazine*. October 10, 2012.

Morris, Wesley. *Boston Globe*. October 11, 2012.

Orndorf, Brian. *Blu-ray.com*. October 11, 2012.

Putman, Dustin. *DustinPutman.com*. October 11, 2012.

Tobias, Scott. *AV Club*. October 11, 2012.

Vaux, Rob. *Mania.com*. October 12, 2012.

TRIVIA

Screenwriter C. Robert Cargill has admitted that the name of the character Ellison Oswalt, played by Ethan Hawke, was inspired by author Harlan Ellison and comedian Patton Oswalt.

SKYFALL

Box Office: $304.2 million

Bond is back and looks better than ever. After an uncharacteristically long gap of four years (due to the bankruptcy and restructuring of studio MGM) following 2008's lackluster *Quantum of Solace*, the longest-running film franchise in cinema history returns with the intensity it so memorably regained in *Casino Royale* (2006) and an aesthetic splendor previously unseen in the series.

Casino Royale, the first film to feature Daniel Craig as Bond, was fantastic, ranking among the very best Bonds ever. A franchise reboot, the key to *Royale's* success was re-humanizing Bond and reining in the cartoonish excesses of a 50-year-old franchise with twenty-three films under its belt. For many decades, a viewer could say, without exaggeration, that the only thing that distinguished one Bond film from another was the villain since everything else (Bond's super hero character, the women, the gadgets, the world domination plot, etc.) remained exactly the same from one film to the next. *Casino Royale* did something different with Bond. Craig's Bond was more human, more conflicted and more psychologically vulnerable than any of his predecessors. This Bond got blood on his suit and seemed to at least be vaguely aware that beating men to death on a daily basis might take a mental toll. *Casino Royale's* script gave Craig, easily the best actor to play Bond, the space to make an actual character out of 007. The stakes were lower too. Refreshingly, *Casino Royale's* plot did not involve the threat of lasers raking the earth from the moon or an insane megalomaniac engineering the submergence of the world's landmass under the ocean to create an undersea kingdom. Instead, Bond was concerned with trying to turn an arms dealer by beating him at poker. *Casino Royale* was the rare reboot that was actually welcome and needed, returning the character to his roots and grounding him in something resembling reality. *Casino Royale* also actually cared about being a good film, something that sadly had not been a concern of the series in a very long time.

Skyfall also cares about being a good film and what it brings to the table is the best director the franchise has ever seen and by far the best production values of any Bond. Indeed, the true star of *Skyfall* is the dark, rich palette of the legendary cinematographer Roger Deakins. Past Bond films have, for the most part, been workmanlike productions with little concern about their appearance. With *Skyfall,* there is finally a Bond film that is as beautiful as its protagonist and the women he encounters. Indeed, the best scene in the film is a breathtakingly beautiful shot of Bond and a baddie fist-fighting silhouetted against a dazzling, screen-engulfing neon sign on a Shanghai skyscraper. Deakins' lens renders images as pedestrian as the exterior of a Shanghai night club or the Scottish countryside with such hypnotizing beauty that the viewer wishes the projectionist would pause the film allowing more time to drink it all in. When is the last time the best part of a Bond film was an aesthetic aspect? Indeed, when have aesthetics ever even been a factor in Bond films? Deakins' superb work is complemented by innovative, occasionally-even-daring (at least by the standards of the franchise) direction from Sam Mendes. Past Bond films have lacked innovative directors out of either risk aversion on the part of producers or lack of interest from top tier talent (a favorite parlor game of Bond aficionados is imagining the Quentin Tarantino Bond, the Martin Scorsese Bond, the Christopher Nolan Bond, etc.). With Mendes, Bond for the first time has a truly artistic director at the helm and it shows.

Nowhere is this more evident than in the memorable introduction of the film's villain, Raoul Silva (Javier Bardem). A former MI6 operative turned terrorist, Silva has stolen the identities of undercover agents and is slowly releasing their identities to the world to torture his former employer, M (Judi Dench). Compared to the world-dominating ambitions of most Bond villains, Silva's motives are refreshingly modest and realistic. Silva is a burned agent out for vengeance against M who he believes sold him out to the enemy. Tortured and left for dead he wants payback. Bond, hot on his trail, is captured by Silva's agents and taken to his villainous headquarters, the deserted Japanese island city of Hashima. As Bond sits, tied to a chair in the foreground, an elevator in the distant background of a cavernous room slowly descends. In one glorious, uninterrupted shot the elevator comes to a stop, the doors open and a gleeful Silva slowly strolls towards Bond, getting larger and larger as he nears Bond and the viewer. It is a mark of the conventionality of the series' past direction that what would be a relatively modest directorial flourish in most other films is here electrifying. Bardem more than matches Mendes' unconventionality with a superb, gloriously over-the-top performance. Sporting ridiculous bleach-blonde hair, a dandyish yellow suit and the giggly demeanor of a private joke that is simply agony to keep to himself, he unbuttons Bond's shirt and fondles his chest, asking with breathy amusement "Oh, dear, what does the training manual say about this?" When is the last time male rape was a possibility in a Bond film? Bardem's Silva is a creepy and magnetic masterpiece, easily the strangest and most intriguing Bond villain ever.

Skyfall is as close to an art film as any Bond film has come to be in its direction, cinematography, art direction, production design and actors but its script (written by Neal Purvis, Robert Wade—responsible for the last five Bond films—and John Logan) is, while certainly superior to many of Bond's past films, disappointingly routine. This is evident in Bardem's performance in which the immensely talented actor makes his character interesting *despite* what the script gives him to play (a run-of-the mill Bond villain). He succeeds fantastically but the contrast between the wildly unique character he has created and the largely routine dialogue he is required to utter and predictable plot action he is required to engage in is telling. Imagine if Bardem was

supplied with a script as daring as his acting. (Anton Chigurh of *No Country for Old Men* comes to mind [2007]). The script also does not give Craig anything surprising to say or do, failing to capitalize on the unpredictability and psychological complexity introduced in *Casino Royale*. In *Skyfall* Bond threatens to ossify back into the generic, one-note superhero that *Casino Royale* did so much to do away with. The film even manages to squander its wonderful island fortress setting. Easily one of the most memorable and haunting settings in the series' history (made all the more so by the fact that it is real), one expected, indeed was eagerly anticipating, spending the remainder of the film there with the abducted Bond and his flamboyant nemesis. Instead, after just a few short minutes and a couple of tantalizing shots of the abandoned-overnight city, Bardem is quickly apprehended by MI6 and brought back to boring old London, where he quickly escapes and attempts to assassinate M in a parliamentary hearing room. The film is redeemed somewhat in the location department by the great setting of its climax, Bond's childhood home, a lonely country estate in the Scottish highlands (the titular *Skyfall*), but it pales in comparison to the haunting grandeur of Silva's island ghost town.

The challenge for any series (all the more so for the oldest and longest running franchise in cinematic history) is how to make itself fresh while not forsaking the elements which made it enjoyable in the first place. Bond is a 50-year-old commercial franchise so one can understand a reluctance to mess with its highly lucrative formula but *Casino Royale* demonstrated that taking chances with the Bond formula can pay off both artistically and commercially and *Skyfall* innovates so successfully in every aspect of its production except its writing that it is difficult not to wish for it to go all the way. Indeed *Skyfall* does so much so well that it presents the viewer with a dilemma in evaluating the film. Does one accept the Bond tropes as fixed and enjoy the magnificent artistic innovation that *Skyfall* achieves around their margins or does one greedily demand that the artistic innovation be applied throughout, tossing the tropes out the window? Every Bond viewer eventually reaches the point in which the desire for innovation outweighs the affection for the tropes and that point has come to pass for this viewer.

Nate Vercauteren

CREDITS

James Bond: Daniel Craig
M: Judi Dench
Silva: Javier Bardem
Gareth Mallory: Ralph Fiennes

Eve: Naomie Harris

Severine: Berenice Marlohe

Q: Ben Whishaw

Clair Dowar: Helen McCrory

Origin: United Kingdom, United States

Language: English

Released: 2012

Production: Barbara Broccoli, Michael G. Wilson; Eon Productions; released by Columbia Pictures

Directed by: Sam Mendes

Written by: Neal Purvis; Robert Wade; John Logan

Cinematography by: Roger Deakins

Music by: Thomas Newman

Sound: Karen M. Baker; Per Hallberg

Editing: Stuart Baird

Art Direction: Chris Lowe

Costumes: Jany Temime

Production Design: Dennis Gassner

MPAA rating: PG-13

Running time: 143 minutes

REVIEWS

Dargis, Manohla. *New York Times*. November 7, 2012.

DeBruge, Peter. *Variety*. October 14, 2012.

Ebert, Roger. *Chicago Sun-Times*. November 7, 2012.

Longworth, Karina. *Village Voice*. November 7, 2012.

Morris, Wesley. *Boston Globe*. November 7, 2012.

Newman, Kim. *Empire*. October 17, 2012.

Phipps, Keith. *AV Club*. November 7, 2012.

Sharkey, Betsy. *Los Angeles Times*. November 7, 2012.

Smith, Kyle. *New York Post*. November 7, 2012.

Uhlich, Keith. *Time Out New York*. November 6, 2012.

QUOTES

James Bond: "Some men are coming to kill us. We're going to kill them first."

TRIVIA

In 50 year history of the James Bond franchise, *Skyfall* is only the second film in which Bond suffers a gunshot wound.

AWARDS

Oscars 2012: Song ("Skyfall"), Sound FX Editing

British Acad. 2012: Orig. Score

Golden Globes 2013: Song ("Skyfall")

Nominations:

Oscars 2012: Cinematog., Orig. Score, Sound

British Acad. 2012: Actor—Supporting (Bardem), Actress—Supporting (Dench), Cinematog., Film Editing, Production Design, Sound

Screen Actors Guild 2012: Actor—Supporting (Bardem)

SLEEPWALK WITH ME

> *When your subconscious has to do the work for you.*
> —Movie tagline

> *A comedy for anyone who ever had a dream. And then jumped out a window.*
> —Movie tagline

Box Office: $2.3 million

On one hand, adapting material from stage or the page to the screen is not easy. Much is often lost in translation. On the other, a good story is a good story.

In his debut as a filmmaker and leading man, comedian Mike Birbiglia gives the latter hand the edge. The co-writer/co-director/star of *Sleepwalk with Me* turns his 2010 book *Sleepwalk with Me and Other Painfully True Stories*, which originated from his acclaimed off-Broadway, one-man show, into a film that effectively embodies Birbiglia's on-stage persona: personable, funny and almost laid-back to a fault.

It may sound strange that a movie about a dangerous sleeping disorder could be called laid-back. In fact, much of *Sleepwalk with Me* revolves not around the harm that Matt Pandamiglio (Birbiglia) may cause himself and others while sleepwalking but denial, a problem that is even more consistently present in his life. Faced with the decision of going to the doctor or eating dinner, Matt eats dinner. Though he knows moving in with his girlfriend Abby (Lauren Ambrose) may not be the best idea, he does it anyway, as if going with the flow will somehow work in his favor. He maintains this philosophy as the two drift apart as a result of the time Matt spends on the road, pursuing a fledgling comedy career of which Abby is extremely supportive. If she knew about his temptations on the road, she likely would not be so in favor of his usage of time, but even without the attentions of women on tour Matt struggles to devote much of himself to his better half when given the opportunity to drive hundreds of miles and earn meager pay for a short, often-unsuccessful performance.

Though the character has a different name, Birbiglia is essentially playing himself, and his everyman comic sensibilities transfer well to film. (This may also simply be a factor of playing himself, a reason that almost all TV sitcoms built around comedians, whether it is Jerry Seinfeld or Kevin James or Ray Romano, find the stars' persona on the show largely reflecting their attitude as a stand-up rather than requiring them to act a part they may not know.) As *Sleepwalk with Me* opens, Matt addresses the audience, quipping that the following story is true, even though people frequently do not believe him. Would people believe it if he said it louder, he wonders? Of course that would change nothing, but this is one of many points in the film when Matt's sheepish, endearing sense of humor makes him a winning character, even when he ultimately makes one selfish and ill-advised decision after another.

Like a large percentage of adult men in movies of the last decade (often played by Will Ferrell or John C. Reilly), Matt is unready for the rites of passage that other people his age embrace. Abby, who is the rare cinematic woman to have more interest in sex than her man, wants to know their 8-year relationship may lead to marriage some day; Matt, like an overgrown kid, instead focuses on questions such as, "Where do you buy cereal?" So it is not much of a surprise when Matt begins hitting the road and nurturing his writing and performing skills as a stand-up, with greater interest in his own interests than his life as part of a pair. "I think to be a comedian you have to be a little bit delusional," Matt claims. He means it in terms of the self-affirmation needed to deflect rejection and audience disinterest, but this recognition proves to be why he puts his relationship and his own health at risk: Matt would rather get a laugh than fix the problem that led to the joke.

Because Matt pays little attention to Abby, *Sleepwalk with Me* likewise fails to appropriately acknowledge her role in the story. Matt learns that Abby puts up with him out of concern for his feelings, but the film neglects to communicate Abby's feelings and perspective as their relationship is reduced to phone calls while her boyfriend constantly puts his own schedule and interests ahead of her own. Far better visualized is Matt's dreams. Anyone watching him may see a man showering in his clothes or standing on a dresser; while sleepwalking, these entertaining sequences show, Matt thinks he is being pummeled with pizza sauce or climbing an Olympic podium to accept a medal. Appearing as a fellow touring comic, Marc Maron gets a good laugh when his character tells Matt that dreams are like movies—meant to be watched, not participated in as they happen.

Consequently, as his sleepwalking episodes grow more damaging, the movie becomes a likable account of how long it will take a man to recognize that his problems will get the best of him if he does not address them first. (Not that long; the easily digestible film runs only 76 minutes.) This narrative plays out onscreen many times per year, particularly when dealing with addiction (see the overrated Denzel Washington vehicle *Flight*.) If Matt is addicted to anything, it is the dedication it takes to make it as a comedian, and his experiences on the road ring true. This ranges from his rocky shows—including one that requires him to host a lip-syncing contest and his developing style that eventually results in Matt addressing his own problems on stage—to the financial concerns that make the tour borderline senseless. Paid $23 after a show, he stands up to a club employee and insists that he not be charged $7 for the chicken fingers he consumed. For most comedians trying to make a name for themselves, $7 means a lot

more than it does to the few who are successful enough for the public to actually know who they are.

Of course, Matt does not do it for the money, really. To the tune of the Backstreet Boys' *I Want It That Way* (1999), he jumps on a motel bed, overjoyed at the experience of being out on the road, doing what he wants to do. He is not a man without major issues, and *Sleepwalk with Me* shows how they pretty much all blow up in his face. In that moment, though, Matt discovers how rewarding it is to follow his dreams when they do not lead him out the window.

Matt Pais

CREDITS

Matt Pandamiglio: Mike Birbiglia
Abby: Lauren Ambrose
Frank: James Rebhorn
Linda: Carol Kane
Janet: Cristin Milioti
Origin: United States
Language: English
Released: 2012
Production: Jacob Jaffke, Ira Glass; Sleepwalkers Anonymous; released by IFC Films
Directed by: Mike Birbiglia; Seth Barrish
Written by: Mike Birbiglia; Seth Barrish; Joe Birbiglia; Ira Glass
Cinematography by: Adam Beckman
Music by: Andrew Hollander
Sound: Tom Efinger
Music Supervisor: Anthony Roman; Lilah Wilson
Editing: Geoffrey Richman
Art Direction: Shiloh Kidd
Costumes: Ciera Wells
Production Design: Tania Bijlani
MPAA rating: PG-13
Running time: 90 minutes

REVIEWS

Byrge, Duane. *Hollywood Reporter*. August 11, 2012.
Debruge, Peter. *Variety*. August 11, 2012.
Ebert, Roger. *Chicago Sun-Times*. August 29, 2012.
Longworth, Karina. *Village Voice*. August 21, 2012.
Morris, Wesley. *Boston Globe*. August 30, 2012.
Rabin, Nathan. *AV Club*. August 11, 2012.
Persall, Steve. *Tampa Bay Times*. October 17, 2012.
Scott, Mike. *New Orleans Times-Picayune*. September 7, 2012.
Schwarzbaum, Lisa. *Entertainment Weekly*. August 22, 2012.
Williams, Joe. *St. Louis Post-Dispatch*. September 14, 2012.

QUOTES

Matt Pandamiglio: "I really feel like our whole lives, no matter how low our self esteem gets, there's a part of us that thinks, 'I have a secret, special skill that no one knows about.' And, eventually, we meet someone who's like, 'You have a secret, special skill.' And you're like, 'I know! So do you!' And that's love."

TRIVIA

Comedian Mike Birbiglia lost 20 pounds to play the role he based on himself.

SMASHED

Box Office: $376,597

The story of an addict overcoming his or her dependency is usually the stuff of a movie-of-the-week melodrama, but the flipside is that it is also a chance for an actor to stretch out and go through the typical character arc of being completely messed up in the first half and fully recovered and enlightened by the film's end. Some obvious examples are *Clean and Sober* (1988), *When A Man Loves A Woman* (1994) and *28 Days* (2000). Of course, the character does not always come out the other side with greater wisdom, as in *Leaving Las Vegas* (1995), *Requiem For A Dream* (2000) or *Shame* (2011), in which case the movie can either come across as a severe cautionary tale or the story of someone completely losing hope and/or a strong sense of identity.

In *Smashed,* the struggle is divided between two people, a young married couple who work during the day and drink heavily at night. At the start of the film, Charlie (Aaron Paul) and Kate Hannah (Mary Elizabeth Winstead) wake up in their bed after a bender and look at the puddle of urine on the mattress as just another inconvenience for their lifestyle. She has to go to work. He can stay home and work his own hours as a freelance writer. Kate works as a 2nd grade teacher where she takes a quick swig from a flask before heading in. She has boundless enthusiasm when she interacts with her students (probably too much) and when she suddenly vomits in the middle of a lesson, one of her students asks if she is pregnant, to which she replies yes.

That same night, Kate leaves the bar early and meets a woman outside who needs a lift home. On the way there, she produces a crack pipe and encourages Kate to give it a try. Against her better judgment even as an alcoholic, Kate gives in and finds herself waking up the next morning on the street with a group of homeless dregs. She wanders home and finally admits to Charlie, "I don't think I can do this anymore...Drinking leads to everything stupid that I do." At work, one of her co-

workers, Dave (Nick Offerman), recognizes her behavior as an addict since he was an addict himself once. "I used to drink cocaine," he says. He hands her his Alcoholic Anonymous chip as a way of encouraging her to get help.

Eventually, after nights of getting belligerent and urinating on the floor of a liquor store that will not sell her booze after hours, she gives in and attends her first meeting. She instantly makes a friend and sponsor in Jenny (Octavia Spencer), who claims to have substituted alcohol with food. The meetings seem to help Kate with recovery, but her husband Charlie has yet to take any steps for himself and has deemed the whole institution of AA as a waste of time. The further Kate gets away from their lifestyle, though, the closer she gets to seeing their marriage is doomed if she is the only one making an effort. A trip to see her alcoholic mother (Mary Kay Place) does not help matters much.

As often happens in these kinds of movies, an outside relationship ensues, but *Smashed* takes an interesting twist. Dave is clearly attracted to Kate and he makes it known in the most verbally inappropriate way that the mere sight of him, even when he sincerely apologizes, gives her nothing but the creeps throughout the rest of the film. To add to the complications at work, the more sober she gets, the harder it is for her to maintain this ruse about being pregnant. Her newfound need to be honest with everyone around her ends up having dire consequences. James Ponsoldt's screenplay underscores the notion that quitting drinking is the easy part. It is the fallout from such a change that is never talked about in AA until it actually happens.

Ponsoldt, who also directed the film, makes some interesting narrative choices, some of which keep the film from being completely successful. Coming in at just about 85 minutes, the film feels a bit rushed, especially with the scenes involving Kate's mother, who offers Kate and Charlie Bloody Marys as soon as they arrive. The visit never seems to amount to much more than over-explaining how Kate got this way. And while the blackout in the third act during a dramatic moment that flashes forward a year later is effective, Ponsoldt's need to be trendy with the overused device of ambiguity in which one character asks an important question and the movie ends before the answer is given, is disappointing and, like many other indie movies before it, feels like a crutch.

Still, there is much to be admired about *Smashed*. Winstead's performance is at its best when she is sober. She plays drunk a little too broadly at times. Paul is, of course, good, but given his stint on the brilliant TV series *Breaking Bad*, in which he plays a meth dealer who also becomes an addict, this hardly seems like much of a stretch. Andy Cabic and Eric D. Johnson's score also adds a nice effect, putting the viewer into the heads of these two troubled people who see their life as a happy-go-lucky experience until the bottom falls out. There are unexpectedly funny moments in this film as well as some expectedly painful ones.

Collin Souter

CREDITS

Kate Hannah: Mary Elizabeth Winstead
Charlie Hannah: Aaron Paul
Jenny: Octavia Spencer
Dave Davies: Nick Offerman
Principal Barnes: Megan Mullally
Origin: United States
Language: English
Released: 2012
Production: Jennifer Cochis, Jonathan Schwartz, Andrea Sperling, Zygi Wilf; Super Crispy Entertainment; released by Sony Pictures Classics
Directed by: James Ponsoldt
Written by: James Ponsoldt; Susan Burke
Cinematography by: Tobias Datum
Music by: Andy Cabic; Eric D. Johnson
Sound: Ryan Collins
Music Supervisor: Tiffany Anders
Editing: Suzanne Spangler
Art Direction: Sarah M. Pott
Costumes: Diaz
Production Design: Linda Sena
MPAA rating: R
Running time: 85 minutes

REVIEWS

Bernard, Linda. *Toronto Star*. October 25, 2012.
Covert, Colin. *Minneapolis Star Tribune*. October 25, 2012.
Ebert, Roger. *Chicago Sun-Times*. October 18, 2012.
Morris, Wesley. *Boston Globe*. October 25, 2012.
Neumaier, Joe. *New York Daily News*. October 11, 2012.
Rabin, Nathan. *AV Club*. October 11, 2012.
Rea, Steven. *Philadelphia Inquirer*. October 25, 2012.
Sachs, Ben. *Chicago Reader*. October 18, 2012.
Schwarzbaum, Lisa. *Entertainment Weekly*. January 27, 2012.
Smith, Kyle. *New York Post*. October 12, 2012.

QUOTES

Kate Hannah: "Why is the coffee so much better when you make it?"
Charlie Hannah: "Because I make it with love, and I also make it with bacon."

TRIVIA

The film was shot in a total of nineteen days.

AWARDS

Nominations:
Ind. Spirit 2013: Actress (Winstead)

SNOW WHITE AND THE HUNTSMAN

The fairytale is over.
    —Movie tagline

Box Office: $155.3 million

"You're so cute, I could just eat you up!" is an expression that countless parents have gushed while gazing upon their offspring, but the monstrous mother in the original version of *Snow White* by the Brothers Grimm would have meant it literally rather than lovingly. Her heart was not overflowing with adoration but jealous anger when she was told by the mirror on the wall that her daughter had supplanted her as the fairest of them all, leading the woman to not only order Snow White's death but also the girl's lungs and liver for a subsequent salted snack. Nineteenth-century tykes were apparently wide-eyed in more ways than one as they listened to this story of a murderous mom, inching warily toward the other side of the bed as the fairy tale being read to them hit a little too close to home. Thus, the woman was distanced to being a wicked stepmother by the Grimms in order to lessen insecurities. Since this alteration, others have made their own changes, and those behind *Snow White and the Huntsman* are no exception. The Grimm's protagonist was a helpless nincompoop who was lucky she was so comely and a good cook, otherwise the dwarves would have tired of having to revive this dim damsel in distress every time she was nearly fooled into the hereafter by her envious elder. However, this latest *Snow White* is likened to an exquisite rose that defiantly hangs on in spite of the onset of forbidding, wintry weather, a heroine destined to be revered as much—if not more—for her dauntless fortitude as her striking appearance. Yet what one ironically remembers most about *Snow White and the Huntsman* are the marvelous sights rather than its story's substance.

Even before a voiceover can intone "Once upon a time," there is an arresting, near-monochromatic shot of a castle's formal garden shrouded in a cloak of snow, at once captivatingly lovely, frigidly bleak, and full of foreboding. A glimpse of the contrastingly-vibrant red rose leads meaningfully to viewers' first look at its human equivalent, a cheery Snow White (played at first by Raffey Cassidy) in the springtime of her life. This image is, like the girls' happiness, quickly blotted out by the death of her beloved mother the Queen, which is followed by the highly impressive, intriguing and ominous sequence featuring the attack of mysterious dark soldiers who shatter into shards of black glass when opposed. They arrive with another character who is extraordinary to behold, particularly because she is played by Charlize Theron, an actress who has been provided by nature with her own very special effect.

While *Snow White and the Huntsman* is clearly endeavoring to impress with its own look, nothing compares to the lengths this adaptation's villainess will go in order to do the same. Bewitching the king (Noah Huntley) with her beauty, it takes seductive sorceress Ravenna (Theron) a single day to replace the chains on her wrists with a ring on her finger. He is merely the means to a bitterness-fueled end: on their wedding night, she imperiously mounts the unsuspecting, aroused monarch and then mercilessly usurps him with something deadly in his drink and a dagger to his heart. However, Ravenna has also been poisoned, her mother having convinced her that the only way a woman can hope to control her destiny in a man's world is by manipulating those men with spellbinding sex appeal that is to be maintained at all cost. Thus, for example, there is the striking image of Ravenna arising from a bath of milk as thick as paint, and the unsettling scene in which she magically sucks the youthfulness out of a girl in a terrifying form of rejuvenation through inhalation. "You're Never Too Old To Be Young, "a song written for Walt Disney's classic *Snow White and the Seven Dwarfs* (1937), cannot help but come to mind.

Raging Ravenna is terrifying, but one is to understand that she is also terrified, not simply a horrifyingly-vain woman seething with resentment against fickle men and jealous of fresher faces, but a woman who has been tragically saddled with a ferociously-desperate, essential need to preserve her pulchritude. Having solely focused for so long on that outward appearance, perhaps she realizes how little is left within upon which she might fall back. No wonder this new Queen is so unnerved when the male-voiced mirror (which oozes down onto the floor and then up into the form of a molten man reminiscent of 1991's *Terminator 2*) undermines her with the assertion that she no longer boasts the loveliest face around. More than a few viewers will think that the mirror must be cracked when it declares Theron's Ravenna less fetching than the Snow White now played as a young woman by Kristen Stewart in her trademark sullen fashion. In any event, the Queen buys into it enough to order her brother Finn (Sam Spruell), a

character whose spirit, countenance and coif are all exceedingly odious, to bring her the heart of the stepdaughter she imprisoned years ago, as gobbling it will grant Ravenna immortality during which she will enjoy undiminished, unrivaled beauty.

Fortunately, Snow White escapes, which, to borrow the title of the Stephen Sondheim musical about all sort of fairy tales, takes viewers wonderfully *Into the Woods*. There, they encounter two marvelous, magical realms that actually linger longer in the memory than either of the film's leading ladies. The first is the disconcerting Dark Forest, a baleful, looming tangle of seemingly-charred trees with branches that appear eerily-intent on seizing passersby. Dead birds and the hideous bugs that feed upon them cover the ground. This shiver-inducing site supposedly derives strength from a person's weakness, and seems to groan as it malignantly lays in wait. The second is the enchanting, sunbathed Sanctuary, a contrastingly lush green spot filled with colorful flowers, winking mushrooms, charming fairies that emerge from inside happily-chirping birds, and an ethereal, intricately-horned white stag that bursts into butterflies when attacked. So scenery is not only strikingly chewed by Theron, but also wondrously displayed.

Made on a budget of $170 million, the film grossed $155 million domestically before more than doubling that overseas. Critical reaction was mixed. This *Snow White* came up with revisions like a hard-drinking, gruff, lost soul of a Huntsman (charismatic Chris Hemsworth) who joins forces with her in retaliation for the cunning Queen's manipulation of this widower's grief. It also offers up eight dwarves that are nothing like Disney's adorable mini-masterpieces, and they are all not only underdeveloped physically but also as characters. (What does make them special, however, is once again the effects: Bob Hoskins, Ian McShane, et. al., have either been digitally-compressed, or had their faces superimposed over those of dwarf doubles.) Finally, Snow White is turned into an inspiring, intrepid, armor-clad avenger who (not entirely credibly) leads a revolt that frees the deteriorating kingdom from a monarch who has been as toxic as the story's iconic apple. Yet, the most distinctive thing about this dark retelling remains the brilliant flashes of ocular interest, not surprising considering that director Rupert Sanders (here making his feature film debut) has excelled at grabbing attention while making commercials. He seems to have failed, however, if he wanted moviegoers to heatedly debate whether Stewart's character should choose the hunky Huntsman or Prince William (Sam Claflin) in a sequel. If her being kissed by two handsome guys failed to bring the *Twilight* series to mind, the actress' unfortunate affair with Sanders that (at least temporarily) broke up her relationship with Robert Pattinson did.

David L. Boxerbaum

CREDITS

Snow White: Kristen Stewart
Queen Ravenna: Charlize Theron
The Huntsman: Chris Hemsworth
Prince William: Sam Claflin
Beith: Ian McShane
Muir: Bob Hoskins
Gort: Ray Winstone
Nion: Nick Frost
Duir: Eddie Marsan
Coll: Toby Jones
Finn: Sam Spruell
Origin: United States
Language: English
Released: 2012
Production: Palak Patel, Joe Roth, Sam Mercer; Roth Films; released by Universal Pictures
Directed by: Rupert Sanders
Written by: Hossein Amini; Evan Daugherty; John Lee Hancock
Cinematography by: Greig Fraser
Music by: James Newton Howard
Sound: Craig Henighan
Editing: Conrad Buff
Costumes: Colleen Atwood
Production Design: Dominic Watkins
MPAA rating: PG-13
Running time: 128 minutes

REVIEWS

Bowles, Scott. *USA Today*. May 31, 2012.
Burr, Ty. *Boston Globe*. May 30, 2012.
Ebert, Roger. *Chicago Sun-Times*. May 30, 2012.
Gleiberman, Owen. *Entertainment Weekly*. May 30, 2012.
Lowry, Brian. *Variety*. May 31, 2012.
Morgenstern, Joe. *Wall Street Journal*. May 31, 2012.
O'Sullivan, Michael. *Washington Post*. May 31, 2012.
Phillips, Michael. *Chicago Tribune*. May 31, 2012.
Pinkerton, Nick. *Village Voice*. May 29, 2012.
Pols, Mary. *Time*. May 31, 2012.

QUOTES

Queen Ravenna: "I was ruined by a king like you once. I replaced his queen. An old woman. And in time I too would have been replaced. Men use women. They ruin us and when they are finished with us they toss us to the dogs like scraps."

TRIVIA

Charlize Theron dropped out of *J. Edgar* to do this movie.

AWARDS

Golden Raspberries 2012: Worst Actress (Stewart)
Nominations:
Oscars 2012: Costume Des., Visual FX
British Acad. 2012: Costume Des.

SOUND OF MY VOICE

Box Office: $408,015

Sound of My Voice opens with two people arriving at a house at night where they are blindfolded, handcuffed, put into another automobile and taken to another house. There, they take showers and are given new clothes to wear—plain, white clothes. When they arrive in the basement of this house, they are greeted by the owners with a complex secret handshake. There are two other people who are also arriving on this evening. They are given a special instruction: "No sudden movements. The first night is always the hardest." This is undoubtedly a cult. The white robes, the secret handshakes, and the leader, a beautiful, charismatic woman named Maggie (Brit Marling) who walks around with an oxygen tank, are all dead giveaways. Why would anyone join?

It turns out that the two new arrivals are would-be documentary filmmakers who are there to infiltrate and expose the cult. Peter (Christopher Denham) and Lorna (Nicole Vicius) have managed to convince the cult leaders that their message has moved them and touched them enough to want to be involved. The leaders suspect nothing. Peter wears glasses, which are made to simply house a microscopic camera that will film all the meetings and rituals of the cult. The glasses will only film if the transmitter is within 50 feet, so Peter swallows the transmitter. The purposes of making the film are personal to Peter, whose mother was in a cult similar to this. Peter works as a substitute teacher by day where one of his students, a young girl, becomes a point of interest to Maggie.

Who is Maggie? She claims to be from the year 2054. She narrates to the audience a flashback sequence in which she is wandering the streets of Los Angeles naked with no ID and without any memory of how she got there. She gets taken in by a cult leader who is still with them today. She needs the oxygen tank because she is severely allergic to the present day air, which also has to do with why there are plants being grown in the house. Yet, when she is asked by a curious member of the cult to sing a song from the future, she ends up singing a song by The Cranberries from back in the '90s. Peter, nevertheless, becomes compromised by the cult and the status of the film project comes into question.

Brit Marling also co-wrote this film with director Zal Batmanglij and it shares some of the same themes and traits as her last screenplay/staring role, *Another Earth* (2011). In that film, she played a woman who (along with the rest of the world) faced the prospect of a planet just like Earth hovering in the sky getting closer and closer to this planet Earth and with the potential of having another person just like her living life on that planet. *Sound of My Voice* shares with that film the same sense of a yearning for an identity and a connection with someone, anyone, even one's self. The character of Peter in *Sound of My Voice* is in denial over the cult's hold on him. He lost his mom to a cult. It stands to reason that Maggie becomes a mother figure to him.

Marling and her co-writers have also employed science fiction into their storylines without calling too much attention them as "sci-fi." *Another Earth* was about another planet lurking in earth's orbit, but the film was not out to be a sci-fi movie with a twist ending. It was after something bigger. Philosophical questions about existence reminiscent of Andrey Tarkovskiy's *Solaris* (1971) and Carl Sagan's novel (and to a lesser degree, the 1997 film) *Contact* were its real means of telling the story. *Sound of My Voice*, though not quite as successfully, uses the idea of time travel in the same way. The natural question, of course, is whether or not Maggie did, indeed, travel back in time. There are certainly enough clues to prove she is full of it, but the movie's Macguffin (the little girl) leaves even more clues that she is definitely in her own world. She probably legitimately believes she did travel back in time.

Sound of My Voice has a lot going for it during most of its duration. Denham and Vicius are a convincing couple and Marling makes Maggie into a compelling and almost empathetic figure. Director Batmanglij keeps the atmosphere cool and sterile without calling too much attention to style. The film's main problem comes at the end, which utilizes an all-too-trendy ambiguous ending, which is often used as a crutch when a story has nowhere to go and the writers believe it is better to send an audience out of the theater arguing than to actually take them somewhere. A film should earn its right to an ambiguous ending. *Another Earth* did. *Sound of My Voice* leaves a lot of unanswered questions while spouting out some vague platitudes about choice and destiny. It is a disappointing coda to a film that had the potential to be just as thought-provoking had it actually come up with a more solid ending.

Collin Souter

CREDITS

Peter: Christopher Denham
Lorna: Nicole Vicius
Maggie: Brit Marling
Origin: United States
Language: English
Released: 2011
Production: Brit Marling, Hans Ritter, Shelley Surpin, Skyscraper Films; released by Fox Searchlight Pictures
Directed by: Zal Batmanglij
Written by: Brit Marling; Zal Batmanglij
Cinematography by: Rachel Morrison
Music by: Rostam Batmanglij
Sound: Will Riley
Editing: Tamara Meem
Costumes: Sarah de Sa Rego
Production Design: Scott Enge
MPAA rating: R
Running time: 86 minutes

REVIEWS

Ebert, Roger. *Chicago Sun-Times.* May 10, 2012.
Edelstein, David. *New York Magazine.* April 23, 2012.
Goodykoontz, Bill. *Arizona Republic.* May 18, 2012.
Howell, Peter. *Toronto Star.* May 10, 2012.
Kennedy, Lisa. *Denver Post.* May 11, 2012.
Lumenick, Lou. *New York Post.* April 27, 2012.
Morgenstern, Joe. *Wall Street Journal.* April 26, 2012.
O'Hehir, Andrew. *Salon.com.* April 28, 2012.
O'Sullivan, Michael. *Washington Post.* April 27, 2012.
Rodriguez, Rene. *Miami Herald.* May 24, 2012.

QUOTES

Peter Aitken: "Somewhere in the valley, there is a woman living in a basement. She's actually amassing followers. these people believe that she will actually lead them to salvation, or whatever. And yes, she's dangerous—but we have to see this thing through. All the way."

AWARDS

Nominations:

Ind. Spirit 2013: Actress—Supporting (Marling), First Feature

SPARKLE

Celebrate the legend.
        —Movie tagline

Box Office: $24.4 million

Sparkle is a film about a young woman who, despite

the sweet and innocent facade that she presents to one and all, will do virtually anything to achieve success in her chosen field—"anything" in this case ranging from lying to family members to exploiting someone else's drug habit to committing a major felony, no matter how inadvertent it might have been, and allowing someone else to take the rap. Since the story revolves around the music industry, she is, of course, the heroine of the piece and is rewarded for her bad behavior by having all of her wishes come true. If the film had at least acknowledged the fact that the end triumph was less the result of hard work, talent and determination than of self-serving behavior, the exploitation of others and a lot of plain luck, it might have made for an interesting story. However, this remake of the 1976 musical cult favorite is inexplicably hell-bent on being an inspirational saga of one young woman's triumph over adversity and the end result, despite the sordid nature of some of the material, is a blandly inspirational bore that is destined to be remembered only because of the untimely demise of co-star Whitney Houston a few months before its theatrical release.

Set in Detroit in 1968 (about a decade further in time than the original), the film stars former *American Idol* winner Jordin Sparks as Sparkle, a would-be songwriter living at home with her two sisters under the overprotective watch of her devout mother (Whitney Houston), a one-time singer whose career was derailed by drink and drugs and who is hell-bent on making sure that neither Sparkle nor her other daughters, the rebellious Sister (Carmen Ejogo) and the studious Dolores (Tika Sumpter), go down the same wayward path that she once did. However, with the help of friend Stix (Derek Luke), the three sisters surreptitiously form a singing group, with the sexy Sister taking lead while Sparkle writes the tunes and sings backup, and they soon find themselves becoming a local sensation. Before long, the dark side of fame rears its ugly head in the form of Satin (Mike Epps), a Richard Pryor-like comedian who swoops in on Sister and introduces her to drugs and the back of his hand. Eventually, the group self-destructs after an audition for a major label goes really bad thanks to Sister's excesses and Sparkle is forced to go it alone and give voice to her work.

The original *Sparkle,* which marked the feature directorial debut of celebrated editor Sam O'Steen and the screenwriting debut of celebrated costume designer Joel Schumacher, was no masterpiece by any means but it is easy to see why it went on to become a cult favorite over the years. The screenplay may have been little more than a fusion of showbiz movie cliches and bits and pieces stolen from the rise and fall of The Supremes, but it had a snap to it that resonated with its target audience. The cast, including the then-unknown Irene Cara, Philip

Michael Thomas and Lonette McKee, made up for what they lacked in experience with energy, enthusiasm and raw charisma, especially in McKee's electrifying portrayal of the self-destructive Sister. Most importantly, the music by Curtis Mayfield, although it did not sound especially accurate to the period it was meant to represent, was still filled with solid tunes. Although the two films tell roughly the same story in the broad strokes, the elements that enlivened the original are nowhere to be found this time around and their absence is keenly felt throughout.

Most of the rough edges found the first time around have been smoothed over into a bland bunch of nothing that tries to replace the darker stuff with spiritual uplift that it has not earned, and which leaves more than a few plot threads dangling in the aftermath. Additionally, one might expect that moving the time frame up to the late sixties might add some resonance to the material but the real world hardly ever seems to intrude on the proceedings. (There is some stuff about Martin Luther King Jr. in the background of the early scenes that is then abruptly dropped from the proceedings.) In the lead role, Jordin Sparks is pretty, sings well, and has a killer smile but when it comes to following in the thespian footsteps of her fellow *American Idol* winners, she is much closer to Kelly Clarkson than Jennifer Hudson—whenever she is doing anything other than singing, she comes across like a deer in headlights. As for the newer music (a couple of songs from the original have been reused), the only thing that it has in common with the original is that this film too fails to properly represent the period it is meant to be set in—instead of a variation of the socially conscious stuff that was just beginning to emerge from Motown at that time, most of the tunes sound like they could be outtakes from an Alicia Keys album in 2012.

Of course, these complaints about *Sparkle* are all academic because the only element of real interest to audiences, both present and future, is the appearance of Whitney Houston in a role that was meant to help launch a comeback and which instead proved to be her swan song. Her presence is by far the most compelling thing about the film but not always for the right reasons. She often looks and sounds a bit worse for wear and while that is how her character is supposed to be, the line between real and reel life gets very blurry, especially when she recites dialogue that now contains an unfortunate subtext in the wake of her passing ("Hasn't my life served as enough of a cautionary tale for you?" being the most wince-inducing of the bunch). However, when she finally steps front and center to perform the gospel tune "His Eye is on the Sparrow," the film finally catches fire because while her voice does betray the ravages brought upon it by time and personal excesses, it also demonstrates in genuinely hair-raising fashion that Houston could still pull it together when she needed to and the fact that it would prove to be one of her final recordings only makes it all the more powerful. This is definitely a standout moment and it is too bad that is was not in the service of a film that deserved it.

Peter Sobczynski

CREDITS

Sparkle: Jordin Sparks
Sister: Carmen Ejogo
Delores: Tika Sumpter
Emma: Whitney Houston
Satin: Mike Epps
Stix: Derek Luke
Reverend Bryce: Michael Beach
Origin: United States
Language: English
Released: 2012
Production: Bishop T.D. Jakes, Debra Martin Chase, Curtis Wallace, Salim Akil, Mara Brock Akil; TDJ Enterprises, Stage 6 Films; released by Sony Pictures Entertainment
Directed by: Salim Akil
Written by: Mara Brock Akil
Cinematography by: Anastas Michos
Music by: Salaam Remi
Sound: Jay Nierenberg
Editing: Terilyn Shropshire
Costumes: Ruth E. Carter
Production Design: Gary Frutkoff
MPAA rating: PG-13
Running time: 116 minutes

REVIEWS

Barker, Andrew. *Variety*. August 16, 2012.
Dujsik, Mark. *MarkReviewsMovies.com*. August 16, 2012.
Ebert, Roger. *Chicago Sun-Times*. August 17, 2012.
Goss, William. *Film.com*. August 16, 2012.
Holden, Stephen. *New York Times*. August 16, 2012.
Hornaday, Ann. *Washington Post*. August 17, 2012.
Lybarger, Dan. *Kansas City Active*. August 26, 2012.
Orndorf, Brian. *Blu-Ray.com*. August 16, 2012.
Pais, Matt. *RedEye*. August 16, 2012.
Puig, Claudia. *USA Today*. August 16, 2012.

TRIVIA

Raven-Symone was at one time considered for the role of Sparkle Williams.

STEP UP REVOLUTION
(Step Up 4)

One step can change your world.
—Movie tagline

Box Office: $35.1 million

That the *Step Up* franchise has been at all successful defies a certain amount of logic. The first installment, starring a younger and not so fully beef-caked Channing Tatum, developed enough of a cult following, despite the film's weak plot, Tatum's awkward take on popping and locking, and some pretty flat acting, that a sequel and then a 3-D segment were green lit. Both follow-ups were panned by critics, but audiences kept buying tickets, so, obviously, a fourth movie was necessary. That fourth film is *Step-Up: Revolution,* a self-aware *Dirty Dancing* meets *Save The Last Dance* hybrid that, although not offering anything revolutionary in terms of story, does deliver the goods where it counts: sexy leads and awesome dance numbers.

Revolution takes viewers to Miami, a "fresh" setting that, in reality, just gives the production license to put as many of the female cast and every extra in bikinis (the guys just take their shirts off a lot). The star-crossed lovers at the center of this drama are Sean (played by Mixed Martial Artist Ryan Guzman) and Emily (Kathryn McCormick, a *So You Think You Can Dance* alum). He is a self-taught hip-hopper from the block who works as a waiter for a posh beachfront Miami hotel. Sean is not just a good dancer though; he is also an artist who used his mad skills to co-found The Mob, a flash mob outfit that hopes to make its fortune through YouTube hits. Emily is the privileged daughter of a real estate tycoon and a by-the-books ballerina. She has got great technique, but no originality. Sean breaks the rules, Emily follows them. If their meet-cute dance off is any indication, they are perfect for one another.

Of course, Emily wants nothing more than to break free from the high-class restraints that have made her life of privilege so difficult: who wants designer clothes when you cannot dance outside the lines? Sean, by contrast, could use a little focus. His flash mob racket needs a plan if it is going to get him noticed; an overnight YouTube sensation is not what it used to be. Luckily, Emily's father gives the couple the push they need by selecting Sean's working-class neighborhood as the site for his new high-end hotel development. Emily rebels against her father by joining Sean's rag tag group, while also suggesting that Sean use dance as a form of protest. It is a win-win for all: The Mob gets a worthy project and Emily gets a tutorial in street dance.

On a story level, *Revolution* asks that its audience suspend all of their collective disbelief. Do not ask how a group of underemployed misfits can afford the lofty price tag of some of the stunts they pull. How do they acquire costumes, high end video gear, and top scale effects? The movie never bothers to even ask much less answer the question. How do they also possess the project management skills to, for example, break into posh art galleries and camouflage their dancers into the gallery's works of art? Who knows? And do not even think of wondering how this international United Colors of Benetton group got together in the first place. What limited time writer Amanda Brody has between extended music videos she uses to try to add depth to a huge array of secondary characters, build a conceivable conflict for Sean and Emily, and make viewers believe that they have real chemistry. Do not be deceived, despite her efforts, *Revolution* does not boast the show-stealing cast of earlier hits like *Pitch Perfect* (2012), nor does it possess the everything-on-the-line tension of cult faves like *Drumline* (2002), or even the life-altering romance of *Save The Last Dance* (2001). But that is OK because *Revolution* has two things working in its favor: that Guzman and McCormick can act (in a relative sense) and that director Scott Speer knows the audience only cares about the dancing.

There will not be any awards handed out to the cast of *Revolution,* but both Guzman and McCormick possess an ease in front of the camera that elevates them beyond the label of "just dancers." Guzman in particular has the potential for mainstream heartthrob given the right opportunities. But the real gems of *Revolution* are the one-upping, electric, mind-bending dance routines—inconceivable as they may be. From the initial scene, where The Mob ties up Ocean Drive by dancing on high-bouncing low riders, to the big finale, when the group disrupts the groundbreaking ceremony of Emily's father's latest development with dancers than bend at impossible angles, it is hard not to want get up and join them. *Revolution* throws everything from break dancing to salsa at the audience and each routine brims with contagious energy. As long as *Step Up* keeps dancing, the audience will follow.

Joanna Topor MacKenzie

CREDITS

Sean: Ryan Guzman

Jason: Stephen Boss
Claire: Megan Boone
Emily: Kathryn McCormick
Vladd: Chadd Smith
Origin: United States
Language: English, Spanish
Released: 2012
Production: Erik Feig, Jennifer Gibgot, Garrett Grant, Adam Shankman, Patrick Wachsberger; Offspring Entertainment; released by Summit Entertainment
Directed by: Scott Speer
Written by: Duane Adler; Amanda Brody
Cinematography by: Karsten Gopinath
Music by: Aaron Zigman
Sound: Michael J. Benavente
Music Supervisor: Buck Damon
Editing: Matthew Friedman; Avi Youabian
Art Direction: Charles Daboub, Jr.; Caleb B. Mikler
Costumes: Rebecca Hofherr
Production Design: Carlos Menendez
MPAA rating: PG-13
Running time: 99 minutes

REVIEWS

Dowd, A. A. *Time Out New York.* July 28, 2012.
Gonzalez, Ed. *Slant Magazine.* July 25, 2012.
Nicholson, Amy. *Boxoffice Magazine.* July 26, 2012.
O'Connell, Sean. *Washington Post.* July 26, 2012.
Ogle, Connie. *Miami Herald.* July 27, 2012.
Olsen, Mark. *Los Angeles Times.* July 26, 2012.
Rea, Hillary. *Philadelphia Inquirer.* July 26, 2012.
Steinberg, Stephanie. *Boston Globe.* July 26, 2012.
Stewart, Sara. *New York Post.* July 27, 2012.
Willmore, Alison. *Movieline.* July 25, 2012.

TRIVIA

Adam G. Sevani/Moose, Mari Koda/Kido, and Chadd Smith/Vladd make a cameo and have their own dance scene in the film.

T

TAKE THIS WALTZ
(Take this Waltz: Une histoire d'amour)

Box Office: $1.2 million

A young woman walks around her kitchen. She is baking muffins, she is barefoot, and she seems content. Once she gets them in the oven, she rests on the floor to wait for them to be done and gives an ever brief look towards the camera as if to say, "this is the life we have chosen." Easily the opening scene to *Take This Waltz* can be read as a picture-perfect rendition of the mid-20th century housewife cooking for her man and left with little to do afterwards but to raise children. As the film takes place in the next century, writer-director Sarah Polley introduces viewers to the idea that the more things change, the more they stay the same.

The woman in the kitchen is Margot (Michelle Williams). She is in her early 20s and is married to Lou (Seth Rogen), who is writing a cookbook on the various methods to prepare chicken, which is a meal they appear to have every night. Margot meets Daniel (Luke Kirby), who engages Margot in conversation when they meet by chance on one of her business trips. Despite her aversion to "connections"—more a phobia of airport schedules than with people—there is a clear liking between the two of them. When they discover they actually live right across the street from each other she immediately blurts out, "I'm married," not just for him to keep his distance but also as a blunt reminder to herself.

The seed is planted in Margot's mind though and it begins to grow like a cancer. Her relationship with Lou is more playful than sexual and there is some discomfort when the two schools are mingled. Lou's sister, Geraldine (Sarah Silverman), is a very good friend of Margot's and also a recovering alcoholic. Each is now teetering on a wagon they so desperately want to control. Margot cannot help but want to be in Daniel's company, accepting afternoon invitations for drinks and conversations that cross the line into metaphorical unfaithfulness. Their dance has the outward appearance of a waltz but the inner rumblings of a Lambada Tango and the future of everyone's happiness hangs on their every move.

Polley is not merely challenging the fundamental struggles of monogamy but also the general bill of goods that romantic comedies with their homogenized happy endings have sold through cinema for far too long. Though many will think of her work as part of a disintegrating marriage in *Blue Valentine* (2010), in a film called *The Baxter* (2005), Michelle Williams played the rebound girl of a man whose life appeared to mirror the typical schlubs who are often discarded as the third wheel when a better option comes along. Now she is the anti-heroine at the center of a fantasy of her own making. Margot with her pixie haircut and goofy mannerisms practically is the Meg Ryan for a new generation. Only when this one comes across what she believes might be her destiny she is more conscious of the consequences involved and if she follows through the audience most certainly will too.

"I don't want to hurt him," Margot emotionally says at one point, referring to the very Baxter she is potentially making out of Lou, whose biggest sin—like most rom-com husbands—is that he is a bit on the boring side. And nothing breeds contempt like complacency.

Across the street, Margot and Daniel are masquerading as adults playing a childhood game of how close they can get to one another without actually touching. Her request for a breakdown on what their passion-filled encounter would be like fulfills her as much as it would any male imagining her in a Penthouse Forum letter. Alternately, Polley and Williams unashamedly show viewers every inch of Margot's naked body but mostly in an asexual manner just getting into the shower or going to the toilet in front of her husband. When Margot and Lou do have sex they are fully covered, only removing their clothing under the blankets. Any male fantasy connected with locker room shower scenes gets their chance with an extended washing with Williams, Silverman and another friend. As the scene progresses though, the nudity on display takes a backseat to the conversation of how every shiny new thing in our lives eventually comes around to being simply old again. Never has this theory been visualized with a more exemplary punch to the gut than a montage that, unfortunately for Margot, is not a fantasy.

Michelle Williams is so good at balancing on this tightrope between perceived happiness and indecision. As magnificent as she was in finding the human side to what could have easily been a Marilyn Monroe impersonation in *My Week With Marilyn* (2011), this is an ever more challenging performance that in many viewers' minds will come off as unsympathetic. Rogen also masterfully contributes to that particularly when he is forced to confront the situation and heartbreakingly reveals the punchline to a joke he had been planning for the next fifty years. Polley's script does not favor sides here in the way most love triangles are forced to create a villain to make the choices easier. She packages Margot as a bundle of insecurity that believes she knows where the line is but continues to inch her way towards crossing it. Her revelation of the courage it takes to seduce her husband is not a referendum on Lou's appearance or even her feelings for him but a suggestion of the inexperience that she entered into this union with in the first place.

Take This Waltz could prove to be a wearisome experience for those who have had their heart broken in a million pieces or exasperating to those who would rather see Margot strangled than fulfilled. It is a hill of beans if taken in story form alone, but the greater implications that Polley pursues within that narrative are staggeringly profound and meaningful. Looking too deeply in-between the human interaction and reactions, one can easily miss the wonderful visuals she has constructed with cinematographer Luc Montpellier: The bright colors and dreamy haze of the opening to an underwater ballet in a pool once the setting for a colorful joke now turning sour up to the time lapse montage

that spins Margot into the next phase of her life. Polley's coup de grace though may be her use of the cliched carnival ride set to the tune that accompanied the very first video on MTV, the jukebox of a new generation. Viewers will never hear The Buggles' *Video Killed the Radio Star* again without thinking about its nostalgic lyrics about nostalgia and a past forgotten in favor of new toys. Staring down Margot's burgeoning ecstasy while riding the Scrambler and her teasing of getting close to Daniel—in a ride practically designed to mash its passengers into one another—is exciting, sexy, suspenseful and sad all at the same time. Never sadder though than the film's final shot which encompasses the isolation of heartbreak, disappointment and the bird-in-the-hand realization that the only true practice of monogamy is just being alone.

Erik Childress

CREDITS

Margot: Michelle Williams
Lou: Seth Rogen
Daniel: Luke Kirby
Geraldine: Sarah Silverman
Karen: Jennifer Podemski
Origin: Canada, Japan, Spain
Language: English
Released: 2011
Production: Susan Cavan, Sarah Polley; released by Joe's Daughter
Directed by: Sarah Polley
Written by: Sarah Polley
Cinematography by: Luc Montpellier
Music by: Jonathan Goldsmith
Sound: Jane Tattersall
Music Supervisor: Jody Colero
Editing: Christopher Donaldson
Art Direction: Aleksandra Marinkovich
Costumes: Lea Carlson
Production Design: Matthew Davies
MPAA rating: R
Running time: 116 minutes

REVIEWS

Ebert, Roger. *Chicago Sun-Times*. July 12, 2012.
Erbland, Kate. *Film School Rejects*. June 30, 2012.
Phillips, Michael. *Chicago Tribune*. July 12, 2012.
Goss, William. *Film.com*. June 29, 2012.
Levy, Shawn. *Oregonian*. July 18, 2012.
Lybarger, Dan. *KC Active*. August 10, 2012.
Pfeiffer, Mark. *Reel Times: Reflections on Cinema*. July 19, 2012.

Rooney, David. *Hollywood Reporter*. October 19, 2012.
Scott, A. O. *New York Times*. June 28, 2012.
Wilmore, Alison. *Movieline*. June 28, 2012.

QUOTES

Geraldine: "Life has a gap in it. It just does. You don't go crazy trying to fill it."

TRIVIA

In 2009, the script was listed in *The Black List*, an annual publication that names the best unproduced screenplays within the year it is published.

TAKEN 2

> *First they took his daughter. Now they're coming for him.*
> —Movie tagline

> *They want revenge, They chose the wrong guy.*
> —Movie tagline

Box Office: $139.9 million

Unlike anything ever seen in those heartwarming Bell System commercials of yore, Bryan Mills (Liam Neeson) picked up a phone in *Taken* (2009) and icily vowed to do much more than merely reach out and touch someone who was kidnapping his daughter, Kim (Maggie Grace). "I will find you and I will kill you," was the sure, pointed end to the ex-CIA op's steely promise, even though, as he admitted at the start, "I don't know who you are. I don't know what you want." When producer Luc Besson sat down with Robert Mark Kamen to devise the screenplay for a sequel, they knew exactly who they would be targeting and what was desired based upon *Taken*'s surprising take: made on a modest budget of $25 million, the potent, pulpy production went on to gross nearly ten times that much worldwide. Moviegoers were asking for it, it seemed to the writing team, and thus they, along with the Albanian baddies, were going to get it—again. What the scribes basically ended up doing is merely phoning in more of the same, formulating a follow-up that often seemed more like a remake to many viewers. While those responsible had more dollars at their disposal this time, they utilized less sense.

For the Mills' own good if not for that of the franchise, an unquestionably sensible course of action to be taken at the conclusion of *Taken 2* would be the revocation of every last passport in the family's possession. In *Taken*, detrimentally-trusting yet somehow still virginal Kim's trip to France did not have being snatched and sold as a sex slave to a rich, revolting sheik on its itinerary, but she was barely out of the terminal at

Charles de Gaulle before that abhorrent activity was added against her will by sneaky Albanian white slavers. This nightmarish scenario was especially successful in creating primal alarm and outrage within parents, although no one reacted as strongly as Kim's aforementioned father, who took the breath away from viewers and villains alike when he became one desperately-driven, astonishingly-ferocious American in Paris. Now, two years after Bryan's rivetingly-relentless, vicariously-satisfying scum slayings, his once-and-possibly-future-wife Lenore (Famke Janssen) and once-but-no-longer-credibly-teenaged-daughter Kim (Grace is in her late twenties) have just joined him in Turkey when their plans for rest and relaxation are abruptly aborted by revenge. This time it is mom and dad who are titularly taken, as Murad (Rade Serbedzija), father of the evildoer Bryan had sensationally electrocuted in the first film, has seethingly sworn to carry out his own retributive unpleasantness. If every Mills makes it home yet again in one piece (and at one point Murad threatens to send Lenore back in many), it might not be the worst thing if these trouble-prone travelers are at least temporarily gripped by an agoraphobic fear of stepping outdoors.

Having retrieved his daughter in the nick of time before her purity could be spoiled by those with bad intentions at the end of *Taken*, Bryan starts off the sequel by over-protectively fetching Kim from the clutches of her loving boyfriend (Luke Grimes). (Mills is unfazed by guys pointing loaded guns at him, but what a horny teenager might be aiming to do to his daughter triggers a pronounced gulp.) Her savior has clearly become a smotherer, able to track her every move—amorous or otherwise—with a GPS device he has secretly implanted in her phone. Not as well-hidden is Bryan's desire to be reinstalled in Lenore's heart, and he senses an opportunity when she tearfully reveals her unhappiness with Husband No. 2. Bryan says to let him know if there is anything he can do, but as bonding leads to brutality overseas, it quickly seems clear that there is ridiculously little he cannot. Immediately sensing that the cab in which he and Lenore are riding is being followed, Bryan swiftly but calmly comes up with a dauntingly-detailed plan for her escape. He reveals contortionistic abilities as a captive, maneuvering a small cell phone from his sock up to his shackled hands. Calling Kim, he once again authoritatively imparts complex instructions, enabling her to triangulate his whereabouts with merely a map, a shoelace, a Sharpie, and his own sharp-earned estimation of the distance between himself and the exploding grenades with which she periodically peppers surprisingly-nonchalant Istanbul. (Kim had earlier escaped onto a ledge outside her hotel room, and during this scene that induced eye-rolling, scoffs and titters, believability went out the window, as well.) Once free, Bryan winds up imperviously prevailing over any and all attackers and returns to rescue the lovely Lenore, whose looks remain surprisingly unaltered after being slashed, hooded, and hung upside down to drip blood like a butchered cow carcass. As trouble began, Lenore had groaned, "I can't believe this is happening!" It did not take many viewers much longer to feel the same way. Silliness kills suspense, and it is mighty tough for involvement to survive incredulity.

It certainly helps Bryan that his swarthy, stubbled foes are so ludicrously inept. Knowing Bryan's formidable potency, tenacity and capacity from the events of *Taken*, they should certainly have looked upon a captive Bryan as bound and determined, and yet he is lackadaisically guarded. When multiple miscreants attack Bryan in one scene, they basically do so one at a time, like deli customers willing to wait in an orderly fashion until their number is up. Guard dogs nearly get laryngitis trying to warn these overtly-oblivious folk that Bryan is sneaking up to end their entranced watching of a televised soccer game with sudden death. When they do aim to fire, they helpfully hesitate just long enough to allow sure-shooting Bryan to pick them off. Grizzled leader Murad cannot help but emit a brief, less-than-fearsome groan when he sits down, sounding half-dead before Bryan completes his condition. If Albanian criminals failed to form an anti-defamation league after the first film, they surely must have done so after *Taken 2*.

At least as glaringly inept as these Albanian avengers is *Taken 2*'s self-surnamed director Olivier Megaton. He poorly stages and shoots fights and chase scenes, including one in which struggling student driver Kim is in every sense under the gun to develop the most extreme of skills. Kinetic camera movements and chaotic cutting are more likely to cause confusion, consternation, and headaches than excitement. While *Taken 2*'s careening cars likely needed a retread, the movie-going public deserved much better. Although Bryan may be doing "what I do best," one wishes his portrayer would return to devoting his own proven proficiency to projects that are laudable and not just lucrative. There were hopeful signs of this possibility when Neeson expressed sentiments that echoed his character's assertion of being "tired of it all." The fact that the $45 million-budgeted film grossed millions more than its predecessor sparked talk of another installment. However, without the serious actor who unexpectedly became an action flick star late in life, *Taken 3* is unlikely to be nearly as successful as Kim's third driving test.

David L. Boxerbaum

CREDITS

Bryan Mills: Liam Neeson
Lenore: Famke Janssen
Kim: Maggie Grace
Murad: Rade Serbedzija
Sam: Leland Orser
Casey: Jon(athan) Gries
Bernie: D.B. Sweeney
Jamie: Luke Grimes
Origin: United States, France
Language: English
Released: 2012
Production: Luc Besson; Europacorp, M6 Films, Grive Prods.; released by 20th Century Fox Film Corp.
Directed by: Olivier Megaton
Written by: Luc Besson; Robert Mark Kamen
Cinematography by: Romain Lacourbas
Music by: Nathaniel Mechaly
Sound: Frederic Dubois
Editing: Camille Delamarre; Vincent Tabaillon
Art Direction: Nanci B. Roberts
Costumes: Pamela Lee Incardona
Production Design: Sebastien Inizan
MPAA rating: PG-13
Running time: 92 minutes

REVIEWS

Anderson, John. *Wall Street Journal*. October 4, 2012.
Bowles, Scott. *USA Today*. October 4, 2012.
Corliss, Richard. *Time*. October 8, 2012.
Ebert, Roger. *Chicago Sun-Times*. October 4, 2012.
Gant, Charles. *Variety*. October 5, 2012.
Genzlinger, Neil. *New York Times*. October 4, 2012.
Hornaday, Ann. *Washington Post*. October 4, 2012.
Morris, Wesley. *Boston Globe*. October 4, 2012.
Nicholson, Amy. *Boxoffice Magazine*. October 3, 2012.
Phillips, Michael. *Chicago Tribune*. October 4, 2012.

QUOTES

Bryan Mills: "If I kill you, your other sons will come and seek revenge?"
Murad: "They will."
Bryan Mills: "And I will kill them too."

TRIVIA

Diego Boneta and Xavier Samuel both auditioned for the role that eventually went to Luke Grimes.

TED

Ted is coming.
—Movie tagline

Box Office: $218.8 million

For a movie that is often raunchy and mean-spirited, *Ted* contains a sweet back-story: When John (Mark Wahlberg) was a kid, he had trouble making friends. So like any lonely eight-year-old child with a devoted stuffed animal who keeps him calm during thunderstorms, John wishes for his teddy bear Ted to come to life. Decades after John's wish comes true, after Ted (voiced by Seth MacFarlane) becomes a national phenomenon and then just a drug-using, no-longer-famous slob of a roommate, John and Ted still sing their special "Thunder Buddies" song to keep the long-time friends from getting scared during the storm. The tune's profanity does not get in the way of its charm.

Other than his role as John's defender from scary weather, Ted no longer really pulls his weight. Like a much more foul-mouthed version of Walter in *The Muppets* (2011), Ted has become a third wheel, and John's girlfriend Lori (Mila Kunis, reuniting with Wahlberg after 2008's *Max Payne*) wants John to ask Ted to move out so the human pair can progress in their lives together. John clearly has mixed feelings, but his history with Ted and the fun they can still have together—which does no favors for John's professional life—makes it difficult to request that the former toy now let his 35-year-old best friend grow up.

Anyone who knows MacFarlane's sensibilities from TV's *Family Guy* (1999) or *American Dad!* (2005) or *The Cleveland Show* (2009) should not be surprised that the tender bond between John and Ted exists among a flurry of bad taste and non sequiturs in *Ted*, a film that just barely works in spite of its smugness. In fact, MacFarlane's lack of perspective about his own impulses is clear early on in his feature directing/co-writing debut when Ted watches *Jack and Jill* (2011) with four prostitutes. (That one of the women defecates on the floor is irrelevant but still worth mentioning.) Ted, who possesses quite a significant sex drive despite having no genitalia, calls Adam Sandler's comedy "unwatchable." He is right, but MacFarlane seems completely oblivious to the fact that both *Jack and Jill* and *Ted* are full of homophobic jokes and contain varying degrees of obsession with farting and cracks at the expense of people who are overweight. While Sandler always plays Jewish stereotypes for laughs, *Ted* contains numerous jokes that act as if anti-Semitism is funny. MacFarlane really should not condescend to a comedian who falls prey to the same poor judgment that he does.

Obviously, MacFarlane does not exactly put much thought into his targets. In *Ted* he takes aim at Corey Feldman, Taylor Lautner and Sinead O'Connor, who are such low-hanging fruit the jokes may as well be coated in grass. If someone advised MacFarlane to pass on these gags, he could probably deliver a clever and consistently funny film. At times, the energetic, sporadically inspired *Ted* is a riot, such as when Ted, doing something with his co-worker (Jessica Barth) at the grocery store that should make the food beneath them unsellable, utters in the heat of the moment, "Stick your finger in the loop of my tag." When John rattles off as many "white trash" names as possible in an attempt to guess the name of Ted's hook-up—her name is Tami-Lynn, by the way—, it is an example of MacFarlane's hyperactive imagination landing on a joke that just plain works on screen.

Something that never works, however, is the creepy guy (Giovanni Ribisi, who made life unpleasant for Wahlberg earlier in 2012 with *Contraband*) who has long fixated on Ted. The twisted nature of this subplot does not fit with the (frequently dirty) lightness of the rest of the film, and it feels shoehorned in merely because MacFarlane had nothing else to do with the story. He should have worked to flesh out Lori, since MacFarlane assumedly knows from working with Kunis on *Family Guy* that she is far too good a comic actress to be saddled with such a bland girlfriend role. In *Ted* she is mostly asked to repeat her performance in 2011's *Friends with Benefits*. There are certainly worse things to see twice, but Kunis deserves to work with a filmmaker who does not see female characters as an after-thought.

She and Wahlberg do ensure Lori and John make a good couple, though, a must for any movie that wants viewers to care if the characters can stay on track for the long haul. Their romance never really takes front and center in *Ted*, whose jokes arrive so fast and often that the moderate success rate works in its favor, but it helps balance things out when the film takes a detour, such as a dream sequence that recalls *Anchorman* (2003) or an absurd party scene in which Ted winds up fighting a duck named James Franco. That is not joke writing, it is just randomness for the sake of randomness, which also goes for Ted's personal friendship with veteran actor Tom Skerritt (who appears as himself).

Yet even if *Ted*, one of the year's biggest hits, often feels like the Seth MacFarlane one-man show, the movie is always funny enough not to fly off the rails. Sure, it is unlikely that society would ever truly get used to a teddy bear that operates like a human, no matter how many years it has been since Johnny Carson interviewed him. Despite his questionable, frequently intolerant sense of humor, Ted remains a welcome presence in the film, at least enough that viewers can understand why John would have trouble putting his and Ted's childish behavior behind him.

Many people struggle to adapt their friendships from youth into adulthood, and that cannot be easy with a teddy bear for a best friend. That concept works in *Ted*, but John dealing that challenge would absolutely be funnier and more fun if the furry guy was not such a racist.

Matt Pais

CREDITS

John Bennett: Mark Wahlberg
Lori Collins: Mila Kunis
Rex: Joel McHale
Donny: Giovanni Ribisi
Guy: Patrick Warburton
Tanya: Laura Vandervoort
Ted: Seth McFarlane (Voice)
Origin: United States
Language: English, French, Spanish
Released: 2012
Production: Jason Clark, John Jacobs, Scott Stuber, Seth McFarlane, Wellesley Wild; Fuzzy Door, Bluegrass Films, Smart Entertainment; released by Universal Pictures
Directed by: Seth McFarlane
Written by: Seth McFarlane; Alec Sulkin; Wellesley Wild
Cinematography by: Michael Barrett
Music by: Walter Murphy
Sound: Elliott L. Koretz
Editing: Jeff Freeman
Art Direction: E. David Cosier
Costumes: Debra McGuire
Production Design: Stephen Lineweaver
MPAA rating: R
Running time: 106 minutes

REVIEWS

Burr, Ty. *Boston Globe*. June 28, 2012.
Ebert, Roger. *Chicago Sun-Times*. June 27, 2012.
McCarthy, Todd. *Hollywood Reporter*. June 23, 2012.
Persall, Steve. *Tampa Bay Times*. July 1, 2012.
Pols, Mary. *Time*. June 28, 2012.
Puig, Claudia. *USA Today*. June 28, 2012.
Rabin, Nathan. *AV Club*. June 27, 2012.
Rea, Stephen. *Philadelphia Inquirer*. June 28, 2012.
Schaeger, Nick. *Slant Magazine*. June 26, 2012.
Scott, A. O. *New York Times*. June 28, 2012.

QUOTES

Narrator: "Now if there's one thing you can be sure of, it's that nothing is more powerful than a young boy's wish. Except an Apache helicopter. An Apache helicopter has machine guns and missiles. It is an unbelievably impressive complement of weaponry, an absolute death machine."

TRIVIA

The film was shipped to theaters under the title "Thunder Buddies."

AWARDS

Nominations:

Oscars 2012: Song ("Everybody Needs a Best Friend")

10 YEARS

*Who got fat? Who didn't change? Who got rich?
Who got hot?*
—Movie tagline

Box Office: $203,373

The typical reunion comedy or drama usually has a lot of narrative hurdles to overcome before settling into a multi-character storyline. Chief among these is the exposition necessary to set everyone in the audience straight on who these people are, where they came from and why their journey will be worth taking by the film's end. It is a lot to establish in just ten or fifteen minutes, but if the characters are charming enough and the script economizes itself in a way that keeps the audience engaged, the result can be a breezy piece of entertainment probably inspired by real-life people and events as experienced by the person who wrote the script. At worst, it can be a narcissistic and self-indulgent chore, such as *I Melt With You* (2011), in which case a miserable time will be had by all.

Fortunately, Jaime Linden's directorial debut *10 Years* is a well-cast, unpretentious and pleasant surprise. The film centers on a ten-year reunion of a group of mostly white, good looking, seemingly middle class people who went to Lake Howell High School and are finding (as people often do in these films) that they have not really grown up as much as they thought they would. Confessions are made, the truth reveals itself, and the final rite of passage for twenty-something adolescence ends up being a life changer for most involved. The movie goes through the usual motions of these kinds of films, but not without occasionally having something interesting to say.

First, there is Jake (Channing Tatum) and his girlfriend Jess (Jenna Dewan-Tatum). Jake and Jess have been seeing each other for three years. Jake has not yet proposed marriage even though he has a wedding ring in the glove compartment of his car. He is simply waiting for the right spontaneous moment. Jess tags along with Jake to this reunion and is often the subject of many speculative conversations between he and his friends. There is also Cully (Chris Pratt) and his wife Sam (Ari Graynor), who have settled into a typical suburban family household with two kids. Cully has never really embraced this lifestyle and seems trapped by it since he is, at heart, a childish buffoon.

The most financially successful of the group is Marty (Justin Long), a Wall Street broker who is still single and maybe looking to rekindle a relationship with Anna (Lynn Collins), who was the life of the party back in the day and who is trying her best to be so at the reunion. Competing for her attention is the affable and awkward AJ (Max Minghella), who has a tendency to show off pictures of his new boat when others are showing off their kids. And there is also Reeves (Oscar Isaac), who went on to become a somewhat famous singer-songwriter and who spends much of the movie in the pleasant company of Elise (Kate Mara), who never made much of an impression on anybody back in high school.

There are more plot threads and characters here, but the core of this reunion is made up of the male leads and their dilemmas. Cully was a bully in high school and spends much of the movie trying to make amends, but ends up regressing the more he drinks while his wife watches and ponders just how much longer she has to live with the mistake she made in marrying him. Jake is taken aback by the presence of Mary (Rosario Dawson), with whom he had a past that involved a meaningful incident on prom night and struggles with his attraction toward her while in the presence of his current girlfriend. Mary is accompanied by her current boyfriend Paul (Ron Livingston) who does not mingle well in this setting.

All of these plot threads flow in and out rather seamlessly, thanks in large part to the appealing cast (this must have been a great looking group of seniors). Long and Minghella are a funny pair of guys who are competing more for their own personal self-worth and validation than for the heart of a woman. Pratt is perfectly cast as Cully, the obnoxious bore whose own self-worth slowly decays the more he tries to go against his own nature. Channing Tatum, who also co-produced the film, is wisely cast along with his real-life wife Jenna Dewan-Tatum, giving the two main characters a believability that gets the movie going on the right foot at the outset. The entire cast as a whole does a good job of making these people and their bond to one another seem authentic.

10 Years is not a particularly ambitious movie. Linden will not receive any strong notices for visual style here, but as a writer and director of actors, he shows some promise. He has a good ear for making scripted dialogue seem genuine and his cast is up to the task of improvising where necessary. There is a very funny scene in which the male characters are in a car getting high and talking about how to get out of having awkward conversations at a reunion. But in the end, Linden's script is about looking ahead during a time when one is supposed to look back and wonder how they got there. The question is inevitably and wisely asked, "Why spend so much time looking back when there is so much to look forward to?"

Collin Souter

CREDITS

Jake: Channing Tatum
Jess: Jenna Dewan-Tatum
Mary: Rosario Dawson
Marty: Justin Long
AJ: Max Minghella
Reeves: Oscar Isaac
Cully: Chris Pratt
Sam: Ari Graynor
Elise: Kate Mara
Anna: Lynn Collins
Garrity: Brian Geraghty
Olivia: Aubrey Plaza
Origin: United States
Language: English
Released: 2012
Production: Marty Bowen, Reid Carolin, Wyck Godfrey, Channing Tatum; Iron Horse, 33 and Out Productions, EG Productions, Boss Media, Temple Hill Entertainment; released by Anchor Bay Entertainment Inc.
Directed by: Jamie Linden
Written by: Jamie Linden
Cinematography by: Steven Fierberg
Music by: Chad Fischer
Sound: Jay Nierenberg
Music Supervisor: Season Kent
Editing: Jake Pushinsky
Art Direction: RA Arancio-Parrain
Costumes: Trayce Gigi Field
Production Design: Kara Lindstrom
MPAA rating: PG-13
Running time: 100 minutes

REVIEWS

Anderson, Melissa. *Village Voice.* September 11, 2012.
Biancolli, Amy. *San Francisco Chronicle.* September 20, 2012.
Goldstein, Gary. *Los Angeles Times.* September 13, 2012.
Goodykoontz, Bill. *Arizona Republic.* September 20, 2012.
Holden, Stephen. *New York Times.* September 13, 2012.
O'Sullivan, Michael. *Washington Post.* September 21, 2012.
Schager, Nick. *Time Out New York.* September 11, 2012.
Schwarzbaum, Lisa. *Entertainment Weekly.* September 5, 2012.
Weitzman, Elizabeth. *New York Daily News.* September 17, 2012.
Willmore, Allison. *AV Club.* September 13, 2012.

TRIVIA

Actors Chris Pine, Anna Faris, Megan Fox, and Taylor Momsen were all considered for various roles in the early stages of production.

THAT'S MY BOY
(I Hate You, Dad)
(Donny's Boy)

The story of a child...and his son.
—Movie tagline

Everyone has a teenage crush...Donny's went a little too far.
—Movie tagline

Box Office: $36.9 million

Adam Sandler tried to do drama. The former *Saturday Night Live* funnyman who found unprecedented and consistent success in his cinematic ventures tried to do something different with Paul Thomas Anderson, who seemed to know the psychosis of his comic creations better than anyone. Critics loved *Punch-Drunk Love* (2002) but his fans avoided it. He tried again with another acclaimed director, James L. Brooks, with *Spanglish* (2004) and the film grossed about as much as the opening weekend of one of his wacky comedies. Mike Binder's *Reign Over Me* (2007) and Judd Apatow's *Funny People* (2009) also were failures, sending Sandler into complete regression. After one of the biggest successes of his career, *Grown Ups* (2010), he delivered one of the very worst, *Just Go With It* (2011). When trailers surfaced for *Jack and Jill* (2011) with Sandler playing the dual role of his twin sister, internet satirists created videos placing George C. Scott in the same screening room he watched the infamous snuff film of *Hardcore* (1979) which led to the immortal protest "turn it OFF!" It is a cry for help that is equally appropriate for *That's My Boy*, as it now seems clear that Sandler has given up on drama or any effort at all.

Back in 1984, teenage Donny Berger began carrying on an affair with his teacher, Mary (Eva Amurri). After they are caught and she is sent to jail, it is revealed that she is pregnant with Donny's child. The taboo relationship turns the boy into a national celebrity which he relishes, but once the clock runs out on his fifteen minutes, the ensuing years as a bad father eventually catch up. Flash-forward to present day, where his son, Todd (Andy Samberg), is successful and about to marry further into money with the lovely Jamie (Leighton Meester).

Adult Donny (Adam Sandler), meanwhile, owes a wealth of back taxes to the IRS and only a few days to pay it to avoid jail. A TV producer offers him enough money to cover the debt if only he can arrange a reunion interview with Todd and the still incarcerated Mary. So it's off to his son's wedding weekend to not so delicately hit him up for the money. As Donny is supposed to have died in a car accident, per Todd's stories, he plays himself off as an old friend who begins to either offend or shockingly ingratiate himself amongst the future in-laws.

Spurred perhaps by a recent spate of successful R-rated comedies, *That's My Boy* ups the vulgarity level from Sandler's usual PG-13 base and attempts to even outdo the line established by contemporaries like Apatow, Adam McKay and Peter and Bobby Farrelly. If the statutory rape and pedophilia of a prologue is not shocking enough, the reunion of father and son leads to fist fights with priests, infidelity amongst in-laws and even closer family members, and the progression of *There's Something About Mary's* (1998) "hair gel" gag.

Never to suggest any such topics are off-limits for comedy, but it requires either a touch of delicacy of which Sandler and his regular cohorts are incapable, a connection to characters forced into such uncomfortable situations or something that contains a satiric truth that underscores how shockingly outrageous it all is. Just having swearing, nudity and cameo appearances by taboo subject matter does not fit the bill. Seth MacFarlane gets criticized for the seeming randomness of his provocateur humor on TV's *Family Guy* and feature directorial debut, *Ted* (2012), but it is usually cloaked in the kind of satire audiences are afraid to risk offending with their own voices. When one of his characters punches a priest, there is a reason beyond the shock value.

There is little else to say about *That's My Boy* that has not already been said about the very worst of Sandler's career. Sandler is doing one of his wacky voices that would demand a replacement in an animation recording studio. Samberg, a solid satirist in his own right, is forced to play the discomforted straight man. Rooting through the memory of a nearly full two-hour film that drains quickly from active memory, it is near impossible to remember any specific line or reaction that produces any sort of chuckle. Though it must have garnered a couple since even with all its effort focused on pratfalls and gross-out situations, the film is not as wholly offensive or foully incompetent as *I Now Pronounce You Chuck & Larry* and *Just Go With It*, Sandler's worst films. If there is any silver lining to *That's My Boy*, it is that it was a box office failure. Even in Sandler's normally golden summer release pattern, the film grossed less than *Funny People* and *Spanglish*. So maybe this is a step in the right direction after all.

Erik Childress

CREDITS

Donny: Adam Sandler
Todd: Andy Samberg
Jamie: Leighton Meester

Father McNally: James Caan

Chad: Milo Ventimiglia

Gerald: Blake Clark

Himself: Vanilla Ice

Origin: United States

Language: English, French, Spanish

Released: 2012

Production: Allen Covert, Heather Parry, Jack Giarraputo, Adam Sandler; Happy Madison Productions; released by Columbia Pictures

Directed by: Sean Anders

Written by: David Caspe

Cinematography by: Brandon Trost

Music by: Rupert Gregson-Williams

Sound: Elmo Weber; Russell Farmarco

Music Supervisor: Kevin Grady

Editing: Tom Costain

Production Design: Aaron Osborne

MPAA rating: R

Running time: 116 minutes

REVIEWS

Fragoso, Sam. *Fan the Fire.* September 18, 2012.

Gleiberman, Owen. *Entertainment Weekly.* June 15, 2012.

Kenigsberg, Ben. *ReelViews.* September 5, 2012.

Lybarger, Dan. *KC Active.* July 1, 2012.

Nusair, David. *Reel Film Reviews.* June 23, 2012.

Pfeiffer, Mark. *Reel Times: Reflections on Cinema.* June 20, 2012.

Rabin, Nathan. *AV Club.* June 14, 2012.

Rocchi, James. *MSN Movies.* June 16, 2012.

Snider, Eric D. *Film.com.* June 15, 2012.

Tobias, Scott. *NPR.* June 14, 2012.

QUOTES

Jamie: "Oh my god! I just found my wedding dress covered in barf! And something else!"

TRIVIA

Rex Ryan has a cameo in this movie playing a Patriots fan. In real life, he is the head coach of the New York Jets, who are the chief rivals of the Patriots.

AWARDS

Golden Raspberries 2012: Worst Actor (Sandler), Worst Screenplay

Nominations:

Golden Raspberries 2012: Worst Director (Anders), Worst Ensemble Cast, Worst Picture, Worst Support. Actor (Vanilla Ice)

THIN ICE
(The Convincer)

Greetings from Kenosha, WI! Where ordinary folks can make a killing.
—Movie tagline

Box Office: $790,421

Thin Ice is one of those thrillers that is not quite a thriller, a comedy that is not quite a comedy, and a drama that feels lost at sea. This is also one of those movies where the less one says about the storyline, the better. It is best to keep the description of the plot as mundane as possible. *Thin Ice* is not a bad movie and one could maybe take pleasure in the big reveals the movie dishes out, but if one starts to think too much about it, the whole thing starts to unravel. Just what is an audience member supposed to take away from this besides "huh...didn't see that coming?"

The story concerns an insurance salesman named Mickey Prohaska (Greg Kinnear) who lives in Wisconsin and travels to seminars where he is a motivational speaker to all other insurance salesmen. While at a hotel, two key plot points take place: 1. Mickey meets Bob Egan (David Harbour), who has been hired at a big firm. Mickey offers him more money to come work for him. Bob eventually accepts. 2. Mickey meets a drunk woman who seduces him and disappears the next day with his cash. These two plot points do not throw the storyline into any kind of tailspin. Rather, they are mere story devices to keep the viewer interested, for what follows is hardly the stuff of edge-of-your-seat suspense.

Bob and Mickey meet the elderly and naive Gorvy (Alan Arkin) who lives in a dilapidated house in rural Wisconsin. Gorvy does not have much to insure, but Mickey eventually sells him on the idea that his house is worth more than he ever imagined. One day, a violin repairman pays Gorvy a visit and drops off a violin he believes is Gorvy's. Mickey learns the violin is worth $25,000, but decides to hide that piece of information from Gorvy and offers to buy the violin from him for a mere sum. Mickey has child support to pay and is running out of money. His secretary Carla (Michelle Arthur) keeps a sharp eye on all of Mickey's finances and if Mickey can buy himself some time, keep up this ruse and get the $25,000 from an interested collector, his problems will be over.

But of course, nothing happens as he hoped. A violin expert and repairman (Bob Balaban) insists that the violin is worth even more than $25,000 and that it was delivered to the wrong person and he wants it back. Kinnear haggles and tries to pass off an ordinary violin as a real collector's item and he eventually finds himself in over his head as he tries to pass off lie after lie about violins, insurance, and how much or how little money he has.

Problems escalate when Gorvy and his friend have a security system installed in the house. The installer is an unstable thief named Randy (Billy Crudup) who catches Mickey in the act of trying to steal the violin out of the house. Mickey catches Randy in the act of stealing and calls him on it. It is at this point where *Thin Ice* takes a grizzly turn and now the story involves a dead body as well as all these other seemingly mundane plot points. The movie goes from a seriously dull sequence of events to an all-too-familiar story of dead bodies, blackmail and greed.

The cast helps keep the movie afloat. Kinnear seems to be in his own element here as a hapless guy who can sell winter coats in Africa while still being just clueless and spineless enough to be led around in a sticky situation. Arkin is also playing a role that seems to be tailored for him, a man who is stuck in another era and is none too happy about being lured into this one. Crudup is the only one here who is trying on a new mode. His is not a character anybody wants to be in a room with for more than a minute or two. His long, contemplative silences as he digests the current situation are eventually punctuated by fits of rage where the object of his anger is probably the person standing next to him. All of these actors are doing good work here, but one has to wonder if the effort is really worth it.

The film was written by Jill and Karen Sprecher and directed by Jill. If the movie works or does not work, it is only partially their doing. *Thin Ice* was taken away from them by the studio and was re-cut, re-structured, given a voice-over and flashbacks. The Sprechers also wrote and directed *13 Conversations About One Thing* (2001), a movie that had one of those multiple characters/multiple storyline structures where the stories are all linked together by a uniting theme. Their intentions for *Thin Ice* will hopefully be realized someday, but in its current form, it remains a mildly interesting movie that never truly comes alive even when its surprises are revealed. It aspires to be in the same vein as the Coen Brothers' *Fargo* (1996) and the comparisons are inevitable, but that will most likely dominate the conversation.

Collin Souter

CREDITS

Mickey Prohaska: Greg Kinnear
Gorvy Hauer: Alan Arkin
Randy: Billy Crudup
Jo Ann Prohaska: Lea Thompson
Bob Egan: David Harbour
Leonard Dahl: Bob Balaban
Origin: United States
Language: English
Released: 2012
Production: Mary Frances Budig, Elizabeth Redleaf, Christine Kunewa Walker; Spare Room Productions, Werc Werk Works; released by ATO Pictures
Directed by: Jill Sprecher
Written by: Jill Sprecher; Karen Sprecher
Cinematography by: Dick Pope
Music by: Jeff Danna
Sound: John Sims
Editing: Lee Percy
Art Direction: Kelly Hemenway
Costumes: Tere Duncan
Production Design: Jeffrey Schoen
MPAA rating: R
Running time: 114 minutes

REVIEWS

Burr, Ty. *Boston Globe*. April 5, 2012.
Covert, Colin. *Minneapolis Star Tribune*. February 16, 2012.
Ebert, Roger. *Chicago Sun-Times*. February 23, 2012.
Gleiberman, Owen. *Entertainment Weekly*. February 15, 2012.
Guzman, Rafer. *Newsday*. February 17, 2012.
Murray, Noel. *AV Club*. February 16, 2012.
O'Sullivan, Michael. *Washington Post*. April 6, 2012.
Rea, Steven. *Philadelphia Inquirer*. February 16, 2012.
Scott, A. O. *New York Times*. February 16, 2012.
Smith, Kyle. *New York Post*. February 17, 2012.

TRIVIA

The violin shop featured in the film, Dahl Violins, is an actual violin shop in downtown Minneapolis. In the film, the shop is supposed to be located in Chicago. However, when Mickey and Randy break into the shop at night, the skyline featured in the scene's initial shot is obviously Minneapolis.

THINK LIKE A MAN

Let the mind games begin.
—Movie tagline

Box Office: $91.5 million

Every once in a while, a studio looking for the next possible breakout hit will buy the screen rights to a best-selling self-help book on the theory that the legions of people buying such pop psychology pap will be equally willing to pay more money to see them brought to life at the local bijou. The trouble is that since these books generally do not have anything resembling a traditional story structure, they then have to invent some kind of narrative through line for the material that will somehow encapsulate the key points that readers embraced in the first place. Needless to say, the films that have emerged in this peculiar sub-genre have mostly been ghastly all-star affairs like *He's Just Not That Into You* (2009) and *What to Expect When You're Expecting* (2012). Frankly, the best one of the bunch remains the early Woody Allen comedy *Everything You Ever Wanted to Know About Sex (but was afraid to ask)* (1972) and even *that* one is usually regarded as one of his lesser efforts.

Because of the prior history of this particular style of filmmaking, most observers presumably gave little thought to *Think Like a Man*, a romantic comedy inspired by *Act Like a Lady, Think Like a Man*, the best-selling book of advice penned by comedian Steve Harvey, when it hit theaters during the normally lackluster spring season. Furthermore, they presumably chalked up its surprisingly strong showing at the box-office as more evidence that a chronically underserved audience will turn out in droves for anything that looks as though it might be up their alley. Truth be told, while the film is no comedic masterpiece by any stretch of the imagination and its insights into the human heart range from the crashingly predictable to the downright insipid, it is a moderately amusing work that is better than it frankly has any right to be and one whose appeal stretches out further than its presumed target audience.

The film follows the intertwining romantic misadventures of a quartet of friends and the women in their lives. Michael (Terrence J.) still has not cut the apron strings binding him to his demanding mother (Jenifer Lewis), much to the consternation of his current girlfriend, single mother Candace (Regina Hall). Dominic (Michael Ealy) is a starry-eyed dreamer who cannot hold a job and who is dating driven businesswoman Lauren (Taraji P. Henson), who does not realize that the reason he was behind the wheel of a fancy car when they met was because he was supposed to be parking it. Jeremy (Jerry Ferrara) is a goof whose refusal to grow up and join the adult world is beginning to wear thin on longtime girlfriend Kristen (Gabrielle Union). Zeke (Romany Malco) is an all-around player who has fallen for Mya (Megan Goode), who has just sworn off one-night stands and plans to abstain from sex until she knows that she has met the right guy. Conflict arises when the women all buy and read Steve Harvey's book in order to use his advice about how men think in order to get them to act how they want them to behave. Eventually, the men stumble upon their secret and start using the secrets contained within the sacred tome as

well before everyone receives their pre-ordained happy endings.

To say that *Think Like a Man* is a bit on the convoluted side would be a massive understatement. Between the four main stories, the numerous sequences of the various characters discussing dating strategies and the frequent kibitzing by Cedric (Kevin Hart), who pops up now and then to offer comments about strippers, jokes about his ex-wife and the occasional bit of narration, the screenplay by Keith Merryman and David A. Newman is so overloaded with characters and incidents that it sometimes feels like a marathon of *Love, American Style* episodes. Perhaps if one of the story lines had been dropped, the others might have had a little more time to breathe and play out at a more relaxed pace. Instead, it tries to jam too much material into its framework and winds up clocking in at over two hours, a running time far too extended for a film of this sort.

Another aspect that gets really aggravating over time is the way that the film often feels like an extended commercial for the book rather than its own separate entity. To judge solely from how it is presented here, Harvey's work is more popular than the *Fifty Shades of Grey* and *Hunger Games* trilogies combined—the kind that would choose Oprah's book club instead of the other way around—more profound than the collected writings of Plato and Dear Abby and hardly a scene or two goes by without someone on the screen singing its praises. In addition, virtually every time a character turns on the television, Harvey is there to deliver more words of wisdom.

And yet, if one can somehow push these flaws to the side, *Think Like a Man"* does contain some modest virtues of note. For one thing, it has a game and likable cast who manage to pump some life into the proceedings even during the most hackneyed moments. For another, while the film is not consistently funny by any means, it does contain enough big laughs scattered throughout (including one hilariously nasty jab at Tyler Perry) to convince most viewers that it is a successful comedy. Most of these come courtesy of Kevin Hart, who has the advantage of not being burdened with one of the story lines that no one cares about and just drifting in to take his shots before retreating to the background once again. *Think Like a Man* is not a great comedy by any means and there is nothing about it that would inspire the average viewer to watch it again or begin waiting in anticipation for the already-announced *Think Like a Man 2*. However, if all one wants from a romantic comedy is a few charming actors and a few good lines, this is a film that more or less delivers the goods, provided that one can wade through all the book plugs, of course.

Peter Sobczynski

CREDITS

Dominic: Michael Ealy
Jeremy: Jerry Ferrara
Mya: Meagan Good
Candace: Regina Hall
Cedric: Kevin Hart
Lauren: Taraji P. Henson
Kristen: Gabrielle Beauvais
Gina: Arielle Kebbel
Himself: Steve Harvey
Origin: United States
Language: English, Chinese, Korean
Released: 2012
Production: William Packer; Rainforest Films; released by Screen Gems
Directed by: Tim Story
Written by: Keith Merryman; David Newman
Cinematography by: Larry Blanford
Music by: Christopher Lennertz
Sound: Michael J. Benavente
Music Supervisor: Spring Aspers
Editing: Peter S. Elliot
Art Direction: Charlie Campbell
Costumes: Salvador Perez
Production Design: Chris Cornwell
MPAA rating: PG-13
Running time: 122 minutes

REVIEWS

Corliss, Richard. *Time*. April 19, 2012.
Ebert, Roger. *Chicago Sun-Times*. April 19, 2012.
Hornaday, Ann. *Washington Post*. April 20, 2012.
Orndorf, Brian. *BrianOrndorf.com*. April 19, 2012.
Pais, Matt. *RedEye*. April 19, 2012.
Puig, Claudia. *USA Today*. April 19, 2012.
Rabin, Nathan. *AV Club*. April 19, 2012.
Saltz, Rachel. *New York Times*. April 19, 2012.
Snider, Eric D. *Film.com*. April 20, 2012.
Tallerico, Brian. *HollywoodChicago.com*. April 20, 2012.

QUOTES

Cedric: "What do you call the three rings of marriage? Engagement ring, wedding ring and suffering."

TRIVIA

Dominic (Michael Ealy) talks about the movie *For Colored Girls*

and says the psycho drops his kids out of the window. Ealy played the character who did that.

THIS IS 40

The sort-of sequel to "Knocked Up."
—Movie tagline

Box Office: $67.5 million

Judd Apatow burst from TV (where he pioneered influential, critical hits like *The Larry Sanders Show, Freaks & Geeks,* and *Undeclared*) into film with critically-acclaimed hits *The 40 Year Old Virgin* (2005) and *Knocked Up* (2007), which made superstars of Steve Carell and Seth Rogen, respectively. Apatow seemed to have a gift with turning the personal into the humorous, using fictional characters to comment on real-life, relatable dilemmas like first love, first sex, first pregnancy, and so on. He looked likely to become the next Woody Allen or Mel Brooks, a comedic director who appealed to audiences and critics alike. Sadly, neither group has really taken to his last two works, 2009's bloated *Funny People* and 2012's truly disappointing *This is 40,* the most dishonest, unfunny work of Apatow's career to date. The writer/director who once tapped something truthful has delivered a bloated, dishonest piece of work that is only redeemed by expectedly strong work from stars Leslie Mann and Albert Brooks. It concerns one to think that success may have elevated Apatow to a level socially and economically that has drained him of the relatable quality that once defined his oh-so-promising work.

Pete (Paul Rudd) and Debbie (Leslie Mann) are happily married with two kids (Mann's real-life children with Apatow, Maude and Iris Apatow). Like most people approaching middle-age, their sex life has started to wane and Pete seems to enjoy spending time on the toilet with his iPad more than anything but his need for a little peace and quiet is understandable as his girls approach adolescence like runaway trains. Overall, Pete and Debbie seem like good parents, living a good life, and *This is 40* is about one of those troublesome chapters in married life when problems from various departments mount up simultaneously. One thing Apatow does get right is that troubles in real life usually arise when multiple spinning plates start crashing instead of just one or two. The significant problem is that the "spinning plates" in Pete and Debbie's life do not feel genuine. They feel like the product of a screenwriter and not borne of the truth needed for this film to work. People like Debbie and Pete do not withhold the drastic, life-changing secrets that Apatow's script requires them to do so unless they are total sociopaths or miserable in their marriage and Apatow does not set up either of those possibilities.

As the title makes clear and Hollywood loves to portray, Debbie is having trouble dealing with the big 4-0. She tells everyone that her impending birthday is really 38 and even gets caught at the gynecologist having told them different ages on forms over the years. Falsifying medical paperwork quickly becomes an afterthought when Debbie finds out that she is expecting a third child, something she and Pete thought physically impossible. As Sadie and Charlotte, her two daughters, continue to fight more frequently and become obsessed with modern technology (as most kids in the '10s do), Debbie sticks her head in the sand regarding a third offspring, not telling Pete she is even pregnant, something that only happens in the movies but allows for some stunningly generic misunderstandings and a predictable third-act confession.

Pete has some incredible secrets of his own. Not only is his record label about to financially collapse (and given the fact that Debbie owns a clothing store and Pete has a failing independent record label, the palatial home the two inhabit adds to the falsity of the film) but he is betting it all on a comeback for aging rocker Graham Parker. When he is not betting it all on Parker (despite the protestations of a fellow co-worker played by Chris O'Dowd), he is giving massive amounts of money to his layabout father (Albert Brooks), who has remarried and just had triplets.

If Pete and Debbie's secrets sound like plenty of plot for one movie, it is just the start for Apatow. He weighs down his storytelling with subplots involving Debbie's staff at her store (and how a bookish character played by Charlyne Yi is convinced that her co-worker played by Megan Fox is stealing), throws in Jason Segel as a personal trainer for some comic relief, finds a cameo for *Bridesmaids* (2011) (which Apatow produced) star Melissa McCarthy, and even adds another parental subplot as Debbie tries to reconnect with her distant dad (John Lithgow). Parenthood (both the character's roles as mother and father and how they deal with their own patriarchs) is the major theme of *This is 40*, an odd choice for a writer/director to make in trying to tell a common story about middle-age.

All of these talented people would be enough to carry most movies over the screenwriting humps but there is such a lack of honesty at the core of this film that it sucks nearly all of them in. There are couples who hide massive, life-changing secrets like pregnancies or the fact that they gave $80,000 to their father against their wife's wishes but those couples are massively dysfunctional. It is truly disappointing that Apatow felt the need to blow up believable behavior into contrived,

cliched movie plotting. None of it feels genuine. When Debbie yells at her daughter's bully, when Pete inexplicably hides his business problems from his completely supportive wife, when Debbie goes out clubbing with Megan Fox—all of it reeks of insincerity. In fact, there is a better movie in the over-130-minute *This is 40* that cuts Megan Fox and Graham Parker's roles entirely. Maybe Segel too.

To be fair, the problems with *This is 40* are on a larger scale and it is performance that nearly save it from them. Mann throws herself into her largest role with typical gusto and pitch-perfect comic timing. It is the little moments between Mann and her daughters that actually resonate the most strongly since they feel the most truthful. Mann is a great, underrated actress, who deserves more sizable roles like this one. Brooks completely delivers as well as his father-son arc is arguably the film's most believable. A late scene in which Brooks is allowed to play off Lithgow as the two parenting styles are contrasted is the film's best on a dramatic level and it is largely because of how much Brooks delivers within it.

It would be so easy to just dismiss *This is 40* entirely but the frustration is amplified because of how clearly one can see the great movie buried in this one. Cut the film by an hour (it is cinematically insane that *40* is longer than *Argo* [2012]) and concentrate on the truthful little things instead of foisting unrealistic plot points on the characters. Audiences fell in love with Steve Carell in *Virgin* and Seth Rogen in *Knocked Up* because they saw something of themselves in these lovable man-children. That is the crucial element missing this time. Well, and it just is not very funny.

Brian Tallerico

CREDITS

Pete: Paul Rudd
Debbie: Leslie Mann
Sadie: Maude Apatow
Charlotte: Iris Apatow
Jason: Jason Segel
Desi: Megan Fox
Oliver: John Lithgow
Origin: United States
Language: English
Released: 2012
Production: Barry Mendel, Clayton Townsend, Judd Apatow; Apatow Productions, Forty Productions; released by Universal Pictures
Directed by: Judd Apatow
Written by: Judd Apatow
Cinematography by: Phedon Papamichael

Music by: Jon Brion
Sound: George H. Anderson
Music Supervisor: Jonathan Karp
Editing: Brent White
Art Direction: Andrew Max Cahn
Costumes: Leesa Evans
Production Design: Jefferson Sage
MPAA rating: R
Running time: 134 minutes

REVIEWS

Baca, Ricardo. *Denver Post*. December 21, 2012.

Dujsik, Mark. *Mark Reviews Movies*. December 21, 2012.

Hall, Corey. *Metro Times*. December 27, 2012.

Honeycutt, Kirk. *HoneycuttsHollywood.com*. December 22, 2012.

Long, Tom. *Detroit News*. December 21, 2012.

O'Sullivan, Michael. *Washington Post*. December 21, 2012.

Puig, Claudia. *USA Today*. December 20, 2012.

Simon, Brent. *Shared Darkness*. December 29, 2012.

Tobias, Scott. *NPR*. December 20, 2012.

Westhoff, Jeffrey. *Northwest Herald*. January 4, 2013.

QUOTES

Barry: "That's the one thing you don't do. You don't tell her you took Viagra. I'm pretty sure that's on the warning label."

TRIVIA

Sadie is a big fan of the television show *Lost* and the character Jack (Matthew Fox) is repeatedly shown on screen. In *Knocked Up*, Ben is very disparaging with regards to Matthew Fox, saying there is nothing interesting about him.

THIS MEANS WAR

It's spy against spy.
—Movie tagline

Box Office: $54.8 million

When Pat Benatar sang in 1983 that love is a battlefield, she was being metaphorical. She was not actually imagining that the pursuit of romantic fulfillment would unfold in the wake of car chases, gunfights and explosions.

However, that is what happens in *This Means War*, a strange action-comedy-romance hybrid that occasionally succeeds in one department or another and ultimately does not quite succeed in any of them. Front and center are two guys who would seem to have no trouble finding a woman: FDR (Chris Pine) and Tuck (Tom Hardy) have been like brothers for their entire lives, and an assumedly well-paying job as CIA agent partners has the already-dapper dudes up to their ears in snazzy clothing. Yet when each guy meets Lauren (Reese Witherspoon), a lonely consumer product tester who only joins online dating site It'sFate.net when her insufferable friend Trish (Chelsea Handler) creates a profile for her, they act as if they have found the possible love of their life.

Obviously, this becomes an inconvenience between best friends and colleagues. Though it will not inspire confidence in viewers about the way that government resources are used, *This Means War* generates some of its zippiest bits of fun as Tuck and FDR, while temporarily banned from field work after a particularly conspicuous public incident in Hong Kong, use CIA tracking devices and assign fellow operatives to follow the other man's courtship of Lauren. Meanwhile, this woman struggles with her developing feelings for two people at the same time while totally unaware that her suitors not only know each other, but have the resources to use, say, a tranquilizer dart to sabotage his rival's date. (This happens to the tune of Beastie Boys' song "Sabotage," indicating the film's low level of imagination.)

Unfortunately, the mindless fun rarely last more than a few minutes without an interruption from stupidity that is too aggressive too ignore. This starts early, in fact, when Tuck and FDR's supervisor Collins (Angela Bassett) informs them, "Remember, this mission is covert." As opposed to what, those CIA missions during which agents are free to inform the public and the media about all relevant strategies and enemies? Unless a policy is in place that dictates agents can tweet about one mission per week, Collins, it is probably not necessary to tell specially trained, highly skilled CIA experts that they need to keep things quiet. That level of forehead-smacking foolishness returns frequently in the form of Trish, whose average comment goes something like, "Men are going to respond to that cameltoe." With a friend like Trish, who constantly mocks her overweight husband when she is not using Cheetos to turn him on, it is no wonder Lauren has a warped perspective on relationships.

As the romantic complications play out, FDR and Tuck are also being hunted by Heinrich (Til Schweiger), a standard Eastern European baddie out for revenge following the death of his brother during the aforementioned Hong Kong mission. This subplot barely has the energy to lick the boots of the *Die Hard* (1988) series from which its villains and agenda feel significantly cribbed. Not that Heinrich or actual CIA work is meant to be the focus of *This Means War*. The movie spends much more time on its central love triangle than on the jobs that each man routinely hides from every woman he meets. FDR claims to be a cruise ship captain; Tuck says that he is a travel agent, leading even his ex Katie [Abigail Spencer] to gullibly note that Tuck is the only travel agent she has ever known who actually travels for work. None of the women in the film are particularly savvy, which may be why Lauren never suspects foul play when both FDR and Tuck adjust their behavior and interests (like art and classic cars) to cater specifically to comments she has recently made in their absence. Worse, she ultimately does not even seem to care that not only has she been massively deceived for the entire time she has known both men, but that no matter who she (seemingly arbitrarily) chooses, he will likely spend every work day risking his life. This is probably not something most girlfriends want to learn about a relatively new boyfriend. Though Lauren initially loves Tuck's British accent and later complains that he is British, so this woman does not seem to have a clear idea of what she wants in the first place.

That any of this nonsense plays out with some charm reflects nicely on each of the three leads, who bring a spunk and swagger to material that certainly is not as clever or effortless as it thinks it is. Witherspoon and her smile have been illuminating romantic comedies for more than a decade; Pine and Hardy, on the other hand, both justify their rising leading man status by effectively balancing between arrogance and vulnerability without making their characters too unlikable. Yes, they are shamelessly lying to a woman they supposedly care about, but the actors' work suggests that FDR and Tuck both have their hearts in the right place and will do right by Lauren if she just gives them the chance.

Director McG delivers action sequences that are interchangeable with any other big-budget CIA story, so it is fortunate that, with minimal excitement to be found, *This Means War* has a few characters who remain appealing in spite of their flaws. One scene in particular, when Tuck takes Lauren to an empty arena to swing from a flying trapeze, achieves the sort of quiet romanticism that really does not fit into a film with this much crass dialogue and forgettable action. "Sometimes falling is the best part," Tuck says to Lauren before sharing their first kiss. Corny? Certainly. But talented actors can make corny cool, and more moments like this might have made *This Means War* a surprisingly light winner, rather than a movie whose divergent instincts never stop sparring.

Matt Pais

CREDITS

Lauren: Reese Witherspoon
FDR Foster: Chris Pine

Tuck: Thomas Hardy
Trish: Chelsea Handler
Heinrich: Til Schweiger
Katie: Abigail Spencer
Collins: Angela Bassett
Joe: John Paul Ruttan
Origin: United States
Language: English
Released: 2012
Production: Simon Kinberg, Robert Simonds, Will Smith, Simon Kinberg; Overbrook Entertainment, Robert Simonds Productions; released by 20th Century-Fox
Directed by: McG
Written by: Timothy Dowling; Simon Kinberg
Cinematography by: Russell Carpenter
Music by: Christophe Beck
Sound: Derek Vanderhorst
Editing: Nicolas De Toth; Jesse Driebusch
Art Direction: Kendelle Elliott; Eric Fraser
Costumes: Sophie de Rakoff
Production Design: Martin Laing
MPAA rating: R
Running time: 97 minutes

REVIEWS

Berardinelli, James. *ReelViews*. February 15, 2012.
Dargis, Manohla. *New York Times*. February 16, 2012.
Hornaday, Ann. *Washington Post*. February 16, 2012.
Jones, J. R. *Chicago Reader*. February 16, 2012.
Morris, Wesley. *Boston Globe*. February 16, 2012.
Persall, Steve. *Tampa Bay Times*. February 15, 2012.
Pols, Mary. *Time*. February 16, 2012.
Puig, Claudia. *USA Today*. February 16, 2012.
Rickey, Carrie. *Philadelphia Inquirer*. February 16, 2012.
Willmore, Alison. *Movieline*. February 16, 2012.

QUOTES

Trish: "Don't choose the better guy, choose the guy that's gonna make you the better girl."

TRIVIA

Sam Worthington, Colin Farrell, Justin Timberlake, and Seth Rogen were all considered for the lead roles in this film, but Chris Pine and Tom Hardy were eventually cast.

THIS MUST BE THE PLACE

A former rock star is hunting down a Nazi criminal. This could be his greatest hit.
—Movie tagline

Box Office: $143,979

All Hollywood actors seem to play the clown at least once. Such often undeniably bad decisions come in the shape of integrity-questioning comedies like when Sylvester Stallone did *Rhinestone* (1984) or *Stop! Or My Mom Will Shoot* (1992) or when Clint Eastwood did *Pink Cadillac* (1989). Sean Penn, who once flirted with that Farrelly Brothers' *Three Stooges* movie (2012), finally puts on his own clown makeup with *This Must Be the Place*. But, as the bombastic Penn lacks any understanding of subtlety to nearly any acting project he comes across, this is not Leoncavallo's *Pagliacci*. This is a fiery-airliner-suicide bomb ready to crash into the art house, with pilot Penn setting himself on fire for all to watch. Even when playing a soft-spoken character with nothing much to say, the actor shows desperation for attention.

In the film, Penn plays Cheyenne, an ex-Goth rocker living with his wife Jane (Frances McDormand) in Ireland. He returns to America to attend the funeral of his estranged father. While at the service, he discovers the story of a man named Aloise Lange who humiliated his father back in World War II, and has since taken up a quiet ex-Nazi life somewhere in America. With the help of Mordecai Midler (Judd Hirsch), Cheyenne decides to hunt down the man by retracing the clues left in his father's journal. This leads him on a road trip across the country where he encounters Lange's wife (Joyce Van Patten), his daughter (Kerry Condon), and, finally, Lange (Heinz Leiven) himself.

While dressed up as this Robert Smith-looking fellow with heavy white make-up, red lipstick, and large pitch-black hair, Penn shows that he is aware of the goofiness of this character. Cheyenne even says the statement, "We all play the fool sometimes.". To this film's dismay, however, such conveyance of smartness does not make this role any less pathetic. Every line that he whimpers, which comes with a small whisper and an often-blank face, is more successful as a joke against Penn and/or this movie than an emotional sentiment. *This Must Be the Place* is most memorable for its freak show moments, which it can not spin its favor. And yet this movie plays it seriously, as does Penn, convinced there is something to be said in this bizarre story in which general sense is not one of its common features.

Like its central character, *This Must Be the Place* is enigmatic to the bone, a thoroughly odd movie. The movie toys with the concept of serendipity, while also throwing in surreal images in its projected world of realism that seem to lack the potential for explanation (like when a massive bottle of beer blocks Cheyenne on the

road, or when an old man rolls by Cheyenne in a parking lot, riding a hayride-like vehicle).

One has to be fair to Penn, however. There is at least one scene in which the bizarre emotional work he is intending for does build up to something, and of course it is a moment in which Penn is howling and screaming with pain, as he opens himself wide to David Byrne about what is really going on in his mind. Although it is in Penn's wheelhouse, it is better than the blank nothingness he provides as the rest of Cheyenne, a frustrating character with only brushes of the hair used to physically express thought.

In a too-bizarre-to-spoil appearance that is perfectly weird for such a movie as *This Must Be the Place*, Harry Dean Stanton does appear in the movie briefly in the third act, when things start to heat up, and also gets even weirder (if such was possible). His screen-time is low, but the veteran actor does show some giddiness in a wild monologue that he gives about rolling suitcases (a favorite item of Cheyenne's). It is just one of many surreal moments in which the film toys with coincidence, only to just look entirely silly.

More likable than most people in the movie, McDormand moves in and out of the picture as Cheyenne's wife, who adds some of the dreamier aspects to the movie that the script is not so clear on. McDormand has a little sunshine as the balance to Cheyenne's chaos, but she does not have any bit of character herself. Most of all, she is meant to serve as an image of a spouse as a caretaker, with little emotional result.

With the man given a prominent cameo in which Cheyenne proclaims him a genius, David Byrne of The Talking Heads contributes bits to the score of the film, which gives it more of an upbeat, late '80s attitude than one may expect (especially considering the anchoring that Penn's Robert Smith imitation would be doing). Fans of The Talking Heads will get to see Byrne on-screen in his pure glory, wearing white on white, performing "This Must Be the Place" himself, before a young boy sings it with Penn again later.

The cinematography in the film has its own attitude, constantly creating images that have more immediacy than anything happening with the story. Often the camera takes delight in empty space, which puts the movie's unique, revolving locations (suburbs to countryside, to frozen lake) into use. At times, such wideness (and with a lot of tracking shots) does not really serve any grand poetic purpose, but it certainly is not affected by the numbness that reaches other parts of the movie.

A wacky anti-comedy played with serious-face art house intentions, *This Must Be the Place* might make more sense if it were put into the hands of Disney auteurs like Walt Becker (*Wild Hogs* [2007], *Old Dogs*

[2009]) or Raja Gosnell (*Beverly Hills Chihuahua* [2008]). The movie has the makings for such, including a road trip set up about a middle-aged man embarking on a personal journey. With its bizarre execution and general aura of pity, this movie does not speak beyond the same levels that *Old Dogs* opines about the effects of old age, or the necessity to keeping one's drugs under control. If a little kid were to kick a soccer ball into Cheyenne's groin in this film, it would not be out of place. It would likely be considered artful.

Nick Allen

CREDITS

Cheyenne: Sean Penn
Jane: Frances McDormand
Mordecai Midler: Judd Hirsch
Mary: Eve Hewson
Rachel: Kerry Condon
Robert Plath: Harry Dean Stanton
Dorothy Shore: Joyce Van Patten
Himself: David Byrne
Ernie Ray: Shea Wigham
Richard: Liron Levo
Jeffery: Simon Delaney
Origin: United States
Language: English, Hebrew
Released: 2012
Production: Mario Spedaletti, Nicola Giuliano, Francesca Cima, Andrea Occhipinti; Lucky Red, Medusa Film, Irish Film Board; released by The Weinstein Company
Directed by: Paolo Sorrentino
Written by: Paolo Sorrentino; Umberto Contarello
Cinematography by: Luca Bigazzi
Music by: David Byrne; William Oldham
Sound: Srdjan Kurpjel
Editing: Cristiano Travaglioli
Art Direction: Dooner
Costumes: Karen Patch
Production Design: Stefania Cella
MPAA rating: R
Running time: 118 minutes

REVIEWS

Burr, Ty. *Boston Globe.* November 8, 2012.
Covert, Colin. *Minneapolis Star Tribune.* November 8, 2012.
Ebert, Roger. *Chicago Sun-Times.* November 15, 2012.
Lane, Anthony. *New Yorker.* October 25, 2012.
LaSalle, Mick. *San Francisco Chronicle.* November 8, 2012.
Linden, Sheri. *Los Angeles Times.* November 1, 2012.
McCarthy, Todd. *Hollywood Reporter.* May 20, 2012.
Morgenstern, Joe. *The Wall Street Journal.* November 1, 2012.
Rainer, Peter. *Christian Science Monitor.* November 2, 2012.
Weissberg, Jay. *Variety.* May 21, 2011.

QUOTES

Cheyenne: "At this particular moment I'm trying to fix up a sad boy and a sad girl, but it's not easy. I suspect that sadness is not compatible with sadness."

TRIVIA

"This Must Be the Place" was the original title for Sam Mendes summer comedy *Away We Go.*

A THOUSAND WORDS

He only has 1,000 words left to discover what matters the most.
—Movie tagline
Make every word count.
—Movie tagline
Nothin' but a good time.
—Movie tagline

Box Office: $18.5 million

In the modern movie star era, perhaps no one actor has personified the timeless role of the "motor mouth" with more style and success than Eddie Murphy. From Reggie Hammond to Axel Foley up to his self-parodying rendition of Jerry Lewis' Buddy Love, Murphy's ability to out-syllable anyone in a scene may have made him a character but it was the laughter he generated and communicated with an audience that immortalized him. As the years passed and Murphy removed a certain vocabulary from his R-rated repertoire down to more accessible PG-13 territory and even the family-friendly PG zone, the laughter began to fade as did his appeal when he was seen rather than merely heard as an animated donkey. It should come as no surprise then that a film trying to take away his once presumed greatest asset would result in his most symbolic of cinematic failures.

Here Murphy plays Jack McCall, a literary agent who prides himself on being able to talk anyone into a deal. Business to him is a great success, but the personal relationships in his life are another matter. He is a jerk to his assistant, Aaron (Clark Duke), who wants nothing more than to emulate his boss and become an agent. The valet outside his office just wants him to review his manuscript, which is tough since Jack is prone to reading only the first and last five pages before deciding on a bestseller. His wife, Caroline (Kerry Washington), wants nothing more than to take their new son to a more baby-proof environment without unguarded pools and large cliff drops. Ironically, Jack does not need many words to knock back all of their dreams.

Jack is more concerned at this time with signing new age guru, Dr. Sinja (Cliff Curtis), and his new book which, naturally, he has not read. In the course of making the deal at his ashram, Jack cuts himself on a tree and is then reminded of one's own destiny to not blame the tree or something or other that goes in one ear and out the other. When that same tree magically uproots itself in Jack's backyard he is anything but speechless, but may need to rethink that reaction. It turns out that whenever Jack says a word, a single leaf will fall off. When all the leaves fall off, the tree will die along with Jack.

Conveniently, after wasting several words and leaves, Jack is provided an explanation for his plight by the new age doctor. While an audience can grasp the concept early on and no doubt be counting down the best they can just how much time Jack has left, the doctor tells us that he still is left with just the right round-number of leaves to give the film its title. Now that the story has painted itself out of that corner, it is time to recognize that in order for this film to work at all, the rules of comedy need to be thoroughly established. Not only can Jack not speak words, the tree has closed the loopholes to even write or express himself.

Former *Seinfeld* and *Saturday Night Live* writer Steve Koren clearly would like this film to follow through with the mix of outrageous screwball fantasy with sentimentality that mixed so well in *Groundhog Day* (1993) and even *Liar Liar* (1997). Koren had even tried before as the writer of similar vehicles for Jim Carrey (*Bruce Almighty* [2003]) and Adam Sandler (*Click* [2006]) to far less success. Yet nothing in his past comes close to the simplistically uninspired treatment of an acorn idea never given a chance to grow into something worthy of Murphy's talents or audience attention. Murphy has never been known as a physical humorist—unless you count the added pounds of prosthetics he has hauled around playing multiple characters. Director Brian Robbins, also responsible for *Norbit* (2008), has tried turning him into one though with *Meet Dave* (2007)—where Murphy played the outer shell of a human spaceship—and, in *A Thousand Words*, the director sporadically uses it as a desperate crutch when left without his true skills. With Jack's psychic link to the tree, a climbing squirrel causes him to itch and attacking the tree produces bodily harm. When insecticide produces a chemical reaction in his body during an important meeting, the soundtrack brings the joke home by playing Afroman's "Because I Got High," which was funny for about one-and-a-half verses back in 2000.

That is par for the course for a movie filmed back in 2008 and delayed for over three years due to studio break-ups and someone there with the due diligence to hold this monstrosity from the public for as long as possible. References to the Atkins diet, a Chili's rib song, crazy Britney Spears, and Hannah Montana selling out concert halls are all on display. Even worse, none seem like actual jokes. A high-concept comedy like *A Thousand Words* needs to maintain its connection to reality around the fantastical elements to truly succeed. The idea of using pre-recorded devices to do business is a clever and potentially funny one if it were not for the follow-up solution which involves an entire office with an apparent mandate that each worker be required to have a talking toy on their desk.

When Robbins, Koren and Murphy all give up on the jokes though, the film takes a dreadful turn for the ultra-maudlin. Without coming close to earning the conciliatory tone that Jack adopts, the audience is subjected to one touchy-feely moment after another—including one with his Alzheimer's-afflicted mother (Ruby Dee)—that wants to be held up as a mirror to Bill Murray's similar turn in *Groundhog Day*, but is as phony as being forced to apologize at gunpoint.

Erik Childress

CREDITS

Jack McCall: Eddie Murphy
Caroline McCall: Kerry Washington
Tyler McCall: Emanuel Ragsdale
Aaron Wiseberger: Clark Duke
Samantha Davis: Allison Janney
Dr. Sinja: Clifford Curtis
Angela McCall: Ruby Dee
Origin: United States
Language: English
Released: 2012
Production: Nicolas Cage, Alain Chabat, Stephanie Danan, Norm Golightly, Brian Robbins, Brian Robbins; DreamWorks SKG, Saturn Films, Varsity Pictures; released by Paramount Pictures
Directed by: Brian Robbins
Written by: Steve Koren
Cinematography by: Clark Mathis
Music by: John Debney
Sound: Elliott L. Koretz
Music Supervisor: Madonna Wade-Reed
Editing: Ned Bastille
Art Direction: Angela Stauffer
Costumes: Mary Vogt
Production Design: Clay A. Griffith

MPAA rating: PG-13
Running time: 91 minutes

REVIEWS

Dowd, A. A. *Time Out New York*. March 9, 2012.
Ebert, Roger. *Chicago Sun-Times*. March 8, 2012.
Ebiri, Bilge. *Vulture*. March 9, 2012.
Gire, Dann. *Daily Herald*. March 8, 2012.
Goss, William. *Film.com*. March 9, 2012.
Nusair, David. *Reel Film Reviews*. March 28, 2012.
Orndorf, Brian. *eFilmCritic*. March 13, 2012.
Putman, Dustin. *DustinPutman.com*. March 9, 2012.
Robinson, Tasha. *AV Club*. March 8, 2012.
Swietek, Frank. *One Guy's Opinion*. March 11, 2012.

QUOTES

Aaron Wiseberger: "I went to community college, and that was only because my grandma was sleeping with the dean."

TRIVIA

After a disastrous opening in the Syates, a release for the film in the United Kingdom was dropped, despite cinemas and trailers already advertising its release. The film was released direct-to-video, as it was in several other European countries.

AWARDS

Nominations:

Golden Raspberries 2012: Worst Actor (Murphy), Worst Picture, Worst Screenplay

360

Everything comes full circle.
—Movie tagline

Box Office: $100,343

There are a certain number, breed and class of films which often get a critical pass from professional writers and arthouse habitues alike—folks afraid of appearing "not to get it." Owing to both its pedigree and thematically stamped subject matter, *360* is emblematic of that type of movie.

A technically polished but quite leaden ensemble drama based very loosely on Arthur Schnitzler's play *La Ronde*, the movie is penned by twice-Oscar-nominated writer Peter Morgan and helmed by Fernando Meirelles, who received a Best Director Academy Award nomination for his work on *City of God* (2003). Spanning six countries (and a couple languages) in interweaving the stories of characters whose connections only become apparent over time, *360* is comprised of some interesting vignettes, but it is cold, calculating and fairly dramatically inert. Like a more mannered and achingly self-satisfied version of *Babel* (2006), it is a film that can be admired, certainly, but also one that diminishes upon reflection—a work less than the sum of its parts.

Writ large, *360*'s topical exploration focuses on infidelity and divorce, and the nature of romantic attraction. In Vienna, a British auto executive, Michael (Jude Law), finds his arrangements to meet up with a Slovakian prostitute, Mirka (Lucia Siposova), interrupted by a chatty German busybody (Moritz Bleibtreu). Back in London, Rose (Rachel Weisz) is having a fling with Brazilian Rui (Juliano Cazarre), whose girlfriend Laura (Maria Flor) is fed up with his infidelity, and splits. On a flight back home, Laura crosses paths with a British man, John (Anthony Hopkins), and a recently paroled sex offender, Tyler (Ben Foster). The former is traveling for very sad reasons related to his daughter, while the latter is desperately fighting urges still present inside of him with the help of a prison counselor, Fran (Marianne Jean-Baptiste). Meanwhile, an Algerian Muslim dentist living in Paris (Jamel Debbouze) struggles with his fascination over a married Russian employee, Valentina (Dinara Drukarova), whose husband Sergei (Vladimir Vdovichenkov) works as a driver and courier of contraband for a hotheaded gangster (Mark Ivanir).

Morgan's screenplay shares a good deal in common with his script for *Hereafter* (2010), another thematic disquisition which utilized seemingly discrete storylines and focused more on grief instead of matters of the heart. Here the gambit feels like more of a reach, though. It is true that moments of *360* punch through, and the film, even at 110 minutes, does not so much bore as just merely sag. It is too well crafted, acted and generally erudite to elicit outright dismissal.

But *360* is definitely illustrative of the differences between literature and cinema, and why some ideas and works do not particularly translate well to the other medium. *La Ronde* (also known as *Reigen*) is a frequently utilized source material, having been made into film versions by most notably Max Ophuls, but also Roger Vadim and Otto Schenk, among others. The text puts human fallibility, sexual morals and class ideology in the crosshairs, achieving social commentary by way of their mixture. That framework allows for a lot. *360*, though, lacks pop and breadth of characterization—crucial qualities for an ensemble.

The film goes out of its way to work down a checklist of crossed boundaries (religion, ethnicity, socioeconomic status, etcetera) that might be explored to deeper effect in a novel or play, but there is a crushing dullness and similarity to many of the characters. Despite their significant differences, the characters—or at least their manifested personalities—feel like variations on shades of grey. Persistently drab and banal dialogue ("I can't do this anymore," "You only live once") also does them no favors. All of this combines for a feeling of contrivance and pretension substituting for profundity. In reality, *360* is but a more somber, self-serious, differently focused version of some far more commercial-minded ensemble piffle like *What To Expect When You're Expecting* (2012). Its putative chief message—take the fork in the road—is something that could be communicated more dynamically in a variety of ways.

The film's more recognizable, veteran faces—Hopkins, Law, Weisz and Foster—are all skilled enough to communicate inner turbulence and conflict in effective short strokes. Flor, too, makes a solid impression. Still, *360* is not really a work that could be legitimately be called an "actors' showcase." Apart from an extended monologue at an Alcoholics Anonymous meeting by Hopkins, *360* does not deliver cathartic or grandly memorable scenes so much as quiet, modulated conversation pieces—work that could be used in acting classes years hence as sides, but not in solo auditions.

Meirelles' film works best, then, as a sort of piecemeal director's reel; inventive transitional editing and gorgeous cinematography, from Daniel Rezende and Adriano Goldman, respectively, stress the filter of gravity and artfulness through which *360* is processed. Given that its stories unfold in a wide variety of cities across the globe, the film makes use of an abundance of airplanes (to underscore the transitional nature of life), while Meirelles also employs mirrors and mirrored surfaces in great quality (and quantity), one supposes to further highlight the duality of mankind—the public faces we sometimes slip on to mask private turmoil, and the theoretical parallel versions of temporal reality that exist for important choices unmade, or made differently.

The smooth contours of its technical achievement notwithstanding, even *360*'s most ardent admirers must resort to looping invocations of its intent and scope rather than stirring praise for its emotional impact or any crafty puzzlebox revelations. Instead, many critics and perhaps most viewers will watch *360* and take its obvious desire to make a significant statement about life as evidence that it succeeded. "Interesting," they will say, not wanting to sound dumb. But that is misguided; *360* has the magisterial air of an emperor, to be sure, but not the robes to back that stature.

Brent Simon

CREDITS

Michael Daly: Jude Law

Rose Daly: Rachel Weisz
John: Anthony Hopkins
Tyler: Ben Foster
Rocco: Johannes Krisch
Algerian Man: Jamel Debbouze
Valentina: Dinara Drukarova
Origin: United Kingdom, Austria, France, Brazil
Language: English, German, Arabic, French, Russian, Portuguese
Released: 2012
Production: Andrew Eaton, David Linde, Chris Hanley, Danny Krausz, Emanuel Michael; BBC Films, Unison Films; released by Magnolia Pictures
Directed by: Fernando Meirelles
Written by: Peter Morgan
Cinematography by: Adriano Goldman
Sound: Ingo Pusswald
Editing: Daniel Rezende
Production Design: John Paul Kelly
MPAA rating: R
Running time: 115 minutes

REVIEWS

Biancoli, Amy. *San Francisco Chronicle*. August 9, 2012.
Dargis, Manohla. *New York Times*. August 9, 2012.
Debruge, Peter. *Variety*. February 23, 2012.
Duralde, Alonso. *The Wrap*. August 2, 2012.
Gleiberman, Owen. *Entertainment Weekly*. August 1, 2012.
Honeycutt, Kirk. *Hollywood Reporter*. March 8, 2012.
Linden, Sheri. *Los Angeles Times*. March 8, 2012.
O'Hehir, Andrew. *Salon.com*. August 2, 2012.
Taylor, Ella. *NPR*. August 2, 2012.
Willmore, Alison. *AV Club*. August 2, 2012.

QUOTES

John: "Run into someone cute. Never done this kind of thing before, but you only live once, how many chances do we get?"

TRIVIA

Karl Markovics was originally set to play Rocco but had to drop out due to a scheduling conflict, he was replaced by Johannes Krisch.

THE THREE STOOGES

Just say Moe.
—Movie tagline
Before there was Jackass, there was Dumbass.
—Movie tagline

It's rated PG, so you can bring your parents!
    —Movie tagline

Box Office: $44.3 million

What sounded like one of the worst movies ideas in recent history has the virtue of proving naysayers wrong, but the handicap of trying to follow a tough act. The original Three Stooges were timeless, offering up slapstick on a par with the greatest practitioners in cinema history. It really is just fine to talk about The Three Stooges being on a par with Charlie Chaplin or Buster Keaton. But while the new incarnation pays proper homage, and gets some laughs of its own, it stops short of achieving much else, settling instead to play with the tools the trio left behind. Countless Stooge gags are utilized and some not unwelcome sentiment is generated, but this is a film destined to go down as a curiosity, at worst a bullet-dodge by the Farrelly Brothers whose reputation for making good-but-not-great films persists, and, at best, a well-intentioned, simplistic love letter to the greatest comedic trio in movie history.

The film borrows a central plot element from *The Blues Brothers* (1980). After growing up in an orphanage the boys discover it will soon be foreclosed. They set out with the nuns' blessing to make a fortune in an attempt to save their childhood home. Along the way they wind up involved, inadvertently, in a murder plot, get asked to star in a reality TV show, and leave a constant trail of destruction. They also rediscover their filial devotion to one another and save the orphanage.

Performances here are often a joy to behold. Sean Hayes (Larry), Will Sasso (Curly), and Chris Diamantopoulos (Moe) virtually channel the Stooges and are, by far the best thing about the film. The supporting cast is fun as well. Sofia Vergara and Stephen Collins are great as the conniving couple that convinces the hapless trio to take part in the murder plot, though Vergara steals the show with her willingness to make fun of her own curvaceous assets when a rat climbs down her cleavage during a key bit of schtick. This is just one example but it makes the point. The cast was game here to engage in some pretty gonzo slapstick, make fun of themselves, and get laughed at for their troubles.

One notable misstep, however, is the waste of Larry David who is forced to wear a nun's habit as the character Sister Mary-Mengele, the only nun at the orphanage who fails to understand why everyone else loves the Stooges. The idea of David in a habit is funny but his role is badly written giving him little to do but rage and pratfall, which hardly plays to his strengths. The rest of the convent—Jane Lynch as Mother Superior, Jennifer Hudson as Sister Rosemary, and Kate Upton as Sister Bernice—are largely asked to play it straight while the guys goof off around them. It works

but it would have been at least equally interesting to see them a tad busier. Better is the always dependable character actor Brian Doyle-Murray who plays Monsignor Ratlife with a condescending but ultimately upended air.

The least well realized aspect of the film has to do with Moe's involvement in a reality show starring real life *Jersey Shore* participants Mike 'The Situation' Sorrentino, Nicole 'Snooki' Polizzi and Jenni 'JWoww' Farley. These minor TV celebrities are not up to even the minor challenges of reacting to the chaos around them coming across instead as modern imitators of the Stooges aesthetic. What sounds like a perfect opportunity for satire is treated far too tamely. The real problem may be that the Farrellys have turned in a family movie here and the Jersey Shore crowd, much less any sophisticated sense of satire, simply has no business in it. In fact the whole film feels a tad strained by the pressure the filmmakers inevitably felt to keep this kid friendly. When laughs do come they generally involve safe humor that merely echoes the Stooges past glory even if those echoes are strong. Strange then that they also miss the boat on a number of gags that would have seemed de rigueur. They pass up the chance to have a full scale pie fight at an upscale lawn party. The writers fail to make use of the cherished line "Dr. Howard, Dr. Fine. Dr. Howard" when the script has gone to the trouble of placing the boys at a hospital where they hideout posed as medical personnel. The most startling failure is the almost complete lack of humor fitting into the Ow! category. Almost none of the pratfalls, even the ones that get solid laughs, are based in anything truly visceral. Without the squirm factor something important is missing.

All of the above noted, viewers might decide to take a pass. But Stooge fans take note. In the eighty or so years since the debut of the first Stooges short *Soup To Nuts* (1930) The Three Stooges have endured an awful lot of ignominy. They were badly treated by Columbia Pictures and others who used them to make millions and they suffered countless physical issues related to their comedic pratfalls. They suffer very little here. Instead, the experience of watching this film, even when it fails to accomplish simple goals, is at least grin-inducing, heartfelt, and often a little nostalgic. Add in a few belly laughs and the participants have good reason to feel proud. After all, what the Stooges were best at was making what they did look so easy.

Dave Canfield

CREDITS

Larry: Sean P. Hayes

Curly: Will Sasso
Moe: Chris Diamantopoulos
Mother Superior: Jane Lynch
Lyndia: Sofia Vergara
Sister Rosemary: Jennifer Hudson
Mr. Harter: Stephen Collins
Sister Mary-Mengele: Larry David
Origin: United States
Language: English, French, Spanish
Released: 2012
Production: Bradley Thomas, Charles B. Wessler, Peter Farrelly, Bobby Farrelly; Wessler Entertainment, Comedy III Entertainment Inc., Conundrum Entertainment; released by 20th Century Fox Film Corp.
Directed by: Bobby Farrelly; Peter Farrelly
Written by: Bobby Farrelly; Peter Farrelly; Mike Cerrone
Cinematography by: Matthew F. Leonetti
Music by: John Debney
Sound: Wayne Lemmer
Music Supervisor: Manish Raval; Tom Wolfe
Editing: Sam Seig
Art Direction: Amy Wheeler
Costumes: Denise Wingate
Production Design: Arlan Jay Vetter
MPAA rating: PG
Running time: 92 minutes

REVIEWS

Corliss, Richard. *Time*. April 12, 2012.
Ebert, Roger. *Chicago Sun-Times*. April 12, 2012.
Dargis, Manohla. *New York Times*. April 12, 2012.
Debruge, Peter. *Variety*. April 12, 2012.
Denby, David. *The New Yorker*. April 23, 2012.
Howell, Peter. *Toronto Star*. April 13, 2012.
McCarthy, Todd. *Hollywood Reporter*. April 12, 2012.
Puig, Claudia. *USA Today*. April 12, 2012.
Snider, Eric D. *Film.com*. April 13, 2012.
Travers, Peter. *Rolling Stone*. April 13, 2012.

QUOTES

Teddy: "So, you boys on Facebook? I'll poke you. Better yet, I'll tweet you."
Curly: "Oh! Tweet us to dinner? Soitenly!"

TRIVIA

The orphanage in the film is shown to be founded in 1934, the same year the Three Stooges began their series of shorts for Columbia Pictures, which continued until 1958.

TIM AND ERIC'S BILLION DOLLAR MOVIE

Box Office: $201,436

It might seem the first, most important question about any comedy is simply, "Is it funny?" Yet there have

always been film makers, comedy writers, and performers who have pushed the boundary not just of what is or is not in good taste, but what constitutes "humor." In recent years, the "anti-humor" movement has resurged to the point that these days some comedic films work very hard not to be funny at all. *Tim and Eric's Billion Dollar Movie* is such an endeavor. Written and directed by the performing team of Tim Heidecker and Eric Wareheim, the feature-length film expands on the absurdist crudity and post-modern buffoonery the two honed over for three years on their cult television show *Tim and Eric Awesome Show, Great Job!*, part of The Cartoon Network's Adult Swim programming.

For their first movie, the pair play aggressively ignorant versions of themselves: two disastrously overconfident would-be filmmakers who spend a billion dollars of a shady corporation's money in order to make a three-minute film called *Diamond Jim,* starring what turns out to be a Johnny Depp impersonator. (Most of the budget was spent on the title character's diamond-covered coat, while the rest went to fueling Tim and Eric's newly lavish lifestyle.) Broke and threatened with grievous legal, financial, and physical consequences, the failed fictional filmmakers form a new market-consultation business and take over the operation of a decrepit shopping mall, assured by its sleazy owner (Will Ferrell) they will indeed pocket a billion dollars from the deal. (Also on hand is impressively game actress Twink Kaplan as Eric's love interest and other bigger-name regulars from the *Tim and Eric* television show, including John C. O'Reilly, Will Forte, and Zach Galifianakis.)

All of this—the premise, the conflict, the possible solution—is served with nothing but winking irony. Cliched targets include the film industry, shopping malls, and hollowly synergistic business scams that run on empty self promotion. However, in using things such as pseudo-science religions, theme restaurants, 1990s corporate training films, and heart-warming After School Specials as grist for their mill, Heidecker and Wareheim are out to mock exactly the kind of films that do so, satirizing comedy as much if not more than anything else. That makes *Tim and Eric's Billion Dollar Movie* something of a slippery Ouroboros, the snake eating more and more of its own tail until either nothing is left to laugh at or everything is.

As is often the case when a sketch show makes the leap to the big screen, the film only uses its flimsy, worn-down plot as place to hang a series of short comedic bits, each more nonsensical (and often offensive) than the last. Employing a surreal "innocence" that sometimes feels as if David Lynch had decided to write a farce, Heidecker and Wareheim specialize in a sort of prancing inanity, with lame punch lines often repeated ad nauseum, daring you to push past them into some sort of transcendent observation about the pact between writer-performer and his or her audience. The old vaudeville saw, "Make 'em laugh" is still in play, but here the audience is meant to laugh at how intentionally unfunny it all is.

More often than not this also means pushing the limits of ugliness, crudity, and gags based on bodily functions and over-the-top violence. Again, the idea is to get a cheap laugh out of such extremism while passing it off as meta-commentary on the trend toward gross-out laughs. With scenes doused in deeply uncomfortable awkwardness, or bodily fluids, or both, that can make parts of *Tim and Eric's Billion Dollar Movie* feel like an endurance test. From the filmmaker's point of view, however, if you are not disgusted by or objecting to at least one thing then you have not fully experienced their film.

That is not to say the film is darkly nihilistic—instead it is brightly nihilistic. It bounds happily along, tossing out a variety of comic bits willy nilly as it goes, with Heidecker and Wareheim serving their subversion with a smiling, over-lit faux cheer that itself becomes part of the commentary. To get back to the original question, yes there are laughs in *Tim and Eric's Billion Dollar Movie*—the jokes and anti-jokes are aimed and flung so far and wide, some of them are bound to stick, whatever the viewer's tastes.

Of course random absurdity and deconstructive surrealism can become their own rut, and the challenge is to keep the original Tim and Eric show's staccato, hit-and-miss two-minute bursts of satiric, sick-puppy silliness working for ninety minutes. However much the viewer might applaud Heidecker and Wareheim's fearless commitment to boundary pushing, eventually a feature-length comedy has to hold itself together enough to follow through on some sort of idea. The secret of the Monty Python films was they dressed themselves in the illusion of anarchy, yet had something to say even if the message-delivery mechanism was sometimes invisible amid the chaos.

Tim and Eric's Billion Dollar Movie does not deliver any message other than self-loathing contempt for its own kind. However, that in itself can be seen as meaning, and to ask whether the film is contemptibly lazy, tedious, and inept or instead laudably subversive, transgressive, and revolutionary is to miss the point: That by embracing the former it hopes to be the latter. Whether all that anti-humor meta-irony works for an individual viewer depends on how willing he or she is to forgive the film's sloppy failings and slovenly attention to its own intentions in the name of supporting daring

comedy (or anti-comedy). That also goes for the extent to which a viewer of *Tim and Eric's Billion Dollar Movie* is amused, nauseated, or bored. Most likely it will be an ever-whirling combination of all three.

Locke Peterseim

CREDITS

Himself: Tim Heidecker
Himself: Eric Wareheim
Earle Swinter: William Atherton
Tommy Schlaaang: Robert Loggia
Chef Goldblum: Jeff Goldblum
Dr. Doone Struts: Ray Wise
Origin: United States
Language: English
Released: 2012
Production: Ben Cosgrove, Will Ferrell, Chris Hency, Dave Kneebone, Tim Heidecker; Abso Lutely, Bobby Weisman Caterers, Funny or Die, Gary Sanchez Prods., Twenty9Twenty9 Productions; released by Magnet Releasing, Magnolia Pictures
Directed by: Tim Heidecker; Eric Wareheim
Written by: Tim Heidecker; Eric Wareheim
Cinematography by: Rachel Morrison
Music by: David Wood
Sound: Trip Brock
Music Supervisor: David Wood
Editing: Daniel Haworth; Doug Lussenhop
Art Direction: Melanie Mandl
Costumes: Diana Contreras
Production Design: Rosie Sanders
MPAA rating: R
Running time: 94 minutes

REVIEWS

Addiego, Walter. *San Francisco Chronicle*. March 2, 2012.
Baumgarten, Marjorie. *Austin Chronicle*. March 2, 2012.
Ebert, Roger. *Chicago Sun-Times*. February 29, 2012.
Ebiri, Bilge. *Vulture*. March 2, 2012.
Gilsdorf, Ethan. *Boston Globe*. March 2, 2012.
O'Sullivan, Michael. *Washington Post*. March 2, 2012.
Pinkerton, Nick. *Village Voice*. February 29, 2012.
Rabin, Nathan. *AV Club*. January 27, 2012.
Webster, Andy. *New York Times*. March 2, 2012.
Whipp, Glenn. *Los Angeles Times*. March 2, 2012.

QUOTES

Serious Announcer: "If you look at Tim and Eric's show, one of the wonderful things about them was how absurd the right and left turns are; one piece to another. But yeah, this has a story. An absurd story."

There are no opening credits, but a fake one crediting Tim and Eric in the film-within-the-film, *Diamond Jim.*

TO ROME WITH LOVE

Box Office: $16.7 million

When a director is as prolific as Woody Allen, who has made an average of one movie a year for the last forty or so years, they will inevitably repeat themselves. At this point in his career, Allen has begun to repeat the theme of the magical European city populated by eccentrics where anything is possible. In the past decade, Allen has moved his New York sensibilities abroad and has now chosen to compose his cinematic love letters to London, Barcelona, Paris, and, now, Rome. The characters, their dilemmas, and Allen's themes have not changed much. Only the backdrops have changed color and now, occasionally, there are subtitles. At times, Allen still finds something new to say, as he did with *Midnight In Paris* (2011), where he confronted the theme of nostalgia and all its trappings, but for the most part, Allen stays within his comfort zone, which can be both a burden and a relief.

With his latest, *To Rome with Love,* Allen populates his comedy with multiple characters within multiple storylines, a device he has employed before, only this time, the stories do not interact. They are told as though the film were in shuffle mode. This means that Allen has to come up with four ways in which he can either repeat the same old material or surprise the audience. Allen has said that he never thinks about his older films or even his latest ones; that he is already thinking about the next film before the latest is in the can. Surprisingly, *To Rome with Love* actually addresses the notion of working well into your twilight years only to come up artistically short. Perhaps not surprisingly, Allen plays the character who must deal with that problem.

The film opens with a traffic conductor breaking the fourth wall and telling the audience that he sees stories everywhere in Rome and it is his job to keep everything moving. The first story introduced is that of Hayley (Alison Pill) and Michelangelo (Flavio Parenti), a couple who are about to get married. Hayley's parents, Phyllis (Judy Davis) and Jerry (Woody Allen), are flying in to meet Michelangelo for the first time. Allen plays his usual nebbish and it seems at first the story will be about overcoming his stubbornness and accept the new member of the family. But then Phyllis and Jerry meet Michelangelo's parents and find that Michelangelo's dad, Giancarlo (Fabio Armiliato), has an amazing opera singing voice, which he only uses when singing in the

shower. Jerry tries to convince Giancarlo to use his talent for something great rather than just keeping it under wraps. It takes some persuading, but Jerry, who has just retired from a long career in producing avant-garde performance art, eventually convinces Giancarlo to sing to a captive audience.

There is also the story of Sally (Greta Gerwig) and Jack (Jesse Eisenberg), a young couple who are studying in Rome (of course, he is an aspiring architect). One day, Jack is out walking about when he meets John (Alec Baldwin), himself a famous architect who has sold out making mini-malls. They get to talking and soon Jack invites him to his place to meet Sally, who has a friend coming in from out of town. This friend, Monica (Ellen Page), is an out-of-work actress who has just broken up with someone. Sally has insecurities that Jack will eventually fall for Monica because all men do. As they explore the city together, John becomes an all-knowing critic of Jack and all his perceptions of Monica and other women. He becomes a figment of Jack's imagination, but nothing John says is untrue.

Perhaps the least interesting story concerns a newlywed couple named Antonio (Alessandro Tiberi) and Milly (Alessandra Mastronardi), who are awaiting a visit from Antonio's Aunt and Uncle who have never met Milly. It is crucial that Milly wins the approval of the relatives since Anotnio will soon be working in their firm. Two mix-ups occur: The first concerns Milly who goes out to run an errand, but gets completely lost in Rome thanks to the locals who keep giving her confusing directions. The other mishap concerns a prostitute named Anna (Penelope Cruz), who is mistakenly sent to Antonio and Milly's hotel room. She fully plans to seduce Antonio regardless and when his relatives walk in on them, he and Anna must now pretend to be newlyweds. Meanwhile, Milly wanders onto a movie set where she meets some of her favorite movie stars and ends up entangled with one of them.

Finally, the kind of short story that Allen often excels at is that of an unexplainable phenomenon. This is the story of Leopoldo (Roberto Benigni), a family man so average and seemingly insignificant that he cannot even enter a conversation without someone telling him that his opinion is never really necessary. Suddenly, without warning, he becomes famous. There are paparazzi outside his house waiting to hear his next word and to see his every move. When he is finally interviewed on a morning talk show, the questions are as banal as "What did you have for breakfast this morning?" and "Did you shave before or after breakfast?" Nobody can explain to him why, but he soon becomes the toast of Rome just for being himself.

The stories seem to be unified by the theme of normalcy versus celebrity, a theme Allen has touched on before, most notably with *Stardust Memories* (1980), *The Purple Rose of Cairo* (1985), *Radio Days* (1987) and *Celebrity* (1998). Woody Allen's character here is trying to turn a normal, modest guy with a singing hobby into an opera sensation. Ellen Page's character is an actress who will eventually move onto fame and fortune if she gets her big break. If she does, relationships will be impossible to navigate. Alessandra Mastronardi 's character finds herself involved with a celebrity whose life will become a scandal if she becomes too involved. And Benigni's character is the obvious focal point of the theme, in which someone can become famous just for being famous. Allen seems to be making a point that all forms of celebrity involve being corrupt and that it is better to just live your life under the radar.

Allen has been lauded in the past for creating strong, interesting female characters. Unfortunately, here, that is not the case. Gerwig and Page are playing Allen female archetypes; Gerwig is the safe, uninteresting woman who might soon get dumped and Page is the ingenue that is supposed to be a sexual dynamo and irresistible to all men who lay eyes on her. Cruz plays a hooker with—what else?—a heart of gold who helps Antonio get in touch with his more sexual nature while in the same story Alessandra Mastronardi plays a woman who will sleep with a dangerous guy with a gun within minutes of meeting him. Davis plays the reactive role to Woody Allen's one-liners and is even used at one point as a human shield against an angry relative with a sharp knife. Benigni's wife is just a wife. And at some point, as often happens in Allen's movies, a woman needs a man to teach her about all manner of culture or, in this case, architecture.

Still, there are laughs to be found here and this movie in no way represents the nadir of Allen's career (that was back in the 2000's with *The Curse of the Jade Scorpion* [2001], *Hollywood Ending* [2002], *Cassandra's Dream* [2007]and *Whatever Works* [2009], to name just a few). The manner in which Jerry convinces Giancarlo to sing in front of an audience is one of his funniest story elements in recent memory, even though he lets the joke run too long. Baldwin has some memorable moments as well in the film's most fully realized storyline, even if he has done it before. The problem is that the film lacks any real momentum to keep it afloat. The storylines feel like ideas that had nowhere really to go. They all serve a theme, but the comedic suspense that Allen has been good at in the past is nowhere to be found.

To Rome with Love was the follow-up to Allen's biggest commercial and critical hit in well over a decade. *Midnight In Paris* became the highest-grossing movie of his career and even earned him his third Academy Award for screenwriting (his fifteenth nomination overall). The expectation that he could repeat this kind of success a year later seems unreasonable, especially this late in his career. But it did help make him relevant again and at least there is a reason to look forward to his movies. *To Rome with Love* will not win or lose any fans, but it does show that he is still interested in playing with the form of filmmaking and storytelling. It may not be his most innovative film (far from it), but it does show signs of life that had too long been missing in the previous decade. Like his character in this film, he cannot seem to bear the thought of retiring and it is hard to imagine the real Woody Allen doing so anytime soon.

Collin Souter

CREDITS

Jerry: Woody Allen
Phyllis: Judy Davis
John: Alec Baldwin
Leopoldo: Roberto Benigni
Jack: Jesse Eisenberg
Monica: Ellen Page
Sally: Greta Gerwig
Anna: Penelope Cruz
Hayley: Alison Pill
Michelangelo: Flavio Parenti
Antonio: Alessandro Tiberi
Milly: Alessandra Mastronardi
Giancarlo: Fabio Armiliato
Luca Salta: Antonio Albanese
Origin: Italy, United States
Language: English
Released: 2012
Production: Letty Aronson, Stephen Tenenbaum, Giampaolo Letta; Medusa Film; released by Sony Pictures Classics
Directed by: Woody Allen
Written by: Woody Allen
Cinematography by: Darius Khondji
Sound: Maurizio Argentien
Editing: Alisa Lepselter
Costumes: Sonia Grande
Production Design: Anne Seibel
MPAA rating: R
Running time: 112 minutes

REVIEWS

Denby, David. *New Yorker.* June 26, 2012.
Ebert, Roger. *Chicago Sun-Times.* June 28, 2012.
Edelstein, David. *New York Magazine.* June 18, 2012.

Gleiberman, Owen. *Entertainment Weekly*. June 20, 2012.

LaSalle, Mick. *San Francisco Chronicle*. June 28, 2012.

O'Sullivan, Michael. *Washington Post*. June 29, 2012.

Orr, Christopher. *The Atlantic*. June 29, 2012.

Packham, Chris. *Village Voice*. June 19, 2012.

Smith, Kyle. *New York Post*. June 22, 2012.

Sobczynski, Peter. *eFilmcrtitic.com*. June 28, 2012.

QUOTES

Jack: "It's incredible that the Colosseum is still standing after thousands of years. You know, Sally and I have to re-tile the bathroom every six months."

TRIVIA

Both Aaron Johnson and Robert Pattinson auditioned for a role in the film.

TOTAL RECALL

Is it real, is it recall?
—Movie tagline

What is real?
—Movie tagline

Box Office: $58.9 million

In many of the late Phillip K. Dick's visionary science-fiction novels and short stories, characters struggle with paranoid suspicions about their identity, the validity of the "real" world around them, and their purpose in a life that may or may not be their own. Director Len Wiseman's *Total Recall* has no such issues with its own identity—it knows exactly what it is and what it is for.

Technically this is a remake of Paul Verhoeven's 1990 slab of over-the-top sci-fi action and Arnold Schwarzenegger's groaning word- and gun-play, itself a broad adaptation of Dick's 1966 short story "We'll Remember It for You Wholesale." Verhoeven and Schwarzenegger's combination of post-'80s ultra-violence and Dick's mind-twisting paranoia somehow comes out ahead of its thick-headed parts. For better or (mostly) worse, however, Wiseman's *Total Recall* sticks to its prosaic purpose as a competently made, visually kinetic, PG-13 gloss on the original film's heady, R-rated bombast. The new movie vaguely entertains or at least distracts from scene to scene, but it never seems to lose sight of the fact that it exists primarily to fill a release date in August's cinematic back room. Even though *Total Recall* 2012 arrived in theaters at a time that felt ripe for a speculative riff on class warfare teetering on the brink of uprising and on the confusion of self in the face of numerous artificial-but-social online escapes, any

such social-economic-political potential is set aside for the all-too familiar, non-stop rhythms of nearly every other contemporary action film.

Colin Farrell steps into the Schwarzenegger role: Douglas Quaid, a late-21st-century blue-collar stiff whose attempt to buy the mentally implanted experience of a vacation getaway accidentally unlocks the hidden memories of his other life as a former revolution-minded secret agent. Where the 1990 movie ended up on Mars, Wiseman stays put on Earth—all the way to its center, in fact, thanks to a giant elevator tram called The Fall that carries lowly factory grunts like Quaid from their densely packed urban squalor environs in The Colony (a massive, concrete-towered company town formerly known as Australia), through the Earth's core, to London, the shiny last bastion of the elite job creators where the laborers build the very robots that will replace them. (The rest of the planet has been conveniently rendered unlivable by environmental collapse and nuclear warfare, leaving The Fall's daily commute as nifty a visual gimmick as it is a physical and logical howler. *Total Recall* asks its audience to not only suspend disbelief but forget such a thing as disbelief ever existed.)

In a shift from Schwarzenegger's pumped-up mugging, Farrell plays Quaid with the sort of moody, broody, somewhat puzzled angst the Irish actor has made his trademark. Kate Beckinsale (the real-life wife of director Wiseman) is Quaid's ersatz "wife" turned Javert-like pursuer, and Jessica Biel plays his revolutionary dream-girl savior—but good luck trying to tell the two very physically similar actresses apart in all the slam-bang chaos. (Say what you will of Quaid, he seems to have a "type" when it comes to the ladies.) Talented genre thespians Bryan Cranston and Bill Nighy are also on hand, on opposite sides of the cause, but they and the film's leads are little more than cogs in the film's steely, blue-gray, action machinery.

As orchestrated and overseen with polished, journeyman workmanship by Wiseman, that machinery clanks steadily along, with no real ideas (other than the aforementioned super-commute Fall), and no discernable style beyond today's standard monochromatic mix of grit and jitter-cam. For all its brawny, post-eighties silliness, Verhoeven's original film—written by Ronald Shusett and Dan O'Bannon—genuinely embraced a few of Dick's brainier, mind-trippier ideas. Such "who am I?" questions are only fleetingly raised in this new movie (scripted by Kurt Wimmer and Mark Bomback) before being set aside for more running, jumping, and shooting. Packed with both visual and aural noise (including plenty of high-tech CGI whatsits and labored winks at the original film), *Total Recall* 2012 pushes ahead on a blunt-force determination to overwhelm without engaging. It asks nothing more of viewers than that they give up an overlong 118 minutes of their lives with the promise that the time spent will be quickly and easily forgotten.

Audiences and critics tended to agree: This *Total Recall* underperformed at the North American box office (though it did better worldwide) and mostly garnered below-average reviews along the general lines of "harmless, but unnecessary." Amy Biancolli of the *San Francisco Chronicle* wrote, "this revamped *Total Recall* is a bland thing—bloodless, airless, humorless, featureless." Though not everyone was unimpressed: *Salon.com*'s Andrew O'Hehir felt, "Wiseman has made his own movie, one that invents its own grim version of the human future (and comes marginally closer to Dick's original story) and doesn't try to rinse the original from our brains."

Locke Peterseim

CREDITS

Douglas Quaid/Hauser: Colin Farrell
Chancellor Vilos Cohaagen: Bryan Cranston
Melina: Jessica Biel
Lori: Kate Beckinsale
Kuato: Bill Nighy
McClane: John Cho
Harry: Bokeem Woodbine
Bergen: Currie Graham
Marek: Will Yun Lee
Origin: United States
Language: English
Released: 2012
Production: Toby Jaffe, Neal H. Moritz; Original Film, Total Recall, Prime Focus, Rekall Productions; released by Columbia Pictures
Directed by: Len Wiseman
Written by: Kurt Wimmer; Mark Bomback
Cinematography by: Paul Cameron
Music by: Harry Gregson-Williams
Sound: Stephen Hunter Flick
Editing: Christian Wagner
Costumes: Sanja Milkovic Hays
Production Design: Patrick Tatopoulos
MPAA rating: PG-13
Running time: 121 minutes

REVIEWS

Biancolli, Amy. *San Francisco Chronicle*. August 2, 2012.
Burr, Ty. *Boston Globe*. August 3, 2012.
Chaney, Jen. *Washington Post*. August 3, 2012.
Corliss, Richard. *Time*. August 2, 2012.
O'Hehir, Andrew. *Salon*. August 2, 2012.

Packham, Chris. *Village Voice*. August 1, 2012.
Phillips, Michael. *Chicago Tribune*. August 2, 2012.
Scott, A. O. *New York Times*. August 2, 2012.
Tobias, Scott. *AV Club*. August 2, 2012.
Turan, Kenneth. *Los Angeles Times*. February 2, 2012.

QUOTES

Three-Breasted Woman: "Trust me, baby, you're gonna wish you had three hands."

TRIVIA

The one shot fight scene was performed by Colin Farrell himself and was shot twenty-two times before Farrell did it perfectly.

AWARDS

Nominations:

Golden Raspberries 2012: Worst Support. Actress (Biel)

TRISHNA

Box Office: $240,381

The idea to move Thomas Hardy's 1891 novel *Tess of the d'Urbervilles* to present-day India in *Trishna* is not as much of a catchy gimmick as it may seem on first glance. Writer and director Michael Winterbottom seems to feel that leaving Hardy's woe begotten heroine in 19th-Century England—as so many film versions have done, including Roman Polanski's *Tess* (1979) and a BBC television miniseries (2008)—would be to make yet another period drama where the sets and costumes, not the characters and themes, become the focus.

Instead, modern India, with its still-strong traditional distinctions about class and the role and rights of women (not to mention cultural standards of female "purity") proves rich ground for giving Hardy's *Tess*, written at a time when England's cultural mores were more restrictive, fresh thematic energy. Winterbottom has always been an excitingly eclectic film maker, restless and roving in both his on-screen eye and his taste in projects, and this is his third Hardy film after the Victorian-set *Jude* (1996) (from *Jude the Obscure*) and the American-Western styled *The Claim* (2000) (from *The Mayor of Casterbridge*). That makes it easier to trust the director in his most recent Hardy endeavor.

And for a while, that trust feels well-placed. Even though British and American films about the India of today have proliferated in recent years (some might say on the back of a cinematic fad), the English Winterbottom dives right in with a fluid, hand-held verisimilitude and the swagger of a curious mind and eye. *Trishna* does not focus on or fetishize a single, stereotypical angle (poverty-ridden India, exotic India, historical India, religious India)—instead, the film seems to show and embrace them as many of them as possible. Even the ins and outs of the pop-ubiquitous Bollywood culture is woven into Winterbottom's cinematic tapestry.

The basic story is still Hardy's, with some major plot points and characters condensed from novel to screen. Tess here is Trishna (the strikingly attractive Freida Pinto), a young woman born into urban poverty and working hard to support her family and ailing, controlling father. As in the novel, Trishna is swept into love and out of her difficult economic circumstances, bringing her both opportunity and misfortune. However, Winterbottom has combined the book's two love interests, Angel Clare and Alec d'Urberville, into one charming, handsome young heir to a hotel fortune: Jay (Riz Ahmed). The move is tricky, and possibility frustrating to Hardy devotees—after all, in the novel Angel is Tess' real, honest love, while Alec is the caddishly manipulative aristocrat who brings her misery. But it works in *Trishna* not as a time-saving device, but because melding the two forces pulling at Tess' heart into one man makes a strong point. A century ago, Hardy needed both men to show the range of male behavior, but today it is easier for audiences to accept more human complexity and duplicity in a single character. As nicely played by Ahmed, the cocky Jay appears both genuinely decent at the start and later coldly cruel.

Winterbottom works hard to keep all this humming along, mixing the story's ingrained melodrama (with romantic scenes set against lovely natural vistas, complete with lovely flora and fauna and Indian pop love songs on the soundtrack) with the gritty, dusty naturalism of poverty-stricken modern India. And yet, *Trishna* slowly, steadily loses momentum, eventually falling into a languid stasis rather than entrancing and enthralling the viewer.

The problem, it turns out, is Pinto. While the Indian actress' loveliness is well-suited to the character—an attractive innocent whose guilelessness is taken advantage of and misused—Pinto has always been a light-impact performer, not prone to asserting herself onto a role. With Trishna already a passive character in her own story, the match-up proves a regrettable one. Pinto's might intend to paint layers of nuance into the character with an understated approach, but the actress does not get her performance to that level of sophisticated subtlety. Trishna the heroine should seem adrift, buffeted by the social, economic, and emotional forces around her, but unfortunately it is Pinto the actress who appears lost.

Even as Jay increasingly debases Trishna, further sullying and tarnishing her natural beauty with his sexual and emotional demands and driving her to extreme measures, the audience cannot help but feel as if it is watching Winterbottom watch Pinto watch the character's actions. Such a remove means the film never fully draws the viewer into either Trishna's early hopes and happiness nor her eventual pain and desperation, and without that connection there is no story and thus no dramatically dynamic film. Though still an interesting endeavor, Winterbottom's admirable effort limps to its conclusion having fallen short of both literary expectations and cinematic potential.

In North America, *Trishna* had a limited art-house release in late July, but failed to make a mark at the box office, even by small-picture standards. Critical reaction was mixed. *Movieline*'s Stephanie Zacharek applauded the results, noting, "The dialogue here is mostly improvised—this is a casual, hip-pocket approach to a revered classic—but Winterbottom keeps the story moving deftly." Ty Burr of the *Boston Globe* was less impressed. "Why... is this film so uninvolving?" Burr wrote. "A sumptuously shot melodrama of a country girl's seduction and betrayal, *Trishna* should move the soul and engage the tear-ducts, yet it passes by as distant as it is lovely."

Locke Peterseim

CREDITS

Trishna: Freida Pinto
Jay: Riz Ahmed
Jay's father: Roshan Seth
Origin: United Kingdom
Language: English, Hindi
Released: 2011
Production: Melissa Parmeter, Michael Winterbottom; Head Gear Films; released by Sundance Selects
Directed by: Michael Winterbottom
Written by: Michael Winterbottom
Cinematography by: Marcel Zyskind
Music by: Shigeru Umebayashi
Sound: Will Whale
Editing: Mags Arnold
Costumes: Niharika Khan
Production Design: David Bryan
MPAA rating: R
Running time: 113 minutes

REVIEWS

Adams, James. *The Globe and Mail*. July 20, 2012.

Bradshaw, Peter. *The Guardian*. March 8, 2012.

Burr, Ty. *Boston Globe*. July 20, 2012.

Dargis, Manohla. *New York Times*. July 12, 2012.

Ebert, Roger. *Chicago Sun-Times*. July 18, 2012.

Hornaday, Ann. *Washington Post*. July 20, 2012.

LaSalle, Mick. *San Francisco Chronicle*. July 19, 2012.

Schenker, Andrew. *Slant Magazine*. April 17, 2012.

Willmore, Alison. *AV Club*. July 12, 2012.

Zacharek, Stephanie. *Movieline*. July 11, 2012.

TROUBLE WITH THE CURVE

Whatever life throws at you.
    —Movie tagline

Box Office: $35.8 million

Hallowed hitter Ted Williams claimed that he could see the rotation of a baseball's seams as it hurtled towards the plate, enabling him to know in advance what type of pitch was headed his way. Countless boys to big leaguers have lamented that they were not blessed with Williams' key acuity, left to merely fantasize about what it would be like to be the sharp-eyed legend. Akin to indulging in such daydreams, watching *Trouble with the Curve* gives one the opportunity to feel like Williams in the batter's box, as it is exceedingly easy to anticipate exactly what is on the way time and time again. While aspiring sluggers would consider this an ability to be an asset, more than a few moviegoers did not enjoy possessing it while viewing this modestly-engaging, well-acted, but hackneyed and woefully-predictable film.

Keenness of both sight and foresight are essential for those assigned to spot which young ballplayers are most likely to mature into major league game changers. Late in his long and much-lauded career, Atlanta Braves scout Gus Lobel (Clint Eastwood) still has the latter but is losing the former due to macular degeneration and glaucoma, conditions which are making it increasingly challenging to discern talent—along with everything else. (Point-of-view shots let the audience experience what he is up against.) Not only is his vision dwindling but his prostate is enlarging, making Gus's attempts to urinate qualify for the baseball term of long relief. The passage of time, on the other hand, along with its resulting ravages, are clearly things this crusty codger would much rather have been impeded. Nevertheless, Eastwood's Gus seems determined to grit his teeth and defiantly stare down debility with one of those patented, potent Clint squints.

While Gus has not been able to prevent time's ability to change him, he has thus far been able to avoid changing with the times, especially when it comes to predicting prospects' potential. It is made clear that Gus is not just old but old school, a scout who still trusts his gaze and his gut over some computer's newfangled statistical analysis. "Anyone who uses a computer doesn't know a damn thing about this game," Gus emphatically growls with disgusted dismissiveness. Thus, it is easy to see how he could be thought of as an aged anachronism by front office whippersnapper know-it-alls who have eschewed eyeballing like Phillip Sanderson (Matthew Lillard), a wily weasel who would be pushing even harder for Gus's retirement if he knew that the touted tools of the man's trade are not as sharp as they used to be. In last year's *Moneyball*, veteran scouts like Gus suffered from a lack of vision in the figurative sense if no other, portrayed as myopic, extinction-ready dinosaurs irksomely in the way of Billy Beane's progressive sabermetrics. However, this film will ultimately vindicate the stubbornly-old-fashioned and supposedly-obsolete, proving that the wizened can provide indispensible wisdom.

Determined to avoid being put out to pasture, Gus keeps his mouth shut about his condition and his ears open, listening for distinctive sounds during play that will clearly tell him what a blur now obscures. What is plainly visible is the concern of Pete Klein (John Goodman), the ballclub's chief of scouting and the friend who loyally goes to bat for Gus. With a crucial draft looming, Pete gets the struggling scout's estranged daughter Mickey (enjoyably-effective Amy Adams) to extend a helping hand across the heretofore unbridgeable chasm that has long existed between father and daughter. She says that she has "picked up a few things growing up," and at least as deep and sustained as the love of baseball she has gotten from Gus is the bitterly-painful puzzlement with which she has been saddled since the age of six when he shunted her off to relatives and boarding school after her mother died. Despite this, not to mention the fact that she is preparing for a make-or-break case on the cusp of attaining the partner position for which she has long bucked, this daughter seen earlier walking off in an understandable huff from her exasperatingly insensitive dad now dutifully marches down to North Carolina to assist him—and take one last swing at reconciliation. Everyone should sense that Mickey will not strike out.

While this baseball-themed film does not feature a cornfield like *Field of Dreams* (1989), it is nonetheless corny. That can be comforting, but some may have wound up agreeing with Gus that "Being comfortable is overrated." The film's banal, sappy TV movie-esque nature was disappointing to many, but nothing compares to its disheartening obviousness. The film bats viewers over the head with blatant parallels between the baseball scout and the daughter he named after a Yankee great, making the point that they are actually kindred spirits who are destined to team up once again. Mickey exhibits her own scouting acumen and is a font of trivia about the National Pastime. Gus thinks she is stubborn, to which Mickey retorts, "I wonder where I get it?" He is peeved that she has deemed him in need of assistance; she keeps declaring that she can take care of herself. Both have wholeheartedly thrown themselves into work while cautiously maintaining a safe emotional distance in their personal lives. Attempts are being made to undermine both back at their respective offices as Gus and Mickey struggle under the gun to prove that they have got what it takes. He resists the push to embrace repugnantly-arrogant high school hotshot Bo Gentry (Joe Massingill) as the Braves' No. 1 pick just because he "looks good on paper," while Mickey balks when feeling pressured by a boyfriend's analysis of their relationship: "This isn't one of those things you can just put on paper!" Is there any question that Johnny (sufficiently charming Justin Timberlake), a Red Sox scout whose promising pitching career was aborted by a blown-out arm, will wind up being a better match when he contrastingly expresses a willingness to wait "as long as it takes"? (Try to ignore that they have little chemistry, though.)

There is no last minute trickiness to the trajectory of anything in *Trouble with the Curve*. Gus' value is reaffirmed, while a justly-deflated Sanderson is fired. This scout with diminished sight and his daughter finally see eye to eye, after a melodramatic, nightmare-foreshadowed revelation that too-tidily lets Gus off the hook for his hurtful behavior. (Notice the utilization of a *Dirty Harry* clip.) Mickey and Johnny surmount a misunderstanding and end up in a promising clinch. Gentry is thrown by the commupance satisfyingly dealt him by the admirably-modest, powerfully-armed peanut vendor-turned-pitching phenom whom he had earlier belittled. (The nuts are surely easier to swallow than the far-fetched nature of this uplift, or attorney-turned-agent Mickey's claim that her law career had merely been an attempt to garner Gus's admiration.)

Things probably would have been better off in Eastwood's experienced, skilled hands than in those of longtime collaborator but first-time director Robert Lorenz and rookie screenwriter Randy Brown. The role of authoritative, good-hearted but gruff Gus undeniably fits Eastwood like a well-worn mitt, and there is certainly fun in watching Clint be Clint. Yet, for Eastwood's first screen appearance since portraying yet another crusty man softened by a young woman in *Gran Torino* (2008), one was hoping for a home run instead of something so run of the mill. Made on a budget of $60 million, *Trouble with the Curve* grossed about $36 million. For

many critics and moviegoers, the trouble with the film is that it failed to offer up a single unforeseen curve.

David L. Boxerbaum

CREDITS

Gus: Clint Eastwood
Mickey: Amy Adams
Johnny Flanagan: Justin Timberlake
Pete Klein: John Goodman
Phillip Sanderson: Matthew Lillard
Max: Ed Lauter
Vince: Robert Patrick
Billy Clark: Scott Eastwood
Origin: United States
Language: English
Released: 2012
Production: Clint Eastwood, Robert Lorenz; Malpaso Productions; released by Warner Bros.
Directed by: Robert Lorenz
Written by: Randy Brown
Cinematography by: Tom Stern
Music by: Marco Beltrami
Sound: Walt Martin
Editing: Gary D. Roach
Art Direction: Patrick M. Sullivan, Jr.
Costumes: Deborah Hopper
Production Design: James Murakami
MPAA rating: PG-13
Running time: 111 minutes

REVIEWS

Burr, Ty. *Boston Globe*. September 20, 2012.
Chang, Justin. *Variety*. September 17, 2012.
Corliss, Richard. *Time*. September 20, 2012.
Denby, David. *New Yorker*. October 7, 2012.
Ebert, Roger. *Chicago Sun-Times*. September 19, 2012.
Hammond, Pete. *Boxoffice Magazine*. September 17, 2012.
Hornaday, Ann. *Washington Post*. September 21, 2012.
McCarthy, Todd. *Hollywood Reporter*. September 17, 2012.
Morgenstern, Joe. *Wall Street Journal*. September 20, 2012.
Phillips, Michael. *Chicago Tribune*. September 20, 2012.

QUOTES

Gus: "Anybody who uses computers doesn't know a damn thing about this game."

TRIVIA

This is the first film Clint Eastwood has starred in that he has not directed himself since 1993's *In the Line of Fire*.

THE TURIN HORSE
(A torinoi lo)

Box Office: $56,097

Bela Tarr's *The Turin Horse* is an invitation more than a film. It is something to be experienced, to challenge, to exasperate. In order to be experienced, the daunting invitation must be accepted. The mysteries it contains are myriad, the power with which it makes them manifest undeniable. Ultimately, it comes and goes making no apologies for itself. In this last sense, *The Turin Horse* is most like life. It seeks almost no justification from the viewer, emerging as masterful cinema that blurs the line between life and art, asking questions that are unanswerable even as they refuse to stop haunting the soul.

An old man with one good arm and his daughter live a secluded existence out in a one-room mud hut, eating only potatoes and utterly dependent on a series of things that fail them one-by-one as the film's two-and-a-half hour runtime spools out. While an endless gale roars outside, stripping the landscape bare of all but the heartiest scrub, the pair fights dwindling resources with a routine that approaches religious ritual. Dressing, starting a fire, eating, readying a wagon—all offer a sense of continuity if not grace to the harsh realities of their lives. In effect, *The Turin Horse* barely tells a story at all, choosing instead to pick up the pair at a seemingly random point and follow them for a number of days through their abject poverty. No one and nothing changes.

Yet it is almost unthinkable not to read meaning into the sparse visuals. A harness dropping off a cart to the dust could represent loss, weakness, or even death. A figure staring wide-eyed and silent out of a window into the desolation could mean the same. In startlingly beautiful moments, the camera fills the screen completely with wood planking, or a freshly-washed, white shirt. Rarely have images been so ready to be invested with the viewer's meaning. Tarr and cinematographer Fred Kelemen go a step further in compressing shots, creating an intense claustrophobia as characters are framed by doorways, pools of light, and close-ups that seem to leech nobility out of their very brows.

The photography itself is richly detailed, bringing to life the grime and grit and sweat in a rough-hewn world. Tarr has spent his career making films devoid of special effects in the sense audiences understand them today. But his landscape and characters here seem lifted from some alien purgatory, dust seems to flow out of the screen; viewers can almost feel the wind. This is a film that evokes dark wonder in the midst of mundanity.

The Turin Horse is based on an oft-told story about the German philosopher Friedrich Nietzsche who is said to have gone mad in the late 1800s while intervening on behalf of a dray horse being savagely beaten by its owner. Falling into the street, exhausted by grief, he remained in a mentally crippled state until his death just over a decade later. Tarr has taken up the tale of the wagon master and the horse not as an apologist for animal abuse but as a mute witness to the heavy hand of the cosmos, fallen and falling on man and beast alike. Using the horse and the man as a starting point, writer director Tarr along with longtime collaborator and co-writer Laszlo Krasznahorkai and his lifetime companion and co-director Agnes Hranitzky fashion a tableau in a mere thirty scenes that, without denying the possibility of hope, forces the viewer to answer for any hope they may have that life in the face of suffering has meaning.

So resolute is the filmmaking team in their goal of simply shaping time that it is almost impossible to speak of the writing or the performances here. The success lies in the fact that both seem barely noticeable. Through it all, the characters plod, sometimes shakily, but with determination. They are cyphers, speaking little, revealing almost nothing of their inner life, faces sanded flat by gale winds and misfortune.

One atypical sequence sees the duo visited by a neighbor who, after begging some liquor, delivers a sad soliloquy on the decaying state of the world; "to touch is to defile" he says. It is the only time the film introduces another character and it is tempting to ascribe it as an attempt to write Nietzsche himself into the story. The old man rejects the nihilistic assessment of his neighbor but Tarr himself gives viewers no respite. The man leaves and things are as they always were; bad and getting worse.

The horse refuses to pull the wagon. The well suddenly goes dry. The fire goes out. In one scene, escape seems immanent. Yet, even there, Tarr tortures viewers with the mundane. The wagon must be brought out, the harnesses secured, the horse led, as time passes like some mocking thing. Suddenly, it dawns that nothing hints of where the duo may be heading. The film leaves the implication that it very well may not matter.

Perhaps the horse himself is the best witness of all. He is beaten at one point, barely batting an eye. The film begins with him lurching out of the shadows pulling a cart, accompanied to Mihaly Vi's dirge like hurdy-gurdy score as if on a death march or accompanying a funeral procession. He is a servant, a tool, a faceless, willing and sandblasted sufferer. When he stops eating three days into the film it comes as no surprise and yet there is never a sure sense of death over him. He is surrounded on all sides but keeps going even when there is no dignity, not even that afforded to beasts.

Tarr has said that this is his last film. If so, one can hardly imagine a more powerful way to end a career. He is a master not just of the long take but of the sense of cinema as a feeling, an immersion made of the same stuff as those who view it. For Tarr, that stuff is symbiotically intertwined with the cosmos rather than just resident in it. How appropriate then to make a film that ends in the swirling dust as he contemplates how poor a home fallen earth makes for man.

Dave Canfield

CREDITS

Origin: France, Germany, Hungary, Switzerland, United States
Language: English, Hungarian
Released: 2011
Production: Gabor Teni, Ruth Waldburger, Martin Hagemann, Juliette Lepoutre, Marie-Pierre Macia; Zero Fiction Film, Movie Partners in Motion Film, TT Filmmuhely, Vega Film; released by The Cinema Guild
Directed by: Bela Tarr; Agnes Hranitzky
Written by: Bela Tarr; Laszlo Krasznahorkai
Cinematography by: Fred Kelemen
Music by: Mihaly Vig
Sound: Gabor ifj. Erdelyi
Editing: Agnes Hranitzky
MPAA rating: Unrated
Running time: 146 minutes

REVIEWS

Andrew, Geoff. *Time Out.* April 7, 2011.
Bennett, Ray. *Hollywood Reporter.* February 15, 2011.
Feeney, Mark. *Boston Globe.* June 28, 2012.
Fuchs, Cynthia. *PopMatters.* April 6, 2012.
Jenkins, Mark. *NPR.* February 9, 2012.
Merry, Stephanie. *Washington Post.* March 16, 2012.
O'Heir, Andrew. *Salon.com.* February 3, 2012.
Pinkerton, Nick. *Village Voice.* February 7, 2012.
Romney, Jonathan. *Screen International.* April 7, 2012.
Scott, A. O. *New York Times.* February 9, 2012.

QUOTES

Bernhard: "Theirs is the moment...nature, infinite silence."

TRIVIA

The film was Hungary's official submission to the Best Foreign Language Film category of the 84th Academy Awards.

21 JUMP STREET

The only thing getting blown tonight is their cover.
—Movie tagline

They're too old for this shift.
—Movie tagline

They thought the streets were mean. Then they went back to high school.
—Movie tagline

Box Office: $138.4 million

There are television shows that find a natural transition into becoming a big-screen movie. Many of them are of the action and fantasy variety that can easily supplant their adventures into a two-hour narrative without losing their core basis. *21 Jump Street* was one of the first big hits of the infant FOX network. Starting in 1987, it is now remembered more today for launching the career of a young Johnny Depp than for any particular greatness or originality. Even at the time, there were a number of films launching themselves with the same premise of baby-faced cops going back to high school to solve crimes. Though it certainly did not take 25 years to erase the memories of *Under Cover* (1987), *Plain Clothes* (1988) and even Jon Cryer's stockbroker-on-the-run film, *Hiding Out* (1987), when the creative well runs dry in Hollywood old ideas become new again. Certainly is the attempt with *21 Jump Street* which, in recognizing the show's antiquated appeal and innate camp factor, has chosen to go the route of *Starsky & Hutch* (2004) and *The Brady Bunch Movie* (1995) and have a little goof on it. Determining the exact route of that goof though is a case even the original detectives would have trouble solving by the end of an hour.

Seven years ago, Morton Schmidt (Jonah Hill) and Greg Jenko (Channing Tatum) were on different paths in high school. One was the awkward geek and the other a popular jock. When they enroll in the police academy and discover they have something to learn from each other's strengths it is a newfound friendship. After a bust goes bad through the most basic of officer errors, they are reassigned to "a canceled undercover police program from the '80s" revamped "for modern times." There is a new synthetic drug killing students and since they are white, "people care." The mission is simple: "Infiltrate the dealers. Find the supplier," even if their angry black Captain (Ice Cube) has to tell them three times.

Things go wrong from the start when the detectives are mistakenly assigned to the wrong class loads. Jenko is put into all the honors classes with the smart kids while Schmidt is forced to endure his own humiliation with the theater crowd. Not all is lost though as they quickly discover the school dealer in Eric (Dave Franco) and Schmidt takes a liking to his friend, Molly (Brie Larson). In their efforts to fit in and discover the identity of the supplier, the undercover brothers proceed to break every rule (and law) they are warned about and even have a close encounter with the drug experience itself to ramp up the silliness and accentuate the monotony of the film's gags.

By the time the script has barely finished establishing its particular plot points, it is easy to forget the film has even the thinnest of connections to its source. This makes a direct parody a rather difficult feat since any good one (or just one in name) brings a twisted wink to material that once took itself seriously. In the absence of something specific, a broader net is cast to approach satire. The aforementioned loud captain and other police movie cliches (such as a high-speed chase sequence with an idea lifted from *The Naked Gun* [1988]) are introduced, but the manner in which directors Phil Lord and Chris Miller awkwardly call attention to them threaten to turn the whole affair into the sort of bottom-feeding spoofs like *Epic Movie* (2007) and *Meet the Spartans* (2008) by untalented hacks Jason Friedberg and Aaron Seltzer.

"The guys in charge of this stuff lack creativity and are completely out of ideas. So all they do now is recycle (stuff) from the past and expect us not to notice," so says Schmidt and Jenko's superior as an unfortunate establishment of the rest of the film's humor. A half-semester of a high school health class that shows nothing but the film, *Superbad* (2006), does not have as many mentions of penis as this film. When Tatum's Jenko is not voicing his vulgar displeasure at everything from Glee to science, seemingly every other gag either directly references or simulates a genitalia-based sex act. The drama teacher yells out "Can someone tell me where my Peter is," referring to his Neverland-based leading man. A bad guy has an unfortunate incident involving his own appendage. Even Schmidt's mom is called another variation of penis. The adherence to this singular brand of humor is so consistent and unflinching that it would not be surprising if it was part of Schmidt and Jenko's undercover dossier. The abundance of penis jokes are particularly sad because a third act surprise is so nicely revealed and perfectly handled that it is nearly worth the build-up alone.

21 Jump Street shows greater potential when it introduces a more direct commentary on the modern day high school experience. Having the partners swap their personal popularity demons is clever enough but attaching it to an evolutionary cycle or precisely what makes one cool in a green, geek-driven society is an idea that never needed the blanket of a nostalgic television show to succeed.

The film is certainly not without a few laughs. Channing Tatum affably throws himself into another role trying to shake the beefcake stereotype and Jonah Hill has a habit of making even the stalest jokes sound interesting. Too bad the film and its flaccid tally of genuine laughs could not stick to its own story long enough to get the job done.

Erik Childress

CREDITS

Schmidt: Jonah Hill
Jenko: Channing Tatum
Capt. Dickson: Ice Cube
Molly Tracey: Brie Larson
Domingo: DeRay David
Eric Molson: Dave Franco
Mr. Walters: Rob Riggle
Officer Judy Hoffs: Holly Robinson Peete
Tom Hanson: Johnny Depp
Officer Doug Penhall: Peter DeLuise
Officer Dennis Booker: Richard Grieco
Origin: United States
Language: English
Released: 2012
Production: Stephen J. Cannell, Neal H. Moritz; Metro-Goldwyn-Mayer Pictures, Original Film, Relativity Media, Stephen J. Cannell Productions; released by Columbia Pictures
Directed by: Phil Lord; Chris Miller
Written by: Michael Bacall
Cinematography by: Barry Peterson
Music by: Mark Mothersbaugh
Sound: Geoffrey G. Rubay
Editing: Joel Negron
Art Direction: Thomas Valentine
Costumes: Leah Katznelson
Production Design: Peter Wenham
MPAA rating: R
Running time: 109 minutes

REVIEWS

Bayer, Jeff. *Scorecard Review*. April 1, 2012.
Gonsalves, Rob. *eFilmCritic*. April 30, 2012.
Goss, William. *Film.com*. March 16, 2012.
Hornaday, Ann. *Washington Post*. March 16, 2012.
Levy, Shawn. *Oregonian*. March 15, 2012.
Lybarger, Dan. *KC Active*. March 18, 2012.
McGranaghan, Mike. *Aisle Seat*. March 16, 2012.
Nusair, David. *Reel Film Reviews*. March 28, 2012.
Sachs, Ben. *Chicago Reader*. March 15, 2012.
Snider, Eric D. *EricDSnider.com*. March 15, 2012.

QUOTES

Schmidt: [referring to a wall in his parents' house displaying many photos of him as a youth] "It looks like I died in a car crash and you never got over me."

TRIVIA

Emma Stone was considered for the lead female role but had to drop out the running due to *The Amazing Spider-Man*.

THE TWILIGHT SAGA: BREAKING DAWN, PART 2

Forever.
—Movie tagline

The epic finale that will live forever.
—Movie tagline

Box Office: $292.2 million

Near the end of 2011, fans were treated to the final installment of the *Harry Potter* films. The epic children's franchise faced a few early missteps, but recent films deftly embraced the good vs. evil battle at the heart of the saga, leading the ever-maturing actors into dark and twisted plotlines that left audiences marveling at the books' on-screen adaptations. The second act of *Harry Potter and The Deathly Hallows, Part 2* (2011), the final Potter film, was no exception. It plunged these beloved characters into the battle of their lives, complete with breathtaking fight scenes and marvelous CGI, and rewarded viewers by playing out the highly anticipated epilogue true to book. It was the perfect end to a beloved series. Unfortunately, the same cannot be said for the *Twilight* franchise and its final film, *Breaking Dawn—Part 2*.

When viewers last left tweendome's favorite couple, Edward (Robert Pattinson) had just turned the love of his immortal life, Bella (Kristen Stewart), into a vampire. She, of course, had perished after giving birth to her half-vamp baby girl, perversely named Renesmee. The opening moments of *Breaking Dawn Part 2* play out like a middle schooler's naive romantic notions about true love: Edward marvels at the new Bella, her orange eyes and her bouncy auburn hair, unable to keep his hands off her. The rest of the film follows suit, embracing their togetherness, and disregarding plot elements and real life intrusions when they threaten to take away from the focus of the film: Edward and Bella playing house (they even get a house of their own, a cozy cottage right out of a Restoration Hardware catalogue). It conveniently turns out that Bella is a super newbie vampire. She can handily control the cravings for human blood that plagued Jasper in the early *Twilight* films, she inherently knows how to fight, and she possesses a runway model perfection that her human self lacked. What is better, she and Edward do not get tired or hungry which means

that they can focus on what is really important—marathon vampire sex. Thank goodness their immortal status keeps any strong parenting vibes at bay, otherwise they would be forced to actually spend time with their child instead of doing it (the only quasi authentic parenting moment comes when Bella rips Jacob a new one when he confesses he is forever tied to Renesmee). It is also convenient that Bella's father does not ask any questions about where Bella has been hiding or how she came to adopt a niece that seems to quadruple in size every time he sees her.

The cold-blooded duo is snapped back to a kind of reality when the Volturi, the cloaked coven that keeps tabs on the vamps worldwide, learns of Renesmee's existence. Believing that she is an "immortal child" (aka that Bella and Edward turned a human child for their own pleasure) the tantrums of which have felled whole villages throughout history, the Volturi decide that Renesmee must be destroyed. This, finally, should be the moment where *Breaking Dawn* revs up the tension, preparing the Cullens for the fight of their life, but anyone familiar with the books knows that author Stephanie Meyer does not write conflict. Still, director Bill Condon tries to spice things up by (spoiler alert), adding a full-on Volturi vs. Cullen battle scene to the film's end, complete with beheadings, many deaths, and ferocious werewolf maulings.

It should be noted that Condon's attempt to liven up the movie ultimately gets more laughs than genuine "oohs" and "ahhs." The groundwork is there, but he is tied to the franchise's hardcore fanbase who only want to see Edward murmuring sweet nothings into Bella's ear, and prisoner to past films that never elevated characterization past Pattinson's tight lips and Stewart's pained expressions. *Breaking Dawn Part 2* hold true to its predecessors, offering stilted dialogue, half-hearted plotting and uneven voice-overs to fill in obvious holes. It is hard not to wonder what might have happened if *Twilight* was offered a true departure, if Condon or one of his predecessors could have taken a page from the *Harry Potter* adaptations and offered audiences a worthy meditation on the perils of inter-species love, not to mention the ramifications of the supernatural and natural worlds rubbing up against one another. In the end, just like all the films in the series, *Breaking Dawn Part 2* never goes past the surface of Meyer's bizarre love triangle relegating the future box set to college sorority houses for "take a shot every time Jacob or Edward take their shirts off" drinking games.

Joanna Topor MacKenzie

CREDITS

Bella Swan Cullen: Kristen Stewart

Edward Cullen: Robert Pattinson
Jacob Black: Taylor Lautner
Renesmee Cullen: Mackenzie Foy
Irina: Maggie Grace
Aro: Michael Sheen
Dr. Carlisle Cullen: Peter Facinelli
Esme Cullen: Elizabeth Reaser
Alice Cullen: Ashley Greene
Origin: United States
Language: English
Released: 2012
Production: Wyck Godfrey, Stephenie Meyer, Karen Rosenfelt; Sunswept Entertainment, Temple Hill Entertainment; released by Summit Entertainment
Directed by: Bill Condon
Written by: Melissa Rosenberg
Cinematography by: Guillermo Navarro
Music by: Carter Burwell
Sound: Dane A. Davis
Editing: Virginia Katz
Costumes: Michael Wilkinson
Production Design: Richard Sherman
MPAA rating: PG-13
Running time: 115 minutes

REVIEWS

Anderson, Melissa. *Village Voice*. November 15, 2012.
Berardinelli, James. *ReelViews*. November 16, 2012.
Bradshaw, Peter. *The Guardian*. November 14, 2012.
Ebiri, Bilge. *New York Magazine*. November 15, 2012.
Morris, Wesley. *Boston Globe*. November 15, 2012.
O'Sullivan, Michael. *Washington Post*. November 15, 2012.
Phillips, Michael. *Chicago Tribune*. November 15, 2012.
Puig, Claudia. *USA Today*. November 15, 2012.
Travers, Peter. *Rolling Stone*. November 15, 2012.
Uhlich, Keith. *Time Out New York*. November 15, 2012.

QUOTES

Bella Cullen: "Now you know. Nobody's ever loved anybody as much as I love you."
Edward Cullen: "There's one exception."

TRIVIA

The end credits are those for the entire series, not just this installment.

AWARDS

Golden Raspberries 2012: Worst Actress (Stewart), Worst Director (Condon), Worst Ensemble Cast, Worst Picture, Worst Remake/Sequel, Worst Support. Actor (Lautner)

Nominations:

Golden Raspberries 2012: Worst Actor (Pattinson), Worst Screenplay, Worst Support. Actress (Greene)

2 DAYS IN NEW YORK

Box Office: $633,210

Cultures clash in the screwball comedy *2 Days in New York,* an unexpected sequel to Julie Delpy's *2 Days in Paris* (2007), an arthouse semi-hit that revealed the international star to be deft at conveying the way relationships built between two people with very different backgrounds can lead to problems. In that film, Adam Goldberg played the cultural interloper, the American who goes to France with girlfriend Marion (Delpy) and is startled by her continued connection with ex-lovers and a few other secrets along the way. Five years later, perhaps inspired by the creative success of another unexpected sequel on her resume in *Before Sunset* (2004), Delpy revisits a character that hardly anyone expected to see again, bringing Marion to New York and allowing her unique family to be the tourists in the comedy equation. Of course, there's another man stuck in the middle, a few more sex jokes, some drug humor, and a sentimental streak, all of which adds up to a film that features some nicely observed characters but not enough consistency of tone to gel into what it could have been. The charismatic cast and Delpy's deft touch with them makes for a comedy that is likable enough without being anything more than that faint praise.

Marion has left her boyfriend from the first film but kept the son created by that relationship and she has moved to New York, where she has fallen in love with an outspoken radio talk show host named Mingus (Rock), seemingly named mostly for the related jokes about how his moniker reminds some of the word for oral sex. For two days, Marion's father Jeannot (Delpy's real-life papa Albert Delpy), sister Rose (Alexia Landeau), and sister's boyfriend Manu (Alex Nahon) come to the Big Apple for a visit. Chaos ensues; very French chaos. The humor is broad and screwball, as one would expect from a French comedy, only it takes place on U.S. shores. Somehow coming off both as surly and jovial in a way only a Frenchman who refuses to shower can do, Jeannot is a hard one for Mingus to figure out even as he wants to impress him. Mingus is less interested in pleasing Manu, who invites over a drug dealer in front of the entire family and makes casually racist comments without much thought. And Mingus is thrown off even further by the fact that Rose does not often wear clothing.

In the film's most interesting family dynamic, the arrival of Rose seems to set off some bizarre family rivalry in Marion. The two fight constantly and Marion somewhat snaps, telling an elaborate series of lies to neighbors Bella (Kate Burton) and Ron (Dylan Baker) about a brain tumor that does not exist. There is a bizarre but well-defined sense of competition between Marion and Rose, as the latter even goes as far as to suggest that Marion's son has autism, as if that would be her fault if he did. The best parts of *2 Days in New York* do not merely go with the fish out of water aspect that a lot of filmmakers have explored throughout movie history but how said fish impact their new environment and the people in it. It really is just a vacation for Jeannot, Manu, and Rose. It is what their vacation does to the people in New York—Marion and Mingus—that makes the film interesting.

Like many films of this type, the characters in *2 Days in New York* do get a little exhausting by the end of the film. It is a fine line for filmmakers to walk in that characters designed to annoy protagonists can often just end up annoying audiences at the same time (so many Hollywood holiday comedies violate this rule, perhaps none more so than the horrendous *Little Fockers* [2010]). The film also falters when it tries to get emotionally heavy in the final act. A few of the twists of the climax feel forced, but then again this is another common trait of the French screwball comedy—tacked-on emotional stakes to ground the final reel in a way that separates it from the others.

As for performance, Julie Delpy has long been one of international cinema's most likable actresses and that has not changed a bit with her doing triple duty as writer and director as well. Her amenable good nature rubs off on Chris Rock, who has not been this naturally likable in years. This may very well be his best performance to date, at least since *Nurse Betty* (2000). Casting her real father as her cinematic one may have been the obvious choice but Delpy draws a charming performance from her pop. The cast works all around, even an effective cameo by Vincent Gallo as himself in the final act.

2 Days in New York could have just been yet another comedy about how foreigners sometimes respond awkwardly to American culture but Delpy wisely plants her screwball behavior in the most relatable arena of all—family. It is not just about how people act differently in a different country but how that behavior has a ripple effect on those who love them. Delpy's comedy could have been more refined and less manipulative in its final act but vacations often end on a sour note.

Brian Tallerico

CREDITS

Marion: Julie Delpy

Mingus: Chris Rock
Jeannot: Albert Delpy
Rose: Alexia Landeau
Manu: Alex Nahon
Ron: Dylan Baker
Bella: Kate Burton
Origin: France
Language: English
Released: 2012
Production: Scott Franklin, Christophe Mazodier, Julie Delpy; Polaris Films; released by Magnolia Pictures
Directed by: Julie Delpy
Written by: Julie Delpy; Alexia Landeau
Cinematography by: Lubomir Bakchev
Music by: Julie Delpy
Sound: Gert Janssen
Editing: Isabelle Devinck
Costumes: Rebecca Hofherr
Production Design: Judy Rhee
MPAA rating: R
Running time: 91 minutes

REVIEWS

Ebiri, Bilge. *New York Magazine.* August 10, 2012.
Kohn, Eric. *indieWIRE.* August 9, 2012.
Phillips, Michael. *Chicago Tribune.* August 16, 2012.
Pinkerton, Nick. *Village Voice.* August 7, 2012.
Pols, Mary. *Time.* August 9, 2012.
Robinson, Tasha. *AV Club.* August 8, 2012.
Rose, Steve. *The Guardian.* July 20, 2012.
Scott, A. O. *New York Times.* August 9, 2012.
Smith, Neil. *Total Film.* July 20, 2012.
Travers, Peter. *Rolling Stone.* August 9, 2012.

QUOTES

Rose: "America is cool! Can I sell my soul too?"

2016: OBAMA'S AMERICA

Love him or hate him, you don't know him.
    —Movie tagline

Box Office: $33.4 million

The general bias that one takes into a movie, whether as a professional critic or a casual observer, usually doubles when it comes to documentaries. The age-old taboo that one must never discuss religion or politics amongst friends then triples amongst films which take such a favorable or negative position on them. The liberal left has had Michael Moore as their champion for years tackling gun control, health care and President

George W. Bush head on at feature length while the conservative right has mainly made movies directly refuting those assertions to mostly lesser and more petty degrees. Right-leaning feature films such an *An American Carol* (2008) and *Atlas Shrugged: Part I* (2011) also hardly met the quality control standards and genuine entertainment value from the Frank Capra era up to *The American President* (1995), *Primary Colors* (1998) and HBO's *Game Change* (2012). One of the great pleasures about movies is to occasionally be presented with a different point of view; an opportunity to open eyes to an ideology or perspective that truly conveys what it means to see both sides of the story. When a film is as constructively sloppy and disgracefully omissive as this one, it is more likely to send people deeper into their own private holes muttering to themselves, "why bother?"

The documentary is the brainchild of conservative author and commentator, Dinesh D'Souza. He spends ten minutes providing viewers with his credentials to kick off a film that purports, as the title implicates, to be about the future. Having assured the audience of his Ivy League education, being an advisor to Ronald Reagan, and public debater of Jesse Jackson, Dinesh casually lists his coincidental connections to Barack Obama. Then not so casually introduces the race card. Indian by birth, Dinesh recalls his first party at Stanford where the white students ("very often pony-tailed guys") marveled at all the ethnic food, using an actor whose motivation is to imply ignorance.

As subtly jarring as this is, it is not dwelled upon in order for D'Souza to get to the root of his theory that Obama's Presidency is a march towards an "anticolonial" ideology that he learned from his father. What is Dinesh's proof? Naturally, the key is in the title of Obama's autobiography, *Dreams From My Father*. Notice how it says "From" and not "Of?" Dinesh wonders "how can he be so influenced by a father not being around?" Viewers are taken through a long-winding timeline of Barack Obama Sr., centered around whom he fathered children with and when. As an absentee father in President Obama's life, the young Barack was nevertheless fostered with stories of his father's greatness. Dinesh interviews a psychologist who suggests the hostile association that fatherless children often grow up to have. In the case of this "airbrushed father" though, they suggest that Obama went the other way, embracing his father's political leanings after being cut off from his stepdad who shared more capitalist sentiments towards oil companies and battled communists as a member of the Indonesian Army.

Dinesh D'Souza, as are many who would rather airbrush their own facts to fit their theories, shows his cards all too often. And not just as a commentator. As a filmmaker he is certainly provided no help by co-director John Sullivan; neither of which has the general knowhow of pure aesthetics in how to sell their premise even if its complete fiction. Interviews are often intercut with D'Souza bopping his cocked head in agreement and then setting up edited conversations with the subjects saying "I think that's possible" and "you're right." For all an experienced media observer knows, they are responding to questions about the Cubs winning it all and the world being round. In one ludicrously contrived set-up, D'Souza is on the phone talking with someone about Obama's ties to Frank Marshall Davis, a political activist whose FBI file has apparently been repressed by the liberal media during Obama's rise to power. As Davis' Communist ties are laid out, viewers are witness to one camera in the subject's home and another in Dinesh's. While they speak on the phone. This is such a ludicrously conceived recreation that whatever kernel of fact might come out of it is buried under the more nagging question of why one of them could not have flown in to see the other since a camera crew clearly was.

Racism will reveal its ugly head once again though, perhaps as part of Dinesh's continued desire to debate Jesse Jackson, who claims that hatred has gone underground in America. That claim is peppered with a staged bit involving a black man first being abandoned at a bar and then presented a birthday cake by all the white patrons who gave him a standing ovation. This is Dinesh's foreshadowing to his later assertion that white people voted for Obama to prove they are not racist—while D'Souza's own racism is up front for the world to revel in. See, Reverend Jackson, you were wrong.

D'Souza's embarrassing tactics and theories truly come to a head as he tracks down Barack's half-brother, George Obama, in Africa. Dinesh comments that his living conditions compare to "something out of Slumdog Millionaire", although this particular strategy is more akin to something out of the National Enquirer when they knock down a celebrity for ignoring a member of their family. D'Souza does everything possible to try and beat George into confessing that Barack has abandoned him. Great credit goes to George for not taking the bait.

Stunning that D'Souza would even keep such an exchange in the film, especially when he is so good at cutting out the facts in-between his convenient truths. America's debt has risen from five trillion to over sixteen since the Clinton administration, but those eight years under George W. Bush and the bailout that economists said worked are ignored leaving the fault on Obama's doorstep. D'Souza reports nonsense like that Obama is "weirdly sympathetic to Muslim jihadists" and has done nothing to prevent Iran from obtaining nuclear capabilities. But nothing mentioned about the sanctions placed upon Iran nor the ordering of the strike that killed Osama Bin Laden. Perhaps the loosest and pettiest of all D'Souza's claims is also the most fractured. Yes it is true that a bust of British Prime Minister Winston Churchill was removed from the Oval Office; a symbol Dinesh states is representative of Obama's anti-colonialism stance. But it was not removed under Obama's authority since the loaner was already scheduled to be removed well before Obama ever took office. Another bust of Churchill currently remains in Barack's private residence.

Michael Moore released *Fahrenheit 9/11* (2004) with the pure intent of preventing a second term for George W. Bush. So it is only fair game that the other side would choose to try their luck in the heat of the 2012 campaign. *2016: Obama's America,* after little promotion and no invitations extended to members of the press—who were later accused of ignoring the film entirely—was expanded into theaters during the week of the Republican National Convention. After a few weeks, it became the highest grossing documentary of the year and the fourth highest ever. (*Fahrenheit 9/11* is the all-time leader with more than three-and-a-half times its numbers.) Moore has also not been above smoothing over some of his factual connections in his films, mostly to nail home a point that was already factual without the further hammering. Dinesh D'Souza is not a filmmaker. And, based on his debut alone, is not much of truth-teller either.

Erik Childress

CREDITS

Himself: Dinesh D'Souza
Herself: Dr. Alice Dewey
Himself: Willy Kauai
Himself: Dr. Paul Kengor
Himself: Barack Obama
Origin: United States
Language: English
Released: 2012
Production: Ann Balog; released by Obama's America Foundation
Directed by: Dinesh D'Souza; John Sullivan
Written by: Dinesh D'Souza; John Sullivan
Music by: Calvin Jones; Greg Kellogg
Editing: Simon James; Michael Thomas; Victoria Sillano
Art Direction: Colin Warde
MPAA rating: PG
Running time: 87 minutes

REVIEWS

Campbell, Christopher. *Movieline.* August 31, 2012.

Feeney, Mark. *Boston Globe.* August 31, 2012.
Hickman, Jonathan W. *Daily Film Fix.* August 31, 2012.
Kendrick, James. *Q Network Film Desk.* September 4, 2012.
Leydon, Joe. *Variety.* August 3, 2012.
Medley, Tony. *Tolucan Times.* August 29, 2012.
O'Hehir, Andrew. *Salon.com.* August 30, 2012.
O'Sullivan, Michael. *Washington Post.* August 31, 2012.
Rea, Steven. *Philadelphia Inquirer.* August 27, 2012.
Webster, Andy. *New York Times.* August 13, 2012.

QUOTES

Dinesh D'Souza: "My journey to America can be traced back to the independence of India, the land of my fathers."

TYLER PERRY'S GOOD DEEDS

(Good Deeds)

Wesley Deeds is about to discover the person he was meant to be.
—Movie tagline

Box Office: $35 million

The difficulty in critically approaching many of Tyler Perry's films—especially the more dramatic-leaning ones that do not feature him cross-dressing as his larger-than-life comic character Madea—is trying to weigh the writer, director, and actor's seemingly heartfelt desire to impart homey life lessons against a name-in-the-title oversized ego and ambition that is in inverse proportion to his sub-par film-making skills.

That is certainly the case with *Tyler Perry's Good Deeds,* an inert Madea-less drama that feels simultaneously smothered by earnest intentions and bloated by self-importance. Whichever side of this paradox the viewer feels wins out, the film itself remains pithed; hollowed out of both entertainment value and emotional honesty but filled with heavy-handed pretension.

There has never been much to recommend Perry technically as a film director. He is infamous for the flat look, static staging, and clunky, stop-start flow of his movies, as well as their over-reaching melodramatic bombast. Often, however, Perry's cinematic shortcomings can be forgiven because he clearly cares more about his characters than where to place the camera. Perry got his start writing and producing plays that were more like tent revivals than theater, designed to amuse, enrapt, and morally enrich a broad audience. In the more than a dozen feature films he has directed, Perry has not toned down his style much or added significant cinematic nuances. But many of those films have other elements—humor, music, or strong messages—to recommend them, if not as cinema, at least as populist entertainment.

Tyler Perry's Good Deeds comes up short across the board. In one of his rare non-Madea starring roles, Perry himself plays Wesley Deeds, a kind, wealthy, workaholic CEO driving himself to be "good"—that is, to predictably live up to everyone else's expectations of him, including his domineering mother (Phylicia Rashad) and all-but-arranged high-class fiance (Gabrielle Union). Deeds' carefully lifeless daily routine is driven by altruistic ambition: He is one of those super-rich people who inherited money, but continue striving to make it because it is a measure of hard work and a life lived correctly.

Into that world, which includes a ne'er-do-well prodigal brother (Brian White), comes Lindsey (Thandie Newton), a suddenly homeless single mother who works as a custodian in Deeds' corporate headquarters and diligently struggles to provide for her movie-adorable young daughter (Jordenn Thompson). Naturally, Lindsey and Deeds find each other and each begins helping the other change their bleak financial and emotional situations. Despite Deeds' engagement, a platonic affection also grows.

When not in Madea's wig and muumuu, Perry the actor is as much a non-presence on the screen as he is stylistically behind the camera. He is a tall man, but without Madea as a bullhorn for his id, Perry comes off shy and receding, as if he is embarrassed by his oversized physical presence. As Deeds, that translates to a hulking passivity both physical and corporate—the CEO seems ashamed of his good fortune and success. The character's reticence is not a deal breaker—a better, more dynamic and nuanced performer might have made something out of Deeds, but Perry's shocking lack of charisma (from the man who created Madea, a creature bursting with rude charisma) acts as a drag on any attempt to create any sort of chemistry with Newton.

In an attempt to keep things jumping, Perry the screenwriter throws nearly every imaginable family and business cliche crisis into the mix. (At one point, feuding family members are literally trapped in an elevator with each other.) Some of these contrivances resonate, like Lindsey and her daughter's frightening nights in homeless shelters, but most of the time Perry seems to almost fetishize hardship, wrapping interpersonal conflicts so thick in swelling, melodramatic music that they cease to feel real but instead are sanitized for viewing at a theatrical distance. The uniform result is almost offensive in the way it ascribes equal amounts of emotional weight and importance to both Lindsey's

scrambling desperation to survive on the street and Wesley's upper-class ennui.

Perry seems to unabashedly embrace this sort of safely dramatic overkill in order to get across to a wide audience his messages about love, family, morality, hope, responsibility, and hard work. There is something admirable about that genuine desire to enlighten, even with the broad of strokes the director uses. But when a film feels as ironically lifeless as *Good Deeds*, the lessons are lost under all the yawning. Deeds wants to be good, and Perry wants to make a film about being good, but those seemingly sincere quests drain the film of all personality. One imagines that watching *Tyler Perry's Good Deeds* is a lot like having dinner with Wesley Deeds: pleasant, harmless, perhaps even educational, but excruciatingly dull. This time out, Perry is so sure he is saying something audiences need to hear that he has forgotten to make them want to listen.

Tyler Perry's Good Deeds was given a wide theatrical release in late February and earned $35 million, making it one of his lowest-opening films, but that was still respectable against its economical budget. Perry has never been a critical favorite and *Good Deeds* was no exception. "*Good Deeds* honors goodness, which isn't at all a bad thing, and it's not without moments of genuine feeling," observed David Dewitt for the *New York Times*. "But by the film's end, after watching a seemingly infinite number of dour close-ups of sober self-evaluation, I felt bludgeoned by thesis-driven dialogue and noble intentions." On the other hand, Rob Humanick of *Slant Magazine* wrote, "Arguably Perry's best film yet, *Good Deeds* is a poignant quotidian reflection on those most basic and frequently unanswered, even unasked questions: Who are we, where do we come from, and where we are going?"

Locke Peterseim

CREDITS

Wesley Deeds: Tyler Perry
Lindsey Wakefield: Thandie Newton
Natalie: Gabrielle Beauvais
Wilimena Deeds: Phylicia Rashad
Walter Deeds: Brian White
Heidi: Rebecca Romijn
John: Eddie Cibrian
Mark Freeze: Jamie Kennedy
Ariel: Jordenn Thompson
Origin: United States
Language: English
Released: 2012
Production: Ozzie Areu, Paul Hall, Tyler Perry; Tyler Perry Studios; released by Lionsgate

Directed by: Tyler Perry
Written by: Tyler Perry
Cinematography by: Alexander Grusynski
Music by: Aaron Zigman
Sound: Mike Wilhoit
Music Supervisor: Joel High
Editing: Maysie Hoy
Art Direction: Gentry L. Akens, II
Costumes: Johnetta Boone
Production Design: Ina Mayhew
MPAA rating: PG-13
Running time: 110 minutes

REVIEWS

Adams, Sam. *AV Club*. February 24, 2012.
Baumgarten, Marjorie. *Austin Chronicle*. March 2, 2012.
Cole, Stephen. *The Globe and Mail*. February 24, 2012.
Dewitt, David. *New York Times*. February 24, 2012.
Ebiri, Bilge. *Vulture*. February 24, 2012.
Gilchrist, Todd. *Box Office Magazine*. February 24, 2012.
Goodykoontz, Bill. *Arizona Republic*. February 24, 2012.
Humanick, Rob. *Slant Magazine*. February 24, 2012.
Morris, Wesley. *Boston Globe*. February 25, 2012.
Willmore, Alison. *Movieline*. February 24, 2012.

TRIVIA

Actresses Thandie Newton and Rebecca Romijn were born on the exact same day: November 6, 1972.

AWARDS

Nominations:

Golden Raspberries 2012: Worst Actor (Perry), Worst Director (Perry)

U

UNDEFEATED

Box Office: $562,218

During the five-year run of NBC's spectacular drama *Friday Night Lights*, coach Eric Taylor (Kyle Chandler) never said, in these exact words, that football reveals character rather than building it. Yet it is a statement with which he would surely agree.

In the tremendously moving documentary *Undefeated*, Manassas High School head coach Bill Courtney will remind viewers of coach Taylor as Courtney continuously reiterates to his players the importance of character and its ability to bring them success both on the field and off. He is not exactly preaching to the choir. At the beginning of the film, as Courtney begins his seventh season volunteering with the team, the coach recalls incidents of the past two weeks: Two starting players have been shot and are no longer in school. Another two players were caught fighting in front of a coach. The starting center was arrested for shooting someone in the face with a BB gun. Few sports fans would call that the start to a promising season, and Courtney states that in a job like this, it is often a commitment to a few players that keeps frustrated coaches coming back.

In this case, one of those players is O.C. Brown, a senior lineman who tops 300 pounds but runs with the speed of a man half his size. He receives recruiting letters from top-tier football programs like the University of Auburn, but O.C. will need to elevate his grades if he wants to be considered eligible for the college part of college football. The other is senior Montrail "Money" Brown (no relation), an undersized right tackle who

knows that his 3.8 grade point average, not his athletics, will be the ticket to his future. Money's father passed away when he was thirteen, and one look at the sadness that often lingers in his eyes reflects the impact this has had on the young man, who lives with his grandma and has never been outside North Memphis. In one of the film's most revealing scenes, Money holds up a pet turtle and describes how turtles' hard outer shell and soft, vulnerable insides represent humans. This type of sensitive comment does not exactly go along with the stereotype of the average football player.

On some level, the goal throughout *Undefeated* rests on Courtney guiding his team toward winning its first playoff game in the school's 110-year history. However, as with many films in which sports serve as a metaphor for life, directors T.J. Martin and Dan Lindsay capture Courtney's efforts to simply keep his players on the team and out of trouble. Junior linebacker Chavis Daniels returns to the team after spending fifteen months in a youth penitentiary. Courtney notes that Chavis, whose father is not in the picture, has anger issues but does not elaborate on what caused his hiatus from school and the team. Soon, Chavis blows up at Money during a team meeting, calling Money "gay" and telling his teammate to get away from him. Money leaves the room and goes home. When Courtney goes to Money's house—noting on the way there that this is not part of the job description, even though he does not know what the job description is—Money tells his coach that he thought he and Chavis were friends. Courtney simply thanks one of his favorite players for leaving before tempers flared up again and strongly encourages him to return.

Throughout *Undefeated*, Courtney serves as a father figure to young men without one at home. Courtney's motivation could not be clearer; his father left when he was four years old, and he recalls scoring the winning touchdown in ninth grade, only to feel the loneliness of watching his teammates walk off the field as their fathers carried their equipment for them. So Courtney devotes most of his time and effort to guiding his players, despite having a wife and four kids at home and recognizing that he has little "emotional capital" left for his family. The movie, intent on emphasizing determination over collateral damage, goes a bit easy as it avoids exploring any consequences of Courtney's priorities. *Undefeated* also does not offer a fully satisfying discussion of the controversy when an assistant coach allows O.C. to live with him and his family so O.C. can be tutored and work toward earning the necessary score of sixteen on his ACTs to attend college. Some townspeople lament that only athletically-promising African-American students receive this kind of special treatment from white educators, and the film's minimal exploration of this opinion suggests the feeling that helping someone is at least better than helping no one.

What happens as a result of Courtney's volunteer work, though, is nothing short of extraordinary. This is not just because he takes a team, formerly called a "Whipping boy" in the local paper and perceived as unable to come from behind, and turns them into a group of guys who excel in the second half of games, in one case coming back from a 20-0 halftime deficit to win 28-20. In fact, Manassas allows its first opponent of the year to return the season's opening kickoff for a touchdown, and they lose that game. It is a long time until they lose again, one of many indications of how much their off-field work translates to on-field drive and unity.

Early in the film, Courtney brings in a former NFL player from north Memphis to tell the kids that they need to "think outside your circumstances," focusing on their own future rather than possible roadblocks like having relatives in jail and one or both parents who did not graduate from college. These situations are not the kids' fault, Courtney later points out, which is a difficult thing for high school students to realize but one that clearly sinks in as a result of their coaches' guidance. After suggesting earlier that he felt no bond with Money, Chavis, after returning from a suspension, later delivers to the entire team a speech in which he praises Money's persistence and strength, especially in the face of an injury that threatens to keep him off the field for the rest of the season. Chavis' words reflect a remarkable adjustment in character, as does his decision to change his number from zero—a demonstration that he has no

sense, Chavis says—to thirty-five. By playing for a man who believes that Chavis has not yet wasted all of his opportunities to prove his worth, the young man steps up in ways that have nothing to do with football. And in this fast-paced, uplifting documentary, the happy tear-inducing result to Money's dreams of going to college is nothing if not a heart-warming testament to the tremendous teamwork that can come from perseverance and karma.

Matt Pais

CREDITS

Himslef: Bill Courtney
Himself: Montrail "Money" Brown
Himself: Chavis Daniels
Himself: O.C. Brown
Origin: United States
Language: English
Released: 2011
Production: Seth Gordon, Ed Cunningham, Rich Maddlemas, Dan Lindsay, Glen Zipper; Five Smooth Stones Prods., Level 22, Spitfire Pictures; released by Weinstein Co.
Directed by: T.J. Martin; Daniel Lindsay
Cinematography by: T.J. Martin; Daniel Lindsay
Music by: Michael Brook; Dan McMahon; Miles Nielsen
Sound: Elmo Weber
Editing: T.J. Martin; Daniel Lindsay
MPAA rating: Unrated
Running time: 113 minutes

REVIEWS

Covert, Colin. *Minneapolis Star Tribune.* March 20, 2012.
Dargis, Manohla. *New York Times.* February 16, 2012.
Ebert, Roger. *Chicago Sun-Times.* March 1, 2012.
Hornaday, Ann. *Washington Post.* March 16, 2012.
Howell, Peter. *Toronto Star.* March 1, 2012.
Jones, J. R. *Chicago Reader.* March 8, 2012.
Long, Tom. *Detroit News.* March 16, 2012.
Morris, Wesley. *Boston Globe.* March 15, 2012.
Puig, Claudia. *USA Today.* February 16, 2012.
Rea, Steven. *Philadelphia Inquirer.* March 1, 2012.

TRIVIA

Was rejected by the prestigious Sundance festival in 2012, but was accepted and shown at the South By Southwest Festival in Austin where it was bought for distribution and went on to win the Oscar for Best Documentary.

AWARDS

Oscars 2011: Feature Doc.

UNDERWORLD: AWAKENING

(Underworld: New Dawn)
(Underworld 4: Awakening)

Vengeance returns.
—Movie tagline

Box Office: $62.3 million

If there is anything to be said about *Underworld: Awakening,* the latest entry in the action-horror franchise that has somehow made it to four installments without inspiring any trace of recognizable public enthusiasm, it is that it is so devoid of anything even remotely of interest to all but the most easily entertained that it, like its predecessors, it will also disappear from memory by the time the credits roll. As always, this is more than a bit odd because one would think that a film centered on a centuries-old battle between vampires and werewolves and centering on a fabulous-looking babe in a leather cat-suit kicking ludicrously-choreographed ass would stick in the mind for a little while. And yet, despite such seemingly sure-fire ingredients, the film, like its predecessors, is such a dully-executed drag that the only memorable thing about it is the absolute lack of anything memorable on display.

Having wisely sat out the previous entry, the pointless prequel *Underworld: Rise of the Lycans* (2010), Kate Beckinsale returns to the franchise as vampiric death-dealer Selene. After a prologue that desperately tries to bring viewers up to speed with the increasingly-convoluted back story, the plot kicks off with her waking up in a strange lab after having been cryogenically frozen for the past twelve years. During that time, the once-secret war between vampires and werewolves somehow became public (possibly because of the way the two sides seemed to take out entire city blocks during their scuffles) and humans have begun eradicating both sides and driving the scattered remaining creatures into hiding. It turns out that she was busted out by a child named Eve (India Eisley) who turns out to be Selene's daughter with her now-missing werewolf lover (apparently Scott Speedman had better things to do) and is just beginning to discover her own awesome powers. These powers attract the interest of the remaining Lycans and it is up to Selene, along with the help of a hunky vampire (Theo James, in the kind of role that might normally be filled by the likes of Screen Gems utility player Cam Gigadent) and a human cop (Michael Ealy), to battle the various Lycans (including one jumbo-sized version), rescue Eve from their clawed clutches, and uncover a massive conspiracy that most viewers will have figured out long before Selene has finished thawing out.

Underworld: Awakening is one of those movies in which so much technical effort has been put forth to so little effect that it is a wonder that the cast and crew were able to summon up the inner strength and intestinal fortitude to return to the set day after day. The story is brief but pointless and so incredibly preposterous and ponderous that it feels more like an exceptionally weak fan-fiction piece than a professionally-produced screenplay and the dialogue is so awful at times ("Yes, yes...your Lycan lover, long dead...") that it is a blessed relief that there are maybe forty to fifty total lines in the whole film. The direction, by a duo of Swedish newcomers billed as Marlind & Stein, is clunky and devoid of energy, especially during the clumsily-handled fight scenes and their use of 3D—already a questionable choice for a film that is set almost entirely in darkness—demonstrates the kind of questionable elan that is usually associated with the likes of Dr. Tongue. As for the performances, Beckinsale—never a particularly warm or empathetic actress even on her best days—somehow manages to come across as way too chilly and remote for her own good, which is funny since she is, after all, playing a recently thawed-out vampire. Among the other performers, the least impressive and most tragically inept of the bunch is Stephen Rea as a scientist who has been working for years on a vaccine—he goes through the entire thing with the kind of excessively hangdog expression that you sometimes see on actors who have finally realized that Neil Jordan can only make so many movies and that they have to do something to keep dinner on the table.

Like its predecessors, *Underworld: Awakening* is so drab and dour that whatever junky charm it might have possessed is slowly and excruciatingly drained away before our eyes—this one may be the most egregious of the sorry lot in this regard. (If it accomplishes nothing else—and it does not—a film like this can at least help one better appreciate the comparative charms of the equally silly but infinitely more entertaining *Resident Evil* franchise.) In fact, there is only one moment that contains the kind of screw-loose ingenuity that the film so desperately needs—a bit where Selene shoves her hand into the chest of another vampire in order to get his heart beating again (odd, since a vampire is already technically dead and theoretically lacking a fully functioning heart in the first place). She succeeds and brings the lifeless hulk back to life. Too bad she could not do the same for the rest of the film.

Peter Sobczynski

CREDITS

Selene: Kate Beckinsale

Michael Corvin: Scott Speedman
Jacob: Stephen Rea
Quint: Kris Holden-Ried
David: Theo James
Eve: India Eisley
Thomas: Charles Dance
Detective Sebastian: Michael Ealy
Origin: United States
Language: English
Released: 2012
Production: Gary Lucchesi, Tom Rosenberg, Richard S. Wright, Len Wiseman; Lakeshore Entertainment; released by Screen Gems
Directed by: Mans Marlind; Bjorn Stein
Written by: J. Michael Straczynski; Len Wiseman; John Hlavin; Allison Burnett
Cinematography by: Scott Kevan
Music by: Paul Haslinger
Sound: Michael Babcock
Music Supervisor: Eric Craig; Brian McNelis
Editing: Jeff McEvoy
Art Direction: Martina Javorova; Gary Myers
Costumes: Monique Prudhomme
Production Design: Claude Pare
MPAA rating: R
Running time: 88 minutes

REVIEWS

Corliss, Richard. *Time*. January 20, 2012.

Gibron, Bill. *Filmcritic.com*. January 20, 2012.

Howell, Peter. *Toronto Star*. January 21, 2012.

Leydon, Joe. *Variety*. January 23, 2012.

Orndorf, Brian. *BrianOrndorf.com*. January 20, 2012.

Pinkerton, Nick. *Village Voice*. January 20, 2012.

Robinson, Tasha. *AV Club*. January 20, 2012.

Tallerico, Brian. *HollywoodChicago.com*. January 20, 2012.

Webster, Andy. *New York Times*. January 22, 2012.

Weinberg, Scott. *FEARnet*. February 1, 2012.

QUOTES

Selene: "The Vampire and Lycans clan have been at war for centuries before I was born, their endless conflict hidden from the human world. I was turned by a Vampire. And given the strength to avenge my family against the Lycans. And I was good at it. Then I found Michael Corvin, a human that was neither turned by Vampire nor Lycan, but a hybrid of the two. And everything changed. Allies turned enemies, and Vampire elders I had protected for now six centuries now wanted me dead. We retaliated, killed the elders, and for a brief moment of time, we were safe. But then a new darkness arose."

TRIVIA

This is the first film in the series to be in Real-D 3D and Imax 3D.

V

V/H/S

This collection is killer.
—Movie tagline

Box Office: $100,345

V/H/S is an easy film to judge but not an easy film to dissect. Like any anthology it has segments that work and ones that pass by with a yawn. Being helmed as it is by several of the hottest young horror directors working today gives fans the right to expect more than they get here but before enumerating the project's flaws it bears mention that this is an exceedingly ambitious bit of storytelling. Not only is it an anthology but one composed entirely of found footage and obvious attempts are made to stretch that mode of presentation into something special. The failures involve use of camera, and just plain bad acting, scripting and plotting but along the way some haunting images and ideas emerge. Horror fans should take note and schedule a viewing. Parts of *V/H/S* are likely to stand the test of time while others will at least survive as interesting footnotes in the careers of several up-and-coming directors.

The narrative that sets the stage for all the others is "Tape 56," which follows a group of young thieves into a house where a simple snatch-and-run mission becomes complicated when they find an old man dead in front of a TV and bank of VCRs. As the group ransacks the house finding more and more videotapes (they were supposed to pick up just one) others take up where the old man left off putting tapes into the various machines and settling in to see what on earth had him so interested. As a framing device it has potential but never

feels anything but thrown together and viewers may well wonder if the film would have been better without it. The real shame is that the segment is co-written by Simon Barett (*Dead Birds* [2004]), who recently penned the fabulous and as yet unreleased *You're Next* (2011), and the equally compelling *A Horrible Way to Die* (2010) with segment co-writer and director Adam Wingard.

The great first segment, "Amateur Night," by David Bruckner who had previously written and directed the excellent *The Signal* (2007), puts the camera in the hands of a group of drunken frat boys whose night of liquor and lust is interrupted when they bring the wrong girl back to their hotel room. What happens next is genuinely shocking and disturbing not so much because of the level of violence (sexual and otherwise) but because the characters come to embody raw human urges and anxieties using the monstrous and abject as metaphors. This is boy meets girl at its most honest and dangerous.

But things go generally downhill from there, failing to generate nearly the same level of tension. Ti West's (*The House of the Devil* [2009], *The Innkeepers* [2012]), "Second Honeymoon" features a young couple rekindling love via a trip out west only to have their revelry interrupted by a mysterious stranger whose increased intrusions lead, unsurprisingly, to violence and a final-moment twist. The horrendous "Tuesday the 17th" pays homage to slasher movies as a group of friends discover they have been brought out to the woods by a member of their party under false pretenses. Bad camerawork here makes this short almost impossible to watch and the dialogue is wooden beyond belief. Writer director Glenn McQuaid, who had previously written and directed the very good *I Sell The Dead* (2008) fails to do anything notable here and is also hampered by a cast that fails to deliver on even simple scares and a truly dumb idea for a monster.

The last two segments nearly save *VHS*. In fact, the truth is they probably do. "The Sick Thing That Happened to Emily When She Was Younger" follows a young couple keeping in touch via Webcam. Directed by noted indie mumblecore king Joe Swanberg, the tale offers a genuinely nasty use of stationary cam in which the viewer is constantly having to worry about what is going on just outside the frame. Lastly, the surprisingly dynamic "10/31/98" follows four friends to a Halloween bash who, instead, wind up in the middle of a secret occult rite where they are beset by demonic forces. The camerawork is very strong here, swooping and swirling in a manner that is rarely encountered in found footage films. The effect is a controlled one and all the more eerie for it.

The history of short-form horror onscreen is an interesting one, dating all the way back to the very good *Dead of Night* (1945), in which a group of people feel compelled to tell each other the stories outlined by their nightmares. Ever since then the subgenre has continued to add worthy additions. *Black Sabbath* (1963), *Tales From the Crypt* (1972), and *Creepshow* (1982) are impossible to ignore here. Yet even those shows fail to deliver across the board, showcasing how, even at their best, great creators like Mario Bava and George Romero sometimes end up making *meh* movies. Granted its very real high points, *V/H/S* is occasionally scary as hell or at least as scary as those goofy old tapes still laying around in storage since the 1980s. As found footage develops into its own small cult cinema genre *V/H/S* will more than likely rise above the herd of an awful lot of very bad found footage movies that will someday be competing with it for everyone's nostalgia.

Dave Canfield

CREDITS

Gary: Calvin Reeder
Zak: Lane Hughes
Brad: Adam Wingard
Sam: Joe Swanberg
Stephanie: Sophia Takal
Lily: Hanna Fierman
Matt: Matt Battinelli-Olpin
Origin: United States
Language: English
Released: 2012
Production: Roxanne Benjamin, Gary Binkow, Brad Miska; Bloody Disgusting, The Collective; released by Magnet Releasing

Directed by: Adam Wingard; Joe Swanberg; Matt Battinelli-Olpin; David Bruckner; Tyler Gillett; Justin Martinez; Glenn McQuaid; Chad Villella; Ti West; Simon Barrett; Radio Silence
Written by: David Bruckner; Tyler Gillett; Justin Martinez; Glenn McQuaid; Chad Villella; Ti West; Brad Miska; Simon Barrett; Nicholas Tecosky; Radio Silence
Cinematography by: Adam Wingard; Tyler Gillett; Justin Martinez; Eric Branco; Andrew Droz Palermo; Victoria K. Warren; Michael J. Wilson
Sound: Owen Granich-Young; Brett Hinton
Music Supervisor: Dan Dixon; Hilary Yarbrough
Editing: Adam Wingard; Joe Swanberg; Matt Battinelli-Olpin; David Bruckner; Tyler Gillett; Glenn McQuaid; Ti West; Joe Gressis
Art Direction: Raymond Carr; Roger Vianna; Lanie Faith Marie Overton
Costumes: Liz Vastola
MPAA rating: R
Running time: 116 minutes

REVIEWS

Catsoulis, Jeannette. *New York Times*. October 4, 2012.
Cavallo, Alexandra. *Boston Phoenix*. October 2, 2012.
Clift, Tom. *Moviedex*. August 8, 2012.
Diones, Bruce. *New Yorker*. October 1, 2012.
Ebert, Roger. *Chicago Sun-Times*. October 4, 2012.
Longworth, Katrina. *Village Voice*. October 2, 2012.
Lyne, Charlie. *Ultra Culture*. April 29, 2012.
Nusair, David. *Reel Film Reviews*. July 21, 2012.
O'Connell, Sean. *Washington Post*. October 5, 2012.
O'Hehir, Andrew. *Salon.com*. October 3, 2012.

QUOTES

Lily: "I like you."

THE VOW

Box Office: $125 million

For better or worse is put to the ultimate test for hipster poster couple Paige (Rachel McAdams) and Leo (Channing Tatum) when a car accident wipes the last five years from Paige's memory in the opening scene of *The Vow*. Gone is the free-spirited sculptor who would listen to loud angry girl music in her studio and secretly feed the stray cat that roamed the alley behind their shared picture-perfect boho loft. The Paige that wakes from a short, medically-induced coma is a sweater-wearing wasp-y suburbanite convinced she is still in law school and engaged to her preppy college sweetheart (Scott Speedman). Not only does she not recognize the hunky beatnik trapped in the body of an ex-male stripper in front of her claiming to be her husband, she cannot believe she voted for Obama...or that he won. One could easily mistake director Michael Sucsy's film as some kind of late-night TV political parody: brain injury can turn even the most hard core liberal into a rich, uptight republican! To offset this reaction, Sucsy plays *The Vow* like a bedtime story for adults. Sure, the movie is based on true events, but even its director knows that a not-even-amnesia-can-keep-us-apart love story is the stuff of legend, clearly reserved for princesses and dashing knights.

From the instant Sucsy's camera swoops down on the couple on a snowy Chicago sidewalk it is as though the city is being viewed through a whimsical lens. The Chicago Paige and Leo encounter on the night of the accident is covered in a whispy white fluff untouched by cars or pedestrians, an impossible urban landscape, but one that this fated love-happy couple embraces. The city sparkles, full of hidden treasures, cafes, hole-in-the-wall Cuban joints, reserved, it seems, just for the two of them. Sucsy's Chicago is their magical kingdom. The twist of fate that changes their lives forever is akin to the bad luck of a poisoned apple, turning Paige into an imprisoned princess and Leo into a knight, except he is clad in cowl-neck sweaters and girl jeans.

On the surface, *The Vow* can be chalked up to a collection of cliches. Leo and Paige meet-cute, move in even cuter and get married so cute little bunnies in teacups would roll their eyes. But Tatum and McAdams sign on to Sucsy's vision and own their part in this sweet narrative, ready to make a believer out of any scrooge in the audience. Because pre- and post-amnesia Paige could have easily fallen into a hackneyed portrayal of opposites, it is nice to see McAdams showcase Paige's struggle to figure out who she is with honesty. It is easy to think of this as Leo's story since he is the one doing the winning back. But McAdams does not let the audience forget that Paige was dealt a raw deal in this set-up. She plays the confused thirty-something with a lovely combination of openness (even if her wide-eyed looks of confusion hint a little too much at an innocent damsel in distress), despite the urge to cling to what her brain tells her she knows, and fear at embracing the new unknown. Still, it is notable that, ultimately, Paige is cast as the girl in need of saving—as opposed to a girl given a strange second chance of sorts. The expansive, four-person writing team behind *The Vow* does not even hint that Paige's pre-Leo life is worth considering. Her parents are one-dimensional, wealthy liars and her ex-fiance is a callous player. Paige needs Leo to rescue her from suburban hell; she just does not know it yet. By turn, Tatum plays knight errant Leo with a perfect mix of vulnerability and determination. He is brave in the face of the unknown, but is not afraid to cry. He is, all in all, a perfect prince. Leo is as committed to his wife as he is to his career as a manager of a recording studio. He refuses to believe that anyone would want to record music at home on their iMac just like he believes that somewhere in the mojito drinking sorority girl he met in the hospital is the Paige he married. So he doggedly matches wits with Paige's straight-laced father, wins over her Lake Forest snobby family, out-smarts her college fiance, and reminds Paige why she fell for him in the first place. The last item is the hardest won, of course, and involves wacky dates that go well, surprise parties that do not, and a mess of emotional baggage that overwhelms the both of them. But Tatum plays his quest so earnestly it is hard not to be swept up in this charming, if unlikely, fairy tale.

Joanna Topor MacKenzie

CREDITS

Paige: Rachel McAdams
Leo: Channing Tatum
Jeremy: Scott Speedman
Bill Thornton: Sam Neill
Rita Thornton: Jessica Lange
Origin: United States
Language: English
Released: 2012
Production: Gary Barber, Roger Birnbaum, Jonathan Glickman, Paul Taublieb; Spyglass Entertainment; released by Screen Gems
Directed by: Michael Sucsy
Written by: Michael Sucsy; Abby Kohn; Marc Silverstein
Cinematography by: Rogier Stoffers
Music by: Michael Brook; Rachel Portman
Sound: Tim Chau
Music Supervisor: Stephanie Diaz-Matos; Randall Poster
Editing: Melissa Kent; Nancy Richardson
Art Direction: Brandt Gordon
Costumes: Alex Kavanagh
Production Design: Kalina Ivanov
MPAA rating: PG-13
Running time: 104 minutes

REVIEWS

Anderson, Jeffrey M. *Combustible Celluloid*. February 10, 2012.
Hall, Corey. *Metro Times*. February 10, 2012.
Jones, Kimberley. *Austin Chronicle*. February 17, 2012.
Pinkerton, Nick. *Village Voice*. February 10, 2012.
Promaikis, Joseph. *Movies for the Masses*. February 17, 2012.
Reed, Rex. *New York Observer*. February 14, 2012.
Roeper, Richard. *RichardRoeper.com*. February 10, 2012.

Rozen, Leah. *The Wrap*. February 10, 2012.
Schwarzbaum, Lisa. *Entertainment Weekly*. February 10, 2012.
Willmore, Alison. *Movieline*. February 10, 2012.

QUOTES

Leo: "Life's all about moments, of impact and how they changes our lives forever. But what if one day you could no longer remember any of them?"

TRIVIA

Some of the purses shown in the movie were designed by Imperfect Indulgence, a Canadian handbag designer.

WANDERLUST

Leave your baggage behind.
—Movie tagline

Box Office: $17.5 million

George (Paul Rudd) and Linda (Jennifer Aniston) are taking their next big step as a couple signing the paperwork on a New York studio apartment (or "micro-loft.") Before the ink can even dry, however, George's company is opened up to federal indictment and Linda has seen her work on an environmental documentary (involving dying penguins) rejected by HBO. No longer able to afford their newfound luxury, the pair pack-up everything and swallow their pride for a second chance under the thumb of George's well-to-do braggart brother (Ken Marino). When a growing case of car ride fever comes over them, they stop at the nearest bed-and-breakfast. When they are greeted down a dark road by a buck nude wanderer (Joe Lo Truglio), their panic forces them to stay at the commune known as Elysium.

More a collection of hippies than a nudist colony, Elysium nevertheless promotes an understanding of free love that is surely a selling point above its messages of tranquility and truth. George and Linda quickly adapt to their new surroundings (aided in part to some mind-expanding drugs) and are both charmed by the teachings of Elysium's spiritual guru, Seth (Justin Theroux), whose cultural references suggest he has been out of touch for a couple of decades. It does not take long for each of them to recognize which of their needs are not being fulfilled in their new home—even just within their own relationship—and the allure of their new brothers and sisters begins to turn sour. Things are

further complicated when developers of a new casino show up to once again prove that no home is safe in this economy.

The fish-out-of-water scenario is peppered with the brand of reactionary oddness that comes with the territory of trying to identify with anti-society exiles. *Wanderlust* mines a lot of laughs from this, not just with the interaction of their new peace-loving outsiders but with George's relatives who may have assimilated but still seek happiness through booze, affairs, and talking down to the lower classes. Michaela Watkins casually and hilariously voices her displeasure as George's sister-in-law through the microphone of a margarita glass. Things prove to be not so easy in Elysium either as attempts to flush the anger out of their bodies (figuratively, not literally as George reminds them) leads to actual moments of clarity. Then further discomfort and privacy issues arise.

In their last collaboration, David Wain and Ken Marino (part of MTV's cult sketch series, *The State*) turned ultra-charming Paul Rudd into a short-fused pessimist in *Role Models* (2008) and his brand of reflexive humor is put to even greater use here. Without trying to be mean or judgmental, Rudd instead allows George to turn into a burning fuse of insecurity at his surroundings and what he keeps losing in the face of change. Theroux also does hysterical work as Elysium's unknowingly egotistical sage. It is unfortunate that the film's women were not allowed more time. Kathryn Hahn, Kerri Kenney-Silver, and Lauren Ambrose all get effective moments, but the front-and-center ladies are more forgettable. Malin Akerman remains just a pretty face and sexual object that hypnotizes viewers into forgetting how little there is going on underneath in her portrayals. More disappointing is Jennifer Aniston, who has proven to be a more than apt comedic presence with the right material but is reduced in the second half to being just an adapted instigator for Rudd's impending meltdown.

None of *Wanderlust*'s flaws can deny the pure laugh quotient that it builds up throughout. Wain is too on target to just deliver a series of shock gags and is certainly more interested in behavior and satire in his films. Even a seemingly independent bit involving a morning show commentary on an Elysium protest is too dead-on in its portrait of an unqualified and sexist elite to feel random. Rudd's work, some of the funniest he's done in an already impressive body of comedy, is alone worth a look. *Role Models* might feel like a more complete film—with certainly a better final act—but *Wanderlust*'s laughs and statement about where yuppies are and where they are headed may just be greater.

Erik Childress

CREDITS

George: Paul Rudd
Linda: Jennifer Aniston
Seth: Justin Theroux
Karen: Kathryn Hahn
Eva: Malin Akerman
Almond: Lauren Ambrose
Wayne: Joe Lo Truglio
Carvin: Alan Alda
Rick: Ken Marino
Origin: United States
Language: English
Released: 2012
Production: Judd Apatow, Paul Rudd, Ken Marino, David Wain; A Hot Dog, Apatow Productions, Relativity Media; released by Universal Pictures
Directed by: David Wain
Written by: David Wain; Ken Marino
Cinematography by: Michael Bonvillain
Music by: Craig (Shudder to Think) Wedren
Sound: George H. Anderson
Music Supervisor: Jonathan Karp
Editing: David Moritz; Robert Nassau
Costumes: Debra McGuire
Production Design: Aaron Osborne
MPAA rating: R
Running time: 98 minutes

REVIEWS

Bayer, Jeff. *Scorecard Review*. February 27, 2012.

Dargis, Manohla. *New York Times*. February 23, 2012.
Edelstein, David. *New York Magazine*. February 27, 2012.
Fine, Marshall. *Hollywood & Fine*. February 24, 2012.
McGranaghan, Mike. *Aisle Seat*. February 24, 2012.
Nusair, David. *Reel Film Reviews*. March 23, 2012.
Patches, Matt. *Hollywood.com*. February 24, 2012.
Rabin, Nathan. *AV Club*. February 23, 2012.
Rocchi, James. *BoxOffice Magazine*. February 23, 2012.
Snider, Eric D. *EricDSnider.com*. February 24, 2012.

QUOTES

Linda: "So what do you do when it rains?"
Seth: "I drink the nourishment that Gaia is feeding me through her cloud teats."

TRIVIA

Despite being naked throughout the film, actor Joe Lo Truglio wore a prosthetic penis. Most of the cast ran up to him and touched it as a joke after showing up on set.

THE WATCH
(Neighborhood Watch)

Got Protection?
    —Movie tagline

Box Office: $35.4 million

The Watch was an idea that once showed great promise. The film started as a script named *Neighborhood Watch* co-written by Seth Rogen and Evan Goldberg, who had previously scribed *Superbad* (2007). From there, the project wrangled in three actors with experience in blockbuster comedies (Ben Stiller, Vince Vaughn, and Jonah Hill), and even the director, Akiva Schaffer, had earned credit for writing and directing many popular shorts for *Saturday Night Live*, along with his helming of Andy Samberg's first lead film, *Hot Rod* (2007).

And then, controversy complicated the silly comedy's marketing when an unarmed young man named Trayvon Martin was murdered on February 26, 2012 by George Zimmerman, who was coordinator for his neighborhood watch in his Florida gated community. This sparked a debate about the racial stereotypes, along with the paranoia of the "other" in a suburban neighborhood. Nevertheless, a film like *Neighborhood Watch* due to be released five months after the incident, had to change its US title to simply *The Watch* while working against any current sensitivities audience members may have concerning a story of a neighborhood watch taking their own course of action against suspicious outsiders.

In this sci-fi buddy comedy, Ben Stiller plays proud suburbanite Evan, who has become extremely involved in his community of Glenview, Ohio. Amongst starting many clubs like Running Club and Spanish Club, he has also been promoted to manager of his local Costco store, a position that he carries with great pride. Perhaps this over-activeness in the community is to cover up the shame he feels at home—he cannot get his wife Abby (Rosemarie DeWitt) pregnant.

When one of Evan's employees, a night security guard, is mysteriously murdered with his skin removed from his body, Evan is inspired to investigate the death himself, and start a neighborhood watch to protect the citizens of Glenview. He is joined by outgoing father Bob, (Vince Vaughn), troubled police academy dropout Franklin (Jonah Hill) and new neighbor Jamarcus (Richard Ayoade). Despite Evan's organization with the group's first meeting, the men are not swayed into taking the idea of a neighborhood watch beyond an excuse to hang out with other men.

The rest of the town does not take Evan's neighborhood watch seriously, either. Snooty cop Sgt. Bressman (Will Forte) laughs in their face when they are on watch at the scene of the crime, and a skater kid (Johnny Pemberton) lures them to a football field simply to throw eggs at them.

The neighborhood watch collectively takes its work seriously when they discover a giant orb in the countryside, which shoots a destructive laser whenever the four of them put all of their fingers in it. Unsure of where the orb came from, their curiosities are answered when they soon after meet a violent alien face-to-face. This has the protective quartet searching for other extra terrestrials in Glenview, entertaining suspicions about many of those around them.

The script's story is thoroughly dinky, and does not gather any speed until a secret is revealed that sends the neighborhood watch on a mission to save the world. Even then, the movie's slim action scenes are too simple, and the jokes within them are flat. There are three co-writers listed in the credits, but one would not know that from watching this film, especially witnessing actors like Stiller and Hill riff their way out of a scene with many moments in *The Watch* that emphasize its sloppy construction. In terms of showing respect to previous science fiction movies, homages to previous successors like *Alien* (1979) and *Close Encounters of the Third Kind* (1977) feel obligatory, as if they were thrown in the film to observe reverence to its smarter ancestors. If this movie were considered most of all to be an homage to *Ghostbusters* (1984), a film that *The Watch* owes most of its structure to, it would be an embarrassment more than anything.

As satisfied as *The Watch* may be with utilizing filmmaking in a sense much lighter than something like *Tree of Life* (2012) it regardless becomes apparent that the script is simply not funny. Stripped of his quirky dryness that made *Hot Rod* a unique gem of the *Napoleon Dynamite* (2004) era, Schaffer, working on a much bigger scale, has nothing to work with here but a melee of product placement and the overheating of Vince Vaughn's motor mouth, working from a script that constantly refers to the act of sodomy in hopes of achieving a raunchy laugh. Like the film's resignation to let Vaughn lead the comedy of the movie, *The Watch's* entire humor is lazy. Along with using raunchy words for cheap laughs, such weak wackiness is indicated by the ironic usage of gangster rap over images of suburbia, something that *Office Space* did in 1999, amongst many other comedies after it.

Stiller rarely finds the right sarcasm with his character Evan, hitting only once or twice an amusing sweetness in a person so committed to his cause (as in with a shirt that he wears in the beginning that says "No More Murders"). With Hill and Ayoade proving to be harmless, if not operational members, Vaughn is the film's weakest link, and unfortunately its bluntest object. Vaughn provides nothing to the comedy but aimless chaos, looking to earn a laugh because he talks about nesting dolls or man caves in a progressively loud, hyper manner.

Despite its desire to be "ruder, cruder, and lewder" (according to its DVD marketing), in the scheme of the raunchy comedy landscape, *The Watch* plays its comedy far too safe, relying on boardroom calculations that say which particular naughty words have worked best in previous movies. Letting down its creative forces and subsequently its audience, *The Watch* lazily banks on the idea that another joke about sodomy will be funny for at least one more time.

With its nearly absent marketing campaign and subsequent dismal domestic box office numbers, moviegoers might have been made to think that the potential of *The Watch* suffered from nightmarish timing. In actuality, there is nothing to blame for its disappointing failure but itself.

Nick Allen

CREDITS

Evan: Ben Stiller
Bob: Vince Vaughn
Franklin: Jonah Hill
Jamarcus: Richard Ayoade
Abby: Rosemarie DeWitt

Sgt. Bressman: Will Forte

Origin: United States

Language: English, French, Spanish

Released: 2012

Production: Shawn Levy, Tom McNulty; 21 Laps
Entertainment, Ingenious Film Partners; released by 20th
Century-Fox

Directed by: Akiva Schafer

Written by: Evan Goldberg; Seth Rogen; Jared Stern

Cinematography by: Barry Peterson

Music by: Christophe Beck

Sound: Wayne Lemmer

Music Supervisor: George Drakoulias

Editing: Dean Zimmerman

Costumes: Wendy Chuck

Production Design: Doug Meerdink

MPAA rating: R

Running time: 102 minutes

REVIEWS

Burr, Ty. *Boston Globe.* July 26, 2012.

Chang, Justin. *Variety.* July 26, 2012.

Guzman, Rafer. *Newsday.* July 26, 2012.

Hornaday, Ann. *Washington Post.* July 26, 2012.

Legel, Laremy. *Film.com.* July 26, 2012.

Long, Tom. *Detroit News.* July 26, 2012.

Moore, Roger. *McClatchy-Tribune News Service.* July 26, 2012.

Myers, Randy. *San Jose Mercury News.* July 25, 2012.

Sharkey, Betsy. *Los Angeles Times.* July 26, 2012.

Tobias, Scott. *NPR.* July 26, 2012.

QUOTES

Bob: "You know what, pal? If being overly aggressive and a
little bit snippy was a crime, I'd be making a citizen's arrest
right now."

TRIVIA

The movie was originally titled "Neighborhood Watch," but
was changed due to sensitivity over the Trayvon Martin
shooting in Florida.

WEST OF MEMPHIS

Box Office: $141,928

The fourth major documentary to cover this 18-
plus-year miscarriage of justice, *West of Memphis* offers a
powerful and definitive look at a case that has drawn attention from millions worldwide. Produced by Peter
Jackson and Fran Walsh, as well as documentary subjects
Damien Echols and his wife, this is must-see viewing

and easily one of the best documentaries of 2012. In
1993, three young men, Jessie Misskelley, age 17, Jason
Baldwin, age 16, and Damien Echols, age 18, were arrested for the torture and murder of three eight-year-old
boys: Steve Branch, Michael Moore and Christopher
Byers. Their quick conviction, on scant, highly circum-
stantial evidence and a forced confession, tainted the
case so badly that it became the subject of a stunning
trio of HBO documentaries, *Paradise Lost: The Child
Murders at Robin Hood Hills* (1996), *Paradise Lost: Revelations* (2000), and the recent *Paradise Lost 3:Purgatory*
(2011), all directed by noted documentarian team Joe
Berlinger and Bruce Sinofsky. The first two documentaries were so effective in establishing reasonable doubt,
and even casting suspicion elsewhere, that an ever-
growing group of supporters, who staged regular protests
and contributed to a defense fund, had little doubt the
revelations uncovered would finally lead to the release of
the men who had been dubbed the West Memphis
Three. But as the years dragged on, it became clear that,
if anything, Arkansas officials had dug their heels in,
refusing to even consider whether or not they might
have got it wrong. The three prisoners became folkloric
figures, adorning t-shirts, and inspiring an ever-growing
legion of supporters to fight for their release.

Enter Hollywood heavy hitters Peter Jackson and
Fran Walsh. The powerhouse duo, frustrated by lack of
movement in the case, got in touch with Lorri Davis,
who had met and married death row defendant Damien
Echols, and now led efforts to secure a new trial.
Convinced the whole story had not been told, the
production team collaborated with Oscar nominated
documentary director Amy Berg (*Deliver Us From Evil*
[2006]) to hire private detectives, finally fully interview
all the family members, and pursue much-needed
modern DNA testing of evidence. But as Berg covered
the defense team's relentless pursuit of the truth she was
also witness to a startling legal denouement. In early
2011, the men were perfunctorily released by the state
of Arkansas which offered them the opportunity to use
the controversial and little known Alford plea in which
defendants may assert their innocence but plead guilty
because they believe it to be in their best interest. If that
sounds mealy-mouthed it is far less so than the reasons
offered up by the state for the use of the statute. When
pressed, the prosecutors actually admit that they used
the statute simply because a new trial (which the
defendants undoubtedly would have received) would
likely lead to the defendant's release.

Even without Berg at the helm this was likely to be
compelling. But over the course of a whopping two and
a half hours virtually every person involved in the case
in any major way is interviewed and offered the chance
to give their opinion, offer up reminisces and even

change their story if they want. In one sequence, a self-appointed occult "expert" admits that the police looked to him as an authority simply because he was the only person they knew of who knew anything about the occult at all. In another, a prosecutor, on video tape, willfully misleads a jury about the location in which a weapon was found. Crowds jeer at and threaten the defendants on the day of their arrest as they are led from the police station and a series of endless civic hysterias are paraded out as part of the news media. *West of Memphis* is a vast showcasing of how the systems around the case broke down, and stayed broken through the passage of decades, even when the right thing to do should have been obvious to everyone involved. Bureaucratic and police incompetence, arrogance and crass ambition on the part of public officials, media manipulation, and cultural bigotry are exposed here.

Though much of the above is in line with the material offered up previously by Berlinger and Sinofsky, Berg's work differs greatly in the time she spends highlighting the human side of the story. That human side is also what trips her up in assembling material and deciding how to present all the participants. The lead prosecutor in the case comes off as a particularly noxious careerist, obviously influenced in his judgment by what would most protect his own political hide. The police emerge as well-meaning but ill-prepared to deal with a crime of this magnitude. The relatives of the victims show amazing bravery in their willingness to tell their stories yet again, often with much restraint and humility when it comes to assessing blame. Where the problems start is in discovery of new DNA evidence that points the finger at one of the victim's stepfathers. Left with just that DNA evidence any average viewer would want answers but the film goes about buttressing its clear accusation via unsubstantiated anecdotal remarks that descend firmly into the realm of hearsay. More convincing is the reaction to that evidence by the accused, who to this date has yet to account for his whereabouts during the hours the crimes were committed and is even heard harassing his only alibi witness on the phone. None of this provides an open and shut case but it does showcase two important things. One is that family members were never looked at seriously as potential suspects. The other is that any investigator should have a ton of questions to direct at the individual in question if only the state of Arkansas would follow through.

A lot of celebrity supporters get camera time here and have taken somewhat of a beating from reviewers as talking heads. The plain truth is that most, if not all of those interviewed, have been intimately involved in the efforts to publicize and free the West Memphis Three and have continued relationships with the men far beyond what would normally be expected in situations like this. They are in short, friends, in every sense of the word with unique perspectives on how they came to be involved in the story that has fascinated so many.

West of Memphis has opened up important new lines of inquiry for future investigation but it also spends a lot of time with the three men accused. The question Berg was in the best position to tackle was just how life can have any meaning for these three men now that they have been released but not exonerated legally. Under the plea agreement they may not sue the state of Arkansas or profit in any way from their story. Eighteen years later, what they are to make of their lives is summed up beautifully by Echols, who talks of wanting nothing more than to just be somewhere, where he is not known for anything other than being himself. Berg uses a number of beautiful flourishes to buttress the poetic angle the film takes on the men and their search for inner as well as outer freedom. It is this deeply touching, very effective material that makes the rest of the story slightly easier to swallow. There are not always satisfactory answers to the hardest questions life can throw but there is often meaning to be found outside the struggle. Friendship, love, loyalty, and forgiveness are on ample display amongst the West Memphis Three and their supporters. Perhaps, this is the best evidence; the final nail in the coffin. No despairing recriminations, just the simple desire to get on with life in an unjust world, and ignore the stingy bureaucrats and incompetent enforcers who claim to speak for truth, justice, and whatever passes for the American way in systems lost to corruption.

Dave Canfield

CREDITS

Origin: United States

Language: English

Released: 2012

Production: Lorri Davis, Peter Jackson, Fran Walsh, Amy Berg; Disarming Films, Wing Nut Films; released by Sony Pictures Classics

Directed by: Amy Berg

Written by: Amy Berg; Billy McMillin

Cinematography by: Maryse Alberti; Ronan Killeen

Music by: Nick Cave; Warren Ellis

Sound: Brent Burge; Chris Ward

Editing: Billy McMillin

MPAA rating: R

Running time: 147 minutes

REVIEWS

Bell, Mark. *FilmThreat.* December 16, 2012.

DeFore, John. *Hollywood Reporter.* January 20, 2012.

Erbland, Kate. *Film School Rejects*. February 1, 2012.
Holmes, Linda. *NPR*. September 7, 2012.
Hughes, David. *Empire Magazine*. December 17, 2012.
Kemp, Phillip. *Total Film*. November 23, 2012.
McWeeny, Drew. *HitFix*. January 21, 2012.
Merin, Jennifer. *About.com*. December 16, 2012.
Murray, Noel. *AV Club*. January 22, 2012.
Smithey, Cole. *ColeSmithey.com*. November 28, 2012.

AWARDS

Nominations:

British Acad. 2012: Feature Doc.
Writers Guild 2012: Documentary Screenplay

WHAT TO EXPECT WHEN YOU'RE EXPECTING

I can't wait to meet my baby.
—Movie tagline

You pee on a stick. It's pretty idiot proof.
—Movie tagline

If I knew I'd have a rack like this, I would've gotten knocked up years ago.
—Movie tagline

I'm calling bull$#!

. Pregnancy sucks.
—Movie tagline

I just have all this extra energy. Plus I'm like crazy horny.
—Movie tagline

There is no judging in "dudes group."
—Movie tagline

It's too late to pull out now.
—Movie tagline

Box Office: $41.2 million

The book, *What to Expect When You're Expecting* by Heidi Murkoff, is a generations-old right of passage for expectant mothers. When that plus sign pops up in the window of the home pregnancy test, it is a crap shoot if one is supposed to call a doctor or head to the bookstore to pick up a copy of the evergreen self-help tome. So it makes sense that someone finally realized the book's film potential, right? Bestsellers of all genres are an often mined source for movie fodder (committed readers are thought to translate into eager filmgoers) but catchy title aside, a month-by-month guide to all things pregnancy seems like an odd choice for a screenplay. Was the hope to capitalize on the nacent—and off-kilter—self-help

subgenre led by meta-infomercial *Think Like A Man* (2012)? Or was the idea to supplant the printed word with a visual guide and have expectant mothers and wannabe expectant mothers look to the crib notes film version as a primer for childbearing and skip the bookstore altogether? If it is the former, then *What to Expect* will do more to sink the burgeoning genre than bolster it (not good news for *Men Are From Mars, Women Are From Venus,* which is currently in development). However, the latter is a pretty safe bet considering that the movie acts as more of a highlight reel for Murkoff's book than a coherent story cast with compelling characters.

What to Expect follows the conception adventures of several couples each acting as the poster child for a specific pregnancy-related issue, as well as excited and overwhelmed parents to-be. There is the beautiful, exotic, arty couple (Jennifer Lopez and Rodrigo Santoro) who cannot conceive naturally and have turned to international adoption to make their family dreams come true; a *Dancing With The Stars*-esque performer (Matthew Morrison) and his TV personality weight loss guru girlfriend (Cameron Diaz), who get pregnant by accident and have to deal with her advanced maternal age; two young food truck chefs (Anna Kendrick and Chace Crawford) who do double duty as spokesmodels for both unprotected one-night stands and the emotional fall-out from miscarriage; and, finally, a Murkoff-lite baby expert (Elizabeth Banks) whose years-long conception journey/resulting pregnancy is a collection of worst-case scenarios from the book (Banks' character is plagued by everything from gas to canckles to an unplanned c-section). All this might be bearable for the boutique shop owner turned breastfeeding motivational speaker, if her husband (Ben Falcone) was not in perpetual competition with his retired race car driver dad (Dennis Quaid) whose bubbly younger wife effortlessly becomes pregnant with twins and manages to look good in a bikini for the whole nine months.

On the outskirts of all this preggo drama, screenwriters Heather Hach and Shauna Cross add a dads-only play group that meets in an Atlanta park to dissect the nitty-gritty of parenting. Pushing strollers, strapped to newborns a la Zach Galifianakis in *The Hangover* (2009), they pride themselves on a *Fight Club* (1999) approach to their membership and, thanks to Chris Rock, provide most of the laughs in the story—unfortunately they come at the expense of his character's young son who manages to time and time again survive his father's cliched neglectful parenting.

Hach and Cross get points for trying to weave the multiple storylines together in an organic way. Inspired by emsemble romantic comedies like *Valentines Day* (2010), *What to Expect* characters bump into each other on the sidewalk, buy tasty treats from other characters' food trucks, and turn out to be distantly related to each other. Conscious of the limited screen time relegated to each character and the repercussions of said allocation, the film punches up the emotional impact with a tear jerker soundtrack that really drives home just how much pregnancy/adoption is changing each couples' lives. Plus, the end product—tiny, adorable babies—are impossible to resist heart-warmers designed by nature to make even the most jaded moviegoer a little gooey.

The rest of the plot, however, is a bit lackluster. "Pregnancy can be funny, too" the film shouts as pregnant women puke in public and freak out over epidurals. And do not forget that fathers are irresponsible, and, when left to their own devices, will pick up the wrong kid from day care! There may be some truth to both statements, but both storylines have been played out before, and even with an eager energetic cast, they just feel tired. Plus, no matter how hard it tries, *What to Expect* cannot let go of its self-help guide source. The undercurrent of medical factoids are palpable and it is obvious that "Every pregnancy is different" was the tag line on set. As much as the film banks off the universality of the emotional journey to parenthood that the readers of Murkoff book must have experienced, the lack of any real introspection fails to make the film approachable.

Joanna Topor MacKenzie

CREDITS

Jules: Cameron Diaz
Holly: Jennifer Lopez
Wendy: Elizabeth Banks
Marco: Chace Crawford
Skyer: Brooklyn Decker
Gary: Ben Falcone
Rosie: Anna Kendrick
Evan: Matthew Morrison
Ramsey: Dennis Quaid
Vic: Chris Rock
Alex: Rodrigo Santoro
Davis: Joe Manganiello
Craig: Thomas Lennon
Kara: Wendi McLendon-Covey
Origin: United States
Language: English, Spanish
Released: 2012
Production: Mike Medavoy, David Thwaites, Arnold W. Messer; Alcon Entertainment, Phoenix Pictures; released by Lionsgate
Directed by: Kirk Jones

Written by: Shauna Cross; Heather Hach
Cinematography by: Xavier Perez Grobet
Music by: Mark Mothersbaugh
Sound: Lon Bender; Glenn Morgan
Music Supervisor: John Houlihan; P.J. Bloom
Editing: Michael Berenbaum
Art Direction: James F. Truesdale
Costumes: Karen Patch
Production Design: Andrew Laws
MPAA rating: PG-13
Running time: 110 minutes

REVIEWS

Burr, Ty. *Boston Globe.* May 17, 2012.
Ebert, Roger. *Chicago Sun-Times.* May 17, 2012.
Goss, William. *Film.com.* May 18, 2012.
Howell, Peter. *Toronto Star.* May 17, 2012.
Jones, J. R. *Chicago Reader.* May 24, 2012.
LaSalle, Mick. *San Francisco Chronicle.* May 17, 2012.
Roeper, Richard. *RichardRoeper.com.* May 17, 2012.
Scott, A. O. *New York Times.* May 17, 2012.
Sharkey, Betsy. *Los Angeles Times.* May 17, 2012.
Travers, Peter. *Rolling Stone.* May 17, 2012.

QUOTES

Wendy: "I just wanted the glow. The one that they promise you on the cover of those magazines. Well, I'm calling it—pregnancy sucks. Making a human being is really hard. I have no control over my body or my emotions."

TRIVIA

Based on the popular series of pregnancy guides by the same name with more than 14.5 million books sold through 2011.

AWARDS

Nominations:

Golden Raspberries 2012: Worst Support. Actress (Decker), Worst Support. Actress (Lopez)

WHERE DO WE GO NOW?

(Et maintenant on va ou?)

Box Office: $531,997

An international co-production and Lebanon's official Best Foreign Language Film selection for the 84th Academy Awards, writer-director-star Nadine Labaki's *Where Do We Go Now?* juggles comic fantasy and politicized drama in telling a story of religious strife held at bay by the better angels of women's nature. Pitched, as its title might suggest, somewhere between alarm and cautious optimism, it is wryly funny and sad at the same time, peddling a vital message of tolerance and coexistence.

Its commingled tonalities do not always quite mesh on a functionally narrative level, but if one sticks with the movie there is some off-kilter delight that cuts against erroneous notions of foreign films which tackle big social issues being necessarily staid and stuffy affairs. Given a very targeted arthouse release by distributor Sony Pictures Classics, aimed at especially an older urban demographic, the movie pulled in just over $500,000 during its domestic theatrical run.

Set in an indeterminate time, Labaki's movie unfolds in a remote Lebanese village, virtually sealed off from its surroundings and accessible only via a thin bridge in severe disrepair. There, church and mosque stand side by side, and Christians and Muslims live amongst one another. The women, whose friendships more naturally transcend the religious fault lines of their community, act as a collective leavening influence, managing and rerouting the testosterone-fueled energy and impulses of the men in their village. Widowed Christian cafe owner Amale (Labaki) and Muslim handyman Rabih (Julian Farhat) nurse a bit of a mutual crush.

Soon, though, news of religious violence from the outside world—delivered via the town's sole television—starts to darken everyone's mood and engender bickering. A series of accidents and misunderstandings ensue, and when a terrible tragedy befalls one of the children who serves as an errand boy to a nearby city, the village is pushed closer to getting caught up in a sectarian bloodbath.

As the child's grief-stricken mother, concerned about the potentially bloodthirsty response of some fellow family members, attempts to keep his death a secret, headstrong Yvonne (Yvonne Maalouf) feigns a miracle connection and chat with God. Then that television gets destroyed. Soon the women turn to increasingly fanciful ploys to maintain their town's hermetic remove, landing upon distractions by way of pot-infused pastries and belly dancing, the latter courtesy of a busload of Ukrainian strippers the women pool their money together to hire to pretend to be stranded.

While true that it deals in specific situations more than abstractions, *Where Do We Go Now?* still works best if one accepts it as the working draft of a kind of cinematic treatise—or a flavored, chewable children's vitamin. There is a message here, but the packaging is of paramount concern to Labaki. Her film is the comedically infused flipside of something like the Academy Award-nominated Best Foreign Language film *Ajami* (2010), or any number of other Middle Eastern-set tales of religious conflict and sectarian strife.

While it cycles through plenty of entertaining schemes of distraction hatched by the women, Labaki and her screenwriting collaborators (chiefly Jihad Hojeily and Rodney Al Haddad, with the additional credited assistance of Thomas Bidegain) are not much interested in digging down into the lasting consequences of these acts. Likewise, the movie's gender politics are necessarily broad, in order to support the conceit, which puts a twist on the classic comedy *Lysistrata*. The film therefore takes on the feeling of a cutesy serial, punctuated here and there by some serious anger.

A tone of cheeky moralizing is its main aim, so *Where Do We Go Now?* takes a while to get into, and additionally lags some in the middle, suffering from ill-conceived scenes that pull viewers away from the crux of the story. The ideas and effort often trump Labaki's big picture execution, in other words.

Mostly middling critical reaction (the film hovered around 50 percent on Rotten Tomatoes) focused on this clashing of styles—in which melodrama, cross-cultural romance, musical and even satire were blended together in a not always convincing goulash. Emblematic of more negative opinions is Stephen Rea's review from the *Philadelphia Inquirer*, in which he wrote that "time passes with a sense that nothing is really happening until suddenly too much happens all at once."

Labaki's film mixes in non-professionals alongside working actors, with mixed results that, when they do work, give *Where Do We Go Now?* a charged sense of spontaneity and energy. Labaki and the slyly amusing Maalouf are particularly engaging. Other roles, though, would have benefited from more traditional casting.

Cinematographer Christopher Offenstein's work leans toward the naturalistic, but notably reaches for stylized, impressionistic sentiment on a couple occasions, notably in a striking cafe fantasy sequence built around Labaki and Farhat's stolen sidelong glances at one another. The music, meanwhile, from composer Khaled Mouzanar, Labaki's off-screen husband, never lets a sense of hopefulness out of its earshot, even during the story's grimmer moments.

While many other likeminded films achieve a greater dramatic resonance by reflecting reality, there is also a dour, suffocating quality to some of those tales. *Where Do We Go Now?* does not suffer from that problem, and is a welcome reprieve from stuffy, stern "message cinema." It is buoyant in the face of tough circumstance, and consisting of jangled, tangled tonalities—just like real life, where we do not get to pick all our neighbors and choose the moments and means by which crises are introduced into our lives.

Brent Simon

CREDITS

Takla: Claude Baz Moussawbaa
Afaf: Leyla Hakim
Amale: Nadine Labaki
Yvonne: Yvonne Maalouf
Saydeh: Antoinette Noufaily
Rabih: Julian Farhat
Origin: France, Lebanon, Egypt, Italy
Language: English, Russian, Arabic
Released: 2011
Production: Anne-Dominique Toussaint, Nadine Labaki; Pathe; released by Sony Pictures Classics
Directed by: Nadine Labaki
Written by: Nadine Labaki; Sam Mounier; Jihad Hojeily; Thomas Bidegain; Rodney Al Haddid
Cinematography by: Cristophe Offenstein
Music by: Khaled Mouzannar
Sound: Gwennole Le Borgne
Editing: Veronique Lange
Costumes: Caroline Labaki
Production Design: Cynthia Zahar
MPAA rating: PG-13
Running time: 110 minutes

REVIEWS

Burr, Ty. *Boston Globe.* May 24, 2012.
Duralde, Alonso. *The Wrap.* May 11, 2012.
Gleiberman, Owen. *Entertainment Weekly.* May 9, 2012.
Holden, Stephen. *New York Times.* May 10, 2012.
Jenkins, Mark. *NPR.* May 10, 2012.
Morgenstern, Joe. *Wall Street Journal.* May 10, 2012.
Olsen, Mark. *Los Angeles Times.* May 10, 2012.
Rea, Stephen. *Philadelphia Inquirer.* May 31, 2012.
Toppman, Lawrence. *Charlotte Observer.* July 26, 2012.
Willmore, Alison. *Village Voice.* May 8, 2012.

QUOTES

Takla: "Fate is a great provider."

TRIVIA

This film is the highest grossing Arabic speaking release in the territory of Lebanon.

THE WOMAN IN BLACK

Do you believe in ghosts?
—Movie tagline

Box Office: $54.3 million

When a film so carefully follows nearly every trick and telltale plot device of its genre, it can either be dismissed as a derivative knock off or embraced as a loving homage. Set around the turn of the 20th century, the English haunted-house film *The Woman in Black* invites both responses, but while few of its spooky jolts are fresh, they are still solidly unnerving and eventually deliciously terrifying.

Directed by James Watkins, *The Woman in Black* is adapted by Jane Goldman from Susan Hill's 1983 novel. (Previous incarnations include a long-running 1987 stage version and a 1989 British television movie.) Arthur Kipps (Daniel Radcliffe) is a grieving widower, father, and lawyer on a last-chance assignment to a remote seaside English village where he is tasked with tying up the will and estate of a recently deceased older woman. Upon arrival, however, Kipps is faced with familiar horror-film trappings such as ill-mannered villagers who want him gone, secrets no one wants to talk about, and a harrowing rash of local children dying. There follow furtive looks and psychic fits and eventually unearthly apparitions—not surprisingly, the title character turns out to be a vengeful spirit on the prowl. Watkins serves up all this with a blue-gray dread, surrounding the proceedings with black wrought-iron fences, billowing white drapes, and a thick layer of sinister fog.

One of the film's overt visual pleasures is the deceased's majestically decrepit mansion. Known as Eel Marsh House, the dwelling is a smorgasbord for lovers of Gothic dilapidation, cobwebs and dust covers, spookily clanging children's toys, and creaking rocking chairs. Adding to its decaying grandeur—and giving *The Woman in Black* spectacularly melancholy vistas—is that the home and its accompanying graveyard sit atop a sometime island, isolated by a vast, muddy wasteland marsh that floods at high tide.

Eel Marsh House acts as a microcosm of the film's entire approach: The haunted locale is a blatant fright-film construction, a straightforward, un-winking genre archetype. Likewise, *The Woman in Black* makes no bones about digging up and dusting off some very familiar set pieces, especially when it comes time to get things bumping and rattling in the old shack. Watkins is not out to subvert or play these tried and tested tropes for irony—he lovingly respects and takes them seriously.

That is not surprising, considering *The Woman in Black*'s release is part of the 21st-century revival of Hammer Films, the once-venerable British genre studio known in the 1950s and 1960s for its devotion to classic horror trappings, including iconic Gothic settings. Combining the tactics and surroundings of those British ghost stories and with the visual tricks of modern Japanese supernatural thrillers, Watkins executes his chills with Hammer virtuoso. He uses the dark hallways, claustrophobic close-ups, and ghastly images to compound the menace, showing restraint in parceling out the thrills at a steadily building pace, but not shying away from big scares.

The Woman in Black also has something to say subtextually about the Horror Gaze—for Kipps the very act of looking and seeing the supernatural further perpetuates the story's body count. ("He saw her" becomes an impressively foreboding phrase.) As such, the film is full of dark figures glimpsed at a distance and pale visages in windows, reminding gore-jaded viewers that something moving slowly closer can be much more disturbing than in-your-face jolts. (Though there are plenty of those as well.)

The acting is suitably dutiful, if secondary to the atmosphere. Radcliffe is no powerhouse, but he does mournful earnestness and broken emotional isolation easily. It helps that his harmlessly reactive non-presence is aided considerably by thespian pros like Ciaran Hinds as the town's upper-class skeptic ("Superstitious rubbish!" he harrumphs with blustering denial) and Janet McTeer as his more haunted and spiritualistic wife. (The script makes useful hay off the seance fads of the era.)

More interested in mood and shadows than shock and gore, *The Woman in Black* takes its time loading up its terrors. For much of the running, the filmmakers play the movie's subtle, eerie elements with impressive skill, and despite its by-the-book familiarity, the film has plenty of genuinely frightening bits, including a bloodcurdling climactic payoff that comes at the audience in an almost giddy rush of shivers. The only problem is that, aforementioned last flourish aside, once Kipps starts solving the mystery in the final act, the film sheds much of its wonderfully single-minded focus on creeping out the audience and loses its narrative and character moorings. The once-taut plot suddenly goes wobbly, and people behave like characters in a ghost tale. If the story had hung in there with the film's otherwise masterful tone, *The Woman in Black* might have been one for the ages. As is, it is still an enjoyable, old-school pulse-quickener for a dark and stormy night.

Locke Peterseim

CREDITS

Arthur Kipps: Daniel Radcliffe
Mr. Daily: Ciaran Hinds
Mrs. Daily: Janet McTeer
Fisher: Shaun Dooley
Stella Kipps: Sophie Stuckey
Mr. Bentley: Roger Allam

Alice Drablow: Alisa Khazanova
Jennet Humfrye: Liz White
Nathaniel Drablow: Ashley Foster
Origin: British Virgin Islands
Language: English
Released: 2012
Production: Richard Jackson, Simon Oakes, Brian Oliver; Alliance Films, Hammer Film Productions, Talisman Films, U.K. Film Council; released by CBS Films
Directed by: James H. Watkins
Written by: Jane Goldman
Cinematography by: Tim Maurice-Jones
Music by: Marco Beltrami
Sound: Ben Barker
Editing: Jon Harris
Art Direction: Paul Ghirardani
Costumes: Keith Madden
Production Design: Kave Quinn
MPAA rating: PG-13
Running time: 95 minutes

REVIEWS

Corliss, Richard. *Time*. February 2, 2012.
Dargis, Manohla. *New York Times*. February 2, 2012.
Ebert, Roger. *Chicago Sun-Times*. February 2, 2012.
Edelstein, David. *Vulture*. February 2, 2012.
Linden, Sheri. *Los Angeles Times*. February 2, 2012.
O'Sullivan, Michael. *Washington Post*. February 3, 2012.
Phillips, Michael. *Chicago Tribune*. February 2, 2012.
Phipps, Keith. *AV Club*. February 2, 2012.
Rodriguez, Rene. *Miami Herald*. February 2, 2012.
Stevens, Dana. *Slate*. February 2, 2012.

QUOTES

Daily: "I believe the most rational mind can play tricks in the dark."

TRIVIA

The music boxes and mechanical toys in the nursery scenes were not created for the movie, but were genuine antique toys from the period, loaned to the production by a collector.

WON'T BACK DOWN

If you can't beat the system...change it.
—Movie tagline

Box Office: $5.3 million

Some critics decided to follow the money in their assessment of *Won't Back Down*, which seems entirely counterproductive to a worthwhile analysis of the content of the movie. Yes, the movie was distributed by Walden Media, which is owned by Philip Anschutz, who supports conservative ideas of educational reform (e.g., varying degrees of privatization of the public education system), yet that hardly defines the content of the movie (Walden Media also distributed the documentary *Waiting for "Superman"* [2010], another politically divisive film that, despite that controversy, still painted an effectively desperate portrait of the public education system in the United States). Besides, the money does not matter when the best argument against the political position the movie holds is the movie itself.

Won't Back Down offers no solid understanding of the so-called "parent trigger" laws, which allow parents to petition for a change in the administration of a public school. The screenplay by Brin Hill and director Daniel Barnz is hazy at best about what kind of change will result from the protagonists' quest to "take over" control of their local public school, save for the vaguely feel-good notion that parents will somehow be in control of their children's education. The screenplay is heavy with details about the formal process to implement the parent trigger—called a "fail-safe" option in the movie—ensuring that the audience understands just how impossible the odds against the story's protagonists are. Instead, the audience is left with an important and overwhelming question of what exactly they are rooting for the heroines to do.

The movie centers around the parent of a child in a school in Pittsburgh and one of the teachers at the school. The parent is Jamie Fitzpatrick (Maggie Gyllenhaal), a single mother who works two jobs to make ends meet. Her 8-year-old daughter Malia (Emily Alyn Lind) has dyslexia; she was enrolled at a private school until Jamie was no longer able to pay for the tuition. Malia is struggling at her current school, especially since her teacher (Nancy Bach) spends time she should be teaching on her cell phone and refuses to spend time after school helping Malia. The teacher tells Jamie that the school day and, along with it, her workday end at 3 p.m.

Malia's teacher is the only one in the movie that represents a legitimately horrible educator; the rest are either exceptional teachers or simply worried about what a change to the school would mean for their jobs. One of the former is Nona Alberts (Viola Davis), who is also the mother of a child with special learning needs. She and Jamie meet while both attempt to have their children enrolled at a local charter school by "winning" a lottery. The school's principal (Ving Rhames) offers the first of many soapbox speeches from characters that paint them and the position for which they stand in the

best or worst light possible. The principal of the school, for example, gives a rousing speech about the aid a charter school can provide for children, while the head of the teachers union (Ned Eisenberg) offers a cynical tirade about how unions do not have the best interest of students at heart (the sentiment is based upon a quote of questionable origin).

Jamie and Nona team up to canvass the school district for signatures from parents to implement the fail-safe option by going door-to-door and holding a rally (another excuse for another speech), while Nona attempts to gather the support of her fellow teachers. Michael Perry (Oscar Isaac) is one of those teachers and an inevitable romantic interest for Jamie. Michael supports her cause in theory but cannot do so in practice; he sees the necessity of a union to protect teachers' interests. Whatever change Jamie hopes to bring about would end that protection for the teachers at the school.

For all the movie's blatant politicking, it does—perhaps inadvertently—make a fine case in favor of teachers unions, or at least the movie makes a more coherent argument for them than it does for the parent trigger laws that it clearly endorses. Union reps, such as the one who gives the speech and Evelyn Riske (Holly Hunter), do not fare so well. Evelyn appears to genuinely care about the teachers she represents, although there is an unfortunate and blatantly manipulative scene in which she attempts to bribe Jamie with a place for Malia at a prestigious school that serves only to place her character in a negative light.

The only genuine bright spot is a school board member played by Marianne Jean-Baptiste, a no-nonsense politician who refuses to accept hollow rhetoric from any side of an issue. Given the screenplay's inability to hold those qualities itself, it is only a matter of time before her character becomes the tool of the plot—a particularly manipulative meeting of the school board that comes down to one final vote on Jamie and Nona's crusade, which is yet another reason for a string of speeches from the participants.

Beyond whatever political leanings the movie might have, its ultimate downfall is its lack of a legitimately human story. The characters exist solely as mouthpieces for one position or another, and the few human touches the screenplay affords them (Nona's marriage is collapsing, and a mistake from her past threatens to put the entire cause in jeopardy) feel calculated. One could say these blatant manipulations undermine the movie's central argument, but, again, that would falsely imply that the movie has a cognizant argument to make in the first place. *Won't Back Down* does itself and the important topic of education reform no favors.

Mark Dujsik

CREDITS

Jamie Fitzpatrick: Maggie Gyllenhaal
Nona Alberts: Viola Davis
Michael Perry: Oscar Isaac
Breena Harper: Rosie Perez
Principal Thompson: Ving Rhames
Charles Alberts: Lance Reddick
Olivia Lopez: Marianne Jean-Baptiste
Principal Holland: Bill Nunn
Malia Fitzpatrick: Emily Ann Lind
Cody Alberts: Dante Brown
Evelyn Riske: Holly Hunter
Origin: United States
Language: English
Released: 2012
Production: Mark Johnson; Gran Via, Walden Media; released by 20th Century Fox Film Corp.
Directed by: Daniel Barnz
Written by: Daniel Barnz
Cinematography by: Roman Osin
Music by: Marcelo Zarvos
Sound: James Emswiller
Music Supervisor: Linda Cohen
Editing: Kristina Boden
Art Direction: Gary Kosko
Costumes: Luca Mosca
Production Design: Rusty Smith
MPAA rating: PG
Running time: 121 minutes

REVIEWS

Burr, Ty. *Boston Globe*. September 27, 2012.
Covert, Colin. *Minneapolis Star Tribune*. September 27, 2012.
O'Hehir, Andrew. *Salon.com*. September 26, 2012.
Osenlund, R. Kurt. *Slant Magazine*. September 26, 2012.
Putman, Dustin. *DustinPutman.com*. September 25, 2012.
Rabin, Nathan. *AV Club*. September 27, 2012.
Scott, A. O. *New York Times*. September 27, 2012.
Taylor, Ella. *NPR*. September 26, 2012.
Weitzman, Elizabeth. *New York Daily News*. September 27, 2012.
Willmore, Alison. *Movieline*. September 27, 2012.

QUOTES

Jamie Fitzpatrick: "I've just never been able to talk smart people into doing things before."

THE WORDS

There's more than one way to take a life.
—Movie tagline

Box Office: $11.5 million

It is remarkably easy to think of a few choice words for Brian Klugman and Lee Bernthal's drama *The Words,* starring Bradley Cooper, Zoe Saldana, Jeremy Irons, Dennis Quaid, and Olivia Wilde. Inert, pretentious, uninteresting, dull, inconsistent, and just stupid come to mind before anything positive. Cooper will never forget 2012 as it is the year that catapulted the long-underrated actor from below-the-radar status to A-list with his Oscar-nominated work in *Silver Linings Playbook* (2012). He is lucky that *The Words* will be made even more of an afterthought in comparison and become little more than a trivia answer—"What was the truly horrendous movie Bradley Cooper made the same year he got his first Academy Award nomination?"

Cooper's lead character actually only exists in a story within a story, one that is being read by Clay Hammond (Quaid), a successful author reading passages from his latest novel in front of a rapt audience of fans that includes the jaw-droppingly gorgeous and flirtatious Daniella (Wilde). Hammond's story is that of another writer named Rory Jansen (Cooper) and his lovely wife Dora (Saldana). The pair is relatively happy but Rory cannot reconcile his inability to crack his potential as a literary luminary and it has begun to eat away at him. He has been rejected by publishers and his dreams have been mocked by his father (J.K. Simmons). In one the film's many false constructs, Rory considers giving up after only two years (a matter of minutes in the world of writing, where anyone worth their printed word knows years of hard work are required before any sort of breakthrough). Rory becomes petulant (and deeply unlikable)—walking out on dinners with friends, whining, and generally complaining that his dreams may not come true.

Just when he needs it, the universe drops a gift into Rory's lap. He finds a manuscript in an old French briefcase and the work is a piece of absolute art. The stories within the text are mesmerizing and Rory takes them as his own, becoming a hot new literary superstar. The spotlight on Rory is bright enough that the original author (Irons) notices and catches up with the film's sullen hero.

One of many problems with *The Words* is a complete and total absence of anyone worth caring about in the slightest. Rory is annoying, Dora disappears at the whim of the bad screenwriting, and Daniella and Clay are stunningly vapid. They are meant to, in many ways, be the audience's translation of the in-movie text. Is this really Clay's story? Why is Daniella so interested in him and it? As they become a bigger part of the action in the final act, the film truly suffers. Late scenes between Quaid and Wilde are among the most embarrassingly written and performed in any film in 2012.

Sadly, one almost wishes the truly awful scenes of the final act were more prominent because most of *The Words* is just dismally boring. It is pretentious, false drama with no center and ambiguous character motivations. It is a film that deals with a hot-button topic (plagiarism has taken on new life when everything can be checked on a smart phone) but then has nothing really to say about it. Ultimately, it is a film with interesting questions about credit and creativity that could have worked in the more forgiving narrative world of the printed word and it seems likely that *The Words* started life as a short story or a proposal for a novella. That would have allowed viewers to get in the heads of Clay, Dora, Rory, and Daniella in ways that the movie just does not offer. And so none of them feel real or genuine in any way. It is a film that, like a pretentious wannabe writer, telegraphs how important it thinks it is without ever once proving it.

Dumped into theaters as unceremoniously as possible on Labor Day 2012, audiences and critics generally avoided or loathed *The Words*. Lou Lumenick of *The New York Post* summed it up best when he wrote, "Bradley Cooper's funniest movie since *The Hangover*—unfortunately, unintentionally, this time...." Audiences were just as unforgiving as the film opened in 4th place and only crawled to just over $11 million domestically, probably making a few executives at CBS Films wonder what they saw in it at the 2012 Sundance Film Festival to make them pick it up in the first place. Every year, there are a few Sundance films that never make it out of Park City. *The Words* should have been one of them in 2012.

Brian Tallerico

CREDITS

Clay Hammond: Dennis Quaid
Rory Jansen: Bradley Cooper
The Old Man: Jeremy Irons
Dora Jansen: Zoe Saldana
Daniella: Olivia Wilde
Mr. Jansen: J.K. Simmons
Origin: United States
Language: English
Released: 2012
Production: Michael Benaroya, Tatiana Kelly, Jim Young; Animus Films, Serena Films; released by CBS Films
Directed by: Brian Klugman; Lee Sternthal
Written by: Brian Klugman; Lee Sternthal
Cinematography by: Antonio Calvache
Music by: Marcelo Zarvos
Sound: Joel Dougherty

Music Supervisor: Laura Katz
Editing: Leslie Jones
Costumes: Simonetta Mariano
Production Design: Michele Laliberte
MPAA rating: PG-13
Running time: 96 minutes

REVIEWS

Bayer, Jeff. *The Scorecard Review.* September 11, 2012.
Chaney, Jen. *Washington Post.* September 7, 2012.
Fine, Marshall. *Hollywood & Fine.* September 7, 2012.
Morris, Wesley. *Boston Globe.* September 6, 2012.
Puig, Claudia. *USA Today.* September 6, 2012.
Rea, Steven. *Philadelphia Inquirer.* September 6, 2012.
Sharkey, Betsy. *Los Angeles Times.* September 6, 2012.
Stevens, Dana. *Slate.* September 6, 2012.
Taylor, Ella. *NPR.* September 6, 2012.
Verniere, James. *Boston Herald.* September 7, 2012.

QUOTES

Mr. Jansen: "Another part of being a man, no matter how painful it might be, is accepting your own limitations."

TRIVIA

Rosamund Pike auditioned for the role that eventually went to Olivia Wilde.

WRATH OF THE TITANS
(Clash of the Titans 2)

Feel the wrath.
—Movie tagline
On March 30th, go to hell.
—Movie tagline

Box Office: $83.7 million

Wrath of the Titans comes two years after the release of a couple of things that were rather dreadful to behold: *Clash of the Titans* (2010) and its Kraken. The latter of that appalling pair was a mythical monster hell-bent on laying waste to ancient Argos during the former, a film that seemed just as ferociously determined to waste the time and money of moviegoers everywhere. The original *Clash of the Titans* (1981) combined some A-list actors like Laurence Olivier and Maggie Smith with B-movie charm (not infrequently veering toward camp), and predominantly lingers in the memory due to the delightfully-transportive stop-motion effects of the great Ray Harryhausen. His hand-molded creature creations seemed old-fashioned even then. Yet they still came wonderfully alive, and so, in turn, did the imaginations of captivated viewers. The idea was to enchantingly draw the audience in rather than blow them away, the conviction being that newfangled effects may come off as spectacular but do not necessarily seem more special.

Those behind the 2010 remake had something very different in mind, with heroic Perseus and his pals pointing their swords at the most cutting-edge, sensationally-animated opposition. However, the degree of one's escapist exhilaration is not necessarily a mere function of how frequent, extended, chaotic, or cacophonous the action sequences are, and, in spite of being steroidally pumped-up, this second *Clash* (and Sam Worthington's lead performance) seemed fairly flat. The critically-rebuked film went on to bilk millions worldwide from its testosterone-fueled target audience, and thus sandaled feet pushed the pedal to the metal and greed propelled things forward toward more Greek. As Queen Andromeda (fetching Rosamund Pike) asserts in *Wrath,* "We humans hope when there is no hope, and believe when believing is idiotic." However, even with a new director and different screenwriters on board this time around, what has been arrived at is disappointingly just more of the same.

"A calamity is coming" Zeus (Liam Neeson) forebodingly intones early on. It seems that the people of Greece have gotten uppity, defiantly turning their noses up at the gods instead of continuing to reverently bow their heads. This paucity of prayer has consequently sapped the order-preserving strengths of the neglected and dismayed deities, to the point where these immortals might soon be anything but. Desperately wanting to avoid being stamped with an expiration date, under-handed god of the underworld Hades (Ralph Fiennes) foolhardily latches on to promises of eternal life that are schemingly whispered in his ears by Kronos, the pandemonium-prone King of the Titans who was long ago overthrown and imprisoned by the Olympian gods he had fathered. Wisely wary Zeus insists that Kronos would break his promise the instant he is allowed to break free from confinement, after which Armageddon will surely follow. Nevertheless, Hades proceeds to seize Zeus (the sibling he still resents for tricking him underground to be abhorred by all mortals) and transfuse his supreme powers into Kronos. It sure seems unlikely that the potentially-terrifying Titan will merely go on to good-naturedly and gratefully keep his word instead of unleashing a nightmarish onslaught that could end the world.

Zeus had previously tried to garner the assistance of his son Perseus (Worthington again), who is part-god, part-human and, unfortunately for his father, wholly uninterested. Since valiantly and ultimately triumphantly

taking a crack at the Kraken ten years prior, the demi-god is now admirable in his desire to simply fish and attentively parent his own son, young Helius (John Bell). Perseus's concern is for preserving his prosaic way of life rather than the weakened and worried deities, as they had not saved his wife nor other loved ones. Thus, he emphatically turns his well-muscled back on Zeus, and a deaf ear to his father's insistence that, if Kronos gets loose, the fisherman will unavoidably have much bigger fish to fry. Indeed, as soon as Hades teams up with Ares (Edgar Ramirez), Zeus's vicious and volatile other son who resentfully fumes that Perseus was always favored, and the aforementioned transfer of power to Kronos begins, the necessity to fight both literally and figuratively hits home for this story's reluctant hero when an immense and pyromaniacal Chimera attacks his village and, even more unacceptably, his beloved Helius. Enlisting the mini-skirted military might and pluck of Andromeda and the incorrigible demigod Agenor, heading off to save his father and the world from gargantuanly-grumpy Grandpa Kronos.

All this talk about difficult relationships between fathers and sons and sibling rivalry never comes off as profoundly heartfelt or thought-provoking: the only truly deep thing in *Wrath* is the Tartarus prison to which Perseus and his allies intrepidly descend. The true focus here is not on kinship but rather on thunderous kineticism. *Wrath* is the kind of 3D spectacle for which glasses are handed out as one enters the theater and hearing aids should be handed out as one leaves. Despite all the din and derring-do, the film is, like its leaden lead, surprisingly dull. Perseus may be put forth as the film's gallant hero, but Worthington once again lacks the potent presence to make the audience root and fear for him.

Upon passing his sizeable sword to his ten-year-old offspring with obvious symbolic significance, Perseus is assured by Helius that it is not too heavy. While the weapon may not be, many thought that the film certainly was. When Zeus turns to Hades and fraternally implores, "Let's have some fun!" as the battle is waged against a colossal, lava-slinging Kronos, many moviegoers were reminded of a key element that had been in decidedly short supply throughout *Wrath.* At least Kebbell and Bill Nighy as demi-demented fallen god Hephaestus are able to add moments of mild comic relief.

Largely dismissed by critics, *Wrath of the Titans* cost $25 million more to make than its 2010 predecessor, yet grossed only about half as much in the U.S. and $191.5 million less worldwide. "One day, somebody's gonna have to make a stand," declared Perseus's adopted father, Spyros, back in *Clash.* "One day, somebody's gonna have to say, *"'Enough!'"* Praise the gods, perhaps that day has come.

David L. Boxerbaum

CREDITS

Perseus: Sam Worthington
Queen Andromeda: Rosamund Pike
Argenor: Toby Kebbell
Hephaestus: Bill Nighy
Zeus: Liam Neeson
Ares: Edgar Ramirez
Hades: Ralph Fiennes
Poseidon: Danny Huston
Origin: United States
Language: English
Released: 2012
Production: Basil Iwanyk, Polly Johnson; Legendary Pictures, Thunder Road Pictures; released by Warner Bros.
Directed by: Jonathan Liebesman
Written by: Dan Mazeau; David Leslie Johnson; Steven Knight
Cinematography by: Ben Davis
Music by: Javier Navarrete
Sound: Dominic Gibbs
Editing: Martin Walsh
Costumes: Jany Temime
Production Design: Charles Wood
MPAA rating: PG-13
Running time: 99 minutes

REVIEWS

Barker, Andrew. *Variety*. March 28, 2012.
Corliss, Richard. *Time*. March 29, 2012.
Ebert, Roger. *Chicago Sun-Times*. March 28, 2012.
Gleiberman, Owen. *Entertainment Weekly*. March 29, 2012.
Holcomb, Mark. *Village Voice*. March 31, 2012.
McCarthy, Todd. *Hollywood Reporter*. March 28, 2012.
Morgenstern, Joe. *Wall Street Journal*. March 29, 2012.
Olsen, Mark. *Los Angeles Times*. March 29, 2012.
O'Sullivan, Michael. *Washington Post*. March 29, 2012.
Puig, Claudia. *USA Today*. March 29, 2012.
Russo, Mark. *Boston Globe*. March 29, 2012.
Schager, Nick. *Boxoffice Magazine*. March 28, 2012.
Travers, Peter. *Rolling Stone*. March 30, 2012.
Webster, Andy. *New York Times*. March 29, 2012.

QUOTES

Andromeda: *"We may not be gods. But we do what people say can't be done, we hope when there isn't any, whatever odds we face, we prevail."*

TRIVIA

This film was sent to the cinemas under code name *"Torn Between."*

AWARDS

Nominations:

Golden Raspberries 2012: Worst Support. Actor (Neeson)

WRECK-IT RALPH

This November, he's exploring new worlds, he's meeting new friends...he's got one chance to play the hero.
—Movie tagline

The story of a regular guy just looking for a little wreck-ognition.
—Movie tagline

This holiday season comes a story for everyone who ever needed a restart on life.
—Movie tagline

When the game is over, a new world comes to life.
—Movie tagline

Get ready for a new kind of hero.
—Movie tagline

When the game is over, the fun begins.
—Movie tagline

When the arcade closes, the fun begins.
—Movie tagline

Box Office: $186.7 million

If *Wreck-It Ralph* wrecks anything, it is the notion that Disney will always lag behind its partners at Pixar in the animation imagination department. Not that it takes terribly much at this point. After fifteen consecutive years without a sizable disappointment, Pixar hit its lowest point in 2011 with the shameful cash-in *Cars 2*, while in 2012 the studio's first princess story *Brave* confronted familiar lessons with creativity that never rose above the routine. Still, the visual and narrative playfulness of *Wreck-It Ralph* marks a step forward of sorts for Disney, which has not delivered a strong animated effort without Pixar's help in years.

To be fair, *Wreck-It Ralph* does resemble the *Toy Story* (1995) concept of what non-living entertainment items do when the people they entertain are not around. Yet *Wreck-It Ralph* also deserves bonus points for incorporating a recent trend in family films (villains who no longer want to be seen as evil, a key element in 2010 in both *Megamind* and *Despicable Me*) and appearing fresh anyway. Nine-foot tall, six hundred-plus pound

Ralph (voiced by John C. Reilly) has had it with the social stigmas attached to his line of work. For thirty years he has served as the bad guy in the videogame "Fix It Felix, Jr.," in which Felix the carpenter (Jack McBrayer) earns the admiration and friendship of an apartment building's residents everyday as he repairs the damage Ralph causes. Ralph's reward for his work: A lonely post-work life, when he trudges off to the nearby dump to sleep against a stump, on top of a pile of bricks. That is not glory; that is discomfort.

As Ralph knows from the support group he attends, in which classic video game villains like Bowser of *Super Mario Brothers* and Zangief of *Street Fighter* meet to establish a support system for each other, just because he is a bad guy does not mean that he is, so to speak, a bad guy. "I am bad, and that's good" goes the mantra of characters just doing what they are programmed to do. Fortunately for Ralph, in *Wreck-It Ralph* characters are able to move between games, traveling through power cords as if they were tiny tunnels through which the virtual world commutes to and from the office. If characters die inside their own game, no worries; the game will start over and they will be fine. If characters die outside their game, Sonic the Hedgehog reminds them in the gaming world's central station, they will not regenerate. Ignoring this risk, Ralph hops over to "Hero's Duty", a game where soldiers and their leader (Jane Lynch) battle cyborq-esque bugs while the human player competes for a medal. If Ralph wins the medal, he thinks, then Felix and everyone else back home will see that so-called bad guys can win medals too. Perhaps then they will see Ralph differently and invite him to parties and treat him like one of the gang, not just the guy employed to destroy their home on a daily basis.

This story could wither without lively visuals, but *Wreck-It Ralph*, the feature directorial debut by Rich Moore (*Futurama*, *The Simpsons*) delivers a world as engaging as a video game without the boredom that comes from watching someone else playing. Never staying in one place for very long but never succumbing to an overly manic sense of pace, the film moves from one game to the next with agility and verve, especially when Ralph winds up in "Sugar Rush", a candy go-kart game in which he meets perky Vanellope (Sarah Silverman). She is eager to join the ranks of the game's go-kart racers, even as the other inhabitants of this candy-covered society—imagine a Willy Wonka video game designed by Katy Perry—insist she is merely an unwanted glitch in the system. Like Ralph, Vanellope feels left out, and their initially rocky relationship gives way to a sweet tale of characters realizing that their inclusion will come not from their own change of behavior but others discovering what they are missing.

If only *Wreck-It Ralph* were funnier. The script by Phil Johnston (*Cedar Rapids* [2011]) and Jennifer Lee fares far better when it is endearing (such as when Ralph, told to make his momma proud in "Hero's Duty", shouts "I love my momma!") rather than childish (numerous jokes are made confusing "duty" and "doody"). The film also introduces a difficult moral question—is it right to prevent someone from following their dreams if the thing they want most may get them killed?—only to back away in favor of a more clear-cut story of clear-cut heroes and villains.

No bother. The 3-D is too effortlessly amusing, particularly in a glorious and surprisingly moving scene in which Ralph and Vanellope use a machine that helps them bake a go-kart. The tale of a big galoot winning over those not predisposed to dislike him taps into the danger of group think while working within traditional family movie tropes about friendship and identity. (Though most films targeted at little ones do not include a message about the importance of taking pride in a job despite a lack of positive feedback. This may be more useful for the maligned work ethic of millennials.) *Wreck-It Ralph* may not end with as much exhilaration as it begins, but it easily one-ups recent efforts like *Tangled* (2010) in the film's ability to deliver a product for kids and older viewers alike without feeling like a vapid retread of the same old lessons solely for the purposes of merchandising. Certainly young ones may be motivated to buy toy replicas of Ralph and Vanellope and the flamboyant King Candy (Alan Tudyk), but they may also want Q*bert and an old version of "Burger Time."

At a time when video games are only growing more intense—Ralph even notes during "Hero's Duty." "When did video games become so violent and scary?"—that sincere nostalgia for simpler, friendlier virtual communication easily earns a medal of its own.

Matt Pais

CREDITS

Wreck-It Ralph: John C. Reilly (Voice)

Vanellope von Schweetz: Sarah Silverman (Voice)

Fix-It Felix: Jack McBrayer (Voice)

Sergeant Calhoun: Jane Lynch (Voice)

King Candy: Alan Tudyk (Voice)

Origin: United States

Language: English

Released: 2012

Production: Clark Spencer; Walt Disney Animation Studios; released by Walt Disney Pictures

Directed by: Rich Moore

Written by: Jennifer Lee; Phil Johnston
Music by: Henry Jackman
Sound: Frank E. Eulner
Music Supervisor: Tom MacDougall
Editing: William Caparella
Art Direction: Ian Gooding
MPAA rating: PG
Running time: 101 minutes

REVIEWS

Burr, Ty. *Boston Globe.* November 1, 2012.
Ebert, Roger. *Chicago Sun-Times.* October 31, 2012.
Goodykoontz, Bill. *Arizona Republic.* November 3, 2012.
Phillips, Michael. *Chicago Tribune.* November 1, 2012.
Pols, Mary. *Time.* November 1, 2012.
Puig, Claudia. *USA Today.* November 1, 2012.
Rickey, Carrie. *Philadelphia Inquirer.* November 1, 2012.
Robinson, Tasha. *AV Club.* October 31, 2012.
Scott, A. O. *New York Times.* November 1, 2012.
Semley, John. *Slant Magazine.* October 28, 2012.

QUOTES

Wreck-It Ralph: "I'm bad, and that's good. I will never be good, and that's not bad. There's no one I'd rather be than me."

TRIVIA

Unlike most animated films, the principal actors regularly recorded audio sessions together in the same room, a situation which led to a lot of improvisation.

AWARDS

Nominations:

Oscars 2012: Animated Film
Golden Globes 2013: Animated Film

WUTHERING HEIGHTS

Box Office: $100,915

The criticisms inevitably launched at Andrea Arnold's audacious adaptation of Emily Bronte's classic 1847 novel evoke memories of the backlash against Terrence Malick's *The Tree of Life* (2011). It is too slow, too subdued, and does not contain nearly enough plot. At least Arnold spared these irascible viewers of CGI dinosaurs. More than anything, these complaints indicate a lack of adventurousness on the part of moviegoers desiring to have everything handed to them on a take-out platter. If that is the way that they prefer

their cinematic morsels to be served, then they have a great many other screen versions of *Wuthering Heights* to choose from, beginning with William Wyler's Oscar-nominated classics.

The leading man of Wyler's film, Laurence Olivier, has a key feature in common with the actors who have inherited the role in subsequent years, including Timothy Dalton, Ralph Fiennes, and Tom Hardy. They all have white skin, which is in stark contrast to Bronte's original character of Heathcliffe, described in the book as "dark-skinned." Arnold's controversial decision to cast a black actor as Heathcliffe makes her film far more faithful to Bronte's vision while illuminating the racism that fuels the discrimination he faces at the titular gloomy English moorland.

Yet this is merely one detail that sets Arnold's picture apart from past filmic incarnations of the familiar yarn. Instead of getting bogged down in long-winded dialogue passages buckling under the weight of over-wrought sentiment, Arnold portrays the hormonal bond between two would-be lovers in near-wordless passages of arresting naturalistic beauty. In purely visual terms, the first hour or so of Arnold's film is the most captivating screen romance since Jane Campion's *Bright Star* (2010). She captures the sensuality reverberating beneath the shared gazes of young Heathcliffe (Solomon Glave) and Catherine (Shannon Beer) without collapsing into creepy prurience.

Nudity is suggested on multiple occasions, but never witnessed in full. Consider the initial encounter between Heathcliffe and Catherine at the farmhouse owned by stern Mr. Earnshaw (Paul Hilton). The religiously devout patriarch has decided that it would be the duty of an upstanding Christian to have the orphaned boy live with his family. Yet Heathcliffe is treated with hostility the instant he walks through the door and is quickly stripped of his clothes for a forcible scrub-down. The eyes of Earnshaw's rebellious daughter, Catherine, peer out from behind a door, spying on the stranger in his nakedness as he becomes gradually aware of her presence. Later, Catherine is seen pulling on her nightgown as Heathcliffe watches, thus implying that she undressed in front of him.

Of course, there is more to this near-coupling than sexual lust. Catherine is perhaps the only person ever to show Heathcliffe a shred of tenderness and compassion. With his eyes blurred by the harsh sunlight and his body knocked to the ground by Earnshaw's hot-headed son, Hindley (Lee Shaw), Catherine is the one to pull him back on his feet. They run across the moor with wild abandon, basking in the roar of a monstrous wind while savoring their fleeting illusion of independence. Cinematographer Robbie Ryan's decision to shoot the film in a classical 1.33:1 aspect ratio is appropriate, since the claustrophobia of their societally imposed prison quickly entraps them within separate cells. Some critics have argued that this stylistic flourish neuters the plot's emotional impact a la Joe Wright's *Anna Karenina* (2012), but this claim could not be further from the truth.

Ryan's vivid close-ups, often viewed from Heathcliffe's perspective, magnify the countless sublime details destined to haunt his mind in later years. He allows the audience to feel the strands of Catherine's hair as they glide across Heathcliffe's face or the coldness of her tongue as it licks the bloody scars on his back left by a slave driver's lash. Inexpressive actors may have killed Arnold's meticulously textured mood, but her two pint-sized leads are splendid discoveries. Glave has a commanding screen presence reminiscent of a young Sidney Poitier, while Beer nails the fragility of an enraptured heart. The look of desire that materializes on her face as Heathcliffe playfully pins her to the ground is destined to haunt viewers long after the credits have rolled.

Alas, the second half of Arnold's film is more problematic, relying too heavily on expository dialogue while recasting the central roles with adult actors so far removed from their young counterparts that they hardly seem like the same characters. Perhaps that is why editor Nicolas Chaudeurge felt compelled to include so many flashbacks in order to evoke the magic of the film's earlier passages. Whereas Beer's Catherine exuded earthy accessibility, Kaya Scodelario (the ravishing beauty best known for BBC's *Skins*) is lensed as an ethereal object of desire as unattainable as Daisy in *The Great Gatsby* or Estella in *Great Expectations*. Of course, this is in keeping with Catherine's transformation into a socially acceptable lady, but Scodelario does not have enough screen time to adequately convey the spiritually wounded woman concealed within the polished costumes.

As for James Howson's Heathcliffe, he remains a frustrating enigma whose off-screen transition into a gentleman is left maddeningly unexplained. Like most filmmakers tackling Bronte's novel, Arnold avoids exploring chapters 18 through 34, which detail Heathcliffe's cold-blooded methods of revenge against the Earnshaw family, though she does include shades of his embittered cruelty, such as when he hangs the family dog. The emotional heart of the film's somewhat underwhelming final hour turns out to be Nichola Burley as Isabella, the smitten sister of Catherine's husband, Edgar (James Northcote), who becomes a strategic object of manipulation for the cold-blooded Heathcliffe.

Regardless of its flaws, this is still a pleasingly chilled corker of a tone poem, as physical and visceral as Arnold's previous features, *Fish Tank* (2009) and *Red Road*

(2006). It does precisely what Wright's *Karenina* had so dearly strived to do: revitalize a time-worn classic of literature. At its best, Arnold's *Wuthering Heights* translates Bronte's words into an exhilarating pictorial roadmap of a human heart wedged delicately between ecstasy and despair. Bronte's language is scarcely utilized, but it is felt in every frame.

Matt Fagerholm

CREDITS

Catherine Earnshaw: Kaya Scodelario
Heathcliff: James Howson
Hindley Earnshaw: Lee Shaw
Young Catherine: Shannon Beer
Young Heathcliff: Solomon Glave
Mr. Earnshaw: Paul Hilton
Ellen Dean: Simone Jackson
Isabella Linton: Nichola Burley
Edagr Linton: James Northcote
Frances Earnshaw: Amy Wren
Joseph: Steve Evets
Origin: United Kingdom
Language: English
Released: 2012
Production: Douglas Rae, Kevin Loader, Robin Bernstein; released by Ecosse Films
Directed by: Andrea Arnold
Written by: Andrea Arnold; Olivia Hetread
Cinematography by: Robbie Ryan
Sound: Nicolas Becker
Editing: Nicolas Chaudeurge
Art Direction: Christopher Wyatt
Costumes: Steven Noble
Production Design: Helen Scott
MPAA rating: Unrated
Running time: 129 minutes

REVIEWS

Burr, Ty. *Boston Globe*. October 18, 2012.
Lanthier, Joseph Jon. *Slant Magazine*. October 1, 2012.
Lyttelton, Oliver. *The Playlist*. October 4, 2012.
O'Hehir, Andrew. *Salon.com*. October 6, 2012.
Phillips, Michael. *Chicago Tribune*. November 29, 2012.
Phipps, Keith. *AV Club*. October 3, 2012.
Rothkopf, Joshua. *Time Out New York*. October 2, 2012.
Schwarzbaum, Lisa. *Entertainment Weekly*. October 3, 2012.
Sharkey, Betsy. *Los Angeles Times*. October 12, 2012.
VanDenburgh, Barbara. *Arizona Republic*. October 23, 2012.

TRIVIA

Casting director Gail Stevens and her team held open calls and wandered the streets of Leeds, Sheffield, York, and Bradford looking for likely Heathcliffs.

Y

YOUR SISTER'S SISTER

A comedy about doing the right thing with the wrong person.
—Movie tagline

Box Office: $1.6 million

Jack and Hannah have just met. They are about as far removed from an ideal coupling as one could possibly imagine. He is a disheveled young man reeling from the death of his less-than-beloved brother. She is an embittered lesbian fresh off a failed seven-year-relationship. Yet on one inebriated morning, this unlikely pair's mutual pain and desire for a connection leads to fleeting, gloriously awkward encounter in the sack.

Such is the set-up for the fourth feature by Lynn Shelton, a filmmaker skilled in pushing sexual boundaries with endearing humanism. Just as her 2009 effort *Humpday* subverted the bromance genre by exploring the homoerotic tendencies of heterosexual men, *Your Sister's Sister* illuminates the bisexuality of people otherwise comfortable in their orientation. Yet that is merely one ingredient in its richly layered smorgasbord of authentically messy human relationships. Few modern provocateurs are as gifted at breaking taboos without damaging the accessibility of their work.

One reason Shelton's films work as well as they do is their peerless casting. Mark Duplass, the "mumblecore" poster child best known for helming 2005's marvelously bittersweet anti-romance, *The Puffy Chair*, has subsequently proven to be one of the most reliably engaging actors in recent cinema (his filmography already includes such diverse titles as *Safety Not Guaranteed* [2012] and *Zero Dark Thirty* [2012]). He projects earthy masculin-

ity devoid of the airbrushed polish that causes many a studio-approved everyman to resemble flesh-colored mannequins. As Jack, Duplass cloaks his character's wounds in angry indifference while still managing to salvage his puppy dog charm.

Enter Iris, Jack's longtime friend, played by the radiantly compassionate Emily Blunt. She valiantly holds her tongue during the increasingly squirm-inducing memorial gathering for Jack's departed brother. When the heartfelt reminiscence of a friend (Mike Birbiglia in a pitch-perfect cameo) is venomously tweaked by Jack, Iris decides that enough is enough. She orders him to stay at her family's isolated cabin for a few days in order to get his bearings. That is where Jack accidentally encounters Iris' half-sister, Hannah, played by Rosemarie DeWitt in one of the finest supporting performances of 2012.

Resisting every cliched approach to a very tricky role, DeWitt nails her character's lethal hybrid of self-pity and self-loathing that leads her to grab hold of an opportunity without considering its repercussions. Shelton allows Jack and Hannah's early morning conversation to unfold in simple, stationary shots devoid of the jagged movement and quick zooms that have marred some of Duplass's recent directorial efforts. Shelton's painstaking focus on dialogue and performances is Bermanesque without falling into the trap of pretension. At its best, *Your Sister's Sister* plays like a night of first-rate theatre in which the viewer is afforded the best seat in the house.

Once Iris enters the cabin for an impromptu visit, it soon becomes apparent that she has deeper feelings for Jack than Hannah would have ever expected. Misunderstandings start mounting on top of last-second deceptions as Shelton takes perverse pleasure in lingering in the multitude of delicious ironies as they materialize one after another. A few moments tip dangerously close toward slapstick-prone, *Three's Company* territory, as Jack douses himself with a ridiculous amount of water to appear as if he just came back from a jog. Yet for the most part, Shelton's improv-based script is more evocative of vintage Woody Allen than subpar sitcoms. DeWitt and Blunt masterfully portray the catharsis of a familial bond tinged with the pain of intimacy that cuts too deep. All three of these characters know each other all too well.

Consistent throughout the picture is the theme of family or the lack thereof, typified by the moment when a lonely Jack passes a Thanksgiving sign while aboard on his creaky bicycle. The bond between Shelton's troubled trio breaks so many conventions that it occasionally threatens to spiral into chaos. DeWitt's performance erupts into a hurricane of conflicted emotions during the film's riveting climax, which unfortunately leads to an all-too tidy denouement. Yet the strength of the film's final minutes is the extent of what is left off-screen. Shelton is less interested in the specifics of her characters' future than whether or not they are prepared to face it. As unforgettably proven by Sean Durkin's *Martha Marcy May Marlene* (2011), an ambiguous cut to black resonates with far more satisfying results than a protracted fade-out.

This is the sort of small-scale gem that becomes more impressive the more one learns about its backstory. Shelton's constrained 12-day shooting schedule hit a disastrous obstacle when one of the film's leading ladies, Rachel Weisz, dropped out of the project, thus leaving the director to find an immediate replacement for Hannah. Despite having little to no background in improvisation, DeWitt flew to the set and made the most out of the three days allotted for her to prepare for the role. The fact that she returned for Shelton's next project, *Touchy Feely* (2013), is a testament to the triumphant brew of spontaneous chemistry that took place on the set of *Your Sister's Sister*. It sets a high water mark for any filmmaker attempting to honestly portray the dimensions and impulsive foibles of the human heart.

Matt Fagerholm

CREDITS

Al: Mike Birbiglia
Hannah: Rosemarie DeWitt
Iris: Emily Blunt
Jack: Mark Duplass
Origin: United States
Language: English
Released: 2011
Production: Steven Schardt; Ada Films; released by IFC Films
Directed by: Lynn Shelton
Written by: Lynn Shelton
Cinematography by: Benjamin Kasulke
Music by: Vinny Smith
Sound: Vinny Smith
Music Supervisor: Mel Eslyn; Sandy Wilson
Editing: Nat Sanders
Production Design: John Lavin
MPAA rating: R
Running time: 90 minutes

REVIEWS

Chang, Justin. *Variety*. April 4, 2012.
Crocker, Jonathan. *Total Film*. June 21, 2012.
Ebert, Roger. *Chicago Sun-Times*. June 13, 2012.
Fujishima, Kenji. *Slant Magazine*. June 9, 2012.
Jones, J. R. *Chicago Reader*. June 13, 2012.
Kohn, Eric. *indieWIRE*. June 10, 2012.
Lane, Anthony. *New Yorker*. June 22, 2012.
Puig, Claudia. *USA Today*. June 28, 2012.
Schwarzbaum, Lisa. *Entertainment Weekly*. June 13, 2012.
Scott, A. O. *New York Times*. June 14, 2012.

TRIVIA

This film was shot in just twelve days and was largely improvised.

AWARDS

Nominations:

Ind. Spirit 2013: Actress—Supporting (DeWitt)

Z

ZERO DARK THIRTY

The greatest manhunt in history.
—Movie tagline

*For ten years one woman never stopped searching
for the most wanted man in history.*
—Movie tagline

Box Office: $91.9 million

Kathryn Bigelow's *Zero Dark Thirty* opens with a title card of that fateful September day in 2001 and the audio of phone calls from panicked people still trapped inside the towers. No one likes to be reminded of images from those moments, but the voice mail messages sound like the ghosts of a time that still haunts the national consciousness. How can people, particularly those directly affected by the losses in those hours, move on when the ramifications of it are felt everyday through regulations, an ongoing war against terror and the general fear that lingers that it could one day happen again? Like any compromise in finding the bare minimum that will satisfy people, revenge is certainly a dish best served cold. The team behind *The Hurt Locker* (2009) have certainly found a cinematic way to do that and maybe all too well for our own good.

From the sounds of over three-thousand lives snuffed out that morning, Bigelow's film flashes inside a detainee cell two years later where anger is still very much alive in CIA interrogator Dan (Jason Clarke). With an Al-Qaeda money-handler chained up, he repeats his most stringent rule—"When you lie, I hurt you." Witness to both physical torture and mental humiliation is CIA analyst Maya (Jessica Chastain), clearly uncomfortable with the methods being used to extract

information. She does not question or second-guess Dan. Instead, her frustration grows in not getting the next dot on the trail connected. When the prisoner appeals to her as the apparent good-cop in the room, she tells him bluntly "You can help yourself by being truthful." Maya is not going to settle for anything less until she finds Osama Bin Laden.

Her journey for the truth will take her all over the world, searching for the underlings in Bin Laden's network. One of her few friends turns out to be another female colleague (Jennifer Ehle); the two start off contentious but quickly bond as they witness—in some cases first-hand—the continuing string of terror attacks against civilians. In the wake of little progress, her biggest adversary turns out to be the regional CIA ambassador (Kyle Chandler), who, like everyone, is under tremendous pressure from his superior (Mark Strong) to produce results. For eight years, Maya's search leads toward many cold trails and colleagues unwilling to follow through on her theories. But when the inhabitants of a heavily suspicious residence in Pakistan raise a few eyebrows, it is only a matter of time before the greenlight is given on the most infamous Navy SEAL mission ever.

Prior to the grand payoff that anyone not living in a cave knows full well is coming, *Zero Dark Thirty* takes viewers through the not-so-grand period of the hunt for the man, who became the most wanted target for nearly a decade. Director Kathryn Bigelow and screenwriter Mark Boal are not afraid to get their hands dirty, plunging us directly into interrogation methods that have drawn strong criticism even from those who still had not seen the film. Politicians, still irksome over the thought that torture was used to extract information, went so far as to ask the filmmakers to redact those scenes from the final print. While certainly harsh in their presentation, at no point do Bigelow and Boal make any succinct connection between these early scenes with Clarke and the endgame of the eventual extraction of Bin Laden's life. This film no more embraces the concept of torture than *Schindler's List* (1993) advocated Nazism and genocide. These are things that happened, for better or worse, and this film's unwavering manner of not offering commentary on it is a part of the cold approach that makes it equally riveting and less superior than other films of its ilk.

Boal has constructed his film in the standard structure of a police procedural. The target is established, a top cop is presented who will turn a case into a lifelong obsession, opposition is provided on her own team, and it all leads to a final showdown in a house. Chastain's Maya, while reportedly based on a real-life character, feels more like Clarice Starling from *The Silence of the Lambs* (1991) or Claire Danes' Carrie Mathison from TV's *Homeland* (only without the emotional baggage of either). Unless it is a direct reaction to being in the line of fire, either literally or figuratively from her superiors, Maya suppresses nearly all human characteristics aside from frustration. Though the film has the semblance of an arc for her, it is never quite clear if this is a woman putting on a brave face in the aftermath of horror or truly the confident crusader who can stand in front of a room full of men announcing herself as the twelve-lettered mask of justice that she describes herself as. Not every decision and emotion needs to be documented. Liam Neeson's Oskar Schindler did not announce his grand shift in his chess-play with the Nazi party, but when he shed tears over what he could have done it was a tear for every life lost and everyone who could do nothing. Maya's single tear at the end feels like one just for herself.

Whether culled from the classified headlines or an amalgam of those at the forefront of the Bin Laden hunt, the more interesting connection with Maya could just be to the very director bringing her to life. Kathryn Bigelow has made a career within the genres generally populated and embraced by men. Though she did bring a feminine slant to psycho-thriller *Blue Steel* (1990), everything else on her resume—from the vampire western mash-up *Near Dark* (1987) to bank-robbing surfing film *Point Break* (1991) with the tagline "100 pure adrenaline" to the award-winning *The Hurt Locker* that made her the first woman in history to grab the Best Director Oscar—hardly reads as the kind of touchy-feely rom-com emotional dramedys often stereotypically ascribed to female filmmakers. Maya is similarly a solo woman in a guy's world, not the girl who sleeps her way to the top—as Bigelow's brief marriage to James Cameron might imply for some—producing solid results to very little direct success. Watching her exasperated at the waiting game it takes before she can get the greenlight to pursue her next big move could be read as any period of Bigelow's career—particularly after the financial failure of *Strange Days* (1995)—until she finally went her own way and rode an independently-produced mission about soldiers defusing bombs to glory. In many ways, like Maya, Bigelow's entire career has been leading up to the moment where she finally gets to kill the biggest, baddest villain several generations have known. And when the moment finally arrives, it does not seem nearly as satisfying as it might have ten years ago.

"Do you realize what you just did," asks a member of the SEAL team after the killshot heard round the world has been applied. The question is an important one and the answer even moreso depending on the context. The accomplished mission, eight years after a ship banner proclaimed it so, might bring some sense of closure to those who lost loved ones on 9/11. Maybe it is a simple high-five moment that provides heroic gratification to a few people, if not only one man, to tell their grandkids that they were the one to pull the trigger. In the course of *Zero Dark Thirty*, it is merely a signal that closure to the movie is right around the corner.

As a procedural, Bigelow's direction and pacing is spot-on. The manner in which an audience is involved in this manhunt could probably be achieved by virtually anyone though and, aside from the final raid, nothing comes close to matching the tension of any one of the vignettes of *The Hurt Locker*. Neither matched are the personalities behind the mission. Despite confident turns by Jason Clarke, Mark Strong, and, at times, Chastain, none can really match the obsessive personality of Jeremy Renner's William James. The need to do their job comes second to the more vital question of precisely why they are doing these jobs; a question that is only mildly raised as an occasional afterthought. Mark Boal's screenplay avoids this kind of background context that could have brought greater perspective to a search that was a combination of tremendous cross-continental legwork, political interference and, occasionally, downright incompetence. One major sequence, in particular, involving the meeting of a high-ranking enemy operative is a failure in both truth and fiction. Despite its apparent real-life outcome, the manner in which it is staged is cliched cinema, tried and true, with smart people doing dumb things at the worst possible time and nobody considering the endgame in a job where the worst happens every day. It is an exceptionally awful, telegraphed scene.

The manner of flaws to be found can be attributed to Boal's script which contains at least one cliche for every declassified first-hand account. Keeping nearly all manner of politics and overview away from the film, just as he did in *The Hurt Locker*, is not an unfair approach and puts the onus on the viewer to form their own intelligence. But it prevents the film from being on par with a film like *Munich* (2005), with its eye-for-an-eye vengeance and the whys behind it were felt well beyond its final shot. In-between the brutality of its opening and the waiting game around Washington, *Zero Dark Thirty*'s step-by-step procedural does not share the same kind of verbal thrust found in *All the President's Men* (1976) or *The Insider* (1999) nor driving home the shared obsession of David Fincher's true-crime timeline thriller, *Zodiac* (2007). For pure visceral in-the-moment thrills, it is unfair to compare it directly to Paul Greengrass' exemplary *United 93* (2006), though tacking on its two hours as a prologue to Bigelow's film would provide the necessary context lacking within the drive of Boal's second act. When the call does comes through that it is time to get America's proverbial white whale, it is near impossible to not feel a chill. Everything has been leading to this moment and if it is the only thing one comes out of the theater remembering—well then mission accomplished.

Erik Childress

CREDITS

Dan: Jason Clarke
Maya: Jessica Chastain
Joseph Bradley: Kyle Chandler
George: Mark Strong
Patrick: Joel Edgerton
Justin: Chris Pratt
Origin: United States
Language: English
Released: 2012
Production: Megan Ellison, Kathryn Bigelow, Mark Boal; First Light Productions, Annapurna Prod.; released by Columbia Pictures
Directed by: Kathryn Bigelow
Written by: Mark Boal
Cinematography by: Greig Fraser

Music by: Alexandre Desplat
Sound: Paul N.J. Ottosson
Music Supervisor: John Bissell
Editing: William Goldenberg; Dylan Tichenor
Art Direction: Rod McLean
Costumes: George L. Little
Production Design: Jeremy Hindle
MPAA rating: R
Running time: 157 minutes

REVIEWS

Berardinelli, James. *ReelViews*. December 18, 2012.
Dargis, Manohla. *New York Times*. December 17, 2012.
Edelstein, David. *New York Magazine*. December 10, 2012.
Fine, Marshall. *Hollywood & Fine*. December 19, 2012.
Kenny, Glenn. *MSN Movies*. December 17, 2012.
Morgenstern, Joe. *Wall Street Journal*. December 20, 2012.
Phillips, Michael. *Chicago Tribune*. January 3, 2013.
Sawin, Chris. *Examiner.com*. December 22, 2012.
Tobias, Scott. *AV Club*. December 18, 2012.
Vaux, Rob. *Mania.com*. December 20, 2012.

QUOTES

Maya: "I'm going to smoke everyone involved in this op and then I'm going to kill bin Laden."

TRIVIA

Rooney Mara was originally cast in the lead role, but had to drop out and was replaced by Jessica Chastain.

AWARDS

Oscars 2012: Sound FX Editing
Golden Globes 2013: Actress—Drama (Chastain)
Writers Guild 2012: Orig. Screenplay
Nominations:
Oscars 2012: Actress (Chastain), Film, Film Editing, Orig. Screenplay
British Acad. 2012: Actress (Chastain), Director (Bigelow), Film, Film Editing, Orig. Screenplay
Directors Guild 2012: Director (Bigelow)
Golden Globes 2013: Director (Bigelow), Film—Drama, Screenplay
Screen Actors Guild 2012: Actress (Chastain)

List of Awards

Academy Awards

Film: *Argo*

Animated Film: *Brave*

Director: Ang Lee (*Life of Pi*)

Actor: Daniel Day-Lewis (*Lincoln*)

Actress: Jennifer Lawrence (*Silver Linings Playbook*)

Supporting Actor: Christoph Waltz (*Django Unchained*)

Supporting Actress: Anne Hathaway (*Les Miserables*)

Original Screenplay: Quentin Tarantino (*Django Unchained*)

Adapted Screenplay: Chris Terrio (*Argo*)

Cinematography: Claudio Miranda (*Life of Pi*)

Editing: William Goldenberg (*Argo*)

Art Direction: Rick Carter and Jim Erickson (*Lincoln*)

Visual Effects: Bill Westenhofer, Guillaume Rocheron, Erik De Boer, and Donald Elliott (*Life of Pi*)

Sound: Andy Nelson, Mark Paterson, and Simon Hayes (*Les Miserables*)

Sound Editing: Per Hallberg and Karen M. Baker (*Skyfall*) and Paul N.J. Ottosson (*Zero Dark Thirty*)

Makeup: Lisa Westcott and Julie Dartnell (*Les Miserables*)

Costume Design: Jacqueline Durran (*Anna Karenina*)

Original Score: Mychael Danna (*Life of Pi*)

Original Song: "Skyfall" (Adele and Paul Epworth *Skyfall*)

Foreign Language Film: *Amour*

Documentary, Feature: *Searching for Sugar Man*

Documentary, Short Subject: *Inocente*

Short Film, Animated: *Paperman*

Short Film, Live Action: *Curfew*

British Academy of Film & Television Awards

Animated Film: *Brave*

Film: *Argo*

Outstanding British Film: *Skyfall*

Director: Ben Affleck (*Argo*)

Original Screenplay: Quentin Tarantino (*Django Unchained*)

Adapted Screenplay: David O. Russell (*Silver Linings Playbook*)

Actor: Daniel Day-Lewis (*Lincoln*)

Actress: Emmanuelle Riva (*Amour*)

Supporting Actor: Christoph Waltz (*Django Unchained*)

Supporting Actress: Anne Hathaway (*Les Miserables*)

Editing: Billy Goldenberg (*Argo*)

Cinematography: Claudio Miranda (*Life of Pi*)

Production Design: Eve Stewart and Anna Lynch-Robinson (*Les Miserables*)

Costume Design: Jacqueline Durran (*Anna Karenina*)

Makeup: Lisa Westcott and Julie Dartnell (*Les Miserables*)

Sound: Andy Nelson, Mark Paterson, and Simon Hayes (*Les Miserables*)

Visual Effects: Bill Westenhofer, Guillaume Rocheron, Erik De Boer, and Donald Elliott (*Life of Pi*)

Music: Thomas Newman (*Skyfall*)

Outstanding Debut by a British Writer, Director, or Producer: Bart Layton and Dimitri Doganis (*The Imposter*)

Best Documentary Film: *Searching for Sugar Man*

Foreign Film: *Amour*

Short Animation: *The Making of Longbird*

Short Film: *Swimmer*

Directors Guild of America Awards

Outstanding Directorial Achievement in Motion Pictures: Ben Affleck (*Argo*)

Outstanding Directorial Achievement in Documentary: Malik Bendjelloul (*Searching for Sugar Man*)

Golden Globes

Film, Drama: *Argo*

Film, Musical or Comedy: *Les Miserables*

Animated Film: *Brave*

Director: Ben Affleck (*Argo*)

Actor, Drama: Daniel Day-Lewis (*Lincoln*)

Actor, Musical or Comedy: Hugh Jackman (*Les Miserables*)

Actress, Drama: Jessica Chastain (*Zero Dark Thirty*)

Actress, Musical or Comedy: Jennifer Lawrence (*Silver Linings Playbook*)

Supporting Actor: Christoph Waltz (*Django Unchained*)

Supporting Actress: Anne Hathaway (*Les Miserables*)

Screenplay: Quentin Tarantino (*Django Unchained*)

Score: Mychael Danna (*Life of Pi*)

Song: "Skyfall" (Adele and Paul Epworth, *Skyfall*)

Foreign Language Film: *Amour*

Golden Raspberry Awards

Worst Picture: *The Twilight Saga: Breaking Dawn - Part 2*

Worst Director: Bill Condon (*The Twilight Saga: Breaking Dawn - Part 2*)

Worst Actor: Adam Sandler (*That's My Boy*)

Worst Actress: Kristen Stewart (*Snow White and the Huntsman* and *The Twilight Saga: Breaking Dawn - Part 2*)

Worst Supporting Actor: Taylor Lautner (*The Twilight Saga: Breaking Dawn - Part 2*)

Worst Supporting Actress: Rihanna (*Battleship*)

Worst Screenplay: David Caspe (*That's My Boy*)

Worst Screen Couple: Taylor Lautner and Mackenzie Foy (*The Twilight Saga: Breaking Dawn - Part 2*)

Worst Prequel, Remake, Rip-Off or Sequel: *The Twilight Saga: Breaking Dawn - Part 2*

Worst Screen Ensemble: The Entire Cast *The Twilight Saga: Breaking Dawn - Part 2*

Independent Spirit Awards

Film: *Silver Linings Playbook*

First Film: *The Perks of Being a Wallflower*

Director: David O. Russell (*Silver Linings Playbook*)

Actor: John Hawkes (*The Sessions*)

Actress: Jennifer Lawrence (*Silver Linings Playbook*)

Supporting Actor: Matthew McConaughey (*Magic Mike*)

Supporting Actress: Helen Hunt (*The Sessions*)

Screenplay: David O. Russell (*Silver Linings Playbook*)

First Screenplay: Derek Connolly (*Safety Not Guaranteed*)

Cinematography: Ben Richardson (*Beasts of the Southern Wild*)

Foreign Film: *Amour*

Documentary: *The Invisible War*

Truer than Fiction Award: *The Waiting Room*

Robert Altman Award: *Starlet*

John Cassavetes Award: *Middle of Nowhere*

Screen Actors Guild Awards

Actor: Daniel Day-Lewis (*Lincoln*)

Actress: Jennifer Lawrence (*Silver Linings Playbook*)

Supporting Actor: Tommy Lee Jones (*Lincoln*)

Supporting Actress: Anne Hathaway (*Les Miserables*)

Ensemble Cast: *Argo*

Writers Guild of America Awards

Original Screenplay: Mark Boal (*Zero Dark Thirty*)

Adapted Screenplay: Chris Terrio (*Argo*)

Documentary Screenplay: Malik Bendjelloul (*Searching for Sugar Man*)

Obituaries

Ian Abercrombie (September 11, 1934–January 26, 2012). Born in Grays, Essex, England, Ian Abercrombie got his start on the British stage as a child actor during World War II, moving to the United States at the age of 17. He was still a very young actor when he made his stage debut across from Jason Robards in 1955. Many years later, Abercrombie would become something of an icon in the sci-fi/Comic-Con community, appearing as Alfred Pennyworth in TV's *Birds of Prey,* in Sam Raimi's *Army of Darkness* (1993), and voicing several characters in the Lucas-verse, including Palpatine in the animated *Clone Wars* TV series and film (2008). He would also voice the role in video games based on *Star Wars* along with a lot of other voice work in games and animated films. Major credits include *The Ice Pirates* (1984), *Twin Peaks* (1992), *Addams Family Values* (1993), *The Lost World: Jurassic Park* (1997), *Inland Empire* (2006), and *Rango* (2011). Many TV fans will most fondly remember Abercrombie as Elaine's boss from the sixth season of *Seinfeld*. He passed away from kidney failure at the age of 77.

Bob Anderson (September 15, 1922–January 1, 2012). Born in Gosport, Hampshire, England, Bob Anderson would become arguably the most important fencer in the history of cinema, using his experience as an English Olympic fencer to work on films that required swordplay, including work with Errol Flynn, Sean Connery, Johnny Depp, Antonio Banderas, and the actors in the *Star Wars* franchise. His film career began when he coached Flynn for his work in *The Master of Ballantine* (1953) and continued through stunt work and fight choreography on classics like *The Guns of Navarone* (1961), *From Russia with Love* (1963), and *Barry Lyndon* (1975). Arguably his most influential work would come after that film with Stanley Kubrick as George Lucas tapped him to coordinate lightsaber choreography for his *Star Wars* (1977) films. He would work regularly in major films for his whole career, including *Highlander* (1986), *The Princess Bride* (1987), *The Three Musketeers* (1993), *The Mask of Zorro* (1998), *Pirates of the Caribbean:*

The Curse of the Black Pearl (2003), *The Lord of the Rings* (2001-03) trilogy, and even this year's *The Hobbit: An Unexpected Journey* (2012).

R.G. Armstrong (April 7, 1917–July 27, 2012). American actor and playwright Robert Golden Armstrong, Jr. was born in Pleasant Grove, Alabama, where he grew up on a farm that would clearly influence his classically American approach to acting and filmmaking. He actually worked with Andy Griffith at the University of North Carolina in Chapel Hill before making his debut on Broadway in *Cat on a Hot Tin Roof*. His first film appearance was in *Garden of Eden* in 1954 but he would spend most of his career in TV westerns in the 1950s and 1960s, hitting all of the major ones, including *Gunsmoke, Rawhide,* and *Maverick*. TV would be his major source of work for decades but Sam Peckinpah saw the film potential in the actor, casting him in several films, including *Ride the High Country* (1962), *Major Dundee* (1965), *The Ballad of Cable Hogue* (1970), and *Pat Garrett and Billy the Kid* (1973). Other major film credits include *El Dorado* (1966), *Race with the Devil* (1975), *Heaven Can Wait* (1978), *Reds* (1981), *Children of the Corn* (1984), *Predator* (1987), and *Dick Tracy* (1990). He died at the age of 95 in his California home, survived by four children from his first of three marriages.

Luke Askew (March 26, 1932–March 29, 2012). With his distinctive name and manner, the Macon, Georgia-born Luke Askew was a familiar face to moviegoers in the 1960s and 1970s through a number of supporting roles, usually of a villainous manner. He made his debut in the controversial Otto Preminger drama *Hurry Sundown* (1967) and followed that up with appearances in many films, including *Cool Hand Luke* (1967), *Easy Rider* (1969), *The Great Northfield Minnesota Raid* (1972), *Pat Garrett and Billy The Kid* (1973), and *Rolling Thunder* (1977). He last worked on several episodes of the popular HBO drama *Big Love* and passed away in Portland, Oregon on March 26.

Zina Bethune (February 17, 1945–February 12, 2012). Born in New York City, Bethune started her performance career as a formal ballet dancer, trained at George Balanchine's School of American Ballet. She was dancing with the New York City Ballet at the age of 14, transitioning to TV work in the 1950s and 1960s. She appeared with Harvey Keitel in Martin Scorsese's first feature film, *Who's That Knocking at My Door* (1967) but did almost all of her work on television and the stage. She was killed in a hit-and-run accident at the age of 67.

Ernest Borgnine (January 24, 1917–July 8, 2012). One of Hollywood's most beloved and venerable icons, the Connecticut-born Ernest Borgnine had actually spent ten years serving in the Navy before even thinking about getting into acting. After the usual summer stock appearances, he made his Broadway debut in 1949 in the hit show *Harvey* and made his first screen appearance a couple of years later in *Whistle at Eaton Falls* (1951). His big breakthrough came with his performance as the nasty Sgt. Fatso Judson in the hit film version of *From Here to Eternity* (1953) and he followed that up two years later with his performance as the shy and lovelorn butcher in *Marty* (1955), a role that would win him the Academy Award for Best Actor. Although he would go on to achieve great success on television as the star of the long-running sitcom *McHale's Navy*, he continued to be a regular presence on the big screen and among his many credits include such classics as *The Catered Affair* (1956), *The Oscar* (1966), *The Dirty Dozen* (1967), *The Legend of Lylah Clare* (1968), *The Wild Bunch* (1969), *Willard* (1971), *The Poseidon Adventure* (1972), *Emperor of the North* (1973), *Escape from New York* (1981), *Merlin's Shop of Mystical Wonders* (1996), and *Gattaca* (1997). He continued to act well into his nineties and even won a new generation of fans as the voice of Mermaid Man on the animated series *Spongebob Squarepants*. After completing what would turn out to be his last film, *The Man Who Shook the Hand of Vincente Fernandez* (2012), he passed away at the age of 95 from renal failure.

Ray Bradbury (August 22, 1920–June 5, 2012). Born in Waukegan, Illinois, Bradbury became one of the leading authors of science-fiction of his time with the 1950 publication of his short story collection *The Martian Chronicles*. It was perhaps inevitable that he would try his fortunes in Hollywood but never quite managed to achieve the same level of success. He was one of the writers of the B-movie favorite *It Came from Outer Space* (1953) and then penned the screenplay for John Huston's flawed screen version of *Moby Dick* (1956). Over the years, his works would be adapted countless times for both the movies and television—the most notable being *The Beast from 20,000 Fathoms* (1953), *Fahrenheit 451* (1966), and *A Sound of Thunder* (2005)—but few managed to effectively capture the voice that enchanted generations of readers, though the underrated *Something Wicked This Way Comes* (1983) came the closest. Bradbury passed away in Los Angeles on June 5.

Peter Breck (March 13, 1929–February 6, 2012). Joseph Peter Breck became a household name with two iconic TV Western roles in *Maverick* and *The Big Valley*. Robert Mitchum was such a fan of Breck's work in dozens of TV Westerns that he offered him a co-starring role in 1958's

Thunder Road. That part earned him even more TV work, appearing on dozens of series in the 1950s and 1960s. His first film starring role was in 1962's *Lad, A Dog* and would appear in *Shock Corridor* (1963) and *The Crawling Hand* (1963) on the big screen but never make anywhere near the impact he did on the small one, where he worked all the way up to the 2000s. He was survived by his wife Diane.

Frank Cady (September 8, 1915–June 8, 2012). Forever remembered as Sam Drucker across three iconic 1960s TV series—*Petticoat Junction*, *Green Acres*, and *The Beverly Hillbillies*. Before that, Cady made minor waves in film, having small roles in major works like *Father of the Bride* (1950), *The Asphalt Jungle* (1950), *When Worlds Collide* (1951), *Ace in the Hole* (1951), *Rear Window* (1954), and *The Bad Seed* (1956). He would be most remembered however for his iconic TV work, playing the same character across nearly three hundred episodes over all three shows. He would work regularly in TV but typecasting made it difficult for him to break back into film. He died at his home at the age of 96.

Harry Carey Jr. (May 16, 2012–December 27, 2012). The son of actors Harry and Olive Carey, it was perhaps inevitable that Carey would choose to follow in their footsteps. He got his first big break when Howard Hawks cast him in the western classic *Red River* (1948) and that was followed with a leading role in *3 Godfathers* (1948), the film that would start off a long association with director John Ford that would include *She Wore A Yellow Ribbon* (1949), *Rio Grande* (1950), *The Wagon Master* (1950), *Mr. Roberts* (1955), *The Long Gray Line* (1955), *The Searchers* (1956), *Two Rode Together* (1961), and *Cheyenne Autumn* (1964). He would go on to appear in over 100 movies, ranging in quality from *Rio Bravo* (1959) to *Billy the Kid Vs. Dracula* (1966) and in later years, he would find work with a new generation of filmmakers, often playing off his iconic presence, in films such as *Nickelodeon* (1976), *The Long Riders* (1980), *Gremlins* (1984), *Back to the Future III* (1990), and *Tombstone* (1993). Carey passed away in California on December 27, 2012.

Leonardo Cimino (November 4, 1917–March 3, 2012). Born in Manhattan to a tailor father, Leonardo Cimino began his career by studying violin at Juilliard but would go on to be a regular performer on stage, film, and television. After serving in the Army and landing in the second wave of soldiers at the invasion of Normandy, Cimino returned to the U.S. and studied dance with Martha Graham. He made his Broadway debut in 1946 and was a fixture there for the next four decades, appearing in nearly 20 productions. Major film roles naturally came with performances in *Stardust Memories* (1980), *Dune* (1984), *Moonstruck* (1987), *The Freshman* (1990), *Q&A* (1990), *Hudson Hawk* (1991), *Waterworld* (1995), and *Before the Devil Knows You're Dead* (2007). The actor passed away of chronic obstructive pulmonary disease in New York at the age of 95.

Gary Collins (April 30, 1938–October 13, 2012). Known more for his television work, including a stint as talk-show host, Gary Ennis Collins was a household name for most of his career, appearing regularly on TV in the 1960s and 1970s and hosting the Miss America Pageant for the bulk of the 1980s. After making a name for himself with regular TV work in the 1960s, Collins tried to transition to film, appearing in *Angel in My Pocket* (1969) and *Airport* (1970), but he made most of his fortune in film as a talk-show host and regular TV guest star. He hosted *Hour Magazine* from 1980-88 and *The Home Show* from 1989-94. He married a former Miss America, Mary Ann Mobley from 1967, and stayed with her until his death in 2012 from natural causes.

Hal David (May 25, 1921–September 1, 2012). American lyricist Hal David was born in New York, New York and is best remembered for his work with Burt Bacharach and Dionne Warwick. Much of David's work with composer Bacharach would translate to hit pop music but a few of their tunes were crafted for films, including Oscar nominations for the title songs from *What's New Pussycat?* (1965) and *Alfie* (1965), "The Look of Love" from *Casino Royale* (1967), "Raindrops Keep Fallin' on My Head" from *Butch Cassidy and the Sundance Kid* (1969), which won the Academy Award. David also worked on two other Bond themes—"We Have All the Time in the World" from *On Her Majesty's Secret Service* (1969) and the title song from *Moonraker* (1979). Hal David passed away from a stroke at the age of 91.

Tom Davis (August 13, 1952–July 19, 2012). Along with longtime partner Al Franken, Davis helped to change the face of American comedy in 1975 when the two were hired as members of the inaugural writing staff of the long-running late-night comedy show *Saturday Night Live*. After leaving the show in 1980 (though he would continue to write for it intermittently until 2003), he worked on a number of television specials and, with Franken, co-wrote and co-starred in the unsuccessful comedy *One More Saturday Night* (1985). Later on, he and Dan Aykroyd co-wrote the screenplay for *Coneheads* (1993), a film vehicle for the hugely popular alien characters that they created for *SNL*. In later years, he served as an interview subject for numerous books and documentaries on the history of *SNL* and in 2009, he would publish the best-selling memoir *39 Years of Short-Term Memory Loss: The Early Days of SNL From Someone Who Was There*. Davis passed away on July 19, 2012 of cancer.

Richard Dawson (November 20, 1932–June 2, 2012). He will live on eternally on the Game Show Network but *Family Feud* host Richard Dawson (born Colin Lionel Emm in Gosport, England) also had notable roles in film and television. Before the *Feud* (which he hosted from 1976-85 and 1994-95 and forever in reruns), Richard Dawson worked regularly in television and cinema. He had small roles in *The Longest Day* (1962) and *King Rat* (1965) before really making waves as Cpl. Peter Newkirk on the hit show *Hogan's Heroes* from 1965-71. Regular TV appearances and his massive success as a game show host would follow but Dawson would make one more splash in film, parodying himself as the host of a futuristic game show in 1987's *The Running Man*.

Phyllis Diller (July 17, 1917–August 20, 2012). Born in Lima, Ohio, Diller was just an ordinary housewife when she decided at the age of 37 to pursue a career in stand-up comedy, a profession that was almost unheard of for women at the time, and continued with it until her retirement in 2002. She was an immediate success in the field and broke ground for virtually every woman who would enter the field. Although primarily known for her appearances on the stage and on television—most notably alongside Bob Hope—she made the occasional screen appearance as well, beginning with a brief appearance in *Splendor in the Grass* (1961). She appeared in three of Hope's later films—*Boy Did I Get a Wrong Number* (1966), *Eight on the Lam* (1967), and *The Private Navy of Sgt. O'Farrell* (1968)—as well as others such as *Pink Motel* (1982) and *Pucker Up and Bark Like a Dog* (1990). In later years, she concentrated largely on voiceover work, most notably in *A Bug's Life* (1998), and would also pop up in various documentaries about the world of comedy including *The Aristocrats* (2005). Diller passed away on August 20, 2012.

Michael Clarke Duncan (December 10, 1957–September 3, 2012). Born in Chicago in 1957, gentle giant Michael Clarke Duncan would make waves in comedy and drama before passing away at a startlingly young age (54) at his home in Los Angeles, California, the victim of a heart attack. Duncan worked physical labor jobs to support his single mother and family when he was younger and ended up as the bodyguard for some notable celebrities in the 1990s, including Will Smith, LL Cool J, and the Notorious B.I.G.. He played a bouncer in small rols in some films (including *Bulworth* [1998] and *A Night at the Roxbury* [1998]) but broke through in Michael Bay's *Armageddon* (1998) before really becoming a household name in *The Green Mile* (1999), which earned Duncan an Oscar nomination for Best Supporting Actor. His acclaim for that work allowed him steady parts in the 2000s, including *The Whole Nine Yards* (2000), *Planet of the Apes* (2001), *The Scorpion King* (2002), *Daredevil* (2003), *The Island* (2005), *Sin City* (2005), *Talladega Nights: The Ballad of Ricky Bobby* (2006), and *Green Lantern* (2011).

Charles Durning (February 28, 1923–December 24, 2012). One of the most underrated and gifted character actors of all time, Charles Edward Durning was a fixture in film, television, and theatre for half-a-century, earning two Oscar nominations and a Tony. The fourth of ten children born in Highland Falls, New York, Durning lost five siblings to scarlet fever and smallpox as children. He was drafted into the Army at the age of 21, serving in World War II, where he participated in the invasion of Normandy. In his time in service for his country, he earned the Silver Star, Bronze Star, and three Purple Heart medals. He worked regularly in film, television, and theatre from the 1960s through the 2010s, earning nine Emmy nominations, two Academy Award nominations (for *The Best Little Whorehouse in Texas* [1982] and *To Be or Not to Be* [1983]), a Tony, and a Lifetime Achievement Award from the Screen Actors Guild in 2008. His breakthrough came in the beloved *The Sting* (1973), which led to memorable roles in, not including his Academy Award-nominated two-fer, *Dog Day Afternoon* (1975), *The Fury* (1978), *North Dallas Forty* (1979), *The Muppet Movie* (1979), *Tootsie* (1982), *The Man with one Red Show* (1985), *Dick Tracy* (1990), *The Hudsucker Proxy* (1994), *O Brother, Where Art Thou?* (2000), *State and Main* (2000), and recurring TV roles on *Evening Shade* and *Rescue Me*. He passed away at the age of 89 of unknown causes at his home in Manhattan, New York, and the actor was buried at Arlington National Cemetery in honor of his amazing military service.

Nora Ephron (May 19, 1941–June 26, 2012). Nominated three times for the Academy Award for writing, Nora Ephron was one of the most influential screenwriters of her generation, forever impacting the way that Hollywood looked at the potential for the romantic comedy and how they treated the genre's audience. The daughter of two screenwriters (Henry and Phoebe Ephron) and sister to another (Delia, with whom Nora sometimes worked), Nora Ephron was surrounded by screenwriting. After graduating from Wellesley College in 1962, Ephron worked as an intern at the White House occupied by President John F. Kennedy before getting a job at the *New York Post.* She became a notable columnist for *Esquire* before helping then-husband Carl Bernstein rewrite the script for *All the President's Men* (1976). Her rewrites reportedly were not used but she used that script to help her get work in the 1970s and her career quickly took off. She first found fame writing two Oscar-nominated roles for Meryl Streep in *Silkwood* (1983) and *Heartburn* (1986). The former earned Ephron her first of three nods as well, followed by 1989's *When Harry Met Sally.* and 1993's *Sleepless in Seattle,* which she also directed. Other credits include *My Blue Heaven* (1990), *Michael* (1996), *You've Got Mail* (1998), *Bewitched* (2005), and *Julie & Julia* (2009). Ephron surprisingly succumbed to pneumonia, a complication related to acute myeloid leukemia, a disease that the writer/director had been afflicted with for years but not shared with most people.

Chad Everett (June 11, 1936–July 24, 2012). Born Raymon Lee Cramton in South Bend, Indiana, Chad Everett appeared in more than 40 films and television series but will be best remembered as Dr. Joe Gannon on CBS's *Medical Center* for the better part of the 1970s. He had a notable film career but it was the guest starring he did in TV that really made him a fixture in the medium for decades, all the way through to a 2012 appearance on ABC's *Castle.* Notable films on the Everett resume include *Made in Paris* (1966), *The Singing Nun* (1966), *First to Fight* (1967), *Airplane II: The Sequel* (1982), *Psycho* (1998), *Mulholland Dr.* (2001), and *Wake Up, Ron Burgundy* (2004), the DVD release of alternate takes and deleted scenes from *Anchorman* (2004). He succumbed to lung cancer after a lengthy battle at the age of 76.

James Farentino (February 24, 1938–January 24, 2012). Often typecast as tough guys, New York actor James Farentino was a fixture in American television and film for four decades, amazing almost 100 credits. Farentino was born and raised in New York and appeared in a number of hit TV series in the 1950s and 1960s, getting his biggest role as a lead in the NBC hit *The Bold Ones* from 1969 to 1972. He continued regular small-screen work, landing an Emmy nomination for his work in the mini-series *Jesus of Nazareth* (1978) and working all the way through the 1990s with recurring roles in *ER* and *Melrose Place.* Notable film roles included *The Final Countdown* (1980), *Dead & Buried* (1981), *Her Alibi* (1989), and *Bulletproof* (1997). He was married four times, including to his final wife, Stella Farentino, since 1994.

William Finley (September 20, 1940–April 14, 2012). Born and raised in Manhattan, Finley attended Columbia University, and that is where he made the acquaintance of

fellow student and budding filmmaker Brian De Palma. Finley would go on to make appearances in a number of De Palma's early groundbreaking films including *Murder a la Mod* (1968), *The Wedding Party* (1969), *Dionysus* (1970), *Sisters* (1973), the title role in the cult classic *Phantom of the Paradise* (1974), *The Fury* (1978), and *Dressed to Kill* (1980). Finley also lent his oddball presence to such quirky films as *Eaten Alive* (1977), *Simon* (1980), *The Funhouse* (1981), and *Silent Rage* (1982) before largely disappearing from the business for more than a decade. In later years, he made the occasional unheralded appearance and reunited with De Palma for a brief but memorable performance in *The Black Dahlia* (2006). This would prove to be his final screen appearance and he passed away from complications following surgery on April 14.

Ben Gazzara (August 28, 1930–February 3, 2012). Iconic character actor and beloved collaborator with some of the most influential filmmakers of all time, Biagio Anthony Gazzarra (he lost one of the "r"s when he changed his stage name to Ben) was born in New York to Italian immigrants. After difficulty in school, he went to City College of New York to become an electrical engineer before feeling the draw of the New School and their Dramatic Workshop. From there, he leapt to TV with a few guest appearance in the mid-1950s, and really broke through on Broadway, creating the role of Brick in *Cat on a Hot Tin Roof* in 1955, among others. His film breakthrough came in 1959 when he appeared in Otto Preminger's beloved and wildly influential *Anatomy of a Murder* (1959) and he really did not stop acting after that role. He would land a pair of Emmy nominations for his work on *Run for Your Life* in the 1960s while also working on films like *Young Doctors* (1961), *A Rage to Live* (1965), and *The Bridge at Remagen* (1969). Working with friend John Cassavetes, Gazzara became most iconic in the films they made together like *Husbands* (1970), *The Killing of a Chinese Bookie* (1976), and *Opening Night* (1977). Notable roles in the final decades of his career included parts in *Road House* (1989), *The Spanish Prisoner* (1997), *The Big Lebowski* (1998), *Happiness* (1998), *Summer of Sam* (1999), and *Dogville* (2003). Gazzara was diagnosed with throat cancer in 1999 and passed away from pancreatic cancer in New York in 2012.

Andy Griffith (June 1, 1926–July 3, 2012). He will forever be canonized for the iconic television show that bore his name (and its catchy theme song) but Andy Samuel Griffith had a notable film career as well, particularly in his break-through role in the excellent *A Face in the Crowd* (1957). While his two TV hits, *The Andy Griffith Show* (1960-68) and *Matlock* (1986-95), made him an icon of that medium, he never gave up big screen acting, appearing in films into the new millennium. Griffith, who grew up so poor that he used a dresser drawer as a cradle as an infant, first found fame through Ira Levin's *No Time for Sergeants,* which starts as an episode of the anthology TV series *The United States Steel Hour* in 1955, moved to Broadway, where it earned Griffith a Tony nomination, and eventually became an acclaimed film in 1958. There, Griffith met Don Knotts, and the rest would be TV history. After transitioning to the small screen in his two iconic roles and a series of telefilms in the 1970s, Griffith rarely went back to the big screen, although film historians would come to regard his work on Elia Kazan's *A Face in the Crowd* as woefully underrated, probably due to the typecasting faced by Griffith after his show. Other notable film roles include *Spy Hard* (1996) and a fantastic supporting turn in Adrienne Shelley's *Waitress* (2007). Andy Griffith passed away in July 2012 from a heart attack, survive by his third wife, Cindy Knight.

Larry Hagman (September 21, 1931–November 23, 2012). Although the son of actress Mary Martin would achieve his greatest fame on television, first as the co-star of the sitcom *I Dream of Jeannie* and later as the infamous J.R. Ewing in the long-running soap opera *Dallas*, Hagman also made several significant big-screen appearances as well. Among the highlights of his silver screen career are his performances in *Fail-Safe* (1964), *Harry & Tonto* (1974), *Stardust* (1974), *Superman* (1978), *S.O.B.* (1981), *Nixon* (1995), and *Primary Colors* (1998). He even stepped behind the camera at one point to direct the immortal sequel *Beware The Blob* (1972) to very little acclaim. After surviving a period of ill health brought on by hard living that culminated with a well-publicized liver transplant in 1995, Hagman worked only occasionally and in 2012, he returned to the role that made him an international celebrity when he joined the cast of a television revival of *Dallas*. He was in the process of shooting the second season of the show when he succumbed to complications from treatment for throat cancer on November 23.

Marvin Hamlisch (June 2, 1944–August 6, 2012). The New York-born composer of many critically and commercially successful musical pieces for the stage and screen got his start in Hollywood by contributing tunes to films such as *Ski Party* (1965) and *Batman* (1967) before being hired to compose his first full score for *The Swimmer* (1968). Before long, he would hook up with fellow New Yorker Woody Allen to score his first two movies, *Take the Money and Run* (1969) and *Bananas* (1971). In 1973, he composed the score and title tune for *The Way We Were* and adapted the music of Scott Joplin for the score of *The Sting* and won Oscars for each, making him the first person to win three Academy Awards in the same year. After that, he would continue to write music for films such as *The Spy Who Loved Me* (1977), *The Fan* (1981), *Frankie & Johnny* (1991) and *The Mirror Has Two Faces* (1996) and collaborated on the long-running Broadway hit *A Chorus Line*. He later returned to film music when Steven Soderbergh hired him to compose the cheerfully retro score for *The Informant* (2009). One of the few people to win the Emmy, Grammy, Oscar, and Tony (with a Pulitzer Prize for good measure), Hamlisch passed away in Los Angeles on August 6.

Levon Helm (May 26, 1940–April 19, 2012). The drummer and singer for the popular rock group The Band, who first became famous as Bob Dylan's backup group when he made the controversial decision to go electric in 1965 and then went on to record a number of hit albums between 1968-1976, made his first on-screen appearance in *The Last Waltz* (1978), Martin Scorsese's chronicle of the group's final concert in 1976. A few years later, he made his acting debut when he was hired to play Loretta Lynn's father in the hit biopic *Coal Miner's Daughter* (1980) and would make appearances over the ensuing years in such films as *The Right Stuff* (1983), *Smooth Talk* (1985), *Feeling Min-*

nesota (1996), *Fire Down Below* (1997), *Shooter* (2007), and *In the Electric Mist* (2009). During this time, he continued to record intermittently, both as a solo artist and with a partially reformed Band, and even after a throat cancer scare in 1998 that threatened to permanently rob him of his voice, he continued to perform and record until he was once again diagnosed with throat cancer in February, 2012. Helm would succumb to cancer on April 19.

Sherman Hemsley (February 1, 1938–July 24, 2012). Another actor who passed in 2012 who was known primarily for film but also made a notable mark in cinema, Sherman Alexander Hemsley was born in Philadelphia, PA in 1938, dropping out of school and joining the Air Force in the 1950s. After leaving the force, Hemsley moved to New York and attended the Academy of Dramatic Arts. He was performing on Broadway when he took the call from Norman Lear that would change his life. He was asked to play George Jefferson in a few episodes of *All in the Family* (1971-79) and then transitioned the character to his own show, *The Jeffersons* (1973-85), which was one of the biggest hits of its generation. He found another TV success in NBC's *Amen* (1986-91) and yet another as a voice actor on ABC's *Dinosaurs* (1991-94). Film roles include parts in *Love at First Bite* (1979), *Stewardess School* (1986), *Mr. Nanny* (1993), *Jane Austen's Mafia!* (1998), *Screwed* (2000), and *American Pie Presents: The Book of Love* (2009). He passed away from cancer at the age of 74 at his home in El Paso, Texas.

Henry Hill (June 11, 1943–June 12, 2012). New York mobster Henry Hill, Jr. will forever be iconized as his story became the basis for the highly-acclaimed and beloved Martin Scorsese film *GoodFellas* (1990), adapted from Nicholas Pileggi's book *Wiseguy: Life in a Mafia Family*. While the film detailed Hill's climb in the NYC Italian Mafia and how he turned on the Lucchese crime family, turning on captains Paul Vario and James Burke in FBI informant testimony, it was a simple heart attack that killed one of the most legendary mobsters in movie history.

Bill Hinzman (October 24, 1936–February 5, 2012). Samuel William Hinzman had a very limited film career but will forever be remembered as he played the first zombie, the one in the cemetery, in George A. Romero's massively influential *Night of the Living Dead* (1968). He also played roles in *Legion of the Night* (1985), *Santa Claws* (1996), and *Evil Ambitions* (1996) and directed *The Majorettes,* (1986) and *Flesheater,* (1988). The horror icon passed away from cancer in Pennsylvania at the age of 75.

Celeste Holm (April 29, 1917–July 15, 2012). An Academy Award winner for her work in *Gentleman's Agreement* (1947), Celeste Holm was one of the most beloved actresses of the 1940s and 1950s, influencing generation of performers who would come later. Holm started acting at a young age, performing in school productions at the University High School for Girls in Chicago before becoming a stage actress in the 1930s. She appeared in several stage productions before breaking through on Broadway in the original staging of the classic *Oklahoma!* (1943). Her stage success earned her a contract with 20th Century Fox and it quickly paid off with her Oscar-winning role that led to more major parts in films like *Come to the Stable* (1949, Oscar-nominated), *All About Eve* (1950, Oscar-nominated), *The*

Tender Trap (1955), and *High Society* (1956). She would work regularly in film and television for the rest of her career (including parts in *Tom Sawyer* [1973], *The Private Lives of J. Edgar Hoover* [1977], *Three Men and a Baby* [1987], and *Still Breathing* [1997]) but never quite find the fame she did in the 1940s and 1950s. Holm was married five times, the final union to Frank Basile, 46 years younger, who she wed in 2004 until her death from a heart attack in July 2012.

Whitney Houston (August 9, 1963–February 11, 2012). Once cited as the most awarded female act of all time, Whitney Elizabeth Houston was one of the most beloved singers of the 1980s and 1990s, transitioning seamlessly into film roles before allowing addiction to get the better of her career and take her at far-too-young an age. Her breakthrough album, "Whitney Houston" came in 1986 and broke records with seven #1 singles and stayed at #1 itself for 14 weeks. It won the Grammy for Album of the Year and became a definitive album of the 1980s. Her follow-up, "Whitney" came the next year and essentially matched its predecessor's success, selling 20 million copies worldwide. Movie offers reportedly rolled in as Houston became a household name around the world but she carefully chose her debut role in *The Bodyguard* (1992), which made a fortune and gave her one of the biggest smash hit singles of her career. Only three big screen film roles would follow, *Waiting to Exhale* (1995), *The Preacher's Wife* (1996), and what was supposed to be her comeback role, *Sparkle* (2012), which was released posthumously. Whitney Houston struggled with addiction through the 1990s and 2000s, passing away on February 11, 2012 in her bathtub at the Beverly Hilton Hotel after using cocaine, marijuana, Xanax, Benadryl, and Flexeril. The Grammy Awards that same week became an impromptu tribute to one of the biggest female musicians of all time and one of the most cautionary tales of what drug use can do to talent.

John Ingle (May 7, 1928–September 16, 2012). Best-known for his work on *General Hospital* in the 1990s, John Ingle did not even start acting until he was in his fifties. He parlayed his success on *GH* into work on *Big Love* and *The Drew Carey Show*, bolstering a resume that included work in films like *True Stories* (1986), *Heathers* (1988), *Robocop 2* (1990), *Repossessed* (1990), *Death Becomes Her* (1992), *The Land Before Time* (1994), *Batman & Robin* (1997), and *Hostage* (2005). John Ingle married Grace-Lynne Martin in 1954 and they were together for nearly six decades with Ingle's wife passing away seven months before he did.

Eiko Ishioka (July 12, 1938–January 21, 2012). Thanks to her work on such projects as the official poster for Expo '70 and album covers for performers like Miles Davis, Ishioka was already one of Japan's leading designers when Paul Schrader hired her to help design the sets and costumes for his controversial 1985 film *Mishima: A Life In Four Chapters* (1985). Her efforts won her a special award for Artistic Contribution at that year's Cannes Film Festival and she went on to work on the hit Broadway musical *Miss Saigon*, for which she received Tony nominations for Costume Design and Scenic Design. She returned to the world of film when Francis Ford Coppola hired her to design the costumes for *Bram Stoker's Dracula* (1992) and her eye-popping creations won her an Oscar for costume

design. With the exception of *Theresa: The Body of Christ* (2007), the remainder of her film work would be in collaboration with director Tarsem Singh, with whom she would collaborate on *The Cell* (2000), *The Fall* (2006), *Immortals* (2011), and *Mirror Mirror* (2012), the latter of which was released two months after her death from pancreatic cancer on January 21 and for which she would receive a posthumous second Oscar nomination.

Kathryn Joosten (December 20, 1939–June 2, 2012). Born Kathryn Rausch, Kathryn Joosten found her greatest fame at the end of her life, winning two Emmys for her work as Karen McCluskey on ABC's *Desperate Housewives*. Joosten did not even start acting until in her forties, working in community theater in Illinois in the 1980s. She took to acting late in life, even being hired to perform at Disney World in the early 1990s before moving to Hollywood and starting a notable string of TV guest appearances on dozens of major shows in the decade, eventually landing her first key role as Mrs. Landingham on *The West Wing*. She was all over TV again in the 2000s before joining the cast of *Housewives,* for which she won Guest Actress in a Comedy Series Emmys in 2005 and 2008. She was upgraded to Supporting Actress for the show's final season and earned an Emmy nod there as well. Film work was much less consistent than TV but Joosten did appear in *Cheaper by the Dozen 2* (2004), *Wedding Crashers* (2005), and *Alvin and the Chipmunks: The Squeakquel* (2009).

Erland Josephson (June 15, 1923–February 25, 2012). Born in Stockholm in 1923, Erland Josephson was a Swedish actor and author who will be forever remembered for his work with some of the most notable auteurs of all time—Ingmar Bergman, Andrei Tarkovsky, and Theodoros Angelopoulos. Josephson also had a notably resilient career, working for seven decades with notable roles in *The Magician* (1958), *Cries and Whispers* (1972), *Scenes From a Marriage* (1973), *The Magic Flute* (1975), *Fanny and Alexander* (1982), *Ulysses' Gaze* (1995), and *Saraband* (2003). Josephson also published dozens of novels, short stories, and volumes of poetry.

Alex Karras (July 15, 1935–October 10, 2012). Indiana-born Alexander George Karras made the often-difficult transition from sports to acting look easy with beloved appearances in Mel Brooks' *Blazing Saddles* (1974) and as one of the leads on *Webster* (1983-1989), one of the most successful television programs of the 1980s. After twelve seasons as a defensive tackle with the Detroit Lions in the 1950s and 1960s, Karras retired from the NFL in 1971 at the age of 35, transitioning to film before his retirement, first appearing in *Paper Lion* (1968), playing himself. Acting became a full-time job after the NFL as Karras appeared on TV shows and TV films before his memorable cameo as Mongo in Mel Brooks' beloved comedy. That same year, Karras became a commentator on ABC's *Monday Night Football* but returned to film with a memorable role in *Porky's* (1982) with his wife Susan Clark, who would also star with Karras in *Webster*. Karras also appeared in *Victor Victoria* (1982) and *Against All Odds* (1984) before making his fortune with *Webster*, after which he essentially retired from the public eye, popping up every once in a while in a football context and playing a small role in Vincent Gallo's *Buffalo '66* (1998). Karras was one of a wave of retired NFL players who accused the organization of not doing enough to protect its retired athletes. He passed away from kidney failure at the age of 77.

David Kelly (July 11, 1929–February 12, 2012). Irish actor David Kelly was well-known in his home country for regular television work but will be most remembered internationally for playing Grandpa Joe in the beloved *Charlie and the Chocolate Factory* (2005) and a key role in *Waking Ned* (1998). Kelly began acting when he was a child in Ireland, appearing on stage in Dublin in the 1950s. He transitioned to BBC productions in the 1960s and 1970s, including a memorable role on *Fawlty Towers* (1975-79). *Waking Ned* really brought Kelly to a much larger international audience, including the attention of Tim Burton, who cast him in the key role in his remake. Other film credits late in life included parts in *Agent Cody Banks 2* (2004), *Laws of Attraction* (2004), and *Stardust* (2007). Kelly was survived by his wife Laurie Morton and two children, David and Miriam.

Zalman King (May 23, 1942–February 3, 2012). A true jack-of-all-trades, the Trenton-born King first achieved fame in 1969 as the star of the television legal drama *The Young Lawyers* and of such cult films as *Some Call It Loving* (1973), *The Passover Plot* (1976) and *Blue Sunshine* (1978). He then moved to working behind the camera, first as a producer on the Alan Rudolph films *Roadie* (1980) and *Endangered Species* (1982) and then as one of the screenwriters of the controversial film *9 1/2 Weeks* (1986). Although the latter film was not a theatrical success, it was enormously popular on home video and inspired him to write, direct and produce such beloved exercises in soft-core erotica as *Two Moon Junction* (1988), *Wild Orchid* (1989), *Wild Orchid II: Two Shades of Blue* (1991), and *Delta of Venus* (1995). These films would also prove to be popular on home video but his greatest success would come when he developed the popular late-night cable anthology series *Red Shoe Diaries* in 1992. Although rarely treated with anything but scorn by critics, his work did find a large and appreciative audience, especially amongst female viewers, and he continued working until he passed away in Santa Monica, California on February 3.

Jack Klugman (April 27, 1922–December 24, 2012). Like so many celebrities who passed away in 2012, Jacob Joachim Klugman will be most remembered for his iconic television work on the shows *The Odd Couple* (1970-75) and *Quincy, M.E.* (1976-83), which made Klugman a household name and earned him numerous award nominations and trophies (he also memorably appeared in four episodes of the original *The Twilight Zone*). Before his television work, he had a notable film career in works like *12 Angry Men* (1957), *Days of Wine and Roses* (1962), *The Detective* (1968), and *The Split* (1968). Film roles would be more infrequent after his small-screen success but Klugman did appear in *Dear God* in 1996 and popped up on TV through the 2000s. Klugman was a heavy smoker and became a symbol of the degenerative properties of that addiction after being diagnosed with throat cancer in 1974 and losing a vocal cord to the disease in 1989, forever giving him a raspy voice. Despite his battle with the diseases, Jack Klugman

made it to 90, dying on Christmas Eve at his home in Woodland Hills, CA, survived by his two sons and two grandchildren.

Sylvia Kristel (September 28, 1952–October 18, 2012). Blessed with unconventional beauty and an undeniable screen presence, the Dutch-born Kristel became an international sex symbol when she was hired by fashion photographer Just Jaeckin to star in *Emmanuelle* (1974), his screen version of the popular novel charting an innocent young woman's sexual awakening. Stressing soft-core steaminess to hard-core graphicness, the film was an enormous hit around the world and Kristel would suit up (so to speak) for the inevitable *Emmanuelle II* (1975) and *Emmanuelle III* (1978). At this point, she made a move towards mainstream acceptance in films such as *The Fifth Musketeer* (1979), *The Concorde Airport '79* (1979), *The Nude Bomb* (1980), and an adaptation of *Lady Chatterly's Lover* (1981) that saw her reunite with Jaeckin for the first time since *Emmanuelle*. When those proved to be unsuccessful at the box-office, she appeared in the low-budget sexploitation comedy *Private Lessons* (1981) and when it became a huge hit, she followed it up with the similar *Private School* (1983). After her next move towards the mainstream, *Mata Hari* (1985), failed to catch on, she returned to Europe and made numerous appearances on film and television in the ensuing years and directed the acclaimed *Topor And Me* (2004), a short film chronicling the life and work of her friend, artist Roland Topor. Her last film was *Two Sunny Days* (2010) and she passed away on October 18 from cancer.

Johnny Lewis (October 29, 1983–September 26, 2012). Jonathan Kendrick Lewis was just beginning his young career when an accidental fall took his life during a controversial investigation of an assault with which he may have been involved. He may be most remembered for his role on FX's hit *Sons of Anarchy* but he also appeared in several films, including roles in *Raise Your Voice* (2004), *Underclassmen* (2005), *Aliens vs. Predator: Requiem* (2007), *One Missed Call* (2008), and *The Runaways* (2010). Johnny Lewis had been arrested three times in the last two years of his life and was reportedly suffering from mental health and addiction issues when he was released from an L.A. County Jail in September 2012, shortly before his brutal death. He was found dead with an 81-year-old named Catherine Davis and is reportedly a posthumous suspect in her passing in what police theorize was a fight gone horribly wrong. He reportedly fell or jumped from her patio and died at the age of 28.

George Lindsey (December 17, 1928–May 6, 2012). Yet another TV icon who passed away in 2012, George Smith Lindsey will forever be remembered as Goober Pyle from *The Andy Griffith Show*, *Mayberry R.F.D.*, and *Hee Haw* although he had a few film roles in his acting career as well. After acting school and parts on Broadway, Lindsey moved to regular TV guest star work before landing the role that would change his life on *The Andy Griffith Show*. After his massive success on TV, Disney called and Lindsey was a regular voice actor in several of the canonic films—*The Aristocats* (1970), *Robin Hood* (1973), and *The Rescuers* (1977). Lindsey passed away at the age of 83 in Nashville, TN.

Herbert Lom (September 11, 1917–September 27, 2012). Born Herbert Karel Angelo Kuchacevic ze Schluderpacheru, Czech actor Herbert Lom moved to the United Kingdom and began his acting career there. He usually played villains over the six decades he remained in the profession and will be most remembered for creating Chief Inspector Charles Dreyfus in *A Shot in the Dark* (1964) and subsequent films in the *Pink Panther* franchise. He actually began acting much earlier, first appearing as Napoleon in *The Young Mr. Pitt* in 1942 (and he would play the role again in *War and Peace* [1956]) before transitioning to several key stage roles, including the original London production of *The King and I,* where Lom created the part of the King of Siam. That success (it ran for years) helped him land key roles in 1950s and 1960s classics like *The Ladykillers* (1955), *Fire Down Below* (1957), *Spartacus* (1960), *El Cid* (1961), *Mysterious Island* (1961), and the Hammer version of *The Phantom of the Opera* (1962). The *Pink Panther* films would make Lom most iconic but he also appeared in several other major works, including *Murders in the Rue Morgue* (1971), *And Then There Were None* (1974), *The Dead Zone* (1983), *King Solomon's Mines* (1985), *Ten Little Indians* (1989), and *The Pope Must Die* (1991). Herbert Lom passed away at the age of 95.

Richard Lynch (February 12, 1940–June 19, 2012). Born in Brooklyn in 1940, Richard Lynch would become one of the most recognizable bad guy faces of B-grade horror in the 1980s and beyond, all the way through Rob Zombie's *Halloween* (2007). He was also a staple of the sci-fi genre, although more regularly on TV than in film, most notably on iconic shows like *Battlestar Galactica* and *Star Trek: The Next Generation.* He began acting in the 1960s, playing a heavy in first film role in *Scarecrow* (1973) and the typecasting stuck. He won a Saturn Award for work in *The Sword and the Sorcerer* (1982) and would go on to appear in films like *Bad Dreams* (1988), *Little Nikita* (1988), *Alligator II: The Mutation* (1991), *Trancers II* (1991), *Puppet Master III: Toulon's Revenge* (1991), and *Werewolf* (1996). He passed away at the age of 72 in his home in Yucca Valley, CA.

Chris Marker (July 29, 1921–July 29, 2012). French writer/director Christian Francois Bouche-Villeneuve, who was credited as Chris Marker in his work, is most well-known for his small selection of films that he chose to direct but is often included with the Left Bank Cinema movement, one that included Alain Resnais, Agnes Varda, Henri Colpi, and Armand Gatti. His film *La jetee* (1962) was the inspiration for Terry Gilliam's beloved *Twelve Monkeys* (1995). Marker was a journalist and photographer before shooting his first 16mm documentary, *Olympia 52* (1952) about the Helsinki Olympic Games. He worked with Resnais on *Statues Also Die* (1953) and served as assistant director on the filmmaker's *Night and Fog* (1955). He worked on other documentaries before the short film *La jetee,* a piece about an experiment in time travel that consists of only filmed photographs. Other notable works include *A Grin Without a Cat* (1977), *San Soleil* (1983), and *AK* (1985), the filmmaker's essay on the great Akira Kurosawa.

Ralph McQuarrie (June 13, 1929–March 3, 2012). Although he originally served as a conceptual designer for Boeing, McQuarrie eventually made the move to Hollywood and managed to contribute his talents to some of the most popular films made during the 1970s and 1980s. His work first appeared in the landmark film *Star Wars* (1977) and then turned up in such smash hits as *Close Encounters of the Third Kind* (1977), *The Empire Strikes Back* (1980), *Raiders of the Lost Ark* (1981), *E.T. The Extra-Terrestrial* (1982), *Return of the Jedi* (1983), *Cocoon* (1985)—for which he received the Academy Award for Visual Effects— *Star Trek IV: The Voyage Home* (1986) and *batteries not included* (1986). After working on the surreal horror item *Nightbreed* (1990), McQuarrie retired from films and passed away in Berkeley, California on March 3.

Russell Means (November 10, 1939–October 22, 2012). Notable Native American rights activist Russell Charles Means was a member of the Oglala Sioux tribe and turned his prominence in the American Indian Movement into a film career in his fifties, appearing in numerous films, including his debut in *The Last of the Mohicans* (1992). Easily identifiable as a political and social leader, Means transitioned easily and appeared in a surprising number of movies nearly back to back in the 1990s, including Michael Mann's *Mohicans,* Oliver Stone's *Natural Born Killers* 1994), and the TV film adaptation of *Buffalo Girls* (1995). He also voiced a central character in Disney's *Pocahontas* (1995) and *Pocahontas II: Journey to a New World* (1998). Parts seems to dry up as quickly as they came but Means was always a prominent figure in his cause and acted all the way to the end, appearing 2013's Cinemax TV series *Banshee.* He passes away at the age of 73 after reportedly being diagnosed with inoperable esophageal cancer in 2011.

Patricia Medina (July 19, 1919–April 28, 2012). Born to a Spanish father and English mother in Liverpool, England, Patricia Paz Maria Medina may never have been a household name but she worked regularly from the 1940s to 1960s, most prolifically in a series of period melodramas in the 1950s with Louis Hayward—*Fortunes of Captain Blood* (1950), *The Lady and the Bandit* (1951), *Lady in the Iron Mask* (1951), and *Captain Pirate* (1952). After that string of films (and a role in Orson Welles' *Mr. Arkadin* [1955]), Medina saw most of her big-screen work dry up but she did appear on television in the 1950s and 1960s. Medina was also notable for being the wife of the legendary Joseph Cotton, who she was married to from 1960 till his death in 1994. When she passed, she was interred next to him in Virginia.

Lupe Ontiveros (September 17, 1942–July 26, 2012). While she worked for decades, Lupe Ontiveros found most of her fame late in life, primarily after the massive critical acclaim and Independent Spirit Award nomination received for her work in Mike White's *Chuck and Buck* (2000). To be fair, Ontiveros had delivered major performances before her late renaissance in the 2000s, most notably in Gregory Nava's *El Norte* (1983), *The Goonies* (1985), *Dolly Dearest* (1992), *Mi Familia* (1995), *Selena* (1997), and *As Good as it Gets* (1997). She often played maids or other typically Hispanic roles but she was a notable activist for getting better parts for Hispanic actors and actresses. Major roles in the 2000s included *Storytelling* (2001), *Real Women Have Curves* (2002), *This Christmas* (2007), and *Our Family Wedding*

(2010). She also memorably appeared on several episodes of ABC's *Desperate Housewives* (2004-12) and starred on CBS's failed sitcom *Rob!* (2012). Ontiveros passed away after a battle with liver cancer, survived by her husband and three sons.

Morgan Paull (December 15, 1944–July 17, 2012). Born in New York City in 1944, Morgan Paull will be best remembered for the role of Holden in Ridley Scott's influential *Blade Runner* (1982). Other notable film credits in his brief career include roles in *Patton* (1970), *The Swarm* (1978), *Norma Rae* (1979), *The Apple Dumpling Gang Rides Again* (1979), and *Out Cold* (1989). Paull passed away from stomach cancer in Ashland, Oregon, survived by his fourth wife Jenny Elam and his two daughters.

Frank Pierson (May 12, 1925–July 22, 2012). Writer/director Frank Pierson worked consistently from the 1940s through the 2010s, even producing several episodes of AMC's critically-beloved *Mad Men*. He was nominated for the Academy Award for screenwriting three times and they are three iconic films—*Cat Ballou* (1965), *Cool Hand Luke* (1967), and *Dog Day Afternoon* (1975), for which Pierson won the Oscar. Pierson started writing for television in the 1950s before very successfully transitioning to film. He also worked on the Barbra Streisand remake of *A Star is Born* (1976), which he wrote and directed, and wrote the scripts for *In Country* (1989) and *Presumed Innocent* (1990). Most of his directorial work came in the form of TV movies. Frank Pierson also made a mark as the President of the Writers Guild of America from 1981 to 1983 and again from 1993 to 1995 and the President of the Academy of Motion Picture Arts and Sciences from 2001 to 2005. Late in life, he was a teacher at the Sundance Institute and Artistic Director of the American Film Institute. He passed away from natural causes in July at his home in Los Angeles, survived by his wife Helene and two children.

Deborah Raffin (March 13, 1953–November 21, 2012). Deborah Raffin had a brief period in the spotlight in the 1970s, appearing in the divisive *Touched by Love* (1981), a film that earned the star both a Golden Globe nomination for Best Actress and a Razzie Award nomination for Worst Actress. Outside of that film, she had a relatively brief career. Other credits include *Once is Not Enough* (1975), *The Sentinel* (1977), *Claudia* (1985), *Death Wish 3* (1985), *Grizzly II* (1987), and *Scanners II: The New Order* (1991). She did regular work on television, appearing in the hit mini-series *Noble House* (1988), *7th Heaven* (1996-2005), and *The Secret Life of the American Teenager* (2008-2010). Deborah Iona Raffin passed away at the young age of 59 from leukemia.

Carlo Rambaldi (September 15, 1925–August 10, 2012). Born in Vigarano Mainardo, Emilla Romagna, Italy, Carlo Rambaldi became one of top visual effects artists in the film industry. After starting in Italy creating effects for such low-budget horror films as *Bay of Blood* (1971) and *A Lizard in a Woman's Skin* (1971)—it is said that his work on the latter involving the illusion of dog mutilation was so convincing that director Lucio Fulci was threatened with a two-year prison sentence for animal cruelty until Rambaldi produced his work in court to prove it was all fake. Within a few years, his effects were found in such major films as *King Kong* (1976), *Close Encounters of the Third Kind*

(1977), *Possession* (1981), and *Dune* (1984) and won Oscars for his work in creating the title creatures for the smash hits *Alien* (1979) and *E.T.* (1982). After *Primal Rage* (1988), a horror film directed by his son, Vittorio, he retired from the industry and returned to Italy, where he passed away in Lamezia Terme, Calabrio on August 10th.

Martin Richards (March 11, 1932–November 26, 2012). Winner of the Oscar for *Chicago* 2002), Martin Richards had a very short career as a film backer but still managed a few notable credits in his brief time. Other than the only musical to win Best Picture in the 2000s, Richards produced *Some of My Best Friends Are* (1971), *The Boys From Brazil* (1978), *The Shining* (1980), and *Fort Apache the Bronx* (1981). He also did a lot of work producing on Broadway and helped found Broadway Cares/Equity Fights AIDS with his wife Mary Lea Johnson Richards. He passed away at the age of 80 from cancer.

J. Michael Riva (June 28, 1948–June 7, 2012). The grandson of the legendary Marlene Dietrich, Riva found his calling behind the camera and would go on to be one of the leading production designers of his time. His first project was *I Never Promised You A Rose Garden* (1978) and he continued on through such varied and increasingly elaborate projects as *Halloween II* (1981), *The Adventures of Buckaroo Banzai: Across the Eighth Dimension* (1984), and *The Goonies* (1985) before receiving his first and only Oscar nomination for his work on *The Color Purple* (1985). From then on, he worked steadily on such high-profile projects as *Lethal Weapon* (1987), *Tango & Cash* (1989), *Congo* (1995), *Evolution* (2001), *Spider-Man 3* (2007), *Iron Man* (2008), *Iron Man 2* (2010), and *The Amazing Spider-Man* (2012). He died in New Orleans on June 7 of complications from a stroke, six months before the release of his final film, *Django Unchained* (2012).

Lina Romay (June 25, 1954–February 15, 2012). Born Rosa Maria Almirall Martinez in Barcelona, Spain, Romay (who took her name from a featured singer from Xavier Cugat's band) was working as an actress on the stage when she met cult filmmaker Jess Franco in the early 1970s. She made her screen debut in a minor role in Franco's *La Maladicionde Frankenstein* (1972) and soon became his leading lady in nearly a hundred deliriously lurid examples of Eurosleaze with such titles as *Female Vampire* (1973), *Barbed Wire Dolls* (1976), *Die Marquise vonn Sade* (1976), and *Wanda the Wicked Warden* (1977). In later years, while continuing to work almost exclusively with Franco (whom she formally married in 2008) as an actress, she branched out into directing, writing and editing as well under a number of pseudonyms. Romay died in Spain of cancer on February 15.

Ann Rutherford (November 2, 1917–June 11, 2012). Therese Ann Rutherford played dozens of roles but made her biggest impact on film history by co-starring as Scarlett O'Hara's sister in *Gone with the Wind* (1939). Born in Vancouver to a silent film actress named Lucille Mansfield, Ann Rutherford was fated to act. She started working in radio before quickly jumping to film in *Waterfront Lady* (1935) at the age of seventeen. She signed a contract with MGM in the 1930s, appearing in *A Christmas Carol* (1938) and *Pride and Prejudice* (1940). She will also be well remembered for her work with Mickey Rooney in a series of films based on the character Andy Hardy, including *You're Only Young Once* (1937) and *Andy Hardy's Double Life* (1942). She worked with Red Skelton in a series of films for MGM that included *Whistling in the Dark* (1941), *Whistling in Dixie* (1942), and *Whistling in Brooklyn* (1943). After continued success in the 1940s, including *The Secret Life of Walter Mitty* (1947), Ann Rutherford retired in 1950 at just 33, making the rare TV appearance in the decades that would follow. She passed away in June in Beverly Hills, survived by her daughter, stepdaughter, and two grandsons.

Andrew Sarris (October 31, 1928–June 28, 2012). One of the leading names in American film criticism during its heyday in the Sixties and Seventies, the Brooklyn-born Sarris was a leading proponent of what became known as the auteur theory through such seminal works as the 1962 article "Notes on the Auteur Theory" (which inspired the equally famous Pauline Kael rebuttal "Circles and Squares") and the 1968 book *American Cinema: Directors and Directing 1929-1968*. His reviews appeared in such outlets as *The Village Voice* and *The New York Observer,* where he worked until his retirement in 2009, and he also published numerous books, including *Confessions of a Cultist, The Primal Screen* and *Politics and Cinema*. Married to fellow film critic Molly Haskell since 1969, the two lived in Manhattan, where he died on June 20 of a stomach infection.

Harris Savides (September 28, 1957–October 9, 2012). One of the most notable cinematographers of the 1990s and 2000s, Harris Savides helped define the visual aesthetic of David Fincher, and worked with Gus Van Sant, Martin Scorsese, Wong Kar Wai, Ridley Scott, Woody Allen, and Sofia Coppola. He was nominated for several awards in his career, including five times for the Independent Spirit Award and once for the BAFTA. In further evidence of the Academy's general incompetence, he was never nominated for the Oscar. Savides cut his cinematic teeth on music videos, shooting some of the most iconic clips of all time, including Michael Jackson's "Scream," Madonna's "Rain," Fiona Apple's "Criminal," Nine Inch Nails' "Closer," and R.E.M's "Everybody Hurts." His first film cinematography credit came in 1996's *Heaven's Prisoners* and he may be best remembered for the six films he shot for Gus Van Sant— *Finding Forrester* (2000), *Gerry* (2002), *Elephant* (2003), *Last Days* (2005), *Milk* (2008), and *Restless* (2011). Other notable credits include *The Game* (1997), *Birth* (2004), *Zodiac* (2007), *American Gangster* (2007), *Margot at the Wedding* (2007), *Whatever Works* (2009), *Greenberg* (2010), and *Somewhere* (2010). Savides passed away far too young when brain cancer took him at 55. He is survived by his wife and daughter.

Tony Scott (June 21, 1944–August 19, 2012). British film director and producer Tony Scott, younger brother to Oscar winner Ridley Scott, surprisingly passed away in Los Angeles after jumping from the Vincent Thomas Bridge in San Pedro. His stunning death was ruled a suicide and rumors circulated that Scott had untreatable cancer but the coroner revealed that not to be the case. The reason for Scott's suicide is as-yet-undetermined. In his decades in the business, Tony Scott made a notable mark and influence on his industry, perhaps no more so than when Don Simpson and Jerry Bruckheimer hired Scott to direct the Tom Cruise

vehicle *Top Gun* (1986), which became one of the highest-grossing and most iconic films of the 1980s. It was not Scott's first film, to be fair, and history has been kind to *The Hunger* (1982) with David Bowie and Catherine Deneuve, but Cruise's breakthrough film was Scott's breakthrough as well. Sadly, Scott's potential nosedived a bit with critically-lambasted films like *Beverly Hills Cop II* (1987), *Revenge* (1990), *Days of Thunder* (1990), and *The Last Boy Scout* (1991). He turned more arthouse with the Quentin Tarantino-written *True Romance* (1993), arguably the most critically acclaimed and artistically successful film that Scott directed in his career. He went back to the mainstream with 1995's *Crimson Tide,* which started a working relationship with Denzel Washington, who would also star in Scott's *Man on Fire* (2004), *DÇjÖ vu* (2006), *The Taking of Pelham 123* (2009), and *Unstoppable* (2010). Other directorial credits include *The Fan* (1996), *Enemy of the State* (1998), *Spy Game* (2001), and *Domino* (2005). Scott's quick-cut, music video style was often derided by critics but led to numerous box office smashes and influenced the form in ways for which the director was never appropriately credited. Tony Scott also founded Scott Free, a production company, with his brother and was responsible behind the scenes for several major TV shows and films. Tony Scott was married three times, the last to Donna Wilson in 1994. He is survived by twin sons, Frank and Max.

Robert B. Sherman (December 19, 1925–March 5, 2012). American songwriter Robert Bernard Sherman was responsible for music that defined a generation, working on several key Disney films and even writing the most notable theme park song in the history of the world—"It's a Small World (After All)." After serving in World War II at the age of 17 (where he helped liberate Dachau and received two Battle Stars along with other medals for his service), he began writing songs with his brother Richard and the guidance of his father Al Sherman, himself a songwriter. Walt Disney was attracted to the Sherman Brothers after they wrote a hit song for Annette Funicello and hired them to write the theme park song. They moved from that to *Mary Poppins* (1965), for which they won two Academy Awards, writing "Feed the Birds," "Supercalifragilisticexpialidocious," and "Chim Chim Cher-ee." Robert Sherman earned nine Academy Award nominations in his career but never won after *Mary Poppins*. Other films for which the Sherman Brothers were nominated were *Chitty Chitty Bang Bang* (1969), two for *Bedknobs and Broomsticks* (1972), *Tom Sawyer* (1974), two for *The Slipper and the Rose* (1978), and *The Magic of Lassie* (1979). They worked on numerous classic Disney and other company's animated films in terms of score and original song, including *The Parent Trap* (1961), *The Jungle Book* (1967), *The Aristocats* (1970), *Charlotte's Web* (1973), *The Many Adventures of Winnie the Pooh* (1977), and *Snoopy, Come Home* (1972). Sherman is also credited with writing *The Adventures of Tom Sawyer* (1973), *The Adventures of Huckleberry Finn* (1974), *The Slipper and the Rose,* and more. Robert B. Sherman is in the Songwriters Hall of Fame.

Sage Stallone (May 5, 1976–July 13, 2012). The son of Sasha Czack and the legendary Sylvester Stallone appeared in a few of his father's films, most notably playing Rocky Balboa's son in *Rocky V* (1990). He also worked with dear old dad on *Daylight* (1996) before moving to more obscure roles in indie productions and B-movies. He passed away at the age of twenty-six of a heart attack.

Danny Steinmann (January 7, 1942–December 18, 2012). An unabashed purveyor of pure cinematic sleaze, the New York City-born Steinmann made his directorial debut with the hard-core pornographic feature *High Rise* (1973) under the nom de plume Danny Stone and would use another assumed name, Peter Foleg, on his next feature, *The Unseen* (1980), after being dissatisfied with the end results. After his next film, the gory Lina Blair revenge thriller *Savage Streets* (1984), he was hired to direct *Friday the 13th V: A New Beginning* (1985), the fifth installment of the hugely popular slasher film franchise. A troubled production that found little favor even with fans of the series, due to the odd conceit of being a *Friday the 13th* film in which (Spoiler Alert!) the killer turned out to be someone merely pretending to be Jason Voorhees, this proved to be Steinmann's swan song in the industry and despite rumors of projects in development (including a proposed sequel to *Last House on the Left* (1972)), he never directed another film. Steinmann passed away in Los Angeles on December 18.

Mel Stuart (September 2, 1928–August 9, 2012). Born Stuart Solomon in New York City, Mel Stuart directed one of the most beloved children's films of all time—*Willy Wonka & the Chocolate Factory* (1971). The cousin of Marvel legend Stan Lee, Stuart directed a few films and TV shows but never came close to the fame he found with *Willy Wonka*. Other credits include *If It's Tuesday, This Must Be Belgium* (1969), *I Love My Wife* (1970), *Wattstax* (1974), and *Mean Dog Blues* (1978). He passed away from cancer at his Beverly Hills home in August of 2012.

Susan Tyrrell (March 18, 1945–June 16, 2012). Born Susan Jillian Creamer, Tyrrell was Oscar-nominated for Best Supporting Actress for her work as Oma in John Huston's *Fat City* (1972) and made a memorable impact in John Waters' *Cry-Baby* (1990). Tyrrell worked in theater for a long time before transitioning to film in 1971's *Shoot Out,* which brought her to the attention Huston, who gave her the actress's most notable role (and caused controversy in later years when Tyrrell accused Huston of using the casting couch to hire the actress). Tyrrell became a tough-chick icon in the 1970s and 1980s, starring in dozens of B-movies and making regular TV appearances and many of the hit shows of the day. Notable credits include *Catch My Soul* (1974), *The Killer Inside Me* (1976), *Andy Warhol's Bad* (1977), *Forbidden Zone* (1982), *Angel* (1984), *Avenging Angel* (1985), *From a Whisper to a Scream* (1987), *Tapeheads* (1988), *Big Top Pee-wee* (1988)m, *Powder* (1995), *Poison Ivy: The New Seduction* (1997), and *Masked and Anonymous* (2003). Tyrell lost both of her legs in 2000 due to essential thrombocythemia and passed away at the age of 67 in 2012.

Gore Vidal (October 3, 1925–July 31, 2012). Although best-known as one of the most celebrated authors and playwrights of his time, Vidal also dabbled from time to time in the world of film, though rarely with much success. There were attempts to bring his work to the screen with results ranging from such adequate efforts as *The Left-Handed Gun* (1958) and *The Best Man* (1964) to the perplexing *Visit to a Small Planet* (1960), which saw his caustic satire transformed into a goofy vehicle for Jerry

Lewis to the legendarily disastrous *Myra Breckenridge* (1970). Vidal's own screen efforts were also a mixed bag—he worked on the scripts for such popular titles as *The Catered Affair* (1956), *Ben Hur* (1959), and *Suddenly Last Summer* (1959) but he was so appalled by what happened to his screenplay for the pornographic epic *Caligula* (1979) when producer Bob Guccione got a hold of it that he took his name off the project entirely even though it had originally been sold around the world as *Gore Vidal's Caligula*. In the end, Vidal's greatest success in the movies would be as an actor—after receiving acclaim for his performance as a well-meaning liberal senator in *Bob Roberts* (1992), he would make appearances in *With Honors* (1994), *The Shadow Conspiracy* (1996), *Gattaca* (1997), *Igby Goes Down* (2002), and *Shrink* (2009). Vidal died of pneumonia on July 31.

Yvette Wilson (March 6, 1964–June 14, 2012). Yet another deceased celebrity of 2012 who will be better remembered for television work than film, Yvette Wilson will be best remembered for work on the sitcoms *Moesha* and *The Parkers*. Before passing away from cervical cancer at the age of 48, Wilson appeared in several urban-skewing films, including *Poetic Justice* (1993), *House Party 3* (1994), *Friday* (1995), and *Don't Be a Menace to South Central While Drinking Your Juice in the Hood* (1996).

William Windom (September 28, 1923–August 16, 2012). Known primarily for his TV work, including an Emmy-winning turn on *My World and Welcome to It* (1969), memorable episodes of *The Twilight Zone* and *Night Gallery,* and a recurring role on *Murder, She Wrote*. After serving in World War II, Windom began acting, finding his first notable film role as Mr. Gilmer in the beloved *To Kill a Mockingbird* (1962). He went on to more regular TV work but also memorably appeared in *The Detective* (1968), *Brewster McCloud* (1970), *The Mephisto Waltz* (1971), *Escape from the Planet of the Apes* (1971), *The Man* (1972), *She's Having a Baby* (1988), *Sommersby* (1993), and *Miracle on 34th Street* (1994). William Windom passed away from congestive heart failure, survived by Patricia Tunder Windom, four children, and four grandchildren.

Isuzu Yamada (February 5, 1917–July 9, 2012). Japanese actress Isuzu Yamada was a regular collaborator with several of her country's most notable directors, including working with Akira Kurosawa on a trio of influential films—*The Lower Depths* (1957), *Throne of Blood* (1957), and *Yojimbo* (1961). Yamada also appeared in the legendary Yasujiro Ozu's *Tokyo Twilight* (1957), working more in television and on stage after her renaissance in the 1950s. In 1995, Yamada received a Special Award from the Chairman of the Japan Academy and was named a Person of Cultural Merit by the Japanese government in 1993. In 2000, she became the first actress to receive the Order of Culture from the Emperor of Japan.

Adam Yauch (August 5, 1964–May 4, 2012). While the world of music will forever remember Adam Yauch as a founding member of The Beastie Boys, he also made a notable impact in the film world when he co-founded Oscilloscope Laboratories with THINKFilm exec David Fenkel. Notable films released by Oscilloscope include *Wendy and Lucy* (2008), *Kisses* (2008), *The Messenger* (2009), *The Maid* (2009), *Howl* (2010), *Meek's Cutoff*

(2011), *Exit Through the Gift Shop* (2011), *Bellflower* (2011), *We Need to Talk About Kevin* (2011), *Hello I Must Be Going* (2012), and *Wuthering Heights* (2012). In 2009, Yauch was diagnosed with cancer of his lymph node. He fought for years, but succumbed in May of 2012, forever leaving his impact musically and with a film production company artistically thriving.

Richard D. Zanuck (December 13, 1934–July 13, 2012). American film producer Richard Darryl Zanuck only has one Oscar for his production of *Driving Miss Daisy* (1989) but was notably involved in dozens of major films throughout his career, including some of the most beloved of all time. Born in Los Angeles, CA in 1934, Zanuck studied at Stanford, beginning work with 20th Century Fox before he had even graduated. His first credit was in 1959 with *Compulsion* and he quickly rose to prominence in the industry, producing *The Sound of Music* (1965) and even serving as President of Fox in the 1960s. In the 1970s, Zanuck formed The Zanuck/Brown Company with David Brown at Universal Pictures and produced Steven Spielberg's *The Sugarland Express* (1974) and *Jaws* (1975). The company produced numerous hit films and Zanuck worked notably with Tim Burton later in life, producing six of the director's films—*Planet of the Apes* (2001), *Big Fish* (2003), *Charlie and the Chocolate Factory* (20050, *Sweeney Todd: The Demon Barber of Fleet Street* (2007), *Alice in Wonderland* (2010), and *Dark Shadows* (2012). Other notable credits include *The Eiger Sanction* (1975), *Jaws 2* (1978), *The Verdict* (1982), *Cocoon* (1985), *Target* (1985), *Deep Impact* (1998), *True Crime* (1999), *Yes Man* (2008), and *Clash of the Titans* (2010). Zanuck passed away in 2012 after a heart attack.

Selected Film Books of 2012

Alger, Jed, Travis Knight, Chris Butler, and Sam Fell. *The Art and Making of ParaNorman.* Chronicle Books LLC, 2012. The LAIKA film from writer/directors Chris Butler and Sam Fell, nominated for the Oscar for Best Animated Feature Film, is explored in this behind-the-scenes coffee table book with concept art, character sketches, artwork, and details on the stop-motion process that drove the critical and commercial hit's production.

Ascher, Steven and Edward Pincus. *The Filmmaker's Handbook: A Comprehensive Guide for the Digital Age: 2013 Edition.* Penguin Group Incorporated, 2012. A heavily updated version of the "Bible" for video and film production that is used in film schools around the world with more details on the digital age and how it is impacting the form.

Belton, John. *American Cinema/American Culture.* McGraw-Hill Companies, Inc., 2012. How does film impact culture and vice versa? The exhaustive answer to that question attempts to capture how the two have been intrinsically woven since the dawn of celluloid.

Bordwell, David and Kristin Thompson. *Film Art: An Introduction with Connect Access Card.* McGraw-Hill Companies, Inc. 2012. An updated edition of the timeless textbook used in so many film studies classes. This edition, which contains more than 1,000 frame enlargements, also offers buyers access to online multimedia and digital tools to help with film production.

Boyle, Bill. *The Visual Mindscape of the Screenplay.* All That Sky Productions, 2012. The author offers more advice for blossoming screenwriters looking for the way to turn their grand ideas into scripted realities.

Bronson, Fred. *The Sound of Music Family Scrapbook.* Applause Theater Book Publishers, 2012. Few films have as devoted of a following as the story of the von Trapps and hills alive with the sound of music. This book approaches the much-chronicled production from the angle of the von Trapp children with the seven actors who played the family

offering their anecdotes on the making of the classic musical for the first time.

Burlingame, Jon. *The Music of James Bond.* Oxford University Press, USA, 2012. Every James Bond film up to 2012's *Skyfall* gets its own chapter, with the primary focus, of course, being on the iconic theme songs of the longest-running franchise in film history.

Burton, Richard and Chris Williams. *The Richard Burton Diaries.* Yale University Press, 2012. If you're dead long enough and were famous enough, someone will reprint your personal diaries. And so the personal writings of the legendary actor, which run from 1939 to 1983, the year before his death, are included here, offering insight into the life of one of the most beloved actors of all time.

Calvisi, Daniel P. *Story Maps: How to Write a GREAT Screenplay.* Act Four Screenplays, 2012. A Story Analyst in Hollywood offers yet another take crafting a hit script by analyzing a few recent smash hits, including *The Social Network* (2010), *The Dark Knight* (2009), and *Black Swan* (2010).

Castelli, Jean-Christophe. *The Making of Life of Pi: A Film, a Journey.* HarperCollins Publishers, 2012. An associate producer on *Life of Pi* (2012) and longtime collaborator with Ang Lee chronicles the making of the Oscar-winning film in this volume with over 275 photographs and illustrations of the first 3-D film to win the Academy Award for Best Director.

Corrigan, Timothy and Patricia White. *The Film Experience: An Introduction.* Bedford/St. Martin's, 2012. A Professor of Cinema Studies, English, and History of Art at the University of Pennsylvania and a Professor of Film and Media Studies at Swarthmore College team up to offer yet another tome that promises to turn the average movie goer into a critical viewer of the form.

Dance, Robert. *Hollywood Unseen: Photographs from the John Kobal Foundation.* Antique Collectors Club Dist., 2012.

Publicity images from the essential Hollywood film studios of the golden age—Columbia, Paramount, MGM, Universal, Warner Brothers, RKO, and Twentieth Century Fox—comprise this appreciation of the machine that helped turn the city of angels into the capital of moviemaking worldwide.

Davis, Gretchen and Mindy Hall. *The Makeup Artist Handbook: Techniques for Film, Television, Photography, and Theatre.* Taylor & Francis, 2012. Having worked on major Hollywood productions, the two authors offer advice from the front line of the competitive and complex world of makeup art, including devoted advice to how makeup has changed in the world of HD filmmaking.

De La Hoz, Cindy. *Elizabeth Taylor: A Shining Legacy on Film.* Running Press Book Publishers, 2012. Yet another book about one of the most famous actresses of all time that chronicles the entire career of a Hollywood legend.

DK Publishing. *Disney Pixar Cars: Character Encyclopedia.* DK Publishing, 2012. An exhaustive list and encyclopedia for the die-cast cars that have been sold to tie-in with *Cars* (2006), *Cars 2* (2011), and TV's *Car Toons* with a character profiled for more than 250 animated and collectible cars.

DK Publishing. *Disney Pixar Character Encyclopedia.* DK Publishing, 2012. More promotional propaganda tied into the Pixar empire with about 200 Disney Pixar characters, including Sully, Nemo, WALL-E, and Woody. Up to date through the 2012 offering, *Brave,* the Oscar winner for Best Animated Feature Film.

DK Publishing. *James Bond: 50 Years of Movie Posters.* DK Publishing, 2012. Packaged with two exclusive prints and tied to the fiftieth anniversary of the longest-running film franchise of all time, this volume chronicles the marketing materials for 007 throughout history, including not just official posters but foreign ones, discarded concepts, lobby cards and more from virtually every country where Bond movies have screened.

Douma, Jesse. *Hollywood Screenwriting Directory Fall 2012: A Specialized Resource for Discovering Where & How to Sell Your Screenplay.* F+W Media, Inc., 2012. Where do you sell your amazing new screenplay that is sure to be a hit? This is the directory to guide the way, created from three decades of working behind the scenes and verifying contact information for the people who sign the deals that oil the Hollywood machine.

Duncan, Paul. *The James Bond Archives.* Taschen America, LLC, 2012. Another volume tied to the fiftieth anniversary of the most legendary spy in cinema history with a massive volume that promises details on the production of every film in the 007 series to date from *Dr. No* (1962) to *Skyfall* (2012). EON Productions opened their archives for stills, production materials, storyboards, etc.

Ebert, Roger. *Roger Ebert's Movie Yearbook 2013: 25th Anniversary Edition.* Andrews McMeel Publishing, 2012. The annual edition of the Pulitzer Prize-winning film critic's yearbook of collected reviews.

The Editors of Entertainment Weekly. *Twilight: The Complete Journey.* Time Home Entertainment, Inc., 2012. A compendium of magazine articles about *The Twilight Saga* from the editors of the entertainment periodical who made

a fortune covering one of the biggest blockbuster series of the modern era.

The Editors of LIFE Books. *LIFE 50 Years of James Bond.* Time Home Entertainment, Inc., 2012. Another magazine, another franchise compendium. With the arrival of the 50th anniversary of James Bond, *LIFE Magazine* collects articles about the series from *Dr. No* (1962) to *Skyfall* (2012).

Edson, Eric. *The Story Solution: 23 Actions All Great Heroes Must Take.* Michael Wiese Productions, 2012. A film and TV writer with four decades of experience in the field offers his take on how to arc a protagonist through a successful screenplay.

Fisher, Jude. *The Hobbit: An Unexpected Journey Visual Companion.* Houghton Mifflin Harcourt, 2012. With more than 100 color photos from the film and details on the making of Peter Jackson's epic work along with a fold-out map charting Bilbo's journey, this is a tie-in to the Warner Bros. hit epic.

Franklin, DeVon and Tim Vandehey. *Produced by Faith: Enjoy Real Success without Losing Your True Self.* Howard Books, 2012. Vice President of Production for Columbia Pictures, a division of Sony Pictures Entertainment, offers readers a guide to maintaining faith and a commitment to God while navigating the sinful waters of the world of filmmaking.

Fry, Jason and Paul R. Urquhart. *Star Wars: The Essential Guide to Warfare.* Random House Publishing Group, 2012. Combat, spaceships, interstellar treaties—the rules of warfare have been an essential part of the massive universe created by George Lucas and this one of many companion books to the most beloved film sci-fi series of all time addresses that aspect of the mythology.

Greenberger, Robert. *Star Trek: The Complete Unauthorized History: To Boldly Go Where No Fan Has Gone Before.* Voyageur Press, 2012. A tome that promises to blend the anecdotal history of the making of the six television series and eleven feature films with the base that has truly kept the franchise vital—the hardcore fans.

Hammett, Kirk and Steffan Chirazi. *Too Much Horror Business: The Kirk Hammett Collection.* Abrams Image, 2012. Kirk Hammett, the lead guitarist for Metallica, one of the most successful rock bands of all time, reveals his personal collection of movie memorabilia from the entire history of the horror genre, including Bela Lugosi's annotated script for *Dracula* (1931), the bunny suit from *Donnie Darko* (2001), and much more.

Janisse, Kier-La. *House of Psychotic Women: An Autobiographical Topography of Female Neurosis in Horror and Exploitation Films.* FAB Press, 2012. An examination of the subgenre of horror films in which women go crazy, often falling victim to their own neuroses, and how these films reflect on Hollywood's view of the female gender.

Jesser, Jody Duncan, Janine Pourroy, Michael Caine, and Christopher Nolan. *The Art and Making of The Dark Knight Trilogy.* Harry N. Abrams, Inc., 2012. A companion piece to *The Dark Knight Rises* (2012) with pages of pictures, artwork, and details on the making of Christopher Nolan's entire Batman trilogy (with *Batman Begins* [2005] and *The Dark Knight* [2008]).

John Wayne Enterprises, Patricia Bosworth, Ron Howard, and Martin Scorsese. *John Wayne: The Legend and the Man: An Exclusive Look Inside Duke's Archives.* PowerHouse Books, 2012. Another collection of film stills, backstage photos, and snapshots that serves as the first exclusively authorized photographic record of his life. This version also includes many personal photos from family albums and friends.

Jones, Jenny M. *The Big Lebowski: An Illustrated, Annotated History of the Greatest Cult Film of All Time.* Voyageur Press, 2012. A making-of volume on the legendary 1998 Joel and Ethan Coen film that did not have much of a ripple commercially or creatively when it was first released but became an international cult hit over the years.

Kaufman, J.B. *The Fairest One of All: The Making of Walt Disney's Snow White and the Seven Dwarfs.* Weldon Owen Reference, Inc., 2012. The 75th anniversary of Disney's beloved *Snow White and the Seven Dwarfs.* (1937) is celebrated with this companion that was approved by and created with the Walt Disney Family Foundation. It includes never-before-published facts and art.

Kaufman, J.B. *Snow White and the Seven Dwarfs: The Art and Creation of Walt Disney's Classic Animated Film.* Weldon Owen Reference, Inc., 2012. A visual representation of the history and production of the beloved children's classic on its 75th anniversary that includes rarely seen concept sketches, background paintings, and cels.

Kenworthy, Christopher. *Master Shots Vol. 1, 2nd Edition: 100 Advanced Camera Techniques to get an Expensive Look on Your Low-Budget Movie.* Michael Wiese Productions, 2012. A guide to the techniques that new filmmakers can use to make their own films by disguising their low budget with high-caliber camerawork.

Knoll, John and J.W. Rinzler. *Creating the Worlds of Star Wars: 365 Days.* Harry N. Abrams, Inc., 2012. The Visual Effects Supervisor for *Star Wars, Episode I: The Phantom Menace* (1999) and the subsequent films in George Lucas' prequel trilogy brings his story to print with this volume of the *365 Days* series that covers all six films and the creation of their worlds through models, sets, props, and computer animation.

Koenig, David. *Danny Kaye: King of Jesters.* Bonaventure Press, 2012. A behind-the-scenes look at the creation of Danny Kaye's most beloved films ever with never-before-published anecdotes and photos.

Korkis, Jim, Bob McLain, and Diane Disney Miller. *The Revised Vault of Walt: Unofficial, Unauthorized, Uncensored Disney Stories Never Told.* Bob McLain Media, 2012. An update of the author's 2010 book with five brand-new stories to add to this compendium of tales about Walt Disney films, Disney theme parks, and the empire built around a more complex history than its publicity machine might have fans believe.

Korkis, Jim, Floyd Norman and Bob McLain. *Who's Afraid of the Song of the South? And Other Forbidden Disney Stories.* Bob McLain Media, 2012. The author of *The Vault of Walt* examines Disney's most controversial film, *Song of the South* (1946), a deeply-racist film that has not been released in any form by Disney since 1986. He also includes ten other tales of controversial chapters in the Disney history.

Lancaster, Kurt. *DSLR Cinema: Crafting the Film Look with Large Sensor Video Cameras.* Taylor & Francis, 2012. The self-explanatory title says it all as the author focuses on video-capable DSLR cameras and how to use them to produce film.

Landau, Neil. *The Screenwriter's Roadmap: 21 Ways to Jump-start Your Story.* Taylor & Francis, 2012. The author, an established script doctor, interviews some of Hollywood's most successful screenwriters in an effort to provide a guide to successful screenwriting. Writers interviewed include Scott Z. Burns, Tony Gilroy, David Koepp, Eric Roth, David S. Goyer, and many more.

Landis, Deborah Nadoolman. *Filmcraft: Costume Design.* Taylor & Francis, 2012. Sixteen of the world's leading costume designers, including Academy Award winners Aggie Guerard Rodgers, Janty Yates, and Liny Hemming, are interviewed in an attempt to offer buyers a window into one of the most important aspects of film production.

Landis, Deborah Nadoolman. *Hollywood Sketchbook.* HarperCollins Publishers, 2012. The Founding Director of the David C. Copley Center for Costume Design at the UCLA School of Theater, Film, and Television offers an array of first-person anecdotes from collectors, archivists, illustrators, and designers in an effort to celebrate one hundred years of costume design and illustration.

Langley, Travis, Dennis O'Neill, and Michael Uslan. *Batman and Psychology: A Dark and Stormy Knight (Wiley Psychology & Pop Culture).* John Wiley & Sons, Inc., 2012. Professor of Psychology at Henderson State University and organizer for the Comic Arts Conference who speaks regularly at the San Diego Comic-Con offers his analysis of what the Batman character says about the workings of the human mind with an emphasis on Christopher Nolan's trilogy, timed for the release of *The Dark Knight Rises* (2012).

Lear, Norman and Rob Reiner. *The Princess Bride: A Celebration.* Rizzoli, 2012. A collection of memorabilia from the archives of the cultdom around and production of one of the most beloved films of the 1980s, Rob Reiner's *The Princess Bride* (1987). Bills itself as the first and only official companion to the film as the production gave the author access to behind-the-scenes photographs, script pages, production designs, and more.

Lerew, Jenny, John Lasseter, Brenda Chapman, and Mark Andrews. *The Art of Brave.* Chronicle Books LLC, 2012. A showcase for the Oscar-winning film with color scripts, storyboards, character studies, environment art, sculpts, and more, with a foreword by the film's directors and a preface by Chief Creative Officer John Lasseter.

Lucasfilm, Nancy Reagin, and Janice Liedl. *Star Wars and History.* John Wiley & Sons, Incorporated, 2012. Yet another book that examines the legacy and historical importance of the franchise created by George Lucas that has spawned literally hundreds of companion volumes.

LucasFilm Ltd, Steven Heller, and Howard Roffman. *Star Wars Art: Illustration.* Harry N. Abrams, Inc., 2012. Co-Chair MFA Design, School of Visual Arts offers his visual take on the George Lucas universe.

Malkiewicz, Kris. *Film Lighting: Talks with Hollywood's Cinematographers and Gaffers.* Touchstone, 2012. A first-hand examination of lighting in film using advice from experts in the field like Oscar-winning cinematographers Dion Beebe, Russell Carpenter, Robert Elswitt, Mauro Fiore, Janusz Kaminski, Wally Pfister, Haskell Wexler, and Vilmos Zsigmond.

Malone, Maggie, Jennifer Lee, John Lasseter, and Rich Moore. *The Art of Wreck-It Ralph (The Art of Disney).* Chronicle Books LLC, 2012. Featuring a foreword by the director and a preface by John Lasseter, this companion to the Oscar-nominated film includes character sketches, storyboards, visual development paintings, color scripts and more.

Maltin, Leonard. *Leonard Maltin's 2013 Movie Guide: The Modern Era.* Penguin Group, 2012. The legendary critic offers his annual year book with more than 16,000 capsule movie reviews and more than 300 new entries.

Mattera, Jason. *Hollywood Hypocrites.* Threshold Editions, 2012. A Talk Radio host from New York offers his conservative viewpoint on how liberal Hollywood performers and filmmakers do not live up to their oft-publicized political and moral views.

McCabe, Bob, Jody Revenson, and Moira Squier. *Harry Potter Page to Screen: The Complete Filmmaking Journey (Collector's Edition).* Brilliance Audio, 2012. This massive collection of several books in one promises to be the ultimate word on the hit film franchise and runs nearly a thousand dollars for the buyer.

Mendez, Antonio and Matt Baglio. *Argo: How the CIA and Hollywood Pulled Off the Most Audacious Rescue in History.* Penguin Group, 2012. Timed to coincide with the release of Ben Affleck's Best Picture-winning film, this work offers the true story of how Tony Mendez engineered the rescue of the "House Guests," the six Americans who escaped the Iranian hostage crisis.

Miller-Zarneke, Tracey. *The Art and Making of Hotel Transylvania.* Titan, 2012. The writer of several companion books timed with animated films offers yet another one with over 400 pieces of concept art, character sketches, storyboards, and digital art, along with interviews with key filmmakers and crew.

Moore, Sir Roger. *Bond on Bond: Reflections on 50 Years of James Bond Movies.* The Lyons Press, 2012. The second man to play James Bond returns to discuss his involvement in the 50-year-old series, including hundreds of iconic images and many unseen photos from the author's personal collection.

Nolan, Christopher. *The Dark Knight Trilogy: The Complete Screenplays with Storyboards.* Hal Leonard Corporation, 2012. At nearly six hundred pages, this volume lives up to its title, including the screenplays and storyboards for *Batman Begins* (2005), *The Dark Knight* (2008), and *The Dark Knight Rises* (2012).

O'Neill, Terry. *All About Bond.* Evans Mitchell Books, 2012. A photographer who started on the set of *Goldfinger* (1963) recalls his time with the series and how he photographed five Bonds and more than 20 Bond girls. It includes more than 100 photographs.

Pauley, Jim and Leonard Maltin. *The Three Stooges: Hollywood Filming Locations.* Santa Monica Press, 2012. A recollection of the sets and filming locations for The Three Stooges short films between 1934 and 1958 with archival photographs, many of which are rare and previously unpublished.

Robb, Brian J, James P. Blaylock, and Jonathan Clements. *Steampunk: The Illustrated History of Fantastical Fiction, Fanciful Film and Other Victorian Visions.* Voyageur Press, 2012. An examination of how the Steampunk movement has been reflected in fiction and film, including the works of Alan Moore, Hayao Miyazaki, and Philip Pullman.

Rogers, Paul. *Name That Movie: 100 Illustrated Movie Puzzles.* Chronicle Books LLC, 2012. Filled with visual brain teasers based on a 100 classic films with six line drawings, delivered in sequence, this small book is good for puzzle lovers and movie fans.

Rollyson, Carl. *Hollywood Enigma: Dana Andrews.* University of Mississippi Press, 2012. The lesser-known actor is profiled in this book that celebrates the work he's done with legends like Joan Crawford, Elizabeth Taylor, Greer Garson, Merle Oberon, Linda Darnell, Susan Hayward, Maureen O'Hara, and Gene Tierney. The author is a professor of journalism at Baruch College, CUNY.

Salisbury, Mark and Ridley Scott. *Prometheus: The Art of the Film.* Titan, 2012. The author used to be the editor of *Empire* magazine and now produces companion books for major films. This one includes an introduction by the director, production art, and behind-the-scenes photos.

Sarantakes, Nicholas Evan. *Making Patton: A Classic War Film's Epic Journey to the Silver Screen.* University Press of Kansas, 2012. An associate professor of strategy at the U.S. Naval War College and author of several books about twentieth century warfare takes his exhaustive approach to the 1970 classic film about General George S. Patton, which won seven Oscars, including Best Picture and Best Actor.

Schickel, Richard and Steven Spielberg. *Steven Spielberg: A Retrospective.* Sterling, 2012. With chapters on every film in Steven Spielberg's career, up through 2012's *Lincoln*, Schickel offers commentary on one of the most important filmmakers of all time, complete with over 250 dynamic images.

Schmidt, Christel. *Mary Pickford: Queen of the Movies.* University Press of Kentucky, 2012. An historian devoted to the legendary Mary Pickford offers another analysis of the star's history created in conjunction with the Library of Congress that includes photographs, stills, and more than two hundred color and black and white illustrations.

Sellers, Michael D. *John Carter and the Gods of Hollywood.* Universal Media, 2012. The subtitle of this behind-the-scenes tome really says it all—The True Story of What Went Wrong with Disney's John Carter and Why Edgar Rice Burroughs' Original Superhero Isn't Dead Yet.

Sheen, Martin, Emilio Estevez, and Hope Edelman. *Along the Way: The Journey of a Father and Son.* Free Press, 2012. A dual memoir by Martin Sheen and Emilio Estevez inspired by their work together on *The Way* (2012) and the path they took along the legendary Camino de Santiago pilgrimage path.

Sibley, Brian. *The Hobbit: An Unexpected Journey Official Movie Guide.* Houghton Mifflin Harcourt, 2012. Pretty self-explanatory tome with hundreds of behind-the-scenes photos of the actors, locations, sets, creatures, and costumes from Peter Jackson's 2012 return to Middle Earth.

Smith, Kevin. *Tough Sh*t: Life Advice from a Fat, Lazy Slob Who Did Good.* Penguin Group, 2012. The writer/director who loves to talk offers more advice on how to "make ten movies with no discernible talent."

Snider, Brandon T. *The Dark Knight Manual: Tools, Weapons, Vehicles and Documents from the Batcave.* Insight Editions LLC, 2012. A fictional approach to Christopher Nolan's Batman trilogy that offers fans of the series the documents used by Bruce Wayne to create the tools of his trade, including sketches, diagrams, and other "top-secret documents."

Surrell, Jason. *Avengers: The Art of Marvel's The Avengers.* Marvel Enterprises, Inc., 2012. A keepsake volume to celebrate Joss Whedon's smash blockbuster, *Marvel's The Avengers* (2012) with concept art, full-color photographs, excerpts from the script, and exclusive interviews with the cast and crew.

Sutherland, Jean-Anne and Kathryn M. Feltey. *Cinematic Sociology: Social Life in Film.* SAGE Publications, 2012. An Associate Professor at the University of North Carolina approaches film from a sociological approach with this volume designed for teachers looking for textbooks for classes.

Taylor, Matt. *Jaws: Memories from Martha's Vineyard.* Titan, 2012. A coffee table book filled with copious archival material from the time that Steven Spielberg's *Jaws* (1975) descended on Martha's Vineyard.

Thomson, David. *The Big Screen: The Story of the Movies.* Farrar, Straus and Giroux, 2012. The legendary author of *The New Biographical Dictionary of Film* approaches the entire history of the form.

Vaz, Mark Cotta. *The Host: The Official Illustrated Movie Companion.* Little, Brown & Company, 2012. Stephenie Meyer, the author of the books that became *The Twilight Saga,* tries for cinematic gold twice with the 2013 release of an adaptation of *The Host* from director Andrew Niccol. The adaptation was released early to build anticipation.

Vaz, Mark Cotta, Paul Levitz, and Nathan Crowley. *Batmobile: The Complete History.* Insight Editions LLC, 2012. A chronicle of the legendary automobile and how it developed both on the comic book page and through cinematic adaptations like Christopher Nolan's trilogy.

Viers, Ric. *The Location Sound Bible: How to Record Professional Dialog for Film and TV.* Michael Wiese Productions, 201. The author of *The Sound Effects Bible* moves outside and offers basic and advanced techniques that should help sound technicians get work in film and television.

Welch, Bob. *52 Little Lessons from It's a Wonderful Life.* Thomas Nelson, Inc., 2012. A lesson for every week from the beloved 1946 Frank Capra classic that plays in constant rotation around the holidays.

Weta Workshop. *The Hobbit: An Unexpected Journey Chronicles: Art & Design.* HarperCollins Publishers, 2012. Packed with more than 1,000 images of concept artwork, photographs, and development paintings that helped guide the design of the 2012 Peter Jackson blockbuster.

Whedon, Joss and Drew Goddard. *The Cabin in the Woods: The Official Visual Companion.* Titan, 2012. With in-depth interviews, production art, and hundreds of color photos, Drew Goddard's highly-acclaimed horror/comedy gets a lavish companion tie-in.

Williams, Greg. *Bond on Set: Filming Skyfall.* DK Publishing, Inc., 2012. A photojournalist was allowed access to the production of Sam Mendes' hit film and produced this companion piece to the mega-blockbuster with candid shots of the stars and sequences.

Wills, David. *Audrey: The 60s.* HarperCollins Publishers, 2012. Few film icons have as many books devoted to them as Audrey Hepburn—this is another. This one includes work by the photographers who helped create her image.

Windham, Ryder, Chris Reiff, and Chris Trevas. *The Millennium Falcon Owner's Workshop Manual: Star Wars (Haynes Manuals).* Random House Publishing Group, 2012. A fictional manual to a fictional machine offers yet another approach to the legendary spaceship first made famous in George Lucas' *Star Wars* (1977).

Director Index

Andrew Adamson (1966-)
Cirque du Soleil: Worlds Away

Ben Affleck (1972-)
Argo

Salim Akil
Sparkle

Woody Allen (1935-)
To Rome with Love

Sean Anders
That's My Boy

Paul Thomas Anderson (1970-)
The Master

Paul W.S. Anderson (1965-)
Resident Evil: Retribution

Wes Anderson (1969-)
Moonrise Kingdom

Mark C. Andrews
Brave

Peter Andrews (1963-)
See *Steven Soderbergh*

Judd Apatow (1967-)
This Is 40

Michael Apted (1941-)
Chasing Mavericks

Nikolaj Arcel
A Royal Affair

Andrea Arnold
Wuthering Heights

Jacques Audiard (1952-)
Rust and Bone

David Ayer (1972-)
End of Watch

Kyle Balda
Dr. Seuss' The Lorax

Daniel Barnz
Won't Back Down

Simon Barrett
V/H/S

Seth Barrish
Sleepwalk with Me

Michael J. Bassett
Silent Hill: Revelation 3D

Zal Batmanglij
Sound of My Voice

Matt Battinelli-Olpin
V/H/S

Juan Antonio Bayona (1975-)
The Impossible

Timur Bekmambetov
Abraham Lincoln: Vampire
Hunter

William Brent Bell
The Devil Inside

Malik Bendjelloul
Searching For Sugar Man

Bruce Beresford (1940-)
Peace, Love & Misunderstanding

Amy Berg
West of Memphis

Peter Berg (1964-)
Battleship

Luc Besson (1959-)
The Lady

Kathryn Bigelow (1952-)
Zero Dark Thirty

Mike Birbiglia (1978-)
Sleepwalk with Me

Ole Bornedal
The Possession

David Bowers (1970-)
Diary of a Wimpy Kid: Dog
Days

Dan Bradley
Red Dawn

David Bruckner
V/H/S

Ken Burns (1953-)
The Central Park Five

Sarah Burns
The Central Park Five

Tim Burton (1960-)
Dark Shadows
Frankenweenie

Chris Butler
ParaNorman

Leos Carax (1960-)
Holy Motors

Joe Carnahan (1969-)
The Grey

Joseph Cedar
Footnote

Nuri Bilge Ceylan
Once Upon a Time in Anatolia

Agnieszka Holland (1948-)
  In Darkness

Tom Hooper (1972-)
  Les Miserables

Agnes Hranitzky
  The Turin Horse

Jon Hurwitz (1977-)
  American Reunion

Peter Jackson (1961-)
  The Hobbit: An Unexpected
  Journey

Benoit Jacquot (1947-)
  Farewell, My Queen

Nicholas Jarecki
  Arbitrage

Rian Johnson (1973-)
  Looper

Kirk Jones (1963-)
  What to Expect When You're
  Expecting

Henry Joost
  Paranormal Activity 4

Bess Kargman
  First Position

Lawrence Kasdan (1949-)
  Darling Companion

Nicole Kassell
  A Little Bit of Heaven

Tony Kaye (1952-)
  Detachment

Christopher Kenneally
  Side by Side

Chris Kentis (1962-)
  Silent House

Alison Klayman
  Ai Weiwei: Never Sorry

Brian Klugman (1975-)
  The Words

David Koepp (1964-)
  Premium Rush

Hirokazu Kore-eda (1962-)
  I Wish

Baltasar Kormakur (1966-)
  Contraband

Lee Toland Krieger
  Celeste & Jesse Forever

Alex Kurtzman (1973-)
  People Like Us

Ken Kwapis (1957-)
  Big Miracle

Nadine Labaki
  Where Do We Go Now?

Laura Lau
  Silent House

Bart Layton
  The Imposter

Ang Lee (1954-)
  Life of Pi

Spike Lee (1957-)
  Red Hook Summer

Stephanie Leger
  Lockout

Asger Leth
  Man on a Ledge

Barry Levinson
  The Bay

Ben Lewin (1946-)
  The Sessions

Jonathan Liebesman (1976-)
  Wrath of the Titans

Todd Lincoln (1976-)
  The Apparition

Jamie Linden
  10 Years

Daniel Lindsay
  Undefeated

Richard Linklater (1960-)
  Bernie

Jane Lipsitz
  Katy Perry: Part of Me

Peter Lord (1953-)
  The Pirates! Band of Misfits

Phil Lord
  21 Jump Street

Robert Lorenz
  Trouble with the Curve

Todd Louiso (1970-)
  Hello I Must Be Going

Sam Lowry (1963-)
  See Steven Soderbergh

Kevin MacDonald (1967-)
  Marley

John Madden (1949-)
  The Best Exotic Marigold Hotel

Javier Mariscal
  Chico & Rita

Mans Marlind (1969-)
  Underworld: Awakening

T.J. Martin
  Undefeated

Justin Martinez
  V/H/S

Steve Martino
  Ice Age: Continental Drift

James Mather
  Lockout

Mike McCoy
  Act of Valor

Martin McDonagh
  Seven Psychopaths

Seth McFarlane (1973-)
  Ted

McG (1968-)
  This Means War

Tom McGrath
  Madagascar 3: Europe's Most
  Wanted

David McMahon
  The Central Park Five

Glenn McQuaid
  V/H/S

Christopher McQuarrie (1968-)
  Jack Reacher

James McTeigue
  The Raven

Olivier Megaton
  Taken 2

Fernando Meirelles (1955-)
  360

Sam Mendes (1965-)
  Skyfall

Roger Michell (1957-)
  Hyde Park on Hudson

Chris Miller (1975-)
  21 Jump Street

Jason Moore
  Pitch Perfect

Rich Moore
  Wreck-It Ralph

Dror Moreh
  The Gatekeepers

Gabriele Muccino (1967-)
  Playing for Keeps

Oliver Nakache
  The Intouchables

Daniel Nettheim
  The Hunter

Mark Neveldine (1973-)
  Ghost Rider: Spirit of Vengeance

Screenwriter Index

Peter Farrelly (1957-)
    The Three Stooges
Pablo F. Fenjves (1956-)
    Man on a Ledge
Will Fetters
    The Lucky One
Dan Fogelman
    The Guilt Trip
Christopher D. Ford
    Robot & Frank
Robbie Fox
    Playing for Keeps
Ciaran Foy
    Citadel
David France
    How to Survive a Plague
Rebecca Frayn (1962-)
    The Lady
Ron Fricke
    Samsara
Jason Fuchs (1986-)
    Ice Age: Continental Drift
Alex Garland (1970-)
    Dredd
John Gatins
    Flight
Peter Gaulke
    The Babymakers
Tyler Gillett
    V/H/S
Dan Gilroy (1959-)
    The Bourne Legacy
Tony Gilroy (1956-)
    The Bourne Legacy
Scott Gimple
    Ghost Rider: Spirit of Vengeance
Ira Glass
    Sleepwalk with Me
Drew Goddard
    The Cabin in the Woods
Evan Goldberg (1982-)
    Goon
    The Watch
Jane Goldman (1970-)
    The Woman in Black
Bobcat Goldthwait (1962-)
    God Bless America
Todd Graff (1959-)
    Joyful Noise

Seth Graham-Smith (1976-)
    Abraham Lincoln: Vampire
        Hunter
    Dark Shadows
Seth Grossman
    A Late Quartet
Lars Gudmestad
    Headhunters
Davis Guggenheim (1964-)
    Safe House
Brian Gunn
    Journey 2: The Mysterious Island
Mark Gunn
    Journey 2: The Mysterious Island
Aaron Guzikowski
    Contraband
Heather Hach
    What to Expect When You're
        Expecting
Dan Hageman
    Hotel Transylvania
Kevin Hageman
    Hotel Transylvania
John Lee Hancock (1957-)
    Snow White and the Huntsman
Michael Haneke (1942-)
    Amour
Shawn Harwell
    The Campaign
Ronald Harwood (1934-)
    Quartet
Leslye Headland
    Bachelorette
Peter Hedges (1962-)
    The Odd Life of Timothy Green
Tim Heidecker
    Tim and Eric's Billion Dollar
        Movie
Rasmus Heisterberg
    A Royal Affair
Chris Henchy
    The Campaign
Olivia Hetread
    Wuthering Heights
Lee Hirsch
    Bully
John Hlavin
    Underworld: Awakening
Erich Hoeber
    Battleship

Jon Hoeber
    Battleship
Seth Hoffman
    Ghost Rider: Spirit of Vengeance
Jihad Hojeily
    Where Do We Go Now?
Skip Hollandsworth
    Bernie
Jon Hurwitz (1977-)
    American Reunion
Peter Jackson (1961-)
    The Hobbit: An Unexpected
        Journey
Benoit Jacquot (1947-)
    Farewell, My Queen
Kevin James (1965-)
    Here Comes the Boom
Nicholas Jarecki
    Arbitrage
Ian Mackenzie Jeffers
    The Grey
David Leslie Johnson
    Wrath of the Titans
Rian Johnson (1973-)
    Looper
Kurt Johnstad
    Act of Valor
Phil Johnston
    Wreck-It Ralph
Rashida Jones (1976-)
    Celeste & Jesse Forever
Zoe Lister Jones
    Lola Versus
Amy Jump
    Kill List
Robert Mark Kamen
    Taken 2
John Kamps
    Premium Rush
Lawrence Kasdan (1949-)
    Darling Companion
Meg Kasdan
    Darling Companion
Zoe Kazan (1983-)
    Ruby Sparks
Jason Keller (1971-)
    Mirror Mirror
Christopher Kenneally
    Side by Side

Katie Anne Naylon
  For a Good Time, Call...

Oleg Negin
  Elena

Richard Nelson (1950-)
  Hyde Park on Hudson

David Newman (1937-2003)
  Think Like a Man

William Nicholson (1948-)
  Les Miserables

Keiko Niwa
  The Secret World of Arrietty

Christopher Nolan (1970-)
  The Dark Knight Rises

Jonathan Nolan (1976-)
  The Dark Knight Rises

Roberto Orci (1973-)
  People Like Us

Brian Patrick O'Toole
  Atlas Shrugged II: The Strike

Ol Parker (1969-)
  The Best Exotic Marigold Hotel

Jeremy Passmore
  Red Dawn

Cinco Paul
  Dr. Seuss' The Lorax

Ben Pearson
  Blue Like Jazz

Oren Peli
  Chernobyl Diaries

Zak Penn (1968-)
  The Avengers

Tyler Perry (1969-)
  Madea's Witness Protection
  Tyler Perry's Good Deeds

Matthew Peterman (1975-)
  The Devil Inside

John Petro
  The Cold Light of Day

Sarah Polley (1979-)
  Take This Waltz

James Ponsoldt
  Smashed

Theresa Preston
  October Baby

Steve Purcell
  Brave

Neal Purvis (1961-)
  Skyfall

Josh Radnor (1974-)
  Liberal Arts

Billy Ray
  The Hunger Games

Karen Ray
  One for the Money

Todd Richman
  How to Survive a Plague

John Ridley (1965-)
  Red Tails

Jose Rivera (1955-)
  On the Road

Seth Rogen (1982-)
  The Watch

Melissa Rosenberg (1962-)
  The Twilight Saga: Breaking
  Dawn, Part 2

Michael R. Roskam
  Bullhead

Gary Ross (1956-)
  The Hunger Games

Eli Roth (1972-)
  The Man with the Iron Fists

David O. Russell (1959-)
  Silver Linings Playbook

Ry Russo-Young
  Nobody Walks

Ulf Ryberg
  Headhunters

RZA (1966-)
  The Man with the Iron Fists

Gabe Sachs
  Diary of a Wimpy Kid: Dog
  Days

Ira Sachs (1965-)
  Keep the Lights On

Kario Salem (1955-)
  Chasing Mavericks

Shane Salerno
  Savages

Sergio G. Sanchez (1973-)
  The Impossible

Duke Sandefur
  Atlas Shrugged II: The Strike

Alvin Sargent (1931-)
  The Amazing Spider-Man

Lorene Scafaria
  Seeking a Friend for the End of
  the World

Jeff Schaffer
  The Dictator

Hayden Schlossberg (1978-)
  American Reunion

Duncan Scott
  Atlas Shrugged II: The Strike

Jason Segel (1980-)
  The Five-Year Engagement

Hannah Shakespeare
  The Raven

David F. Shamoon
  In Darkness

Lynn Shelton
  Your Sister's Sister

Dax Shepard (1975-)
  Hit and Run

Stacy Sherman
  One for the Money

Radio Silence
  V/H/S

Marc Silverstein
  The Vow

Juliet Snowden
  The Possession

Joel Soisson
  Piranha 3DD

Todd Solondz (1960-)
  Dark Horse

Paolo Sorrentino
  This Must Be the Place

Jon Spaihts
  Prometheus

Jill Sprecher
  Thin Ice

Karen Sprecher
  Thin Ice

Jon Stalberg, Jr.
  High School

Sylvester Stallone (1946-)
  The Expendables 2

Andrew Stanton (1965-)
  John Carter

Andrew Steele
  Casa de mi Padre

Jared Stern
  The Watch

Lee Sternthal
  The Words

Whit Stillman (1952-)
  Damsels in Distress

Cecil Stokes
  October Baby

Cinematographer Index

Barry Ackroyd (1954-)
Contraband

Remi Adefarasin (1948-)
The Cold Light of Day

Javier Aguirresarobe (1948-)
The Five-Year Engagement

Maryse Alberti (1954-)
West of Memphis

Maxime Alexandre (1971-)
Silent Hill: Revelation 3D

Gonzalo Amat (1974-)
The Devil Inside

Mitchell Amundsen (1958-)
High School
Premium Rush
Red Dawn

John Andreas Andersen
Headhunters

Peter Andrews (1963-)
See Steven Soderbergh

Thierry Arbogast (1957-)
The Lady

John Aronson
Red Tails

John Bailey (1942-)
Big Miracle

Thimios Bakatakis
Keep the Lights On

Lubomir Bakchev
2 Days in New York

Florian Ballhaus (1965-)
Hope Springs

Michael Barrett (1970-)
Ted

Miroslaw Baszak
House at the End of the Street

Bojan Bazelli (1957-)
Rock of Ages

Adam Beckman
Sleepwalk with Me

Ross Berryman (1954-)
Atlas Shrugged II: The Strike

Luca Bigazzi (1958-)
This Must Be the Place

Larry Blanford
Think Like a Man

Christopher Blauvelt
Nobody Walks

Sean Bobbitt
Hysteria

Michael Bonvillain
Wanderlust

Eric Branco
V/H/S

Eigil Bryld
Not Fade Away

Don Burgess (1956-)
Flight

David Byrd (1933-2001)
Joyful Noise

Antonio Calvache
The Words

Paul Cameron (1958-)
Man on a Ledge
Total Recall

Russell Carpenter (1950-)
A Little Bit of Heaven
This Means War

Chris Cassidy
Side by Side

Caroline Champetier (1954-)
Holy Motors

Chi Ying Chan
The Man with the Iron Fists

Enrique Chediak
Intruders

Danny Cohen
Les Miserables

Lol Crawley (1974-)
Hyde Park on Hudson

Jeff Cronenweth (1962-)
Hitchcock

Stefan Czapsky
Safe

Tobias Datum
Smashed

Ben Davis (1962-)
The Best Exotic Marigold Hotel
Seven Psychopaths
Wrath of the Titans

John de Borman (1954-)
Quartet

Matthew F. Leonetti (1941-)
  The Three Stooges
Andrew Lesnie (1956-)
  The Hobbit: An Unexpected
    Journey
Matthew Libatique (1969-)
  Ruby Sparks
Daniel Lindsay
  Undefeated
Matthew Lloyd
  Robot & Frank
Sam Lowry (1963-)
  See Steven Soderbergh
Julio Macat (1959-)
  Pitch Perfect
Glen MacPherson (1957-)
  Resident Evil: Retribution
Mihai Malaimare, Jr.
  The Master
Anthony Dod Mantle (1955-)
  Dredd
Alain Marcoen
  The Kid with a Bike
T.J. Martin
  Undefeated
Justin Martinez
  V/H/S
Eduardo Martinez Solares
  For Greater Glory
Igor Martinovic
  Silent House
James Mather
  Lockout
Clark Mathis
  A Thousand Words
Tim Maurice-Jones
  The Woman in Black
Sam McCurdy
  The Collection
Michael McDonough (1967-)
  Darling Companion
Seamus McGarvey (1967-)
  Anna Karenina
  The Avengers
Glen McPherson (1957-)
  See Glen MacPherson
Phil Meheux (1941-)
  Here Comes the Boom
Peter Menzies, Jr.
  Playing for Keeps

Anastas Michos
  Sparkle
Dan(iel) Mindel (1958-)
  John Carter
  Savages
Claudio Miranda
  Life of Pi
Luc Montpellier
  Take This Waltz
Reed Morano (1977-)
  The Magic of Belle Isle
Rachel Morrison
  Sound of My Voice
  Tim and Eric's Billion Dollar
    Movie
Guillermo Navarro (1955-)
  The Twilight Saga: Breaking
    Dawn, Part 2
Ramsay Nickell (1963-)
  Casa de mi Padre
Christopher Norr
  Sinister
Josh Nussbaum
  The Bay
Cristophe Offenstein
  Where Do We Go Now?
Daryn Okada (1960-)
  American Reunion
Atsushi Okui
  The Secret World of Arrietty
Tristan Oliver
  ParaNorman
Yaron Orbach
  Fun Size
Tim Orr (1968-)
  Seeking a Friend for the End of
    the World
Roman Osin (1961-)
  Won't Back Down
Andrew Droz Palermo
  V/H/S
Phedon Papamichael (1962-)
  This Is 40
Andrij Parekh (1971-)
  Dark Horse
Frank Passingham
  The Pirates! Band of Misfits
Daniel Pearl (1951-)
  The Apparition
Ben Pearson
  Blue Like Jazz

Barry Peterson
  21 Jump Street
  The Watch
Wally Pfister (1961-)
  The Dark Knight Rises
Ronald Plante
  Monsieur Lazhar
Bill Pope (1952-)
  Chasing Mavericks
  Men in Black 3
Dick Pope (1947-)
  Bernie
  Thin Ice
Rodrigo Prieto (1965-)
  Argo
Declan Quinn (1957-)
  Being Flynn
  Neil Young Journeys
William Rexer
  Friends with Kids
Ben Richardson
  Beasts of the Southern Wild
Robert Richardson (1955-)
  Django Unchained
Anthony B. Richmond (1942-)
  Diary of a Wimpy Kid: Dog
    Days
Eliot Rockett
  The Innkeepers
Laurie Rose
  Kill List
Danny Ruhlmann
  The Raven
Robbie Ryan
  Wuthering Heights
Linus Sandgren (1972-)
  Promised Land
Anthony Savini
  The Central Park Five
Roberto Schaefer
  The Paperboy
Yaron Scharf
  Footnote
Tobias Schliessler
  Battleship
Brian Schulz
  Brooklyn Castle
John Schwartzman (1960-)
  The Amazing Spider-Man
Dean Semler (1943-)
  Parental Guidance

Editor Index

Greg Hayden
  The Dictator

Malcolm Hearn
  Side by Side

Jason Hellmann
  The Grey

Evan Henke
  For a Good Time, Call...

Emma E. Hickox
  Rock of Ages

Robin Hill
  Kill List

Scott Hill
  Here Comes the Boom

Kathryn Himoff
  Joyful Noise

Masahiro Hirakubo
  Bel Ami

David Hopper
  God Bless America

Niven Howie
  The Raven
  Resident Evil: Retribution

Maysie Hoy
  Madea's Witness Protection
  Tyler Perry's Good Deeds

William Hoy
  Abraham Lincoln: Vampire
    Hunter

Agnes Hranitzky
  The Turin Horse

Andrew Hulme
  The Imposter

Joe Hutshing
  Savages

Simon James
  2016: Obama's America

Leslie Jones
  The Master
  The Words

Michael Kahn
  Lincoln

Bess Kargman
  First Position

Brian A. Kates
  Killing Them Softly

Brad Katz
  The Babymakers

Virginia Katz
  The Twilight Saga: Breaking
    Dawn, Part 2

Tony Kearns
  Citadel

Melissa Kent
  The Vow

William Kerr
  The Five-Year Engagement

Eric Kissack
  The Dictator

Joe Klotz
  The Paperboy

Hirokazu Kore-eda (1962-)
  I Wish

Justin Krish
  The Pirates! Band of Misfits

Stephane Lafleur
  Monsieur Lazhar

Joe Landauer
  Safety Not Guaranteed

Veronique Lange
  Where Do We Go Now?

Lisa Lassek
  The Avengers
  The Cabin in the Woods

Brian David Lazarte
  Katy Perry: Part of Me

Chris Lebenzon
  Dark Shadows

Kasper Leick
  A Royal Affair

Robert Leighton
  People Like Us

Alisa Lepselter
  To Rome with Love

Michael Levine
  The Central Park Five

Stuart Levy
  Savages

Daniel Lindsay
  Undefeated

Susan Littenberg
  Lola Versus

Victor Livingston
  The Queen of Versailles

Mike Long
  Side by Side

Sam Lowry (1963-)
  See *Steven Soderbergh*

Steven Lui
  Dr. Seuss' The Lorax

Doug Lussenhop
  Tim and Eric's Billion Dollar
    Movie

Devin C. Lussier
  Piranha 3DD

Mark Magidson
  Samsara

Mary Jo Markey
  The Perks of Being a Wallflower

Alex Marquez
  Savages

Pamela Martin
  Hitchcock
  Ruby Sparks

T.J. Martin
  Undefeated

Anna Mass
  Elena

Rie Matsuhara
  The Secret World of Arrietty

Tom McArdle
  Hello I Must Be Going

Jeff McEvoy
  Underworld: Awakening

Padraic McKinley
  Playing for Keeps

Billy McMillin
  West of Memphis

Peter McNulty
  The Master

Glenn McQuaid
  V/H/S

Tamara Meem
  Sound of My Voice

Kevin Messman
  Dark Horse

Michael R. Miller
  Liberal Arts

Todd E. Miller
  The Expendables 2

Steve Mirkovich
  House at the End of the Street

Tim Mirkovich
  The Devil Inside

Stephen Mirrione
  The Hunger Games

Andrew Mondshein (1962-)
  The Odd Life of Timothy Green

Nick Moore
  Mirror Mirror

Matthew Sterling
Blue Like Jazz

Mark Stevens
The Collection

Jason Stewart
God Bless America

Kevin Stitt
Jack Reacher
Man on a Ledge

Crispin Struthers
Silver Linings Playbook

Joe Swanberg
V/H/S

Vincent Tabaillon
Taken 2

Troy Takaki
Diary of a Wimpy Kid: Dog Days

Arthur Tarnowski
Deadfall

Michael Thomas
2016: Obama's America

Frederic Thoraval
Safe
Sinister

Dylan Tichenor (1968-)
Lawless
Zero Dark Thirty

Tara Timpone
Friends with Kids

David Trachtenberg
Casa de mi Padre

Cristiano Travaglioli
This Must Be the Place

Michael Tronick
Act of Valor

Lindsay Utz
Bully

Bernat Vilaplana
The Impossible

Anders Villadsen
The Possession

Christian Wagner
Total Recall

Tyler H. Walk
How to Survive a Plague

Martin Walsh
Wrath of the Titans

John W. Walter
Nobody Walks

Scott Waugh
Act of Valor

Steven Weisberg
Hope Springs

Andrew Weisblum
Moonrise Kingdom

Juliette Welfing
The Hunger Games

Juliette Welfling
Rust and Bone

Ti West
The Innkeepers
V/H/S

Dirk Westervelt
Cirque du Soleil: Worlds Away

Brent White
This Is 40

Monika Willi
Amour

Adam Wingard
V/H/S

Jeffrey Wolf
Bachelorette

Sidney Wolinsky
Not Fade Away

Gabriel Wyre
High School

Aaron Yanes
The Bay

Avi Youabian
Step Up Revolution

Dan Zimmerman
Deadfall

Dean Zimmerman
The Watch

Don Zimmerman
Men in Black 3

Eric Zumbrunnen
John Carter

Art Director Index

Michael Ahern
  Arbitrage

Gentry L. Akens, II
  Tyler Perry's Good Deeds

RA Arancio-Parrain
  10 Years

Grant Armstrong
  Les Miserables

Alan Au
  Here Comes the Boom

Dilek Yapkuoz Ayaztuna
  Once Upon a Time in Anatolia

Peter Baran
  Lola Versus

Guy Barnes
  Cirque du Soleil: Worlds Away

Rodney Becker
  Bernie

Curt Beech
  Lincoln

Greg Berry
  The Dictator

Kevin Bird
  The Magic of Belle Isle

Max Boas
  Rise of the Guardians

Didac Bono
  The Impossible

Edward S. Bonutto
  Red Lights

Peter Borck
  Argo

Shane Boucher
  House at the End of the Street

Dennis Bradford
  Contraband

Simon Bright
  The Hobbit: An Unexpected
    Journey

Andrew Max Cahn
  This Is 40

Charlie Campbell
  Think Like a Man

Dustin Cardwell
  For a Good Time, Call...

Raymond Carr
  V/H/S

Steve Carter
  Salmon Fishing in the Yemen

Scott Coates
  Big Miracle

John Collins
  The Hunger Games

Kevin Constant
  End of Watch

Sarah Contant
  Gone

E. David Cosier
  Ted

Gina B. Cranham
  Red Dawn

David Crank
  Lincoln

Bill Crutcher
  Hysteria

Emmanuelle Cuillery
  Holy Motors

Adrian Curelea
  Ghost Rider: Spirit of Vengeance

Kelly Curley
  Seeking Justice

Charles Daboub, Jr.
  Step Up Revolution

Bob Danyla
  Playing for Keeps

Katya Debear
  Silent House

Ross Dempster
  The Grey

Christopher R. DeMuri
  Darling Companion

Christopher Dileo
  Magic Mike

Dooner
  This Must Be the Place

Henry Dunn
  Not Fade Away

Nash Dunnigan
  Ice Age: Continental Drift

Kendelle Elliott
  This Means War

Douglas Fick
  The Collection

Lauren Fitzsimmons
   Fun Size

Stan Flint
   The Bay

Eric Fraser
   This Means War

Beat Frutiger
   Abraham Lincoln: Vampire
      Hunter

Pablo Maestre Galli
   Safe House

Jason Garner
   Paranormal Activity 4

Martin Gendron
   On the Road

Paul Ghirardani
   The Woman in Black

Elliott Glick
   American Reunion

Ian Gooding
   Wreck-It Ralph

Brian Goodwin
   Damsels in Distress

Brandt Gordon
   The Vow

W. Steven Graham
   A Little Bit of Heaven
   Men in Black 3

Eric Guillon
   Dr. Seuss' The Lorax

James Hambidge
   John Carter

Lisa B. Hammond
   Safety Not Guaranteed

Aaron Haye
   Battleship

Ryan Heck
   Being Flynn

Jonathan Hely-Hutchinson
   Safe House

Kelly Hemenway
   Thin Ice

David Hewlette
   Blue Like Jazz

Bruce Robert Hill
   Journey 2: The Mysterious Island

David Hindle
   The Deep Blue Sea

Shira Hockman
   Safe House

Julie Ann Horan
   Kill List

Anthony Ianni
   Silent Hill: Revelation 3D

Rumiko Ishii
   A Late Quartet

Martina Javorova
   Underworld: Awakening

Shannon Jeffries
   Madagascar 3: Europe's Most
      Wanted

John R. Jensen
   Parental Guidance

Johnny Jos
   High School

John B. Josselyn
   The Five-Year Engagement

Paul D. Kelly
   The Lucky One

Shiloh Kidd
   Sleepwalk with Me

Jindrich Koci
   Red Tails

Gary Kosko
   Won't Back Down

Scott Kuzio
   The Innkeepers
   Liberal Arts

Michele Laliberte
   Deadfall

David Lazan
   Flight
   The Guilt Trip

Mando Lopez
   Nobody Walks

Chris Lowe
   Dark Shadows
   Skyfall

Ron Lukas
   Hotel Transylvania

Melanie Mandl
   Tim and Eric's Billion Dollar
      Movie

Aleksandra Marinkovich
   Take This Waltz

Naaman Marshall
   Casa de mi Padre

Dawn Masi
   Dark Horse

Nicki McCallum
   Salmon Fishing in the Yemen

Leslie McDonald
   Lincoln

Rod McLean
   Zero Dark Thirty

Yann Megard
   Rust and Bone

Caleb B. Mikler
   Step Up Revolution

Laura Miller
   Keep the Lights On

Dane Moore
   Madea's Witness Protection

Niall Moroney
   Anna Karenina

Christa Munro
   Jack Reacher

Desma Murphy
   Project X

Scott P. Murphy
   Battleship

Gary Myers
   Underworld: Awakening

Inigo Navarro
   Haywire
   Intruders

Jim Oberlander
   Haywire

Patrick O'Connor
   Chronicle

Lanie Faith Marie Overton
   V/H/S

Sarah Pasquali
   The Deep Blue Sea

Matt Perry
   The Pirates! Band of Misfits

Erik Polczwartek
   Safe House

Serban Porupca
   Ghost Rider: Spirit of Vengeance

Sarah M. Pott
   Smashed

Anna Rackard
   Haywire

Mark Raggett
   Hyde Park on Hudson

Tom Reta
   The Cabin in the Woods
   Red Dawn

Greg Richman
   Butter

Music Director Index

Adam Anders
  Rock of Ages

Tiffany Anders
  Nobody Walks

Michael Andrews
  The Five-Year Engagement
  Jeff, Who Lives at Home

Peer Astrom
  Rock of Ages

Cyrille Aufort
  A Royal Affair

Alexandre Azaria
  Lockout

Chris Bacon
  Atlas Shrugged II: The Strike

Angelo Badalamenti (1937-)
  A Late Quartet

Roque Banos (1968-)
  Intruders

Samuel Barber
  The Deep Blue Sea

Erran Baron Cohen
  The Dictator

Tyler Bates
  Killer Joe

Rostam Batmanglij
  Sound of My Voice

Beacon Street Studios
  Casa de mi Padre

Jeff Beal (1963-)
  The Queen of Versailles

Christophe Beck
  The Guilt Trip
  The Watch

Christophe Beck (1972-)
  Pitch Perfect
  This Means War

Marco Beltrami (1966-)
  Deadfall
  The Sessions
  Trouble with the Curve
  The Woman in Black

Trond Bjerknaes
  Headhunters

Terence Blanchard (1962-)
  Red Tails

Stuart Bogie
  How to Survive a Plague

Ramachandra Borcar
  Goon

Kathryn Bostic
  Middle of Nowhere

Jon Brion (1963-)
  ParaNorman
  This Is 40

Michael Brook (1952-)
  The Perks of Being a Wallflower
  Undefeated
  The Vow

David Buckley
  Gone

T-Bone Burnett (1948-)
  The Hunger Games

Carter Burwell (1955-)
  Seven Psychopaths
  The Twilight Saga: Breaking
    Dawn, Part 2

David Byrne
  This Must Be the Place

Andy Cabic
  Smashed

Nick Cave (1957-)
  Lawless
  West of Memphis

Charlie Clouser (1963-)
  The Collection

Elia Cmiral (1957-)
  Piranha 3DD

Cecile Corbel
  The Secret World of Arrietty

Bruno Coulais (1954-)
  Farewell, My Queen

Zach Cowie
  Celeste & Jesse Forever

Jeff Danna (1964-)
  Silent Hill: Revelation 3D
  Thin Ice

Mychael Danna (1958-)
  Life of Pi

Marcello De Francisci
  Samsara

Lakshman Joseph De Saram
  Bel Ami

John Debney (1956-)
  Alex Cross
  A Thousand Words
  The Three Stooges

Deborah Lurie
    Fun Size
    Katy Perry: Part of Me
    One for the Money
Dario Marianelli (1963-)
    Anna Karenina
    Quartet
    Salmon Fishing in the Yemen
Bob Marley (1945-1981)
    Marley
Robert Nesta Marley (1945-1981)
    See Bob Marley
Cliff Martinez (1954-)
    Arbitrage
Heather McIntosh
    Compliance
Dan McMahon
    Undefeated
Nathaniel Mechaly (1972-)
    Taken 2
Daniel Meir
    The Gatekeepers
Alan Menken (1949-)
    Mirror Mirror
Mateo (Matt) Messina
    Butter
Ryan Miller
    Safety Not Guaranteed
Paul Mills
    October Baby
Mark Mothersbaugh (1950-)
    Hotel Transylvania
    Safe
    21 Jump Street
    What to Expect When You're
        Expecting
Khaled Mouzannar
    Where Do We Go Now?
Walter Murphy (1952-)
    Ted
John Nau
    Bachelorette
Javier Navarrete
    Wrath of the Titans
Thomas Newman (1955-)
    The Best Exotic Marigold Hotel
    Skyfall
Mikkel E.G. Nielsen
    A Royal Affair
Miles Nielsen
    Undefeated

Anne Nikitin
    The Imposter
William Oldham (1970-)
    This Must Be the Place
Ab Ovo
    The Gatekeepers
Heitor Pereira
    A Little Bit of Heaven
Adam Peters
    Savages
Rachel Portman (1960-)
    Bel Ami
    The Vow
John Powell (1963-)
    Dr. Seuss' The Lorax
    Ice Age: Continental Drift
Amit Poznansky (1974-)
    Footnote
Aria Prayogi
    The Raid: Redemption
A.R. Rahman (1966-)
    People Like Us
Salaam Remi
    Sparkle
Victor Reyes (1962-)
    Red Lights
Graham Reynolds (1971-)
    Bernie
Justin Rice
    Bully
J. Peter Robinson (1945-)
    Seeking Justice
Ben Romans
    The Devil Inside
Daniel Romer
    Beasts of the Southern Wild
Christian Rudder
    Bully
Arthur Russell (1908-)
    Keep the Lights On
Arthur Wolseley Russell (1908-)
    See Arthur Russell
Billy Ryan
    Side by Side
Brendan Ryan
    Side by Side
RZA (1966-)
    The Man with the Iron Fists
Jonathan Sadoff
    Seeking a Friend for the End of
        the World

Jeremy Sams (1957-)
    Hyde Park on Hudson
Anton Sanko
    The Possession
Gustavo Santaolalla (1951-)
    On the Road
David Sardy
    End of Watch
    Ghost Rider: Spirit of Vengeance
    Premium Rush
Brian Satz
    Brooklyn Castle
Claude-Michel Schonberg
    Les Miserables
Danny Seim
    Blue Like Jazz
Eric Serra (1959-)
    The Lady
Marc Shaiman (1959-)
    The Magic of Belle Isle
    Parental Guidance
Theodore Shapiro (1971-)
    The Campaign
    Hope Springs
    The Pirates! Band of Misfits
Ed Shearmur (1966-)
    The Babymakers
Edward Shearmur
    Diary of a Wimpy Kid: Dog
        Days
Howard Shore (1946-)
    Cosmopolis
    The Hobbit: An Unexpected
        Journey
Clinton Shorter (1971-)
    Contraband
Alan Silvestri (1950-)
    The Avengers
    Flight
Rob Simonsen (1978-)
    Seeking a Friend for the End of
        the World
Vinny Smith
    Your Sister's Sister
Michael Stearns
    Samsara
Diego Stocco
    Chernobyl Diaries
Marc Streitenfeld
    The Grey
    Prometheus

Performer Index

Christopher Abbott
    Hello I Must Be Going

Alon Aboutboul (1965-)
    The Dark Knight Rises

Amy Acker (1976-)
    The Cabin in the Woods

Amy Adams (1974-)
    The Master
    On the Road
    Trouble with the Curve

CJ Adams
    The Odd Life of Timothy Green

Ben Affleck (1972-)
    Argo

Casey Affleck (1975-)
    ParaNorman (V)

Riz Ahmed (1982-)
    Trishna

Malin Akerman (1978-)
    Wanderlust

Doni Alamsyah (1978-)
    The Raid: Redemption

Antonio Albanese (1964-)
    To Rome with Love

Alan Alda (1936-)
    Wanderlust

Jay Ali
    Darling Companion

Roger Allam (1953-)
    The Woman in Black

Brady Allen
    Paranormal Activity 4

Isabelle Allen
    Les Miserables

Joan Allen (1956-)
    The Bourne Legacy

Woody Allen (1935-)
    To Rome with Love

Marshall Allman (1984-)
    Blue Like Jazz

Nansi Aluka
    The Bay

Mathieu Amalric (1965-)
    Cosmopolis

Lauren Ambrose (1978-)
    Sleepwalk with Me
    Wanderlust

Christian Ameri
    The Intouchables

John Amos (1941-)
    Madea's Witness Protection

Joe Anderson
    The Grey

Fernanda Andrade (1984-)
    The Devil Inside

Peter Andrews (1963-)
    See *Steven Soderbergh*

Michael Angarano (1987-)
    Haywire

Jennifer Aniston (1969-)
    Wanderlust

Nonso Anozie
    The Grey

Iris Apatow
    This Is 40

Maude Apatow
    This Is 40

Tomas Arana (1959-)
    The Dark Knight Rises

Randall Archer
    The Collection

Moises Arias
    The Secret World of Arrietty (V)

Alan Arkin (1934-)
    Argo
    Thin Ice

Pedro Armendariz, Jr. (1940-2011)
    Casa de mi Padre

Fabio Armiliato
    To Rome with Love

Richard Armitage (1971-)
    The Hobbit: An Unexpected
    Journey

Will Arnett (1970-)
    The Secret World of Arrietty (V)

Nora Arnezeder
    Safe House

Tom Arnold (1959-)
    Hit and Run
    Madea's Witness Protection

Patricia Arquette (1968-)
    Girl in Progress

Tadanobu Asano (1973-)
Battleship

Nelson Ascencio (1964-)
The Hunger Games

Lior Loui Ashkenazi
Footnote

William Atherton (1947-)
Tim and Eric's Billion Dollar
Movie

Dan Aykroyd (1952-)
The Campaign

Richard Ayoade
The Watch

De'Adre Azziza
Red Hook Summer

Diedrich Bader (1966-)
Atlas Shrugged II: The Strike

Sayed Badreya
The Dictator

Madhur Bahadur (1933-)
See Madhur Jaffrey

Dylan Baker (1958-)
2 Days in New York

Kathy Baker (1950-)
Big Miracle

Sarah Baker
The Campaign

Bob Balaban (1945-)
Thin Ice

Alec Baldwin (1958-)
Rise of the Guardians (V)
Rock of Ages
To Rome with Love

Christian Bale (1974-)
The Dark Knight Rises

Rochelle Ballantyne
Brooklyn Castle

Eric Bana (1968-)
Deadfall

Antonio Banderas (1960-)
Haywire
Ruby Sparks

Elizabeth Banks (1974-)
The Hunger Games
Man on a Ledge
People Like Us
Pitch Perfect
What to Expect When You're
Expecting

Shlomo Bar-Aba
Footnote

Javier Bardem (1969-)
Skyfall

Aneurin Barnard (1987-)
Citadel

Milton Barnes
Silent Hill: Revelation 3D

Adam Barnett
Silent House

Dallas Barnett
Cirque du Soleil: Worlds Away

Sacha Baron Cohen (1971-)
The Dictator
Les Miserables
Madagascar 3: Europe's Most
Wanted (V)

Tara Lynne Barr
God Bless America

Drew Barrymore (1975-)
Big Miracle

Justin Bartha (1978-)
Dark Horse

Alison Bartlett (1971-)
The Innkeepers

Jay Baruchel (1982-)
Cosmopolis
Goon

Bailey Bass
A Little Bit of Heaven

Charlotte Bass
A Little Bit of Heaven

Angela Bassett (1958-)
This Means War

Kathy Bates (1948-)
A Little Bit of Heaven

Matt Battinelli-Olpin
V/H/S

Jean Battiste
Beasts of the Southern Wild

Dave Bautista (1969-)
The Man with the Iron Fists

Claude Baz Moussawbaa
Where Do We Go Now?

Michael Beach (1963-)
Sparkle

Simon Russell Beale (1961-)
The Deep Blue Sea

Sean Bean (1959-)
Mirror Mirror
Silent Hill: Revelation 3D

Gabrielle Beauvais (1973-)
Flight
Think Like a Man
Tyler Perry's Good Deeds

Xavier Beauvois
Farewell, My Queen

Hugo Becker
Damsels in Distress

Kate Beckinsale (1973-)
Contraband
Total Recall
Underworld: Awakening

Shannon Beer
Wuthering Heights

Jason Beghe (1960-)
Atlas Shrugged II: The Strike

Jamie Bell (1986-)
Man on a Ledge

Kristen Bell (1980-)
Big Miracle
Hit and Run

Gil Bellows (1967-)
House at the End of the Street

Roberto Benigni (1952-)
To Rome with Love

Annette Bening (1958-)
Ruby Sparks

Manu Bennett (1969-)
The Hobbit: An Unexpected
Journey

Wes Bentley (1978-)
Gone
The Hunger Games

Ingrid Bolso Berdal
Chernobyl Diaries

Jenica Bergere
Safety Not Guaranteed

Xander Berkeley (1958-)
Seeking Justice

Gael Garcia Bernal (1978-)
Casa de mi Padre
A Little Bit of Heaven

Halle Berry (1968-)
Cloud Atlas

Paul Bettany (1971-)
The Avengers (V)

Demian Bichir (1963-)
Savages

Jessica Biel (1982-)
 Hitchcock
 Playing for Keeps
 Total Recall

Jason Biggs (1978-)
 American Reunion

Jean-Luc Bilodeau
 Piranha 3DD

Juliette Binoche (1964-)
 Cosmopolis

Mike Birbiglia (1978-)
 Sleepwalk with Me
 Your Sister's Sister

Taner Birsel (1959-)
 Once Upon a Time in Anatolia

Jack Black (1969-)
 Bernie

Ruben Blades (1948-)
 For Greater Glory
 Safe House

Selma Blair (1972-)
 Dark Horse

Cate Blanchett (1969-)
 The Hobbit: An Unexpected
 Journey

Kirby Bliss Blanton (1990-)
 Project X

Tempestt Bledsoe (1973-)
 ParaNorman (V)

Brian Blessed (1937-)
 The Pirates! Band of Misfits (V)

Moon Bloodgood (1975-)
 The Sessions

Emily Blunt (1983-)
 The Five-Year Engagement
 Looper
 Salmon Fishing in the Yemen
 Your Sister's Sister

Matt Bomer (1977-)
 Magic Mike

Diego Boneta (1990-)
 Rock of Ages

Helena Bonham Carter (1966-)
 Dark Shadows
 Les Miserables

Megan Boone (1983-)
 Step Up Revolution

Zachary Booth
 Keep the Lights On

Kyle Bornheimer
 Bachelorette

Marcin Bosak (1979-)
 In Darkness

Stephen Boss
 Step Up Revolution

Devon Bostick (1991-)
 Diary of a Wimpy Kid: Dog
 Days

Katrina Bowden
 Piranha 3DD

Alice Braga (1983-)
 On the Road

Russell Brand (1975-)
 Rock of Ages

Jay Brazeau (1945-)
 The Possession

Kyle Harrison Breitkopf
 Parental Guidance

Ben Brey
 The Grey

Beau Bridges (1941-)
 Hit and Run

Alison Brie (1982-)
 The Five-Year Engagement

Will Brill
 Not Fade Away

Connie Britton (1968-)
 Seeking a Friend for the End of
 the World

Jim Broadbent (1949-)
 Cloud Atlas

Adam Brody (1980-)
 Damsels in Distress
 Seeking a Friend for the End of
 the World

Adrien Brody (1973-)
 Detachment
 High School

Josh Brolin (1968-)
 Men in Black 3

Dante Brown
 Won't Back Down

Jefferson Brown
 Silent Hill: Revelation 3D

Jonathan Daniel Brown
 Project X

Jules Brown
 Red Hook Summer

Marcus Lyle Brown
 Seeking Justice

Montrail 'Money' Brown
 Undefeated

O.C. Brown
 Undefeated

W. Earl Brown (1963-)
 The Sessions

Daniel Bruhl (1978-)
 Intruders

Joy Bryant (1976-)
 Hit and Run

Brooke Bundy (1944-)
 The Hunger Games

MyAnna Buring
 Kill List

Jason Burke
 October Baby

Robert John Burke (1961-)
 Safe

Nichola Burley
 Wuthering Heights

Carol Burnett (1933-)
 The Secret World of Arrietty (V)

Ed Burns
 Man on a Ledge

Edward Burns (1968-)
 Alex Cross
 Friends with Kids

Ty Burrell (1967-)
 Butter

Kate Burton (1957-)
 Liberal Arts
 2 Days in New York

Steve Buscemi (1957-)
 Hotel Transylvania (V)

Gary Busey (1944-)
 Piranha 3DD

Matthew Bush (1986-)
 High School
 Piranha 3DD

Gerard Butler (1969-)
 Chasing Mavericks
 Playing for Keeps

Calvin O. Butts, III
 The Central Park Five

Thomas Jefferson Byrd (1960-)
 Red Hook Summer

David Byrne (1952-)
 This Must Be the Place

James Caan (1939-)
 Detachment
 That's My Boy

Rob Corddry (1971-)
    Butter
    Seeking a Friend for the End of
        the World

Emayatzy Corinealdi
    Middle of Nowhere

Abbie Cornish (1982-)
    Seven Psychopaths

Jean-Michel Correia
    Rust and Bone

James Cosmo (1948-)
    Citadel

Nikolaj Coster-Waldau (1970-)
    Headhunters

Marion Cotillard (1975-)
    The Dark Knight Rises
    Rust and Bone

Jason Cottle
    Act of Valor

Tom Courtenay (1937-)
    Quartet

Bill Courtney
    Undefeated

Randy Couture (1963-)
    The Expendables 2

Brian Cox (1946-)
    The Campaign

Joe Coyle
    Promised Land

Daniel Craig (1968-)
    Skyfall

Bryan Cranston (1956-)
    Argo
    John Carter
    Red Tails
    Rock of Ages
    Total Recall

Chace Crawford (1985-)
    Peace, Love & Misunderstanding
    What to Expect When You're
        Expecting

Jermaine Crawford (1992-)
    Damsels in Distress

Terry Crews (1968-)
    The Expendables 2

Joseph Cross (1986-)
    Lincoln

Russell Crowe (1964-)
    Les Miserables
    The Man with the Iron Fists

Suzan Crowley
    The Devil Inside

Billy Crudup (1968-)
    Thin Ice

Connor Cruise
    Red Dawn

Tom Cruise (1962-)
    Jack Reacher
    Rock of Ages

Penelope Cruz (1974-)
    To Rome with Love

Billy Crystal (1947-)
    Parental Guidance

Brett Cullen (1956-)
    The Dark Knight Rises
    The Guilt Trip
    Red Dawn

Liam Cunningham (1961-)
    Safe House

Vincent Curatola
    Killing Them Softly

Clifford Curtis (1968-)
    A Thousand Words

John Cusack (1966-)
    The Paperboy
    The Raven

Michael Hall D'Addario
    People Like Us

Willem Dafoe (1955-)
    The Hunter
    John Carter

Alan Dale (1947-)
    A Little Bit of Heaven

James Badge Dale (1978-)
    The Grey

Matt Damon (1970-)
    Promised Land

Charles Dance (1946-)
    Underworld: Awakening

Hugh Dancy (1975-)
    Hysteria

Jeanne Dandoy
    Bullhead

Chavis Daniels
    Undefeated

Blythe Danner (1944-)
    Detachment
    Hello I Must Be Going
    The Lucky One

Paul Dano (1984-)
    Being Flynn
    Looper
    Ruby Sparks

Ted Danson (1947-)
    Big Miracle

James D'Arcy (1975-)
    Hitchcock

Dexter Darden
    Joyful Noise

Madison Davenport (1996-)
    The Possession

DeRay David
    21 Jump Street

Keith David (1954-)
    Cloud Atlas

Larry David (1947-)
    The Three Stooges

Embeth Davidtz (1965-)
    The Amazing Spider-Man

Morgana Davies
    The Hunter

Jason Davis
    A Little Bit of Heaven
    Seeking Justice

Judy Davis (1956-)
    To Rome with Love

Kristin Davis (1965-)
    Journey 2: The Mysterious Island

Viola Davis (1952-)
    Won't Back Down

Rosario Dawson (1979-)
    10 Years

Rebecca Dayan
    Celeste & Jesse Forever

Daniel Day-Lewis (1957-)
    Lincoln

Cecile de France (1975-)
    The Kid with a Bike

Robert De Niro (1943-)
    Being Flynn
    Red Lights
    Silver Linings Playbook

Frank Deal
    The Bay

Jamel Debbouze (1975-)
    360

Brooklyn Decker
    Battleship
    What to Expect When You're
        Expecting

Ruby Dee (1924-)
  A Thousand Words

Dane DeHaan (1987-)
  Chronicle

Benicio Del Toro (1967-)
  Savages

Simon Delaney
  This Must Be the Place

Albert Delpy
  2 Days in New York

Julie Delpy (1969-)
  2 Days in New York

Peter DeLuise (1966-)
  21 Jump Street (C)

Judi Dench (1934-)
  The Best Exotic Marigold Hotel
  Skyfall

David Dencik (1974-)
  A Royal Affair

Christopher Denham
  The Bay
  Sound of My Voice

Johnny Depp (1963-)
  Dark Shadows
  21 Jump Street (C)

Bruce Dern (1936-)
  Django Unchained

Laura Dern (1966-)
  The Master

Tena Desae
  The Best Exotic Marigold Hotel

Robert Desiderio (1951-)
  Liberal Arts

William Devane (1939-)
  The Dark Knight Rises

Adam DeVine
  Pitch Perfect

Danny DeVito (1944-)
  Dr. Seuss' The Lorax (V)

Jenna Dewan-Tatum
  10 Years

Dr. Alice Dewey
  2016: Obama's America

Rosemarie DeWitt (1974-)
  A Little Bit of Heaven
  Nobody Walks
  The Odd Life of Timothy Green
  The Watch
  Your Sister's Sister

Egon Di Mateo
  The Kid with a Bike

Rick Dial (1955-2011)
  Bernie

Chris Diamantopoulos
  The Three Stooges

Dimitri Diatchenko
  Chernobyl Diaries

Alyssa Diaz
  Red Dawn

Cameron Diaz (1972-)
  What to Expect When You're
  Expecting

Leonardo DiCaprio (1974-)
  Django Unchained

Robert Diggs (1966-)
  See *RZA*

Garret Dillahunt (1964-)
  Looper

David Dinkins
  The Central Park Five

Peter Dinklage (1969-)
  Ice Age: Continental Drift (V)
  A Little Bit of Heaven

Nina Dobrev
  The Perks of Being a Wallflower

Vincent D'Onofrio (1959-)
  Sinister

Kether Donohue
  The Bay

Martin Donovan (1957-)
  Silent Hill: Revelation 3D

Tate Donovan (1963-)
  Argo

Shaun Dooley
  The Woman in Black

Thomas Doret
  The Kid with a Bike

Larry Dotson
  Bernie

Michael Douglas (1944-)
  Haywire

Ann Dowd
  Compliance

Robert Downey, Jr. (1965-)
  The Avengers

Fran Drescher (1957-)
  Hotel Transylvania (V)

Dinara Drukarova (1976-)
  360

Dinesh D'Souza (1961-)
  2016: Obama's America

Olivia Taylor Dudley
  Chernobyl Diaries

Clark Duke
  A Thousand Words

Stephen Dunham (1964-2012)
  Paranormal Activity 4

Kirsten Dunst (1982-)
  Bachelorette
  On the Road

Mark Duplass (1976-)
  Darling Companion
  People Like Us
  Safety Not Guaranteed
  Your Sister's Sister

Kevin Durand (1974-)
  Cosmopolis
  Resident Evil: Retribution

Lena Durham (1986-)
  The Innkeepers

Clea DuVall (1977-)
  Argo

Robert Duvall (1931-)
  Jack Reacher

Jim Dwyer
  The Central Park Five

Trine Dyrholm (1972-)
  A Royal Affair

Michael Ealy (1973-)
  Think Like a Man
  Underworld: Awakening

Clint Eastwood (1930-)
  Trouble with the Curve

Scott Eastwood
  Chasing Mavericks
  Trouble with the Curve

Megalyn Echikunwoke
  Damsels in Distress

Joel Edgerton (1974-)
  The Odd Life of Timothy Green
  Zero Dark Thirty

Pobo Efokoro
  Brooklyn Castle

Zac Efron (1987-)
  Dr. Seuss' The Lorax (V)
  Liberal Arts
  The Lucky One
  The Paperboy

Jesse Eisenberg (1983-)
  To Rome with Love

India Eisley (1993-)
  Underworld: Awakening

Carmen Ejogo (1975-)
  Alex Cross
  Sparkle

Idris Elba (1972-)
  Ghost Rider: Spirit of Vengeance
  Prometheus

Shannon Elizabeth (1973-)
  American Reunion

Jacqueline Emerson
  The Hunger Games

India Ennenga (1994-)
  Nobody Walks

Mike Epps (1970-)
  Sparkle

Yilmaz Erdogan (1967-)
  Once Upon a Time in Anatolia

Ato Essandoh (1972-)
  Django Unchained

Philip Ettinger
  Compliance

Chris Evans (1981-)
  The Avengers

Luke Evans (1979-)
  The Raven

Alice Eve (1982-)
  Men in Black 3
  The Raven

Rupert Everett (1959-)
  Hysteria

Steve Evets
  Wuthering Heights

Patrick Fabian (1964-)
  Atlas Shrugged II: The Strike

Peter Facinelli (1973-)
  The Twilight Saga: Breaking
    Dawn, Part 2

Ben Falcone
  What to Expect When You're
    Expecting

Julian Farhat
  Where Do We Go Now?

Anna Faris (1976-)
  The Dictator

Vera Farmiga (1973-)
  Safe House

Colin Farrell (1976-)
  Seven Psychopaths
  Total Recall

Mia Farrow (1945-)
  Dark Horse

Michael Fassbender (1977-)
  Haywire
  Prometheus

Alexia Fast
  Jack Reacher

Nat Faxon
  The Babymakers

Katie Featherston (1982-)
  Paranormal Activity 4

Oded Fehr (1970-)
  Resident Evil: Retribution

Mohamed Fellag (1950-)
  Monsieur Lazhar

Tom Felton (1987-)
  The Apparition

Craig Ferguson (1962-)
  Brave (V)

Jay Ferguson (1943-)
  The Lucky One

Jerry Ferrara
  Think Like a Man

Conchata Ferrell (1943-)
  Frankenweenie (V)

Will Ferrell (1968-)
  The Campaign
  Casa de mi Padre

America Ferrera (1984-)
  End of Watch

Pam Ferris (1948-)
  The Raven

Sally Field (1946-)
  The Amazing Spider-Man
  Lincoln

Ralph Fiennes (1962-)
  Skyfall
  Wrath of the Titans

Hanna Fierman
  V/H/S

Albert Finney (1936-)
  The Bourne Legacy

Isla Fisher (1976-)
  Bachelorette
  Rise of the Guardians (V)

Caitlin Fitzgerald
  Damsels in Distress

Emma Fitzpatrick
  The Collection

Dax Flame
  Project X

Audrey Fleurot
  The Intouchables

Claire Foley
  Sinister

Mikkel Boe Folsgaard
  A Royal Affair

Jane Fonda (1937-)
  Peace, Love & Misunderstanding

Will Forte (1970-)
  The Watch

Ashley Foster
  The Woman in Black

Ben Foster (1980-)
  Contraband
  360

Kerry Fox (1966-)
  Intruders

Matthew Fox (1966-)
  Alex Cross

Megan Fox (1986-)
  The Dictator
  Friends with Kids
  This Is 40

Jamie Foxx (1967-)
  Django Unchained

Mackenzie Foy
  The Twilight Saga: Breaking
    Dawn, Part 2

Jon Francis (1957-)
  See Jon(athan) Gries

Dave Franco (1985-)
  21 Jump Street

Kirk Franklin
  Joyful Noise

Mourad Frarema
  Rust and Bone

Martin Freeman (1971-)
  The Hobbit: An Unexpected
    Journey
  The Pirates! Band of Misfits (V)

Morgan Freeman (1937-)
  The Dark Knight Rises
  The Magic of Belle Isle

Nick Frost (1972-)
  Snow White and the Huntsman

Emma Fryer
  Kill List

Isabelle Fuhrman (1997-)
  The Hunger Games

Emma Fuhrmann
  The Magic of Belle Isle

Benno Furmann (1972-)
  In Darkness

Dan Futterman (1967-)
  Hello I Must Be Going
Sarah Gadon (1987-)
  Cosmopolis
M.C. Gainey (1948-)
  Django Unchained
Nichole Galicia
  Django Unchained
Zach Galifianakis (1969-)
  The Campaign
John Galvin
  Brooklyn Castle
Michael Gambon (1940-)
  Quartet
James Gandolfini (1961-)
  Killing Them Softly
  Not Fade Away
Victor Garber (1949-)
  Argo
Andy Garcia (1956-)
  For Greater Glory
Andrew Garfield
  The Amazing Spider-Man
Jeff Garlin (1962-)
  ParaNorman (V)
Jennifer Garner (1972-)
  Butter
  The Odd Life of Timothy Green
Brad Garrett (1960-)
  Not Fade Away
Michael Gaston (1962-)
  Big Miracle
Rafi Gavron (1989-)
  Celeste & Jesse Forever
Ari Gaynor
  Celeste & Jesse Forever
Jordan Gelber
  Dark Horse
Kiniko Gelman (1966-)
  The Hunger Games
Brian Geraghty (1974-)
  Flight
  10 Years
Richard Gere (1949-)
  Arbitrage
Gina Gershon (1962-)
  Killer Joe
Greta Gerwig
  Damsels in Distress
  Lola Versus
  To Rome with Love

Paul Giamatti (1967-)
  Cosmopolis
  Rock of Ages
Marla Gibbs (1946-)
  Madea's Witness Protection
Maya Gilbert
  Middle of Nowhere
Joe Gilgun
  Lockout
Jared Gilman
  Moonrise Kingdom
Solomon Glave
  Wuthering Heights
Brendan Gleeson (1954-)
  The Pirates! Band of Misfits (V)
  The Raven
  Safe House
Domhnall Gleeson (1983-)
  Anna Karenina
Philip Glenister (1963-)
  Bel Ami
Scott Glenn (1942-)
  The Bourne Legacy
Miriam F. Glover
  Django Unchained
Walton Goggins (1971-)
  Django Unchained
  Lincoln
Whoopi Goldberg (1955-)
  A Little Bit of Heaven
Jeff Goldblum (1952-)
  Tim and Eric's Billion Dollar
    Movie
Rick Gomez (1972-)
  The Apparition
Selena Gomez (1992-)
  Hotel Transylvania (V)
Meagan Good (1981-)
  Think Like a Man
Caroline Goodall (1959-)
  The Cold Light of Day
Cuba Gooding, Jr. (1968-)
  Red Tails
John Goodman (1952-)
  Argo
  Flight
  ParaNorman (V)
  Trouble with the Curve
Zachary Gordon (1998-)
  Diary of a Wimpy Kid: Dog
    Days

Joseph Gordon-Levitt (1981-)
  The Dark Knight Rises
  Lincoln
  Looper
  Premium Rush
Burn Gorman (1974-)
  The Dark Knight Rises
Elliott Gould (1938-)
  Ruby Sparks
Dana Michelle Gourrier
  Django Unchained
Maggie Grace (1983-)
  Lockout
  Taken 2
  The Twilight Saga: Breaking
    Dawn, Part 2
Currie Graham (1967-)
  Total Recall
Holliday Grainger (1988-)
  Bel Ami
Ionut Grama
  The Devil Inside
Hugh Grant (1960-)
  Cloud Atlas
  The Pirates! Band of Misfits (V)
Macy Gray (1967-)
  The Paperboy
Ari Graynor (1983-)
  For a Good Time, Call...
  10 Years
Cee-Lo Green (1975-)
  Hotel Transylvania (V)
Eva Green (1980-)
  Dark Shadows
Ashley Greene (1987-)
  The Apparition
  Butter
  The Twilight Saga: Breaking
    Dawn, Part 2
Bruce Greenwood (1956-)
  Flight
  For Greater Glory
Judy Greer (1971-)
  Jeff, Who Lives at Home
  Playing for Keeps
Clark Gregg (1964-)
  The Avengers
Richard Grieco (1965-)
  21 Jump Street (C)
Jon(athan) Gries (1957-)
  Taken 2

Frank Grillo (1963-)
  End of Watch
  The Grey

Luke Grimes (1984-)
  Taken 2

Agnieszka Grochowska (1979-)
  In Darkness

Marc-Andre Grondin
  Goon

Pierre Gruno
  The Raid: Redemption

Mario Guerra
  Chico & Rita (*V*)

Julianna Guill
  The Apparition

Sienna Guillory (1975-)
  Resident Evil: Retribution

Luis Guzman (1956-)
  Journey 2: The Mysterious Island

Ryan Guzman
  Step Up Revolution

Jake Gyllenhaal (1980-)
  End of Watch

Maggie Gyllenhaal (1977-)
  Hysteria
  Won't Back Down

Lukas Haas (1976-)
  Contraband

Harry Hadden-Paton (1981-)
  The Deep Blue Sea

Kathryn Hahn (1974-)
  Wanderlust

Leyla Hakim
  Where Do We Go Now?

Lutz Halbhubner
  Cirque du Soleil: Worlds Away

Jackie Earle Haley (1961-)
  Dark Shadows
  Lincoln

Philip Baker Hall (1931-)
  People Like Us

Regina Hall (1970-)
  Think Like a Man

Melinda Page Hamilton
  God Bless America

Jon Hamm (1971-)
  Friends with Kids

Armie Hammer (1986-)
  Mirror Mirror

Chelsea Handler
  Fun Size
  This Means War

Colin Hanks (1977-)
  The Guilt Trip
  High School

Tom Hanks (1956-)
  Cloud Atlas

Alyson Hannigan (1974-)
  American Reunion

David Harbour (1974-)
  Thin Ice

Marcia Gay Harden (1959-)
  Detachment

Omari Hardwick (1974-)
  Middle of Nowhere

Thomas Hardy (1977-)
  The Dark Knight Rises
  Lawless
  This Means War

Tom Hardy (1977-)
  See Thomas Hardy

Kit Harington (1986-)
  Silent Hill: Revelation 3D

Woody Harrelson (1962-)
  The Hunger Games
  Seven Psychopaths

Ed Harris (1949-)
  Man on a Ledge

Jared Harris (1961-)
  Lincoln

Naomie Harris (1976-)
  Skyfall

Rachael Harris (1968-)
  Diary of a Wimpy Kid: Dog
    Days

Wood Harris (1969-)
  The Babymakers
  Dredd

Kevin Hart (1980-)
  Think Like a Man

Max Hart
  Katy Perry: Part of Me

Steve Harvey (1956-)
  Think Like a Man

Isao Hashizume
  I Wish

David Hasselhoff (1952-)
  Piranha 3DD (*C*)

Maddie Hasson
  God Bless America

Anne Hathaway (1982-)
  The Dark Knight Rises
  Les Miserables

Ethan Hawke (1971-)
  Sinister

John Hawkes (1959-)
  Lincoln
  The Sessions

Salma Hayek (1966-)
  Here Comes the Boom
  The Pirates! Band of Misfits (*V*)
  Savages

Sean P. Hayes (1970-)
  The Three Stooges

Kara Hayward
  Moonrise Kingdom

Lena Headey (1976-)
  Dredd

Pat Healy (1971-)
  Compliance
  The Innkeepers

Bella Heathcote
  Dark Shadows
  Not Fade Away

Garrett Hedlund (1984-)
  On the Road

Kevin Heffernan (1968-)
  The Babymakers

Tim Heidecker
  Tim and Eric's Billion Dollar
    Movie

Katherine Heigl (1978-)
  One for the Money

Ed Helms (1974-)
  Dr. Seuss' The Lorax (*V*)
  Jeff, Who Lives at Home

Evan Helmuth
  The Devil Inside

Chris Hemsworth (1983-)
  The Avengers
  The Cabin in the Woods
  Red Dawn
  Snow White and the Huntsman

Liam Hemsworth (1990-)
  The Expendables 2
  The Hunger Games

Christina Hendricks (1975-)
  Detachment

Rachel Hendrix
  October Baby

Aksel Hennie (1975-)
  Headhunters

David Henrie (1989-)
  The Secret World of Arrietty (*V*)

Dwight Henry
  Beasts of the Southern Wild

Lenny Henry (1958-)
  The Pirates! Band of Misfits (*V*)

Taraji P. Henson (1970-)
  Think Like a Man

Werner Herzog (1942-)
  Jack Reacher

Eve Hewson
  This Must Be the Place

Tom Hiddleston
  The Avengers
  The Deep Blue Sea

Jonah Hill (1983-)
  Django Unchained
  21 Jump Street
  The Watch

Paul Hilton
  Wuthering Heights

Ciaran Hinds (1953-)
  Ghost Rider: Spirit of Vengeance
  John Carter
  The Woman in Black

Ashley Hinshaw (1988-)
  Chronicle

Emile Hirsch (1985-)
  Killer Joe

Judd Hirsch (1935-)
  This Must Be the Place

Edwin Hodge (1985-)
  Red Dawn

Philip Seymour Hoffman (1967-)
  A Late Quartet
  The Master

Hal Holbrook (1925-)
  Lincoln
  Promised Land

Kris Holden-Ried
  Underworld: Awakening

Tom Holland
  The Impossible

Claire Holt (1988-)
  Blue Like Jazz

James Hong (1929-)
  Safe

Anthony Hopkins (1937-)
  Hitchcock
  360

Casey Hopper
  Katy Perry: Part of Me

Cody Horn
  End of Watch
  Magic Mike

Bob Hoskins (1942-)
  Snow White and the Huntsman

Julianne Hough (1988-)
  Rock of Ages

Whitney Houston (1963-2012)
  Sparkle

Terrence Howard (1969-)
  Red Tails

James Howson
  Wuthering Heights

Cooper Huckabee (1951-)
  Django Unchained

Vanessa Anne Hudgens (1988-)
  Journey 2: The Mysterious Island

Jennifer Hudson (1981-)
  The Three Stooges

Kate Hudson (1979-)
  A Little Bit of Heaven

Lane Hughes
  V/H/S

Charlie Hunnam (1980-)
  Deadfall

Helen Hunt (1963-)
  The Sessions

Holly Hunter (1958-)
  Won't Back Down

Isabelle Huppert (1955-)
  Amour

Adil Hussain
  Life of Pi

Danny Huston (1962-)
  Hitchcock
  Wrath of the Titans

Jack Huston (1982-)
  Not Fade Away

Josh Hutcherson (1992-)
  The Hunger Games
  Journey 2: The Mysterious Island
  Red Dawn

Anna Hutchison (1986-)
  The Cabin in the Woods

Ice Cube (1969-)
  21 Jump Street

Rhys Ifans (1968-)
  The Amazing Spider-Man
  The Five-Year Engagement

Celia Imrie (1952-)
  The Best Exotic Marigold Hotel

Jeremy Irons (1948-)
  The Words

Oscar Isaac (1980-)
  For Greater Glory
  10 Years
  Won't Back Down

Gregory Itzin (1948-)
  Lincoln

Zeljko Ivanek (1957-)
  Seven Psychopaths

Mark Ivanir (1968-)
  A Late Quartet

Hugh Jackman (1968-)
  Butter
  Les Miserables
  Rise of the Guardians (*V*)

Samuel L. Jackson (1948-)
  The Avengers
  Django Unchained

Simone Jackson
  Wuthering Heights

Oliver Jackson-Cohen (1986-)
  The Raven

Oscar Jaenada
  The Cold Light of Day

Madhur Jaffrey (1933-)
  A Late Quartet

Kevin James (1965-)
  Here Comes the Boom
  Hotel Transylvania (*V*)

Lennie James (1965-)
  Lockout

Theo James (1984-)
  Underworld: Awakening

Allison Janney (1960-)
  Liberal Arts
  A Thousand Words

Famke Janssen (1964-)
  Taken 2

Marianne Jean-Baptiste (1967-)
  Won't Back Down

Richard Jenkins (1953-)
  The Cabin in the Woods
  Darling Companion
  Jack Reacher
  Killing Them Softly
  Liberal Arts

Byron Jennings
  Lincoln

Ashley Jensen (1969-)
  Hysteria

Scarlett Johansson (1984-)
  The Avengers
  Hitchcock

Aaron Johnson (1990-)
  See Aaron Taylor-Johnson

Brian Johnson
  The Devil Inside

Caryn Johnson (1955-)
  See Whoopi Goldberg

Caryn E. Johnson (1955-)
  See Whoopi Goldberg

Caryn Elaine Johnson (1955-)
  See Whoopi Goldberg

Don Johnson (1949-)
  Django Unchained

Dwayne 'The Rock' Johnson (1972-)
  Journey 2: The Mysterious Island

Jake M. Johnson
  Safety Not Guaranteed

Karl Johnson (1948-)
  The Deep Blue Sea

Caleb Landry Jones
  Contraband

Felicity Jones (1984-)
  Hysteria

January Jones (1978-)
  Seeking Justice

Rashida Jones (1976-)
  Celeste & Jesse Forever

Richard T. Jones (1972-)
  Atlas Shrugged II: The Strike

Toby Jones (1967-)
  The Hunger Games
  Red Lights
  Snow White and the Huntsman

Tommy Lee Jones (1946-)
  Hope Springs
  Lincoln
  Men in Black 3

Zoe Lister Jones
  Lola Versus

Jeremy Jordan (1973-)
  Joyful Noise

Michael B. Jordan (1987-)
  Chronicle

Samuel Joslin
  The Impossible

Milla Jovovich (1975-)
  Resident Evil: Retribution

Victoria Justice (1993-)
  Fun Size

Adhir Kalyan
  High School

Carol Kane (1952-)
  Sleepwalk with Me

Willy Kauai
  2016: Obama's America

Zoe Kazan (1983-)
  Ruby Sparks

Diane Keaton (1946-)
  Darling Companion

Arielle Kebbel (1985-)
  Think Like a Man

Toby Kebbell (1982-)
  Wrath of the Titans

Catherine Keener (1961-)
  A Late Quartet
  Peace, Love & Misunderstanding

Devin Kelley
  Chernobyl Diaries

Mark Kelly (1973-)
  The Do-Deca-Pentathlon

Michael Kelly (1969-)
  Chronicle

Anna Kendrick (1985-)
  End of Watch
  ParaNorman (V)
  Pitch Perfect
  What to Expect When You're
    Expecting

Dr. Paul Kengor
  2016: Obama's America

Jamie Kennedy (1970-)
  Tyler Perry's Good Deeds

Mimi Kennedy (1949-)
  The Five-Year Engagement

Irrfan Khan (1962-)
  The Amazing Spider-Man
  Life of Pi

Alisa Khazanova (1974-)
  The Woman in Black

Anupam Kher (1955-)
  Silver Linings Playbook

Nicole Kidman (1966-)
  The Paperboy

Julia Kijowska (1981-)
  In Darkness

Kirin Kiki
  I Wish

Richard Kind (1956-)
  Argo

Ben Kingsley (1943-)
  The Dictator

Joel Kinnaman (1979-)
  Lola Versus

Greg Kinnear (1963-)
  Thin Ice

Terry Kinney (1954-)
  Promised Land

Luke Kirby (1978-)
  Take This Waltz

Justin Kirk (1969-)
  Nobody Walks

Langley Kirkwood (1973-)
  Dredd

Taylor Kitsch (1981-)
  Battleship
  John Carter
  Savages

Martin Klebba (1969-)
  Project X

Chris Klein (1979-)
  American Reunion

Kevin Kline (1947-)
  Darling Companion

Alexis Knapp (1989-)
  Pitch Perfect
  Project X

Herbert Knaup (1956-)
  In Darkness

Keira Knightley (1985-)
  Anna Karenina
  Seeking a Friend for the End of
    the World

Johnny Knoxville (1971-)
  Fun Size

Ed Koch
  The Central Park Five

Boris Kodjoe (1973-)
  Resident Evil: Retribution

David Koechner (1962-)
  Hotel Transylvania (V)
  Piranha 3DD

Evgeniya Konushkina
  Elena

Fran Kranz (1983-)
  The Cabin in the Woods

John Krasinski (1979-)
    Big Miracle
    Nobody Walks
    Promised Land

Lenny Kravitz (1964-)
    The Hunger Games

Johannes Krisch
    360

Kris Kristofferson
    Deadfall

Kris Kristofferson (1936-)
    Joyful Noise

Diane Kruger (1976-)
    Farewell, My Queen

Mila Kunis (1983-)
    Ted

Stephen Kunken
    The Bay

Sebastian La Cause
    Keep the Lights On

Nadine Labaki
    Where Do We Go Now?

Shia LaBeouf (1986-)
    Lawless

Jennifer LaFleur
    The Do-Deca-Pentathlon

Frank Lammers (1972-)
    Bullhead

Katherine LaNasa (1966-)
    The Campaign

Martin Landau (1931-)
    Frankenweenie (V)

Alexia Landeau
    2 Days in New York

Lowell Landes
    Beasts of the Southern Wild

Nathan Lane (1956-)
    Mirror Mirror

Eric Lange (1973-)
    Blue Like Jazz

Jessica Lange (1949-)
    The Vow

Frank Langella (1940-)
    Robot & Frank

Bouli Lanners
    Rust and Bone

Brie Larson (1989-)
    21 Jump Street

Ed Lauter (1940-)
    Trouble with the Curve

Taylor Lautner (1992-)
    The Twilight Saga: Breaking
        Dawn, Part 2

Denis Lavant (1961-)
    Holy Motors

Jude Law (1972-)
    Anna Karenina
    Rise of the Guardians (V)
    360

Jennifer Lawrence
    House at the End of the Street
    The Hunger Games
    Silver Linings Playbook

Sharon Lawrence (1963-)
    Middle of Nowhere

Cung Le
    The Man with the Iron Fists

Denis Leary (1957-)
    The Amazing Spider-Man
    Ice Age: Continental Drift (V)

Virginie Ledoyen (1976-)
    Farewell, My Queen

Alexondra Lee (1975-)
    Paranormal Activity 4

Christopher Lee (1922-)
    Frankenweenie (V)
    The Hobbit: An Unexpected
        Journey

Spike Lee (1957-)
    Red Hook Summer

Will Yun Lee (1971-)
    Total Recall

James LeGros (1962-)
    Big Miracle

John Leguizamo (1964-)
    Ice Age: Continental Drift (V)
    One for the Money

Victoria Leigh
    Sinister

Thomas Lennon (1969-)
    The Dark Knight Rises
    What to Expect When You're
        Expecting

Anne LeNy
    The Intouchables

Devan Leos
    Madea's Witness Protection

Logan Lerman (1992-)
    The Perks of Being a Wallflower

Liron Levo (1972-)
    This Must Be the Place

Eugene Levy (1946-)
    American Reunion
    Goon
    Madea's Witness Protection

Jane Levy (1989-)
    Fun Size

Micah Lewensohn
    Footnote

Elise Lhomeau
    Holy Motors

Bingbing Li (1973-)
    Resident Evil: Retribution

Jet Li (1963-)
    The Expendables 2

Landon Liboiron
    Girl in Progress

Matthew Lillard (1970-)
    Trouble with the Curve

Htun Lin
    The Lady

Emily Ann Lind
    Won't Back Down

Thure Lindhardt (1974-)
    Keep the Lights On

Hamish Linklater (1976-)
    Lola Versus

Richard Linklater (1960-)
    Side by Side

Laura Linney (1964-)
    Hyde Park on Hudson

Erica Linz
    Cirque du Soleil: Worlds Away

Ray Liotta (1955-)
    Killing Them Softly

Peyton List (1998-)
    Diary of a Wimpy Kid: Dog
        Days

John Lithgow (1945-)
    The Campaign
    This Is 40

Lucy Liu (1968-)
    Detachment
    The Man with the Iron Fists

Blake Lively (1987-)
    Savages

Ron Livingston (1968-)
    The Odd Life of Timothy Green

Christopher Lloyd (1938-)
    Piranha 3DD

Robert Loggia (1930-)
    Tim and Eric's Billion Dollar
        Movie

Noah Lomax
    Playing for Keeps

Justin Long (1978-)
    For a Good Time, Call...
    10 Years

Eva Longoria (1975-)
    For Greater Glory

Jennifer Lopez (1970-)
    Ice Age: Continental Drift (*V*)
    What to Expect When You're
        Expecting

Pilar Lopez de Ayala (1978-)
    Intruders

Sam Louwyck
    Bullhead

Aiden Lovekamp
    Paranormal Activity 4

Sam Lowry (1963-)
    See *Steven Soderbergh*

Isabel Lucas
    Red Dawn

William Lucking (1942-)
    Contraband

Alexander Ludwig
    The Hunger Games

Derek Luke (1974-)
    Sparkle

Diego Luna (1979-)
    Casa de mi Padre
    Contraband

Dolph Lundgren (1959-)
    The Expendables 2

Noemie Lvovsky (1964-)
    Farewell, My Queen

Elena Lyadova
    Elena

David Lynch (1946-)
    Side by Side

Jane Lynch (1960-)
    The Three Stooges
    Wreck-It Ralph (*V*)

Melanie Lynskey (1977-)
    Hello I Must Be Going
    The Perks of Being a Wallflower
    Seeking a Friend for the End of
        the World

Natasha Lyonne (1979-)
    American Reunion

Toni Lysaith
    Red Hook Summer

Yvonne Maalouf
    Where Do We Go Now?

Hayes Macarthur
    The Babymakers
    Bachelorette

Christopher Macdonald
    The Collection

Kelly Macdonald (1977-)
    Anna Karenina
    Brave (*V*)

Matthew MacFadyen (1974-)
    Anna Karenina

Anthony Mackie (1979-)
    Abraham Lincoln: Vampire
        Hunter
    Man on a Ledge

Kyle MacLachlan (1959-)
    Peace, Love & Misunderstanding

Shirley MacLaine (1934-)
    Bernie

Carrie Maclemore (1987-)
    Damsels in Distress

Laine MacNeil
    Diary of a Wimpy Kid: Dog
        Days

Peter MacNichol (1954-)
    Battleship

Synnove Macody Lund
    Headhunters

William H. Macy (1950-)
    The Sessions

Bailee Madison (1999-)
    Parental Guidance

Virginia Madsen (1963-)
    The Magic of Belle Isle

Koki Maeda
    I Wish

Oshiro Maeda
    I Wish

John Magaro
    Liberal Arts
    Not Fade Away

Billy Magnussen
    Damsels in Distress

Romany Malco (1968-)
    A Little Bit of Heaven

Paula Malcomson (1970-)
    The Hunger Games

Aasif Mandvi (?-1966)
    Dark Horse
    Premium Rush
    Ruby Sparks

Joe Manganiello (1976-)
    Magic Mike
    What to Expect When You're
        Expecting

Leslie Mann (1972-)
    ParaNorman (*V*)
    This Is 40

Thomas Mann (1991-)
    Fun Size
    Project X

Kate Mara (1983-)
    10 Years

Adam Marcello
    Katy Perry: Part of Me

Daniel Marcovich
    Footnote

Ken Marino (1968-)
    Wanderlust

Nadezhda Vasilievna Markina
    Elena

Annika Marks
    The Sessions

Bob Marley (1945-1981)
    Marley

Robert Nesta Marley (1945-1981)
    See *Bob Marley*

Brit Marling (1982-)
    Arbitrage
    Sound of My Voice

Berenice Marlohe (1979-)
    Skyfall

Sean Marquette (1988-)
    High School

Eddie Marsan (1968-)
    Snow White and the Huntsman

James Marsden (1973-)
    Bachelorette
    Robot & Frank

Jason Marsden (1975-)
    Blue Like Jazz

Ailsa Marshall (1978-)
    Act of Valor

Logan Marshall-Green
    Prometheus

Jesse L. Martin (1969-)
    Joyful Noise

Joel David Moore (1977-)
Gone

Julianne Moore (1961-)
Being Flynn

Esai Morales (1962-)
Atlas Shrugged II: The Strike

Joseph Moreau
Katy Perry: Part of Me

Chloe Grace Moretz (1997-)
Dark Shadows

Bonnie Morgan
The Devil Inside

Danny Morgan
On the Road

Jeffrey Dean Morgan (1966-)
Peace, Love & Misunderstanding
The Possession
Red Dawn

Matthew Morrison
What to Expect When You're
Expecting

David Morse (1953-)
The Odd Life of Timothy Green

Viggo Mortensen (1958-)
On the Road

Samantha Morton (1977-)
Cosmopolis
John Carter

Wunmi Mosaku
Citadel

Carrie-Anne Moss (1970-)
Silent Hill: Revelation 3D

Elisabeth (Elissabeth, Elizabeth, Liz)
Moss (1982-)
Darling Companion
On the Road

Anson Mount (1973-)
Safe

Megan Mullally (1958-)
Smashed

Dermot Mulroney (1963-)
Big Miracle
The Grey

Olivia Munn (1980-)
The Babymakers
Magic Mike

Cillian Murphy (1976-)
The Dark Knight Rises
Red Lights

Donna Murphy (1958-)
Dark Horse

Eddie Murphy (1961-)
A Thousand Words

Haley Murphy
Silent House

Bill Murray (1950-)
Hyde Park on Hudson
Moonrise Kingdom

Joel Murray (1963-)
God Bless America

Alex Nahon
2 Days in New York

Yu Nan
The Expendables 2

Liam Neeson (1952-)
Battleship
The Dark Knight Rises
The Grey
Taken 2
Wrath of the Titans

Sam Neill (1948-)
The Hunter
The Vow

Sophie Nelisse
Monsieur Lazhar

Tim Blake Nelson (1965-)
Detachment

Tim Blake Nelson (1965-)
Big Miracle
Lincoln

Franco Nero (1942-)
Django Unchained

Emilien Neron
Monsieur Lazhar

Kathryn Newton
Paranormal Activity 4

Thandie Newton (1972-)
Tyler Perry's Good Deeds

Ne-Yo (1982-)
Red Tails

Thomas Ian Nicholas (1980-)
American Reunion

Rachel Nichols (1980-)
Alex Cross

Julianne Nicholson (1971-)
Keep the Lights On

Jackson Nicoll
Fun Size

Bill Nighy (1949-)
The Best Exotic Marigold Hotel
Total Recall
Wrath of the Titans

Chuck Norris (1939-)
The Expendables 2

James Northcote
Wuthering Heights

Edward Norton (1969-)
The Bourne Legacy
Moonrise Kingdom

Antoinette Noufaily
Where Do We Go Now?

Bill Nunn (1953-)
Won't Back Down

Barack Obama (1961-)
2016: Obama's America

Barack H. Obama (1961-)
See Barack Obama

Barack Hussein Obama (1961-)
See Barack Obama

Barry Obama (1961-)
See Barack Obama

Frances O'Connor (1967-)
The Hunter

Joe Odagiri (1976-)
I Wish

Marissa O'Donnell
Peace, Love & Misunderstanding

Chris O'Dowd
Friends with Kids

Gregoire Oestermann
The Intouchables

Nick Offerman (1970-)
Casa de mi Padre
Smashed

Catherine O'Hara (1954-)
Frankenweenie (*V*)

Nene Ohtsuka
I Wish

Dayo Okeniyi
The Hunger Games

Gary Oldman (1958-)
The Dark Knight Rises
Lawless

Elizabeth Olsen (1989-)
Liberal Arts
Peace, Love & Misunderstanding
Red Lights
Silent House

Jason O'Mara
One for the Money

Eman Xor Ona
Chico & Rita (*V*)

Aubrey Plaza (1984-)
  Safety Not Guaranteed
  10 Years

Jesse Plemons (1988-)
  The Master

Tim Plester (1970-)
  Lockout

Jennifer Podemski
  Take This Waltz

Amy Poehler (1971-)
  The Secret World of Arrietty (*V*)

Kevin Pollak (1958-)
  The Magic of Belle Isle

Imogen Poots
  A Late Quartet

Brigitte Poupart
  Monsieur Lazhar

Chris Pratt (1979-)
  The Five-Year Engagement
  10 Years
  Zero Dark Thirty

Jennifer Price
  October Baby

Danielle Proulx (1952-)
  Monsieur Lazhar

Jonathan Pryce (1947-)
  Hysteria

Bill Pullman (1953-)
  Lola Versus

Lucy Punch (1977-)
  A Little Bit of Heaven

James Purefoy (1964-)
  John Carter

Ella Purnell
  Intruders

Dennis Quaid (1954-)
  Playing for Keeps
  What to Expect When You're
    Expecting
  The Words

Jack Quaid (1992-)
  The Hunger Games

Simon Quaterman
  The Devil Inside

Queen Latifah (1970-)
  Ice Age: Continental Drift (*V*)
  Joyful Noise

Daniel Radcliffe (1989-)
  The Woman in Black

Josh Radnor (1974-)
  Liberal Arts

Jonathan Raggett
  The Lady

Emanuel Ragsdale
  A Thousand Words

Leven Rambin (1990-)
  Chasing Mavericks
  The Hunger Games

Cierra Ramirez (1995-)
  Girl in Progress

Edgar Ramirez (1977-)
  Wrath of the Titans

Efren Ramirez (1973-)
  Casa de mi Padre

James E. Ransome (1961-)
  Red Hook Summer

Noomi Rapace (1979-)
  Prometheus

David Rasche (1944-)
  Men in Black 3

Phylicia Rashad (1949-)
  Tyler Perry's Good Deeds

Victor Rasuk (1984-)
  Being Flynn

Navi Rawat (1977-)
  The Collection

Tania Raymonde (1988-)
  Blue Like Jazz

Stephen Rea (1946-)
  Underworld: Awakening

Elizabeth Reaser (1975-)
  Liberal Arts
  The Twilight Saga: Breaking
    Dawn, Part 2

James Rebhorn (1948-)
  Sleepwalk with Me

Lance Reddick (1969-)
  Won't Back Down

Eddie Redmayne (1982-)
  Les Miserables

Calvin Reeder
  V/H/S

Keanu Reeves (1964-)
  Side by Side (*N*)

Vincent Regan (1965-)
  Lockout

Tara Reid (1975-)
  American Reunion

John C. Reilly (1965-)
  Wreck-It Ralph (*V*)

Kelly Reilly (1977-)
  Flight

James Remar (1953-)
  Django Unchained

Jeremie Renier (1981-)
  The Kid with a Bike

Jeremy Renner (1971-)
  The Avengers
  The Bourne Legacy

Jean Reno (1948-)
  Alex Cross

Gloria Reuben (1964-)
  Lincoln

Debbie Reynolds (1932-)
  One for the Money

Ryan Reynolds (1976-)
  Safe House

Ving Rhames (1961-)
  Piranha 3DD
  Won't Back Down

Rhianna (1988-)
  Battleship

Kim Rhodes
  Atlas Shrugged II: The Strike

Giovanni Ribisi (1974-)
  Contraband
  Ted

Christina Ricci (1980-)
  Bel Ami

Brett Rice (1954-)
  Hope Springs

Denise Richards (1972-)
  Madea's Witness Protection

Joely Richardson (1965-)
  Red Lights

Andy Richter (1966-)
  Madagascar 3: Europe's Most
    Wanted (*V*)

Rob Riggle
  Big Miracle
  Dr. Seuss' The Lorax (*V*)
  21 Jump Street

Sam Riley (1980-)
  On the Road

Fergus Riordan
  Ghost Rider: Spirit of Vengeance

Emmanuelle Riva (1927-)
  Amour

Emilio Rivera (1961-)
  Act of Valor

David Schwimmer (1966-)
   Madagascar 3: Europe's Most
    Wanted (*V*)

Edith Scob (1937-)
   Holy Motors

Kaya Scodelario
   Wuthering Heights

Martin Scorsese (1942-)
   Side by Side

Adam Scott (1973-)
   Bachelorette
   Friends with Kids
   The Guilt Trip

Campbell Scott (1962-)
   The Amazing Spider-Man

Seann William Scott (1976-)
   American Reunion
   Goon
   Ice Age: Continental Drift (*V*)

Tom Everett Scott (1970-)
   Parental Guidance

Kristin Scott Thomas (1960-)
   Bel Ami
   Salmon Fishing in the Yemen

Kyra Sedgwick (1965-)
   Man on a Ledge
   The Possession

Jason Segel (1980-)
   The Five-Year Engagement
   Jeff, Who Lives at Home
   This Is 40

Rade Serbedzija (1946-)
   Taken 2

Andy Serkis (1964-)
   The Hobbit: An Unexpected
    Journey (*V*)

Nestor Serrano (1957-)
   Act of Valor

Roshan Seth (1942-)
   Trishna

Rufus Sewell (1967-)
   Abraham Lincoln: Vampire
    Hunter

Lea Seydoux (1985-)
   Farewell, My Queen

Amanda Seyfried (1985-)
   Gone
   Les Miserables

Yara Shahidi
   Butter

Michael Shannon (1974-)
   Premium Rush

Molly Shannon (1964-)
   Hotel Transylvania (*V*)

Suraj Sharma
   Life of Pi

Lee Shaw
   Wuthering Heights

Vinessa Shaw (1976-)
   Big Miracle

Alia Shawkat (1989-)
   Ruby Sparks

Wallace Shawn (1943-)
   A Late Quartet

Martin Sheen (1940-)
   The Amazing Spider-Man

Michael Sheen (1969-)
   The Twilight Saga: Breaking
    Dawn, Part 2

Dax Shepard (1975-)
   Hit and Run

Sam Shepard (1943-)
   Darling Companion
   Killing Them Softly
   Safe House

Sherri Shepherd (1970-)
   One for the Money

Rade Sherbedgia (1946-)
   See *Rade Serbedzija*

Willow Shields (2000-)
   The Hunger Games

Amy Shiels
   Citadel

William Shimell
   Amour

Matt Shively
   Paranormal Activity 4

Martin Short (1950-)
   Frankenweenie (*V*)

Grant Show (1962-)
   The Possession

Elisabeth Shue (1963-)
   Chasing Mavericks
   Hope Springs
   House at the End of the Street

Sarah Silverman (1970-)
   Take This Waltz
   Wreck-It Ralph (*V*)

Alicia Silverstone (1976-)
   Butter

J.K. Simmons (1955-)
   Contraband
   The Words

Johnny Simmons
   The Perks of Being a Wallflower

Heather Alicia Simms
   Red Hook Summer

Jeremy Sisto (1974-)
   Robot & Frank

Alexander Skarsgard (1976-)
   Battleship

Stellan Skarsgard (1951-)
   The Avengers

Krzysztof Skonieczny (1983-)
   In Darkness

Jean Smart (1959-)
   Hope Springs

Michael Smiley
   Kill List

Andrey Smirnov (1941-)
   Elena

Brandon Smith (1952-)
   Bernie

Chadd Smith
   Step Up Revolution

Lois Smith (1930-)
   The Odd Life of Timothy Green

Mackenzie Brooke Smith
   God Bless America

Maggie Smith (1934-)
   The Best Exotic Marigold Hotel
   Quartet

Sheridan Smith
   Quartet

Will Smith (1968-)
   Men in Black 3

Willow Smith
   Dr. Seuss' The Lorax (*V*)

Yeardley Smith (1964-)
   High School

Kodi Smit-McPhee (1996-)
   ParaNorman (*V*)

Cobie Smulders (1982-)
   The Avengers

Brittany Snow (1986-)
   Pitch Perfect

Steven Soderbergh (1963-)
   Side by Side

Barry Soetoro (1961-)
   See *Barack Obama*

Karan Soni
   Safety Not Guaranteed

Sissy Spacek (1949-)
Deadfall

David Spade (1964-)
Hotel Transylvania (*V*)

Rafe Spall (1983-)
Life of Pi
Prometheus

Jordin Sparks (1989-)
Sparkle

Scott Speedman (1975-)
Underworld: Awakening
The Vow

Abigail Spencer
Chasing Mavericks
This Means War

Octavia Spencer
Smashed

Stephen Spinella (1956-)
Lincoln

Sam Spruell
Snow White and the Huntsman

Sylvester Stallone (1946-)
The Expendables 2

Sebastian Stan (1983-)
The Apparition
Gone

Harry Dean Stanton (1926-)
The Avengers
This Must Be the Place

Jason Statham (1972-)
The Expendables 2
Safe

Imelda Staunton (1956-)
The Pirates! Band of Misfits (*V*)

David Steen (1954-)
Django Unchained

Paprika Steen (1964-)
Keep the Lights On

Amandla Stenberg (1998-)
The Hunger Games

Eric Sheffer Stevens
Silent House

Josh Stewart (1977-)
The Collection

Kristen Stewart (1990-)
On the Road
Snow White and the Huntsman
The Twilight Saga: Breaking
Dawn, Part 2

Riley Thomas Stewart (2002-)
The Lucky One

Julia Stiles (1981-)
Silver Linings Playbook

Ben Stiller (1965-)
Madagascar 3: Europe's Most
Wanted (*V*)
The Watch

Rachael Stirling (1977-)
Salmon Fishing in the Yemen

Emma Stone (1988-)
The Amazing Spider-Man

Peter Stormare (1953-)
Lockout

Yvonne Strahovski (1982-)
The Guilt Trip

David Strathairn (1949-)
The Bourne Legacy
Lincoln

Meryl Streep (1949-)
Hope Springs

Barbra Streisand (1942-)
The Guilt Trip

Elaine Stritch (1925-)
ParaNorman (*V*)

Freddie Stroma
Pitch Perfect

Jeremy Strong
Lincoln
Robot & Frank

Mark Strong (1963-)
John Carter
Zero Dark Thirty

Don Stroud (1937-)
Django Unchained

Sophie Stuckey
The Woman in Black

Michael Stuhlbarg
Hitchcock
Lincoln
Men in Black 3

Jim Sturgess (1978-)
Cloud Atlas

Tom Sturridge (1985-)
On the Road

Jason Sudeikis (1975-)
The Campaign

Tika Sumpter (1980-)
Sparkle

Daniel Sunjata (1971-)
The Dark Knight Rises
Gone
One for the Money

Donald Sutherland (1934-)
The Hunger Games

Mena Suvari (1979-)
American Reunion

Joe Swanberg
V/H/S

D.B. Sweeney (1961-)
Atlas Shrugged II: The Strike
Taken 2

Taylor Swift (1989-)
Dr. Seuss' The Lorax (*V*)

Tilda Swinton (1961-)
Moonrise Kingdom

Omar Sy
The Intouchables

Wanda Sykes (1964-)
Ice Age: Continental Drift (*V*)

Tabu
Life of Pi

Charlie Tahan
Frankenweenie (*V*)

Sophia Takal
V/H/S

Amber Tamblyn (1983-)
Django Unchained

Russ Tamblyn (1934-)
Django Unchained

Ayush Tandon
Life of Pi

Meagan Tandy
Piranha 3DD

Firat Tanis (1975-)
Once Upon a Time in Anatolia

Quentin Tarantino (1963-)
Django Unchained

Joe Taslim (1981-)
The Raid: Redemption

Channing Tatum (1980-)
Haywire
Magic Mike
10 Years
21 Jump Street
The Vow

Lili Taylor (1967-)
Being Flynn

Noah Taylor (1969-)
Lawless

Aaron Taylor-Johnson (1990-)
Anna Karenina
Savages

Miles Teller (1987-)
Project X

Juno Temple (1989-)
The Dark Knight Rises
Killer Joe

David Tennant (1971-)
The Pirates! Band of Misfits (*V*)

Lee Terjesen (1965-)
Red Tails

Alexandre Tharaud
Amour

Charlize Theron (1975-)
Prometheus
Snow White and the Huntsman

Justin Theroux (1971-)
Wanderlust

David Thewlis (1963-)
The Lady

Max Thieriot (1988-)
House at the End of the Street

Olivia Thirlby (1986-)
Being Flynn
Dredd
Nobody Walks

Eddie Kaye Thomas (1980-)
American Reunion

Emma Thompson (1959-)
Brave (*V*)
Men in Black 3

Jordenn Thompson
Tyler Perry's Good Deeds

Kenan Thompson (1978-)
The Magic of Belle Isle

Lea Thompson (1962-)
Thin Ice

Tracie Thoms (1975-)
Looper

Uma Thurman (1970-)
Bel Ami
Playing for Keeps

Alessandro Tiberi
To Rome with Love

Justin Timberlake (1981-)
Trouble with the Curve

Analeigh Tipton (1988-)
Damsels in Distress

Marisa Tomei (1964-)
Parental Guidance

Lorraine Toussaint (1960-)
Middle of Nowhere

John Travolta (1954-)
Savages

Adam Trese (1969-)
Silent House

Jean-Louis Trintignant (1930-)
Amour

Joe Lo Truglio
Wanderlust

Colleen Trussler
October Baby

Stanley Tucci (1960-)
The Hunger Games

Chris Tucker (1972-)
Silver Linings Playbook

Alan Tudyk (1971-)
Wreck-It Ralph (*V*)

Tamara Tunie (1959-)
Flight

James Tupper
Playing for Keeps

Aisha Tyler (1970-)
The Babymakers

Liv Tyler (1977-)
Robot & Frank

Cicely Tyson (1933-)
Alex Cross

Deborah Kara Unger (1966-)
Silent Hill: Revelation 3D

Johann Urb (1977-)
Resident Evil: Retribution

Karl Urban (1972-)
Dredd

Iko Uwais
The Raid: Redemption

Muhammet Uzuner (1964-)
Once Upon a Time in Anatolia

Jean-Claude Van Damme (1961-)
The Expendables 2

Carice van Houten (1976-)
Intruders

Joyce Van Patten (1934-)
This Must Be the Place

Courtney B. Vance (1960-)
Joyful Noise

Laura Vandervoort (1984-)
Ted

Vanilla Ice (1967-)
That's My Boy

Nia Vardalos (1962-)
For a Good Time, Call...

Vince Vaughn (1970-)
The Watch

Alex Veadov
Act of Valor

Milo Ventimiglia (1977-)
That's My Boy

Armand Verdure
Rust and Bone

Sofia Vergara (1972-)
The Three Stooges

Elizabeth Vicary
Brooklyn Castle

Nicole Vicius
Sound of My Voice

Alicia Vikander
Anna Karenina
A Royal Affair

Julie Vorus
The Do-Deca-Pentathlon

Mark Wahlberg (1971-)
Contraband
Ted

Tom Waits (1949-)
Seven Psychopaths

Amr Waked (1973-)
Salmon Fishing in the Yemen

Rhys Wakefield
Nobody Walks

Christopher Walken (1943-)
Dark Horse
A Late Quartet
Seven Psychopaths

Benjamin Walker (1982-)
Abraham Lincoln: Vampire
Hunter

Dreama Walker
Compliance

Polly Walker (1966-)
John Carter

Quvenzhane Wallis
Beasts of the Southern Wild

Kate Walsh (1967-)
The Perks of Being a Wallflower

M. M. Emmet Walsh (1935-)
The Odd Life of Timothy Green

Julie Walters (1950-)
Brave (*V*)

Christoph Waltz (1956-)
Django Unchained

Patrick Warburton (1964-)
Ted

Eric Wareheim
    Tim and Eric's Billion Dollar
        Movie

Denzel Washington (1954-)
    Flight
    Safe House

Kerry Washington (1977-)
    Django Unchained
    A Thousand Words

Mia Wasikowska (1989-)
    Lawless

Emily Watson (1967-)
    Anna Karenina

Emma Watson (1990-)
    The Perks of Being a Wallflower

Naomi Watts (1968-)
    The Impossible

Jacki Weaver (1947-)
    Silver Linings Playbook

Sigourney Weaver (1949-)
    The Cold Light of Day
    Red Lights

Hugo Weaving (1959-)
    Cloud Atlas
    The Hobbit: An Unexpected
        Journey

Mark Webber (1980-)
    For a Good Time, Call...

Steven Weber (1961-)
    A Little Bit of Heaven

Rachel Weisz (1971-)
    The Bourne Legacy
    The Deep Blue Sea
    360

Justin Welborn
    Blue Like Jazz

Titus Welliver (1961-)
    Argo
    Man on a Ledge

Dominic West (1969-)
    John Carter

Samuel West (1966-)
    Hyde Park on Hudson

Jennifer Westfeldt (1970-)
    Friends with Kids

Jonny Weston
    Chasing Mavericks

Shea Whigham (1969-)
    Silver Linings Playbook

Ben Whishaw (1980-)
    Skyfall

Betty White (1922-)
    Dr. Seuss' The Lorax (*V*)

Brian White (1973-)
    The Cabin in the Woods
    Tyler Perry's Good Deeds

Julie White
    Hello I Must Be Going
    Lincoln

Liz White
    The Woman in Black

Dondre T. Whitfield (1969-)
    Middle of Nowhere

Bradley Whitford (1959-)
    The Cabin in the Woods

Mae Whitman (1988-)
    The Perks of Being a Wallflower

Johnny Whitworth (1975-)
    Ghost Rider: Spirit of Vengeance

Emily Wickersham
    Gone

Robert Wieckiewicz (1967-)
    In Darkness

Dianne Wiest (1948-)
    Darling Companion
    The Odd Life of Timothy Green

Shea Wigham
    This Must Be the Place

Kristen Wiig (1973-)
    Friends with Kids

Olivia Wilde (1984-)
    Butter
    Deadfall
    People Like Us
    The Words

Craig Steven Wilder
    The Central Park Five

Tristan Wilds
    Red Tails

Tom Wilkinson (1948-)
    The Best Exotic Marigold Hotel

Fred Willard (1939-)
    The Magic of Belle Isle

Jesse Williams
    The Cabin in the Woods

Michelle Williams (1980-)
    Take This Waltz

Olivia Williams (1968-)
    Anna Karenina
    Hyde Park on Hudson

Treat Williams (1952-)
    A Little Bit of Heaven

Bruce Willis (1955-)
    The Cold Light of Day
    The Expendables 2
    Looper
    Moonrise Kingdom

Jake Wilson
    Citadel

Rebel Wilson (1986-)
    Bachelorette
    Pitch Perfect

Penelope Wilton (1946-)
    The Best Exotic Marigold Hotel

Michael Wincott (1959-)
    Hitchcock

Adam Wingard
    V/H/S

Debra Winger (1955-)
    Lola Versus

Henry Winkler (1945-)
    Here Comes the Boom

Mare Winningham (1959-)
    Mirror Mirror

Mary Elizabeth Winstead (1984-)
    Abraham Lincoln: Vampire
        Hunter
    Smashed

Ray Winstone (1957-)
    Snow White and the Huntsman

Ray Wise (1947-)
    Tim and Eric's Billion Dollar
        Movie

Reese Witherspoon (1976-)
    This Means War

Collette Wolfe (1980-)
    The Babymakers

Nat Wolff (1994-)
    Peace, Love & Misunderstanding

James Wolk (1985-)
    For a Good Time, Call...

Elijah Wood (1981-)
    Celeste & Jesse Forever
    The Hobbit: An Unexpected
        Journey

Bokeem Woodbine (1973-)
    Total Recall

Jonathan Woodhouse
    The Lady

Finn Woodlock
    The Hunter

Tom Wopat (1951-)
    Django Unchained

Sam Worthington (1976-)
  Man on a Ledge
  Wrath of the Titans
Amy Wren
  Wuthering Heights
Daniel Wu (1974-)
  The Man with the Iron Fists
Anton Yelchin (1989-)
  The Pirates! Band of Misfits (V)
Michelle Yeoh (1962-)
  The Lady
Burhan Yildiz
  Once Upon a Time in Anatolia

Neil Young (1945-)
  Neil Young Journeys
Rick Yune (1971-)
  The Man with the Iron Fists
Alma Zack
  Footnote
Steve Zahn (1968-)
  Diary of a Wimpy Kid: Dog
    Days
Igor Zaripov
  Cirque du Soleil: Worlds Away
Roschdy Zem (1965-)
  The Cold Light of Day

Catherine Zeta-Jones (1969-)
  Playing for Keeps
  Rock of Ages
Steve Zissis
  The Do-Deca-Pentathlon
  Jeff, Who Lives at Home
Michal Zurawski (1979-)
  In Darkness
Ayelet Zurer (1969-)
  Darling Companion
Chris Zylka (1985-)
  The Amazing Spider-Man
  Piranha 3DD

Subject Index

3-D Movies
The Amazing Spider-Man
Dr. Seuss' The Lorax
Dredd
Ghost Rider: Spirit of Vengeance
Ice Age: Continental Drift
John Carter
Men in Black 3
Piranha 3DD
The Pirates! Band of Misfits
Prometheus
Wrath of the Titans

Action-Adventure
Act of Valor
The Amazing Spider-Man
Argo
Battleship
Big Miracle
The Bourne Legacy
Chronicle
The Cold Light of Day
Contraband
The Dark Knight Rises
Friends with Kids
Gone
The Grey
Haywire
Kill List
Man on a Ledge
Premium Rush
The Raid: Redemption
Safe
Safe House
Savages

Seeking Justice
Taken 2
Underworld: Awakening

Action-Comedy
Casa de mi Padre
Hit and Run
One for the Money
This Means War
21 Jump Street

Adapted from a Book
Alex Cross
Anna Karenina
Atlas Shrugged II: The Strike
Bel Ami
Cloud Atlas
Cosmopolis
Dr. Seuss' The Lorax
John Carter
Life of Pi
Rise of the Guardians
The Secret World of Arrietty
Total Recall
Trishna
The Twilight Saga: Breaking
    Dawn, Part 2
The Woman in Black

Adapted from a Fairy Tale
Mirror Mirror
Snow White and the Huntsman

Adapted from a Play
The Deep Blue Sea
Killer Joe

Adapted from a Story
Total Recall

Adapted from an Article
The Sessions

Adapted from Comics
Dredd

Adapted from Television
Dark Shadows
21 Jump Street

Adolescence
High School
House at the End of the Street

Adoption
The Three Stooges

African America
Beasts of the Southern Wild
Madea's Witness Protection

Aging
The Best Exotic Marigold Hotel
Hope Springs
Robot & Frank
Trouble with the Curve

AIDS/HIV
How to Survive a Plague

Aircraft or Air Travel

Flight
The Grey
Red Tails

Alcoholic Beverages

Lawless
Smashed

Alcoholism

Flight
The Master
People Like Us
Smashed

Alien Beings

Battleship
Prometheus
The Watch

American South

Beasts of the Southern Wild
The Campaign
Joyful Noise
The Lucky One

Amusement Parks

Piranha 3DD

Animals

The Grey
Ice Age: Continental Drift

Animation & Cartoons

Brave
Chico & Rita
Dr. Seuss' The Lorax
Hotel Transylvania
Ice Age: Continental Drift
Madagascar 3: Europe's Most
Wanted
ParaNorman
The Pirates! Band of Misfits
Rise of the Guardians
The Secret World of Arrietty

Arctic or Antarctic Regions

Ice Age: Continental Drift

Art or Artists

Ai Weiwei: Never Sorry

Asia

The Lady

Asian-American Culture

The Lucky One

Baltimore

The Raven

Baseball

Trouble with the Curve

Bicycling

Premium Rush

Biography

The Imposter
The Lady
Lincoln

Biography: Music

Marley

Biography: Show Business

Hitchcock

Black Culture

Red Tails
Think Like a Man
Tyler Perry's Good Deeds

Books or Bookstores

Cosmopolis

Bounty Hunters

Ghost Rider: Spirit of Vengeance
One for the Money

Business or Industry

Atlas Shrugged II: The Strike
Cosmopolis
Resident Evil: Retribution
Step Up Revolution

Canada

Neil Young Journeys

Cancer

Marley

Carnivals or Circuses

Madagascar 3: Europe's Most
Wanted

Childhood

Dark Shadows
Diary of a Wimpy Kid: Dog
Days
Ghost Rider: Spirit of Vengeance
The Odd Life of Timothy Green
ParaNorman
The Possession
Safe
The Secret World of Arrietty

Children

Beasts of the Southern Wild
Citadel
I Wish
Paranormal Activity 4

China

Ai Weiwei: Never Sorry
The Man with the Iron Fists

Christianity

Blue Like Jazz

Civil War

Abraham Lincoln: Vampire
Hunter
Lincoln

College

Blue Like Jazz
Damsels in Distress
Footnote
Liberal Arts

Comedy

The Babymakers
Butter
The Campaign
For a Good Time, Call...
God Bless America
High School
Project X
Robot & Frank
10 Years
Thin Ice
To Rome with Love
2 Days in New York

Comedy-Drama

The Best Exotic Marigold Hotel
Blue Like Jazz
Darling Companion
Jeff, Who Lives at Home
Liberal Arts
Salmon Fishing in the Yemen
Silver Linings Playbook
Think Like a Man
A Thousand Words
Your Sister's Sister

Computers

V/H/S

Concert Films

Neil Young Journeys

Confidence Games

Thin Ice

Conspiracies or Conspiracy Theories

The Bourne Legacy

Contract Killers

Alex Cross

Looper

Crime Drama

Arbitrage

Bullhead

Contraband

The Dark Knight Rises

End of Watch

Headhunters

Killer Joe

Lawless

Man on a Ledge

Once Upon a Time in Anatolia

The Raven

Safe

Safe House

Savages

Crime or Criminals

Lawless

Seven Psychopaths

Dance

Step Up Revolution

Dance--Ballet

First Position

Deadly Viruses

Resident Evil: Retribution

Demons or Wizards

The Devil Inside

Detroit

Sparkle

Devils

Ghost Rider: Spirit of Vengeance

Divorce

Hello I Must Be Going

I Wish

Peace, Love & Misunderstanding

360

Doctors

A Royal Affair

Doctors or Nurses

Darling Companion

Hysteria

Documentary Films

Ai Weiwei: Never Sorry

First Position

How to Survive a Plague

The Imposter

The Invisible War

Marley

Neil Young Journeys

The Queen of Versailles

Samsara

Searching For Sugar Man

Side by Side

Dogs

Darling Companion

Seven Psychopaths

Domestic Abuse

Sparkle

Drama

Atlas Shrugged II: The Strike

Beasts of the Southern Wild

Compliance

The Deep Blue Sea

Detachment

Farewell, My Queen

The Lucky One

Promised Land

Smashed

Step Up Revolution

360

Tyler Perry's Good Deeds

Drug Abuse

Casa de mi Padre

End of Watch

Flight

Keep the Lights On

Sparkle

Drugs

High School

Marley

Peace, Love & Misunderstanding

Ecology or Environment

Big Miracle

Dr. Seuss' The Lorax

Education or Schooling

Detachment

I Wish

Won't Back Down

Engagement

The Five-Year Engagement

That's My Boy

Tyler Perry's Good Deeds

Entertainment Industry

Rock of Ages

Sparkle

Europe

Madagascar 3: Europe's Most Wanted

Family

The Cold Light of Day

Darling Companion

Friends with Kids

Fun Size

I Wish

Killer Joe

Ruby Sparks

Silver Linings Playbook

Wrath of the Titans

Your Sister's Sister

Family Comedy

Diary of a Wimpy Kid: Dog Days

The Do-Deca-Pentathlon

Madea's Witness Protection

The Odd Life of Timothy Green

Peace, Love & Misunderstanding

That's My Boy

A Thousand Words

Family Drama

Dark Horse

Footnote

I Wish

People Like Us

Sparkle

Trouble with the Curve

Family Films

The Odd Life of Timothy Green

Family Reunions

Dark Shadows

Horror Anthology
V/H/S

Horror Comedy
Piranha 3DD

Hostages
Lockout

Hotels or Motels
The Best Exotic Marigold Hotel
Hotel Transylvania
The Innkeepers

Immigration
Monsieur Lazhar

India
The Best Exotic Marigold Hotel
Trishna

Infants
Friends with Kids

Insurance
Thin Ice

Inteligence Service Agencies
Act of Valor
Argo
The Bourne Legacy
The Cold Light of Day
Safe House
This Means War

International Relations
Haywire

Interviews
The Imposter
Marley
Side by Side

Islands
Journey 2: The Mysterious Island
Moonrise Kingdom

Italy
The Devil Inside
To Rome with Love

Journalism
Big Miracle

Judaism
In Darkness

Kidnappers or Kidnappings
Act of Valor
The Cold Light of Day
Savages
Seven Psychopaths

Law or Lawyers
Dredd
Once Upon a Time in Anatolia
The Woman in Black

Little People
Mirror Mirror
Snow White and the Huntsman

Live Action/Animation Combinations
Ted

London
Hysteria

Los Angeles
End of Watch
Hit and Run
People Like Us
Ruby Sparks
Seven Psychopaths
Side by Side

Louisiana
Beasts of the Southern Wild

Male Domestic Employees
The Dark Knight Rises

Marriage
Celeste & Jesse Forever
Darling Companion
Friends with Kids
Headhunters
Hitchcock
The Lady
The Queen of Versailles
Smashed
To Rome with Love
Wanderlust

Martial Arts
Hope Springs
The Man with the Iron Fists
The Raid: Redemption

Mass Media
To Rome with Love

The Meaning of Life
Jeff, Who Lives at Home

Memphis
Undefeated

Men
The Expendables 2
Magic Mike
Men in Black 3
Think Like a Man
The Watch

Mental Health
Citadel
Silver Linings Playbook

Mexico
Act of Valor
Casa de mi Padre
Savages

Miami
Step Up Revolution

Middle East
The Dictator
Salmon Fishing in the Yemen

Military: Foreign
Red Dawn

Military: Navy
Act of Valor
Battleship

Missing Persons
The Amazing Spider-Man
Gone

Mistaken Identity
The Amazing Spider-Man
Total Recall

Montreal
Monsieur Lazhar

Mothers
Won't Back Down

Motorcycles
Ghost Rider: Spirit of Vengeance

Rescue Missions

Argo
Big Miracle
Journey 2: The Mysterious Island
Lockout
Safe
Wrath of the Titans

Reunions

10 Years

Revenge

The Expendables 2
Seeking Justice

Road Trips

Hit and Run
Seeking a Friend for the End of
    the World

Robots & Androids

Prometheus
Robot & Frank

Romance

Anna Karenina
Bel Ami
Casa de mi Padre
Celeste & Jesse Forever
The Deep Blue Sea
Hotel Transylvania
Joyful Noise
Keep the Lights On
Middle of Nowhere
A Royal Affair
Savages
10 Years
This Means War
To Rome with Love
Trishna
The Words
Your Sister's Sister

Romantic Comedy

Celeste & Jesse Forever
The Five-Year Engagement
Hello I Must Be Going
Hysteria
Moonrise Kingdom
Ruby Sparks
This Means War
What to Expect When You're
    Expecting

Roommates

For a Good Time, Call...

Royalty

Brave
Farewell, My Queen
Mirror Mirror
A Royal Affair
Snow White and the Huntsman

Russia/USSR

Anna Karenina
Chernobyl Diaries

Salespeople

Thin Ice

Satire or Parody

Butter
Casa de mi Padre
God Bless America
Tim and Eric's Billion Dollar
    Movie

Science Fiction

The Avengers
Battleship
Chronicle
Cloud Atlas
Dredd
The Hunger Games
John Carter
Lockout
Looper
Men in Black 3
Prometheus
Resident Evil: Retribution
Robot & Frank
Total Recall
The Watch

Science or Scientists

Salmon Fishing in the Yemen

Scotland

Brave

Serial Killers

Gone
The Raven
V/H/S

Sex or Sexuality

The Babymakers
Bel Ami
For a Good Time, Call...
Hello I Must Be Going
Hysteria
Keep the Lights On
The Sessions
360
Trishna

Sexual Abuse

Compliance
Red Hook Summer

Sibling Rivalry

The Do-Deca-Pentathlon

Slice of Life

The Kid with a Bike

Soccer

Playing for Keeps

Space Exploration or Outer Space

Lockout
Prometheus

Spain

The Cold Light of Day

Spies and Espionage

The Cold Light of Day
Savages
Skyfall
Taken 2

Spies or Espionage

Haywire
Total Recall

Sports

The Do-Deca-Pentathlon

Sports Documentaries

Undefeated

Sports--General

Playing for Keeps

Stepparents

Journey 2: The Mysterious Island

Strippers

Magic Mike

Suburban Dystopia

Butter

Suicide

Monsieur Lazhar

Super Heroes

The Amazing Spider-Man
The Avengers

Title Index

This cumulative index is an alphabetical list of all films covered in the volumes of the *Magill's Cinema Annual*. Film titles are indexed on a word-by-word basis, including articles and prepositions. English leading articles (A, An, The) are ignored, as are foreign leading articles (El, Il, La, Las, Le, Les, Los). Acronyms appear alphabetically as if regular words. Common abbreviations in titles file as if they are spelled out. Proper names in titles are alphabetized beginning with the individual's first name. Titles with numbers are alphabetized as if the numbers were spelled out. When numeric titles gather in close proximity to each other, the titles will be arranged in a low-to-high numeric sequence. Films reviewed in this volume are cited in bold; films reviewed in past volumes are cited with the *Annual* year in which the review was published. Original and alternate titles are cross-referenced to the American release title. Titles of retrospective films are followed by the year, in brackets, of their original release.

A

A corps perdu. *See* Straight for the Heart.

A. I.: Artificial Intelligence 2002

A la Mode (Fausto) 1995

A Lot Like Love 2006

A Ma Soeur. *See* Fat Girl.

A nos amours 1984

Abandon 2003

ABCD 2002

Abduction 2012

Abgeschminkt! *See* Making Up!.

About a Boy 2003

About Adam 2002

About Last Night... 1986

About Schmidt 2003

Above the Law 1988

Above the Rim 1995

Abraham Lincoln: Vampire Hunter 2013

Abrazos rotos, Los. *See* Broken Embraces.

Abre Los Ojos. *See* Open Your Eyes.

Abril Despedacado. *See* Behind the Sun.

Absence of Malice 1981

Absolute Beginners 1986

Absolute Power 1997

Absolution 1988

Abyss, The 1989

Accepted 2007

Accidental Tourist, The 1988

Accompanist, The 1993

Accordeur de tremblements de terre, L'. *See* Piano Tuner of Earthquakes, The.

Accused, The 1988

Ace in the Hole [1951] 1986, 1991

Ace Ventura: Pet Detective 1995

Ace Ventura: When Nature Calls 1996

Aces: Iron Eagle III 1992

Acid House, The 2000

Acqua e sapone. *See* Water and Soap.

Across the Tracks 1991

Across the Universe 2008

Act of Valor 2013

Acting on Impulse 1995

Action Jackson 1988

Actress 1988

Adam 2010

Adam Sandler's 8 Crazy Nights 2003

Adam's Rib [1950] 1992

Adaptation 2003

Addams Family, The 1991

Addams Family Values 1993

Addicted to Love 1997

Addiction, The 1995

Addition, L'. *See* Patsy, The.

Adjo, Solidaritet. *See* Farewell Illusion.

Adjuster, The 1992

Adjustment Bureau, The 2012

Adolescente, L' 1982

Adoration 2010

All's Fair 1989

All-American High 1987

Allan Quatermain and the Lost City of Gold 1987

Alley Cat 1984

Alligator Eyes 1990

Allnighter, The 1987

Almost an Angel 1990

Almost Famous 2001

Almost Heroes 1999

Almost You 1985

Aloha Summer 1988

Alone. *See* Solas.

Alone in the Dark 2006

Alone with Her 2008

Along Came a Spider 2002

Along Came Polly 2005

Alpha and Omega 2011

Alpha Dog 2008

Alphabet City 1983

Alpine Fire 1987

Altars of the World [1976] 1985

Alvin and the Chipmunks 2008

Alvin and the Chipmunks: Chip-wrecked 2012

Alvin and the Chipmunks: The Squeakquel 2010

Always (Jaglom) 1985

Always (Spielberg) 1989

Amadeus 1984, 1985

Amanda 1989

Amantes. *See* Lovers.

Amantes del Circulo Polar, Los. *See* Lovers of the Arctic Circle, The.

Amants du Pont Neuf, Les 1995

Amateur 1995

Amateur, The 1982

Amazing Grace 2008

Amazing Grace and Chuck 1987

Amazing Panda Adventure, The 1995

Amazing Spider-Man, The 2013

Amazon Women on the Moon 1987

Ambition 1991

Amelia 2010

Amelie 2002

Amen 2004

America 1986

American, The 2011

American Anthem 1986

American Beauty 2000

American Blue Note 1991

American Buffalo 1996

American Carol, An 2009

American Chai 2003

American Cyborg: Steel Warrior 1995

American Desi 2002

American Dream 1992

American Dreamer 1984

American Dreamz 2007

American Fabulous 1992

American Flyers 1985

American Friends 1993

American Gangster 2008

American Gothic 1988

American Haunting, An 2007

American Heart 1993

American History X 1999

American in Paris, An [1951] 1985

American Justice 1986

American Me 1992

American Movie 2000

American Ninja 1984, 1991

American Ninja 1985

American Ninja II 1987

American Ninja III 1989

American Outlaws 2002

American Pie 2000

American Pie 2 2002

American Pop 1981

American President, The 1995

American Psycho 2001

American Reunion 2013

American Rhapsody, An 2002

American Stories 1989

American Splendor 2004

American Summer, An 1991

American Taboo 1984, 1991

American Tail, An 1986

American Tail: Fievel Goes West, An 1991

American Teen 2009

American Wedding 2004

American Werewolf in London, An 1981

American Werewolf in Paris, An 1997

American Women. *See* The Closer You Get.

America's Sweethearts 2002

Ami de mon amie, L'. *See* Boyfriends and Girlfriends.

Amin: The Rise and Fall 1983

Amistad 1997

Amityville Horror, The 2006

Amityville II: The Possession 1981

Amityville 3-D 1983

Among Giants 2000

Among People 1988

Amongst Friends 1993

Amor brujo, El 1986

Amores Perros 2002

Amos and Andrew 1993

Amour 2013

Amour de Swann, Un. *See* Swann in Love.

Amours d'Astrée et de Céladon, Les. *See* Romance of Astree and Celadon, The.

Amreeka 2010

Anaconda 1997

Analyze That 2003

Analyze This 2000

Anastasia 1997

Anchorman: The Legend of Ron Burgundy 2005

Anchors Aweigh [1945] 1985

And God Created Woman 1988

...And God Spoke 1995

And Life Goes On (Zebdegi Edame Darad) 1995

And Nothing but the Truth 1984

And Now Ladies and Gentlemen 2004

And the Ship Sails On 1984

And You Thought Your Parents Were Weird 1991

And Your Mother Too. *See* Y tu mama tambien.

Andre 1995

Android 1984

Broken Vessels 1999

Broken Wings 2005

Bronson 2010

Bronx Tale, A 1993

Brooklyn Castle 2013

Brooklyn's Finest 2011

Brother (Balabanov) 1999

Brother (Kitano) 2001

Brother Bear 2004

Brother from Another Planet, The 1984

Brother of Sleep 1996

Brotherhood of the Wolf 2003

Brothers 2006

Brothers 2010

Brothers, The 2002

Brothers Bloom, The 2010

Brothers Grimm, The 2006

Brother's Keeper 1993

Brother's Kiss, A 1997

Brothers McMullen, The 1995

Brothers Solomon, The 2008

Brown Bunny, The 2005

Brown Sugar 2003

Browning Version, The 1995

Bruce Almighty 2004

Bruce Lee Story, The. *See* Dragon.

Brüno 2010

Bu-Su 1988

Bubba Ho-Tep 2004

Bubble 2007

Bubble Boy 2002

Buche, La [2000] 2001

Buck 2012

Bucket List, The 2009

Buckminster Fuller: Thinking Out Loud 1996

Bucky Larson: Born to Be a Star 2012

Buddy 1997

Buddy Boy 2001

Buddy Buddy 1981

Buddy System, The 1984

Buena Vista Social Club, The 2000

Buffalo 66 1999

Buffalo Soldiers 2004

Buffy the Vampire Slayer 1992

Bug 2008

Bug's Life, A 1999

Bugsy 1991

Building Bombs 1995

Bull Durham 1988

Bulldog Drummond [1929] 1982

Bulletproof (Carver) 1988

Bulletproof (Dickerson) 1996

Bulletproof Heart 1995

Bulletproof Monk 2004

Bullets Over Broadway 1995

Bullhead 2013

Bullies 1986

Bullshot 1985

Bully 2002

Bully 2013

Bully Project, The. *See* Bully.

Bulworth 1999

Bum Rap 1988

'Burbs, The 1989

Burglar 1987

Burglar, The 1988

Buried 2011

Buried on Sunday 1995

Burke and Hare 2012

Burke and Wills 1987

Burlesque 2011

Burn After Reading 2009

Burnin' Love 1987

Burning Plain, The 2010

Burning Secret 1988

Burnt by the Sun 1995

Bushwhacked 1995

Business of Fancydancing, The 2003

Business of Strangers, The 2002

Busted Up 1987

Buster 1988

But I'm a Cheerleader 2001

Butcher Boy, The 1999

Butcher's Wife, The 1991

Butter 2013

Butterfield 8 [1960] 1993

Butterflies 1988

Butterfly 2003

Butterfly Effect 2005

Buy and Cell 1988

Buying Time 1989

By Design 1982

By the Sword 1993

Bye Bye Blue Bird 2001

Bye Bye Blues 1990

Bye Bye, Love 1995

C

Cabaret Balkan 2000

Cabeza de Vaca 1992

Cabin Boy 1988

Cabin Fever 2004

Cabin in the Woods, The 2013

Cabinet of Dr. Ramirez, The 1995

Cable Guy, The 1996

Cache 2007

Cactus 1986

Caddie [1976] 1982

Caddyshack II 1988

Cadence 1991

Cadillac Man 1990

Cadillac Records 2009

Cafe Ole 2001

Cafe Society 1997

Cage 1989

Cage aux folles III, La 1986

Cage/Cunningham 1995

Caged Fury 1984

Cairo Time 2011

Cal 1984

Calendar 1995

Calendar Girl 1993

Calendar Girls 2004

Calhoun. *See* Nightstick.

Call Me 1988

Calle 54 2002

Caller, The 1987

Calling the Shots 1988

Came a Hot Friday 1985

Cameron's Closet 1989

Camilla 1995

Camille Claudel 1988, 1989

Camorra 1986

Chained Heat 1983

Chairman of the Board 1999

Challenge, The 1982

Chamber, The 1996

Chambermaid of the Titanic, The 1999

Chameleon Street 1991

Champion [1949] 1991

Champions 1984

Chan Is Missing 1982

Chances Are 1989

Change-Up, The 2012

Changeling 2009

Changing Lanes 2003

Changing Times 2007

Chansons d'amour, Les. *See* Love Songs.

Chantilly Lace 1995

Chaos 2004

Chaos. *See* Ran.

Chaos Theory 2009

Chaplin 1992

Character 1999

Chariots of Fire 1981

Charlie and the Chocolate Factory 2006

Charlie Bartlett 2009

Charlie St. Cloud 2011

Charlie's Angels 2001

Charlie's Angels: Full Throttle 2004

Charlie Wilson's War 2008

Charlotte Gray 2003

Charlotte's Web 2007

Charm Discret de la Bourgeoisie, Le. *See* The Discreet Charm of the Bourgeoisie.

Chase, The 1995

Chasers 1995

Chasing Amy 1988

Chasing Liberty 2005

Chasing Mavericks 2013

Chasing Papi 2004

Chateau, The 2003

Chateau de ma mere, Le. *See* My Mother's Castle.

Chattahoochee 1990

Chattanooga Choo Choo 1984

Che 2010

Cheap Shots 1991

Cheaper by the Dozen 2004

Cheaper by the Dozen 2 2006

Cheatin' Hearts 1993

Check Is in the Mail, The 1986

Checking Out 1989

Cheech & Chong Still Smokin' 1983

Cheech & Chong's The Corsican Brothers 1984

Cheetah 1989

Chef in Love, A 1997

Chelsea Walls 2003

Chere Inconnue. *See* I Sent a Letter to My Love.

Chéri 2010

Cherish 2003

Chernobyl Diaries 2013

Cherry Orchard, The 2003

Cherry Pink. *See* Just Looking.

Chevre, La. *See* Goat, The.

Chi bi. *See* Red Cliff.

Chicago 2003

Chicago Joe and the Showgirl 1990

Chicago 10 2009

Chicken Hawk: Men Who Love Boys 1995

Chicken Little 2006

Chicken Run 2001

Chico & Rita 2013

Chief Zabu 1988

Chihwaseon: Painted Fire 2003

Child, The 2007

Child's Play 1988

Child's Play II 1990

Child's Play III 1991

Children of a Lesser God 1986

Children of Heaven, The 2000

Children of Men 2007

Children of Nature 1995

Children of the Corn II 1993

Children of the Revolution 1997

Chile, la Memoria Obstinada. *See* Chile, Obstinate Memory.

Chile, Obstinate Memory 1999

Chill Factor 2000

Chilled in Miami. *See* New In Town.

Chimes at Midnight. *See* Falstaff.

China Cry 1990

China Girl 1987

China Moon 1995

China, My Sorrow 1995

China Syndrome, The [1979] 1988

Chinese Box 1999

Chinese Ghost Story II, A 1990

Chinese Ghost Story III, A 1991

Chipmunk Adventure, The 1987

Chloe 2011

Chocolat (Denis) 1989

Chocolat (Hallstrom) 2001

Chocolate War, The 1988

Choke 2009

Choke Canyon 1986

Choose Me 1984, 1985

Chopper 2002

Chopper Chicks in Zombie Town 1991

Chopping Mall 1986

Choristes, Les. *See* Chorus, The.

Chorus, The 2006

Chorus Line, A 1985

Chorus of Disapproval, A 1989

Chosen, The 1982

Christine 1983

Christine F. 1982

Christmas Carol, A 2010

Christmas Story, A 1983

Christmas Tale, A 2009

Christmas with the Kranks 2005

Christopher Columbus: The Discovery 1992

Chronicle 2013

Chronicles of Narnia: Prince Caspian, The 2009

Chronicles of Narnia: The Lion, the Witch and the Wardrobe, The 2006

Chronicles of Narnia: The Voyage of the Dawn Treader, The 2011

Chronicles of Riddick, The 2005

Chronos 1985

Cold Feet (Van Dusen) 1984

Cold Fever 1996

Cold Heaven 1992

Cold Light of Day, The 2013

Cold Moon 1995

Cold Mountain 2004

Cold Souls 2010

Cold Steel 1987

Coldblooded 1995

Collapse 2010

Collateral 2005

Collateral Damage 2003

Collection, The 2013

Collector, The 2010

College Road Trip 2009

Colombiana 2012

Colonel Chabert 1995

Colonel Redl 1985

Color Adjustment 1995

Color Me Kubrick 2008

Color of Money, The 1986

Color of Night 1995

Color Purple, The 1985

Colorado Territory [1949] 1985

Colors 1988

Colpo di Luna. *See* Moon Shadow.

Combat Shock 1986

Combination Platter 1995

Come and Get It [1936] 1981

Come Back to the Five and Dime Jimmy Dean, Jimmy Dean 1982

Come See the Paradise 1990

Come Undone 2002

Comebacks, The 2008

Comedian Harmoniest: Six Life Stories, The 1995

Comedy of Power 2008

Comfort and Joy 1984

Comfort of Strangers, The 1991

Comic Book Confidential 1988

Coming to America 1988

Commandments 1997

Commando 1985

Commando Squad 1987

Comme une image. *See* Look at Me.

Commitments, The 1991

Committed 2001

Common Bonds 1995

Communion 1989

Como Agua Para Chocolate. *See* Like Water for Chocolate.

Company, The 2005

Company Business 1991

Company Man 2002

Company Men, The 2011

Company of Strangers, The. *See* Strangers in Good Company.

Company of Wolves, The 1985

Competition [1963] 1985

Complex World 1995

Compliance 2013

Complot, Le. *See* To Kill a Priest.

Compromising Positions 1985

Con Air 1997

Conan O'Brien Can't Stop 2012

Conan the Barbarian 1982

Conan the Barbarian 2012

Conan the Destroyer 1984

Conceiving Ada 2000

Concert, The 2011

Coneheads 1993

Confessions of a Dangerous Mind 2003

Confessions of a Shopaholic 2010

Confessions of a Teenage Drama Queen 2005

Confidence 2004

Confidences trop intimes. *See* Intimate Strangers.

Confidentially Yours 1984

Confusion of Genders 2004

Congo 1995

Connie and Carla 2005

Consenting Adults 1992

Conspiracy Theory 1997

Conspirator, The 2012

Conspirators of Pleasure 1997

Constant Gardener, The 2006

Constantine 2006

Consuming Passions 1988

Contact 1997

Contagion 2012

Conte d'Automne. *See* Autumn Tale.

Conte de Noël, Un. *See* Christmas Tale, A.

Conte de printemps. *See* Tale of Springtime, A.

Conte d'Hiver. *See* Tale of Winter, A.

Contender, The 2001

Continental Divide 1981

Contraband 2013

Control 2008

Control Room 2005

Convent, The 1995

Conviction 2011

Convicts 1991

Convincer, The. *See* Thin Ice.

Convoyeurs Attendent, Les. *See* The Carriers Are Waiting.

Coogan's Bluff [1968] 1982

Cook, the Thief, His Wife, and Her Lover, The 1990

Cookie 1989

Cookie's Fortune 2000

Cookout, The 2005

Cool as Ice 1991

Cool Dry Place, A 2000

Cool Runnings 1993

Cool School, The 2009

Cool World 1992

Cooler, The 2004

Cop 1987

Cop and a Half 1993

Cop Land 1997

Cop Out 2011

Copie conforme. *See* Certified Copy.

Cops and Robbersons 1995

Copycat 1995

Coraline 2010

Core, The 2004

Coriolanus 2012

Corky Romano 2002

Corporation, The 2005

Corpse Bride. *See* Tim Burton's Corpse Bride.

Corrina, Corrina 1995

Corruptor, The 2000

Cujo 1983

Cup, The 2001

Cup Final 1992

Curdled 1996

Cure, The 1995

Cure in Orange, The 1987

Curious Case of Benjamin Button,
The 2009

Curious George 2007

Curly Sue 1991

Current Events 1990

Curse of the Golden Flower 2007

Curse of the Jade Scorpion, The 2002

Curse of the Pink Panther 1983

Cursed 2006

Curtains 1983

Cut and Run 1986

Cutthroat Island 1995

Cutting Edge, The 1992

Cyborg 1989

Cyclo 1996

Cyclone 1987

Cyrano de Bergerac 1990

Cyrus 2011

Czlowiek z Marmuru. *See* Man of
Marble.

Czlowiek z Zelaza. *See* Man of Iron.

D

Da 1988

Da Vinci Code, The 2007

Dad 1989

Dad On the Run 2002

Daddy and the Muscle Academy
1995

Daddy Day Camp 2008

Daddy Day Care 2004

Daddy Nostalgia 1991

Daddy's Boys 1988

Daddy's Dyin' 1990

Daddy's Little Girls 2008

Dadetown 1996

Daffy Duck's Quackbusters 1988

Dakhtaran-e Khorshid. *See* Daughters
of the Sun.

Dakota 1988

Damage 1992

Damned in the U.S.A. 1992

Damned United, The 2010

Damsels in Distress 2013

Dan in Real Life 2008

Dance Flick 2010

Dance Maker, The 2000

Dance of the Damned 1989

Dance with a Stranger 1985

Dance with Me 1999

Dancer in the Dark 2001

Dancer, Texas Pop. 81 1999

Dancer Upstairs, The 2004

Dancers 1987

Dances with Wolves 1990

Dancing at Lughnasa 1999

Dancing in the Dark 1986

Dangerous Beauty 1999

Dangerous Game (Ferrara) 1995

Dangerous Game (Hopkins) 1988

Dangerous Ground 1997

Dangerous Liaisons 1988

Dangerous Lives of Altar Boys, The
2003

Dangerous Love 1988

Dangerous Method, A 2012

Dangerous Minds 1995

Dangerous Moves 1985

Dangerous Woman, A 1993

Dangerously Close 1986

Daniel 1983

Danny Boy 1984

Danny Deckchair 2005

Danny the Dog. *See* Unleashed.

Dante's Peak 1997

Danton 1983

Danzon 1992

Daredevil 2004

Darfur Now 2008

Darjeeling Limited, The 2008

Dark Backward, The 1991

Dark Before Dawn 1988

Dark Blue 2004

Dark Blue World 2002

Dark City

Dark Crystal, The 1982

Dark Days 2001

Dark Eyes 1987

Dark Half, The 1993

Dark Horse 2013

Dark Knight, The 2009

Dark Knight Rises, The 2013

Dark Obsession 1991

Dark of the Night 1986

Dark Shadows 2013

Dark Star [1975] 1985

Dark Water 2006

Dark Wind, The 1995

Darkest Hour, The 2012

Darkman 1990

Darkness 2005

Darkness, Darkness. *See* South of
Reno.

Darkness Falls 2004

Darling Companion 2013

D.A.R.Y.L. 1985

Date Movie 2007

Date Night 2011

Date with an Angel 1987

Daughter of the Nile 1988

Daughters of the Dust 1992

Daughters of the Sun 2001

Dauntaun Herozu. *See* Hope and
Pain.

Dave 1993

Dave Chappelle's Block Party 2007

Dawn of the Dead 2005

Day After Tomorrow, The 2005

Day I Became a Woman, The 2002

Day in October, A 1992

Day of the Dead 1985

Day the Earth Stood Still, The 2009

Daybreakers 2011

Dayereh. *See* Circle, The.

Daylight 1996

Days of Glory 2008

Days of Thunder 1990

Days of Wine and Roses [1962] 1988

Daytrippers, The 1997

Dazed and Confused 1993

Dragonball: Evolution 2010

Dragonfly 2003

Dragonheart 1996

Dragonslayer 1981

Draughtsman's Contract, The 1983

Dream a Little Dream 1989

Dream Demon 1988

Dream for an Insomniac 1999

Dream House 2012

Dream Lover (Kazan) 1986

Dream Lover (Pakula) 1995

Dream of Light 1995

Dream Team, The 1989

Dream With the Fishes 1997

Dreamcatcher 2004

Dreamchild 1985

Dreamer: Inspired by a True Story
    2006

Dreamers, The 2005

Dreamgirls 2007

Dreamlife of Angels, The 2000

Dreams. *See* Akira Kurosawa's
    Dreams.

Dreams with Sharp Teeth 2009

Dreamscape 1984

Dredd 2013

Drei Sterne. *See* Mostly Martha.

Dresser, The 1983

Dressmaker, The 1988

Drifter, The 1988

Drifting 1984

Drillbit Taylor 2009

Drive 1992

Drive 2012

Drive Angry 2012

Drive Me Crazy 2000

Driven 2002

Driving Miss Daisy 1989

Drole de Felix. *See* Adventures of Fe-
    lix, The.

Drop Dead Fred 1991

Drop Dead Gorgeous 2000

DROP Squad 1995

Drop Zone 1995

Drowning by Numbers 1988

Drowning Mona 2001

Drugstore Cowboy 1989

Drumline 2003

Drunks 1997

Dry Cleaning 2000

Dry White Season, A 1989

D3: The Mighty Ducks 1996

Duchess, The 2009

Duchess of Langeais, The 2009

Duck Season 2007

Ducktales, the Movie 1990

Dude, Where's My Car? 2001

Dudes 1987

Dudley Do-Right 2000

Due Date 2011

Duel in the Sun [1946] 1982, 1989

Duet for One 1986

Duets 2001

D.U.I. 1987

Dukes of Hazzard, The 2006

Dulcy [1923] 1981

Duma 2006

Dumb and Dumber 1995

Dumb and Dumberer: When Harry
    Met Lloyd 2004

Dummy 2004

Dune 1984

Dungeons & Dragons 2001

Dunston Checks In 1996

Duolou Tianshi. *See* Fallen Angels.

Duplex 2004

Duplicity 2010

Dust Devil: The Final Cut 1995

Dutch 1991

Dying Gaul, The 2006

Dying Young 1991

Dylan Dog: Dead of Night 2012

E

E la nave va. *See* And the Ship Sails
    On.

Eagle, The 2012

Eagle Eye 2009

Eagle vs. Shark 2008

Earth 2001

Earth 2010

Earth Girls Are Easy 1989

Earthling, The 1981

East Is East 2001

East is Red, The 1995

Eastern Promises 2008

East-West 2002

Easy A 2011

Easy Money 1983

Easy Virtue 2010

Eat a Bowl of Tea 1989

Eat and Run 1986

Eat Drink Man Woman 1995

Eat Pray Love 2011

Eat the Rich 1988

Eating 1990

Eating Raoul 1982

Ebro Runs Dry, The 1993

Echo Park 1986

Echoes 1983

Echoes of Paradise 1989

Eclipse, The 2011

Ed 1996

Ed and His Dead Mother 1993

Ed Wood 1995

Eddie 1996

Eddie and the Cruisers 1983

Eddie and the Cruisers II 1989

Eddie Macon's Run 1983

Eddie Murphy Raw 1987

Eden 1999

Edes Emma, Draga Bobe: Vazlatok,
    Aktok. *See* Sweet Emma, Dear
    Bobe: Sketches, Nudes.

Edge, The 1997

Edge of Darkness 2011

Edge of Heaven, The 2009

Edge of Sanity 1989

Edge of Seventeen 2000

Edith and Marcel 1984

Edith's Diary 1986

Ed's Next Move 1996

Edtv 2000

Educating Rita 1983

Education, An 2010

Education of Little Tree, The 1997

Edukators, The 2006

Frequency 2001

Fresh 1995

Fresh Horses 1988

Freshman, The 1990

Freud [1962] 1983

Frida 2003

Friday 1995

Friday After Next 2003

Friday Night 2004

Friday Night Lights 2005

Friday the 13th 2010

Friday the 13th, Part III 1982

Friday the 13th, Part IV 1984

Friday the 13th, Part VI 1986

Friday the 13th Part VII 1988

Friday the 13th Part VIII 1989

Fried Green Tomatoes 1991

Friend of the Deceased, A 1999

Friends & Lovers 2000

Friends With Benefits 2012

Friends with Kids 2013

Friends with Money 2007

Fright Night 1985

Fright Night 2012

Frighteners, The 1996

Fringe Dwellers, The 1987

From Beyond 1986

From Dusk Till Dawn 1996

From Hell 2002

From Hollywood to Deadwood 1988

From Paris With Love 2011

From Prada to Nada 2012

From Swastikas to Jim Crow 2001

From the Hip 1987

Front, The [1976] 1985

Frosh: Nine Months in a Freshman Dorm 1995

Frost/Nixon 2009

Frozen 2011

Frozen Assets 1992

Frozen River 2009

Fruhlingssinfonie. *See* Spring Symphony.

Fruit Machine, The 1988

Fu-zung cen. *See* Hibiscus Town.

Fucking Amal. *See* Show Me Love.

Fugitive, The 1993

Full Blast 2001

Full Frontal 2003

Full Metal Jacket 1987

Full Monty, The 1997

Full Moon in Paris 1984

Full Moon in the Blue Water 1988

Full of It 2008

Fun Down There 1989

Fun Size 2013

Fun With Dick and Jane 2006

Funeral, The 1987

Funeral, The (Ferrara) 1996

Funny About Love 1990

Funny Bones 1995

Funny Farm (Clark) 1983

Funny Farm (Hill) 1988

Funny Games 2009

Funny People 2010

Furry Vengeance 2011

Further Adventures of Tennessee Buck, The 1988

Future, The 2012

G

Gabbeh 1997

Gabriela 1984

Gabrielle 2007

Gaby—A True Story 1987

Gadjo Dilo 1999

Gake no une no Ponyon. *See* Ponyo.

Galactic Gigolo 1988

Galaxy Quest 2000

Gallipoli 1981

Gambler, The 2000

Game, The 1989

Game, The 1997

Game Plan, The 2008

Game 6 2007

Gamer 2010

Gamin au velo, Le. *See* Kid with a Bike, The.

Gandhi 1982

Gang-Related 1997

Gangs of New York 2003

Gangster No. 1 2003

Garage Days 2004

Garbage Pail Kids Movie, The 1987

Garbo Talks 1984

Garde a vue 1982

Garden, The 1995

Garden State 2005

Gardens of Stone 1987

Garfield 2005

Garfield: A Tail of Two Kitties 2007

Gas Food Lodging 1992

Gate, The 1987

Gate II 1992

Gatekeepers, The 2013

Gattaca 1997

Gaudi Afternoon 2002

Gay Divorcee, The [1934] 1981

Gegen die Wand. *See* Head-On.

Genealogies D' Un Crime. *See* Genealogies of a Crime.

Genealogies of a Crime 1999

General, The 1999

General's Daughter, The 2000

Genghis Blues 2000

Gentilezza del tocco, La. *See* Gentle Touch, The.

Gentle Touch, The 1988

Gentlemen Broncos 2010

Gentlemen Don't Eat Poets 1997

Gentlemen's Agreement [1947] 1989

Genuine Risk 1990

George A. Romero's Diary of the Dead. *See* Diary of the Dead.

George A. Romero's Land of the Dead 2006

George Balanchine's The Nutcracker 1993

George of the Jungle 1997

George's Island 1991

Georgia 1988

Georgia 1995

Georgia Rule 2008

Germinal 1993

Geronimo 1993

Gerry 2004

Get Back 1991

Get Bruce! 2000

Get Carter 2001

Get Crazy 1983

Get Him to the Greek 2011

Get Low 2011

Get on the Bus 1996

Get Over It! 2002

Get Real 2000

Get Rich or Die Tryin' 2006

Get Shorty 1995

Get Smart 2009

Getaway, The 1995

Geteilte Liebe. *See* Maneuvers.

Getting Away with Murder 1996

Getting Even 1986

Getting Even With Dad 1995

Getting It Right 1989

Getting to Know You 2001

Gettysburg 1993

G-Force 2010

Ghare Bhaire. *See* Home and the World, The.

Ghost 1990

Ghost and the Darkness, The 1996

Ghost Dad 1990

Ghost Dog: The Way of the Samurai 2000

Ghost in the Shell II: Innocence 2005

Ghosts of Girlfriends Past 2010

Ghost Rider 2008

Ghost Rider: Spirit of Vengeance 2013

Ghost Ship 2003

Ghost Writer, The 2011

Ghosts Can't Do It 1990

Ghosts of Mississippi 1996

Ghosts…of the Civil Dead 1988

Ghost Story 1981

Ghost Town 1988

Ghost Town 2009

Ghost World 2002

Ghosts of Mars. *See* John Carpenter's Ghosts of Mars.

Ghostbusters 1984

Ghostbusters II 1989

G.I. Jane 1997

G.I. Joe: The Rise of Cobra 2010

Giant [1956] 1993, 1996

Gift, The (Lang) 1983

Gift, The (Raimi) 2001

Gift From Heaven, A 1995

Gig, The 1986

Gigli 2004

Ginger Ale Afternoon 1989

Ginger and Fred 1986

Ginger Snaps 2002

Gingerbread Man, The 1999

Giornata speciale, Una. *See* Special Day, A.

Giovane Toscanini, II. *See* Young Toscanini.

Girl Cut in Two, A 2009

Girl from Paris, The 2004

Girl in a Swing, The 1988

Girl in the Picture, The 1986

Girl in Progress 2013

Girl, Interrupted 2000

Girl Next Door, The 2001

Girl Next Door, The (Greenfield) 2005

Girl on the Train, The 2011

Girl 6 1996

Girl Talk 1988

Girl Who Kicked the Hornet's Nest, The 2011

Girl Who Played with Fire, The 2011

Girl with a Pearl Earring 2004

Girl with the Dragon Tattoo, The 2011

Girl with the Dragon Tattoo, The 2012

Girl with the Hungry Eyes, The 1995

Girl with the Red Hair, The 1983

Girlfight 2001

Girlfriend Experience, The 2010

Girls Can't Swim 2003

Girls School Screamers 1986

Girls Town 1996

Give My Regards to Broad Street 1984

Giving, The 1992

Gladiator (Herrington) 1992

Gladiator (Scott) 2001

Glamazon: A Different Kind of Girl 1995

Glamour 2002

Glaneurs et la Glaneuse, Les. *See* Gleaners and I, The.

Glass House, The 2002

Glass Menagerie, The 1987

Glass Shield, The 1995

Gleaming the Cube 1989

Gleaners and I, The 2002

Glee: The 3D Concert Movie 2012

Glengarry Glen Ross 1992

Glimmer Man, The 1996

Glitter 2002

Gloire de mon pere, La. *See* My Father's Glory.

Gloomy Sunday 2004

Gloria (Cassavetes) [1980] 1987

Gloria (Lumet) 2000

Glory 1989

Glory Road 2007

Gnomeo & Juliet 2012

Go 2000

Go Fish 1995

Go Now 1999

Goal! The Dream Begins 2007

Goat, The 1985

Gobots 1986

God Bless America 2013

God Doesn't Believe in Us Anymore 1988

God Grew Tired of Us 2008

God Is Great, I'm Not 2003

God Is My Witness 1993

God Said "Ha"! 2000

Goddess of 1967, The 2003

Godfather, Part III, The 1990

Gods and Generals 2004

Gods and Monsters 1999

Gods Must Be Crazy, The 1984

Gods Must Be Crazy II, The 1990

God's Will 1989

Godsend 2005

Godzilla 1985 1985

Godzilla 1997

Godzilla 2000 2001

Gohatto. *See* Taboo.

Goin' to Chicago 1991

Going All the Way 1997

Going Berserk 1983

Going the Distance 2011

Going Undercover 1988

Goin' South 1978

Gold Diggers: The Secret of Bear Mountain 1995

Golden Bowl, The 2002

Golden Child, The 1986

Golden Compass, The 2008

Golden Gate 1995

Golden Seal 1983

Goldeneye 1995

Gomorrah 2010

Gone 2013

Gone Baby Gone 2008

Gone Fishin' 1997

Gone in Sixty Seconds 2001

Gone With the Wind [1939] 1981, 1982, 1997

Gong fu. *See* Kung Fu Hustle.

Gonza the Spearman 1988

Good Boy! 2004

Good Burger 1997

Good Bye Cruel World 1984

Good Bye, Lenin! 2005

Good Deeds. *See* Tyler Perry's Good Deeds.

Good Evening, Mr. Wallenberg 1995

Good German, The 2007

Good Girl, The 2003

Good Hair 2010

Good Luck Chuck 2008

Good Man in Africa, A 1995

Good Marriage, A. *See* Beau Mariage, Le.

Good Morning, Babylon 1987

Good Morning, Vietnam 1987

Good Mother, The 1988

Good Night, and Good Luck 2006

Good Old Fashioned Orgy, A 2012

Good Shepherd, The 2007

Good Son, The 1993

Good, the Bad, the Weird, The 2011

Good Thief, The 2004

Good Weather, But Stormy Late This Afternoon 1987

Good Will Hunting 1997

Good Woman, A 2007

Good Woman of Bangkok, The 1992

Good Work. *See* Beau Travail.

Good Year, A 2007

Goodbye, Children. *See* Au Revoir les Enfants.

Goodbye Lover 2000

Goodbye, New York 1985

Goodbye People, The 1986

Goodbye Solo 2010

GoodFellas 1990

Goods: Live Hard, Sell Hard, The 2010

Goods: The Don Ready Story, The. *See* Goods: Live Hard, Sell Hard, The.

Goofy Movie, A 1995

Goon 2013

Goonies, The 1985

Gordy 1995

Gorillas in the Mist 1988

Gorky Park 1983

Gorky Triology, The. *See* Among People.

Gosford Park 2002

Gospel 1984

Gospel According to Vic 1986

Gossip 2001

Gossip (Nutley) 2003

Gost 1988

Gotcha! 1985

Gothic 1987

Gothika 2004

Gout des Autres, Le. *See* Taste of Others, The.

Gouttes d'Eau sur Pierres Brulantes. *See* Water Drops on Burning Rocks.

Governess 1999

Goya in Bordeaux 2001

Grace Is Gone 2008

Grace of My Heart 1996

Grace Quigley 1985

Gracie 2008

Graffiti Bridge 1990

Gran Fiesta, La 1987

Gran Torino 2009

Grand Bleu, Le. *See* Big Blue, The (Besson).

Grand Canyon 1991

Grand Canyon: The Hidden Secrets 1987

Grand Chemin, Le. *See* Grand Highway, The.

Grand Highway, The 1988

Grand Illusion, The 2000

Grand Isle 1995

Grande Cocomero, Il. *See* Great Pumpkin, The.

Grandfather, The 2000

Grandma's Boy 2007

Grandview, U.S.A. 1984

Grass Harp, The 1996

Gravesend 1997

Graveyard Shift. *See* Stephen King's Graveyard Shift.

Gray Matters 2008

Gray's Anatomy 1997

Grease [1978] 1997

Grease II 1982

Great Balls of Fire! 1989

Great Barrier Reef, The 1990

Great Buck Howard, The 2010

Great Day In Harlem, A 1995

Great Debaters, The 2008

Great Expectations 1999

Great Mouse Detective, The 1986

Great Muppet Caper, The 1981

Great Outdoors, The 1988

Great Pumpkin, The 1993

Great Raid, The 2006

Great Wall, A 1986

Great White Hype, The 1996

Greatest, The 2011

Greatest Game Ever Played, The 2006

Greatest Movie Ever Sold, The. *See* POM Wonderful Presents: The Greatest Movie Ever Sold.

Greedy 1995

Hans Christian Andersen's Thumbelina 1995

Hansel and Gretel 1987

Hanussen 1988, 1989

Happening, The 2009

Happenstance 2002

Happily Ever After 1993

Happily Ever After 2006

Happily N'Ever After 2008

Happiness 1999

Happy Accidents 2002

Happy End 2001

Happy Endings 2006

Happy Feet 2007

Happy Feet Two 2012

Happy '49 1987

Happy Gilmore 1996

Happy Hour 1987

Happy New Year 1987

Happy, Texas 2000

Happy Times 2003

Happy Together 1990

Happy Together 1997

Happy-Go-Lucky 2009

Happythankyoumoreplease 2012

Hard Candy 2007

Hard Choices 1986

Hard Core Logo 1999

Hard Eight 1997

Hard Hunted 1995

Hard Promises 1992

Hard Rain 1999

Hard Target 1993

Hard Ticket to Hawaii 1987

Hard Times 1988

Hard to Hold 1984

Hard to Kill 1990

Hard Traveling 1986

Hard Way, The (Badham) 1991

Hard Way, The (Sherman) 1984

Hard Word, The 2004

Hardball 2002

Hardbodies 1984

Hardbodies II 1986

Hardware 1990

Harlem Nights 1989

Harley Davidson and the Marlboro Man 1991

Harmonists, The 2000

Harold & Kumar Escape from Guantanamo Bay 2009

Harold & Kumar Go to White Castle 2005

Harriet Craig [1950] 1984

Harriet the Spy 1996

Harrison's Flowers 2003

Harry and Son 1984

Harry and the Hendersons 1987

Harry Brown 2011

Harry, He's Here to Help. *See* With a Friend Like Harry.

Harry Potter and the Chamber of Secrets 2003

Harry Potter and the Deathly Hallows: Part 1 2011

Harry Potter and the Deathly Hallows: Part 2 2012

Harry Potter and the Goblet of Fire 2006

Harry Potter and the Half-Blood Prince 2010

Harry Potter and the Order of the Phoenix 2008

Harry Potter and the Prisoner of Azkaban 2005

Harry Potter and the Sorcerer's Stone 2002

Harry, Un Ami Qui Vous Veut du Bien. *See* With a Friend Like Harry.

Hart's War 2003

Harvard Man 2003

Harvest, The 1995

Hasty Heart, The [1949] 1987

Hatchet Man, The [1932] 1982

Hatchet II 2011

Hatouna Mehuheret. *See* Late Marriage.

Haunted Honeymoon 1986

Haunted Mansion, The 2004

Haunted Summer 1988

Haunting, The 2000

Haunting in Connecticut, The 2010

Hauru no ugoku shiro. *See* Howl's Moving Castle.

Haute tension. *See* High Tension.

Hav Plenty 1999

Havana 1990

Hawk, The 1995

Hawks 1988

Haywire 2013

He Got Game 1999

He Liu. *See* River, The.

He Loves Me...He Loves Me Not 2004

He Said, She Said 1991

Head Above Water 1997

Head in the Clouds 2005

Head Office 1986

Head of State 2004

Head On 2000

Head-On 2006

Head Over Heels 2002

Headhunters 2013

Heads or Tails 1983

Hear My Song 1991

Hear No Evil 1993

Hearat Shulayim. *See* Footnote.

Hearing Voices 1991

Heart 1987

Heart and Souls 1993

Heart Condition 1990

Heart in Winter, A. *See* Coeur en hiver, Un.

Heart Like a Wheel 1983

Heart of a Stag 1984

Heart of Dixie 1989

Heart of Midnight 1989

Heart of the Game, The 2007

Heartaches 1982

Heartbreak Hotel 1988

Heartbreak Kid, The [1972] 1986

Heartbreak Kid, The (Farrelly/Farrelly) 2008

Heartbreak Ridge 1986

Heartbreaker 1983

Heartbreakers 2002

Heartburn 1986

Heartland 1981

Hitcher, The 1986

Hitcher, The (Meyers) 2008

Hitchhiker's Guide to the Galaxy, The 2006

Hitman 2008

Hitman, The 1991

Hoax, The 2008

Hobbit: An Unexpected Journey, The 2013

Hobo with a Shotgun 2012

Hocus Pocus 1993

Hodejegerne. *See* Headhunters.

Hoffa 1992

Holcroft Covenant, The 1985

Hold Back the Dawn [1941] 1986

Hold Me, Thrill Me, Kiss Me 1993

Holes 2004

Holiday [1938] 1985

Holiday, The 2007

Holiday Inn [1942] 1981

Hollow Man 2001

Hollow Reed 1997

Hollywood Ending 2003

Hollywood Homicide 2004

Hollywood in Trouble 1986

Hollywood Mavericks 1990

Hollywood Shuffle 1987

Hollywood Vice Squad 1986

Hollywoodland 2007

Holy Blood. *See* Santa Sangre.

Holy Innocents, The 1985

Holy Man 1999

Holy Motors 2013

Holy Rollers 2011

Holy Smoke 2000

Holy Tongue, The 2002

Hombre [1967] 1983

Home Alone 1990

Home Alone II: Lost in New York 1992

Home Alone III 1997

Home and the World, The 1985

Home at the End of the World, A 2005

Home for the Holidays 1995

Home Free All 1984

Home Fries 1999

Home Is Where the Heart Is 1987

Home of Our Own, A 1993

Home of the Brave 1986

Home on the Range 2005

Home Remedy 1987

Homeboy 1988

Homegrown 1999

Homer and Eddie 1990

Homeward Bound 1993

Homeward Bound II: Lost in San Francisco 1996

Homework 1982

Homework. *See* Art of Getting By, The.

Homicide 1991

Homme et une femme, Un. *See* Man and a Woman, A.

Hommes et des dieux, Des. *See* Of Gods and Men.

Hondo [1953] 1982

Honey 2004

Honey, I Blew Up the Kid 1992

Honey, I Shrunk the Kids 1989

Honeybunch 1988

Honeydripper 2008

Honeymoon Academy 1990

Honeymoon in Vegas 1992

Honeymooners, The 2006

Hong Gaoliang. *See* Red Sorghum.

Honky Tonk Freeway 1981

Honkytonk Man 1982

Honneponnetge. *See* Honeybunch.

Honor Betrayed. *See* Fear.

Honorable Mr. Wong, The. *See* Hatchet Man, The.

Honour of the House 2001

Hoodlum 1997

Hoodwinked 2007

Hoodwinked Too! Hood vs. Evil 2012

Hook 1991

Hoop Dreams 1995

Hoosiers 1986

Hoot 2007

Hop 2012

Hope and Glory 1987

Hope and Pain 1988

Hope Floats 1999

Hope Springs 2013

Horrible Bosses 2012

Horror Show, The 1989

Hors de prix. *See* Priceless.

Hors la Vie 1995

Horse of Pride, The 1985

Horse Whisperer, The 1999

Horseman on the Roof, The 1996

Horton Hears a Who! *See* Dr. Seuss' Horton Hears a Who!

Host, The 2008

Hostage 2006

Hostel 2007

Hostel: Part II 2008

Hot Chick, The 2003

Hot Dog...The Movie 1984

Hot Fuzz 2008

Hot Pursuit 1987

Hot Rod 2008

Hot Shots! 1991

Hot Shots! Part Deux 1993

Hot Spot, The 1990

Hot to Trot 1988

Hot Tub Time Machine 2011

Hotel Colonial 1987

Hotel De Love 1997

Hotel for Dogs 2010

Hotel New Hampshire, The 1984

Hotel Rwanda 2005

Hotel Terminus 1988

Hotel Transylvania 2013

Hotshot 1987

Hottest State, The 2008

Hound of the Baskervilles, The 1981

Hours, The 2003

Hours and Times, The 1992

House 1986

House II 1987

House Arrest 1996

House at the End of the Street 2013

House Bunny, The 2009

I Love You 1982

I Love You, Beth Cooper 2010

I Love You, Don't Touch Me 1999

I Love You, I Love You Not 1997

I Love You, Man 2010

I Love You Phillip Morris 2011

I Love You to Death 1990

I, Madman 1989

I Married a Shadow 1983

I Now Pronounce You Chuck and Larry 2008

I Only Want You to Love Me 1995

I Ought to Be in Pictures 1982

I Remember Mama [1948] 1981

I, Robot 2005

I Saw the Devil 2012

I Sent a Letter to My Love 1981

I Served the King of England 2009

I Shot Andy Warhol 1996

I Spit on Your Grave 2011

I Spy 2003

I Stand Alone 2000

I Still Know What You Did Last Summer 1999

I, the Jury 1982

I Think I Do 2000

I Think I Love My Wife 2008

I Want to Go Home 1989

I Want Someone to Eat Cheese With 2008

I Was a Teenage Zombie 1987

I Went Down 1999

I Wish 2013

I Woke Up Early the Day I Died 2000

Ice Age 2003

Ice Age: Continental Drift 2013

Ice Age: Dawn of the Dinosaurs 2010

Ice Age: The Meltdown 2007

Ice Harvest, The 2006

Ice House 1989

Ice Pirates, The 1984

Ice Princess 2006

Ice Rink, The 2001

Ice Runner, The 1993

Ice Storm, The 1997

Iceman 1984

Icicle Thief, The 1990

Ideal Husband, An 2000

Identity 2004

Identity Crisis 1989

Ides of March, The 2012

Idiocracy 2007

Idiots, The [1999] 2001

Idle Hands 2000

Idlewild 2007

Iedereen Beroemd! *See* Everybody's Famous!

If Looks Could Kill 1991

If Lucy Fell 1996

If You Could See What I Hear 1982

Igby Goes Down 2003

Ignorant Fairies 2002

Igor 2009

Iklimler. *See* Climates.

Il y a longtemps que je t'aime. *See* I've Loved You So Long.

Ill Testimone dello Sposo. *See* Best Man, The.

I'll Be Home for Christmas 1999

I'll Do Anything 1995

I'll Sleep When I'm Dead 2005

Illtown 1999

Illuminata 2000

Illusionist, The 2007

Illusionist, The 2011

Illustrious Energy 1988

Ils se Marient et Eurent Beaucoup D'Enfants. *See* Happily Ever After.

I'm Dancing as Fast as I Can 1982

I'm Going Home 2003

I'm No Angel [1933] 1984

I'm Not There 2008

I'm Not Rappaport 1997

I'm Still Here 2011

I'm the One That I Want 2001

Imagemaker, The 1986

Imaginarium of Doctor Parnassus, The 2010

Imaginary Crimes 1995

Imaginary Heroes 2006

Imagine 1988

Imagine Me & You 2007

Imagine That 2010

Immediate Family 1989

Immortal Beloved 1995

Immortals 2012

Imperative 1985

Importance of Being Earnest, The 1995

Importance of Being Earnest, The (Parker) 2003

Imported Bridegroom, The 1991

Impossible, The 2013

Imposter, The 2013

Impostor 2003

Impostors 1999

Impromptu 1991

Impulse (Baker) 1984

Impulse (Locke) 1990

In a Better World 2012

In a Shallow Grave 1988

In America 2004

In and Out 1997

In Bloom. *See* Life Before Her Eyes, The.

In Bruges 2009

In Country 1989

In Crowd, The 2001

In Custody 1995

In Dangerous Company 1988

In Darkness 2013

In Dreams 2000

In Fashion. *See* A la Mode.

In God's Hands 1999

In Good Company 2006

In Her Shoes 2006

In-Laws, The 2004

In Love and War 1997

In My Country 2006

In Our Hands 1983

In Praise of Love 2003

In the Army Now 1995

In the Bedroom 2002

In the Company of Men 1997

In the Cut 2004

In the Heat of Passion 1992

In the Heat of the Night [1967] 1992

In the Land of Blood and Honey 2012

In the Land of the Deaf 1995

In the Land of Women 2008

In the Line of Fire 1993

In the Loop 2010

In the Mirror of Maya Deren 2004

In the Mood 1987

In the Mood for Love 2002

In the Mouth of Madness 1995

In the Name of the Father 1993

In the Name of the King: A Dungeon Seige Tale 2009

In the Realms of the Unreal 2006

In the Shadow of Kilimanjaro 1986

In the Shadow of the Moon 2008

In the Shadow of the Stars 1992

In the Soup 1992

In the Spirit 1990

In the Valley of Elah 2008

In This World 2004

In Time 2012

In Too Deep 2000

In Weiter Ferne, So Nah! *See* Faraway, So Close.

Incendies 2012

Inception 2011

Inchon 1982

Incident at Oglala 1992

Incident at Raven's Gate 1988

Incognito 1999

Inconvenient Truth, An 2007

Incredible Hulk, The 2009

Incredible Journey, The. *See* Homeward Bound.

Incredibles, The 2005

Incredibly True Adventures of Two Girls in Love, The 1995

Incubus, The 1982

Indecent Proposal 1993

Independence Day 1996

Indian in the Cupboard, The 1995

Indian Runner, The 1991

Indian Summer 1993

Indiana Jones and the Kingdom of the Crystal Skull 2009

Indiana Jones and the Last Crusade 1989

Indiana Jones and the Temple of Doom 1984

Indigènes. *See* Days of Glory.

Indochine 1992

Inevitable Grace 1995

Infamous 2007

Infernal Affairs 2005

Infinity 1991

Infinity (Broderick) 1996

Informer, The [1935] 1986

Informant!, The 2010

Informers, The 2010

Inglourious Basterds 2010

Inkheart 2010

Inkwell, The 1995

Inland Empire 2007

Inland Sea, The 1995

Inner Circle, The 1991

Innerspace 1987

Innkeepers, The 2013

Innocent, The 1988

Innocent, The 1995

Innocent Blood 1992

Innocent Man, An 1989

Innocent Sleep, The 1997

Innocents Abroad 1992

Inside I'm Dancing. *See* Rory O'Shea Was Here.

Inside Job 2011

Inside Man 2007

Inside Monkey Zetterland 1993

Insider, The 2000

Insidious 2012

Insignificance 1985

Insomnia (Skjoldbjaerg) 1999

Insomnia (Nolan) 2003

Inspector Gadget 2000

Instant Karma 1990

Instinct 2000

Intacto 2004

Intermission 2005

Internal Affairs 1990

International, The 2010

Interpreter, The 2006

Interrogation, The 1990

Interrupters, The 2012

Intersection 1995

Interview 2008

Interview with the Vampire 1995

Intervista 1993

Intimacy 2002

Intimate Relations 1997

Intimate Strangers 2005

Into the Abyss 2012

Into the Blue 2006

Into the Night 1985

Into the Sun 1992

Into the West 1993

Into the Wild 2008

Intolerable Cruelty 2004

Intouchables, The 2013

Intruders 2013

Invaders from Mars 1986

Invasion! *See* Top of the Food Chain.

Invasion, The 2008

Invasion of the Body Snatchers [1956] 1982

Invasion U.S.A. 1985

Inventing the Abbotts 1997

Invention of Love 2001

Invention of Lying, The 2010

Invictus 2010

Invincible 2003

Invincible 2007

Invisible, The 2008

Invisible Circus 2002

Invisible Kid, The 1988

Invisible War, The 2013

Invitation au voyage 1983

Invitation to the Dance [1956] 1985

I.Q. 1995

Iris 2002

Irma la Douce [1963] 1986

Irma Vep 1997

Iron Eagle 1986

Iron Eagle II 1988

Iron Giant, The 2000

Iron Lady, The 2012

Iron Man 2009

Iron Man 2 2011

Iron Maze 1991

Iron Triangle, The 1989

Iron Will 1995

Ironweed 1987

Irreconcilable Differences 1984

Irreversible 2004

Is Anybody There? 2010

Ishtar 1987

Island, The 2006

Island of Dr. Moreau, The 1996

Isn't She Great 2001

Istoriya As-Klyachimol. *See* Asya's Happiness.

It Could Happen to You 1995

It Couldn't Happen Here 1988

It Had to Be You 1989

It Happened One Night [1934] 1982

It Happened Tomorrow [1944] 1983

It Might Get Loud 2010

It Runs in the Family 2004

It Takes Two 1988

It Takes Two 1995

Italian for Beginners 2002

Italian Job, The 2004

Italiensk for Begyndere. *See* Italian for Beginners.

It's a Wonderful Life [1946] 1982

It's Alive III 1987

It's All About Love 2005

It's All Gone Pete Tong 2006

It's All True 1993

It's Complicated 2010

It's Kind of a Funny Story 2011

It's My Party 1996

It's Pat 1995

It's the Rage 2001

Ivan and Abraham 1995

I've Heard the Mermaids Singing 1987

I've Loved You So Long 2009

J

J. Edgar 2012

Jack 1996

Jack and His Friends 1993

Jack and Jill 2012

Jack and Sarah 1996

Jack Frost 1999

Jack Goes Boating 2011

Jack Reacher 2013

Jack the Bear 1993

Jackal, The 1997

Jackass Number Two 2007

Jackass 3D 2011

Jacket, The 2006

Jackie Brown 1997

Jackie Chan's First Strike 1997

Jacknife 1989

Jackpot 2002

Jack's Back 1988

Jacob 1988

Jacob's Ladder 1990

Jacquot of Nantes 1993

Jade 1995

Jagged Edge 1985

J'ai epouse une ombre. *See* I Married a Shadow.

Jailhouse Rock [1957] 1986

Jake Speed 1986

Jakob the Liar 2000

James and the Giant Peach 1996

James Cameron's Sanctum. *See* Sanctum.

James' Journey to Jerusalem 2005

James Joyce's Women 1985

Jamon, Jamon 1993

Jane Austen Book Club, The 2008

Jane Eyre 1996

Jane Eyre 2012

January Man, The 1989

Japanese Story 2005

Jarhead 2006

Jason Goes to Hell 1993

Jason X 2003

Jason's Lyric 1995

Jawbreaker 2000

Jaws: The Revenge 1987

Jaws 3-D 1983

Jay and Silent Bob Strike Back 2002

Jazzman 1984

Je Rentre a la Maison. *See* I'm Going Home.

Je tu il elle [1974] 1985

Je vous salue, Marie. *See* Hail Mary.

Jean de Florette 1987

Jeanne Dielman, 23 Quai du Commerce, 1080 Bruxelles [1976] 1981

Jeepers Creepers 2002

Jeepers Creepers 2 2004

Jeff, Who Lives at Home 2013

Jefferson in Paris 1995

Jeffrey 1995

Jekyll and Hyde…Together Again 1982

Jennifer Eight 1992

Jennifer's Body 2010

Jerky Boys 1995

Jerome 2001

Jerry Maguire 1996

Jersey Girl 2005

Jerusalem 1996

Jesus of Montreal 1989

Jesus' Son 2000

Jet Lag 2004

Jet Li's Fearless 2007

Jetsons 1990

Jewel of the Nile, The 1985

JFK 1991

Jigsaw Man, The 1984

Jim and Piraterna Blom. *See* Jim and the Pirates.

Jim and the Pirates 1987

Jiminy Glick in Lalawood 2006

Jimmy Hollywood 1995

Jimmy Neutron: Boy Genius 2002

Jimmy the Kid 1983

Jindabyne 2008

Jingle All the Way 1996

Jinxed 1982

Jiro Dreams of Sushi 2013

Jit 1995

Jo-Jo at the Gate of Lions 1995

Jo Jo Dancer, Your Life Is Calling 1986

Kamilla and the Thief 1988

Kandahar 2002

Kandyland 1988

Kangaroo 1987

Kangaroo Jack 2004

Kansas 1988

Kansas City 1996

Karakter. *See* Character.

Karate Kid, The 1984

Karate Kid, The 2011

Karate Kid: Part II, The 1986

Karate Kid: Part III, The 1989

Kari-gurashi no Arietti. *See* Secret World of Arrietty, The.

Kate & Leopold 2002

Katy Perry: Part of Me 2013

Kazaam 1996

Kazoku. *See* Where Spring Comes Late.

Keep, The 1983

Keep the River On Your Right: A Modern Cannibal Tale 2002

Keep the Lights On 2013

Keeping Mum 2007

Keeping the Faith 2001

Keeping Up with the Steins 2007

Kerouac, the Movie 1985

Key Exchange 1985

Keys of the Kingdom, The [1944] 1989

Keys to Tulsa 1997

Khuda Gawah. *See* God Is My Witness.

Kick-Ass 2011

Kickboxer 1989

Kickboxer II 1991

Kicked in the Head 1997

Kickin' It Old Skool 2008

Kicking and Screaming (Baumbach) 1995

Kicking & Screaming 2006

Kid, The. *See* Vie en Rose, La.

Kid & I, The 2006

Kid Brother, The 1987

Kid Colter 1985

Kid in King Arthur's Court, A 1995

Kid Stays in the Picture, The 2003

Kid with a Bike, The 2013

Kidnapped 1987

Kids 1995

Kids Are All Right, The 2011

Kids in the Hall: Brain Candy, The 1996

Kids in America. *See* Take Me Home Tonight.

Kika 1995

Kikujiro 2001

Kill Bill: Vol. 1 2004

Kill Bill: Vol. 2 2005

Kill List 2013

Kill Me Again 1989

Kill Me Later 2002

Kill the Irishman 2012

Kill-Off, The 1990

Killer Elite 2012

Killer Image 1992

Killer Inside Me, The 2011

Killer Instinct 1995

Killer Joe 2013

Killer Klowns from Outer Space 1988

Killer of Sheep 2008

Killer Party 1986

Killers 2011

Killing Affair, A 1988

Klling Fields, The 1984

Killing Floor, The 1995

Killing of a Chinese Bookie, The [1976] 1986

Killing of John Lennon, The 2009

Killing Them Softly 2013

Killing Time 1999

Killing Time, The, 1987

Killing Zoe 1995

Killpoint 1984

Killshot 2010

Kindergarten Cop 1990

Kindred, The 1987

King, The 2007

King Arthur 2005

King and I, The 2000

King David 1985

King Is Alive, The 2002

King Is Dancing, The 2002

King James Version 1988

King Kong [1933] 1981

King Kong 2006

King Kong Lives 1986

King Lear 1987

King of Comedy, The 1983

King of Jazz [1930] 1985

King of Kong: A Fistful of Quarters, The 2008

King of Masks, The 2000

King of New York 1990

King of the Children 1988

King of the Hill 1993

King Ralph 1991

King Solomon's Mines 1985

Kingdom, Part 2, The 1999

Kingdom, The 1995

Kingdom, The 2008

Kingdom Come 2002

Kingdom of Heaven 2006

Kingpin 1996

Kings and Queen 2006

King's Ransom 2006

King's Speech, The 2011

Kinjite 1989

Kinky Boots 2007

Kinsey 2005

Kipperbang 1984

Kippur 2001

Kiss Before Dying, A 1991

Kiss Daddy Good Night 1987

Kiss Kiss Bang Bang 2006

Kiss Me a Killer 1991

Kiss Me Goodbye 1982

Kiss Me, Guido 1997

Kiss Me, Stupid [1964] 1986

Kiss of Death 1995

Kiss of the Dragon 2002

Kiss of the Spider Woman 1985

Kiss or Kill 1997

Kiss, The 1988

Kiss the Girls 1997

Kissed 1997

Kisses 2011

Last of the Dogmen 1995

Last of the Finest, The 1990

Last of the Mohicans, The 1992

Last Orders 2003

Last Party, The 1993

Last Resort 1986

Last Resort 2002

Last Rites 1988

Last Samurai, The 2004

Last Seduction, The 1995

Last September, The 2001

Last Shot, The 2005

Last Song, The 2011

Last Starfighter, The 1984

Last Station, The 2010

Last Straw, The 1987

Last Supper 1996

Last Temptation of Christ, The 1988

Last Time I Committed Suicide, The 1997

Last Time I Saw Paris, The [1954] 1993

Last Summer in the Hamptons 1995

Last Wedding 2003

Lat den rätte komma in. *See* Let the Right One In.

Latcho Drom 1995

Late August, Early September 2000

Late Chrysanthemums [1954] 1985

Late for Dinner 1991

Late Marriage 2003

Late Quartet, A 2013

Late Summer Blues 1987

Latin Boys Go to Hell 1997

Latter Days 2005

L'Auberge Espagnole 2004

Laurel Canyon 2004

Law Abiding Citizen 2010

Law of Desire, The 1987

Law of Enclosures, The 2002

Lawn Dogs 1999

Lawless 2013

Lawless Heart 2004

Lawnmower Man, The 1992

Lawnmower Man 2: Beyond Cyberspace 1996

Lawrence of Arabia [1962] 1990

Laws of Attraction 2005

Laws of Gravity 1992

Layer Cake 2006

L' Ecole de la chair. *See* School of Flesh, The.

Leading Man, The 1999

League of Extraordinary Gentlemen, The 2004

League of Their Own, A 1992

Lean on Me 1989

Leap of Faith 1992

Leap Year 2011

Leatherface 1990

Leatherheads 2009

Leave It to Beaver 1997

Leave to Remain 1988

Leaves of Grass 2011

Leaving Las Vegas 1995

Leaving Normal 1992

Lebanon 2011

Lebedyne ozero. *See* Swan Lake.

Leben der Anderen, Das. *See* Lives of Others, The.

Lectrice, La. *See* Reader, The.

Leela 2003

Left Hand Side of the Fridge, The 2002

Legal Eagles 1986

Legally Blonde 2002

Legally Blonde 2: Red, White & Blonde 2004

Legend 1986

Legend of Bagger Vance, The 2001

Legend of Billie Jean, The 1985

Legend of 1900 2000

Legend of Rita, The 2002

Legend of the Guardians: The Owls of Ga'Hoole 2011

Legend of Wolf Mountain, The 1995

Legend of Zorro, The 2006

Legends 1995

Legends of the Fall 1995

Leggenda del Pianista Sull'oceano, La. *See* Legend of 1900.

Legion 2011

Lemon Sisters, The 1990

Lemon Sky 1987

Lemony Snicket's A Series of Unfortunate Events 2005

Leo Tolstoy's Anna Karenina 1997

Leolo 1993

Leon the Pig Farmer 1995

Leonard Part VI 1987

Leopard Son, The 1996

Leprechaun 1993

Leprechaun II 1995

Les Miserables 2013

Les Patterson Saves the World 1987

Less Than Zero 1987

Let Him Have It 1991

Let It Come Down: The Life of Paul Bowles 2000

Let It Ride 1989

Let Me In 2011

Let the Right One In 2010

Let's Fall in Love. *See* New York in Short: The Shvitz and Let's Fall in Love.

Let's Get Lost 1988

Let's Make Friends. *See* I Love You, Man.

Let's Spend the Night Together 1983

Lethal Weapon 1987

Lethal Weapon 2 1989

Lethal Weapon 3 1992

Lethal Weapon 4 1999

Letter to Brezhnev 1986

Letters from Iwo Jima 2007

Letters to Juliet 2011

Leviathan 1989

Levity 2004

Levy and Goliath 1988

Ley del deseo, La. *See* Law of Desire, The.

L'heure d'été. *See* Summer Hours.

Liaison Pornographique, Une. *See* Affair of Love, An.

Liam 2002

Lianna 1983

Liar, Liar 1997

Liar's Moon 1982

Liberal Arts 2013

Libertine, The 2007

L'ivresse du pouvoir. *See* Comedy of Power.

Lizzie McGuire Movie, The 2004

Ljuset Haller Mig Sallskap. *See* Light Keeps Me Company.

Lo sono l'amore. *See* I Am Love.

Loaded 1996

Local Hero 1983

Lock, Stock, and Two Smoking Barrels 2000

Lock Up 1989

Lockout 2013

Locusts, The 1997

Lodz Ghetto 1989

Lola 1982

Lola La Loca 1988

Lola Rennt. *See* Run, Lola, Run.

Lola Versus 2013

Lolita 1999

London Kills Me 1992

Lone Runner, The 1988

Lone Star 1996

Lone Wolf McQuade 1983

Lonely Guy, The 1984

Lonely Hearts (Cox) 1983

Lonely Hearts (Lane) 1995

Lonely in America 1991

Lonely Lady, The 1983

Lonely Passion of Judith Hearne, The 1987

Lonesome Jim 2007

Long Day Closes, The 1993

Long Dimanche de Fiancailles, Un. *See* Very Long Engagement, A.

Long Good Friday, The 1982

Long Gray Line, The [1955] 1981

Long Kiss Goodnight, The 1996

Long Live the Lady! 1988

Long, Long Trailer, The [1954] 1986

Long Lost Friend, The. *See* Apprentice to Murder.

Long Walk Home, The 1990

Long Way Home, The 1999

Long Weekend, The 1990

Longest Yard, The 2006

Longshot, The 1986

Longshots, The 2009

Longtime Companion 1990

Look at Me 2006

Look Who's Talking 1989

Look Who's Talking Now 1993

Look Who's Talking Too 1990

Lookin' to Get Out 1982

Looking for Comedy in the Muslim World 2007

Looking for Richard 1996

Lookout, The 2008

Looney Tunes: Back in Action 2004

Loong Boonmee raluek chat. *See* Uncle Boonmee Who Can Recall His Past Lives.

Looper 2013

Loophole 1986

Loose Cannons 1990

Loose Connections 1988

Loose Screws 1986

L'ora di religione: Il sorriso di mia madre. *See* My Mother's Smile.

Lorax, The. *See* Dr. Seuss' The Lorax.

Lord of Illusions 1995

Lord of the Flies 1990

Lord of the Rings: The Fellowship of the Ring 2002

Lord of the Rings: The Return of the King 2004

Lord of the Rings: The Two Towers 2003

Lord of War 2006

Lords of Discipline, The 1983

Lords of Dogtown 2006

Lords of the Deep 1989

Lorenzo's Oil 1992

Loser 2001

Losers, The 2011

Losin' It 1983

Losing Isaiah 1995

Loss of a Teardrop Diamond, The 2010

Loss of Sexual Innocence 2000

Lost and Delirious 2002

Lost and Found 2000

Lost Angels 1989

Lost Boys, The 1987

Lost City, The 2007

Lost Highway 1997

Lost in America 1985

Lost in La Mancha 2004

Lost in Siberia 1991

Lost in Space 1999

Lost in Translation 2004

Lost in Yonkers. *See* Neil Simon's Lost in Yonkers.

Lost Moment, The [1947] 1982

Lost Prophet 1995

Lost Souls 2001

Lost Weekend, The [1945] 1986

Lost Words, The 1995

Lost World, The 1997

Lottery Ticket 2011

Lou, Pat, and Joe D 1988

Louder Than a Bomb 2012

Louis Bluie 1985

Louis Prima: The Wildest 2001

Loulou 1981

Love Actually 2004

Love Affair 1995

Love After Love 1995

Love Always 1997

Love and a .45 1995

Love and Basketball 2001

Love and Death in Long Island 1999

Love and Human Remains 1995

Love and Murder 1991

Love and Other Catastrophes 1997

Love and Other Drugs 2011

Love & Sex 2001

Love at Large 1990

Love Child, The 1988

Love Child: A True Story 1982

Love Come Down 2002

Love Crimes 1992

Love Don't Cost a Thing 2004

Love Field 1992

Love Guru, The 2009

Love Happens 2010

Love in Germany, A 1984

Love in the Afternoon [1957] 1986

Love in the Time of Cholera 2008

Men 1999

Men at Work 1990

Men Don't Leave 1990

Men in Black 1997

Men in Black II 2003

Men in Black 3 2013

Men in Tights. *See* Robin Hood.

Men of Honor 2001

Men of Respect 1991

Men Who Stare at Goats, The 2010

Men with Brooms 2003

Men with Guns 1999

Menace II Society 1993

Ménage 1986

Men's Club, The 1986

Mephisto 1981

Mercenary Fighters 1988

Merchant of Venice, The 2006

Merci pour le Chocolat 2003

Mercury Rising 1999

Mermaids 1990

Merry Christmas. *See* Joyeux Noel.

Merry Christmas, Mr. Lawrence 1983

Merry War, A 1999

Mesrine 2011

Mesrine: Killer Instinct. *See* Mesrine.

Mesrine: Public Enemy #1. *See* Mesrine.

Message in a Bottle 2000

Messenger, The 1987

Messenger, The 2010

Messenger: Joan of Arc, The 2000

Messenger of Death 1988

Messengers, The 2008

Metallica: Some Kind of Monster 2005

Metalstorm: The Destruction of Jarred-Syn 1983

Metamorphosis: The Alien Factor 1995

Meteor Man, The 1993

Metro 1997

Metroland 2000

Metropolitan 1990

Mexican, The 2002

Mi Vida Loca 1995

Mia Eoniotita ke Mia Mers. *See* Eternity and a Day.

Miami Blues 1990

Miami Rhapsody 1995

Miami Vice 2007

Michael 1996

Michael Clayton 2008

Michael Collins 1996

Michael Jackson's This Is It 2010

Mickey Blue Eyes 2000

Micki & Maude 1984

Micmacs 2011

Microcosmos 1996

Middle Men 2011

Middle of Nowhere 2013

Midnight (Leisen) 1986

Midnight (Vane) 1989

Midnight Clear, A 1992

Midnight Crossing 1988

Midnight in the Garden of Good and Evil 1997

Midnight in Paris 2012

Midnight Run 1988

Midsummer Night's Sex Comedy, A 1982

Midwinter's Tale, A 1996

Mies Vailla Menneisyytta. *See* Man Without a Past, The.

Mifune 2001

Mighty, The 1999

Mighty Aphrodite 1995

Mighty Ducks, The 1992

Mighty Heart, A 2008

Mighty Joe Young 1999

Mighty Macs, The 2012

Mighty Morphin Power Rangers: The Movie 1995

Mighty Quinn, The 1989

Mighty Wind, A 2004

Mike's Murder 1984

Mikey and Nicky 1984

Milagro Beanfield War, The 1988

Mildred Pierce [1945] 1986

Miles from Home 1988

Milk 2009

Milk and Honey 1989

Milk & Honey 2006

Milk Money 1995

Millennium 1989

Millennium Mambo 2003

Miller's Crossing 1990

Million Dollar Baby 2005

Million Dollar Hotel, The 2002

Million Dollar Mystery 1987

Million to Juan, A 1995

Millions 2006

Mimic 1997

Mina Tannenbaum 1995

Mindhunters 2006

Mindwalk 1991

Ministry of Vengeance 1989

Minner. *See* Men.

Minority Report 2003

Minotaur 1995

Minus Man, The 2000

Mio Viaggio in Italia. *See* My Voyage to Italy.

Miracle 2005

Miracle, The 1991

Miracle at St. Anna 2009

Miracle Mile 1988, 1989

Miracle on 34th Street 1995

Miracle Woman, The (1931) 1982

Miral 2012

Mirror, The 2000

Mirror Has Two Faces, The 1996

Mirror Mirror 2013

Mirrors 2009

Misadventures of Mr. Wilt, The 1990

Mischief 1985

Miserables, The 1995

Miserables, The 1999

Misery 1990

Misfits, The [1961] 1983

Mishima 1985

Misma luna, La. *See* Under the Same Moon.

Misplaced 1995

Misplaced 1989

Miss Congeniality 2001

Miss Congeniality 2: Armed and Fabulous 2006

Monument Ave. 1999

Moolaade 2005

Moon 2010

Moon in the Gutter 1983

Moon Over Broadway 1999

Moon over Parador 1988

Moon Shadow [1995] 2001

Moonlight and Valentino 1995

Moonlight Mile 2003

Moonlighting 1982

Moonrise Kingdom 2013

Moonstruck 1987

More Than A Game 2010

Morgan Stewart's Coming Home 1987

Moriarty. *See* Sherlock Holmes.

Morning After, The 1986

Morning Glory 1993

Morning Glory 2011

Morons from Outer Space 1985

Mort de Mario Ricci, La. *See* Death of Mario Ricci, The.

Mortal Kombat 1995

Mortal Kombat II: Annihilation 1997

Mortal Thoughts 1991

Mortuary Academy 1988

Morvern Callar 2003

Mosca addio. *See* Moscow Farewell.

Moscow Farewell 1987

Moscow on the Hudson 1984

Mosquito Coast, The 1986

Most Dangerous Game, The [1932] 1985

Most Dangerous Man in America: Daniel Ellsberg and the Pentagon Papers, The 2011

Most Fertile Man in Ireland, The 2002

Most Wanted 1997

Mostly Martha 2003

Mother 1996

Mother 2011

Mother, The 2005

Mother and Child 2011

Mother Lode 1983

Mother Night 1996

Mother Teresa 1986

Motherhood 2010

Mothering Heart, The [1913] 1984

Mother's Boys 1995

Mothman Prophecies, The 2003

Motorama 1993

Motorcycle Diaries, The 2005

Moulin Rouge 2002

Mountain Gorillas 1995

Mountains of Moon 1990

Mountaintop Motel Massacre 1986

Mouse Hunt 1997

Mouth to Mouth 1997

Movers and Shakers 1985

Moving 1988

Moving the Mountain 1995

Moving Violations 1985

MS One: Maximum Security. *See* Lockout.

Much Ado About Nothing 1993

Mui du du Xanh. *See* Scent of Green Papaya, The.

Mujeres al borde de un ataque de nervios. *See* Women on the Verge of a Nervous Breakdown.

Mulan 1999

Mulholland Drive 2002

Mulholland Falls 1996

Multiplicity 1996

Mumford 2000

Mummy, The 2000

Mummy Returns, The 2002

Mummy: Tomb of the Dragon Emperor, The 2009

Munchie 1995

Munchies 1987

Munich 2006

Muppets, The 2012

Muppet Christmas Carol, The 1992

Muppets from Space 2000

Muppet Treasure Island 1996

Muppets Take Manhattan, The 1984

Mur, Le. *See* Wall, The.

Murder at 1600 1997

Murder by Numbers 2003

Murder in the First 1995

Murder One 1988

Murderball 2006

Murderous Maids 2003

Muriel's Wedding 1995

Murphy's Law 1986

Murphy's Romance 1985

Muse, The 2000

Muses Orphelines, Les. *See* Orphan Muses, The.

Music and Lyrics 2008

Music Box 1989

Music for the Movies: Bernard Herrmann 1995

Music From Another Room 1999

Music of Chance, The 1993

Music of the Heart 2000

Music Tells You, The 1995

Musime si Pomahat. *See* Divided We Fall.

Musketeer, The 2002

Must Love Dogs 2006

Mustang: The Hidden Kingdom 1995

Musuko. *See* My Sons.

Mutant on the Bounty 1989

Mute Witness 1995

Mutiny on the Bounty [1962] 1984

My African Adventure 1987

My American Cousin 1986

My Apprenticeship. *See* Among People.

My Architect 2005

My Baby's Daddy 2005

My Beautiful Laundrette 1986

My Best Fiend 2000

My Best Friend 2008

My Best Friend Is a Vampire 1988

My Best Friend's Girl 1984

My Best Friend's Girl 2009

My Best Friend's Wedding 1997

My Big Fat Greek Wedding 2003

My Bloody Valentine 3D 2010

My Blue Heaven 1990

My Blueberry Nights 2009

My Boss's Daughter 2004

My Boyfriend's Back 1993

Near Dark 1987

Nebo nashevo detstva. *See* Sky of Our Childhood, The.

Necessary Roughness 1991

Ned Kelly 2005

Needful Things 1993

Negotiator, The 1999

Neighborhood Watch. *See* Watch, The.

Neil Simon's Lost in Yonkers 1993

Neil Simon's The Odd Couple 2 1999

Neil Simon's The Slugger's Wife 1985

Neil Young: Heart of Gold 2007

Neil Young Journeys 2013

Nell 1995

Nell Gwyn [1934] 1983

Nelly & Mr. Arnaud 1996

Nemesis 1993

Nenette et Boni 1997

Neon Bible, The 1995

Nervous Ticks 1995

Net, The 1995

Nettoyoge a Sec. *See* Dry Cleaning.

Never Again 2003

Never Back Down 2009

Never Been Kissed 2000

Never Cry Wolf 1983

Never Die Alone 2005

Never Let Me Go 2011

Never Say Never Again 1983

Never Talk to Strangers 1995

Never too Young to Die 1986

Neverending Story, The 1984

Neverending Story II, The 1991

New Adventures of Pippi Longstocking, The 1988

New Age, The 1995

New Babylon, The [1929] 1983

New Eve, The 2001

New Guy, The 2003

New In Town 2010

New Jack City 1991

New Jersey Drive 1995

New Kids, The 1985

New Life, A 1988

New Moon. *See* Twilight Saga: New Moon, The.

New Nightmare. *See* Wes Craven's New Nightmare.

New Rose Hotel 2000

New World, The 2006

New Year's Day 1989

New Year's Eve 2012

New York, I Love You 2010

New York in Short: The Shvitz and Let's Fall in Love 1995

New York Minute 2005

New York, New York [1977] 1983

New York Stories 1989

Newsies 1992

Newton Boys, The 1999

Next 2008

Next Best Thing, The 2001

Next Big Thing, The 2003

Next Day Air 2010

Next Friday 2001

Next Karate Kid, The 1995

Next of Kin 1989

Next Stop Greenwich Village [1976] 1984

Next Stop Wonderland 1999

Next Summer 1986

Next Three Days, The 2011

Next Year if All Goes Well 1983

Niagara Falls 1987

Niagara, Niagara 1999

Nice Girls Don't Explode 1987

Nicholas Nickleby 2003

Nick and Jane 1997

Nick & Norah's Infinite Playlist 2009

Nick of Time 1995

Nico and Dani 2002

Nico Icon 1996

Niezwykla podroz Balthazara Kobera. *See* Tribulations of Balthasar Kober, The.

Night and Day 1995

Night and the City 1992

Night at the Museum 2007

Night at the Museum: Battle of the Smithsonian 2010

Night at the Roxbury, A 1999

Night Catches Us 2011

Night Crossing 1982

Night Falls on Manhattan 1997

Night Friend 1988

Night Game 1989

Night in Heaven, A 1983

Night in the Life of Jimmy Reardon, A 1988

Night Listener, The 2007

'night, Mother 1986

Night of the Comet 1984

Night of the Creeps 1986

Night of the Demons II 1995

Night of the Hunter, The [1955] 1982

Night of the Iguana, The [1964] 1983

Night of the Living Dead 1990

Night of the Pencils, The 1987

Night of the Shooting Stars, The 1983

Night on Earth 1992

Night Patrol 1985

Night Shift 1982

Night Song [1947] 1981

Night Visitor 1989

Night Watch 2007

Night We Never Met, The 1993

Nightbreed 1990

Nightcap. *See* Merci pour le Chocolat.

Nightfall 1988

Nightflyers 1987

Nighthawks 1981

Nighthawks II. *See* Strip Jack Naked.

Nightmare at Shadow Woods 1987

Nightmare Before Christmas, The 1993

Nightmare on Elm Street, A 2011

Nightmare on Elm Street, A 1984

Nightmare on Elm Street: II, A 1985

Nightmare on Elm Street: III, A 1987

Nightmare on Elm Street: IV, A 1988

Nightmare on Elm Street: V, A 1989

Nightmares III 1984

Obsluhoval jsem anglického krále. *See* I Served the King of England.

O.C. and Stiggs 1987

Oceans 2011

Ocean's Eleven 2002

Ocean's Thirteen 2008

Ocean's Twelve 2005

Oci Ciornie. *See* Dark Eyes.

October Baby 2013

October Sky 2000

Octopussy 1983

Odd Life of Timothy Green, The 2013

Odd Man Out [1947] 1985

Oedipus Rex 1995

Oedipus Rex [1967] 1984

Oedipus Wrecks. *See* New York Stories.

Of Gods and Men 2012

Of Human Bondage [1946] 1986

Of Love and Shadows 1996

Of Men and Mavericks. *See* Chasing Mavericks.

Of Mice and Men 1992

Of Unknown Origin 1983

Off Beat 1986

Off Limits 1988

Off the Menu: The Last Days of Chasen's 1999

Office Killer 1997

Office Party 1989

Office Space 2000

Officer and a Gentleman, An 1982

Official Story, The 1985

Offret. *See* Sacrifice, The.

Oh God, You Devil 1984

O'Hara's Wife 1982

Ojos de Julia, Los. *See* Julia's Eyes.

Okuribito. *See* Departures.

Old Dogs 2010

Old Explorers 1991

Old Gringo 1989

Old Joy 2007

Old Lady Who Walked in the Sea, The 1995

Old School 2004

Oldboy 2006

Oleanna 1995

Oliver and Company 1988

Oliver Twist 2006

Olivier Olivier 1993

Omen, The 2007

On Deadly Ground 1995

On Golden Pond 1981

On Guard! 2004

On the Edge 1986

On the Line 2002

On the Other Side. *See* Edge of Heaven, The.

On the Road 2013

On the Town [1949] 1985

On Valentine's Day 1986

Once 2008

Once Around 1991

Once Bitten 1985

Once More 1988

Once Were Warriors 1995

Once Upon a Crime 1992

Once Upon A Forest 1993

Once Upon a Time in America 1984

Once Upon a Time in Anatolia 2013

Once Upon a Time in Mexico 2004

Once Upon a Time in the Midlands 2004

Once Upon a Time…When We Were Colored 1996

Once We Were Dreamers 1987

Ondine 2011

One 2001

One, The 2002

One and a Two, A. *See* Yi Yi.

One Crazy Summer 1986

One Day 2012

One Day in September 2001

One False Move 1992

One Fine Day 1996

One Flew over the Cuckoo's Nest [1975] 1985, 1991

One for the Money 2013

One from the Heart 1982

One Good Cop 1991

One Hour Photo 2003

101 Dalmatians 1996

101 Reykjavik 2002

102 Dalmatians 2001

187 1997

112th and Central 1993

127 Hours 2011

One Magic Christmas 1985

One Missed Call 2009

One More Saturday 1986

One More Tomorrow [1946] 1986

One Nation Under God 1995

One Night at McCool's 2002

One Night Stand 1997

One Shot. *See* Jack Reacher.

One Tough Cop 1999

One True Thing 1999

Onegin 2000

Ong Bak: The Beginning. *See* Ong Bak 2.

Ong Bak 2 2010

Onimaru. *See* Arashi Ga Oka.

Only Emptiness Remains 1985

Only the Lonely 1991

Only the Strong 1993

Only the Strong Survive 2004

Only Thrill, The 1999

Only When I Laugh 1981

Only You 1995

Open Doors 1991

Open Range 2004

Open Season 2007

Open Water 2005

Open Your Eyes 2000

Opening Night 1988

Opera 1987

Operation Condor 1997

Operation Dumbo Drop 1995

Opportunists, The 2001

Opportunity Knocks 1990

Opposite of Sex, The 1999

Opposite Sex, The 1993

Orange County 2003

Orchestra Seats. *See* Avenue Montaigne.

Parsifal 1983

Parsley Days 2001

Parting Glances 1986

Partisans of Vilna 1986

Partners 1982

Party Animal 1985

Party Girl 1995

Party Line 1988

Party Monster 2004

Pascali's Island 1988

Pass the Ammo 1988

Passage, The 1988

Passage to India, A 1984, 1990

Passages 1995

Passed Away 1992

Passenger 57 1992

Passion (Duncan) 2001

Passion (Godard) 1983

Passion d'amore 1984

Passion Fish 1992

Passion in the Desert 1999

Passion of Martin, The 1991

Passion of Mind 2001

Passion of the Christ, The 2005

Passion Play 2012

Passion to Kill, A 1995

Passionada 2003

Pastime 1991

Patch Adams 1999

Patch of Blue, A [1965] 1986

Pathfinder 1990

Pathfinder 2008

Pathology 2009

Paths of Glory [1957] 1991

Patinoire, La. *See* Ice Rink, The.

Patriot, The 2001

Patriot Games 1992

Patsy, The 1985

Patti Rocks 1987

Patty Hearst 1988

Paul 2012

Paul Blart: Mall Cop 2010

Paul Bowles: The Complete Outsider 1995

Paulie 1999

Pauline a la plage. *See* Pauline at the Beach.

Pauline and Paulette 2003

Pauline at the Beach 1983

Paura e amore. *See* Three Sisters.

Pavilion of Women 2002

Pay It Forward 2001

Payback 2000

Paycheck 2004

PCU 1995

Peace, Love, & Misunderstanding 2013

Peace, Propaganda & The Promised Land 2006

Peaceful Air of the West 1995

Peacemaker, The 1997

Pearl Harbor 2002

Pearl Jam Twenty 2012

Pebble and the Penguin, The 1995

Pecker 1999

Pee-wee's Big Adventure 1985

Peggy Sue Got Married 1986

Pelican Brief, The 1993

Pelle Erobreren. *See* Pelle the Conqueror.

Pelle the Conquered 1988

Pelle the Conqueror 1987

Penelope 2009

Penitent, The 1988

Penitentiary II 1982

Penitentiary III 1987

Penn and Teller Get Killed 1989

Pennies from Heaven 1981

People I Know 2004

People Like Us 2013

People on Sunday [1929] 1986

People Under the Stairs, The 1991

People vs. George Lucas, The 2012

People vs. Larry Flynt, The 1996

Pepi, Luci, Bom 1992

Percy Jackson & the Olympians: The Lightning Thief 2011

Perez Family, The 1995

Perfect 1985

Perfect Candidate, A 1996

Perfect Getaway, A 2010

Perfect Host, The 2012

Perfect Man, The 2006

Perfect Match, The 1987

Perfect Model, The 1989

Perfect Murder, A 1999

Perfect Murder, The 1988

Perfect Score, The 2005

Perfect Son, The 2002

Perfect Storm, The 2001

Perfect Stranger 2008

Perfect Weapon, The 1991

Perfect World, A 1993

Perfectly Normal 1991

Perfume: The Story of a Murderer 2008

Perhaps Some Other Time 1992

Peril 1985

Peril en la demeure. *See* Peril.

Perks of Being a Wallflower, The 2013

Permanent Midnight 1999

Permanent Record 1988

Persepolis 2009

Personal Best 1982

Personal Choice 1989

Personal Services 1987

Personal Velocity 2003

Personals, The 1983

Persuasion 1995

Pervola, Sporen in die Sneeuw. *See* Tracks in the Snow.

Pest, The 1997

Pet Sematary 1989

Pet Sematary II 1992

Pete Kelly's Blues [1955] 1982

Peter Ibbetson [1935] 1985

Peter Pan 2004

Peter Von Scholten 1987

Peter's Friends 1992

Petit, Con. *See* Little Jerk.

Petite Bande, Le 1984

Petite Veleuse, La. *See* Little Thief, The.

Peyote Road, The 1995

Phantasm II 1988

Phantom, The 1996

Pollock 2001

Poltergeist 1982

Poltergeist II 1986

Poltergeist III 1988

POM Wonderful Presents: The Greatest Movie Ever Sold 2012

Pomme, La. *See* Apple, The.

Pompatus of Love, The 1996

Ponette 1997

Pontiac Moon 1995

Ponyo 2010

Ponyo on the Cliff by the Sea. *See* Ponyo.

Pooh's Heffalump Movie 2006

Poolhall Junkies 2004

Pootie Tang 2002

Popcorn 1991

Pope Must Die, The 1991

Pope of Greenwich Village, The 1984

Porgy and Bess [1959] 1992

Porky's 1982

Porky's II: The Next Day 1983

Pornographic Affair, An. *See* Affair of Love, An.

Porte aperte. *See* Open Doors.

Portrait Chinois 2000

Portrait of a Lady, The 1996

Poseidon 2007

Positive I.D. 1987

Posse 1993

Possession 2003

Possession, The 2013

Possible Worlds 2001

Post Coitum 1999

Post Coitum, Animal Triste. *See* Post Coitum.

Post Grad 2010

Post Grad Survival Guide, The. *See* Post Grad.

Postcards from America 1995

Postcards from the Edge 1990

Poster Boy 2007

Postman, The (Radford) 1995

Postman, The (Costner) 1997

Postman Always Rings Twice, The 1981

Potiche 2012

Pound Puppies and the Legend of Big Paw 1988

Poupees russes, Les. *See* Russian Dolls.

Poussière d'ange. *See* Angel Dust.

Powaqqatsi 1988

Powder 1995

Power 1986

Power, The 1984

Power of One, The 1992

Powwow Highway 1988

Practical Magic 1999

Prairie Home Companion, A 2007

Prancer 1989

Prayer for the Dying, A 1987

Prayer of the Rollerboys 1991

Preacher's Wife, The 1996

Precious: Based on the Novel 'Push' by Sapphire 2010

Predator 1987

Predator II 1990

Predators 2011

Prefontaine 1997

Prelude to a Kiss 1992

Premium Rush 2013

Premonition 2008

Prenom, Carmen. *See* First Name, Carmen.

Presidio, The 1988

Presque Rien. *See* Come Undone.

Prestige, The 2007

Presumed Innocent 1990

Pret-a-Porter. *See* Ready to Wear.

Pretty Baby [1978] 1984

Pretty in Pink 1986

Pretty Persuasion 2006

Pretty Woman 1990

Prettykill 1987

Prey for Rock and Roll 2004

Priatiel Pakoinika. *See* Friend of the Deceased, A.

Price Above Rubies, A 1999

Price of Glory 2001

Price of Milk 2002

Priceless 2009

Prick Up Your Ears 1987

Pride 2008

Pride and Glory 2009

Pride and Prejudice 2006

Priest 1995

Priest 2012

Priest of Love 1981

Primal Fear 1996

Primary Colors 1999

Primary Motive 1995

Prime 2006

Prince and Me, The 2005

Prince of Darkness 1987

Prince of Egypt, The 1999

Prince of Pennsylvania, The 1988

Prince of Persia: The Sands of Time 2011

Prince of the City 1981

Prince of Tides, The 1991

Princess Academy, The 1987

Princess and the Frog, The 2010

Princess and the Goblin, The 1995

Princess and the Warrior, The 2002

Princess Bride, The 1987

Princess Caraboo 1995

Princess Diaries, The 2002

Princess Diaries 2, The 2005

Principal, The 1987

Principio da Incerteza, O. *See* Uncertainty Principle, The.

Prison 1988

Prisoners of the Mountain 1998

Prisoners of the Sun 1991

Private Fears in Public Places 2008

Private Function, A 1985

Private Investigations 1987

Private Life of Sherlock Holmes, The [1970] 1986

Private Lives of Pippa Lee, The 2010

Private Parts 1997

Private School 1983

Private Worlds [1935] 1982

Prize Winner of Defiance, Ohio, The 2006

Prizzi's Honor 1985

Problem Child 1990

Rage of Honor 1987

Raggedy Man 1981

Raggedy Rawney, The 1988

Raging Angels 1995

Raging Fury. *See* Hell High.

Ragtime 1981

Raid: Redemption, The 2013

Raiders of the Lost Ark 1981

Rain 2003

Rain. *See* Baran.

Rain Killer, The 1990

Rain Man 1988

Rain Without Thunder 1993

Rainbow Brite and the Star Stealer 1985

Rainbow, The 1989

Raining Stones 1995

Raintree County [1957] 1993

Rainy Day Friends 1985

Raise the Red Lantern 1992

Raise Your Voice 2005

Raisin in the Sun, A [1961] 1992

Raising Arizona 1987

Raising Cain 1992

Raising Helen 2005

Raising Victor Vargas 2004

Rambling Rose 1991

Rambo 2009

Rambo: First Blood Part II 1985

Rambo III 1988

Ramona 1995

Ramona and Beezus 2011

Rampage 1987, 1992

Rampart 2012

Ran 1985

Random Hearts 2000

Rango 2012

Ransom 1996

Rapa Nui 1995

Rapid Fire 1992

Rappin' 1985

Rapture, The 1991

Raspad 1992

Rasputin [1975] 1985

Rat Race 2002

Ratatouille 2008

Ratboy 1986

Rat's Tale, A 1999

Ratcatcher 2001

Rate It X 1986

Raven, The 2013

Ravenous 2000

Raw Deal 1986

Rawhead Rex 1987

Ray 2005

Rayon vert, Le. *See* Summer.

Razorback 1985

Razor's Edge, The 1984

Re-Animator 1985

Read My Lips 2003

Reader, The 1988, 1989

Reader, The 2009

Ready to Rumble 2001

Ready to Wear 1995

Real Blonde, The 1999

Real Genius 1985

Real McCoy, The 1993

Real Men 1987

Real Steel 2012

Real Women Have Curves 2003

Reality Bites 1995

Reaping, The 2008

Rear Window [1954] 2001

Reason to Believe, A 1995

Rebel 1986

Rebound 2006

[Rec] 2 2011

Reckless 1984

Reckless 1995

Reckless Kelly 1995

Reckoning, The 2005

Recruit, The 2004

Recruits 1986

Red 1995

Red 2011

Red Cliff 2010

Red Corner 1997

Red Dawn 1984

Red Dawn 2013

Red Dragon 2003

Red Eye 2006

Red Firecracker, Green Firecracker 1995

Red Heat 1988

Red Hill 2011

Red Hook Summer 2013

Red Lights 2013

Red Planet 2001

Red Riding Hood 2012

Red Riding Trilogy, The 2011

Red Riding: 1980. *See* Red Riding Trilogy, The.

Red Riding: 1983. *See* Red Riding Trilogy, The.

Red Riding: 1974. *See* Red Riding Trilogy, The.

Red Road 2008

Red Rock West 1995

Red Scorpion 1989

Red Sonja 1985

Red Sorghum 1988

Red State 2012

Red Surf 1990

Red Tails 2013

Red Violin, The 1999

Redbelt 2009

Redl Ezredes. *See* Colonel Redl.

Reds 1981

Redwood Pigeon 1995

Reefer and the Model 1988

Ref, The 1995

Reflecting Skin, The 1991

Reform School Girls 1986

Regarding Henry 1991

Regeneration 1999

Reign of Fire 2003

Reign Over Me 2008

Reindeer Games 2001

Reine Margot, La. *See* Queen Margot.

Rejuvenator, The 1988

Relax, It's Just Sex 2000

Relentless 1989

Relic, The 1997

Religion Hour, The. *See* My Mother's Smile.

Religulous 2009

Rob Roy 1995

Robert A. Heinlein's The Puppet Masters. *See* Puppet Masters, The.

Robin Hood 1991

Robin Hood 2011

Robin Hood: Men In Tights 1993

Robocop 1987

Robocop II 1990

Robocop III 1993

Robot & Frank 2013

Robot Jox 1990

Robot Stories 2005

Robots 2006

Rock, The 1996

Rock-a-Doodle 1992

Rock 'n Roll Meller. *See* Hellbent.

Rock Hudson's Home Movies 1995

Rock of Ages 2013

Rock School 2006

Rock Star 2002

Rock the Boat 2000

Rocker, The 2009

Rocket Gibraltar 1988

Rocket Man 1997

Rocket Science 2008

Rocketeer, The 1991

RocknRolla 2009

Rocky III 1982

Rocky IV 1985

Rocky V 1990

Rocky Balboa 2007

Roger and Me 1989

Roger Corman's Frankenstein Unbound 1990

Roger Dodger 2003

Roi Danse, Le. *See* King Is Dancing, The.

Rois et reine. *See* Kings and Queen.

Rok spokojnego slonca. *See* Year of the Quiet Sun, A.

Role Models 2009

Roll Bounce 2006

Rollerball 2003

Rollercoaster 2001

Rolling Stones at the Max 1991

Roman de gare 2009

Roman Holiday [1953] 1989

Roman Polanski: Wanted and Desired 2009

Romance 2000

Romance of Astree and Celadon, The 2009

Romance of Book and Sword, The 1987

Romancing the Stone 1984

Romantic Comedy 1983

Romeo 1989

Romeo and Julia 1992

Romeo is Bleeding 1995

Romeo Must Die 2001

Romper Stomper 1993

Romuald et Juliette. *See* Mama, There's a Man in Your Bed.

Romulus, My Father 2009

Romy & Michelle's High School Reunion 1997

Ronin 1999

Rooftops 1989

Rookie, The 1990

Rookie, The 2003

Rookie of the Year 1993

Room with a View, A 1986

Roommate, The 2012

Roommates 1995

Rory O'Shea Was Here 2006

Rosa Luxemburg 1987

Rosalie Goes Shopping 1990

Rosary Murders, The 1987

Rose Garden, The 1989

Rosencrantz and Guildenstern Are Dead 1991

Rosewood 1997

Rosie 2000

Rouge of the North 1988

Rough Cut 1982

Rough Magic

Roughly Speaking [1945] 1982

Rouille et d'os, De. *See* Rust and Bone.

'Round Midnight 1986

Rounders 1999

Rover Dangerfield 1991

Row of Crows, A. *See* Climate for Killing, A.

Roxanne 1987

Roy Rogers: King of the Cowboys 1995

Royal Affair, A 2013

Royal Tenenbaums, The 2002

Royal Wedding [1951] 1985

Rubin and Ed 1992

Ruby 1992

Ruby in Paradise 1993

Ruby Sparks 2013

Rude Awakening 1989

Rudo y Cursi 2010

Rudy 1993

Rudyard Kipling's the Second Jungle Book 1997

Rugrats Go Wild! 2004

Rugrats in Paris: The Movie 2001

Rugrats Movie, The 1999

Ruins, The 2009

Rules of Attraction, The 2003

Rules of Engagement 2001

Rum Diary, The 2012

Rumba, La. *See* Rumba, The.

Rumba, The 1987

Rumble Fish 1983

Rumble in the Bronx 1996

Rumor Has It... 2006

Rumpelstiltskin 1987

Run 1991

Run, Fatboy, Run 2009

Run Lola Run 2000

Run of the Country, The 1995

Runaway Bride 2000

Runaway Jury 2004

Runaway Train 1985

Runaways, The 2011

Rundown, The 2004

Rundskop. *See* Bullhead.

Runestone, The 1992

Running Brave 1983

Running Free 2001

Running Hot 1984

Running Man, The 1987

Running on Empty 1988

Schindler's List 1993

Schizo 2006

Schizopolis 1997

School Daze 1988

School for Scoundrels 2007

School of Flesh, 432

School of Rock 2004

School Spirit 1985

School Ties 1992

Schtonk 1995

Schultze Gets the Blues 2006

Science des reves, La. *See* Science of Sleep, The.

Science of Sleep, The 2007

Scissors 1991

Scooby-Doo 2003

Scooby-Doo 2: Monsters Unleashed 2005

Scoop 2007

Scorched. *See* Incendies.

Scorchers 1995

Score, The 2002

Scorpion 1986

Scorpion King, The 2003

Scorta, La 1995

Scotland, PA 2003

Scott Pilgrim vs. the World 2011

Scout, The 1995

Scream 1996

Scream 4 2012

Scream 2 1997

Scream 3 2001

Scream of Stone 1995

Screamers 1996

Screwed 2001

Scrooged 1988

Se, jie. *See* Lust, Caution.

Sea Inside, The 2005

Sea of Love 1989

Sea Wolves, The 1982

Seabiscuit 2004

Search and Destroy 1995

Search for Signs of Intelligent Life in the Universe, The 1991

Searching for Bobby Fischer 1993

Searching for Sugar Man 2013

Season of Dreams 1987

Season of Fear 1989

Season of Men, The 2003

Season of the Witch 2012

Seasons 1995

Second Best 1995

Second Chance, The 2007

Second Sight 1989

Second Skin 2003

Second Thoughts 1983

Secondhand Lions 2004

Secret Admirer 1985

Secret Garden, The 1993

Secret in Their Eyes, The 2011

Secret Life of Bees, The 2009

Secret Life of Walter Mitty, The [1947] 1985

Secret Lives of Dentists, The 2004

Secret Love, Hidden Faces. *See* Ju Dou.

Secret of Kells, The 2011

Secret of My Success, The 1987

Secret of NIMH, The 1982

Secret of Roan Inish, The 1995

Secret of the Sword, The 1985

Secret Places 1985

Secret Policeman's Third Ball, The 1987

Secret Window 2005

Secret World of Arrietty, The 2013

Secretariat 2011

Secretary 2003

Secreto de sus ojos, El. *See* Secret in Their Eyes, The.

Secrets 1984

Secrets & Lies 1996

Seduction, The 1982

See No Evil 2007

See No Evil, Hear No Evil 1989

See Spot Run 2002

See You in the Morning 1989

Seed of Chucky 2005

Seeing Other People 2005

Seeker: The Dark Is Rising, The 2008

Seeking a Friend for the End of the World 2013

Seeking Justice 2013

Segunda Piel. *See* Second Skin.

Selena 1998

Self Made Hero, A 1998

Semi-Pro 2009

S'en Fout la Mort. *See* No Fear, No Die.

Sender, The 1982

Senna 2012

Sensations 1988

Sense and Sensibility 1995

Sense of Freedom, A 1985

Senseless 1999

Sentimental Destiny 2002

Sentinel, The 2007

Separate Lies 2006

Separate Vacations 1986

Separation, A 2012

Seppan 1988

September 1987

September Dawn 2008

September Issue, The 2010

Serendipity 2002

Serenity 2006

Sgt. Bilko 1996

Seraphim Falls 2008

Serbuan maut. *See* Raid: Redemption, The.

Serial Mom 1995

Series 7: The Contenders 2002

Serious Man, A 2010

Serpent and the Rainbow, The 1988

Servants of Twilight, The 1995

Serving Sara 2003

Sesame Street Presents: Follow That Bird 1985

Session 9 2002

Sessions, The 2013

Set It Off 1996

Set Me Free 2001

Seto uchi shonen yakyudan. *See* Mac-Arthur's Children.

Seunlau Ngaklau. *See* Time and Tide.

Seven 1995

Seven Hours to Judgement 1988

Seven Men from Now [1956] 1987

Stranger Than Fiction 2007

Stranger than Paradise 1984, 1986

Strangers, The 2009

Stranger's Kiss 1984

Strangers in Good Company 1991

Strangers with Candy 2007

Strapless 1990

Straw Dogs 2012

Strawberry and Chocolate 1995

Strayed 2005

Streamers 1983

Street Fighter 1995

Street Fighter: The Legend of Chun-Li 2010

Street Kings 2009

Street Smart 1987

Street Story 1989

Street Trash 1987

Street Wars 1995

Streets 1990

Streets of Fire 1984

Streets of Gold 1986

Streetwalkin' 1985

Streetwise 1985

Strictly Ballroom 1993

Strictly Business 1991

Strictly Propaganda 1995

Strike It Rich 1990

Striking Distance 1993

Strip Jack Naked (Nighthawks II) 1995

Stripes 1981

Stripped to Kill 1987

Stripped to Kill 2 1989

Stripper 1986

Striptease 1996

Stroker Ace 1983

Stryker 1983

Stuart Little 2000

Stuart Little 2 2003

Stuart Saves His Family 1995

Stuck On You 2004

Student Confidential 1987

Stuff, The 1985

Stupids, The 1996

Submarine 2012

Substance of Fire, The 1996

Substitute, The 1996

Suburbans, The 2000

Suburban Commando 1991

Suburbia 1984

subUrbia 1997

Subway 1985

Subway to the Stars 1988

Such a Long Journey 2001

Sucker Punch 2012

Sudden Death 1985

Sudden Death 1995

Sudden Impact 1983

Sudden Manhattan 1997

Suddenly, Last Summer [1959] 1993

Suddenly Naked 2002

Sugar 2010

Sugar & Spice 2002

Sugar Cane Alley 1984

Sugar Hill 1995

Sugar Town 2000

Sugarbaby 1985

Suicide Kings 1999

Suitors, The 1989

Sukkar banat. *See* Caramel.

Sullivan's Pavilion 1987

Sum of All Fears, The 2003

Sum of Us, The 1995

Summer 1986

Summer Camp Nightmare 1987

Summer Catch 2002

Summer Heat 1987

Summer Hours 2010

Summer House, The 1993

Summer Lovers 1982

Summer Night with Greek Profile, Almond Eyes, and Scent of Basil 1987

Summer of Sam 2000

Summer Palace 2009

Summer Rental 1985

Summer School 1987

Summer Stock [1950] 1985

Summer Story, A 1988

Summertime [1955] 1990

Sunchaser 1996

Sunday 1997

Sunday in the Country, A 1984

Sunday's Child 1989

Sunday's Children 1995

Sunset 1988

Sunset Boulevard [1950] 1986

Sunset Park 1996

Sunshine 2001

Sunshine (Boyle) 2008

Sunshine Cleaning 2010

Sunshine State 2003

Super 2012

Super, The 1991

Super 8 2012

Super Mario Bros. 1993

Super Size Me 2005

Superbad 2008

Supercop 1997

Superfantagenio. *See* Aladdin.

Supergirl 1984

Superhero Movie 2009

Superman II 1981

Superman III 1983

Superman IV 1987

Superman Returns 2007

Supernova 2001

Superstar 1991

Superstar 2000

Sur 1988

Sur Mes Levres. *See* Read My Lips.

Sure Fire 1993

Sure Thing, The 1985

Surf II 1984

Surf Nazis Must Die 1987

Surf Ninjas 1993

Surf's Up 2008

Surfwise 2009

Surrender 1987

Surrogate, The. *See* Sessions, The.

Surrogates 2010

Surveillance 2010

Survival Quest 1990

Survival of the Dead 2011

Tasogare Seibei. *See* Twilight Samurai, The.

Taste of Others, The 2002

Tatie Danielle 1991

Taxi 2005

Taxi Blues 1991

Taxi nach Kairo. *See* Taxi to Cairo.

Taxi to Cairo 1988

Taxi to the Dark Side 2009

Taxi to the Toilet. *See* Taxi Zum Klo.

Taxi Zum Klo 1981

Taxing Woman, A 1988

Taxing Woman's Return, A 1989

Tea in the Harem 1986

Tea With Mussolini 2000

Teachers 1984

Teacher's Pet: The Movie. *See* Disney's Teacher's Pet.

Teaching Mrs. Tingle 2000

Team America: World Police 2005

Tears of the Sun 2004

Ted 2013

Ted and Venus 1991

Teen Witch 1989

Teen Wolf 1985

Teenage Mutant Ninja Turtles 1990

Teenage Mutant Ninja Turtles (2007). *See* TMNT.

Teenage Mutant Ninja Turtles II 1991

Teenage Mutant Ninja Turtles III 1993

Teeth 2009

Telephone, The 1988

Tell No One 2009

Telling Lies in America 1997

Témoins, Les. *See* Witnesses, The.

Temp, The 1993

Tempest 1982

Tempest, The 2011

Temporada de patos. *See* Duck Season.

Temps qui changent, Les. *See* Changing Times.

Temps qui reste, Les. *See* Time to Leave.

Temps Retrouve. *See* Time Regained.

Temptress Moon 1997

Ten 2004

Ten Things I Hate About You 2000

10,000 B.C. 2009

10 to Midnight 1983

10 Years 2013

Tenacious D in the Pick of Destiny 2007

Tender Mercies 1983

Tenebrae. *See* Unsane.

Tenue de soiree. *See* Menage.

Tequila Sunrise 1988

Terminal, The 2005

Terminal Bliss 1992

Terminal Velocity 1995

Terminator, The 1984

Terminator Salvation 2010

Terminator 2 1991

Terminator 3: Rise of the Machines 2004

Termini Station 1991

Terminus. *See* End of the Line.

Terms of Endearment 1983

Terri 2012

Terror Within, The 1989

Terrorvision 1986

Tess 1981

Test of Love 1985

Testament 1983

Testimony 1987

Tetro 2010

Tetsuo: The Iron Man 1992

Tex 1982, 1987

Texas Chainsaw Massacre, The (Nispel) 2004

Texas Chainsaw Massacre, Part II, The 1986

Texas Chainsaw Massacre: The Beginning, The 2007

Texas Comedy Massacre, The 1988

Texas Killing Fields 2012

Texas Rangers 2003

Texas Tenor: The Illinois Jacquet Story 1995

Texasville 1990

Thank You and Good Night 1992

Thank You for Smoking 2007

That Championship Season 1982

That Darn Cat 1997

That Night 1993

That Old Feeling 1997

That Sinking Feeling 1984

That Thing You Do! 1996

That Was Then...This Is Now 1985

That's Entertainment! III 1995

That's Life! 1986, 1988

That's My Boy 2013

The au harem d'Archi Ahmed, Le. *See* Tea in the Harem.

Thelma and Louise 1991

Thelonious Monk 1988

Then She Found Me 2009

Theory of Flight, The 1999

There Goes My Baby 1995

There Goes the Neighborhood 1995

There Will Be Blood 2008

There's Nothing Out There 1992

There's Something About Mary 1999

Theremin: An Electronic Odyssey 1995

They All Laughed 1981

They Call Me Bruce 1982

They Drive by Night [1940] 1982

They Live 1988

They Live by Night [1949] 1981

They Might Be Giants [1971] 1982

They Still Call Me Bruce 1987

They Won't Believe Me [1947] 1987

They're Playing with Fire 1984

Thiassos, O. *See* Traveling Players, The.

Thief 1981

Thief, The 1999

Thief of Hearts 1984

Thieves 1996

Thin Blue Line, The 1988

Thin Ice 2013

Thin Line Between Love and Hate, A 1996

Thin Red Line, The 1999

Thing, The 1982

Thing, The 2012

Thing Called Love, The 1995

Things Are Tough All Over 1982

Things Change 1988

Things to Do in Denver When You're Dead 1995

Things We Lost in the Fire 2008

Think Big 1990

Think Like a Man 2013

Third World Cop 2001

Thirst 2010

Thirteen 2004

13 Assassins 2012

Thirteen Conversations About One Thing 2003

Thirteen Days 2001

Thirteen Ghosts 2003

13 Going On 30 2005

Thirtieth Floor, The 2000

Thirtieth Warrior, The 2000

30 Days of Night 2008

30 Minutes or Less 2012

35 Shots of Rum 2011

Thirty Two Short Films About Glenn Gould 1995

Thirty-five Up 1992

37, 2 le Matin. *See* Betty Blue.

Thirty-six Fillette 1988

This Boy's Life 1993

This Christmas 2008

This Is Elvis 1981

This Is 40 2013

This is My Father 2000

This is My Life 1992

This Is Spinal Tap 1984

This Is It. *See* Michael Jackson's This Is It.

This Means War 2013

This Must Be the Place 2013

This Side of the Truth. *See* Invention of Lying, The.

This World, Then the Fireworks 1997

Thomas and the Magic Railroad 2001

Thomas Crown Affair, The 2000

Thomas in Love 2002

Thor 2012

Those Who Love Me Can Take the Train 2000

Thou Shalt Not Kill 1988

Thousand Acres, A 1997

Thousand Pieces of Gold 1991

Thousand Words, A 2013

Thrashin' 1986

Three Amigos 1986

Three Brothers 1982

Three Burials of Melquiades Estrada, The 2007

Three…Extremes 2006

3:15 1986

Three for the Road 1987

Three Fugitives 1989

300 2008

360 2013

3-Iron 2006

Three Kinds of Heat 1987

Three Kings 2000

Three Lives & Only One Death 1996

Three Madeleines, The 2001

Three Men and a Baby 1987

Three Men and a Cradle 1986

Three Men and a Little Lady 1990

Three Monkeys 2010

Three Musketeers, The 1993

Three Musketeers, The 2012

Three Ninjas Kick Back 1995

Three Ninjas 1992

Three O'Clock High 1987

Three of Hearts 1993

Three Seasons 2000

Three Sisters 1988

Three Stooges, The 2013

3 Strikes 2001

3:10 to Yuma 2008

3000 Miles to Graceland 2002

Three to Get Ready 1988

Three to Tango 2000

Three Wishes 1995

Threesome 1995

Threshold 1983

Through the Eyes of the Children. *See* 112th and Central.

Through the Olive Trees 1995

Through the Wire 1990

Through the Window 2001

Throw Momma from the Train 1987

Thumbelina. *See* Hans Christian Andersen's Thumbelina.

Thumbsucker 2006

Thunder Alley 1986

Thunderbirds 2005

Thunderheart 1992

THX 1138 [1971] 1984

Thy Kingdom Come…Thy Will Be Done 1988

Tian di ying xiong. *See* Warriors of Heaven and Earth.

Tian Yu. *See* Xiu Xiu: The Sent Down Girl.

Ticket to Ride. *See* Post Grad.

Tideland 2007

Tie Me Up! Tie Me Down! 1990

Tie That Binds, The 1995

Tieta of Agreste 2000

Tiger Warsaw 1988

Tigerland 2002

Tiger's Tale, A 1987

Tigger Movie, The 2001

Tightrope 1984

Til' There Was You 1997

Till Human Voices Wake Us 2004

Tillman Story, The 2011

Tillsammans. *See* Together.

Tim and Eric's Billion Dollar Movie 2013

Tim Burton's Corpse Bride 2006

Time After Time 1983

Time and Tide 2002

Time Bandits 1981

Time Code 2001

Time for Drunken Horses, A 2001

Time Indefinite 1995

Time Machine, The (Pal) [1960] 1983

Time Machine, The (Wells) 2003

Time of Destiny, A 1988

Time of Favor 2002

Time of the Gypsies 1990

Time Out 2003

Time Regained 2001

Time to Die, A 1991

Time to Kill, A 1996

Time to Leave 2007

Time Traveler's Wife, The 2010

Time Will Tell 1992

Timebomb 1992

Timecop 1995

Timeline 2004

Timerider 1983

Timothy Leary's Dead 1997

Tin Cup 1996

Tin Men 1987

Tinker Tailor Soldier Spy 2012

Titan A.E. 2001

Titanic 1997

Tito and Me 1993

Titus 2000

TMNT 2008

To Be or Not to Be 1983

To Begin Again. *See* Volver a empezar.

To Die For 1989

To Die For 1995

To Die Standing (Crackdown) 1995

To Gillian on Her 37th Birthday 1996

To Kill a Mockingbird [1962] 1989

To Kill a Priest 1988

To Live 1995

To Live and Die in L.A. 1985, 1986

To Protect Mother Earth 1990

To Render a Life 1995

To Return. *See* Volver.

To Rome with Love 2013

To Sir with Love [1967] 1992

To Sleep with Anger 1990

To Wong Foo, Thanks for Everything! Julie Newmar 1995

Todo Sobre Mi Madre. *See* All About My Mother.

Together 2002

Together 2004

Tokyo Pop 1988

Tokyo-Ga 1985

Tom and Huck 1995

Tom and Jerry 1993

Tom & Viv 1995

Tomb Raider. *See* Lara Croft: Tomb Raider.

Tomboy 1985

Tombstone 1993

Tomcats 2002

Tommy Boy 1995

Tomorrow [1972] 1983

Tomorrow Never Dies 1997

Tomorrow's a Killer. *See* Prettykill.

Too Beautiful for You 1990

Too Hot to Handle [1938] 1983

Too Much 1987

Too Much Sleep 2002

Too Much Sun 1991

Too Outrageous! 1987

Too Scared to Scream 1985

Too Soon to Love [1960]

Tooth Fairy 2011

Tootsie 1982

Top Dog 1995

Top Gun 1986

Top of the Food Chain 2002

Top Secret 1984

Topio stin omichi. *See* Landscape in the Mist.

Topsy-Turvy 2000

Tora-San Goes to Viena 1989

Torajiro Kamone Uta. *See* Foster Daddy, Tora!

Torch Song Trilogy 1988

Torinoi lo, A. *See* Turin Horse, The.

Torment 1986

Torn Apart 1990

Torn Curtain [1966] 1984

Torque 2005

Torrents of Spring 1990

Tortilla Soup 2002

Total Eclipse 1995

Total Recall 1990

Total Recall 2013

Totally F***ed Up 1995

Toto le heros. *See* Toto the Hero.

Toto the Hero 1992

Tottering Lives 1988

Touch 1997

Touch and Go 1986

Touch of a Stranger 1990

Touch of Evil [1958] 1999

Touch of Larceny, A [1959] 1986

Touch the Sound 2006

Touching the Void 2005

Tough Enough 1983

Tough Guys 1986

Tough Guys Don't Dance 1987

Tougher than Leather 1988

Touki-Bouki 1995

Tourist, The 2011

Tous les matins du monde 1992

Toward the Within 1995

Tower Heist 2012

Town, The 2011

Town and Country 2002

Town is Quiet, The 2002

Toxic Avenger, The 1986

Toxic Avenger, Part II, The 1989

Toxic Avenger, Part III, The 1989

Toy, The 1982

Toy Soldiers (Fisher) 1984

Toy Soldiers (Petrie) 1991

Toy Story 1995

Toy Story 3 2011

Toy Story 2 2000

Toys 1992

Trace, The 1984

Traces of Red 1992

Track 1988

Tracks in the Snow 1986

Trade 2008

Trade Winds [1939] 1982

Trading Hearts 1988

Trading Mom 1995

Trading Places 1983

Traffic 2001

Tragedia di un umo ridiculo. *See* Tragedy of a Ridiculous Man.

Tragedy of a Ridiculous Man 1982

Trail of the Lonesome Pine, The. *See* Waiting for the Moon.

Trail of the Pink Panther 1982

Turbo: A Power Rangers Movie, 1997

Turbulence, 1997

Turin Horse, The 2013

Turistas 2007

Turk 182 1985

Turn It Up 2001

Turner and Hooch 1989

Turning Paige 2003

Turtle Beach 1995

Turtle Diary 1985, 1986

Turtles are Back...In Time, The. *See* Teenage Mutant Ninja Turtles III.

Tuxedo, The 2003

TV Set, The 2008

Twelfth Night 1996

Twelve 2011

Twelve Monkeys 1995

Twelve O'Clock High [1949] 1989

12 Rounds 2010

Twenty Bucks 1993

20 Dates 2000

28 Weeks Later 2008

25th Hour 2003

24 Hour Party People 2003

24 Hours. *See* Trapped.

21 Grams 2004

TwentyFourSeven 1999

24 Hour Woman 2000

28 Days 2001

28 Days Later 2004

28 Up 1985

2046 2006

Twenty-ninth Street 1991

Twenty-one 1991

21 Jump Street 2013

2012 2010

21 2009

27 Dresses 2009

Twice Dead 1988

Twice in a Lifetime 1985

Twice upon a Time 1983

Twilight 1999

Twilight 2009

Twilight of the Cockroaches 1990

Twilight of the Ice Nymphs 1999

Twilight Saga: Breaking Dawn, Part 1, The 2012

Twilight Saga: Breaking Dawn, Part 2, The 2013

Twilight Saga: Eclipse, The 2011

Twilight Saga: New Moon, The 2010

Twilight Samurai, The 2005

Twilight Zone: The Movie 1983

Twin Dragons 2000

Twin Falls Idaho 2000

Twin Peaks: Fire Walk with Me 1992

Twin Town 1997

Twins 1988

Twist 1993

Twist and Shout 1986

Twisted 2005

Twisted Justice 1990

Twisted Obsession 1990

Twister 1990

Twister 1996

Two Bits 1995

Two Brothers 2005

Two Can Play That Game 2002

2 Days in New York 2013

2 Days in Paris 2008

2 Days in the Valley 1996

Two Evil Eyes 1991

Two Family House 2001

2 Fast 2 Furious 2004

Two for the Money 2006

Two Girls and a Guy 1999

200 Cigarettes 2000

Two If By Sea 1996

Two Jakes, The 1990

Two Lovers 2010

Two Moon Junction 1988

Two Much 1996

Two Ninas 2002

Two of a Kind 1983

Two Small Bodies 1995

2016 Obama's America 2013

2010 1984

Two Weeks Notice 2003

Twogether 1995

Tycoon 2004

Tyler Perry's Daddy's Little Girls. *See* Daddy's Little Girls.

Tyler Perry's Good Deeds 2013

Tyler Perry's I Can Do Bad All By Myself. *See* I Can Do Bad All By Myself.

Tyler Perry's Madea Goes to Jail. *See* Madea Goes to Jail.

Tyler Perry's Meet the Browns 2009

Tyler Perry's Why Did I Get Married?. *See* Why Did I Get Married?

Tyler Perry's Why Did I Get Married Too? *See* Why Did I Get Married Too?

Tyrannosaur 2012

Tyson 2010

U

U-571 2001

UFOria 1986

Ugly, The 1999

Ugly Truth, The 2010

UHF 1989

Ulee's Gold 1997

Ultraviolet 2007

Ulysses' Gaze 1995

Un Air de Famille 1999

Unaccompanied Minors 2007

Unbearable Lightness of Being, The 1988

Unbelievable Truth, The 1990

Unborn, The 1991

Unborn, The 2010

Unbreakable 2001

Uncertainty Principle, The 2003

Uncle Boonmee Who Can Recall His Past Lives 2012

Uncle Buck 1989

Uncommon Valor 1983

Unconquering the Last Frontier 2002

Undead 2006

Undefeated 2013

Undefeated, The 2012

Under Cover 1987

Under Fire 1983

Under Hellgate Bridge 2002

Under Siege 1992

Under Siege II: Dark Territory 1995

Verdict, The 1982

Vermont is for Lovers 1995

Verne Miller 1987

Veronica Guerin 2004

Veronika Voss 1982

Very Annie Mary 2003

Very Long Engagement, A 2005

Vertical Limit 2001

Vertical Ray of the Sun, The 2002

Vertigo [1958] 1996

Very Bad Things 1999

Very Brady Sequel, A 1996

Very Harold & Kumar 3D Christmas, A 2012

Very Thought of You, The 2000

Vesnicko ma strediskova. *See* My Sweet Little Village.

Veuve de Saint-Pierre, La. *See* Widow of Saint-Pierre, The.

V/H/S 2013

Via Appia 1991

Viaggio d'amore. *See* Journey of Love.

Vibes 1988

Vice Squad 1982

Vice Versa 1988

Vicky Cristina Barcelona 2009

Victim [1961] 1984

Victor/Victoria 1982

Victory 1981

Victory. *See* Vincere.

Videodrome 1983

Vie Apres l'Amour, La. *See* Life After Love.

Vie continue, La 1982

Vie de Boheme, La 1995

Vie en Rose, La 2008

Vie est rien d'autre, La. *See* Life and Nothing But.

Vie est un long fleuve tranquille, La. *See* Life Is a Long Quiet River.

Vie Promise, La. *See* Promised Life, The.

Vierde Man, De. *See* 4th Man, The.

View from the Top 2004

View to a Kill, A 1985

Village, The 2005

Village of the Damned 1995

Ville est Tranquille, La. *See* Town is Quiet, The.

Vince Vaughn's Wild West Comedy Show: 30 Days & 30 Nights— Hollywood to the Heartland 2009

Vincent and Theo 1990

Vincere 2011

Violets Are Blue 1986

Violins Came with the Americans, The 1987

Violon Rouge, Le. *See* Red Violin, The.

Viper 1988

Virgen de los Sicanos, La. *See* Our Lady of the Assassins.

Virgin Queen of St. Francis High, The 1987

Virgin Suicides, The 2001

Virtuosity 1995

Virus 2000

Vision Quest 1985

Visions of Light 1993

Visions of the Spirit 1988

Visit, The 2002

Visiting Hours 1982

Visitor, The 2009

Visitor, The. *See* Ghost.

Vital Signs 1990

Volcano 1997

Volere, Volare 1992

Volunteers 1985

Volver 2007

Volver a empezar 1982

Vor. *See* Thief, The.

Vow, The 2013

Voyage du ballon rouge, Le. *See* Flight of the Red Balloon.

Voyager 1992

Voyages 2002

Voyeur 1995

Vroom 1988

Vulture, The 1985

Vzlomshik. *See* Burglar, The.

W

W. 2009

Wackness, The 2009

Waco: The Rules of Engagement 1997

Wag the Dog 1997

Wagner 1983

Wagons East! 1995

Wah-Wah 2007

Waist Deep 2007

Wait for Me in Heaven 1990

Wait Until Spring, Bandini 1990

Waiting... 2006

Waiting for Gavrilov 1983

Waiting for Guffman 1997

Waiting for 'Superman' 2011

Waiting for the Light 1990

Waiting for the Moon 1987

Waiting to Exhale 1995

Waitress 1982

Waitress (Shelly) 2008

Waking Life 2002

Waking Ned Devine 1999

Waking the Dead 2001

Walk Hard: The Dewey Cox Story 2008

Walk in the Clouds, A 1995

Walk Like a Man 1987

Walk on the Moon, A 1987

Walk on the Moon, A (Goldwyn) 2000

Walk the Line 2006

Walk to Remember, A 2003

Walker 1987

Walking and Talking 1996

Walking After Midnight 1988

Walking Dead, The 1995

Walking Tall 2005

Wall, The 1986

Wall Street 1987

Wallace & Gromit: The Curse of the Were-Rabbit 2006

WALL-E 2009

Wall Street: Money Never Sleeps 2011

Waltz Across Texas 1983

Waltz with Bashir 2009

Wandafuru raifu. *See* After Life.

Wanderlust 2013

What a Girl Wants 2004

What About Bob? 1991

What Dreams May Come 1999

What Happened to Kerouse? 1986

What Happened Was... 1995

What Happens in Vegas 2009

What Just Happened 2009

What Lies Beneath 2001

What Planet Are You From? 2001

What the (Bleep) Do We Know? 2005

What Time Is It There? 2002

What to Expect When You're Expecting 2013

What Women Want 2001

Whatever 1999

Whatever It Takes (Demchuk) 1986

Whatever It Takes (Raynr) 2001

Whatever Works 2010

What's Cooking? 2001

What's Eating Gilbert Grape 1993

What's Love Got To Do With It 1993

What's the Worst That Could Happen? 2002

What's Your Number? 2012

When a Man Loves a Woman 1995

When a Stranger Calls 2007

When Brendan Met Trudy 2002

When Did You Last See Your Father? 2009

When Father Was Away on Business 1985

When Harry Met Sally 1989

When in Rome 2011

When Love Comes 2000

When Nature Calls 1985

When Night is Falling 1995

When the Cat's Away 1997

When the Party's Over 1993

When the Whales Came 1989

When the Wind Blows 1987

When We Were Kings 1997

When Will I Be Loved 2005

Where Angels Fear to Tread 1992

Where Are the Children? 1986

Where Do We Go Now? 2013

Where Spring Comes Late 1988

Where the Boys are '84 1984

Where the Day Takes You 1992

Where the Green Ants Dream 1985

Where the Heart Is (Boorman) 1990

Where the Heart Is (Williams) 2001

Where the Heart Roams 1987

Where the Money Is 2001

Where the Outback Ends 1988

Where the River Runs Black 1986

Where The Rivers Flow North 1995

Where the Truth Lies 2006

Where the Wild Things Are 2010

Wherever You Are 1988

While You Were Sleeping 1995

Whip It 2010

Whispers in the Dark 1992

Whistle Blower, The 1987

Whistleblower, The 2012

White 1995

White Badge 1995

White Balloon, The 1996

White Boys 2000

White Chicks 2005

White Countess, The 2006

White Dog 1995

White Fang 1991

White Fang II: Myth of the White Wolf 1995

White Girl, The 1990

White Hunter, Black Heart 1990

White Man's Burden 1995

White Material 2011

White Men Can't Jump 1992

White Mischief 1988

White Nights 1985

White Noise 2006

White of the Eye 1987, 1988

White Oleander 2003

White Palace 1990

White Ribbon, The 2010

White Rose, The 1983

White Sands 1992

White Sister, The [1923] 1982

White Squall 1996

White Trash 1992

White Winter Heat 1987

Whiteout 2010

Who Framed Roger Rabbit 1988

Who Killed the Electric Car? 2007

Who Killed Vincent Chin? 1988

Who Knows? *See* Va Savoir.

Who Shot Pat? 1992

Whole Nine Yards, The 2001

Whole Ten Yards, The 2005

Whole Wide World, The 1997

Whoopee Boys, The 1986

Whore 1991

Who's Afraid of Virginia Wolf? [1966] 1993

Who's Harry Crumb? 1989

Who's That Girl 1987

Who's the Man? 1993

Whose Life Is It Anyway? 1981

Why Did I Get Married? 2008

Why Did I Get Married Too? 2011

Why Do Fools Fall In Love 1999

Why Has Bodhi-Dharma Left for the East? 1995

Why Me? 1990

Why We Fight 2007

Wicked Lady, The 1983

Wicked Stepmother 1989

Wicker Man, The [1974] 1985

Wicker Man, The 2007

Wicker Park 2005

Wide Awake 1999

Wide Sargasso Sea 1993

Widow of Saint-Pierre, The 2002

Widows' Peak 1995

Wife, The 1996

Wigstock: the Movie 1995

Wilbur Wants to Kill Himself 2005

Wild, The 2007

Wild America 1997

Wild at Heart 1990

Wild Bill 1995

Wild Bunch, The [1969] 1995

Wild Duck, The 1985

Wild Geese II 1985

Wild Grass 2011

Wild Hearts Can't Be Broken 1991

Wild Hogs 2008

Wild Horses 1984

Wild Life, The 1984

Wild Man Blues 1999

Wild Orchid 1990

Wild Orchid II: Two Shades of Blue 1992

Wild Pair, The 1987

Wild Parrots of Telegraph Hill, The 2006

Wild Reeds 1995

Wild Thing 1987

Wild Things 1999

Wild Thornberrys Movie, The 2003

Wild West 1993

Wild West Comedy Show. *See* Vince Vaughn's Wild West Comedy Show: 30 Days & 30 Nights— Hollywood to the Heartland.

Wild Wild West 2000

Wildcats 1986

Wilde 1999

Wilder Napalm 1993

Wildfire 1988

Willard 2004

William Shakespeare's A Midsummer's Night Dream 2000

William Shakespeare's Romeo & Juliet 1996

William Shakespeare's The Merchant of Venice. *See* Merchant of Venice, The.

Willow 1988

Wilt. *See* Misadventures of Mr. Wilt, The.

Wimbledon 2005

Win. *See* Vincere.

Win a Date with Tad Hamilton 2005

Win Win 2012

Wind 1992

Wind, The [1928] 1984

Wind in the Willows, The 1997

Wind the Shakes the Barley, The 2008

Wind Will Carry Us, The 2001

Window Shopping 1995

Window to Paris 1995

Windtalkers 2003

Windy City 1984

Wing Commanders 2000

Winged Migration 2004

Wings of Desire 1988

Wings of the Dove 1997

Winner, The 1997

Winners, The 2000

Winners Take All 1987

Winnie the Pooh 2012

Winslow Boy, The 2000

Winter Guest, The 1997

Winter Meeting [1948] 1986

Winter of Our Dreams 1982

Winter Passing 2007

Winter People 1989

Winter Solstice 2006

Winter Tan, A 1988

Winter War, The. *See* Talvison.

Winter's Bone 2011

Wiping the Tears of Seven Generations 1995

Wired 1989

Wired to Kill 1986

Wirey Spindell 2001

Wisdom 1986

Wise Guys 1986

Wisecracks 1992

Wish You Were Here 1987

Wishmaster 1997

Witchboard 1987

Witches, The 1990

Witches of Eastwick, The 1987

With a Friend Like Harry 2002

With Friends Like These... 2006

With Honors 1995

With Love to the Person Next to Me 1987

Withnail and I 1987

Without a Clue 1988

Without a Paddle 2005

Without a Trace 1983

Without Evidence 1996

Without Limits 1999

Without You I'm Nothing 1990

Witless Protection 2009

Witness 1985

Witness for the Prosecution 1986

Witness to a Killing 1987

Witnesses, The 2009

Wittgenstein 1995

Wizard, The 1989

Wizard of Loneliness, The 1988

Wizard of Oz, The [1939], 1999

Wo De Fu Qin Mu Qin. *See* Road Home, The.

Wo Die Gruenen Ameisen Traeumen. *See* Where the Green Ants Dream.

Wo Hu Zang Long. *See* Crouching Tiger, Hidden Dragon.

Wolf 1995

Wolfen 1981

Wolfman, The 2011

Woman, Her Men, and Her Futon, A 1992

Woman, The 2012

Woman in Black, The 2013

Woman in Flames, A 1984

Woman in Red, The 1984

Woman in the Moon 1988

Woman in the Window, The [1944] 1982

Woman Next Door, The 1982

Woman on the Beach, The [1947] 1982

Woman's Pale Blue Handwriting, A 1988

Woman's Tale, A 1991

Wombling Free [1979] 1984

Women, The 2009

Women in Trouble 2010

Women on the Verge of a Nervous Breakdown 1988

Women's Affair 1988

Wonder Boys 2001

Wonderful Days. *See* Sky Blue.

Wonderful, Horrible Life of Leni Riefenstahl, The 1995

Wonderland (Saville) 1989

Wonderland (Winterbottom) 2001